HORSES
AND
HORSEMANSHIP

(Animal Agriculture Series)

Cover Photo
Mrs. J. Austin Du Pont
driving her Welsh Ponies
(Courtesy, Welsh Pony & Cob
Society of America,
Winchester, VA)

ABOUT THE AUTHOR

Marion Eugene Ensminger completed B.S. and M.S. degrees at the University of Missouri, and the Ph.D. at the University of Minnesota. Dr. Ensminger served, in order, as Manager of the Dixon Springs Agricultural Center (University of Illinois), Simpson, Illinois; and on the staffs of the University of Massachusetts, the University of Minnesota, and Washington State University. Dr. Ensminger also served as Consultant, General Electric Company, Nucleonics Department, and as the first President of the American Society of Agricultural Consultants. Since 1964, Dr. Ensminger has served as President of Agriservices Foundation, Clovis, California, a nonprofit foundation serving world agriculture in the area of World Food, Hunger, and Malnutrition.

Among Dr. Ensminger's many honors and awards are: Distinguished Teacher Award, American Society of Animal Science; the "Ensminger Beef Cattle Research Center" at Washington State University, Pullman, named after him in recognition of his contributions to the University; Faculty-Alumni Award of the University of Missouri; Outstanding Achievement Award of the University of Minnesota; Distinguished Service Award of the American Medical Association (with Mrs. Ensminger); Honorary Professor, Huazhong Agricultural College, Wuhan, China; Doctor of Laws (LL.D.) conferred by the National Agrarian University of Ukraine; and an oil portrait of him was placed in the 300-year-old gallery of the famed Saddle and Sirloin Club, Lexington, Kentucky.

In 1995, Cuba honored Dr. Ensminger by making him an Honorary Member of the Cuban Association of Animal Production; presenting him the 30th anniversary Gold Medal of the Institute of Animal Science, at Havana; making him an Honorary Guest Professor of the Agricultural University (ISCAH), at Havana; and making him an Honorary Guest Professor of the University of Camaguey, Camaguey, Cuba.

In 1995, Dr. Ensminger received the Distinguished Teacher Award, the highest honor of the National Association of Colleges and Teachers of Agriculture (NACTA).

In May 1996, Iowa State University awarded Dr. Ensminger the honorary degree, Doctor of Humane Letters, for "extraordinary achievements in animal science, education, and international agriculture."

In July 1996, Dr. Ensminger was the recipient of the International Animal Agriculture Bouffault Award, Paris, France, and the American Society of Animal Science.

Dr. Ensminger founded the International Ag-Tech Schools, which he directed for more than 50 years. He has directed schools, lectured, and/or conducted seminars in 70 countries. Dr. Ensminger is the author of more than 500 scientific articles, bulletins, and feature articles; and he is the author or co-author of 21 books, which are in several languages and used all over the world. He waives all royalties on the foreign editions of his books in order to help the people. The whole world is Dr. Ensminger's classroom.

HORSES
AND
HORSEMANSHIP

(Animal Agriculture Series)

by

M. E. Ensminger, B.S., M.A., Ph.D.

SEVENTH EDITION

INTERSTATE PUBLISHERS, INC.
Danville, Illinois

HORSES AND HORSEMANSHIP, Seventh Edition.
Copyright © 1999 by Interstate Publishers, Inc. All rights
reserved. Printed in the United States of America.

Editions:
First 1951
Second 1956
Third 1963
Fourth 1969
Fifth 1977
Sixth 1990
Seventh 1999

LIBRARY OF CONGRESS CATALOG CARD NO. 96-79329

ISBN 0-8134-3115-8

1 2 3
4 5 6
7 8 9

To
the memory of
my beloved brother,
Garnett Atwell "Buck" Ensminger,
who loved life, people, and horses.

PREFACE TO THE SEVENTH EDITION

Through the ages, horses have transformed travel, warfare, economics, culture, social organizations, political boundaries, and languages.

This seventh edition of *Horses and Horsemanship* presents two recent schools of thought, each by highly reputable authorities and each well documented, relative to the time and place of the first domestication of horses. Until now, it was generally accepted that horses were first domesticated about 2000 B.C.

An archeological discovery reported in 1991 (*Nature*, Vol. 350, March 28, 1991) placed the earliest domestication and use of horses at 4000 B.C. in the Ukrainian steppes (a treeless level prairie). Not so, according to the Greek historian, Horodotus and Near Eastern Records. They report (*National Geographic*, Vol. 190, No. 3, Sept., 1996, pp. 54-79) that in the 7th century B.C. the Scythian nomads of Central Asia were the first to domesticate and mount horses. These discoveries are important because the history and development of horses and people are inseparable. Wherever humans have left their footprints in their long climb from barbarism to civilization, the footprints of horses are beside them. Without doubt, further research and discoveries by archeologists and historians will pinpoint both the time and place of the domestication and use of horses.

Throughout, the seventh edition of *Horses and Horsemanship* imparts assurance that the human values in the horse industry are being preserved in the current age of biotechnology. The unique thing about the horse business, not found in any other industry, is that it is a people's business, and a way of life for many.

This generation has more money to spend and more leisure time in which to spend it than any population in history. A shorter workweek, increased automation, and the continued recreation and sports surge, with emphasis on physical fitness and the out-of-doors, assure a bright future for horses.

The horse industry is big and important business as evidenced by the following statistics: Annually, in the mid-1990s, it was a $15.2 billion industry; 258,434 youths were involved in 4-H horse and pony programs; there were 14,000 sanctioned horse shows; and 42.6 million people went to U.S. horse races and wagered an estimated $14 billion.

In the 17 western range states, an estimated 500,000 horses will continue to be the cow ponies of the west, furnishing needed assistance to ranchers.

This seventh edition of *Horses and Horsemanship* (1) tells how genetic wizardry, called biotechnology, is involving every facet of horse production; (2) describes and pictures several minor breeds of horses; (3) portrays draft horses and mules as still the show; and (4) details the new and more liberal AI and embryo transfer rules of the horse breed registry associations.

I am grateful to all those who contributed so richly to this seventh revision of *Horses and Horsemanship*. The following horse specialists provided critiques of the entire book, and made many valuable suggestions: Lee Eaton, noted Thoroughbred breeder, Eaton Sales, 4454 Mt. Horeb, Lexington, KY 40511, with whom I consulted frequently relative to the entire book. David E. McGlothlin, Manager, Horse Division, Harris Farms, Coalinga, California; and Sid Huntley, Quarter Horse breeder, Santa Ynez, California. Dr. Melissa T. Hines, DVM, Ph.D., Department of Veterinary Clinical Sciences, Washington State University, Pullman, Washington, co-authored Chapter 15, Horse Health, Disease Prevention, and Parasite Control; and Ms. Carla Wennberg, Equine Science Instructor, the University of Georgia, Athens, authoritatively reviewed Chapter 17, Horsemanship. Audrey H. Ensminger provided invaluable professional help, book design, and layout; Joan Wright processed my Missouri hieroglyphics and the voluminous correspondence through a computer; and Randall and Susan Rapp were par excellence in typesetting and proofreading. Additionally, a host of breed registry associations, colleges, companies, and individuals provided pictures and made other notable contributions, which are acknowledged throughout the book.

M. E. Ensminger
Clovis, California, 1998

REFERENCES

In addition to *Horses and Horsemanship*, the following books by M. E. Ensminger are available from Interstate Publishers, Inc., P. O. Box 50, Danville, IL 61832:

Animal Science
Animal Science Digest
Beef Cattle Science
Dairy Cattle Science
Feeds & Nutrition
Feeds & Nutrition Digest
Poultry Science
Sheep and Goat Science
Stockman's Handbook, The
Stockman's Handbook Digest
Swine Science

The *Stockman's Handbook* and *Stockman's Handbook Digest* are modern "how to do it" books which contain under one cover, the pertinent things that livestock producers need to know in the daily operation of their farms and ranches. They cover the broad field of animal agriculture, concisely and completely, and whenever possible, in tabular and outline form.

Animal Science and *Animal Science Digest* present a perspective or panorama of the far-flung livestock industry; *Feeds & Nutrition* and *Feeds & Nutrition Digest* cover the entire gamut of animal feeds and nutrition; and each of the specific class-of-livestock books presents specialized material pertaining to the class of animals indicated by the title.

OTHER SELECTED REFERENCES

Title of Publication	Author(s)	Publisher
Book of the Horse, The	Consultant Editor: P. Macgregor-Morris	G. P. Putnam's Sons, New York, NY, 1979
Breeding and Raising Horses, Ag. Hdbk. No. 394	M. E. Ensminger	Agricultural Research Service, USDA, Washington, DC, 1972
Complete Book of the Horse, The	Ed. by E. H. Edwards C. Geddes	Ward Lock Limited, London, England, 1974
Equine Pathology	J. M. Rooney J. L Robertson	Iowa State University Press, Ames, IA, 1996
Every Horse Owners' Cyclopedia	Ed. by R. McClure	I-Tex Publishing Company, Inc., Huntsville, TX, 1971
Fair Exchange	H. S. Finney	Charles Scribner's Sons, New York, NY, 1974

First Horse	R. Hapgood	Chronicle Books, San Francisco, CA, 1972
Harper's Encyclopedia for Horsemen: The Complete Book of the Horse	L. Taylor	Harper & Row, Publishers, New York, NY, 1973
Horse, The	J. M. Kays	A. S. Barnes and Co., Inc., Cranbury, NJ, 1969
Horse, The	P. D. Rossdale	The California Thoroughbred Breeders Association, Arcadia, CA, 1972
Horse, The	J. W. Evans, *et al.*	W. H. Freeman and Company, New York, NY, 1990
Horse Breeding Farm, The	L. C. Willis	A. S. Barnes & Co., Inc., Cranbury, NJ, 1973
Horse Care	F. Harper	Popular Library, New York, NY, 1966
Horse Management	Ed. by J. Hickman	Academic Press, San Diego, CA, 1987
Horses—a practical and scientific approach	M. Bradley	McGraw-Hill Book Company, New York, NY, 1981
Horse Science Handbook, Vols. 1-3	Ed. by M. E. Ensminger	Agriservices Foundation, Clovis, CA, 1963, 1964, and 1966
Horseman's Encyclopedia, The	M. C. Self	A. S. Barnes & Co., Inc., Cranbury, NJ, 1963
Horsemanship and Horse Care, Ag. Info. Bull. No. 353	M. E. Ensminger	Agricultural Research Service, USDA, Washington, DC, 1972
Horsemanship & Horsemastership	G. Wright	Doubleday & Company, Inc., Garden City, NY, 1962
Horses and Horsemanship	L. E. Walraven	A. S. Barnes & Co., Inc., New York, NY, 1970
Horses Health, The, from A to Z	P. D. Rossdale	David & Charles Publishers, Great Britain, 1989
Horses, Horses, Horses	M. E. Ensminger	M. E. Ensminger, Clovis, CA, 1965
Horses & Tack	M. E. Ensminger	Houghton Mifflin Company, Boston, MA, 1991
Horses: Their Selection, Care and Handling	M. C. Self	A. S. Barnes & Co., Inc., New York, NY, 1943
Horses of Today	H. H. Reese	Wood & Jones, Pasadena, CA, 1956
Light Horse Management, An Introduction to	R. C. Barbalace	Caballus Publishers, Fort Collins, CO, 1974
Light Horses, Farmers' Bull. No. 2127	M. E. Ensminger	Agricultural Research Service, USDA, Washington, DC
Saddle Up!	C. E. Ball	J. B. Lippincott Co., Philadelphia, PA, 1970
Shetland Pony, The	L. F. Bedell	Iowa State University Press, Ames, IA, 1959
Shetland Pony, The	M. C. Cox	Adam & Charles Black, Ltd., London, England, 1965
Stud Managers Course Lectures		Stud Managers Course, University of Kentucky, Lexington, KY, intermittent years since 1951
Stud Managers' Handbook, The	Ed. by M. E. Ensminger	Agriservices Foundation, Clovis, CA, annually since 1965
Summerhays' Encyclopedia for Horsemen	R. S. Summerhays	Frederick Warne and Co., Inc., New York, NY, 1966
Veterinary Encyclopedia for Horsemen	Staff of Equine Research Publications	Equine Research Publications, Grapevine, TX, 1975
Western Horse Behavior and Training	R. W. Miller	Doubleday & Company, Inc., Garden City, NY, 1975

CONTENTS

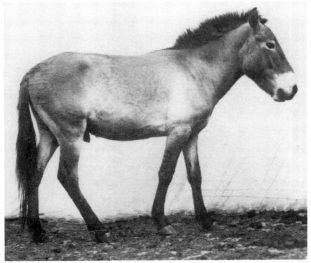

1

HISTORY AND DEVELOPMENT OF THE HORSE INDUSTRY

Przewalski horse, the original wild horse, maintained itself during some 60 million years of evolution. It was last seen in the wild in 1968 in southwestern Mongolia, along the border with China. (Courtesy, New York Zoological Society, New York, NY)

Wherever humans have left their footprints in their long ascent from barbarianism to civilization, the footprints of horses and people are inseparable; they are part of each other. Without the horse, people would neither be what, nor where, they are today.

EVOLUTION OF THE HORSE

Fossil remains prove that members of the horse family roamed the plains of America (especially what is now the Great Plains area of the United States) during most of Tertiary time, beginning about 58 million years ago. Yet no horses were present on this continent when Columbus discovered America in 1492. Why they perished, only a few thousand years before, is still one of the unexplained mysteries of evolution. As the disappearance was so complete and so sudden, many scientists believe that it must have been caused by some contagious disease or some fatal parasite. Others feel that perhaps it was due to multiple causes, including (1) climatic changes, (2) competition, and/or (3) failure to adapt. Regardless of why horses disappeared, it is known that conditions in America were favorable for them at the time of their reestablishment by the Spanish conquistadores, less than 500 years ago.

Through fossil remains, it is possible to reconstruct the evolution of the horse (see Table 1-1), beginning with the ancient 4-toed ancestor, the *Eohippus* (meaning *dawn horse*). This was a small animal, scarcely more than a foot high, with 4 toes on the front feet and 3 toes on the hind feet, and with slender legs, a short neck, and even teeth. It was well adapted to traveling in and feeding on the herbage of swamplands.

TABLE
EVOLUTION OF HORSES AS

Eras	Periods	Epochs	Approximate Duration in Years	Approximate Number of Years Since Beginning	General Characteristics
Cenozoic (recent life) Age of Mammals and Angiosperms	Quaternary	Recent	12,000±	12,000±	Post-Glacial Age. Rise of modern humankind, *Homo sapiens*. Development of complex cultures and civilizations. Domestication of animals.
		Pleistocene (Gr. *pleistos*, most + *kainos*, recent)	1,000,000	1,000,000	Ice Age: 4 major advances. Evolution of primitive humankind. Neanderthal, Heidelberg, Peking, Java, etc. Mammoth, mastodon, great sloth, saber-tooth tiger, etc. 90-100% modern species. Rise of Alps and Himalayas.
	Tertiary	Pliocene (Gr. *pleion*, more + *kainos*)	11,000,000	12,000,000	Mammals increase in size. 50-90% modern species.
		Miocene (Gr. *meion*, less *kainos*)	16,000,000	28,000,000	The "Golden Age" of mammals. Luxuriant grasses; culmination of plains-dwelling mammals. 20-40% modern species.
		Oligocene (Gr. *oligos*, little + *kainos*)	10,000,000	38,000,000	Modern mammals predominate over primitive ones. 10-15% modern species.
		Eocene (Gr. *eos*, dawn + *kainos*)	20,000,000	58,000,000	Archaic mammals, the advent of the horse. 1-5% modern species.
		Paleocene	17,000,000	75,000,000	The beginning of the age of mammals. Great development of the angiosperms. 1% modern species.

[1]In some cases, other genera might well be listed, but the leading ones of the respective epochs are given here.

Gradually, the descendants of *Eohippus* grew in size and changed in form, evolving into a 3-toed animal known as *Mesohippus*, which was about 24 inches in height or about the size of a Collie dog. Further changes continued, transforming the animal from a denizen of the swamp to a creature capable of surviving in the forest and finally to one adapted to the prairie. In terms of conformation, the animal grew taller.

1-1
DECIPHERED FROM THE FOSSIL RECORD[1]

The Horse

Equus (Modern Horse; *Equus* is Latin for horse). Beginning about 25,000 years ago, during the Paleolithic (Old Stone Age), people hunted horses and used them as a source of food. They were probably the last of the common domestic animals to be domesticated. This domestication is thought to have occurred toward the end of the Neolithic (New Stone Age) about 5,000 years ago. The horse was returned to the "New World" by the Spanish conquistadores less than 500 years ago.

Equus (Modern Horse); One large functional toe on each foot with the two side toes reduced to mere splint bones and entirely nonfunctional. The horse reached the climax of its evolutionary development with *Equus*. Several known species in North America. Most of these were the size of small ponies but one fully equaled the greatest of modern draft horses. However, in the Americas they died out toward the end of the Pleistocene Epoch, perhaps due to multiple causes, including (1) climatic changes, (2) competition, (3) epidemic, and/or (4) failure to adapt. Fortunately, however, horses had found a land bridge (probably via Alaska and Siberia) into the Old World, where they survived to become a servant and friend to humans. They had entered the Old World by this same route at other times in the Tertiary past.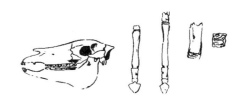

Pliohippus (Gr. *pleion*, more + *hippos*, horse). First one-toed horse, the side toes being reduced to splints. High-crowned grazing type teeth. Pony size. This was the immediate and virtually full-grown forerunner of *Equus*. Also *Hipparion* (Gr. dim of *hippos*; a pony), a three-toed grazer, and several other genera.

Merychippus (Rudimentary horse; Gr. *Meryx*, ruminant + *hippos*, horse). Three toes on each foot with the middle much heavier than the others which failed to touch the ground. A slim, graceful animal about the size of a Shetland Pony, whose teeth were high crowned and hard surfaced, suitable for eating grass. Thus *Merychippus* was thoroughly adapted to life on the prairie. Also *Protohippus* (Gr. *Protos*, first, primordial + *hippos*) generally similar to *Merychippus*, *miohippus* (Gr. *Meion*, less + *hippos*) with foot structure like *Merychippus* but with short-crowned, browsing teeth; *Parahippus* (Almost, nearly *hippos*) and others.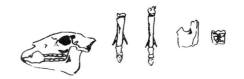

Mesohippus (Gr. *meso*, in the middle, intermediate-*hippos*). Three toes on each foot with the middle toe distinctly larger and a fourth toe on the front foot reduced to a splint, all touched the ground and shared in carrying the animal's weight. Teeth low crowned, probably for browsing. *Mesohippus* was about the size of a Collie dog with longer legs and a straighter back than its tiny Eocene forerunner. Also its intelligence and agility increased.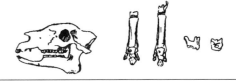

Eohippus (Gr. *eos*, dawn-*hippos*). Four functional toes on the front foot, one larger than the others, with a fifth reduced to a splint; the hind foot had 3 functional toes and a splint. *Eohippus* was a small, graceful animal, scarcely more than a foot high with a slender face, an arched back, short neck, slender legs and a long tail, adapted for living in swamps. Also *Orohippus* (Gr. *oros*, mountain-*hippos*), having foot structure like *Eohippus* but without vestigal splints, and *Epihippus* (Gr. *epi*, upon, among—*hippos*).

Prehorse. The 5 toes (one a splint) on the forefeet of *Eohippus* indicate that its ancestor probably had 5 toes all around, but no 5-toed horse has yet been found. The ancestors of the horse were probably primitive 5-toed ungulates, perhaps similar to some primitive Condylarth.

The teeth grew longer, stronger, and more roughened to suit the gradual changes to grazing on the prairie. The cannon bones—metacarpals and metatarsals—lengthened; the middle toe (or third toe) grew longer and stronger, forming a hoof; and the other toes (second and fourth toes) gradually disappeared except for vestiges, the slender bones known as splints, under the skin. The transformation in length and structure of foot made for greater speed over prairie type of terrain, thereby enabling the animal to feed farther and farther from water, and providing for greater safety in its struggle to survive. The horse is an excellent example, therefore, of the slow adaptation of animal life to changing conditions in environment, climate, food, and soil. The animal was transformed from one adapted to a swamp type environment to one adapted to the prairie.

Though all horses eventually perished in the New World and none were present on the continent when America was discovered, fortunately some of these animals had long before emigrated to Asia and Europe at a time when there was a land bridge connecting Alaska and Siberia (now Bering Strait). These emigrants formed the sturdy wild European stock from which the horse family of today descended, and this stock also populated Africa with its asses and zebras.

From Table 1-1, it can be seen that the evolution of the horse covered a period of approximately 58 million years, but that people hunted horses as recently as 25,000 years ago and domesticated them a mere 5,000 years ago, and that the Spanish conquistadores returned them to the New World less than 500 years ago.

ORIGIN AND DOMESTICATION OF THE HORSE[1, 2, 3, 4, 5]

The origin and domestication of the horse is clouded in more obscurity than its evolutionary development. Moreover, the early use of horses transformed travel, warfare, economics, culture, social organizations, political boundaries, and languages.

There are two recent schools of thought, each by highly reputable authorities and each well documented, relative to the time and place of the first domestication of horses. Until now, it was generally

accepted that horses were first domesticated about 2000 B.C.

■ *The school of thought based on archaeological discovery reported in 1991, placing the earliest domestication and use of horses at 4000 B.C. in the Ukrainian steppes (a treeless level prairie).*[3]

■ *The school of thought crediting the Scythian nomads of Central Asia as being the first to domesticate and use horses in the 7th century, B.C.*[4]

Without doubt, further research and discoveries by archaeologists and historians will pinpoint both the time and place of the domestication and use of horses. In the meantime the fascinating story based on present evidence follows.

According to the Greek historian, Herodotus, along with Near Eastern records, in the 7th century B.C. the Scythian nomads of Central Asia were the first to domesticate and mount horses.

The Scythians, who were accomplished horsemen, were bearded men, with dark deep-set eyes, weather-beaten faces, and long wind-snarled hair. They are credited with the invention of the chief items of riding gear—the bridle and saddle. The Scythians used horses for mounts, draft animals, milk, and meat, and for waging war. They were fierce fighters; they charged at the gallop, shooting deadly arrows from their bows, scalping their victims and making drinking cups from their skulls.

The Scythians devoted much time and attention to their horses and ornamented all their trappings. Bridles were provided with metal bits and metal cheekpieces. Saddles consisted of two felt cushions mounted on wooden frames. But metal stirrups were unknown to the Scythians. Women traveled with their children in covered wagons with solid wheels and tongue, pulled by horses, mules, or oxen.

Archaeological evidence of the Scythians is scanty. But during the first half of the 7th century grazing land in Central Asia was hard to come by due to competition, perhaps accentuated by a severe drought. Instead of fighting for their grazing rights, the Scythians migrated westward in search of better pastures and people to conquer. En route, they pillaged Nineveh, Babylon, and Palestine.

When the Scythians reached the Ukrainian steppe (a treeless, level prairie), they found a sea of grass spreading before them, a dream realm for horsemen and keepers of cattle, sheep, and goats.

At their height in the 4th century B.C., an estimated half a million Scythians ruled most of modern-day Ukraine and the plains of southern Russia. Also, the Greeks and the Scythians were trading partners.

But during the last half of the 4th century B.C., this flourishing culture waned and Scythian herds and flocks began to decline. Some experts suspect drought

[1]*Academic American Encyclopedia*, Vol. 17, p. 167

[2]*Encyclopaedia Britannica*, Vol. 16, pp. 438-442.

[3]*Nature*, Vol. 350, March 28, 1991, by Jared M. Diamond.

[4]*National Geographic*, Vol. 190, No. 3, Sept., 1996, pp. 54-79, by Mike Edwards, Assistant Editor.

[5]*World Book*, Vol. 17, p. 208.

and overgrazing; others cite hordes of Samaritans invading from the east; and still others feel that the increasing sedentary lifestyle undermined the Scythians nomad spirit, leading to cultural collapse. Yevgeny Chernenko, Ukraine's most respected archeologist, says: "The truth is, we simply don't know what happened."

Mysteriously, the Scythians disappeared from history by the 3rd century A.D. leaving only tales of their courage and cruelty—and imposing tombs (mounds called Kurgans) lavishly provisioned for eternity, including horses and grooms.

■ **Expansion of horses**—Although the Egyptians—the most advanced civilization of the day—had domesticated and used the ass from the earliest times, horses were wholly unknown to them until the dynasty of the Shepherd Kings, who entered Egypt from Asia in 1680 B.C. It is reported that, thereafter, the horse was much favored in Egypt.

Presence of the horse seems to have prompted the invention of the chariot, a type of vehicle drawn by horses that the Egyptians used in war and other pursuits. The Bible also relates that when Joseph took

Fig. 1-2. Distinguished young Greek in fashionable riding habit. Bowl painting 500 B.C. Though the Greeks were accomplished equestrians, at this time the use of the saddle and stirrups appears to have been unknown to them. (Courtesy, the Bettmann Archive)

his father's remains from Egypt back to Canaan "there went up with him both chariots and horsemen."[6] It is probable that the Egyptians were largely responsible for the spread of domesticated horses to other countries.

There were no horses in Arabia during the early period when they were flourishing in Egypt. But horses and chariots were used in Greece at least a thousand years before Christ, to judge from the account of their use in the siege of Troy. It is also interesting to note that the first and most expert equestrians of Greece, the Thessalonians, were colonists from Egypt. As evidence that the Greeks were accomplished in the use of horses, it might be pointed out that they developed the snaffle bit at an early period. Also, one of their number is said to have originated the axiom "No foot, no horse." Yet, the use of the saddle and stirrups appears to have been unknown in Greece at this time.

From Greece, the horse was later taken to Rome and from there to other parts of Europe. The Romans proved to be master equestrians. They invented the curb bit. According to historians, when Caesar invaded Britain, about 55 B.C., he took horses with him. Although there were other horses in Britain at the time of the Roman occupation, Eastern breeding was probably greatly infused at this time—thus laying the foundation for the Blood Horse of today.

The Arabs, strangely enough, did not use horses

Fig. 1-1. Joseph using horses in his move to Egypt (about 1500 B.C.), from a miniature painting in the Bible of the Counts of Toggenburg, 16th Century. (Courtesy, the Bettmann Archive)

<hr />

[6]Genesis 50:9.

to any extent until after the time of Mohammed (570 to 632 A.D.), depending on camels before that time. As evidence of this fact, it is noted that in the 7th Century after Christ, when Mohammed attacked the Koreish near Mecca, he had but two horses in his whole army; and at the close of his murderous campaign, although he drove off 24,000 camels and 40,000 sheep and carried away 24,000 ounces of silver, not one horse appeared in his list of plunder. This would seem to indicate rather conclusively that Arabia, the country whose horses have done so much to improve the horses of the world, was not the native home of the horse and that the Arabs did not use horses until after the time of Christ.

Of course, it seems incredible that all the various breeds, colors, and types of draft, light, and pony horses should have descended from a common, wild ancestor. Rather, there were probably many different wild stocks giving descent to domestic horses.

THE WILD HORSE OF ASIA

The wild horses of Asia, which are sometimes referred to as the Oriental light-legged horses, were of Asiatic origin, tracing to a wild horse (now extinct) of the Asiatic deserts. Historic evidence indicates that this group of horses gave rise to most of the swift and slenderly built breeds of modern times. The Arabian, the Barb, and the Turk are all descendants of these animals; and, in turn, the Thoroughbred originated from these stocks.

THE WILD HORSE OF EUROPE

The European wild horse, sometimes referred to as the European forest type, continued to live in the forests of Germany and Scandinavia until historic times; and wild horses are believed to have lived in the Vosges Mountains on the western border of Alsace until the year 1600. One of the pagan practices of the ancient German tribes was the sacrifice of horses and the eating of their meat at religious feasts. To this day one may find a relic of horse worship in the horse skulls set on the gables of houses and barns in southern Germany.

The European wild horse was the wild black horse of Flanders. This was a stocky animal that possessed considerably more size and scale than the Oriental type. This draft type was native to Western Europe at the time of the Roman invasion. It was the forerunner of the Great War Horse of the Middle Ages. The latter, in turn, fathered the modern draft breeds.

Not all wild horses of Europe were large, however, for small, shaggy animals were native to northern

Fig. 1-3. Horses vary in size and use. The Shetland Pony foal (left) is thought to have descended from the small, shaggy, wild stock of northern Europe; whereas the draft horse (right) is thought to have descended primarily from the ponderous, wild black horse of Flanders. (Courtesy, Iowa State University, Ames)

Europe. They were strong and hardy and required less feed than other types of horses. These animals are thought to be the progenitors of the Shetland Pony.

THE TARPAN

Though now extinct in the wild, the Tarpan—a small dun-colored, genuine wild species of horse—was formerly abundant everywhere in southern Russia and Central Asia. These animals were hated by the farmers because they devoured their crops, and especially because the Tarpan stallions constantly recruited domestic mares for their wild bands. For these reasons, they were killed off by the Russians. The last wild Tarpan alive in the wild, a mare, was killed the latter part of the 1800s when she was chased off a cliff. The last pure Tarpan died in a Russian zoo in 1909.

Fortunately, the history of the Tarpans did not end in 1909. Several naturalists and zoologists recreated Tarpans by regrouping their genetic material and bred them back into existence. In order to preserve and protect the purity of the bloodlines, the American Tarpan Studbook Association was formed in 1971.

Tarpans stand between 12 and 14 hands at the withers, with 13-2 hands being considered ideal. They are stockily built. Their necks are very thick; their hoofs are large and resilient and should never be shod. In winter, Tarpan coats change to an off-white color.

Today, there is an adoptive program for Tarpans designed to help save the breed. Anyone interested in adopting a Tarpan(s) should contact the American Tarpan Studbook Association, 1225 Hwy. 11 South, Hillsboro, GA 31038.

Fig. 1-4. Weanling Tarpan filly. (Courtesy, American Tarpan Studbook Assn., Hillsboro, GA)

PRZEWALSKI HORSE

The Przewalski horse, named after the Russian explorer, Przewalski, who rediscovered them in the northwestern corner of Mongolia, in 1879, maintained itself during some 60 million years of evolution, in Europe and Asia. It was last seen in the wild in 1968 in southwestern Mongolia, along the border with China. Today, it is almost certainly extinct in the wild. However, about 700 Przewalski horses are maintained in captivity. It is a small, stockily built, and distinctly yellowish horse, with an erect mane and no forelock. There is usually a dark stripe on the shoulders and down the middle of the back. In the wild, Przewalski horses separated into bands, seldom more than 40 in number, with a stallion leader in each group. When crossed on domestic horses, the hybrids are fertile, which proves that Przewalski horses are very closely related to the domestic horse.

ORIGIN AND DOMESTICATION OF THE DONKEY

The two species of the horse family that have been tamed are *Equus caballus*, the horse, and *Equus asinus*, the ass or donkey. The history of the domestic donkey is as clear as that of the horse is obscure. Donkeys were first domesticated in Egypt, where they served people from earliest times. Good figures of them appear on slates of the 1st Dynasty, about 3400 B.C. Domestic donkeys are descended from the wild donkey (the Nubian wild ass) of North Africa, a species which became extinct about 1980. Because of the frequent tendency to have stripes on the legs, however, some zoologists also think that the domestic donkey is related to the Somali wild ass of Africa.

From Egypt, the use of the domestic donkey spread into southwestern Asia sometime prior to the year 1000 B.C. The Bible first refers to the ass in relating how Abraham, the patriarch of the Old Testament, rode one of these animals from Beersheba to Mount Mordah. Every child is familiar with the fact that Jesus rode into Jerusalem on an ass. This mode of transportation was not unusual at the time of Christ, for donkeys were then the common saddle animals throughout the Near East.

As is generally known, the donkey is commonly used in this country in the production of mules.[7] Mules have been known from very ancient times, as we learn from the accounts of the Trojan War.

Fig. 1-5. A Mongolian wild ass in the Gobi desert in Asia. (Courtesy, American Museum of Natural History, New York, NY)

---

[7]In recent years, some miniature donkeys are being used as pets in the U.S.

POSITION OF THE HORSE IN THE ZOOLOGICAL SCHEME

The following outline shows the basic position of the domesticated horse in the zoological scheme:

Kingdom *Animalia*: Animals collectively; the Animal Kingdom.

Phylum *Chordata*: One of approximately 21 phyla of the animal kingdom, in which there is either a backbone (in the vertebrates) or the rudiment of a backbone, the chorda.

Class *Mammalia*: Mammals, or warm-blooded, hairy animals that produce their young alive and suckle them for a variable period on a secretion from the mammary glands.

Order *Perissodactyla*: Nonruminant hoofed mammals, usually with an odd number of toes, the third digit the largest and in line with the axis of the limb. This suborder includes the horse, tapir, and rhinoceros.

Family *Equidae*: The members of the horse family may be distinguished from the other existing perissodactyla (rhinoceros and tapir) by their comparatively more slender and agile build.

Genus Equus: Includes horses, asses, and zebras.

Species *Equus caballus*: The horse is distinguished from asses and zebras by the longer hair of the mane and tail, the presence of the "chestnut" on the inside of the hind leg, and by other less constant characters such as larger size, larger hoofs, more arched neck, smaller head, and shorter ears.

USES OF HORSES

The name *horse* is derived from the Anglo-Saxon, *hors*, meaning swiftness; and the word horseman comes from the Hebrew root *to prick or spur*.[8] These early characterizations of the horse, within themselves, tell somewhat of a story. Perhaps the very survival of the wild species was somewhat dependent upon its swiftness, which provided escape from both beast and human. The Hebrew description of a horseman was obviously assigned after the horse had been domesticated and ridden.

---

[8]The Jews were forbidden by divine authority to use horses. In fact, they were required to hamstring horses captured in war.

The various uses that people have made of the horse down through the ages, in order of period of time, are (1) as a source of food, (2) for military purposes, (3) in the pastimes and sports of the nations, (4) in agricultural and commercial pursuits, and (5) for recreation and sport.

THE HORSE AS A SOURCE OF FOOD

The first role of the horse in the odyssey of humans was as a source of food. During the Paleolithic (Old Stone) Age, horses were hunted. This was prior to their domestication. These earliest records date back to some 25,000 years ago. Perhaps the best-preserved record of this type consists of the cracked and dismembered bones of horses, mostly young animals, found around old campsites. One bone heap of this sort is at Solutre, in the Rhone Valley in southern France. It is estimated that this one campsite contains the remains of 100,000 horses.

Following domestication, which is thought to have occurred sometime toward the end of the New Stone Age, it is reasonable to surmise that mares were milked for human food—a practice still followed in certain parts of the world. Mares may give up to 4½ gallons of milk per day.[9] Also, the use of horses for meat still persists in many parts of the world, including France, Belgium, and Switzerland. But the intimate association of horses and people in many parts of the world, including in the United States, developed into a companionship, resulting in a taboo against eating horseflesh.

THE HORSE FOR MILITARY PURPOSES

Unfortunately, not long after domestication of horses, people used them for waging war. About 1500 B.C., Pharaoh pursued the Israelites to the Red Sea, using chariots and horses.[10] This would seem to imply that the Egyptian army used horses, both as cavalry and to draw vehicles.

During the glamorous days of the knight in armor, horses of size, strength, and endurance were essential. The Great Horse of medieval times was the knight's steed. Usually stallions were used. Often the knight and his armor weighed 350 to 425 lb. During the Crusades and for several centuries after, the clad-in-

---

[9]Mares of mature weights of 600, 800, 1,000, and 1,200 lb may produce 36, 42, 44, and 49 lb of milk daily, respectively.

[10]Exodus 14:7.

THROUGH THE AGES

Fig. 1-6. The horse in *allegory*: A winged figure, clad in a crimson cloak with a striped shawl around her waist, is shown standing on a small island in the middle of a lake. In her left hand, she holds a branch; and in her right hand, a silken cord which is wound around the neck of a white stallion prancing beside her. In the foreground, a siren swims in the water; and in the background can be seen a boat and birds flying above the distant rocky shore. (Courtesy, National Gallery of Art, Kress Collection, Washington, DC)

Fig 1-8. The horse in *allegory*: "Triumph of Chastity." Chastity represented by a young woman holding a palm, stands on top of a pedestal on a car drawn by two unicorns. Before her kneels a cupid with clipped wings, his hands holding the bow and arrows that have been taken from cupid. They are preceded by another young woman holding a banner emblazoned with an ermine (weasel). In the background, is a landscape with a view of a town on the shores of a lake. (Courtesy, National Gallery of Art, Kress Collection, Washington, DC)

Fig. 1-7. Bronze horse-drawn cart, with a round canopy and a covered front. This was part of 230 artifacts of the Eastern Han Dynasty (25 A.D.-220 A.D.) discovered in a large brick tomb in China in 1969. (Photo by A.H. Ensminger)

Fig. 1-9. The flying horse of Kansu, shown at the rack. This bronze horse of the Eastern Han Dynasty (25 A.D.-220 A.D.) was discovered in China in 1969. The horse is floating through the air, with three feet off the ground. The right hind foot is on a bird, which conveys the message that the horse racks faster than the bird can fly. (Photo by A.H. Ensminger)

armor type of warrior relied upon sheer weight to beat down the enemy.

The deeds of great warriors, mounted on their favorite chargers, were long perpetuated in marble or bronze. Every schoolchild vividly associates Alexander the Great with his charger, Bucephalus; Napoleon with his famous horse, Marengo; the Duke of Wellington with his favorite mount, Copenhagen; George Washington, receiving the surrender of Cornwallis' army at Yorktown, with his handsome mount, Nelson; and General Grant with his horse, *Cincinnatus.*

Many people are under the erroneous impression that no horses were used in World War II. Nothing could be further from the truth. But this is another story, to be related at the end of this chapter.

THE HORSE IN THE PASTIMES AND SPORTS OF NATIONS

As early as 1450 B.C., the sports-loving Greeks introduced the horse in the Olympic games, in both chariot and horse races. The most celebrated of these events was held at Olympia every fourth year in honor of Jupiter. However, because of the scarcity of horses, very few were used in early contests. Classes were divided according to age—and sometimes sex—and the distance of the course was approximately four miles.

Fig. 1-10. Chariot driven through Pompeii. The horse-drawn chariot was used by the sports-loving Greeks in chariot races, as well as in war and other pursuits. (Courtesy, The Bettmann Archive)

For these important events, the Greeks trained both themselves and their horses. The chariot races were even provided with settings to tempt the charioteers to daring deeds. Most of the chariots were low, two-wheeled, narrow track vehicles.

THE HORSE IN AGRICULTURAL AND COMMERCIAL PURSUITS

For many years following domestication, horses were used for purposes of war and sport. Their use in pulling loads and tilling the soil is a comparatively recent development.

There is no evidence to indicate that the horse was used in Europe to draw the plow prior to the 10th century, and oxen remained the common plow animal in England until the end of the 18th century. Remains of ancient art show conclusively that, long after domestication of the horse, the ox and the camel continued as the main source of agricultural power and transportation, respectively.

Fig. 1-11. Draft teams waiting their turn at the watering tank during noon rest. (Courtesy, J. C. Allen & Son, Inc., West Lafayette, IN)

It is interesting to note that heavier draft-type animals had their development primarily in those countries in which Caesar campaigned in western Europe, including England. Without doubt, the improved roads that the Romans constructed during their long occupation were largely instrumental in encouraging the breeding of heavier horses capable of drawing heavier loads. The Great Horse served as the progenitor of the draft horse of agriculture.

Fig. 1-12. Horses and riders on the trail. (Courtesy, American Saddlebred Horse Assn., Lexington, KY)

THE HORSE FOR RECREATION AND SPORT

In 1993, recreation spending in the United States consumed an average of 8.8% of personal income, or an amount equal to 304 billion dollars. The combination of available money, leisure time, and emphasis on the out-of-doors has created great interest in light horses for recreation and sport. As a result, the race crowds are big, the bridle paths in the city parks are being lengthened each year, the game of polo is expanding, riding to hounds is sharing its glamour with greater numbers, people of all walks of life enjoy the great horse shows throughout the land, and saddle clubs are springing up everywhere. This trend will continue.

INTRODUCTION OF HORSES AND MULES TO, AND EARLY HISTORY IN, THE UNITED STATES

It has been established that most of the evolution of the horse took place in the Americas, but this animal was extinct in the Western World at the time of Columbus' discovery, and apparently extinct even before the arrival of the Indians some thousands of years earlier.

Columbus first brought horses to the West Indies on his second voyage in 1493. Cortez brought Spanish horses with him to the New World in 1519 when he landed in Mexico (16 animals were the initial contingent, but approximately 1,000 head more were subsequently imported during the 2-year conquest of Mexico). Horses were first brought directly to what is now the United States by de Soto in the year 1539. Upon his vessels, he had 237 horses. These animals traveled with the army of the explorer in the hazardous journey from the Everglades of Florida to the Ozarks of Missouri. Following de Soto's death and burial in the upper Mississippi 3 years later, his followers returned by boats down the Mississippi, abandoning many of their horses.

One year following de Soto's landing in what is now Florida, in 1540, another Spanish explorer, Coronado, started an expedition with an armed band of horsemen from Mexico, penetrating to a point near the boundary of Kansas and Nebraska.

Beginning about 1600, the Spaniards established a chain of Christian missions among the Indians in the New World. The chain of missions extended from the eastern coast of Mexico up the Rio Grande, thence across the mountains to the Pacific Coast. Each mission brought animals, including horses, from the mother country.

There are two schools of thought relative to the source of the foundation stock of the first horses of the American Indians, and the hardy bands of Mustangs—the feral horses of the Great Plains. Most historians agree that both groups were descended from animals of Spanish (Arabian) extraction. However, some contend that their foundation stock came from the abandoned and stray horses of the expeditions of de Soto and Coronado, whereas others claim that they were obtained chiefly from Santa Fe, an ancient Spanish mission founded in 1606. It is noteworthy that Santa Fe and other early Spanish missions were the source of the Spanish Longhorn cattle, thus lending credence to the theory that the missions were the source of foundation horses for the Indians and the wild bands of Mustangs.

Much romance and adventure is connected with the Mustang, and each band of wild horses was credited with leadership by the most wonderful stallion ever beheld by humans. Many were captured, but the leaders were always alleged to have escaped by reason of speed, such as not possessed by a domesticated horse. The Mustang multiplied at a prodigious rate. In one high luxuriant bunchgrass region in the state of Washington, wild horses thrived so well that the region became known as "Horse Heaven," a name it bears even today.

The coming of the horse among the Indians increased the strife and wars between the tribes. Following the buffalo on horseback led to greater infringement upon each other's hunting grounds, which had ever been a cause for war. From the time the Indians came into possession of horses until the country was taken over by the white people there was no peace among the tribes.

Later, animals of both light- and draft-horse breeding were introduced from Europe by the colonists. For many years, however, sturdy oxen continued to draw the plows for turning the sod on many a rugged New England hillside. Horses were largely used as pack animals, for riding, and later for pulling wagons and stagecoaches. It was not until about 1840 that the buggy first made its appearance.

Six mares and two stallions were brought to Jamestown in 1609, these being the first European importations. Some of these animals may have been eaten during the period of near starvation at Jamestown, but importations continued; and it was reported in 1611 that a total of 17 horses had been brought to this colony.

The horse seems to have been much neglected in early New England, as compared with cattle and sheep. This is not surprising, inasmuch as oxen were universally used for draft purposes. Roads were few in number; speed was not essential; and the horse

Fig 1-13. A covered wagon, drawn by horses. This was a common method of transportation in this country prior to the advent of the railroad and the motor vehicle. (Photo by Ewing Galloway, New York, NY)

had no meat value like that of cattle. Because of the great difficulty in herding horses on the commons, they were usually hobbled. Despite the limited early-day use of the horse, the colonists must have loved them, because, very early, the indiscriminate running of stallions among the mares upon the commons was recognized as undesirable. Massachusetts, before 1700, excluded from town commons all stallions "under 14 hands high and not of comely proportion."[11]

Even before horses found much use in New England, they became valuable for export purposes to the West Indies for work in the sugar mills. In fact, this business became so lucrative that horse stealing became a common offense in New England in the 18th Century. Confiscation of property, public whippings, and banishment from the colony constituted the common punishments for a horse thief.

As plantations materialized in Virginia, the need for easy-riding saddle horses developed, so that the owners might survey their broad estates. Racing also became a popular sport among the Cavaliers in Virginia, Maryland, and the Carolinas—with the heat races up to four miles being common events. The plantation owners took considerable pride in having animals worthy of wearing their colors. So great was the desire to win that by 1730 the importation of English racehorses began.

George Washington maintained an extensive horse- and mule-breeding establishment at Mount Vernon. The President was also an ardent race fan, and riding to hounds was a favorite sport with him. As soon as Washington's views on the subject of mules became known abroad, he received some valuable breeding

---

[11]Thompson, J. W., *History of Livestock Raising in the United States, 1607-1860*, Agricultural History Series No. 5, USDA, Nov. 1942.

stock through gifts. In 1787, the Marquis de Lafayette presented him with a jack and some jennets of the Maltese breed. The jack, named Knight of Malta, was described as a superb animal, of black color, with the form of a stag and the ferocity of a tiger. In 1795, the King of Spain gave Washington a jack and two jennets that were selected from the royal stud at Madrid. The Spanish jack, known as Royal Gift, was 16 hands high, of a gray color, heavily made, and of a sluggish disposition. It was said that Washington was able to combine the best qualities of the two gift jacks, especially through one of the descendants named Compound. General Washington was the first to produce mules of quality in this country, and soon the fame of these hardy hybrids spread throughout the South.

The Dutch, Puritan, and Quaker colonists to the north adhered strictly to agricultural pursuits, frowning upon horse racing. They imported heavier types of horses. In Pennsylvania, under the guidance of William Penn, the farmers prospered. Soon their horses began to improve, even as the appearance and fertility of their farms had done. Eventually, their large horses were hitched to enormous wagons and used to transport freight overland to and from river flatboats and barges along the Ohio, Cumberland, Tennessee, and Mississippi rivers. Both horses and wagons were given the name *Conestoga*, after the Conestoga Valley, a German settlement in Pennsylvania. The Conestoga wagon[12] was the forerunner of the prairie schooner, and before the advent of the railroad it was the freight vehicle of the time. It was usually drawn by a team of six magnificent Conestoga horses, which were well groomed and expensively harnessed. At one time, the Conestoga horses bid to become a new breed—a truly American creation. However, the railroads replaced them, eventually driving them into permanent oblivion. Other breeds were developed later, but this is another story.

■ **Protection of wild horses and burros**—There were approximately two million wild horses roaming the U.S. western rangelands from 1800 to 1900. By 1971, wild horses and burros had almost been hunted to extinction. At this point and period of time, the plight of the wild horses and burros caught the attention of Velma Johnson, affectionately known as "Wild Horse

---

[12]It is noteworthy that the American custom of driving to the right of the road, instead of to the left as is the practice in most of the world, is said to have originated among the Conestoga wagon drivers of the 1750s. The drivers of these 4- and 6-horse teams either sat on the left wheel horse or on the left side of the seat, the better to wield their whip hand (the right hand) over the other horses in the team. Also, when two Conestoga drivers met, they pulled over to the right so that, sitting on the left wheel horse or on the left side of the seat, they could see that the left wheels of their wagons cleared each other. Lighter vehicles naturally followed the tracks of the big Conestoga wagons.

Fig. 1-14. Conestoga freight wagon drawn by six Conestoga horses, in front of a country inn. These improved horses and large wagons were both given the name Conestoga, after the Conestoga Valley, a German settlement in Pennsylvania. The advent of the railroads drove the Conestoga horses into oblivion, and the Conestoga wagon was succeeded by the prairie schooner. (Courtesy, The Bettmann Archive)

Annie," the first president of the International Society for the Protection of Mustangs and Burros (ISPMB), who was instrumental in her 30-year campaign to save wild horses and burros from eradication in the United States by promoting the passage of a federal law known as PL92-195, The Wild Free-Roaming Horse and Burro Act. Today, the Bureau of Land Management is mandated by law to protect America's wild horses and burros. The following registry gives recognition to America's wild horses and burros that have been removed from federal lands: International Society for the Protection of Mustangs and Burros, 6212 E. Sweetwater Avenue, Scottsdale, AZ 85254.

PONY EXPRESS

The Pony Express was a mail service, operated as a private venture under contract, which carried U.S. mail on horseback from St. Joseph, Missouri to Placerville, California, in the days before railways or telegraph. It was started in 1861, and it had a brief existence of but 18 months before it was supplanted by a telegraph line. The riders' steeds were, of course, not ponies but fleet horses. The horses were stationed at points 10 to 15 miles apart, and each rider rode 1 to 7 animals successively, covering about 75 miles before passing the pouch to his successor. There were 80 riders, some 420 horses, and 190 relay stations. Riders were paid $25 per week.

The fastest trip ever made was in 7 days and 17 hours, when Lincoln's first inaugural address was carried to the West Coast. But the normal schedule was

Fig. 1-15. The statue of the Pony Express which stands in the St. Joseph, Missouri, Civic Center. It was erected in 1940, when the Postal Department honored the riders of the Pony Express with a commemorative postage stamp. (Courtesy, St. Joseph Museum, St. Joseph, MO)

8 days, which was about 24 days faster than the schedule of Butterfield's Overland Stage line on the southern route. The maintenance of this schedule through the wilderness, often in blinding snows and howling storms and in the face of Indian dangers, won for the service a fame that has not diminished with the passing of time.

The Pony Express lost money. The average charge for sending a letter during the period was $3, but it cost about $16 per letter to operate the service; thus, the private venture lost $13 per letter, and it is estimated that the Pony Express cost its backers $390,000.

Despite its short life, the Pony Express was credited with many important contributions, not the least of which was its help in keeping East and West joined together during the early crucial days of the Civil War. A 7,200-lb. life-size bronze statue of a Pony Express rider and his mount stands in St. Joseph's Civic Center in Missouri. It was unveiled on April 20, 1940, when the Postal Department honored the riders of the Pony Express with a commemorative postage stamp.

THE STORY OF HORSES AND MULES IN WORLD WAR II; THE REMOUNT SERVICE

Once the bulwark of armies—its numbers often deciding the issue of conflict—the horse in World War II was practically jeeped, tanked, and trucked out of his long-held place of importance in military history. Despite the unparalleled mechanization, however, horses played an indispensable role on many fronts during the great struggle for freedom. It is an old cavalry axiom that a horse can go wherever people can travel, a feat which even the Army's famous little jeep could not accomplish.

The use of horses in World War II reached its greatest proportion in the Russian Army. Long famous for its Cossacks and centuries of cavalry tradition, Russia had, in 1940, about 200,000 horses in cavalry and 800,000 more in artillery, draft, and pack. It is also estimated that the U.S.S.R. had two mounted armies available for combat. The Russian cavalry is credited with playing a decisive role in the defense of both Moscow and Stalingrad—striking swift, devastating blows, then quickly withdrawing and melting into the forests and countryside. The full story of the role played by the Russian Cossacks may never be known.

Germany and Japan also recognized the place of the horse in modern warfare. According to the most reliable sources available, the Germans at one time had 50,000 horses for cavalry use and approximately 910,000 draft and pack animals. The Japanese—constantly building up their horse units in China, where large areas were prohibitive to motor vehicles—probably had a cavalry force of 50,000 horses with an additional 300,000 in use for draft and pack purposes.

The U.S. Army had relatively few horses during World War II—only about 25,000 for cavalry use and 12,000 for draft and pack—but these units performed magnificently in combat. The 26th Cavalry fought a brilliant delaying action on Luzon; and both horses and mules were used in the Burma and Italian campaigns, which were conducted through jungles and over mountains where no vehicle of any sort could go.

On the civilian front, the contribution of horses and mules, though less spectacular than on the field of battle, were nonetheless substantial. Though statistics show a continued gradual but steady decline in horse and mule numbers throughout the war years, perhaps figures alone do not tell the true story. With the rationing of critical rubber and gasoline, the diverting of iron and steel to war production, and the consequent shortage of equipment—all resulting in a scarcity of mechanized power—there is little doubt that the horses and mules on farms in the United States were utilized to the maximum to help carry the major load of farm production.

The Remount Service, which was established by Act of Congress in 1921, was transferred to the U.S. Department of Agriculture on July 1, 1948, following which the program was liquidated. At the time of the transfer, approximately 700 remount stallions were in service throughout the country.

In summary, it may be said that the relentless wheels of progress took away from horses their role in both agriculture and war. But horses are rising to a more happy position in contributing to the fields of recreation and sport.

SELECTED REFERENCES

Title of Publication	Author(s)	Publisher
Animals and Men	H. Dembeck	The American Museum of Natural History, The Natural History Press, Garden City, NY, 1965
Appaloosa: The Spotted Horse in Art and History	F. Haines	University of Texas Press, Austin, TX, 1963
Asiatic Wild Horse, The	E. Mohr trans. by D. M. Goodall	J. A. Allen & Co. Ltd., London, England, 1971
Encyclopaedia Britannica		Encylopaedia Britannica, Inc., Chicago, IL
Evolution of the Horse	W. D. Matthew S. H. Chubb	American Museum of Natural History, New York, NY, 1921
First Horsemen, The	F. Trippett	Time-Life Books, New York, NY, 1974
History of Domesticated Animals, A	F. E. Zuener	Harper & Row, Publishers, Inc., Great Britain, 1963
History of Thoroughbred Racing in America	W. H. Robertson	Prentice-Hall, Inc., Englewood Cliffs, NJ, 1965
Horse, The, through fifty centuries of civilization	A. Dent	Phaidon Press Limited, London, England, 1974
Horses	G. G. Simpson	Oxford University Press, New York, NY, 1951
Horses in America	F. Haines	Thomas Y. Crowell Company, New York, NY, 1971
Horses and Americans	P. D. Strong	Frederick A. Stokes Company, New York, NY, 1939
Horses and Horsemanship Through the Ages	L. Gianoli	Crown Publishers, Inc., New York, NY, 1969
Horses of Today	H. H. Reese	Wood & Jones, Pasadena, CA, 1956
Horse Today—and Tomorrow, The?	K. Jeschko H. Lange	Arco Publishing Company, Inc., New York, NY, 1972
Kinships of Animals and Man	E. Adams	McGraw-Hill Book Company, Inc., New York, NY, 1955
Natural History of the Horse, The	J. Clabby	Weidenfeld and Nicolson, London, England, 1976
Our Friendly Animals and Whence They Came	K. P. Schmidt	M. A. Donohue & Co., Chicago, IL, 1938
Principles of Classification and a Classification of Mammals, The, Vol. 85	G. G. Simpson	American Museum of Natural History, New York, NY, 1945
Wild Horse of the West, The	W. D. Wyman	University of Nebraska Press, Lincoln, NE, 1945

The author of this book was the first American to see this artifact after it was unearthed and placed on exhibit, at which time the Chinese labeled it as the "Galloping Horse of Kanzu." Dr. Ensminger corrected the gait for the Chinese—pointing out that the flying horse is *racking* (single footing). A rack is a fast, flashy, four-beat gait in which each foot meets the ground separately, at equal intervals. This was among the artifacts found in a tomb of the late Eastern Han Dynasty, 25 AD to 220 AD. (Photo by Audrey Ensminger)

2

DISTRIBUTION, ADAPTATION, AND THE FUTURE OF THE HORSE INDUSTRY

For the most part, the future of the horse is in the fields of recreation and sport and as the cow pony of the West. This shows former President Ronald Reagan of the United States and King Hassan II of Morocco on horseback in Virginia. (Courtesy, Michael Evans, The White House, Washington, DC)

Since prehistoric times, there has been nearly worldwide distribution of horses. Moreover, effective use of horses has constantly progressed, especially from the standpoint of improvement in the equipment to which they were attached for the purpose of drawing loads.

After horses were domesticated and no longer hunted down and killed for meat, they were used to carry riders and support goods upon their strong backs. In an effort to provide transportation for a longer load than could be fastened directly to the back of the horse, an ingenious person devised a basketlike arrangement which was fitted between two long poles. One end of these poles rested on the back of the horse and the other end was dragged on the ground to the rear. In an effort to reduce the resistance of this vehicle and permit the carrying of still heavier loads, the poles were supported on a wooden axle and two wheels made of wood, thus inventing a two-wheeled cart. Next, leather harness was developed, transferring the pull from the back of the horse to the better-adapted shoulders. Then, came the four-wheeled, self-supporting vehicle with improved axles made of iron instead of wood; and, finally, steel wheels with pneumatic tires mounted on ball bearings, evolved.

But the passing of the horse as a source of power is recognized. A century ago, muscles provided 94% of the world's energy needs; coal, oil, and waterpower provided the other 6%. Today, the situation is reversed in the developed nations. They now obtain 94% of their energy needs from coal, oil, natural gas, and waterpower, and only 6% from the muscle power of people and animals.

WORLD DISTRIBUTION OF HORSES AND MULES

At a very early date and throughout the world, the versatility and adaptation of horses were recognized. They were unexcelled in carrying riders comfortably and swiftly on long journeys; they possessed a long life of usefulness; and, above all, they were intelligent. Despite all these virtues, in some areas horses have been unable to replace patient "roughage-burning" oxen and water buffalo. To this day, oxen are still the main source of power on farms in such densely populated countries as India, Pakistan, and China, in many Near Eastern and African countries, and in some countries in Latin America; and water buffalo are the main source of power in rice-producing areas, because of their ability to work in muddy paddy fields. In the more isolated portions of the New England states, oxen are occasionally used, and stoneboat-pulling contests are a great attraction at the New England fairs.

Members of the ass family (mules and donkeys) are distributed in the warmer regions of the world, where they still occupy a rather important place among the animals used for both pack and draft purposes.

Table 2-1 shows the size and density of the horse population of the important horse countries of the world. As noted, world horse numbers totaled 58,158,000 in 1994. The decline in world horse numbers since 1938 can be attributed chiefly to the mechanization of agriculture. For example, the number of tractors in use in agriculture in the world in 1993

totaled 25,703,904 compared with fewer than 2 million in 1939.

Fig. 2-1 shows the 10 leading horse countries of the world in 1994. As noted, by rank they are: China, United States, Mexico, Brazil, Argentina, Ethiopia, Russian Federation, Mongolia, Colombia, and Kazakhstan.

WORLD HORSE NUMBERS

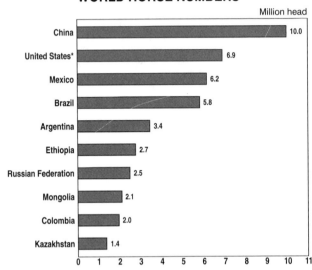

*United States horse numbers are for 1996, and from the American Horse Council News release of December 11, 1996.

Fig. 2-1. Ten leading horse countries of the world, 1994. (Based on data from *FAO Production Yearbook 1994*, The United Nations, Rome, Vol. 48, pp. 187–188.)

TABLE 2-1
LEADING HORSE-PRODUCING COUNTRIES OF THE WORLD

Country	Horses[1]	Human Population[2]	Size of Country		Horses per Capita[3]	Horses per	
	(thousands)	*(thousands)*	*(sq mi.)*	*(sq km)*		*(sq mi.)*	*(sq km)*
China	9,960	1,203,097	3,696,100	*9,609,860*	0.0008	2.7	*1.0*
United States[4]	6,900[4]	263,200[4]	3,787,428	*9,847,313*	0.026	1.82	*0.7*
Mexico	6,191	93,986	756,066	*1,965,772*	0.07	8.2	*3.1*
Brazil	5,800	160,737	3,286,500	*8,544,900*	0.04	1.8	*0.7*
Argentina	3,369	34,293	1,073,518	*2,791,147*	0.09	3.1	*1.2*
Ethiopia	2,750	55,979	437,794	*1,138,264*	0.05	6.3	*2.4*
Russian Federation	2,500	149,909	6,592,800	*17,141,280*	0.02	0.4	*0.1*
Mongolia	2,100	2,494	604,800	*1,572,480*	0.8	3.5	*1.3*
Colombia	2,000	36,200	440,831	*1,146,161*	0.06	4.5	*1.7*
Kazakhstan	1,400	17,377	1,049,200	*2,727,920*	0.08	1.3	*0.5*
World total	58,158	5,734,000	57,900,000	*150,540,000*	0.01	1.0	*0.4*

[1]*FAO Production Yearbook 1994*, The United Natioins, Rome, Vol. 48, pp. 187–188. The horse figures are for 1994.

[2]*The World Almanac and Book of Facts 1996*, pub. by Funk & Wagnalls Corp., Mahwah, NJ.

[3]Horses per capita computed from most recent census figures available.

[4]United States horse numbers from American Horse Council News release of December 11, 1996. United States human population from *Ensminger's World Book*, 1996, page 6.

GROWTH AND DECLINE OF U.S. HORSE AND MULE PRODUCTION

The golden age of the horse extended from the Gay Nineties to the mechanization of agriculture—to the advent of the automobile, truck, and tractor. During this era, everybody loved the horse. The town livery stable, watering trough, and hitching post were trademarks of each town and village. People wept when the horse fell on the icy street, and they jailed people who beat or mistreated horses. The oat bag, carriage, wagon, buggy whip, axle grease, horseshoe, and horseshoe nail industries were thriving and essential parts of the national economy. Every school child knew and respected the village blacksmith.

Fig. 2-3. Horse-drawn covered wagons. This photograph was taken when making the film for the "Covered Wagon," founded on Emerson Hough's novel of the same name. When the news was spread that gold had been discovered in California, the Oregon Trail split in half, one part branching off to the south while the other part turned north toward Oregon. Improved roads and the advent of the motor vehicle have practically eliminated horses from the highways and city streets. (From Ewing Galloway)

Fig. 2-2. Until about 1925, most work was "muscle powered."

Bobtailed Hackneys attached to high-seated rigs made a dashing picture as they pranced down the avenue; they were a mark of social prestige. A few memorable dinner parties of the era were even staged on horseback, with the guests lining up in exclusive restaurants astride their favorite mounts. One of the most notable of these horseback bashes was staged in Louis Sherry's restaurant, corner of Fifth Avenue and 44th Street, New York City, on March 28, 1903, with Cornelius K. G. Billings—racing enthusiast, Chicago utilities heir, and self-styled "American Horse King"—as host (see Fig. 2-4). To publicize his newly opened $200,000 stable at 196th Street and Fort Washington Road (now Fort Tryon Park), Mr. Billings converted the grand ballroom of Sherry's into a woodland paradise by means of $10,000 worth of full-scale scenic props, artificial foliage, potted palms, and a tanbark floor covering—borrowed, at Mr. Sherry's in-

sistence, from the Barnum and Bailey Circus. Thirty-six mystified horses were conveyed up to the ballroom by freight elevators, and the guests—members of the New York Riding Club—attired in white ties and tails, and gingerly astride their favorite mounts, drank and ate to the merriment of music, while their steeds munched oats, and costumed lackeys cleaned up behind them. Miniature tables were attached to the saddle pommels (drive-in style), and apprehensive waiters dressed in riding attire served drink after drink, and course after course, topped off by Jack Horner pies—huge, ornamental concoctions which, when cut open, revealed a covey of nymphs in their birthday suits. Only one guest fell off his horse.

In 1900, the automobile was still the plutocrat's plaything, and the truck and tractor were unknown. Most of the expensive 8,000 cars in the country at the time were either imported or custom-built. Tires cost about $40 each, and lasted only 2,000 miles. Few really loved the auto. Complaints were made of the noise they made; laws were enacted against their going through the city parks; and people split their sides with laughter when autos had to be pushed uphill or got stuck in the mud.

Then, in 1908, Henry Ford produced a car to sell at $825. The truck, the tractor, and improved highways followed closely in period of time. Horses did not know it at the time, but their days were numbered. As shown in Fig. 2-5 and Table 2-2, the passing of the horse age

Fig. 2-4. Horseback dinner in Louis Sherry's restaurant in New York City, hosted by Cornelius K. G. Billings, 1903. (Photo by Byron, The Byron Collection, Museum of the City of New York)

and the coming of the machine age went hand in hand; as tractor and truck numbers increased, horse and mule numbers declined.

The number of horses in the United States increased up to 1915, at which time there was a record number of 21,431,000 head (horses only; not including mules). Horse population expanded with the growth and development of farms.

Mules on farms slowly but steadily increased in numbers for 10 years after horses began their decline, reaching a peak in 1925 at 5,680,897 head. Mule numbers decreased proportionately less rapidly than horses because of their great use in the deep South where labor was cheaper and more abundant and the farms smaller in size.

In 1915—the peak year, there were 26,493,000 horses and mules, combined, on farms and ranches in the United States and an additional 2,000,000 head in cities. By January 1, 1960, the census showed that there were only 3,089,000 head of horses and mules on the nation's farms and ranches (not counting suburban owned horses and those kept on parcels under 10 acres in size)—the lowest number ever recorded.

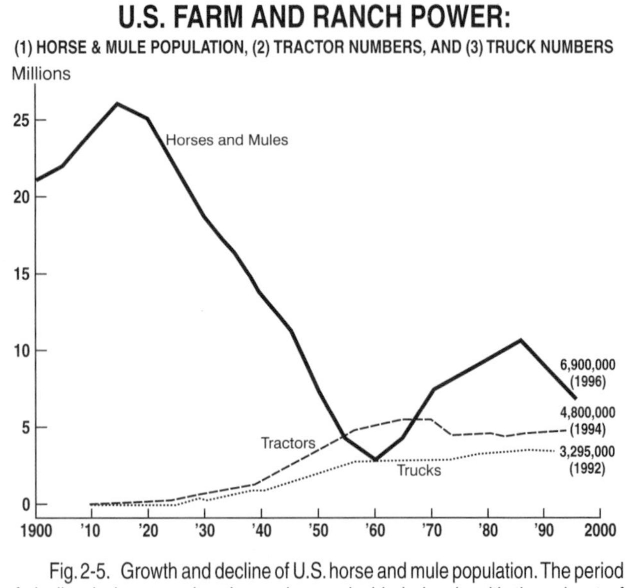

U.S. FARM AND RANCH POWER:
(1) HORSE & MULE POPULATION, (2) TRACTOR NUMBERS, AND (3) TRUCK NUMBERS

Fig. 2-5. Growth and decline of U.S. horse and mule population. The period of decline in horse and mule numbers coincided closely with the advent of mechanized power, especially the tractor and truck. (Source: USDA)

TABLE 2-2
U.S. FARM AND RANCH (1) HORSE AND MULE POPULATION,
(2) TRACTOR NUMBERS, AND (3) TRUCK NUMBERS,
FROM 1900 TO 1996

Year	Horses and Mules[1]	Number of Tractors (including garden)[2]	Number of Trucks[3]
1900	21,531,635	—	—
1905	22,077,000	—	—
1910	24,042,882	1,000	0
1915	26,493,000	25,000	25,000
1920	25,199,552	246,083	139,169
1925	22,081,520	503,933	459,000
1930	18,885,856	920,021	900,385
1935	16,676,000	1,048,000	890,000
1940	13,931,531	1,567,430	1,047,084
1945	11,629,000	2,422,000	1,490,000
1950	7,604,000	3,610,000	2,207,000
1955	4,309,000	4,692,000	2,701,000
1960	3,089,000	5,138,000	3,110,000
1965	4,580,000	5,486,000	3,030,000
1970	7,668,000	5,424,000	2,984,000
1975	8,568,000	4,469,000	3,032,000
1980	9,663,000	4,752,000	3,344,000
1985	10,581,000	4,676,000	3,380,000
1990	5,267,000	4,749,000	3,437,000[4]
1994		4,800,000	3,295,000[5]
1996	6,900,000		

[1]From 1900 to 1960, USDA sources; from 1960 to 1990, *FAO Production Yearbooks*, United Nations; 1996 from American Horse Council news release December 11, 1996.

[2]From 1910 to 1985, USDA sources; 1990 and 1994, *FAO Production Yearbooks*, United Nations.

[3]1910 to 1985 from USDA sources.

[4]For year 1987, *Agricultural Statistics 1995–96*, Table 535.

[5]For year 1992, *Agricultural Statistics 1995–96*, Table 535.

Ironical as it may seem, the development of manufacturing and commerce was responsible for both the rise and fall of the horse and mule industry of the United States. The early growth of American industry created a large need for horses to transport the raw and manufactured goods and to produce needed agricultural products for those who lived in the cities and villages. With further scientific developments—especially the invention of the tractor and truck—the horse was replaced, first ever so slowly, but then rapidly and drastically.

Today, very few horses are found on city streets. The old-time livery stable has long since passed out of existence; draft horses are seldom hitched to dray wagons; and horses hitched to a delivery wagon or to a plow are almost a novelty.

Draft horses and mules were the victims of mecha-nization—farming changed. But light horses came up fast in the fields of recreation and sport.

The two leading states in horse numbers, by rank, are: Texas and California.

PRESENT STATUS OF THE U.S. HORSE INDUSTRY

The unique thing about the horse business, not found in any other industry, is the human values back of it. It's a people's business, and a way of life for many.

Also, the U.S. horse industry is big and important business. The following facts and figures attest to the magnitude of the industry.[1]

■ There are 6.9 million horses in the United States, over 70% of which are involved in showing or recreation.

■ The horse industry produces goods and services valued at $25.3 billion. Thus, it is about the same size as such major industries as the apparel manufacturing industry and the motion picture industry, in terms of the value of goods and services produced.

■ The industry has a $112.1 billion impact on the U.S. economy when the multiplier effect of spending by industry suppliers and employees is taken into account.

■ 7.1 million people are involved in the industry as horse owners, service providers, employees, and volunteers. Many more participate as spectators.

■ The industry provides directly 338,500 full-time equivalent jobs. Spending by suppliers and employees generates additional jobs, for a total employment impact of approximately 1.4 million full-time equivalent jobs.

■ The median income of horse-owning families is around $60,000. Horse ownership is broad-based among income classes with 38% of the owners under $50,000 of income and 21% over $100,000.

■ The horse industry pays approximately $1.9 billion in taxes to all levels of government.

(Also see Chapter 19, section headed "Impact of the U.S. Horse Industry" for additional facts and figures.)

[1]From American Horse Council news release December 11, 1996. The study was commissioned by the American Horse Council Foundation with major funding support from the Jockey Club, the American Quarter Horse Association, Breeders Cup Limited, and the Kentucky Thoroughbred Association.

Fig. 2-6. UF Fasitraz, winner of the Arabian English Pleasure class at the U.S. Nationals, ridden by Sara Jane Skone, and owned by Brian Skone of Grantville, Georgia. (Courtesy, Arabian Horse Registry of America, Inc., Westminster, CO)

Fig. 2-7. A field of pacers rounds the turn at the Red Mile in Lexington, Kentucky. (Courtesy, The United States Trotting Assn., Columbus, OH)

Despite the magnitude of the industry, U.S. horse owners suffer appalling losses. They are—

1. Spending millions of dollars on needless concoctions, and many caretakers are using unbalanced and deficient rations.

2. Producing only a 50% foal crop, which means that they are keeping two mares a whole year to produce one foal.

3. Keeping too many stallions for producing too few foals.

4. Maintaining horse breeding establishments that return little or nothing on investment.

5. Retiring an appalling number of horses from tracks, shows, and other uses due to unsoundnesses.

6. Losing through inefficiency and deaths millions of dollars due to diseases and parasites.

Such wanton losses prompt the question: If the horse industry is so good, why not better?

Fig. 2-8. An attractive horse farm. (Courtesy, Kentucky Department of Public Information, Frankfort, KY)

FUTURE OF THE HORSE INDUSTRY

This generation has more money to spend and more leisure time in which to spend it than any population in history. A shorter workweek, increased automation, and the continued recreation and sports surge, with emphasis on physical fitness and the out-of-doors, will require more horses.

It is expected that the estimated 500,000 horses in the 17 western range states will continue to hold their own. Even the Jeep is not sufficiently versatile for use in roping a steer on the range. It is reasonable to assume, therefore, that the cow pony will continue to furnish needed assistance to ranchers in the West.

Horse racing will continue to be a popular spectator sport, although there will be increased competition for the recreation and sports dollar in the years ahead.

In the final analysis, the dominant factors that will determine the future of the horse industry are (1) the need for the cow pony, and (2) the use of horses for recreation and sport.

Horse production will, in common with most businesses, encounter increasing competition in the years ahead. Competition will be keen for land, labor, and capital, as well as from other sports.

Skilled management and production programs geared to produce horses that meet more exacting market demands will be the two essential ingredients for success. Also, it will require greater skill and understanding of fundamental relationships to take care of highly bred, sensitive animals in forced production.

Never has there been so much reason to have confidence in, and to be optimistic about, the future. The years ahead will be the most rewarding in the history of the horse industry.

Fig. 2-9. Count The Spots, Paint Horse, winner of the National Cutting Horse Association (NCHA) National Championship. (Courtesy, American Paint Horse Assn., Ft. Worth, TX)

HORSE RESEARCH

The Age of Research was ushered in with World War II. Now we are in the biotechnology age, and all industry, big and little—including the horse business—must be geared to it. Other animal industries have long been cognizant of new frontiers possible through research. But horse research has lagged, with the result that we have just begun to apply science, automation, and technology to light horses.

Fig. 2-10. Horses will continue to be used for recreation and sport. This shows an Appaloosa jumper in action and well ridden. (Courtesy, *Appaloosa Journal*, Moscow, ID)

There is every reason to believe that today's research will be reflected in a host of tomorrow's advances—that many of today's horse problems will be solved through research. Indeed, horse research should be expanded. More specifically, and among other things, we need to know the following in the horse business:

1. We need to know how to modernize rations and effect savings in costs; we need to eliminate needless concoctions and unbalanced and deficient rations.

2. We need to know how to rectify appalling and costly sterility and reproductive failures; we need to produce more than a 50% foal crop.

3. We need to know how to bring mares in heat at will.

4. We need to improve the technology (a) for freezing and storing stallion semen, and (b) for freezing, transporting, and transplanting equine embryos.

5. We need to know more about the relationship between soil fertility, plant nutrients, and horses.

6. We need to know how to provide laborsaving buildings and equipment—how to automate the horse business. Seventy-five percent of horse work is still hand labor, one-third of which could be eliminated by mechanization and modernization.

7. We need to know how to improve upon the control of diseases and parasites.

8. We need to know how to increase the durability and useful life of a horse—in racing, in showing, and in breeding; we need to lessen the appalling number of horses that are retired from tracks, shows, and other uses due to unsoundnesses.

9. We need to know how to make a fair return on capital invested in horse breeding establishments.

We must remember, however, (1) that horse research is both slow and costly, and (2) that other industries have long liberally supported research costs with no assistance from the taxpayer, simply including them as a normal part of their operating costs. In addition to individual owners contributing to the support of research programs, the time has arrived when racehorse owners should review where racing dollars go. Perhaps a liberal proportion of racing revenue which now goes into the treasuries of states having pari-mutuel betting should be earmarked for horse research, teaching, and extension. Otherwise, there is grave danger of starving "the goose that laid the golden egg."

Finally, it should be emphasized that research can make the information available, but it is still up to each individual to secure and apply the results. "You can lead a horse to water, but you can't make him drink." Nevertheless, in the years ahead equestrians will not be able to cling to horse-and-buggy methods while the rest of industry forges ahead. For sheer survival, they must use science and technology.

SELECTED REFERENCES

Title of Publication	Author(s)	Publisher
Agricultural Statistics		U.S. Department of Agriculture, Washington, DC, annual
American Horse Industry Handbook	Staff	American Horse Council, Washington, DC, 1993
Breeding and Raising Horses, Ag. Hdbk. No. 394	M. E. Ensminger	U.S. Department of Agriculture, Washington, DC, 1972
"Changes in Horse Numbers as Related to Farm Mechanization, Recreation, and Sport"	B. G. Stark	Thesis, Washington State University, Pullman, WA, 1960
Economic Impact of the U.S. Horse Industry, The		The American Horse Council, Washington, DC, 1987
FAO Yearbook		Food and Agriculture Organization of the United Nations, Rome, Italy, annual
Horse Industry Directory	Staff	American Horse Council, Washington, DC, 1996
Horsemanship and Horse Care, Ag. Info. Bull. No. 353	M. E. Ensminger	U.S. Department of Agriculture, Washington, DC, 1972
Horses in America	F. Haines	Thomas Y. Crowell Company, New York, NY, 1971
Light Horses, Farmers, Bull. No. 2127	M. E. Ensminger	U.S. Department of Agriculture, Washington, DC, 1965
Power to Produce: Yearbook of Agriculture, 1960		U.S. Department of Agriculture, Washington, DC, 1960
Statistical Abstracts of the United States		U.S. Department of Commerce, Bureau of the Census, Washington, DC, annual
World Almanac and Book of Facts		Funk & Wagnalls Corp., Mahwah, NJ

FUNCTIONAL ANATOMY OF THE HORSE

Anatomically, horses are well adapted to carrying riders and supporting heavy loads upon their strong backs. This shows Fjord Horses being used as packhorses in the rugged mountains of Montana. (Courtesy, Jane Exon-Equine Photography, Laramie, WY)

Anatomically, horses are well adapted to pulling heavy loads from their shoulders. This shows a Fjord Horse pulling a heavy load. (Courtesy, Pam McWethy, Norwegian Fjord Horse Registry, Acworth, NJ)

The anatomy of the horse is adapted to two primary functions or uses: (1) to carrying riders and supporting packs upon their strong backs, and (2) to pulling heavy loads from their shoulders.

This chapter is for the purpose of relating the structure of the horse to the desired functions and usefulness. Broadly speaking, one type of animal is required for slow, heavy, draft purposes, and quite another for recreation and sport. This is really the distinction between draft and light horse breeds. However, further and very fundamental differences in structure fit the respective types and breeds for more specific purposes. Thus, the Thoroughbred running horse possesses certain hereditary structural characteristics which better fit it for speed and endurance than for usage as a five-gaited saddle horse. For the same reason, hunters are seldom obtained from among American Saddle Horses. In general, these structural differences between different types of horses are as marked as the fundamental differences between human weight lifters and 10-second runners. Yet, it must be pointed out that, regardless of the usage to which the animal is put, equestrians universally emphasize the importance of good heads and necks, short couplings, strong loins, and good feet and legs.

Fig. 3-1. The legendary Thoroughbred stallion, Secretariat, demonstrating the functional anatomy that made him a Triple Crown winner. (Courtesy, Dell Hancock Photography, Claiborne Farm, Paris, KY)

SKELETON OF THE HORSE

The skeleton of the horse consists of 205 bones, as follows:

Vertebral column 54
Ribs 36
Sternum 1
Skull (including auditory ossicles) 34
Thoracic limbs 40
Pelvic limbs 40
    Total 205

VERTEBRAL COLUMN

The vertebral column consists of an average of 18 coccygeal (tail) vertebrae. In addition, the vertebral column consists of 7 cervical (neck) vertebrae, 18 dorsal (back), 6 lumbar (loin), and 5 sacral (croup) vertebrae.

In horses of the correct conformation, the lower line of the dorsal vertebrae (commonly referred to as the backbone) is arched slightly upward. The degree to which the backbone is arched in different horses varies greatly. If the arch is extreme, the animal is referred to as "roach backed"; whereas if the backbone

sags very markedly, the animal is known as "sway-backed." Either of these conditions represents a weakness in conformation and is objectionable.

Desired height at the withers and proper topline are obtained through variation in the length of the spinous processes which project upward from the vertebrae. Thus, the structure at this point is of especial importance in the saddle horse, determining the desirability of the seat.

There is a close correlation between the length of the individual vertebrae and the length of the component parts of the entire animal. Thus, an animal with long vertebrae has a long neck, back, loin, croup, and tail. Within limits, length is desired. For example, the longer neck on a saddle horse gives the desired effect of "much horse in front of the rider." On the other hand, a very long back and loin are objectionable, denoting lack of strength. Apparent length of back may be alleviated by having a sloping shoulder, with the upper end joining the back at the rear part of the withers.

RIBS

There are usually 18 pairs of ribs in the horse, but a nineteenth rib on one side or both is not at all rare. Eight pairs are known as true ribs, joining the

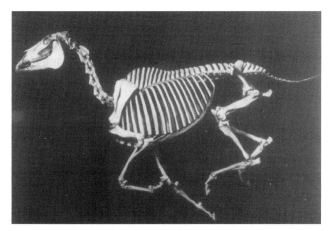

Fig. 3-2. Skeleton of the famous American racehorse Sysonby, showing action at the run. This illustration shows how the bones act as levers as (1) the hind legs are drawn up beneath the body, then moved forward preparatory to straightening out and propelling the horse forward with a long stride typical of great running horses, and (2) the front legs sustain a tremendous jar as the horse lands. The run is a four-beat gait where the feet strike the ground separately; first one hind foot, then the other hind foot, then the front foot on the same side as the first hind foot, then the other front foot which decides the lead. (Courtesy, The American Museum of Natural History, New York, NY)

Fig. 3-3. Skeleton of horse and human. It can be seen that (1) the knee joint in the horse is the counterpart of the wrist joint in the human; (2) the stifle joint in the horse is the counterpart of the knee joint in the human; and (3) the hock joint in the horse is the counterpart of the ankle joint in the human. (Courtesy, The American Museum of Natural History, New York, NY)

segments of the sternum or breastbone; whereas the remaining 10 pairs are floating, merely overlapping and being attached to one another. The seventh and eighth ribs are longest, with the back ribs much shorter.

A capacious chest and middle, which is desirable in all horses, is obtained through long, well-sprung ribs. Such a structural condition allows for more room for the vital internal organs, and experienced horse handlers know that such horses eat better and stand up under more hard work.

STERNUM

The sternum or breastbone of the horse is composed of eight segments, the whole of which is shaped somewhat like a canoe. There are indentures in the sides for the reception of the cartilages extending from the ribs.

SKULL

The skull encloses the brain and the most important organs of sense. It consists of 34 bones, mostly flat, which yield and overlap at points of union at the time of birth, thus making for greater ease of parturition.

The size of the head should be proportionate to the size of the horse, and the shape true to the characteristics of the breed or type represented. Thus, the Thoroughbred possesses a broad forehead, with the face gradually tapering from the forehead to the muzzle, giving the animal an intelligent and alert expression.

The lower jaw should always be strong and well defined, with good width between the branches so as not to compress the larynx when the neck is flexed.

The mature male horse has 40 teeth, and the female 36. Animals of each sex possess 24 molars or grinders and 12 incisors or front teeth. In addition, the male has 4 tushes or pointed teeth, and sometimes these occur in females.

The young animal, whether male or female, has 24 temporary or milk teeth. These include 12 incisors and 12 molars.

THORACIC LIMBS

This includes all the bones of the foreleg; namely, the scapula, humerus, radius and ulna, 7 or 8 carpal bones, cannon bone and 2 splint bones, 2 sesamoid bones, large pastern bone, small pastern bone, navicular bone, and coffin bone. The correctness of these bones determines the action and consequent usefulness and value of the animal. Since the front feet maintain about 60% of the horse's weight and are subject to great concussion, they should receive careful attention.

The scapula, humerus, radius, and ulna are enclosed in heavy muscles which move them; whereas the parts of the leg below the knee are motivated by long tendons.

The carpal bones collectively comprise the knee of the horse, which corresponds to the wrist in humans. The knee should be broad, deep, straight, clean-cut, strongly supported, and free from soft fluctuating swellings. The cannons should be wide, flat, and clean with large, sharply defined, cordlike tendons.

The degree of slope of the pasterns is closely associated with that of the shoulders, and moderate slope (about 45°) to these parts of the anatomy—the scapula and large and small pastern bones—is desirable. Oblique shoulders and pasterns aid in producing elastic springy action and absorb concussions or jars much better than short, straight pasterns and straight shoulders—thereby lessening the possibility of an unsoundness.

The set to the front legs should also be true. When viewed from the front, a vertical line dropped from the point of the shoulder should fall upon the center of the knee, cannon, pastern, and foot. When viewed from the side, a vertical line dropped from the center of the elbow joint should fall upon the center of the knee and fetlock and strike the ground just back of the hoof.

PELVIC LIMBS

The pelvic limbs, embracing 40 bones, are the horse's chief means of propulsion forward. The stifle and hock joints will be discussed separately under this heading.

The stifle joint of the horse corresponds to the knee in the human. Excepting for an occasional dislocation of the patella (a condition known as stifled), this joint is not subject to much trouble.

The hock is the most important single joint of the horse, probably being the seat of more serious unsoundnesses than any other part of the body—among them bone spavins, bog spavins, curbs, and thoroughpins. The hock should be wide, deep, flat, clean, hard, strong, well supported, and correctly set with prominent points.

The rear pasterns should be similar to the front ones, although they may be slightly less sloping (a 50° angle being satisfactory for the hind foot).

The set to the hind legs should be such that, when viewed from the rear, a vertical line dropped from the point of the buttock will fall upon the center of the hock, cannon, and foot. When viewed from the side, this vertical line should touch the point of the hock and run parallel with the back of the cannon.

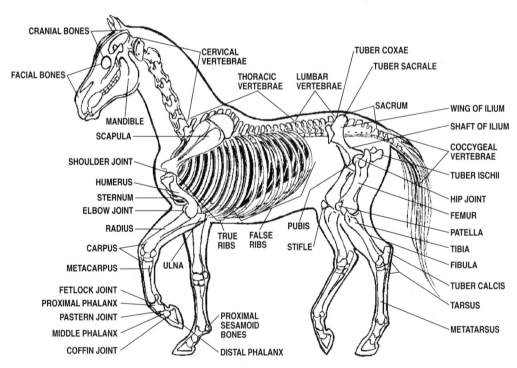

Fig. 3-4. Skeleton of horse.

ANATOMY OF THE FOOT

When it is realized that the horse has been transplanted from its natural roving environment and soft, mother-earth footing to carrying and drawing loads over hard, dry-surfaced topography by day and then stabled on hard, dry floors at night, it is not surprising that foot troubles are commonplace. Nor are these troubles new. The Greeks alluded to them in the age-old axiom, "No foot, no horse."

In order to lessen foot troubles, and to permit intelligent shoeing, knowledge of the anatomy of a horse's foot, pasterns, and legs is necessary.

PARTS OF THE FOOT

Table 3-1 gives pertinent facts about each part of the foot, whereas Fig. 3-5 illustrates the parts.

TABLE 3-1
PARTS OF THE HOOF

The Parts	Description	Functions	Comments
The four major parts:			
Bones	They are: Long pastern bone Short pastern bone Coffin bone Navicular bone	Provide framework of the foot and facilitate locomotion.	Long pastern bone lies entirely above the hoof. Only lower end of short pastern bone is within hoof.
Elastic structure	Consists of: Lateral cartilages Plantar cushion	Overcomes concussion or jar when the foot strikes the ground.	Normally, heel expands about 1/16 in. on each side of foot.
Sensitive structure, called the corium or pododerm	Consists of: Coronary band Perioplic ring Sensitive laminae Sensitive sole Sensitive frog	Furnishes nutrition to corresponding part of hoof.	All 5 parts are highly sensitive and vascular.
Horny wall	The outer horny covering	Encloses and protects the sensitive parts beneath.	
The exterior of the hoof:			
Horny wall	The basic shell and wearing surface of the foot.	Protects: there is no feeling in the wall of the foot until the area of the coronary band is reached.	The horny wall extends vertically from the edge of the hair around the front and sides of the foot, then turns in upon itself at the heel, forming the bar which extends forward toward the center.
Perioplic ring	The seat where periople is produced.	Produces periople, the varnishlike substance that covers the outer surface of the wall and seals it from excess drying.	The wall of a normal foot consists of about 1/4 water, by weight.
White line	The juncture of the wall and horny sole. It is about 1/8 in. wide.	Serves as the farrier's "red light," beyond (toward the inside of the foot) which nails should not go.	A nail past the white line may either enter the sensitive structure or produce pressure, with resulting lameness.
Horny frog	The V-shaped pad in the middle of the sole.	Compresses under weight, and transmits pressure to the elastic structures. Aids blood circulation, absorbs concussion, and prevents slippage.	Without this normal pressure, the hoof has a tendency to shrink and become dormant, with contracted feet and unsoundness resulting.
Commissures	The deep grooves on both sides of the frog.	Give elasticity.	Thrush is often found in the commissures.
Horny sole	The bottom of the foot. It is a thick (about 3/8 in.) plate or horn which grows out from the fleshy sole.	Protects the foot from the bottom. Nature didn't intend that the horny sole should carry weight, for it is convex in shape so that most of the weight rests on the wall and frog area.	The sensitive sole is directly under the horny sole. Pressure on the horny sole area will usually produce lameness.
Bars	The horny protrusions that lie along the frog between the commissures and the sole.	Help support the foot and keep it open at the heels.	

(Continued)

TABLE 3-1 (Continued)

The Parts	Description	Functions	Comments
The perimeter sections:			
Inside and outside toe Quarters Heel		(See Fig. 3-5)	

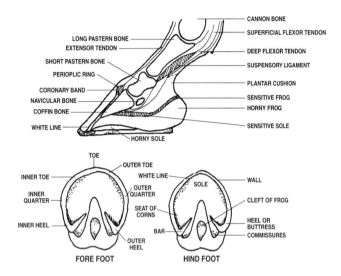

HOW THE HOOF GROWS

The hoof grows downward and forward. A complex system of arteries, veins, and nerves inside the outer structure provides for its growth. The average rate of growth of the horny portions of the hoof (wall, sole, and frog) is ⅛ to ¼ in. per month.

Fig. 3-5. Parts of the foot.

SELECTED REFERENCES

Title of Publication	Author(s)	Publisher
Anatomy and Conformation of the Horse	G. B. Edwards	Dreenan Press Ltd., Croton-on-Hudson, NY, 1973
Anatomy of the Domestic Animals	S. Sisson	W. B. Saunders Company, Philadelphia, PA, 1953
Anatomy of the Horse, The	R. F. Way D. G. Lee	J. B. Lippincott Co., Philadelphia, PA, 1965
Anatomy and Physiology of Farm Animals	R. D. Frandson	Lea & Febiger, Philadelphia, PA, 1965
Dukes' Physiology of Domestic Animals, Eleventh Edition	Ed. by M. J. Swenson	Cornell University Press, Ithaca, NY, 1993
Horse Industry Handbook	Staff	American Horse Council, Washington, DC, 1993
Horseshoeing Theory and Hoof Care	L. Emery J. Miller N. Van Hoosen	Lea & Febiger, Philadelphia, PA, 1977
Horse Structure and Movement, The	R. H. Smythe rev. by P. C. Goody	J. A. Allen & Co., London, England, 1972
Lameness in Horses	O. R. Adams	Lea & Febiger, Philadelphia, PA, 1966
Leg at Each Corner, A	N. Thelwell	E. P. Dutton & Co., Inc., New York, NY, 1963
Mechanics of the Horse, The	J. R. Rooney	Robert E. Krieger Publishing Co., New York, NY, 1980
Points of the Horse	M. H. Hayes	Arco Publishing Co., Inc., New York, NY, 1969
Principles of Horseshoeing, The	D. Butler	Doug Butler, Maryville, MO, 1985

SELECTING AND JUDGING HORSES

EA Novelle, many times Dressage Champion, an Arabian, owned by Charles and Suzzane Stuart, ridden by Sandi Chohany, owned by Charles and Suzzane Stuart. (Photo by Bruce Kuehl; print courtesy, Arabian Horse Trust, Westminster, CO)

The great horse shows throughout the land have exerted a powerful influence in molding the types of certain breeds of horses. Other breeds have been affected primarily through selections based on performance, such as the racetrack. It is realized, however, that only a comparatively few animals are subjected to the scrutiny of experienced judges or to trial on the racetrack. Rather, the vast majority of them are evaluated—bought and sold—by persons who lack experience in judging, but who have a practical need for an animal and take pride in selecting and owning a good horse. Before buying a horse, the amateur should enlist the help of a competent equestrian.

PARTS OF A HORSE

In selecting and judging horses, parts are usually referred to, rather than to the individual as a whole. It is important, therefore, to master the language that describes and locates the different parts of a horse. In addition, it is necessary to know which of these parts are of major importance; that is, what compara-

tive evaluation to give the different parts. Nothing so quickly sets a real equestrian apart from a novice as a thorough knowledge of the parts and the language used in describing them. Fig. 4-1 shows the parts of a horse.

HOW TO SELECT A HORSE

As with other classes of farm animals, any one or a combination of all four of the following methods may serve as bases for selecting horses: (1) individuality, (2) pedigree, (3) show-ring winnings, and/or (4) performance testing. One must also be aware of the fact that environment, including feeding and training, plays a tremendously important part in the individuality and performance of a horse.

SELECTION BASED ON INDIVIDUALITY

In addition to obtaining a sound horse of desirable

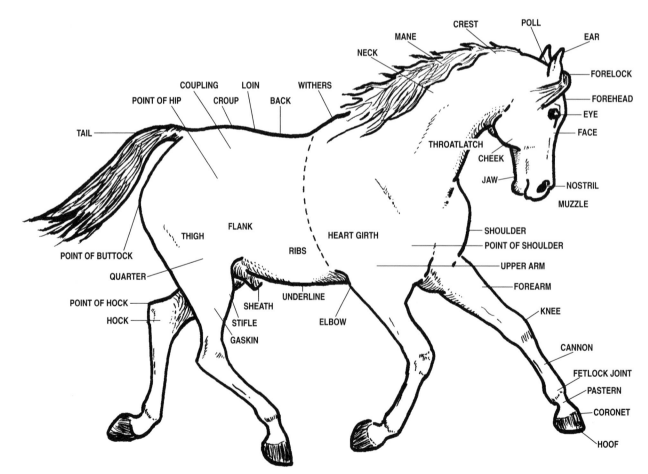

Fig. 4-1. Parts of a horse. The first step in preparation for judging horses consists in mastering the language that describes the different parts of the animal.

conformation, consideration should be given to the following points:

1. The mount should be purchased within a price range that the rider can afford.

2. The amateur or child should have a quiet, gentle, well-broken horse that is neither headstrong nor unmanageable. The horse should never be too spirited for the rider's skill.

3. The size of the horse should be in keeping with the size of the rider. A very small child should have a small horse or pony, whereas a heavy person should have a horse of the weight-carrying type. An exceedingly tall person also looks out of place if not mounted on a horse with considerable height.

4. Usually the novice will do best to start with a 3-gaited horse and first master the 3 natural gaits before attempting to ride a horse executing the more complicated 5 gaits, should a 5-gaited horse be desired.

5. Other conditions being equal, the breed and color of horse may be decided on the basis of preference.

6. The mount should be well suited to the type of work to be performed.

ALL-BREED HORSE SCORECARD

First, a horse must conform to the specific type which fits it for the function it is to perform. Second, the horse should be true to the characteristics of the breed that it represents. The use of a scorecard is a good way in which to make sure that (1) no part is overlooked, and (2) proper weight or value is assigned to each part.

A scorecard is a listing of the different parts of an animal, with a numerical value assigned to each according to its relative importance. Fig. 4-2 shows an All-breed Horse Scorecard, developed by the author. Breed characteristics may be, and are, considered in this scorecard.

Selection on the basis of individuality and performance alone is still the best single method for obtaining suitable horses, whether they be used for heavy harness, light harness, saddle, or pony purposes. In other words, the individuality of the horse, its phenotype, is closely correlated with its performance. However, if the animals are selected for breeding purposes, additional criteria—pedigree, record of both the individual and near relatives, progeny if the animal is old enough and has produced, family name, etc.—should be taken into consideration. Also, show-ring winnings may be helpful.

SELECTION BASED ON PEDIGREE

The Arabians were the first livestock breeders to trace the lineage of their animals, often memorizing many generations of the pedigree. Moreover, they accorded particular importance to the dam's side of the heritage, a practice that still persists in certain breeds of livestock today as evidenced by the family names tracing to certain great females many generations removed.

If the pedigree is relatively complete in terms of records of performance (speed, show winnings, etc.) of the ancestors, particularly those close up, it can be of very great usefulness in providing a safer basis for selection. A pedigree of this type is of value in predicting (1) the usefulness of the individual (whether it be for racing under the saddle or jumping, etc.) and (2) the probable prepotency as a breeding animal.

Pedigree selection is of special importance where animals are either too thin or so young that their individual merit cannot be ascertained with any degree of certainty. Then, too, where selection is being made between animals of comparable individual merit, the pedigree may be the determining factor.

SELECTION BASED ON SHOW-RING WINNINGS

Breeders of pleasure horses have long used show-ring records as a basis of selection. Because training plays such an important part in the performance and show-ring winnings of pleasure horses, however, it is likely that this basis of selection is less valuable from a breeding standpoint than with any other class of animals. At the same time, the show record may be a most valuable criterion in indicating the utility value of the horse.

SELECTION BASED ON PERFORMANCE TESTING

Although selection based on the basis of progeny testing is the most infallible tool available to the horse breeder, it must be pointed out that the following limitations exist:

1. Because of relatively few offspring, it is difficult to apply it to females.

2. Even with males, a progeny testing rating cannot be obtained until late in life, after sufficient offspring have been born and have reached an age when they can be tested.

3. There is the hazard that the stallion being

tested will be bred to only a few select mares and that only the top offspring will be tested.

4. Training and feeding play such a major part in the development of horses that it is always difficult to separate out environmental from hereditary influences.

Performance testing is easy to apply because it is an individual matter. In fact, most racehorses used for breeding purposes are first performance tested on the track.

Perhaps it might be added that the progressive

	POINTS or %	NAME and/or No. of Horse	NAME and/or No. of Horse	NAME and/or No. of Horse	NAME and/or No. of Horse
BREED TYPE . . . . The breed is distinguished by its unique combination of style and beauty. COLOR: In keeping with the breed. HEIGHT AT MATURITY: Proper height; extremes undesirable. WEIGHT AT MATURITY: Proper weight; extremes undesirable.	15				
FORM . . . . STYLE AND BEAUTY: Attractive, good carriage, alert, refined, symmetrical, and all parts nicely blended together. BODY: Nicely turned, long, well-sprung ribs; heavily muscled. BACK AND LOIN: Short and strong, wide, well muscled, and short coupled. CROUP: Long, level, wide, muscular, with a high-set tail. REAR QUARTERS: Deep and muscular. GASKIN: Heavily muscled. WITHERS: Prominent, and of the same height as the high point of the croup. SHOULDERS: Deep, well laid in, and sloping (about a 45° angle). CHEST: Fairly wide, deep, and full. ARM AND FOREARM: Well muscled.	35				
FEET AND LEGS . . . . LEGS: Correct position and set (when viewed from front, side, and rear). PASTERNS: Long, sloping (about a 45° angle). FEET: In proportion to size of horse, good shape, wide and deep at heels, dense texture of hoof. HOCKS: Deep, clean-cut, and well supported. KNEES: Broad, tapering gradually into cannon. CANNONS: Clean, flat, with tendons well defined.	15				
HEAD AND NECK . . . . Alertly carried, showing style and character. HEAD: Well proportioned to rest of body, refined, clean-cut, with chiseled appearance; broad, full forehead with great width between eyes; ears medium sized, well carried and attractive; eyes large and prominent. NECK: Long and nicely arched, clean-cut about the throatlatch; with head well set on, gracefully carried.	10				
QUALITY . . . . Clean, flat bone; well defined and clean joints and tendons, and fine skin and hair.	10				
ACTION . . . . WALK: Easy, springy, prompt, balanced, a long step, with each foot carried forward in a straight line, feet lifted clear of the ground. TROT: Prompt, straight, elastic, balanced, with hocks carried closely, and high flexion of knees and hocks.	15				
DISCRIMINATION: Any abnormality that affects the serviceability of the horse.					
DISQUALIFICATION: Blindness (except by injury), bone spavin, stifled, stringhalt, cryptorchid.					
TOTAL SCORE	100				

Fig. 4-2. All-breed horse scorecard.

breeder will continue to use all four methods of selection—individuality, pedigree, show-ring winnings, and production testing—but with increasing emphasis upon the latter method.

JUDGING HORSES

The discussion that follows represents a further elucidation of the first point discussed under selection—individuality. But, in addition to individual merit, the word judging implies the comparative appraisal or placing of several animals.

Judging horses, like all livestock judging, is an art, the rudiments of which must be obtained through patient study and long practice. Successful equestrians are usually competent judges. Likewise, shrewd traders are usually masters of the art, even to the point of deception.

Accomplished livestock producers generally agree that horses are the most difficult to judge of all classes of farm animals. In addition to considering conformation—which is the main criterion in judging other farm animals—action and numerous unsoundnesses are of paramount importance.

QUALIFICATIONS OF A GOOD HORSE JUDGE

The essential qualifications that a good horse judge must possess, and the recommended procedure to follow in the judging assignment, are as follows:

1. **Knowledge of the parts of a horse.** This consists in mastering the language that describes and locates the different parts of a horse (see Fig. 4-1). In addition, it is necessary to know which of these parts are of major importance; that is, what comparative evaluation to give to the different parts.

2. **A clearly defined ideal or standard of perfection.** Successful horse judges must know what they are looking for. That is, they must have in mind an ideal or standard of perfection.

3. **Keen observation and sound judgment.** Good horse judges possess the ability to observe good conformation and performance, as well as defects, and to weigh and evaluate the relative importance of the various good and bad features.

4. **Honesty and courage.** Good horse judges must possess honesty and courage, whether it be in making a show-ring placing or in conducting a breeding and selling program. For example, it often requires considerable courage to place a class of animals without regard to (a) winnings in previous shows, (b) ownership, and (c) public applause. It may take even greater courage and honesty within oneself to discard

a costly stallion or mare whose progeny have failed to measure up.

5. **Logical procedure in examining.** There is always great danger of beginners making too close an inspection; they often get "so close to the trees that they fail to see the forest."

Good judging procedure consists in the following three steps: (a) observing at a distance and securing a panoramic view where several horses are involved, (b) seeing the animals in action, and (c) inspecting close up. Also, it is important that a logical method be used in viewing an animal from all directions (front view, rear view, and side view), and in judging its action and soundness—thus avoiding overlooking anything and making it easier to retain the observations that are made.

6. **Tact.** In discussing either (a) a show-ring class, or (b) horses on a farm or ranch, it is important that judges be tactful. Owners are likely to resent any remarks which indicate that their animals are inferior.

DO'S AND DON'TS FOR CONTEST HORSE JUDGES

College judging classes, FFA students, 4-H Club members, and other prospective horse judges should first become thoroughly familiar with the six qualifications of a good judge as outlined in the previous section. Next, they should observe the following do's and don'ts:

1. **Do's:**
   a. Make certain how the class is numbered, and keep the numbers straight.
   b. Get a clear picture of the class and of each individual animal in mind, so that they will be remembered.
   c. Keep in a position of vantage, where the class can be seen at all times; usually this means some distance away rather than too close.
   d. Make placings on the basis of the big things.
   e. Make certain that the card is filled out completely and correctly, and that the correct numbers are kept in mind.
   f. If permissible, make concise notes that will assist in recalling each individual in the class; record such things as distinctive color markings, outstanding faults, etc.
   g. When giving reasons, use good poise and look the judge in the eye.
   h. State reasons clearly, and with conviction and confidence.
   i. Give reasons in a logical sequence; give the major reasons first.
   j. Use terms appropriate to the class of ani-

mals; for example, use breeding terms in a breeding class.

k. Use comparative and descriptive terms in giving reasons. Avoid such vague terms as "good," "better," and "best."

l. Concede or grant good points and faults, regardless of the placing of the animal.

2. **Don'ts:**

a. Don't act on hunches; if the first placing is arrived at after due consideration and in a logical manner, stick to it.

b. Don't place animals on the basis of small, relatively unimportant characters.

c. Don't destroy self-confidence and self-respect by discussing the class with others before giving reasons.

d. Don't pay attention to what you overhear others say about a class; be an independent judge.

e. Don't give wordy and meaningless reasons.

f. Don't bluff, if you don't know the answer to a question, say so.

JUDGING PROCEDURE FOR BREEDING OR HALTER CLASSES

It is suggested that the beginner proceed as follows:

1. Master the nomenclature of the animal—the parts (see Fig. 4-1).

2. Have an ideal in mind, and be able to recognize both desirable characteristics and common faults (see Fig. 4-5).

3. Follow a procedure in examining, such as is indicated in Table 4-1; namely (a) front view, (b) rear view, (c) side view, (d) action, and (e) soundness. This applies to breeding or halter classes in particular.

4. Rank or place animals of each class on each of the points listed under "what to look for," keeping in mind the "ideal type" and "common faults" (see Fig. 4-5).

5. Rank or place the animals according to their consistent rating on all points, especially the most important ones (see Table 4-1).

JUDGING PROCEDURE FOR PERFORMANCE CLASSES

Custom decrees somewhat different show-ring procedure in judging different classes. Halter classes are first examined while lined up side by side, or while being led in a circle and later inspected while moved one at a time; whereas performance classes are first examined with the entire class in action, and later lined up for close inspection. In judging performance classes, the officials should be thoroughly familiar with, and follow, the show rules—either local or the American Horse Shows Association, Inc., whichever applies. If the judge is in doubt as to what is expected of a performance class, he/she should seek the advice of the steward.

After a judge has inspected a light horse performance class, both in action and when lined up, it is considered entirely proper to request that certain animals be pulled out again and put through their gaits. Fig. 4-4 shows the common method of examining a three-gaited Saddle Horse performance class.

WHAT TO LOOK FOR

A horse must first conform to the specific type which fits it for the function it is to perform. Secondly, the horse should be true to the characteristics of the breed that it represents. Regardless of type or breed, however, Fig. 4-5 shows certain desirable and undesirable characteristics in horses, and Table 4-1 is a judging guide.

GOOD HEAD, NECK, AND SHOULDERS

The head should be well proportioned to the rest of the body, refined and clean-cut, with a chiseled appearance. A broad, full forehead with great width between the eyes indicates intelligence. A straight face is usually preferable to a concave profile or a convex one (Roman nose), the former suggesting a timid disposition and the latter strong will power. The jaw should be broad and strongly muscled. There should be great width between large, clear eyes; and the ears

Fig. 4-3. A Quarter Horse class being judged. (Courtesy, American Quarter Horse Assn., photo by Wyatt McSpadden)

TABLE 4-1
JUDGING GUIDE FOR LIGHT HORSES[1]

Procedure for Examining, and What to Look for	Ideal Type	Common Faults
Front View:		
 Fig. 4-6	 Fig. 4-7	 Fig. 4-8
1. Head.	1. Head well proportioned to rest of body; refined, clean-cut, with chiseled appearance; broad, full forehead with great width between the eyes; jaw broad and strongly muscled; ears medium sized, well carried and attractive.	1. Plain headed.
2. Sex character.	2. Refinement and femininity in the broodmare; boldness and masculinity in the stallion.	2. Mares lacking femininity; stallions lacking masculinity.
3. Chest capacity.	3. A deep, wide chest.	3. A narrow chest.
4. Set to the front legs.	4. Straight, true, and squarely set.	4. Crooked front legs.
Rear View:		
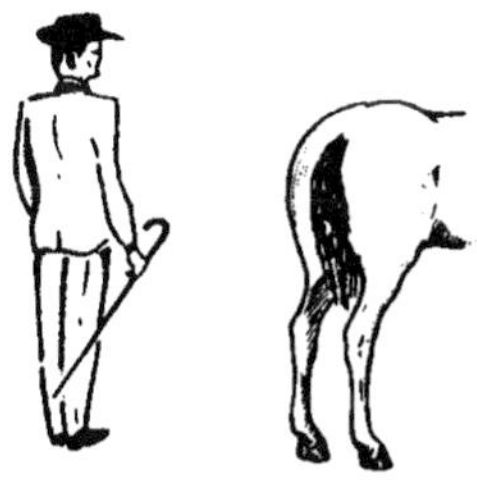 Fig. 4-9	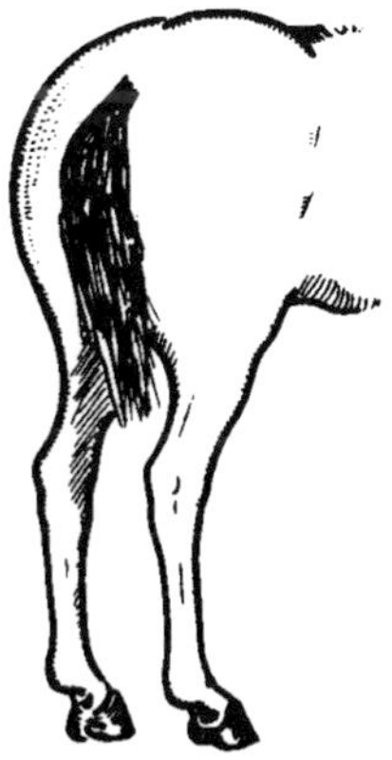 Fig. 4-10	 Fig. 4-11
1. Width of croup and through rear quarters.	1. Wide and muscular over the croup and through the rear quarters.	1. Lacking width over the croup and muscling through the rear quarters.
2. Set to the hind legs.	2. Straight, true, and squarely set.	2. Crooked hind legs.

(Continued)

TABLE 4-1 (Continued)

Procedure for Examining, and What to Look for	Ideal Type	Common Faults
Side View: Fig. 4-12	 Fig. 4-13	 Fig. 4-14
1. Style and beauty.	1. High carriage of head, active ears, alert disposition and beauty of conformation.	1. Lacking style and beauty.
2. Balance and symmetry.	2. All parts well developed and nicely blended together.	2. Lacking balance and symmetry.
3. Neck.	3. Fairly long neck, carried high; clean-cut about the throatlatch; with head well set on.	3. A short, thick neck; ewe-necked.
4. Shoulders.	4. Sloping shoulders (about 45° angle).	4. Straight in the shoulders.
5. Topline.	5. A short, strong back and loin, with a long, nicely turned and heavily muscled croup, and a high, well-set tail; withers clearly defined and of the same height as the high point of croup.	5. Swaybacked; steep croup.
6. Coupling.	6. A short coupling as denoted by the last rib being close to the hip.	6. Long in the coupling.
7. Middle.	7. Ample middle due to long, well-sprung ribs.	7. Lacking middle.
8. Rear flank.	8. Well let down in the rear flank.	8. High cut rear flank or "wasp waisted."
9. Arm, forearm, and gaskin.	9. Well-muscled arm, forearm, and gaskin.	9. Light-muscled arm, forearm, and gaskin.
10. Legs, feet, and pasterns.	10. Straight, true, and squarely set legs; pasterns sloping about 45°; hoofs large, dense, and wide at the heels.	10. Crooked legs; straight pasterns, hoofs small, contracted at the heels, and shelly.
11. Quality.	11. Plenty of quality, as denoted by clean, flat bone, well-defined joints and tendons, refined head and ears, and fine skin and hair.	11. Lacking quality.
12. Breed type (size, color, shape of body and head, and action true to the breed represented).	12. Showing plenty of breed type.	12. Lacking breed type.

(Continued)

TABLE 4-1 (Continued)

Procedure for Examining, and What to Look for	Ideal Type	Common Faults
Soundness:		
1. Soundness, and freedom from defects in conformation that may predispose unsoundness.	1. Sound, and free from blemishes.	1. Unsound; blemished (wire cuts, capped hocks, etc.).
Action:[2]		
 1. At the walk.	1. Easy, prompt, balanced; a long step, with each foot carried forward in a straight line; feet lifted clear of the ground.	1. A short step, with feet not lifted clear of the ground.

Fig. 4-15

 2. At the trot.	2. Rapid, straight, elastic trot, with the joints well flexed.	2. Winging, forging, and interfering.

Fig. 4-16

3. At the canter.	3. Slow collected canter, which is readily executed on either lead.	3. Fast and extended canter.

[1]The illustrations for this table were prepared by Prof. R. F. Johnson.

[2]The three most common gaits are given here. Five-gaited horses must perform two additional gaits. In selecting for gait, (1) observe horse at each intended gait, and (2) examine trained horses while performing at use for which they are intended.

①

"Walk your horses"

②

"Trot your horses"

Fig. 4-4. Diagram showing the customary procedure in examining a 3-gaited Saddle Horse in the show-ring. The animal herein is shown (1) walking, (2) trotting, (3) cantering, and (4) lined up. Traditionally, the judge or judges work from the center of the ring, while the ringmaster requests the riders to execute the different gaits.

③ *"Canter, please — canter"*

④ *"Line up — please"*

Fig. 4-4 (continued). Three-gaited horses are expected to walk, trot, and canter. Five-gaited horses must perform 2 additional gaits; namely, (a) slow gait (which is the stepping pace in the show-ring), and (b) the rack. In addition to performing the gaits with perfection, both 3- and 5-gaited horses should possess desirable conformation, perfect manners, and superior style and animation. (Drawings by Prof. R. F. Johnson)

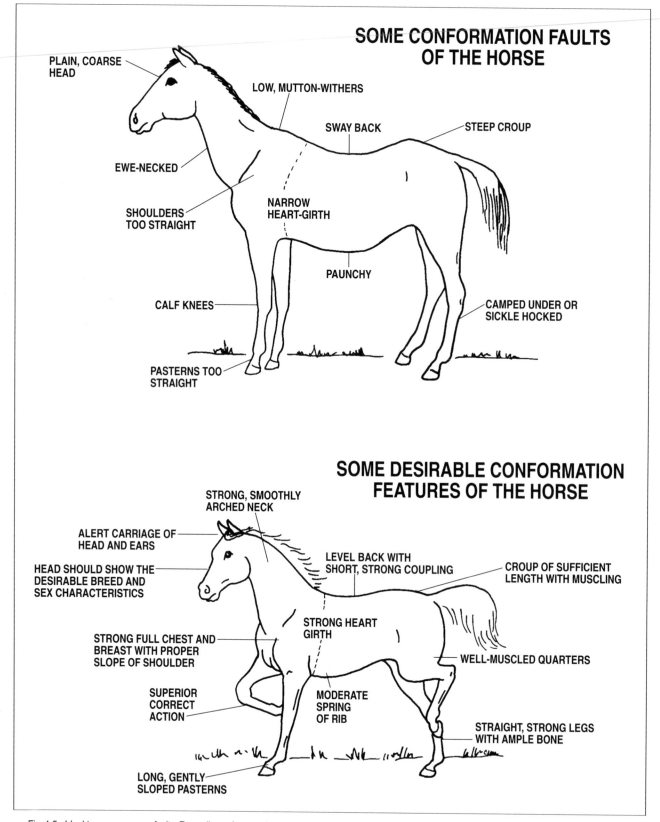

Fig. 4-5. Ideal type vs common faults. Regardless of type or breed, certain desirable characteristics should be present in all horses. The successful horse judge must be able to recognize both the desirable characteristics and the common faults, and the relative importance of each.

should be of medium size, well carried and active. The neck should be fairly long. It should be carried high, slightly arched, lean and muscular, and clean-cut about the throatlatch, with the head set on. Also, the neck should neatly join long, oblique, smooth shoulders. The head and neck of the animal should show sex character—boldness and masculinity in the stallion and refinement and femininity in the broodmare.

A STRONG, HEAVILY MUSCLED TOPLINE, WITH A SHORT BACK AND LOIN AND A LONG LEVEL CROUP

The topline should include a short, strong back and loin, with a long, nicely turned and heavily muscled croup, and a high, well-set tail. The withers should be rather clearly defined and of the same height as the hips. Good withers and oblique shoulders make for a better seat in riding horses. Moreover, a sloping shoulder is usually associated with sloping pasterns and more springy, elastic action. The back and loin muscles help sustain the weight of the rider, lift the forequarters of the horse, and strengthen the arch of the back of the horse in motion. A desirable short coupling is obtained when the last rib is close to the hip.

AMPLE CHEST AND MIDDLE

Ample chest and middle due to long, well-sprung ribs is desired. A deep, wide chest and large, full heart girth—together with a good middle—provide needed space for vital organs and indicate a strong constitution and good feeding and staying qualities. All horses should be fairly well let down in the hind flank, though racehorses in training may show much less depth at this point than other types of horses. Even with racehorses, however, the extremely high-cut, so-called "wasp-waisted" ones will not endure heavy racing. Moreover, racehorses usually deepen materially in the rear flank with age or higher condition.

WELL-MUSCLED ARM, FOREARM, AND GASKIN

The muscles of the arm, forearm, and gaskin should be well developed. Since little or no fat can be placed upon the forearm and gaskin, these areas are a good indication of the muscular development of the entire animal, even when horses are in high condition. The powerful muscles of the croup, thigh, and gaskin give the animal ability to pull, jump, or run.

CORRECT LEGS, FEET, AND PASTERNS

There has long been a saying "no foot, no horse." After all, the value of horses lie chiefly in their ability to move, hence the necessity of good underpinning. The legs should be straight, true, and squarely set; the bone should be well placed and clearly defined. The pasterns should be sloping; the feet large and wide at the heels. (See Figs. 4-17 and 4-18.)

The hock should be large, clean, wide from front to back, deep, clean-cut, and correctly set. The knee

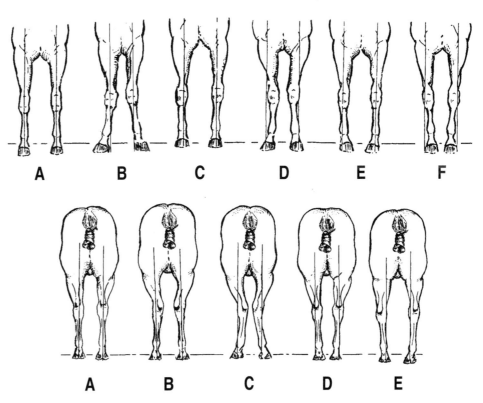

Fig. 4-17. The proper and faulty conformation of the forelegs (top) when viewed from the front, and the hind legs (bottom) when viewed from the rear. *The forelegs:* A, represents correct conformation; B, knock-kneed and splay-footed (forefeet toes out/heels in); C, bowed legs with offset cannons; D, knock kneed, with toes pointing outward; E, pigeon toed (toes pointing in); F, base narrow. *The hind legs:* A, represents correct conformation; B, slightly cow hocked and toed out; C, badly cow-hocked; D, hind legs set too close together; E, pigeon toed. The direction of the leg and the form of the foot are very important in the horse.

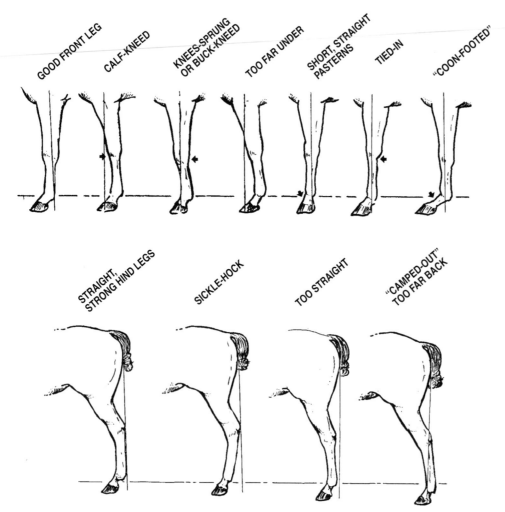

Fig. 4-18. The proper and faulty conformation of (top) the forelegs when viewed from the side, and (bottom) the hind legs when viewed from the side. *Top row, the forelegs:* The illustration on the extreme left shows correct conformation; the illustrations to the right of it show the common faults as labeled. *Bottom row, the hind legs:* The illustration on the extreme left shows correct conformation; the illustrations to the right of it show the common faults as labeled.

SOUNDNESS

The horse should be serviceably sound, and in the young animal there should be no indication of defects in conformation that may predispose unsoundnesses. Horse judges must first know and recognize the normal structure and function before attempting to determine unsoundnesses. Practically speaking, *an unsoundness is any deviation in form or function that interferes with the usefulness of the individual; whereas, a blemish is an abnormality which may detract from the appearance of an animal, but which does not affect its serviceability.* The latter includes wire-cut scars, capped hocks, etc.

CONSIDERATIONS WHEN BUYING A HORSE

Horses may be, and are, bought and sold at auction and private treaty.

Professionals find horse auctions useful, as a place to buy or sell. Although many fine horses are bought and sold at sales, there is little opportunity to "try them out." So, when buying at auction, the nonprofessional should seek the help of a reputable dealer or agent.

Private treaty buying and selling generally involves negotiations of a buyer with a breeder or dealer. Many reputable breeders or dealers will let the prospective buyer take a horse home to try out. Also, many sellers are quite willing to allow the prospective buyer to have a veterinarian examine the horse for soundness.

The price is always of considerable importance. Although a high price may be justified for superior breeding and performing horses, sound judgment should always prevail.

In addition to price and desirable conformation, there should be style and beauty, balance and symmetry, an abundance of quality, an energetic yet man-

should be deep from front to rear, wide when viewed from the front, straight, and taper gradually into the leg. Since the hock and knee joints of the horse are subject to great wear and are the seat of many unsoundnesses, they should receive every attention.

GOOD ACTION

Although the degree of action of the horse will vary somewhat with the type (speed, show, and saddle), the usefulness of all horses is dependent upon their action and their ability to move in various types of racing, driving, hunting, riding, polo, etc. In all types and breeds, the motion should be straight and true with a long, swift, and elastic stride.

Fig. 4-19. Horse auction in progress. This shows a yearling Thoroughbred in the ring at the Select Yearling Sale at Keeneland, Lexington, Kentucky. Note the electrically operated record above the auctioneers, identifying the animal in the ring as Hip number 257, and giving the sale price—$1,050,000. The sales topper was consigned by Gainesway Farm and purchased by H. Nakamura. (Courtesy, Keeneland, Thoroughbred Racing Sales)

ageable disposition, freedom from vices, good wind, suitable age, freedom from disease, and proper condition. The buyer should also be on the alert for possible misrepresentations. As these factors should receive careful consideration when buying a horse, a separate section is devoted to each of them.

STYLE AND BEAUTY

This has reference to the attractiveness with which the horse displays itself at all times. Good carriage of the head, active ears, an alert, active disposition, and beauty of conformation are factors contributing to the style of the horse. This quality is especially important in heavy harness, fine harness, and saddle horses.

BALANCE AND SYMMETRY

Balance and symmetry refers to the harmonious development of all parts. With the full development of all important parts, which are nicely blended together, the horse will present an attractive appearance.

QUALITY

Quality is denoted by clean, flat bone, well-defined joints and tendons, refined head and ears, and fine skin and hair. Good quality in the horse indicates easy keeping and good endurance.

AN ENERGETIC YET MANAGEABLE DISPOSITION

Both sexes and all types of horses should at all times display energetic yet manageable dispositions. The disposition of a horse, whether good or bad, is usually considered as being a product of both inheritance and environment. Regardless of the cause of a nasty disposition, one should avoid purchasing such an animal. Superb manners and disposition are especially important in all types of pleasure horses.

FREEDOM FROM VICES

Although not considered as unsoundnesses, such stable vices as cribbing, weaving, tail rubbing, kicking, stall walking, stall trotting, and halter pulling do detract from the value of a horse. But vices are not confined to actions in the stall. Some horses object to taking a bit in their mouths; others are touchy about their ears; still others jump when an attempt is made to place a saddle or harness on their backs. Any of these traits is objectionable.

GOOD WIND

Good wind is imperative. Defects of wind may be easily detected by first moving the animal at a rapid gait for some distance, then suddenly bringing it to a stop and listening in near proximity to the head. Unsound animals are usually noisy in breathing.

SUITABLE AGE

Horses are usually considered as being in their prime between the ages of 3 and 8. Since younger horses are still growing and becoming hardened, many 2- and 3-year-olds do not stand up under heavy racing or other use. Although the market value begins to depreciate when they reach their eighth year, they may be useful in performing certain services until they are well over 20 years old.

FREEDOM FROM DISEASES

In transporting horses, there is always the possible exposure to the many ills to which they are subject. Sometimes these prove to be of sufficiently serious nature as to make working impossible at a time when the animals are most needed; and occasionally they even prove fatal. It must also be remembered that such diseases as contracted may very likely spread to the

Fig. 4-20. World Champion Hunter Hack, Fabulous Dun Bar, a Buckskin. (Courtesy, International Buckskin Horse Assn., Shelby, IN)

other horses on the farm and even in the community, thus exposing them to the same risk.

CONDITION

Both productive ability and endurance are lowered by either a thin, run-down condition or an over-fat and highly fitted condition. A good, vigorous, thrifty condition is conducive to the best work and breeding ability, and horses so fitted attract the eye of the prospective buyer. However, extremes in feeding and lack of exercise are to be avoided in purchasing a horse for either work or breeding. It must be remembered that fat will cover up a multitude of defects. In buying valuable mares or stallions, the purchaser should insist on having a health certificate signed by a licensed veterinarian. Such examination should also show that the reproductive organs are normal and healthy.

MISREPRESENTATIONS

The inexperienced person is especially likely to encounter misrepresentations as to age, soundness,

vices, and the training and working ability of the horse. Perhaps knowing the seller as well as the horse is the best preventative of this sort of thing. Also, a prepurchase examination by a licensed veterinarian is recommended.

COLORS AND MARKINGS OF HORSES

Izaak Walton, in *The Compleat Angler*, says, "There is no good horse of a bad color." Yet, within certain breeds, some colors are preferred, or even required, whereas others are undesirable or even constitute disqualifications for registry. Also, a good equestrian needs a working knowledge of horse colors and patterns because it is the most conspicuous feature by which a horse can be described or identified.

BODY COLORS

The five basic horse body colors and their descriptions follow:

1. **Bay.** Bay is a mixture of red and yellow. It

includes many shades, from a light yellowish tan (light bay) to a dark, rich shade which is almost brown (dark bay); a bay horse usually has a black mane and tail and black points.

2. **Black.** A black horse is completely black, including the muzzle and flanks. If there is doubt as to whether a horse is dark brown or black, one should note the color of the fine hairs on the muzzle and the hair on the flanks; tan or brown hairs at these points indicate that the horse is not a true black, but a seal brown.

3. **Brown.** A brown horse is almost black, but can be distinguished by the fine tan or brown hairs on the muzzle or flanks.

4. **Chestnut (sorrel).** A chestnut horse is basically red. The shades vary from light washy yellow (light chestnut) to a dark liver color (dark chestnut), between which come the brilliant red gold and copper shades. Normally, the mane and tail of a chestnut horse are the same shade as the body, although they may be lighter in color; these are termed a flaxen mane and tail. Chestnut color is never accompanied by a black mane and tail.

5. **White.** A true white horse is born white and remains white throughout its life. A white horse has snow-white hair, pink skin, and brown eyes (rarely blue).

In addition to the five basic horse colors given, there are five major variations to these coat colors; namely:

1. **Dun (buckskin).** A dun horse has a yellowish color of variable shading from pale yellow to a dirty canvas color; the horse also has a stripe down its back.

2. **Gray.** A gray horse has a mixture of white and black hairs. Sometimes gray is difficult to distinguish from black at birth, but grays get lighter with age.

3. **Palomino.** Palomino is a golden color (the color of a newly minted gold coin, or three shades lighter or darker), with a light-colored mane and tail (white, silver, or ivory).

4. **Pinto (calico or paint).** Pinto is a Spanish word, meaning "painted." The Pinto horse is characterized by irregular colored and white areas, as (a)

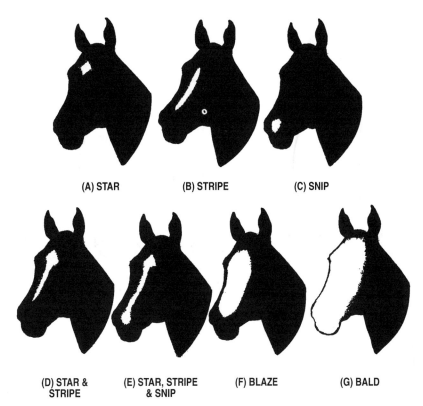

(A) STAR **(B) STRIPE** **(C) SNIP**

(D) STAR & STRIPE **(E) STAR, STRIPE & SNIP** **(F) BLAZE** **(G) BALD**

Fig. 4-21. The head markings of horses. A, *Star* is any white mark on the forehead located above a line running from eye to eye; B, *stripe* is a narrow white marking that extends from about the line of the eyes to the nostrils; C, *snip* is a white mark between the nostrils or on the lips; D, *star and stripe* includes both a star and a stripe; E, *star, stripe, and snip* includes all three of these marks—star, stripe, and snip; F, *blaze* is a broad, white marking covering almost all of the forehead but not including the eyes or nostrils; G, *bald* is a bald, or white, face including the eyes and nostrils, or a partially white face. (Drawing by Prof. R. F. Johnson)

piebald (white and black), and (b) skewbald (white and any color other than black).

5. **Roan.** A roan horse has a mixture of white hairs intermingled with one or more basic colors, as (a) white with bay (red roan), (b) white with chestnut (strawberry roan), and (c) white with black (blue roan).

HEAD MARKINGS

When identifying an individual horse, it is generally necessary for one to be more explicit than to refer to body color only; for example, it may be necessary to further identify the dark sorrel as the one with the blaze face. The most common head markings are shown in Fig. 4-21.

LEG MARKINGS

Leg markings are usually used, along with head markings, to describe a horse. The most common leg markings are shown in Fig. 4-22.

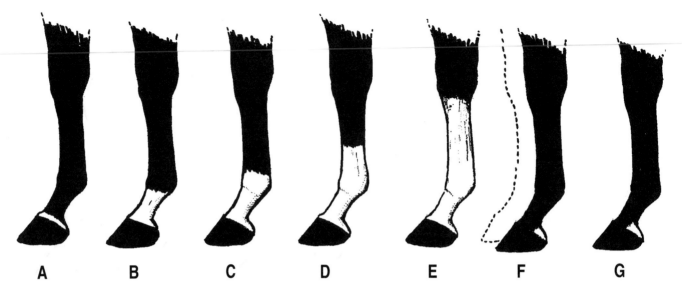

A   B   C   D   E   F   G

Fig. 4-22. Most common leg markings. A, *coronet*—a white strip covering the coronet band; B, *pastern*—white extends from the coronet to and including the pastern; C, *ankle*—white extends from the coronet to and including the fetlock; D, *half stocking*—white extends from the coronet to the middle of the cannon; E, *stocking*—white extends from the coronet to the knee. When the white includes the knee, it is known as a full stocking; F, *white outside heels*—both heels are white; G, *white outside heel*—outside heel only is white.

SELECTED REFERENCES

Title of Publication	Author(s)	Publisher
Anatomy and Conformation of the Horse	G. B. Edwards	Dreenan Press Ltd., Croton-on-Hudson, NY, 1973
Breeding and Raising Horses, Ag. Hdbk. No. 394	M. E. Ensminger	Agricultural Research Service, USDA, Washington, DC, 1972
Color of Horses, The	B. K. Green	Northland Press, Flagstaff, AZ, 1974
Determining the Age of Farm Animals by Their Teeth, Farmers, Bull. No. 1721		U.S. Department of Agriculture, Washington, DC
Fair Exchange	H. S. Finney	Charles Scribner's Sons, New York, NY, 1974
Horse Buyer's Guide, The	J. K. Posey	A. S. Barnes & Co., Inc., Cranbury, NJ, 1973
Horse Industry Handbook	Staff	American Horse Council, Washington, DC, 1993
Horsemanship and Horse Care, Ag. Info. Bull. No. 353	M. E. Ensminger	Agricultural Research Service, USDA, Washington, DC, 1972
Horses: Their Selection, Care & Handling	M. C. Self	A. S. Barnes & Co., Inc., New York, NY, 1943
Judging Manual for American Saddlebred Horses	J. Foss	American Saddle Horse Breeders Association, Louisville, KY, 1973
Lameness in Horses, Second Edition	O. R. Adams	Lea & Febiger, Philadelphia, PA, 1966
Livestock Judging, Selection and Evaluation, Fourth Edition	R. E. Hunsley W. M. Beeson	Interstate Publishers, Inc., Danville, IL, 1992
Points of the Horse, Seventh Revised Edition	M. H. Hayes	Arco Publishing Co., Inc., New York, NY, 1969
Rule Book		The American Horse Shows Association, Inc., New York, NY, annual
Stockman's Handbook, The, Seventh Edition	M. E. Ensminger	Interstate Publishers, Inc., Danville, IL, 1992

DETERMINING THE AGE AND HEIGHT OF HORSES

In the glory days of the Roman Empire, it was discovered that as the horse aged the gums receded, the teeth slanted to the front, and cups and dental star changed appearance and shape in time. So, a custom and cliche were born! Soon horse buyers were determining a horse's age by examining its teeth. (Courtesy, Kentucky Department of Public Information, Frankfort, KY)

Establishing the age of horses through the appearance of the teeth is not new. Apparently it was known in ancient days. It is not surprising, therefore, to find that the old saying, "Do not look a gift horse in the mouth," is attributed to Saint Jerome, a Father of the Latin Church and papal secretary in the 5th Century, who used this expression in one of his commentaries.

Physical changes within the body are constant. As they affect the general outward appearance and disposition of the horse within certain limits, it is possible by mere general appearance to estimate the age of the animal. Changes in the teeth, however, afford a much more accurate method.

There is nothing mysterious about determination of the age by the teeth. In horses up to 5 years of age, it is simply a matter of noting the number of permanent and milk teeth present. From 6 to 12 years, the number of cups or indentations in the incisor teeth is used; whereas the age of horses beyond 12 years may be estimated by studying the cross section and slant of the incisor teeth. It must be realized, however, that theoretical knowledge is not sufficient and that anyone who would become proficient must also have practical experience. The best way to recognize age is to examine the teeth in horses of known ages.

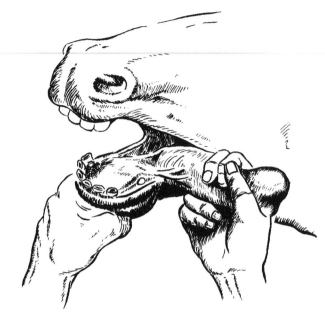

Fig. 5-1. How to look a horse in the mouth. With the tongue held in one hand and the lower jaw grasped with the other hand, you can look at the teeth for as long as you like. (Drawing by Prof. R. F. Johnson)

THE IMPORTANCE OF AGE

As the productive life of the horse is comparatively brief and the height of its usefulness is even more limited, the market value of the animal increases rather sharply with maturity and then decreases beyond eight years of age. On the other hand, for many purposes horses are quite useful up to 12 years of age or longer.

JANUARY 1 BIRTH DATE

Regardless of when a foal is born, its birth date is always considered as January 1. Thus, a foal born May 1, 1995, will be 10 years old on January 1, 2005. This is done from the standpoint of racing and showing. As a result, those who race or show make every effort to have foals arrive as near January 1 as possible, thereby getting the advantage of more growth than animals born later in the year. This is especially important in the younger age groups; for example, when racing or showing a two-year-old.

OLDEST HORSE

Authentic records of very old horses are hard to come by. *Old Bill*, a horse owned throughout his lifetime by a Mr. Petrie, of Edinburgh, Scotland, lived to age 62, according to B. S. Dystra, hippologist, of Holland.[1]

_____

[1]*American Shetland Pony Journal*, Nov. 1969, p. 25.

An ex-Italian Army horse, *Topolino*, was foaled on February 24, 1909, and died in February, 1960, at the age of 51.

Old Nellie, a black mare of draft breeding, raised by a Missouri farmer, was 53 years and 8 months old when she died in 1969.

Since the average life-span of a horse is about one-third the life expectancy of a person in the United States, in terms of human life a 50-year-old horse would be equivalent to a 150-year-old person.

But the average horse lives only 25 years, which is comparable to the human lifespan of 75 years.

NUMBERS AND TYPES OF TEETH

The mature male horse has a total of 40[2] teeth; whereas the young animal, whether male or female, has 24. These are listed in Table 5-1.

TABLE 5-1
NUMBERS AND TYPES OF TEETH

Number of Teeth of Mature Animal	Number of Teeth of Young Animal	Types of Teeth
24	12	Molars or grinders.
12	12	Incisors or front teeth (the 2 central incisors are known as middle incisors, centrals, pinchers, or nippers; the next 2—one on each side of the nippers—are called intermediates; and the last—or outer pair—the corners).
4	None	Tushes or pointed teeth. These are located between the incisors and the molars in the male.

As the tushes are usually not present in the mare, the mature female may be considered as having a total of 36 teeth rather than 40 as in the male.

The knowledgeable equestrian is also aware of the difference between permanent and temporary teeth. The temporary or milk teeth are smaller, much whiter, and have a distinct neck at the junction of the crown and fang, which is at the gum line. After their eruption, the permanent teeth may be distinguished from the temporary teeth by their greater size, darker color, a broader neck showing no constriction, and greater width from side to side.

The permanent incisor teeth of young horses five

_____

[2]Quite commonly, a small pointed tooth, known as a *wolf tooth*, may appear in front of each first molar in the upper jaw, thus increasing the total number of teeth to 42 in the male and 38 in the female. Less frequently, two more wolf teeth in the lower jaw increase the total number of teeth in the male and female to 44 and 40, respectively.

to seven years of age are elliptical or long from side to side; whereas when the animal becomes older, these teeth become triangular, with the apex of the triangle pointed upward. As the animal advances still more in age, the teeth become more slanting. Instead of curving to approach a right angle with the jaws, they slant outward.

From 5 to 12 years of age the wearing surface of the cups is the most reliable indication of age. At fairly regular intervals, according to age, the cups disappear with wear.

Table 5-2 illustrates and describes how to determine the age of horses by the teeth.

TABLE 5-2
HANDY GUIDE TO DETERMINING THE AGE OF HORSES BY THE TEETH[1]

Drawing of Teeth	Age of Animal	Description of Teeth	
 Fig. 5-2	At birth or before 10 days of age	First or central upper and lower incisors appear.	
 Fig. 5-3	4 to 6 weeks of age	Second or intermediate upper and lower incisors appear.	Appearance of temporary teeth
 Fig. 5-4	6 to 10 months	Third or corner upper and lower incisors appear.	
 Fig. 5-5	1 year of age	Crowns of central incisors show wear.	
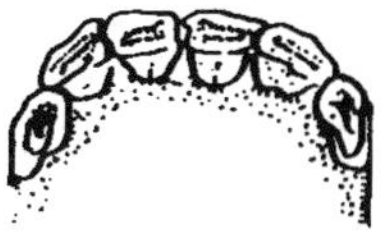 Fig. 5-6	1½ years of age	Intermediate incisors show wear.	Wear of temporary teeth
 Fig. 5-7	2 years of age	All temporary incisors show wear.	

(Continued)

TABLE 5-2 (Continued)

Drawing of Teeth	Age of Animal	Description of Teeth	
 Fig. 5-8	2½ years of age	First of central incisors appear.	
 Fig. 5-9	3½ years of age	Second or intermediate incisors appear.	Appearance of permanent teeth
 Fig. 5-10	4½ years of age	Third corner incisors appear.	
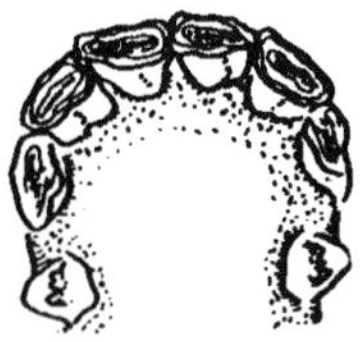 Fig. 5-11	4 to 5 years of age (in male)	Canines appear.	
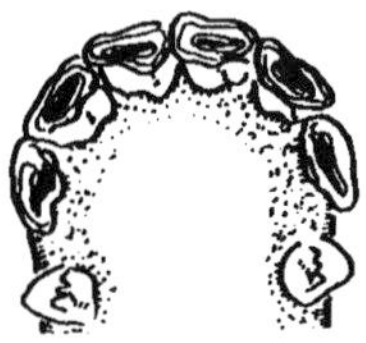 Fig. 5-12	5 years of age	Cups in all incisors.	Wear of permanent teeth
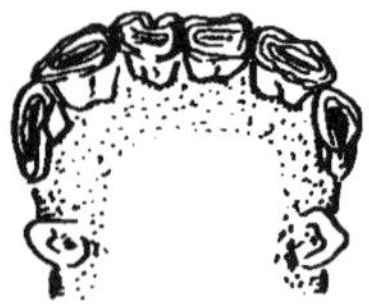 Fig. 5-13	6 years of age	Cups worn out of lower central incisors.	

(Continued)

TABLE 5-2 (Continued)

Drawing of Teeth	Age of Animal	Description of Teeth	
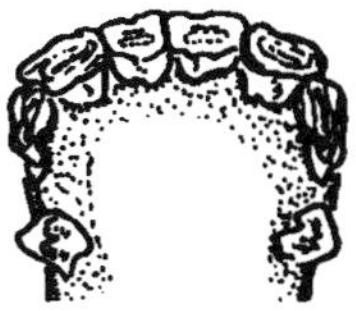 Fig. 5-14	7 years of age	Cups also worn out of lower intermediate incisors.	
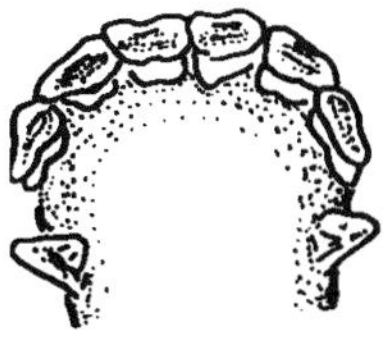 Fig. 5-15	8 years of age	Cups worn out of all lower incisors, and dental *star* appears on lower central and intermediate pairs.	
 Fig. 5-16	9 years of age	Cups also worn out of upper central incisors, and dental *star* appears on upper central and intermediate pairs.	Wear of permanent teeth
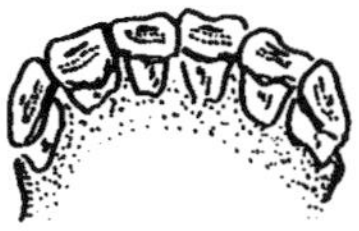 Fig. 5-17	10 years of age	Cups also worn out of upper intermediate incisors and dental *star* is present on all incisors both upper and lower.	
 Fig. 5-18	11 years of age	Cups worn out of all upper and lower incisors, and dental *star* approaches center of cups.	
 Fig. 5-19	12 years of age	No cups. *Smooth mouthed.*	

[1]The illustrations for this table were prepared by Prof. R. F. Johnson.

STRUCTURE OF THE TOOTH

The tooth consists of an outside cement and a second layer of a very hard enamel followed by the dentine and a dark center known as the pulp. The enamel passes up over the surface of the teeth and extends inward, forming a pit. The inside and bottom of the pit, which is blackened by feed, constitutes the *mark* or *cup*. As the rims of these cups disappear through wear, two distinct rings of enamel remain, one around the margin of the tooth and the other around the cup. With wear, the cups become smaller—first more oval or rounding in shape, then triangular and more shallow, and they finally disappear completely. Further wear on the table or grinding surface of the tooth exposes the tip of the pulp canal or cavity in the center of the tooth. The exposed tip of this canal, which appears between what is left of the cup and the front of the tooth, is known as the *dental star*. The gradual wearing and disappearance of the cups according to a rather definite pattern in period of time enables the experienced equestrian to judge the age of the animal with a fair degree of accuracy up to 12 years.

A summary showing the changes in teeth according to usual age intervals is given in Table 5-2.

After 12 years of age, even the most experienced equestrian cannot determine accurately the age of an animal. It is known, however, that with more advanced age the teeth change from oval to triangular and that they project or slant forward more and more each year (see Fig. 5-21).

It must also be realized that the environment of the animal can very materially affect the wear on the teeth, often making it impossible to determine accurately the age of animals. For example, the teeth of horses raised in a dry, sandy area will show more than normal wear. Thus, the 5-year-old western horse may have a 6- or even 8-year-old mouth. The unnatural wear resulting in the teeth of cribbers, or animals with parrot mouth or undershot jaw, also makes it difficult to estimate age.

TEMPORARY TOOTH   PERMANENT TOOTH

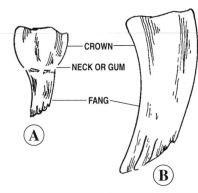

CROWN

NECK OR GUM

FANG

(A)

(B)

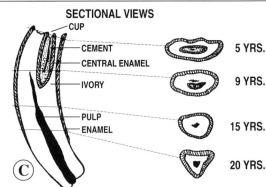

SECTIONAL VIEWS

CUP

CEMENT

CENTRAL ENAMEL   5 YRS.

IVORY   9 YRS.

PULP

ENAMEL   15 YRS.

(C)   20 YRS.

Fig. 5-20. The horse's tooth. A, temporary lower pincher tooth; B, permanent lower pincher tooth. Temporary or milk teeth are smaller and much whiter than permanent teeth, and constricted at the gum line (neck). C, longitudinal section of a permanent lower middle pincher tooth; and cross section of permanent lower middle pincher teeth at different age levels. These drawings show why, with advancing age, the teeth of the horse (1) slant out toward the front, (2) change in wearing surface as noted in the cross-sectional shape, (3) change in shape of cups and in the time of disappearance of the cups, and (4) change in appearance and shape of the dental star. (Drawing by Prof. R. F. Johnson)

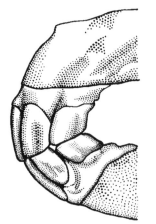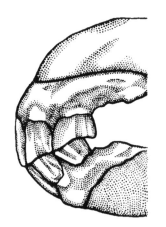

Fig. 5-21. Side view of horse's mouth at 5, 7, and 20 years. Note that as the horse advances in age, the teeth change from nearly perpendicular to slanting sharply toward the front. (Drawing by Prof. R. F. Johnson)

FLOATING TEETH

Sometimes the teeth of horses develop sharp edges. Rectifying the situation by filing off the sharp edges is known as floating.

TAMPERED OR "BISHOPED" TEETH

Occasionally, unscrupulous horse traders endeavor to make the amateur a victim of their trade tricks, especially through tampering with the teeth. As very young horses increase in value to a certain stage, the milk teeth are sometimes pulled a few months before they would normally fall out. This hastens the appearance of the permanent teeth and makes the animal appear older.

Bishoping is the practice of artificially drilling, burning, or staining cups in the teeth of older horses in an attempt to make them sell as young horses. The experienced equestrian can detect such deception because the ring of enamel that is always present around the natural cup cannot be reproduced. This makes the practice more difficult than counterfeiting money. Moreover, the slanting position and triangular shape of the teeth of an older animal cannot be changed. An experienced equestrian should always be called upon to make an examination if there is any suspicion that the teeth have been tampered with.

MEASURING HORSES

The normal measurements pertinent to a horse are: (1) height, (2) weight, (3) girth, and (4) bone.

HEIGHT

The height of a horse is determined by standing the animal squarely on a level area and measuring the vertical distance from the highest point of its withers to the ground. The unit of measurement used in expressing the height is the *hand*, each hand being 4 inches. Thus, a horse measuring 62 in. is said to be 15-2 hands (15 hands and 2 inches) high. Animals standing less than 14-2 (meaning 14 hands and 2 in.) are classed as ponies.

Instead of actually measuring by calipers or tape, the experienced equestrian deftly estimates the height of a horse in relation to his/her own stature. Thus, by knowing the exact height from the ground to the level of his/her own eyes, the equestrian can stand opposite the front limbs of the horse, look to the highest point of the withers, and estimate the height very quickly and accurately.

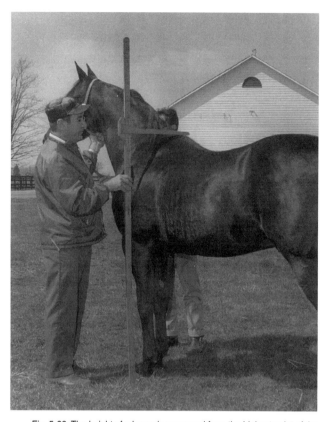

Fig. 5-22. The height of a horse is measured from the highest point of the withers to the ground. The experienced equestrian deftly estimates the height of a horse in relation to his/her own stature, and does not use any measuring device. (Courtesy, The United States Trotting Assn., Columbus, OH)

WEIGHT

The weight of a horse is best determined by placing the animal on a properly balanced scale. The weight is recorded in pounds.

GIRTH

The girth is a measurement of the circumference of the chest behind the withers and in front of the back. A large girth is desired because it indicates ample space for such vital organs as the heart and lungs.

BONE

The size of the bone is usually determined by placing a tape measure around the cannon bone halfway between the knee and fetlock joints. The reading is recorded in inches.

SELECTED REFERENCES

Title of Publication	Author(s)	Publisher
Breeding and Raising Horses, Ag. Hdbk. No. 394	M. E. Ensminger	Agricultural Research Service, USDA, Washington, DC, 1972
Determining the Age of Farm Animals by Their Teeth, Farmers' Bull. No. 1721		U.S. Department of Agriculture, Washington, DC
Horse Industry Handbook	Staff	American Horse Council, Washington, DC, 1993
Horsemanship and Horse Care, Ag. Info. Bull. No. 353	M. E. Ensminger	Agricultural Research Service, USDA, Washington, DC, 1972
Judging Manual for American Saddlebred Horses	J. Foss	American Saddle Horse Breeders Association, Louisville, KY, 1973.
Livestock Judging, Selection and Evaluation, Fourth Edition	R. E. Hunsley W. M. Beeson	Interstate Publishers, Inc., Danville, IL, 1993
Points of the Horse, Seventh Edition	M. H. Hayes	Arco Publishing Co., Inc., New York, NY, 1969
Stockman's Handbook, The, Seventh Edition	M. E. Ensminger	Interstate Publishers, Inc., Danville, IL 1992

6

UNSOUNDNESSES AND STABLE VICES

In the wild, soundness was essential for survival, and there were no stable vices. (After a painting by Ernest Grisét. Courtesy, Smithsonian Institution)

An integral part of selecting and judging horses is the ability to recognize the common blemishes and unsoundnesses and to rate the importance of each. Also, equestrians should be knowledgeable relative to the scientific diagnosis and treatment of blemishes and unsoundnesses.

Today, X-rays and ultrasound complement each other in diagnosing injuries; X-rays for detecting bone injuries, and ultrasound for detecting tissue injuries. Today, too, various types of steroids are used to increase muscle mass and eliminate pain from creaky joints. Researchers and practitioners caution, however, that the potential reproductive harm may far outweigh whatever good might accrue.

DISTINCTION BETWEEN BLEMISHES AND UNSOUNDNESSES

Technically speaking, any abnormal deviation in structure or function constitutes an unsoundness. From a practical standpoint, however, a differentiation is made between those abnormalities that do and those that do not affect the serviceability of a horse. Thus, the following definitions usually apply:

1. *Blemishes include those abnormalities that do not affect the serviceability of a horse.* Such unsightly things as wire cuts, rope burns, nail punctures, shoe boils, capped hocks, etc., are generally placed under this category.

2. *Unsoundnesses include those more serious abnormalities that affect the serviceability of the horse.*

CAUSES OF UNSOUNDNESSES

Unsoundnesses may be caused by any one or various combinations of the following:

1. An inherent or predisposing weakness.
2. Subjection of the horse to strain and stress far beyond the capability of even the best structure and tissue.

3. Accident and injury.
4. Nutritional deficiencies, particularly minerals.

Unsoundnesses that can be definitely traced to the latter three causes should not be considered as hereditary. Unless one is very positive, however, serious unsoundnesses should always be regarded with suspicion in the breeding animal. Probably no unsoundness is actually inherited, but the fact that individuals may inherit a predisposition to an unsoundness through faulty conformation cannot be questioned.

LOCATION OF COMMON BLEMISHES AND UNSOUNDNESSES

Fig. 6-1 and the accompanying outline give the body location of the common blemishes and unsoundnesses. As would be suspected, the great preponderance of troubles affect the limbs.

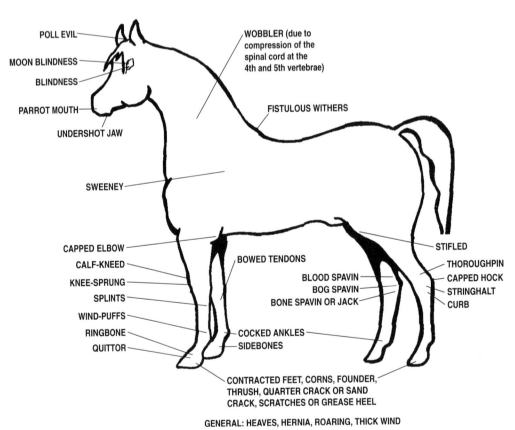

Fig. 6-1. Location of points of common unsoundnesses in horses.

I. Head:
1. Blindness
2. Moon blindness (periodic ophthalmia)
3. Parrot mouth and undershot jaw
4. Poll evil
5. Wobblers

II. Withers and shoulders:
1. Fistulous withers
2. Sweeney

III. Front limbs:
1. Bowed tendons
2. Calf-kneed
3. Cocked ankles
4. Knee-sprung
5. Ringbone
6. Shoe boil
7. Splints
8. Wind-puffs

9. Contracted feet
10. Corns
11. Navicular disease
12. Founder or laminitis
13. Quarter crack or sand crack
14. Quittor
15. Scratches or grease heel
16. Sidebones
17. Thrush
} Front Feet

IV. Rear limbs:
1. Cocked ankles
2. Ringbone
3. Stifled
4. Stringhalt
5. Wind-puffs

6. Blood spavin
7. Bog spavin
8. Bone spavin or jack
9. Capped hock
10. Curb
11. Thoroughpin
} Hocks

12. Contracted feet
13. Corn
14. Founder or laminitis
15. Quarter crack or sand crack
16. Quittor
17. Scratches or grease heel
18. Thrush
} Hind Feet

V. General:
1. Heaves
2. Hernia or rupture
3. Roaring
4. Thick wind

DESCRIPTION AND TREATMENT OF COMMON BLEMISHES AND UNSOUNDNESSES

The following brief description and treatment pertain to the common blemishes and unsoundnesses of different body areas.

UNSOUNDNESSES OF THE HEAD AND NECK

The most serious unsoundnesses of the head are those that affect the sight of the animal; namely, blindness and moon blindness. In addition, poll evil is very serious, and the parrot mouthed and undershot jaw conditions are most undesirable.

BLINDNESS

Partial or complete loss of vision is known as blindness. Either or both eyes may be affected. A blind horse usually has very erect ears and a hesitant gait. Frequently, blindness also can be detected by the discoloration of the eye. Further and more certain verification can be obtained by moving the hand gently in close proximity to the eye.

MOON BLINDNESS (OR PERIODIC OPHTHALMIA)

Moon blindness (or periodic ophthalmia) is a cloudy or inflamed condition of the eye which disappears and returns in cycles that are often completed in about a month. Because many people formerly believed the cycle to be related to changes of the moon, it was given the name of *moon blindness*.

The causes of moon blindness are unknown, but it appears that it may result from several conditions. Experiments initiated at the Front Royal Remount Depot, beginning in 1943, showed that, in some cases, it is a nutritional deficiency disease, caused by a lack of riboflavin.[1] Today, much evidence exists that leptospirosis may cause periodic ophthalmia. Also, some cases appear to be caused by the presence of the parasite *Filaria equina* within the eye, or from a reaction to systemic parasitism elsewhere in the body. Other investigations have suggested that periodic

---

[1]In the Front Royal experiments, when crystalline riboflavin was added to the ration at the rate of 40 mg per horse per day, no new cases of periodic ophthalmia developed.

ophthalmia is a reaction of the eye to antigens from repeated streptococcal infections.

PARROT MOUTH AND UNDERSHOT JAW

Both parrot mouth and undershot jaw are hereditary imperfections in the way in which the teeth come together. In parrot mouth, or overshot jaw, the lower jaw is shorter than the upper jaw. The reverse condition is known as undershot jaw.

POLL EVIL

This is an inflamed condition in the region of the poll (the area on top of the neck and immediately behind the ears). It is usually caused by bruising the top of the head. The swelling, which may be on one or both sides, usually contains pus or a straw-colored fluid. At first the affected area is hot and painful, but later the acute symptoms of inflammation subside. Treatment, which should be handled by a veterinarian, consists in establishing proper drainage and removing all dead tissue. In addition to surgery, some veterinarians claim that recovery is hastened by injections of a specially prepared bacterin. Poll evil is slow to yield to treatment, and it may break out again after it is thought to be cured.

WOBBLERS

There are many neurologic diseases in horses. Number one on the list is Cervical Vertebral Stenotic Myelopathy (CVM), commonly known as wobblers, which primarily affects long-necked horses such as the Thoroughbred. Smaller individuals and ponies are not affected. The symptoms appear in young equines anywhere from birth to three years of age. Afflicted males outnumber afflicted females 3 to 1. In the early stages, it is difficult to detect wobblers. It begins with hindlimb incoordination, evidenced by dragging of the toes and errors in the rate, range, force, and direction of movement; and generally the condition worsens. The clinical signs are primarily damage to the white matter of the cervical spinal cord. All available evidence suggests that wobblers is an hereditary condition. Medical treatment and surgery have been used with mixed results. Economically,. it may not be practical to treat wobblers either medically or surgically. Also, because the abnormality is thought to be genetic, using such animals for breeding purposes is questionable.

Number two on the list of neurologic diseases of horses is Equine Protozoal Myeloencephalitis (EPM). Current thinking is that EPM is transmitted between two hosts—opossums becoming infected by eating dead birds (many birds serve as intermediate hosts) and recontaminating the environment in a cyclical manner over and over again. The horse ingests the parasites which go to its brain and spinal cord. However, EPM has not yet been reproduced experimentally in horses, and the entire life cycle of *S. falcatula* (organisms obtained from opossums and birds) has not been completed in the laboratory.

UNSOUNDNESSES OF THE WITHERS AND SHOULDERS

Though less frequent in occurrence than the unsoundnesses of the feet, the conditions of the shoulders known as fistulous withers and sweeney are very injurious to animals which are affected.

FISTULOUS WITHERS

Fistulous withers is an inflamed condition in the region of the withers. *Brucella abortus*, and occasionally *B. suis*, can be isolated from the fluid aspirated from the unopened bursa, and outbreaks of brucellosis in cattle have followed contact with horses with open bursitis. Fistula and poll evil are very similar except for location. As in poll evil, therefore, treatment for fistulous withers, which should be handled by a veterinarian, consists in establishing proper drainage and removing all dead tissue.

Fig. 6-2. Horse with fistulous withers. (Courtesy, University of Pennsylvania)

SWEENEY

A depression in the shoulder due to atrophied muscles is known as sweeney. Sweeney is caused by nerve injury. No known treatment will restore the nerve, but it is possible to fill in the depression by injecting irritants into the affected area.

UNSOUNDNESSES OF THE LIMBS

Although they are confined to a relatively small proportion of the anatomy of the horse, there appears to be hardly any limit to the number of unsoundnesses that may affect the front limbs. The major unsoundnesses of this type will be discussed briefly.

BLOOD SPAVIN

Blood spavin is a varicose vein enlargement which appears on the inside of the hock, but immediately above the location of bog spavin. No successful treatment for blood spavin is known.

BOG SPAVIN

Bog spavin is a filling of the natural depression on the inside and front of the hock. A bog spavin is much larger than a blood spavin. Common treatments include removal of excess fluid, corticosteroid injections into the joint capsule, liniment, and pressure bandages. Massage several times daily will reduce the swelling. Even if treatment is successful, bog spavin swellings have a tendency to recur.

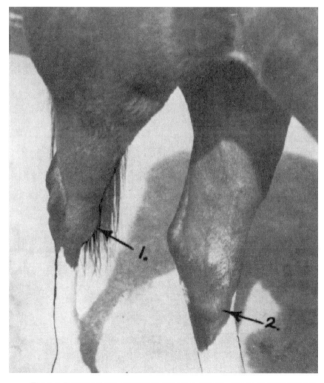

Fig. 6-3. Bog spavin on right hock (No. 1) and bone spavin on left hock (No. 2). Bog spavin is a filling of the natural depression on the inside and front of the hock. Bone spavin is a bony enlargement that appears on the inside and the front of the hock at the point where the base of the hock tapers into the cannon part of the leg.

BONE SPAVIN (OR JACK SPAVIN)

Bone spavin (or jack spavin) is a bony enlargement that appears on the inside and front of the hock at the point where the base of the hock tapers into the cannon part of the leg. It is one of the most destructive conditions affecting the usefulness of a horse. The lameness is most evident when the animal is used following rest. A hereditary weakness—together with such things as bruises, strains, and sprains—appears to cause bone spavin. Rest seems to be the most important treatment. Additional therapy involves easing the pain by corrective shoeing or surgically fusing the joint, depending on the extent of the bone spavin.

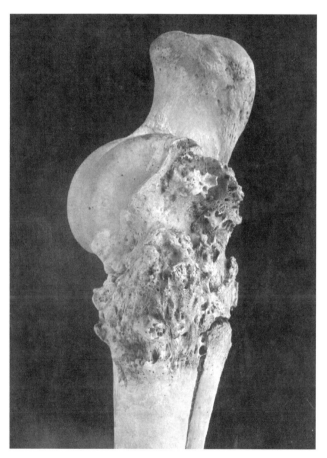

Fig. 6-4. Bone (or jack) spavin, showing the extra bone formation (exostosis) of the metatarsal and tarsal bones. This is a medial, or inside, view of the hock area. (Photo by J. C. Allen & Son, West Lafayette, IN)

BOWED TENDONS

Enlarged tendons behind the cannon bones, in both the front and hind legs, are called bowed tendons. Descriptive terms of *high* and *low* bow are used by equestrians to denote the location of the injury; the high bow appears just under the knee and the low bow just above the fetlock. This condition is often brought about by severe strains, such as heavy training or racing. When bowed tendons are pronounced, more or less swelling, soreness, and lameness are present.

Prompt treatment of a bowed tendon can make the difference between return to work and retirement. If the horse is some distance from the stable, as is often the case for horses that are racing or in training, a very tight bandage should be applied immediately in order to lessen the massive hemorrhage in, and blood flow to, the affected area. Any bandage will work. If a tourniquet is used, it should be removed at 20 minute intervals, then reapplied.

As soon as the horse is in the stable, the bandage should be removed and the leg put in ice for several hours. If the horse has been iced for about 12 hours, the veterinarian may apply a cast from the knee to the hoof and administer steroids. The first cast is usually replaced by the second cast in 7 to 10 days; and the second cast is usually left on for 2 to 3 weeks.

After a month of the above treatments (bandage, ice, steroids, and casts), further healing will be up to nature. Tendons heal slowly, so about a year will be required for complete healing.

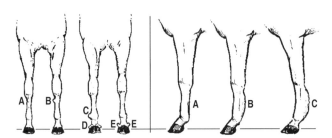

Fig. 6-5. Unsoundness of the front limbs. *Left*—Front legs of the horse, as viewed from the front: **A**, sound leg; **B**, splint; **C**, wind-puffs; **D**, ringbone; and **E**, sidebones. *Right*—Front legs of the horse, as viewed from the side: **A**, sound leg; **B**, bowed tendon; and **C**, filled tendon.

BUCKED SHINS

Bucked shins refers to a temporary racing unsoundness. For the most part, it occurs in the forelimbs (rarely in the hind limb; and it is peculiar to two-year-olds, although occasionally a three-year-old that did little campaigning at two will fall victim to the condition. It usually strikes early in the final stages of preparation to race or early in the racing career. It is a very painful inflammation of the periosteum (bone covering) along the greater part of the front surface of the cannon bone, caused by constant pressure from concussion during fast works or races. Afflicted horses become very lame and are very sensitive when the slightest

pressure is applied about the shins; many horses will almost lie down to keep a person from touching the sore area.

Rest for a minimum of one month from training is important until the soreness and inflammation have disappeared. The acute inflammation may be relieved by cold water bandages, poultices, antiphlogistic packs, or corticosteroids. *Note:* The prognosis is good if enough rest is given.

CALF-KNEED

Standing with knees too far back, directly opposite to buck-kneed or knee-sprung, is called *calf-kneed*.

CAPPED HOCK

Capped hock is an enlargement at the point of the hock; it is usually caused by bruising. Daily painting of the enlargement with tincture of iodine may help to diminish it. Though it may be unsightly, capped hock need not be considered serious unless it interferes with the work of the horse. Successful reduction of the swelling depends on prompt and persistent treatment, with antiphlogistic applications, before the fluid has a chance to form the fibrinous tissue in the sheath or bursa. Once the cap has set or become fibrinous, all that can be done is to remove any inflammation present, and then, by a series of blisters, attempt to cause resorption (reduction in size).

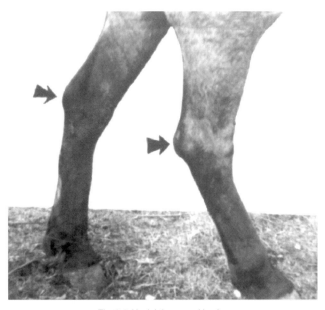

Fig. 6-6. Unsightly capped hocks.

COCKED ANKLES

Cocked ankles refers to horses that stand bent forward on the fetlocks in a cocked position. This condition can be corrected by proper trimming, allowing the toes to grow out while keeping the heels trimmed. However, where cocked ankles are of nutritional origin (as a result of the rickets syndrome), they should be treated by correcting the causative nutritional deficiency or imbalance.

CONTRACTED FEET

This condition, known as contracted, most often occurs in the forefeet and is characterized by a drawing in or contracting at the heels (see Fig. 6-7). A tendency toward contracted feet may be inherited, but improper shoeing usually aggravates the condition. Paring, removal of shoes, or use of special shoes constitutes the best treatment.

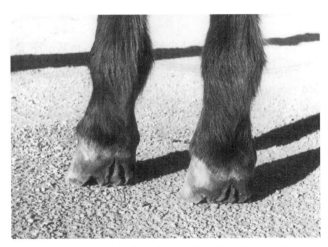

Fig. 6-7. Contracted heels on forefeet. (Courtesy, *Western Horseman*, Colorado Springs, CO)

CORNS

A bruise to the soft tissue underlying the horny sole of the foot—which manifests itself in a reddish discoloration of the sole immediately below the affected area—is known as a corn. Fast work on hard and rough roads, flat soles, weakened bars, and poor shoeing may cause corns. Paring, special shoeing, poulticing, sanitation, and rest constitute the best treatment.

CURB

Curb is the name given to the condition in which there is a fullness at the rear of the leg and below the point of the hock. This fullness is due to enlargement of the ligament or tendon. The condition is caused by anything that brings about a thickening in the ligament, tendon, or skin of this region so as to cause a deviation in the straight line that normally extends from the point of the hock to the fetlock. If the condition is due to acute inflammation, cold packs and rest are indicated. Little can be done to overcome a curb that is due to poor conformation.

Fig. 6-8. Curb. (Courtesy, Michigan State University)

FOUNDER (OR LAMINITIS)

Founder (or laminitis) is a serious ailment of the fleshy laminae. It strikes many horses each year; worse yet, there is no cure. Founder may be caused by (1) overeating (grain, or lush legume or grass known as *grass founder*), (2) overwork, (3) giving animals too much cold water when they are hot, or (4) inflammation of the uterus following foaling. All feet may be affected, but the front feet are more susceptible. Prompt treatment by a competent veterinarian will usually prevent permanent injury. Until the veterinarian arrives, the horse may be given great relief by applying cold applications to the feet. This may be accomplished by wrapping the feet with burlap bags saturated with cold water or by standing the horse in a foot bath. If the condition is neglected, chronic laminitis will develop and will cause dropping of the hoof soles and a turning up of the toe walls.

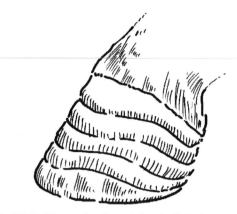

Fig. 6-9. Hoof of a foundered horse. In founder, the foot undergoes structural changes. As it grows down, successive rings appear and it becomes deformed through a bulging or dropped sole, and the horse walks on the heels with a shortened stride. (Drawing by Prof. R. F. Johnson)

FRACTURED FIBULA

Most cases of acute or chronic lameness due to fibula fractures are found on the racetrack.

The fibula is a small, long bone extending along the back side of the tibia from the stifle downward. The upper end articulates with the end of the tibia and the lower end eventually becomes fused with this same bone. In young horses, only the upper third is visible on X-ray plates, because the long, thin shaft has not changed from cartilage to bone. In older horses, the entire length is easily seen on X-ray plates.

The fracture of the fibula causes lameness of the stifle, hip, and back. Horses in training are able to negotiate turns well, but they tend to turn sideways (away from the injured leg) on the straight. An X-ray examination is the only conclusive way to arrive at a diagnosis.

Fibular fracture is caused by undue stress, a strain, or a blow—from (1) sudden starts from off-balanced positions at the starting gate, (2) sudden stops or propping, (3) bad racetracks, (4) sudden shifting of weight in rearing or shying, (5) being cast in the stall, or (6) kicks or collisions. Also, faulty nutrition may be a causative factor in some cases.

Rest is usually an effective treatment for fractures of the fibula. However, fractured fibula may be treated by surgical removal of the bone fragment.

GRAVEL

Gravel is usually caused by penetration of the protective covering of the hoof by small bits of gravel or dirt. Access to the sensitive tissue is usually gained at the *white line* or junction of the sole and wall, where the horn is somewhat softer. Once in the soft tissue inside the wall or sole, bacterial infection carried by the foreign material develops rapidly, producing pus and gas that create pressure and intense pain in the foot. In untreated cases, it breaks out at the top of the coronary band and the pus and gas are forced out through this opening.

Treatment consists in (1) opening the pathway used by the gravel or dirt going into the foot, thus draining the pus at the bottom and relieving the pressure, (2) administering antitoxin, and (3) protecting the opening from further infection.

KNEE-SPRUNG

The condition of being over in the knees, or with the knees protruding too far forward, is known as *knee-sprung* or *buck-kneed*.

NAVICULAR DISEASE

Navicular disease is an inflammation of the small navicular bone and bursa of the front foot. It is often impossible to determine the exact cause of the disease. Affected animals go lame; have a short, stubby stride; and usually point the affected foot when standing. Few animals completely recover from the disease. Treatment consists in special shoeing. In cases of persistent or severe lameness, unnerving may be performed by a veterinarian, who can destroy sensation in the foot.

OSSELETS

Osselets, like bucked shins, are primarily an affliction of younger horses and the result of more strain or pressure from training or racing than the immature bone structure can stand. However, osselets are not so common among two-year-olds as bucked shins.

Osselets is a rather inclusive term used to refer to a number of inflammatory conditions around the ankle joints. Generally it denotes a swelling that is fairly well defined and located slightly above or below the actual center of the joint, and, ordinarily, a little to the inside or outside of the exact front of the leg. When touched, it imparts the feeling of putty or mush, and it may be warm to hot. The pain will be in keeping with the degree of inflammation as evidenced by swelling and fever. Afflicted horses travel with a short, choppy stride and show evidence of pain when the ankle is flexed.

Standard treatment consists in stopping training and rest at the first sign that the condition is developing. Additionally, the inflammation may be reduced by (1) cold water bandages, (2) ice packs, (3) antiphlogistic packs, (4) poultices, and/or (5) corticosteroid injections.

POPPED KNEE

Popped knee (so named because of the sudden swelling that accompanies it) is a general term describing inflammatory conditions affecting the knees. It is due either to (1) sprain or strain of one or more of the extensive group of small but important ligaments that hold the bones of the knee in position, or (2) damage to a joint capsule, followed by an increase in the amount of fluid within the capsule and a distension or bulging out between the overlying structure. Of course, faulty conformation of the knees contributes largely to the breaking down of some individuals.

Horses suffering severe popped knees rarely are able to regain a degree of soundness that will allow them to return to the racing form shown before the injury. The common treatments include (1) prolonged rest, (2) removal of excess fluid from the joint, and (3) intra-articular injection of a corticosteroid.

QUARTER CRACK (OR SAND CRACK)

A vertical split in the horny wall of the inside of the hoof (in the region of the quarter), which extends from the coronet or hoof head downward, is known as *quarter crack* or *sand crack*. It is seldom found in the hind legs. When the crack is on the forepart of the toe, it is termed toe crack. This condition usually results from the hoof being allowed to become too dry and brittle or from improper shoeing. Special shoeing or clamping together of the cracks is the usual treatment. Growth of new horn may be encouraged by application of a counterirritant (*e.g.*, tincture of iodine).

Fig. 6-11. Quittor on right hind foot. This is a deep-seated running sore at the coronet or hoof head. It causes severe lameness.

of the third phalanx. It results in severe lameness. The infection may arise from a puncture wound, corns, and sand cracks; or it may be carried in the bloodstream. Quittor is usually confined to the forefeet, but it sometimes occurs in the hind feet. Drainage and antiseptics may relieve the condition, although surgery by a veterinarian may be necessary.

RINGBONE

Ringbone is a bony growth on the pastern bone

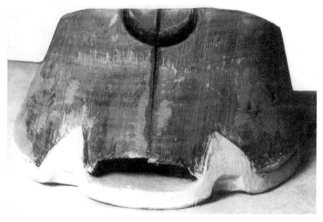

Fig. 6-10. Hoof showing sand crack and one method of treatment. (Courtesy, Michigan State University)

QUITTOR

Quittor is a deep-seated running sore at the coronet or hoof head caused by necrosis of the cartilage

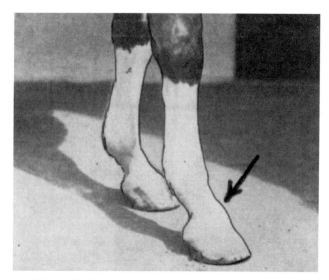

Fig. 6-12. Ringbone on the right foot. This is a bony growth on the pastern bone, generally on the forefoot, although occasionally the hind foot is affected.

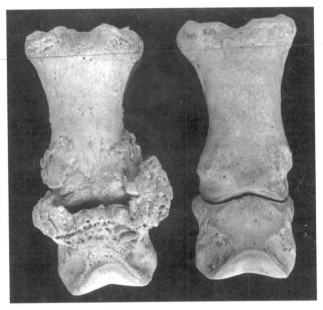

Fig. 6-13. Ringbone on the pastern, showing the extra bone formation, in corallike masses, on the surface of the first and second phalanges. (Photo by J. C. Allen & Son, West Lafayette, IN)

generally of the forefoot, although occasionally the hind foot is affected. The condition usually causes a lameness, accompanied by a stiff ankle. This condition generally follows severe straining, blows, sprains, or improper shoeing. Treatment consists of complete rest, cold and astringent applications, and radiation therapy in the early stages. Anti-inflammatory medication may relieve the signs of lameness. Neurectomies (severing of the nerves) are sometimes performed to alleviate the pain.

SCRATCHES (OR GREASE HEEL)

Scratches or grease heel is a mangelike inflammation of the posterior surfaces of the fetlocks, most frequently confined to the hind legs. Treatment consists in placing the affected animal in clean quarters, clipping closely all hair on the affected areas, cleaning with mild soap and water, and applying astringent, antiseptic substances at regular intervals.

SESAMOID FRACTURES

The sesamoids are two pyramidlike bones that form a part of the fetlock or ankle joints (on both front and rear legs) and articulate with the posterior part of the lower end of the cannon bone. They lie imbedded in ligaments and cartilage which form a bearing surface over which the flexor tendons glide.

The fracture of these fragile little bones is more frequent than has been supposed.

Treatment may be either (1) surgical, or (2) casting of the leg, depending on the size and type of fracture.

SHOE BOIL (OR CAPPED ELBOW)

Shoe boil is a soft, flabby swelling caused by an irritation at the point of the elbow, hence the common name *capped elbow*. The two most common causes of this unsoundness are injury from the heel calk of the shoe and injury from contact with the floor. Affected animals may or may not go lame, depending upon the degree of inflammation and the size of the swelling. If discovered while yet small, shoe boil may be successfully treated by daily applications of tincture of iodine and the use of the shoe boil boot or roll. This latter is strapped about the pastern in such a manner as to keep the heel from pressing upon the elbow while the horse is in a recumbent position. For treatment of large shoe boils, surgery by a veterinarian may be necessary, but such treatment is not always successful. Some equestrians report good results from the use of ligature which is passed around the neck of the swelling and tightened each day until circulation is stopped and the whole mass sloughs off.

SIDEBONES

Sidebones are ossified lateral cartilages immediately above and toward the rear quarter of the hoof head. They occur most commonly in the forefeet. Lameness may or may not be present. The condition may occur on one or both sides of the foot, or on one or both front feet. This is perhaps the most common unsoundness of the feet of horses.

Sidebones may be partially or entirely of genetic origin; or the condition may result from running or working horses on pavement or other hard surface. Sidebones may also develop following sprains, cracks, quittor, or other injuries. Treatments vary and are not always successful. Temporary relief from fever and soreness can usually be obtained through the application of cold-water bandages. If the horse is lame, corrective shoeing is the usual treatment, to allow the quarters to expand.

SPLINTS

Splints are abnormal bony growths found on the cannon bone, usually on the inside surface, but occasionally on the outside. They are most common on the front legs. When found on the hind cannon, they are generally on the outside. Splints may enlarge and interfere with a ligament and cause irritation and lameness. Their presence detracts from the appearance of the animal, even when there is no lameness. When found on young horses, they often disappear. Local use of steroids delays the consolidation process. All treatments must include at least 30 days of complete rest. If the bone growth encroaches on the suspensory ligament, surgery may be necessary.

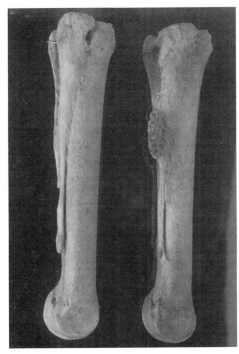

Fig. 6-14. Two cannon (forelimb) bones. The left one is normal. The right one shows a splint on the median, or inside, involving the second and third metacarpal bones. (Photo by J. C. Allen & Son, West Lafayette, IN)

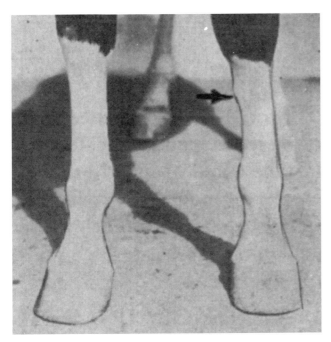

Fig. 6-15. Splints on the left front leg.

STIFLED

The stifle corresponds to the knee in humans. A horse is said to be stifled when the patella (or kneecap) slips out of place temporarily and locks in a location above and to the inside of its normal location. Technically, this condition is known as dorsal patellar fixation. Sometimes it is possible to place the patella back in normal position manually. However, the most effective treatment is surgery, known as medial patellar desmotomy, which consists in removal of one of the ligaments which attach the patella. Surgery will correct most cases.

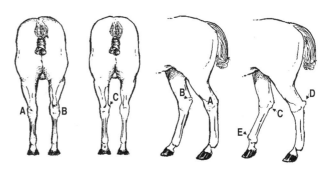

Fig. 6-16. Unsoundnesses of the rear limbs. *Left*—Hind legs of the horse as viewed from the rear; **A**, sound leg; **B**, bog spavin; **C**, bone spavin. *Right*—Hind legs of the horse, as viewed from the side: **A**, sound legs; **B**, thoroughpin; **C**, curb; **D**, capped hock; and **E**, cocked ankle.

STRINGHALT

Stringhalt is characterized by excessive flexing of the hind legs. It is most easily detected when backing a horse. The condition may be cured or greatly relieved by a surgical operation on the lateral extensor tendon. An incision is made over the tendon on the outside of the leg just below the hock, and about 2 in. of the tendon is removed. Prognosis following surgery is guarded—not all cases respond.

SUSPENSORY LIGAMENT SPRAIN

The suspensory ligament is situated over the back leg and passes over the fetlock or ankle joint, both in the fore and hind legs. Its principal function is to support the fetlock. This ligament is frequently the object of severe strain; the swelling begins just above the ankle and extends obliquely downward and forward over the sides of the ankle. Should the injury be further up on the leg, the exact location at first may appear obscure as the ligament is covered by the flexor tendons.

When the suspensory ligament is affected, the swelling will be found right up against the bone. If it is the flexor tendons that are involved, the swelling will be farther back near the surface on the back of the leg.

The front legs are more frequently affected than the hind legs, except in the Standardbred breed, where suspensory ligament injury most commonly occurs in the hind legs.

THOROUGHPIN

Thoroughpin is a puffy condition in the web of the hock. It can be determined by movement of the puff, when pressed, to the opposite side of the leg. Rest is indicated. If the veterinarian sees the need, the area can be drained and corticosteroids injected two to three times a week until the swelling subsides.

THRUSH

Thrush is a disease of the frog of the horse's foot, caused by unsanitary conditions along with anaerobic bacteria, which produces a foul smell.

Prevention consists in sanitary conditions and cleaning the hooves daily.

Most cases will respond to sanitation, accompanied by trimming away the affected frog, using an old toothbrush and scrubbing the affected area with soap and water, drying the hoof thoroughly, and applying to the infected area such agents as 10% formalin, equal parts of phenol and iodine, or tincture of iodine.

WIND-PUFFS (OR WINDGALLS)

Windgalls or puffs are an enlargement of the fluid sac (bursa) located immediately above the pastern joints on the fore and rear legs. They are usually the result of too fast or hard road work, especially on hard surfaces. Treatment is not necessary if there is no lameness. Decreased work will usually suffice. If there is lameness, the veterinarian will usually treat by (1) applying local heat, (2) draining off the excess synovial fluid, and (3) injecting corticosteroids locally.

GENERAL UNSOUNDNESSES OF THE HORSE

Hernia and certain abnormal respiratory conditions are classed as general unsoundnesses. These unsoundnesses greatly lower the usefulness and value of affected animals.

HEAVES

Heaves is a difficulty in forcing air out of the lungs. It is characterized by a jerking of the flanks (double-flank action) and coughing after drinking cold water. There is no satisfactory treatment, although affected animals are less bothered if turned to pasture, if used only at light work, if the hay is sprinkled lightly with water at the time of feeding, or if the entire ration is pelleted. Sometimes, the veterinarian may prescribe atropine, corticosteroids, or antihistamines to relieve distress.

HERNIA (OR RUPTURE)

Hernia (or rupture) refers to the protrusion of any internal organ through the wall of its containing cavity, but it usually means the passage of a portion of the intestine through an opening in the abdominal muscle. Umbilical, scrotal, and inguinal hernias are fairly common in young foals.

An umbilical hernia may be present at birth or may develop soon thereafter. In the majority of cases, the condition corrects itself. If surgery becomes necessary, it is usually postponed until after weaning.

A scrotal hernia, which may be noticed at birth or shortly thereafter, will usually correct itself also, although such natural correction may require several weeks' time. Nevertheless, it is well to advise the veterinarian of the trouble.

ROARING

An animal that makes a roaring sound when respiration is speeded up with exercise is said to be a *roarer*. The condition causes a roaring sound when afflicted animals inhale, and cannot get enough air.

The cause of roaring is unknown. It usually affects horses over 15 hands tall; ponies are seldom affected. An estimated 80% of Thoroughbreds may be affected.

Several surgical procedures are used for the condition, with the results ranging from totally effective to 70% effective.

THICK WIND

Difficulty in breathing is known as *thick wind*.

RACING UNSOUNDNESSES

Experienced trainers estimate that one-third of the horses in training require treatment in one form or another.

The author surveyed a select group of Thoroughbred, Standardbred, and Quarter Horse breeders. This study revealed the following reasons, by rank and percentages, for retiring horses from racing:

Rank	Thoroughbred	Standardbred	Quarter Horse	Three Breeds Combined
1.	Bowed tendons (23%)	Bowed tendons (34%)	Bowed tendons (27%)	Bowed tendons (25%)
2.	Osselets (21%)	Splint (14%)	Bucked shin (18%)	Knee injury (16%)
3.	Knee injury (20%)	Fractured fibula (12%)	Knee injury (12%)	Osselets (16%)
4.	Splint (6%)	Curb (5%)	Fractured sesamoid (9%)	Bucked shin (7%)
5.	Bucked shin (5%)	Knee injury (5%)	Osselets (8%)	Splint (7%)
6.	Fractured sesamoid (4%)	Suspensory ligament (4%)	Splint (5%)	Fractured sesamoid (5%)
7.	Sand crack (3%)	Osselets (3%)	Suspensory ligament (2%)	Fractured fibula (3%)
8.	Fractured fibula (2%)	Ringbone (2%), Parasites (2%)	Sand crack (2%)	Sand crack (2%)
9.	Suspensory ligament (1%)	Sidebones (2%)	Shoulder injury (2%), Arthritis (2%)	Suspensory ligament (2%)
10.	Other (15%)	Other (11%)	Other (13%)	Other (17%)

UNSOUNDNESS, INJURY OR DISEASE FOR ALL THREE BREEDS
(RANKED ORDER)

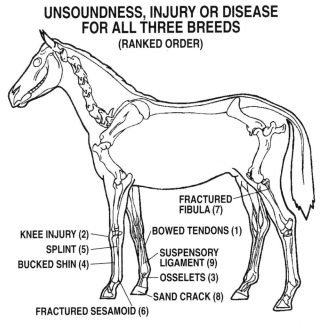

KNEE INJURY (2)
SPLINT (5)
BUCKED SHIN (4)
FRACTURED SESAMOID (6)
FRACTURED FIBULA (7)
BOWED TENDONS (1)
SUSPENSORY LIGAMENT (9)
OSSELETS (3)
SAND CRACK (8)

Fig. 6-17. Most common causes, by rank for retiring horses (composite of Thoroughbred, Standardbred, and Quarter Horse breeds) from racing.

VICES

Vices are difficult to suspect for they are often present in the most handsome and lovable creature. Some vices are vicious and dangerous to people and other animals; others inflict punishment upon the offender; and still others merely use energy wastefully. Regardless of the type of vice, it is undesirable and to be avoided. In general, vices may be divided into two classifications: stable vices, and other vices.

COMMON STABLE VICES

As the name would indicate, stable vices are those which are observed in confinement. Perhaps many of these have arisen because of the unnaturalness of stable conditions.

BOLTING

Bolting is the name given to the habit that ravenous horses have of eating too fast. This condition may be controlled by adding chopped hay to the grain ration or by placing some large, round stones, as big or bigger than baseballs, in the feed box.

CRIBBER

A horse that has the vice of biting or setting the teeth against some object, such as the manger, while sucking air is known as a cribber. This causes a bloated appearance and hard keeping; and such horses are more subject to colic. The best approach is to assure adequate exercise and to pasture the horse. The common remedy for a cribber is a strap buckled around the neck in a way that will compress the larynx when the head is flexed, but that will not cause any discomfort when the horse is not indulging in the vice. A surgical operation to relieve cribbing has been developed and used with some success.

HALTER PULLING

Halter pulling refers to pulling back on the halter rope when tied in the stable.

KICKING

Occasionally, unusual excitement or injury will cause the so-called gentle horse to kick. However, a true stable kicker appears to have no other excuse than the satisfaction of striking something or somebody with its hind feet.

TAIL RUBBING

Persistent rubbing of the tail against the side of the stall or other objects is objectionable. The presence of parasites may cause animals to acquire this vice. Installation of a tail board or electric wire may be necessary in breaking animals of this habit. A tail board is a board projecting from the wall of the stall high enough to strike just below the point of the buttock, instead of the tail, of the rubbing horse.

WEAVING

A rhythmical swaying back and forth while standing in the stall is called weaving.

OTHER VICES

Other vices that are often difficult to cope with and which detract from the value of the animal are: balking, backing, rearing, shying, striking with the front feet, a tendency to run away, and objection to harnessing, saddling, and grooming. Many of these vices originate with incompetent handling; nevertheless, they may be difficult to cope with or correct. This is especially true in older animals, thus lending credence to the statement, "You can't teach an old horse new tricks."

SELECTED REFERENCES

Title of Publication	Author(s)	Publisher
Anatomy and Conformation of the Horse	G. B. Edwards	Dreenan Press Ltd., Croton-on-Hudson, NY, 1973
Anatomy of the Horse, The	R. P. Way D. G. Lee	J. B. Lippincott Co., Philadelphia, PA, 1965
Anatomy and Physiology of Farm Animals	R. D. Frandsen	Lea & Febiger, Philadelphia, PA, 1965
Equine Medicine and Surgery	Ed. by J. F. Bone, *et al.*	American Veterinary Publications, Inc., Wheaton, IL, 1963
Equine Pathology	J. R. Rooney J. L. Robertson	Iowa State University Press, Ames, IA, 1996
First Aid Hints for the Horse Owner	W. E. Lyon	Collins, London, England, 1950
Horse Health, The, from A to Z	P. D. Rossdale S. M. Wreford	Billings & Sons, Ltd., Worcester, England, 1989
Horse Industry Handbook	Staff	American Horse Council, Washington, DC, 1993
Horse, The	J. M. Kays	A. S. Barnes & Co., Inc., Cranbury, NJ, 1969
Horse Owner's Vet Book, The	E. C. Straiton	J. B. Lippincott Co., Philadelphia, PA, 1973
Horsemanship and Horse Care, Ag. Info. Bull. No. 353	M. E. Ensminger	U.S. Department of Agriculture, Washington, DC, 1972
Horseshoeing Theory and Hoof Care	L. Emery J. Miller N. Van Hoosen	Lea & Febiger, Philadelphia, PA, 1977
Horses' Injuries	C. L. Strong	Arco Publishing Co., Inc., New York, NY, 1973
How to Select a Sound Horse, Farmer's Bull. No. 779	H. H. Reese	U.S. Department of Agriculture, Washington, DC, 1949
Lame Horse, The	J. R. Rooney	A. S. Barnes & Co., Inc., Cranbury, NJ, 1974
Lameness in Horses	O. R. Adams	Lea & Febiger, Philadelphia, PA, 1967
Merck, Veterinary Manual, The, Seventh Edition	Staff	Merck & Co., Inc., Rahway, NJ, 1991
Progress in Equine Practice	Ed. by E. J. Catcott J. M. Smithcors	American Veterinary Publications, Inc., Wheaton, IL, 1966
TV Vet Horse Book	TV Vet	Farming Press Ltd., Ipswich, Suffolk, England, 1971
Veterinary Encyclopedia	H. M. Vale, DVM, Editor	Equine Research Publications, Grapevine, TX, 1975
Veterinary Notebook	W. R. McGee	The Blood Horse, Lexington, KY, 1958
Veterinary Notes for Horse Owners	M. H. Hays	Arco Publishing Co., Inc., New York, NY, 1972
Veterinary Notes for the Standardbred Breeder	W. R. McGee	United States Trotting Assn., Columbus, OH

Lipizzan horse literally flying through the air. The stallion is doing the *Capriole*, a movement resembling the leaping, twisting, fighting, and frolicking of high-spirited horses in pastures. (Courtesy, Spanish Riding School, Wels, Austria)

In the wild state, the horse executed four natural gaits—the walk, trot, pace, and gallop or run. Under domestication, these gaits have been variously modified, and additions have been made through (1) type, (2) breeding and selection, and (3) schooling.

RELATION OF TYPE TO ACTION

Regardless of the use to which horses are put, certain points in conformation are stressed—for example, a shapely, clean-cut head with a large, clear eye; a strong, heavily muscled topline; heavy muscling in the forearm and gaskin; and correct set to the feet and legs. Yet, certain differences in conformation better adapt the animal for use in specific types of work—as draft animals, gaited saddle horses, running horses, heavy harness horses, or hunters, etc. These differences are often as marked as those in the build of the 10-second track person and the champion wrestler. The thickness, massiveness, and low station of the draft horse are points of conformation that adapt it to power at the walk; whereas the angular form, relatively long legs, well-muscled hindquarters, and close-to-the-ground action of the Thoroughbred constitute form conducive to great speed at the run. But many less exaggerated differences exist. Thus, a horse with straight shoulders and short, straight pasterns is almost certain to be short and choppy in its action, and a very widefronted conformation often predisposes paddling.

RELATION OF BREEDING AND SELECTION TO ACTION

The relation of breeding and selection to action becomes obvious in a group of weanlings of mixed breeding. Upon starting across a field, some amble off in a rhythmic running walk, nodding their heads as they go; others travel high enough to clear the tops of the daisies; still others break away in an easy gallop. Each of these three types of action is executed with equal ease and naturalness. The first weanlings described are Tennessee Walking Horses, the second are Hackneys, and the third are Thoroughbreds. In each of these breeds, the distinctive way of going has been accomplished through years of breeding and selection.

RELATION OF SCHOOLING TO ACTION

If the offspring of Man O' War and six of the fastest mares ever to grace the tracks had merely worked on laundry trucks until six years old, and if at that time they had suddenly been placed upon a racetrack—without prior training or other preparation—the immediate results would have been disappointing. Their natural aptitude in conformation and breeding would

not have been enough. Schooling and training would still have been necessary in order to bring out their inherent ability. No horse—whether it be used for saddle, race, or other purposes—reaches a high degree of proficiency without an education.

On the other hand, it must be emphasized that it is equally disappointing to spend money in educating a colt for purposes to which it is not adapted. It is difficult, for example, to train a Hackney as a five-gaited park hack; and it is equally unsatisfactory to school a born Standardbred to the high action of the heavy harness horse.

It should also be pointed out that horses, like people, are likely to revert to an untrained status if placed in an improper environment—despite type, breeding, and early schooling. Thus, an inexperienced rider may, through ignorance, allow the most beautifully trained 5-gaited park hack to revert to a very ordinary mount. Proper and frequent handling is necessary if a horse of this training is to retain the five distinct gaits which are executed in a proud and collected manner. For this reason, the less experienced rider often rightfully prefers and will pay more for a three-gaited saddle horse than for a five-gaited one.

GAITS

A gait is a particular way of going, either natural or acquired, which is characterized by a distinctive rhythmic movement of the feet and legs. In proper show-ring procedure, horses are brought back to a walk each time before being called upon to execute a different gait. An exception is made in five-gaited classes, where the rack may be executed from the slow gait.

WALK

The walk is a natural, slow, flat-footed, four-beat gait, the latter meaning that each foot takes off from and strikes the ground at a separate interval. It should be springy, regular, and true.

On the draft horse, in which class of animals it constitutes the most important gait, the walk should be executed as a powerful stride; whereas the American Saddle Horse displays what is known as a proud walk, which calls for high action and attractiveness in contrast to power.

TROT

The trot is a natural, rapid, two-beat, diagonal gait in which the front foot and the opposite hind foot take

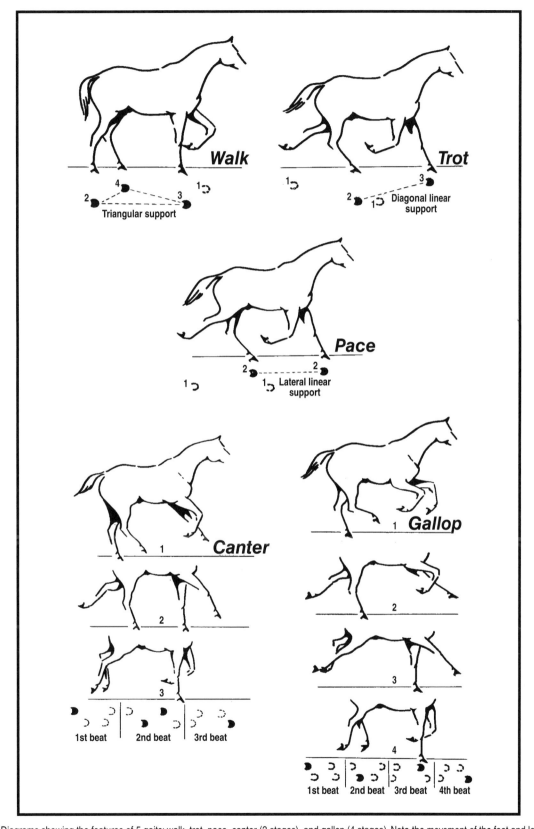

Fig. 7-1. Diagrams showing the features of 5 gaits; walk, trot, pace, canter (3 stages), and gallop (4 stages). Note the movement of the feet and legs of each gait (above), and the support base and beat of the feet (below). (Drawing by Prof. R. F. Johnson)

Fig. 7-2. Trotter, *Greyhound*, Standardbred harness racehorse, trotted the mile in 1:55¼. With a stride exceeding 27 ft, Greyhound was often referred to as the "Silver Groomed Flyer." (Courtesy, United States Trotting Assn., Columbus, OH)

Fig. 7-3. At the lope, showing the right lead (as opposed to the left lead). (Courtesy, *Appaloosa News*, Moscow, ID)

off at the same split second and strike the ground simultaneously. There is a brief moment when all four feet are off the ground and the horse seemingly floats through the air.

This gait varies considerably according to breed and training. The trot of the Standardbred is characterized by the length and rapidity of the individual strides; whereas the trot of the Hackney shows extreme flexion of the knees and hocks that produces a very high-stepping show gait.

CANTER, LOPE

The canter is a slow, restrained, three-beat gait in which the two diagonal legs are paired, thereby producing a single beat which falls between the successive beats of the other unpaired legs. The canter imposes a special wear on the leading forefoot and its diagonal hind foot. It is important, therefore, that the lead should be changed frequently; and in a well-trained horse, this shift is easily made at the will of the rider. In the show-ring, the lead should be toward the inside of the ring. It is changed by reversing the direction of travel (when the ringmaster calls for "reverse and canter").

It is a common saying among saddle horse enthusiasts that "a horse should canter all day in the shade of an apple tree." This is but another way of emphasizing that this gait should be executed in such a slow, collected manner that the animal may perform in a relatively small circle.

The lope is the western adaptation of a very slow canter. It is a smooth, slow gait in which the head is carried low.

RUN OR GALLOP

The run or gallop is a fast, four-beat gait where the feet strike the ground separately; first one hind foot, then the other hind foot, then the front foot on the same side as the first hind foot, then the other front foot which decides the lead. There is a brief interval in which all four feet are off the ground. In executing the gallop, the propulsion is chiefly in the hindquarters, although the forequarters sustain a tremendous jar as the horse lands. The gallop is the fastest gait of both the wild horse and the Thoroughbred racehorse.

Fig. 7-4. Run (or gallop), showing only the right hind foot on the ground. (Courtesy, *The Florida Horse*, Ocala, FL)

PACE

The pace is a fast, two-beat gait in which the front and hind feet on the same side start and stop simultaneously. The feet rise very little above the ground level. There is a split second when all four feet are off the ground and the horse floats forward through the air.

The pace is faster than the trot but not so fast as the run or gallop. It was a popular gait in the early history of England, but it lost favor soon after the development of the Thoroughbred. The pace allows for a quick getaway with a burst of speed, but it produces an objectionable side or rolling type of motion. The pace is not suited to travel in mud or snow, as a smooth, hard footing and easy draft are necessary for its best execution.

Fig. 7-5. Pacer, *Cam's Card Shark*, 1994 Harness Horse of the Year, showing the feet on the same side starting and stopping simultaneously. (Courtesy, United States Trotting Assn., Columbus, OH)

STEPPING PACE (OR SLOW PACE)

This is the preferred slow gait for five-gaited show horses. It is a modified pace in which the objectionable side or rolling motion of the true pace is eliminated because the two feet on each side do not move exactly together. Instead, it is a four-beat gait with each of the four feet striking the ground separately. In the takeoff, the hind and front feet start almost together, but the hind foot touches the ground slightly ahead of the front foot on the same side, and each foot strikes the ground separately.

FOX TROT

The fox trot is a slow, short, broken type of trot in which the head usually nods. In executing the fox trot, the horse brings each hind foot to the ground an instant before the diagonal forefoot. This gait is accepted as a slow gait, but it is not so popular as the stepping pace.

RUNNING WALK

The running walk is a four-beat gait in which all four feet strike the ground separately at regular intervals. The hindfoot overstrikes the footprint left by the lateral forefoot by 18 to 50 in., giving the motion a smooth, gliding effect. It is characterized by a bobbing or nodding of the head, a flopping of the ears, and a snapping of the teeth in rhythm with the movement of the legs. The running walk is easy on both horse and rider. It is the all-day business gait of the South and is executed at a speed of 6 to 8 miles per hour. This is a necessary gait in Plantation Walking Horses.

RACK

The rack (formerly, but now incorrectly, called single-foot) is a fast, flashy, unnatural, four-beat gait in which each foot meets the ground separately at equal intervals; hence, it was originally known as the *single-foot*, a designation now largely discarded. The rack is easy on the rider but hard on the horse. However, it is without doubt the most popular gait in the American show-ring, being fast, brilliant, and flashy. On the tanbark, great speed at the rack is requested by giving the command, "rack on."

TRAVERSE OR SIDE STEP

The traverse or side step is simply a lateral movement of the animal to the right or left as desired, without moving forward or backward. This trick will often assist in (1) lining up horses in the show-ring, (2) opening and closing gates, and (3) taking position in a mounted drill or a posse.

COMMON DEFECTS IN WAY OF GOING

The feet of an animal should move straight ahead and parallel to a center line drawn in the direction of travel. Any deviations from this way of going constitute defects.

CROSS-FIRING

Cross-firing, a defect in the way of going, is generally confined to pacers and consists of a scuffling on the inside of the diagonal fore and hind feet.

DWELLING

Dwelling, most noticeable in trick-trained horses, consists of a distinct pause in the flight of the foot, as though the stride were completed before the foot reaches the ground.

FORGING

The striking of the forefoot by the toe of the hind foot is known as forging.

INTERFERING

The striking of the fetlock or cannon by the opposite foot that is in motion is known as interfering. This condition is predisposed in horses with base-narrow, toe-wide, or splayfooted standing positions.

LAMENESS

Lameness is a defect that can be detected when the affected foot is favored when standing. In action, the load on the ailing foot is eased, and there is characteristic bobbing of the head of the horse as the affected foot strikes the ground.

PADDLING

Throwing the front feet outward as they are picked up is known as paddling. This condition is predisposed in horses with toe-narrow or pigeon-toed standing positions.

POINTING

Perceptible extension of the stride with little flexion is called pointing. This condition is likely to occur in the Thoroughbred and Standardbred breeds—animals bred and trained for great speed with a long stride.

POUNDING

Pounding is a condition in which there is heavy contact with the ground in contrast to the desired light, springy movement.

ROLLING

Excessive lateral shoulder motion, characteristic of horses with protruding shoulders, is known as rolling.

SCALPING

Scalping is that condition in which the hairline at the top of the hind foot hits the toe of the forefoot as it breaks over.

SPEEDY CUTTING

Speedy cutting is a condition of a horse at speed in which a hind leg above the scalping mark hits against the shoe of a breaking-over forefoot. In trotters, legs on the same side are involved. In pacers, diagonal legs are involved.

STRINGHALT

Stringhalt is characterized by excessive flexing of the hind legs. It is most easily detected when backing a horse.

TRAPPY

A short, quick, choppy stride is known as trappy. This condition is predisposed in horses with short, straight pasterns and straight shoulders.

WINDING OR ROPE-WALKING

A twisting of the striding leg around in front of the supporting leg so as to make contact in the manner of a rope-walking artist is known as winding or rope-walking. This condition most often occurs in horses with very wide fronts.

WINGING

Winging is an exaggerated paddling, particularly noticeable in high-going horses.

SELECTED REFERENCES

Title of Publication	Author(s)	Publisher
Anatomy and Conformation of the Horse	G. B. Edwards	Dreenan Press Ltd., Croton-on-Hudson, NY, 1973
Breeding and Raising Horses, Ag. Hdbk. No. 394	M. E. Ensminger	Agriculture Research Service, USDA, Washington, DC, 1972
Horse Industry Handbook	Staff	Horse Industry Council, Washington, DC, 1993
Horse, The	D. J. Kays rev. by J. M. Kays	A. S. Barnes & Co., Inc., Cranbury, NJ, 1969
Horse Buyer's Guide, The	J. K. Posey	A. S. Barnes & Co., Inc., Cranbury, NJ, 1973
Horse Structure and Movement, The	R. H. Smythe rev. by P. C. Goody	J. A. Allen & Co., London, England, 1972
Horsemanship	Mrs. A. W. Jasper	Boy Scouts of America, New Brunswick, NJ, 1963
Horsemanship and Horse Care, Ag. Info. Bull. No. 353	M. E. Ensminger	Agriculture Research Service, USDA, Washington, DC, 1972
Horsemanship and Horsemastership	Ed. by G. Wright	Doubleday & Company, Inc., Garden City, NY, 1962
Horseshoeing Theory and Hoof Care	L. Emery J. Miller N. Van Hoosen	Lea & Febiger, Philadelphia, PA, 1977
Horses: Their Selection, Care and Handling	M. C. Self	A. S. Barnes & Co., Inc., Cranbury, NJ, 1943
Judging Manual for American Saddlebred Horses	J. Foss	American Saddle Horse Breeders Association, Louisville, KY, 1973
Lameness in Horses, Second Edition	O. R. Adams	Lea & Febiger, Philadelphia, PA, 1966
Leg at Each Corner, A	N. Thelwell	E. P. Dutton & Co., Inc., New York, NY, 1963
Livestock Judging, Selection, and Evaluation, Fourth Edition	R. E. Hunsley W. M. Beeson	Interstate Publishers, Inc., Danville, IL, 1992
Practical Dressage for Amateur Trainers	J. M. Ladendorf	A. S. Barnes & Co., Inc., Cranbury, NJ
Rule Book		The American Horse Shows Association, Inc., New York, NY, annual
Saddle Up!	C. E. Ball	J. B. Lippincott Co., Philadelphia, PA, 1970
Spanish Riding School, The	H. Handler	McGraw-Hill Book Co., Ltd., Maidenhead, England, 1972

The horse in action. (Courtesy, North American Morab Horse Assn., Hilbert, WI)

TYPES AND CLASSES OF LIGHT HORSES ACCORDING TO USE

Cigar galloped into history July 13, 1996, in the Arlington Citation Challenge, Chicago, in his 16th consecutive win, bringing his career record bankroll to $8,819,815. (Photo by Barbara D. Livingston, Horse Racing Photography, P.O. Box 5163, Saratoga Springs, NY 12866; with the permission of CMG Worldwide, Inc., and Allen Paulson, *Cigar's* owner)

The improvement of horses dates back to the time when people first domesticated them and sought to improve them more nearly to fulfill their needs. Through selection, different types and breeds evolved, better adapted to different uses and better meeting different human desires. (See Table 8-1.)

Today, horses are classified according to weight, size, build, and use as light horses, draft horses, or ponies.

Light horses stand 14-2 to 17 hands high, weigh 900 to 1,400 lb, and are used primarily for riding, driving, or racing, or for utility purposes on the farm. Light horses generally are more rangy and are capable of more action and greater speed than draft horses.

Draft horses stand 14-2 to 17-2 hands high, weigh 1,400 lb or more, and are used primarily for drawing loads and other heavy work.

TABLE 8-1
LIGHT HORSE SUMMARY

Type	Primary Use	Breeds	
Riding Horses and Ponies	Three-gaited saddle horses . . .	American Saddlebred Andalusian Appaloosa Arabian Half Saddlebred Hanoverian Hungarian Horse Irish Draught Horse Lipizzan Morab Morgan	National Show Horse Paint Horse Palomino Pintabian Pinto Arabian Pinto Horse Quarter Horse Spanish-Barb Spotted Saddle Horse Thoroughbred Trakehner
	Gaited horses	American Saddlebred Missouri Fox Trotting Horse National Show Horse	Paso Fino Peruvian Paso Tennessee Walking Horse
	Stock horses	Grades, crossbreds, or following purebreds: American Mustang Appaloosa Buckskin Chickasaw Cracker Horse Galiceno Hungarian Horse	 Morgan Paint Horse Pinto Horse Quarter Horse Spanish-Barb Spanish Mustang Thoroughbred
	Ponies for riding	American Walking Pony Connemara Pony Pony of the Americas Quarter Pony	Shetland Pony Swedish Gotland Horse Welara Pony Welsh Pony and Cob
Racehorses[1]	Running racehorses	Appaloosa Arabian Thoroughbred	
	Quarter racehorses	Quarter Horse	
	Harness racehorses (trotters and pacers)	Standardbred Trottingbred	
Driving Horses and Ponies	Driving horses: Harness horses	Hackney	
	Fine harness horses	American Saddlebred (predominantly, although other breeds are also used)	
	Roadsters	Standardbred	
	Driving ponies:	Hackney	
	Harness show ponies	Shetland Pony	
	Heavy harness ponies	Welsh Pony and Cob	
All-purpose Horses and Ponies	Family horses/ponies	American Bashkir Curly American Gotland Horse Blazer Horse Cleveland Bay	Dales Pony Exmoor Pony Haflinger Norwegian Fjord Horse
Sport Horses	Dressage Hunters/Jumpers Three-day eventing Endurance trials . . . . Polo Parade horses	Akhal-Teke American Creme and American White Lipizzan Selle Francias Thoroughbred Trakehner Warmbloods: American, Belgian, Dutch, Swedish	
Miniature Horses and Donkeys	Driving	Miniature Horse	
	Pets	Miniature Donkey	

[1]In a few states, Appaloosa and Arabian horses are also being raced under saddle.

Ponies stand under 14-2 hands high and weigh 500 to 900 lb. Not every small horse is a pony, however. Some small horses are merely small animals of established light horse breeds; others are nondescript runts. In ponies, there is a distinct conformation; in miniature, they are either of draft horse, heavy harness horse, or saddle or harness horse type. The breeding, feeding, care, and management are essentially the same for ponies as for larger light horses; the only differences result from their diminutive size. The discussion which follows in this chapter will be limited to light horses and ponies.

In no class of animals have so many diverse and distinct types been developed as in the horse. The descendants of the Oriental light-legged horse have, for generations, been bred and used for riding and driving purposes—first as the chariot and riding horses of Persia, Egypt, Greece, and Arabia; later as the running horse of England; and finally for purposes of recreation and sport in the United States and throughout the world. In due time, further refinements in breeding light horses were made, and these animals were adapted for more specific purposes. In this manner, light horses well adapted to the primary purposes listed in Table 8-1 have evolved. Of course, most horses can be, and are, trained for more than one use.

In attempting to produce animals to meet these specific purposes, new breeds of light horses have been created. In certain cases, however, the particular use or performance is so exacting that only one breed appears to be sufficiently specialized; for example, in running races the Thoroughbred is used almost exclu-

Fig. 8-2. Combined Driving Events require horses with strength, endurance, and winning dispositions. These traits are represented by Lisa Singer and her Morgan pair, *Avalon Avante Garde* and *Meadowgreen Treasure*, while navigating a marathon hazard. Following this event, the team represented the U.S. at the 1995 World Pairs Driving Championship in Poland, where they won the U.S. Pairs Driving Championship (1994). (Courtesy, American Morgan Horse Assn., Shelburne, VT)

sively,[1] and harness races are now synonymous with the Standardbred breed.

RIDING HORSES AND PONIES

Riding horses have many and varied uses, but, as the name indicates, they are all ridden. They may have a very definite utility value, as is true of stock horses, or they may be used chiefly for purposes of recreation and sport. For the latter use, training, manners, and style are of paramount importance, although durability and efficiency are not to be overlooked in any horse.

THREE- AND FIVE-GAITED SADDLE HORSES

Long after the development of the New England town, the opening up of roads along the Eastern Seaboard, and the development of the buggy and the popularity of the roadster type of horse, the states of Virginia, West Virginia, Kentucky, Tennessee, and Missouri still consisted of large plantations under the ownership of southern gentlemen. Roads were few and far between, and travel was largely on horseback over the most natural paths that could be found. Thus, there was need for a horse that would carry the plantation

Fig. 8-1. Dressage, executed by Morgan pony, *Quivira Encounter*. Note the collection, balance, and forward movement. (Courtesy The American Morgan Horse Association, Shelburne, VT)

---

[1]Except for Quarter Horse races, and races limited to certain other breeds.

owners with dignity befitting their station in life and with the least distress possible to both rider and horse. As the plantation owners rode over their broad estates, easy gaits were a necessity. Such was the need, and out of this need arose the beautiful American Saddlebred horse.

Animals qualifying as either three- or five-gaited saddle horses in the leading American horse shows are generally of American Saddlebred breeding, a truly American creation.[2] Occasionally, however, animals of the other light horse breeds are trained to execute the five gaits. It must also be remembered that the vast majority of American horses of all breeds are of the three-gaited variety and that only a relatively small proportion of these animals are ever exhibited. Instead, most of the three-gaited horses are used for pleasure riding.

The gaits of three-gaited horses are: the walk, the trot, and the canter. In addition to performing these same gaits, the five-gaited horse must possess a slow gait and the rack. The slow gait may be either the running walk, fox trot, or stepping pace (slow pace); but for show purposes only the stepping pace is accepted. In the show-ring, generally the judge requests that five-gaited horses execute the gaits in the following order: the walk, the trot, the slow gait, the rack, and the canter.

Whether an animal is three-gaited or five-gaited is primarily a matter of training. Current custom decrees that three-gaited horses be shown with the mane shaved, and the tail full-length and flowing (formerly, the tails of three-gaited horses were clipped or sheared for a short distance from the base). Custom decrees that five-gaited horses be shown with braided manes and full-length tails. Also, because of the speed at which five-gaited horses are expected to perform at the trot and the rack, they are permitted to wear quarter boots to protect the heels of the front feet, a practice which is forbidden in three-gaited classes.

Both three- and five-gaited horses are shown under saddle; and each may be shown in combination classes, in which they must perform both in harness and under saddle. Also, five-gaited horses (but not three-gaited horses) may be shown in a third division; namely, in fine harness classes.

In combination classes, the entries enter the ring hitched to an appropriate four-wheeled vehicle, with the saddle and bridle hidden in the back of the rig. The judge works the class both ways of the ring, then lines them up in the center for inspection and backs each horse in order to test its manners. Next the judge orders that the entries be unhitched, unharnessed,

---

[2]Herein reference is made to the Saddlebred Horse Division as described by The American Horse Shows Association, and not to the several performance classes in which three-gaited horses of various breeds compete.

Fig. 8-3. A three-gaited American Saddlebred. Note the shaved mane and the full-length and flowing tail—as custom decrees. (Photo by Jamie Donaldson. Courtesy, American Saddlebred Horse Assn., Lexington, KY)

Fig. 8-4. A five-gaited horse performing at the trot. Note the braided mane and full-length tail—as custom decrees. Note, too, the quarter boots protecting the front feet. (Photo by Jamie Donaldson. Courtesy, American Saddlebred Horse Assn., Lexington, KY)

saddled, bridled, and worked under saddle both ways of the ring. Finally, the horses are again lined up in the center of the ring, and each animal is backed under saddle.

A fine harness horse is exactly what the name implies—a fine horse presented in fine harness. The entire ensemble is elegant, and represents the ultimate in grace and charm.

Fine harness horses are penalized if driven at excessive speed. Combination horses, especially five-gaited ones, should be driven at a more speedy trot than fine harness horses.

In addition to executing the gaits with perfection, both three- and five-gaited animals should possess the following characteristics:

1. **Superior conformation,** in which the principal requirements are:

    a. Graceful lines obtained through a fairly long, arched neck; short, strong back and loin with a good seat; a nicely turned croup; a smartly carried, flowing tail; and a relatively long underline.

    b. A shapely and smart head.

    c. Nicely sloping shoulders and pasterns.

    d. Symmetry and blending of all parts.

    e. Quality, as evidenced by a clean-cut, chiseled appearance throughout, and soundness.

    f. Style, alertness, and animation, sometimes said to be comparable to that of a "peacock."

2. **Perfect manners,** which include form, training, and obedience—those qualities that make for a most finished performance.

3. **Superior action,** including an elastic step, high action, and evidence of spirit and dash.

WALKING HORSES

This particular class of horses is largely comprised of one breed—the Tennessee Walking Horse.[3]

Horses of this type were first introduced into Tennessee by the early settlers from Virginia and the Carolinas. For many years, the plantation owners of middle Tennessee—men who spent long hours daily in supervising labor from the saddle—selected and bred animals for their easy, springy gaits, good dispositions, and intelligence. Particular stress was placed upon the natural gait known as the running walk and upon the elimination of the trot. Thus, the three gaits that evolved in the walking horse (also called Plantation Walking Horse) were: the walk, the running walk, and the canter.

At the running walk there is a characteristic nodding of the head. Sometimes there is also a flopping of the ears and a snapping of the teeth while the animal is in this rhythmic movement. Walking horses are also noted for their wonderful dispositions. Their easy gaits and superb dispositions make them an ideal type of horse for the amateur rider or the professional society person who rides infrequently.

Fig. 8-5. *He's Puttin' On The Ritz*, 1996 World Grand Champion Tennessee Walking Horse, trained and ridden by Sammy Day, owned by William B. and Sandra Johnson, Atlanta, Georgia. (Courtesy, *Voice Magazine*, Lewisburg, TN)

STOCK HORSES

Stock horses constitute the largest single class of light horses of this country; there are approximately 500,000 of them in use in the 17 range states. They are the cow ponies of the West.

Usually, stock horses are of mixed breeding. Most generally they are descended from the Mustang—the feral horse of the United States. Subsequently, Mus-

Fig. 8-6. A cutting horse in action, separating a cow from the herd and preventing its return. This event is one of the most popular tests of the inherent "cow sense" of a horse. (Photo by Midge Ames Photography, Citrus Heights, CA. Courtesy, David E. McGlothlin, Harris Farms, Coalinga, CA)

---

[3]A more detailed description of this and other breeds may be found in Chapter 10.

tang mares were mated to sires of practically every known light horse breed—especially Thoroughbreds and Quarter Horses. Stallions of the Palomino, Morgan, Arabian, and other breeds have also been used. Such grading-up has improved the size, speed, and perhaps the appearance of the cow pony, but most equestrians will concede that no amount of improved breeding will ever produce a gamier, hardier, and more durable animal than the Mustang. In addition to being game and hardy, the stock horse must be agile, surefooted, fast, short coupled, deep, powerfully muscled, durable, and possess good feet and legs. Above all, the cowboy insists that his pony be a good companion and possess "cow sense."

SPORT HORSES
(See also Table 8-1)

In addition to racing, horses are used for many equine sports, including dressage, hunters/jumpers, three-day eventing, endurance trials, polo, and parade horses. Purebreds, crossbreds, and grades of the following breeds are well adapted for use in the equine sport events herewith described: Akhal-Teke, American Creme and American White, Lipizzan, Selle Francais, Thoroughbred, Trakehner, and Warm Bloods.

■ **Dressage**—*Dressage is the guiding of a horse through natural maneuvers without emphasis on the use of reins, hands, and feet.*

The term dressage comes from the French verb meaning *to train.* After the horse has learned to respond to the simple directions of moving forward or backward, turning, changing gait, and halting, equestrians who wish to develop the horse's strength, willingness, and agility as much as possible continue training by giving special exercises to develop these traits. This training is called dressage.

All of the movements described as dressage or training movements are based on natural movements of the horse while at liberty. Thus, by watching horses (especially young horses) in a corral, they will be seen to execute with ease changes from one gait to another, sudden halts, changes of the leading leg at the canter when changing direction, and such intricacies of the *Haute Ecole* as the pirouette, the piaffe, the passage, and the pesade. Why, then, must a horse be trained to do these things if it already knows how? There are two reasons: (1) the horse must learn to balance itself under the weight of the rider, and (2) the horse must learn to do these movements when so requested by the rider.

In dressage competition, the horse is exhibited in a series of demanding, often spectacular, required movements. The horse appears to flow over the ground with relaxed strides while the rider's signals to the

horse remain invisible. In the musical freestyle competition, when the required moves are performed to music, the horses appear to be dancing.

■ **Hunters/Jumpers**—*The hunter is that type of horse used in following the hounds in fox hunting.* The sport is traditional in England, and each year it is sharing its glamour with more people in the United States.

The hunter is not necessarily of any particular breeding, but Thoroughbred blood predominates. The infusion of some cold blood (draft breeding) is often relied upon in order to secure greater size and a more tractable disposition.

In addition to being of ample size and height, hunters must possess the necessary stamina and conformation to keep up with the pack. They must be able to hurdle with safety such common field obstacles as fences and ditches. The good hunter, therefore, is rugged, short coupled, and heavily muscled throughout.

Fig. 8-7. *Sacred Melody*, 1995 APHA World Champion Amateur Working Hunter. (Courtesy, American Paint Horse Assn., Ft. Worth, TX)

All hunters are jumpers to some degree, but high jumpers are not necessarily good hunters. To qualify as hunters, horses must do more. They must execute many and varied jumps over a long period of time.

Jumpers are a nondescript group, consisting of all breeds and types; the only requisite is that they can jump. In the show-ring, an unsoundness does not penalize a jumper unless it is sufficiently severe to be considered an act of cruelty.

■ **Three-day eventing**—The 1912 Stockholm Olympic Games pioneered in *Three-Day Eventing.* Currently,

Fig. 8-8. The jumper, *Margo*, a Trakehner, ridden by Ian Silitch, competing in Grand Prix Show Jumping at Upperville, Virginia. (Courtesy, American Trakehner Assn., Newark, OH)

in the Olympics, this is a multidiscipline competition, held over a three-day period in which the same horse-and-rider combination compete in dressage, cross-country jumping over fixed jumps at specified speeds, and stadium jumping over fences that can easily be knocked down. *Eventing* tests all the skills of both horse and rider—suppleness for dressage, courage for running cross-country, and smartness for stadium jumping. The unique characteristic of *Eventing* is that it features horse-and-rider combinations rather than individual athletes—it's a test of the ultimate in teamwork.

■ **Endurance trials (rides)**—*Competitive tests designed to test the stamina of horses are known as endurance trials.* The riders must take their horses over a prescribed course, which is usually of rugged terrain, and which may require anywhere from one to three days to cover. The time for the different courses varies according to the topography, elevation, and footing. Regular tests (temperature, pulse, respiration, etc.) are made at intervals.

One of the best known endurance rides is the Tevis Cup Ride, held at Auburn, California each August. It is 100 miles and over extremely rough terrain. The time limit is 24 hours, and there are three mandatory rest stops of one hour each. During the rest stops, the veterinarians check the pulse, respiration, and temperature of each horse, both at the beginning and the end of the hour, so as to determine whether its rate of recovery is satisfactory. There are two kinds of competition in the Tevis Cup Ride: (1) a race over the 100-mile course, and (2) the best-conditioned

horse that completes the ride within the 24-hour period.

Generally over 200 competitors start on the Tevis Cup Ride and about 160 (or 80%) finish. The winning horse makes the ride in approximately 11 hours.

Fig. 8-9. Tevis Cup competitor going over "Cougar Rock" near Auburn, California. (Photo by Charles E. Barieau, Auburn, CA)

■ **Polo**—*As the name would indicate, polo mounts are horses that are particularly adapted for use in playing the game of polo.* This game, which was first introduced into this country in 1876, is played by four mounted players on each team. The object is to drive a wooden ball between goal posts at either end of a playing field 300 yards long and 120 to 150 yards wide. Long-handled regulation mallets are used to drive the ball.

At the time the game was first introduced into the United States, there was a decided preference for ponies under 13-2 hands in height. Later, horses up to 14-2 hands were accepted, and more recently horses up to 15-2 and over have been used.

Although very similar to the hunter in type, polo mounts are generally smaller in size. They must be quick and clever in turning, and they must be able to dodge, swerve, or wheel while on a dead run. They must like the game of polo and be able to follow the ball.

The polo mount is trained to respond to the pressure of the reins on the neck, so that the rider may be free to guide it with only one hand. Up to 5 or 6 years is required to complete the schooling of a polo horse, and as many as 4 to 6 mounts may be used by each player in a single game—all of which contributes to the expensiveness of the sport.

Fig. 8-10. An excellent polo mount. Note the pronounced Thoroughbred type. (Courtesy, United States Polo Assn., New York, NY)

Polo ponies are usually of mixed breeding, but most of them are predominantly Thoroughbred. Type and training, together with native ability and intelligence, are the primary requisites.

■ **Parade horses**—*Parade horses are horses of any breed, cross, or color used under elaborate Western, Mexican, or Spanish equipment in parades.* Attractive colors and good manners are important. Parade horses are shown at an animated walk and a parade gait. The latter is a prancing cadenced trot at not to exceed five miles per hour.

Fig. 8-11. Parade horse—a Morgan Horse. (Courtesy, American Morgan Horse Assn., Shelburne, VT)

PONIES FOR RIDING

Several pony breeds are used for riding; among them, the Connemara, Gotland Horse, Pony of Americas, Shetland, and Welsh. Also, the smaller animals failing to meet the minimum height requirements of the American Saddlebred, Appaloosa, Quarter Horse, and Tennessee Walking Horse breeds are registered as Saddlebred Pony, Appaloosa Pony, Quarter Pony, and Walking Pony, respectively.

In the 1950s, the Welsh Pony and the Tennessee Walking Horse were crossed to create the American Walking Pony. In the 1960s, the Shetland and Hackney breeds were crossed to produce the Saddlebred type of pony. In 1980, the Welara Pony Society was formed to register the breed created by crossing the Arabian and Welsh breeds.

Ponies are children's mounts. So, in addition to their small size, they should possess the following characteristics: (1) gentleness, (2) sound feet and legs, (3) symmetry, (4) good eyes, (5) endurance, (6) intelligence, (7) patience, (8) faithfulness, and (9) hardiness. Above all, they must be kind and gentle in disposition.

Fig. 8-12. Child and pony; the right size for each other.

RACEHORSES

The term *racehorse* refers to a horse that is bred and trained for racing.

According to historians, the Greeks introduced horse racing in the Olympic Games in 1450 B.C. Also, it is reported that a planned horse race of consequence was run in England in 1377 A.D., between animals owned by Richard II and the Earl of Arundel. The sporting instinct of people being what it is, it is reasonable to surmise, however, that a bit of a contest was staged the first time that two proud mounted equestrians chanced to meet.

The development of horse racing in Britain dates from the 17th Century, although it is known to have taken place much earlier. Records exist of racing during the Roman occupation; and during the reign of Henry II races took place at Smithfield, which was the great London horse market at the time. But it was in the reign of James I that racing first began to be an organized sport. He took a great liking to Newmarket, where he had a royal palace and a racecourse built. Also, he established public races in various parts of the country.

Fig. 8-13. Kentucky's historic Churchill Downs, familiar to millions of people all over the world. The Kentucky Derby—first run in 1875, now run the first Saturday of each May—is one of the most beautiful and exciting contests in all of the world of sport. (Courtesy, Kentucky Department of Public Information, Frankfort, KY)

The famous Rowley Mile Course at Newmarket, the home of English flat racing, is named after Charles II. "Old Riley" was his nickname, after his favorite riding horse by that name. Charles II loved racing; he rode in matches, founded races called the Royal Plates, and sometimes adjudicated in the disputes.

The Jockey Club came into existence at Newmarket in 1752, with many rich and influential men among its members. It gradually became the governing body of English racing.

Today, three types of horse races are run: (1) running races (including steeplechase races), (2) quarter races, and (3) harness races. For the most part, each type of race is dominated by one breed. Thus, in running races, it's Thoroughbreds; in quarter races, it's Quarter Horses; and in harness races, it's Standardbreds. However, on a limited basis, and in a few

states, Appaloosa and Arabian horses are now being raced under saddle.

RACING COLORS

The Jockey Club assigns colors to racing stables. They may be assigned for one year, or they may be assigned for a lifetime. Sometimes colors are reassigned when no longer in use, but this is not the case with the colors of very famous stables. Jockeys must wear the colors assigned to the stable.

RACING ATTENDANCE

Approximately 42.6 million people attended U.S. horse races at tracks in 1994, and wagered an estimated $14 billion.[4]

RACING RECORDS

In running races (Thoroughbreds), the all-time records at 1⅜ mile (11 F) on dirt and turf are:

1⅜ mile (11 F) on dirt:
Timely Warning (6 yr) at Aqueduct in 1991 under 112 lb; 2:14 min.

1⅜ mile (11 F) on turf:
With Approval (4 yr) at Belmont in 1990 under 118 lb; 2:10 ⅕ min.

In quarter races (Quarter Horses), *Evening Snow* set the U.S. record for a quarter mile (440 yards) at 20.94 in 1996.

In harness racing (Standardbreds), *Pine Chip* holds the world's trotting record for a mile at 1:51 minutes, which was established in 1994; and *Silver Almahurst* set the world's pacing record for a mile at 1:50.4 minutes in 1993.

RUNNING RACEHORSES

Racehorses used for running (an extended gallop) under the saddle are now confined almost exclusively to one breed, the Thoroughbred. On the other hand, the Thoroughbred breed (including both purebreds and crossbreds) has been used widely for other purposes, especially as polo mounts and hunters.

Although trials of speed had taken place between horses from the earliest recorded history, the true and

---

[4]*Horse Industry Directory*, 1996, p.4, American Horse Council, Washington, DC.

unmistakable foundation of the Thoroughbred breed as such traces back only to the reign of Charles II, known as the "father of the British turf."

Although the length of race, weight carried, and type of track have undergone considerable variation in recent years, the running horse always has been selected for speed and more speed at the run. The distinguishing characteristics of the running horse, as represented by the Thoroughbred, are the extreme refinement, oblique shoulders, well-made withers, heavily muscled rear quarters, straight hind legs, and close travel to the ground.

Fig. 8-14. A running (Thoroughbred) race at Hollywood Park, Inglewood, California. (Courtesy, *The Florida Horse*, Ocala, FL)

QUARTER RACEHORSES

Quarter racing has become an increasingly popular sport. For the most part, races of this type are confined to animals of the Quarter Horse breed, which animals derived their name and initial fame for their extraordinary speed at distances up to a quarter mile. Although the great majority of Quarter Horses are used to work cattle and never appear on the racetrack, the proponents of quarter racing advocate the racetrack as a means of proving animals. Performance, so they argue, is the proof of whether or not a horse can do the job for which it is bred. Thus, quarter racing is used as a breed proving ground for the Quarter Horse, for in racing the fundamental quality of speed can be accurately measured and recorded in such a way that the performance of horses in all parts of the country can be compared.

HARNESS RACEHORSES (TROTTERS AND PACERS)

Prior to the advent of improved roads and the automobile, but following the invention of the buggy, there was need for a fast, light-harness type of horse. This horse was used to draw vehicles varying in type from the light roadster of the young gallant to the dignified family carriage. In the process of meeting this need, two truly American breeds of horse evolved—the Morgan and the Standardbred. The first breed traces to the foundation sire, *Justin Morgan*; and the latter to *Hambletonian 10*, an animal which was line bred to imported *Messenger*.

As horse-and-buggy travel passed into permanent oblivion, except for recreation and sport, the Standardbred breeders wisely placed greater emphasis on the sport of racing; whereas the Morgan enthusiasts directed their breeding programs toward transforming their animals into a saddle breed.

The early descendants of *Messenger* were sent over the track, trotting (not galloping) under the saddle; but eventually the jockey races in this country came to be restricted to a running type of race in which the Thoroughbred was used. With this shift, qualifying standards—a mile in 2:30 at the trot and 2:25 at the pace when hitched to the sulky—were set up for light harness races; and those animals so qualifying were registered.[5] The pneumatic-tire racing vehicles, known as sulkies, were first introduced in 1892. With their use

Fig. 8-15. *Peace Corps*, driven by John Campbell, the richest trotter ever with career earnings of $4,907,307. (Courtesy, The United States Trotting Assn., Columbus, OH)

---

[5]On January 1, 1933, registration on performance alone was no longer granted, and registration of both sire and dam was required. The qualifying standards were initiated in 1879.

that year, the time was reduced nearly 4 seconds below the record of the previous year. Thus, were developed harness racing and the Standardbred breed of horses, which today is the exclusive breed used for this purpose.

Trotters and pacers are of similar breeding and type, the particular gaits being largely a matter of training. In fact, many individuals show speed at both the trot and the pace. It is generally recognized, however, that pacers are handicapped in the mud, in the sand, or over a rough surface.

The Standardbred breed—like the Thoroughbred—also found other uses, as driving horses in roadster classes, delivery horses, and general utility horses. By way of comparison with the Thoroughbred, the Standardbred possesses a more tractable disposition, is smaller, longer bodied, closer to the ground, heavier-limbed, and sturdier in build. The latter characteristic is very necessary because harness races are usually "heat races"—for example, the best two out of three races.

In the beginning, horses of this type found their principal use in harness races at county and state fairs. However, in recent years pari-mutuel harness racing has been established at a number of tracks. Today, harness racehorses are almost exclusively of the Standardbred breed.

DRIVING HORSES AND PONIES

At the present time, driving horses and ponies are used chiefly for purposes of recreation. According to the specific use made of them, driving horses are classified as hackneys, fine harness horses, roadsters, or ponies.

HACKNEYS

Horses of the Hackney type were very popular during the Victorian era in England, where they were known as heavy harness horses. The vehicles drawn were of heavy construction and elegant design, and logically and artistically the harness had to be heavy, too.

In this country during the Gay Nineties, bobtailed Hackneys attached to high-seated rigs made a dashing picture as they pranced down the avenue.

At one time, there were several heavy harness breeds, but at present all except the Hackney have practically ceased to exist in America. In this country, therefore, the Hackney is now the heavy harness breed; and the American Horse Shows Association officially refers to show classifications as Hackneys rather than as Heavy Harness Horses.

The Hackney is elegance in action. Today, Hackneys are shown in the following divisions:

1. The Hackney/harness (or longtail) pony must be 12-2 hands or under at the withers, and must be shown with a long mane and an undocked tail (see Fig. 8-16).

Fig. 8-16. *Ballet*, World Grand Champion Hackney Harness Pony in Louisville, Kentucky, in 1995. (Photo by Doug Shiflet Photography, Courtesy, Ed Frickey, Lafayette, IN)

2. The Hackney (or cobtail) division is for ponies measuring over 12-2 but under 14-2 hands at the withers. These ponies must be shown with the appearance of a shortened tail and a braided mane.

3. The Hackney Roadster ponies are for speedsters of the Hackney breed. They are shown hitched to a two-wheeled road bike with their drivers wearing racing silks. (see Fig. 8-17).

4. Leisure driving division. These ponies may be longtail or cobtail, and they are shown with unbraided manes and tails, hitched to an appropriate pleasure vehicle (see Fig. 8-18).

5. The combined driving. This is a three-day trial comparable to eventing under saddle. The combined driving components are dressage, marathon, and cones course.

Hackneys should possess the following distinguishing characteristics:

■ **Beauty**—Beauty is obtained through graceful, curved lines; full-made form; and high carriage.

■ **High action**—Animals of this type are bred for high hock and knee action, but skilled training, bitting, and shoeing are necessary for their development. In the show-ring, heavy harness horses must be able to fold

Fig. 8-17. *Aisle Party*, World Champion Amateur Road Pony 1996. (Photo by Macklin. Courtesy, Ed Frickey, Lafayette, IN)

Fig. 8-18. *Bristol Fashion*, Reserve World Champion Hackney, Pleasure Driving Division, 1996. (Photo by Jamie Donaldson. Courtesy, Ed Frickey, Lafayette, IN)

FINE HARNESS HORSES

A fine harness horse is exactly what the name implies—a fine horse presented in fine harness. The entire ensemble is elegant and represents the ultimate in grace and charm.

Fig. 8-19. Fine harness horse, 1993 and 1994 World's Grand Champion, *Be Happy*. (Photo by Jamie Donaldson. Courtesy, American Saddle Horse Assn., Lexington, KY)

In the show-ring, fine harness horses are, according to the rules of the American Horse Shows Association, limited to the American Saddlebred breed. In some shows, however, other breeds are exhibited in fine harness classes. Fashion decrees that fine harness horses shall be shown wearing long mane and tail and drawing a four-wheeled vehicle, preferably a small buggy with wire wheels, but without top, or with top drawn. Light harness with a snaffle bit is required. Fine harness horses are shown at an animated park trot and at an animated walk.

ROADSTERS

The sport of showing a roadster originated in the horse and buggy era. It was founded upon the desire to own an attractive horse that possessed the necessary speed to pass any of its rivals encountered upon the city or county thoroughfares.

In the show-ring, roadsters are generally shown in either or both (1) roadster to bike, or (2) roadster to road wagon or buggy classes. The latter are hitched singly or in pairs. Some shows also provide a class or classes[6] for roadsters under saddle. In all divi-

their knees, flex their hocks, and set their chins. "Woodenlegged" horses cannot take competition.

■ **Manners and temperament**—Perfection in the manners and disposition of pleasure horses of this type is a requisite of first rank.

■ **Color**—Seal brown, brown, bay, and black colors are preferred in heavy harness horses. White stockings are desired for the purposes of accentuating high action.

_____

[6]In many of the larger shows, a roadster appointments class is provided. Appointments are listed in the A.H.S.A. Rule Book.

Fig. 8-20. Roadster to bike—a Standardbred driven by Sam Brannon, Georgetown, Kentucky. (Photo by Jamie Donaldson. Courtesy, Sam Brannon)

sions—whether shown to bike or buggy, or under saddle—entries must trot; pacing is barred.

Originally, roadster classes included animals of both Standardbred and Morgan extraction. In recent years, however, the Morgan has developed in the direction of the saddler. Today the *Rule Book* of the American Horse Shows Association lists two divisions for roadsters: (1) Roadster Division, for Standardbred and Standardbred-type horses; and (2) Roadster Ponies, for ponies under 12-2 hands (50 in. and under).

Particular stress is placed in roadster show classes upon the manners, style, and beauty of conformation, combined with speed. In striking contrast to heavy harness classes, the roadster is shown hitched to very light vehicles permitting fast travel.

Custom decrees that roadsters shall enter the ring at a jog-trot, and work the wrong way (clockwise) of the track first. After jogging for a brief time, usually the judge asks that they perform the road gait, then jog again (all clockwise of the ring). Then, in succession, the judge asks them to reverse, jog, road gait, and turn on or trot at speed. Lastly, they are called to the center of the ring for inspection in a standing position, at which time the judge usually tests their manners by asking the drivers, in order, to back their horses.

PONIES FOR DRIVING

The best harness show ponies are vest-pocket editions of fine harness horses; that is, they possess the same desirable characteristics, except that they are in miniature. According to the rules of the American Horse Shows Association, harness show ponies may be of any breed or combination of breeds; the only

requisite is that they must be under 12-2 hands in height. Three breeds produce more animals that qualify under this category; namely, the Shetland, Welsh, and Hackney breeds.

Three breeds produce animals that qualify as ponies; namely, the Hackney, Welsh, and Shetland breeds. The Hackney is generally exclusively of the harness type, but the Welsh and Shetland breeds are used either under saddle or in harness. In the major horse shows of the land, the latter two breeds may be exhibited in harness, but in practical use they are children's mounts.

Fig. 8-21. American Shetland Pony performing in the fine harness division. (Courtesy, *The American Shetland Pony Journal*, Lafayette, IN)

ALL-PURPOSE HORSES AND PONIES

All-purpose horses are horses that are used for riding, driving, and/or draft purposes. They may be

Fig. 8-22. All-purpose Norwegian Fjord Horses, on Skoal Farm, Gilmanton Iron Works, New Hampshire. (Courtesy, Norwegian Fjord Horse Registry, Acworth, NJ)

used for pleasure riding, carriage horses, jumpers, hunters, trail riders, stock horses, or for light draft purposes. They are family-type horses, suitable for both children and adults. Because of their versatility, they are especially well adapted for use by suburban and part-time farm families. The following breeds are extolled as all-purpose horses and ponies; American Bakshir Curly, American Gotland Horse, Haflinger, and Norwegian Fjord Horse.

MINIATURE HORSES AND DONKEYS

The Miniature Horse is a scaled-down model of a full-size horse, and not a dwarf. The American Miniature Horse Association, which was organized in 1978, stipulates that a Miniature Horse cannot exceed 34 in. at the withers. Some people keep Miniature Horses as pets. Others exhibit them as driving horses, in single pleasure and roadster driving classes. Still others exhibit them in multiple hitches, pulling miniature wagons, stage coaches, carriages, and other vehicles. Although they can pull a pretty good load, because of their small size only a small child can ride them.

Donkeys, which are small members of the ass family, *Equus asinus*, were domesticated in Egypt, where they were first ridden and used as pack animals about 3400 B.C. Like the horse, donkeys vary in size. Miniature Mediterranean donkeys, native of Sardinia and Sicily, are under 38 in. high, and are used as pets. Sometimes, they are hitched to specially made small vehicles.

Fig. 8-23. Miniature Horse, Hemlock Brook Egyptian King, champion stallion, 31¼ in. in height. Owned by Bob and Sandy Erwin, NFC Miniature Horse Farm, Waitesboro, Texas. (Courtesy, American Miniature Horse Association, Burleson, TX)

Fig. 8-24. Miniature donkey. (Courtesy, Daniel Langfeld, Omaha, NE)

SELECTED REFERENCES

Title of Publication	Author(s)	Publisher
American Horse Shows Association Rule Book, The	Staff	American Horse Shows Assn., New York, NY, 1996–1997
America's Quarter Horses	P. Laune	Doubleday & Company, Inc., Garden City, NY, 1973
Breeding and Raising Horses, Ag. Hdbk. No. 394	M. E. Ensminger	U.S. Department of Agriculture, Washington, DC, 1972
Encyclopedia of the Horse, The	Ed. by C. E. Hope G. N. Jackson	The Viking Press, New York, NY, 1973

From Dawn to Destiny	F. Jennings	The Thoroughbred Press, Inc., Lexington, KY, 1962
Harper's Encyclopedia for Horsemen: The Complete Book of the Horse	L. Taylor	Harper & Row, Publishers, New York, NY, 1973
History of Horse Racing, The	R. Longrigg	Stein and Day Publishers, New York, NY, 1972
History of Thoroughbred Racing in America, The	W. H. Robertson	Prentice-Hall, Inc., Englewood Cliffs, NJ, 1964
Horse, The	D. J. Kays rev. by J. M. Kays	A. S. Barnes & Co., Inc., Cranbury, NJ, 1969
Horse America Made, The	L. Taylor	American Saddle Horse Breeders Association, Louisville, KY, 1961
Horse Industry Directory	Staff	American Horse Council, Washington, DC, 1996
Horse Industry Handbook	Staff	American Horse Council, Washington, DC, 1993
Horseman's Encyclopedia, The	M. C. Self	A. S. Barnes & Co., Inc., Cranbury, NJ, 1963
Horsemanship and Horse Care, Ag. Info. Bull. No. 353	M. E. Ensminger	Agriculture Research Service, USDA, Washington, DC, 1972
Horsemanship and Horsemastership	Ed. by G. Wright	Doubleday & Company, Inc., Garden City, NY, 1962
Light Horses, Farmers' Bull. No. 2127	M. E. Ensminger	Agricultural Research Service, USDA, Washington, DC, 1965
Shetland Pony, The	L. F. Bedell	Iowa State University Press, Ames, IA, 1959
Shetland Pony, The	M. C. Cox	Adam and Charles Black Ltd., London, England, 1965
Steeplechasing	J. Hislop	J. A. Allen & Co., Ltd., London, England, 1970
Summerhays' Encyclopaedia for Horsemen	R. S. Summerhays	Frederick Warne & Co., Inc., New York, NY, 1966
Trotting Horse of America, The	H. Woodruff	University Press; Welch, Bigelow, & Co., Cambridge, MA, 1871
Using the American Quarter Horse	L. N. Sikes	The Saddlerock Corporation, Houston, TX, 1958

Exmoor stallion, *Devon's New Decade*. (Courtesy, Marlyn Exmoors, Amherst, Nova Scotia, Canada.

TYPES AND CLASSES
OF WORK HORSES
AND MULES

How it used to be done! This shows a horse-drawn reaper, successor to the cradle. The reaper, with its two-person crew (one riding the horse, and the other raking the cut grain from the reaper) could cut as much grain as 4 to 5 men with cradles. (Courtesy, International Harvester, Chicago, IL)

As with light horses, similar distinct types—though smaller in number—evolved in the draft horse. From the ponderous beast of Flanders, used as foundation stock, the Great War Horse of the Middle Ages was developed; the Great War Horse, in turn, served as the forerunner of the draft horse of commerce and agriculture. Further and eventual refinement through breeding and selection adapted the draft animals to many and diverse uses, most of which have subsequently passed into oblivion with mechanization. For example, expressers—fast-stepping, delivery-type horses in great demand during the early part of the present century—are seldom seen in the United States at the present time.

During their heyday, certain distinct types of mules were also bred. The type of mule desired was largely controlled through the selection of certain types of mares for breeding purposes.

Today, draft horses and mules are of negligible importance, and types, classes, and market terms are primarily of historic interest. They're reminiscent of an era of horse power, in agriculture and commerce, of the village blacksmith, of few improved roads, and of little automation.

WORK HORSES

Although marked differences in size and weight exist among work horses, all of them are used for power. So, they must be heavy, and they must possess a deep, broad, compact, muscular form suited to the pulling of a heavy load at the walk. A detailed description of a draft type animal is as follows: It should have plenty of size, draftiness, and substance. The head should be shapely and clean-cut, the eyes large and clear, and the ears active. The chest should be especially deep and of ample width. The topline should include a short, strong back and loin, with a long, nicely turned, and well-muscled croup, and a well-set tail. The middle should be wide and deep, and there should be good depth in both fore and rear flanks. Muscling should be heavy throughout, especially in the forearm and gaskin; the shoulder should be sloping; the legs should be straight, true, and squarely set; the bone should be strong and flat and show plenty of quality. The pasterns should be sloping and the feet should be large and have adequate width at the heels and toughness in conformation. With this splendid draft type, there should be style, balance, and symmetry; an abundance of quality; an energetic yet manageable disposition; soundness; and freedom from disease. The action should be straight and true, with a long, swift, and elastic stride, both at the walk and the trot.

HISTORICAL CLASSIFICATION OF WORK HORSES

During the first half of the 1900s, the classification of work horses according to the use to which they were put, including the range in height and weight, was as shown in Table 9-1 and as defined in this section. Today, this classification is no longer used. It is of historic interest only.

TABLE 9-1
MARKET CLASSIFICATION OF WORK HORSES

Class	Range in Height	Range in Weight	
	(hands)	*(lb)*	*(kg)*
Draft horses	16 to 17–2	1,600 upward	*726 upward*
Wagon horses	15–2 to 16–2	1,300 to 1,600	*590 to 726*
Farm chunks	15 to 16	1,300 to 1,400	*590 to 635*
Southerners	14–2 to 15–2	600 to 1,100	*272 to 499*

■ **Draft horses**—Draft horses stood from 16 to 17-2 hands in height and weighed from 1,600 lb upward. They represented the ultimate in power type. Formerly, draft-type horses of quality and style were used on

Fig. 9-1.   Draft horses being used to collect maple sap at a maple sugar camp in Northeastern United States. This was the common practice during the first half of the 20th century. (Courtesy, J. C. Allen and Son, Inc., West Lafayette, IN)

farms and city streets, but these have long since been replaced by tractors and trucks.

■ **Wagon horses**—Wagon horses were intermediate in weight and height between the drafter and the chunk, and they had more action than either. They weighed from 1,300 to 1,600 lb and stood from 15-2 to 16-2 hands in height. Wagon horses were formerly used on milk and laundry wagons.

■ **Farm chunks**—These were chunky, "small-sized" drafters standing 15 to 16 hands in height and weighing from 1,300 to 1,400 lb.

■ **Southerners**—Southerners were small, plain type animals that were formerly used in the South. They usually stood from 14-2 to 15-2 hands and weighed from 600 to 1,100 lb.

MODERN CLASSIFICATION OF WORK HORSES

Currently, the modern classification of draft horses consists primarily of two categories; draft horses, and all-purpose (utility) horses.

DRAFT HORSES

Today, few draft horses are used on farms or city streets. The most glamorous use of the "gentle giants" is in six- and eight-horse hitches for exhibition purposes—a type of advertising. Also, horse-pulling contests are great attractions at fairs throughout the country.

Fig. 9-2. Percheron stallion, *Misty Valley Mountaineer*, owned by Hostetler Bros. Fredericktown, Ohio. (Courtesy, Percheron Horse Assn. of America, Fredericktown, OH)

Fig. 9-3. A horse-pulling contest always draws a good crowd, as this event did in 1928. (Courtesy, J. C. Allen and Son, Inc., West Lafayette, IN)

ALL-PURPOSE (UTILITY) HORSES

All-purpose horses are used for light draft purposes, and as pleasure horses—for riding and driving. They usually have less depth of body and longer legs than draft horses; thus, they are better able to jog along at the trot. In addition to being versatile, it is desirable that all-purpose horses be attractive—an important requisite when they are used as pleasure horses.

Fig. 9-4. American Cream draft horses, owned by Earl Hammond, Goshen, Indiana, making hay. (Photo by Robert Mischka. Courtesy, American Cream Draft Horse Assn., Charles City, IA)

All-purpose horses are especially well adapted for use on small farms and in suburban areas, where they are needed for both work and pleasure.

MULES

It has been correctly said that the mule is without pride of ancestry or hope of posterity. He is a hybrid, being a cross between two species of the family *Equidae*—the *caballus* or horse and the *asinus* or ass.[1] Like most hybrids, the mule is seldom fertile.

The use of the mule in the United States was first popularized by two early American statesmen, George Washington and Henry Clay. The first jack to enter this country, of which there is authentic record, was presented by the King of Spain to General Washington in 1787, shortly after the close of the Revolutionary War. Other importations followed; and from that day until mechanization, the hardy mule furnished the main source of animal power for the South. In comparison with the horse, the mule (1) withstands higher temperatures; (2) endures less experienced labor; (3) adapts its eating habits to either irregularity or self-feeding with little danger of founder or digestive disturbances; (4) works or stables in lower areas without head injury (the mule lowers its head when the ears touch an object, whereas a horse will throw its head upward under similar conditions); (5) encounters less foot trouble, wire cuts, etc.; and (6) maneuvers about without harm to itself.

Although the mule resembles its sire, the jack,

---

[1]The cross between a jennet and a stallion is known as a hinny. The mule and the hinny are indistinguishable.

Fig. 9-5. Percheron mare and her mule foal.

Fig. 9-6. A near-perfect model of a young jack. Note his heavy bone, well-set legs, and good head and ears.

more than its dam, the desired conformation is identical to that described for the horse; perhaps the one exception is that more stress is placed upon the size, set, and quality of the ear. The most desirable mules must be of good size and draftiness, compact and heavily muscled; must show evidence of plenty of quality; must stand on correct feet and legs; and must be sound. As the natural tendency of the mule is to be lazy and obstinate, an active, energetic disposition is sought.

HISTORICAL CLASSIFICATION OF MULES

During the first half of the 1900s, the classification of mules according to the use to which they were put, including the range in height and weight, was as shown in Table 9-2, and as defined in this section. But this classification was obsoleted with the decline in the use and numbers of mules; today, it is of historic interest only.

TABLE 9-2
MARKET CLASSIFICATION OF MULES

Class	Range in Height	Range in Weight	
	(hands)	(lb)	(kg)
Draft	16 to 17–2	1,200 to 1,600	545 to 726
Sugar	16 to 17	1,150 to 1,300	522 to 590
Farm	15–2 to 16	900 to 1,250	409 to 568
Cotton	13–2 to 15–2	750 to 1,100	341 to 499
Pack and mining . . .	12 to 16	600 to 1,350	272 to 613

Draft mules—Draft mules were the finest mules in type and quality, weighed from 1,200 to 1,600 lb, and stood 16 to 17-2 hands in height.

Sugar mules—Sugar mules derived their name from their most common usage prior to mechanization; they were the sugar plantation mules of the South.

Farm mules—Farm mules were those purchased for use on farms. These mules were often plainer looking, thinner in flesh, and showed less evidence of quality than draft mules.

Cotton mules—As the name indicates, mules of this type were once used primarily by cotton growers in the South, to plant, cultivate, and harvest the cotton crop.

Pack and mine mules—Pack mules were used for transport work—carrying heavy loads on their backs—in very rough or wooded country not accessible to vehicles.

MODERN CLASSIFICATION OF MULES

The modern classification of mules is as follows:

DRAFT MULES

These are the largest mules. They are produced by mating draft mares to jacks. Belgian mares are popular for the production of mules, because they

Fig. 9-7. A classy sorrel draft mule, sired by a Mammoth jack and out of a Belgian mare. Owned by Kathy Berrens, Puyallup, Washington. (Courtesy, The American Donkey and Mule Society, Denton, TX)

produce sorrel mules, which are highly prized. However, Clydesdale, Percheron, Shire, and Suffolk mares produce excellent draft mules, also. Draft mules weigh from 1,100 to 1,600 lb and stand 15 to 17 hands high.

PACK/WORK MULES

Pack and work mules are produced by mating medium sized draft mares (purebreds, crossbreds, or grades of the draft breeds) to a jack. They are smaller than draft mules; they weigh from 800 to 1,250 lb and stand 13 to 16 hands high. Pack mules are used to

transport goods and/or people, frequently to areas not accessible by vehicles.

The size and conformation of work mules differ according to the type of work, but all of them are built for heavy work.

Fig. 9-9. A work mule. These mules are generally plainer looking, thinner in flesh, and show less evidence of quality than draft mules.

SADDLE AND DRIVING MULES

Saddle and driving mules are produced by mating pleasure horses to a jack. They vary in size, from small to large, but all of them are of pleasure type.

Most of these mules have easy gaits and are used

Fig. 9-8. Pack mules in use in rough country not accessible to motor vehicles. (Courtesy, Mary C. Roeser, Mammoth Lake Packout Outfit, Mammoth Lake, CA 93564; Courtesy, Mrs. Betsy Hutchins, Secretary-Editor, The American Donkey and Mule Society, Denton, TX)

Fig. 9-10. An excellent type of saddle mule produced by mating a Thoroughbred mare to a jack of the Mammoth breed. Owned by Susan and Sally Skinner, Mira Loma, California. (Courtesy, American Donkey and Mule Society, Inc., Denton, TX)

for riding. Some are used for driving; and still others are used for jumping.

MINIATURE MULES AND DONKEYS

Fig. 9-11. Spotted Asses, *Wxicof Windy* and *Wxicof Flopodopolos*, Champion jenny and Champion gelding (mother and son), at the 1996 American Council of Spotted Asses National Show held in Shelbyville, Tennessee; bred, owned, and shown by Coreen Eaton, Wxicof Wooly Woods, Wentyville, Missouri. (Courtesy, Coreen Eaton)

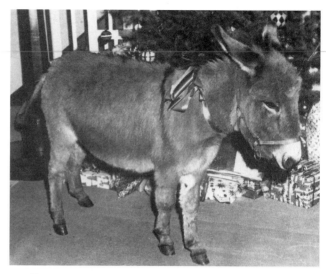

Fig. 9-12. Miniature donkey. (Courtesy, Miniature Donkey Registry of the United States, Inc., Omaha, NE. Presently, the American Donkey and Mule Society, Denton, TX)

Miniature mules are produced by mating pony mares to a very small jack. Fifty inches is considered the maximum height for miniature mules. Miniature donkeys, which were originally imported from Sicily and Sardinia, must be under 36 in. at the withers. Miniature mules and donkeys are used as pets/companions, and for driving. Sometimes they are ridden by small children.

As would be expected, there is considerable spread in value between mules within each class—depending on conformation, quality, temperament, condition, action, soundness, and age. Mare mules usually outsell horse mules. The most desirable age is between 4 and 8 years, and sorrel mules are most popular.

SELECTED REFERENCES

Title of Publication	Author(s)	Publisher
Gentle Giants	R. Whitlock	Lutterworth Press, Guildford and London, England, 1976
History of American Jacks and Mules	F. C. Mills ed. by H. L. Hall	Hutch-Line, Inc., Hutchinson, KS, 1971
History of the Percheron Horse, A	A. H. Sanders W. Dinsmore	Breeder's Gazette Print, Chicago, IL, 1917
Horse Industry Directory	Staff	American Horse Council, Washington, DC, 1996
Horse, The	D. J. Kays rev. by J. M. Kays	A. S. Barnes & Co., Inc., Cranbury, NJ, 1969
People with Long Ears	R. Borwick	Cassell & Company Ltd., London, England, 1970
Percheron Horse, The	M. C. Weld	O. Judd Co., New York, NY, 1886

10

BREEDS OF
LIGHT HORSES

Memorial to *Justin Morgan*, the foundation sire of the first family of American horses. (Courtesy, The American Morgan Horse Assn., Shelburne, VT)

Contents   *Page*

Contents   *Page*

Contents	Page

Contents	Page

A breed of horses may be defined as *a group of horses having a common origin and possessing certain well-fixed, distinctive, uniformly transmitted characteristics that are not common to other horses.*[1]

There is scarcely a breed of horses that does not possess one or more distinctive breed characteristics in which it excels all others. Moreover, any one of several breeds is often well adapted to the same use. To amateurs, this is most confusing; so, they are prone to inquire as to the best breed. Certainly, if any strong preference exists, it should be an important factor, though it is recognized that certain breeds are better adapted to specific purposes.

It is noteworthy that most of the breeds of light horses are American creations. There are two primary reasons for this; namely, (1) the diverse needs and uses for which light horses have been produced, and (2) the fact that many people of wealth have bred light horses.

RELATIVE POPULARITY OF BREEDS OF LIGHT HORSES

Table 10-1 shows the latest available annual registrations (for 1994 or 1995 unless otherwise stipulated), and total registrations to date of the various breeds of light horses.

---

[1]Sometimes people construe the write-up of a breed of livestock in a book or in a USDA bulletin as an official recognition of the breed. Nothing could be further from the truth, for no person or office has authority to approve a breed. The only legal basis for recognizing a breed is contained in the Tariff Act of 1930, which provides for the duty-free admission of purebred breeding stock provided they are registered in the country of origin. But the latter stipulation applies to imported animals only.

In this book, no *official* recognition of any breed is intended or implied. Rather, the author has tried earnestly, and without favoritism, to present the factual story of the breeds in narrative and pictures. In particular, such information relative to the new and/or less widely distributed breeds is needed, and often difficult to secure.

TABLE 10-1
ANNUAL (1994 OR 1995) AND TOTAL REGISTRATIONS SINCE BREED REGISTRY STARTED OF LIGHT HORSES IN U.S. BREED ASSOCIATIONS

Breed	Annual (1994 or 1995) Registrations	Total Registrations (since breed registry started)
Quarter Horse	128,352	2,777,860
Thoroughbred	35,200	1,483,957
Paint Horse	34,846	320,949
Arabian	17,625	825,098
Purebred	12,962	514,498
Half Arabian	4,495	301,973
Anglo-Arabian	168	8,627
Standardbred	12,204	716,466
Appaloosa	10,104	568,331
Tennessee Walking Horse	9,376	314,695
Palomino	3,157	92,590
The Palomino Horse Assn.	1,664	51,564
Palomino Horse Breeders of America	1,493	41,026
Morgan	3,038	135,000
Missouri Fox Trotting Horse	2,821	46,537
American Saddlebred	2,738	228,322
Paso Fino	2,036	25,969
Haflinger	1,755	13,150
Haflinger Assn. of America	1,000	7,000
Haflinger Registry of North America	755	6,150
Peruvian Paso	1,712	23,278
Am. Assn. of Owners & Breeders of Peruvian Horses	772	11,072
Peruvian Paso Horse Registry of North America	940	12,206
Shetland Pony	1,200	150,000
Miniature Horse	NA	30,000
Pony of the Americas	1,120	42,000
Buckskin	921	17,500
Welsh Pony & Cob	715	36,952
National Show Horse	610	11,467
Trakehner	465	8,117
Hanoverian	450	5,000

(Continued)

TABLE 10-1 (Continued)

Breed	Annual (1994 or 1995) Registrations	Total Registrations (since breed registry started)
National Spotted Horse	436	3,996
Andalusian (two associations)	355	1,903
Dutch Warmblood	315	3,000
Pinto Horse	290	1,420
Pinto Arabian	200	300
Iberian Warmblood	207	207
American Bashkir Curly	163	875
American Part Blooded	147	14,450
Mustang	136	
American Mustang Assn.	NA	242
N. Am. Mustang Assn. & Reg. . . .	NA	260
Spanish Mustang Registry	136	2,320
Selle Francais	110	635
Half Saddlebred	107	2,874
Lipizzan	95	953
Welara Pony	93	423
Hungarian	30	800
Norwegian Fjord Horse	21	424
Spanish Barb	18	421
American Walking Pony	15	300
American White & Creme	11	3,754
Pintabian	11	32
Swedish Gotland	10	500
Exmoor Pony	5	34
Dales Pony	2	34
American Warmblood	NA	1,500
Morab	NA	730
Cracker Horse	NA	242
Irish Draught Horse	NA	23

The recent annual figures reflect the current popularity and numbers of the respective breeds, although it is recognized that one year's data fails to show trends, and that new breeds have few numbers in the formative period.

AKHAL-TEKE

The Akhal-Teke is an ancient breed. Originally, it was used as war mounts. Later, it was used for racing. Today, it is used in equine sports.

ORIGIN AND NATIVE HOME

The Akhal-Teke breed originated in the U.S.S.R., in Southern Turkmenia by the "Teke" tribe, on the "Akhal" oasis. As the chief mount of the Turkoman warriors for centuries, the Akhal-Teke developed great stamina; and from the harsh desert environment, it developed the ability to withstand great extremes in temperature, along with periods of privation of feed and water.

EARLY AMERICAN IMPORTATIONS

The first American purchases of an Akhal-Teke, a stallion and a mare, were made in Moscow, U.S.S.R., in 1978; following which these two animals were imported into the United States—the stallion in 1979, and the mare in 1980. Other importations followed.

AKHAL-TEKE CHARACTERISTICS

Fig. 10-1. Akhal-Teke stallion, *Sengar*, owned by The Akhal-Teke Stud, Staunton, Virginia. (Courtesy, Shenandoah Farm, Staunton, VA)

The Akhal-Teke is a desert-bred horse, with a light, elegant build. It has a long, tapering face, wide nostrils, large eyes, mobile ears; a long, straight neck; a short, sparse mane and forelock; sloping shoulders; prominent withers; a long, lean, narrow, and sinewy body; a pronounced croup; long legs, muscular forearms, strong hocks, and dense hooves; and gliding, elastic action. Akhal-Tekes are 15 to 15-2 hands high; weigh 900 to 1,000 lb; and are of quiet temperament.

ADAPTATION AND USE

The Akhal-Teke is used in all competitive equine sports, including endurance trials, dressage, and jumping.

PRESENT STATUS OF THE BREED

The Akhal-Teke Registry Association of America was formed in 1983.

The Russians now consider the Akhal-Teke as genetic material of exceptional value.

The breed is quite rare, with fewer than 2,000 purebred animals existing worldwide. The largest population of about 1,400 Akhal-Tekes is in the U.S.S.R. The second largest number, comprising about 200 head, is in Germany; and the third largest number, about 100 head, is in the United States.

AMERICAN BASHKIR CURLY

The long, curly coat of hair, for which the American Bashkir Curly is noted, makes them especially well adapted to extremely cold weather, such as exists in their native home—the eastern slopes of the Ural Mountains of the U.S.S.R.

ORIGIN AND NATIVE HOME

Horses with curly hair are known to have been raised for centuries by the people of Bashkiria on the eastern slopes of the Ural Mountains; hence, the name Bashkir. In this rugged climate, the Bashkiri people depended upon their horses for transportation, clothing, meat, and milk. In their native land, mares give 3 to 6 gallons of milk per day, which is highly prized. In addition to being consumed as fresh milk, cream, and butter, it makes a delicious cheese. Also, the milk is fermented to make a drink called *koumiss*, which the natives drink both as an intoxicating liquor and for medicinal purposes. History also records that the nomadic Mongols rode curly horses.

The modern history of curly horses in America began in 1898, when Peter Damele of Ely, Nevada, cut three curly animals from a herd of wild horses in the Peter Hanson Mountain Range. Most of today's curly horses trace to Damele ranch breeding.

Thus, the Bashkir Curly originated in the U.S.S.R. How and when these curly animals came to the United States is clouded in obscurity. Although they were known to have existed on a Nevada ranch as early as 1898, the American Bashkir Curly Registry was not formed until August 14, 1971.

AMERICAN BASHKIR CURLY CHARACTERISTICS

Fig. 10-2. American Bashkir Curley mare. (Courtesy, American Bashkir Curly Registry, Ely, NV)

The curly coat, with corkscrew mane and wavy tail, is the most unique characteristic of the breed. The mane hair, and often the tail hair, falls out completely each summer and grows back during the winter. In build, Curlies are medium size and chunky, somewhat resembling the early-day Morgan in conformation. The breed is noted for small nostrils, a gentle disposition, and heavy milking. Many of the animals have a natural fox-trot gait. All colors are accepted. Horses weighing in excess of 1,350 lb or having faulty conformation are disqualified for registry.

ADAPTATION AND USE

The American Bashkir Curly is used as a pleasure horse and for utility purposes—including light draft work. Because of their ruggedness, endurance, and gentle dispositions, they make ideal family trail horses and children's mounts.

PRESENT STATUS OF THE BREED

The American Bashkir Curly has two primary things going for it: (1) the nostalgia imparted by its ancient origin in the Soviet Union, and (2) a curly coat of hair, not possessed by any other breed.

AMERICAN CREME HORSE

This is a color breed, rather than a distinctive type.

ORIGIN AND NATIVE HOME

Pale cream horses have been around for a very long time, primarily in Oregon and Washington. However, they were not given breed status until 1970, at which time the American Albino Association, Inc., established a separate American Creme Horse Division for their registration.

AMERICAN CREME HORSE CHARACTERISTICS

Fig. 10-3. American Creme Horse, owned by Vanessa Jenkins, La Farayrio, France. (Courtesy, International American Albino Assn., Naper, NE)

The following color classifications of American Creme Horses are registered:

A—Body ivory white, mane white (lighter than body), eyes blue, skin pink.

B—Body cream, mane darker than body, cinnamon buff to ridgeway, eyes dark.

C—Body and mane of the same color, pale cream, eyes blue, skin pink.

D—Body and mane of same color, sooty cream, eyes blue, skin pink.

Combinations of the above classifications are also acceptable.

The American Creme Horse may possess the characteristics of any breed.

Pink eyes or any color other than ivory white or cream are disqualifications.

Both horses and ponies are accepted for registry; animals above 14-2 hands are classed as horses, those below 14-2 are classed as ponies.

ADAPTATION AND USE

American Creme horses are used as pleasure horses, for exhibition purposes, as parade and flag bearer horses, and as stock horses.

PRESENT STATUS OF THE BREED

Both the American Creme Horse and the American White Horse are registered and well promoted by the International American Albino Association, Naper, Nebraska, with separate divisions provided for each. It's an attractive breed, but numbers are limited.

AMERICAN MUSTANG

The American Mustang traces to the wild horses of the North American plains, which were descended from Spanish stock.

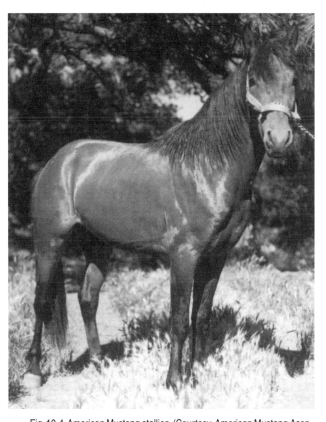

Fig. 10-4. American Mustang stallion. (Courtesy, American Mustang Assn., Yucaipa, CA)

ORIGIN AND NATIVE HOME

American Mustang horses originated along the Barbary Coast of North Africa; from here they were taken to Spain by the conquering Moors, propagated in Andalusia, and brought to America by the conquistadors. The American Mustang Association was formed in 1962.

AMERICAN MUSTANG CHARACTERISTICS

They may be any color, but they must be between 13-2 and 15 hands high. Animals under 13-2 hands or over 15 hands are disqualified for registry.

ADAPTATION AND USES

American Mustangs are used for show, pleasure riding, trail riding, endurance trials, stock horses, and jumping.

PRESENT STATUS OF THE BREED

Although the American Mustang is of ancient origin, the breed registry is relatively new and numbers are limited. The breed enthusiasts are wisely promoting its historic origin, along with its hardiness and versatility.

AMERICAN SADDLEBRED
(See Plates 1, 23, and 24)

The American Saddlebred is distinctly an American creation. With at least passable roads in the East, the breeding of harness horses was centered in this area, particularly in the vicinity of New York and Philadelphia. Farther inland, however, roads were few and far between, and horses' backs afforded the chief means of transportation. The early residents of Kentucky, Tennessee, Virginia, and West Virginia selected animals with easy, lateral, ambling gaits, finding these to be most desirable to ride over plantations and hilly and rolling grazing areas, especially on long journeys.

ORIGIN AND NATIVE HOME

The creation of the American Saddlebred had its unplanned beginning with the settlement of the plantations of southeastern United States. Later, Missouri-ans took up the breeding of easy-gaited saddle horses. These southern pioneers, who never rode with short stirrups and who regarded posting as a heathenish invention of the English, very early selected and imported ambling types of horses from Canada and the New England states. Canada at that time had a sturdy little horse which paced, known as the Canadian pacer. Animals of the Thoroughbred breed and what later proved to be the forerunners of the Morgan and Standardbred breeds were also infused. The type of horse demanded was one that could travel long distances without distress to either the horse or the rider and which possessed beauty, speed, tractability, intelligence, courage, durability, longevity, and versatility (adapted to harness use if desired). Conditions calling for horses of this type prevailed throughout the states mentioned, beginning with the earliest settlement. It is not surprising, therefore, that the men, women, and children of this area became equestrians.

The amalgamation of diverse blood continued and with it constant selection for the desired qualities, particularly adaptability to easy riding gaits. Eventually, the plantation owners fixed on a definite and beautiful type, even though it was not to be known as a breed until many years later, since no breed registry association was formed until 1891.

The modern American Saddlebred now traces most of its origins to a Thoroughbred four-mile race stallion, *Denmark* (foaled in 1839). Although this horse did not achieve great fame on the track, his races were said to be characterized by unusual stamina and gameness. *Denmark* left numerous progeny, but his most notable offspring was *Gaine's Denmark*, out of a natural ambler of native stock, known as the Stevenson mare. Many have credited this mare with being of greater foundation importance than *Denmark* himself. Certainly the Stevenson mare supplied the genetic basis for the gaits so easily attained by her descendants. To *Denmark*, however, credit must be given for courage, breediness, shoulders, fineness of head and neck, clean dense bone, and quality of the sons and daughters of many subsequent generations. In considering the diverse breeding of the native stock from which the breed sprung, including the Stevenson mare—and without in any way minimizing the influence of the Thoroughbred—one might even conclude that the American Saddlebred is indebted to the Canadian Pacer for its easy riding gaits; to the Morgan for docility, beauty, and animation; and to the Standardbred for a good trot.

In 1901, the American Saddlebred Horse Association approved a list of 10 stallions entitled to rank as the great foundation sires of the breed. There can be little question, however, that *Denmark*, largely through his illustrious son, *Gaine's Denmark*, was the greatest of all.

AMERICAN SADDLEBRED CHARACTERISTICS

Fig. 10-5. American Saddlebred, *The Right Stuff*. (Avis Photo. Courtesy, American Saddlebred Horse Assn., Lexington, KY)

The chief distinguishing characteristic of horses of this breed is their ability to furnish an easy ride with great style and animation. Park hacks may be either three- or five-gaited, the choice being largely a matter of preference and training. Walk-trot-canter horses are known as three-gaited; whereas animals possessing the rack, and a show-gait in addition (running walk, fox trot, or slow pace), are known as five-gaited.

Custom decrees that three-gaited American Saddlebreds be shown with shaved mane and full-length and flowing tail; and that five-gaited horses be shown with braided mane and full-length tail, and that boots protect the front feet.

Members of the breed are usually bay, brown, chestnut, gray, black, or golden in color. Most of them stand from 15 to 16 hands in height and weigh from 1,000 to 1,200 lb.

The American Saddlebred is noted for a beautiful head carried on a long, graceful neck; for a short, rounded back, a level croup, and a high-set tail; and for proud action. The entire ensemble is without a peer when it comes to style, spirit, and animation. At the same time, members of the breed are docile, intelligent, and tractable.

ADAPTATION AND USE

The American Saddlebred is now used almost exclusively as three- or five-gaited saddle horses, primarily as pleasure horses—either on the bridle paths or in the show-ring.

Fine harness show horses come from the American Saddlebred, and it has been said that horses of this breed meet the demand for combination horses better than any other group. Animals of American Saddlebred extraction are occasionally used as stock horses, jumpers, and for other light horse purposes; but their versatility does not approach that of the Thoroughbred. They are primarily a park hack, for which use they are preeminent.

PRESENT STATUS OF THE BREED

Well-trained American Saddlebreds of good type have enjoyed a broad demand at good prices for many years. This demand has come mostly from city people who use the saddle horse for purposes of pleasure, recreation, and exercise. Although representatives of the breed are found in every state, Kentucky and Missouri continue as the great breeding centers.

AMERICAN WALKING PONY
(See Plate 7)

The American Walking Pony is a pony (under 14-2 hands) with the running walk gait.

ORIGIN AND NATIVE HOME

The breed originated near Macon, Georgia, in 1968; from a foundation cross of Tennessee Walking Horse and Welsh Pony.

AMERICAN WALKING PONY CHARACTERISTICS

American Walking Ponies must perform the running walk gait.

There is no coat color stipulation. Since it is a cross between the Welsh Pony and the Tennessee Walking Horse, the colors of both parent breeds occur—bay, chestnut, gray, black, brown, white, palomino, and paint. They range in height from 13 to 14-2 hands.

Appaloosa color is not accepted for registry.

Fig. 10-6. American Walking Pony. (Courtesy, American Walking Pony Assn., Macon, GA)

ADAPTATION AND USE

They are used for pleasure riding, and as mounts for children or small adults

PRESENT STATUS OF THE BREED

The American Walking Pony is a relatively new breed with limited numbers.

AMERICAN WARMBLOOD

Warmbloods were first brought to the United States about 1970, primarily from Germany, Sweden, and Holland. Subsequently, the Warmbloods went their separate ways, with the formation of different breeds and different breed registries. The American Warmbloods, which are registered by the American Warmblood Society, Phoenix, Arizona, only registers horses that are involved in the four sports supported by the United States Equestrian Team; namely, dressage, show jumping, combined training, and combined driving. The American Warmblood may be of any breed or combination of breeds, except they cannot be 100% hot-bloods (*i.e.*, Arabian or Thoroughbred) or 100% cold-bloods (of draft horse breeding). Also, for registration, the American Warmblood must satisfy one of the following five performance test requirements: sport horse in-hand, dressage, combined training, combined driving, show jumping.

Like the American Warmblood Society, the American Warmblood Registry, Tallahassee, Florida, con-

tends that Warmbloods are highly intermingled and, therefore, do not necessarily represent distinct breeds. Rather they are various types of the Warmblood breed. But the American Warmblood Registry differs from the American Warmblood Society in that they do not limit registration to horses involved in the four sports supported by the U.S. Equestrian Team. Rather, they promote the American Warmblood as a super athlete with a kind and easy-going temperament, suited for both the professional and amateur competitor. The American Warmblood Registry was established in 1981.

AMERICAN WHITE HORSE
(See Plates 8 and 45)

The American White Horse is a color breed with snow-white hair.

ORIGIN AND NATIVE HOME

The breed originated on White Horse Ranch, Naper, Nebraska. It traces to the white stallion, Old

Fig. 10-7. American White champion mare, *Charmin Snow Mist.* (Courtesy, International American Albino Assn., Naper, NE)

King, of unknown pedigree, foaled in 1906, which the White Horse Ranch purchased in Illinois.

In 1936, the White Horse Ranch owners—Caleb R. Thompson and his wife, Ruth E. White Thompson—organized the American Albino Horse Club.

Presently, both the American White Horse and The American Creme Horse are registered by the International American Albino Association, Naper, Nebraska, with separate divisions provided for each.

AMERICAN WHITE HORSE CHARACTERISTICS

American White Horses have snow-white hair, as white as clean snow, with pink skin. The eyes are light blue, dark blue (near black), brown, or hazel, but never pink. Both horses and ponies are accepted for registry; animals above 14-2 hands are classed as horses, those below 14-2 are classed as ponies.

ADAPTATION AND USE

American White Horses are used as pleasure horses. Their snow-white color makes them very attractive as trained horses for exhibition purposes and as parade and flag bearer horses.

PRESENT STATUS OF THE BREED

Numbers are limited, but the breed is attractive and well promoted.

ANDALUSIAN
(See Plate 41)

Although the Andalusian traces its origin to the cave dwellers of the Mesolithic Age, in the mountains of the Iberian Peninsula, about 8,000 years ago, it is little known in America. This obscurity is attributed to the embargo, which was placed on the breed by the government of Spain and continued for over a century.

ORIGIN AND NATIVE HOME

Andalusian horses originated in Spain. The Spanish call the breed Español; the Portuguese call it Lusitano. The American Andalusian Horse Association was founded in the 1960s. All purebred Andalusians must trace to the Registration Books of the Spanish Army.

EARLY AMERICAN IMPORTATIONS

Since the lifting of the Spanish embargo in the 1960s, limited numbers of purebred Andalusians have been imported into the United States.

ANDALUSIAN CHARACTERISTICS

In type, the Andalusian resembles the Arabian, except that they are not dish-faced. Whites, grays, and bays are the most common colors, but there are a few

Fig. 10-8. Andalusian stallion. (Courtesy, The American Andalusian and Lusitano Horse Assn., Sykesville, MD)

blacks, roans, and chestnuts.

ADAPTATION AND USE

Andalusian horses are used for bullfighting, parade, dressage, jumping, and pleasure riding.

PRESENT STATUS OF THE BREED

Currently, the breed is being registered and promoted by two associations; the American Andalusian and Lusitano Horse Association and the International Andalusian and Lusitano Horse Association. In 1996, there were an estimated 1,200 purebred Andalusians in the United States. The proud owners of Andalusians consider their horses priceless.

Animals not tracing to the Spanish Registry, which is supervised by the Army in Spain, are not eligible for registry.

APPALOOSA
(See Plate 29)

The Appaloosa played a major role in the Indian wars and in the development of the early-day livestock industry of northwestern United States.

ORIGIN AND NATIVE HOME

Appaloosa horses originated in the United States—in Oregon, Washington, and Idaho—from animals that first came from Fergana, Central Asia.

Ancient art attests to the fact that spotted horses are as old as recorded history. Without doubt, the ancestors of the Appaloosa were introduced into Mexico by the early Spanish explorers. Eventually (about 1730), through trading, wars, and capturing strays, the Nez Percé tribe of American Indians came into possession of some of these spotted horses. The Indians were pleased with these colorful mounts and greatly increased their numbers on their fertile ranges in northeastern Oregon, southeastern Washington, and the bordering area in Idaho. Eventually, these horses came to be known as the Appaloosa, which name is said to be derived from the word *Palouse*, which in turn came form the French word *peluse*, meaning grassy sward. The rolling Palouse country was formerly covered by virgin prairie, but it is now world-famous wheat and pea country.

For many years, most of the Appaloosa horses were owned by the Nez Percé tribe, but the War of 1877 resulted in their being scattered throughout the West. Finally, on December 30, 1938, the Appaloosa Horse Club was organized for the purpose of preserving and promoting the breed.

APPALOOSA CHARACTERISTICS

Fig. 10-10. Appaloosa mare and foal. (Photo by Alice Coleman. Courtesy, Appaloosa Horse Club, Moscow, ID)

Fig. 10-9. Appaloosa stallion, *Pete McCue*, owned by Dr. W. R. Jacobs, M.D., Lewiston, Idaho; and ridden by Jesse Redheart, a full-blooded Nez Percé Indian. Note (1) that the horse is wearing a war bridle (Himpaiein), a type of chin rein; (2) that the Indian rider is wearing a bonnet of Golden Eagle feathers, of a type denoting the rank of the warrior; and (3) that the rider is seated on a blanket, for the Nez Percé did not use saddles. Other standard equipment of the Nez Percé included a buffalo hide shield, a bow and arrows. This entry won first in the Appaloosa Mounted Costume Class (a horse show class originated by the author of this book) in the Washington State University Horse Show. (Courtesy, Washington State University)

Appaloosas show many variations and combinations of unusual coat patterns. They may be black, bay, brown, chestnut, white with dark spots over the loin and hips, white with dark spots over the entire body, or mottled dark and white or with white spots over a dark body. The eye is encircled by a white sclera, the same as the human eye; and the hoofs are striped vertically black and white.

Any one of the following constitute a disqualification and make the animal ineligible for registry: Under 14 hands high after five years of age; parrot mouth or undershot jaw unless gelded or spayed; cryptorchid or monorchid, or sired by a cryptorchid or a monorchid; paint or pinto markings; gray or non-Appaloosa roan, or the progeny of a gray or non-Appaloosa roan; or draft pony, albino, Pinto, or Paint breeding.

ADAPTATION AND USE

Though once used for war, racing, and buffalo hunting, Appaloosas are now used for stock horses, pleasure horses, parade mounts, and racehorses.

PRESENT STATUS OF THE BREED

In recent years, the Appaloosa has made great strides—increasing in both quality and numbers.

Much credit for the present status of the Appaloosa breed is due to the dedicated efforts of George B. Hatley, longtime executive secretary of the Appaloosa Horse Club, Inc., who served the club without compensation for many years.

The Appaloosa Horse Club provides *permanent registry* for animals out of registered parents whose applications are accompanied by four recent colored photographs and the scheduled fee. Additionally, animals originally registered in the *tentative registry* can be advanced to *permanent registry* by any one of the following procedures:

1. When the sire and dam of a horse registered in the *tentative* category have both been permanent, the owner should send the *tentative certificate of registration*, four recent colored photographs, and the proper fee to the Appaloosa registry and request that the application be changed to *permanent*.

2. By meeting the following production requirement: When a stallion has sired 12 regular registered foals, or a mare has produced three regular registered foals, it is eligible for advancement to permanent. So, the owner should then complete the application for advancement, and send it along with four recent color photographs and the proper fee to the Appaloosa Horse Club.

3. Stallions that are *tentative registered* and later gelded will be transferred to *permanent* only if all requirements are met for regular registration. The same applies to mares that are spayed.

ARABIAN

Many writers have credited the Arabs with having first domesticated the horse, but this is not the case. The preponderance of evidence favors the belief that the foundation stock of the Arabian horse was obtained many centuries following their domestication from either the Egyptians or the Libyan tribes of northern Africa.

In addition to purebred Arabians, there are Half-Arabians and Anglo-Arabs, both of which are registered by the International Arabian Horse Association, Denver, Colorado, with eligibility as shown in Table A-17 of the Appendix of this book.

Additionally, parti-colored Arabians, half or purebred Arabians, with excessive white markings, are registered by the Association of Parti-Colored Arabians, 37680 S.E. Fall Creek Rd., Estacada, OR 97023.

ORIGIN AND NATIVE HOME

The Arabian, oldest breed of horses and the fountainhead of all the other light horse breeds, was developed in the desert country of Arabia, from which it derives its name. Regardless of the clouded obscurity that surrounds the early origin of the breed, it is generally recognized that, through long and careful mating, the Arabs produced a superior type of horse which would carry them swiftly and safely over long stretches of sandy soil and at the same time withstand deprivations in feed and water to a remarkable degree. As the Bedouins of the desert were a warring, pilfering tribe, the very safety of their lives often depended upon a swift escape. Such was the need, and out of this

Fig. 10-11. Arabian Native Costume Class. (Courtesy, International Arabian Horse Assn., Denver, CO)

need was developed the Arabian horse. Legend has it that at night the Arabs would often steal semen from a highly prized stallion owned by an enemy tribe and inseminate their mares therefrom. This was the first artificial insemination of farm animals.

It is easy to understand how the environmental conditions surrounding the development of the Arabian breed could and did give rise to myth and exaggerated statements as to the speed, endurance, docility, and beauty of the breed. At one moment, the Arabs were cruel to their mounts; then again they would shower them with kindness. During the latter moments, they were inclined to remark, "Go and wash the feet of your mare and drink the water thereof."

EARLY AMERICAN IMPORTATION

The Arabian stallion, *Ranger*, was imported into Connecticut in 1765. *Ranger* was the sire of the gray charger ridden by General Washington in the Revolutionary War. Throughout the 19th Century, many other notable importations followed, all of which gave a good account of the breed and encouraged other purchases.

The Arabian Horse Registry of America was established in 1908.

Fig. 10-12. Arabian. Photo by Johnny Johnston. (Courtesy, Arabian Horse Trust, Westminster, CO)

ARABIAN CHARACTERISTICS

The distinctive characteristics of the Arabian breed are: medium to small in size, a beautiful head, short coupling, docility, great endurance, and an airy way of going. The usual height is from 14 to 15-1 hands and the weight from 850 to 1,100 lb. A typical Arabian has a beautiful head, broad at the forehead and tapering toward the nose; a dished face; short alert ears; large clear eyes that are set wide apart; large nostrils; and deep, wide jaws. The Arabian also possesses an anatomical difference in comparison with other breeds, having one less lumbar (back) vertebra and one or two fewer vertebrae in the tail. In conformation, the Arabian breed is further noted for proud carriage of the head on a long and graceful neck; well-sloped shoulders and pasterns; a short back and loin; well-sprung ribs, and high, well-set tail; deep quarters; and superior quality of underpinning without any tendency to appear leggy.

The predominating colors are bay, gray, and chestnut, with an occasional white or black. According to an old Arab proverb, "The fleetest of horses is the chestnut, the most enduring the bay, the most spirited the black, and most blessed the white." White marks on the head and legs are common, but purebred Arabians are never piebald, skewbald, or spotted—circus and movie information to the contrary. The skin is always black, no matter what the coat color.

The better horses in Arabia, consisting of a relatively small number of animals owned by the tribes in the interior desert, have always been bred and raised in close contact with the families of their masters and are renowned for affection, gentleness, and tractability.

ADAPTATION AND USE

The Arabian was primarily developed as a saddle horse, a use which still predominates. They are also used as stock, show, race, and pleasure horses.

Generally animals of this breed are trained and used at the three gaits—walk, trot, and canter. Occasionally, however, purebred Arabians are trained to execute five gaits to perfection. Animals of this breed are easily broken to make a safe, although not a fast, driver in light harness.

The Arabian has made an invaluable contribution in the development of most all breeds, adding to their courage, endurance, quality, intelligence, docility, and beauty. It is no exaggeration to say that the prepotent blood of the Arabians has refined and improved all those breeds with which it has been infused.

PRESENT STATUS OF THE BREED

At the present time, no great number of high-class Arabians remain in the country of their origin. In addition, World Wars I and II devastated many of the better breeding establishments of Europe. Thus, the future preservation of the breed would appear to rest primarily with American breeders.

BELGIAN WARMBLOOD

The Belgian Warmblood was developed over several decades by selectively breeding Belgium's finest cavalry and other light horses to Thoroughbreds, Anglo-Arabs, and other European warmbloods (Hanoverian, Holsteiner, Selle Francais, and Dutch). Today, the modern Belgian Warmblood is a sporthorse as well as an ideal riding horse. As a sporthorse, Belgian Warmbloods excel in show jumping, eventing, and dressage.

The Belgian Warmblood first entered the North American show scene in the 1970s. The North American District of the Belgian Warmblood Association was established in 1987; and the first inspection by the Belgian verband of breeding horses was held in 1988.

BLAZER HORSE

The Blazer Horse is one man's dream—the dream of Neil Hinck of Star, Idaho. It's Neil Hinck's ideal western horse.

ORIGIN AND NATIVE HOME

As a boy and young adult, Neil Hinck seldom found the qualities that he desired in a horse. So, he proceeded to develop his own breed. He selected foundation animals possessing the desirable characteristics of what he termed "the ultimate western horse." He achieved his goal in 1959 with the birth of *Little Blaze*, which was designated as the foundation animal of the Blazer Horse breed. The Blazer Horse Association was organized in 1967.

BLAZER HORSE CHARACTERISTICS

The Blazer Horse is a gentle disposition/superior conformation breed, both traits of which are requisites for registration. They cannot be under 13 hands or over 15 hands at maturity. A Blazer Horse can be solid colored as long as the skin is not white. White skin is allowed on the legs below the top of the knees and

Fig. 10-13. *Little Blaze*, the foundation sire of the Blazer Horse, at 28 years of age. (Courtesy, Blazer Horse Assn., Star, ID)

hocks and on the face. White/glass eyes are disqualifications. Permanent registration is not attainable before age two.

ADAPTATION AND USE

The Blazer Horse is very versatile. They excel in and out of the arena, in endurance trials, jumping, pulling, cutting, roping, or as pleasure horses. They are an all-around western horse with stamina, grace, beauty, intelligence, and a heart to please.

PRESENT STATUS OF THE BREED

In 1995, 150 Blazer Horses were registered, bringing the total registrations since the breed registry was formed in 1967 to 1,050.

BUCKSKIN
(See Plate 25)

Buckskin horses are buckskin-colored—a shade of yellow that may range from gold to nearly brown. The color description may vary with the person describing it, but horses of these general hues or patterns have long enjoyed high favor among western ranchers.

ORIGIN AND NATIVE HOME

Buckskin horses originated in the United States, largely from horses of Spanish extraction.

BUCKSKIN CHARACTERISTICS

Fig. 10-14. World Champion golden Buckskin. (Courtesy, International Buckskin Horse Assn., Shelby, IN)

Coat colors are buckskin, dun, red dun, or grulla (mouse-dun). The International Buckskin Horse Association lists the following added color characteristics: dorsal stripe, leg barring, shoulder stripe or shadowing, black ear tips, cobwebbing on face, and/or frosted mane and tail.

The Buckskin is primarily a color breed, with no particular type favored. It is important, however, that each animal be a good specimen of the type represented.

Disqualifications for registration are:

1. **American Buckskin Registry Association:** Palominos, chestnuts, sorrels, or bays with dorsal stripe; draft type; blue or glass eyes; white spots on body (indicating Pinto or Appaloosa blood) or white markings above knees or hocks.

2. **International Buckskin Horse Association:** Excessive white; showing Paint, Pinto, or Appaloosa characteristics. Also, the International Buckskin Horse Association does not accept draft type horses or ponies.

ADAPTATION AND USE

Buckskins are used as stock horses, pleasure horses, and show horses.

PRESENT STATUS OF THE BREED

Horses of buckskin color have always been popular in the West, especially as stock horses.

CHICKASAW

The Chickasaw horse is one of two breeds of horses developed by American Indians (American Indians also developed the Appaloosa).

ORIGIN AND NATIVE HOME

Chickasaw horses were developed by the Chickasaw Indians of Tennessee, North Carolina, and Oklahoma, from horses of Spanish extraction.

CHICKASAW CHARACTERISTICS

The breed is characterized by a short head and ears; a short back; a short neck; square, stocky hips; a low-set tail; a wide chest; and great width between the eyes. The preferred height is from 53 to 59 in. Coat colors are bay, black, chestnut, gray, roan, sorrel, and palomino.

ADAPTATION AND USE

Chickasaw horses are used primarily as cow ponies.

PRESENT STATUS OF THE BREED

The Chickasaw horse is one of the less populous breeds.

In a letter dated September 1, 1995, The Chickasaw Horse Assn., Inc., Love Valley, North Carolina, reported that they are on an "inactive status."

CLEVELAND BAY
(See Plate 9)

The Cleveland Bay takes its name from the Cleveland district of Yorkshire, England, where it originated, and from its color, which is invariably solid bay with black legs, mane, and tail. It is the oldest established breed of English horses. During the 19th century, thousands of Cleveland Bays were bred to Thoroughbreds to produce The Yorkshire Coach Horse.

EARLY AMERICAN IMPORTATIONS

Cleveland Bays were imported into the United States as early as 1820. The Cleveland Bay Society of America was organized in 1885. Around 1900, Cleveland Bays were used as general purpose horses—for driving and farm work. Subsequently, they were imported for two purposes: (1) to cross on Thoroughbreds to obtain heavyweight hunters; and (2) to cross on heavy draft mares to produce an active type of farm horse. The need for farm horses has passed, but heavyweight hunters are still in demand.

CLEVELAND BAY CHARACTERISTICS

Fig. 10-15. Cleveland Bay colt, *Chakola's M'Lord Beethoven*, at two years of age. (Photo by Jane E. Scott. Courtesy, Cleveland Bay Horse Society of North America)

The coat color is always solid bay on the body and black on the legs. These horses are larger than most light horse breeds; they weigh from 1,150 to 1,400 lb.

Animals are disqualified for registration if they are any color but bay, although a few white hairs on the forehead are permissible.

ADAPTATION AND USE

Cleveland Bays are used for riding, driving, and utility work. They also are used in crossbreeding to produce heavyweight hunters. It is noteworthy that the Cleveland Bay breed was chosen by William Cody, America's Buffalo Bill, for his Wild West Shows.

The Cleveland Bay is an endangered breed, with fewer than 500 purebreds worldwide and only 53 in North America. The registry is maintained and supervised by the Cleveland Bay Society of Great Britain.

CONNEMARA PONY
(See Plate 10)

The Connemara Pony is Ireland's gift to the equine world.

ORIGIN AND NATIVE HOME

Connemara Ponies originated on the west coast of Ireland where, for generations, subsistence under the most difficult conditions produced a hardy breed. Although the exact origin of the Connemara is unknown, legend has it that Andalusian, Spanish Barb, and Arabian horses were crossed on hardy, native ponies to produce the ancestors of the Connemara.

EARLY AMERICAN IMPORTATIONS

The first Connemara Ponies for breeding purposes were imported to the United States in 1951.

The American Connemara Society was formed in 1956.

CONNEMARA PONY CHARACTERISTICS

These ponies are heavy boned, hardy and docile.

Fig. 10-16. Connemara Pony mare, *Aladdin's Rhiannow*. (Courtesy, American Connemara Society, Winchester, VA)

They range rather widely in height; hence, the American Connemara Society registers in two sections: Section 1, "pony" 13 to 14-2 hands; section 2, "small horse," over 14-2 hands.

Coat colors usually are gray, black, bay, dun, brown, or cream, and occasionally roan or chestnut.

Animals are disqualified for registration if they are piebald, skewbald, or cream with blue eyes.

ADAPTATION AND USE

Connemara Ponies are great jumpers. Additionally, they are used for most other riding purposes. They are unexcelled as advanced children's mounts and for riding by small adults.

PRESENT STATUS OF THE BREED

The Connemara is a new and less populous breed in the United States. However, it is increasing in popularity and numbers.

CRACKER HORSE

The Cracker Horse got its name from the Cracker people who used it, and the Cracker people got their name from the loud cracking whips they used in herding and penning the wily Spanish cattle.

ORIGIN AND NATIVE HOME

The history of the Cracker Horse is much older than its name. The ancestors of the Cracker Horse were introduced into what is now Florida in 1521, when the Spanish explorer, Ponce de Leon, on his second Florida trip, brought horses, cattle, and other livestock. Similar introductions by other Spanish explorers and colonists continued well into the next century. Feral horse herds from escaped and liberated animals were molded and tempered by nature.

First the Indians, and later the pioneers, began to use the Spanish horses. They were hardy and well adapted to the Florida climate and environment; and they excelled as working cow ponies.

Genetically, the Cracker Horse descends from the Iberian Horse of early 16th century Spain and includes the blood of the North African Barb, the Spanish Sorraia, and the Andalusian.

CRACKER HORSE CHARACTERISTICS

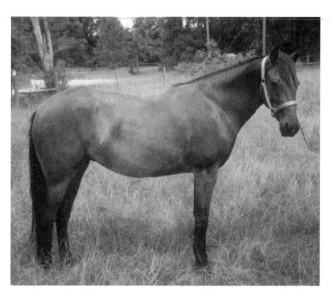

Fig. 10-17. *Fiddle*, a Cracker mare owned by Sam Getzen. (Courtesy, Florida Cracker Horse Assn., Inc., Newberry, FL)

Cracker Horses are from 13-2 to 15 hands high and weigh from 750 to 950 lb. They are noted for their unusual strength and endurance, herding instinct, quickness, and fast walking gait.

Many of them have a running walk. Cracker Horse colors include all colors common to horses, with solid colors, roans, and grays predominating.

ADAPTATION AND USE

Although best known for their talents at working cattle, Cracker Horses were often pressed into service as buggy horses, and sometimes they were the only horse power for family farms well into the 20th century.

In 1989 the Florida Cracker Horse Association was formed for the preservation and perpetuation of the Cracker Horse as a distinct and unique Colonial Spanish breed of horses. But Cracker Horses are still very few in number, only 242 have been registered to date. Almost without exception Cracker Horses are range bred and raised.

DALES PONY AND EXMOOR PONY
(See Plate 11 for Dales Pony; and see Plate 12 for Exmoor Ponies)

Both of these pony breeds are registered and promoted by the Canadian Mountain & Moorland Society, Amherst, Nova Scotia, Canada. *Note*: These are two separate breeds, registered and promoted by the same society; hence, they are accorded separate listings in this section.

ORIGIN AND NATIVE HOME

Dales Pony originated in Northeast England. Exmoor Pony originated in Southwest England.

DALES PONY AND EXMOOR PONY CHARACTERISTICS

■ **Dales Pony Characteristics**—Under 14-2 hands. *Colors*: Black, brown, some grey, a few bay. White markings only as a star, snip, and/or fetlocks of hind legs.

Fig. 10-18. Dales Pony stallion, Black Robbie. (Courtesy, Canadian Mountain & Moorland Society, Amherst, Nova Scotia, Canada.)

■ **Exmoor Pony**—Stallions and geldings not exceeding 12-3 hands at any age; and mares not exceeding 12-2 hands at any age. *Colors*: Bay, brown, or dun; mealy nose; no white markings.

ADAPTATION AND USE

Both Dales Pony and Exmoor Pony are adapted to, and used for, riding and pulling which ponies of their respective sizes can perform.

Fig. 10-19. Exmoor stallion, owned by Marlyn Exmoors, Amherst, Nova Scotia, Canada. (Courtesy, Dales and Exmoor Ponies, Inc., Amherst, Nova Scotia, Canada)

PRESENT STATUS OF THE BREEDS

■ **Dales Pony**—In 1994, The Canadian Mountain & Moorland Society registered six ponies, bringing their total registrations since their formation in 1993 to 22.

■ **Exmoor Pony**—In 1994, The Canadian Mountain & Moorland Society registered four ponies, bringing their total registrations since their formation in 1993 to 29.

DUTCH WARMBLOOD

The Dutch Warmblood is a sport horse, bred for international competition in jumping, dressage, eventing, and driving. The breed has made a meteoric rise to prominence in the international equestrian world in recent years.

The Dutch Warmblood originated in The Netherlands, where they were selectively bred for good conformation, good action, superior performance, and soundness.

The modern Dutch Warmblood evolved from two native Dutch breeds—the Gelderlander and the Groningen. The Gelderlander was a stylish horse of medium size, commonly chestnut with flashy white markings; while the Groningen was a larger and heavier breed than the Gelderlander, and frequently black. In the heyday of coach horses, there was likely infusion of Norfolk Trotter, Yorkshire Coach, and Cleveland Bay. Later, there was infusion of Thoroughbreds, Holsteiners, and Trakehners. Even today, Dutch Warmbloods continue to be influenced by imported breeding, but

Fig. 10-20. Dutch Warmblood, *Wula*, ridden by Candice Scholm. (Courtesy, North American Department of the Royal Dutch Warmblood Studbook of the Netherlands, Winchester, OR)

The Netherlands continue to treasure and cultivate the special qualities of temperament, adaptability, and soundness.

Although the word *breed* denotes to most horsemen a closed studbook, it has a different connotation in the European Warmbloods. In The Netherlands, *breed* refers to the "breeding area" as much as the strict purity of the bloodlines. Each breeding area sets its own breeding goals. Today in Holland there are three distinct types:

1. **The Riding horse type**, which are the most numerous and internationally important. This is the sport horse, famed as jumpers, dressage horses, combined driving, and vaulting horses.

2. **The "Tvigpaard-type**,*"* an elegant carriage horse shown like the American Fine Harness Horse.

3. **"Bassistype" or basic type**, a versatile horse, used for riding, driving, and farm work.

The Dutch Warmblood is increasing in U.S. numbers. In 1995, the North American Department of The Royal Dutch Warmblood Studbook of The Netherlands registered 315 horses, bringing its total to 3,000 since its formation in 1983.

GALICENO

The Galiceno lays claim to being the ancestor of the Mustang—the feral horse of western United States.

ORIGIN AND NATIVE HOME

Galiceno horses originated in Galicia, a province in northwestern Spain. Horses of this lineage were first brought to America by the conquistadors.

EARLY AMERICAN IMPORTATION

Galiceno horses were officially introduced as a breed into the United States in 1958. Two Texans, in search of a new breed that could double (1) as a small pleasure horse, and (2) as a good stock horse, met their need by importing Galicenos from Mexico.

The Galiceno Horse Breeders Association was organized in 1959.

GALICENO CHARACTERISTICS

Fig. 10-21. Galiceno mare, Champion in 1995, owned by Kandice Hanshew, Godley, Texas. (Courtesy, Galiceno Horse Breeders Assn., Godley, TX)

The most common coat colors are bay, black, chestnut (sorrel), dun (buckskin), gray, brown, or palomino. Solid colors prevail. Animals of pinto or albino color are disqualified for registry.

At maturity, Galiceno horses must be between 12 and 13-2 hands high.

Cryptorchids and monorchids are not eligible for registration unless gelded.

ADAPTATION AND USE

The Galiceno is adapted to and used as a stock horse and for pleasure riding, barrel racing, cutting, jumping, and Spanish Fiesta.

PRESENT STATUS OF THE BREED

The Galiceno is one of the less populous breeds.

HACKNEY
(See Plate 2)

The Hackney is the lone survivor of the five breeds of heavy harness or carriage horses. In fact, except for the Hackney, the other breeds of this type are now practically extinct in the United States and are of historic interest primarily.

ORIGIN AND NATIVE HOME

The very name *Hackney*, and its abbreviated derivative *Hack*, is suggestive of the type and adaptation of this breed, denoting both a general-purpose horse and the vehicle which it draws.

The breed originated in Norfolk and adjoining counties on the eastern coast of England. Here, in the first half of the 18th Century, was developed a trotting type of horse that was fast and that would go a distance, known as the Norfolk Trotter. It was this native stock with Thoroughbred infusion from which the Hackney was later derived. In this period, roads and vehicles were few and primitive, so that these Norfolk Trotters were used chiefly under saddle. Well-authenticated records exist of travel at the rate of 17 miles per hour over ordinary roads.

The real beginning of the Hackney breed is traced to a stallion known as *Blaze*,[2] a Thoroughbred foaled in 1773 and a grandson of the immortal *Darley Arabian*, the latter being the most noted of the foundation sires of the Thoroughbred breed. *Blaze* and his noted son, *Old Shales* (foaled in 1755), produced a remarkably valuable riding and driving horse when crossed on the native stock of Norfolk.

The early formative period of the Hackney was before the advent of either the carriage or the railroad. Thus, these sturdy foundation animals were first used under saddle and were even employed for some light agricultural purposes. It was not uncommon in that era to see a farmer riding to market with his spouse behind him on a pillion.[3] Such use called for attractive animals with adequate size and substance and the ability to trot long distances at a fair speed.

With the development and use of the British hackney coaches of the 18th Century, the Hackney became specialized for driving purposes. It soon became the leading harness horse of the world. With this specialized use and its increased popularity with the aristocracy of England, the Hackney's naturally high, trappy action was cultivated. As many of the vehicles were heavy, animals with size and a robust conformation were demanded. With it all, graceful, curved form, beauty, and style were emphasized. In brief, the quality and performance of the harness horse became an indication of social prestige.

EARLY AMERICAN IMPORTATIONS

The first Hackney pony imported to America was *239 Stella*, brought to Philadelphia by Mr. A. J. Cassatt in 1878. In 1891, Mr. Cassatt and other Hackney enthusiasts founded the American Hackney Horse Society.

It was not until the era of the Gay Nineties that any great numbers were brought over. At this time, a boom in Hackneys developed in this country as prancing carriage horses became characteristic of the avenues traversed by the wealthy in the eastern cities.

HACKNEY CHARACTERISTICS

In size, the Hackney varies more than any other breed, ranging from 12 to 16 hands. The small Hackney pony, under 14-2 hands in height, and the larger animals are registered in the same stud book. When used in a pair for a lady's phaeton, smaller animals are preferred. Because of the weight of the vehicle,

Fig. 10-22. Hackney harness pony. (Courtesy, American Hackney Horse Society, Lexington, KY)

---

[2]The same *Blaze* from whom imported *Messenger*, the foundation sire of the Standardbred, was descended. Thus, on the sire's side the Hackney and Standardbred were of similar origin, but the native mares which served as foundation stock for the respective breeds and the objectives sought were very different.

[3]A seat or cushion which was placed behind the gentleman's saddle.

however, a larger animal is necessary when driven single. As would be expected with the wide range in height of the breed, Hackneys vary considerably in weight, from 800 to 1,200 lb.

Typical Hackneys are relatively short-legged horses, rather robust in conformation; heavy in proportion to their height; smooth and gracefully curved in form, with symmetry and balance; and upheaded, clean-cut, alert, and stylish to a high degree. High natural action—which is accentuated by skilled training, bitting, and shoeing—is perhaps their most distinguishing feature.

In any one show, a Hackney pony may be shown in only one of the following four sections, according to The American Horse Shows Association Rule Book, 1996–1997: (1) Hackney short or bob tail and a tightly braided mane, (2) Hackney harness long tail, (3) Hackney roadster, or (4) Hackney harness pleasure driving pony.

Chestnut, bay, and brown are the most common colors found in the Hackney breed, although roans and blacks are seen. Regular white marks are rather common and are even desired for purposes of accentuating high action.

Animals of piebald or skewbald color are not eligible for registry.

ADAPTATION AND USE

The Hackney is the harness horse par excellence for both the show-ring and park driving. Many hunters and jumpers are half-bred Hackneys, a cross which gives animals of the desired size.

Today, the Hackney is essentially a show animal, noted for superb quality, beautiful condition, and spirited high action. When drawing a proper vehicle devoid of shiny parts (which serve to blind the spectators), the well-trained Hackney is a wonderful spectacle to behold.

PRESENT STATUS OF THE BREED

The nearer the street surfaces approach perfection for automobile traffic, the less satisfactory they are for use by horses. Thus, at the present time, the use of the Hackney is almost exclusively confined to the show-ring. On the tanbark, the high-stepping horses are still the show, and, to many, their appearance is reminiscent of the Gay Nineties.

HAFLINGER
(See Plates 13 and 46)

Haflingers are noted for versatility; they are used for all the purposes for which light horses and draft horses are used. They are *family horses*.

ORIGIN AND NATIVE HOME

The Haflinger is a very old breed, named after the village of Hafling, which was part of Austria at the end of World War I, now a part of Italy. The breed can be traced to one stallion, named *Folie*, which resulted from crossing an Arabian stallion on a native mountain mare.

EARLY AMERICAN IMPORTATIONS

The first Haflingers were imported from Austria to the United States in 1958 by Temple Smith, of the Temple Steel and Temple Farms, Wadsworth, Illinois.

HAFLINGER CHARACTERISTICS

Fig. 10-23. Haflinger stallion owned by Meadowlane Farm, Hemlock, Michigan. (Courtesy, Haflinger Assn. of America, Hemlock, MI)

The Haflinger is a relatively small, stocky horse, standing from 13 to 14-3 hands high. It is noted for beauty, strength, vitality, intelligence, and a good disposition. The color is chestnut, ranging from honey blond to dark chocolate, with white or flaxen mane and tail.

ADAPTATION AND USE

The Haflinger is remarkably well adapted for either work or pleasure. In its early development in Europe, the emphasis was on draft purposes. But, in both Austria and the United States, the current trend is to select and breed taller and lighter bodied horses, more suitable for pleasure riding and other light horse purposes.

PRESENT STATUS OF THE BREED

There are two U.S. breed registries: The Haflinger Association of America was established in 1976; and the Haflinger Registry of North America was established in 1983.

U.S. Haflinger owners continue the Austrian practice of naming animals according to the lines of the stallions and mares. For example, all names of colts (male foals) must begin with the first letters of the stallion's name. Likewise, all names of filly foals must begin with the first letter of the mare's name. This practice contributes to the ease of maintaining the identity of family lines.

HALF SADDLEBRED
(See Plate 14)

As implied by its name, one parent, either sire or dam, of a Half Saddlebred must be an American Saddlebred duly registered in the American Saddlebred Horse Association.

ORIGIN AND NATIVE HOME

The Half Saddlebred Registry of America was founded in the United States in 1971.

HALF SADDLEBRED CHARACTERISTICS

The registry association refers to the Half Saddlebred as a horse for all "reasons"; as an innovator and utility breed. To date, 32 different breed crosses with American Saddlebred stallions or mares have been recorded by The Half Saddlebred Registry of America. Obviously, these crosses result in Half Saddlebreds of many types and uses.

ADAPTATION AND USE

The registry association reports that, due to their

Fig. 10-24. Half Saddlebred (a Saddlebred/Andalusian gelding) shown hitched to a Gentleman's Phaeton; owned and driven by Henry Zum Felde, Wauslon, Ohio. (Courtesy, The Half Saddlebred Registry of America, Coshocton, OH)

diverse breeding and adaptation, individual Half Saddlebred horses excel as a trail horse, endurance horse, jumper, dressage, barrel racing, cutting, reining, and cow pony. Above all, they are well adapted as a child's mount.

PRESENT STATUS OF THE BREED

In 1994, 107 Half Saddlebred horses were registered, making for a total of 2,874 horses registered since the breed registry was formed in 1971.

HANOVERIAN
(See Plate 15)

Approximately 70% of the horses of Germany are Hanoverians, and it is the most numerous light horse breed in Europe.

ORIGIN AND NATIVE HOME

The Hanoverian breed originated in the Hanover section of Germany, beginning in 1732. An Englishman went to Hanover and became its Prince. Later, he returned to England and became King George II. But, during his stay in Germany, he assembled outstanding individuals of certain breeds for the purpose of developing a superior horse for military use, with emphasis on size, intelligence, and temperament. Out of this effort evolved the Hanoverian breed of horses.

The American Hanoverian Society was incorporated in 1978.

EARLY AMERICAN IMPORTATION

The date of the first Hanoverian importations is clouded in obscurity. In the 1960s and early 1970s, sufficient animals were imported to prompt the formation of a breed registry.

HANOVERIAN CHARACTERISTICS

Fig. 10-25. Hanoverian stallion, *Donavan.* (Courtesy, The American Hanoverian Society, Lexington, KY)

Hanoverian horses are big and powerful. Many of them stand 16-2 hands or better and weigh 1,200 lb or more. They combine nobility, size, and strength in a unique way.

ADAPTATION AND USE

In Europe, Hanoverian horses are used for riding, driving (carriage horses), hunting, jumping, dressage and utility purposes. In the United States, the breed is used for all light horse purposes, especially for hunting, jumping, and dressage.

PRESENT STATUS OF THE BREED

The U.S. and German Hanoverian breeding organizations put potential breeding stallions through a rigorous inspection and performance testing process before certifying them for breeding purposes. Only 0.6% of Hanoverian foals ever become fully licensed stallions, enabling them to sire Hanoverian foals eligible for registry.

HUNGARIAN HORSE

The Hungarian Horse is a very old breed in Hungary, where it is without a peer as a cavalry mount, and where it is involved in every conceivable equine use—including horse racing.

ORIGIN AND NATIVE HOME

Hungarian Horses originated in Hungary, the product of generations of selective breeding extending back to the conquering Magyars (Hungarians) at the end of the 9th Century, who brought with them swift and sturdy horses of Asiatic origin.

EARLY AMERICAN IMPORTATIONS

Hungarian Horses were brought to the United States at the close of World War II (in 1945), as spoils of war. They were auctioned off at the U.S. Remount Station, Ft. Reno, Oklahoma.

The Hungarian Horse Association of the United States was formed in September, 1966.

Fig. 10-26. The late Margit Sigray Bessenyey, Hungarian breeder, of Hamilton, Montana, in native Hungarian csikos (cowboy) costume, holding a Hungarian Horse. The csikos rides on a girthless saddle and carries a long whip. (Photo by Ernst Peterson, Hamilton, MT; courtesy, Mrs. Bessenyey)

HUNGARIAN HORSE CHARACTERISTICS

These horses possess a unique combination of style and beauty, with ruggedness.

The coat may be any color, either broken or solid.

Animals are disqualified for registration if they are cryptorchids or have glass eyes.

ADAPTATION AND USE

The primary uses of Hungarian Horses in the United States are: stock horses, cutting horses, pleasure horses, trail riding, hunters, and jumpers.

Fig. 10-28. Irish Draught Horse—a mare. Contrary to the name, this is a light horse breed. (Courtesy, Irish Draught Horse Society of North America, Sidney, BC, Canada)

Fig. 10-27. Hungarian stallion, *Taltos*, who stood at stud at Cookslee Ranch, Anselmo, Nebraska. (Courtesy, Hungarian Horse Assn., Anselmo, NE)

PRESENT STATUS OF THE BREED

A few purebred Hungarian Horse breeders, each with limited numbers, control the destiny of the Hungarian Horse in the United States. The breed has given a good account of itself, as stock horses and pleasure horses, and in competitive events.

IRISH DRAUGHT HORSE
(See Plate 16)

The Irish Draught Horse is a light horse breed, not a draft horse as implied by the name. The North American Draught Horse Society evolved following the importation of frozen semen from select Irish Draught Horse stallions in 1994.

In 1995, there were only a total of 23 registered Irish Draught Horses in North America. AI and embryo transfer are accepted. As yet, there are no specified

color markings. Obvious Clyde breeding or five-gaited crosses are not accepted for registry.

LIPIZZAN
(See Plate 17)

Most horse lovers rightfully associate the Lipizzan breed with the Spanish Riding School, near Vienna, Austria, where representatives of the breed are superbly trained and exhibited.

ORIGIN AND NATIVE HOME

The Lipizzan traces to the year 1504, at which time Andalusian stallions were crossed on Spanish-Barb mares. It was recognized as a breed by Prince Maximillian in 1564. In 1580, 6 stallions and 27 mares were shipped to the village of Lipizza, in what is now Yugoslavia, from which the breed got its name.

The Spanish Riding School was established in 1735 by the Hapsburg King of Spain, Charles VI, who had lost his Spanish Kingdom to Phillip V. During the closing days of World War II, in 1945, horse-loving General Patton of the United States interceded to save the Lipizzan horses for posterity. They were moved to another location, where they remained for the next 10 years. Thence, they were returned to Vienna in 1955.

EARLY AMERICAN IMPORTATIONS

Lipizzan horses were first imported from Austria by Evelyn L. Dreitzler, Raflyn Farms, Snohomish, WA, in 1960.

Currently, there are two breed registry associations: the Lipizzan Assn. of North America and the United States Lipizzan Registry.

LIPIZZAN CHARACTERISTICS

Lipizzan horses are noted for graceful movements, placid nature, high knee action, and a remarkable memory. As high school and dressage horses, they are without a peer.

Fig. 10-29. Lipizzan three-year-old filly, owned by Silver Meadow Farm, Johnstown, Ohio. (Courtesy, Lipizzan Assn. of North America, Johnstown, OH)

Most mature animals of the breed are white. But Lipizzan foals are born dark (brown or gray), then turn white at 4 to 6 years of age. About one in 600 remains black or brown throughout life. When the latter happens it is considered good luck.

ADAPTATION AND USE

The suitability of the Lipizzan for dressage and high school horses is well known. However, the same qualities that make them stellar performers—placid nature, tractability, stamina, action, and a remarkable memory—also make them ideal pleasure horses (either English or Western), jumpers, stock horses, and horses for trail riding.

PRESENT STATUS OF THE BREED

At the present time, there are Lipizzans in Austria, Yugoslavia, Hungary, Czechoslovakia, and the United States.

Presently, there are an estimated 3,000 Lipizzans in the world today, only about 600 of which are producing broodmares.

MINIATURE HORSE
(See Plates 3 and 43)

The Miniature Horse is a small model of a full-sized horse; it is not a dwarf or a freak.

ORIGIN AND NATIVE HOME

The Miniature Horse is a new breed, with an old history. Miniature horses were used in England and Northern Europe to pull ore carts in the coal mines, as early as 1765. They were also bred as pets for some of the royal families of Europe. Some of these small horses were brought to the United States in the late 19th century and used in the mines of West Virginia and Ohio. Miniature horses of the Falabella breed, no taller than 34 in., have been bred by Maria Angelica Falabella of Argentina for many years.

Fig. 10-30. Miniature Horse, *Little Blue Boy*, a stallion standing 30 in. tall. (Courtesy, Flying W Farms, Piketon, OH)

The American Miniature Horse Association, Inc. was organized in July, 1978.

MINIATURE HORSE CHARACTERISTICS

The Miniature Horse cannot exceed 34 in. high at the withers. Miniatures are of two types: (1) the more refined Arabian type, and (2) the heavier Quarter Horse type. All colors are accepted.

ADAPTATION AND USE

Some people keep Miniature Horses as pets. Others exhibit them as driving horses, in single pleasure and roadster driving classes. Still others exhibit them in multiple hitches, pulling miniature wagons, stage coaches, carriages and other vehicles.

PRESENT STATUS OF THE BREED

The breed has enjoyed great popularity and rapid growth. Presently, three associations are registering Miniature Horses. The American Miniature Horse Association, the largest of the three, registered 6,500 horses in 1994, bringing their total registrations since the registry was formed to 52,000.

MISSOURI FOX TROTTING HORSE

The Missouri Fox Trotting Horse is noted for the fox-trot, a slow gait in which the head usually nods and in which the horse brings each hind foot to the ground an instant before the diagonal forefoot.

ORIGIN AND NATIVE HOME

This breed originated in the Ozarks of Missouri. In 1948, the Missouri Fox Trotting Horse Breed Association was founded at Ava, Missouri.

MISSOURI FOX TROTTING HORSE CHARACTERISTICS

The Missouri Fox Trotting Horse is distinguished by the fox-trot gait, which is performed by walking in front and trotting behind. Sorrel is the most common color, but any color is accepted.

Animals are disqualified for registration if they cannot fox-trot.

Fig. 10-31. *Delta's Secret Magic*, Missouri Fox Trotting Horse, owned by Double Doc Ranch, Cody, Wyoming. (Courtesy, Missouri Fox Trotting Horse Breed Assn., Ava, MO)

ADAPTATION AND USE

Missouri Fox Trotting Horses are used primarily as pleasure horses, stock horses, and for trail riding.

PRESENT STATUS OF THE BREED

The breed must compete with such old and well-established breeds as the American Saddlebred and the Tennessee Walking Horse for a place in the horse world. But the breed is doing all right as evidenced by registering 2,821 horses in 1994, bringing their total since their founding in 1948 to 46,537.

MORAB

The Morab resulted from fusing the Arabian and the Morgan, breeds whose characteristics genetically complemented each other, to give a unique and versatile new breed.

ORIGIN AND NATIVE HOME

Although Morgan X Arabian crosses were made in the early 1800s, the name *Morab* was not coined until the 1920s, when William Randolph Hearst became involved in a breeding program for his horses. He crossed Arabian stallions on Morgan mares to produce horses for use on his San Simeon ranch in California.

The modern Morab is predominantly Morgan and Arabian, although it may be part Thoroughbred.

MORAB CHARACTERISTICS

Fig. 10-32. Morab stallion, *Jericho's Mr. Chauvinist*, 1994 and 1995 Morab Horse of the Year. (Courtesy, International Morab Breeders Assn., Eagle, WI)

The breed possesses the muscular strength and ruggedness of the Morgan and the refinement and beauty of the Arabian. Morabs average about 15 hands in height.

Animals are disqualified if they have breed characteristics other than Morgan, Arabian, and Thoroughbred; if they have albino, appaloosa, paint, or pinto color; or if they are under 14 hands at maturity.

ADAPTATION AND USE

Morabs are used for show, pleasure riding, endurance rides, and ranch work.

PRESENT STATUS OF THE BREED

The breed is new, and there are few registered animals. The North American Morab Horse Association, which was formed in 1984, registered a total of 730 Morabs through its first 11 years. In 1996, it was estimated that there were approximately 320 living registered Morabs in North America. However, this did not include an estimated 50,000 horses in the United States of similar breeding—animals produced by, or descended from, Arabian X Morgan crosses.

MORGAN
(See Plate 44)

The Morgan is known as the first family of American horses. The early development of the breed took place in the New England states, thus giving the eastern section of the country primary credit for founding three light horse breeds.

ORIGIN AND NATIVE HOME

The origin of the Morgan breed was a mere happenstance, and not the result of planned effort on the part of the breeders to produce a particular breed of horse which would be adapted to local conditions. Whatever may be said of the greatness of *Justin Morgan*, he was the result of a chance mating—one of nature's secrets for which there is no breeding formula. In fact, it may be said that had a British general downed his liquor in his own parlor and had a Springfield, Massachusetts, farmer been able to pay his debts, the first family of American horses might never have existed. Legend has it that, one evening during the Revolutionary War, Colonel De Lancey, commander of a Tory mounted regiment, rode up to an inn at King's Bridge and after hitching his famous stallion, *True Briton*, to the rail, went into the inn for some liquid refreshments, as was his custom. While the Colonel was celebrating with liquor and song, the Yankees stole his horse, later selling the animal to a farmer near Hartford Connecticut. The whimsical story goes on to say that *True Briton* later sired the fuzzy-haired colt that was to be christened after his second owner, Justin Morgan.

According to the best authorities, Mr. Morgan, who first lived for many years near Springfield, Massachusetts, moved his family to Randolph, Vermont, in 1788. A few years later, he returned to Springfield to collect a debt. But instead of getting the money, he bartered for a three-year-old gelding and a two-year-old colt of Thoroughbred and Arabian extraction. The stud colt, later named after the new owner as was often the custom of the day, became the noted horse, *Justin Morgan*, the progenitor of the first famous breed of horses developed in America.

Justin Morgan was a dark bay with black legs, mane, and tail. His head was shapely; his dark eyes were prominent, lively, and pleasant; his wide-set ears were small, pointed, and erect; his round body was short backed, close ribbed, and deep; his thin legs were set wide and straight, and the pasterns and shoulders were sloping; his action was straight, bold, and vigorous; and his style was proud, nervous, and imposing. *Justin Morgan* was a beautifully symmetrical, stylish, vibrant animal—renowned for looks, manners, and substance. It was claimed of him that he could outrun for short distances any horse against which he was matched. He was a fast trotter, a great horse on parade under saddle, and he could out-pull most horses weighing several hundred pounds more.

Justin Morgan lived his 32 years (1789–1821) in an era of horses rather than in an era of power machinery. The westward expansion had been limited; roads and trails were in the raw, as nature had left them, and were often impassable even with a horse and buggy. Virgin forest had to be cleared, and the tough sod of the prairie had to be broken. These conditions called for an extremely versatile type of horse—one that could pull a good load on the farm, could be driven as a roadster, could be raced under saddle, and could be ridden in a parade. *Justin Morgan* and his progeny filled this utility need in a most remarkable manner. In due time, in 1893 to be exact, many years following the death of the foundation sire and after a decade of exhaustive research, Colonel Joseph Battell published Volume I of the American Morgan Horse Register. Such was the beginning of preservation of the lineage of the breed—a registry assignment now handled under the same name by the American Morgan Horse Association.

MORGAN CHARACTERISTICS

With shifts in use, it is but natural to find considerable variation in the size of present-day Morgans. Yet throughout the vicissitudes of time and shifts in

emphasis that have occurred during the past hundred years, Morgan horses to an amazing degree have continued to have certain unique characteristics which distinguish them as a breed.

The height of representative animals ranges from 14-2 to 16 hands, with the larger animals now given preference by most equestrians. The average Morgan weighs from 800 to 1,200 lb. Standard colors are bay, brown, black, and chestnut; and white markings are not uncommon.

In conformation, the breed has retained most of the characteristics attributed to the foundation sire. With greater emphasis on use under saddle, however, modern Morgans are inclined to be more upstanding, to have longer necks, and to possess more slope to their shoulders and pasterns. Regardless of type changes, the breed continues to be noted for easy keeping qualities; stamina, docility, beauty, courage, and longevity. The presence of only five lumbar vertebrae in many Morgans is attributed to the use of Arabian breeding.

Animals with walleye (lack of pigmentation of the iris) or with blue eyes, or with natural white markings above the knee or hock except on the face, are disqualified for registry.

ADAPTATION AND USE

In the early formative period of the breed, the Morgan was thought of as a general purpose type of animal—for use in harness racing, as roadsters, on the farm, on the avenue, in the park, on the range, and on the trail. With the development of mechanization, many of these needs passed into oblivion. The more progressive breeders, fully cognizant of the change in needs, took stock of the breed's inherent possibilities and shifted their efforts in breeding and selection to the production of a superior riding horse. At the present time, therefore, it is not surprising to find that there is considerable variation in emphasis in different sections of the United States. In the West, the Morgan is primarily a stock horse; whereas in the East the emphasis is upon the Morgan as a saddle horse, particularly for general country use and for recreational purposes over the hundreds of miles of trails.

The number of purebred Morgans today is no criterion of the true importance of the breed. Their influence has literally extended to the entire horse population of the continent. Morgan blood was used in laying the foundation for many breeds. The leading Standardbred families of today are a fusion of Hambletonian lines with the Morgan—*Axworthy*, *Mako*, and *Peter the Great* all carried Morgan blood in their veins. Likewise, the American Saddlebred is indebted to the Morgan, for the Peavine and Chief families both con-

Fig. 10-33. Morgan stallion, *Man About Town*, Grand Champion Stallion at the 1995 New England Regional Championship. (Photo by Lorie. Courtesy, American Morgan Horse Assn., Shelburne, VT)

tained Morgan ancestry. *Allen*, the foundation sire of the Tennessee Walking Horse, was a great grandson of a Morgan, *Vermont Black Hawk.*

PRESENT STATUS OF THE BREED

During the period of transition and shift in emphasis from a utility and harness type of horse to use under the saddle, the registration of Morgan horses declined, and the identity of many registered animals was lost. This greatly reduced the number of available breeding animals to use as a base for the rapid expansion of breeding interest that occurred beginning in the late 1930s.

In 1907, Colonel Battell—an admirer, breeder, and founder of the Register of Morgan Horses—presented to the U.S. Department of Agriculture what became known as the United States Morgan Horse Farm, near Middlebury, Vermont. Colonel Battell's primary objective in presenting the farm to the federal government was that of providing a place upon which the breed could be perpetuated and improved. Though it would appear ironical today, it was also rumored that the old gentleman was disturbed with the high taxes of the period and had decided that the only way to beat the government was to give his holdings to the United States. Regardless of the possible latter objective, it must be agreed that the U.S. Morgan Horse Farm was a powerful influence in perpetuating and improving the Morgan breed. Effective July 1, 1951, by authorization of the U.S. Congress, the United States Morgan Horse Farm was transferred without cost to the Vermont Agricultural College.

NATIONAL SHOW HORSE
(See Plate 18)

The National Show Horse was created from an Arabian/Saddlebred cross to meet a need for a beautiful show horse with athletic ability, and for new excitement and incentives in the show-ring.

ORIGIN AND NATIVE HOME

By the 1970s, Arabian/Saddlebred crosses had become a show favorite and consistent winners in the Half-Arabian performance and halter classes.

The National Show Horse Registry was conceived and incorporated by Gene La Croix, a prominent Arabian breeder, in 1981. The young breed grew quickly. By 1982, 156 stallions were nominated as NSHR sires, and 975 horses were registered. During its beginning in 1982, and for a brief period between November 1,

1983, and January 15, 1984, the NSHR allowed a period of open registration in order to create a pool of foundation horses for the new breed.

Today, the registry has specific rules regarding the types of horses that can be used to produce National Show Horses. To be eligible for registration as a National Show Horse, a foal must be sired by a *NSHR Nominated Sire*, which may be a purebred Arabian, Saddlebred, or National Show Horse. To qualify as a *Nominated Sire*, the owner must pay a $6,000 fee, and the stallion must be approved by the NSHR Board of Directors. Nominated Sires may produce eligible NSHR foals and are eligible for prize money based on the winnings of their get in the show-ring.

NSHR eligible foals can be produced by breeding a nominated stallion to a registered Arabian, Saddlebred, or National Show Horse mare, but the resulting foal must have at least 25%, but less than 100% Arabian blood.

NATIONAL SHOW HORSE CHARACTERISTICS

Fig. 10-34. National Show Horse. (Photo by Bob Moseder. Courtesy, National Show Horse Registry, Louisville, KY)

The National Show Horse combines the beauty, refinement, and stamina of the Arabian and the size and high-stepping action of the Saddlebred. The ideal National Show Horse is long-necked, pretty-headed, and relatively short-backed, with long legs and a high, animated trot.

ADAPTATION AND USE

The goal of the breed founders was to produce the ideal show horse. They set out to (1) create a horse with great show-ring appeal, (2) develop a prize money system that would make it financially rewarding for exhibitors to show their horses, and (3) design a breed suitable for amateurs to ride and participate in the show-ring.

PRESENT STATUS OF THE BREED

In 1994, 562 National Show Horses were registered, and a total of 11,400 had been registered since recording started in 1982. Thus the breed appears to be firmly established and filling a need.

NORWEGIAN FJORD HORSE

The Norwegian Fjord Horse is a small, but powerful, all-purpose family horse—versatile and gentle.

ORIGIN AND NATIVE HOME

The Norwegian Fjord Horse is thought to be the oldest breed of domestic horses. In color and build, they resemble Przewalski Horse, the wild horse of Asia, from which it is believed to be descended. The first records of the Fjord-like horses are found in Viking sagas and on ancient horse artifacts, dating as early as 700 A.D. In Norway, they have been selectively bred for more than 2,000 years.

EARLY AMERICAN IMPORTATIONS

Warren Delano, whose nephew was President Franklin Delano Roosevelt, was the first to import Fjord horses into the United States; he brought a stallion and six mares from Bergen, Norway in 1900. The next importation of Fjords, consisting of three stallions and three mares, was made by Mrs. Josephine Mills of the Broadmore Hotel, Colorado Springs, Colorado, in 1955. Other importations followed.

NORWEGIAN FJORD HORSE CHARACTERISTICS

Fjordings (as their fond owners call them) are dun colored (ranging from light to dark), with a dorsal stripe, dark bars on the legs, and dark hooves, eyes,

Fig. 10-35. Norwegian Fjord stallion, *King Gjestar*, owned by Nancy Clow, Nancy's Fjord Horses, Buffalo, Wyoming. (Courtesy, Jane Exon Equine Photography, Laramie, WY)

and ear tips. They range in height from 13 to 14-2 hands. The body is compact and muscular.

ADAPTATION AND USE

Throughout Europe, the Norwegian Fjord Horse is used for riding, driving, and draft purposes. With more and more tractors on European farms, the Fjords have been used increasingly as pleasure horses. In the United States, Fjord Horses are used for draft, carriage, pleasure riding, jumping, dressage, and trail riding.

PRESENT STATUS OF THE BREED

The Norwegian Fjord Horse Registry of North America was formed in 1980, for the purpose of preserving the genetic purity of, and promoting, the breed. Although there are few Fjords in the United States, the breed has given a good account of itself. It is noted for its versatility and gentleness.

PAINT HORSE
(See Plate 6)

The words *paint* and *pinto* are synonymous—both refer to spotted or two-tone horses with body markings of white and another color. However, when used to refer to breed registry associations, the words take on different meaning. The American Paint Horse Association is devoted strictly to the stock type horse and bases its registry on the blood of registered Paints, Quarter Horses, and Thoroughbreds; whereas the International Pinto Sportshorse Registry and the National Pinto Horse Registry register pinto colored horses of any background; and the Pinto Horse Association of America promotes the Pinto breed. Thus, the Paint Horse represents a combination of breeding, conformation, and color, whereas the Pinto is primarily a color breed.

ORIGIN AND NATIVE HOME

Paint Horses originated in the United States. The American Paint Stock Association was formed in 1962. In 1965, this association combined with the American Paint Quarter Horse Association to establish the American Paint Horse Association.

PAINT HORSE CHARACTERISTICS

Fig. 10-36. Paint mare and foal. (Courtesy, American Paint Horse Assn., Ft. Worth, TX)

Paint Horses are distinguished by two color patterns—they may be either overo or tobiano. Tobiano are most numerous (there are about four tobianos to one overo).

Figure 10-37 illustrates the two patterns.

Overo   **Tobiano**

Fig. 10-37. Coat patterns. Overo (left) and tobiano (right).

Coat colors are white plus any other color, but the coloring must be a recognizable paint. No discrimination is made against glass, or light-colored eyes.

Animals are disqualified for registration unless they have natural white markings above the knees or hocks, except on the face; if they have Appaloosa coloring or breeding; if they are adult horses under 14 hands high; or if they are five-gaited horses.

ADAPTATION AND USE

Paint Horses are used as stock horses, pleasure horses, and for showing and racing.

PRESENT STATUS OF THE BREED

The breed is gaining popularity and numbers. In 1994, a total of 27,549 Paint Horses were registered,

Fig. 10-38. American Paint Horse World Champion Junior Cutting Horse, *Solo Lee*, exhibited by Ernest Wilson, owned by Lynn Strickland. (Photo by Gail Bates. Courtesy, American Paint Horse Assn., Ft. Worth, TX)

bringing the total registrations since the breed registry was started to 286,103.

PALOMINO
(See Plates 19 and 26)

The word *palomino* correctly implies a horse of a golden color with white, silver, or ivory mane and tail. Originally, Palominos were not considered either a breed or a type, but simply a color. Today, animals of palomino color and meeting certain other stipulations may be recorded in one of three registry associations, one of which is for Palomino ponies 14 hands or under.

ORIGIN AND NATIVE HOME

Palomino horses originated in the United States, from animals of Spanish extraction.

When, in the course of the Mexican War—which ended in 1848, over 100 years ago—the United States acquired what is now the state of California, many attractive golden-colored horses of good type were found in the new territory.

According to the best records available, these animals were first introduced from Spain to the New World beginning with Cortez, in 1519, and their introduction was continued by other Spanish explorers. Evidently these horses had long been bred for color in Spain, being used exclusively as the distinctive mounts of the royal family, the nobility, and high military officials. In Spain these golden-colored animals were known as "The Horse of the Queen," and their use by commoners was forbidden. It is also known that the Spaniards obtained the golden horse from Arabia and Morocco, but further than this its origin is clouded in obscurity.

In the early days of California, Palominos were extremely popular. Spanish gentlemen took pride in ownership of these beautiful mounts, which were also used as the racehorses in early California. However, with the importation of the Thoroughbred and other horses of light horse extraction from the Eastern Seaboard and Europe, the golden horse was threatened with extinction. Only in recent years has its popularity again come to the fore, finally resulting in the formation of three breed registry associations—the Palomino Horse Association, which was incorporated in 1936; the Palomino Horse Breeders of America, which was organized in 1941; and the Palomino Ponies of America for Palominos 14 hands or under.

PALOMINO CHARACTERISTICS

Fig. 10-39. Palomino exhibited by Jeannie Young. (Courtesy, Palomino Horse Breeders of America, Tulsa, OK)

The Palomino must be golden in color (the color of a newly minted gold coin or three shades lighter or darker), with a light-colored mane and tail (white, silver, or ivory, with not more than 15 percent dark or chestnut hair in either). White markings on the face or below the knees or hocks are acceptable. The skin and eyes shall be dark or hazel. The usual height range is from 14-2 to 16 hands and the weight from 1,000 to 1,200 lb. As might be expected, in an attempt to form a new breed with a color requirement as first and foremost, considerable variation in type exists.

Some authorities feel that the palomino color may be unfixable—that it cannot be made true breeding, no matter how long or how persistent the effort. (See discussion relative to Incomplete Dominance in Chapter 12.) Further, there appears to be ample theory—substantiated by practical observation—to indicate that palomino colored foals may be produced by any of the following four types of matings:

1. Palomino X Palomino resulting in the production of foals in the ratio of 1 chestnut:2 Palominos:1 albino.[4]

2. Palomino X chestnut producing foals in the ratio of 1 chestnut:1 Palomino.

3. Palomino X albino, producing foals in the ratio of 1 Palomino:1 albino.

---

[4]The term *albino* as herein used is familiar to equestrians, but it does not refer to a true albino as exists in white mice, rats, and rabbits.

4. Chestnut X albino, producing only Palomino foals.

As indicated, when palomino mares are bred to a palomino stallion, the foals are, on the average, of the following colors: half of them are palominos, one-fourth of them chestnut, and one-fourth of them albinos. Also, it is noteworthy that chestnut X albino matings produce only palomino foals.

■ **The Palomino Horse Association lists the following disqualifications:** Buckskin, chocolate, or sorrel color; blue or chalk eyes; a dorsal stripe along the spine; horses with white or dark spots to indicate Pinto, Appaloosa, or Paint background; horses with known Albino breeding; or horses with the characteristics of draft horses.

■ **The Palomino Horse Breeders of America lists the following disqualifications:** A dorsal stripe of brown or black along the spine, zebra stripes around the legs or across the wither, or patches of white hair with underlying pink or light skin, unless caused by injury.

ADAPTATION AND USE

Palominos are used as stock, parade, pleasure, saddle, and fine harness horses.

PRESENT STATUS OF THE BREED

It is to the credit of the breed associations and the breed enthusiasts that they have done a wonderful job in selling the public on the beauty of the Palomino. They have accepted palomino colors from among the light horse breeds and have wisely admonished the breeders themselves to improve the type.

■ **Palomino Horse Association (PHA) registration requirements**—First, the PHA requires that the horse be a golden color, and 14-1 hands to 17 hands high. Next, based on submitting four good colored pictures with the application for registry, with the option of inspection by the PHA, Palomino horses registered in the same breed associations as are accepted by the PHBA may be registered in the PHA.

■ **Palomino Horse Breeders of America (PHBA) registration requirements**—First, the PHBA requires that the horse be a Palomino in color. Next, if the Palomino is registered in one of the following breed registries, the horse shall not be inspected: American Morgan Horse Association, American Quarter Horse Association, American Saddlebred Horse Association, Arabian Horse Registry, International Arabian Horse Association, Jockey Club, or Tennessee Walking Horse Breeders and Exhibitors Association.

PASO FINO

In the United States, there are two offshoots of Paso horses, the Paso Fino and the Peruvian Paso, with registration and promotion by different breed registries.

ORIGIN AND NATIVE HOME

Paso Fino horses originated in the Caribbean area, where they have existed for over 400 years. They have been registered in stud books in Peru, Puerto Rico, Cuba, and Columbia.

The Paso Fino Horse Association was founded in 1972 under the name Paso Fino Owners and Breeders Association.

PASO FINO CHARACTERISTICS

First and foremost, the Paso Fino is characterized by the paso gait, essentially a broken pace—lateral (not a diagonal) gait. The sequence of the movement of the hooves is: right rear, right fore, left rear, and left

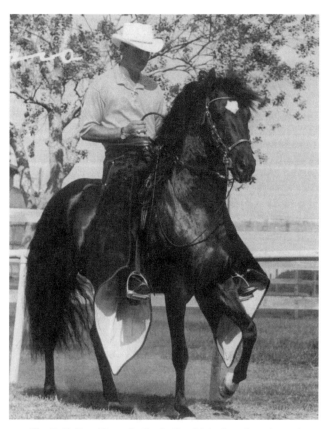

Fig. 10-40. Paso Fino, reflecting its Spanish heritage through proud carriage, grace, and elegance. (Courtesy, Paso Fino Horse Assn., Plant City, FL)

fore; with the hind foot touching the ground a fraction of a second before the front foot. When performed on a hard surface, a definite 1, 2, 3, 4 beat can be heard. The paso gait is performed at three speeds: (1) paso fino, which is the classic show-ring gait, performed with the horse fully balanced and collected; (2) paso corto, which is a more relaxed form of the gait and is commonly referred to as the natural paso gait; and (3) paso largo, which is the speed form of the gait. Additionally, Paso Finos walk and canter; hence, they are three-gaited horses.

The coat may be any color, although solid colors are preferred. Bay, chestnut, or black with white markings are most common. Occasionally, palominos and pintos appear. They range in height from 13-2 to 15-2 hands.

ADAPTATIONS AND USE

Paso Finos are used as pleasure, cutting, and parade horses and for endurance riding and drill team work.

PRESENT STATUS OF THE BREED

The breed is very popular, and numbers are increasing. In 1995, 2,036 Paso Finos were registered, bringing the total number registered since the formation of the breed registry to a total of 25,969.

PERUVIAN PASO

The Peruvian Paso is original only to Peru. In this respect, it should not be confused with the Paso Fino breeds, whose ancestors were scattered throughout the Caribbean area.

ORIGIN AND NATIVE HOME

The Peruvian Paso is descended from three breeds brought to Peru by the Spanish conquistadors—the Andalusian, the Barb, and the Friesian. No other blood, other than these three original breeds, was ever introduced into the Peruvian Paso breed.

EARLY IMPORTATION

The first importation to the United States of Peruvian horses of any consequence was made in the 1960s. Prior to that time, the breed was practically unheard of in North America.

PERUVIAN PASO CHARACTERISTICS

Fig. 10-41. Peruvian Paso stallion. (Courtesy, Drs. McCormick, Calistoga, CA)

One of the trademarks of the breed is the piso, or gait, a natural (inborn), smooth, four-beat, lateral gait—in essence, a broken pace. It does not give the rider either the vertical movement of the trot or the lateral motion of the pace. It is recognized as the smoothest ride in the horse world. Another trademark of the Peruvian Paso is that it is the only breed in the world that does the *termino*, a graceful, flowing movement in which the forelegs are rolled to the outside as the horse strides forward, much like the arm motions of a swimmer. This showy action gives the Peruvian Paso the appearance of always being *on parade*. It is a completely natural gait. It is not a wing or paddle; it originates in the shoulder. The action of the Peruvian is completely natural. It is not induced or aided in any way by artificial training or devices. In both Peru and the United States, Peruvian horses are shown without shoes and with a short, natural hoof.

Mature Peruvian Pasos average about 14 to 15-1 hands high and weigh 900 to 1,200 lb.

Peruvian horses come in all basic, solid colors, as well as grays, roans, and palominos, with some rather striking variations of these colors.

The American Association of Owners and Breeders of Peruvian Paso Horses disqualifies horses with more than 25% body white, including on the legs and head.

The Peruvian Paso Horse Registry of North America disqualifies for registry cryptorchids, monorchids, and albino animals.

Additionally, there are two part-blood registries: the Peruvian Part-Blood Registry is open to horses, ponies, or mules which are at least 50% Peruvian Paso, with at least one parent a registered Peruvian Paso.

The Peruvian Paso Part-Blood Registry registers only mares, geldings, and mules, one parent of which must be a registered Peruvian Paso.

ADAPTATION AND USE

The primary uses of Peruvian horses are: pleasure horses, parade horses, and endurance horses.

PRESENT STATUS OF THE BREED

In 1994, the two full-blooded Peruvian Paso associations registered a total of 1,222 horses. The demand for these horses exceeds the supply.

PINTABIAN
(See Plate 20)

The Pintabian (pronounced pin-tay-bee-an) is a new breed characterized by its Arabian type and tobiano markings. It was developed by crossing tobianos back to purebred Arabians until a relatively pure strain of spotted horses was developed. They carry more than 99% Arabian blood.

PINTO ARABIAN

Pinto Arabians must have one-fourth or more Arabian blood and be spotted.

The American Pinto Arabian Registry was established in 1991. The registry association states that "Pinto Arabians give breeders the opportunity to combine what is best from several different breeds as long as the resulting foals have pinto coloring and some Arabian blood in the pedigree." Among the several different breeds that have gone into the make-up of the Pinto Arabian are: American Saddlebred, Paint Horse, Pinto Horse, Tennessee Walking Horse, Thoroughbred, and Warmbloods. Purebred Pinto Arabians have only shown the overo color pattern. Part blood

Fig. 10-42. Pinto Arabian stallion, *Excalibur Incognito*, two years of age, tobiano pattern, an Arabian X Tennessee Walking Horse cross, owned by Excalibur Arabians and Pintos. (Photo by D. L. Brinkley. Courtesy, American Pinto Arabian Registry, Ennis, TX)

Pinto Arabians show all the usual pinto color patterns with the tobiano being dominant.

PINTO HORSE[5]

The word *pinto* refers to a spotted horse, a description first applied to the spotted descendants of the horses of the Spanish conquerors.

Pinto Horses are also referred to as *piebalds* (English term for black-and-white pinto), *skewbalds* (English term for all pintos other than black-and-white in color), and *paints* (a term of old American West translating *pinto*—a derivation of the Spanish word *pintado*, meaning painted).

ORIGIN AND NATIVE HOME

The Pinto breed originated in the United States, from horses of Spanish ancestry. Spotted or Pinto horses first arrived in the New World with the Spanish conquistadors. From that day forward, animals of this color played a leading role in the development of the

---

[5]The words *pinto* and *paint* are synonymous—both refer to spotted or two-toned horses with body markings of white and another color. However, the Pinto Horse, which is registered by the National Pinto Horse Registry and the Pinto Horse Association of America, embraces all types and breeds, whereas the Paint Horse, which is registered by The American Paint Horse Association, is limited to stock type and to registered animals of the Paint, Quarter Horse, and Thoroughbred breeds.

West. Many of them were captured and used as the highly prized riding horses of the American Indians. Later, they were found among the feral horses of the West; and, most important, through the years many of them have been used as stock horses.

PINTO CHARACTERISTICS

Fig. 10-43. Pinto mare, *Miss Super Chick*, Champion Halter Mare, a bay overo. (Courtesy, Pinto Horse Assn. of America, Ft. Worth, TX)

The most distinctive characteristic of the Pinto Horse is its color. The ideal Pinto possesses a 50-50 color pattern distribution. However, the patterns and markings are extremely varied and are found in many colors ranging from predominantly white to the predominantly dark-colored horse. Horses with less than 50-50 percentage of markings will be accepted. But a Pinto must have noticeable markings on the body, not including the face and legs. Glass eyes are a part of Pinto lineage and are not to be discounted.

There are two basic patterns or markings, called *tobiano* and *overo* (see Fig. 10-37 under "Paint Horse").

Most tobianos have color on the head, chest, flanks, and some in the tail. The legs are nearly always white, and the white markings extend over the back. The edges of the markings are usually fairly smooth and rounded.

The overo often has jagged or lacy-edged white markings, mostly on the midsection of the body and neck area. The white rarely crosses the backline; legs are usually a color rather than white. There is more variation of pattern with overos than with tobianos.

The following three types of Pinto Horses are raised:

1. **Stock-type.** This is a Western horse, with Quarter Horse breeding and conformation, suitable for use on the range or for competing in Western show events.

2. **Saddle type.** This is a saddle or parade type, with American Saddlebred breeding and conformation, suitable for parades, gaited events, fine harness competition, or for park riding.

3. **Pleasure type.** Most pleasure-type Pintos carry Arabian or Morgan breeding. This is the versatile Pinto, suitable for all events, either English or Western.

Animals with Appaloosa ancestry or color, or of known draft horse breeding, are ineligible for registry. Animals with pony breeding of any kind are eligible for registry only in the Pony Division of the Pinto Horse Association of America.

ADAPTATION AND USE

The adaptation and use of the Pinto Horse is well summarized in the following statement which appears in the *Stud Book*, Vol. 4:[6] "There is the Pinto pony—long the pride and joy of millions of American youth. We find Pintos, too, among the cow ponies and polo ponies, jumpers, hunters, and other sporting types. Again, among the pleasure types such as trail horses, hacks, and particularly parade horses, the pinto enjoys wide and deserved popularity." In brief, the Pinto is adapted for use for any light horse purpose, but it is especially superb as a show, parade, novice, stock horse, and pleasure animal.

PRESENT STATUS OF THE BREED

The breed enthusiasts have never attempted to dominate other breeds nor to make wild claims for their representatives. Rather, they are wisely attempting to preserve, improve, and extend the use of horses of a color whose development has gone hand in hand with the transformation of America itself.

The Pinto Horse Association of America, Inc., maintains the following types of registries:

1. **Tentative Registration.** This is for foals. They become eligible for permanent registry at two years of age if they meet the standards.

2. **Permanent Registration Division.** Horses recorded herein must be two years of age, 14 hands or over, and of acceptable conformation, quality, refinement, and color.

3. **Premium Registration.** This division is for the

---

[6] "The Pinto's Place Now and in the Future," Official Stud Book and Registry, The Pinto Horse Society, Vol. 4, December 31, 1945, pp. 13 and 14.

purpose of encouraging and recording the breeding of fine Pintos. The registration certificate is so marked.

4. **Approved Breed Division.** The Approved Breed Division is for the purpose of establishing pure-bred Pinto bloodlines for future generations of Pintos.

5. **Solid Color Breeding Stock Division.** The Solid Color Stock Division provides for solid color horses with Pinto Horse Association registered ancestry.

6. **Pony Registry.** The Pony Registry provides registration for Pintos under 14 hands (56 in.).

The Pinto Horse Association of America registered 3,000 horses in 1994, bringing its total number of horses registered since its formation to 79,500.

PONY OF THE AMERICAS

The Pony of the Americas (POA) is an all-around pleasure horse that is small enough for a child but large enough for a teenager.

ORIGIN AND NATIVE HOME

The Pony of the Americas is, as the name indicates, a pony breed that originated in America. The registry, known as the Pony of the Americas Club, Inc. (POAC), was formed in 1954, with headquarters in Mason City, Iowa; with Mr. Leslie L. Boomhower, an able lawyer and equestrian, as the first executive secretary.

PONY OF THE AMERICAS CHARACTERISTICS

The Pony of the Americas is a happy medium of Arabian and Quarter Horse in miniature, ranging in height from 46 in. to 54 in., with appaloosa coloring. It's a Western-type small horse.

Ponies possessing any of the following characteristics are disqualified for registry: (1) pinto, paint, or albino color, or pinto, paint, or albino sire or dam; and (2) white markings with underlying light skin above each leg at the top of the knees and top of the hocks, behind a line running from the center of each ear to the corner of each side of the mouth, or on the lower lip above a line running from one corner of the mouth to the other corner. POAs that mature over the 56 in. maximum or under the 46 in. minimum (six years of age) are eligible for transfer to the breeding stock only category of the Registry. POAs foaled solid colored with no visible Appaloosa color can be registered as breeding stock, also.

Fig. 10-44. Becki Belcher, Pembroke, Georgia, riding *Hauling Oats* in the 1995 International Show. (Courtesy, POA Club, Indianapolis, IN)

ADAPTATION AND USE

The primary use of the Pony of the Americas is for mounts for juniors who have outgrown Shetlands but who are not ready for horses.

PRESENT STATUS OF THE BREED

More than 42,000 Pony of the Americas have been registered since the breed was founded in 1954. Also, through selective breeding, the POA has changed from looking like a pony to looking like a small horse.

The registry consists of the following four categories:

1. **Tentative.** Ponies having at least one POA parent, visible Appaloosa color and characteristics, and five years or younger.

2. **Permanent.** Ponies having at least one POA parent, visible Appaloosa color and characteristics, six years and older, 46 in. to 56 in. (Tentative ponies must advance to permanent status at six years of age or lose registered status.)

3. **ID Blue Papers.** Foals having at least one POA parent, no visible Appaloosa type color, breeding stock only.

4. **ID Pink Papers.** This is for tentatively registered ponies that mature under 46 in. or over 56 in., breeding stock only.

QUARTER HORSE
(See Plate 34)

The earliest form of horse racing in America—particularly in Maryland, Virginia, and the Carolinas—was through necessity usually over a quarter-mile track. The topography and the wilderness were such as to make difficult the construction of formal racetracks. Rather, small race paths were literally hewn out of the wilderness. Many of these courses were down the main street of town, as this was the only straight and cleared stretch available. To race over these tracks, the pioneers selected sturdy stock possessed of a great burst of speed at short distances.

ORIGIN AND NATIVE HOME

Quarter Horses originated in the United States.

Although the breed registry association did not come into existence until 1940, the Quarter Horse had its beginning some 300 years earlier with the crude quarter-mile race paths of pioneer days. Those heavily muscled, sturdy animals, best adapted to rugged courses in matched races, were to serve as the foundation stock of a now popular western breed. With the advent of the Thoroughbred and the construction of the formal racetracks of greater length in the East, Quarter Horse racing stock was pushed to the West and Southwest. In the range states these rugged animals continued to flourish for quarter racing, and they endeared themselves as the ideal cow pony.

There are two schools of thought relative to the ancestry of the Quarter Horse: (1) that the foundation stock consisted of the native mares of Spanish extraction in Virginia, Maryland, and the Carolinas which were mated to Thoroughbred stallions; and (2) that little or no Thoroughbred blood was infused, for—so it is argued—the foundation of the Quarter Horse was laid a hundred years before the first Thoroughbred horse was imported to America in 1730.

It is known that the early improvement of the Quarter Horse and that of the Thoroughbred were closely associated. Perhaps the truth of the matter is that certain animals contributed notably to each breed.

Most authorities recognize as the Quarter Horse patriarch, the imported Thoroughbred stallion *Janus* (1756–1780), a tested four-mile racer in England. It is reported that *Janus'* progeny were unexcelled for a great burst of speed over short distances, and, like their sire, they were sturdy in build and possessed powerful muscling in the hindquarters.

Since there was no Quarter Horse registry prior to 1940, it is incredible that the purity of the breed could have been maintained through more than 300 years of an unplanned beginning. Suffice it to say that

the distinctive breed that evolved at the end of this period is ample evidence of the superior quality of the blood infused through the years—regardless of its source.

Steel Dust, the most famous of all Quarter Horses, made his debut in Texas around the middle of the 19th century. Until his fame became known, it was said that he nearly bankrupted a certain Texas community in which he first appeared in a matched race with a notorious racer of the day. In commenting on the influence of *Steel Dust* in molding the breed, Robert Denhart[7] states that, "Every horse trader who has not recently joined a church will modestly admit that his horses are direct descendants of Steel Dust." There are some 11 prominent families listed in the Stud Book and Registry, most of which either originated in or were introduced in Texas.

QUARTER HORSE CHARACTERISTICS

Fig. 10-45. Quarter Horse mares and foals. (Courtesy, The Foundation Quarter Horse Registry, Akron, CO)

Quarter Horses are powerfully built, but modern animals no longer have the once-sought *bulldog build*. Although a well-muscled horse is desired, the moderate type is more useful than the muscle-bound type. Also, certain families are being selected for racing—for great speed at short distances. The latter approach the build of the Thoroughbred, but they possess more substance.

The head is somewhat short and is distinct because of the small alert ear. The neck is well developed, the back and loin short and heavily muscled, the forearms and rear quarters are well muscled, and the legs relatively short. The entire ensemble is such as to make the Quarter Horse an ideal stock horse—an

---

[7] *The Quarter Horse—A History*, The American Quarter Horse Association Stud Book and Registry, Vol. I, 1941, p. 18.

animal that is agile and speedy, capable of outrunning any "critter." Also, the Quarter Horse possesses sufficient weight and power to hold a heavy steer when roped and has a calm disposition even in the roundup.

The most predominant colors of the breed are chestnut, sorrel, bay, and dun. Palominos, blacks, browns, roans and copper-colored animals, however are not uncommon.

Animals are disqualified for registration if they have Paint, Pinto, Appaloosa, or albino coloring. Also, no animal having white markings or underlying light skin beyond the following locations is eligible for registration: (1) white above a knee or hock, (2) white back of a line from the ear to the corner of the mouth, or (3) white on the lower lip above a line connecting the two corners of the mouth.

ADAPTATION AND USE

Quarter Horses are adapted and used chiefly for two purposes: (1) for quarter-mile racing, and (2) for cow ponies. Thus, it follows that there are two schools of thought as to the best method of testing the performance of Quarter Horses: (1) to race them up to distances of a quarter-mile; and (2) to work cattle with them. Advocates of the first method are interested primarily in speed and racing, whereas advocates of the second method are interested chiefly in a superior cow pony. Perhaps some combination of the two criteria is desirable in most Quarter Horses.

PRESENT STATUS OF THE BREED

Despite the decline in the horse and mule population since the 1930s, the stock horse will always remain on the western range. Even the versatile Jeep does not threaten to take over the job of roping a steer. Also, Quarter Horse racing is increasing in popularity. Thus, the future of the Quarter Horse breed seems assured.

The Official Stud Book of the American Quarter Horse Association consists of two parts:

1. **Numbered**, composed of—

a. Horses foaled January 1, 1962, or later, and issued numbered certificates by the AQHA.

b. Horses foaled prior to January 1, 1962, and issued permanent certificates by the AQHA.

c. Horses foaled prior to January 1, 1962, and issued tentative certificates by the AQHA.

2. **Appendix**, composed of—

a. **New Appendix**, for horses foaled on or after January 1, 1962.

b. **Old Appendix**, for horses foaled prior to January 1, 1962.

(1) All foals of 1961 and prior years in the Old Appendix shall have the same rights and privileges of securing a number as they have had prior to January 1, 1962; by (a) having both parents acquire an AQHA number equivalent to a Permanent number, unless this individual previously has been rejected on conformation inspection, or (b) by qualifying for one of the Registers of Merit that is not limited (such as age or amateur status of contestant), or by passing conformation inspection.

(2) Any stallion or mare listed in the Old Appendix, which cannot advance because of lack of bloodlines, Quarter Horses conformation, or inability to qualify for a Register of Merit, is eligible to compete in any approved performance event. Foals may not be registered, however, from any stallion or mare in this category.

(3) Any gelding listed in the Old Appendix is eligible to compete in any approved class (halter or performance) contest, or racing event.

The American Quarter Horse Association registered 105,017 horses in 1994 bringing its total number registered since its formation in 1940 to 3,300,000.

SELLE FRANCAIS

For many years, and especially since World War II, the French have pursued an aggressive breeding program with the goal of producing a superior sport

Fig. 10-46. *Heisman*, Selle Francais stallion, performing in the 1992 Barcelona Olympics; owned by Sale Johnson, W. H. G. R. Farm, New York, NY. (Courtesy, North American Selle Francais Horse Association, Winchester, VA)

horse, a horse that would excel in the three equestrian Olympic disciplines—show jumping, three-day eventing, and dressage. Toward this end, they selectively crossed the sturdy native Normandy horses, and horses from other regions of France, on Thoroughbreds. By continuing to infuse Thoroughbreds in the Selle Francais, they achieved their ideal: a big horse with good movement capable of covering ground—a horse with the conformation of a big-boned Thoroughbred and a calm temperament. Today, the Thoroughbred influence in the Selle Francais is decreasing due to the number of exceptional Selle Francais stallions.

The Selle Francais is an elegant sport horse, athletically versatile and with a phenomenal record in the World Equestrian Games since the 1990s. The North American Selle Francais Horse Association, Winchester, Virginia, registered 110 horses in 1994, bringing their total registrations to 635 since their formation in 1990.

SHETLAND PONY

There are two types of Shetlands—the *Classic* and the *Modern*.

ORIGIN AND NATIVE HOME

The Shetland Pony is native to the Shetland Isles, which lie 100 miles north of Scotland, parallel with central Norway, and not more than 400 miles from the Arctic Circle. Historic records give evidence that the breed was located in this rugged area as early as the 6th century A.D. This qualifies the breed as one of the oldest in existence. Centuries of survival in the rigors of the northland climate and on sparse vegetation have endowed the breed with that hardiness for which it is justly famed.

EARLY AMERICAN IMPORTATIONS

The first importations of Shetlands to the United States took place about the middle of the 19th century. Large numbers of subsequent importations followed.

The American Shetland Pony Club was organized in 1888.

SHETLAND PONY CHARACTERISTICS

Today, the American Shetland Pony Club promotes two types of ponies: The *classic type*, which is somewhat short and chunky; and the *modern type*, which is rather fine boned, long-necked, and high going.

■ **The Classic Shetland Pony**—It has the classic beauty of the time-honored breed. No Classic Shetland should exceed 46 in. While uncrossed with other breeds, the Classic is still somewhat more refined than its stocky ancestors in the Shetland Islands.

Fig. 10-47. Classic American Shetland Pony, two-times National Grand Champion Gelding. (Photo by Lisa. Courtesy, *The Journal*, Warrensville, IL)

Classics posses substance, muscle and bone, without coarseness. Also, they have a certain amount of refinement about the ears, head, throatlatch, and neck. Short, sharp, erect ears, prominent eyes and a refined jaw all contribute to the Classic Shetland's beauty. Classics can be of any color, either solid or mixed. Today, both beautiful solid color Shetlands and flashy, spotted animals are popular.

By nature, the Classic Shetland is docile and gentle. Because of their personalities, these elegant, but sturdy, ponies are extremely versatile. Classics are used as working ponies and pets as well as in the show-ring. In competition, Classics are shown in hand where they are judged on conformation, style, and soundness. Many are driven in pleasure, hitch, carriage or obstacle classes, or are used under saddle in pleasure, rein, or parade classes. Often, they are ridden by children in lead line classes or are used in costume classes. Also, Classic Shetlands may pull a wagon, hitch, or be used as a working pony.

■ **The Modern American Shetland**—The Modern Shetland is more refined and more animated than the Classic Shetland. It combines the historic hardiness of the Classic with an outcross of an animated and refined pony breed such as the Hackney to achieve refinement and action. Modern American Shetlands are long-necked and fine-boned and have a distinct, spirited personality that lends itself well to the show-ring.

Fig. 10-48. Modern American Shetland Pony, Hall-of-Fame Roadster Pony. (Photo by Macklin. Courtesy, *The Journal*, Warrensville, IL)

Modern Shetlands come in any color, solid or mixed, are neat and well-made, and should not exceed 46 in. in height. They should have neat, refined ears, heads, and necks as well as prominent, wide-set eyes.

Modern Shetlands are shown in two height divisions—under 43 in. and 43 to 46 in. They are shown in breeding/halter classes or in performance classes which include roadster, harness, and pleasure driving. They should have good conformation and high, easy action, airy, and freely coordinated on all four corners of the pony. A good headset, superb carriage, and high action most often define a great Modern Shetland performance pony.

ADAPTATION AND USE

The Classic American Shetland Pony is versatile, with the temperament and personality to become a lifelong friend.

The spirited Modern American Shetland is a natural show pony, with high-stepping action, great energy, and style in the show-ring—beautiful to behold on the tanbark. It is well suited for the professional horse-exhibitor. When well trained, they may be shown by amateurs, ladies, or children—even in children's costume classes and barrel racing.

PRESENT STATUS OF THE BREED

Wherever there are children, Shetland Ponies will continue to be in demand. It is likely that more and more Shetlands will come to provide healthful outdoor recreation for the boys and girls of America.

Shetlands in the United States are registered by the American Shetland Pony Club in Peoria, Illinois. Two types of Shetlands are registered and promoted:

the *Classic*, and the *Modern*. In 1995, a total of 1,200 ponies of the two types were registered, making for a total of more than 150,000 since the U.S. breed registry was formed.

In 1972, the American Shetland Pony Club opened the American Miniature Registry to provide services for Miniatures. Miniatures can be either *Division A, 34 in. or under*, or *Division B, 34 to 38 in.*

SPANISH-BARB
(See Plate 21)

The unique thing about the Spanish-Barb is the genetic phenomenon of 5 lumbar vertebrae and 17 thoracic vertebrae found in the breed.

ORIGIN AND NATIVE HOME

The Barb horse was taken from Africa to Spain with the conquest of Spain by the Moors in 711 A.D. From Spain, they were taken to Cuba in 1511, to Mexico in 1519, to southwestern United States in 1540, and to Florida in 1565. The Spanish-Barb Breeders Association was organized in 1972.

SPANISH-BARB CHARACTERISTICS

Spanish-Barbs are small horses (the standard height is 13-3 to 14-3 hands), with short couplings, deep bodies, good action, and without extreme mus-

Fig. 10-49. Spanish-Barb champion halter stallion, *Gran Talisman*, owned by Southwind Farm, Saucier, Mississippi. (Courtesy, Spanish-Barb Breeders Assn., Terry, MS)

cling. All colors are represented in the breed, but dun, grulla, sorrel, and roan are most common. A dorsal stripe and zebra markings occur in all duns and grullas and in some sorrels.

ADAPTATION AND USE

Spanish-Barbs are used for cow ponies, Western riding, English riding, and packhorses.

PRESENT STATUS OF THE BREED

The Spanish-Barb horse is in the hands of people who believe in both (1) the historical importance of the breed, and (2) the exceptional capabilities of the breed. Because of the past efforts of a handful of dedicated people, the Spanish-Barb has survived into the 20th Century. These ardent supporters will continue to perpetuate the breed.

■ **The Wilbur-Cruce Mission Strain of Colonial Spanish Horse**—In a report dated September 1990, to the members of the American Minor Breed Conservatory (AMBC), which headquarters at Pittsboro, North Carolina, Dr. Phillip Sponenberg, Technical Chairman, AMBC, told of the rescue of a herd of old-type Spanish horses on the Wilbur-Cruce Ranch in Arizona. These horses traced directly to the high-quality stock used to supply the mission chain from Mexico to Arizona during the late 1600s and the early 1700s. In 1995, 38 of these horses were registered in a separate division of the Spanish-Barb Breeders Association, where they are observing the same rules and disqualifications as the Spanish-Barb.

SPANISH MUSTANG
(See Plate 30)

The Spanish Mustang descends from the feral horse that once roamed the plains of North America.

ORIGIN AND NATIVE HOME

The Spanish Mustang originated in the United States. They trace to the feral and the semiferal (Indian-owned) horses of Barb and Andalusian ancestry that were brought to America by the Spanish conquistadors in the early 1500s and 1600s. Beginning about 1925, Robert E. Brislawn, Sr., and his brother, Ferdinand L. Brislawn, began gathering pure Spanish Mustangs. To retain the purity of the strain, The Spanish

Mustang Registry, Inc., was founded in 1957, at Sundance, Wyoming.

SPANISH MUSTANG CHARACTERISTICS

Fig. 10-50. Spanish Mustang Stallion, raised on Medicine Spring Ranch, Finley, Oklahoma, Gilbert H. Jones, owner. (Courtesy, Southwest Spanish Mustang Assn.)

Spanish Mustangs run the whole gamut of equine colors, including all the solid colors and all the broken colors. They stand 13-2 to 15-2 hands; and some have 5 to 5½ lumbar vertebrae.

ADAPTATION AND USE

Spanish Mustangs are used for cow ponies, Western riding, English riding, packhorses, and trail horses.

PRESENT STATUS OF THE BREED

Spanish Mustang breeders are dedicated to perpetuating the breed. They appear to be making progress.

SPOTTED SADDLE HORSE

As the name indicates, animals of this breed are spotted and saddle horses. With their loud colors and easy gaits, Spotted Saddle Horses are popular in trail rides, parades, and horse shows.

ORIGIN AND NATIVE HOME

Colorful spotted horses were first brought to the United States by the early Spaniards. Also, spotted saddle horses were not uncommon in the foundation animals of the American Saddlebred and the Tennessee Walking Horse breeds.

On October 24, 1979, a group of breeders met in Murfreesboro, Tennessee and formed the National Spotted Saddle Horse Association, to collect, record, and preserve the pedigrees of the Spotted Saddle Horse.

SPOTTED SADDLE HORSE CHARACTERISTICS

Spotted Saddle Horses range in height from 14 to 16 hands, with an average of about 15 hands. In addition to color, the breed is characterized by its ruggedness, intelligent eyes, fox-type ears, surefootedness, and good disposition. Spotted Saddle Horses must be gaited.

ADAPTATION AND USE

In addition to being used as a pleasure mount and jumper, the registry association promotes the breed as a bird-dog mount, and for use by coon hunters in rugged mountain terrain.

PRESENT STATUS OF THE BREED

During the first 10 years after the registry was formed, 3,996 horses were registered. Thus, the breed appears to be off to a good start. Four pictures must accompany the application for registration.

STANDARDBRED
(See Plate 35)

Both the Standardbred and the American Saddlebred are the result of a Thoroughbred cross on native mares; both are truly American creations—the former developing as a road horse in the East and the latter as a saddle horse of the southern plantations. In each case, the descendants of one Thoroughbred individual dominated the breed. *Messenger*, imported in 1788, largely shaped the Standardbred through his great grandson, *Hambletonian 10*; whereas Denmark, foaled in 1839, largely determined the destiny of the American Saddlebred through his illustrious son, *Gaine's*

Denmark. Despite these similarities in background, two very different breeds evolved because of (1) the differences in the native mares bred, and (2) selection as influenced by the respective ends in view. In the case of the Standardbred, the native foundation mares were trotters or pacers adapted to fast driving in harness; whereas the native mares used in molding the American Saddlebred were amblers, easy to ride.

ORIGIN AND NATIVE HOME

The Standardbred horse originated in the United States. Originally developed for road driving and racing, it descended from five sources: (1) the Thoroughbred, (2) the Norfolk Trotter or Hackney, (3) the Arabian and Barb, (4) the Morgan, and (5) certain pacers of mixed breeding. In the beginning, this breed was often referred to as the American Trotter, but this designation is now discarded because the breed embraces both trotters and pacers, all of which are registered in the same association. The name *Standardbred* is derived from the fact that, beginning in 1879, eligibility for registration was based on the ability of the animal to trot the mile at 2:30 or pace the same distance at 2:25. Today, a record performance is no longer a prerequisite to registration—it is merely necessary that animals be the offspring of recorded sires and dams.[8]

The great pillar of the Standardbred was *Rysdyk's Hambletonian*, or *Hambletonian 10* (the latter designating his Standard number in Vol. IV of the Register). This great stallion, foaled in 1849, carried the blood of *Messenger*, a gray Thoroughbred stallion imported from England to Philadelphia in 1788 at the age of eight, and *Bellfounder*, a Norfolk Trotter or Hackney, foaled in England in 1815 and imported to Boston in 1822. No breed can boast of a greater sire than *Hambletonian 10*. During his 21 years in the stud, he sired 1,321 foals, and so famous did he become by virtue of the speed of his get that his service fee was placed at $500.

STANDARDBRED CHARACTERISTICS

In general, animals of this breed are smaller, longer bodied, less leggy and possess less quality than the Thoroughbred, but they show more substance and ruggedness and they possess a more tractable disposition. The head, ears, and bone show less refinement, and the hind legs are not quite so straight as in the Thoroughbred. Standardbred animals attain speed through ability to extend themselves into long

---

[8]On January 1, 1933, registration on performance alone was no longer granted, and registration of both sire and dam was required.

Fig. 10-52. Harness racing at a county fair. (Courtesy, The United States Trotting Assn., Columbus, OH)

Fig. 10-51. The immortal *Hambletonian 10* (also known as *Rysdyk's Hambletonian*), the descendent of *Messenger* who solidified the Standardbred breed. William Rysdyk, a poor farmhand, purchased him as a suckling colt, along with his dam, for $125. *Hambletonian 10* never raced. He began his stud career at 2 and lived to the age of 27, during which time he earned approximately $500,000 for his owner. Today, it is estimated that 99% of the trotters and pacers in America trace to this great sire. (Courtesy, The United States Trotting Assn., Columbus, OH)

strides, repeated rapidly, because of the long forearm and long, narrow muscles.

In weight, the Standardbred ranges from 900 to 1,300 lb, and in height from 15 to 16 hands, with the average being around 15-2 hands. Bay, brown, chestnut, and black are the most common colors; but grays, roans, and duns are found.

Though possessing a common ancestry, some families produce a much larger proportion of pacers than others. Many individuals show speed at both gaits. Shoeing and training are also important factors in determining whether an animal shall be a trotter or a pacer.

ADAPTATION AND USE

As previously indicated, the Standardbred was primarily originated as a trotting horse and for the purpose of providing a superior road horse in the days of the horse and buggy. It was first put under saddle and eventually into harness hitched to a sulky. With the coming of improved highways and the automobile, the progressive breeders, ever alert to new developments, turned their attention almost exclusively to the production of a speedy harness racehorse—either at the trot or the pace. The gameness and stamina of the Standardbred is unexcelled, thus adapting him to race heats wherein it is necessary that he go mile after mile at top speed. Animals of this breed are also

exhibited as light harness horses in the great horse shows of the land.

The early foundation of the Standardbred contributed to the development of the American Saddlebred and the Tennessee Walking Horse. Many hunters are also of Standardbred extraction. It may be said that the Standardbred has proved to be a valuable utility horse—animals of such extraction having speed, endurance, and a tractable disposition.

PRESENT STATUS OF THE BREED

It is quite likely that new harness racetracks will be developed; and with their development, a limited increase in numbers of Standardbreds may be expected. Further improvements in both conformation and speed may be expected, also.

The Standardbred breed has the unique distinction of being one of the few breeds of livestock that the United States has exported rather than imported. Many good specimens of the breed have been shipped to Russia, Austria, Germany, and Italy.

In addition to registering animals both of whose parents are recorded in the United States Trotting Association, any horse sired by a registered horse may be accepted for racing purposes as follows:

Non-Standardbred: Any horse may be registered as Non-Standard if an application is filed showing satisfactory identification of the horse for racing purposes. This identification may be accomplished by furnishing the name, age, sex, sire, dam, color, and markings; also required is a history of the previous owners, if any. A mating certificate must accompany this application, showing the sire to be some type of a registered horse. Any owner standing a non-standard stallion for service must include the fact it is non-standard in all advertisements of such service.

THE DAN PATCH STORY

Dan Patch was a great Standardbred horse whose exploits took place soon after the turn of the century, from 1902 to 1910. In 1906, he paced the fastest mile ever, in 1:55, at the Minnesota State Fair. That record stood until 1938. But it was not recognized, because a windshield was pulled in front of the sulky to break the wind. But to the 93,000 rabid fans who witnessed the feat, and to his worshippers everywhere, the record stood.

The great horse's owner, Will Savage, was a fabulous and colorful character. Will and Dan belonged to each other, when winning—yes, even in death. Mr. Savage made headlines of a sort when he paid $60,000 for the six-year-old Standardbred pacer in 1902. Even his friends referred to the deal as "Savage's folly." But subsequent events proved how wrong they were.

Fig. 10-53. Dan Patch. (Courtesy, United States Trotting Assn., Columbus, OH)

Dan Patch brought fame and fortune to his master, and to himself. A railroad line—The Dan Patch Line—was named after him. There were also Dan Patch sleds, coaster wagons, cigars, washing machines (a two-minute performer like Dan), and shoes for kiddies. Mr. Savage built the great horse an empire, surroundings befitting his station in life. The stable was equipped with modern living quarters for 60 caretakers. Two racetracks were constructed—the best mile strip ever built, and a covered half-miler with 8,400 panes of glass. Even during a Minnesota blizzard, Dan and his stablemates could train in comfort—and style.

Dan Patch was the idol of his day—the Babe Ruth, the Bing Crosby, and the Beatles. People came to see him, as they do any other notable. Lili Langtry, the famous actress, arranged to have her train stopped near Dan's so that she could go to his private car for a visit. Men vied for his shoes, women fought to pluck hair from his mane and tail, small boys played Dan Patch in the backyard, and people wept when he became ill.

The town of Hamilton changed its name to Savage, in honor of the man who had put it on the map.

But there was more than a platonic relationship between horse and owner—there was something almost supernatural between Dan and Will. On July 4, 1916, Dan Patch and Will Savage both took ill on the same day. Those keeping vigil over the horse saw him snuff out his last race—the race with life itself—on July 11. He died at age 20. Thirty-two hours later, Dan's master, Will Savage, was dead at age 57. Both were buried at the same hour; Mr. Savage in Lakewood Cemetery, and Mr. Patch under the shade of an oak tree on the bank of the Minnesota River.

SWEDISH GOTLAND HORSE (American Gotland Horse)

The Gotland, a small horse dating from prehistoric times in Sweden, is an all-purpose horse, suitable for children and medium-sized adults.

ORIGIN AND NATIVE HOME

The breed originated on the Swedish island of Gotland, a part of Sweden.

EARLY AMERICAN IMPORTATIONS

Gotland Horses were first imported to the United States in 1957.

SWEDISH GOTLAND HORSE CHARACTERISTICS

Coat colors are bay, brown, black, dun, chestnut, roan, or palomino, and some leopard and blanket markings. They average about 51 in. high, with a range of 11 to 14 hands.

Pintos and animals with large white markings are disqualified for registration.

The Gotland is a versatile small horse noted for its intelligence, gentleness, tolerance, and good disposition.

Fig. 10-54. Gotland mare and foal. (Photo by Leslie Bebensee. Courtesy, The American Livestock Breeds Conservancy, Pittsboro, NC)

ADAPTATION AND USE

Swedish Gotland Horses are used for harness racing (trotting), as pleasure horses and jumpers, as stock horses, and as riding horses for children and medium-sized adults.

PRESENT STATUS OF THE BREED

There are approximately 8,000 Gotlands in the world, mostly in Sweden. There are fewer than 50 Gotlands in North America.

SWEDISH WARMBLOOD

In the 12th century, the Danish archbishops held

Fig. 10-55. Swedish Warmblood stallion, *Flying Flamingo*. (Courtesy, Swedish Warmblood Assn. of North America, Coupeville, WA)

a heavily fortified stronghold with mounted troops at Flyinge, Sweden. In 1658, following the peace treaty at Roskilde, the Swedish King Carl X Gustaf ordered that a royal stud be established at Flyinge, Sweden. Centuries of skillful breeding resulted in the creation of the Swedish Warmblood.

With the founding of the equestrian Olympic Games by Swedish horseman Clarence Von Rosen in 1912, Swedish horses were very successful—especially in Dressage and Three-Day Eventing.

The Swedish Warmblood is one of the oldest warmblood breeds in the world. For centuries the breed has been developed for riding, whereas, between world wars, most of the other warmblood breeds were bred primarily as agricultural draft horses. The military selected stallions that would produce comfortable and reliable horses for the army, carefully infusing Thoroughbred and other warmblood stallions for new genes. Farmers owned the mares and the army bought the suitable offspring.

The Swedish Warmblood Association was formed in 1928.

Elegance, combined with excellent gaits and a positive attitude, jumping ability, and the capacity to absorb training, makes the Swedish Warmblood well suited for international equestrian sports—dressage in particular. Swedish horses have won medals in most every Olympic Game since 1912, most often in Dressage, but also in Combined Training.

In the United States, the Swedish Warmblood is promoted by the Swedish Warmblood Association of North America, P. O. Box 1587, Coupeville, WA 98239.

TENNESSEE WALKING HORSE
(See Plates 22 and 27)

Today, the Tennessee Walking horse is synonymous with the Plantation Walking Horse, as the latter show-ring classification is constituted by this one breed. In the early formative period of the breed, animals of the walk, running walk, and canter variety were referred to as Plantation Walking Horses because the southern owners and overseers used this type of animal in riding over their estates daily. They liked these animals because of their stamina and comfortable gaits.

ORIGIN AND NATIVE HOME

The Tennessee Walking Horse was at home in the Middle Basin of Tennessee for more than a hundred years prior to the formation of a breed registry in 1935. Like other American breed creations, the Tennessee Walking Horse is of composite origin. Yet, through constant breeding and selection, distinct characteristics evolved, molding the horse into an entity of its own. The sturdy native saddle stock of Tennessee accompanied the early settlers from Virginia. According to the best authorities, the breed represents an amalgamation of the Thoroughbred, Standardbred, Morgan, and American Saddlebred breeds, together with whatever else may have constituted the native stock. Thus, throughout a century or more of meticulous breeding, the Tennessee Walking Horse came to possess some of the endurance and upstanding qualities of the Thoroughbred, the substance and sturdiness of the Standardbred, the graceful lines and docility of the Morgan, and the style and beauty of the American Saddlebred.

The real patriarch, or foundation sire, of the Tennessee Walking Horse was a stallion known as *Allan F-1*, sometimes called *Black Allan* because of his color. This horse, of mixed Standardbred and Morgan ancestry, foaled in 1886, proved to be a progenitor of remarkable prepotency when crossed on native mares. Moreover, his offspring carried on. Thus, in many respects, the origin of the Tennessee Walking Horse is not unlike the development of the Morgan.

The Tennessee Walking Horse Breeders' and Exhibitors' Association was organized in 1935.

Fig. 10-56. Tennessee Walking Horse stallion, *Prides Genius*, a former World Junior Grand Champion, bred and owned by Harlinsdale Farm, Franklin, Tennessee. At the end of 1995, *Prides Genius* ranked third in the all-time sire rating of the Tennessee Walking Horse breed. (Courtesy, Harlinsdale Farm, Franklin, TN)

TENNESSEE WALKING HORSE CHARACTERISTICS

In comparison with the American Saddlebred, the average member of the Tennessee Walking Horse breed is larger, stouter, and more rugged. Also, it is plainer about the head, shorter necked, carries the head lower, and possesses more massiveness about the body and quarters. Although it has less style and elegance, the Tennessee Walking Horse excels the American Saddlebred when it comes to temperament and disposition. It has been referred to as the "gentleman of the equines."

The Tennessee Walking Horse averages around 15-2 hands in height and weighs from 1,000 to 1,200 lb. A great array of colors exists, including sorrel, chestnut, black, roan, white, bay, brown, gray, and golden. White markings on the feet and legs are common.

The three gaits characterizing the breed are all natural gaits. They are free and easy and are called the flat-footed walk, the running walk, and the canter. Particular emphasis is placed upon the running walk, an all-day gait which is executed at a speed of 6 to 8 miles per hour. It is started like the flat-footed walk and is a diagonally opposed foot movement. As the speed is increased, the hind foot usually oversteps the

front track from a few to as many as 18 inches. This gives the rider a gliding sensation.

ADAPTATION AND USE

Although the Tennessee Walking Horse arose as the business or plantation horse of Tennessee and the South, it is now largely a pleasure horse. Because of its gentle manner and easy gaits, it is an ideal horse for the amateur or the person who rides infrequently. The experienced equestrian, likewise, enjoys these same traits.

PRESENT STATUS OF THE BREED

Because of the many sterling qualities of the breed, especially its fine disposition and the easy-on-the-rider running walk, the Tennessee Walking Horse has established a wide niche for itself in the horse world.

THOROUGHBRED
(See Plates 4, 32, and 33)

The term *Thoroughbred* is applied properly only

to a breed of running racehorse developed originally in England. It should not be confused with nor used synonymously with the designation purebred, an adjective used to denote the pure lineage of any breed of livestock regardless of class or breed. Today, the Thoroughbred has become the equine synonym for speed and racing quality.

Part-Thoroughbreds may be registered in the American Remount Association Part Thoroughbred Stud Book, Inc., Middleburg, Virginia. It has seven different sections, with eligibility as given in Table VIII-1 of the Appendix of this book.

ORIGIN AND NATIVE HOME

The history of the Thoroughbred, as we think of it today, had its beginning in the 17th Century, though the Oriental lineage of the breed is as old as civilization itself. The nature of people being what it is, there was racing wherever there were horses. However, the real molding of the fleet light horse in England became a necessity with the shift from medieval warfare—in which the fighting unit consisted of a mounted knight in full armor—to the use of arrows and finally gunpowder. Speed and stamina became imperative. Simultaneously, interest in horse racing in England was greatly accelerated. As early as the reign of Henry VIII, a royal stud was established.

The real impetus to the development of a superior English running horse, however, had its beginning under Charles II, who reigned from 1660 to 1685. King Charles imported a number of outstanding Barb mares for the royal stable. Upon the descendants of this improved foundation stock were subsequently crossed 3 immortal stallions known respectively as: the *Byerly Turk*, imported in 1689; the *Darley Arabian*, imported in 1706; and the *Godolphin Arabian*, brought from Paris in 1724. From these three illustrious sires sprang three male lines: Matchem, tracing to the Godolphin Arabian; Eclipse, tracing to the Darley Arabian; and Herod, tracing to the Byerly Turk. Such was the development of the Thoroughbred, a breed predominantly of Arabian, Barb,[9] and Turk[10] extraction; though it may have in its veins the blood of the Galloway, Scotch Pony, and Highland Dun—animals used for cart or draft purposes, and "heaven only knows what else."

The first edition of the General (English) Stud Book was published in 1793.

---

[9]The Barbs were native to the Barbary States of northern Africa. They were more rugged than the Arabian but lacked the quality, refinement, and the beauty of the latter.

[10]The Turk horse was found chiefly in Anatola and only to a limited extent in Turkey. These animals were noted for docility and beauty, but they lacked the vigor and endurance of the Arabian.

EARLY AMERICAN IMPORTATIONS

The first Thoroughbred imported to America was the 21-year-old stallion, *Bulle Rock*, by *Darley Arabian* and out of a dam by *Byerly Turk*, arriving in Virginia in 1730. Governors Ogle and Sharpe of Maryland made subsequent importations between 1747 and 1755. The Revolution interrupted the growth of Thoroughbred breeding, but at its close the stream of importations was reestablished. New racetracks were built, and the breed became firmly entrenched in America.

All the U.S. Thoroughbreds are registered in the Jockey Club, established in 1894. Membership in the Club is by election. Consisting of about 95 members, it is probably the most exclusive club in the world.

THOROUGHBRED CHARACTERISTICS

Fig. 10-57. *Moscow Ballet*, a group III stakes-winning son of the great *Nijinsky II*, is a leading California sire standing at Harris Farms near Coalinga, California. His progeny have earned nearly $7,000,000, and he has sired four California champions. (Courtesy, David E. McGlothlin, Horse Division, Harris Farms, Coalinga, CA)

Thoroughbreds are bay, brown, chestnut, black, or, less frequently, gray in color. White markings on the face and legs are common. Animals of this breed range in height from 15 to 17 hands, with an average of around 16 hands. In racing trim, the Thoroughbred may weigh from 900 to 1,025 lb, whereas stallions in breeding condition may approach 1,400 lb.

The build of the Thoroughbred shows the speed type in the extreme. The body is long, deep chested, rather narrow, upstanding, and often a bit angular. This horse possesses a high degree of quality and refinement throughout. The head is small and well proportioned, with a straight face, small neat ear, and fine throttle. The shoulders and pastern are sloping, and the thigh and quarter are powerfully muscled. The temperament is active and energetic, being of the racy or highly nervous variety. The action of most Thoroughbreds is characterized by going low and pointed at the trot but executing the gallop or run to perfection.

ADAPTATION AND USE

As a running racehorse, the Thoroughbred is without a peer. Yet, it is noteworthy that a considerable number of Thoroughbreds foaled in the United States are never raced, and many that are raced never win.

Many excellent horses of straight- or part-Thoroughbred breeding have excelled as gaited saddle horses, stock horses, polo mounts, hunters, and cavalry mounts. No other breed of horses has found such diverse use and adaptation. Because of the almost incredible adaptation of the Thoroughbred and the use of its blood in producing new breeds, the breed has been referred to as the "essential oil of horse flesh."

It must be realized, however, that many of the new breeds that evolved from a Thoroughbred foundation have now reached such a high state of perfection that an outcross to the Thoroughbred might now be a step backward. Such is the status of the American Saddlebred, the Tennessee Walking Horse, and the Standardbred—when it comes to their respective performances as three- and five-gaited park hacks, plantation walking horses, and harness racers. But until other or new breeds become better adapted and more important, the blood of the Thoroughbred will continue to predominate in the production of polo mounts and hunters.

PRESENT STATUS OF THE BREED

Racing and the unquestioned value of the Thoroughbred for crossbreeding purposes, assure the breed a bright future.

About one-third of the nation's Thoroughbreds are bred in Kentucky.

THE MAN O' WAR STORY

Ask people on the street—people who may never have gone to a race—to name the greatest horse of all time and chances are that they'll say, Man O' War. If there is any absolute against which greatness in a horse may be measured, it is the legendary Man O' War. "Big Red," as he was known, seemed to have limitless speed. Only once in his 21 starts did his machine-like power fail to propel him first across the

Fig. 10-58. The legendary *Man O' War*, one of the greatest racehorses of all time. (Courtesy, the Jockey Club, New York, NY)

finish line; that was when he was beaten by the aptly named *Upset* at Saratoga on August 13, 1919, after an unfortunate start. As if to redress that wrong, *Man O' War* trounced *Upset* with authority the next three times they met. In 8 times of his 11 starts as a three-year-old, he broke either a track record or world's record.

Man O' War was born in 1917. Samuel D. Riddle bought him as a yearling at the Saratoga sale on August 17, 1918, for $5,000.

During his career, talented writers and eloquent speakers extolled him with such superlatives as "look of eagles" and "living flame." But it fell to his groom, Will Harbut, who had quite a way with words as well as with horses, to devise the most fitting description of all. "*Man O' War*," as Will never tired of telling the thousands who came to see him, "was the mostest horse that ever was." During his lifetime, more visitors went to see *Man O' War* than Mammoth Cave.

Physically, *Man O' War* was a glowing chestnut, almost red, standing 16 hands 1⅝ in. He measured 71¾ in. at the girth and weighed 1,100 lb in training. As a stallion, his weight reached 1,370 lb. He was unusually long bodied and powerfully muscled in the gaskins. Estimates of his stride varied anywhere from 25 to 28 ft, although, oddly enough, it was never officially measured.

When training, Big Red's morning came early. He was given his first meal at 3:30 a.m. At 7:30 a.m., he was brushed and massaged; the bandages that he wore at all times except when in action were removed, and his legs were washed; his face, eyes, and nostrils were sponged; and he was given a rubdown with a soft cloth. After work on warm days, he was washed; then he was rubbed thoroughly, his feet were cleaned and dressed, and he was left to rest in his stall. He was fond of his caretaker; he liked to snatch his hat and carry it around as he showed off for visitors.

Most Thoroughbred horses share a universal birthday—January 1. But Big Red was different! At Faraway Farms, near Lexington, where he spent most of his life, his actual foaling date, March 29, was duly observed as a special occasion. He received telegrams, carrots, and other tokens of recognition from all over the country.

The great horse, who was the first to command $5,000 service fee, was maintained largely for private use. He sired over 300 offspring who won over 1,200 races and earned more than $3.5 million.

Big Red died in 1947, at the age of 30, Ira Drymon, as the Thoroughbred Club's representative, delivered the eulogy before the 2,000 people assembled, and over a nationwide radio hookup. As taps were sounded and the mammoth coffin of polished oak containing the body of *Man O' War* was lowered to his final resting place, men, women and children wept unashamedly.

The *Man O' War* legend continues on, for he lived and died and won a lasting name and fame—a rare achievement by any beast, or human.

TRAKEHNER
(See Plate 31)

The Trakehner has gained popularity in the United States hand in hand with increased interest in combined training and dressage.

ORIGIN AND NATIVE HOME

The breed originated in Trakehner, East Prussia in 1732. It evolved from the blending of the indigenous Prussian horses, Thoroughbreds, and Arabians.

The American Trakehner Association was formed in September, 1974.

TRAKEHNER CHARACTERISTICS

Although the breeding goals have changed through the years to meet the needs of the time, generally speaking, the emphasis has been on the development of a horse with the size of the Thoroughbred, but more rugged and possessing the elegance of the Arabian.

ADAPTATION AND USE

The breed is superbly adapted to, and used for,

Fig. 10-59. Trakehner mare, *Mischka*, owned by Christian Guernon, Melbourne, Quebec. (Courtesy, American Trakehner Assn., Newark, OH)

dressage, combined training, and for jumper and hunter classes.

PRESENT STATUS OF THE BREED

The Trakehner is new to the United States. However, a bright future is predicted for this big, sound athlete and good-looking horse of quiet and sensible nature, particularly on the American horse show scene, in dressage and combined training, and in hunter and jumper classes.

WELARA PONY

The Welara Pony evolved from a Welsh X Arabian cross. It resembles a miniature coach horse.

ORIGIN AND NATIVE HOME

Although many equestrians have long admired Welsh X Arabian crossbreds, there was no breed registry to promote the stylish ponies resulting from this breeding. So, in 1981, a small group of horse fanciers, most of whom were either Welsh or Arabian breeders, joined together to form the Welara Pony Society; and on January 15, 1981, they officially opened the registry.

WELARA PONY CHARACTERISTICS

The Welara Pony resembles a miniature coach horse, except that it is more refined, and it has a higher

Fig. 10-60. Welara Pony mare, *Lady B*. (Courtesy, American Welara Pony Society, Yucca Valley, CA)

ably since Saxon times in England, these horses have ranged in bands, living a vagabond existence on the sparse vegetation. Under these conditions only the more rugged, thrifty, and agile animals survived. In more recent years, improvement has been wrought by annually rounding up the semiwild, nomadic bands and selecting the stallion leader for each.

EARLY AMERICAN IMPORTATIONS

The first Welsh Ponies to be imported to America of which there is record were 20 head brought over by George Brown of Aurora, Illinois. Subsequent, but infrequent, importations followed.

The Welsh Pony and Cob Society of America was established in 1907.

WELSH PONY CHARACTERISTICS

tail carriage, a more animated gait, and a more natural arched neck. Any color, except Appaloosa, is acceptable for registry. Welara Ponies range from 46 to 58 in. in height. The Welara is noted for its beauty.

ADAPTATION AND USE

The Welara is most commonly used for fine harness, English pleasure, halter, hunter, and native costume classes. Also the Welara has been hugely successful in competitive trail rides.

PRESENT STATUS OF THE BREED

The Welara Pony is a new breed with limited numbers. So, one of the main goals of the registry is to greatly increase the number of breeders and animals, followed by sponsoring more shows and events for Welara Ponies.

WELSH PONY AND COB
(See Plate 28)

The Welsh breed is especially recommended for use by older children who have outgrown the use of a Shetland—children up to 15 years of age.

ORIGIN AND NATIVE HOME

The Welsh is native to the rough mountainous country of Wales. Here for unknown generations, prob-

Fig. 10-61. Welsh Pony. (Courtesy, Welsh Pony and Cob Society of America, Winchester, VA)

Present-day Welsh Ponies are usually gray, roan, black, bay, brown, or chestnut; though cream, dun, and white colors are found. In fact, any color except piebald and skewbald is eligible for registry. Large white areas on the body are not accepted.

Representative animals range from 10 to 14 hands in height. In build, the modern Welsh Pony may be described as a miniature coach horse, being more upstanding than the Shetland. Individuals of this breed should possess good heads and necks, short coupling, plenty of muscling, and substance of bone; and with it all, there should be considerable speed and action at the trot and unusual endurance.

ADAPTATION AND USE

Welsh Ponies are unexcelled as advanced children's mounts, for riding by small adults, and for such other general purposes as are within their size limitations. Among their uses are: as roadsters, and for harness shows, racing, trail riding, parades, stock cutting, and hunting.

PRESENT STATUS OF THE BREED

Although it is not likely that great numbers of Welsh Ponies will ever be found in America, they will always fill a need. With the greater emphasis on physi-cal fitness, it is quite likely that present numbers in America will be increased.

The Welsh Pony and Cob Society of America maintains the following divisions, according to height stipulations:

1. **The Welsh Mountain Pony.** Section A of the Stud Book, for Welsh not exceeding 12-2 hands.
2. **The Welsh Pony.** Section B of the Stud Book, for Welsh not to exceed 14-2 hands.
3. **The Welsh Pony (Cob type) and the Welsh Cob.** Sections C and D of the Stud Book, respectively. Section C is for Welsh not exceeding 13-2 hands, without lower limit. Section D is for Welsh exceeding 13-2 hands with no upper limit on height.

SELECTED REFERENCES

Title of Publication	Author(s)	Publisher
America's Quarter Horses	P. Lavne	Doubleday & Company, Inc., Garden City, NY, 1973
Appaloosa	F. Haines	Amon Carter Museum of Western Art, Fort Worth, TX, 1963
Appaloosa Horse, The	F. Haines G. B. Hatley R. Peckinpah	R. G. Bailey Printing Company, Lewiston, ID, 1957
Arabian Horse Breeding	H. H. Reese	Borden Publishing Co., Los Angeles, CA, 1953
Breeding and Raising Horses, Ag. Hdbk. No. 394	M. E. Ensminger	Agricultural Research Service, USDA, Washington, DC, 1972
Breeds of Livestock, The	C. W. Gay	The Macmillan Company, New York, NY, 1918
Breeds of Livestock in America	H. W. Vaughan	R. G. Adams and Company, Columbus, OH, 1937
Foundation Sires of the American Quarter Horse	R. M. Denhart	University of Oklahoma Press, Norman, OK, 1976
History of Thoroughbred Racing in America	W. H. P. Robertson	Prentice-Hall, Inc., Englewood Cliffs, NJ, 1965
Horse America Made, The	L. Taylor	American Saddle Horse Breeders Association, Louisville, KY, 1944
Horse Industry Handbook	Staff	American Horse Council, Washington, DC, 1993
Horsemanship and Horse Care, Ag. Info. Bull. No. 353	M. E. Ensminger	Agricultural Research Service, USDA, Washington, DC, 1972
Horses, Their Selection, Care, and Handling	M. C. Self	A. S. Barnes & Co., Inc., New York, NY, 1943
Horses of Today	H. H. Reese	Wood & Jones, Pasadena, CA, 1956
Kellogg Arabians, The	H. H. Reese G. B. Edwards	Borden Publishing Co., Los Angeles, CA, 1958

King Ranch Quarter Horses, The	R. M. Denhardt	University of Oklahoma Press, Norman, OK, 1978
Light Horse Breeds, The	J. W. Patten	A. S. Barnes & Co., Inc., New York, NY, 1960
Light Horses, Farmers' Bull. No. 2127	M. E. Ensminger	U.S. Department of Agriculture, Washington, DC, 1965
Modern Breeds of Livestock, Fourth Edition	H. M. Briggs D. M. Briggs	The Macmillan Company, New York, NY, 1980
Morgan Horse Handbook, The	J. Mellin	Stephen Green Press, Brattleboro, VT, 1973
Pinto, The		Yearbook and Studbook of the Pinto Horse Association of America, 1958–59
Shetland Pony, The	L. F. Bedell	The Iowa State University Press, Ames, IA, 1959
Shetland Pony, The	M. C. Cox	Adam & Charles Black, London, England, 1965
Stockman's Handbook, The, Seventh Edition	M. E. Ensminger	Interstate Publishers, Inc., Danville, IL, 1992
Study of Breeds, The	T. Shaw	Orange Judd Company, New York, NY, 1912
Types and Breeds of Farm Animals	C. S. Plumb	Ginn and Company, Boston, MA, 1920
World Dictionary of Breeds, Types, and Varieties of Livestock, A, Third Edition	I. L. Mason	Commonwealth Agricultural Bureaux, Farnham House, Farnham Royal, Slough, Bucks, England, 1988
World of Pinto Horses, A	Ed. by R. D. Greene	The Pinto Horse Association of America, San Diego, CA, 1970

Also, breed literature pertaining to each breed may be secured by writing to the respective breed registry associations (see Sec. VIII, Appendix, for the name and address of each association).

11

BREEDS OF DRAFT HORSES; JACKS AND DONKEYS

A finely trained mule jumping without use of a bridle. (Courtesy, The American Donkey and Mule Society, Denton, TX)

Today, the pure breeds of draft horses are primarily of historical interest. Nevertheless, it is noteworthy that registration numbers have increased in recent years, reflecting nostalgia rather than energy shortage. For those registry associations active and reporting, Table 11-1 shows the registration numbers of draft horses by breeds in 1994, and in total registrations since the respective breed registries were formed.

The breeds of draft horses here considered are the American Cream Draft Horse, Belgian, Clydesdale, Percheron, Shire, and Suffolk. Regardless of the distinct breed trademarks and the virtues ascribed to each breed, all are characterized by great massiveness—their adapted field of utility being the drawing of heavy loads at a comparatively slow gait, usually at the walk.

Power rather than speed is desired. In order to possess this power, draft horses should be blocky or compact, low set or short legged, and sufficiently heavy to enable them to throw the necessary weight into the collar to move a heavy load and at the same time maintain a secure footing. This calls for horses around 16 to 17 hands in height and weighing not less than 1,600 lb.

All of the modern draft breeds of horses, regardless of color or breed or later infusions of other breeding, rest upon a Flemish foundation—the large, coarse, black, hairy, and sluggish horse which, from a very early time, existed in the low-lying sections of what is now Belgium, France, Holland, and Germany. Thus, the draft breeds were of European origin, whereas the light horse breeds were of Oriental extraction.

Battle chariots, drawn by heavy horses and used to convey armored troops who fought on foot, were encountered by the Roman legions under Caesar when he invaded England in the year 55 B.C. Later, these ponderous beasts, imposing in height and bulk, were known as the Great Horses of the Middle Ages.

These animals were the cavalry mounts of the heavily armored knights when they rode forth to battle for king and country, and at times to enforce their views of religion upon unbelievers in general and Mohammedans in particular. They had to be large and powerful in order to carry the immense weight of their riders, their arms, and their armor—including eventually the armor of both the horse and the rider. Often the combined weight of their load was up to 450 lb.

Finally, in the 19th Century, when the use of armor in warfare was abandoned after invention and adoption of gunpowder by the fighting nations and when the development of agriculture and commerce received new impetus, the Great Horse served as the foundation for the draft breeds as we know them today. Lighter horses came into use for riding and the Great Horse was relegated to pulling the cart and the plow and to hauling timber, coal, and other industrial materials.

RELATIVE POPULARITY OF BREEDS OF DRAFT HORSES

Table 11-1 shows the 1994 and total registrations to date of the various breeds of draft horses and classes of jacks/donkeys/mules, as reported by those breed registries that were active and responded at that time. As noted, the draft registry associations are doing little business.

TABLE 11-1
ANNUAL AND TOTAL REGISTRATIONS
OF DRAFT HORSES, JACKS, DONKEYS, AND MULES
IN U.S. BREED ASSOCIATIONS

Breed	Annual (1994 or 1995) Registrations	Total Registrations Since Breed Registry Started
Belgian	3,400	150,000
Percheron	2,100	275,300
Shire	562	11,400
Clydesdale	407	15,000
Suffolk	80	3,766
American Cream Draft Horse	18	94
Miniature Donkeys	1,516	18,855
American Donkeys	771	
Mules	172	1,950
Race Mules	24	—
Spotted Asses	116	1,208

AMERICAN CREAM DRAFT HORSE
(See Plate 36)

This is a relatively new breed, which originated in the United States

ORIGIN AND NATIVE HOME

The American Cream Draft Horse is unique because it is the only draft breed to originate in the United States. The breed descended from a mare of unknown ancestry, in central Iowa during the early part of the twentieth century. Offspring of this cream-colored, foundation mare were mated to animals of the established draft breeds, thereby increasing numbers and improving the type and quality while retaining the cream color.

About 1935, a few men began linebreeding and inbreeding with the objective of establishing a distinct breed. In 1944, the American Cream Horse Association was organized and granted a charter by the State of Iowa. In 1950, the breed was recognized by the Iowa Department of Agriculture.

AMERICAN CREAM DRAFT HORSE CHARACTERISTICS

The distinguishing characteristic of the breed is the color, which is cream, with white mane and tail, pink skin, and amber eyes (foals are born with nearly

Fig. 11-1. American Cream Draft Horse stallion, *ClarAnn Dick*, owned by ClarAnn Farms, Charles City, Iowa. (Courtesy, American Cream Draft Horse Assn., Charles City, IA)

white eyes, which darken and turn to amber at maturity). Some white markings are considered desirable.

The American Cream Draft Horse is classified as a medium draft breed. At maturity, mares weigh 1,600 to 1,800 lb, and stallions from 1,800 to 2,000 lb. Animals of the breed are noted for their good dispositions.

PRESENT STATUS OF THE BREED

Although limited in numbers, this unique American-created draft breed is registered and promoted by the American Cream Draft Horse Association, 2065 Noble Avenue, Charles City, IA 50616-9108.

BELGIAN

The Belgian breed made marked progress in this country, considering that so few animals were imported prior to the beginning of the 20th Century. Belgian stallions were especially valuable in improving the draftiness of the native stock on which they were crossed.

ORIGIN AND NATIVE HOME

The Belgian breed originated in Belgium, from which country it derives its name. The agricultural needs of this low-lying country were such as to require a horse of size and bulk. So far as is known, no Oriental blood was fused with the native stock. Thus, it may be concluded that the Belgian breed is directly and exclusively descended from the old Flemish ancestry—indigenous to the country of its origin. Even today, the great massiveness of the Belgian breed more nearly resembles the Flemish horse than does any other breed.

The Belgian Draft Horse Society was founded in 1886. In their native country, the breeding of Belgians was promoted by the government, which annually awarded prizes and subsidies to the best animals in the various provinces. Also, stallions that stood for public service had to be approved by a commission appointed by the government.

EARLY AMERICAN IMPORTATIONS

The first importation of the Belgian to the United States was made in 1886 by Dr. A. G. Van Hoorebeke of Monmouth, Illinois, but the breed attracted little attention until 1900. Thus, the introduction of the breed was more recent than that of the Percheron, Clydes-

dale, and Shire. Despite their late entry into this country, however, Belgians gave a good account of themselves.

The American Association of Importers and Breeders of Belgian Draft Horses was organized in 1887. In 1937, the name of the registry was changed to the Belgian Draft Horse Corporation of America.

BELGIAN CHARACTERISTICS

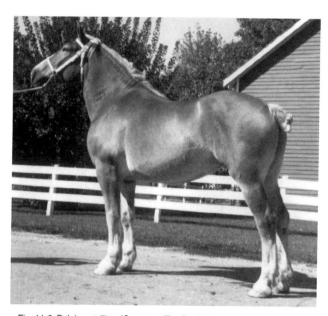

Fig. 11-2. Belgian stallion. (Courtesy, *The Draft Horse Journal*, Waverly, IA)

Bay, chestnut, and roan are the most common colors, but browns, grays, and blacks are occasionally seen. Many Belgians have flaxen manes and tails and white-blazed faces. Mature stallions stand from 15-2 to 17 hands in height and weigh 1,900 to 2,200 lb, or more.

The Belgian is noted for its draftiness—being the widest, deepest, most compact, most massive, and lowest set of any draft breed. Formerly, the breed was likely to be severely criticized for having small round hoofs, round bones, short thick necks, and lack of refinement. But it is to the everlasting credit of the American breeders that these defects have been largely overcome.

The Belgian is extremely quiet, docile, and patient. The action is powerful, though less springy and high than found in the Clydesdale and Percheron. Because of their great width in front, many Belgians roll or paddle somewhat.

PRESENT STATUS OF THE BREED

The Belgian breed is registered and promoted by the Belgian Draft Horse Corporation of America, P.O. Box 335, Wabash, IN 46992. Currently, the annual registration of Belgians is the highest of the draft breeds (see Table 11-1).

CLYDESDALE
(See Plate 38)

Like all classes and breeds of livestock of Scotch origin—including Ayrshire, Aberdeen-Angus, Galloway, and Highland cattle, and Cheviot and Black-faced Highland sheep—the Clydesdale breed of horses is distinctive for style, beauty, and action.

ORIGIN AND NATIVE HOME

This Scotch breed of draft horses derives its name from the valley of the River Clyde, an area popularly known as Clydesdale, located in the County of Lanark, Scotland.

The breed is of mixed origin, and the early history is more or less obscure. It is probable that the blood of both Flemish and English horses entered quite largely into the breed during its early formative period. Rather frequent importations of horses of Flemish extraction from England and the low countries were made, thus giving the Scotch Clydesdale and the English Shire and Suffolk similar ancestry. However, the breeders in the respective countries had very different notions as to what constituted a desirable draft animal, and their selections were governed accordingly, the Scotch placing particular emphasis upon style and action.

The British breed registry, known as the Clydesdale Horse Society of Great Britain and Ireland, was established in 1877.

EARLY AMERICAN IMPORTATIONS

The first Clydesdales brought to North America were probably imported into Canada by the Scotch who settled there. Beginning in the early 1870s, Clydesdales were imported into the United States, both via Canada and direct from Scotland. The American Clydesdale Horse Association was organized in 1879.

CLYDESDALE CHARACTERISTICS

The Clydesdale is not so heavy as the Shire,

Fig. 11-3. Clydesdale stallion, *THV Jaster*, owned by Jim and Betty Groves, Pecatonica, Illinois. (Courtesy, Clydesdale Breeders' Assn. of the United States, Pecatonica, IL)

Belgian, or Percheron. Average representatives of the breed are also more rangy and lack the width and compactness of the other draft breeds. Mature stallions in average condition weigh from 1,700 to 1,900 lb and stand from 16 to 17 hands in height.

No other breed of draft horses equals the Clydesdale in style and action. The breed is noted for a prompt walk, with a good snappy stride and a short trot, and the hocks are well flexed and carried close together. Good, clean, flat bone; well-set, fairly long and sloping pasterns; and a moderate amount of fine feather or long hair at the rear of the legs below the knees and hocks is characteristic. Sometimes, in America, the breed has been criticized for lack of width and depth of body and for having too much feather and too much white. Usually, Americans do not fancy too much white on the face and legs in any breed of horses, and they object to the feather or long hair about the fetlocks because of the difficulty in keeping the legs and feet free from mud and snow. Bay and brown with white markings are the most characteristic colors, but blacks, grays, chestnuts, and roans are occasionally seen.

For show use in a six-horse hitch on the tanbark, a well-matched, carefully trained, and expertly handled hitch of Clydesdales is unexcelled. Their flowing white fetlocks and high action give them a picturesque appearance.

PRESENT STATUS OF THE BREED

The Clydesdale breed is registered and promoted

by the Clydesdale Breeders of the U.S.A., 17378 Kelley Road, Pecatonica, IL 61063)

PERCHERON
(See Plate 39)

During the draft horse era, the Percheron was the most widely distributed of all draft breeds.

ORIGIN AND NATIVE HOME

The Percheron horse originated in northwestern France, in the ancient district of La Perche, an area about one-fifteenth the size of the state of Iowa. The native stock was primarily of Flemish extraction upon which there was a subsequent and rather liberal infusion of Arab blood.

Although early records are lacking, it is known that with the defeat of the Saracens (the Moors from North Africa) at Tours and Poitiers, France, in 732 A.D. by Charles Martel, the Arab, Barb, and Turk horses upon which the Moors were mounted—mostly stallions as was the custom of the day—fell into the hands of the Franks and were eventually distributed throughout the country. The successful Crusaders of the 12th, 13th, and 14th Centuries also brought back stallions as spoils of war from Palestine, and this again furnished a direct, though unplanned, infusion of Oriental blood. Thus, on a coldblood base, the Flemish horse, repeated top crosses of Oriental blood were made. Finally, in about 1870, a systematic effort was made to transform the mixture into a true type. Eventually, the Percheron breed evolved, and the Percheron Society of France was organized in 1883.

EARLY AMERICAN IMPORTATIONS

American importations of Percherons began about 1840, but it was not until the early 1850s that any great numbers came over. *Brilliant 1271*, a black stallion foaled in 1877 and imported in 1881, is recognized as the most famous and prepotent animal of the breed ever imported. Other importations followed, and the center of interest in the breed came to be located in the Corn Belt.

The United States breed registry, originally known as the Percheron-Norman Horse Association, was formed in 1876, seven years earlier than its counterpart in France.

PERCHERON CHARACTERISTICS

Fig. 11-4. Percheron mare, *Blue Ribbon Farms Garnet*, foaled April 30, 1993, owned by Albert and Karen Cleve, Farmington, Missouri. (Courtesy, Percheron Horse Assn. of America, Fredericktown, OH)

Most commonly, Percherons are black or gray (the latter being a probable Arab inheritance); but bays, browns, chestnuts, and roans are occasionally seen. Fully 90%, however, are black or gray.

Mature stallions stand from 16-1 to 16-3 hands in height and weigh from 1,900 to 2,100 lb. In size, the Percheron is intermediate between the larger Shire and Belgian and the smaller Clydesdale and Suffolk. In comparison with other draft breeds, the Percheron is noted for its handsome, clean-cut head; good action (being surpassed in style and action only by the Clydesdale); excellent temperament; and longevity.

PRESENT STATUS OF THE BREED

Presently, the breed is being registered and promoted by the Percheron Horse Association of America, P.O. Box 141, Fredericktown, OH 43019-0141.

SHIRE

England originated and developed two breeds of draft horses, the Shire and the Suffolk. Originally, the Shire was known by various names, such as the Great Horse, War Horse, Cart Horse, Old English Black Horse, Lincolnshire Cart Horse, etc.

ORIGIN AND NATIVE HOME

The Shire breed was originated on the low, marshy

Fig. 11-5. Robert Bakewell (1726–1795), English livestock breeder. He contributed greatly to the improvement of the Shire. (Obtained for the author by Sir John Hammond from the Royal Agricultural Society of England)

EARLY AMERICAN IMPORTATIONS

Shire horses were first imported to London, Ontario, Canada, in 1836. A gray stallion, known as *Columbus*, was imported to Massachusetts prior to 1844. Small scattered importations followed, but no great numbers came over until 1880. In 1885, the American Shire Breeders' Association was organized. Two years later, in 1887, more than 400 Shires were imported. Very early, horse breeders became aware of the fact that Shire stallions were unsurpassed in their ability to beget draft horses from mares lacking in size and bone.

SHIRE CHARACTERISTICS

Fig. 11-6. Shire stallion, *Admergill Prince*. (Courtesy, The American Shire Horse Assn., Davis, CA)

lands of east central England, particularly in Lincolnshire and Cambridgeshire; hence, comes the name *Shire*.

The great size and bulk of this breed are derived directly from the Great Horse of the Middle Ages, of which Shires are held to be the nearest living reproductions. As previously indicated, the Great Horse was in turn descended from the ponderous black Flemish horse which existed in Great Britain long before the Christian era, more than 2,000 years ago.

In the year 1066, England was conquered by an army of Normans led by William the Conqueror. This marked the beginning of improvement in the native draft stock of England. Importations of horses followed from France, Germany, and the low countries. Centuries later, Robert Bakewell (1726–1795), known as the first great improver of livestock, contributed to the further improvement of the Shire—as well as to that of Leicester sheep and Longhorn cattle. Bakewell imported from Holland several mares which were mated to native stallions, and selected and perpetuated the better offspring therefrom. During Bakewell's era, the Shire was molded as a draft horse for agriculture and commerce, the use of armor in warfare having been abandoned. Thus, the development and improvement of the Shire breed antedate that of any other breed of draft horses.

The Shire Horse Society of England was organized in 1878. In addition to recording the lineage of animals, it, along with the livestock shows of England, did much to improve the Shire horse.

Today, Shires are much larger horses than their ancestors that were used by the mounted warriors of old. They are equaled in weight only by the Belgian. Shire stallions in fair condition weighing 2,000 lb or over are comparatively common. In height, representatives of this breed stand from 16 to 17-2 hands. They are less compact or more rangy than the Belgian and taller than any other draft breed.

In the formative period of the breed, it was faulted for its heavy bone, feather, lack of quality and refinement, shelly-textured hoofs, sluggish temperament, and excessive white markings; but breeders made marked progress in overcoming these objections.

The common colors are bay, brown, and black with white markings; although grays, chestnuts, and roans are occasionally seen.

PRESENT STATUS OF THE BREED

Presently, the breed is being registered and promoted by The American Shire Horse Association, 35380 County Road 31, Davis, CA 95616. The American Shire Horse Association registered 123 horses in 1995 and it has registered about 2,400 horses since the formation of the breed registry in 1885.

SUFFOLK

The Suffolk is unique among draft breeds in that (1) it was developed exclusively as a farm workhorse and not for use on city streets, and (2) all animals of the breed are chestnut in color, this color being recessive. Often the breed is referred to as the Suffolk Punch, a name descriptive of the *punched-up* conformation of the old-fashioned animals of this breed.

ORIGIN AND NATIVE HOME

The native home of the Suffolk is in the county of Suffolk, on the eastern coast of England, bordering the North Sea. The origin of the breed is unknown, but horses of similar characteristics are known to have existed in Suffolk for many centuries. Although proof is lacking, it is claimed that Norman stallions were crossed on native mares of Suffolk County 500 years ago. Also, it has been conjectured that the chestnut color of the breed is due to a cross with Norwegian horses brought in by the early Norse invaders. It is known, however, that from a very early period these animals were produced in Suffolk by farmers and for farming purposes. It is said that every well-bred Suffolk of today is descended from a bright colored chestnut stallion foaled in 1768, and owned by a Mr. Crisp of Ufford.

The Suffolk Horse Society of Great Britain published the first volume of the Suffolk Stud Book in 1880.

EARLY AMERICAN IMPORTATIONS

Suffolks were first imported into the United States in the early 1880s, followed by limited subsequent importations. They were never available in large numbers, the area devoted to their production being rather limited and there being an active demand for them at home and in the British Dominions.

The American Suffolk Horse Association was formed in 1911.

SUFFOLK CHARACTERISTICS

Fig. 11-7. Suffolk mare, *Lil' Wonder*, owned by Sarah Fryer/Bob Oswald, Monroe, Washington. (Courtesy, American Suffolk Horse Assn., Ledbetter, TX)

The Suffolk is smaller than other drafters. Average animals weigh from 1,600 to 1,800 lb and range in height from 15-2 to 16-2 hands. Occasionally, a mature stallion may weigh 2,000 lb or more, but such weight is not characteristic of the breed.

Suffolk horses are always chestnut in color, varying from light to dark, often with cream-colored mane and tail. When white markings occur, they are likely to be unobtrusive. Aside from color, the distinguishing characteristics of the breed include their close-to-the-ground and chunky build, smooth rotund form, and clean-boned leg devoid of the feather characteristic of the other two British draft breeds.

Although small in size, the Suffolk is celebrated for courage and willingness to work, and excellent disposition. The story goes that in their native land the courage and strength of Suffolk horses was often tested by contests involving the hitching of individual animals or teams to an immovable object, such as a tree—with the winner being determined by the number of efforts the animal or animals made in throwing themselves into the collar and pulling with all their might at the command.

The Suffolk never gained wide popularity in this country, primarily because of lack of size and lightness of bone.

PRESENT STATUS OF THE BREED

Presently, the breed is being registered and promoted by the American Suffolk Horse Association, 4240 Goehring Road, Ledbetter, Texas.

ASSES

Biologists designate the ass as *Equus asinus*; the horse as *Equus caballus*. The males of the ass family are known as jacks; the females as jennets. Compared with the horse, the ass is smaller; has shorter hairs on the mane and tail; does not possess the chestnuts on the inside of the hind legs; has much longer ears; has smaller, deeper hoofs; possesses a louder and more harsh voice, called a bray; is less subject to founder or injury; is more hardy and has a longer gestation period—jennets carry their young about 12 months. Small asses are commonly called donkeys or burros.

BREEDS OF ASSES

Currently, the following breeds of asses are recognized and registered in the United States:

Mammoth
Standard (and Large Standard)
Miniature Donkey
Mules
Race Mules

All five of the breeds of asses listed above are registered by The American Donkey and Mule Society, Inc., 2901 North Elm Street, Denton, TX 76201, which was founded in 1967. Its simple registry rules are: (1) AI and embryo transfer allowed; (2) no stipulations relative to marking or identifying animals; and (3) animals with ¼ in. or more overshot or undershot jaw (bite), and jacks over age two with one testicle retained, or both testicles retained (a cryptorchid), are disqualified for registry.

The American Donkey and Mule Society publishes *The Brayer Magazine*, which goes to the membership quarterly.

MAMMOTH

Mammoth is the largest of the ass breeds. Jacks should be 56 in. high and up; and jennets should be 54 in. and up. Mammoth jacks are crossed on draft horse mares to produce draft mules.

Mammoth has its own breed registry, which is:

American Mammoth Jack Stock Registry
6513 W. Laurel Road
London, KY 40741

Fig. 11-8. Mammoth jennet, owned by Brigitte A. Lange, Sulphur Run Farm, Elk Horn, Kentucky. (Courtesy, The American Donkey and Mule Society, Denton, TX)

Fig. 11-9. Draft mule, owned by Dr. Gary Potter. (Courtesy, The American Donkey and Mule Society, Denton, TX)

Also, Mammoth can be registered in The American Donkey and Mule Society, Inc., 2901 North Elm Street, Denton, TX 76201

The Mammoth breed is a blend of several breeds of jack stock originally imported into the United States in the 1800s from Southern Europe, mostly from the area bordering on the Mediterranean. The imported breeds included: Catalonian, Andalusian, Majorica, Maltese, Poitou, and Italian. The best foundation sire brought to the United States was a jack named *Mammoth*, imported from Catalonia, Spain in 1819; this accounts for the name *Mammoth* being given to the largest and best bred breed of the ass family in the United States.

STANDARD (and Large Standard)

Standard jacks range from 36 to 48 in. tall; and Large Standards from 48 to 56 in. tall. Standard jacks are crossed on small mares and ponies to produce mules for driving and pets. Large Standard jacks are used to produce riding mules. Standard and Large Standard jacks and jennets may be registered in The American Donkey and Mule Society, Inc., 2101 North Elm Street, Denton, TX 76201, which was established in 1967.

MINIATURE DONKEY

The Miniature Donkey Registry of the United States was established in 1958. The original breed registry was for donkeys 36 in. or under. They have

Fig. 11-10. *Snow White*, white miniature jennet, owned by Elain Spear, Miami, Florida. (Courtesy, The American Donkey and Mule Society, Denton, TX)

the patience of Job; hence, they make great pets for children.

MULES

The American Mule Registry was established by The American Donkey and Mule Society, Inc., 2101 North Elm Street, Denton, TX 76201, in 1967. It registers the following mule breeds:

Draft, from draft type mares
Pack and work, from large work type mares
Saddle, from riding type mares
Miniature, up to 50 in. tall, from pony and
  miniature mares

(Also see Chapter 9, Types and Classes of Work Horses and Mules, the section on "Mules.")

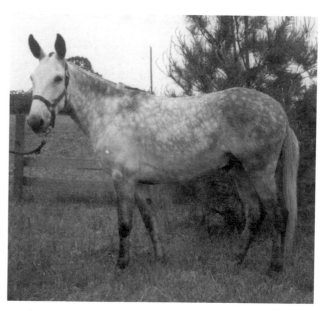

Fig. 11-11. Saddle mule, owned by Dean Hudson, Asheboro, North Carolina. (Courtesy, The American Donkey and Mule Society, Denton, TX)

RACE MULES

In 1995, The American Mule Registry was established by The American Donkey and Mule Society, Inc., 2101 North Elm Street, Denton, TX 76201, established a registry for race mules. In 1994, they registered 24 race mules.

SPOTTED ASSES

Spotted asses, *Equus asinus*, share a common origin and domestication with all donkeys, which is detailed in Chapter 1, under the heading "Origin and Domestication of the Donkey." However, Spotted

Asses, characterized by being spotted, are an American creation. In 1995, 116 Spotted Asses were registered, bringing the current registered numbers to 1,208. Spotted Asses are registered by the American Council of Spotted Asses, Inc., Box 121, New Melle, MO 63355.

Fig. 11-12. Two-month-old Spotted Jack, Large Standard/Mammoth breeding. (Courtesy, Coreen Eaton, Wxicof Wooly Woods, 914 Riske Lane, Wentzville, MO 63385)

SELECTED REFERENCES

Title of Publication	Author(s)	Publisher
Draft Horse Handbook, EB 1135	L. C. Luce J. B. Johnson	Washington State University, Pullman, WA, 1982
History of American Jacks and Mules	F. C. Mills	Hutch-Line, Inc., Hutchinson, KS, 1971
History of the Percheron Horse, A	A. H. Sander W. Dinsmore	Breeder's Gazette, Sanders Publishing Co., Chicago, IL, 1917
Horse Industry Directory	Staff	American Horse Council, Washington, DC, 1996
Modern Breeds of Livestock, Fourth Edition	H. M. Briggs D. M. Briggs	Macmillan Publishing Co., Inc., New York, NY, 1980
People with Long Ears	R. Borwick	Cassell & Company Ltd., London, England, 1970
Percheron Horse, The	M. C. Weld	O. Judd Co., New York, NY, 1886
World Dictionary of Livestock Breeds	I. L. Mason	C-A-B International, Wallingford, Oxon, U.K., 1988

12

BREEDING HORSES

Being born and born alive is the first essential of horse breeding. This shows a newborn Hungarian foal taking the first faltering steps. (Photo by Ernst Peterson. Courtesy, Bitteroot Stock Farm, Hamilton, MT)

Horses will continue to be bred so long as they (1) provide recreation and sport, and (2) serve the livestock industry of the West. It is important, therefore, that both the student and the progressive equestrian be familiar with the breeding of horses.

PART I.
SOME PRINCIPLES OF HORSE GENETICS

Nature ordained that genetics be applied to horse breeding long before there were geneticists. Prior to the domestication of horses, there was natural selection for speed and stamina because one of the most important defense mechanisms of the horse was to

Fig. 12-1. Standardbred mares and foals on pasture at Winback Farm, Chesapeake City, Maryland. (Courtesy, The United States Trotting Assn., Columbus, OH)

outrun his enemies. Natural selection was probably very effective in improving speed and endurance since the slower horses were eliminated by their enemies. To the extent that faster horses were speedy because of the genes that they carried, each succeeding generation would average faster than the previous generation because many of the slower horses would not have become parents.

It is noteworthy, too, that through the years, many horse breeders have been practicing genetics as they concerned themselves with the art of breeding, even though they may not have been cognizant of it. Their guiding concept of heredity was that "like begets like." That the application of this principle over a long period of time has been effective in modifying horse types becomes evident from a comparison of present-day horses. Thus, the speed of the modern Thoroughbred—coupled with his general lithe, angular build and nervous temperament—is in sharp contrast to the slow, easy gaits and the docility of the Missouri Fox Trotting Horse. Yet, there is good and substantial evidence to indicate that both breeds descended from a common ancestry. Because of the diversity of genes carried by the original parent stock, it has been possible, through selection, to evolve with two distinct breeds—one highly adapted to fast running at extended distances and the other to a slow gait. Also, through selection accompanied by planned matings, this same parent stock has been altered into horses especially adept as hunters, jumpers, stock horses, polo mounts, three- and five-gaited park hacks, harness racehorses, etc.

Eighteenth century breeders made a tremendous contribution in pointing the way toward horse improvement before Mendel's laws became known to the world in the early part of the 20th century. As knowledge of genetics developed, there evolved an understanding of the science that underlies the art of horse breeding.

The application of the science of genetics to the art of breeding proceeded rather rapidly in cattle, sheep, swine, and poultry. But, for many years, no such progress was made in the application of science to the art of horse breeding. As a result, little scientific work was done on the genetics of the horse. Today, this situation is being righted. The art and the science of horse breeding are being brought together; bridges are being established between those on the scientific side and those on the art side. With the experiences of the earlier horse breeders to guide us, along with our present knowledge of genetics and physiology of reproduction, progress should now be much more certain and rapid. In the past, horse breeding has been an art. In the future, it is destined to be both an art and a science.

SOME FUNDAMENTALS OF HEREDITY IN HORSES

The author has no intention of covering all of the diverse field of genetics and animal breeding. Rather, he will present a condensation of a few of the known facts in regard to the field and briefly summarize their application to horses.

Obviously, heredity in horses is identical in principle with that in other farm animals and humans. Because of the difficulty in conducting breeding experiments with horses (due to their greater cost, slower reproductive rate, etc.), however, less applied knowledge of genetics is available in the equine field. Also, it is fully recognized that such systems of breeding as inbreeding and grading up are seldom deliberately planned and followed in horse breeding; yet the enlightened horse breeder should be fully informed relative to them.

THE GENE AS THE UNIT OF HEREDITY

Genes determine all the hereditary characteristics of animals, from the body type to the color of the hair. They are truly the fundamental unit of genetics.

The bodies of animals are made up of millions or even billions of tiny cells, microscopic in size. Each cell contains a nucleus in which there are a number of pairs of bundles, called chromosomes. In turn, the chromosomes carry pairs of minute particles, called genes, which are the basic hereditary material. The nucleus of each body cell of horses contains 32 pairs of chromosomes,[1] or a total of 64, whereas there are perhaps thousands of pairs of genes. These genes determine all the hereditary characteristics of living animals. Thus, inheritance goes by units rather than by blending of two fluids, as our grandfathers thought.

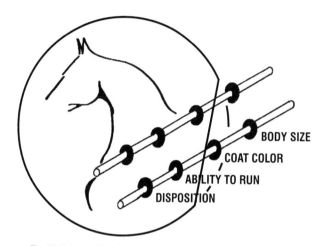

Fig. 12-2. A pair of bundles, called chromosomes, carrying minute particles, called genes. The genes determine all the hereditary characteristics of living animals, from length of leg to body size. (Drawing by Prof. R. F. Johnson)

The modern breeder knows that the job of transmitting qualities from one generation to the next is performed by the germ cells—a sperm from the male and an ovum or egg from the female. All animals, therefore, are the result of the union of two such tiny cells, one from each of its parents. These two germ cells contain the basis of all the anatomical, physiological, and psychological characters that the offspring will inherit.

In the body cells of an animal, each of the chromosomes is duplicated; whereas in the formation of the sex cells, the egg and the sperm, a reduction division occurs and only one chromosome and one gene of each pair goes into a sex cell. This means that only half the number of chromosomes and genes present in the body cells of the animal go into each egg and sperm, but each sperm or egg cell has genes for every characteristic of its species. As will be explained later, the particular half that any one germ cell

---

[1]Cattle have 60 chromosomes; sheep have 54; and swine have 40.

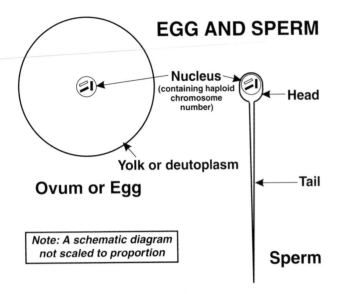

EGG AND SPERM

Nucleus
(containing haploid
chromosome
number)

Head

Yolk or deutoplasm

Ovum or Egg

Tail

*Note: A schematic diagram
not scaled to proportion*

Sperm

Fig. 12-3. Egg and sperm. The parent germ cells, the egg from the female and the sperm from the male, unite and transmit to the offspring all the characters that it will inherit.

gets is determined by chance. When mating and fertilization occur, the single chromosomes from the germ cell of each parent unite to form new pairs, and the genes are again present in duplicate in the body cells of the embryo.

With all possible combinations in 32 pairs of chromosomes (the species number in horses) and the genes that they bear, any stallion or mare can transmit over one billion different samples of its own inheritance; and the combination from both parents make possible one billion times one billion genetically different offspring. It is not strange, therefore, that no two animals within a given breed (except identical twins from a single egg split after fertilization) are exactly alike. Rather, we can marvel that the members of a given breed bear as much resemblance to each other as they do.

Even between such closely related individuals as full sisters, it is possible that there will be quite wide differences in size, growth rate, temperament, conformation, speed, and in almost every conceivable character. Admitting that many of these differences may be due to undetected differences in environment, it is still true that in such animals much of the variation is due to hereditary differences. A stallion, for example, will sometimes transmit to one offspring much better inheritance than he does to most of his get, simply as the result of chance distribution of the genes that go to different sperm at the time of the reproductive division. Such differences in inheritance in offspring have been called both the hope and the despair of the livestock breeder.

If an animal gets similar determiners or genes

from each parent, it will in turn produce a uniform set of offspring,[2] because any half of its inheritance is just like any other half. For example, regardless of what combination of chromosomes go into a particular germ cell, it will be just like any other egg or sperm from the same individual. Such animals are referred to as being homozygous. Unfortunately, few, if any, of our animals are in this pure hereditary state at the present time; instead of being homozygous, they are quite heterozygous. This explains why there may be such wide variation within the offspring of any given sire or dam. The wise and progressive breeder recognizes this fact, and insists upon the production records of all get rather than those of just a few meritorious individuals.

Variations between the offspring of animals that are not pure or homozygous is not to be marveled at, but is rather to be expected. No one would expect to draw exactly 20 sound apples and 10 rotten ones every time a random sample of 30 was taken from a barrel containing 40 sound ones and 20 rotten ones, although on the average—if enough samples were drawn—about that proportion of each could be expected. Individual drawings would of course vary rather widely. Exactly the same situation applies to the relative numbers of good and bad genes that may be present in different germ cells from the same animal. Because of this situation, the mating of a mare with a fine track record to a stallion that on the average transmits relatively good performance will not always produce a foal of a merit equal to that of its parents. The foal could be markedly poorer than the parents or, happily, it could in some cases be better than either parent.

Selection and closebreeding are the tools through which the horse breeder may obtain stallions and mares whose chromosomes and genes contain similar hereditary determiners—animals that are genetically more homozygous.

GENES SELDOM CHANGE

Gene changes are technically known as mutations. A mutation may be defined as *a sudden variation which is later passed on through inheritance and which results from changes in a gene or genes.* Not only are mutations rare, but they are prevailingly harmful. For all practical purposes, therefore, the genes can be thought of as unchanged from one generation to the next. The observed differences between animals are usually due to different combinations of genes being present rather than to mutations. Each gene probably changes only about once in each 100,000 to 1,000,000 animals produced.

---

[2]Unless it is homozygous for a simple recessive and is mated to an animal that is heterozygous for that trait.

Once in a great while a mutation occurs in a farm animal, and it produces a visible effect in the animal carrying it. These animals are commonly called *sports*. Such sports are occasionally of practical value.

Gene changes can be accelerated by exposure to X rays, radium, ultraviolet light, and several other mutagenic agents. Such changes may eventually be observed in the offspring of both the people and animals of Japan that were exposed to the atom bombs unleashed in World War II.

SIMPLE GENE INHERITANCE (QUALITATIVE TRAITS)

In the simplest type of inheritance, only one pair of genes is involved, Thus, a pair of genes may be responsible for the color of body hair in horses. This situation can be illustrated by the pedigree of the Thoroughbred stallion, *Whirlaway*.

```
                                          Blanford
                                          (Brown—Bb)
                    *Blenheim II
                    (Brown)³  . . . . .   Malva
                                          (Brown—Bb)
Whirlaway  . . .
(Chestnut—bb)
                                          Sweep
                                          (Brown—Bb)
                    Dustwhirl
                    (Black—Bb)  . . .     Ormonda
                                          (Chestnut—bb)
```

In reality, the fixation of coat color in horses may not be so simple as expected. The idea that certain basic colors may have a rather simple explanation of inheritance should not alter the fact that other genes or contributing factors may play an important role, through their influence on basic schemes. Other color patterns and shades, of more complex nature, may exhibit an almost unreal influence when crossed with the more simple genotypes. The action of certain dilution genes is, without doubt, responsible for various shades of basic colors; this is amply portrayed, for example, by the many and varied hues of chestnut (sorrel) color.

Also, it should be borne in mind that the various gene contributions and colors will appear in the offspring in the expected proportions only when relatively large numbers are concerned. The possible gene combinations, therefore, are governed by the laws of chance, operating in much the same manner as the results obtained from flipping coins. For example, if a

penny is flipped often enough, the number of heads and tails will come out about even. However, with the laws of chance in operation, it is possible that out of any four tosses one might get all heads, all tails, or even three to one.

Other possible examples of simple gene inheritance in horses (sometimes referred to as qualitative traits) might include eye color and the set of the ears on the head.

DOMINANT AND RECESSIVE FACTORS

In the example of horse colors shown in Fig. 12-4, the phenomenon of *dominance* is illustrated. In this type of expression, a factor or gene has its full effect regardless of whether it is present with another like itself or paired with a recessive gene. Thus, black is dominant to chestnut; hence, when a pure black stallion is crossed on a chestnut mare, all of the offspring will be black. The resulting black is not genotypically pure, however; it is Bb, where B stands for the dominant black and b for the recessive chestnut. This black animal will produce germ cells carrying black and chestnut genes in equal proportion. Then if an F_1 stallion is crossed on F_1 mares, the F_2 population will, on the average, consist of three blacks to one chestnut. The chestnut—being a recessive—will be pure for color; that is, the mating of two chestnut horses will produce chestnut offspring, which is the situation in the Suffolk breed of draft horse where all animals of the breed are chestnuts. Of the three blacks in the F_2, however, only one is pure black (with the genetic constitution BB). The other two will be Bb in genetic constitution, and will produce germ cells carrying b and B in equal proportion.

It is clear, therefore, that a dominant character may cover up a recessive. Hence, a horse's breeding performance cannot be recognized by its phenotype (how it looks), a fact of great significance in practical breeding.

As can be readily understood, dominance often makes the task of identifying and discarding all animals carrying an undesirable recessive factor a difficult one. Recessive genes can be passed on from generation to generation, appearing only when two animals, both of which carry the recessive factor, happen to mate. Even then, only one out of four offspring produced will, on the average, be homozygous for the recessive factor and show it.

Assuming that a hereditary defect or abnormality has occurred in a herd and that it is recessive in nature, the breeding program to be followed to prevent or minimize the possibility of its future occurrence will depend somewhat on the breeding of the animals involved—especially on whether they are grade or purebred. In an ordinary grade herd of horses, the

---

³This is not shown as (Bb) because some brown stallions mated to chestnut mares produce no chestnut offspring. Rather, it is suggested that the brown of *Blenheim II* was a modified black.

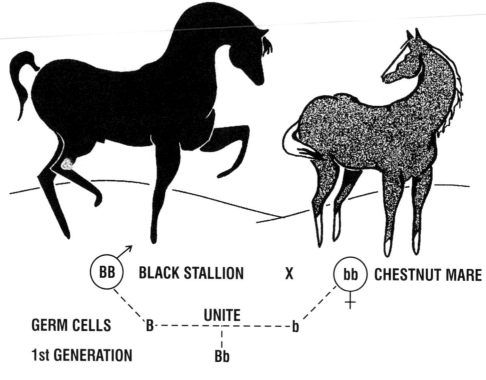

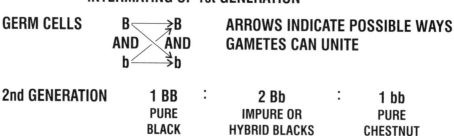

2nd GENERATION

1 BB	:	2 Bb	:	1 bb
PURE BLACK		IMPURE OR HYBRID BLACKS		PURE CHESTNUT

Fig. 12-4. An example of gene inheritance in horses. Note—

1. That each horse has at least a pair of genes for color, conveniently represented by symbols.
2. That each reproduction cell (egg or sperm) contains but one of each pair.
3. That the Bb genotypes, in the F_1 generation, can vary in the degree of blackness, thus tending to resemble the one black parent.
4. That the F_2 generation has the ratio of three blacks to one chestnut (phenotypically). The Bb's may be black or shading into brown.
5. That the pure blacks and certain hybrid blacks may not be distinguished on the basis of appearance, because the B gene obscures the b gene in varying degrees.
6. That the chestnut (bb) is quite likely the only pure color, in this example, that can be detected on sight.

breeder can usually guard against further reappearance of the undesirable recessive by using an outcross (unrelated) sire within the same breed or by crossbreeding with a sire from another breed. With this system, the breeder is fully aware of the recessive being present, but action has been taken to keep it from showing up.

On the other hand, if such an undesirable recessive appears in a purebred herd, the action should be more drastic. Reputable purebred breeders have an obligation, not only to themselves, but to their custom-

ers. Purebred animals must be purged of undesirable genes and lethals. This can be done by:

1. Eliminating those stallions and mares that are known to have transmitted the undesirable recessive character.
2. Eliminating both the abnormal and phenotypically normal offspring produced by these sires and dams (approximately half of the normal animals will carry the undesirable character in the recessive condition).

3. In some instances, breeding a young stallion to a number of females known to carry the gene for the undesirable recessive, thus making sure that the young sire is free of the recessive.

Such action in a purebred herd is expensive, and it calls for considerable courage. Yet it is the only way in which horses can be freed from such undesirable genes.

INCOMPLETE DOMINANCE

In some cases, dominance is neither complete nor absent, but incomplete or partial and expressed in a variety of ways. Perhaps the best-known case of this type in horses is the palomino color.

Genetic studies of the Palomino indicate that the color is probably unfixable—that it cannot be made true breeding, no matter how long or how persistent the effort.[4] Further, there appears to be ample theory—substantiated by practical observation—to indicate that palomino foals may be produced by any one of several types of matings (see discussion relative to Palomino characteristics, in Chapter 10).

Certain investigations[5] have revealed that the palomino color is due to the interaction of three pairs of genes; namely, bb = homozygous chestnut, Dd = heterozygous dilution, and AA or Aa = either homozygous or heterozygous bay coat pattern, resulting in the chestnut color bb being diluted to a cream or golden body color by Dd (DD animals being very pale or almost white). If it is assumed that the Palomino's color depends on the Dd gene pair being heterozygous, the Palomino color cannot breed true.

MULTIPLE GENE INHERITANCE (QUANTITATIVE TRAITS)

Relatively few characters of economic importance in horses are inherited in as simple a manner as the ones just described. Rather, important characters— such as speed—are due to many genes; thus, they are called multiple-gene characters. Because such characters show all manner of gradation—from high to low performance, for example—they are sometimes referred to as quantitative traits. Thus, quantitative inheritance refers to the degree to which a characteristic is inherited; for example, all Thoroughbred horses can run and all inherit some ability to run, but it is the degree to which they inherit the ability which is important.

In quantitative inheritance, the extremes (either good or bad) tend to swing back to the average. Thus, the offspring of a world-record stallion and a world-record mare is not apt to be as good as either parent. Likewise, and happily so, the progeny of two very mediocre parents will likely be superior to either parent.

Estimates of the number of pairs of genes affecting each economically important characteristic vary greatly, but the majority of geneticists agree that for most such characters 10 or more pairs of genes are involved. Growth rate in a foal, therefore, is affected by (1) the animal's appetite or feed consumption; (2) the efficiency of assimilation—that is, the proportion of the feed eaten that is absorbed into the bloodstream; and (3) the use to which the nutrients are put after assimilation—for example, whether they are used for growth or fattening. This example indicates that such a characteristic as growth rate is controlled by many genes and that it is difficult to determine the mode of inheritance of such characters.

HEREDITY AND ENVIRONMENT

A beautiful horse, standing deep in straw and with a manger full of feed before him, is undeniably the result of two forces—heredity and environment (with the latter including training). If turned out to pasture, an identical twin to the beautiful horse would present an entirely different appearance. By the same token, optimum environment could never make a champion out of a horse with scrub ancestry.

These are extreme examples and they may be applied to any class of farm animals; but they do

Fig. 12-5. This growthy/healthy foal is the product of two forces—heredity and environment. (Courtesy, American Andalusian Horse Assn., Springfield, OH)

---

[4]Castle, W. E., and King, F. L., "New Evidence on Genetics of Palomino Horses," *The Journal of Heredity*, 42:60-64, 1951.

[5]*Ibid.*

emphasize the fact that any particular animal is the product of heredity and environment. Stated differently, heredity may be thought of as the foundation, and environment as the structure. Heredity has already made its contribution at the time of fertilization, but environment works ceaselessly away until death. Generally horse trainers believe that heredity is most important, whereas horse owners believe that environment—particularly training—is most important, especially if they lose a race. Actually, qualitative traits (such as hair and eye color) are affected little by environment; whereas quantitative traits (such as ability to run) may be affected greatly by environment.

Experimental work has long shown conclusively enough that the vigor and size of animals at birth is dependent upon the environment of the embryo from the minute the ovum or egg is fertilized by the sperm, and now we have evidence to indicate that newborn animals are affected by the environment of the egg and the sperm long before fertilization has been accomplished. In other words, perhaps due to storage of factors, the kind and quality of the ration fed to young, growing females may later affect the quality of their progeny. Generally speaking, then, environment may inhibit the full expression of potentialities from a time preceding fertilization until physiological maturity has been attained.

It is generally agreed, therefore, that maximum development of characters of economic importance—growth, body form, speed, etc.—cannot be achieved unless there are optimum conditions of nutrition and management.

Admittedly, after looking over an animal or studying its production record, a breeder cannot with certainty know whether it is genetically a high or low producer. There can be no denying the fact that environment—including feeding, management, and disease—plays a tremendous part in determining the extent to which hereditary differences that are present will be expressed in animals. Yet, it would appear to be more difficult to estimate the possible effect of degree of suboptimal development than it would be to make selections on the basis of optimum environment.

Within the pure breeds of livestock—managed under average or better than average conditions—it has been found that, in general, only 15 to 30% of the observed variation in a characteristic is actually brought about by hereditary variations. To be sure, if we contrast animals that differ very greatly in heredity—for example, a champion horse and a scrub—90% or more of the apparent differences in type may be due to heredity. The point is, however, that extreme cases such as the one just mentioned are not involved in the advancement within improved breeds of horses. Here the comparisons are between animals of average or better than average quality, and the observed differences are often very minor.

The problem of the progressive breeder is that of selecting the very best animals available genetically—these to be parents of the next generation. The fact that only 15 to 30% of the observed variation is due to heredity, and that environmental differences can produce misleading variations, makes mistakes in the selection of breeding animals inevitable. However, if the purebred breeder has clearly in mind a well-defined ideal and adheres rigidly to it in selecting breeding stock, some progress can be made by selection, especially if mild inbreeding is judiciously used as a tool through which to fix the hereditary material.

HERITABILITY OF PERFORMANCE

Relatively little scientific work has been done on the heritability of performance of horses—on the genetics of working ability, racing ability, cutting ability, jumping ability, etc. As a result, the horse is the last of farm animals to which the science of genetics has been added to the art of breeding. Nevertheless, breeders have selected for performance. For example, the Thoroughbred horse has been selected and bred for speed and stamina for 300 years. Because more often than not the best horse wins, the breeding of the best to the best has resulted in improvement of the track performance of the Thoroughbred horse over the centuries.

The underlying genetic principle which determines the success of mating the best to the best is based upon the assumption that the phenotypes of the best for a given trait, such as speed, are due to simple additive-type genes without regard to family relationships. On the other hand, when a breeder plans matings on the basis of a nick, family or pedigree relationships receive careful consideration.

The underlying genetic principle in making an outcross is that the members of the unrelated strains or families will bring together genes which will act in a complementary fashion to produce hybrid vigor in the offspring for the traits desired.

Differences in the performance ability (working, racing, cutting, jumping) are due to two major forces—heredity and environment. Success in selecting superior breeding animals for each of these traits depends entirely upon how accurately we are able to partition the differences in performance capacity of horses into causes due to the environment and causes due to heredity.

The important environment factors in determining the overall performance of horses are nutrition (both prenatal and postnatal), health care, quality of training, ability of the handler (teamster, rider), and injuries.

An important genetic principle is that traits as such are not inherited. Rather, what is inherited is the ability to respond to a given set of environmental conditions in order to produce a trait with a measurable effect.

The key to continued genetic improvement in the performance of a horse, such as the racing capacity of the Thoroughbred, rests essentially on two factors: (1) the magnitude of the heritable component (additive genes) of performance (racing) capacity, and (2) the accuracy with which the breeder can identify those individuals which are truly genetically superior to their contemporaries.

Essentially, the breeding value of a horse is the fraction of the differences that will be transmitted to the progeny. The most straightforward measure of this is the heritability of the trait. It follows that an estimate of heritability of a trait is one of the most important considerations in formulating an effective program of improvement through breeding. Reliable estimates on the heritability of performance traits in horses are limited in comparison with other species. Nevertheless, further and important knowledge has been accumulated in recent years. Some heritability estimates follow:

■ **Working ability**—In most countries, work horses, as distinct from light horses (sporting breeds), still make up the bulk of the population. In France, for example, only 15% of the horse population consists of the sporting breeds.

The main measure of the working ability in a horse is pulling power. This performance trait has been estimated to have a heritability of 26%.[6]

■ **Racing ability**—Racing performance can be measured in different ways; by purses earned, time per unit distance, handicap weight, or Timeform ratings or other year-end handicaps. In a 1971 study, the Texas Agriculture Experiment Station[7] determined the racing ability of individual horses through a computer comparison of the number of lengths (one length = 8 ft) the horse would win or lose to other horses in a typical race. For this unique study, each horse was given a rating called the *Performance Rate*. Theoretically, it was assumed that the average horse would have a Performance Rate of zero. Then, in an average race, a horse with a Performance Rate of +12 would, theoretically, finish 12 lengths in front of the average horse. Likewise, a horse whose Performance Rate was −12 would, theoretically, finish 12 lengths behind the average horse and 24 lengths behind one with a +12 Performance Rate.

The Texas Station study included all three-year-

olds that raced on North American tracks in 1971. It involved 6,458 fillies and 7,113 colts and geldings, which were sired by 3,228 different stallions. Statistical analysis of the data showed that racing ability is about 40% heritable. This means that, on the average, about 40% of the difference in racing superiority of one horse over another is due to difference in heredity. The remaining 60% is due to difference in environment— nutrition, state of health, and abilities of trainers and jockeys.

So, after nearly three centuries of selection for speed and stamina, it should still be possible to improve the racing performance of Thoroughbred horses through selection of superior stock for future parents.

■ **Cutting ability**—Based on a study made by the Texas Station, the cutting ability of horses is less than 10% heritable.[8] Obviously, training is most important in determining cutting ability.

■ **Jumping ability**—Based on a study of steeplechase results in France, involving 3,500 progeny of 326 stallions, the heritability of jumping was estimated to be 18%.[9]

Although the heritability estimates of performance traits in horses above reported are disturbingly low, genes are a permanent, transmissible investment, whereas environmental factors are not. When buying horses, therefore, it is important to know whether you're buying desirable genes or superior environment.

HOW SEX IS DETERMINED

On the average, and when considering a large population, approximately equal numbers of males and females are born in all common species of animals. To be sure, many notable exceptions can be found in individual herds.

Sex is determined by the chromosomal makeup of the individual. One particular pair of the chromosomes is called the sex chromosomes. In farm animals, the female has a pair of similar chromosomes (usually called X chromosomes), whereas the male has a pair of unlike sex chromosomes (usually called X and Y chromosomes). In the bird, this condition is reversed, the female having the unlike pair and the male having the like pair.

The pairs of sex chromosomes separate out when the germ cells are formed. Thus, each of the ova or

[6]Cunningham, Professor E. P., Head of Animal Breeding and Genetics, Dublin University, Ireland, "Equine Genetics," *The Blood-Horse*, Oct. 6, 1975, p. 4210.

[7]Keiffer, Dr. N. M., Geneticist, Texas A&M University, College Station, Texas, "Heritability of Racing Ability," *The Blood-Horse*, Oct. 13, 1975, p. 4292.

[8]Keiffer, Dr. N. M., Geneticist, Texas A&M University, College Station, Texas, *Research Report*, Texas A&M Experiment Station, Dec. 3, 1975.

[9]Cunningham, Professor E. P., Head of Animal Breeding and Genetics, Dublin University, Ireland, "Equine Genetics," *The Blood-Horse*, Oct. 6, 1975, p. 4210.

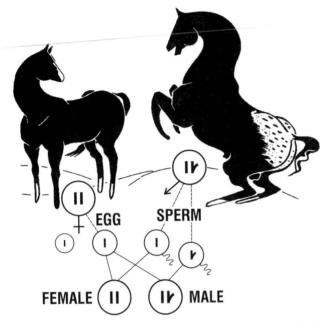

Fig. 12-6. Diagrammatic illustration of the mechanism of sex determination in horses, showing how sex is determined by the chromosomal makeup of the individual. The mare has a pair of like sex chromosomes, whereas the stallion has a pair of unlike chromosomes. Thus, if an egg and sperm of like sex chromosomal makeup unite, the offspring will be a filly; whereas if an egg and sperm of unlike sex chromosomal makeup unite, the offspring will be a colt. (Drawing by Prof. R. F. Johnson)

eggs produced by the mare contain the X chromosome; whereas the sperm of the stallion are of two types, one-half containing the X chromosome and the other half containing the Y chromosome. Since, on the average, the eggs and sperm unite at random, it can be understood that half the progeny will contain the chromosomal makeup XX (female) and the other half XY (male).[10]

LETHALS IN HORSES

The term lethal refers to *a genetic factor that causes death of the animal, either during prenatal life, at birth, or later in life.* Other defects occur which are not sufficiently severe to cause death, but which do impair the usefulness of affected animals.

Many abnormal foals are born each year. Unfortunately, purebred breeders, whose chief business is that of selling breeding stock, are likely to "keep mum" about the appearance of any defective animals in their

---

[10]The scientists' symbols for the male and female respectively, are: ♂ (the sacred shield and spear of Mars, the Roman god of war), and ♀ (the looking glass of Venus, the Roman goddess of love and beauty).

herds because of the justifiable fear that it may hurt their sales.

The embryological development—the development of the young from the time that the egg and sperm unite until the animal is born—is very complicated. Thus, the oddity probably is that so many of the offspring develop normally rather than that a few develop abnormally.

Many such abnormalities (commonly known as monstrosities or freaks) are hereditary, being caused by certain bad genes. Moreover, the bulk of such lethals are recessive and may, therefore, remain hidden for many generations. The prevention of such genetic abnormalities requires that the germ plasm be purged of the bad genes. This means that, where recessive lethals are involved, the breeder must be aware of the fact that both parents carry the gene. For the total removal of the lethals, test matings and rigid selection must be practiced. The best test mating to use for a given stallion consists in mating him to some of his own daughters.

In addition to hereditary abnormalities, there are certain abnormalities that may be due to nutritional deficiencies, or to accidents of development—the latter including those which appear to occur sporadically and for which there is no well-defined reason. When only a few defective individuals occur within a particular herd, it is often impossible to determine whether their occurrence is due to (1) defective heredity, (2) defective nutrition, or (3) merely to accidents of development. If the same abnormality occurs to any appreciable number of animals, however, it is probably either hereditary or nutritional. In any event, the diagnosis of the condition is not always a simple matter.

The following conditions would tend to indicate a **hereditary** defect in horses:

1. If the defect had previously been reported as hereditary in the same breed.
2. If it occurred more frequently within certain families or when there had been inbreeding.
3. If it occurred in more than one season and when different rations had been fed.

The following conditions might be accepted as indications that the abnormality was due to a **nutritional** deficiency:

1. If it had previously been reliably reported to be due to a nutritional deficiency.
2. If it appeared to be restricted to a certain area.
3. If it occurred when the ration of the dam was known to be deficient.
4. If it disappeared when an improved ration was fed.

If there is suspicion that the ration is defective, it should be improved, not only from the standpoint of preventing such deformities, but from the standpoint of good and efficient management.

If there is good and sufficient evidence that the abnormal condition is hereditary, the steps to be followed in purging the herd of the undesirable gene are identical to those for ridding the herd of any other undesirable recessive factor. An inbreeding program, of course, is the most effective way in which to expose hereditary lethals in order that purging may follow. Some of the genetic defects that have been reported in horses are summarized in Table 12-1.

TABLE 12-1
SOME GENETIC DEFECTS OF HORSES

Trait	Description	Probable Mode of Inheritance
Abnormal sex ratio	Ratio of 55 males to 90 females reported in Oldenburger breed of horses. About ½ the males die before birth or during the early stages of prenatal development.	Recessive
Aretesia coli	Closure of colon; often associated with brain defects. Affected foals stand with difficulty, soon develop colic and die. Surgery is unsuccessful.	Recessive
Barker (wanderer, dummy)	Foals completely disoriented at birth or soon thereafter. In severe cases, the animal goes down, followed by violent convulsions. In the latter stage, it emits a sound like a yelping dog; hence, the name barker.	Unknown
Big head	Bony enlargements on both sides of face, below eyes.	Dominant
Blindness	Foals born blind.	Recessive
Cataract	Loss of transparency of the lens of the eye or its capsule.	Recessive
Chestnuts missing	Chestnuts on hind legs missing.	Dominant
Contracted heels	Drawing in or contracting at the heels.	2 pairs of recessive genes
Cryptorchidism	Both testicles small and retained in abdomen.	Dominant
Curly coat	Hair is curly.	Recessive
Fetal membrane defective	Fetal membrane fails to grow and abortion results.	Recessive
Flat feet	Flat sole, and soft keratin.	Recessive .
Foal ataxia	Foal weak legged and can't walk. Dies in 8-14 days.	Recessive
Hernia, scrotal	Intestines pass through inguinal ring into stallions scrotum.	2 pairs of recessive genes
Hernia, umbilical	Intestines protrude through umbilical opening. It usually disappears within the first few months of the foal's life. If the hernia persists, surgical repair may be necessary. The latter is usually very successful.	Recessive
Hydrocephalus	Water on the brain.	Unknown
Hyperkalemic Periodic Paralysis (HYPP)	Intermittent episodes of muscle tremors caused by a muscle membrane defect and associated with irregular concentration of blood potassium.	Dominant
Isoerythrolysis (Haemolytic anemia, or jaundice)	Foals born normal and remain normal until they suckle. After they suckle, they become weak and lethargic, the body temperature drops, and the yellowish discoloration of jaundice appears on the membranes of the mouth and eyes. This condition results from the destruction of the foal's red blood cells by antibodies which the foal ingests from the mother's colostrum.	Unknown
Lameness	Hind legs alternate in lameness; first one, then the other. When acute, movement is difficult.	Dominant
Lethal white	Low fertility; first reported in horses of the Frederiksborg breed, in Denmark.	Unknown
Mallenders	An eczema-like condition of the skin caused by a protozoan parasite. However, there is some evidence that susceptibility to the parasite is inherited.	Recessive
Myopia	Nearsightedness.	Recessive
Parrot mouth	Upper jaw protrudes beyond lower jaw, like the beak of a parrot.	Dominant
Roaring	Wind broken; horse makes a loud noise in drawing air into the lungs.	Recessive
Skin defect	Patches of skin on body without hair. Hoof is sometimes missing, also.	Recessive
Stiff forelegs	Foals born with stiff forelegs.	Recessive
Stringhalt	Excessive flexing of hind legs.	Recessive
Wobbles	Incoordination; weaving gait in the rear legs.	Unknown

HYBRIDS WITH THE HORSE AS ONE PARENT

The mule, representing a cross between the jack (male of the ass family) on the mare (female of the horse family), is the best-known hybrid in the United States. The resulting offspring of the reciprocal cross of the stallion mated to a jennet is known as a *hinny.*

Fig. 12-7. One of the rarest of nature's whims—a colt dropped by a mare mule. The colt, sired by a stallion, was born in St. Martinsville, Louisiana, Nov. 13, 1947. *Lou*—the 21-year-old mother mule—pulled a cane wagon all day on Nov. 12. She was owned by Acie Miller, a St. Martinsville mule trader. The case of this unusual birth was verified by Dr. P. Broussard, D.V.M., New Iberia, Louisiana. (Photo, courtesy, Dr. Broussard)

Rarely have mules proved fertile; only five authentic cases of mare mules producing foals have been reported in the United States. This infertility of the mule is probably due to the fact that the chromosomes will not pair and divide equally in the reduction division.

The offspring of fertile mules are generally horselike in appearance,[11] showing none of the characteristics of the mule's sire (or ass). For the most part, therefore, the eggs (ova) which produce them do not carry chromosomes from the ass; they are pure horse eggs without any inheritance from their maternal grandfathers. This indicates that in the production of eggs in mare mules the reduction division is such that all of the horse chromosomes go to the egg and none to the polar bodies.

It is interesting to project the probability of a horselike animal being produced from a fertile mare mule and a horse sire. Assuming (1) that the offspring is the result of cases where all the horse chromosomes and all the ass chromosomes go to opposite poles in the dam during oogenesis, and (2) that this *horse egg* was fertilized, the chance is 1 in 2^{32}, or 1 in 4,294,967,296. Since this is the number of ways in which the horse's chromosomes may arrange themselves, it speaks highly for the skill of the successful horse breeder.

The zebroid—a zebra X horse hybrid—is rather popular in certain areas of the tropics because of its docility and resistance to disease and heat.

RELATIVE IMPORTANCE OF THE STALLION AND THE MARE

As the stallion can have so many more offspring during a given season or a lifetime than a mare, he is from a hereditary standpoint a more important individual than any one mare so far as the whole herd is concerned, although both the stallion and the mare are of equal importance so far as concerns any one offspring. Because of their wider use, therefore, stallions are usually culled more rigidly than mares, and the breeder can well afford to pay more for an outstanding stallion than for an equally outstanding mare.

Experienced horse breeders have long felt that stallions and their fillies usually resemble each other, and that mares and their colts resemble each other. Some stallions and mares, therefore, enjoy a reputation based almost exclusively on the merit of their sons, whereas others owe their prestige to their daughters. Although this situation is likely to be exaggerated, any such phenomenon that may exist is due to sex-linked inheritance which may be explained as follows:

---

[11]Not all are horselike however. Thus, one of *Old Beck's* (fertile mule owned by Texas A&M College) three offspring was mulelike in appearance.

The genes that determine sex are carried on one of the chromosomes. The other genes that are located on the same chromosome will be linked or associated with sex and will be transmitted to the next generation in combination with sex. Thus, because of sex-linkage, there are more color-blind men than color-blind women. In poultry breeding, the sex-linked factor is used in a practical way for the purpose of distinguishing the pullets from the cockerels early in life, through the process known as *sexing* the chicks. Thus, when a black cock is crossed with barred hens, all the cocks come barred and all the hens come black. It should be emphasized, however, that under most conditions it appears that the influence of the sire and dam on any one offspring is about equal. Most breeders, therefore, will do well to seek excellence in both sexes of breeding animals.

PREPOTENCY

Prepotency refers to the ability of the animal, either male or female, to stamp its own characteristics on its offspring. The offspring of a prepotent stallion, for example, resemble both their sire and each other more closely than usual. The only conclusive and final test of prepotency consists in the inspection of the get.

From a genetic standpoint, there are two requisites that an animal must possess in order to be prepotent: (1) dominance, and (2) homozygosity. All offspring that receive dominant genes will show the effects of those genes in the particular characters which result therefrom. Moreover, perfectly homozygous animals would transmit the same kind of genes to all of their offspring. Although entirely homozygous animals probably never exist, it is realized that a system of inbreeding is the only way to produce animals that are as nearly homozygous as possible.

It should also be emphasized that it is impossible to determine just how important prepotency may be in animal breeding, although many sires of the past have enjoyed a reputation for being extremely prepotent. Perhaps these animals were prepotent, but there is also the possibility that their reputation for producing outstanding animals may have rested upon the fact that they were mated to some of the best females of the breed.

In summary, it may be said that if a given stallion or mare possesses a great number of genes that are completely dominant for desirable type and performance and if the animal is relatively homozygous, the offspring will closely resemble the parent and resemble each other, or be uniform. Fortunate, indeed, is the breeder who possesses such an animal.

NICKING

If the offspring of certain matings are especially outstanding and in general better than their parents, breeders are prone to say that the animals *nicked* well. For example, a mare may produce outstanding foals to the service of a certain stallion, but when mated to another stallion of apparent equal merit as a sire, the offspring may be disappointing. Or sometimes the mating of a rather average stallion to an equally average mare will result in the production of a most outstanding individual both from the standpoint of type and performance.

So-called successful nicking is due, genetically speaking, to the fact that the right combinations of genes for good characters are contributed by each parent, although each of the parents within itself may be lacking in certain genes necessary for excellence. In other words, the animals nicked well because their respective combinations of good genes were such as to complement each other.

The history of animal breeding includes records of several supposedly favorable nicks. Because of the very nature of successful nicks, however, outstanding animals arising therefrom must be carefully scrutinized from a breeding standpoint, because, with their heterozygous origin, it is quite unlikely that they will breed true.

FAMILY NAMES

In animals, depending upon the breed, family names are traced through either the males or the females. Unfortunately, the value of family names is generally grossly exaggerated. Obviously, if the foundation stallion or mare, as the case may be, is very many generations removed, the genetic superiority of this head of family is halved so many times by subsequent matings that there is little reason to think that one family is superior to another. The situation is often further distorted by breeders placing a premium on family names of which there are few members, little realizing that, in at least some cases, there may be unfortunate reasons for the scarcity in numbers.

Such family names have about as much significance as human family names. Who would be so foolish as to think that the Joneses as a group are alike and different from the Smiths? Perhaps, if the truth were known, there have been many individuals with each of these family names who have been of no particular credit to the clan, and the same applies to all other family names.

Family names lend themselves readily to speculation.

Because of this, the history of livestock breeding

has often been blighted by instances of unwise pedigree selection on the basis of not too meaningful family names.

On the other hand, certain linebred families—linebred to a foundation sire or dam so that the family is kept highly related to it—do have genetic significance. Moreover, if the programs involved have been accompanied by rigid culling, many good individuals may have evolved, and the family name may be in good repute.

SYSTEMS OF BREEDING

The many diverse types and breeds among each class of farm animals in existence today originated from only a few wild types within each species. These early domesticated animals possessed the pool of genes, which, through controlled matings and selection, proved flexible. In horses, for example, through various systems of breeding, there evolved animals especially adapted to riding, racing, and driving.

Perhaps at the outset it should be stated that there is no one best system of breeding or secret of success for any and all conditions. Each breeding program is an individual case, requiring careful study. The choice of the system of breeding should be determined primarily by the size and quality of the herd, by the finances and skill of the operator, and by the ultimate goal ahead.

PUREBREEDING

A purebred animal may be defined as *a member of a breed, the animals of which possess a common ancestry and distinctive characteristics; and it is either registered or eligible for registry in that breed.*

The breed association consists of a group of breeders banded together for the purposes of (1) recording the lineage of their animals, (2) protecting the purity of the breed, and (3) promoting the interest of the breed.

The term purebred refers to animals whose entire lineage, regardless of the number of generations removed, traces back to the foundation animals which have been accepted by the breed or to animals which have been subsequently approved for infusion. It should be emphasized that the word purebred does not necessarily guarantee superior type or high productivity. That is to say, the word purebred is not, within itself, magic, nor is it sacred. Many people have found to their sorrow that there are such things as purebred scrubs. Yet, on the average, purebred animals are superior to non-purebreds.

For the breeder with experience and adequate

capital, the breeding of purebreds may offer unlimited opportunities. It has been well said that honor, fame, and fortune are all within the realm of possible realization of the purebred breeder; but it should also be added that only a few achieve this high calling.

Purebred breeding is a highly specialized type of production. Generally speaking, only the experienced breeder should undertake the production of purebreds with the intention of furnishing foundation or replacement stock to other purebred breeders. Although we have had many constructive horse breeders and great progress has been made, it must be remembered that only a few achieve sufficient success to classify as master breeders. However, this need not discourage the small operator—the owner of one mare, or of a few mares—from mating to a good purebred stallion of the same breed, in order to produce some good horses.

INBREEDING

Most scientists divide inbreeding into various categories, according to the closeness of the relationship of the animals mated and the purpose of the matings. There is considerable disagreement, however, as to both the terms used and the meanings that it is intended they should convey. In this book, the following definitions apply:

Inbreeding is the mating of animals more closely related than the average of the population from which they came.

Closebreeding is the mating of closely related animals—such as sire to daughter, son to dam, and brother to sister.

Linebreeding is the mating of animals more distantly related than in closebreeding, and in which the matings are usually directed toward keeping the offspring closely related to some highly admired ancestor—such as half-brother and half-sister, female and grandsire, and cousins.

CLOSEBREEDING

Closebreeding is rarely practiced among present-day horse breeders, though it was common in the foundation animals of most of the breeds. There is good reason why closebreeding is seldom followed with horses, especially racehorses, because (1) experiments with other animals clearly show that closebreeding (inbreeding above a level of about 10%) results in less vigor, and (2) there is not available a desirable outlet for horses of poor type or performance, such as is afforded when discarded cattle, sheep, and swine are marketed for slaughter.

LINEBREEDING

From a biological standpoint, closebreeding and linebreeding are the same thing, differing merely in intensity. In general, closebreeding has been frowned upon by horse breeders, but linebreeding (the less intensive form) has been looked upon with favor in some quarters.

In a linebreeding program, the degree of relationship is not closer than half-brother and half-sister or matings more distantly related—cousin matings, grandparents and grand offspring, etc.

Linebreeding may be practiced in order to conserve and perpetuate the good traits of a certain outstanding stallion or mare. Because such descendants are of similar lineage, they have the same general type of germ plasm and therefore exhibit a high degree of uniformity in type and performance.

In a more limited way, a linebreeding program has the same advantages and disadvantages of a closebreeding program. Stated differently, linebreeding offers fewer possibilities both for good and harm than closebreeding. It is a more conservative and safer type of program, offering less probability of either hitting the jackpot or sinking the ship. It is a middle-of-the-road program that the vast majority of average and small breeders can safely follow to their advantage. Through it, reasonable progress can be made without taking any great risk. A greater degree of homozygosity of certain desirable genes can be secured without running too great a risk of intensifying undesirable ones.

Usually a linebreeding program is best accomplished through breeding to an outstanding sire rather than to an outstanding dam because of the greater number of offspring of the former. If a horse breeder had possession of a great stallion—proven great by the performance records of a large number of his get—a linebreeding program might be initiated in the following way: Select two of the best sons of the noted stallion and mate them to their half-sisters, balancing all possible defects in the subsequent matings. The next generation mating might well consist of breeding the daughters of one of the stallions to the son of the other, etc. If, in such a program, it seems wise to secure some outside blood (genes) to correct a common defect or defects in the herd, this may be done through selecting a few outstanding proved mares from the outside—animals whose get are strong where the herd may be deficient—and then mating these mares to one of the linebred stallions with the hope of producing a son that may be used in the herd.

The small operator—the owner of one mare, or of a few mares—can often follow a linebreeding program by breeding mares to a stallion owned by a large breeder who follows such a program—thus, in effect, following the linebreeding program of the larger breeder.

Naturally, a linebreeding program may be achieved in other ways. Regardless of the actual matings used, the main objective in such a system of breeding is that of rendering the animals homozygous—in desired type and performance—to some great and highly regarded ancestor, while at the same time weeding out homozygous undesirable characteristics. The success of the program, therefore, is dependent upon having desirable genes with which to start an intelligent intensification of these good genes.

It should be emphasized that there are some types of herds that should almost never closebreed or linebreed. These include herds of only average quality.

With purebred herds of only average quality, more rapid progress can usually be made by introducing superior outcross sires. Moreover, were the animals of only average quality they would have a preponderance of bad genes that would only be intensified through a closebreeding or linebreeding program.

OUTCROSSING

Outcrossing is the mating of animals that are members of the same breed but which show no relationship close up in the pedigree (for at least the first four or six generations).

Most of our purebred animals of all classes of livestock are the result of outcrossing. It is a relatively safe system of breeding, for it is unlikely that two such unrelated animals will carry the same undesirable genes and pass them on to their offspring.

Perhaps it might well be added that the majority of purebred breeders with average or below average herds had best follow an outcrossing program, because, in such herds, the problem is that of retaining a heterozygous type of germ plasm with the hope that genes for undesirable characters will be counteracted by genes for desirable characters. With such average or below average herds, an inbreeding program would merely make the animals homozygous for the less desirable characters, the presence of which already makes for their mediocrity. In general, continued outcrossing offers neither the hope for improvement nor the hazard of retrogression of linebreeding or inbreeding programs.

Judicious and occasional outcrossing may well be an integral part of linebreeding or inbreeding programs. As closely inbred animals become increasingly homozygous with germ plasm for good characters, they may likewise become homozygous for certain undesirable characters even though their general overall type and performance remain well above the breed average. Such defects may best be remedied by introducing an outcross through an animal or animals known to be especially strong in the character or characters needing strengthening. This having been accomplished, the wise breeder will return to the original inbreeding or linebreeding program, realizing full well the limitations of an outcrossing program.

GRADING UP

Grading up is that system of breeding in which a purebred sire of a given breed is mated to a native or grade female. Its purpose is to impart quality and to increase performance in the offspring. It is the common system of breeding followed on the western range, where mares of Mustang background are generally graded up by using a purebred stallion of a certain breed (usually either a Quarter Horse or a Thoroughbred), year after year, in producing cow ponies. Likewise, horse owners of the one- to two-mare variety frequently mate their grade mare(s) to a purebred stallion of the same breed, in order to produce hunters, jumpers, pleasure horses, etc.

Naturally, the greatest single step toward improved quality and performance occurs in the first cross. The first generation from such a mating results in offspring carrying 50% of the hereditary material of the purebred parent (or 50% of the *blood* of the purebred parent, as many breeders speak of it). The next generation gives offspring carrying 75% of the blood of the purebred breed, and in subsequent generations the proportion of inheritance remaining from the original scrub parent is halved with each cross. Later crosses will usually continue to increase quality and performance slightly more, though in less marked degree. After the third or fourth cross, the offspring compare very favorably with purebred stock in conformation, and only exceptionally good sires can bring about further improvement. This is especially so if the stallions used in grading up successive generations are derived from the same strain within a breed.

As evidence that horses of high merit may be produced through grading up, examples of champion performers among hunters, jumpers, polo ponies, cow ponies, etc., might be cited.

CROSSBREEDING

Crossbreeding is the mating of animals of different breeds. In a broad sense, crossbreeding also includes the mating of purebred sires of one breed with high-grade females of another breed.

Perhaps in the final analysis, all would agree that any merits that crossbreeding may possess are and will continue to be based on improved seed stock. Certainly from a genetic standpoint, it should be noted

Fig. 12-8. *Syrian's Souvenir*, Crossbred Saddlebred/Arabian/Standardbred stallion shown under saddle. Owned by Jim Coughlin of Hudson, Ohio. (Courtesy, The Half Saddlebred Registry of America, Coshocton, OH)

that crossbred animals generally possess greater heterozygosity than outcross animals—with the added virtue of hybrid vigor. It may also be added that, as in outcrossing, the recessive and undesirable genes remain hidden in the crossbred animal.

On purely theoretical grounds, it would appear that crossbreeding should result in some increase in vigor because the desirable genes from both breeds would be combined and the undesirable genes from each would tend to be overshadowed as recessives.

In summary, it can be said that crossbreeding has a place, particularly from the standpoint of increased vigor, growth rate, efficiency of production, and in the creation of new breeds adapted to certain conditions; but purebreeding will continue to control the destiny of further improvements in horses and furnish the desired homozygosity and uniformity which many horse breeders insist is part of the art of breeding better horses.

RECORD FORMS

An important requisite in any horse breeding program is the keeping of relatively simple but meaningful records. Figs. 12-9a, 12-9b, 12-10a, and 12-10b are record forms developed by the author. One is for the broodmare, and the other is for the stallion. These record forms may be modified somewhat to suit individual needs and desires.

INDIVIDUAL LIFETIME BROODMARE RECORD

Name of mare _____

Number or other identity _____

Birth date _____

Show or performance record _____

_____

_____

Temperament _____
(gentle, nervous, cross)

PHOTO

Bred by _____
(name and address)

Purchased from _____
(name and address)
Date _____ Price _____

Disposal: Sold to _____
(name and address)
Date _____ Price _____

Remarks _____

Production Record of Mares

Year	Sire of foal	Birth date of foal	Temperament of mare at foaling (gentle, nervous, cross)	Foaling (normal, requiring assistance, retained placenta)	Vigor of foal at birth (deformities)	Sex of foal	Identity of foal	Date foal was weaned	Score of foal				Disposal of foal				
									Under 1-year	Yearling	2-year-old	3-year-old	Sold to: (name and address)	Date	Price	Reasons	Remarks

Fig. 12-9a. Individual Lifetime Broodmare Record. (See Fig. 12-9b for reverse side of record form.)

HEALTH RECORD

Date	Immunization					Type of parasite treatment	Other veterinary treatment	Remarks
	Encephalomyelitis	Tetanus	Abortion					

Fig. 12-9b. Individual Lifetime Broodmare Record. (This is the reverse side of Fig. 12-9a.)

INDIVIDUAL YEARLY STALLION BREEDING RECORD

Name of stallion _____

Number or other identity_____

Birth date _____

Show or performance record _____

_____

_____

| PHOTO |

For breeding year of _____

For foaling year of _____

Total number of services _____

No. services/conception _____

Mares in Foal to Stallion

Name of Mare	Date mare was bred				Date foaled	Vigor of foal at birth	Sex of foal	Disposal of foal				Remarks
								Sold to: (name and address)	Date	Price	Reasons	

Fig. 12-10a. Individual Yearly Stallion Breeding Record. (See Fig. 12-10b for reverse side of record form.)

HEALTH RECORD

Date	Immunization			Type of parasite treatment	Semen test	Veterinary Treatment	Remarks
	Encepha-lomyelitis	Tetanus	Other				

Fig. 12-10b. Individual Yearly Stallion Breeding Record. (This is the reverse side of Fig. 12-10a.)

PERFORMANCE TESTING HORSES

The breeders of racehorses have always followed a program of mating animals of proved performance on the track. For example, it is interesting to note that the first breed register which appeared in 1791—known as *An Introduction to The General Stud Book,*—recorded the pedigrees of all the Thoroughbred horses winning important races. In a similar way, the Standardbred horse—which is an American creation—takes its name from the fact that, in its early history, animals were required to trot a mile in 2 minutes and 30 seconds, or to pace a mile in 2 minutes and 25 seconds, before they could be considered as eligible for registry. The chief aim, therefore, of early-day breeders of racehorses was to record the pedigree of outstanding performers rather than all members of the breed.

Thus, Thoroughbred or Standardbred animals bred for racing may be performance tested by timing on the track. The working ability of draft horses may be measured by pulling power on the dynamometer. Less satisfactory tests for saddle horses and harness horses have been devised. However, it is conceivable that actual exhibiting on the tanbark in the great horse

Fig. 12-11. Meeting performance standards on the track was a requisite to registration in the formation of the Standardbred breed. This shows *CR Kay Suzie,* 1995 Harness Horse of the Year. (Courtesy, The United States Trotting Assn., Columbus, OH)

shows of the country may be an acceptable criterion for saddle- and harness-bred animals.

PART II.
SOME PHYSIOLOGICAL ASPECTS OF REPRODUCTION IN HORSES

Horse producers have many reproductive problems, a reduction of which calls for a full understanding of reproductive physiology and the application of scientific practices therein.

REPRODUCTIVE ORGANS OF THE MARE

The mare's functions in reproduction are to (1) produce the female reproductive cells, the eggs or ova; (2) develop the new individual, the embryo, in the uterus; (3) expel the fully developed young at the time of birth or parturition; and (4) produce milk for the nourishment of the young. Actually, the part played by the mare in the generative process is much more complicated than that of the stallion. It is important, therefore, that the modern horse breeder have a full understanding of the anatomy of the reproductive organs of the mare and the functions of each part. Fig. 12-12 shows the reproductive organs of the mare.

The primary sex organ of the mare is the ovary (there are two ovaries). These are somewhat bean-

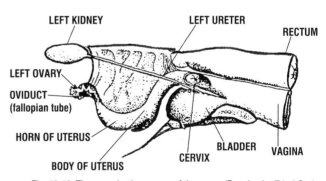

Fig. 12-12. The reproductive organs of the mare. (Drawing by Ethel Gadberry)

shaped organs 2 to 3 in. long. The ovaries produce eggs. Each egg is contained in a bubblelike sack on the ovary, called a follicle. There are hundreds of follicles on every ovary. Generally, the follicles remain in an unchanged state until the advent of puberty, at which time one of them begins to grow through an increase in the follicular liquid within, while the others remain small. The egg is suspended in the follicular fluid. When the follicle is about an inch in diameter (which coincides with the time of mating of mares that are bred), a hormone causes it to rupture and discharge the egg, which process is known as ovulation. The egg is then trapped in a funnel-shaped membrane, called the infundibulum, that surrounds the ovary. The infundibulum narrows into a tube called the oviduct. The oviduct then carries the egg to the uterus, or womb, the largest of the female reproductive organs, where the unborn young (the fetus) will develop. The lining of the uterus is soft and spongy, containing a vast network of blood vessels, which provide a bed for the fertilized egg to settle into and develop. At birth, the heavy layers of muscles of the uterus wall contract with great pressure to force the new animal through the cervix and vagina (birth canal) and out into the new world.

REPRODUCTIVE ORGANS OF THE STALLION

The stallion's functions in reproduction are (1) to produce the male reproductive cells, the sperm or spermatozoa, and (2) to introduce sperm into the female reproductive tract at the proper time. Fig. 12-13 is a schematic drawing of the reproductive organs of the stallion.

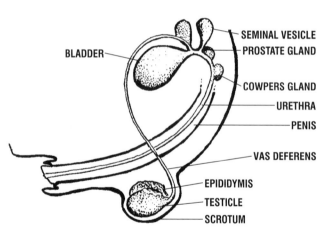

Fig. 12-13. The reproductive organs of the stallion. (Drawing by Ethel Gadberry)

The primary sex organ of the stallion is the testicle (there are two testicles). The testicles produce (1) sperm, and (2) a hormone called testosterone, which regulates and maintains the male reproductive tract in its functional state and is responsible for the masculine appearance and behavior of the stallion.

Sperm production takes place in the seminiferous tubules—a mass of minute, coiled tubules, the inner wall or surface of which produce the sperm. These tubules merge into a series of larger ducts which carry the sperm to a coiled tube called the epididymis. The epididymis is the place where the sperm are stored, and where they mature or ripen.

The testicles and epididymides are enclosed in the scrotum, the chief function of which is thermoregulatory—to maintain the testicles at temperatures several degrees cooler than the body proper.

From the epididymis, the sperm move through a tube, the vas deferens, into the urethra. The urethra has a dual role; it carries (1) urine from the bladder through the penis, and (2) sperm from the junction with the vas deferens to the end of the penis.

Among the urethra are the accessory glands—the prostate, the seminal vesicles, and the Cowper's glands. Their fluids nourish and preserve the sperm, and provide a medium for its transport. The combined sperm and fluid is called semen.

CARE AND MANAGEMENT OF THE STALLION

Although certain general recommendations can be made, it should be remembered that each stallion

Fig. 12-14. Man O'War, Thoroughbred stallion, and his groom, Will Harbut. The legendary Man O'War was one of the greatest horses of all time. (Courtesy, J. C. Skeets Meadows and Keeneland Library, Lexington, KY)

should be studied as an individual, and his care, feeding, exercise, and handling should be varied accordingly.

QUARTERS FOR THE STALLION

The most convenient arrangement for the stallion is a roomy box stall which opens directly into a 2- or 3-acre pasture paddock, preferably separated from the other horses by a double fence. The stall door opening into such a paddock may be left open except during extremely cold weather; this will give the stallion plenty of fresh air, sunshine, and additional exercise.

Fig. 12-15. *Left:* A stallion barn adjacent to a paddock. *Right:* A breeding barn. (Courtesy, California Thoroughbred Breeders Association, Arcadia, CA)

FEEDING THE STALLION

The feed and water requirements of the stallion are adequately discussed in Chapter 13. In addition to this, it may be well to reemphasize that, in season, clean lush pastures produced on fertile soils are excellent for the stallion. Grass is the horse's most natural feed, and it is a rich source of vitamins that are so necessary for vigor and reproduction. Perhaps the ideal arrangement in providing pasture for the stallion is to give him access to a well-sodded paddock.

EXERCISE FOR THE STALLION

Most stud managers feel that regular, daily exercise for the stallion is important. Certainly, it is one of the best ways in which to keep a horse in a thrifty, natural condition.

Stallions of the light-horse breeds are most generally exercised under saddle or hitched to a cart. Thus,

Standardbred stallions are usually jogged 3 to 5 miles daily while drawing a cart. Thoroughbred stallions and saddle stock stallions of all other breeds are best exercised under saddle for from 30 minutes to 1 hour daily, especially during the breeding season. Exercise should not be hurried or hard; the walk and the trot are the best gaits to use for this purpose. After the stallion is exercised, he should be rubbed down and cooled off before he is put up, especially if he is hot. Better yet, the ride should be so regulated at the end that the horse will be brought in cool, in which case he can be brushed off and turned into his corral.

Frequently in light horses, bad feet exclude exercise on roads, and faulty tendons exclude exercise under the saddle. Under such conditions, one may have to depend upon (1) exercise taken voluntarily by the stallion in a large paddock, (2) longeing or exercising on a 30- to 40-ft rope, or (3) leading.

Longeing should be limited to a walk and a trot; and if possible, the stallion should be worked on both hands; that is, made to circle both to the right and to the left. It is also best that this type of exercise be administered within an enclosure. Two precautions in longeing are (1) do not longe a horse when the footing is slippery, and (2) do not pull the animal in such manner as to make him pivot too sharply with the hazard of breaking a leg.

Leading is a satisfactory form of exercise for some stallions if it is not practical to ride them. In leading, a bridle should always be used—never a halter—and one should keep away from other horses and be careful that the horse being ridden is not a kicker.

Where several stallions are exercised, a properly installed mechanical exerciser, similar to a merry-go-round, driven by an electric motor may be used as a means of lessening labor.

The objection to relying upon paddock exercises alone is that the exercise cannot be regulated, especially during inclement weather. Some animals may take too much exercise and others too little. Moreover, merely running in the paddock will seldom, if ever, properly condition any stallion. Nevertheless, a two- or three-acre grassy paddock should always be provided, even for horses that are regularly exercised. Stallions that are worked should be turned out at night and on idle days.

GROOMING THE STALLION

Proper grooming of the stallion is necessary, not only to make the horse more attractive in appearance, but to assist exercise in maintaining the best of health and condition. Grooming serves to keep the functions of the skin active. It should be thorough, with special care taken to keep all parts of the body clean and free from any foulness, but not so rough nor so severe as to cause irritation either of the skin or the temper.

AGE AND SERVICE OF THE STALLION

It should be remembered that the number and kind of foals that a stallion sires in a given season is more important than the total number of services. The number of services allowed during a season will vary with the age, development, temperament, health, and breeding condition of the stallion and the distribution of services. Therefore, no definite best number of services can be recommended for any and all conditions, and yet the practices followed by good stud managers are not far different. All are agreed that excessive service of the stallion may reduce his fertility. Also, it must be realized that two or three services are required for each conception, and that there are breed differences, due primarily to differences in temperament.

A stallion's daily sperm output should be determined as it will give stallion managers a basis for how many potential mares or breedings can be booked during a given period.

Table 12-2 contains recommendations relative to the number of services for stallions of different ages, with consideration given to age and type of mating. Because of their more naturally nervous temperaments, stallions of the light-horse breeds are usually more restricted in services than stallions of the draft-horse breeds. Also, there is a difference between breeds. *Note:* Table 12-2 applies to natural service only. In the United States by the mid-1990s, few popular stallions were limited to natural service only. Most breed registries permitted natural service being aug-

mented (1) by reinforcing with fresh semen, and/or (2) by using cooled semen. Some accepted frozen semen.

The most satisfactory arrangement for the well-being of the stallion is to allow not more than one service each day. With proper handling, however, the mature, vigorous stallion may with certainty and apparently without harm serve two mares in a single day. During the heavy spring breeding season, this may often be necessary. It is a good plan to allow a stallion to rest at least one day a week.

In order to secure higher conception of the mares and yet avoid overwork of the stallion with an excessive number of natural services, most breeders now reinforce each natural service with one artificial insemination. Several of the breed registries stipulate that this must be done at once after natural service, with semen from the stallion performing the natural service on the mare that has just been covered.

Stallions often remain virile and valuable breeders until 20 to 25 years of age, especially if they have been properly handled. However, it is usually best to limit the number of services on a valuable old sire in order to preserve his usefulness and extend his longevity as long as possible.

Occasionally, Thoroughbred and Standardbred stallions are used to a limited extent before retirement to the stud, although many good breeders seem to feel that it is not best to use them until it is time for them to be retired. Saddle horses may be bred to a few mares and still be used in the show-ring. However, sometimes it makes them more difficult to handle.

It frequently happens that a wonderful horse is injured in the midst of his racing career, and while awaiting the next racing season, he is bred to a few mares.

If two services a day are planned with the mature stallion, one should be rather early in the morning and the other late in the afternoon. It is also best not to permit teasing or services immediately before or after feeding the stallion, for this may result in a digestive disturbance, particularly in nervous, fretful individuals.

EXAMINATION OF THE STALLION

The stallion is the key to success in breeding! Hence, he merits a very thorough examination, with special attention given to the following: (1) studying his past breeding record, bearing in mind that the most reliable and obvious indication of potency is a large number of healthy, vigorous foals from a season's service; (2) a general physical examination; (3) special examination of the hind legs for any injuries or problems which may prevent him from mounting mares; (4) checking the feet, and trimming the hoofs if necessary; (5) checking the teeth, and floating if necessary; (6) checking the condition, especially noting if overweight

TABLE 12-2
STALLION MATING GUIDE[1]

Age	No. of Matings/Yr.		Comments
	Hand Mating	Pasture Mating	
2-year-old	10–15	Preferably no pasture mating unless the stallion is prepared for same and certain precautions are taken.	1. Limit the 2-year-old to 2-3 services/week; the 3-year-old to 1 service/day; and 4-year-old or over to 2–3 services/day.
3-year-old	20–40		
4-year-old	40–60		2. A stallion should remain a vigorous and reliable breeder up to 20 to 25 years of age.
Mature horse	50–70		
Over 18 yrs. old	20–40		

[1]There are breed differences. Thus, when first entering stud duty, the average 3-year-old Thoroughbred should be limited to 20 to 25 mares per season, whereas a Standardbred of the same age may breed 25 to 30 mares; and the 4- or 5-year-old Thoroughbred should be limited to 30 or 40 mares, whereas a Standardbred of the same age may breed 40 to 50 mares. Mature stallions of the draft breeds may breed up to 70, or more, mares in a season.

or underweight; (7) checking the respiratory and cardiovascular systems; (8) checking for evidence of arthritis and/or melanomas in older stallions; (9) checking for internal parasites, and treating if necessary; (10) checking libido; (11) checking temperament; and (12) evaluating the semen.

When purchasing a stallion of breeding age, he should be a guaranteed breeder; this is usually understood among reputable breeders.

In order to monitor a stallion during a heavy breeding season, a microscopic examination of the semen may be made by an experienced person. As the stallion dismounts from service, some of the semen is collected in a sterilized funnel by holding the penis over the plugged funnel. A sample of the semen is then strained through sterile gauze, and a small amount is placed on a slide for examination. A great number of active sperm cells is an indication, although not definite assurance, that the stallion is fertile. Some establishments have a regular practice of making such a microscopic examination twice each week during the breeding season. If it is desired to examine a stallion's semen after the breeding season or when a mare is not in season an artificial vagina may be used. When an entire ejaculate is available for study, the four main criteria of quality are (1) semen volume, (2) spermatozoan count, (3) progressive movement, and (4) morphology.

If a stallion is a shy breeder or lacks fertility although one is certain that the feed and exercise have been up to standard, masturbation should be suspected. Some horses are very hard to catch in the act, but generally masturbation can be detected by (1) the shrinkage of the muscles of the loin, and (2) the presence of dried semen on the abdomen or on the back of the front legs. Once this practice is detected or even suspected, corrective measures should be taken. Stalling and turning the horse out where he can see other horses will help in some instances; also, giving the horse more sunshine, grass, and outdoor exercise will help.

STALLION STATIONS

Recently, there has been a trend toward grouping 10 to 20 stallions on a breeding farm, commonly referred to as a Stallion Station. This development has been especially strong in the Thoroughbred, Standardbred, and Quarter Horse breeds.

These highly specialized breeding establishments have the following **advantages**:

1. It makes it convenient for an owner wishing to breed several mares to select from among a number of stallions.

2. It is more practical to employ expert personnel to handle the breeding operations.

3. It usually makes for superior facilities for this specialized purpose.

4. It generally results in a higher percentage of in-foal mares, earlier conception, and more efficient use of the stallion—primarily due to (a) more expert management, examination, and medication if necessary; and (b) improved facilities.

As with all good things, there may be, and sometimes are, **disadvantages**, such as the following:

1. The hazard of spreading contagious diseases is increased where there is a great concentration of horses, thus requiring extreme cleanliness and precautions.

2. There is considerable expense in operating a highly specialized service of this kind.

3. There is difficulty in obtaining a battery of really outstanding sires.

NORMAL BREEDING HABITS OF MARES

Horses have the poorest reproductive performance of all domestic animals, due to the intervention of people with the natural breeding season.

Under domestication, horses are selected for their

Fig. 12-16. Quarter Horse mares and foals on pasture, approaching normal breeding habitats of mares under domestication. (Courtesy, American Quarter Horse Assn., Amarillo, TX)

performance, gait, coat color, and size—well ahead of reproductive efficiency. Moreover, the January 1 birthdate imposed by breed registries has forced horse breeders to breed for January and February foals, which is two months before the natural breeding season. Thus, the low fertility normally encountered under domestication must be caused to a large extent by the relatively artificial conditions under which horses are mated.

So, understanding mare reproductive physiology is paramount to breeding horses today.

AGE OF PUBERTY

Fillies generally start coming in heat when 12 to 15 months of age.

AGE TO BREED MARES

Only exceptionally well-grown fillies should be bred as two-year-olds, so as to foal at three years of age. Under a system of early breeding, the fillies must be fed exceptionally well in order to provide growth for their own immature bodies as well as for the developing fetus. Furthermore, they usually should not be bred the following year. Generally speaking, it is best to breed the mare as a three-year-old so that she will foal when four. Not only will the three-year-old be better grown, but there will not be the handicap of training her while she is heavy in foal.

In selecting a broodmare, it is usually advisable either to obtain a young three- or four-year-old or to make certain of the sure and regular breeding habits of any old mares.

MARE REPRODUCTIVE PHYSIOLOGY

The mare has a seasonally polyestrous type of estrous cycle; which means that, typically, she is receptive to the stallion and ovulates only during certain times of the year.

During the anestrous (nonovulatory) period, most mares show no behavioral signs of sexual receptivity and fail to develop follicles which ovulate. In the northern hemisphere, the anestrous period of the mare occurs most frequently during the winter (mid-November to mid-February). There are exceptions; however, some mares show behavioral signs of sexual receptivity throughout the year, even though they usually do not ovulate in the winter.

During the ovulatory season—from about mid-April to mid-September, unless pregnant—the mare cycles, exhibits sexual receptivity to the stallion on a regular basis, and produces follicles which ovulate. During the ovulatory season, the mare undergoes a series of cycles, each of which is approximately 21 to 23 days in length; with some shorter, and others longer. The estrous cycle is divided into two physiological

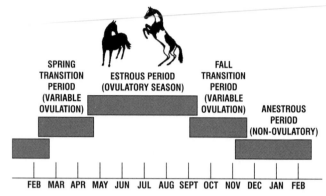

Fig. 12-17. Mare seasonality. From about mid-April to mid-September, the mare cycles and exhibits sexual receptivity to the stallion every 15 to 19 days.

parts: estrus and diestrus. *Estrus refers to the time the mare is in heat and sexually receptive to the stallion; it is the time of follicular maturation and ovulation. Diestrus refers to the longest period (15 to 19 days) of the estrous cycle; it is the time the mare is not receptive to the stallion.* But mares do not always follow a normal cycle—they're erratic!

Estrus usually lasts 3 to 7 days. Ovulation generally occurs 24 to 48 hours prior to the end of estrus. The mare enters diestrus following ovulation and the end of estrus. The follicle that ovulated at the end of the estrus develops into a structure called the corpus luteum (CL). If the mare is not pregnant, the corpus luteum will regress and follicular development will proceed at the end of diestrus. Diestrus usually lasts 15 to 19 days. Some mares may ovulate two follicles during estrus or a second follicle during early diestrus. The occurrence of a second ovulation during or subsequent to estrus may lead to twinning, which is undesirable in the equine species.

The hormones produced by the hypothalamus, anterior pituitary, and ovaries are responsible for both the release of the egg and the behavioral signs of estrus. It follows that management of the ovulatory season requires that those responsible for breeding mares have an understanding of normal hormonal patterns, because many management practices that are utilized to increase conception rates involve action upon these patterns. Normal levels of hormones, along with corresponding ovarian activity, are shown graphically in Fig. 12-18.

Pertinent information relative to each of the hormones listed in Fig. 12-18 follows:

■ **Estrogen**—This is the primary hormone responsible for the characteristic changes that occur in the mare's genital tract in preparation for ovulation and conception, and for causing the mare to show behavioral signs of receptivity to the stallion. It is highest when the mare is in estrus.

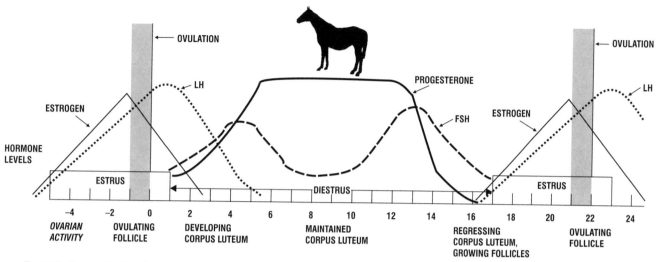

Fig. 12-18. Hormone levels and corresponding ovarian activity in the estrus period of the mare. Estrus (heat) usually lasts 3 to 7 days. The optimum time to breed is 20 to 24 hours before ovulation. (See screened bar areas.) The highest rate of conception may be obtained by serving the mare daily or every other day during the heat period, beginning with the third day.

■ **Leutenizing hormone (LH)**—This is the primary hormone responsible for ovulation. It is highest at ovulation.

■ **Follicle stimulating hormone (FSH)**—This hormone is mainly responsible for ovarian follicular development.

■ **Progesterone**—This hormone, which is produced in the corpus luteum, is primarily responsible for the recognition and maintenance of pregnancy.

Ovulation (day 0) occurs in response to increased levels of LH. If the mare is not pregnant, the corpus luteum (CL) begins to regress in response to prostaglandin (about day 13), with this regression complete by about day 18. Progesterone levels decrease when the CL regresses. About the same time (day 13) FSH levels increase, causing follicular growth in preparation for ovulation of the following estrus (day 19 to 22).

As with different phases of the estrous period, the transition from the anestrous period to the estrous period is due to the changes in hormonal patterns in response to photoperiod. Mares are long-day breeders.

The percentage of ovulating mares increases significantly as the daily photoperiod increases above the 12 hour vernal equinox (March 21), and decreases when daylight decreases in the fall below the 12 hour autumnal equinox (Sept. 21). Generally, the maximum number of naturally ovulating mares occurs during the maximum daylight periods of June.

The estrous cycle may be manipulated for any or all of the following purposes: (1) to enable breeding a mare at a predetermined time, (2) to allow breeding a group of mares within a narrow predetermined time (synchronization of ovulations), and (3) to spread and space ovulations of a group of mares over a relatively prolonged period of time that is most compatible within a given set of managerial conditions (scheduling of ovulations).

Breeding managers are generally concerned with estrous cycle manipulation and estrous detection.

ESTROUS CYCLE MANIPULATION

The two main methods of estrus manipulation are: artificial lighting, and hormonal control.

■ **Artificial Lighting For Mares**—Artificial lighting will result in earlier than normal initiation of the estrous cycle in mares.

Mares are seasonal breeders. Normally, their natural breeding season begins in mid-April and extends to mid-September. During this period, they usually experience regular heat cycles and ovulation every 21 to 22 days.

Seasonal influences on the estrous cycle of the mare are related to length of daylight, nutrition, and climatic factors (i.e., temperature). Length of daylight and nutrition can be controlled. It is noteworthy, too, that the reproductive function in sheep, poultry, and migratory fowl is regulated by the length of daylight.

The ratio of hours of daylight to darkness throughout the year acts on nerves in the region of the pituitary gland, and stimulates or inhibits the release of the follicle-stimulating hormone (FSH). Lengthening the daylight hours activates the pituitary, and causes it to release increasing amounts of the FSH which stimulates ovarian function. Thus, sometime after the daylight period begins to increase, the estrous cycle begins in mares.

Artificial lighting of broodmares enables breeders to bring mares in season about six weeks earlier than normal. By the use of the artificial light technique, a mare that would normally conceive on March 15 may get in foal sometime in February. By avoiding the necessity of skipping a year due to late breeding, this technique may actually result in obtaining two extra foals during the lifetime of a mare.

The procedure consists in using a 200-watt light bulb in a box stall so as to extend the hours of daylight to 16 hours daily. A general rule is that if a newspaper can be read easily in any corner of the stall or corral, the lighting is sufficient. By beginning the light treatment of mares about December 1, they may be bred about February 1.

Table 12-3 may be used as an artificial lighting guide in the northern United States.

Slight adjustments in the schedule given in Table 12-3 will need to be made in different locations, depending upon the sunrise and sunset times of the particular area.

TABLE 12-3
ARTIFICIAL LIGHTING SCHEDULE

Date	A.M.		P.M.	
	Lights On	Lights Off	Lights On	Lights Off
November 1	7:00	8:30	3:30	6:00
November 8	6:45	8:30	3:30	6:00
November 15	6:45	8:30	3:30	6:15
November 22	6:30	8:30	3:30	6:15
November 29	6:30	8:30	3:30	6:30
December 6	6:15	8:30	3:30	6:30
December 13	6:15	8:30	3:30	6:45
December 20	6:00	8:30	3:30	6:45
December 27	6:00	8:30	3:30	7:00
January 3	5:45	8:30	3:30	7:00
January 10	5:45	8:30	3:30	7:15
January 17	5:30	8:30	3:30	7:15
January 24	5:30	8:30	3:30	7:30
January 31	5:30	8:30	3:30	7:45
February 7	5:30	8:30	3:30	8:00
February 14	5:30	8:30	3:30	8:15
February 21	5:30	8:30	3:30	8:30

The following additional points are pertinent to the artificial lighting of mares:

1. While the use of artificial lighting has the greatest benefit on dry or open mares, recent studies indicate that early foaling mares will also respond to added light.

2. For maximum effect, mares should be housed in box stalls rather than sheds. This ensures that each mare is given a similar concentration of light and is kept within about 8 ft of the source. However, flood lights can be used on mares in outside corrals or pens.

3. Mares should not be expected to cycle immediately after being placed under lights. Although the time lapse between the initiation of lighting and estrus will vary between individual mares, it will usually be within the range of 45 to 60 days.

4. Once estrous cycles are initiated by light treatment in mares, their cycles continue in a normal manner.

5. When once put under the lights, mares should be kept under lights until spring. They should not be taken out part way through the season. A change in the lighting exposure program can bring about a severe upset to the established estrous cycle.

6. A regular teasing program accompanied by rectal examination of mares showing estrus is necessary to obtain desired results.

7. One good heat period and ovulation should occur before breeding. The mare can then be bred during the next heat period.

8. Artificial lighting will not increase fertility—it only extends the breeding season. Mares will shed their winter coats earlier, but they exhibit no other physiological changes. They will exhibit heat cycles about six weeks earlier than normal.

■ **Hormonal control of heat in mares**—Several pharmaceutical products are used in the horse industry to maximize conception rates once mares are cycling, with prostaglandin, progesterone, and human chorionic gonadotropin (HCG) heading the list.

1. **Prostaglandin (PGF$_{2a}$).** These hormonelike substances are natural compounds (fatty acids), synthesized in many body tissues. Prostaglandin F$_2$ alpha can be used for regressing the corpus luteum during normal cycles. Mares can be *short cycled* by treatment with prostaglandin F$_2$ alpha or one of its synthetic analogues, provided there is a viable corpus luteum present. Contrary to some opinions, it is not a heat-producing drug. Rather, it causes the corpus luteum to regress, and the mare secretes her own gonadotropins to regulate the ovary and cause a physiological heat. Prostaglandins are most effective when used subsequent to days 6 through 8 after ovulation, potentially reducing the interval from one heat to the next by as much as 8 days. Prostaglandin treatment is most often used on mares which were not bred on the previous cycle, and which have a viable corpus luteum that is suppressing cyclicity. The use of prostaglandin should be under the direct supervision of a veterinarian, both for determination of usage and because of occasional adverse affects. Pregnant women should avoid contact with the drug as it has been shown to cause abortion.

2. **Progesterone.** This hormone can be successfully used to suppress heat during transition into the

ovulatory season in mares which have histories of long and erratic estrous cycles during this time. Progesterone has also been used with less consistent results in an attempt to maintain pregnancy in mares with abortion history.

3. **Human Chorionic Gonadotropin (HCG).** This hormone, which has been used with some success in horse breeding, stimulates follicles to ovulate. It is most often given at the same time the mare is bred. HCG will normally lead to ovulation of a mature follicle within 48 hours, aiding in appointment breeding and helping mares which tend to develop a follicle and fail to ovulate.

4. **Other hormones.** Estrogen, gonadotropin releasing hormone (GnRH), and FSH have been used in an attempt to alter reproductive function. However, the use of these hormones alone on mares has not been as effective as when they are used in other large animal species.

ESTRUS DETECTION

One of the most important, but frequently overlooked, aspects of equine reproduction is estrus (heat) detection. Failure to detect heat and breed at a time conducive to conception are people-causes of infertility in mares. This can be easily corrected with knowledge of how to detect heat.

Palpation and teasing are the two most common management tools used in detection of heat. Most managers use a combination of palpation and teasing for estrus detection and breeding determination. Mares are teased, and those showing signs of estrus are palpated better to define reproductive status.

■ **Palpation**—Rectal palpation, and perhaps ultrasonography, will help define the time of ovulation, and thus aid in mating management. Parameters of follicular size, follicular consistency, cervical size and consistency, as well as uterine tone, can be monitored through rectal palpation. A mare with a large, very soft follicle that has an open cervix and proper uterine tone is ready for breeding. On the other hand, a mare that has no follicles, or that has very small turgid follicles, along with a closed cervix and poor uterine tone, is not ready for breeding.

■ **Teasing**—During the breeding season, most breeding establishments tease the mare daily. The teasing stallion should possess certain qualities that enable him to contribute to a successful breeding season. He must have good temperament, strong libido, and be aggressive enough to encourage outward signs of heat; he must be able to elicit estrus from obstinate mares. An ill-mannered teaser that requires constant restraint is likely to injure mares and/or handlers during the teasing process.

Behavior during estrus is characterized by an obviously receptive attitude toward the stallion. Upon sight or sound of the teasing stallion, mares in good *standing heat* will assume a squatting posture with a raised tail, urinate frequently, and have spasmodic *winking* of the vulva (*i.e.,* eversion of the clitoris). On the other hand, maiden mares, shy mares, or mares with foals may not show strong signs of heat when teased. So, it is important to use skillful observation, patience, and a variety of heat detection techniques. The behavior of mares that are teased when not in heat ranges from neutral to extremely violent.

Mares may be individually teased or placed in teasing pens to allow for group teasing. Also, teasing procedures are very individualistic, depending on the stud manager and the design of the facilities. The most common facilities/methods of teasing follow:

1. **Stall door.** There are two ways in which to use a safe and securely fastened stall door as the partition. The stallion can be led by each mare's stall, or each mare can be led by the stallion's stall. From a labor-saving standpoint, it is best to lead the teasing stallion by each mare's stall, because this method does not require handling each mare.

In stall door teasing, the teasing stallion and mare are introduced by a brief nose-to-nose partition. If the mare is in estrus, she will be receptive toward the stallion. If not, she will likely lay her ears back, squeal, and strike at the stallion. The teaser should be allowed gently to nip and nuzzle the mare, but he should not be allowed to get rough. Sometimes, a little gentle persuasion on the part of the stallion will reveal that an initially resistant mare is actually in heat. The mare is not in heat if she ignores the stallion or remains hostile. Hand teasing provides safety for everyone involved, and allows for individualized attention to every mare.

2. **Teasing wall/solid fence.** The teasing wall can be used in the same manner as the stall door. The wall is constructed of two heavy wooden layers that are heavily padded. The teasing wall allows the stallion to have intimate contact with the mare during the teasing process.

3. **Multiple-teaser pen.** This system involves a large octagonal-shaped teaser pen. The teaser is placed in the center and is surrounded by smaller pens so that several mares can be teased at once.

4. **Teasing chute.** This method consists in using a long chute, which will accommodate several mares at one time. The teasing stallion is led up and down the solid side of the chute to tease. After teasing, the mares can be led through the exit and replaced by another group.

5. **Pasture teasing.** In this system, the teaser stallion is led along the fenceline to tease mares in large pens or in a pasture. Pasture teasing is not

Fig. 12-19. David E. McGlothlin, Manager, Horse Division, Harris Farms, is shown overseeing teasing, using a solid fence for separation of the stallion and mare. (Courtesy, David McGlothlin, Harris Farms, Coalinga, CA)

always effective, because dominant mares may keep timid mares from being adequately teased.

6. **Vasectomy.** This method consists in allowing a vasectomized stallion to run with a band of brood mares, thus providing a natural teasing environment. However, vasectomy teasing has two drawbacks: (1) it may increase the spread of infection between mares via the teasing stallion, and (2) it increases the chances of injury to both the teaser and the mares.

7. **Teasing cage.** This method consists of constructing a teasing cage in one corner of the pasture where the stallion can be released and allowed to tease. In order to be effective, dominant mares must be removed so that timid mares that may be in estrus can have access to the stallion.

There are many teasing techniques, just a few of which have been listed and described. The teasing program is individualistic; it must be developed to meet the specific needs of the breeding farm manager. In whatever teasing program is developed, emphasis should be placed on safety of the horses and personnel involved. It cannot be rushed; each mare must be given time to react.

BREEDING OPERATIONS

No phase of horse production has become more unnatural or more complicated with domestication than the actual breeding operation. It is important, therefore, that those responsible for breeding conduct each operation thereof in such manner as to maximize conception.

CONDITIONING THE MARE FOR BREEDING

Proper conditioning of the mare prior to breeding is just as important as in the stallion. Such conditioning depends primarily upon adequate and proper feed and the right amount of exercise.

For the highest rate of conception, mares should be neither too thin nor too fat; a happy medium in condition makes for best results. It is especially important that one avoid the natural tendency of barren or maiden mares to get too fat.

Time permitting, mares of the light-horse breeds may best be exercised and conditioned by riding under saddle or driving in harness. When these methods are not practical or feasible, permitting a band of mares to run in a large pasture will usually provide a satisfactory amount of exercise.

EXAMINATION OF THE MARE

Ahead of the breeding season, the breeding farm staff should evaluate the maiden, barren, and open mares and prepare them for the breeding season. Each mare should be given a physical examination and cultured for uterine infections. Mares that have uterine infections or other reproductive disorders should be treated. Mares that have a deep-set anus and a vulva that forms a shelf, instead of being nearly vertical as is normal, should be sutured (Caslick operation), to alleviate their vulvas from aspiring air and contaminants into their reproductive tracts. Mares that are overweight should be placed on a diet.

Before accepting outside mares for service, stud managers should check every possible condition with care. They should examine the mare closely and question owners concerning health, last foaling date, breeding record, and similar matters. They should be well acquainted with the symptoms of dourine and other venereal diseases. Even though these diseases are not common in this country, there is always danger of finding them in imported stallions and mares. It is wise to require that barren mares be accompanied by a health certificate signed by a veterinarian. The following types of mares should be rejected:

1. Mares showing the slightest symptoms of venereal disease.

2. Mares that have an abnormal discharge (such as blood or pus) from the vagina, commonly known as the whites.

3. Mares affected with skin diseases and parasites.

4. Mares suffering from high fevers, which accompany colds, strangles, influenza, shipping fever, and pneumonia.

5. Mares that have recently suffered from retained afterbirth.

6. Mares that have suffered lacerations in foaling.

7. Mares that do not show definite signs of heat.

8. Mares under three years of age unless mature and well developed.

9. Mares that have a very narrow or deformed pelvis.

10. Mares that stay in heat incessantly (nymphomaniacs).

11. Mares that are extremely thin or emaciated.

12. Mares that have severe unsoundnesses which may be hereditary.

When mares have been barren over an extended period or when there is the slightest suspicion of infection, it is good protection to require a veterinarian's certificate to the effect that the mare is in a healthy breeding condition.

During the breeding season on most farms, as each mare comes into estrus (as determined by daily teasing), she is given (1) genital organ examination consisting of visual inspection of the cervix and vagina, and (2) a daily palpation per rectum of the uterus and ovaries. The changes in the cervix, vagina, and ovaries are correlated with the behavioral signs of estrus to determine the time to breed; the optimal time is just ahead of ovulation. By use of a teaser and rectal palpation, an experienced stud manager or veterinarian can determine the stage of the estrus cycle.

HAND BREEDING (NATURAL SERVICE)

Where natural service is involved, hand-breeding is undoubtedly the best way in which to breed mares; it is the accepted practice in the better breeding establishments throughout the world. It allows the breeder to record breeding dates and project foaling dates; and it guards against injury to both the stallion and the mare.

In preparation for breeding, the mare's tail is wrapped with either a track bandage, disposable obstetrical sleeve, tube sock, or some other tail covering, followed by washing her external genitalia. Wrapping the tail prevents interference during breeding and prevents hairs from irritating or lacerating the stallion's penis. The mare's hindquarters are thoroughly washed with warm soapy water, always starting with the vulva and washing outward to minimize the chances of recontaminating a clean area. The washing procedure should be repeated three times, following which the area should be rinsed thoroughly with lukewarm water and the hindquarters dried with clean paper towels; again, going from the center outward. The mare is then led to the breeding area and restrained for breeding. Even when the mare is showing standing estrus, breeding hobbles and a twitch should be applied for protection of the stallion.

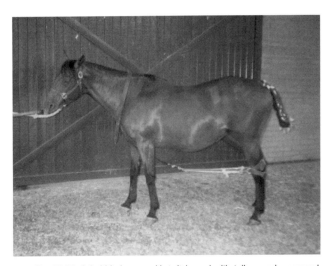

Fig. 12-20. A hobbled mare with twitch, and with tail properly wrapped, ready for service. Hobbles and twitches are used only to protect the stallion as he approaches and dismounts and not in any way to force the mare into submission to service when not ready. (Courtesy, David E. McGlothlin, Manager, Horse Division, Harris Farms, Coalinga, CA)

The stallion should be allowed to tease the mare briefly to encourage the extension of the penis. Then, he should be moved to the wash area, which should be close to the breeding area and in sight of the mare to help stimulate continued expansion of the penis. The stallion's penis is washed with clean, warm water at 100°F until all smegma, debris, and dead skin are removed.

The stallion is then led to the mare's left side at about a 45° angle and allowed to tease the mare in order to achieve a full erection; however, he is not allowed to mount the mare until a full erection is achieved. Usually a slight pull on the lead shank before he shifts his weight to the hind feet is sufficient to prevent mounting. The stallion should not be allowed to savage the mare; he should be reprimanded when necessary. However, excessive correction during breeding should be avoided as it may have serious physiological effects, such as resulting in reduced libido or refusal to mount the mare. Once the stallion mounts, the mare's tail should be pulled to one side, and, if needed, the stallion's penis should be guided for proper intromission. During breeding, the handler of the mare should keep her from moving or walking around. Ejaculation is signaled by flagging of the stallion's tail, or by pulsation along the urethra, which may be detected by holding the base of the penis gently. The stallion should be allowed to rest on the mare for a few seconds, following which he dismounts. As he dismounts, the mare is watched carefully and turned to the left to prevent her from kicking the stallion. The stallion is rewashed before being returned to his stall to prevent possible spreading of disease.

Most breeding farms employ the *jumping* procedure before allowing a valuable stallion to breed a young mare. The mare is restrained, as for regular breeding. Then, a gentle teaser is allowed to approach and mount her. But actual copulation is prevented by diverting the penis of the teaser to one side. This gives the young mare an opportunity to discover what is going to happen and serves as added protection to a valuable stallion.

ARTIFICIAL INSEMINATION (AI)

Artificial insemination is less widely practiced in horses than in dairy cattle. However, beginning about the mid-1990s, most horse breed registry associations liberalized their rules and the use of AI increased.

AI permits more mares to be bred to a stallion, and makes for a higher conception rate; lessens the hazard of transmitting an infection or disease; and lessens the risk of biting and kicking.

■ **Kinds of processed semen.** Three kinds of processed semen are used in horses——fresh, frozen, and cooled.

1. **Fresh stallion semen.** Fresh semen is collected, an extender is usually added, and it may be stored in a refrigerator at a temperature of about 55°F (13°C), and used within 24 hours.

2. **Frozen semen.** Following collection, an extender is added to semen that is to be frozen, and it can be stored indefinitely.

3. **Cooled semen.** Cooled semen is usually extended with at least three parts of extender to one part of semen (as opposed to 1:1 with fresh semen), and used within 24 hours.

Cooled semen is semen that is slowly cooled from body temperature down to 41°F (5°C). Cooled semen is viable for 24 hours. Thus, with cooled semen a mare owner in California may breed to a stallion in Texas, or vice versa, without shipping the mare. Following collection, semen that is to be cooled is evaluated, an extender is added, it is put into a container that gradually cools it down to 41°F *(5°C)*, and placed in a plastic bag. The Equitainor is one of the most popular containers for cooling down semen, although several disposal containers are now on the market.

The recommended count for fresh semen is 500 million motile spermatozoa. With cooled semen, it is 1 billion. Thus, stallion managers need to be aware that if a stallion can normally breed six mares from one collection of fresh semen, that number will be reduced to approximately three mares with cooled semen.

A mare is bred with cooled semen as she would in normal AI; the semen is taken from the container and inserted directly into the mare. There is no need to warm the semen.

Several breeds accept the use of cooled semen. The Warmbloods have used cooled semen for years; and it is presently accepted by the registry associations of the following breeds: Arabians, Tennessee Walking Horses, American Saddlebreds, American Show Horses, Paint Horses, and Standardbreds. Beginning in 1997, the American Quarter Horse Association accepted cooled semen.

■ **Collection**——Semen for artificial insemination in horses may be collected by means of a breeder's bag (condom) or by use of an artificial vagina (AV). An AV provides the best results and lessens contamination. The following three kinds of AVs are available: (1) The FHK model, (2) the Colorado Model, and (3) the Missouri Model. When used, the temperature of an AV should be 108–111°F *(42–44°C)*, achieved through filling the water-container space of the AV with warm water; and the AV should be properly lubricated.

■ **Evaluation**——Following collection, semen is evaluated by three criteria: (1) volume, (2) motility, and (3) concentration. The typical ejaculate volume is about 50 ml, but it may range from 40 to over 150 ml. The sperm concentration ranges from 30 million to 800 million per milliliter, with a total of 6 to 10 billion sperm per ejaculate.

■ **Extended**——Semen may be extended from one to several times, depending on sperm concentration and quality. Numerous extenders are available. Most extenders include egg yolk, milk, milk byproducts, and chemicals to regulate osmolarity and/or pH. Extenders should be prepared on the day of semen collection.

■ **Time of insemination**——The estrous cycle of the mare ranges from 10 to 37 days, but averages 21 to 23 days. Ovulation commonly occurs 24 to 36 hours before the end of heat. The mare should be inseminated about two days before the end of heat to one day after the end of heat. The use of transrectal ultrasound techniques or palpation to determine approaching ovulation will increase the efficiency of sperm usage and conception.

■ **Insemination procedure**——The procedure for inseminating the mare is the same whether using fresh, frozen, or cooled semen. For liquid semen, a syringe attached to a plastic disposable horse breeding tube is frequently used. For frozen semen in straws an insemination gun is commonly used. Prior to insemination, the mare's buttocks and external genitalia should be cleaned and disinfected; and a clean paper towel should be used to wipe the lips of the vulva prior to entry. The inseminator usually uses a shoulder-length disposable plastic glove that is sanitized and lubricated.

BREEDING AFTER FOALING

Mares usually come in heat 7 to 10 days after foaling (known as *foal heat*), with individual mares varying from 3 to 13 days after foaling. Provided that foaling has been extremely normal and there is no discharge or evidence of infection, they may be rebred at this time. Mares not bred at foal heat or not conceiving will come in heat between the 25th and 30th day after foaling.

If any of the following conditions exist, mares should not be rebred at foal heat: placenta retained more than three hours, unhealed lacerations in the cervix or vagina, severe bruises—especially of the cervix, vaginal discharge, lack of tone in the uterus, or the presence of urine in the vagina.

Mares suffering from an infection of the genital tract are seldom settled in service. Besides, the infection may be needlessly spread to the stallion and other mares by such a practice.

BREEDING RECORDS

The keeping of accurate records of each mare's reproductive status is most important. Breeding records, health records, and teasing/palpation records are necessary to assist in attaining maximum productivity. Breeding records should include mare identification, breeding dates, health comments, and expected actual foaling date. Health records should identify the date and description of health care, including the person who administered it. The teasing record should include identification of the mare, teasing dates, teasing codes (an intensity of heat score) corresponding to the teasing dates, and other information such as treatment records and dates bred.

Palpation records should include dates and comments relative to each palpation, teasing scores, and information describing follicular and reproductive tract condition.

Fig. 12-21 is an example of a Teasing and Palpation Record, to which the following codes correspond:

Teasing Code
1-Mare is visibly resistant to stallion
2-Mare is indifferent to stallion
3-Mare is slightly interested in stallion; urinates, winks vulva
4-Mare is greatly interested in stallion; urination, profuse vulva activity
5-Mare is greatly interested in stallion; profuse urination, squatting

Follicular Size
Commonly sized as 10, 20, 30, 40, or 50 millimeters in diameter

Follicular Consistency
T-Turgid
S-Soft
B-Breedable (very soft)
O-Ovulated

Cervix Size
1-10 millimeters
2-20 millimeters
3-30 millimeters
4-40 millimeters
5-50 millimeters

Uterine Tone
Poor, Fair, Good, or Excellent

FERTILIZATION

Generally, the egg is liberated during the period of one day before to one day after the end of heat. Unfortunately, there is no reliable way of predicting the length of heat nor the time of ovulation by palpation—by feeling the ovary (follicle) with the hand through the rectal wall.

The sperm (or male germ cells) are deposited in the uterus at the time of service and from there ascend the reproductive tract. Under favorable conditions, they meet the egg, and one of them fertilizes it in the upper part of the oviduct near the ovary.

A series of delicate time relationships must be met, however, or the egg will never be fertilized. The sperm cells live only 24 to 30 hours in the reproductive tract of the female, and it probably requires 4 to 6 hours for them to ascend the female reproductive tract. Moreover, the egg is viable for an even shorter period of time than the sperm, probably for not more than 4 to 6 hours after ovulation. For conception, therefore, breeding must take place within 20 to 24 hours before ovulation.

As mares usually stay in heat from four to six days, perhaps the highest rate of conception may be obtained by serving the mare daily or every other day during the heat period, beginning with the third day. When many mares are being bred and heavy demands are being made upon a given stallion, this condition may be obtained by reinforcing a natural service with subsequent daily artificial insemination as long as heat lasts. In no case should the mare be bred twice in the same day.

PREGNANCY DETERMINATION

In order to produce as high a percentage of foals as possible and to have them arrive at the time desired, the horse breeder should be familiar with the signs of

HORSES & HORSEMANSHIP

Tease Code

1. Resistance
2. Indifferent
3. Interested
4. Wings vulva, urinates
5. Profuse urination and vulvular activity

T Treated
C Culture
S Speculum
P Palpate
B Bred
Pr Pregnant
F Foaled
A Arrived
D Departed

TS Tease Score
FS Follicle Size
CX Cervix
FC Follicular Consistency

Mare _____ Color _____ Age _____ Farm Number _____

Year ____ Booked to _____ Mare Owner _____

Results of last year's breeding _____

	1	2	3	4	5	6	7	8	9	10	11	12	13	14	15	16	17	18	19	20	21	22	23	24	25	26	27	28	29	30	31
Dec.																															
Jan.																															
Feb.																															
Mar.																															
Apr.																															
May																															
June																															
July																															

Palpation

Date _____ Remarks _____
ts: 1 2 3 4 5
fs: _____ mm.
cx: 1 2 3 4
fc: t c b o
Uterine tone _____

Date _____ Remarks _____
ts: 1 2 3 4 5
fs: _____ mm.
cx: 1 2 3 4
fc: t c b o
Uterine tone _____

Date _____ Remarks _____
ts: 1 2 3 4 5
fs: _____ mm.
cx: 1 2 3 4
fc: t c b o
Uterine tone _____

Date _____ Remarks _____
ts: 1 2 3 4 5
fs: _____ mm.
cx: 1 2 3 4
fc: t c b o
Uterine tone _____

Date _____ Remarks _____
ts: 1 2 3 4 5
fs: _____ mm.
cx: 1 2 3 4
fc: t c b o
Uterine tone _____

Date _____ Remarks _____
ts: 1 2 3 4 5
fs: _____ mm.
cx: 1 2 3 4
fc: t c b o
Uterine tone _____

Fig. 12-21. Teasing and Palpation Record For Mares from *Reproductive Management of the Mare*, OSU Extension Facts, No. 3974.

and tests of pregnancy. This is doubly important when it is recognized that a great many mares may either be shy breeders or show signs of heat even when well advanced in gestation.

By identifying open mares, it is possible (1) to cull mares more intelligently and sharply reduce management costs; and (2) to separate pregnant mares from barren ones, and manage each group more effectively and efficiently. In some cases when a pregnancy test shows that a valuable mare is not in foal, the early diagnosis of her nonpregnant state will allow a veterinarian to initiate an early treatment program to improve her chances of conception the next year.

The signs of pregnancy follow:

1. **The cessation of the heat period.** One of the simplest determinations of pregnancy is the cessation of the heat period—the mare does not exhibit any signs of heat 18 to 20 days after her last ovulation. This may be difficult to determine as well as misleading. Some mares will continue to exhibit the characteristic heat symptoms when in foal; sometimes, they show such pronounced signs of heat that they are given the service of a stallion, which may result in abortion. Other mares may not cycle due to follicular or corpora luteal abnormalities or have silent heat periods in which external signs of estrus are not evident. Because of these situations, other methods of pregnancy are commonly used.

2. **Rectal palpation.** The most widely used method of pregnancy determination is by rectal palpation.

An experienced technician can determine pregnancy (or barrenness) of mares at 98 to 100% accuracy by feeling with the hand through the rectal wall.

Normally, the test is made 18 to 25 days after breeding. When performed by an experienced person, the manual test is quite reliable.

The following procedure is employed by most experienced technicians in making the manual test:

a. The examination is made in surroundings familiar to the mare and in an unhurried manner, as this (a) makes for a minimum of restraint, and (b) avoids roughness.

b. Two helpers are needed; one to twitch the mare, and the other to hold the tail to one side. If the mare objects to the twitch, it is left off.

c. The latex obstetrical sleeve with glove attached is slipped on and lubricated. The rectum is entered and evacuated, the arm is inserted nearly to the shoulder, reaching forward and downward until the ovaries are located (the left ovary is most accessible for the right-handed operators; the right ovary for left-handed operators); and the uterus is gently palpated and massaged. If the mare is 43 to 45 days pregnant, an enlargement approximately the size of a large orange can be located along the bottom of one of the uterine horns.

3. **Ultrasonography.** In recent years, ultrasonography has increased in use in pregnancy determination. This technique can be used to obtain a visual image of the mare's reproductive tract, and thus detection of pregnancy, before palpation is normally performed. Ultrasonography is normally utilized following the 18th day postbreeding, but it can detect pregnancies as early as 13 to 14 days postovulation.

The ultrasound can also be used to detect follicular development, to detect estrus, and to detect reproductive abnormalities.

4. **Blood tests.** Blood tests, involving blood samples taken 40 to 45 days following breeding, give an indication of pregnancy. The disadvantage of blood tests is that the hormone, Equine Chorionic Gonadotropin, is not measurable to a large extent earlier than 40 to 45 days after conception.

GESTATION PERIOD

The average gestation period of mares is 336 days, or a little over 11 months. This will vary, however, with individual mares and may range from 310 to 370 days. A handy rule-of-thumb method that may be used to figure the approximate date of foaling is to subtract 1 month and add 2 days to the date the mare was bred. Hence, a mare bred May 20 should foal April 22 the following year.

CARE OF THE PREGNANT MARE

Barren and foaling mares are usually kept separately because pregnant mares are sedate, whereas barren mares are more likely to run, tease, and kick. Precautions in handling the pregnant mare will be covered in the discussion that follows.

QUARTERS FOR THE MARE

If mares are worked under saddle or in harness, they may be given quarters like those accorded to the rest of the horses used similarly, at least until near parturition time. Idle mares may be best turned out to pasture.

FEEDING THE PREGNANT MARE

The feed and water requirements for the pregnant mare are adequately discussed in Chapter 13, so repetition is unnecessary.

Fig. 12-22. Mare and foal in paddock adjacent to their quarters at Walmac International, Lexington, KY. (Courtesy, Thoroughbred Publications, Inc., Lexington, KY)

EXERCISE FOR THE PREGNANT MARE

The pregnant mare should have plenty of exercise. This may be obtained by allowing a band of broodmares to roam over large pastures in which shade, water, and minerals are available.

Mares of the light-horse breeds may be exercised for an hour daily under saddle or hitched to a cart. When handled carefully, the broodmare may be so exercised to within a day or two of foaling. Above all, when not receiving forced exercise or on idle days, she should not be confined to a stable or small drylot.

CARE AT FOALING TIME

A breeding record should be kept on each mare so that it will be known when she is due to foal. As has been previously indicated, the period of gestation of a mare is about 336 days, but it may vary as much as a month in either direction. Therefore, the careful and observant caretaker will be ever alert and make certain definite preparations in ample time.

The period of parturition is one of the most critical stages in the life of the mare. Through carelessness or ignorance, all of the advantages gained in selecting genetically desirable and healthy parent stock and in providing the very best of environmental and nutritional conditions through gestation can be quickly dissipated at this time. Generally speaking, less difficulty at parturition was encountered in the wild state, when the females of all species brought forth their young in the fields and glens.

WORK AND EXERCISE

Saddle and light-harness mares should be exercised moderately in the accustomed manner. If they are not used, other gentle exercise, such as leading, should be provided. This is especially important if they have not been accustomed to being on pasture and if it is desired to avoid abrupt changes in feeding at this time.

SIGNS OF APPROACHING PARTURITION

Usually the first sign of approaching parturition is a distended udder, which may be observed 2 to 6 weeks before foaling time. About 7 to 10 days before the arrival, there will generally be a marked shrinkage or falling away of the muscular parts of the top of the buttocks near the tailhead and a falling of the abdomen. Although the udder may have filled out previously, the teats seldom fill out to the ends more than 4 to 6 days before foaling; and the wax on the ends of the nipples generally is not present until within 2 to 4 days before parturition. About this time the vulva becomes full and loose. As foaling time draws nearer, milk will drop from the teats; and the mare will show restlessness, break into a sweat, urinate frequently, lie down and get up, etc. It should be remembered, however, that there are times when all signs fail and a foal may be dropped when least expected. Therefore, it is well to be prepared as much as 30 days in advance of the expected foaling time.

PREPARATION FOR FOALING

Approximately one month ahead of foaling, consideration should be given to vaccinating gestating mares. At this time, one prominent California horse farm routinely gives each mare a four-way booster shot against tetanus, influenza, and Western and Eastern encephalomyelitis (sleeping sickness), along with a vaccine for the prevention of strangles. The tetanus booster shot administered at this time forms sufficient antibodies to protect both the mare and the foal (the latter via colostrum). Also, at this time, sutures are removed from sutured (Caslicked) mares; and the feet and teeth receive such attention as necessary.

When signs of approaching parturition seem to indicate that the foal may be expected within a week or 10 days, arrangements for the place of foaling should be completed. Thus, the mare will become accustomed to the new surroundings before the time arrives.

During the spring, summer, and fall months when the weather is warm, the most natural and ideal place for foaling is a clean, open pasture away from other livestock. Under these conditions, there is decidedly less danger of either infection or mechanical injury to the mare and foal. Of course, in following the practice, it is important that the ground be dry and warm. Small paddocks or lots that are unclean and foul with droppings are unsatisfactory and may cause such infectious troubles as navel ill.

During inclement weather, the mare should be placed in a roomy, well-lighted, well-ventilated, comfortable, quiet box stall, free of projections, which should be first carefully cleaned, disinfected, and bedded for the occasion. It is best that the mare be stabled therein at nights a week to 10 days before foaling so that she may become accustomed to the new surroundings. The foaling stall should be at least 12 feet square and free from any low mangers, hay racks, or other obstructions that might cause injury to either the mare or the foal. After the foaling stall has been thoroughly cleaned, it should be disinfected to reduce possible infection. This may be done by scrubbing with boiling hot lye water, made by using 8 oz of lye to 20 gal. of water (one-half this strength of solution should be used in scrubbing mangers and grain boxes). The floors should then be sprinkled with air-slaked lime. Plenty of clean, fresh bedding should be provided at all times.

A foaling stall somewhat away from other horses and with a smooth, well-packed clay floor is preferred. The clay floor may be slightly more difficult to keep smooth and sanitary than concrete or other such surface materials, but there is less danger to the mare and the newborn foal from slipping and falling; and it is decidedly better for the hoofs.

FEEDING AT FOALING TIME

Shortly before foaling, it is usually best to decrease the grain allowance slightly and to make more liberal use of light and laxative feeds, especially wheat bran. If there is any sign of constipation, a wheat bran mash should be provided.

THE ATTENDANT

A good rule for the attendant is to *be near but not in sight*. Some mares seem to resent the presence of an attendant at this time, and they will delay foaling as long as possible under such circumstances. Mares that have foaled previously and which have been properly fed and exercised will usually not experience any difficulty. However, young mares foaling for the first time, old mares, or mares that are either over-fat or in a thin run-down condition may experience considerable difficulty. The presence of the attendant may prevent possible injury to the mare and foal; and, when necessary, the attendant may aid the mare or call a veterinarian.

PARTURITION

The immediate indications that the mare is about to foal are extreme nervousness and uneasiness, lying down and getting up, biting at the sides and flanks, switching of the tail, sweating in the flanks, and frequent urination.

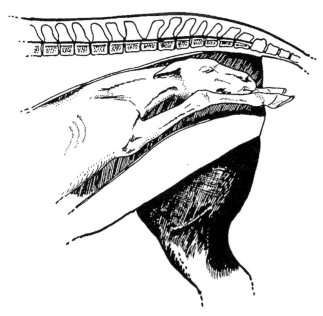

Fig. 12-23. Normal presentation. The back of the fetus is toward the back of the mother, the forelegs are extended toward the vulva with the heels down, and the nose rests between the forelegs.

The first actual indication of foaling is the rupture of the outer fetal membrane, followed by the escape of a large amount of fluid. This is commonly referred to as the rupture of the water bag. The inner membrane surrounding the foal appears next, and labor then becomes more marked.

With normal presentation, a mare foals rapidly, usually not taking more than 15 to 30 minutes. Usually, when the labor pains are at their height, the mare will be down, and it is in this position that the foal is generally born, while the mare is lying on her side with all legs stretched out.

In normal presentation, the front feet, with heels down, come first, followed by the nose which is resting on them, then the shoulders, the middle (with the back up), the hips, and then the hind legs and feet. If the presentation is other than normal, a veterinarian should be summoned at once, for there is great danger that the foal will smother if its birth is delayed. If the feet are presented with the bottoms up, it is a good indication that they are the hind ones, and there is likely to be difficulty.

If after reasonable time and effort have been expended a mare appears to be making no progress in parturition, it is advisable that an examination be made and assistance be rendered before the animal has completely exhausted her strength in futile efforts at expulsion. In rendering any such assistance, the following cardinal features should exist:

1. Cleanliness
2. Quietness
3. Gentleness
4. Perseverence
5. Knowledge, skill, and experience

When parturition is unduly delayed or retarded the fetus often dies from twists or knots in the umbilical cord, or from remaining too long in the passage. In either case, there may be stoppage of fetal circulation or lack of oxygen for the fetus, or both.

If foaling has been normal, the attendant should enter the stable to make certain that the foal is breathing and that the membrane has been removed from its mouth and nostrils. If the foal fails to breathe immediately, artificial respiration should be applied. This may be done by blowing into the mouth of the foal, working the ribs, rubbing the body vigorously, and permitting the foal to fall around. Then after the navel has been treated, the mare and foal should be left to lie and rest quietly as long as possible so that they may gain strength.

BIRTH OF A FOAL

The birth of this foal—from start to finish—took only about 15 minutes. The photos for Figs. 12-24a through 12-24k were taken at approximately one-minute intervals, with the stages of birth indicated by the sequence of letters. The last picture (Fig. 12-24l),

taken 15 minutes after birth, shows *Pocohontas*, the newborn Pony of the Americas foal, with a new-found friend, Debbie.

Fig. 12-24a. (Courtesy, Dean Kenney, Blue Ribbon Ranch, Culver City, CA)

Fig. 12-24d. (Courtesy, Dean Kenney, Blue Ribbon Ranch, Culver City, CA)

Fig. 12-24b. (Courtesy, Dean Kenney, Blue Ribbon Ranch, Culver City, CA)

Fig. 12-24e. (Courtesy, Dean Kenney, Blue Ribbon Ranch, Culver City, CA)

Fig. 12-24c. (Courtesy, Dean Kenney, Blue Ribbon Ranch, Culver City, CA)

Fig. 12-24f. (Courtesy, Dean Kenney, Blue Ribbon Ranch, Culver City, CA)

Fig. 12-24g. (Courtesy, Dean Kenney, Blue Ribbon Ranch, Culver City, CA)

Fig. 12-24j. (Courtesy, Dean Kenney, Blue Ribbon Ranch, Culver City, CA)

Fig. 12-24h. (Courtesy, Dean Kenney, Blue Ribbon Ranch, Culver City, CA)

Fig. 12-24k. (Courtesy, Dean Kenney, Blue Ribbon Ranch, Culver City, CA)

Fig. 12-24i. (Courtesy, Dean Kenney, Blue Ribbon Ranch, Culver City, CA)

Fig. 12-24l. (Courtesy, Dean Kenney, Blue Ribbon Ranch, Culver City, CA)

AFTERBIRTH

To aid in afterbirth (placenta) expulsion and involution of the uterus, immediately after foaling some horse breeding managers give to each foaling mare, except old mares or mares that have had a difficult time foaling, 100 USP units of the hormone oxytocin.

If the afterbirth is not expelled as soon as the mare gets up, it should either be tied up in a knot or tied to the tail of the mare. This should be done so that the foal or mare will not step on it, thereby increasing the danger of inflammation of the uterus and foal founder in the mare. Usually, the afterbirth will be expelled within 1 to 6 hours after foaling. If it is retained for a longer period, or if lameness is evident, the mare should be blanketed, and an experienced veterinarian should be called. Retained afterbirth often causes laminitis, which is recognized by lameness in the mare. This is usually treated by feeding easily digested feed for a period of 36 hours and by applying cold applications to the mare's feet until the condition is relieved.

The afterbirth should always be examined for evidence of infection and to ensure that none of it remains in the mare.

To prevent development of bacteria and foul odors, the afterbirth should be removed from the stall and burned or buried in lime.

As soon as possible after the afterbirth has passed, mares that previously were sutured are resutured (Caslicked).

CLEANING THE STALL

Once the foal and mare are up, the stall should be cleaned, wet, stained, or soiled bedding should be removed. The floor should be sprinkled with lime; and clean, fresh bedding should be provided. Such sanitary measures will be of great help in preventing the most common type of joint ill.

If the weather is extremely cold and the mare hot and sweaty, she should be rubbed down, dried, and blanketed soon after getting on her feet.

FEED AND WATER AFTER FOALING

Following foaling, the mare usually is somewhat hot and feverish. Occasionally, a mare will show symptoms of colic a few minutes after foaling. The abdominal pain is due to contraction of the uterine muscles. Usually, these symptoms last for only a few minutes.

After foaling, the mare should be given small quantities of lukewarm water at intervals, but she should never be allowed to gorge. It is also well to feed lightly and with laxative feeds for the first few days. The very first feed might well be a wet bran mash with a few oats or a little oat meal soaked in warm water. About one-half the usual amount should be fed. Usually, for the first week, no better grain ration can be provided than bran and oats. The quantity of feed given should be governed by the mild flow, the demands of the foal, and the appetite and condition of the mare. Usually the mare can be back on full feed within a week or 10 days after foaling.

OBSERVATION

The good caretaker will be ever alert to discover difficulties before it is too late. If the mare has much temperature (normal for the horse is about 101°F), something is wrong and the veterinarian should be called. As a precautionary measure, the mare's temperature should be taken a day or two after foaling. Any discharge from the vulva should be regarded with suspicion.

POST FOALING EVALUATION

Following each foaling, a post foaling evaluation and record should be made. If the birth was normal and without incident, it should be so stated. If foaling was abnormal, it should be detailed, with such things as the following recorded: abnormal presentation of the fetus (hind feet first, two forelegs but no head, prolonged labor without fetus showing, etc.); size of foal (especially if oversized); weak foal; bruising or tearing; broken ribs; convulsive syndrome; retained afterbirth (length of time retained); laminitis; temperature of the mare (normal is 101°F); infusion and type—if any; and colic.

HANDLING THE NEWBORN FOAL

Immediately after the foal has arrived and breathing has started, it should be thoroughly rubbed and dried with warm towels. Then it should be placed in one corner of the stall on clean, fresh straw. Usually the mare will be less restless if this corner is in the direction of her head. The eyes of a newborn foal should be protected from bright light.

NAVEL CORD

At the time the umbilical cord is ruptured, there is a direct communication from outside the body to some of the vital organs and the blood of the foal. Usually this opening is soon closed by the ensuing swelling and final drying and sloughing-off process. Under natural conditions, in the wild state, there was little danger

Fig. 12-25. A mare and her newborn foal.

of navel infection, but domestication and foaling under confined conditions have changed all this.

To reduce the danger of navel infection (which causes a disease known as joint ill or navel ill), the navel cord of the newborn foal should be treated at once with a solution of 7% tincture of iodine (or Metaphen or Merthiolate may be used). This may be done by placing the end of the cord in a wide mouthed bottle nearly full of tincture of iodine while pressing the bottle firmly against the abdomen. This is best done with the foal lying down. The cord should then be dusted with a good antiseptic powder. Dusting with the powder should be continued daily until the stump dries up and drops off and the scar heals, usually in 3 or 4 days. If an antiseptic powder is not available, air-slaked lime may be used. Any foreign matter that accumulates on the navel should be pressed out, and a disinfectant should be applied.

In 1994, researchers at the California Veterinary Research Laboratory, at Davis, reported that they found 0.5% chlorhexidine (Nolvasan diluted one to four parts water) to be more effective than 7% iodine in treatment of the umbilical cords of newborn foals. Although the 7% iodine was very effective in eliminating bacteria, it dries the stump too quickly, leaving a long tail and occasionally sloughing adjacent skin, providing bacteria access to the bloodstream. This

indicates the need for more research relative to the treatment of the navel cord of newborn foals.

If left alone, the navel cord of the newborn foal usually breaks within 2 to 4 in. from the belly. Under such conditions, no cutting is necessary. However, if it does not break, it should be severed about 2 in. from the belly with clean, dull shears or it may be scraped in two with a knife. Never cut diagonally across. A torn or broken blood vessel will bleed very little, whereas one that is cut directly across may bleed excessively. If severing of the cord is resorted to, it should be immediately treated with iodine.

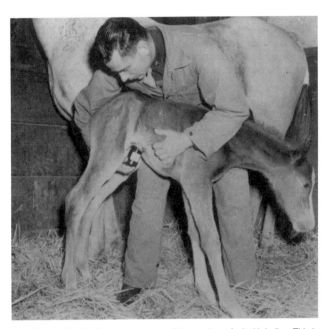

Fig. 12-26. Treating the navel cord of the newborn foal with iodine. This is done by placing the end of the cord in a wide-mouthed bottle nearly full of tincture of iodine while pressing the bottle firmly against the abdomen. (Courtesy, Thoroughbred Breeders Assn., Arcadia, CA)

NAVEL INFECTION (JOINT ILL OR NAVEL ILL)

Although most newborn foal infections are referred to as navel infection—implying that the infection is postnatal, with entrance to the body gained through the umbilical cord after birth—many such troubles are of prenatal origin. In the latter type, infection of the foal takes place in the uterus (womb) of the dam before the foal is born. The infection may either be present in the dam before she is bred, or it may be introduced by the stallion, if he is infected or if he has previously bred other infected mares. If prenatal infection does not result in abortion and the mare carries the fetus to normal term, the foal is often born weak or develops navel ill within a few days and dies; or if it does not die, it becomes a hopeless cripple that must be destroyed.

Under unsanitary conditions, there is also great danger from infections that may enter the bloodstream through the opening of the navel cord prior to the time it has dried up and the scar has healed over. When weather conditions permit foaling in a clean pasture in the fresh air and sunshine, danger of such infection is held to a minimum. On the other hand, foaling in a filthy paddock or stall and with no precautions taken is very likely to result in infection and navel ill. For this reason, when it is necessary to have mares foal in the stall, every precaution should be taken. The stall should be thoroughly cleaned, disinfected, and bedded; and the navel should be treated with iodine immediately after the foal arrives, followed by dusting with a good antiseptic powder several times daily.

Navel infection (joint ill or navel ill) may be recognized by a loss of appetite, soreness, and stiffness in the joints, and a general listlessness of the foal. If this is recognized in the early stages and a veterinarian is called at once, the infected foal may be treated and

Fig. 12-27. Foal with navel infection (joint ill or navel ill). The disease is fatal in about 50% of the cases. Also, a large proportion of the animals that survive are left with deformed joints like the foal pictured. (Courtesy, Dept. of Veterinary Pathology and Hygiene, College of Veterinary Medicine, University of Illinois)

may recover. If, however, the disease has reached the pus-forming stage, very likely it will be fatal. Blood transfusions from the dam to the foal have been given in all types of foal infections, usually with good results. With certain specific types of infections, antibiotics, sulfanilamides, serums, or bacterins may be used successfully; but these should always be administered by a veterinarian. Prevention is decidedly the best protection.

In summary, it may be stated that the practice of sanitation and hygiene, starting with the stallion and broodmare at the time of mating and continuing with the broodmare and young foal at foaling time, usually prevents the most common type of joint ill. In certain areas, particularly those known to be goiterous or semigoiterous, such as the Pacific Northwest, the feeding of stabilized iodized salt to in-foal mares appears to reduce losses from joint ill.

COLOSTRUM

The colostrum is the milk that is secreted by the dam for the first few days following parturition. It differs from ordinary milk in the following aspects:

1. It is more concentrated.
2. It is higher in protein content, especially globulins.
3. It is richer in vitamin A.
4. It contains more antibodies.
5. It has a more stimulating effect on the alimentary tract.

Because of these many beneficial qualities of colostrum, the caretaker should make very certain that the newborn foal secures this first milk.

The strong, healthy foal will usually be up on its feet and ready to nurse within 30 minutes to 2 hours after birth. Occasionally, however, a big awkward foal will need a little assistance and guidance during its first time to nurse. The stubborn foal should be coaxed to the mare's teats (forcing is useless). This may be done by backing the mare up on additional bedding in one corner of the stall and coaxing the foal with a bottle and nipple. The attendant may hold the bottle while standing on the opposite side of the mare from the foal. The very weak foal should be given the mare's first milk even if it must be drawn in a bottle and fed by nipple for a time or two. Sometimes these weak individuals will nurse the mare if steadied by the attendant.

Aside from the difference in chemical composition, the colostrum (the milk yielded by the mother for a short period following the birth of the young) has the following functions:

1. It contains antibodies that temporarily protect

the digestive tract. Because newborn foals are unable to produce antibodies for some time after birth, they must acquire preformed antibodies through colostrum, which is especially high in immune lactoglobulins. To be effective in protection against disease, however, colostrum must be ingested within a few hours after birth, preferably within 15 to 30 minutes, because gut closure occurs about 24 to 30 hours after birth. Subsequently, the foal digests these large molecular weight proteins, with the loss of their immunization properties.

2. It serves as a natural purgative, removing fecal matter that has accumulated in the digestive tract.

This, therefore, explains why mares should not be milked out prior to foaling and why colostrum is important to the newborn foal.

Before allowing the foal to nurse for the first time, it is usually a good practice to wash the mare's udder with a mild disinfectant and to rinse it with clean, warm water.

BOWEL MOVEMENT OF THE FOAL

The regulation of the bowel movement in the foal is very important. Two common abnormalities are constipation and diarrhea or scours.

Impaction in the bowels of the excrement accumulated during the development prior to birth—material called meconium—may prove fatal if not handled promptly. Usually a good feed of colostrum will cause elimination, but not always—especially when foals are from stall-fed mares.

Bowel movement of the foal should be observed within 4 to 12 hours after birth. If by this time there has been no discharge and the foal seems rather sluggish and fails to nurse, it should be given an enema. This may be made by using 1 to 2 quarts of water at blood heat, to which a little glycerin has been added; or warm, soapy water is quite satisfactory. The solution may be injected with a baby syringe (one having about a 3-inch nipple) or a tube and can. This treatment may be repeated as often as necessary until the normal yellow feces appears.

Diarrhea or scours in foals may be associated with infectious diseases or may be caused by unclean surroundings. Any of the following conditions may bring on diarrhea: contaminated udder or teats; nonremoval of fecal matter from the digestive tract; fretfulness or temperature above normal in the mare; an excess of feed affecting the quality of the mare's milk; cold, damp bed, or continued exposure to cold rains. As treatment is not always successful, the best practice is to avoid the undesirable conditions.

Some foals scour during the foal heat of the mare,

Fig. 12-28. Giving an enema to a foal, using a tube and can.

which occurs between the seventh and ninth day following foaling.

Diarrhea is caused by an irritant in the digestive tract that should be removed if recovery is to be expected. Only in exceptional cases should an astringent be given with the idea of checking the diarrhea; and such treatment should be prescribed by the veterinarian.

If the foal is scouring, the ration of the mare should be reduced, and a part of her milk should be taken away by milking her out at intervals or by muzzling the foal for a few hours.

RAISING THE ORPHAN FOAL

Occasionally a mare dies during or immediately after parturition, leaving an orphan foal to be raised. Also, there are times when mares fail to give a sufficient quantity of milk for the newborn foal. Sometimes there are twins. In such cases, it is necessary to resort to other milk supplies. The problem will be simplified if the foal has at least received the colostrum from the dam, for it does play a very important part in the well-being of the newborn young.

If at all possible, the foal should be shifted to another mare. Some breeding establishments regularly follow the plan of breeding a mare that is a good milk producer but whose foal is expected to be of little value. Her own foal is either destroyed or raised on a bottle, and the mare is used as a foster-mother or nurse mare.

Most nurseries keep a supply of colostrum on hand. They remove colostrum from mares that (1) have had dead foals, or (2) produce excess milk, then store it in a freezer for future foals that do not receive colostrum from their dams. When needed, it can be removed from the freezer, heated, and fed. This is an excellent practice.

If no colostrum is available, the foal should be placed on either (1) cow's milk made as nearly as possible of the same composition as mare's milk, or (2) a synthetic milk replacer.

A comparison of cow's milk and mare's milk is given in Table 12-4.

TABLE 12-4
COMPOSITION OF MILK FROM COWS AND MARES[1]

Source	Water	Protein	Fat	Sugar	Ash
	(%)	(%)	(%)	(%)	(%)
Cow	87.17	3.55	3.69	4.88	0.75
Mare	90.78	1.99	1.21	5.67	0.35

[1]USDA Farmers' Bull. No. 803.

As can be observed, mare's milk is higher in percentage of water and sugar than cow's milk and is lower in other components.

For best results in raising the orphan foal, milk from a fresh cow, low in butterfat, should be used. To about a pint of milk, add a tablespoonful of sugar and from 3 to 5 tablespoonfuls of lime water. Warm to body temperature and for the first few days feed about one-fourth of a pint every hour. After 3 or 4 weeks the sugar can be stopped, and at 5 to 6 weeks skimmed milk can be used entirely.

Orphan foals may also be raised on synthetic milk replacer, fed according to the directions of the manufacturer. Here again the situation is simplified if the foal has first received colostrum.

For the first few days, the milk (either cow's milk or milk replacer) may be fed using a bottle and a rubber nipple. Later the foal should be taught to drink from a pail. It is important that all receptacles be kept absolutely clean and sanitary (cleaned and scalded each time), and that feeding be at regular intervals. Grain feeding should be started at the earliest possible time with the orphan foal.

PERCENTAGE OF MARES BRED PRODUCING FOALS

Without question more difficulty is experienced in breeding mares than any other kind of livestock. The percentage of mares bred that actually conceive each year will vary from 40 to a high of 85, with an average probably running less than 50; and some of this number will fail to produce living foals. This means that, on the average, two mares are kept a whole year in order to produce one foal. By contrast, nationally, 88% of all beef cows that are bred, calve; 95% of all ewes, lamb; and 85% of all sows bred, farrow pigs.

The lower percentage conception in mares than in other classes of livestock is due primarily to the following: (1) Research in the field has lagged, (2) an attempt is made to get mares bred in about 4 months instead of 12, (3) the breeding season has been arbitrarily limited to a period (late winter and early spring) that at its best is only about 50% in agreement with nature, and (4) the birth date of horses is computed on a January 1 basis, regardless of how late they may be born.

In the bluegrass country of Kentucky, where there are both experienced breeders and as desirable conditions for breeding as can be secured under domestication, 66% foaling is considered as average for the area.

Recognition of the following facts may help to increase the percentage of foals produced:

1. Mares bred in the late spring of the year are more likely to conceive. If mares are bred out of season, spring conditions should be duplicated as nearly as possible.

2. Mares bred as three- and four-year-olds and kept in regular production thereafter are more likely to conceive and produce living foals.

3. Infections or other unhealthy conditions of either mare or stallion are not favorable for production.

4. More conceptions will occur if the mare is bred at the proper time within the heat period. Usually mares bred just before going out of heat are more likely to conceive.

5. Returning the mare to the stallion for retrial or rebreeding is important.

6. Mares in foal should be fed and cared for properly so as to develop the young. Balance of proteins, minerals, and vitamins is important.

7. It must also be remembered that old mares, overfat mares, or mares in a thin, run-down condition are less likely to be good breeders. Unfortunately, these conditions frequently apply to mares that are bred following retirement from the racetrack or the show-ring.

A shift of the date of birth (the January 1 birthday, for purposes of racing and showing) to somewhere between March 1 and May 1 would improve conception rate and foaling percentage, simply because mares would be bred under more natural and ideal spring conditions. Thus, it would have considerable virtue from the standpoint of the horse producer. On the other side of the ledger, however, it would create problems in racing and in registrations, both here and abroad. Also, such deep-rooted tradition would be difficult to change; in fact, much consideration has been given to the matter from time to time. In the final analysis, therefore, stepping up breeding research is the primary avenue through which the deplorably low percentage foal crop may be improved.

STERILITY OR BARRENNESS IN MARES

Sterility is a condition of infertility. Whatever the cause, there are no cure-alls for the condition. Rather, each individual case requires careful diagnosis and specific treatment for what is wrong. It should be recognized also that there are two types of sterility—temporary and permanent—although no sharp line can be drawn between them.

Regardless of the cause of sterility, it is well to give a word of caution against the so-called *opening up* of mares, which is the practice of inserting the hand and arm into the genital organs for the purpose of rearranging the organs in order to ensure conception. Few laymen, no matter how expert they may classify themselves, have either sufficient knowledge of the anatomy of the mare or appreciation of the absolutely sterile methods necessary in such procedure to be probing about. Moreover, it is only rarely that the reproductive organs are out of place. Unless the opening up is recommended and conducted by a veterinarian, it should not be permitted. When performed by an amateur, or even most would-be experts, it is a dangerous practice that is to be condemned.

TEMPORARY STERILITY

Some causes of temporary sterility are:

1. Lack of exercise, irregular work, and overfeeding accompanied by extremely high condition.
2. Overwork, underfeeding, and an extremely thin and run-down condition.
3. Nutritional deficiencies.
4. Infections of various kinds.
5. Some types of physiological imbalances characterized by such things as cystic ovaries or failure to ovulate at the proper time.

Temporary sterility can be reduced by removing the cause and correcting the difficulty, whatever it may be.

PERMANENT STERILITY

Naturally, permanent sterility is much more serious to the horse breeder. Perhaps the most common causes of permanent sterility are:

1. Old age, which is usually accompanied by irregular breeding and eventual total sterility.
2. Infections in the reproductive tract, usually in the cervix, uterus, or fallopian tubes.
3. Some types of physiological imbalances characterized by such things as cystic ovaries or failure to ovulate at the proper time.
4. Closure of female genital organs.

Sometimes a veterinarian is able to correct the latter two conditions; and, on an extremely valuable breeding mare, it may be worthwhile to obtain such professional service in an effort to bring about conception.

Retained afterbirth or other difficulties encountered in foaling may cause inflammation and infection that will prevent conception as long as the condition exists. There is real danger of spreading the infection if the mare is bred while in such a condition.

NORMAL BREEDING SEASON AND TIME OF FOALING

The most natural breeding season for the mare is in the spring of the year. Usually mares are gaining in flesh at this time; the heat period is more evident; and they are more likely to conceive. Furthermore the spring-born foal may be dropped on pasture—with less danger of infection and with an abundance of exercise, fresh air, and sunshine to aid in its development. Also, there will be good, green, succulent pasture for the mare. Such conditions are ideal.

However, when the demands for using the mares are such that spring foaling interferes and fall or perhaps late-winter foals are desired, plans may be changed accordingly. Under such circumstances, spring conditions should be duplicated at the breeding season. That is, the mare should be fed to gain in flesh, and, if necessary, should be blanketed for comfort.

Also, it must be remembered that the exhibitor will want to give consideration to having the foals dropped at such a time that they may be exhibited to the best advantage. The same applies to the person who desires to sell well-developed yearlings or to race two-year-olds. It is noteworthy, however, that the percentage of barren mares that conceive at an early breeding is markedly lower than is obtained later in the season. Nevertheless, some mares do conceive early in the

Fig. 12-29. Off to a good start! Spring-born and on pasture. (Courtesy, Kentucky Department of Public Information, Frankfort)

year, and even a small percentage is advantageous to some breeders.

HOW TO LOWER THE COST OF RAISING HORSES

Some principles that should receive consideration in lowering the cost of raising horses are:

1. Attain higher fertility in both mares and stallions; secure a higher percent foal crop. With a 50% foal crop, two mares are kept a whole year to raise one foal.

2. Eliminate unnecessary concoctions and drugs, if they are not needed.

3. Begin using the horses moderately at two years of age, at which time their use should more than compensate for the feed cost.

4. Keep all horses of usable age earning their way. Animals that are not necessary or that do not increase in value at a profitable rate are a needless expense.

5. Utilize pastures to the maximum. Such a practice will supply nutritious feeds at a low cost, save time in feeding, reduce labor in caring for the horses, and do away with bedding the stalls and cleaning the barn.

6. Utilize the less salable roughage as much as

possible, particularly during the second and third years.

7. Do not construct or maintain costly quarters for the young, growing horse.

8. Keep animals free from parasites, both internal and external. Feeding parasites is always too costly.

9. Provide least-cost balanced rations, including a balance of proteins, necessary minerals, and vitamins. Also, plenty of good, clean water should be available at all times.

BUYING HORSES OR RAISING FOALS

Where horses are needed, either they must be purchased or foals must be raised. The primary factors to consider in determining whether horses will be bought or foals raised are (1) the experience of the individual, (2) comparative cost, and (3) risks surrounding the introduction of horses.

EXPERIENCE OF THE BUYER/BREEDER

Certainly it must be recognized that the person who would attempt to raise replacements must have more knowledge of horse production than the person buying mature horses. In addition to knowing the regular care and management aspects of horse production, the person who raises replacements must be somewhat familiar with the breeding of horses and rearing of foals.

COMPARATIVE COST

In determining whether horses will be bought or foals raised, the comparative cost of the two methods should be computed. In arriving at such comparative cost figures, the following factors should be remembered:

1. Such figures should be on the basis of animals of equal merit and usefulness for the purpose desired. Consideration should also be given to age and future depreciation.

2. Computing the purchase price on horses should be on the basis of price delivered to the farm. Commission, freight or trucking, and insurance charged should not be overlooked.

3. In computing the cost of raising a foal to usable age, feed prices should be figured on the basis of farm values rather than on actual grain market values.

Fig. 12-30. The cost of raising horses can generally be lowered by utilizing pastures to the maximum. This shows two-year-old Hungarian fillies and geldings on pasture in the Nebraska Sandhills, at Cooksley Ranch, Anselmo, Nebraska. (Courtesy, Hungarian Horse Assn. of America, Anselmo, NE)

RISKS SURROUNDING THE INTRODUCTION OF HORSES

After giving full consideration to the experience of the buyer/breeder and the comparative cost of the two methods, there are still some rather perplexing problems encountered in introducing horses. These difficulties may be summarized as follows:

1. **Misrepresentation.** The inexperienced buyer is likely to encounter misrepresentations as to age, soundness, vices, and the training and usefulness of the horse.

2. **Diseases.** In moving a horse, there is always a possible exposure to the many ills. Sometimes these are of sufficiently serious nature as to make the use of the animal impossible at a time when most needed; occasionally they even prove fatal. Also, it must be remembered that such diseases as are contracted very likely may spread to the other horses on the farm and even to those in the community, thus exposing them to the same risk.

3. **Acclimating.** Horses coming from a distance usually need time to become acclimated before being most useful.

4. **Condition.** In all too many instances, horses brought in for sale and speculative purposes have been made fat for the occasion. Usually such liberal feeding has been made even more harmful through accompanying lack of work and confinement to a stall. Such horses are soft and require a period of gradual fitting for work. Also, it must be remembered that fat will cover up a multitude of defects.

BLOOD TYPING[12]

Horse blood typing was developed at the University of California at Davis during the period 1958–64. It involves a study of the components of the blood which are inherited according to strict genetic rules that have been established in the research laboratory. By determining the genetic *markers* in each blood sample and then applying the rules of inheritance, parentage can be affirmed or denied. To qualify as the offspring of a given mare and stallion, a foal must not possess any genetic markers not present in his alleged parents. If it does, it constitutes grounds for illegitimacy.

Horse blood typing is used for the following purposes:

■ **To verify parentage**—The test is used in instances where the offspring may bear some unusual color markings or carry some undesirable characteristic. Through blood typing, parentage can be verified with 90% accuracy.[13] Although this means that 10% of the cases cannot be settled, it is not possible to do any better than this in human blood typing.

■ **To determine which of two sires**—When a mare has been served by two or more stallions during one breeding season, blood typing can exclude the incorrect stallion and include the correct stallion in over 90% of the cases.

■ **To provide a permanent blood type record for identification purposes**—Two samples of blood are required from each animal to be studied; and the samples must be drawn in tubes and in keeping with detailed instructions provided by the laboratory. In parentage cases, this calls for blood samples from the offspring and both parents; in paternity cases, samples must be taken from the offspring, the dam, and all the sires.

■ **To substitute for fingerprinting**—Much attention is now being given to the idea of utilizing blood typing as a positive means of identification of stolen animals, through proving their parentage.

■ **Blood typing laboratories**—The following laboratories are capable of determining equine parentage:

---

[12]The author expresses his grateful appreciation for the authoritative review accorded this section by Dr. Clyde Stormont, Director of the Serology Laboratory and Professor of Immunogenetics, University of California, Davis, CA.

[13]In a personal communication to the author, Dr. Clyde Stormont, Professor Emeritus, University of California at Davis and owner of Stormont Laboratories, Inc., 1237 E. Beamer St., Suite D, Woodland, California 95695, reported that they have been able to solve approximately 91% of all the parentage cases.

In the United States

Department of Veterinary Sciences
University of Kentucky
102 Animal Pathology Building
Lexington, KY 40546.

Serology Laboratory
School of Veterinary Medicine
University of California
Davis, CA 95616

Stormont Laboratories, Inc.
1237 E. Beamer St., Suite D
Woodland, CA 95695

In Canada

Mann Equitest, Inc.
550 McAdam Road
Mississauga, Ont. L4Z 1P1

DNA TESTING

Parentage is also being determined by DNA testing.
Effective January 1, 1995, both the American Paint Horse Association and the American Quarter Horse Association began recognizing DNA marker genotype as an acceptable method of parentage verification.

DNA testing of Quarter Horses at the University of California by the Davis Veterinary Genetics Lab showed an efficacy of 99.9%, compared to an efficiency of 97 to 98% of blood typing.

REGISTRATION OF FOALS PRODUCED THROUGH ARTIFICIAL INSEMINATION (AI) OR EMBRYO TRANSFER (ET)

Although artificial insemination (AI) was first practiced with horses, some American registry associations frown upon or forbid the practice. Moreover, there is little unanimity of opinion among them so far as their rules and registries apply to the practice. Table 12-5 summarizes the horse association rules relative to registering young produced by AI or ET.

Note: Through AI and ET outstanding stallions and mares can be as close as your nearest airport.

TABLE 12-5
HORSE ASSOCIATION RULES RELATIVE TO REGISTERING
YOUNG PRODUCED BY ARTIFICIAL INSEMINATION (AI) OR EMBRYO TRANSFER (ET)[1]

Breed	Present Rules or Attitude of Registry Association Relative to AI or ET
Light Horses and Ponies:	
Akhal-Teke	AI and ET accepted.
American Bashkir Curly	AI and ET are not sanctioned.
American Creme Horse	AI accepted provided a licensed veterinarian collects the semen, and a licensed veterinarian performs the insemination. ET accepted provided a licensed veterinarian gathers the egg and performs the implant.
American Part-Blooded Horse Registry	AI accepted when customary proof of breeding is provided.
American Saddlebred	AI accepted; and fresh, cooled or frozen semen may be used. The use of frozen semen collected from a stallion that has died or has been castrated will be allowed on calendar year of death or castration. ET accepted. The blood type of the stallion and donor mare must be on file, and the blood type of the foal resulting from ET must be on file. Four foals per year per donor mare may be registered.
American Walking Pony	AI and ET accepted provided collection and insemination are performed by a veterinarian.
American Warmblood	AI and ET accepted.
American White	AI accepted. But must have signed statement of insemination.
Andalusian	The International Association does not register foals produced by AI or by ET. The American Andalusian Horse Association permits AI, but has not addressed the issue of ET.
Anglo-Arabian and Half-Arabian	AI accepted provided (1) stallion licensed by Arabian Horse Registry for AI, and (2) registration certificate is stamped to show animal was AI produced.

(Continued)

TABLE 12-5 (Continued)

Breed	Present Rules or Attitude of Registry Association Relative to AI or ET
Appaloosa	AI accepted provided (1) stallion's blood type is filed with the ApHC, and (2) semen is not stored, shipped, or transported from premises where the stallion is standing. ET accepted, but only one offspring per donor mare per year is eligible for registration unless there are twins. Additionally, ET foals are not eligible for registration unless (1) record owner or lessee notifies Appaloosa Horse Club (ApHC) in writing at least 15 days in advance of intended collection and transfer of fertilized egg, (2) an ApHC representative or ApHC approved veterinarian is present for the collection and transfer, and (3) parentage of resulting foal is verified by blood-typing.
Arabian	AI accepted provided (1) collection of semen from stallion and insemination of mare with this semen take place on the same premises, and (2) semen is not frozen and is used within 72 hours. Effective Jan. 1, 1995, semen collected in the United States or Mexico, or semen imported into the United States or Mexico, could be transported or stored provided stipulated requirements were met. ET accepted provided stipulated requirements are met, but it is limited to registration of one foal per calendar year from one donor mare.
Belgian Warmblood	Both AI and ET accepted; ET with blood typing.
Buckskin	International Buckskin Horse Association, Inc. accepts AI providing foals meet all other registration requirements.
Chickasaw	No rules.
Cleveland Bay	The Cleveland Bay Horse Society of the United Kingdom recognizes AI; and they are now considering ET.
Connemara	AI-produced foals accepted. Semen may be transported frozen or fresh. The Society recommends that the semen be collected, and the insemination be done, by a licensed veterinarian or trained technician.
Dales Pony	AI accepted.
Dutch Warmblood	AI and ET accepted, with blood type to verify parentage.
Exmoor Pony	AI accepted.
Galiceno	AI accepted without rules or restrictions.
Hackney	AI accepted provided insemination takes place on premises where stallion is standing and in presence of owner or party authorized to sign certificate of breeding for stallion. ET accepted with the following stipulations: (1) application for permit filed with the American Hackney Horse Society (AHHS), (2) the blood types of the stallion and donor mare must be on file with the AHHS, (3) the blood type of the foal resulting from ET must be on file with the AHHS, (4) only two foals per donor mare per year may be registered, and (5) a licensed veterinarian must be present during the collection transfer procedure.
Haflinger	The Haflinger Registry of North America accepts AI provided the mare, stallion, and foal are blood typed. Rules governing ET are now being formulated.
Half Saddlebred	AI accepted. But the breed registry form HSRA #122 must be filled out and accompany the application for registration.
Hanoverian	AI accepted, but a licensed veterinarian must issue and sign an insemination certificate which lists and describes the mare inseminated.
Lipizzan	AI and ET accepted. If semen is transported, a licensed veterinarian must perform the insemination and identify the recipient mare. ET must be performed by a licensed veterinarian who shall certify the date, location of transfer, and identity of the recipient mare and donor stallion.
Missouri Fox Trotting Horse	The breed association accepts foals produced by AI. If semen is shipped, stipulations must be followed. The breed registry does not accept foals produced by ET.
Morab	AI and ET require a special permit from the International Morab Breeders Assn. Also, DNA typing required for foal born from transported semen or ET.
Morgan	AI and ET permitted, with stipulations.
Mustang: American Mustang Assn.	AI accepted provided certified authentication is provided by the attending veterinarian of both the mare and stallion. ET not accepted.
N. American Mustang Assn. and Registry	NA
Spanish Mustang Registry	AI and ET accepted.

(Continued)

TABLE 12-5 (Continued)

Breed	Present Rules or Attitude of Registry Association Relative to AI or ET
National Show Horse	AI and ET allowed, with stipulations.
National Spotted Saddle Horse	AI is accepted.
Norwegian Fjord Horse	Neither AI nor ET accepted.
Paint Horse	AI accepted if semen is used within 24 hours of collection, and on premises of collection. Cooled semen (not frozen) may be transported from location of collection provided specified conditions are met. ET accepted provided stipulated conditions are met, including limiting donor mare to one foal registration per year.
Palomino	As "color registries," both Palomino associations recognize the AI and ET rules of the other registry associations in which Palomino horses are registered.
Paso Fino	AI accepted with use of fresh, cooled, or frozen semen; and with stipulations. ET accepted, but it must be so recorded on the Certificate of Registration.
Peruvian Paso	AI and ET accepted under stipulated rules of each registry association.
Pintabian	AI and ET accepted, with permit and blood typing required.
Pinto Arabian	AI and ET accepted provided proper forms are executed.
Pinto Horse	AI accepted provided (1) intent of each AI breeding requested in letter to registrar, (2) a veterinarian (not necessarily the same one for each step) certifies to collection of semen, insemination of mare, and birth of foal; and (3) blood type evidence of parentage, along with foaling date, is furnished. National Pinto Horse Registry does not have any rules relative to ET.
Pony of the Americas	AI on the farm where the stallion is located is approved. But mailing of semen is not allowed. ET accepted, but POA (1) limits it to one mare per year, and (2) requires advance notice, presence of veterinarian, blood typing of foal, and application to register foal within 10 days of birth.
Quarter Horse	AI accepted but semen must be used within 72 hours. If cooled semen is to be transported, both the stallion owner or lessee and the mare owner must sign a certificate. Any foal resulting from the use of transported cooled semen must have its pedigree verified by genetic testing (DNA testing), including sire, dam, and foal and/or by other genetic testing as AQHA deems necessary. ET accepted, but limited to one offspring per mare per calendar year unless two foals are the result of the fertilization of one ovum and both foals are carried by one recipient mare following a single implantation.
Rangerbred	No rules. No request to use AI.
Selle Francais	AI fresh, cooled, or frozen semen accepted. ET accepted, with donor mare limited to three foals per year.
Shetland Pony	No ruling on AI or ET.
Spanish-Barb	AI permitted, but (1) must have prior written approval of the Board, (2) both stallion and mare must be blood-typed, and (3) semen must be used within 48 hours. ET accepted, but (1) must have prior written approval of the Board, and (2) only one ET will be allowed for a mare in one calendar year.
Spanish Mustang	AI accepted, but limited to 100 foals per year. ET accepted, but each mare limited to 3 embryo transplants per year.
Standardbred	A foal conceived by fresh semen shall be eligible for registration. A foal conceived by semen which is frozen, desiccated, or transported off the premises where it is produced is not eligible for registration.
Swedish Gotland Horse	AI and ET accepted.
Swedish Warmblood	Foals from AI (fresh, transported, or frozen) accepted provided parents and foal are blood typed. Foals from ET accepted after verifying parentage by blood typing. However, the number of foals per mare is limited as follows: equal the mare's age in years minus three.
Tennessee Walking Horse	AI accepted provided both parents are blood typed. ET is allowed on the basis of one foal per mare per year.
Thoroughbred	Natural service only. But the immediate AI reinforcement of the stallion's service with a portion of the ejaculate produced by the stallion during such cover is permitted. ET not eligible for registration.

(Continued)

TABLE 12-5 (Continued)

Breed	Present Rules or Attitude of Registry Association Relative to AI or ET
Trakehner	AI on premises with fresh semen must be under the supervision of a licensed veterinarian. When fresh or frozen semen are transported, both the mare and foal must be blood typed; and the insemination must take place under the supervision of a licensed veterinarian. ET accepted provided both donor mare and foal are blood typed. Only one foal per donor per calendar year will be registered.
Welsh Pony and Cob	AI accepted if prior approved and foal DNA typed. ET accepted if prior approved and donor mares limited to four genetic offspring per calendar year; and either fresh or frozen embryos may be used.
Draft Horses:	
American Cream	No rules.
Belgian	AI accepted provided Belgian Assn. has been given advance notice in writing; report of collection, shipment, and insemination is filed in writing with the Belgian registry within 120 days. When chilled semen is used, the Belgian registry may require blood typing of dam and foal. When frozen semen is used, all mares and foals must be blood typed. ET accepted provided both the sire and donor mare are blood typed prior to application of ET permit; and ET permit is submitted by owner of donor mare.
Clydesdale	The following rules apply to semen for off-site use, and to semen collected and frozen for future use: (1) Stallion from which semen is collected must be blood typed, with a copy of the blood type document sent to the registry association; and (2) report of collection, shipment, and insemination resulting in conception must be forwarded to the association within 120 days of breeding. The following rules apply to ET: (1) The association must be notified of the intended collection of the fertilized egg at least 15 days in advance of collection, (2) an association approved veterinarian must be present during the collection and transfer, (3) the resulting foal must have its pedigree verified by blood test of the mare, stallion, and foal, and (4) the association must be notified in writing if embryos are frozen.
Percheron	AI accepted provided semen is obtained from member of the Percheron Horse Assn. or from a reputable breeding establishment; impregnation is by a licensed veterinarian; and the DNA of the stallion whose semen is used is on file with the Percheron Assn. Frozen semen may be used providing the program for handling, freezing, storing, and dispensing are prior approved by the Percheron Assn. ET Percheron foals accepted provided they meet the standard stipulations for registry; the Assn. is notified in writing within 90 days of an attempted ET; and the DNA is submitted for the sire, dam, and foal.
Shire	AI accepted, but mares bred by AI must be reported on the annual stallion report if filed. Registration application forms and registration certificates for foals produced by AI must so indicate. ET accepted. Registration application forms and registration certificates for foals produced by ET must so indicate.
Suffolk	No rules, but favorable toward AI.
Jacks and Donkeys:	
Donkeys	AI and ET accepted without restrictions.
Jacks and Jennets	AI and ET accepted without restrictions.

[1]The AI and ET regulations of breed registries change from time to time. So, anyone wishing to apply these practices should first secure the latest rules from the intended registry association.

SELECTED REFERENCES

Title of Publication	Author(s)	Publisher
Animal Breeding	A. L. Hagedoorn	Crosby Lockwood & Son, Ltd., London, England, 1950
Animal Breeding Plans	J. L. Lush	Collegiate Press, Inc., Ames, IA, 1963
Animal Genetics	F. B. Hutt	The Ronald Press Company, New York, NY, 1964
Arab Breeding in Poland	E. Skorkowski	*Your Pony*, Columbus, WI, 1969
Arabian Horse Breeding	H. H. Reese	Bordon Publishing Company, Los Angeles, CA, 1953
Breeding Better Livestock	V. A. Rice F. N. Andrews E. J. Warwick	McGraw-Hill Book Company, New York, NY, 1953
Breeding and Improvement of Farm Animals	V. A. Rice, *et al.*	McGraw-Hill Book Company, New York, NY, 1967
Breeding and Raising Horses, Ag. Hdbk. No. 394	M. E. Ensminger	U.S. Department of Agriculture, Washington, DC, 1972
Breeding the Racehorse	F. Tesio	J. A. Allen & Co., Ltd., London, England, 1964
Breeding Thoroughbreds	J. F. Wall	Charles Scribner's Sons, New York, NY, 1946
Elements of Genetics, The	C. D. Darlington K. Mather	The Macmillan Company, New York, NY, 1950
Equine Genetics & Selection Procedures	Staff of Equine Research Publications	Equine Research Publications, Dallas, TX, 1978
Equine Reproduction	Edited by I. W. Rowlands W. R. Allen P. D. Rossdale	Blackwell Scientific Publications, Oxford, England, 1975
Equine Reproduction II	Edited by I. W. Rowlands W. R. Allen	Journals of Reproduction and Fertility, Ltd., Cambridge, England, 1979
Farm Animals	J. Hammond	Edward Arnold & Company, London, England, 1952
Genetic Basis of Selection, The	I. M. Lerner	John Wiley & Sons, Inc., New York, NY, 1964
Genetic Principles in Horse Breeding	J. F. Lasley	John F. Lasley, Columbia, MO, 1970
Genetics	M. W. Strickberger	The Macmillan Company, New York, NY, 1968
Genetics and Animal Breeding	I. Johansson J. Rendel	W. H. Freeman and Co. Publishers, San Francisco, CA, 1968
Genetics Is Easy	P. Goldstein	Lantern Press, New York, NY, 1967
Genetics of the Horse	W. E. Jones R. Bogart	Edwards Brothers, Inc., Ann Arbor, MI, 1971
Genetics of Livestock Improvement, Third Edition	J. F. Lasley	Prentice-Hall, Inc., Englewood Cliffs, NJ, 1978
Hammond's Farm Animals	J. Hammond, Jr. I. L. Mason T. J. Robinson	Butler & Tanner, Ltd., Frome and London, England, 1971

Horse, The	J. Warren Evans, *et al.*	W. H. Freeman and Co., New York, NY, 1990
Horse Breeding and Stud Management	H. Wynmalen	J. A. Allen & Co., Ltd., London, England, 1950
Horse Science Handbook, Vols. 1-3	Edited by M. E. Ensminger	Agriservices Foundation, Clovis, CA, 1963, 1964, 1966
Horsemanship and Horse Care, Ag. Info. Bull. No. 353	M. E. Ensminger	U.S. Department of Agriculture, Washington, DC, 1972
How Life Begins	J. Power	Simon and Schuster, Inc., New York, NY, 1965
Lectures, Stud Managers Course		Stud Managers Course, Lexington, KY, intermittant since 1951
Light Horses, Farmers' Bull. No. 2127	M. E. Ensminger	U.S. Department of Agriculture, Washington, DC, 1965
Livestock Improvement	J. E. Nichols	Oliver and Boyd, London, England, 1957
Management of the Stallion for Maximum Reproductive Efficiency, II	B. W. Pickett, *et al.*	Colorado State University, Fort Collins, CO, 1989
Modern Developments in Animal Breeding	J. M. Lerner H. P. Donald	Academic Press, Inc., New York, NY, 1966
Principles of Genetics	I. H. Herskowitz	The Macmillan Company, New York, NY, 1973
Reproduction in Farm Animals, Fourth Edition	E. S. Hafez	Lea & Febiger, Philadelphia, PA, 1980
Reproductive Physiology	A. V. Nalbandov	W. H. Freeman and Co., Publishers, San Francisco, CA, 1958
Science of Genetics, The	G. W. Burns	The Macmillan Company, New York, NY, 1972
Stud Farm Diary, A	H. S. Finney	J. A. Allen & Co., Ltd., London, England, 1973
Stud Managers' Handbooks	Edited by M. E. Ensminger	Agriservices Foundation, Clovis, CA, annually since 1965
Studies on Reproduction in Horses	Y. Nishakawa	Japan Racing Association, Tokyo, Japan, 1959

Quarter Horse mares and foals on good pasture. (Courtesy, American Quarter Horse Association, Amarillo, TX)

TYPES OF LIGHT HORSES

Plate 1. Five-gaited American Saddlebred at the trot. (Photo by Jamie Donaldson. Courtesy, American Saddlebred Horse Assn., Lexington, KY)

Plate 2. Hackney Harness Pony **Trimmed In Brass**, Champion at Lexington, KY, in 1995. (Photo by Doug Shiflet Photography. Courtesy, Ed Frickey, Frickey Farm, Lafayette, IN)

Plate 3. Miniature stallion, NFC **Superman** a National Grand Champion. (Photo by Jock Slatzberg. Courtesy, *The Journal*, Warrensville, IL)

Plate 4. Race horse. Statue of the legendary **Man O'War**. Only once in his 21 starts did his machine-like power fail to propel him first across the finish line.

Plate 5. Reigning, a test of the willingness and responsiveness of the horse to the rider. (Photo by Wyatt McSpadden. Courtesy, American Quarter Horse Assn., Amarillo, TX)

Plate 6. Western Pleasure Horse–a Paint. (Photo by David Stoecklein. Courtesy American Paint Horse Assn., Ft. Worth, TX)

LESS POPULOUS BREEDS

Plate 7. American Walking Pony stallion, BT **Rush For Gold**. (Courtesy, Mrs. Joan Hudson Brown, Macon, GA)

Plate 8. American White Horse, owned by Gail Adams, Blue Grass, IA. (Courtesy, International American Albino Assn., Naper, NE)

Plate 9. Cleveland Bay dam, **Pepperpot Bay** (left), and daughter **Rosedale Atlantic** (right). (Photo by David Field. Courtesy, Cleveland Bay Horse Society of North America, South Windham, CT)

Plate 10. Connemara pony stallion. (Courtesy, American Connemara Pony Society, Winchester, VA)

Plate 11. Dales Pony stallion, **Dartdale Freddie**, owned by Denise and Colin Dunkley, Holyrood, Ontario. (Courtesy, Canadian Mountain and Moorland Society, Amherst, Nova Scotia, Canada)

Plate 12. Exmoor Ponies. (Courtesy Canadian Mountain & Moorland Society, Amherst, Nova Scotia, Canada)

Plate 13. Haflinger mare, **Amsel** NTF, owned by Lynn Cummings, Haslett, MI. (Courtesy, Haflinger Assn. of America, Hemlock, MI)

Plate 14. Half Saddlebred (a Saddlebred/Arabian/Standardbred stallion), Champion Halter stallion owned and shown by Sandra Anderson, North Branch, MN. (Courtesy, The Half Saddlebred Registry of America, Coshocton, OH)

Plate 15. Hanoverian mare, **Donna Elena**, Grand Champion. (Courtesy, The American Hanoverian Society, Lexington, KY)

Plate 16. Irish Draft Horse, Milestone's **Lughnasa Dancer**, dressage horse, owned by Milestone Farm, Goldsboro, NC. (Courtesy, Irish Draft Horse Society, British Columbia, Canada)

Plate 17. Lipizzan, **Pluto Blamora**, shown by Alice Hunter, owned by Silver Meadow Farm. (Courtesy, Lipizzan Assn. of North America, Anderson, IN)

Plate 18. National Show Horse stallion, **Night Of Roses**, leading sire of the National Show Horse Registry. (Courtesy, National Show Horse Registry, Louisville, KY)

Plate 19. Palomino Morab stallion, **Damars Diamond Champ**, shown by Joel and Carrie Boldig, Hi-Fad Middle Branch Morab Farm, Tigerton, WI. (Courtesy, North American Morab Horse Assn., Hilbert, WI)

Plate 20. Pintabian foal. Note the Arabian type and tobiano markings which are characteristic of the breed. (Courtesy, Pintabian Horse Registry, Karlstad, MN 56732)

Plate 21. Spanish-Barb mare, **Las Brisas**, owned by Judith L. Smith, Houston, TX. (Courtesy, Spanish-Barb Breeders Assn., Terry, MS)

Plate 22. Tennessee Walking Horse, **Con Bad News**. (Courtesy Voice Magazine, Lewisburg, TN)

SHOW HORSES

Plate 23. American Saddlebred, three-gaited. (Donaldson Photo, Courtesy, American Saddlebred Horse Assn., Lexington, KY)

Plate 24. American Saddlebred fine harness horse. (Photo by Jamie Donaldson. Courtesy, American Saddlebred Horse Assn., Lexington, KY)

Plate 25. Buckskin. Reserve World Champion, **Dad's Joy**, owned by John Morse, Schoharie, NY. (Courtesy, International Buckskin Horse Assn., Shelby, IN)

Plate 26. Palomino stallion, **C L Legacy**, World Champion, owned by Charles and Linda Cline, Cushing, OK. (Courtesy, Charles Cline)

Plate 27. Tennessee Walking Horse, **He's Puttin' on the Ritz**, 1996 World's Grand Champion, performing at the running walk, trained and ridden by Sammy Day, owned by William B. and Sandra Johnson, Atlanta, GA. (Courtesy, *Voice Magazine*, Lewisburg, TN)

Plate 28. Welsh Cob drawing a cart. (Courtesy, Welsh Pony & Cob Society or America, Winchester, VA)

EQUINE ATHLETES

Plate 29. Appaloosa jumper in action. (Photo by Contemporary Images. Courtesy, Appaloosa Horse Club, Moscow, ID)

Plate 30. Spanish Mustang, **The Cisco Kid** (foreground) owned by Teddi Botham, Cove, OR, in a polo game. (Courtesy, Spanish Mustang Registry, Wilcox, AZ)

Plate 31. Trakehner stallion, **Tarim**, grand prix dressage stallion, owned by Joan Peyton, Avignon Farm, Upperville, VA. (Courtesy, Trakehner Assn., Newark, OH)

Plate 32. Thoroughbred, **Cigar**, foaled April 18, 1990, shown at 10 days of age with his dam, **Solar Slew**, at Country Life Farm, Hartford County, Maryland. Cigar is by **Palace Music**. (Photo by Ellen B. Pons, with the permission of CMG Worldwide, Inc., and Allen Paulson, Cigar's owner.)

HORSE RACING

Plate 33. **Soviet Problem** (on the right) shown here in the $1,000,000 Breeder's Cup Sprint at Churchill Downs in 1994. **Soviet Problem** won 15 of 19 races in her 3-year racing career, with total earnings of $905,546. (Courtesy, Harris Farms, Coalinga, CA)

Plate 34. Quarter Horse race. The most popular Quarter Horse races are 440 yards, or one-quarter mile, which these sprinters cover in 21 seconds. (Photo by Wyatt McSpadden. Courtesy, American Quarter Horse Assn., Amarillo, TX)

Plate 35. Harness racing at historic track, Goshen, New York. (Courtesy, The United States Trotting Assn., Columbus, OH)

DRAFT HORSES AND MULES

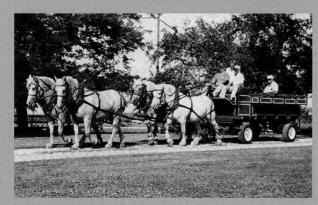

Plate 36. American Cream four-horse hitch. (Courtesy, American Cream Draft Horse Assn., Charles City, IA)

Plate 38. Clydesdale mare, **Solomon's Paulette**, bred and owned by the Max Remus Family, Osborne, KS. (Courtesy, Clydesdale Breeders of the United States, Pecatonica, IL)

Plate 37. Belgian four-horse hitch making hay. (Courtesy, *The Draft Horse Journal*, Waverly, IA)

Plate 39. Percheron horses pulling a plow. Owned by Bill Grimm, Gowanda, NY. (Photo by Race Reflections, West Seneca, NY. Courtesy, Percheron Horse Assn. of America, Fredericktown, OH)

Plate 40. Six-mule hitch driven by Van Seney of Terrebonne, Oregon, pulling a log wagon loaded with 20-ft. logs in the Prineville Oregon Timber Carnival. (From: *1995 Mule Calender*; photo by Deb Seney, Route 1, Box 74, Waitsburg, WA 99361. Courtesy, Mrs. Betsy Hutchins, Secretary-Editor, The American Donkey and Mule Society, Denton, TX)

FOR THE FUN OF IT

Plate 41. Andalusian stallions with riders in correct attire; female riders in Spanish, and male riders in Portuguese. Stallions owned by Dr. and Mrs. Rafael Parra, San Antonio, TX. (Courtesy, International Andalusian Assn., Shoal Creek, AL)

Plate 44. One-horse open sleigh pulled by a Morgan horse. (Photo by Cliff Borchert. Courtesy, The American Morgan Horse Assn., Shelburne, VT)

Plate 42. Exhibition. Royal Canadian Mounted Police. This is a highly trained drill unit, used for exhibition purposes. For many years, horses have had a valuable role in police work. Mounted police are especially effective in dispersing a riotous crowd. (Courtesy, Royal Canadian Mounted Police, Ottawa, Canada

Plate 45. Parade. American White Horse Parade Unit, owned by Mr. and Mrs. George Galgas, Ojai, CA, in the Parade of Roses, Portland, OR, 1994. (Courtesy International American Albino, Assn., Naper, NE)

Plate 43. Miniature Horse shown in harness. The Miniature Horse is a scaled-down full size horse, and not a dwarf. They cannot exceed 34 in. at the wither. (Photo by A. H. Ensminger)

Plate 48. Wedding party happily being transported by a team of Haflinger horses owned by Four "O" Acres, Massillon, OH. (Courtesy, Haflinger Assn. of America, Hemlock, MI)

Feed is the most important influence in the environment of the horse.
(Courtesy, Kentucky Department of Public Information, Frankfort, KY)

13

FEEDING HORSES

Contents

Contents

Feed is the most important influence in the environment of the horse. Unless the horse is fed properly, its maximum potential in reproduction, growth, body form, speed, endurance, style, and attractiveness cannot be achieved.

The following conditions make it imperative that the nutrition of horses be the best that science and technology can devise:

1. **Confinement.** Many horses are kept in stables or corrals most of the time.

2. **Fitting yearlings.** When forcing young equines, it is important to their development and soundness that the ration be nutritionally balanced.

3. **Racing two-year-olds.** In the United States, we race more two-year-olds than any other nation in the world; our richest races are for them. If the nutrient content of the ration is not adequate, there is bound to be more breakdown on the track than with older horses—this is costly.

4. **Stress.** Stress is affected by excitement, temperament, fatigue, number of horses together, previous nutrition, breed, age, and management. Race and show horses are always under stress; and the more tired they are and the greater the speed, the greater the stress. Thus, the ration for race and show horses should be scientifically formulated, rather than based on fads, foibles, and trade secrets. The greater the stress, the more exacting the nutritive requirements.

5. **Horses are unique.** They differ from other farm animals: They have greater value; are kept for recreation, sport and work; are fed for a longer life of usefulness; have a smaller digestive tract; should not carry surplus weight; and are fed for nerve, mettle, animation, and character of muscle.

Also, feed constitutes the greatest single cost item in the horse business.

EVOLUTION OF HORSE PARALLELED ITS FEED

Through fossil remains, it is evident that the evolution of the horse has always paralleled its soil and vegetation. In the beginning little *Eohippus*, which was about the size of a Fox Terrier dog, had four toes on the front foot and three on the hind, had soft teeth, and was adapted to feeding on the herbage of the swamp. Gradually, it grew taller, its teeth grew stronger and harder, its legs grew longer, and all but one toe disappeared, thereby enabling it to feed farther from water and adapting it to the prairies.

It is only natural, in a world so big, that some equines should fare better than others. Thus, the ponderous horse of Flanders, progenitor of the modern draft horse, was the product of fertile soils, a mild

climate, and abundant vegetation; whereas the diminutive, hardy Shetland Pony evolved on the scanty vegetation native to the long, cold winters of the Shetland Isles.

The effect of feed and nutrition as a creative force on horses did not end with their domestication, about 5,000 years ago. At that time, humans replaced nature as keepers of horses, for, from that remote day forward, they assumed primary responsibility for the breeding, feeding, caring, and managing of their charges. When one considers that among wild bands 95% foal crops were common and unsoundnesses were relatively unknown, it's apparent that horses haven't fared so well with humans serving as their providers.

FEEDS, FOIBLES, AND TRADE SECRETS

Hand in hand with the horse boom, the fabulous days of the "hoss doctor"—along with fads, foibles, and trade secrets—returned. At least this has been true in altogether too many cases.

Like Topsy, the light horse industry just grew. There was precious little organized planning. With the passing of the draft horse, the Horse and Mule Association of America was inactivated, the Army Remount Service was stilled, and those great horse specialists of the U.S. Department of Agriculture and our Land Grant Colleges retired and were not replaced.

Conditions were ripe for "fast operators" to make a "quick buck." Many folks with more money than animal knowledge owned horses, and the breeding and using of horses shifted from farms and ranches to suburban areas. As a result, "horse practitioners," whose products and sales pitches were reminiscent of the "medicine men" of old, developed a flourishing business, pawning off on unsuspecting caretakers a myriad of potions, cure-alls, tonics, reconditioners, worm expellers, mineral mixes, vitamin mixes, and feeds of a kind.

Generally speaking, claims were made for increased growth, improved breeding, better development, more speed, and increased stamina; and the feeding directions called for a cup or for 3 or 4 tablespoonsful per horse daily.

But such "horse practitioners" were not entirely to blame. Many owners insist on some kind of treatment; and they'll keep going until they get it. Especially when a horse "starts down," they'll grasp for straws. In such frantic moments, they'll buy and try almost any formula for which claims are made, completely oblivious to the facts (1) that distilled water might do just as much good—and far less harm, and (2) that they are buying losing tickets with their eyes wide open.

Equestrians are also great imitators. They'll single

out some great horse, and, in one way or another, find out what it's getting. Then, they'll get some of the "same stuff" and use it from then 'til doomsday. The author has known caretakers to pay $50 for a gallon of a mysterious concoction, in a green jug, made in some little hamlet in Kentucky. Of course, the fallacy of such imitation—of feeding what the "great horse" got—is that the "name" horse might have been even greater had it been fed properly, and that there must be a reason why there are so few truly great horses. Also, the following searching question might well be asked: Why do many horses start training in great physical shape, only to slow down and lose appetite, and be taken out of training for some rest?

PERTINENT HORSE AND FEED FACTS

There is no panacea in the horse business. Success cannot be achieved through witchcraft or old wives' tales; some merely achieve despite such handicaps. Instead, it calls for the combined best wit, wisdom, and judgment of science, technology, and practical experience.

The horse of today cannot be fed as it was yesterday and be expected to perform as the horse of tomorrow!

The following facts are pertinent to horse feeding, either directly or indirectly, and of importance to equestrians and those who counsel with them:

1. Horse owners are—
    a. Spending millions for concoctions, and unbalanced and deficient rations.
    b. Producing a 50% foal crop. How many cattle producers could afford to keep two cows a whole year to produce one calf?
    c. Retiring an appalling number of horses from tracks, shows, and other uses, due to unsoundness.
    d. Losing millions of dollars through inefficiency and from deaths due to diseases and parasites.
2. Artificial conditions have been created which have caused unsoundnesses. In the wild state, horses roamed the plains in bands, with plenty of outdoor exercise on natural footing and fed on feeds derived from unleached soils, and, they were in unforced production. Today, many horses spend 95% of their time in a stall or corral, are exercised before daylight, forced for early growth and use (being ridden and raced as two-year-olds), and put under great stress when shown, ridden, or raced (when running, horses expend up to 100 times the energy utilized at rest).
3. Remarkable progress has been made in feeding meat animals, as a result of which (a) feed required per pound of gain has been reduced, and (b) rate of gain has been increased. But no such progress has been made in horses; altogether too many of them are being fed the same old oats and same old timothy hay. In fact, many horses of today are being fed about the same as they were a century ago. How many meat animal producers could survive were they to turn back the pages of time and feed as their great, great grandfathers did 100 years ago?

4. Soils have been leached and depleted. This condition has come with the passing of time. Since soil nutrients affect plant nutrients, many horses are being shortchanged nutritionally.

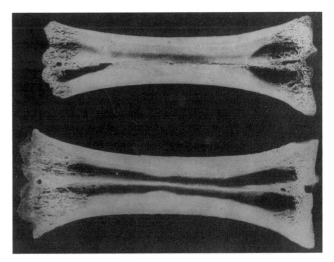

Fig. 13-1. Soil nutrients made the difference! Split bones from two animals of similar breeding and age. Small, fragile, pitted bone (top) obtained from animal pastured on belly-deep grass grown on weathered soil low in mineral content. Big, rugged, strong bone (bottom) from animal grown on moderately weathered, but highly mineralized soil. (Courtesy, University of Missouri)

5. Much can, and will, continue to be done through improved horse breeding, but this takes time. By contrast, improved nutrition makes for immediate results.
6. At one time, nearly all lamenesses in horses were attributed to faulty shoeing. Later, this thought gave way to the traumatism (injury) theory—bone ailments were blamed upon bruising, pounding, and violent exertion. Still others maintain that skeletal troubles are primarily genetic in origin, that they're inherited from the parents.
7. Today, we know that a big head, bulging forehead, weak and crooked legs, enlarged joints, certain faulty conformation, and "ouchiness" are, in a vast majority of cases, deficiency symptoms resulting from improper nutrition. Many of the bone ailments that plague breeders and trainers—the sprains, spavins, splints, and ringbones—are the tragic result of im-

proper skeletal development during the fetal and early growth stages.

8. Grass hays and farm grains are inadequate in quantity and quality of proteins, in certain minerals and vitamins, and in unidentified factors.

9. Horses are the most poorly nourished of all domestic animals from a scientific point of view.

10. Feeding horses for show or racing is more complicated and difficult than feeding any other farm animal. This is primarily because of the stress and strain under which they are put and the absolute necessity for soundness.

11. Equine feed formulations are becoming more complex.

12. The average horse eats 11,000 lb, or 5½ tons, of feed (hay and grain, or equivalent in pasture), each year.

13. Feed storage and labor costs have spiraled.

14. Horses reach maturity at four to five years of age. This means that many are expected to work hard, especially the racing breeds, as mere juveniles. No other animal is subjected to such stress and expected to perform so well at such an early age. This calls for the best in nutrition, so as to assure maximum growth and soundness of muscle and bone.

15. A major problem of breeders of racehorses today is to produce enough sound horses to supply the demand of racetracks.

16. If we are to improve nutrition, it must start with the fertility of the soil; it must be "from the ground up."

17. The grass on the other side of the fence is usually greener. What's more, if it's on a highway shoulder or right-of-way, it's usually more nutritious because of growing on more fertile soil.

18. Much more research has been done on diseases and parasites of horses per se than on their nutrition. Yet, it is recognized that nutrition plays a major role in disease and parasite resistance. This is true of bacterial infections, azoturia, "tying-up," some cases of periodic ophthalmia, and digestive disturbances.

19. The following parallel to the altogether too common breakdown of young horses in training or on the track is noteworthy: When young lambs or young pigs are pushed for daily gains that are twice as rapid as they were 50 years ago without simultaneously meeting their increased and more critical nutrient needs, they usually become crooked legged and crippled, much as happens to young equines that are forced. But, through proper nutrition, we generally alleviate this condition in young lambs and pigs.

20. Horse owners and others, sometimes ask, "If so little nutrition research has been done on horses, how can one formulation or ration be superior to others?" In the judgment of the author, the answer is simple: We have made rapid strides in the fields of animal and human nutrition during the past two decades. These can be used as guides. It's a matter of fitting all these parts together, and, scientifically and practically, adapting them to the horse. It's not unlike the making of a satellite, which necessitates the scientific and practical fitting together of research for a specific purpose.

DIGESTIVE SYSTEM

The alimentary canal proper includes the entire tube extending from the mouth to the anus.

An understanding of the principal parts and functions of the digestive system of the horse is requisite to intelligent feeding.

Fig 13-2 shows the anatomical position of the digestive system of the horse, whereas Table 13-1 and Fig. 13-3 show the comparative structures and sizes of the digestive tracts of farm animals. As noted, the digestive tract of the horse is anatomically and physiologically quite different from that of the ruminant.

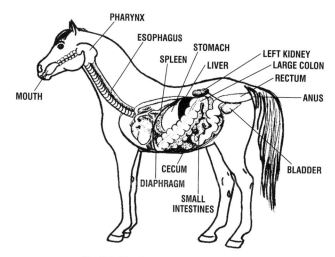

Fig. 13-2. The digestive system of the horse.

TABLE 13-1
PARTS AND CAPACITIES OF DIGESTIVE TRACTS OF HORSE, COW, AND PIG

	Horse[1]	Cow	Pig
	--------- (qt capacity) ---------		
Stomach	8–16	(200)	6–8
Rumen (paunch)		160	
Reticulum (honeycomb) . .		10	
Omasum (manyplies) . . .		15	
Abomasum (true stomach)		15	
Small intestine	48	62	9
Cecum	28–32		
Large intestine	80	40	10

[1]Values for an average horse of 1,000 to 1,200 lb.

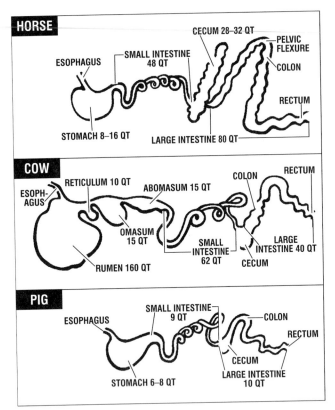

Fig. 13-3. Schematic diagram of digestive tracts of horse, cow, and pig.

MOUTH

The mouth is the first part of the alimentary canal. In the horse, it is long and cylindrical. It includes the teeth (both uppers and lowers—24 molars and 12 incisors in the mature horse), the tongue, and 3 pairs of large salivary glands.

Digestion starts in the mouth. The feed is masticated by the teeth and moistened with saliva. In the mature horse, approximately 85 lb (10 gal.) of saliva are secreted daily. It wets feedstuffs, thereby making for easier passage down the esophagus. In addition, the saliva contains the enzyme ptyalin, which transforms starch into maltose.

The mouth of the horse differs anatomically and physiologically from the ruminant as follows: Horses have upper incisor teeth, ruminants do not; horses masticate feed with the teeth, ruminants are cud chewing; horses secrete a larger volume of saliva, and the saliva of the horse contains ptyalin, whereas the saliva of ruminants is enzyme-free.

ESOPHAGUS

This 50- to 60-in. tube provides passage of feed from the pharynx to the stomach.

STOMACH

The stomach is the enlarged part of the alimentary canal which lies between the esophagus and the small intestine. It holds 8 to 16 qt, but it functions best at two-thirds capacity. The stomach secretes gastric juices by which proteins and fats are broken down.

At the time of eating, feed passes through the horse's stomach very rapidly—so much so that feed eaten at the beginning of the meal passes to the intestine before the last part of the meal is completed.

SMALL INTESTINE

The small intestine is the tube that connects the stomach with the large intestine. On the average, it is about 70 ft long, and 3 to 4 in. thick when distended, with a capacity of about 12 gal.

The small intestines of the horse and the cow have about the same total capacity, although the organ of the cow is nearly twice as long and half as thick.

In the horse, as in the ruminant, the enzymes of the pancreas and liver assist in further breaking down the protein, fats, and sugars which escape breakdown by the gastric juices of the stomach.

LARGE INTESTINE

The large intestine of the horse is divided into the cecum (4 ft long and 1 ft in diameter; contents fluid), great colon (12 ft long and 10 in. in diameter; contents fluid to semifluid), small colon (10 ft long and 4 in. in diameter; contents solid), and rectum.

In the cecum, sometimes called the water gut, digestion (fermentation) continues, limited vitamin synthesis occurs, and nutrients are absorbed.

The great colon is usually distended with food. In it, there is a continuation of the digestion of feed by digestive juices, bacterial action, and absorption of the nutrients.

In the small colon, the contents of the digestive tract become solid and balls of dung are formed.

ANATOMICAL AND PHYSIOLOGICAL DIFFERENCES

The anatomical and physiological peculiarities of the digestive system of the horse are of great significance, nutritionally. In comparison with the cow (a ruminant), the digestive tract of a horse differs as follows.

1. It is smaller (see Table 13-1), with the result

that the horse cannot eat as much roughage as cattle. Not only that, it functions best at two-thirds capacity. Because of its small size, if a horse is fed too much roughage, labored breathing and quick tiring may result. Actually, the horse's stomach is designed for almost constant intake of small quantities of feed (such as happens when a horse is grazing on pasture), rather than large amounts at one time.

2. Without feed, the horse's stomach will empty completely in 24 hours, whereas it takes about 72 hours (3 times as long) for the cow's stomach to empty. At the time of eating, feed passes through the horse's stomach very rapidly—so much so that the food eaten at the beginning of the meal passes into the intestine before the last part of the meal is completed.

3. The cow has four compartments (rumen, reticulum, omasum, and the abomasum or true stomach), whereas the horse has one.

4. There is comparatively little microbial action in the stomach of the horse, but much such action in the stomach (rumen) of the cow. As a result, the horse does not break down more than about 30% of the cellulose of feed, whereas the ruminant breaks down 60 to 70%. Hence, horses cannot handle as much roughage as can ruminants. Also, higher quality (lower cellulose content) forages must be fed to horses.

5. The primary seats of microbial activity in ruminants and horses occupy different locations in the digestive system in relation to the small intestine. In cows (and sheep), the rumen precedes the small intestine; in horses, the cecum follows it. As a result, the efficiency of absorption of nutrients synthesized by the microorganism is likely to be lower in a horse than in a ruminant.

The limited protein synthesis in the horse (limited when compared with ruminants), and the lack of efficiency of absorption due to the cecum being on the lower end of the gut (thereby not giving the small intestine a chance at the ingesta after it leaves the cecum), clearly indicate that horse rations should contain high-quality proteins, adequate in amino acids.

In comparison to a cow, therefore, a horse should be fed less roughage, more and higher quality protein (no urea), and added B vitamins. Actually, the nutrient requirements of a horse more nearly parallel those of a pig than a cow.

FUNCTIONS OF FEEDS

The feed consumed by horses is used for a number of different purposes, the exact usage varying somewhat with class, age, and productivity of the animal. A certain part of the feed is used for the maintenance of bodily functions aside from any useful production. This is known as the maintenance require-

ment. In addition, feed is used to take care of the functions for which horses are kept. Thus, young growing equines need nutrients suitable for building muscle tissue and bone; horses being readied for show or sale need a surplus of energy feeds for formation of fat; broodmares require feed for the development of their fetuses, and, following parturition, for the production of milk; whereas work (or racing) animals use feed to supply energy for work.

MAINTENANCE

A horse differs from an engine in that the latter has no fuel replacement when idle, whereas the horse requires fuel every second of the day, whether it is idle or active.

The maintenance requirement may be defined as a ration which is adequate to prevent any loss or gain of tissue in the body when there is no production. Although these requirements are relatively simple they are essential for life itself. A mature horse must have heat to maintain body temperature, sufficient energy to cover the internal work of the body and the minimum movement of the animal, and a small amount of proteins, minerals, and vitamins for the repair of body tissues.

No matter how quietly a horse may be standing in the stall, it still requires a certain amount of fuel, and the least amount on which it can exist is called its basal maintenance requirement. Even under the best of conditions, about one-half of all the feed consumed by horses is used in meeting the maintenance requirements.

GROWTH

Growth may be defined as an increase in size of bone, muscles, internal organs, and other body parts.

The period of rapid growth of the young horse is one of the most critical in its life and requires the best possible nutrition. Foals attain approximately 90% of their mature height and 75% of their mature weight at 12 months of age (Fig. 13-4), followed by more gradual growth to 5 years of age.[1] Since bones and muscles are a significant part of early growth, proper nutrition is a must for their development. A foal that is severely restricted in nutrients will never reach its genetic potential. Naturally, the growth requirements become increasingly acute when horses are forced for early use, such as the training and racing of a two- or three-year-old.

---

[1]Brody, S., *Bioenergetics and Growth*, Reinhold Publishing Corporation, New York, NY, p. 552; and *A Study of Growth* and *Development in the Quarter Horses*, Bull. No. 546, Louisiana State University.

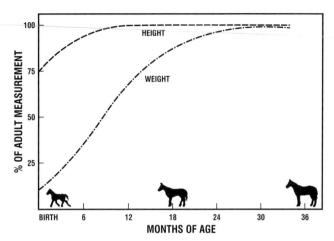

Fig. 13-4. Foals usually attain about 90% of their mature height and about 75% of their mature weight by 12 months of age. Bones and muscles are a significant part of early growth; hence, proper nutrition for young stock is very important.

Growth has been referred to as the foundation of horse production. Breeding animals may have their productive ability seriously impaired if they have been raised improperly. Nor can the most satisfactory performance be expected unless they have been well developed. For example, running horses do not possess the desired speed and endurance if their growth has been stunted or if their skeletons have been injured by inadequate rations during the growth period.

FITTING (FATTENING)

This is the laying on of fat, especially in the tissues of the abdominal cavity and in the connective tissues just under the skin and between the muscles.

Usually, fitting rations contain more energy than do maintenance rations. However, the same formulation may be used for both fitting and maintenance purposes, but with larger quantities being supplied to horses that are being fitted.

In practical fitting rations, higher condition in mature animals is usually obtained through increasing the allowance of feeds high in carbohydrates and fats—a more liberal allowance of grains. Any surplus of protein may also serve for the production of fat, but usually such feeds are more expensive and are not used for economy reasons. In fitting mature horses, very little more proteins, minerals, and vitamins are required than for maintenance. In fitting young, growing animals, however, it is essential that, in addition to supplying more carbohydrates and fats, ample proteins, minerals, and vitamins be provided to meet their accelerated growth.

REPRODUCTION AND LACTATION

Regular and normal reproduction is the basis for profit on any horse breeding establishment. Despite this undeniable fact, it has been estimated that only 40 to 60% of all mares bred actually produce foals. Certainly, there are many causes of reproductive failure, but most scientists are agreed that inadequate nutrition is a major one.

With all species, most of the growth of the fetus occurs during the last third of pregnancy, thus making the reproductive requirements most critical during this period. The ration of the pregnant mare should supply sufficient amounts of protein, minerals, and vitamins.

The nutritive requirements for moderate to heavy milk production are much more rigorous than the pregnancy requirements. There is special need for a rather liberal protein, mineral, and vitamin allowance.

In the case of young, growing, pregnant females, additional protein, minerals, and vitamins, above the ordinary requirements, must be provided; otherwise, the fetus will not develop properly or milk will be produced at the expense of the tissues of the dam.

Fig. 13-5. Lactation increases the nutritional requirements significantly. This shows a broodmare and her newborn foal (1-hour and 25 minutes old). (Courtesy, Kentucky Department of Information, Frankfort, KY)

It is also known that the ration exerts a powerful effect on sperm production and semen quality. Too fat a condition can even lead to temporary or permanent sterility. Moreover, there is abundant evidence that greater fertility of stallions exists under conditions where a well-balanced ration and plenty of exercise are provided.

WORK

In many respects, work requirements are similar to the needs for fitting, both functions requiring high-energy feeds.

For mature horses, not in reproduction, work is performed primarily at the expense of the carbohydrates and fats of the ration—energy that can be supplied in the form of additional grain. Theoretically, the protein is not drawn upon so long as the other nutrients are present in adequate amounts. From a practical standpoint, however, it is usually desirable to feed more proteins than the maintenance requirement, to maintain a protein-calorie ratio in the diet which promotes efficiency of energy utilization. For work animals, the mineral and vitamin requirements are practically the same as for comparable idle animals—except for the greater need for salt because of increased perspiration.

Fig. 13-6. Hard-working barrel racing horse. This requires high-energy feeds, usually supplied by additional grain. (Photo by Wyatt McSpadden. Courtesy, American Quarter Horse Assn., Amarillo, TX)

NUTRIENT NEEDS

Meeting the nutrient needs of horses is a major factor in determining their efficiency and years of service. In the discussion that follows, both requirements and allowances will be covered; and the nutritive needs of the horse will be discussed under the following headings: (1) energy (carbohydrates and fats), (2) protein, (3) minerals, (4) vitamins, and (5) water.

NUTRIENT REQUIREMENTS VS ALLOWANCES

In ration formulation, two words are commonly used—*requirements* and *allowances*. Requirements do not provide for margins of safety. Thus, to feed a horse on the basis of meeting the bare requirements would not be unlike building a bridge without providing margins of safety for heavier than average loads or for floods. No competent engineer would be so foolish as to design such a bridge. Likewise, knowledgeable horse nutritionists provide for margins of safety—they provide for the necessary nutritive allowances. They allow for variations in feed composition; possible losses during storage and processing; day-to-day, and period-to-period, differences in needs of animals; age and size of animal; stage of gestation and lactation; the kind and degree of activity; the amount of stress; the system of management; the health, condition and temperament of the animal; and the kind, quality and amount of feed—all of which exert a powerful influence in determining nutritive needs.

RECOMMENDED NUTRIENT ALLOWANCES

Presently available information indicates that the recommended nutrient allowances given in Table 13-2 will meet the minimum requirements for horses and provide reasonable margins of safety. Additional recommended allowance figures are given in the following tables: Minerals, in Table 13-4; and vitamins, in Table 13-5.

■ **Stress affects nutritive needs**—Stress may be caused by excitement, temperament, fatigue, number of horses together, previous nutrition, breed, age, and management. Race and show horses are always under stress; and the more tired they become and the greater the speed, the greater the stress. Thus, the ration for race and show horses should be scientifically formulated. The greater the stress, the more exacting the nutritive requirements.

■ **Other factors affect nutritive needs**—The feed requirements of horses do not necessarily remain the same from day-to-day or from period-to-period. The age and size of the animal; the stage of gestation or lactation of a mare; the kind and degree of activity; climatic conditions; the kind, quality, and amount of feed; the system of management; and the health, condition, and temperament of the animal are all continually exerting a powerful influence in determining its nutritive needs. How well the caretaker understands,

TABLE 13-2
RECOMMENDED NUTRIENT ALLOWANCES FOR HORSES (TOTAL RATION/AS-FED BASIS)[1]

	Mature Horses (Consuming 25 lb feed/horse/day. Idle horses require less feed and/or consume more roughage than heavily worked horses or lactating mares.)					Young Horses, Based on Mature Weight 1,000 lb				
	Idle Horses/ Light Work/ Moderate Work (1,000 lb Wt)	Heavy Training/ Heavy Work (1,000 lb Wt)	Stallions in Breeding Season (1,000 lb Wt)	Mares, Last 90 Days Gestation (1,000 lb Wt)	Mares, Peak of Lactation (1,000 lb Wt)	Creep Feed (250 lb Body Wt/ 11 lb Feed Daily)	Weanlings (450 lb Body Wt/12 lb Feed Daily)	Yearlings (650 lb Body Wt/13 lb Feed Daily)	2-Yr-Olds & 3-Yr-Olds (800 lb Body Wt/14 lb Feed Daily)	2-Yr-Olds in Light Training (800 lb Body Wt/15 lb Feed Daily)
Digestible Energy:										
TDN[2] . . . . (%)	55	62.50	75	62.50	75	75	75	70	60	65
Mcal per . . . . (lb)	0.8	1.2	1.0	0.90	1.10	1.25	1.25	1.15	1.00	1.10
Mcal per . . . . (kg)[3]	*1.80*	*2.55*	*2.15*	*2.0*	*2.35*	*2.60*	*2.60*	*2.50*	*2.20*	*2.40*
Crude Protein . . . . (%)	9.0	11.0	14.0	13.0	14.0	18.0	16.0	14.0	13.0	13.0
Lysine . . . . (%)	0.25	0.36	0.30	0.32	0.41	0.54	0.55	0.48	0.38	0.41
Major or Macrominerals:										
Salt . . . . (%)	0.75	0.75	0.75	0.75	0.75	0.75	0.75	0.75	0.75	0.75
Calcium . . . . (%)	0.21	0.31	0.26	0.29	0.47	0.62	0.55	0.40	0.28	0.31
Phosphorus . . . . (%)	0.15	0.23	0.19	0.30	0.30	0.34	0.30	0.22	0.15	0.17
Magnesium . . . . (%)	0.08	0.12	0.10	0.10	0.09	0.07	0.07	0.07	0.08	0.09
Potassium . . . . (%)	0.27	0.39	0.33	0.33	0.38	0.27	0.27	0.27	0.27	0.29
Sulfur . . . . (%)	0.15	0.15	0.15	0.15	0.15	0.15	0.15	0.15	0.15	0.15
Trace or Microminerals:										
Cobalt . . . . (ppm)[4]	0.11	0.11	0.11	0.11	0.11	0.11	0.11	0.11	0.11	0.11
Copper . . . . (ppm)	25	25	25	25	30	40	40	30	25	25
Iodine . . . . (ppm)	0.11	0.11	0.11	0.11	0.11	0.11	0.11	0.11	0.11	0.11
Iron . . . . (ppm)	40	60	90	90	90	90	80	60	60	60
Manganese . . . . (ppm)	46	46	46	46	46	46	48	46	46	46
Selenium . . . . (ppm)	0.11	0.11	0.11	0.11	0.11	0.11	0.11	0.11	0.11	0.11
Zinc . . . . (ppm)	80	90	90	100	100	100	100	100	90	90
	(/lb)	(/lb)	(/lb)	(/lb)	(/lb)	(/lb)	(/lb)	(/lb)	(/lb)	(/lb)
Fat-soluble Vitamins in Feed:										
Vitamin A . . . . (IU)	1,045	1,045	1,045	1,569	1,569	1,045	1,045	1,045	1,045	1,045
Vitamin D . . . . (IU)	156	156	156	314	314	419	419	419	419	419
Vitamin E . . . . (IU)	26	41	41	41	41	41	41	41	41	41
Vitamin K . . . . (mg)	0.32	0.32	0.32	0.32	0.32	0.30	0.30	0.30	0.30	0.30
Water-soluble Vitamins in Feed:										
Biotin . . . . (mg)	0.1	0.1	0.1	0.1	0.1	0.1	0.1	0.1	0.1	0.1
Choline . . . . (mg)	20	30	30	30	30	62.5	62.5	62.5	62.5	62.5
Folacin . . . . (mg)	0.8	1.2	1.2	1.2	1.2	3.0	3.0	3.0	3.0	3.0
Niacin . . . . (mg)	10	20.8	10	10	10	10	10	10	10	10
Pantothenic acid . . . . (mg)	10	20.8	10	10	10	10	10	10	10	10
Riboflavin . . . . (mg)	1.6	1.6	1.6	1.6	1.6	1.6	1.6	1.6	1.6	1.6
Thiamin (B-1) . . . . (mg)	1.57	2.61	1.57	1.57	1.57	1.57	1.57	1.57	1.57	1.57
Vitamin B-6 . . . . (mg)	1.0	1.0	1.0	1.0	1.0	0.5	0.5	0.5	0.5	0.5
Vitamin B-12 . . . . (mg)	0.005	0.006	0.006	0.006	0.006	0.007	0.007	0.007	0.007	0.007
Vitamin C (ascorbic acid) . . . (mg)	2.4	4.0	4.0	4.0	4.0	3.75	3.75	3.75	3.75	3.75

[1] Where hay is fed separately, double the amounts shown in this table should be added to the concentrate.

[2] 1 lb TDN = 2 Mcal or 2,000 Kcal.

[3] 1 kg = 2.2 lb or 1,000 g.

[4] 1 ppm (parts per million) = 1 mg/kg.

anticipates, interprets, and meets these requirements usually determines the success or failure of the ration.

No set of instructions, calculator, or book of knowledge can substitute for experience and born horse intuition. Skill and good judgment are essential.

In the discussion that follows, the nutrient requirements and recommended allowances of the horse are discussed under these headings: (1) energy (carbohydrates and fats), (2) protein, (3) minerals, (4) vitamins, and (5) water.

ENERGY

The energy requirements of horses for various activities are hard to develop because it is difficult to express quantitatively the type of exercise, the intensity and duration of work, the condition and training of the animals, the ability and weight of the rider and driver, the degree of fatigue, and the environmental temperature—all of which influence energy requirements. Based on Cornell studies by Pagan, Hintz reported the energy requirements given in Table 13-3. The Cornell researchers found that the amount of energy expended was proportional to the body weight of the riderless horse or the combined weight of the horse plus the rider, and that the amount of energy expended was exponentially related to speed. Additional studies are needed to determine the energy expenditures at speeds faster than the 13 miles per hour reported in Table 13-3.

Fig. 13-7. When racing, horses may require up to 100 times more energy when running than at rest. (Courtesy, *The Quarter Horse Journal*, Amarillo, TX)

The caretaker may base individual horse energy requirements on observation. If the horse is too thin, increase the energy intake; if too fat, decrease energy intake. Generally, increased energy for horses is met by increasing the grain and decreasing the roughage.

Although proteins, fats, and carbohydrates can be used to provide energy for maintenance, work, or fattening of horses, the carbohydrates (primarily grains and roughages) are by far the most important, and fats are next in importance for energy purposes.

CARBOHYDRATES

The carbohydrates are organic compounds composed of carbon, hydrogen, and oxygen. This group includes the sugars, starch, cellulose, gums, and related substances. They are formed in the plant by photosynthesis as follows:

$$6CO_2 + 6H_2O + \text{energy from sun} =$$
$$C_6H_{12}O_6 \text{ (glucose)} = 6O_2$$

On the average, the carbohydrates comprise about three-fourths of all dry matter in plants, the chief source of horse feed. They form the woody framework of plants as well as the chief reserve food stored in seeds, roots, and tubers. When consumed by horses, carbohydrates are used as a source of heat and energy, and any excess of them is stored in the body as fat, or, in part, secreted.

TABLE 13-3
DIGESTIBLE ENERGY REQUIREMENTS FOR
VARIOUS ACTIVITIES OF LIGHT HORSES[1]

Gait	Speed (Miles/Hour)[2]	DE/Hour (Kcal/kg of Wt)[3]
Slow walk	2.2	1.7
Fast walk	3.6	2.5
Slow trot	7.5	6.5
Medium trot	9.3	9.5
Fast trot/slow canter	11.2	13.7
Medium canter	13.0	19.5

[1]Hintz, H. F., "Energy Requirements of Horses," *Feed Management*, Vol. 37, No. 2, Feb. 1986, p. 15.

[2]To convert to metric, see Appendix, Weights and Measures.

[3]Body weight of horse plus weight of rider and tack.

A lack of energy intake may cause slow and stunted growth in foals and loss of weight, poor condition, and excessive fatigue in mature horses. Excess energy may result in obese horses, which are more susceptible to stress and founder and have lowered reproductive efficiency and decreased longevity.

No appreciable amount of carbohydrate is found in the horse's body at any one time, the blood supply of animals being held rather constant at about 0.05 to 0.1% for most animals, but with the pig ranging from 0.05 to 0.25%. However, this small quantity of glucose in the blood, which is constantly replenished by changing the glycogen of the liver back to glucose, serves as the chief source of fuel with which to maintain the body temperature and to furnish the energy needed for all body processes. The storage of glycogen (called "animal starch") in the liver amounts to 3 to 7% of the weight of that organ.

From a feeding standpoint, the carbohydrates consist of nitrogen-free extract (NFE) and fiber. The nitrogen-free extract includes the more soluble, and, therefore, the more digestible, carbohydrates—such as the starches, sugars, hemicelluloses, and the more soluble part of the celluloses and pentosans. Also, NFE contains some lignin. The fiber is that woody portion of plants (or feeds) which is not dissolved out by weak acids and alkalis. Fiber, therefore, is less easily digested. It includes cellulose, hemicellulose, and lignin.

The ability of horses to utilize roughages—to digest the fiber therein—depends chiefly on bacterial action. It is a true symbiotic type of relationship, carried out chiefly by anaerobic bacteria, mostly in the cecum and colon of the horse. This bacterial digestion breaks down the cellulose and pentosans of feeds into usable organic acids (chiefly acetic, propionic and butyric acids).

The fiber of growing pasture grass, fresh or dried, is more digestible than the fiber of most hay. Likewise, the fiber of early cut hay is more digestible than that of hay cut in the late bloom or seed stages. The difference is due to both chemical and physical structure, especially in the presence of certain encrusting substances (notably lignin) which are deposited in the cell wall with age. This is understandable when it is recognized that lignin is the principal constituent of wood, for no one would think of feeding wood to horses.

Since the horse evolved as a grazing animal, its digestive system often has difficulty in handling large quantities of cereal grains (starchy material). Evidence of the horse's difficulty with high grain rations is manifested clinically as founder, colic, and/or loss of appetite. So, to promote normal physiological activity of the gastrointestinal tract, some coarse roughage is necessary; finely ground roughage (or pelleted forage) will not suffice. But the precise amount of fiber needed has not been determined. It is generally recommended that horses be fed 1.0 to 2.0 lb of roughage per 100 lb of body weight, daily. Young horses and working (or running) horses must have rations in which a large part of the carbohydrate content is low in fiber, and in the form of nitrogen-free extract.

FATS

Lipids (fat and fatlike substances), like carbohydrates, contain three elements: carbon, hydrogen, and oxygen. As horse feeds, fats function much like carbohydrates in that they serve as a source of heat and energy and for the formation of fat. Because of the larger portion of carbon and hydrogen, however, fats liberate more heat than carbohydrates when digested, furnishing approximately 2.25 times as much heat or energy per pound on oxidation as do carbohydrates. A smaller quantity of fat is required, therefore, to serve the same function.

The physical and chemical properties of fats are quite variable. From a chemical standpoint, a molecule of fat consists of a combination of three molecules of certain fatty acids with one molecule of glycerol. Fats differ in their melting points and other properties, depending on the particular fatty acids which they contain. Thus, because of the high content of unsaturated acids (such as oleic and linoleic) and acids of low molecular weight, corn fat is a liquid at ordinary temperatures; whereas, because of the high content of stearic and palmitic acids, beef fat is solid at ordinary temperatures.

Unsaturated fatty acids have the ability to take up oxygen or certain other chemical elements. Chemically, these unsaturated acids contain one or more pairs of double bond carbon atoms.

A small amount of fat in the ration is desirable, as fat is the carrier of the fat-soluble vitamins (vitamins A, D, E, and K). There is evidence that some species (humans, swine, rats, and dogs) require certain of the fatty acids. Although the fatty acid requirements of horses have not been settled, it is thought that ordinary farm rations contain ample quantities of these nutrients.

In the past, most caretakers and scientists were of the opinion that horses could not tolerate high-fat diets. However, recent work indicates that they will readily consume 10 to 20% added fat to the ration, without difficulty—and even with benefit.[2] In an endurance trial conducted by the Colorado Station, horses fed fat supplemented rations (9% added fat) outperformed their counterparts that were fed either (1) starch supplemented rations, or (2) protein supplemented rations.[3] Subsequent experiments and experiences indicate that the amount of the energy and the energy density needed in the ration increase dramatically as work intensity increases. Research at Texas A&M University also shows that a high fat diet will

[2]Tyznik, W. J., "Energy for Horses," paper presented at the 1975 California Livestock Symposium.

[3]Slade, L. M., and P. L. Hambleton, "Feeding the Horse for Endurance," *Stud Managers' Handbook*, Vol. 12 edited by M. E. Ensminger, Agriservices Foundation, Clovis, CA, 1976, p. 140.

increase the reproductive and lactation performance of broodmares.

The horse's utilization of feed energy for muscular work involves (1) the production of energy-rich adenosine triphosphate (ATP) from carbohydrates, fats, and proteins by means of oxidative processes, and (2) the contraction of the muscle fibers induced by ATP. When exercising lightly or moderately—at a gait no faster than cantering—the cardiovascular system of the horse can supply enough oxygen to the muscle tissue to permit the complete oxidation of energy sources (ATP) needed for muscle contraction, with little or no formation of lactic acid. This is called *aerobic exercise*. For such exercise, normal rations consisting of grain and hay suffice.

When the exercise of the equine athlete is very intense—as in training, racing, cutting, reining, and polo—and the horse is unable to transport enough oxygen to the muscles to oxidize completely the energy sources (ATP), aerobic capacity is augmented in part by nonoxidative processes. This is called *anaerobic exercise*. Glycogen serves as the primary energy source during anaerobic exercise. But if a sufficient amount of oxygen is not present, large amounts of lactic acid build up, resulting in heavy breathing, fatigue, soreness, and a prolonged recovery period; and the elimination of the lactic acid buildup requires extra oxygen. So, it is theorized (1) that vegetable or animal fats, which provide about 2.25 times as much energy as the carbohydrates, will conserve muscle glycogen for that all important anaerobic period of high energy demand—such as the stretch run; and (2) that a high fat ration will allow the horse to store and maintain higher levels of muscle glycogen, thereby imparting more staying power or endurance.

Also, when a substantial increase in energy (calories) is needed for the high performance horse, energy-dense fats, which contain more than twice as much energy per unit weight as carbohydrate feeds, are safer, lessening founder, colic, and other digestive disturbances. Additionally, when fed 5 to 20% high-quality fat in a properly processed ration, performance horses usually clean up their feed better. As with any ration change, the conversion to a high fat ration should be gradual.

Unsaturated fats—vegetable oils, particularly corn oil or safflower oil—have the added virtue of imparting gloss, or sheen, to the hair when as little as 2 oz (4 tbsp) are fed twice daily. Except for vegetable oils (unsaturated fats) producing an attractive coat, there is no difference between animal and vegetable fats; hence, the choice may be determined by economics—which is the best buy.

Feeds high in fat content are likely to become rancid, and rancid feeds are unpalatable, if not actually injurious in some instances. Thus, when fat is added to the ration, it is important that it be stabilized by the use of an antioxidant. Also, there should be added protein (to maintain the protein-calorie ratio), minerals, and vitamins.

METHODS OF MEASURING ENERGY

One nutrient cannot be considered as more important than another, because all nutrients must be present in adequate amounts if efficient production is to be maintained. Yet, historically, feedstuffs have been compared or evaluated primarily on their ability to supply energy to animals. This is understandable because (1) energy is required in larger amounts than any other nutrient, (2) energy is most often the limiting factor in livestock production, and (3) energy is the major cost associated with feeding animals.

Our understanding of energy metabolism has increased through the years. With this added knowledge, changes have come in both the methods and terms used to express the energy value of feeds.

The methods of measuring the energy value of feedstuffs currently employed in the United States are: (1) total digestible nutrient (TDN), and (2) calorie system.

Each system has its advantages and advocates. Also, both the difficulty in determining energy values of feeds according to the different systems of measurement and the accuracy of the results increase in the order that they are listed above. Nevertheless, more and more feedstuffs are being evaluated in calories, with net energy being the method of choice.

TOTAL DIGESTIBLE NUTRIENTS (TDN)

Total Digestible Nutrients (TDN) is the sum of the digestible protein, fiber, nitrogen-free extract, and fat × 2.25. It has been the most extensively used measure for energy in the United States.

Back of TDN values are the following steps:

1. **Digestibility.** The digestibility of a particular feed for a specific species is determined by a digestion trial.

2. **Computation of digestible nutrients.** Digestible nutrients are computed by multiplying the percentage of each nutrient in the feed (protein, fiber, nitrogen-free extract (NFE), and fat) by its digestion coefficient. The result is expressed as digestible protein, digestible fiber, digestible NFE, and digestible fat. For example, if dent corn contains 8.9% protein of which 77% is digestible, the percent of digestible protein is 6.9.

3. **Computation of total digestible nutrients (TDN).** The TDN is computed by use of the following formula:

$$\% \text{ TDN} = \% \text{ DCP} + \% \text{ DCF} + \% \text{ DNFE} +$$
$$(\% \text{ DEE} \times 2.25)$$

where DCP = digestible crude protein; DCF = digestible crude fiber; DNFE = digestible nitrogen free extract; and DEE = digestible ether extract.

TDN is ordinarily expressed as a percent of the ration or in units of weight (lb or kg), not as a caloric figure.

The main **advantage** of the TDN system is that it has been used for a very long time and many people are acquainted with it.

The main **disadvantages** of the TDN system are:

1. It is really a misnomer, because TDN is not an actual total of the digestible nutrients in a feed. It does not include the digestible mineral matter (such as salt, limestone, and defluorinated phosphate—all of which are digestible); and the digestible fat is multiplied by the factor 2.25 before being included in the TDN figure, because its energy value is higher than carbohydrates and protein. As a result of multiplying fat by the factor 2.25, feeds high in fat will sometimes exceed 100 in percentage TDN (a pure fat with a coefficient of digestibility of 100% would have a theoretical TDN value of 225%—100% × 2.25).

2. It is an empirical formula based upon chemical determinations that are not related to actual metabolism of the animal.

3. It is expressed as a percent or in weight (lb or kg), whereas energy is expressed in calories.

4. It takes into consideration only digestive losses; it does not take into account other important losses, such as losses in the urine, gasses, and increased heat production (heat increment).

5. It overevaluates roughages in relation to concentrates when fed for high rates of production, due to the higher heat loss per pound of TDN in high-fiber feeds.

Because of these several limitations, in the United States the TDN system is gradually being replaced by other energy evaluation systems, particularly net energy. However, due to the voluminous TDN data on many feeds and long-standing tradition, it will continue to be used by many people for a long time to come.

CALORIE SYSTEM

Calories are used to express the energy value of feedstuffs. *One calorie* (always written with a small "c") *is the amount of heat required to raise the temperature of 1 g of water 1°C* (precisely from 14.5 to 15.5°C).

To measure this heat energy, an instrument known as the bomb calorimeter is used, in which the feed (or other substance) to be tested is placed and burned in the presence of oxygen.

Through various digestive and metabolic processes, much of the energy in feed is dissipated as it passes through the animal's digestive system. About 60% of the total combustible energy in grain and about 80% of the total combustible energy in roughage is lost as feces, urine, gases, and heat. These losses are illustrated in Fig. 13-8.

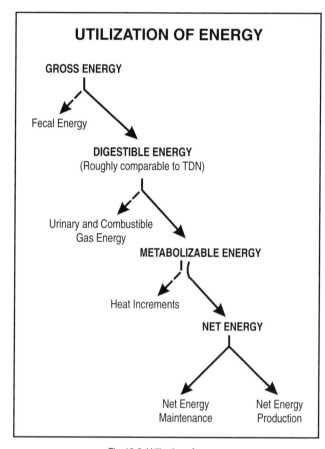

Fig. 13-8. Utilization of energy.

As shown in Fig. 13-8, energy losses occur in the digestion and metabolism of feed. Measures that are used to express animal requirements and the energy content of feeds differ primarily in the digestive and metabolic losses that are included in their determination. Thus, the following terms are used to express the energy value of feeds:

■ **Gross energy (DE)**—*Gross energy represents the total combustible energy in a feedstuff.* It does not differ greatly among feeds, except for those high in fat. For example, 1 lb of corncobs contains about the same amount of GE as 1 lb of shelled corn. Therefore, GE does little to describe the useful energy in feeds.

■ **Digestible energy (DE)**—*Digestible energy is that portion of the GE in a feed that is not excreted in the feces.*

■ **Metabolizable energy (ME)**—*Metabolizable energy represents that portion of the GE that is not lost in the feces, urine, and gas.* Although ME more accurately describes the useful energy in the feed than does GE or DE, it does not take into account the energy lost as heat.

■ **Net Energy (NE)**—*Net energy represents the energy fraction in a feed that is left after the fecal, urinary, gas, and heat losses are deducted from the GE.* The net energy, because of its greater accuracy, is being used increasingly in ration formulations, especially in computerized formulations for large operations.

Although net energy is a more precise measure of the real value of the feed than other energy values, it is much more difficult to determine.

Two systems of net energy evaluation are presently being used. Lofgreen and Garrett[4] developed a system whereby the net energy requirements are listed as dictated by physiological functions—for example, net energy for maintenance NE_m and net energy for gain Ne_g). Also, Moe and Flatt[5] developed a net energy system that compares the physiological function to that of lactation through the use of regression analysis. This value, $NE_{lactation}$, is applicable for all physiological functions.

PROTEIN

For more than a century, proteins and their structural units, the amino acids, have been studied and recognized as important dietary constituents. Proteins are complex organic compounds made chiefly of amino acids, which are present in characteristic proportions for each specific protein. This nutrient always contains carbon, hydrogen, oxygen, and nitrogen, and, in addition, it usually contains sulfur and frequently phosphorus. Proteins are essential in all plant and animal life as components of the active protoplasm of each living cell.

In plants, the protein is largely concentrated in the actively growing portions, especially the leaves and seeds. Legumes also have the ability to synthesize their own proteins from such relatively simple soil and air compounds as carbon dioxide, water, nitrates, and sulfates. Thus, plants, together with some bacteria which are able to synthesize these products, are the original sources of all proteins.

In animals, proteins are much more widely distributed than in plants. Thus, the proteins of the animal body are primary constituents of many structural and protective tissues—such as bones, ligaments, hair, hoofs, skin and the soft tissues which include the organs and muscles. The total protein content of a horse's body ranges from about 10% in very fat mature horses to 20% in thin young foals. By way of further contrast, it is also interesting to note that, except for the bacterial action in the cecum, horses lack the ability of the plant to synthesize proteins from simple materials. They must depend upon plants as a source of dietary protein. In brief, except for the proteins built by the bacterial action in the cecum, they must have amino acids or more complete protein compounds in the ration.

Horses of all ages and kinds require adequate amounts of protein of suitable quality—for maintenance, growth, fattening, reproduction, and work. Of course, the protein requirements for growth, reproduction and lactation are the greatest and most critical.

The protein requirements for work are minimal and are not increased by work load; they're the same for maintenance, medium exercise, and intense exercise, according to researchers at Washington State University.[6] Therefore, the protein requirements for work are essentially the same as the maintenance requirements. Of course, when total feed intake increases to meet the added energy requirements of working horses, total protein intake also increases, even though the percent protein in the ration remains the same.

If more protein is consumed than is needed, the extra protein is broken down by the body and utilized for energy. However, protein is not as effectively and efficiently utilized for energy as are carbohydrates and fats. Furthermore, the byproducts of protein metabolism, such as urea, are excreted in the urine.

A deficiency of protein in the ration of the horse may result in the following deficiency symptoms: depressed appetite, poor growth, loss of weight, reduced milk production, irregular estrus, lowered foal crops, loss of condition, and lack of stamina.

Since the vast majority of protein requirements given in feeding standards meet minimum needs only, the allowances for race, show, breeding, and young animals should be higher. *CAUTION:* Increasing the protein in foal rations to stimulate growth without providing adequate levels of minerals may cause skeletal deformities and leg weaknesses which cannot be reversed.

QUALITY OF PROTEINS

In addition to an adequate quantity of proteins

[4]Lofgreen, G. P., and W. N. Garrett, "A System for Expressing Net Energy Requirements and Feed Values for Growing and Finishing Beef Cattle," *Journal of Animal Science*, Vol. 27, 1968, p. 793.

[5]Moe, P. W., and W. P. Flatt, "Net Energy of Feedstuffs for Lactation," *Journal of Dairy Science*, Vol. 52, 1969, p. 928.

[6]Patterson, P. H., C. N. Coon, and I. M. Hughes, "Protein Requirements for Mature Working Horses," *Journal of Animal Science*, Vol. 61, No. 1, July 1985, p. 187.

being supplied, it is essential that the character of proteins be thoroughly understood. Proteins are very complex compounds with each molecule made up of hundreds of thousands of amino acids combined with each other. The amino acids, of which some 23 are known, are sometimes referred to as the building stones of proteins. Certain of these amino acids can be made by the animal's body to satisfy its needs. Others cannot be formed fast enough to supply the body's needs, and therefore are known as indispensable (or essential) amino acids. These must be supplied in the feed. Thus, rations that furnish an insufficient amount of any of the essential amino acids are said to have proteins of poor quality, whereas those which provide the proper proportions of the various necessary amino acids are said to supply proteins of good quality. In general, animal proteins are superior to plant proteins for monogastric animals (including humans) because they are better balanced in the essential amino acids. For example, zein (a corn protein) is an incomplete plant protein. It is deficient in the essential amino acids lysine and tryptophan. On the other hand, animal proteins are excellent sources of lysine, and many of them (especially milk and eggs) are abundant in tryptophan.

The necessity of each amino acid in the diet of the experimental rat has been thoroughly tested, but less is known about the requirements of large animals or even the human. According to our present knowledge, based largely on work with the rat, the following division of amino acids as indispensable and dispensable seems proper:

Indispensable	Dispensable
Arginine	Alanine
Histidine	Aspartic acid
Isoleucine	Citrulline
Leucine	Cysteine
Lysine	Cystine
Methionine (may be replaced	Glutamic acid
in part by cystine)	Glycine
Phenylalanine	Hydroxyglutamic acid
Threonine	Hydroxyproline
Tryptophan	Norleucine
Valine	Proline
	Serine
	Tyrosine

CECUM SYNTHESIS

In the case of ruminants (cattle and sheep), there is tremendous bacterial action in the paunch. These bacteria build body proteins of high quality from sources of inorganic nitrogen that nonruminants (humans, rats, chickens, swine, poultry, and dogs) cannot use. Farther on in the digestive tract, the ruminant digests the bacteria and obtains good proteins there-

from. Although the horse is not a ruminant, apparently the same bacterial process occurs to a limited extent in the cecum—that greatly enlarged blind pouch of the large intestine of the horse. However, it is much more limited than in ruminants, and the cecum is located beyond the small intestine, the main area for digestion and absorption of nutrients. This points up the fallacy of relying on cecum synthesis in the horse; above all, it must be remembered that little cecum synthesis exists in young equines.

The limited protein synthesis in the horse (as compared with ruminants) and the lack of efficiency of absorption due to the cecum being on the lower end of the gut (thereby not giving the small intestine a chance at the digesta after it leaves the cecum), clearly indicate that horse rations should contain high-quality proteins, adequate in essential amino acids. Most cereal grains, such as oats, corn, or barley, are deficient in lysine, tryptophan, and methionine for optimum growth. Some protein supplements, such as linseed and cottonseed meal, do not contain adequate lysine. Proteins from animal sources (such as dried skimmed milk) and from alfalfa and soybeans are high quality. High-quality protein is especially important for young equines, because cecum synthesis is very limited early in life. So, in practical horse feeding, foals should be provided with some protein feeds of animal origin in order to supplement the protein found in grains and forages. In feeding mature horses, a safe plan to follow is to provide plant protein from several sources, unless a high-quality protein source such as dried skimmed milk or soybean meal is used.

In recognition that lysine is the first limiting amino acid of horses and is thus an indicator of the quality of protein which horses require, the recommended lysine allowance for horses is given in Table 13-2.

There is evidence that nonprotein nitrogen (urea) can be substituted for protein in the ration of the horse, but the conversion to protein is inefficient as compared with ruminants. Up to 5% of the urea in the total ration does not appear to be harmful. Nevertheless, in recognition of the more limited bacterial action in the horse and the hazard of toxicity, most state laws forbid the use of such nonprotein nitrogen sources as urea in horse rations.

The extent to which the horse's ration is supplemented with proteins depends on the age of the horse and on the quality of the forage fed. Growing or lactating animals require somewhat more protein than horses that are idle, gestating, or working. Also, grass hays are generally low in quality and quantity of proteins and require more supplementation than legumes.

PROTEIN POISONING

Some opinions to the contrary, protein poisoning

as such has never been documented. There is no proof that heavy feeding of high-protein feeds to horses is harmful, provided (1) the ration is balanced in all other respects, (2) the animal's kidneys are normal and healthy (a large excess of protein in terms of body needs increases the work of the kidneys for the excretion of the urea), (3) any ration change to high-protein feed is made gradually, as is recommended in any change in feed, and (4) there is adequate exercise and normal metabolism.

Some horses do appear to be allergic to certain proteins or to excesses of specific amino acids, as a result of which they may develop *protein bumps*.

It is recognized that protein in excess of what the body can use tends to be wasted insofar as its specific functions are concerned, since it cannot be stored in any but very limited amounts and must be catabolized. Nevertheless, some wastage of protein in terms of its known functions may be both physiologically and economically desirable in order to (1) maintain the protein reserves, (2) provide an adequate protein-calorie ratio for efficient energy utilization, and (3) assure that protein quality needs are met, despite the marked difference of quality among commonly fed rations.

MINERALS[7]

When we think of minerals for the horse, we instinctively think of bones and unsoundnesses. This is so because (1) a horse's skeleton is very large, weighing 100 lb or more in a full-grown horse, of which more than half consists of organic matter and minerals, and (2) experienced trainers estimate that one-third of the horses in training require treatments for unsoundnesses, in one form or another. But in addition to furnishing structural material for the growth of bones, teeth, and tissues, minerals regulate many of the life processes.

In an amazingly short time after birth, a healthy foal can run almost as fast as its mother—and on legs almost as long. In fact, the cannon bones (the lower leg bones extending from the knees and hocks to the fetlocks) are as long at the time of birth as they will ever be. This indicates that important development of the skeleton takes place in the fetus, before the foal is born. It is evident, therefor, that adequate minerals must be provided the broodmare if the bones of her offspring are to be sound.

The mineral requirements of mares in lactation are even more rigorous than those during gestation. Mares

weighing about 1,000 lb will produce an average of 2 gal., or more, of milk per day throughout the 7-month suckling period. That's a total of 3,612 lb of milk. Since fresh mare's milk contains 0.7% ash, this amount of mare's milk contains 25.28 lb of mineral (3,612 × 0.7% = 25.28). Here's how this phenomenon works: The mare's skeleton is like a bank—people deposit money in a bank, then draw out or write checks on their reserves as needed. So, when properly fed before breeding, in early pregnancy, and when barren, mineral deposits are made in the mare's skeleton. Then at those times when the mineral demands are greater than can be obtained from the feed—the last of pregnancy, and during lactation—the mare draws from the stored reserves in her skeleton. Of course, if there hasn't been proper storage in the mare's skeleton, something must give—and that something is the mother. Nature has ordained that growth of the fetus, and the lactation that follows, shall take priority over the maternal requirements. Hence, when there is a mineral deficiency, the mare's body will be deprived, or even stunted if she is young, before the developing fetus or milk production will be materially affected.

Eighteen mineral elements are known to be required by at least some animal species. They can be divided into the following two groups based on the relative amounts needed in the ration:

Major or Macrominerals	**Trace or Microminerals**
Calcium (Ca)	Iodine (I)
Phosphorus (P)	Manganese (Mn)
Sodium (Na)	Iron (Fe)
Chlorine (Cl)	Zinc (Zn)
Potassium (K)	Copper (Cu)
Magnesium (Mg)	Molybdenum (Mo)
Sulfur (S)	Fluorine (F)
	Chromium (Cr)
	Selenium (Se)
	Silicon (Si)
	Cobalt (Co)

Approximately 70% of the mineral content of the horse's body consists of calcium and phosphorus. About 99% of the calcium and over 80% of the phosphorus are found in the bones and teeth.

Although acute mineral deficiency diseases and actual death losses are relatively rare, inadequate supplies of any one of the essential mineral elements may result in lack of thrift, poor gains, inefficient feed utilization, lowered reproduction, and decreased performance in racing, showing, riding, or whatnot.

Thus, like a thief in the night, subacute mineral deficiencies in horses each year steal away millions of dollars from the horse owners of America, and, for the most part, go unnoticed. Only when the mineral deficiency reaches such proportions that it results in excess emaciation, reproductive failure, or death is it

---

[7]In this section, when reference is made to a National Academy of Sciences recommendation, this implies the following source: *Nutrient Requirements of Horses*, No. 6, 5th rev. ed., National Academy of Sciences, 1989, the latest NRC *Nutrient Requirements of Horses*.

likely to be detected. This does not mean that all 18 mineral elements must always be included in horse mineral supplements. Rather, only the specific minerals that are deficient in the ration—and in the quantities necessary—should be supplied. *Excesses and mineral imbalances are to be avoided.*

At Washington State University, in a study with rabbits, the effect of soil phosphorus—*just one mineral*—on plants, and, in turn, the effects of these plants on animals, was established.[8] Generation after generation, rabbits were fed on alfalfa, with one group receiving hay produced on low-phosphorus soils and the other group eating alfalfa grown on high-phosphorus soils. The rabbits in the low-phosphorus soil-alfalfa group (1) were retarded in growth, (2) required 12% more matings per conception, and (3) had a 47% lower breaking strength of bones than the rabbits on the high-phosphorus soil-alfalfa group. There is reason to believe that soil nutrients can affect horses simi-

Fig. 13-9. Rabbit with bowed legs and enlarged joints resulting from eating alfalfa produced on low-phosphorus soils. There is reason to believe that the same thing happens to horses. (Courtesy, Washington State University)

---

[8]Heinemann, W. W., *et al.*, Wash. Ag. Exp. Sta. Tech. Bull. 24.

larly—in growth, conception, and soundness of bone; but more experimental work on this subject is needed.

The typical horse ration of grass hay and farm grains is usually deficient in calcium, but adequate in phosphorus. Also, salt is almost always deficient; and many horse rations do not contain sufficient iodine and certain other trace elements. Thus, horses usually need special mineral supplements. But they should not be fed either more or less minerals than needed. Also, it is recognized that mineral allowances given with the ration or in a mineral mix should vary according to the mineral content of the soil on which feeds are grown.

The proper development of the bone is particularly important in the horse, as evidenced by the stress and strain on the skeletal structure of the racehorse, especially when racing the two-year-old. Since the greatest development of the skeleton takes place in the young, growing animal, it is evident that adequate minerals must be provided at an early age if the bone is to remain sound.

■ **Metabolic bone disease (MBD)**—In recent years, there has been a great increase in metabolic bone disease in growing horses, especially epiphysitis, contracted tendons, and osteochondritis dissecans (OCD). A brief description of each of these conditions follows:

1. **Epiphysitis.** This is an inflammation of the growth plate of the long bones, primarily found at the lower end of the radius above the knee, but it may be noticeable at the distal tibial and the distal metacarpal and metatarsal bones. Epiphysitis results in a firm and painful swelling.

2. **Contracted tendons.** This involves a shortening of the flexor tendons, causing the heels to be raised and the pasterns to be straight or, in severe cases, to knuckle forward with the horse walking on its toe. Contracted tendons may be present at birth, or they may be acquired during growth.

3. **Osteochondritis dissecans (OCD).** This is a condition in which the cartilage in a growing foal does not properly convert into bone. It may appear in either of two forms: (a) The form in which it is localized in one or a few joints (most commonly the stifle and hock joints, although any joint may be involved), usually without any clinical signs; and (b) the second and less common form, which most commonly affects the more distal limb joints such as pastern and fetlock, although it may affect any joint, including those of the back.

At this time, the cause of the increase in the incidence of the above bone diseases is not entirely clear. However, it appears that the major factors are: (1) rapid growth and excess weight, (2) injury to the epiphysis, (3) nutritional imbalances, (4) genetic predisposition, (5) limited forced exercise, (6) exercise on hard ground, and (7) faulty conformation.

Based on field observations and a study conducted by Ohio State University, involving 384 yearlings raised on 19 breeding farms in Ohio and Kentucky, and including the Thoroughbred, Standardbred, Arabian, and Quarter Horse breeds, there is strong evidence that calcium, phosphorus, copper, and zinc deficiencies/imbalances and/or masking are involved. They reported that the average calcium content of the rations on farms with the fewest skeletal problems was 1.16% ± 0.09 and the phosphorus content was 0.72% ± 0.08.[9]

On the other hand, Krook and Maylin of Cornell University theorize that overfeeding of calcium to the growing horse or the pregnant mare is the primary cause of osteochondrosis in the foal. Their explanation: A dietary calcium overload causes an excessive secretion of the hormone calcitonin which acts directly on the bone of growing horses; calcitonin inhibits (1) the conversion of cartilage to bone, and (2) the resorption of calcium from bone. In the pregnant mare, calcitonin can be transferred through the placenta to the fetus; which might explain how a foal could be born with osteochondrosis. The Cornell scientists also theorize that osteochondrosis would predispose racehorses to fractures. They recommend that alfalfa hay not be fed to pregnant mares and pregnant and growing horses because of its high calcium content, and that calcium be limited to 34 g per horse per day.[10]

Both the Ohio State and Cornell scientists recognize the seriousness of metabolic bone disease. But they differ markedly as to the cause. Ohio State researchers submit strong evidence that deficiencies of calcium, phosphorus, copper, and zinc are the primary causes, whereas the Cornell scientists theorize that high calcium is the main cause.

Further experimental studies are needed. In the meantime, horse owners and caretakers are admonished to practice the old adage: "Use moderation in all things."

Based on experiments (including unpublished work at both Ohio State and Cornell) and experiences, the author recommends (1) that breeders continue to feed alfalfa hay to pregnant mares and growing horses, and (2) that the levels of calcium, phosphorus, copper, iron, manganese, and zinc be in keeping with the recommendations given in Tables 13-2 and 13-4.

A summary of individual mineral functions, deficiency symptoms, sources, and recommended allowances is given in Table 13-4, Horse Mineral Chart. Minerals may be incorporated in the ration in keeping

with the recommended allowances given in this table and in Table 13-2. Additionally, horses should have free access to salt.

The daily requirements and recommended allowances vary with the mature weight, age, and type and level of productivity of the horse. Likewise, the mineral requirements and recommended allowances of the total ration vary with the percent dry matter in the ration, and with the age and the type and level of productivity of the horse.

MAJOR OR MACROMINERALS

The major or macrominerals required by the horse are salt (sodium chloride), calcium, phosphorus, magnesium, potassium, and sulfur.

SALT (SODIUM CHLORIDE)

Salt, which serves as both a condiment and a nutrient, is needed by all classes of animals, but more especially by herbivora (grass-eating animals, like the horse). It may be provided in the form of granulated, rock, or block salt. In general, the form selected is determined by price and availability. It is to be pointed out, however, that it is difficult for horses to eat very hard block and rock salt. This often results in inadequate consumption. Also, if there is much competition for the salt block, the more timid animals may not get their requirements.

Iodized salt should be provided in iodine-deficient areas. Trace-mineralized salt is recommended, because it is a simple, safe means of providing iodine and other trace minerals at only slightly greater cost than common salt.

The horse requires both sodium and chlorine. They are necessary in maintaining the osmotic pressure of body cells (thereby assisting in the transfer of nutrients to the cells and the removal of waste materials). Also, sodium is associated in muscle contraction and is important as one of the main body buffers and in making bile, which aids in the digestion of fats and carbohydrates. Chlorine is required for the formation of the hydrochloric acid in the gastric juice so vital to protein digestion. Generally, the chlorine requirement will be met if the sodium needs are met.

A deficiency of sodium over a long period of time results in depraved appetite, rough coat, reduced growth, and lowered milk production.

Salt should always be available in the stall, paddock, or pasture. Horses will seldom overeat salt when they are allowed free access to it at all times and are given water at frequent intervals. Rather, they will consume only enough to meet their requirements. On the average, a horse needs about 3 oz of salt daily or 1.33 lb per week, although salt requirements vary with

[9]Knight, Debra A., et al., Correlation of Dietary Minerals to Incidence and Severity of Metabolic Bone Disease in Ohio and Kentucky, College of Veterinary Medicine, The Ohio State University; paper presented at the 1985 American Association of Equine Practitioners meeting in Toronto, Canada.

[10]Sellnow, L., "Linking Breakdowns and Diet," The Blood-Horse, May 3, 1986, p. 3162.

Minerals Which May Be Deficient Under Normal Conditions	Conditions Usually Prevailing Where Deficiencies Are Reported	Function of Mineral	Some Deficiency Symptoms	Practical Sources of the Mineral
Major or macrominerals:				
Salt (NaCl)	Negligence, for salt is cheap. The salt requirement is greatly increased under conditions which cause heavy sweating, thereby resulting in large losses of this mineral from the body. Unless it is replaced, fatigue will result. For this reason, when engaged in hard work and perspiring profusely, horses should receive liberal allowances of salt.	Salt serves as both a condiment and a nutrient. Sodium and chlorine help maintain osmotic pressure in body cells, upon which depends the transfer of nutrients to the cells and the removal of waste materials. Sodium is associated with muscle contraction and is important in making bile, which aids in the digestion of fats and carbohydrates. Chlorine is required for the formation of hydrochloric acid in the gastric juice so vital to protein digestion.	In warm or hot weather, work-horses show heat stress. Long-term symptoms of sodium deficiency are depraved appetite, rough hair coat, reduced growth of young animals, and decreased milk production.	Salt provided free-choice, preferably in loose form, or 0.5–1.0% salt added to the ration. It is very difficult for horses to eat very hard block or rock salt. This often results in inadequate consumption. Also, if there is much competition for a salt block, the more timid animals may not get their requirements. Iodized salt should be used in iodine-deficient areas.
Calcium (Ca)	The typical horse ration of grass hay and farm grains—usually deficient in calcium.	Builds strong bones and sound teeth. Very important during lactation. Affects availability of phosphorus. Calcium and phosphorus comprise three-fourths of the ash of the skeleton and from one-third to one-half of the minerals of milk.	A deficiency of calcium in young animals is generally characterized by poorly formed, soft bone, which may bend or bow; and a severe deficiency may cause rickets. A deficiency of calcium in older animals results in porous, fragile bones. Because deficiency conditions may not be completely reversible, prevention is imperative.	Ground limestone or oystershell flour. When both calcium and phosphorus are needed, use steamed bone meal or dicalcium phosphate. Horses absorb 55 to 75% of the calcium in a typical ration.
Phosphorus (P)	Horses grazed on phosphorus-deficient areas or fed for a long period on mature, weathered forage.	Important in the development of bones and teeth. Essential to metabolism of carbohydrates and fats, and enzyme activation.	Rickets in young horses; osteomalacia in mature horses.	Monosodium phosphate, disodium phosphate, or sodium tripolyphosphate. Where both calcium and phosphorus are needed, use steamed bone meal or dicalcium phosphate. Horses absorb 35–55% of the phosphorus in a typical ration.
Magnesium (Mg)	Horses fed high grain-low forage ration, which characterizes most horses at hard work (as in racing and showing). Lactating mares grazing on lush spring pastures low in magnesium or in which Mg is unavailable.	Reduces stress and irritability. Magnesium is important in enzyme systems, bone formation, and calcium and phosphorus metabolism.	Horses under stress are keyed up, high-strung, and jumpy. Foals fed a purified ration deficient in magnesium develop nervousness, muscular tremors, convulsive paddling of the legs and, in some cases, die. Grass tetany.	Magnesium sulfate. Magnesium oxide.
Potassium (K)	When stabled horses are fed high-concentrate rations. Excessive sweating.	Major cation of intracellular fluid where it is involved in osmotic pressure and acid-base balance. Muscle activity. Required in enzyme reaction involving phosphorylation of creatine. Influences carbohydrate metabolism.	Reduced appetite, growth retardation, unsteady gait, general muscle weakness, pica, diarrhea, distended abdomen, emaciation, followed by death. Fatigue. Abnormal electrocardiograms.	Potassium chloride. Roughages usually contain ample potassium.

13-4
CHART

Classes/Function	Nutrient Requirements[1,2]				Nutrient Allowances[1,2]				Comments
	Per Horse Daily	In Ration A-F	Per Ton Ration A-F		Per Horse Daily	In Ration A-F	Per Ton Ration A-F		
	(g)	(%)	(lb)	(kg)	(g)	(%)	(lb)	(kg)	
Maintenance: 1,000-lb (454-kg) horse	85	0.5–1.0	10–20	4.5–9.1	85	0.75	15	6.8	Horses require both sodium and chlorine, but the requirement for chlorine is approximately half that of sodium. Generally, the chlorine requirements will be met if the sodium needs are adequate. Sodium and chlorine are low in feeds of plant origin. There is little danger of overfeeding salt unless a salt-starved animal is suddenly exposed to too much salt, or if liberal amounts of water are not available. Excessive salt intake may result in high water intake, excessive urine excretion, digestive disturbances, or death from salt cramps.
Gestation/Lactation: 1,000-lb (454-kg) mare	85	0.5–1.0	10–20	4.5–9.1	85	0.75	15	6.8	
Growth: 450-lb (204.5-kg) weanling	41	0.5–1.0	10–20	4.5–9.1	41	0.75	15	6.8	
Working: 1,000-lb (454-kg) horse	85	0.5–1.0	10–20	4.5–9.1	85	0.75	15	6.8	
Maintenance: 1,000-lb (454-kg) horse	20	0.175	3.5	1.6	23	0.21	4.1	1.8	The calcium-phosphorus ratio should be maintained close to 1.1:1 although 2:1 is acceptable. Narrower ratios may cause osteomalacia in mature horses. When there is a shortage of calcium in the ration, it is withdrawn from the bones. Feeding excess calcium interferes with the utilization of magnesium, manganese, and iron—and perhaps in the utilization of zinc.
Gestation/Lactation: 1,000-lb (454-kg) mare	56	0.495	9.9	4.5	64	0.57	11.3	5.1	
Growth: 450-lb (204.5-kg) weanling	36	0.66	13.2	6.0	41	0.76	15.1	6.8	
Working: 1,000-lb (454-kg) horse	40	0.35	7.0	3.2	46	0.41	8.1	3.7	
Maintenance: 1,000-lb (454-kg) horse	14	0.125	2.5	1.1	16.1	0.14	2.8	1.3	For the growing horse, the calcium-phosphorus ratio should be maintained close to 1.1:1, although 2:1 is acceptable. The mature horse can tolerate a Ca:P ratio as wide as 4:1 or 5:1 provided adequate levels of phosphorus are available. Excess phosphorus can cause bighead. If plenty of vitamin D is present, the ratio of calcium to phosphorus becomes less important.
Gestation/Lactation: 1,000-lb (454-kg) mare	36	0.315	6.3	2.9	41.4	0.37	7.3	3.3	
Growth: 450-lb (204.5-kg) weanling	19	0.35	7.0	3.2	21.9	0.4	8.0	3.7	
Working: 1,000-lb (454-kg) horse	29	0.255	5.1	2.3	33.4	0.3	5.9	2.7	
Maintenance: 1,000-lb (454-kg) horse	7.5	0.065	1.3	0.6	8.6	0.08	1.5	0.7	Excess of magnesium upsets calcium and phosphorus metabolism. Rations containing 50% forage will likely contain sufficient magnesium for unstressed horses.
Gestation/Lactation: 1,000-lb (454-kg) mare	10.9	0.096	1.92	0.9	12.5	0.11	2.2	1.0	
Growth: 450-lb (204.5-kg) weanling	5.7	0.105	2.1	1.0	6.6	0.12	2.4	1.1	
Working: 1,000-lb (454-kg) horse	15.1	0.135	2.7	1.2	17.4	0.16	3.1	1.4	
Maintenance: 1,000-lb (454-kg) horse	25.0	0.22	4.4	2.0	28.8	0.26	5.1	2.3	A ration that contains at least 50% forage can be expected to meet potassium requirements.
Gestation/Lactation: 1,000-lb (454-kg) mare	46.0	0.405	8.1	3.7	52.9	0.47	9.3	4.2	
Growth: 450-lb (204.5-kg) weanling	18.2	0.335	6.7	3.0	20.9	0.39	7.7	3.5	
Working: 1,000-lb (454-kg) horse	49.9	0.44	8.8	4.0	57.4	0.51	10.1	4.6	

(Continued)

Minerals Which May Be Deficient Under Normal Conditions	Conditions Usually Prevailing Where Deficiencies Are Reported	Function of Mineral	Some Deficiency Symptoms	Practical Sources of the Mineral
Major or macrominerals (continued)				
Sulfur (S)		Sulfur is an integral part of the amino acids methionine and cystine.		
Trace or microminerals				
Cobalt (Co)	Animals grazed in cobalt-deficient areas, such as Australia, Western Canada, and the following states of U.S.: Florida, Michigan, Wisconsin, New Hampshire, Pennsylvania, and New York.	Cobalt is required for the synthesis of vitamin B-12 in the intestinal tract of the horse.	Anemia. Severe weight loss.	Cobaltized mineral mix made by adding cobalt at the rate of 0.2 oz/100 lb (5.7 g/45.4 kg) of salt as cobalt chloride, cobalt sulfate, cobalt oxide, or cobalt carbonate. Also, several good commercial cobalt-containing minerals are on the market.
Copper (Cu)	Suckling foals. Mare's milk, along with milk from other species, is low in copper. Deficiency occurs in regions where soils contain too little copper or where horses are getting an excess of molybdenum, sulfur, or zinc.	Copper, along with iron and vitamin B-12 is necessary for hemoglobin formation, although it forms no part of the hemoglobin molecule (or red blood cells). Closely associated with normal bone development in young growing animals.	Anemia, characterized by fewer than normal red cells and less than normal amount of hemoglobin. Abnormal bone development in young equines, including an increased incidence of epiphysitis, contracted tendons, and osteochondritis dissecans (OCD).	Trace mineralized salt containing copper sulfate or copper carbonate.
Iodine (I)	Iodine-deficient areas or soils (in Northwestern U.S. and in the Great Lakes region) when iodized salt is not fed. Use of feeds that come from iodine-deficient areas.	Iodine is needed by the thyroid gland in making thyroxin, an iodine-containing compound which controls the rate of body metabolism or heat production.	Foals born dead, or very weak with enlarged thyroid glands (goiter) and unable to stand or nurse. Higher than normal incidence of navel ill.	Stabilized iodized salt containing 0.01% potassium iodide (0.0076% iodine). Calcium iodate.
Iron (Fe)	Suckling foals kept away from soil and feed other than milk. Horses subjected to pressure from racing, showing, or other heavy use. Such animals require added iron in their daily ration. Excessive blood loss from a wound or heavy parasite infestation.	Necessary for formation of hemoglobin, an iron-containing compound which enables the blood to carry oxygen. Also, important to certain enzyme systems.	Iron-deficiency anemia, characterized by fewer than normal red cells and less than normal amount of hemoglobin. Anemic horses tire easily. *Note well:* Iron deficiency anemia may also result from heavy parasitization.	Ferrous sulfate administered orally. Trace mineralized salt. Cane molasses. Iron oxide should not be used as a source of iron for horses because it is poorly absorbed.

(Continued)

Classes/Function	Nutrient Requirements[1,2]			Nutrient Allowances[1,2]			Comments
	Per Horse Daily	In Ration A-F	Per Ton Ration A-F	Per Horse Daily	In Ration A-F	Per Ton Ration A-F	
	(g)	(%)	(lb) (kg)	(g)	(%)	(lb) (kg)	
Maintenance: 1,000-lb (454-kg) horse				17.0	0.15	3.0 1.36	The precise sulfur requirement is not known, but an allowance of 0.15% of the total ration appears to be adequate.
Gestation/Lactation: 1,000-lb (454-kg) mare				17.0	0.15	3.0 1.36	If the protein requirement of the ration is met, the sulfur intake will usually be at least 0.15%, which appears to be adequate.
Growth: 450-lb (204.5-kg) weanling				8.2	0.15	3.0 1.36	
Working: 1,000-lb (454-kg) horse				17.0	0.15	3.0 1.36	
			(g/ton)			(g/ton)	
Maintenance: 1,000-lb (454-kg) horse	1.13	0.1	0.091	1.3	0.11	0.104	The disease called *salt sick* in Florida is due to a cobalt deficiency associated with a copper deficiency.
Gestation/Lactation: 1,000-lb (454-kg) mare	1.13	0.1	0.091	1.3	0.11	0.104	The cobalt requirement for horses is very low, for horses have remained in good health while grazing pastures so low in cobalt that ruminants confined to them have died.
Growth: 450-lb (204.5-kg) weanling	0.54	0.1	0.091	0.6	0.11	0.100	
Working: 1,000-lb (454-kg) horse	1.13	0.1	0.091	1.3	0.11	0.104	
Maintenance: 1,000-lb (454-kg) horse	113.4	10.0	9.070	283.4	25	22.675	A copper deficiency in horses has been reported in Australia.
Gestation/Lactation: 1,000-lb (454-kg) mare	113.4	10.0	9.070	340.1	30	27.210	In high-molybdenum areas, more copper may be added to horse rations; but excesses and toxicity should be avoided.
Growth: 450-lb (204.5-kg) weanling	54.4	10.0	9.070	217.7	40	36.280	
Working: 1,000-lb (454-kg) horse	113.4	10.0	9.070	283.4	25	22.675	
Maintenance: 1,000-lb (454-kg) horse	1.13	0.1	0.091	1.3	0.11	0.104	Enlargement of the thyroid gland (goiter) is nature's way of trying to make enough thyroxin (an iodine-containing hormone) when there is insufficient iodine in the feed. Feeding excess iodine continuously will also produce goiter in foals.
Gestation/Lactation: 1,000-lb (454-kg) mare	1.13	0.1	0.091	1.3	0.11	0.104	Iodine deficiency seldom occurs in coastal areas because of the abundance of iodine from spray drift from ocean or sea water.
Growth: 450-lb (204.5-kg) weanling	0.54	0.1	0.091	0.6	0.11	0.100	
Working: 1,000-lb (454-kg) horse	1.13	0.1	0.091	1.3	0.11	0.104	
Maintenance: 1,000-lb (454-kg) horse	453.5	40	36.280	453.5	40	36.280	The horse's body contains about 0.004% iron. Milk is deficient in iron, and the iron content of the mother cannot be increased through feeding iron. Thus, foals should be individually or creep fed as soon as they are old enough. A variable store of both iron and copper is located in the liver and spleen, and some iron is found in the kidneys. Too much iron may be harmful.
Gestation/Lactation: 1,000-lb (454-kg) mare	566.9	50	45.350	1,020.4	90	81.630	
Growth: 450-lb (204.5-kg) weanling	272.1	50	45.350	489.8	90	81.630	
Working: 1,000-lb (454-kg) horse	453.5	40	36.280	680.3	60	54.420	

(Continued)

Minerals Which May Be Deficient Under Normal Conditions	Conditions Usually Prevailing Where Deficiencies Are Reported	Function of Mineral	Some Deficiency Symptoms	Practical Sources of the Mineral
Trace or microminerals (continued)				
Manganese (Mn)	Excess calcium and phosphorus which decreases absorption of manganese.	Essential for normal bone formation (as a component of the organic matrix). Thought to be an activator of enzyme systems. Growth and reproduction.	Poor growth. Lameness, shortening and bowing of legs, and enlarged joints. Impaired reproduction (testicular degeneration of males; defective ovulation of females).	Trace mineralized salt containing 0.25% manganese (or more).
Selenium (Se)	Muscle disorders and lowered serum selenium.		Infertility. Myositis (muscular discomfort or pain).	Forages or grains grown on soils known to have adequate selenium. Sodium selenate. Sodium selenite.
Zinc (Zn)	Feeds low in zinc. Excess calcium may reduce the absorption and utilization of zinc.	Important in many enzyme systems. Required for normal protein synthesis and metabolism. Imparts gloss or bloom to the hair coat.	Rough, dull hair coat. Loss of appetite.	Zinc carbonate. Zinc sulfate.

[1]All "nutrient requirements" given in this table were adapted by the author from *Nutrient Requirements of Horses*, 5th rev. ed., NRC—National Academy of Sciences, the latest NRC *Nutrient Requirements of Horses*. The "nutrient allowances" given in this table represent the author's best judgment based on current research; it is intended that they meet the nutrient requirements, and provide adequate margins of safety in addition.

[2]Feed consumption of a mature 1,000-lb *(454 kg)* horse estimated at 25 lb *(11.36 kg)* per day. Feed consumption of a 450-lb *(204.5-kg)* weanling estimated at 12 lb *(5.45 kg)* per day.

work and temperature. When at hard work during warm weather—conditions accompanied by profuse perspiration and consequent loss of salt in the sweat—even greater quantities may be required. The white, encrusted sides of a horse after work are evidence of the large amount of salt drawn from the body through sweat (2 gm of salt/lb of sweat). Horses at moderate work may lose 50 to 60 grams of salt in the sweat and 35 grams in the urine daily. Unless salt is replaced, the animal will soon exhibit signs of excessive fatigue.

When incorporated in the concentrate ration, salt should be added at a level of 0.5 to 1.0%.

If horses have been salt starved—if they have not previously been fed salt for a considerable length of time—they may overeat, resulting in digestive disturbances and even death from salt cramps. Salt starved animals should first be hand fed salt, and the daily allowance should be increased gradually until they start leaving a little in the mineral box. When this point is reached, self-feeding may be followed.

CALCIUM/PHOSPHORUS

Horses are more apt to suffer from a lack of calcium and phosphorus than from any of the other minerals except salt.

These two minerals comprise about three-fourths of the ash of the skeleton and from one-third to one-half of the minerals of milk.

A deficiency of either calcium or phosphorus will cause rickets in foals.

The following general characteristics of feeds in regard to calcium and phosphorus are important in rationing horses:

1. The cereal grains and their byproducts and

(Continued)

Classes/Function	Nutrient Requirements[1,2]			Nutrient Allowances[1,2]			Comments
	Per Horse Daily	In Ration A-F	Per Ton Ration A-F	Per Horse Daily	In Ration A-F	Per Ton Ration A-F	
	(g)	(%)	(g/ton)	(g)	(%)	(g/ton)	
Maintenance: 1,000-lb (454-kg) horse	453.5	40	36.280	521.5	46	41.720	Most natural feedstuffs are rich in manganese.
Gestation/Lactation: 1,000-lb (454-kg) mare	453.5	40	36.280	521.5	46	41.720	
Growth: 450-lb (204.5-kg) weanling	217.7	40	36.280	250.4	46	41.734	
Working: 1,000-lb (454-kg) horse	453.5	40	36.280	521.5	46	41.720	
Maintenance: 1,000-lb (454-kg) horse	1.13	0.1	0.091	1.3	0.11	0.104	Excess selenium results in selenium poisoning, or alkali disease. In 1987, FDA approved an increase in the maximum allowance of selenium in complete feeds for cattle (beef & dairy), sheep, swine, and poultry from 0.1 ppm to 0.3 ppm.
Gestation/Lactation: 1,000-lb (454-kg) mare	1.13	0.1	0.091	1.3	0.11	0.104	
Growth: 450-lb (204.5-kg) weanling	0.54	0.1	0.091	0.6	0.11	0.100	
Working: 1,000-lb (454-kg) horse	1.13	0.1	0.091	1.3	0.11	0.104	
Maintenance: 1,000-lb (454-kg) horse	453.5	40	36.280	907.0	80	72.560	If zinc in the feed is on the low side, the addition of zinc should improve the hair coat. Excess zinc prevents calcium utilization and produces signs of calcium deficiency. The toxicity level exceeds 1,000 ppm.
Gestation/Lactation: 1,000-lb (454-kg) mare	453.5	40	36.280	1,133.8	100	90.700	
Growth: 450-lb (204.5-kg) weanling	217.7	40	36.280	544.2	100	90.700	
Working: 1,000-lb (454-kg) horse	453.5	40	36.280	1,020.4	90	81.630	

straws, dried mature grasses, and protein supplements of plant origin are low in calcium.

2. The protein supplements of animal origin and legume forage are rich in calcium.

3. The cereal grains and their byproducts are fairly high or even rich in phosphorus, but a large portion of the phosphorus is not readily available.

4. Almost all protein-rich supplements are high in phosphorus. But, here again, plant sources of phosphorus contain much of this element in a bound form.

5. Beet byproducts and dried, mature non-leguminous forages (such as grass hays and fodders) are likely to be low in phosphorus.

6. The calcium and phosphorus content of plants can be increased through fertilizing the soil upon which they are grown.

The availability to the horse of calcium and phosphorus in common feedstuffs is unknown. But the availability of calcium is assumed to be 55 to 75%, and the availability of phosphorus is assumed to be 35 to 55%. Several factors account for this poor absorption, including the Ca:P ratio, level of intake, source of calcium and phosphorus, and the presence of organic inhibitors such as oxalate and phytate. Also, due to poor utilization, the calcium and phosphorus requirements of aged animals (animals over 20 years of age) are higher than for younger animals.

In considering the calcium and phosphorus requirements of horses, it is important to realize that the proper utilization of these minerals by the body is dependent upon three factors: (1) an adequate supply of calcium and phosphorus in an available form; (2) a suitable ration between them; and (3) sufficient vitamin D to make possible the assimilation and utilization of the calcium and phosphorus. If plenty of vitamin D is present (as provided either by sunlight or through the ration), the ratio of calcium to phosphorus becomes less important. Also, less vitamin D is needed when there is a desirable calcium-phosphorus ratio.

Normally, the calcium to phosphorus ratio should be about 1.1:1. However, the ratio varies according to age. For example, older horses can have a calcium-phosphate ratio of 2:1. Provided adequate phosphorus is fed, weanling foals will tolerate a 3:1 ratio and mature horses a 5:1 ratio. It is important, however, to have more calcium than phosphorus—but not too much calcium. Feeding excessive calcium interferes with the utilization of magnesium, manganese, and iron—and perhaps with the utilization of zinc.

The pregnant mare deposits an amount equivalent to 10 to 12% of her body weight in products of conception; and these products contain approximately 1.2% calcium and 0.6% phosphorus. Since most of these minerals are deposited in the bones, and approximately 90% of the bone development occurs during the last 90 days of gestation, about 6 g of calcium and 3 g of phosphorus per day will be deposited during this period in a 1,100-lb pregnant mare.

The calcium and phosphorus requirements for lactation depend on level of production. Milk production varies among mares and with stage of lactation. During peak production, mares will give up to 4½ gal. (38.7 lb/17.6 kg) of milk per day, with each pound containing 0.45 g of calcium and 0.2 g of phosphorus. Thus, a mare producing 4½ gal. of milk per day will deposit 17.4 g of calcium and 7.7 g of phosphorus per day.

Lack of either or both calcium and phosphorus can result in bone disorders, with the type and severity of the disorder dependent upon the age of the animal and the degree and duration of the deficiency. Deficiency in young horses is generally characterized by poorly formed, soft bones, which may bend or bow; and deficiency in older animals, by porous, fragile bones. Because these conditions are not completely reversible, prevention is imperative.

A deficiency of either calcium or phosphorus will cause rickets in foals. Also, there is substantial evidence that lack of calcium and phosphorus, along with deficiencies of copper and zinc, causes epiphysitis, contracted tendons, and osteochondritis dissecans (OCD) in young horses.

Bone disturbances (called osteodystrophia fibrosa, nutritional secondary hyperparathyroidism, osteomalacia, osteoporosis, and Miller's disease) develop in adult horses fed rations containing limited calcium and high phosphorus. The disease develops when rations with a calcium-phosphorus ratio of 0.8:1 are fed for 6 to 12 months, and it progresses rapidly when the ratio is 0.6:1.

After giving consideration to all the above mentioned factors, and after considering the experiments, the author recommends that calcium and phosphorus

be provided to lactating mares and young horses at the levels in the total ration given in Tables 13-2 and 13-4.

Generally speaking, legume forages, such as alfalfa hay or pasture, are rich in calcium; cereal grains and their byproducts—oats, corn, barley, and wheat bran—are fair to good sources of phosphorus; and the protein supplements—linseed meal, soybean meal, and dried skim milk—are good sources of both calcium and phosphorus. So, by selecting and combining the common horse feeds properly, the maintenance needs of most horses can be met. (See Fig. 13-10.)

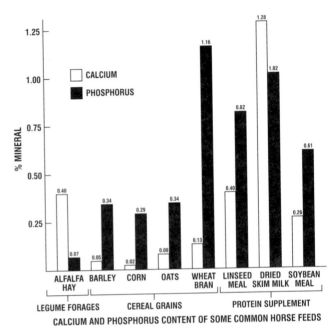

Fig. 13-10. Calcium and phosphorus content of some common horse feeds (as-fed basis).

Where both calcium and phosphorus are needed, the author favors the use of high-quality steamed bone meal for horses, because bone meal contains many ingredients in addition to calcium and phosphorus. It is a good source of iron, manganese, and zinc, and it contains such trace minerals as copper and cobalt. However, it is increasingly difficult to get good bone meal. Some of the imported products are high in fat, rancid, and/or odorous and unpalatable. Where good bone meal is not available, dicalcium phosphate is generally recommended.

Where phosphorus alone is needed, defluorinated rock phosphate, sodium monophosphate, or sodium polyphosphate are the minerals of choice. Sodium monophosphate and sodium polyphosphate are not palatable, hence, it is important that they be combined with more palatable products.

Fig. 13-11. Calcium-phosphorus imbalance. Horse with big head disease (nutritional secondary hyperparathyroidism) resulting from feeding ingredients low in calcium and high in phosphorus, commonly associated with a ration excessively high in wheat bran. Note that the upper jaw is enlarged because calcium is replaced by fibrous connective tissue. (Courtesy, National Academy of Sciences, and College of Veterinary Medicine, Texas A&M University)

MAGNESIUM

Rations containing 50% forage will likely contain sufficient magnesium for unstressed horses, unless the forage is known to be deficient in magnesium. But horses at hard work (as in racing and showing) consume more grain (which is low in magnesium) and less forage. Also, horses being raced or shown, or otherwise stressed, are frequently keyed up, high-strung, and jumpy, similar to the nervousness that characterizes animals and humans known to be suffering from a magnesium deficiency.

In view of the above, it would appear prudent that one-half to two-thirds of the recommended daily magnesium allowance of the horse be added to the ration.

POTASSIUM

Forage-consuming animals generally require about 0.3% of potassium in their rations. A ration that contains at least 50% forage can be expected to meet potassium requirements. However, a horse ration that does not contain roughage, molasses, or oil meals may be deficient in potassium.

Significant amounts of potassium are lost during heavy sweating.

A reduced appetite is an early sign of a potassium deficiency. A severe deficiency may cause muscle tremors and erratic heart beat.

SULFUR

Inorganic sulfur is not known to be an essential dietary constituent of the horse. If the protein requirement of the ration is met, the sulfur intake will usually be at least 0.15%, which appears to be adequate.

TRACE OR MICROMINERALS

The need for trace minerals may be inferred from the many reports on the value of blackstrap molasses (a good source of trace minerals) for horses fed low-quality hays.

Although the horse's requirements for most of the trace minerals are not known, there is evidence that the need is similar to that of other species.

Trace minerals may be supplied (1) as part of either the concentrate or complete ration, and/or (2) in a trace mineralized (TM) salt. When incorporated in the concentrate mix, TM salt should be added at the rate of 1%. When TM salt is fed free-choice, it should be placed in a conveniently located covered mineral box in amounts that will be consumed in not more than 1 to 2 weeks. When remaining in a mineral box longer than this period of time, it may become unpalatable and there may be losses of some elements.

A discussion of each of the trace minerals follows. They are listed alphabetically, and not necessarily in order of importance.

COBALT

Cobalt is required for the synthesis of vitamin B-12 in the intestinal tract of the horse. A lack of cobalt and/or B-12 will result in anemia. However, the cobalt requirement of the horse is very low, for horses have remained in good health while grazing pastures so low in cobalt that ruminants confined to them have died. This means that the cobalt requirement, if any, of the horse is lower than that of ruminants. However, it is noteworthy that anemia in horses has responded to vitamin B-12 treatment; and, of course, B-12 contains cobalt in the molecular structure. Thus, inclusion of cobalt in the ration of horses is in the nature of good insurance.

In different sections of the world, a cobalt deficiency is known as Denmark disease, coast disease, enzootic marasmus, bush sickness, salt sickness, nakuritis, and pining disease.

COPPER

A copper deficiency has been reported in Australia

in horses grazing on pastures low in copper. Also, mare's milk (along with milk from all species) is low in copper; and its copper concentration decreases greatly during the first weeks of lactation. The presence of 5 to 25 ppm of molybdenum in forages causes disturbances in copper utilization in horses. Cornell researchers found that the addition of high levels of molybdenum (27.4 and 107.3 ppm) to the ration decreased copper absorption and retention as a consequence of increased excretion of absorbed copper in bile.[11]

Copper is of special interest to nutritionists because, in addition to its effect on iron metabolism, it is closely associated with normal bone development in young growing animals of all species. Abnormal bone development has been reported in foals on low copper rations.

There are wide species differences in tolerance to copper. Horses are very tolerant to copper, whereas sheep are very sensitive to it. The maximum tolerable levels of copper for growing animals in ppm, according to the National Academy of Sciences, are: horse, 800 ppm; chicken, 300 ppm; swine, 250 ppm; cattle, 100 ppm; and sheep, 25 ppm.

The author's recommended copper allowances are: 30 ppm of the total ration for lactating mares, and 40 ppm for young horses. (See Tables 13-2 and 13-4.)

In high molybdenum areas, it is recommended that the copper level for horses be about five times higher than the normal level.

IODINE

Pregnant mares are very susceptible to iodine deficiency. Where such a deficiency exists, the foals are usually stillborn or so weak that they cannot stand and suck. There is also some evidence to indicate that the incidence of navel ill in foals may be lessened by feeding iodine to broodmares.

Other facts pertinent to iodine for horses follow:

1. **Amount in body and function.** It is estimated that the mature animal body contains less than 0.00004% iodine, but if this minute amount is not maintained in the diet, disaster results. More than half of the total iodine content of the body is located in the thyroid gland of the neck. Iodine, which is secreted by the thyroid gland in the form of thyroxin (an iodine-containing hormone), controls the rate of metabolism of the body.

2. **Iodine deficiencies.** If the soil—and the water and feed crops coming therefrom—is low in iodine, the body is likely to show deficiency symptoms in the form

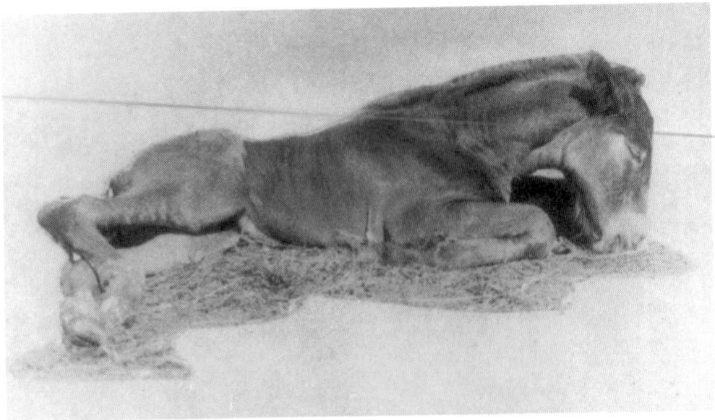

Fig. 13-12. Newborn colt affected with simple goiter due to deficiency of iodine during prenatal period. (Courtesy, Western Washington Agricultural Experiment Station)

of simple goiter, unless an adequate source of iodine is provided artificially. A goiter is simply an enlargement of the thyroid gland, which is nature's way of trying to make enough thyroxin when there is insufficient iodine in the feed. However, iodine-deficiency symptoms are not always evidenced by the appearance of goiter, although this is the most common characteristic of such deficiency in humans, calves, lambs, and kids. In pigs, the outstanding symptom of the deficiency is hairlessness, whereas in foals the only symptom may be extreme weakness at birth, resulting in an inability to stand and suck.

In general, it may be said that goiter is an advanced symptom of iodine deficiency, but that the chief loss is from interference with reproductive processes and the birth of weak, deformed offspring that fail to survive.

Iodine deficiencies are worldwide. In the United States, the northwestern states, the Pacific Coast, and the Great Lakes region are classed as goiter areas.

Fig. 13-13. Goiter in a foal caused by feeding excess iodine. Goiter is usually caused by an iodine deficiency, but it may result from feeding excess iodine over a long period of time. (Courtesy, Dr. D. E. Cooperrider, Chief, Diagnostic Laboratories, Division of Animal Industry, Kissimmee, FL)

[11]Cymbalak, N. F., et al., "Influence of Dietary Molybdenum on Copper Metabolism in Ponies," *The Journal of Nutrition*, Vol. III, No. 1, January 1981, p. 96.

3. **Recommended iodine supplements.** The simplest method of supplying iodine in deficient areas is through use of salt containing (a) 0.01% potassium iodide (0.0076% iodine), or (b) calcium iodate. Most of the salt companies now manufacture stabilized iodized salt. If iodized salt is fed, additional iodine supplementation is unnecessary. Organic iodine supplements, such as kelp, are not any better than iodized salt.

4. **Precautions in feeding iodized salt.** Although iodized salt is an effective preventive measure, no satisfactory treatment has been developed for animals which have developed pronounced deficiency symptoms. In fact, studies with goiter in humans have clearly established that, although iodine is an effective preventative, it may be harmful rather than beneficial as a treatment after the goiter has developed.

Excessive and continued iodine supplementation, such as feeding kelp meal in addition to iodized salt or trace mineralized salt, may cause goiter.

Iodized salt should always be kept in a dry place and it should be kept fresh. It should also be provided in such form and quantities as to ensure an adequate intake of iodine.

IRON

If horses are fed diets that are too low in iron, or in iron and copper, nutritional anemia results.

The National Academy of Sciences estimates the maintenance requirements of the horse for iron at 40 ppm, and the requirements of foals at 50 ppm. However, it has been reported that horses which are subjected to pressure from racing, showing, or other heavy use, require higher levels of iron. To be on the safe side, approximately one-half of the iron requirement of the horse should be added to the ration; and it should be in a biologically available form (iron oxide should not be used as a source of iron for horses because it is poorly absorbed).

Other facts pertinent to iron for horses follow:

1. **Body store of iron and copper at birth.** Nature has planned wisely. Young equines are born with a store of iron and copper in their bodies, which usually suffices until they normally begin to eat feeds which supply these constituents. This is most fortunate, as milk is very low in iron and copper. When young animals are continued on a milk diet for a long period of time, particularly under confined conditions and with little or no supplemental feeds, nutritional anemia will likely develop.

2. **Natural sources of iron.** In obtaining sources of iron, it is well to remember that simple inorganic iron salts, such as ferric chloride, are readily utilized, whereas the iron in the complex organic compounds in the hemoglobin of the blood is much less readily available, if at all. Also, though certain small amounts of iron are very essential, too much of this element in the diet may actually be deleterious—interfering with phosphorus absorption by forming an insoluble phosphate—and rickets may thus result from a diet otherwise adequate.

MANGANESE

Feeds containing 60 to 70 ppm of manganese are recommended, with the higher levels fed to foals, stressed horses, and breeding animals.

Since most natural feedstuffs are rich in manganese, it can be assumed that part of the requirement for this element will be met by the normal ration.

SELENIUM

Selenium is an essential mineral for horses. Deficient animals have muscle disorders and lowered serum selenium.

It is recommended that horse rations contain 0.1 ppm of selenium in the complete feed. Excess selenium above 5 ppm results in selenium poisoning, or alkali disease.

In 1987, FDA approved an increase in the maximum allowance of selenium in complete feeds for cattle (beef and dairy), sheep, swine, and poultry from 0.1 ppm to 0.3 ppm.

ZINC

A level of 80 to 100 ppm of zinc is recommended, with young and highly stressed animals receiving the upper level.

Zinc is necessary for the maintenance and development of skin and hair. Since beautiful hair coats are important in horses, fortifying the daily ration with zinc will prevent any possibility of a zinc deficiency; and if the zinc in the feed is on the low side, it should improve the hair coat.

CHELATED TRACE MINERALS

The word chelate is derived from the Greek *chelae*, meaning a claw or pincerlike organ. Those selling chelated minerals generally recommend a smaller quantity of them (but at a higher price per pound) and extol their "fenced-in" properties.

When it comes to synthetic chelating agents, much needs to be learned about their selectivity toward minerals, the kind and quantity most effective, their mode of action, and their behavior with different species of animals and with varying rations.

It is possible that their use may actually create a mineral imbalance. These answers, and more, should be forthcoming through carefully controlled experiments.

MINERAL IMBALANCES

Having the right balance and forms of minerals can be very important. The more calcium you feed, the more phosphorus you need. The more copper you feed, the more manganese you need.

Also, minerals can be fed in several different forms. For example, iron can be fed as an oxide, sulfite, sulfate, or as a proteinate. Oxides may be absorbed at about 2 to 5%, while sulfites may be absorbed at up to 10%, and sulfates at 25%.

Thus, the requirements of any mineral may be modified (1) by another mineral which enhances or interferes with its utilization, or (2) by the form of the mineral.

From the above, it is apparent that excess fortification of the horse's ration with one or more mineral elements may prove more detrimental than helpful. Thus, caretakers who know and care will avoid harmful imbalances; they will provide minerals on the basis of recommended allowances (see Tables 13-2 and 13-4). Also, when fortifying rations with minerals, consideration should be given to the minerals provided by the ingredients of the normal ration, for it is the total composition of the feed that counts.

FEEDING MINERALS

With the exception of sodium, the self-feeding of the major minerals cannot be relied upon to meet the needs of horses. This is so because horses consume such supplements on the basis of palatability, rather than because of dietary need. As a result, the free-choice intake of minerals among individual horses will vary from too little to too much. Sometimes minerals are incorporated in a salt mix, but salt consumption is erratic and variable according to the sodium content of the feedstuffs being fed. So, the only way to ensure that each horse receives the needed major minerals is to incorporate the proper amounts in the animal's feed and/or water.

Trace minerals may be added to the ration and/or incorporated in the salt. In either case, the amounts and proportions of trace minerals should be selected with care because the improper use of trace minerals can lead to induced deficiencies. Theoretically, the total ration (grain plus forage) should be balanced in trace mineral content, with the trace mineral mix providing only the minerals needed and with each one in the right amount. Of course, this isn't practical. Therefore, a trace mineral mix must contain an array of minerals in adequate levels to meet a wide variety of conditions.

Fortunately, the horse is tolerant to most trace mineral excesses.

When horses are on pasture and no grain or protein supplement is being fed, minerals may be self-fed, usually as either a commercially manufactured mineral block or as a mineral mixture. A suitable home-mixed mineral for self-feeding on pasture may be prepared as follows:

1. **Where the pasture is primarily grass.** Prepare a mixture containing two parts of calcium to one part of phosphorus.

2. **Where the pasture is primarily a legume.** Prepare a mixture containing one part of calcium to one part of phosphorus.

To each of the above mixes, add one-third trace-mineralized salt to provide the microminerals and improve the palatability.

VITAMINS[12]

Until early in the 20th Century, if a ration contained proteins, fats, carbohydrates, and minerals, together with a certain amount of fiber, it was considered to be a complete ration. True enough, the disease known as beriberi made its appearance in the rice-eating districts of the Orient when milling machinery was introduced from the West, having been known to the Chinese as early as 2600 B.C.; and scurvy was long known to occur among sailors fed on salt meat and biscuits. However, for centuries these diseases were thought to be due to toxic substances in the digestive tract caused by pathogenic organisms rather than food deficiencies, and more time elapsed before the discovery of vitamins. Of course, there was no medical profession until 1835, the earlier treatments having been based on superstition rather than science.

Funk, a Polish scientist working in London, first referred to these nutrients as *vitamines*, in 1912. Presumably, the name vitamines alluded to the fact that they were essential to life, and they were assumed to be chemically of the nature of amines (the chemical assumption was later proved incorrect, with the result that the "e" was dropped—hence the word *vitamin*).

The actual existence of vitamins, therefore, has been known only since 1912, and only within the last few years has it been possible to see or touch any of them in a pure form. Previously, they were merely mysterious invisible "little things," known only by their effects. In fact, most of the present fundamental knowledge relative to the vitamin content of both human

---

[12]In this section, when reference is made to a National Academy of Sciences recommendation, this implies the following source: *Nutrient Requirements of Horses*, No. 6, 5th rev. ed., National Academy of Sciences, the latest NRC *Nutrient Requirements of Horses*.

foods and animal feeds was obtained through measuring their potency in promoting growth or in curing certain disease conditions in animals—a most difficult and tedious method. For the most part, small laboratory animals were used, especially the rat, guinea pig, pigeon, and chick.

The lack of vitamins in a horse ration may, under certain conditions, be more serious than a short supply of feed. Deficiencies may lead to failure in growth or reproduction, poor health, and even characteristic disorders known as deficiency diseases.

Unfortunately, there are no warning signals to tell a caretaker when a horse is not getting enough of certain vitamins. But a continuing inadequate supply of any one of several vitamins can produce illness which is very hard to diagnose until it becomes severe, at which time it is difficult and expensive—if not too late—to treat. The important thing, therefore, is to insure against such deficiencies occurring. But caretakers should not shower a horse with mistaken kindness through using shotgun-type vitamin preparations. Instead, the quantity of each vitamin should be based on available scientific knowledge.

It has long been known that the vitamin content of feeds varies considerably according to soil, climatic conditions, and curing and storing.

Deficiencies may occur during periods (1) of extended drought or in other conditions of restriction in diet, (2) when production is being forced, or during stress, (3) when large quantities of highly refined feeds are being fed, or (4) when low-quality forages are utilized.

Although the occasional deficiency symptoms are the most striking result of vitamin deficiencies, it must be emphasized that in practice mild deficiencies probably cause higher total economic losses than do severe deficiencies. It is relatively uncommon for a ration, or diet, to contain so little of a vitamin that obvious symptoms of a deficiency occur. When one such case does appear, it is reasonable to suppose that there must be several cases that are too mild to produce characteristic symptoms but that are sufficiently severe to lower the state of health and the efficiency of production.

Certain vitamins are necessary for the growth, development, health, and reproduction of horses. Deficiencies of vitamins A and D are sometimes encountered. Also, indications are that vitamin E and some of the B vitamins are required by horses. Further, it is recognized that single, uncomplicated vitamin deficiencies are the exception rather than the rule.

High-quality, leafy, green forages plus plenty of sunshine generally give horses most of the vitamins they need. Horses get carotene (which they can convert to vitamin A) and riboflavin from green pasture and green hay not over a year old, and they get vitamin D from sunlight and sun-cured hay. If plenty of green forage and sunlight are not available, the caretaker should get the advice of a nutritionist or veterinarian on the use of vitamin additives to the feed.

Table 13-2 lists the vitamins most commonly involved in horse nutrition; and Table 13-5, Horse Vitamin Chart, gives pertinent information pertaining to each. Although there is no evidence of deficiencies of certain vitamins, it is possible that more of them may be destroyed or used by horses during stress or strain than can be obtained through normal feeds or synthesized by the intestinal microflora of the horse; hence, adding them to the ration may assure maximum performance.

FAT-SOLUBLE VITAMINS

The fat-soluble vitamins, which are stored in the body in appreciable quantities, are vitamin A (carotene), vitamin D, vitamin E, and vitamin K.

VITAMIN A

Vitamin A is strictly a product of animal metabolism, no vitamin A being found in plants. The counterpart in plants is known as carotene, which is the precursor of vitamin A. Because the animal body can transform carotene into vitamin A, this compound is often spoken of as *provitamin A*.

Carotene is the yellow-colored, fat-soluble substance that gives the characteristic color to carrots and to butterfat (vitamin A is nearly a colorless substance). Carotene derives its name from the carrot, from which it was first isolated over 100 years ago. Although its empirical formula was established in 1906, it was not until 1919 that Steenbock, of the University of Wisconsin, discovered its vitamin A activity. Though the yellow color is masked by the green chlorophyll, the green parts of plants are rich in carotene and have high vitamin A value. Also, the degree of greenness in a roughage is a good index of its carotene content, provided it has not been stored too long. Early cut, leafy green hays are very high in carotene.

Vitamin A is not synthesized in the cecum. Thus, it must be provided in the feed, either (1) as vitamin A, or (2) as carotene, the precursor of vitamin A. For horses, 1 mg of beta-carotene is equivalent to 400 IU of vitamin A.

Aside from yellow corn, practically all of the cereal grains used in horse feeding have little carotene or vitamin A value. Even yellow corn has only about one-tenth as much carotene as well-cured hay. Dried peas of the green and yellow varieties and carrots are also valuable sources of carotene.

Studies by the New Jersey Station indicate that the carotene content of alfalfa hay may be more avail-

TABLE
HORSE VITAMIN

Vitamins Which May Be Deficient Under Normal Conditions	Conditions Usually Prevailing Where Deficiencies Are Reported	Function of Vitamin	Some Deficiency Symptoms	Practical Sources of the Vitamin
Fat-soluble vitamins:				
A	Extended drought, bleached hays. Stall feeding where there is little or no green forage or yellow corn. Following great stress, as when race or show horses are put in training. The younger the animal, the quicker vitamin A deficiencies will show up. Mature animals may store sufficient vitamin A to last 6 months.	Promotes growth and stimulates appetite. Assists in reproduction and lactation. Keeps the mucous membranes of respiratory and other tracts in healthy condition. Makes for normal vision. Prevents night blindness.	Loss of appetite, poor growth, reproductive problems, nerve degeneration, night blindness, lachrymation (tears), keratinization of the cornea and skin, uneven and poor hoof development, a predisposition to respiratory infection, incoordination, progressive weakness, convulsive seizures, certain bone disorders, and finicky appetite.	Stabilized vitamin A. Green grass. Green grass or legume hay not over 1 year old. Carrots, yellow corn.
D	Limited sunlight and/or limited sun-cured hay, especially when the horse is kept inside most of the time.	Assimilation and utilization of calcium and phosphorus, necessary in normal bone development—including the bones of the fetus.	Rickets in foals, osteomalacia in mature horses. Both conditions result in large joints and weak bones. Rickets is characterized by reduced bone calcification, stiff and swollen joints, stiffness of gait, irritability, and reduction in serum calcium and phosphorus. Osteomalacia results in bones which soften, become distorted, and fracture easily.	Either vitamin D_2 (the plant form) or D_3 (the animal form) is equally effective for the horse. Exposure to sunlight. Sun-cured hays.
E	More vitamin E may be destroyed or used by horses during times of stress or strain than can be obtained through normal feeds.	As an antioxidant. As an occasional replacement for selenium. Improves reproduction. Prevents anhidrosis.	Lowered breeding performance in both mares and stallions. Anhidrosis—a dry, dull hair coat; elevated temperature; and high blood pressure. Anhidrosis has been successfully treated by the oral administration of 1,000 to 3,000 IU of vitamin E daily.	Alpha-tocopherol acetate, a stable form of vitamin E. Wheat germ meal and wheat germ oil. Green plants. Green hays.
K	Following intestinal disorders.	Concerned with blood coagulation. It converts precursor proteins to the active blood clotting factors.	Increased clotting time of the blood and lowered level of prothrombin.	Green pasture. Well-cured hays. Cereal grains. Milk. Menadione (vitamin K_3)

13-5
CHART

Classes/Function	Nutrient Requirements[1,2]			Nutrient Allowances[1,2]			Comments
	Per Horse Daily	In Ration A-F	Per Ton Ration A-F	Per Horse Daily	In Ration A-F	Per Ton Ration A-F	
	(IU)	*(IU/lb)*	*(IU/ton)*	*(IU)*	*(IU/lb)*	*(IU/ton)*	
Maintenance: 1,000-lb *(454-kg)* horse	22,725	909	1,818,000	26,134	1,045	2,090,700	Vitamin A is not synthesized in the cecum. Hay over 1 year old, regardless of green color, is usually not an adequate source of carotene or vitamin A activity. When deficiency symptoms appear, add stabilized vitamin A to the ration. It is wasteful to feed more vitamin A than is needed. Also exceedingly high levels over an extended period of time may cause bone fragility, hyperostosis, and exfoliated epithelium.
Gestation/Lactation: 1,000-lb *(454-kg)* mare	34,100	1,364	2,728,000	39,215	1,569	3,137,200	
Growth: 450-lb *(204.5-kg)* weanling	10,908	909	1,818,000	12,544	1,045	2,090,700	
Working: 1,000-lb *(454-kg)* horse	22,725	909	1,818,000	26,134	1,045	2,090,700	
Maintenance: 1,000-lb *(454-kg)* horse	3,400	136	272,000	3,910	156	312,800	The vitamin D requirement is less when a proper balance of calcium and phosphorus exists in the ration. When animals are exposed to direct sunlight, the ultraviolet light produces vitamin D from traces of cholesterol in the skin. Stabled horses, exercised in the early morning, will not get sufficient vitamin D in this manner. Too much vitamin D may harm a horse. Vitamin D toxicity is characterized by calcification of the blood vessels, heart, and other soft tissues, and by bone abnormalities. Toxic level of vitamin D has not been established in the horse, but a level 50 times the requirement may be harmful.
Gestation/Lactation: 1,000-lb *(454-kg)* mare	6,825	273	546,000	7,849	314	627,900	
Growth: 450-lb *(204.5-kg)* weanling	4,368	364	728,000	5,023	419	837,200	
Working: 1,000-lb *(454-kg)* horse	3,400	136	272,000	3,910	156	312,800	
Maintenance: 1,000-lb *(454-kg)* horse	575	23	46,000	661	26	52,900	Utilization of vitamin E is dependent on adequate selenium.
Gestation/Lactation: 1,000-lb *(454-kg)* mare	900	36	72,000	1,035	41	82,800	
Growth: 450-lb *(204.5-kg)* weanling	432	36	72,000	497	41	82,800	
Working: 1,000-lb *(454-kg)* horse	900	36	72,000	1,035	41	82,800	
				(mg)	*(mg/lb)*	*(mg/ton)*	
Maintenance: 1,000-lb *(454-kg)* horse				8.0	0.32	640	High levels of vitamin K will overcome bleeding due to dicoumarol. Vitamin K is generally (1) widely distributed in normal feeds, and/or (2) synthesized in adequate amounts by the intestinal microflora of the horse.
Gestation/Lactation: 1,000-lb *(454-kg)* mare				8.0	0.32	640	
Growth: 450-lb *(204.5-kg)* weanling				3.6	0.30	600	
Working: 1,000-lb *(454-kg)* horse				8.0	0.32	640	

(Continued)

TABLE 13-5

Vitamins Which May Be Deficient Under Normal Conditions	Conditions Usually Prevailing Where Deficiencies Are Reported	Function of Vitamin	Some Deficiency Symptoms	Practical Sources of the Vitamin
Water-soluble vitamins:				
Biotin	Sulfa drugs kill intestinal organisms; hence, when they are used an extended period, there may be deficiency of biotin.	Biotin plays an important role in the metabolism of carbohydrates, fats, and proteins.	In all animals, a deficiency of biotin will depress growth and cause a loss of hair and/or a dermatitis.	Alfalfa hay, blackstrap molasses, cottonseed meal, soybean meal, peanut meal, milk, wheat bran, synthetic biotin, and yeast (brewers', torula).
Choline	Ration low in methionine, an amino acid.	Prevention of fatty livers, the transmitting of nerve impulses, and the metabolism of fat.	Slow growth and fatty livers are the deficiency symptoms.	Feed sources, such as alfalfa hay, blackstrap molasses, and cereal grains. Body manufacture of choline from excess of the amino acid methionine. Choline chloride. Choline dihydrogen.
Folacin (Folic Acid)		In all vertebrates, folacin is essential for normal growth and reproduction, for the prevention of blood disorders, and for important biochemical mechanisms in each cell.	Poor growth. Anemia.	Alfalfa hay, the oil meals (soybean, cottonseed, and linseed), skimmed milk, and wheat and wheat byproducts. Synthetic folacin, wheat germ, and yeast (brewers', torula).
Niacin (Nicotinic Acid, Nicotinamide)		Constituent of two important coenzymes. They are involved in the release of energy from carbohydrates, fats, and proteins, and in the synthesis of fatty acids, protein, and DNA.	Reduced growth and appetite. Skin rashes, diarrhea, nerve disorders.	Green alfalfa. Niacin is widely distributed in feeds; fermentation solubles and certain oil meals are especially good sources. Synthetic niacin.
Pantothenic Acid (Vitamin B-3)		Part of coenzyme A, which plays a key role in body metabolism.	Poor growth, skin rashes, poor appetite, nervous disorders.	Safflower meal, blackstrap molasses, wheat bran, and milk. Calcium pantothenate.
Riboflavin (Vitamin B-2)	When green feeds (pasture, hay, or silage) are not available.	Riboflavin has an essential role in the oxidative mechanisms of the cells.	Periodic ophthalmia (or moon blindness), characterized by catarrhal conjunctivitis in one or both eyes, accompanied by photophobia, and lachrymation. Decreased rate of growth and feed efficiency. Porous and weak bones; ligaments and joints impaired.	Green pasture. Green hay. Milk and milk products. Synthetic riboflavin. Yeast.

(Continued)

Classes/Function	Nutrient Requirements[1,2]			Nutrient Allowances[1,2]			Comments
	Per Horse Daily	In Ration A-F	Per Ton Ration A-F	Per Horse Daily	In Ration A-F	Per Ton Ration A-F	
	(mg)	*(mg/lb)*	*(mg/ton)*	*(mg)*	*(mg/lb)*	*(mg/ton)*	
Maintenance: 1,000-lb *(454-kg)* horse				2.5	0.1	200	Biotin is closely related metabolically to folacin, pantothenic acid, and vitamin B-12.
Gestation/Lactation: 1,000-lb *(454-kg)* mare				2.5	0.1	200	
Growth: 450-lb *(204.5-kg)* weanling				1.2	0.1	200	
Working: 1,000-lb *(454-kg)* horse				2.5	0.1	200	
Maintenance: 1,000-lb *(454-kg)* horse				500	20.0	40,000	Choline content of normal feeds is usually sufficient.
Gestation/Lactation: 1,000-lb *(454-kg)* mare				750	30.0	60,000	
Growth: 450-lb *(204.5-kg)* weanling				750	62.5	125,000	
Working: 1,000-lb *(454-kg)* horse				750	30.0	60,000	
Maintenance: 1,000-lb *(454-kg)* horse				20	0.8	1,600	Folacin is widely distributed in horse feeds. Also, folacin is synthesized in the lower gut.
Gestation/Lactation: 1,000-lb *(454-kg)* mare				30	1.2	2,400	
Growth: 450-lb *(204.5-kg)* weanling				36	3.0	6,000	
Working: 1,000-lb *(454-kg)* horse				30	1.2	2,400	
Maintenance: 1,000-lb *(454-kg)* horse				250	10.0	20,000	There is some evidence that niacin is synthesized by the horse. The horse can convert the essential amino acid tryptophan into niacin. Hence, it is important to make certain that the ration is adequate in niacin; otherwise, the horse will use tryptophan to supply niacin needs.
Gestation/Lactation: 1,000-lb *(454-kg)* mare				250	10.0	20,000	
Growth: 450-lb *(204.5-kg)* weanling				250	20.8	41,600	
Working: 1,000-lb *(454-kg)* horse				250	10.0	20,000	
Maintenance: 1,000-lb *(454-kg)* horse				250	10.0	20,000	Grain is very deficient in pantothenic acid. Of all the B vitamins, pantothenic acid is most likely to be deficient under stable (confinement) conditions.
Gestation/Lactation: 1,000-lb *(454-kg)* mare				250	10.0	20,000	
Growth: 450-lb *(204.5-kg)* weanling				250	20.8	41,600	
Working: 1,000-lb *(454-kg)* horse				250	10.0	20,000	
Maintenance: 1,000-lb *(454-kg)* horse	22.8	0.91	1,820	40.0	1.6	3,200	Lack of vitamin B-2 is not the only cause of moon blindness. Sometimes, moon blindness follows leptospirosis, and it may be caused by an allergic reaction.
Gestation/Lactation: 1,000-lb *(454-kg)* mare	22.8	0.91	1,820	40.0	1.6	3,200	
Growth: 450-lb *(204.5-kg)* weanling	10.9	0.91	1,820	19.2	1.6	3,200	
Working: 1,000-lb *(454-kg)* horse	22.8	0.91	1,820	40.0	1.6	3,200	

(Continued)

TABLE 13-5

Vitamins Which May Be Deficient Under Normal Conditions	Conditions Usually Prevailing Where Deficiencies Are Reported	Function of Vitamin	Some Deficiency Symptoms	Practical Sources of the Vitamin
Water-soluble vitamins:				
Thiamin (Vitamin B-1)	Poor-quality hay and grain. When sulfa drugs or antibiotics are given to the horse, the synthesis of B vitamins is impaired. Consumption of bracken fern (*Pteris aquilina*) and horsetail (*Equisetum* spp) will cause thiamin deficiency due to the anti-thiamin compounds that they contain.	In energy metabolism. Without thiamin, there would be no energy. In the working of the peripheral nerves. Promotes appetite and growth.	A thiamin deficiency has been produced experimentally. Decreased feed consumption (loss of weight), anemia, incoordination (especially in the hindquarters), lowered blood thiamin, elevated blood pyruvic acid, enlarged heart, and nervous symptoms.	Wheat and wheat byproducts. Oilseed meals. Oat grain and groats. Thiamin hydrochloride. Yeast (brewers', torula).
Vitamin B-6 (Pyridoxine, Pyridoxal, Pyridoxamine)		In its coenzyme forms, it is involved in a large number of physiologic functions, particularly protein, carbohydrate, and fat metabolism.	No deficiency symptoms of vitamin B-6 have been reported in the horse. So, it is thought to be synthesized in the cecum.	Green pasture, alfalfa hay, wheat bran, wheat germ, and yeast (brewers', torula).
Vitamin B-12 (Cobalamins)	When few, or no feeds of animal origin are fed. Where cobalt is not present in the feed, thereby precluding the synthesis of vitamin B-12 in the gastrointestinal tract.	Coenzyme in several enzyme systems. Closely linked with choline, folacin, and pantothenic acid.	Loss of appetite and poor growth.	Protein supplements of animal origin. Fermentation products. Cobalamins, yeast.
Vitamin C (Ascorbic Acid, Dehydroascorbic Acid)	The vitamin C requirements of fish and humans have been observed to increase in periods of stress. So, it is conjectured that heavily stressed horses may require more vitamin C than they can synthesize.	Formation and maintenance of collagen. More rapid healing of wounds. Sound bones.	No deficiency symptoms in horses noted. In humans and monkeys, scurvy is the main deficiency symptom. Also, in humans sudden death from severe internal hemorrhage and heart failure are always a danger.	Ordinary rations and body synthesis provide adequate vitamin C for horses. Well-cured hays and green pastures are good sources of vitamin C.
Unidentified factors	Since the U.S. foal crop is only around 50%, it is obvious that there is room for improvement somewhere along the line; and perhaps unidentified factors are involved. Also, optimal results with horses during the critical periods (growth, gestation-lactation, and when under stress as in racing or showing) appear to be dependent upon providing unidentified factors through such ingredients as distillers' dried solubles, dehydrated alfalfa meal, condensed fish solubles, brewers' dried yeast, antibiotic fermentation residues, dried whey, and corn fermentation solubles.			

[1]As used herein, the distinction between "nutrient requirements" and "nutrient allowances" is as follows: In nutrient requirements, no margins of safety are included intentionally; whereas in nutrient allowances, margins of safety are provided in order to compensate for variations in feed composition, environment, and possible losses during storage or processing. The nutrient requirements in Table 13-5 were adapted by the author from *Nutrient Requirements of Horses*, 5th rev. ed., NRC-National Academy of Sciences, the latest NRC *Nutrient Requirements of Horses*. The nutrient allowances were developed by the author, based on experiments and experiences; it is intended that they meet the nutrient requirements, and provide adequate margins of safety in addition.

[2]Feed consumption of mature 1,000-lb *(454-kg)* horse estimated at 25 lb *(11.36 kg)* per day. Feed consumption of 450-lb *(204.5-kg)* weanling estimated at 12 lb *(5.45 kg)* per day.

(Continued)

Classes/Function	Nutrient Requirements[1,2]			Nutrient Allowances[1,2]			Comments
	Per Horse Daily	In Ration A-F	Per Ton Ration A-F	Per Horse Daily	In Ration A-F	Per Ton Ration A-F	
	(mg)	(mg/lb)	(mg/ton)	(mg)	(mg/lb)	(mg/ton)	
Maintenance: 1,000-lb *(454-kg)* horse	34.1	1.36	2,720	39.2	1.57	3,140	Thiamin is synthesized in the lower gut of the horse by bacterial action, but there is some doubt as to its sufficiency.
Gestation/Lactation: 1,000-lb *(454-kg)* mare	34.1	1.36	2,720	39.2	1.57	3,140	When neither green pasture nor high-quality roughage is available, thiamin hydrochloride should be added to the ration.
Growth: 450-lb *(204.5-kg)* weanling	16.4	1.36	2,720	18.9	1.57	3,140	Since carbohydrate metabolism is increased during physical exertion, it is important that B-1 be available in
Working: 1,000-lb *(454-kg)* horse	56.8	2.27	4,540	65.3	2.61	5,220	quantity at such times.
Maintenance: 1,000-lb *(454-kg)* horse				25.0	1.0	2,000	Normally, horse rations contain adequate vitamin B-6. Also, it appears to be synthesized in the cecum. Yet, these
Gestation/Lactation: 1,000-lb *(454-kg)* mare				25.0	1.0	2,000	sources may not be adequate for the maximum performance of the horse.
Growth: 450-lb *(204.5-kg)* weanling				6.0	0.5	1,000	
Working: 1,000-lb *(454-kg)* horse				25.0	1.0	2,000	
Maintenance: 1,000-lb *(454-kg)* horse				0.125	0.005	10	It is reported that horses in poor nutritional condition showing anemia respond to the administration of vitamin
Gestation/Lactation: 1,000-lb *(454-kg)* mare				0.150	0.006	12	B-12.
Growth: 450-lb *(204.5-kg)* weanling				0.084	0.007	14	
Working: 1,000-lb *(454-kg)* horse				0.150	0.006	12	
Maintenance: 1,000-lb *(454-kg)* horse				60	2.4	4,800	Dietary need is clearly evident for humans, monkeys, guinea pigs, fruit-eating bats, and bulbul birds. However,
Gestation/Lactation: 1,000-lb *(454-kg)* mare				100	4.0	8,000	vitamin C is probably required by other species, but synthesized in the body; the only question is whether the
Growth: 450-lb *(204.5-kg)* weanling				45	3.75	7,500	horse can synthesize enough vitamin C when under stress.
Working: 1,000-lb *(454-kg)* horse				100	4.0	8,000	

able to the horse and more efficiently converted into vitamin A than the carotene in timothy hay.

Severe deficiency of vitamin A may cause night blindness (impaired adaptation to darkness), lacrimation (tears), keratinization of the cornea and skin, reproductive difficulties, poor or uneven hoof development, difficulty in breathing, incoordination, convulsive seizures, progressive weakness, and poor appetite. There is also some evidence that deficiency of this vitamin may cause or contribute to certain leg bone weaknesses. When vitamin A deficiency symptoms appear, the caretaker should add a stabilized vitamin A product to the ration.

A considerable margin of safety in vitamin A and carotene is provided in the recommended allowances due to the oxidative destruction of these materials in feeds during storage. But, it is wasteful to feed more vitamin A than is needed. Also, feeding exceedingly high levels of vitamin A over an extended period of time may cause bone fragility, hyperostosis, and exfoliated epithelium. When fed as directed, the vast majority of horse feeds won't provide excesses of vitamin A.

Other facts pertinent to vitamin A for horses follow:

1. **Circumstances conducive to vitamin A deficiencies.** The circumstances most conducive to vitamin A deficiencies are (a) extended periods of drought, resulting in the pastures becoming dry and bleached; (b) a long winter feeding period on bleached hays or straws, especially overripe cereal hays and straws; and (c) using feeds which have lost their vitamin A potency as a result of either heat or extended storage (for example, it has been found that alfalfa may lose nine-tenths of its vitamin A value in a year's storage). There is reason to believe that mild deficiencies of vitamin A, especially in the winter and early spring, are fairly common.

Fortunately, horses are able to store vitamin A, primarily in the liver, during periods of abundance to tide them through periods of scarcity. Thus, horses that have been consuming green forage for 4 to 6 weeks usually store sufficient vitamin A in the liver to maintain adequate levels of plasma vitamin A for 3 to 6 months.

It is noteworthy (1) that the absorption of vitamin A is adversely affected by the presence of parasites in the intestinal tract, and (2) that the presence of enough protein of good quality enhances the conversion of carotene to vitamin A.

It is generally believed that stressed horses have a higher vitamin A requirement than those not under stress. Among such stress factors are: racing, showing, fatigue, hot weather, confinement, excitement, and number of animals run together.

The vitamin A requirements for gestating mares may be five times the minimum maintenance requirements. Therefore, unless properly fed, broodmares may become almost depleted of their vitamin A reserves by the end of winter—at a time when vitamin A deficiency could be critical to the rapid development of the fetus.

2. **Measurement of vitamin A potency.** The vitamin A potency (whether due to the vitamin itself, to carotene, or to both) of feeds is usually reported in terms of IU or USP units. These two units of measurement are the same. They are based on the growth response of rats, in which several different levels of the test product are fed to different groups of rats, as a supplement to a vitamin A-free diet which has caused growth to cease. A USP or IU is the vitamin A value for rats of 0.30 microgram of pure vitamin A alcohol, or of 0.60 microgram of pure beta-carotene. The carotene or vitamin A content of feeds is commonly determined by colorimetric or spectroscopic methods.

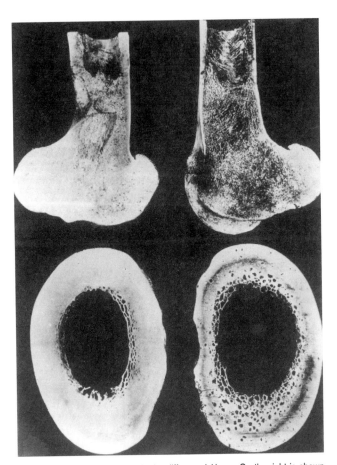

Fig. 13-14. Vitamin A made the difference! *Upper:* On the right is shown the sagittal section of the distal end of the femur of a vitamin A-deficient horse compared to normal bone (left). *Lower:* On the right is shown the cross section of the cannon bone from a vitamin A-deficient horse compared to normal bone (left). (Courtesy, California Agricultural Experiment Station)

VITAMIN D

For horses, both D_2 (the plant form) and D_3 (the

animal form) are equally effective, so there is no need to use some of each.

Foals sometimes develop rickets because of insufficient vitamin D, calcium, or phosphorus. Rickets is characterized by reduced bone calcification, stiff and swollen joints, stiffness of gait, irritability, and reduction in serum calcium and phosphorus. It can be prevented by exposing the animal to direct sunlight as much as possible, by allowing free access to a suitable mineral mixture, or by providing good quality sun-cured hay or luxuriant pasture grown on well-fertilized soil. In northern areas that do not have adequate sunshine, many caretakers provide the foal with a vitamin D supplement.

With vitamin D, as with vitamin A, there is need for adequacy without harmful excesses. Too much vitamin D may harm a horse. Vitamin D toxicity is characterized by calcification of the blood vessels, heart, and other soft tissues, and by bone abnormalities. Also, there is general weakness and loss of body weight. Although the toxic level of vitamin D in the horse has not been established a level 50 times the requirement may be harmful.

The vitamin D requirement is less when a proper balance of calcium and phosphorus exists in the ration.

Other facts pertinent to vitamin D for horses follow:

1. **Vitamin D, and cholesterol and ergosterol.** Most of the commonly used feeds contain little or no vitamin D, yet there is no widespread need for special supplements containing this factor. Fortunately, the skin of horses and many feeds contain provitamins in certain forms of cholesterol and ergosterol, respectively, which, through the action of ultraviolet light (light of such short wave length that it is invisible) from the sun, are converted into vitamin D. These certain forms of cholesterol and ergosterol themselves have no antirachitic effect.

2. **Vitamin D limited in feeds.** Of all the known vitamins, vitamin D has the most limited distribution in common feeds. Very little of this factor is contained in the cereal grains and their byproducts, in roots and tubers, in feeds of animal origin, or in growing pasture grasses. The only important natural sources of vitamin D are sun-cured hay and other roughages. The chief vitamin D rich concentrates include vitamin D_2, vitamin D_3, sun-cured hay, cod and certain other fish liver oils, irradiated cholesterol and ergosterol, and irradiated yeast.

As might be suspected from the preceding discussion, artificially dehydrated hay contains little vitamin D.

3. **Effectiveness of sunlight in producing vitamin D.** The effectiveness of sunlight is determined by the lengths and intensity of the ultraviolet rays which reach the body. It is more potent in the tropics than elsewhere, more potent at noon than earlier or later in the day, more potent in the summer than in the winter, and more potent at high altitudes. The ultraviolet rays are largely screened out by clothing, window glass, clouds, smoke, or dust. Also, some biochemists theorize that the color of the skin of humans is nature's way of regulating the manufacture of vitamin D—that the dark skin of races near the equator filters out excess ultraviolet light. Perhaps color of hair and skin in horses exercises a similar control, although this is not known.

VITAMIN E

Vitamin E, or tocopherol, is associated with reproduction. Also, it prevents and corrects anhidrosis, a condition characterized by a dry, dull hair coat, elevated temperature, high blood pressure, and labored breathing. Anhidrosis has been successfully treated by the oral administration of 1,000 to 3,000 IU of vitamin E daily for one month.

Most practical rations contain liberal quantities of vitamin E, perhaps enough except under conditions of work, stress, or reproduction, or where there is interference with its utilization. Green forages, especially alfalfa, are good sources.

It is now preferable to use milligrams of alpha-tocopherol equivalents as a summation term for all vitamin E activity. However, feed composition tables generally give values in IU, and IU is still used for labeling most feed products.

The requirements for vitamin E are influenced by interrelationships with other essential nutrients—increased by the presence of interfering substances, and spared by the presence of other substances that may be protective or that may assume part of its functions. The recommended allowances of vitamin E are given in Tables 13-2 and 13-5.

VITAMIN K

When vitamin K is deficient, the coagulation time of the blood is increased and the prothrombin level is decreased. This is the main justification for adding this vitamin to the ration of the horse. Also, vitamin K has value in veterinary medicine as an aid in controlling hemorrhages.

WATER-SOLUBLE VITAMINS

The large amounts of water which pass through the horse's body daily tend to carry out the water-soluble vitamins, thereby depleting the supply. Thus, they must be supplied in the horse's ration on a day-to-day basis. All of the water-soluble vitamins except C are known as B vitamins.

Vitamins of the B-complex, particularly biotin,

choline, folacin (folic acid), niacin, pantothenic acid, riboflavin, thiamin (B-1), vitamin B-6 (pyridoxine) and vitamin B-12 may be essential, especially for (1) young horses before the synthesis of the B-complex vitamins by the microflora begins, and (2) horses that are under stress, as in racing and showing.

However, it is not clear which ones are needed, in what quantities they are needed, and as to their status from the standpoint of synthesis and absorption in the horse. Healthy horses usually get enough of them either in natural rations or by synthesis in the intestinal tract. However, when neither green pasture nor high-quality dry forage is available, it may be in the nature of good insurance to provide them, especially for horses that are under stress.

Although some of the B vitamins and unidentified factors are synthesized in the cecum of the horse, it is doubtful that microbial activity is sufficient to meet the need during the critical periods—growth, reproduction, and when animals are subjected to great stress as in showing or racing. Also, there is reason to question the efficacy of absorption this far down the digestive tract; for, in comparison with that of humans and other animals, the cecum is on the wrong end of the digestive tract. Moreover, it is known that horses fed thiamin-deficient rations lose weight, become nervous, and show incoordination in the hindquarters; then, when thiamin is added to the ration, this condition is cured. For these reasons, in valuable horses it is not wise to rely solely on bacterial synthesis. The B vitamins, along with unidentified factors, may be provided by adding to the ration such ingredients as distillers' dried solubles, dried brewers' yeast, dried fish solubles, or animal liver meal; usually through a reputable commercial feed.

BIOTIN

Ordinary equine rations probably contain ample biotin, or horses synthesize all they need. But, in recognition that biotin is required by all species, and that it plays an important role in metabolism of carbohydrates, fats, and proteins, it is possible that adding biotin to the ration of the horse may assure maximum performance. Also, there is some indication that biotin is essential for sound hooves; but it should not be concluded that all hoof problems are due to biotin deficiency. They are not. Actually, several nutrients are known to influence hoof growth—biotin among them. Studies indicate that a complete balanced ration is essential for proper hoof growth. Without doubt, heritability is also a factor.

CHOLINE

Choline is a metabolic essential for building and maintaining cell structure and in the transmission of nerve impulses. Choline deficiency has been produced in rats, dogs, chickens, pigs, and other species. Slow growth is a nonspecific symptom.

The dietary requirement for choline depends on the level of methionine (an amino acid) in the ration. Also, it is noteworthy that all naturally occurring fats contain some choline; however, normal horse feeds are low in fat. Hence, the addition to the ration of 500 mg of choline per day is the recommended allowance for a 1,000-lb horse.

FOLACIN (FOLIC ACID)

There is no single compound vitamin with the name folacin; rather, the term *folacin* is used to designate folic acid and a group of closely related substances which are essential for vertebrates.

Folacin is widely distributed in horse feeds. Also, it is synthesized in the lower digestive tract of the horse. Hence, it is unlikely that a dietary source is required, although a small amount may be in the nature of cheap insurance.

NIACIN (NICOTINIC ACID, NICOTINAMIDE)

Niacin is a collective term which includes nicotinic acid and nicotinamide, both natural forms of the vitamin with equal niacin activity.

Some evidence indicates that niacin is synthesized by the horse. Also, the horse can convert the essential amino acid tryptophan into niacin. Hence, it is important to make certain that the ration is adequate in niacin; otherwise, the horse will use tryptophan to supply niacin needs. Niacin is widely distributed in feeds; fermentation solubles, and certain oil meals are especially good sources. Only a modest addition of niacin to the ration is indicated.

PANTOTHENIC ACID (VITAMIN B-3)

Intestinal synthesis of pantothenic acid has been found to occur in all species studied. In the case of the horse, such synthesis appears to be sufficiently extensive to meet body needs, at least in part. However, of all the B vitamins, pantothenic acid is most likely to be deficient under stable (confinement) conditions. As indicated in Table 13-5, a daily allowance of 250 mg of pantothenic acid is recommended for a 1,000-lb gestating or lactating mare.

RIBOFLAVIN (VITAMIN B-2)

A deficiency of riboflavin may cause periodic ophthalmia (moon blindness), characterized by catarrhal conjunctivitis in one or both eyes, accompanied by photophobia, and lacrimation. Repeated attacks affect the retina, lens, and ocular fluids and cause impaired vision or blindness. But it is known that lack of this vitamin is not the only factor causing this condition. Sometimes moon blindness follows leptospirosis in horses, and it may be caused by a localized hypersensitivity or allergic reaction. Periodic ophthalmia caused by lack of riboflavin may be prevented by feeding green hay and green pasture, supplying feeds high in riboflavin, or by adding crystalline riboflavin to the ration.

Two properties of riboflavin lend support to riboflavin supplementation for the horse: (1) it is destroyed by light, and it is destroyed by heat in an alkaline solution; and (2) body storage is very limited, so day-to-day needs must be provided in the ration.

THIAMIN (VITAMIN B-1)

Vitamin B-1 is synthesized in the lower gut of the horse by bacterial action, but there is some doubt as to its sufficiency and as to the amount absorbed always meeting the full requirements.

A thiamin deficiency has been produced experimentally. It is characterized by loss of appetite, loss of weight, anemia, incoordination (especially of the hind legs), lower blood thiamin, elevated blood pyruvic acid, and dilated and hypertrophied heart.

Vitamin B-1 is required for normal carbohydrate metabolism. Since carbohydrate metabolism is increased during physical exertion, it is important that B-1 be available in quantity at such times.

VITAMIN B-6 (PYRIDOXINE, PYRIDOXAL, PYRIDOXAMINE)

There is no evidence that deficiencies of vitamin B-6 occur in horses on commonly fed rations; and it is not expected that deficiencies should occur in view of the widespread distribution of vitamin B-6 in feedstuffs and the probable synthesis of B-6 in the cecum. Yet, these sources may be adequate to assure maximum performance of the horse. So, the daily supplementation of 25 mg of vitamin B-6 per horse may be in the nature of cheap insurance, especially because of the important role of this vitamin.

Vitamin B-6, in its coenzyme forms, is involved in a large number of physiologic functions, particularly the metabolism of protein, carbohydrate, and fat. Also, it is involved in clinical problems, including (1) anemia that is not iron responsive, (2) kidney stones, and (3) the physiologic demands of pregnancy.

VITAMIN B-12 (COBALAMINS)

It has been reported that horses in poor nutritional

condition showing anemia respond to the administration of vitamin B-12. An allowance of 0.084 mg of B-12 per day is recommended for weanlings.

Vitamin B-12 injections are frequently given to horses to improve performance and to prevent or cure anemia. There is no experimental evidence that such shots are either helpful or harmful.

VITAMIN C (ASCORBIC ACID, DEHYDROASCORBIC ACID)

A dietary need for ascorbic acid is limited to humans, monkeys, guinea pigs, fruit-eating bats, and bulbul birds.

The vitamin is probably required by all other species, including the horse, but is likely synthesized adequately in the body. It is noteworthy, however, that catfish and trout require dietary sources of vitamin C when they are stressed by being raised in extremely crowded conditions. This theory of stress has been carried over to human nutrition. So, it is conjectured that heavily stressed horses may not be able to synthesize sufficient vitamin C for maximum performance; hence, adding the vitamin to the ration may make for added assurance.

VITAMIN IMBALANCES

Experiments have shown that the amounts needed of certain vitamins may be affected by the supply of another vitamin or of some other nutritive essential. Also, it is known that excess fortification of the horse's ration with certain vitamins may prove more detrimental than helpful. Thus, caretakers should avoid harmful imbalances; they should provide vitamins on the basis of recommended allowances. Also, when fortifying with vitamins, consideration should be given to the vitamins provided by the ingredients of the normal ration, for it is the total composition of the feed that counts.

UNIDENTIFIED FACTORS

Since the U.S. foal crop is only around 50%, and since horses under stress (racing, showing, etc.) frequently become temperamental in their eating habits, it is obvious that there is room for improvement in the ration somewhere along the line. Perhaps unidentified factors are involved.

Unidentified factors include those vitamins which the chemist has not yet isolated and identified. For this reason, they are sometimes referred to as the vitamins of the future. There is mounting evidence of the importance of unidentified factors for animals, including humans. Among other things, they lower the incidence of ulcers in humans and swine. For horses, they appear to increase growth and improve feed efficiency and breeding performance when added to rations thought to be complete with regard to known nutrients. The anatomical and physiological mechanism of the digestive system of the horse, plus the stresses and strains to which modern horses are subjected, would indicate the wisdom of adding unidentified factor sources to the ration of the horse. Unidentified factors appear to be of special importance during breeding, gestation, lactation, and growth.

Three highly regarded unidentified factor sources are dried whey product, corn fermentation solubles, and dehydrated alfalfa meal.

Fig. 13-15. Free access to clean, fresh water is desirable. Note that the concrete tank is rounded so as to lessen injuries. (Courtesy, *Equus Magazine*, Gaithersburg, MD)

WATER

Water is one of the most vital of all nutrients. In fact, horses can survive for a longer period without feed than they can without water. The loss of 10% body water will result in disorders; the loss of 20% body water will cause death. But, fortunately, under ordinary conditions water can be readily provided and at little cost.

Water is one of the largest single constituents of the animal body, varying in amount with condition and age. The younger the animal, the more water it contains. Also, the fatter the animal, the lower the water content. Thus, as an animal matures, it requires proportionately less water on a weight basis, because it consumes less feed per unit of weight and the water content of the body is being replaced by fat.

Water performs the following important functions in horses:

1. It is essential for the production of saliva.

2. It is necessary to the life and shape of every cell and is a constituent of every body fluid.

3. It acts as a carrier for various substances, serving as a medium in which nourishment is carried to the cells and waste products are removed therefrom.

4. It assists with temperature regulation in the body, cooling the animal by evaporation from the skin as perspiration.

5. It is necessary for many important chemical reactions of digestion and metabolism.

6. It lubricates the joints, as a constituent of the synovial fluid; it acts as a water cushion for the nervous system, in the cerebrospinal fluid; it transports sound, in the perilymph in the ear; and it is concerned with sight and provides a lubricant for the eye.

Surplus water is excreted from the body, principally in the urine, and to a slight extent in the perspiration, feces, and water vapor from the lungs.

The average horse will drink 10 to 12 gal. of water daily, the amount varying according to weather, amount of work done (sweating), rations fed, and size of horse.

Free access to water is desirable. When this is not possible, horses should be watered at approximately the same times daily. Opinions vary among caretakers as to the proper times and method of watering horses. All agree, however, that regularity and frequency are desirable. Most caretakers agree that water may be given before, during, or after feeding.

Frequent, small waterings between feedings are desirable during warm weather or when the animal is being put to hard use. Do not allow a horse to drink heavily when it is hot, because it may founder; and do not allow a horse to drink heavily just before being put to work.

Automatic waterers are the modern way to provide clean, fresh water at all times—as nature intended. Also, frequent but small waterings avoid gorging. All waterers should have drains for easy cleaning, and should be heated to 40 to 45°F during the winter months in cold regions. Waterers should be available in both stalls and corrals.

FEEDS FOR HORSES

Individual feeds vary widely in feeding value. Oats and barley, for example, differ in feeding value according to the hull content and weight per bushel, and forages vary according to the stage of maturity at which they are cut and how well they are cured and stored. Also, the feeding value of certain feeds is materially affected by preparation.

Regardless of the feeds selected, they should be of sound quality, and not moldy, spoiled, or dusty. This applies to both hay and grain. The careful selection of feeds is more important for horses than for any other class of livestock.

More than one kind of hay makes for appetite appeal. In season, any good pasture can replace part or all of the hay unless work or training conditions make substitution impractical.

Good quality oats and timothy hay always have been considered standard feeds for horses. However, feeds of similar nutritive properties can be interchanged in the ration as price relationships warrant; among them, the grains—corn, barley, wheat, and sorghum; the protein supplement—linseed meal, soybean meal, cottonseed meal, and sunflower meal; and hays of many varieties. Feed substitution makes it possible to obtain a balanced ration at lowest cost.

During the winter months, it is well to add a few sliced carrots to the ration, an occasional bran mash, or a small amount of linseed meal. Also, a bran mash or linseed meal may be used to regulate the bowels.

The proportion of concentrates must be increased and the roughages decreased as energy needs rise with the greater amount, severity, or speed of work. A horse that works at a trot needs considerably more feed than one that works at a walk. For this reason, riding horses in medium to light use require somewhat less grain and more hay in proportion to body weight than horses that are racing. Also, from an esthetic standpoint, large, paunchy stomachs are objectionable on horses that are used for recreation and sport.

In addition to making for a nutritionally complete ration, the following factors should be considered when choosing horse feeds: cost, palatability, preparation, variety, bulk, and laxative or constipating qualities.

For purposes of convenience in the discussion that follows, the author has classed feeds as (1) pasture, (2) hay, (3) silage, (4) concentrates, (5) protein supplements, (6) special feeds and additives, and (7) treats.

PASTURE

The great horse breeding centers of the world—Kentucky, Ireland, and New Zealand, to name three of them—are characterized by good pastures. Yet, it is becoming difficult to provide good pasture for horses, especially in suburban areas. Also, it is recognized that many caretakers are prone to overrate the quality of their grass.

In season and when available, good pastures—pastures that are more than mere gymnasiums for horses—should be provided, especially for idle horses, broodmares, and young stock. In fact, pastures have a very definite place for all horses, with the possible exception of animals at heavy work or in training. Even with the latter, pastures may be used with discretion. Horses in heavy use may be turned to pasture at night or over the weekend. Certainly, the total benefits derived from pasture are to the good, although pasturing may have some laxative effects and produce a greater tendency to sweat.

The use of a temporary or seeded pasture grown in regular crop rotation is recommended instead of a

Fig. 13-16. Mares and foals on good pasture. (Courtesy, Dr. Stephen G. Jackson, University of Kentucky, Lexington)

permanent pasture that may become infested with parasites. However, the parasites in horse pastures can be reduced dramatically by picking up the manure twice a week. An Ohio State University study showed that a pasture routinely cleaned in this manner had 18 times fewer parasites than an uncleaned pasture. Manure can be removed manually or mechanically. In England, a power sweeper is available, consisting of a small tractor fitted with a vacuum pump powered by a tractor or small engine.

Horse pastures should be well drained and not too rough or stony. All dangerous places such as pits, stumps, poles, and tanks should be guarded. Shade, water, and suitable minerals should be available in all pastures.

Most horse pastures can be improved by seeding new and better varieties of grasses and legumes and by fertilizing and management. Also, caretakers need to give attention to supplementing some pastures with additional feed. Early in the season, pastures have a high water content and lack energy. Mature, weathered grass is almost always deficient in protein, with as little as 3% or less, and low in carotene, the precursor of vitamin A. However, these deficiencies can be corrected by proper supplemental feeding.

In addition to the nutritive value of the grass, pasture provides invaluable exercise on natural footing—with plenty of sunshine, fresh air, and lowered feeding costs as added benefits. Feeding on pasture is the ideal existence for young stock and breeding animals.

But pastures should not be taken for granted. Again and again, scientists and practical equestrians have demonstrated that the following desired goals in pasture production are well within the realm of possibility:

■ To produce higher yields of palatable and nutritious forage.

■ To extend the grazing season from as early in the spring to as late in the fall as possible.

■ To provide a fairly uniform supply of feed throughout the entire season.

KINDS OF PASTURE

Broadly speaking, all horse pastures may be classified as either (1) permanent pastures, or (2) seeded and temporary pastures.

1. **Permanent pastures.** Permanent pastures, with proper care, last for many years. They are most commonly found on land that cannot be used profitably for cultivated crops, mainly because of topography, moisture, or fertility. The vast majority of U.S. farms have one or more permanent pastures, and most range areas come under this classification.

2. **Seeded and temporary pastures.** Seeded pastures are used as part of the established crop rotation. They are generally used for two to seven years before plowing.

Temporary pastures are those that are used for a short period—like rye, wheat, or oat pasture. They are seeded for the purpose of providing supplemental grazing during the season when the regular permanent or seeded pastures are relatively unproductive.

PASTURE TABLE—ADAPTED GRASSES/LEGUMES

The specific grass or grass legume mixture will vary from area to area, according to differences in soil, temperature, and rainfall. A complete listing of all adapted and recommended grasses and legumes for horse pastures would be too lengthy for this book. However, Fig. 13-17 shows the 10 generally recognized pasture areas and Table 13-6 shows the most important grasses for each of these areas. In using Table 13-6, bear in mind that many species of forages have wide geographic adaptation, but subspecies or varieties often have rather specific adaptation. Thus, alfalfa, for example, is represented by many varieties which give this species adaptation to nearly all states. Variety then, within species, makes many forages adapted to widely varying climate and geographic areas. The county agricultural agent or state agricultural college can furnish recommendations for the area that they serve.

Five grass species—orchardgrass, reed canarygrass, fescue, smooth bromegrass, and Bermudagrass—account for the major portion of seeded grasses in the United States. The leading legumes are alfalfa, trefoil, lupine, sweet clover, kudzu, and clover.

Sudan and hybrid Sudans in the growing stage should never be grazed by horses, because of the

LEGUMES AND GRASSES ADAPTED TO 10 AREAS OF THE 48 CONTIGUOUS STATES

1. Northern Humid Area
2. Central Humid Area
3. Southern Humid Area
4. Eastern Coastal Area
5. Northern Great Plains Area
6. Southern Great Plains Area
7. Northwest Intermountain Area
8. Southwest Area
9. Northwest Coastal Area
10. California Coastal Area

Fig. 13-17. The 10 generally recognized U.S. pasture areas.

TABLE 13-6
ADAPTED GRASSES AND LEGUMES (INCLUDING BROWSE AND FORBS) FOR HORSE PASTURES, BY 10 GEOGRAPHICAL AREAS OF THE UNITED STATES (SEE FIG. 13-17 FOR GEOGRAPHICAL AREAS)[1]

	Areas of the United States									
Grasses, shrubs, forbs:	**1**	**2**	**3**	**4**	**5**	**6**	**7**	**8**	**9**	**10**
Alfileria (filaree)								x	x	
Bahiagrass (a paspalum)			x	x						
Beardgrass (a bluestem)								x		
Bentgrass	x	x								
Bermudagrass		x	x	x		x		x		x
Bluegrass	x	x			x		x	x		
Bluestem	x	x			x	x		x		
Bristlegrass (a millet)								x		
Bromegrass	x	x			x		x	x	x	
Buckwheat (wild)								x		
Buffalograss					x	x				
Buffelgrass						x				
Chamiza (fourwing saltbush)								x		
Cottontop								x		
Curly mesquite (a Hilaria)						x		x		
Dallisgrass (a paspalum)			x	x						
Dropseed						x		x		
Fescue, tall	x	x	x				x	x	x	x
Foxtail						x			x	
Galleta (a Hilaria)						x		x		
Grama grass	x				x	x		x		
Hardinggrass									x	x
Indiangrass	x	x			x	x				
Indian ricegrass								x		
Indianwheat								x		
Johnsongrass (a sorghum)			x	x		x				
Junegrass					x	x		x		
Kleingrass						x				
Lovegrass	x	x				x		x		
Mesquite (vine; a panicum)						x		x		
Millet	x	x	x	x		x				
Mormon tea (ephedra, jointfir)								x		
Muhly								x		
Needlegrass (needle-and-thread)					x		x			
Oatgrass									x	
Oats	x	x	x	x	x			x	x	x
Orchardgrass	x	x	x	x	x		x	x	x	x
Pangola digitgrass			x	x						
Panicgrass (a panicum)					x		x			
Paragrass (malojillo)				x						
Pea bush								x		
Pearlmillet		x	x	x		x				
Ratany								x		
Redtop	x						x		x	
Reed canarygrass	x	x			x		x		x	
Rescuegrass			x	x				x		
(continued)										
Rhodesgrass			x	x						
Rye	x	x	x	x	x	x		x	x	x
Ryegrass, annual		x	x	x		x			x	
Ryegrass, perennial	x	x	x						x	
Sacaton								x		
St. Augustine grass			x							
Sorghum-Sudan hybrids	x	x	x	x	x	x	x			
Stargrass			x							
Sudangrass	x	x	x	x	x	x	x	x	x	x
Switchgrass (a panicum)	x	x	x		x	x				
Three-awn (wiregrass)								x	x	
Timothy	x	x						x		x
Tobosa (a Hilaria)								x		
Wheat	x	x	x	x	x	x	x		x	x
Wheatgrass							x	x	x	x
Wild-rye							x	x	x	
Winterfat (white sage)									x	
Wintergrass (Texas)								x		
Legumes:										
Alfalfa (lucerne)	x	x	x	x	x	x	x	x	x	x
Alyceclover			x	x						
Black medic (yellow trefoil)		x			x		x			
Bur-clover		x							x	x
Cicer milkvetch	x				x		x			
Clover, alsike	x	x			x		x	x	x	
Clover, arrowleaf		x	x							
Clover, crimson		x	x							
Clover, Hubam (white sweet clover)	x	x						x	x	
Clover, Kura	x	x			x			x		
Clover, Ladino	x	x	x	x			x	x	x	x
Clover, prairie						x		x		
Clover, red	x	x	x	x			x	x	x	
Clover, strawberry						x		x	x	
Clover, subterranean		x	x					x	x	x
Clover, white	x	x	x	x			x	x	x	x
Cowpeas		x	x							
Crownvetch	x	x								
Field pea		x	x			x				
Hairy indigo			x							
Lespedeza (annual)	x	x	x							
Lespedeza (perennial, sericea)	x	x	x							
Peas (flat)								x		
Soybeans	x	x	x	x		x				
Sweet clover	x	x			x	x	x	x		
Trefoil, birdsfoot	x	x	x				x		x	x
Velvet beans		x	x							
Vetch		x	x	x	x	x		x	x	

[1]Authoritative recommendations for this table were made by the following agronomists: J. E. Baylor, Ph.D., Professor Emeritus of Agronomy Extension, The Pennsylvania State University, State College; R. A. Forsberg, Ph.D., *et al.*, Department of Agronomy, University of Wisconsin-Madison; J. R. Forwood, Ph.D., Research Agronomist, USDA-ARS, University of Missouri, Columbia; S. C. Fransen, Ph.D., Forage Agronomist, Western Washington Research and Extension Center, Washington State University, Puyallup; C. S. Hoveland, Ph.D., Professor of Agronomy, Department of Agronomy, The University of Georgia, Athens; W. E. McMurphy, Ph.D., Professor, Department of Agronomy, Oklahoma State University, Stillwater; D. A. Miller, Ph.D., Professor, Department of Agronomy, University of Illinois, Urbana-Champaign; R. R. Smith, Ph.D., Professor, Department of Agronomy, University of Wisconsin, Madison.

hazard of cystitis. This disease, which occurs more frequently in mares than in stallions or geldings, is characterized by continuous urination, mares appearing to be constantly in heat, and incoordination in the gait. Animals seldom recover after either the incoordination or the dribbling of urine become evident. Apparently hay from Sudan or from hybrid Sudans will not produce the same malady.

SUPPLEMENTING PASTURES

Except for idle horses, it is generally advisable to provide supplemental feed for horses that are on pasture. This is so because (1) horses are usually subjected to considerable stress; (2) show, sale, and pleasure horses should have eye appeal—sleek, bloomy hair coats that attract judges, buyers, and all who see them; and (3) young animals are usually forced for early development. Further, it is important not to jeopardize soundness or lower the reproductive ability of breeding animals. Consequently, the nutritive requirements of horses may be more critical than can be met by pasture alone.

SUPPLEMENTING EARLY SPRING GRASS

Turning horses on pasture when the first sprigs of green grass appear will usually make for a temporary deficiency of energy, due to (1) washy (high water content) grasses, and (2) inadequate forage for animals to consume. As a result, owners are often disappointed in the poor condition of horses.

If there is good reason why grazing cannot be delayed until there is adequate spring growth, it is recommended that early pastures be supplemented with grass hay or straw (a legume hay will accentuate looseness, which usually exists under such circumstances), preferably placed in a rack; perhaps with a high-energy concentrate provided, also.

SUPPLEMENTING DRY PASTURE

Dry, mature, weathered, bleached grass characterizes (1) drought periods, and (2) fall-winter pastures. Such cured-on-the-stalk grasses are low in energy, in protein (as low as 3% or less), in carotene—the precursor of vitamin A, and in phosphorus and perhaps certain other minerals. These deficiencies become more acute following frost and increase in severity as winter advances. This explains the often severe loss in condition of horses following the first fall freeze.

In addition to the deficiencies which normally characterize whatever plants are available, dry pasture may be plagued by a short supply of feed.

Generally speaking, a concentrate or supplement is best used during droughts or on fall-winter pastures.

However, when there is an acute shortage of forage, hay or other roughage should be added, also.

PASTURE SUPPLEMENTS

Equestrians face the question of what pasture supplement to use, when to feed it, and how much of it to feed.

In supplying a supplement to horses on pasture, the following guides should be observed:

■ It should balance the diet of the horses to which it is fed, which means that it should supply all the nutrients missing in the forage.

■ It should be fed in such a way that each horse gets its proper proportion, which generally means (1) the use of salt blocks, (2) tying up horses during concentrate feeding when more than one animal is fed in a given pasture, or (3) taking them to their stalls at feeding time.

■ The daily allowance of the supplement should be determined by (1) the available pasture (quantity and quality), and (2) the condition of the horse.

HAY

Through mistaken kindness or carelessness, horses are often fed too much hay or other roughage, with the result that they breathe laboriously and tire quickly. With cattle and sheep, on the other hand, it is usually well to feed considerable roughage. This difference between horses and ruminants is due primarily to the relatively small size of the stomach of the horse in comparison with the fourfold stomach of the ruminant.

Under most conditions, the roughage requirement of horses ranges from 0.5 to 1.0% of body weight, or from 5 to 10 lb of roughage daily for a 1,000-lb horse.

Usually, young horses and idle horses can be provided with an unlimited allowance of hay. In fact, much good will result from feeding young and idle horses more roughage and less grain. But one should gradually increase the grain and decrease the hay as work or training begins.

Racehorses should receive a minimum of roughage, since they need a maximum of energy. When limiting the allowance of roughage, it is sometimes necessary to muzzle greedy horses (gluttons) to prevent them from eating the bedding.

Hay native to the locality is usually fed. However, equestrians everywhere prefer good quality timothy. With young stock and breeding animals especially, it is desirable that a sweet grass-legume mixture of alfalfa hay be fed. The legume provides a source of

Fig. 13-18. Horses are fond of good-quality hay. (Courtesy, *The Quarter Horse Journal*, Amarillo, TX)

high-quality proteins and certain minerals and vitamins.

Horses like variety. Therefore, if at all possible, it is wise to have more than one kind of hay in the stable. For example, timothy may be provided at one feeding and a grass-legume mixed hay at the other feeding. Good caretakers often vary the amount of alfalfa fed, for increased amounts of alfalfa in the ration will increase urination and give a softer consistency to the bowel movements. This means that elimination from the kidneys and bowels can be carefully regulated by the amount of alfalfa feedings. Naturally, such regulation becomes more necessary with irregular use and idleness. On the other hand, in some areas alfalfa is fed as the sole roughage with good results.

The easily recognizable characteristics of hay of high quality are:

1. It is made from plants cut at an early stage of maturity, thus assuring the maximum content of protein, minerals, and vitamins; and the highest digestibility.

2. It is leafy, thus giving assurance of high protein content.

3. It is bright green in color, thus indicating proper curing, a high carotene or provitamin A content (provided it is not over a year old), and palatability.

4. It is free from foreign material, such as weeds and stubble.

5. It is free from must or mold and dust.

6. It is fine stemmed and pliable—not coarse, stiff, and woody.

7. It has a pleasing, fragrant aroma; it "smells good enough to eat."

The most important factor affecting hay quality is the stage of maturity at which it is cut. As the plant matures, the stem-to-leaf ratio increases, the percentage of digestible nutrients (such as protein and calcium) decreases, and the digestibility and voluntary intake decrease. Workers at the Pennsylvania Station cut two hay crops, alfalfa and orchardgrass, on three different dates—June 3, June 13, and June 23—then determined the nutritive value of the hays for horses. Their results are given in Table 13-7.

As shown in Table 13-7, each 10-day delay in the cutting date of both alfalfa and orchardgrass resulted in a decrease in crude protein, an increase in crude fiber, and a lowering of digestibility of energy.

TABLE 13-7
EFFECT OF DATE OF CUTTING ON NUTRITIVE VALUE
OF HAY FED TO HORSES[1]

Hay	Date	Crude Protein	Crude Fiber	Digestibility of Energy
		(%)	*(%)*	*(%)*
Alfalfa	June 3	15.1	28.3	65
	June 13	14.4	32.7	56
	June 23	9.1	38.7	52
Orchardgrass . . .	June 3	14.0	30.9	59
	June 13	10.9	32.3	55
	June 23	6.5	38.0	49

[1]Adapted from Darlington, J. M., and T. V. Herschberger, *Journal of Animal Science*, Vol. 27, No. 6, p. 1573.

ALFALFA (LUCERNE)

Alfalfa is an important, perennial, leguminous forage plant with trifoliate leaves and bluish-purple flowers. It is grown widely, principally for hay. Alfalfa is capable of surviving dry periods because of its extraordinarily long root system, and it is adapted to widely varying conditions of climate and soil. It yields the highest tonnage per acre and has the highest protein content of the legume hays.

Not too many years ago, alfalfa hay was not considered fit feed for a horse. Today, some caretakers are feeding it exclusively, with good results. It averages 15.3% protein, which is of high quality; and it is a good source of certain minerals and vitamins. In addition to being used as a hay, alfalfa is an ingredient of most all-pelleted feeds.

When fed alfalfa hay, horses urinate more than when fed grass hay; and there may be a strong smell of ammonia in the barn because alfalfa is high in nitrogen.

OAT HAY

Oat hay is an excellent feed for horses. It's easy to cure, and horses like it. Early cutting (in the soft dough stage) greatly increases its feeding value, due to the higher protein content. Even though considerable energy is stored in the kernels at maturity, shattering of the grain during harvesting of mature oats results in energy losses and decreased feeding value compared with early-cut hay.

Oat hay is low in protein; hence, its feeding value is greatly enhanced when it is fed with alfalfa or some other legume.

TIMOTHY

Timothy is the preferred hay by most horse owners, although it has become scarce and expensive. Although it may be grown alone, it is commonly seeded in mixtures with medium red or alsike clover.

Timothy is easy to harvest and cure. However, in comparison with hay made from the legumes, it is low in crude protein and minerals, particularly calcium.

As with all other forages, the feeding value of timothy is affected by the stage of growth of the plants at the time of cutting. With increasing maturity, (1) the percentage of crude protein decreases, (2) the percentage of crude fiber increases, (3) the hay becomes less palatable, and (4) the digestibility decreases. However, delaying cutting until timothy has reached full bloom stage, or later, usually results in the highest yields. When both yield and quality are considered, the best results are obtained when timothy is cut for hay at the early bloom stage.

SILAGE

Well-preserved silage of good quality, free from mold and not frozen, affords a highly nutritious succulent forage for horses during the winter months. *Because horses are more susceptible than cattle or sheep to botulism or other digestive disturbances resulting from the feeding of poor silage, nothing but choice, fresh silage should ever be fed.*

Various types of silages may be fed successfully to horses, but corn silage and grass-legume silage are most common. If the silage contains much grain, the concentrate allowance should be reduced accordingly.

Silage should not be used as the only roughage for horses. Usually it should be fed in such quantity as to replace not more than one-third to one-half of the roughage allowance, considering that ordinarily 1 lb of hay is equivalent to approximately 3 lb of wet silage. This means that the silage allowance usually does not exceed 10 to 15 lb daily per head for mature animals, although much larger amounts have been used satisfactorily in some instances. Silage is especially suited for the winter feeding of idle horses, broodmares, and growing foals.

CONCENTRATES

Horses cannot handle as large quantities of roughages as ruminants. When used for heavy work, for pleasure, or for racing they must be even more restricted in their roughage allowance and should receive a higher proportion of concentrates.

Because of less bulk and lower shipping and handling costs, the concentrates used for feeding are less likely to be locally grown than the roughages. Even so, the vast majority of grains fed to horses are homegrown, thus varying from area to area, according to the grain crops best adapted.

Of all the concentrates, heavy oats most nearly meet the needs of horses; and, because of the uniformly good results obtained from their use, they have always been recognized as the leading grain for horses. Corn is also widely used as a horse feed, particularly in the central states. Despite occasional prejudice to the contrary, barley is a good horse feed. As proof of the latter assertion, it is noteworthy that the Arabs—who were good horsemen—fed barley almost exclusively. Also, wheat, wheat bran, and commercial mixed feeds are extensively used. It is to be emphasized, therefore, that careful attention should be given to the prevailing price of feeds available locally, for many feeds are well suited to horses. Often substitutions can be made that will result in a marked saving without affecting the nutritive value of the ration. So, the primary consideration in selecting the cereal grain(s) is the cost per unit of energy.

BARLEY

Barley is the leading horse grain in western United States.

Compared with corn, barley contains somewhat more protein (crude protein; barley 13%; corn 10%) and fiber (due to the hulls) and somewhat less carbohydrate and fat. Like oats, the feeding value of barley is quite variable, due to the wide spread in test weight per bushel. Most equestrians feel that it is preferable to feed barley along with more bulky feeds; for example, 25% oats or 15% wheat bran.

When fed to horses, barley should always be steam rolled or ground coarsely.

BRAN MASH

Feeding a bran mash is the traditional way of regulating the bowels of horses on idle days and at such other times as required.

The mash is prepared by filling a 2- to 2½-gal. bucket with wheat bran, pouring enough boiling hot water over it to make it the consistency of breakfast oatmeal, covering the bucket with a blanket and allowing it to steam until cool, then feeding it to the horse.

Occasionally, when a horse is offered a bran mash for the first time, he may refuse to eat it. When this occurs, the animal may be enticed to eat the mash by either (1) introducing him to a little of it by hand, or (2) sprinkling some sugar, or some other well-liked feed, over it.

CORN (MAIZE)

Corn ranks second to oats as a horse feed. It is palatable, nutritious, and rich in energy-producing carbohydrate and fat, but it has certain very definite limitations. It lacks quality (being especially low in the amino acids, lysine and tryptophan) and quantity of proteins (it runs about 9%), and it is deficient in minerals, particularly calcium.

Corn may be fed to horses on the cob, shelled, cracked, as corn-and-cob meal, or flaked.

DRIED BREWERS' GRAINS

Dried brewers' grains are a byproduct of beer production. They are what is left after the sugar and other solubles have been fermented. Dried brewers' grains are lower in energy and higher in protein and fiber than some other grains; they are a wholesome, nutritious, and palatable feed for horses.

MOLASSES (CANE OR BEET)

Molasses is a byproduct of sugar factories, with cane molasses coming from sugarcane and beet molasses coming from sugar beets. Cane molasses is slightly preferred to beet molasses for horses, although either is satisfactory.

For horses, molasses is 80 to 95% as valuable as oats, pound for pound. However, molasses is used primarily as an appetizer.

In hot, humid areas, molasses should be limited to 5% of the ration; otherwise, mold may develop. Where mustiness is a problem, add calcium propionate to the feed according to the manufacturer's directions.

OATS

Oats are the leading U.S. horse feed. They normally weigh 32 lb per bushel, but the best horse oats are heavier. The feeding value varies according to the hull content and test weight per bushel.

Because of their bulky nature, oats form a desirable loose mass in the stomach, which prevents impaction.

Oats may be rolled, crimped, or fed whole. Hulled oats are particularly valuable in the ration for young foals.

Oat groats, oats with the hull removed, are excellent for foal rations, but they are relatively high in price.

SORGHUM (MILO)

The production of grain sorghum has increased in the United States in recent years; and with more production, increased feeding to horses has followed. Properly used, it is a good horse feed. In comparison with the other commonly used cereal grains fed to horses, sorghum grain is more variable in protein content, less palatable (because of the presence of tannic acid), and has a harder seed. The small, round grain should be steam rolled, coarsely crimped, or coarsely ground.

WHEAT

When the price is favorable, wheat may be fed to horses. In comparison with the other cereal grains, it is higher in protein. Wheat should be rolled or coarsely cracked. In order to lessen the possibility of colic, wheat should be limited to 20% of the concentrate and fed in combination with more bulky feeds.

WHEAT BRAN

Wheat bran is the coarse outer covering of the wheat kernel. It contains a fair amount of protein (averaging about 16%) and a good amount of phosphorus. Bran is valuable for horses because of its bulky nature and laxative properties. Also, it is very palatable. However, high levels of wheat bran have been associated with nutritional secondary hyperparathyroidism (big head disease); attributed to the high phosphorus content of wheat bran, resulting in a calcium/phosphorus imbalance. So, wheat bran should not constitute more than 10 to 15% of the concentrate portion of the ration.

PROTEIN SUPPLEMENTS

The extent to which the horse's ration is supplemented with proteins depends primarily on the age of the horse and on the quality of the forage fed. Growing or lactating animals require somewhat more protein than horses that are idle, gestating, or working. Also, grass hays and farm grains are generally low in quality and quantity of proteins and require more supplementation than legumes.

In practical horse feeding, foals should be provided with some protein feeds of animal origin in order to supplement the proteins found in grains and forages. In feeding mature horses, a safe plan to follow is to provide plant protein from several sources.

In general, feeds of high protein content are more

expensive than those high in carbohydrates or fats. Accordingly, there is a temptation to feed too little protein. On the other hand, when protein feeds are the cheapest—as is often true of cull peas in certain sections of the West—excess quantities of them may be fed as energy feeds without harm, provided the ration is balanced in all other respects. Any amino acids that are left over, after the protein requirements have been met, are deaminated or broken down in the body. In this process, a part of each amino acid is turned into energy, and the remainder is excreted via the kidneys.

The following oil meals are most commonly used as protein supplements for horses: cottonseed meal, linseed meal, soybean meal, sunflower meal, and rapeseed meal (canola meal).

COTTONSEED MEAL

Among the oilseed meals, cottonseed meal ranks second in tonnage to soybean meal.

The protein content of cottonseed meal can vary from about 22% in meal made from undecorticated (unhulled) seed to 60% in flour made from seed from which the hulls have been removed completely. Thus, in screening out the residual hulls, which are low in protein and high in fiber, the processor is able to make a cottonseed meal of the protein content desired—usually 41, 44, or 50%.

Cottonseed meal is low in lysine and tryptophan and deficient in vitamin D, carotene (vitamin A value), and calcium. Also, unless glandless seed is used, it contains a toxic substance known as gossypol, varying in amounts with the seed and the processing. But, it is rich in phosphorus.

Some prejudices to the contrary, good grade cottonseed meal is satisfactory for mature horses. But, because of its deficiency in lysine and tryptophan, young, growing horses do not gain as rapidly or efficiently when fed cottonseed meal as when fed soybean meal.

LINSEED MEAL

Linseed meal is a byproduct of flaxseed following oil extraction by either of two processes: (1) the mechanical process (what is known as the "old process"); or (2) the solvent process ("new process"). If solvent extracted, it must be so designated. Equestrians prefer the mechanical process, for the remaining meal is more palatable, has a higher fat content, and imparts more gloss to the hair coat.

Linseed meal averages about 35% protein content. For horses, the proteins of linseed meal do not effectively make good the deficiencies of the cereal grains—linseed meal being low in the amino acids lysine and tryptophan. Also, linseed meal is lacking in carotene and vitamin D, and is only fair in calcium and the B vitamins. Because of its deficiencies, linseed meal should not be fed to horses as the sole protein supplement.

Because of its laxative nature, linseed meal in limited quantities is a valuable addition to the ration of horses. Also, it imparts a desirable "bloom" to the hair of show and sale animals.

SOYBEAN MEAL

Soybean meal, processed from the soybean, is the most widely used protein supplement in the United States. It is the ground residue (soybean oil cake or soybean oil chips) remaining after the removal of most of the oil from soybeans. The oil is extracted by either of three processes: (1) the expeller process; (2) the hydraulic process; or (3) the solvent process. Although a name descriptive of the extraction process must be used in the brand name, well-cooked soybean meal produced by each of the extraction processes is of approximately the same feeding value.

Soybean meal normally contains 41, 44, or 50% protein, according to the amount of hull removed; and the proteins are of better quality than the other protein-rich supplements of plant origin. It is low in calcium, phosphorus, carotene, and vitamin D.

Soybean meal is satisfactory as the only protein supplement to grain for mature horses, providing a high-quality ground legume is incorporated in the ration and adequate sources of calcium and phosphorus are provided. For foals, it is best that a dried milk byproduct be included.

SUNFLOWER MEAL

The development of high oil-yielding varieties by Russian scientists has stirred worldwide interest in the use of sunflowers as an oilseed crop. Some of these varieties yield over 50% oil.

Sunflower meal (41% protein or better) can be used as a protein supplement for horses provided (1) it is good quality, and (2) care is taken to supply adequate lysine, for sunflower meal is low in this amino acid. When incorporated in well-balanced rations, properly processed sunflower meal of good quality may supply up to one-third of the protein supplement of horses.

RAPESEED MEAL (CANOLA MEAL)

Rape is adapted to cold climates; to northern Europe and Asia, Canada, and Northern United States.

In common with other members of the *Brassica* species, rapeseed contains goitrogenic compounds called glucosinolates. Fortunately, selected cultivars of rape have been developed which are low in glucosinolates. In Canada, the low glosinate cultivars that they developed are called *canola*.

Solvent extracted rapeseed (canola) meal runs about 41-43% protein on a moisture-free basis. It is used as a protein supplement for all animal species, including horses.

UREA

It is recognized that horses frequently consume urea-containing cubes and blocks intended for cattle and sheep, particularly on the western range. Moreover, it appears that mature horses are able to do so without untoward effects. The latter observation was confirmed in one limited experiment[13] in which four horses consumed an average 4.57 lb per day of a urea-containing supplement, or 0.55 lb/head/day of feed urea (262%), for five months. Also, the Louisiana Station[14] did not find urea detrimental or toxic to horses when it constituted up to 5% of the grain ration, with up to 0.5 lb per day of urea consumed. There are reports, however, of urea toxicity in foals, in which bacterial action is more limited than in older horses.

Thus, there is some evidence that non-protein nitrogen (urea) can be substituted for protein in the diet of the horse, but the conversion to protein is inefficient. Up to 5% of urea in the total ration does not appear to be harmful to mature horses. Nevertheless, in recognition of the more limited bacterial action in the horse and the hazard of toxicity—especially to young equines, most state laws forbid the use of such nonprotein nitrogen sources as urea in horse rations.

SPECIAL FEEDS AND ADDITIVES

Special horse feeds may be needed from time to time for promoting growth of young stock, preventing diseases, or imparting bloom and attractiveness.

ANTIBIOTICS

The newer knowledge of antibiotics—products of molds, bacteria, and green plants—dates from the discovery of penicillin by Dr. Alexander Fleming, a British scientist, in 1928.[15] Quite by accident, a stray mold spore floated in the breeze, and landed on a culture plate of bacteria with which Dr. Fleming was working. It inhibited the growth of the bacteria. Dr. Fleming correctly interpreted his observation—the possible value of the mold in the treatment of disease, thus ushering in the antibiotic era. However, penicillin did not come into prominence until 10 years later, and it was not until 1944 that streptomycin, the second most widely known of the antibiotics, was discovered by Waksman, a soil microbiologist, and his colleagues at the New Jersey Station.

Antibiotics are not nutrients; they're drugs. They are chemical substances, produced by molds or bacteria, which have the ability to inhibit the growth of or to destroy other microorganisms.

The author was a member of the research team that conducted the first U.S. study on feeding antibiotics to foals, which study was subsequently used in obtaining Food and Drug Administration (FDA) approval for feeding Aureomycin to foals. This experiment revealed that an 85 milligram level of Aureomycin, fed to foals from 5 days of age to 5 months, produced 22 lb more weight.[16]

Certain antibiotics, at stipulated levels, are approved by the FDA for growth promotion and for the improvement of feed efficiency of young equines up to one year of age. Unless there is a disease level, however, there is no evidence to warrant the continuous feeding of antibiotics to mature horses. Such practice may even be harmful. Hence, where antibiotics are needed for therapeutic purposes, it is best to seek the advice of a veterinarian.

It appears that antibiotics may be especially helpful for young foals which suffer setbacks from infections, digestive disturbances, inclement weather, and other stress factors. Also, horses may benefit from antibiotics (1) when being transported from one location to another—for example, when being moved to a new show or track; (2) when there is a low disease level in the herd; or (3) when mares are foaling.

The poorer the feed, the greater the response from antibiotics; and the poorer the management, the greater the response from antibiotics. It follows, therefore, that there is a temptation to use antibiotics as a "crutch," rather than improve the regimen.

When added to feed, the level of antibiotics should be in keeping with the directions of the manufacturer and with the Food and Drug Administration regulations.

BLOOM-IMPARTING FEEDS

Bloom or gloss is important in horses. But sometimes they lack this desired quality—their hair is dull and dry. Feeding a well-balanced ration will usually

[13]*Veterinary Medicine*, Vol. 58, No. 12, Dec., 1963, pp. 945-946.

[14] "Non-Toxicity of Urea Feeding to Horses," *Veterinary Medicine/Small Animal Clinician*, Nov. 1965.

[15]Actually, the presence of antibiotics was known much earlier than the discovery of penicillin, but no commercial use was made of them.

[16]Wash. Ag. Exp. Sta. Circ. 263, April 1955.

rectify this situation. Also, feeding the following products will make for an attractive, shiny coat:

1. **Corn oil or safflower oil.** Feed at the rate of 2 oz (2 tbsp) per horse twice per day.

2. **Whole flaxseed soaked.** Put a handful of whole flaxseed in a teacup, cover it with water, let it stand overnight, then pour it over the morning feed. Repeat twice each week.

Unless the horse is afflicted with lice, mange, or some other ailment, either of the above treatments will impart bloom or gloss to the coat.

LYSINE

Protein quality is important for horses. Because of more limited amino acid synthesis in the horse than in ruminants, plus the fact that the cecum is located beyond the small intestine—the main area for digestion and absorption of nutrients, it is generally recommended that high quality protein rations, adequate in amino acids, be fed to equines. This is especially important for young equines, because cecal synthesis is very limited in early life.

Fortunately, the amino acid content of proteins from various sources varies. Thus, the deficiencies of one protein may be improved by combining it with another, and the mixture of the two proteins often will have a higher feeding value than either one alone. It is for this reason, along with added palatability, that a considerable variety of feeds in the horse ration is desirable.

Cornell University reported that the addition of lysine to the diet of growing horses increased weight gains, feed consumption, and feed efficiency.

In recognition that lysine is the first limiting amino acid of horses and is thus an indicator of the quality of protein which horses require, the recommended lysine allowance for horses is given in Table 13-2.

MILK BYPRODUCTS

The superior nutritive values of milk byproducts are due to their high-quality proteins, vitamins, a good mineral balance, and the beneficial effect of the milk sugar, lactose. In addition, these products are palatable and highly digestible. They are an ideal feed for young equines and for balancing out the deficiencies of the cereal grains. Most foal rations contain one or more milk byproducts, primarily dried skim milk, with some dried whey and dried buttermilk included at times. The chief limitation to their wider use is price.

MILK REPLACER

As indicated by the name, a milk replacer is a replacement for milk. Such replacers generally contain the following composition: animal or vegetable fat, 17–20%; crude soybean lecithin, 1–2%; skimmed milk solids, 78–82% (10–15% dried whey powder can be included in place of an equivalent amount of skimmed milk solids); plus fortification with minerals and vitamins.

Foals suckling their dams generally develop very satisfactorily up to weaning time. But the most critical period in the entire life of a horse is that space from weaning time (about six months of age) until one year of age. This is especially so in the case of young horses being fitted for shows or sales, where condition is so important. Thus, where valuable weanlings or yearlings are to be shown or sold, the use of a milk replacer may be practical.

TREATS

Horses are fed a great variety of treats. On a government horse breeding establishment in Brazil, the author saw a large, well-manicured vegetable garden growing everything from carrots to melons, just for horses. Also, trainers recognize that most racehorses, which are the *prima donnas* of the equine world, don't "eat like a horse"; they eat like people—and sometimes they're just as finicky. Their menus may include a choice of carrots or other roots, fruit, pumpkins, squashes or melons, sugar or honey, and innumerable other goodies.

Ask equestrians why they feed treats to their horses and you'll get a variety of answers. However, high on the list of reasons will be (1) as appetizers; (2) as a source of nutrients and as conditioners; (3) as rewards; (4) as a means of alleviating obesity (dieting of the horse); or (5) folklore.

TREATS AS APPETIZERS

If a horse doesn't eat his feed, it won't do him any good. Hence feed consumption is important.

Sooner or later, a caretaker is bound to get one of those exasperating equines that just refuses to clean up its feed. Perhaps it will eat a few bites, then stop; or maybe it won't even touch the "stuff." Sometimes this happens to race and show horses that started training in great physical shape, only to lose appetite and have to be taken out of training for rest.

Lots of things can cause finicky eaters; among them, (1) stress and nervousness, (2) an unpalatable and monotonous ration, (3) nutritional deficiencies, (4) poor health, and (5) lack of exercise. Whatever the cause, the condition(s) making for poor feed consumption should be rectified—if it can be determined, and if it is within the power of the caretaker to correct it. Additionally, there should be incorporated in the ration something that the horse really likes—such as carrots or other roots; molasses, sugar, or honey; or sliced fruit.

But treats can be overdone. Hence, a horse should not be permitted to eat too much of any treat, simply because it likes it.

TREATS AS A SOURCE OF NUTRIENTS

Sometimes, even nutritionists overlook the fact that, when evaluated on a dry matter basis, high water content tubers, fruits, and melons have almost the same nutrient value as the cereal grains. This becomes apparent in the following table which gives the energy value on a moisture-free basis of several horse treats compared with barley, corn, oats, and timothy. (See Table 13-8).

TABLE 13-8
ENERGY VALUE OF SEVERAL FEEDS ON A MOISTURE-FREE BASIS

| Feed | Water | Dry Matter | Energy Value (TDN) | |
			As Fed	Moisture-Free Basis
	(%)	(%)	(%)	(%)
Barley	10	90	77	85
Corn	10	90	80	90
Oats	11	89	68	76
Timothy hay, mature	14	86	41	48
Apples	82	18	13	74
Carrots	88	12	10	82
Melons	94	6	5	80
Potatoes	79	21	18	85
Sugar beets	87	13	10	77

Generally speaking, horse treats are not a good buy when evaluated on a cost per unit of nutrient content (protein, energy, etc.) basis. This becomes obvious when it is realized that it takes nearly 7 lb of carrots to equal 1 lb of oats in energy value, primarily because of the difference in water content of the two feeds. Occasionally, such products as carrots are in surplus or not suited for human consumption. At such times, they may be available for as little as $2 to $3 per ton, in which case they are a good buy in comparison with grains. Even then, it is best that they not replace more than 10 to 20% of the normal grain ration. For the most part, however, treats are fed to horses because they possess qualities that cannot be revealed by a chemical analysis—because of their values as appetizers, in aiding digestion, and as conditioners.

TREATS AS REWARDS

The training of horses is based on a system of rewards and punishment. This doesn't mean that the horse is fed a tidbit each time he obeys, or that he is beaten when he refuses or does something wrong.

But horses are big and strong; hence, it's best that they want to do something, rather than have to be forced. Also, too frequent or improper use of such artificial aids as whips, spurs, reins, and bits makes them less effective; worse yet, it will likely make for a mean horse.

Horses appreciate a pat on the shoulder or a word of praise. However, better results may be obtained by working on an equine's greediness—his fondness for such things as carrots or a sugar cube. Also, treats may be used effectively as rewards to teach some specific thing such as posing, or to cure a vice like moving while the rider is mounting; but this should not be overdone.

TREATS TO ALLEVIATE OBESITY

Horses are equine athletes; hence, they should be lean and hard, rather than fat and soft. Obese horses should be avoided because (1) they lack agility, (2) excessive weight puts a strain on the musculoskeletal system, (3) it lowers fertility in broodmares and stallions, (4) fat horses are prone to founder, and (5) overweight horses are more susceptible to azoturia.

Such watery feeds as carrots and melons are filling, but low in calories. This becomes obvious when it's realized that (1) it takes more than 8 lb of fresh carrots to produce 1 lb of dried product, and (2) it takes nearly 7 lb of carrots or over 13 lb of melons to furnish as much energy as 1 lb of oats. Thus, when used as a "salad" for the horse, carrots or melons are as effective as slenderizers for equines as they are for humans.

TREATS FOR FOLKLORE REASONS

Among the bagful of the equestrian's secrets, sometimes the claim is made that apple cider will prolong life, increase vigor, and improve sex drive, fertility, and reproduction. However, there isn't a shred of evidence, based on studies conducted by a reputable experiment station, to substantiate such claims. Of course, it's good to have faith in something; and, too, nature is a wonderful thing. It is estimated that 70 to 80% of all horses with afflictions would recover even without treatment.

APPLES AND OTHER FRUITS

An apple a day is good for a horse, especially

when used as a tidbit or reward. They are very palatable because of their sugar content. However, the feeding of apples can be overdone; many a case of colic, or even death, has resulted from old dobbin's stolen visit to the orchard.

Also, peaches, plums, and pears are occasionally used as treats for the horse. The seeds of stone fruits should always be removed prior to feeding.

CARROTS AND OTHER ROOTS

Carrots are relished by horses. Additionally, they're succulent, and high in carotene and minerals. Each pound of fresh carrots contains 48 milligrams of carotene, which can be converted into 26,640 IU of vitamin A by the young equine, sufficient vitamin A to meet the daily requirement of a 1,000-lb horse. By contrast, 1 lb of timothy hay (mature) provides only 2.1 milligrams of carotene or 1,165 IU, which is only one–twenty-sixth of the daily vitamin A requirement for a 1,000-lb horse. Also, carrots are a good source of minerals; on a dry basis 1 lb contains 0.42% calcium and 0.34% phosphorus, whereas mature timothy hay as fed contains 0.17% and 0.15% of these elements, respectively. Additionally, carrots are high in sugar; on a dry basis they contain 40% sugar (invert), which explains their sweetness.

Caretakers have long fed carrots, especially during the winter months when green feeds are not available, and to horses that are stabled much of the time. They report that 1 to 2 lb of carrots per horse per day will stimulate the appetite, increase growth, assist in reproduction, make for normal vision, and improve the health, coat, and attractiveness of the animal.

Carrots should be cleaned, sliced from end to end in small strips, so as to avoid choking, then mixed with the grain.

Other roots such as parsnips, rutabagas, turnips, potatoes, and sugar beets may be fed to horses in small amounts, provided they are first cut finely enough to avoid choking.

MOLASSES, SUGAR, AND HONEY

The horse has a "sweet tooth"; or at least he readily cultivates a taste for sweets. Hence, when added to the ration, molasses, sugar, and honey make for a "sweet feed," or appetizer. For this reason, small amounts (usually about 5%) of molasses, sugar, or honey are sometimes added to the concentrate mixture for racehorses, show horses, and other finicky eaters. Once a horse becomes accustomed to a sweet feed, it is difficult to eliminate it from the ration; in fact, if the sweets are suddenly deleted, the horse may refuse to eat altogether. Thus, if for any reason sweets must

be taken out of the ration, the change should be very gradual.

Also, sugar cubes are a good and convenient reward, provided too many of them are not used and the tendency of nipping or biting is avoided.

PUMPKINS, SQUASHES, AND MELONS

Pumpkins, squashes, and melons are sometimes used as relish for horses. They contain only 6 to 10% dry matter; hence, their nutritive value on a wet basis is low in comparison with cereal grains. When fed in the usual amounts, their seeds are not harmful to horses, some opinions to the contrary. However, an entire ration of seeds alone is apt to cause indigestion, because of their high fat content.

PALATABILITY OF FEED

Palatability is important, for horses must eat their feed if it is to do them any good. But many horses are finicky simply because they are spoiled. For the latter, stepping up the exercise and halving the ration will usually effect a miraculous cure.

Also, it seems possible that well-liked feeds are digested somewhat better than those which are equally nutritious, but less palatable.

Palatability is particularly important when feeding horses that are being used hard, as in racing or showing. Unless the ration is consumed, such horses will obtain insufficient nutrients to permit maximum performance. For this reason, lower quality feeds, such as straw or stemmy hay, should be fed to idle horses.

Familiarity and habit are important factors concerned with the palatability of horse feeds. For example, horses have to learn to eat pellets, and very frequently they will back away from feeds with new and unfamiliar odors. For this reason, any change in feeds should be made gradually.

Occasionally, the failure of a horse to eat a normal amount of feed is due to a serious nutritive deficiency. For example, if horses are fed a ration made up of palatable feeds, but deficient in one or more required vitamins or minerals, they may eat normal amounts for a time. Then when the body reserves of the lacking nutrient(s) are exhausted, they will usually consume much less feed, due to an impairment of their health and a consequent lack of appetite. If the deficiency is not continued so long that the horses are injured permanently, they will usually recover their appetites if some feed is added which supplies the nutritive lack and makes the ration complete.

PALATABILITY OF THE PROTEIN SUPPLEMENT

Where a protein supplement lacks palatability, the situation can usually be corrected by increasing the salt content of the supplement to 3%. The reasoning back of increasing the salt is this: Whatever the cause of the unpalatability in a supplement may be (particularly if it is one of the ingredients), it is apt to show up more in the supplement than in other feeds, simply because it is more concentrated. The high salt content usually overcomes the unpalatability and adequate consumption follows. Of course, one should not go higher than 2% in a concentrate or in an all-pelleted ration because higher levels of salt are unpalatable, but up to 3% salt in a supplement fed at a level of 1 to 2 lb per horse per day will usually work wonders.

PALATABILITY CHECKLIST

Here is a checklist, along with the author's comments, where there appears to be a palatability problem with a horse feed:

1. **Quality of feeds.** Make very certain on this point. It is almost impossible to detect through a chemical analysis many factors that may lower quality, such as "heated grain" and poor quality hay.

2. **Mustiness.** Again, check with care. Remember that horses can detect mustiness more quickly and easily than people.

3. **Hard pellets.** If pellets are too hard, horses will spit them out.

4. **Flavors.** In some cases, flavors will help in overcoming the lack of palatability due to poor quality feeds, but they will do little to enhance good quality feeds.

5. **Your premix.** Check on the "carrier" and premix ingredients which your feed manufacturer is using in his horse feeds. The author recalls one incident where dried fish meal was being used in a premix as a source of unidentified factors; and an unpalatable ration resulted because of the poor quality of the fish meal in the premix.

6. **The formulation.** Of course, some feeds are more palatable to horses than others. Among the well-liked feeds are wheat bran and molasses, both of which are usually incorporated in horse rations.

DISTANCE LENDS ENCHANTMENT TO FEEDS

Distance lends enchantment! Many equestrians not only believe that there is something magical about certain horse feeds, but they think that they must be grown in a specific area.

For example, timothy hay and oats are frequently extolled on the basis that they are grown in certain "name" areas; they are even referred to as "racehorse oats" or "racehorse timothy hay." Such specialty areas may produce superior products, but their feeding value is generally exaggerated far beyond their price with much of their added cost going for hundreds of miles of transportation and for several handlers.

CHEMICAL ANALYSIS OF FEEDS

Feed composition tables ("book values"), or average analysis, should be considered only guides, because of wide variations in the composition of feeds. For example, the protein and moisture content of milo and hay are quite variable. Wherever possible, especially with large operations, it is best to take a representative sample of each major feed ingredient and have a chemical analysis made of it for the more common constituents—protein, fat, fiber, nitrogen-free extract, and moisture; and often calcium, phosphorus, and carotene. Such ingredients as the oil meals and prepared supplements, which often must meet specific standards, need not be analyzed as often, except as quality control measures.

Despite the recognized value of a chemical analysis, it is not the total answer. It does not provide information on the availability of nutrients to the animal; it varies from sample to sample, because feeds vary and a representative sample is not always easily obtained; and it does not tell anything about the associated effect of feedstuffs. Nor does a chemical analysis tell anything about taste, palatability, texture, undesirable physiological effects such as digestive disturbances, and laxativeness. Thus, one cannot buy feed for horses on the basis of chemical analysis alone. However, a chemical analysis does give a solid foundation on which to start evaluating feeds. Also, with chemical analysis at hand, and bearing in mind that it is the composition of the total feed (the finished ration) that counts, the person formulating the ration can determine more intelligently the quantity of protein to buy, and the kind and amounts of minerals and vitamins to add.

TERMS USED IN ANALYSES AND GUARANTEES

Knowledge of the following terms is requisite to understanding analyses and guarantees:

■ **Dry matter** is found by determining the percentage of water and subtracting the water content from 100%.

■ **Crude protein** is used to designate the nitrogenous constituents of a feed. The percentage is obtained by multiplying the percentage of total nitrogen by the factor 6.25. The nitrogen is derived chiefly from complex chemical compounds called amino acids.

■ **Crude fat** is the material that is extracted from moisture-free feeds by ether. It consists largely of fats and oils with small amounts of waxes, resins, and coloring matter. In calculating the heat and energy value of the feed, the fat is considered 2.25 times that of either nitrogen free extract or protein.

■ **Crude fiber** is the relatively insoluble carbohydrate portion of a feed consisting chiefly of cellulose. It is determined by its insolubility in dilute acids and alkalis.

■ **Ash** is the mineral matter of a feed. It is the residue remaining after complete burning of the organic matter.

■ **Nitrogen-free extract** consists principally of sugars, starches, pentoses and nonnitrogenous organic acids. The percentage is determined by subtracting the sum of the percentages of moisture, crude protein, crude fat, crude fiber, and ash from 100.

■ **Carbohydrates** represent the sum of the crude fiber and nitrogen-free extract.

■ **Calcium** and **phosphorus** are essential mineral elements that are present in feeds in varying quantities. Mineral feeds are usually high in source materials of these elements.

■ **TDN**—The digestible nutrients of any ingredient are obtained by multiplying the percentage of each nutrient by the digestion coefficient. For example, dent corn contains 8.9% protein of which 77% is digestible. Therefore, the percent of digestible protein is 6.9.

The TDN is the sum of all the digestible organic nutrients—protein, fiber, nitrogen-free extract, and fat (the latter multiplied by 2.25).

CALCULATING CHEMICAL ANALYSIS

Most of the larger feed manufacturers maintain strict product control. Among other things, they sample and analyze their feeds from time to time, as a means of satisfying themselves that they are meeting their guarantees.

Smaller manufacturers who do not have their own chemical laboratories usually use a commercial laboratory; or, in some states, the college of agriculture provides a feed testing laboratory service on a nominal charge basis. Caretakers can also check any feed in this same manner.

An actual chemical analysis is always best when it comes to checking a guarantee. However, where the pounds of each ingredient in a mixed feed are known, the chemical analysis can be calculated. Of course, with closed formula feeds this is not possible.

Table 13-9 and the discussion that follows show how to calculate the chemical analysis of a protein supplement for horses.

TABLE 13-9
A HORSE PROTEIN SUPPLEMENT

Ingredients	Lb/1,000-Lb Batch	Lb of Crude Protein	Lb of Fat	Lb of Fiber
	(lb)	(lb)	(lb)	(lb)
Linseed meal	80	28	4.8	6.4
Soybean meal	320	146	4.2	18.9
Dried skimmed milk	50	16.5	0.5	—
Alfalfa meal, 17% dehy	105	18.4	2.7	26.3
Wheat bran	100	16.4	4.5	10.0
Hominy feed	157.5	16.9	10.2	7.9
Molasses (cane)	100	3.0	—	—
Salt	7.5	—	—	—
Dical	42.5	—	—	—
Vit.-trace min. premix	37.5	—	—	—
	1,000.0	245.2	26.9	69.5

Step by step, here's how the calculation in Table 13-9 was done:

1. The ingredients were listed in the first column, followed in the second column with the pounds of each ingredient in a batch (the size batch need not total 1,000 lb; it could be 100 lb; 1 ton, or any other quantity).

2. By using a feed ingredient table, a calculation was made of the number of pounds each of protein, fat, and fiber furnished by each ingredient, this was recorded in the proper column. For example, 80 lb of linseed meal × 35.0% protein = 28 lb of protein in 80 lb of linseed meal.

3. The sum of each column gives the total number of pounds of protein, fat, and fiber in the particular batch.

4. To obtain the percentage of protein, fat, and fiber, each total was divided by the total pounds in the batch as follows:

a. Protein $\dfrac{245.2 \times 100}{1,000}$ = 24.52% protein

b. Fat $\dfrac{26.9 \times 100}{1,000}$ = 2.69% fat

c. Fiber $\dfrac{69.5 \times 100}{1,000}$ = 6.95% fiber

For these percentages, the suggested guarantees would be:

	Guarantee	
	(Min.)	(Max.)
Crude protein	24%	
Fiber		7.5%
Fat	2.5%	

FEED PREPARATION

The physical preparation of cereal grains for horses has been practiced by caretakers for a very long time. Generally speaking, feed is processed in order to increase palatability and digestibility, and to facilitate handling. Basically, grain is either soaked, cooked, ground, rolled (wet or dry), pelleted (cubed), or sprouted; and hay is either fed long, or pelleted (with the grain and hay combined), or cubed.

Pelleted feeds may be prepared from concentrates alone, from forage alone, or from concentrates and forage combined in a complete ration.

A summary relative to each of the common methods of feed preparation for horses follows.

DRY ROLLING, CRIMPING, AND GRINDING

These methods can be and are used in preparing horse feeds. The important thing is to keep the grain as coarse as possible and to avoid fines.

FLAKING

Flaking, which is the modification of steam rolling in which the grain is subjected to steam for a longer period of time, is the preferred method of processing grains for horses. It produces light, fluffy particles, which result in fewer digestive disturbances than any other method of feed preparation.

The flaking process varies according to the grain.

Fig. 13-19. Milo properly steam rolled into dustless flakes. (Courtesy, Dr. Al Lane, Extension Livestock Specialist, The University of Arizona; from *Horse Feeding*, Circular 288, The University of Arizona)

For example, corn is usually steamed for approximately 20 minutes at a temperature of 200°F, with a moisture content of about 18%. The grain that responds the most to flaking is milo, which is generally flaked as follows: the grain is subjected to 20 lb of steam pressure for 20 to 25 minutes, at approximately 205°F; then at 18 to 20% moisture content, it is run through large rollers operated at one-third to one-half capacity and rolled to thin flakes. The end product has a distinct and pleasant aroma, resembling cooked cereal.

HAY CUBES

This refers to the practice of compressing long or coarsely cut hay in cubes or wafers, which are larger and coarser than pellets. Most cubes are about 1¼ in. square and 2 in. long, with a bulk density of 30 to 32 lb per cubic foot. Cubing costs about $5 per ton more than baling.

This method of haymaking is increasing, because it (1) simplifies haymaking, (2) facilitates automation, (3) lessens transportation costs and storage space—cubed roughages require about one-third as much space as when the forage is baled and stacked, and (4) decreases nutrient losses.

From a nutrition standpoint, hay cubes are as satisfactory as hay in any other form (long or baled). However, some equestrians report occasional choking from feeding cubes.

HYDROPONICS (SPROUTED GRAIN)

Hydroponics (or sprouted grain) is the growing of plants with their roots immersed in an aqueous solution containing the essential mineral nutrient salts, instead of in soil. This means that sprouted grain for feed is produced with water and chemicals, without dirt.

The Michigan Agricultural Experiment Station made a study of sprouted oats as a feed for dairy cows. As a result of this experiment, the Michigan scientists concluded as follows:[17]

The cost of sprouted oats was over four times that of the original oats or similar grains. This high cost plus (1) the loss in nutrients during sprouting, (2) the decreased digestibility of sprouted oats, and (3) no observed increase in milk production when sprouted oats were added to an adequate ration indicate that this feed has no justification for being included in any modern dairy ration.

---

[17]Report from *Quarterly Bulletin*, Vol. 44, No. 4, Michigan State University, East Lansing, pp. 654-665.

The findings of the Michigan study are likely to be applicable to other classes of livestock.

Without doubt, sprouted grains will give an assist when added to poor rations—and the poorer the ration, the bigger the boost.

PELLETED COMPLETE FEED

Currently, equestrians are much interested in complete, all-pelleted feed, in which the hay and grain are combined. Compared to conventional long hay and grain concentrate fed separately, all-pelleted feed has the following advantages:

1. It is less bulky and easier to store and handle, thus lessening transportation, building, and labor costs. Pelleted roughage requires one-fifth to one-third as much space as is required by the same roughage in loose or chopped form.

2. Pelleting prevents horses from selectively refusing ingredients likely to be high in certain dietary essentials; each bite is a balanced feed.

3. Pelleting practically eliminates waste; therefore, less pelleted feed is required. Horses may waste up to 20% of long hay. Waste of conventional feed is highest where low quality hay is fed or feed containers are poorly designed.

4. Pelleting eliminates dustiness and lessens the likelihood of heaves.

5. Pellet-fed horses are trimmer in the middle and more attractive because they consume less bulk.

6. Pellets lessen pollution. Pelleting lessens the manure by about 25%, simply because of less wastage and lower feed consumption; hence, it lessens pollution. Since a 1,000-lb horse normally produces about 8 tons of manure, free of bedding, per year, this is an important consideration in the present environment-conscious era. Thus, an all-pelleted ration will result in about 2 tons less manure per horse per year.

The following points are pertinent to the proper understanding and use of all-pelleted rations:

1. One-half-in. pellets are preferred for mature horses and ¼-in. pellets for weanlings and short yearlings. Also, very hard pellets should be avoided; if horses cannot chew them, they will not eat them.

2. The ratio of roughage to concentrates should be higher in all-pelleted rations than when long hay is fed. For most horses, the ratio may range from 60.5% roughage to 39.5% concentrate up to 69% roughage to 31% concentrate.

3. Any horse feed should form a loose mass in the stomach to assure ease of digestion, fewer digestive disturbances, and less impaction. To this end, in a complete all-pelleted ration, such feeds as oats and barley should be crimped or steam rolled but not finely ground. The roughage should be ¼-in. chop or coarser. Otherwise, a couple of pounds of long hay may be fed daily to each horse.

4. Young horses and horses at heavy work need more energy. They should be fed less roughage and more concentrate.

5. When less roughage and more concentrate is fed, horses are likely to be overfed and get too fat if they are idle or at light to medium work. But if the total feed consumption is limited too severely to keep the weight down, the problem of wood chewing is increased because of a lack of physical filling of the digestive tract.

6. When the roughage consists of high-quality legume hay, a higher percentage of roughage may be used than when all or part of the roughage is grass or other nonlegumes.

7. If more energy is needed for racing or young stock on an all-pelleted ration, it can be provided either by increasing the daily allowance of the all-pelleted ration, and/or replacing a portion of the all-pelleted ration with a suitable concentrate or supplement.

8. Because waste is eliminated, less all-pelleted feed is required than conventional feed. For a horse at light work, give 14 to 18 lb of all-pelleted feed daily per 1,000 lb of body weight. Use a feed that contains 51 to 58% total digestible nutrients (TDN). Increase the feed allowance with the severity of work.

9. As with any change in feed, the switch to an all-pelleted ration should be made gradually, otherwise such vices as wood chewing and bolting (eating feed too rapidly) may be induced. At first, continue to offer all the long hay the horse wants and slowly replace the grain portion of the conventional ration with the complete pelleted feed. Increase the pelleted feed by 1 to 2 lb daily and begin gradually lessening the hay. After a few days, the horse usually will stop eating the hay and it can be removed completely from the ration.

10. The feces of pellet-fed horses are softer than the feces of those not fed pellets.

ALL-PELLETED RATIONS AND WOOD CHEWING

Among many equestrians, the feeling persists that horses on all-pelleted rations are more prone to wood chewing than those fed on hay. Perhaps this is true—at least to some degree. But wherever there is wood, some horses will chew it, regardless of what they are fed. This stems from the fact that pellet-fed horses have more time to indulge in vices, simply because they can eat an all-pelleted ration more quickly than where long hay is involved. As a result, they get bored; and, to pass the time, they chew wood. (Also, see later section entitled, "Pica—Wood Chewing.")

PELLETED GRAINS-CONCENTRATES

Grains and other concentrates are sometimes pelleted for the purposes of (1) facilitating mechanization in handling; (2) eliminating fines and dust, and increasing palatability; (3) alleviating sifting out and sorting; (4) increasing feed density; (5) reducing storage space; and (6) making it possible to feed on the ground or in windy areas with little loss.

Pelleting is accomplished by (1) grinding the material finely (and usually steaming it, also), then (2) forcing it through a thick die. Pellets can be made into small chunks or cylinders of different diameters, lengths, and degrees of hardness. Large pellets—especially those large enough to be fed on pasture or range—are commonly called cubes.

The following concentrates may be pelleted: (1) the entire concentrate; (2) the fines only, with the grains flaked; (3) the protein supplement; and (4) pasture supplements.

STEAM ROLLING

If properly done, steam rolling of grains is preferred to grinding for horses. However, there is great variation in steam rolling. Altogether too much steam rolling consists in exposing the grain to steam for 3 to 5 minutes, using a temperature of about 180°F, and adding an unknown amount of moisture. Such processing is little better than dry rolling.

Desirable steam flaking consists of subjecting the grain to steam under atmospheric conditions for 15 to 30 minutes, followed by rolling. This produces a flat flake with 16 to 20% moisture.

Desirable pressure flaking consists of subjecting the grain to steam under pressure for a short time (such as 50 psi for 1 to 2 minutes) and a temperature approaching 300°F, then cooling below 200°F and drying below 20% moisture, followed by rolling.

RATIONS

Correctly speaking, a ration is the amount of feed given to a horse in a day, or a 24-hour period. To most caretakers, however, the word implies the feeds fed to an animal without limitation of the time in which they are consumed.

To supply all the needs of horses—maintenance, growth, fitting, reproduction, lactation, and work—the different classes of horses must receive sufficient feed to furnish the necessary quantity of energy (carbohydrates and fats), protein, minerals, vitamins, and water. A ration that meets all these needs is said to be balanced. More specifically, by definition, *a balanced ration is one which provides an animal the proper proportions and amounts of all the required nutrients for a period of 24 hours.* Moreover, the feed must be palatable—horses must like it. The rations listed in Table 13-10 meet these standards. Also, liberal margins of safety have been provided to compensate for variations in feed composition, environment, possible losses of nutrients during storage, and differences in individual animals.

HOME-MIXED FEEDS

A horse feeding guide is given in Table 13-10. In selecting rations, compare them with commercial feeds. If only small quantities are required or little storage space is available, it may be more satisfactory to buy ready-mixed feeds.

The quantities of feeds recommended in Table 13-10, in the column headed "Daily Allowance," are intended as guides only. For example, the caretaker should increase the feed, especially the concentrates, when the horse is too thin and decrease the feed if it gets too fat.

Sudden changes in the diet should be avoided, especially when changing from a less concentrated ration to a more concentrated one. When this rule of feeding is ignored, digestive disturbances result and the horse goes "off feed." In either adding or omitting one or more ingredients, the change should be made gradually. Likewise, caution should be exercised in turning horses to pasture or in transferring them to more lush grazing.

In general, horses may be given as much non-legume roughage as they will eat. But they must be accustomed gradually to legumes because legumes may be laxative.

In feeding horses, as with other classes of livestock, it is recognized that nutritional deficiencies (especially deficiencies of certain vitamins and minerals) may not be of sufficient proportions to cause clear-cut deficiency symptoms. Yet, such deficiencies without outward signs may cause great economic losses because they go unnoticed and unrectified. Accordingly, sufficient additives (especially minerals and vitamins) should always be present, but care should be taken to avoid imbalances.

SUGGESTED RATIONS

Table 13-10 contains some suggested rations for different classes of horses. This is merely intended as a general guide. The feeder should give consideration to (1) the quality, availability, and cost of feeds; (2) the character and severity of the work; and (3) the age and individuality of the animal.

TABLE 13-10
LIGHT HORSE FEEDING GUIDE[1]

Age, Sex, and Use	Daily Allowance	Kind of Hay	Suggested Grain Rations		
			Rations No. 1	Rations No. 2	Rations No. 3
			(lb)	(lb)	(lb)
Stallions in breeding season (weighing 900 to 1,400 lb)	0.75 to 1.5 lb grain per 100 lb body weight, together with a quantity of hay within same range.	Grass-legume mixed; or one-third to one-half legume hay, with remainder grass hay.	Oats . . . . 55 Wheat . . . . 20 Wheat bran . . . . 20 Linseed meal 5	Corn . . . . 35 Oats . . . . 35 Wheat . . . . 15 Wheat bran 15	Oats 100
Pregnant mares (weighing 900 to 1,400 lb)	0.75 to 1.5 lb grain per 100 lb body weight, together with a quantity of hay within the same range.	Grass-legume mixed; or one-third to one-half legume hay, with remainder grass hay (straight grass hay may be used first half of pregnancy).	Oats . . . . 80 Wheat bran 20	Barley . . . . 45 Oats . . . . 45 Wheat bran 10	Oats . . . . 95 Linseed meal 5
Foals before weaning (weighing 100 to 350 lb with projected mature weights of 900 to 1,400 lb)	0.5 to 0.75 lb grain per 100 lb body weight, together with a quantity of hay within same range.	Legume hay.	Oats . . . . 50 Wheat bran . . . . 40 Linseed meal . . . 10	Oats . . . . 30 Barley . . . . 30 Wheat bran . . . . 30 Linseed meal . . . 10	Oats . . . . 80 Wheat bran 20
			Rations balanced on basis of following assumption: Mares of mature weights of 600, 800, 1,000, and 1,200 lb may produce 36, 42, 44, and 49 lb of milk daily.		
Weanlings (weighing 350 to 450 lb)	1 to 1.5 lb grain and 1.5 to 2 lb hay per 100 lb body weight.	Grass-legume mixed; or one-half legume hay, with remainder grass hay.	Oats . . . . 30 Barley . . . . 30 Wheat bran . . . . 30 Linseed meal 10	Oats . . . . 70 Wheat bran . . . . 15 Linseed meal . . . 15	Oats . . . . 80 Linseed meal . . . 20
Yearlings, second summer (weighing 450 to 700 lb)	Good, luxuriant pastures. (If in training for other reasons without access to pastures, the ration should be intermediate between the adjacent upper and lower groups.)				
Yearlings, or rising 2-year-olds, second winter (weighing 700 to 1,000 lb)	0.5 to 1 lb grain and 1 to 1.5 lb hay per 100 lb body weight.	Grass-legume mixed; or one-third to one-half legume hay, with remainder grass hay.	Oats . . . . 80 Wheat bran 20	Barley . . . . 35 Oats . . . . 35 Bran . . . . 15 Linseed meal . . . 15	Oats 100
Light horses at work; riding, driving, and racing (weighing 900 to 1,400 lb)	Hard use—1.25 to 1.33 lb grain and 1 to 1.25 lb hay per 100 lb body weight. Medium use—0.75 to 1 lb grain and 1 to 1.25 lb hay per 100 lb body weight. Light use—0.4 to 0.5 lb grain and 1.25 to 1.5 lb hay per 100 lb body weight.	Grass hay.	Oats 100	Oats . . . . —70 Corn 30	Oats . . . . 70 Barley 30
Mature idle horses; stallions, mares, and geldings (weighing 900 to 1,400 lb)	1.5 to 1.75 lb hay per 100 lb body weight.	Pasture in season; or grass-legume mixed hay.	(With grass hay, and 0.75 lb of a high-protein supplement daily.)		

[1]With all rations and for all classes and ages of horses, provide free access to a mineral box as follows: (1) *Where the pasture or hay is primarily grass*, use a mixture containing 2 parts of calcium to 1 part of phosphorus; and (2) *where the pasture or hay is primarily a legume*, use a mixture containing 1 part of calcium to 1 part of phosphorus. To each of these mixes, add one-third salt (trace mineralized) to improve acceptability. If preferred, a good commercial mineral may be used. Self-feed salt separately.

AMOUNT OF ROUGHAGE

Actually, a horse does not need any hay. Also, more horses receive too much roughage than not enough, as evidenced by hay bellies (distended digestive tracts), quick tiring, and labored breathing.

Under most conditions, the roughage requirement of horses ranges from 0.5 to 1.0% of body weight, or from 5 to 10 lb of roughage daily for a 1,000-lb horse.

HOW TO BALANCE A RATION[18]

Generally speaking, the rations given in Table 13-10 will suffice, especially if similar feeds are substituted in some cases. However, good equestrians should know how to balance a ration. Then, if the occasion demands, they can do so. Perhaps of even greater importance, they will then be able more intelligently to select and buy rations with informed appraisal, to check on how well their manufacturer (or dealer) is meeting guarantees, and to evaluate the results.

The author has already made clear his position relative to "nutritive requirements" vs "recommended allowances" for horses (see earlier section under "Nutrient Requirements Vs Allowances"). Hence, the stated allowances given in the two examples that follow are his "recommended allowances," and not "minimum requirements."

Two problems are stated here, followed by their solutions—as an exercise on how to balance a ration.

Problem No. 1: Prepare a balanced ration for a 1,000-lb lactating mare, at the peak of lactation.

Step by step, here is how it's done:

1. **Set down the desired allowances.** In order to balance a ration, it is first necessary to know what allowances we wish to meet. Here they are for a 1,000 lb lactating mare (see Table 13-2).

Daily feed	Crude protein	TDN	Calcium	Phosphorus
(lb)	(%)	(%)	(%)	(%)
25	14	75	0.47	0.30

2. **Apply the trial-and-error method.** Next, let us see if we can meet these desired allowances by using a ration of equal parts of oats and timothy hay.

---

[18]For more complete instructions on how to balance rations, including balancing rations by computer and other methods, see *Feeds & Nutrition*, 2nd ed., and *Feeds & Nutrition Digest*, 2nd ed.; chapter 18 in both books.

	Daily feed	Crude protein	TDN	Calcium	Phosphorus
	(lb)	(%)	(%)	(%)	(%)
Timothy hay (late cut) .	12.5	6.8	39	0.36	0.21
Oats	12.5	8.6	36	0.29	0.22
	25.0	7.7	38	0.33	0.22

Upon checking the above with step 1 (the allowances that we wish to meet), it is quite obvious that a ration of equal parts of timothy hay and oats is very unsatisfactory for the 1,000-lb lactating mare; it is much too low in protein, TDN, calcium, and phosphorus. The only requisite that it meets is to provide 25 lb of feed daily.

3. **Let's add some other ingredients.** Oats and timothy hay can be used, provided they are balanced with certain other ingredients. Here's how:

Ingredients	Daily feed	Crude protein	TDN	Calcium	Phosphorus
	(lb)	(%)	(%)	(%)	(%)
Timothy hay (late cut)	8.7	6.8	39	0.36	0.21
Oats	2.0	11.9	65	0.08	0.34
Alfalfa meal sun cured	2.0	20.1	56	2.32	0.24
Corn (Grade No. 2) . .	0.8	8.9	61	0.02	0.29
Molasses (cane)	2.5	4.3	61	1.04	0.42
Linseed meal (solv.) .	2.0	35.7	67	0.40	0.82
Soybean meal (solv.) .	3.0	49.0	75	0.35	0.64
Fat	3.6		209		
Salt	0.1				
Dicalcium phosphate .	0.2			27.00	19.07
Premix min. vit.	0.1				
	25.0	14.4	75.8	0.71	0.46

This is an excellent ration. It contains adequate amounts of protein, TDN, calcium, and phosphorus; and the calcium to phosphorus ratio is a very excellent 1.5:1.

Problem No. 2: A horse breeder grows oats and alfalfa-bromegrass hay. He/she wants to balance these feeds out for a 450-lb weanling, 10 months of age—using 49% soybean oil meal, fat, and ground oyster shell.

Step by step, here is the answer to Problem No. 2:

1. **Set down the desired allowances.** Here they are for a 450-lb weanling (see Table 13-2):

Daily feed	Crude protein	TDN	Calcium	Phosphorus
(lb)	(%)	(%)	(%)	(%)
12	16	75.0	0.55	0.30

2. **Apply the trial-and-error method.** To start with, let's estimate that about 1.5 lb of 49% soybean

oil meal, 1.3 lb of fat, and 0.05 lb of ground oyster shell will balance this ration:

Ingredients	Daily feed (lb)	Crude protein (%)	TDN (%)	Cal-cium (%)	Phos-phorus (%)
Alfalfa-brome hay	4	14.1	45	1.02	0.25
Oats	5.2	11.9	65	0.08	0.34
Fat	1.3		209		
49% soybean meal	1.5	49.0	77	0.25	0.63
Ground oyster shell	0.5			35.85	0.1
	12.05	16	75.4	0.56	0.31

This is a good ration. Note that it meets the protein, TDN (energy), calcium, and phosphorus needs; and that the Ca:P ratio is an acceptable 1.8:2.

FEED SUBSTITUTION TABLE

Successful equestrians are keen students of values. They recognize that feeds of similar nutritive properties can and should be interchanged in the ration as price relationships warrant, thus making it possible at all times to obtain a balanced ration at the lowest cost.

Table 13-11, Feed Substitution Table for Horses, is a summary of the comparative values of the most common U.S. feeds used for horses. In arriving at these values, chemical composition, feeding value, and palatability have been considered.

In using this feed substitution table, the following facts should be recognized:

1. That, for best results, different ages of animals should be fed differently.

TABLE 13-11
FEED SUBSTITUTION TABLE FOR HORSES (AS-FED BASIS)

Feedstuffs	Relative Feeding Value (lb for lb) in Comparison with the Designated Base Feed (in bold italic) Which = 100	Maximum Percentage of Base Feed (or comparable feed or feeds) Which it Can Replace for Best Results	Remarks
GRAINS, BYPRODUCT FEEDS, ROOTS, AND TUBERS:[1] (Low and Medium Protein Feeds)			
Oats	*100*	*100*	The leading grain for horses. The feeding value of oats varies according to the hull content and test weight per bushel. Need not be ground.
Barley	110	100	Most caretakers feel that it is preferable to feed barley along with more bulky feeds; for example, 25% oats or 15% wheat bran. Crush for horses.
Beet pulp, dried	100	33.33	Not palatable to horses.
Beet pulp, molasses, dried	100	33.33	Not palatable to horses.
Brewers' dried grains	100	50	
Carrots	15–25	10	Horses are very fond of carrots.
Corn, No. 2	115	100	Ranks second to oats as a light horse feed.
Corn gluten feed (gluten feed)	100	50	It has a lower value than indicated when forage is of low-protein content.
Distillers' dried grains	90–100	25	
Distillers' dried solubles	90–100	25	
Hominy feed	115	100	
Molasses, beet	85–95	10	In hot, humid areas, molasses should be limited to 5%; otherwise, mold may develop unless an inhibitor is used. Cane molasses is slightly preferred to beet molasses.
Molasses, cane	80–95	10	In hot, humid areas, molasses should be limited to 5%; otherwise, mold may develop unless an inhibitor is used.
Peas, dried	100	40	
Rice (rough rice)	115	50	Grind for horses.

(Continued)

TABLE 13-11 (Continued)

Feedstuffs	Relative Feeding Value (lb for lb) in Comparison with the Designated Base Feed (in bold italic) Which = 100	Maximum Percentage of Base Feed (or comparable feed or feeds) Which it Can Replace for Best Results	Remarks
GRAINS, BYPRODUCT FEEDS, ROOTS, AND TUBERS:[1] (Low and Medium Protein Feeds) (Continued)			
Rye	115	33.33	Higher levels or abrupt changes to rye may cause digestive disturbances. Not palatable.
Sorghum, grain	110–115	85	All varieties have about the same feeding value. Crush for horses.
Wheat	115	50	Wheat should be mixed with a more bulky feed in order to prevent colic.
Wheat bran	100	20	Valuable for horses because of its bulky nature and laxative properties.
Wheat-mixed feed (mill run)	105	20	Excessive quantities will cause colic or other digestive upsets.
PROTEIN SUPPLEMENTS:			
Linseed meal (35%)	*100*	*100*	Linseed meal (old process) is the preferred protein supplement for horses. It is valued because of its laxative properties and because of the sleek hair coat which it imparts.
Brewers' dried grains	65–70	50	
Buttermilk, dried	100	100	May be used in place of dried skimmed milk for foals.
Copra meal (coconut meal); (21%)	90–100	50	
Corn gluten feed (gluten feed)	70	100	
Corn gluten meal (gluten meal)	100	50	Somewhat unpalatable to horses.
Cottonseed meal (41%)	100	100	Satisfactory if limited to amount necessary to balance ordinary rations.
Peanut meal (45%)	100	100	
Peas, dried	75	50	
Skimmed milk, dried	100	100	Especially valuable for young equines; for creep feeding until past weaning.
Soybean meal (41%)	100	100	
Soybeans	100	100	Soybeans should be limited to one-third of the concentrate ration.
Sunflower meal (41%)	100	33.33	Sunflower meal should not constitute more than one-third of the protein supplement for palatability reasons.
Whey, dried	50	50	Whey may be laxative.
DRY FORAGES AND SILAGES:[2]			
Timothy hay	*100*	*100*	The preferred hay of caretakers.
Alfalfa hay, all analyses	133.33	100	Good quality alfalfa hay is excellent for horses. Alfalfa may be ground and pelleted. It provides high-quality proteins, and certain minerals and vitamins. It is somewhat laxative. Contrary to some "old wives' tales," it will not damage the kidneys.
Barley hay	100	100	Lower value if not cut at the early dough stage.
Bromegrass hay	100	100	
Clover hay, crimson	125	100	Crimson clover hay has considerably lower value if not cut at an early stage.

(Continued)

TABLE 13-11 (Continued)

Feedstuffs	Relative Feeding Value (lb for lb) in Comparison with the Designated Base Feed (in bold italic) Which = 100	Maximum Percentage of Base Feed (or comparable feed or feeds) Which it Can Replace for Best Results	Remarks
DRY FORAGES AND SILAGES: (Continued)			
Clover hay, red	125	100	Clover hay should be well cured and free from dust and mold.
Clover-timothy hay	110–115	100	Value of clover-timothy mixed hay depends on the proportion of clover present and the stage of maturity at which it is cut.
Corn fodder	100	50	Preferably fed along with a good legume hay. It is best to shred the fodder.
Corn silage	45–55	33.33–50	
Corn stover	60	50	Preferably fed along with a good legume hay. It is best to shred the stover.
Cowpea hay	110	100	
Grass-legume mixed hay	110–115	100	
Grass-legume silage	45–50	33.33–50	
Grass silage	40–45	33.33–50	
Johnsongrass hay	90–95	100	
Lespedeza hay	115	100	
Oat hay	100	100	Lower value if not cut at the early dough stage.
Orchardgrass	100	100	Should be cut before maturity.
Prairie hay	100	100	
Reed canarygrass	90–95	100	
Sorghum fodder	100	50	Preferably fed along with a good legume hay. It is best to shred the fodder.
Sorghum silage	40–45	33.33–50	
Sorghum stover	60	50	Preferably fed along with a good legume hay. It is best to shred the stover.
Soybean hay	110	100	
Sudangrass hay	90–95	100	
Vetch-oat hay	110–115	100	The higher the proportion of vetch, the higher the value.
Wheat hay	100	100	

[1]Roots and tubers are of lower value than the grain and byproduct feeds due to their higher moisture content.

[2]Well preserved silage of good quality, free from mold and not frozen, affords a highly nutritious succulent forage for horses during the winter months—especially for idle horses, broodmares, and growing colts. Silages are of lower value than dry forages due to their higher moisture content.

2. That individual feeds differ widely in feeding value. Barley and oats, for example, vary widely in feeding value according to the hull content and the test weight per bushel, and forages vary widely according to the stage of maturity at which they are cut and how well they are cured and stored.

3. That nonlegume forages may have a higher relative value to legumes than herein indicated pro-vided the chief need of the animal is for additional energy rather than for supplemented protein. Thus, the nonlegume forages of low value can be used to better advantage for wintering mature horses than for young foals.

On the other hand, legumes may have a higher actual value relative to nonlegumes than herein indicated provided the chief need is for additional protein rather than for added energy. Thus, no protein supplement is necessary for broodmares provided a good quality legume forage is fed.

4. That, based primarily on variable supply and price, certain feeds—especially those of medium protein content, such as brewers dried grains, distillers dried solubles, and peas (dried)—are used interchangeably as (a) grains and byproduct feeds, and/or (b) protein supplements.

5. That the feeding value of certain feeds is materially affected by preparation. The values herein reported are based on proper feed preparation in each case.

For these reasons, the comparative values of feeds shown in the feed substitution table (Table 13-11) are not absolute. Rather, they are reasonably accurate approximations based on average-quality feeds.

PRIMARY COMMERCIAL HORSE FEEDS AND COMMERCIAL MINERALS

In 1995, 116.6 million tons of primary commercial feeds were marketed in the U.S. *A primary feed is a feed mixed with individual feed ingredients, sometimes with the addition of a premix at the rate of up to 100 lb per ton of finished feed.* Of the 116.6 million tons of primary commercial feeds, the following percentages were used for each class of animals:

Poultry	49.99%
Beef cattle/sheep	16.91%
Dairy cattle	13.40%
Swine	12.85%
All others, including horses	6.85%

Horses are not big users of commercial feeds for two reasons: (1) the small number of horses in comparison with most other classes of animals, and (2) most horsemen feed grain, often with a supplement added; and hay.

Commercial mineral mixes are minerals mixed by manufacturers who specialize in the commercial mineral business, either handling minerals alone or a combination of feeds and minerals.

The commercial manufacturer has the distinct advantages of (1) purchasing ingredients (feeds or minerals) in quantity lots, making possible price advantages, (2) economical and controlled mixing, (3) the hiring of scientifically trained personnel for use in determining formulations, and (4) quality control. Most equestrians have neither the know-how nor the quantity of business to provide these services on their own. In fact, due to the small quantities of feed and mineral usually involved and the complexities of horse rations

and minerals, they have more reason to rely on good commercial products than do owners of other classes of farm animals and poultry. Because of these several advantages, commercial feeds and minerals are finding a place of increasing importance in horse feeding.

The nutritive requirements of horses vary according to age, weight, use or demands, growth, stage of gestation or lactation, and environment. Also, part of the horse ration may be homegrown.

Good commercial minerals supply only the specific elements that are deficient, and in the quantities necessary. Excesses and mineral imbalances are avoided.

HOW TO EVALUATE A COMMERCIAL FEED AND A COMMERCIAL MINERAL

There is a difference in commercial feeds and minerals! That is, there is a difference from the standpoint of what a horse owner can purchase with his/her feed or mineral dollars. The smart caretaker will know how to determine what constitutes the best in commercial feeds or minerals for his/her specific needs. The feeder will not rely solely on how the feed looks and smells. The most important factors to consider or look for in buying a commercial feed or mineral are:

1. **The specific needs.** Feed needs vary according to (a) the class, age, and productivity of horses, and (b) whether animals are fed primarily for maintenance, growth, fattening (or show-ring fitting), reproduction, lactation, or work (running).

The mineral requirements of horses are much the same everywhere, although it is recognized that age, pregnancy, and lactation make for differences. Additionally, there are some area differences. For example, the Northern Great Plains and the Southwest are generally recognized as phosphorus-deficient areas—their grasses and hays are usually low in phosphorus. Accordingly, a high-phosphorus mineral is needed for horses in such areas—one containing 10 to 15% phosphorus.

The wise operator will buy different formula feeds and minerals for different needs.

2. **The reputation of the manufacturer.** This may be determined by conferring with the other caretakers who have used the particular product and checking on whether or not the commercial feed or mineral under consideration has consistently met its guarantees. The latter can be determined by reading the bulletins or reports published by the respective state departments in charge of enforcing feed laws.

3. **Flexible formulas.** Feeds and minerals with flexible formulas are usually the best buy. This is because the price of ingredients varies considerably from time to time. Thus, a good feed manufacturer will shift formulas as prices change, in order to give the horse owner the most for the money. This is as it should

be, for (a) there is no one best ingredient, and (b) if substitutions are made wisely, the price of the feed or mineral can be kept down, and the caretaker will continue to get equally good results.

4. **What's on the tag?** Equestrians should be able to study and interpret what's on the feed or mineral tag. Does the product contain what's needed? Fig. 13-20 shows a feed tag taken from a foal ration. The reverse side of this particular tag contained feeding directions.

```
┌─────────────────────────────────────────┐
│           ( B R A N D   X )              │
├─────────────────────────────────────────┤
│         (Net Weight 50 pounds)           │
├─────────────────────────────────────────┤
│         GUARANTEED ANALYSIS              │
│                                          │
│ Crude Protein, not less than ...... 21.00% │
│ Crude Fat, not less than ..........  2.00% │
│ Crude Fiber, not more than ........  9.00% │
│ Ash, not more than ................  9.00% │
│ Added Mineral, not more than ......  3.00% │
│ Calcium, not less than ............  1.00% │
│ Phosphorus, not less than .........  0.75% │
│ Salt, not more than ...............  0.50% │
│ Iodine, not less than .......... 0.00035% │
│ TDN, not less than ............... 68.00% │
└─────────────────────────────────────────┘
```

Ingredients: Rolled Oats, Dried Whey, Soybean Meal, Cottonseed Meal, Linseed Meal, Dehydrated Alfalfa Meal, Wheat Bran, Wheat Shorts, Wheat Flour, Cane Molasses, Bone Meal, Iodized Salt, Distillers Dried Grains with Solubles, Alfalfa Leaf Meal, Condensed Fish Solubles (dried), Brewers Dried Yeast, Streptomycin Mycelia Meal, Vitamin A Palmitate with Increased Stability, Fleischman's Irradiated Dry Yeast (Source of Vitamin D-2), d-Alpha-Tocopherol Acetate (Source of Vitamin E), Choline Chloride, Ferrous Carbonate, Niacin, Calcium Pantothenate (Source of d-Pantothenic Acid), Riboflavin Supplement, Copper Oxide, Manganous Oxide, Thiamin, Sulphur, Menadione Sodium Bisulfate (Source of Vitamin K), Calcium Iodate, Folic Acid, Cobalt Carbonate, Vitamin B-12 Supplement, Preserved withEhtoxyquin (1, 2-dihydro-6-ethoxy-2, 2, 4-trimethyl-quinoline), Anise.

FEEDING DIRECTIONS–SEE OTHER SIDE

Manufactured by
ADAIR MILLING COMPANY
(Address and Phone Number)

Fig. 13-20. Feed tag.

An analysis of Fig. 13-20 reveals the following:

a. The brand or name of the feed.

b. The net weight.

c. The guaranteed analysis, each stated in percent, in minimum crude protein and crude fat; maximum crude fiber, ash, and minerals; minimum calcium and phosphorus; maximum salt; and minimum iodine and TDN. But guaranteed analysis, within itself, will not suffice. For example, on the basis of chemical composition, soft coal (9.06% crude protein) and coffee grounds (11.23% crude protein) are comparable in protein content to many

commonly used grains. Yet, no one would be so foolish as to feed these products to horses.

d. The ingredients, (the constituent material making up the feed) listed in descending order of amounts, by weight. This type of listing aids in making decisions as the possible quality of the feed. For example, if feather meal, which contains 85% protein by analysis, were listed (which it is not in the above feed), it could be concluded that the horse would obtain little nutritional advantage from this type of ration component. All ingredients listed in the above ration are good, and each one appears to contribute needed nutrients.

e. The name, address, and phone number of the manufacturer.

f. The feeding directions on the reverse side.

Many states have slightly different requirements than indicated by the tag just analyzed. Some require both the minimum and maximum percentage of calcium and salt.

By studying this tag, a knowledgeable user can, readily and easily, see what's in the feed and determine if it will meet the requirements of the horse to which it is to be fed. A similar study and analysis can be made of a mineral tag.

5. **What's the best buy?** When buying a feed or mineral, the equestrian should check price against value received.

■ **Best buy in feeds**—One criterion for determining the best buy in horse feeds is the cost per unit protein. (Likewise, one may compare feeds on the basis of cost per unit energy, or on the basis of cost per unit of both protein and energy.)

Example: Two horse feeds are under consideration, which we shall call brand "X" and brand "Y."

Brand X contains 10% crude protein and sells at $5 per hundredweight. How much can you afford to pay for brand Y which has 14% protein (and other likely plus values that we shall discuss later)?

COMPARATIVE VALUES OF FEEDS—BRANDS X AND Y
(Based on Protein Content Alone)

Brand	Crude Protein	Price/cwt	Cost/lb Protein
	(%)	($)	(¢)
X	14	7.00	50
Y	10	5.00	50

This shows that if 10% crude protein horse feed sells at $5 per cwt, one could afford to pay $7 per cwt for a 14% crude protein feed, based on the added value of the protein alone. And that's not all! As a usual thing, if a horse ration is scientifically formulated from the standpoint of quantity of protein, it will also have other plus values, among them:

1. Quality of proteins (the essential amino acids).
2. Energy.
3. Minerals, vitamins, and unidentified factors—which are adequate, without imbalances.
4. Palatability and digestibility. Although horses must like feeds well enough to eat them, it is recognized that—

   a. Palatability is, in part, a matter of habit—of being used to a certain feed. For this reason, changes in horse feeds should be made gradually.

   b. It does not necessarily follow that everything is good for a horse just because he likes it.
5. The end result—superior performance.

In other words, when a ration is deficient in one category—in protein, for example—you're apt to be short-changed all along the line.

■ **Best buy in minerals**—One criterion for determining the best buy in horse minerals is the cost per unit of one or more elements.

Example: Let's assume that the main need is for phosphorus, and that we wish to compare two minerals which we shall call brand "X" and brand "Y." Brand X contains 12% phosphorus and sells at $8.50 per hundredweight, whereas brand Y contains 10% phosphorus and sells for $8.00 per hundredweight. Which is the better buy?

COMPARATIVE VALUES OF MINERALS—BRANDS X AND Y
(Based on Phosphorus Content Alone)

Brand	Phosphorus	Price/cwt	Cost/lb Phosphorus
	(%)	($)	(¢)
X	12	8.50	71
Y	10	8.00	580

Hence, brand X is the better buy, even though it costs 50¢ more per hundred.

One other thing is important: As a usual thing, the more scientifically formulated mineral mixes will have plus values in terms of (a) trace mineral (needs and balance), and (b) palatability (horses will eat just the right amount of a good mineral, but they won't overdo it—due to appetizers, rather than needs).

Commercial mineral mixtures costing 60 to 80¢ per pound of phosphorus are not excessively priced. If the average consumption per horse per month of a mineral mix costing $8.50 per hundredweight is 3 lb, the monthly per head cost will be about 26¢, or less than 1¢ per horse per day.

RESULTS MORE IMPORTANT THAN COST PER BAG

As is true when buying anything—whether it be a suit of clothes, a dinner, or whatnot—horse feed should be bought on a quality basis, rather than what is cheapest—results are more important than cost per bag. If this were not so, one might well buy and feed many cheap products, including sawdust.

Consideration should be given to meeting the specific needs of the horse, with special attention given to providing adequate quantity and quality proteins, minerals, vitamins, unidentified factors, and palatability.

SWEET FEED

Sweet feed refers to a feed to which has been added one or more ingredients that are sweet. Most commonly, it is molasses (approximately 10%); although brown sugar (about 5%) is sometimes used, and occasionally honey.

Horses have a "sweet tooth"; hence, it's not easy to switch them from a sweet feed to what may be a more nutritious ration. Of course, manufacturers of sweet feed would have it that way. Also, it must be remembered that sweet feeds are a way in which feed manufacturers may, should they so desire, make poor quality feed ingredients more appetizing.

Further, and most important, not everything is good for a horse just because he likes it. In this respect an analogy may be made to boys and girls. If given a choice between a well balanced diet and candy, most boys and girls will take the latter; yet, few parents or MDs would be so foolish as to say that sweets are good for them. The same can be said relative to the sweet feeds and concoctions fed to horses.

STATE COMMERCIAL FEED LAWS

Nearly all the states have laws regulating the sale of commercial feeds. These benefit both the horse owner and reputable feed manufacturers. In most states, the laws require that every brand of commercial feed sold in the state be licensed, and that the chemical composition be guaranteed.

Samples of commercial feeds are taken each year, and analyzed chemically in the state's laboratory to determine if manufacturers lived up to their guarantees. Additionally, skilled microscopists examine the sample to ascertain that the ingredients present are the same as those guaranteed. Flagrant violations on the latter point may be prosecuted.

Results of these examinations are generally published, annually, by the state department in charge of such regulatory work. Usually, the publication of the guarantee alongside any short-changing is sufficient to cause the manufacturer promptly to rectify the situation, for such public information soon becomes known to both users and competitors.

Additionally, most commercial feed laws stipulate the following:

■ **Medicated feed tags and labels**—Medicated feeds (those which contain drug ingredients intended or represented for the cure, mitigation, treatment, or prevention of diseases of animals) must also carry the following information in their labeling: (1) the purpose of the medication; (2) directions for the use of the feed; (3) the names and amounts of all active drug ingredients; (4) a warning or caution statement for a withdrawal period when required for the particular drug contained in the feed; and (5) warnings against misuse.

■ **Vitamin product labels**—When a product is marketed as a vitamin supplement per se, the quantitative guarantees (unit/pound) of vitamins A and D are expressed in USP units; of E in IU; and of other vitamins in milligrams per pound.

■ **Mineral product labels**—Some states require that all minerals except salt (NaCl) be quantitatively guaranteed in terms of percentage of the element(s); others require milligrams per pound.

■ **Other rules and regulations**—Generally, the following rules and regulations apply in the different states:

1. The brand or product name must not be misleading.
2. The sliding scale or range (for example 15% to 18% crude protein) method of expressing guarantees is prohibited.
3. Ingredient names are those adopted by the Association of American Feed Control Officials.
4. The term *dehydrated* may precede the name of any product that has been artificially dried.
5. Urea and ammonium salts of carbonic and phosphoric acids cannot be used in horse feeds.

ART OF FEEDING

Feeding horses is both an art and a science. The art is knowing how to feed and how to take care of each horse's individual requirements. The science is meeting the nutritive requirements with the right combination of ingredients.

AMOUNT TO FEED

The main qualities desired in horses are trimness, action, spirit, and endurance. These qualities cannot be obtained with large, paunchy stomachs or lack of energy, which may result from excessive use of roughage. Moreover, a healthy condition is desired, but excess fat is to be avoided. The latter is especially true with horses used for racing, where the carrying of any surplus body weight must be avoided.

The quantity of grain and hay required by horses depends primarily upon the following:

1. The individuality—horses vary in keeping qualities, just as people do. Some horses simply utilize their feed more efficiently than others. A hard keeper will require considerably more feed than an easy keeper when doing the same amount of work.
2. The age, size, and condition of the animal.
3. The kind, severity, regularity, amount, and speed of work performed. With greater speed, the horse requires proportionately greater energy; hence, considerably more concentrate is required when performing work at a trot than at a walk.
4. The weather; for example, under ideal October weather conditions in Missouri, a horse may require 14 lb of 60% TDN feed daily, whereas in the same area, the same horse requires 16 lb daily of the same feed in July and August, and 20 lb in the winter.
5. Kind, quality, and amount of feed.
6. System of management.
7. Health, condition, and temperament of the animal.

When given all the feed that they will consume, mature horses will generally eat an amount equivalent to about 2.5% of their body weight. Growing foals and lactating mares eat more heartily—they'll consume up to 3% of their body weight.

Because the horse has a rather limited digestive capacity, the amount of concentrates must be increased and the roughages decreased when the energy needs rise with greater amount, severity, or speed of work. The following are general guides for the daily ration of horses under usual conditions:

1. **For horses at light work** (1 to 3 hours per day of riding or driving), allow ⅖ to ½ lb of grain and 1¼ to 1½ lb of hay per day per 100 lb liveweight.
2. **For horses at medium work** (3 to 5 hours per day of riding or driving), allow ¾ to 1 lb of grain and 1 to 1¼ lb of hay per 100 lb of liveweight.
3. **For horses at hard work** (5 to 8 hours per day of riding or driving), allow about 1¼ to 1⅓ lb of grain and 1 to 1¼ lb of hay per 100 lb of liveweight.

The recommended feed allowance on the basis of animal weight are equally applicable to equines of all sizes, including ponies and donkeys; simply vary as necessary according to the work performed and the individuality of the animal.

As will be noted from these recommendations, the total allowance of concentrates and hay should be within the range of 2.0 to 2.5 lb daily per 100 lb of liveweight. No grain should be left from one feeding to the next, and all edible forage should be cleaned up at the end of each day.

About 6 to 12 lb of grain daily is an average grain ration for a light horse at medium or light work. Racehorses in training usually consume 10 to 16 lb of grain per day—the exact amount varying with the individual requirements and the amount of work. The hay allowance averages about 1 to 1¼ lb daily per 100 lb liveweight, but it is restricted as the grain allowance is increased. Light feeders should not be overworked.

It is to be emphasized that the quantities of feeds recommended above are intended as guides only. The feeder will increase the allowance, especially the concentrates, when the horse is too thin, and decrease the feed when the horse is too fat.

The regular practice of turning horses to pasture at night, on idle days, and in off-work seasons is good for the health and well-being of the animals and decreases the quantity of grain and hay required. If the horse must be confined to the stall on idle days, the grain ration should be reduced by 50% in order to avoid azoturia or other digestive disturbances. When idle, it is also advisable to add some wheat bran to the ration. A mixture of two-thirds grain and one-third bran is quite satisfactory. Many good caretakers regularly give a feeding of bran, either dry or as a wet mash, on Saturday night.

OVERFEEDING

Overfeeding may result in two consequences: if done suddenly, it may cause founder (laminitis, colic, or enterotoxemia); if prolonged, it will likely result in obesity (too fat). Both are bad.

STARTING HORSES ON FEED

Horses must be accustomed to changes in feed gradually. In general, they may be given as much nonlegume roughage as they will consume. But they must be accustomed gradually to high-quality legumes, which may be very laxative. This can be done by slowly replacing the nonlegume roughage with greater quantities of legumes. Also, as the grain ration is increased, the roughage is decreased.

Starting horses on grain requires care and good judgment. Usually, it is advisable first to accustom them to a bulky type of ration; a starting ration with considerable rolled oats is excellent for this purpose.

The keenness of the appetite and the consistency of the droppings are an excellent index of a horse's capacity to take more feed. In all instances, scouring should be avoided.

FREQUENCY, ORDER, AND REGULARITY OF FEEDING

The grain ration usually is divided into three equal feeds given morning, noon, and night. Because a digestive tract distended with hay is a hindrance in hard work, most of the hay should be fed at night. The common practice is to feed one-fourth of the daily hay allowance at each of the morning and noon feedings and the remaining half at night when the animals have plenty of time to eat leisurely.

Usually the grain ration is fed first and then the roughage. This way, the animals can eat the bulky roughages more leisurely.

Horses learn to anticipate their feed. Accordingly, they should be fed at the same time each day. During warm weather, they will eat better if the feeding hours are early and late, in the cool of the day.

AVOID SUDDEN CHANGES

Sudden changes in diet should be avoided, especially when changing from a less concentrated ration to a more concentrated one. If this rule of feeding is ignored, horses have digestive disturbances and go off-feed. When ingredients are added or omitted, the change should be made gradually. Likewise, caution should be exercised in turning horses to pasture or in transferring them to more lush grazing.

Sometimes caretakers experience difficulty in switching horses from an overly sweet or highly flavored feed to a more nutritious ration. But the end results usually justify the effort.

ATTENTION TO DETAILS PAYS

The successful equestrian pays great attention to details. In addition to maintaining the health and comfort of animals, he/she should also give consideration to their individual likes and temperaments.

It is important to avoid excessive exercise to the point of fatigue and undue stress. Also, rough treatment, excitement, and noise usually result in nervousness and inefficient use of feed.

BOLTING FEED

Horses that eat too rapidly are said to be bolting their feed. It can be lessened by spreading the concentrate thinly over the bottom of a large grain box, so that the horse cannot get a large mouthful; or by placing in the grain box a few smooth stones about the size of baseballs, so that the horse has to work to get feed.

EATING BEDDING

Sometimes gluttonous animals eat their bedding. This is undesirable because (1) most bedding materials are low in nutritional value, and (2) feces soiled bedding adds to the parasite problem. The problem can be alleviated by muzzling the horse.

FEEDING SYSTEMS

Most horses are hand-fed. The grain ration usually is divided into three equal feeds given morning, noon, and night. Because a digestive tract distended with hay is a hindrance in hard work, most of the hay should be fed at night. The common practice is to feed one-fourth of the daily hay allowance at each of the morning and noon feedings and the remaining one-half at night when the animals have plenty of time to eat leisurely.

A few caretakers self-feed high-energy rations, but, sooner or later, they usually founder a valuable horse. Except for the use of reasonably hard salt-protein blocks, salt-free mixes in meal form (never in pellet form), or high-roughage rations, the self-feeding of horses is not recommended.

GENERAL FEEDING RULES

In addition to the guides already mentioned, observance of the following general rules will help avoid some of the common difficulties:

1. Know the approximate weight and age of each animal.

2. Feed by weight of feed, not by volume (volume as determined by a coffee can or marked bucket). Horses do not require a certain volume of feed; rather, they require a certain weight of nutrients based on their body weight.

3. Avoid sudden changes in the ration.

4. Never feed moldy, musty, dusty, or frozen feed.

5. Feed regularly. Horses anticipate their feed.

6. Look for problems at feeding time; don't just dump the feed and run. Look for injuries and abnormalities.

7. Check the feces. Any change in quantity, odor, color, or composition may presage trouble.

8. Inspect the feedbox frequently to see if the horse goes off feed. Feed refusal means (1) the horse

was over-fed, (2) something is wrong with the feed, or (3) the horse is sick.

9. Keep the feed and water containers clean. Scrub them periodically to insure proper sanitation.

10. Do not overfeed. Some horses suffer from obesity, while others suffer from deficiency. Fat horses not receiving adequate exercise are predisposed to colic and founder. An old Arab proverb cautions: "The two greatest enemies of horses are fat and rest."

11. Force aggressive eaters to slow down. Some horses may bolt their feed when fed in deep narrow feed boxes. Their eating may be slowed by scattering the feed in a larger box, or by placing large round stones, bricks, or salt blocks in the feed container.

12. Accord timid eaters solitude to eat. Feed them where it is quiet and they will not be disturbed.

13. Do not feed from the hand; this can lead to nibbling.

14. Exercise stalled horses daily. It improves their appetite, digestion, and overall well being. This may be accomplished by riding, longeing, walking, ponying, swimming, treadmilling.

15. Avoid excessive exercise (to the point of fatigue and stress), rough treatment, noise, and excitement.

16. Do not feed concentrates 1 hour before or within 1 hour after hard work.

17. Feed horses as individuals; consider their likes and temperaments. Learn the peculiarities and desires of each animal because each one is different.

18. Gradually decrease the condition of horses that have been fitted for show or sale. Many caretakers accomplish this difficult task, and yet retain strong vigorous animals, by cutting down gradually on the feed and increasing the exercise.

19. Prevent wood chewing. This habit usually results from boredom, lack of exercise, lack of adequate roughage, or lack of phosphorus; so, alleviate the causes.

20. Make certain that the horse's teeth are sound.

21. Know the signs of a well-fed, healthy horse, any departure from which constitutes a warning signal.

SIGNS OF A WELL-FED AND HEALTHY HORSE

A well-fed and healthy horse is bright-eyed and bushy-tailed. Additional signs of good nutrition and health are: contentment, alertness, eating with relish, normal productivity, sleek coat and pliable/elastic skin, pink eye membranes, normal feces and urine, maintenance of social organization, and normal temperature, pulse rate, and breathing.

FEEDING PLEASURE HORSES

Keeping pleasure horses—horses used for recreation and sport—in peak condition makes for greater satisfaction when they are used.

It is difficult to feed pleasure horses properly because their use is often irregular. Sometimes they are used moderately; at other times they are idle; at still other times they are worked hard over the weekend or on a trail ride.

Most horses used for pleasure are worked lightly, perhaps 1 to 3 hours of riding per day. Others are worked medium hard, as when ridden 3 to 5 hours per day. Still others are worked very hard, as when raced or when ridden 5 to 8 hours per day. The recommended daily feed allowance per 100 lb body weight of pleasure horses in light, medium, and hard use follows:

Lb Daily/100 lb Weight of Horse	Light Use	Medium Use	Hard Use
Hay	1.25–1.5	1–1.25	1–1.25
Grain	0.4–0.5	0.75–1	1.25–1.33

As shown, the roughage content of the ration decreases and the concentrate content increases as the amount of work increases. This is because the digestibility and the efficiency of conversion are greater for high-energy concentrates than for roughages.

Of course, horses differ in temperament and in ease of keeping. Also, no two horses will perform the same amount of work with an equal expenditure of energy, and no two caretakers will get the same amount of work out of the same horse. So, the feed allowance should be increased if the horse fails to maintain condition, and it should be decreased if the animal becomes too fat.

In season, pasture may replace hay, all or in part, according to the quality of the pasture. But the concentrate allowance of the working horse should remain about the same on pasture as in the stable or dry corral. There is a tendency of the pastured working horse to sweat and tire more easily (be soft), probably due to the high water content of green forage.

In addition to forage and grain, pleasure horses should have access to salt and a suitable mineral mix, free choice.

The mineral requirements of the working horse differ from the idle horse mainly in the salt requirements, due to the loss of salt in perspiration.

The vitamin requirements of working horses are approximately the same as those of idle horses, except for the increase in the B complex requirements due to the greater carbohydrate metabolism of the working horse.

FEEDING HORSES IN TRAINING (EQUINE ATHLETES)

Horses in heavy training for specific purposes—such as training for racing, cutting, roping, jumping, or hunting—have a higher nutritional requirement than most pleasure horses. The younger the animal in training, the higher the level of nutrition needed in order to develop and maintain sound legs and build a strong frame and body. Therefore, the level of work, the temperament of the individual, and the age of the horse determine the nutritional needs.

Horses in training will eat about 1½ lb of grain and 1 lb of hay per 100 lb of liveweight.

Fig. 13-21. Cutting horse in action. Such equine athletes have a higher nutritional requirement than most pleasure horses. (Courtesy, American Quarter Horse Assn., Amarillo, TX)

FEEDING RACEHORSES

It is recognized that some unsoundnesses may be inherited, others may be due to accident and injury, and still others may be due to subjecting horses to stress and strain far beyond the capability of even the best structure and tissue. However, nutritional deficiencies appear to be the major cause of unsoundnesses in racehorses.

Racehorses are equine athletes whose nutritive requirements are the most exacting, but the most poorly met, of all animals. This shocking statement is true because racehorses are commonly handled as follows:

1. Started in training very shortly past 18 months of age, which is comparable to an adolescent boy or girl doing sweatshop labor.

2. Moved from track to track under all sorts of conditions.

3. Trained the year around, raced innumerable times each year, and forced to run when fatigued.

4. Outdoors only a short time each day—usually before sunup, with the result that the sun's rays have little chance to produce vitamin D from the cholesterol in the skin.

5. Without opportunity for even a few mouthfuls of grass—a rich natural source of the B vitamins and unidentified factors.

6. Fed oats, grass hay, and possibly bran—produced in unknown areas, and on soils of unknown composition. Such an oats-grass hay-bran ration is almost always deficient in vitamins A and D and the B vitamins, and lopsided and low in calcium and phosphorus.

7. Given a potion of some concoction of questionable value—if not downright harmful.

By contrast, human athletes—college football teams and participants in the Olympics, for example—are usually required to eat at a special training table, supervised by nutrition experts. They are fed the best diet that science can formulate and technology can prepare. It's high in protein, rich in readily available energy, and fortified and balanced in vitamins and minerals.

It's small wonder, therefore, that so many equine athletes go unsound, whereas most human athletes compete year after year until overtaken by age.

Indeed, high strung and highly stressed, racehorses need special rations just as human athletes do—and for the same reasons; and the younger the age, the more acute the need. This calls for rations high in protein, rich in readily available energy, fortified with vitamins, minerals, and unidentified factors—and with all nutrients in proper balance.

A racehorse is asked to develop a large amount of horsepower in a period of one to three minutes. The oxidations that occur in a racehorse's body are at a higher pitch than in an idle or little-worked horse, and, therefore, more vitamins are required.

Also, racehorses are the prima donnas of the equine world; most of them are temperamental, and no two of them can be fed alike. They vary in rapidity of eating, in the quantity of feed that they will consume, in the proportion of concentrate to roughage that they will take, and in response to different caretakers. Thus, for best results, they must be fed as individuals.

During the racing season, the hay of a racehorse should be limited to 7 or 8 lb, whereas the concentrate allowance may range up to 16 lb. Heavy roughage eaters may have to be muzzled, to keep them from eating their bedding. A bran mash is commonly fed once a week.

FEEDING BROODMARES

Regular and normal reproduction is the basis for profit on any horse breeding establishment. However, only 40 to 60% of mares bred produce foals. There are many causes of reproductive failure, but inadequate nutrition is a major one.

Broodmares should be kept in thrifty condition, but they should not be allowed to become too fat nor too thin. Proper feeding begins with conditioning them prior to the breeding season by providing adequate and proper feed and the right amount of exercise.

Gestating mares need a ration that will meet their own body needs plus (1) the needs of the fetus, or (2) furnishing the nutrients required for milk production. If work is also being performed, additional energy feeds must be provided. Moreover, for the young, growing mare additional proteins, minerals, and vitamins, above the ordinary requirements, must be provided; otherwise, the fetus will not develop normally, or milk will be produced at the expense of tissues of the dam. Also, protein deficiency may affect undesirably the fertility of the mare.

Most of the growth of the fetus occurs during the last third of pregnancy, thus the reproductive requirements—especially the requirements for proteins, minerals, and vitamins—are greatest during this period.

As with the females of all species, the nutritive requirements for milk production in the mare are much more rigorous than the pregnancy requirements. It is estimated that, two months following foaling, mares of mature weights of 600, 800, 1,000, and 1,200 lb may produce 36, 42, 44, and 49 lb of milk daily. Thus, it can be appreciated that a mare's feed requirements during the suckling period are not far different from those of a high-producing dairy cow. In general, it is important that the ration of the gestating-lactating mare supply sufficient energy, protein, calcium and phosphorus; and vitamins A and D (the D being provided through the feed if the animal is not exposed to sunlight), and riboflavin.

The correct feeding of a broodmare that is worked is often simpler than the feeding of an idle one, for the condition of the animal can be regulated more carefully under working conditions. In addition to a ration that will meet the maintenance and work requirements largely through high-energy feeds, the working broodmare needs ample protein, calcium, and phosphorus with which to take care of the growth of the fetus and/or milk production.

The broodmare should be fed and watered with care immediately before and after foaling. For the first 24 hours after parturition, she may have a little hay and a limited amount of water from which the chill has been taken. A light feed of bran or a wet bran mash is suitable for the first feed and the following meal may consist of oats or a mixture of oats and bran. A reasonably generous allowance of good-quality hay is permissible after the first day. If confined to the stable, as may be necessary in inclement weather, the mare should be kept on a limited and light grain and hay ration for about 10 days after foaling. Feeding too much grain at this time is likely to produce digestive disturbances in the mare; and even more hazardous, it may produce too much milk, which may cause indigestion in the foal. If weather conditions are favorable and it is possible to allow the mare to foal on a clean, lush pasture, she will regulate her own feed needs most admirably.

In comparison with geldings or unbred mares, the following differences in feeding gestating-lactating broodmares should be observed:

1. A greater quantity of feed is necessary—usually about 20 to 50% more—the highest requirement being during lactation.

2. Dusty or moldy feed and frozen silage should be avoided in feeding all horses, but especially in feeding the broodmare, for such feed may produce complications and possible abortion.

3. More proteins are necessary for the broodmare.

4. More attention must be given to supplying the necessary minerals and vitamins.

5. The bowels should be carefully regulated through providing regular exercise and feeding such laxative feeds as bran, linseed meal, and alfalfa hay.

6. A few days before and after foaling, the ration should be (a) decreased, and (b) lightened by using wheat bran.

7. Regular and ample exercise is a necessary adjunct to proper feeding of the broodmare.

FEEDING STALLIONS

The ration exerts a powerful effect on sperm production and semen quality. In recognition of this fact, the usual advice given worried stallion owners when the stallion is not a sure breeder is to, "reduce the ration and increase the exercise."

In all too many instances, little thought is given to the feeding and caring for the stallion, other than during the breeding season. The program throughout the entire year should be such as to keep the stallion in a vigorous, thrifty condition at all times. Immediately before the breeding season, the feed might very well be increased in quantity so that the stallion will gain in weight. The quantity of grain fed will vary with the individual temperament and feeding ability of the stallion, the work and exercise provided, services allowed, available pastures, and quality of roughage. Usually, this will be between ¾ and 1½ lb daily of the grain

Fig. 13-22. Proper feeding and exercising enhance stallion fertility. (Courtesy, Windfield Farm, Chesapeake City, MD)

mixture per 100 lb weight, together with a quantity of hay within the same range.

During the breeding season, the stallion's ration should contain more protein and additional minerals and vitamins than are given in rations fed work horses or stallions not in service. During the balance of the year (when not in service), the stallion may be provided a ration like that of other horses similarly handled. In season, pastures are an excellent source of both nutrients and exercise.

In addition to the grain and roughage, there should be free access to a mineral supplement and salt. These should be placed in separate compartments of a suitable box. During the winter months or when little work or exercise is provided, the stallion should receive a succulent feed, such as carrots. Also, laxative feeds, such as wheat bran or linseed meal, should be supplied at these times. Plenty of fresh clean water should be provided at all times. Drugs or stock tonics should not be fed in an attempt to increase virility.

Overfitted, heavy stallions should be regarded with suspicion, for they may be uncertain breeders. On the other hand, a poor, thin, run-down condition is also to be avoided.

FEEDING FOALS

Growth is the very foundation of horse production. This is so because horses cannot perform properly or possess the necessary speed and endurance if their growth has been stunted or their skeletons have been injured by inadequate rations during early age. Naturally, these requirements become increasingly acute when horses are forced for early use, such as the training and racing of the two-year-old. Also, unless foals are rather liberally fed when young, they never attain the much desired body form, which is so important where young stock is sold or shown.

As with all young mammals, milk from the dam gives the foal a good start in life. Within 30 minutes to 2 hours after birth, the foal should be up on its feet and getting the colostrum.

But milk is not the perfect food, as once claimed. It is deficient in iron and copper, with the result that suckling young may suffer from anemia. This nutritional deficiency may be prevented, and increased growth, durability, and soundness may be obtained, by feeding foals separate from their dams; either (1) by tying the mare while the foal eats, or (2) by providing a creep for the foals.

The need for a foal feeding program, starting early in life, is due to the decline in mare's milk in both quantity and nutrients following foaling. The Michigan Station[19] reported that the crude protein content of the milk dropped from 19.1% within 30 minutes after birth of the foal, to 3.8% 12 hours later, and 2.2% 2 months later. Also, the gross energy, total solids, ash, magnesium, and sodium in mare's milk were relatively high at birth, but dropped rather abruptly 12 hours later, then declined more slowly.

When the foal is between 10 days and 3 weeks of age, it will begin to nibble on grain and hay. In order to promote thrift and early development and to avoid setback at weaning time, it is important to encourage the foal to eat supplementary feed as early as possible. For this purpose, a low-built grain box should be provided especially for the foal; or, if on pasture, the foal may be creep fed. The choice between individual feeding and creep feeding may be left to the caretaker;

Fig. 13-23. Creep feeding. (Courtesy, Beaufort Cottage Stables, Newmarket, Great Britain)

[19]Ullrey, D. E., *et al., Journal of Animal Science,* Vol. 25, No. 1, pp. 217–222.

the important thing is that foals receive supplemental feed.

A creep is an enclosure for feeding purposes, made accessible to the foal(s), but through which the dam cannot pass. For best results, the creep should be built at a spot where the mares are inclined to loiter. The ideal location is on high ground, well drained, in the shade, and near the place of watering. Keeping the salt supply nearby will be helpful in holding mares near the creep.

It is important that foals be started on feed carefully, and at an early age. At first only a small amount of feed should be placed in the trough each day, any surplus being removed and given to other horses. In this manner, the feed will be kept clean and fresh, and the foals will not be consuming any moldy or sour feed.

Rolled oats and wheat bran, to which a little brown sugar has been added, is especially palatable as a starting ration.

Table 13-12 gives the formulation of an excellent foal ration, which may be either individually fed or creep fed.

TABLE 13-12
FOAL RATION

Ingredients	Percent	Amount in 500-lb Mix	
	(%)	(lb)	(kg)
Corn (flaked)	37.4	187.0	87.9
Soybean meal (41%)	33.0	165.0	74.9
Oats (rolled)	23.0	115.0	52.2
Brewers' yeast	0.5	2.5	1.1
Molasses	3.0	15.0	6.8
Steamed bone meal or dicalcium phosphate	2.0	10.0	4.5
Salt (trace mineralized)	1.0	5.0	2.3
Vitamins A and D premix	0.1	0.5	0.2
Total	100.0	500.0	227.0

Because of the difficulty in formulating and home mixing a foal ration, the purchase of a good commercial feed usually represents a wise investment.

In addition to its grain ration, the foal should be given a good quality hay (preferably a legume), unless it is on good pasture.

Free access to salt and a suitable mineral mixture should be provided. The mineral will be consumed to best advantage if placed in a convenient place and under shelter; or it may be incorporated in the ration. Plenty of fresh water must be available at all times.

When foals are on luxuriant pasture and their mothers are milking well, difficulty may be experienced in getting them to eat. Thus, patience on the part of the caretaker is extremely important. However, foals are curious. Usually, they'll examine a creep. But it may be necessary to start them on the creep ration by first letting them nibble a little feed from the hand.

At 4 to 5 weeks of age, the normal healthy foal should be consuming ½ lb of grain daily per 100 lb of liveweight. By weaning time, this should be increased to about ¾ lb or more per 100 lb liveweight (or 6 to 8 lb of feed/head/day), the exact amount varying with the individual, the type of feed, and the development desired.

Under such a system of care and management, the foal will become less dependent upon its dam, and the weaning process will be facilitated. If properly cared for, foals will normally attain one-half of their mature weight during the first year. Most Thoroughbred and Standardbred breeders plan to have the animals attain full height by the time they are two years of age. However, such results require liberal feeding from the beginning.

It is well recognized that the forced development of race, show, and sale horses must be done expertly if the animals are to remain durable and sound. This calls for particular emphasis on the kind of ration, feed allowance, and exercise.

FEEDING WEANLINGS

The most critical period in the entire life of a horse is that interval from weaning time (about six months of age) until one year of age. Foals suckling their dams and receiving no grain may develop very satisfactorily up to weaning time. However, lack of preparation prior to weaning and neglect following the separation from the dam may prevent the animal from gaining proper size and shape. The primary objective in breeding horses is the economical production of a well-developed, sound individual at maturity. To achieve this result requires good care and management of weanlings.

No great setback or disturbances will be encountered at weaning time provided that the foals have developed a certain independence from proper grain feedings during the suckling period. Generally, weanlings should receive 1 to 1½ lb of grain and 1½ to 2 lb of hay daily per each 100 lb of liveweight. The amount of feed will vary somewhat with the individuality of the animal, the quality of roughage, available pastures, the price of feeds, and whether the weanling is being developed for show, race, or sale. Naturally, animals being developed for early use or sale should be fed more liberally, although it is equally important to retain clean, sound joints, legs, and feet—a condition which cannot be obtained so easily in heavily fitted animals.

Because of the rapid development of bone and muscle in weanlings, it is important that, in addition to

ample quantity of feed, the ration also provides quality proteins, and adequate minerals and vitamins.

FEEDING YEARLINGS

If young animals have been fed and cared for so that they are well grown and thrifty as yearlings, usually little difficulty will be experienced at any later date.

When on pasture, yearlings that are being grown for show or sale should receive grain in addition to grass. They should be confined to their stalls in the daytime during the hot days and turned out at night (because of not being exposed to sunshine, adequate vitamin D must be provided). This point needs to be emphasized when forced development is desired; for, good as pastures may be, they are roughages rather than concentrates.

The winter feeding program for the rising two-year-olds should be such as to produce plenty of bone and muscle rather than fat. From ½ to 1 lb of grain and 1 to 1½ lb of hay should be fed for each 100 lb of liveweight. The quantity will vary with the quality of the roughage, the individuality of the animal, and the use for which the animal is produced. In producing for sale, more liberal feeding may be economical. Access to salt and to a mineral mixture should be provided at all times; or the minerals should be incorporated in the ration. An abundance of fresh, pure water must be available.

FEEDING TWO- AND THREE-YEAR-OLDS

Except for the fact that the two- and three-year-olds will be larger, and, therefore, will require more feed, a description of their proper care and management would merely be a repetition of the principles that have already been discussed for the yearling.

With the two-year-old that is to be raced, however, the care and feeding at this time become matters of extreme importance. Once the young horse is placed in training, the ration should be adequate enough to allow for continued development and to provide necessary maintenance and additional energy for work. This means that special attention must be given to providing adequate proteins, minerals, and vitamins to the ration. Overexertion must be avoided, the animal must be well groomed, and the feet must be cared for properly. In brief, every precaution must be taken if the animal is to remain sound—a most difficult task when animals are raced at an early age, even though the right genetic makeup and the proper environment are present.

Fig. 13-24. Two-year-olds on pasture near Calgary, Alberta, Canada. (Courtesy, *The Quarter Horse Journal*, Amarillo, TX)

FITTING FOR SHOW AND SALE

Each year, many horses are fitted for shows or sales. In both cases, a fattening process is involved, but exercise is doubly essential.

For horses that are being fitted for shows, the conditioning process is also a matter of hardening, and the horses are used daily in harness or under saddle. Regardless of whether a sale or a show is the major objective, fleshing should be obtained without sacrificing action or soundness or without causing filling of the legs and hocks.

In fattening horses, the animals should be brought to full feed rather gradually, until the ration reaches a maximum of about 2 lb of grain daily for each 100 lb of liveweight. When on full feed, horses make surprising gains. Daily weight gains of 4 to 5 lb are not uncommon. Such animals soon become fat, sleek, and attractive. This is probably the basis for the statement that "fat will cover up a multitude of sins in a horse."

Although exercise is desirable from the standpoint of keeping the animals sound, it is estimated that such activity decreases the daily rate of gains by as much as 20%. Because of the greater cost of gains and the expense involved in bringing about forced exercise, most feeders of sale horses limit the exercise to that obtained naturally from running in a paddock.

In comparison with finishing cattle or sheep, there is more risk in fattening horses. Heavily fed horses kept in idleness are likely to become blemished and injured through playfulness, and there are more sick-

TABLE
NUTRITIONAL DISEASES AND

Disease	Species Affected	Cause	Symptoms (and age or group most affected)	Distribution and Losses Caused by
Alkali disease (see selenium poisoning)				
Anemia, nutritional	All warmblooded animals, including humans.	Commonly an iron deficiency, but it may be a deficiency of copper, cobalt, or certain vitamins—especially B-12.	Loss of appetite, poor performance, progressive emaciation and death. Most prevalent in suckling young.	Worldwide. Losses consist of retarded growth and deaths.
Azoturia (hemoglobinuria, Monday morning disease, blackwater, tying up)	Horses.	Sudden exercise, following a day or two of rest during which time the horse has been on full feed, resulting in partial spasm or "tie-up." Thought to be caused by an abnormal amount of glycogen stored in the muscle. As the glycogen breaks down, lactic acid is formed. The lactic acid builds up in the muscle, causing a myocitis which manifests itself as partial spasm, or "tie-up."	Profuse sweating, abdominal distress, wine-colored urine, stiff gait, reluctance to move, and lameness. Finally, animal assumes a sitting position, and eventually falls prostrate on the side.	Worldwide, but the disease is seldom seen in horses on pasture and rarely in horses at constant work.
Colic	Horses.	Internal parasites are the number one cause of colic. Additional causes are improper feeding, working, or watering.	Excruciating pain; and depending on the type of colic, other symptoms are: the horse looking at its belly, distended abdomen, increased intestinal rumbling, violent rolling and kicking, profuse sweating, constipation, and refusal of feed and water.	Worldwide. Colic is the most common ailment among horses and is the leading cause of death.

nesses among liberally fed horses than in other classes of stock handled in a similar manner.

In fitting show horses, the finish must remain firm and hard, the action superb, and the soundness unquestioned. Thus, they must be carefully fed, groomed, and exercised to bring them to proper bloom.

Equestrians who fit and sell yearlings or younger animals may feed a palatable milk replacer or commercial feed to advantage.

NUTRITIONAL DISEASES AND AILMENTS

Nutritional deficiencies may be brought about either by (1) too little feed, or (2) rations that are too low in one or more nutrients. Also, forced production (such as racing two-year-olds) and the feeding of forages and grains which are often produced on leached or depleted soils have created many problems in nutrition. This condition has been further aggravated through the increased confinement of horses, many animals being confined to stalls or lots all or a large part of the year. Under these unnatural conditions, nutritional diseases and ailments have become increasingly common.

Although the cause, prevention, and treatment of most equine nutritional diseases and ailments are known, they continue to plague the horse industry simply because the available knowledge is not put into practice. Moreover, those widespread nutritional deficiencies which are not of sufficient proportions to produce clear-cut deficiency symptoms cause even greater economic losses because they go unnoticed and unrectified.

Unfortunately, there are no warning signals to tell a caretaker when a horse is not getting enough of a certain nutrient. A continuing inadequate supply of any one of several nutrients can produce illness which is very hard to diagnose until it becomes severe, at which time it is difficult and expensive—if not too late—to treat. The important thing, therefore, is to ensure against such deficiencies occurring. But caretakers should not shower a horse with mistaken kindness through using shotgun-type mineral and vitamin preparations. Instead, the quantity of each nutrient should be based on available scientific knowledge.

Table 13-13 contains a summary of the important nutritional diseases and ailments affecting horses.

13-13
AILMENTS OF HORSES

Treatment	Prevention	Remarks
Provide dietary sources of the nutrient or nutrients the deficiency of which is known to cause the condition.	Supply dietary sources of iron, copper, cobalt, and certain vitamins—especially B-12. Keep suckling animals confined to a minimum and provide supplemental feeds at an early age.	Anemia is a condition in which the blood is either deficient in quality or quantity (a deficient quality refers to a deficiency in hemoglobin and/or red cells). Levels of iron in most feeds believed to be ample, since most feeds contain 40 to 400 mg/lb.
Absolute rest and quiet. While awaiting the veterinarian, apply heated cloths or blankets, or hot-water bottles to the swollen and hardened muscles. The veterinarian should determine treatment. In mild cases, he/she may use a tranquilizer or sedative. In severe cases he/she may use muscle relaxers or sodium bicarbonate in solution to readjust the acid balance in the muscles.	Restrict the ration and provide daily exercise when the animal is idle. Give a wet bran mash the evening before an idle day or turn the idle horses to pasture. Some believe that a diuretic (a drug which will increase the flow of urine) will prevent the tie-up syndrome. This is a common treatment of racehorses. Others feel that increased B vitamins will prevent the lactic acid buildup.	The chances of recovery are good for horses that remain standing, are not forced to move after the signs are noticed, and whose pulse returns to normal within 24 hours.
Call a veterinarian. To avoid danger of inflicting self-injury, (1) place the animal in a large, well-bedded stable, or (2) take it for a slow walk. Depending on diagnosis, the veterinarian may use one or more of following: sedatives; laxatives, such as mineral oil; drugs, or surgery.	Parasite control. Proper feeding, working, watering.	Colic is also a symptom of abdominal pain that can be caused by a number of different conditions. For example, bloodworms cause a colic due to damage in the wall of blood vessels. This results in poor circulation to the intestine.

(Continued)

TABLE 13-13

Disease	Species Affected	Cause	Symptoms (and age or group most affected)	Distribution and Losses Caused by
Fescue foot	Horses. Cattle. Sheep.	The fungus, *acremonium coenophialum*, which lives in the leaves, stems, and seeds of tall fescue.	Decrease or absence of milk production, prolonged gestation, abortion, and thickened placenta.	Wherever tall fescue is grown.
Fluorine poisoning (fluorosis)	All farm animals, fish, poultry, and humans.	Ingesting excessive quantities of fluorine through either the feed, air, water, or a combination of these.	Abnormal teeth (especially mottled enamel and excessive wear); abnormal bones (bones become thickened, rough, and soft); stiffness of joints; loss of appetite; emaciation; reduction in milk flow; diarrhea; and salt hunger.	The water in parts of Arkansas, California, South Carolina, and Texas has been reported to contain excess fluoride. Occasionally, throughout the U.S., high-fluorine phosphates are used in mineral mixtures.\n\nAreas near certain industries which heat earthy materials or burn high-fluoride coal may be a problem.
Founder (laminitis) 	Horses. Cattle. Sheep. Goats.	Overeating, (grain; or lush legume or grass—known as "grass founder"), overdrinking, or from inflammation of the uterus following parturition. Also intestinal inflammation.\nToo rapid change in the ration.	Extreme pain, fever (103 to 106° F), and reluctance to move. If neglected, chronic laminitis will develop, resulting in a dropping of the hoof soles and a turning up of the toe walls.	Worldwide.\nActual death losses from founder are not very great, but usefulness may be affected.
Goiter (see iodine deficiency)				
Heaves 	Horses. Mules.	Exact cause unknown, but it is known that the condition is often associated with the feeding of damaged, dusty, or moldy hay.\nIt often follows severe respiratory infection such as strangles.\nProbably an allergy.	Difficulty in forcing air out of the lungs, resulting in a jerking of flanks (double flank action) and coughing. The nostrils are often slightly dilated and there is a nasal discharge.	Worldwide.\nLosses are negligible.
Iodine deficiency (goiter)	All farm animals and humans.	A failure of the body to obtain sufficient iodine from which the thyroid gland can form thyroxin (an iodine-containing hormone).	Foals may be weak.	Northwestern U.S. and the Great Lakes region; also reported in California and Texas.\nAlso goiter areas are scattered all over the world.
Night blindness (nyctalopia)	All farm animals and humans.	Deficiency of vitamin A.	Slow dark adaptation progressing to night blindness.	Worldwide.\nEspecially prevalent during an extended drought, or when winter feeding bleached grass or hay.
Nitrate poisoning (oat hay poisoning; corn stalk poisoning)	Primarily cattle, but it may affect horses and sheep.	Forages (vegetative part) of most grain crops, Sudangrass, and numerous weeds.\nInorganic nitrate or nitrite salts, or fertilizer left where animals have access to them, or where they may be mistaken for salt.\nPond or shallow well into which surface runoff from barnyard or well-fertilized soil drain.	Accelerated respiration and pulse rate; diarrhea; frequent urination; loss of appetite; general weakness; trembling and staggering gait; frothing from mouth; abortion; blue color of the mucous membrane and muzzle due to lack of oxygen in blood; death within 4½ to 9 hours after consuming nitrates.\nA rapid and accurate diagnosis of nitrate poisoning may be made by examining blood. Normal blood is red and becomes brighter when exposed to air, whereas blood from animals toxic with nitrates is a brown color due to formation of methemoglobin.	Excessive nitrate content of feeds is an increasingly important cause of poisoning in farm animals, due primarily to more and more high-nitrogen fertilization. But nitrate toxicity is not new, having been reported as early as 1850, and having occurred in semiarid regions of this and other countries for years.

(Continued)

Treatment	Prevention	Remarks
There is no effective treatment.	Seeding of fungus-free fescue seed. Where fescue foot is a problem, gestating mares should be removed from fescue pasture the last 2 to 3 months of pregnancy.	
Discontinue the use of feeds, water, or minerals containing excessive fluoride. Any damage may be permanent, but animals which have not developed severe symptoms may be helped to some extent if sources of excess fluorine are eliminated.	Avoid the use of feeds, water or mineral supplements containing excessive fluorine. The National Academy of Sciences uses the figure of 60 ppm fluoride as the dietary fluoride tolerance of horses, or dietary level that can be fed without clinical interference with normal performance.	Fluorine is a cumulative poison.
Pending arrival of the veterinarian, the attendant should stand the animal's feet in a cold-water bath. Antihistamines, restricting the diet, use of diuretics, and antiinflammatory agents such as corticosteroids or phenylbutazone, may speed recovery and alleviate serious after effects.	Alleviate the causes; namely, (1) overeating, (2) overdrinking (especially when hot), and/or (3) inflammation of the uterus following parturition. Veterinary attention should be given if mares retain the afterbirth longer than 12 hours.	Unless foundered animals are quite valuable, it is usually desirable to dispose of them following a case of severe founder.
Antihistamine granules can be administered in feed to control coughing due to lung congestion. Affected animals are less bothered if turned to pasture. If used only at light work, if fed an all-pelleted ration, or if the hay is sprinkled lightly with water at feeding.	Avoid the use of damaged feeds. Feed an all-pelleted ration, thereby alleviating dust.	Unlike humans, a horse cannot breathe through its mouth. Basically, heaves is a rupture of some of the alveoli in the lungs, of which the specific cause is unknown. Heaves in horses is similar to emphysema in people.
At the first signs of iodine deficiency, an iodized salt should be fed to all horses. Once the iodine-deficiency symptoms appear in farm animals, no treatment is very effective.	In iodine-deficient areas, feed iodized salt to all horses throughout the year. Salt containing 0.01% potassium iodide is recommended.	The enlarged thyroid gland (goiter) is nature's way of attempting to make sufficient thyroxin under conditions where a deficiency exists. Large excesses of iodine may cause abortions.
Correcting the vitamin A deficiency.	Provide good sources of carotene in the ration, or add stabilized vitamin A to the ration.	High levels of nitrates interfere with the conversion of carotene to vitamin A.
A 4% solution of methylene blue (in a 5% glucose or a 1.8% sodium sulfate solution) administered by a veterinarian intravenously at the rate of 100cc/1000 lb liveweight.	More than 0.9% nitrate nitrogen (dry basis) may be considered as potentially toxic. Feed should be analyzed when in question. Nitrate poisoning may be reduced by (1) feeding high levels of grains and other high-energy feeds (molasses) and vitamin A, (2) limiting the amount of high-nitrate feeds, (3) ensiling forages which are high in nitrates.	Nitrate form of nitrogen does not appear to cause the actual toxicity. During digestion, the nitrate is reduced to nitrite, a more toxic form, 10 to 15 times more toxic than nitrates. In horses, conversion is in the cecum. When nitrate trouble is expected, contact veterinarian or county agent.

(Continued)

Disease	Species Affected	Cause	Symptoms (and age or group most affected)	Distribution and Losses Caused by
Osteomalacia	All farm animals and humans.	Inadequate phosphorus (sometimes inadequate calcium). Lack of vitamin D. Inadequate intake of calcium and phosphorus. Incorrect ratio of calcium to phosphorus.	Phosphorus deficiency symptoms are: depraved appetite (gnawing on bones, wood, or other objects; or eating dirt); lack of appetite, stiffness of joints; failure to breed regularly; and an emaciated appearance. Calcium deficiency symptoms are: fragile bones; reproductive failures; and lowered lactations. Mature animals most affected. Most of the acute cases occur during pregnancy and lactation.	Southwestern U.S. is classed as a phosphorus-deficient area whereas calcium deficient areas have been reported in parts of Florida, Louisiana, Nebraska, Virginia, and West Virginia.
Periodic ophthalmia (moon blindness)	Horses. Mules. Asses.	It may be caused by (1) lack of riboflavin; (2) an autoimmune reaction; (3) an allergic reaction; (4) genetics; (5) leptospirosis, brucellosis, or strangles; (6) parasitic infections; or (7) fungal infections.	Periods of cloudy vision, in one or both eyes, which may last for a few days to a week or two and then clear up; but it recurs at intervals, eventually culminating in blindness in one or both eyes.	In many parts of the world. In the U.S. it occurs most frequently in Northeastern U.S.
Rickets	All farm animals and humans.	Lack of calcium, phosphorus, or vitamin D; or an incorrect ratio of the two minerals.	Enlargement of the knee and hock joints, and the animal may exhibit great pain when moving about. Irregular bulges (beaded ribs) at juncture of ribs with breastbone, and bowed legs. Rickets is a disease of young animals, including foals.	Worldwide. It is seldom fatal.
Salt deficiency (sodium chloride deficiency)	All farm animals and humans.	Lack of salt (sodium chloride).	Loss of appetite, retarded growth, loss of weight, a rough coat, lowered production of milk, and a ravenous appetite for salt.	Worldwide, especially among grass-eating animals.
Salt poisoning (sodium chloride)	All farm animals, including horses, but swine and sheep most frequently affected.	When excess salt is fed after a period of salt starvation. When salt is improperly used to govern self-feeding of concentrates.	Sudden onset—1 to 2 hours after ingesting salt; extreme nervousness; muscle twitching and fine tremors; much weaving and wobbling, staggering, and circling; blindness; weakness; normal temperature; rapid but weak pulse; and very rapid and shallow breathing; diarrhea; death from a few hours to 48 hours.	Salt poisoning is relatively rare.
Selenium poisoning (alkali disease)	All farm animals and humans.	Consumption of plants grown on soils containing high levels of selenium.	Loss of hair from the mane and tail in horses. In severe cases, the hoofs slough off, lameness occurs, feed consumption decreases, and death may occur by starvation.	In certain regions of western U.S.—especially certain areas in South Dakota, Montana, Wyoming, Nebraska, Kansas, and perhaps areas in other states in the Great Plains and Rocky Mountains. Also, in Canada.
Urinary calculi (gravel, stones, water belly)	Horses. Cattle. Sheep. Goats. Mink. Humans.	Unknown, but it seems to be nutritional. Experiments have shown a higher incidence of urinary calculi when there is (1) a high intake of potassium, (2) more phosphorus than calcium in the ration, or (3) a high proportion of beet pulp or grain sorghum in the ration.	Frequent attempts to urinate, dribbling or stoppage of the urine, pain and renal colic. Usually only males affected, the females being able to pass the concretions. Bladder may rupture, with death following. Otherwise, uremic poisoning may set in.	Worldwide. Affected animals seldom recover completely.

(Continued)

Treatment	Prevention	Remarks
Select natural feeds that contain sufficient calcium and phosphorus. Feed a special mineral supplement. If the disease is far advanced, treatment will not be successful.	Feed balanced rations, and allow animals free access to a suitable calcium and phosphorus supplement. Increase the calcium and phosphorus content of feeds through fertilizing the soils.	Calcium deficiencies are much more rare than phosphorus deficiencies in horses.
Antibiotics or corticosteroids administered promptly are helpful in some cases. Immediately (1) change to greener hay or grass, and (2) add riboflavin at the rate of 40 mg/day/animal.	Feed green grass, or well-cured green, leafy hay; or add riboflavin to the ration at the rate of 40 mg per horse per day.	This disease has been known to exist for at least 2,000 years.
If the disease has not advanced too far, treatment may be successful by supplying adequate amounts of vitamin D, calcium, and phosphorus, and/or adjusting the ratio of calcium to phosphorus.	Provide (1) sufficient calcium, phosphorus, and vitamin D, and (2) a correct ratio of the 2 minerals.	Rickets is characterized by a failure of growing bone to ossify or harden properly.
Salt starved animals should be gradually accustomed to salt; slowly increase the hand-fed allowance until the animals may be safely allowed free access to it.	Provide plenty of salt at all times, preferably by free-choice feeding.	Common salt is one of the most essential minerals for grass-eating animals and one of the easiest and cheapest to provide.
Provide large amounts of fresh water to affected animals. Those that cannot and do not drink should be given water via stomach tube, by a veterinarian. The veterinarian may also give (I.V. or intraperitoneally) calcium gluconate to severely affected animals.	If animals have not had salt for a long time, they should be hand fed salt, gradually increasing daily allowance until they leave a little in the mineral box, then self-feed.	Indians and pioneers handed down many legendary stories about huge numbers of wild animals that killed themselves by gorging at a newly found salt lick after having been salt starved for long periods of time.
The effect of chronic selenium toxicity may be reduced by feeding a high protein ration and by use of trace amounts of an arsenic compound. Pasture rotation and use of supplemental feeds from nonselenium areas are practical solutions to the problem. There is no known treatment for acute selenium poisoning.	Abandon areas where soils contain more than 0.5 ppm of selenium, because crops produced on such soils constitute a menace to both animals and humans.	Chronic cases of selenium poisoning occur when animals consume feeds containing 8.5 ppm of selenium over an extended period; acute cases occur on 500 to 1,000 ppm. The maximum level of selenium recommended by FDA is 2 ppm.
Once calculi develops, dietary treatment appears to be of little value. Smooth muscle relaxants may allow passage of calculi if used before rupture of bladder. In horses, bladder calculi must be surgically removed.	Good feed and management appear to lessen the incidence, but no sure preventive is known. Avoid high phosphorus and low calcium. Keep the Ca:P ratio between about 2:1 and about 1:1. Also, avoid high potassium. One to three percent salt in the concentrate ration may help (using the higher levels in the winter when water consumption is normally lower).	Calculi are stonelike concretions in the urinary tract which almost always originate in the kidneys. These stones block the passage of urine.

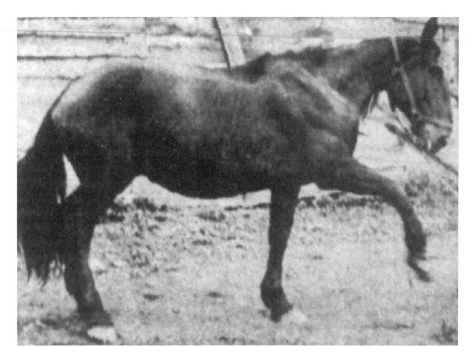

Fig. 13-25. Horse with colic. This digestive disturbance may be caused by feed to which the animal is unaccustomed, sudden changes in the ration, rapid eating, imperfectly cured or damaged feeds, the horse's being worked too soon or too hard after feeding, or gorging on water—especially when warm. (Courtesy, Pitman-Moore, Indianapolis, IN)

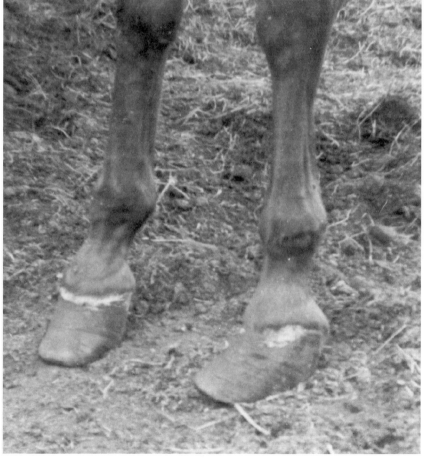

Fig. 13-26. Horse's foot affected with founder, which is most often caused by overeating. (Courtesy, Alex Weinstein, Murrieta, CA)

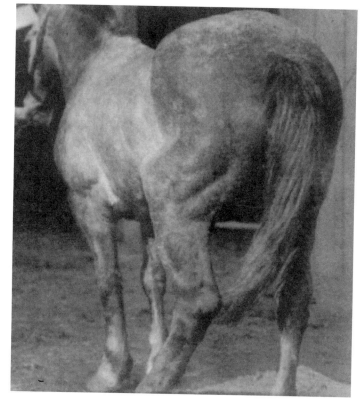

Fig. 13-27. Horse with azoturia, which is generally attributed to faulty metabolism. Prevention lies in restricting the ration and providing daily exercise when the animal is not at work. (Courtesy, Pitman-Moore, Indianapolis, IN)

Fig. 13-28. Osteomalacia of the facial bones in a Hackney. This deficiency disease in mature horses may be caused by (1) a lack of vitamin D, (2) a lack of calcium or phosphorus, or (3) an incorrect ratio of calcium to phosphorus. (Courtesy, College of Veterinary Medicine, University of Illinois)

SELECTED REFERENCES

Title of Publication	Author(s)	Publisher
Animal Science, Ninth Edition	M. E. Ensminger	Interstate Publishers, Inc., Danville, IL, 1991
Breeding and Raising Horses, Ag. Hdbk. No. 394	M. E. Ensminger	Agricultural Research Service, USDA, Washington, DC, 1972
Complete Encyclopedia of Horses, The	M. E. Ensminger	A. S. Barnes & Co., Inc., Cranbury, NJ, 1977 (Now, Oak Tree Publications, San Diego, CA)
Equine Nutrition and Feeding	D. Frape	Longman Scientific & Technical, Essex, England, 1994
Feeding and Care of the Horse	L. D. Lewis	Lea & Febiger, Philadelphia, PA, 1982
Feeding Ponies	W. C. Miller	J. A. Allen & Co., London, England, 1968
Feeds & Nutrition, Second Edition	M. E. Ensminger J. E. Oldfield W. W. Heinemann	The Ensminger Publishing Company, Clovis, CA, 1990
Feeds & Nutrition Digest, Second Edition	M. E. Ensminger J. E. Oldfield W. W. Heinemann	The Ensminger Publishing Company, Clovis, CA, 1990
Horse Feeding and Nutrition	T. J. Cunha	Academic Press, New York, NY, 1980
Horse, The	P. D. Rossdale	The California Thoroughbred Breeders Assn., Arcadia, CA, 1972
Horse, The, Second Edition	J. W. Evans, *et al.*	W. H. Freeman and Co., New York, NY, 1990
Horse Science Handbook, Vols. 1, 2, and 3	Ed. by M. E. Ensminger	Agriservices Foundation, Clovis, CA, 1963, 1964, and 1966
Horsemanship and Horse Care, Ag. Info. Bull. No. 353	M. E. Ensminger	Agricultural Research Service, USDA, Washington, DC, 1972
Horses and Tack, Second Edition	M. E. Ensminger	Houghton Mifflin Company, Boston, MA, 1991
Light Horse Management	R. C. Barbalace	Caballus Publishers, Fort Collins, CO, 1974
Light Horses, Farmers' Bull. No. 2127	M. E. Ensminger	U.S. Department of Agriculture, Washington, DC, 1965
Nutrient Requirements of Horses, No. 6, Fifth Revised Edition	National Research Council	National Academy of Sciences, Washington, DC, 1989
Shetland Pony	L. F. Bedell	Iowa State University Press, Ames, IA, 1959
Stud Managers' Handbook	Edited by M. E. Ensminger	Agriservices Foundation, Clovis, CA

14

BUILDINGS AND EQUIPMENT FOR HORSES

Attractive Tennessee Walking Horse breeding barn on famed Harlinsdale Farm, Franklin, Tennessee. (Courtesy, Bill Harlin)

The primary reasons for having horse buildings and equipment are: (1) to provide a place in which to confine horses and store feed and tack; (2) to modify the environment by controlling temperature, humidity, and other factors; and (3) to provide feed, water, and other facilities for the care of horses. Properly designed, constructed, and arranged facilities make for increased horse comfort and performance, greater efficiency in the use of feed, and less expenditure for labor in the care of horses.

Fig. 14-1. Lunging Ring at Gainesway Farm, Lexington, Kentucky, recipient of the American Institute of Architects Honor Award for Excellence in Design. (Courtesy, Thoroughbred Publications, Lexington, KY)

The effects of technological progress in horse buildings and equipment are everywhere. Yet, there is need for more experimental work pertaining to the basic requirements of such facilities. The most glaring deficiencies pertain to: (1) labor saving devices;[1] (2) flexibility; (3) environmental control—including temperature, humidity, and ventilation; (4) methods of handling excrement; (5) sanitation; (6) safety of animals and caretakers; (7) fire-resistant construction; (8) materials;[2] and (9) cost.

ENVIRONMENTAL CONTROL FOR HORSES

People achieve environmental control through clothing, vacations to resort areas, and air-conditioned homes and cars.

Wild horses were little affected by environment as long as they roamed pastures and ranges. But the domestication of horses and their confinement into smaller spaces changed all this. Building and equipment design became critical.

Environment may be defined as all the conditions, circumstances, and influences surrounding and affecting the growth, development, and production of a living

---

[1]Seventy-five percent of horse work is still hand labor, one-third of which could be eliminated by mechanization and modernization.

[2]Many equestrians complain that metal buildings are unsatisfactory; that they must still be protected with wood, that moisture condensation is a problem, and that they are too hot in the summer and too cold in the winter. Some express preference for concrete blocks. However, the vast majority seem to favor conventional wood construction, despite the greater fire hazard.

thing. In horses, this includes the feed, air temperature, relative humidity, air velocity, wet bedding, dust, light, ammonia buildup, odors, and space requirements. Control, or modifications, of these factors offers possibilities for improving animal performance. There is still much to be learned about environmental control, but the gap between awareness and application is becoming smaller.

Properly designed horse barns and other shelters, shades, insulation, ventilation, air conditioning, fans, and heat lamps can be used to approach the environment that we want. Naturally, the investment in environmental control facilities must be balanced against the expected increased returns; and there is a point beyond which further expenditures for environmental control will not increase return sufficiently to justify the added cost. This point of diminishing returns will differ between sections of the country, quality of the horses (the more valuable the animals, the higher the expenditure for environmental control can be), and operators; and labor and feed costs will enter into the picture, also.

Fig. 14-2. Fan, heat lamps, and sunlight in stall ceiling, all designed to improve the environment and enhance horse comfort, at Happy Valley Farm, Ocala, Florida. (Courtesy, *Thoroughbred Record*, Lexington, KY)

Environmentally controlled buildings are costly to construct, but they make for the ultimate in animal comfort, health, and efficiency of feed utilization. Also, they lend themselves to automation, which results in a saving in labor, and, because of minimizing space requirements, they effect a saving in land cost. Today, environmental control is rather common in poultry and swine housing, and it is on the increase for horses.

Environmental control is of particular importance in horse barn construction, because many horses spend the majority of their lives in stalls—for example, race and show horses may be confined as much as 95% of the time.

Before an environmental system can be designed for horses, it is important to know (1) the heat production of horses, (2) the vapor (moisture) production of horses, (3) the effect of temperature on horses, and (4) the space requirements of horses. This information is as pertinent to designing livestock buildings as nutrient requirements are to balancing rations.

HEAT PRODUCTION OF HORSES

The heat production of horses varies with age, body weight, ration, breed, activity, barn temperature, and humidity at high temperatures. The heat production of any animal is closely related to size and varies approximately as the two-thirds power of the body weight. Table 14-1 may be used as a guide relative to the heat production of horses.

Heat is measured in British thermal units (Btu). One Btu is the amount of heat required to raise the temperature of one pound of water one degree Fahrenheit.

TABLE 14-1
HEAT PRODUCTION OF A 1,000-LB HORSE[1, 2]

Temperature	Heat Production, BTU/hr	Temperature	Heat Production, Kcal/hr
	Total		Total
(°F)		(°C)	
70	1,800–2,500[2]	21	453.6–630

[1]Adapted by the author from *Farm Buildings*, by J. C. Wooley, McGraw-Hill Book Company, Inc., p. 140, Table 24.

[2]Amsby and Kriss, in a paper entitled, "Some Fundamentals of Stable Ventilation," *Journal of Agricultural Research*, Vol. 21, p. 343, list the total heat output as follows: A 1,000-lb horse, 1,500 Btu per hour; a 1,500-lb horse, 2,450 Btu per hour.

VAPOR (MOISTURE) PRODUCTION OF HORSES

Horses give off moisture during normal respiration; and the higher the temperature the greater the moisture. The moisture should be removed from buildings through the ventilation system. When it's cold and this moisture is not removed, it condenses and forms frost. The latter condition is indicative of lack of ventilation, and it may be indicative of insufficient insulation, also. Most building designers govern the amount of winter ventilation by the need for moisture removal. Also, cognizance is taken of the fact that moisture removal in the winter is lower than in the summer; hence, less air is needed. However, lack of heat makes moisture removal more difficult in the wintertime. Table 14-2 gives the information necessary for determining the approximate amount of moisture to be removed.

TABLE 14-2
VAPOR (MOISTURE) PRODUCTION OF A 1,000-LB HORSE[1]

Temperature		Vapor Production	Vapor Production
(°F)	(°C)	(lb/hr)	(kg/hr)
70	21	0.729	0.33

[1]Adapted by the author from *Farm Buildings*, by J. C. Wooley, McGraw-Hill Book Company, Inc., p. 141, Table 25.

As shown in Table 14-2, a horse breathes into the air approximately 17.5 lb, or about 2.1 gal. of moisture per day. For 40 horses, there would be given off 700 lb, or about 84 gal. of water per day. The removal of such a large quantity of moisture, especially in the winter when the barn is closed, is a difficult problem for the designer to solve.

Since ventilation also involves a transfer of heat, it is important to conserve heat in the building to maintain desired temperatures and reduce the need for supplemental heat. In a well-insulated building, mature horses usually produce sufficient heat to provide a desirable balance between heat and moisture; but in cold areas, young animals may require supplemental heat. The major requirement of summer ventilation is temperature control, which requires moving more air than in the winter.

RECOMMENDED ENVIRONMENTAL CONTROL FOR HORSES

The comfort of animals (or people) is a function of temperature, humidity, and air movement. Likewise, the heat loss from animals is a function of these three items.

The prime function of the winter ventilation system is primarily for temperature control. If air in horse barns is supplied at a rate sufficient to control moisture—that is, to keep the inside relative humidity in winter below 75%—then this will usually provide the needed fresh air, help suppress odors, and prevent an ammonia buildup.

Based on currently available information, the author recommends the environmental control given in Table 14-3 for horses.

Thus, until more experimental work is available, based on extrapolating from confinement systems in use for other classes of animals, the author recommends the following environmental conditions for horses:

■ **Temperature**—A range of 50 to 75°F is satisfactory, with 55°F considered optimum. Until a newborn foal is dry, it should be warmed to 75 to 80°F. This can be done with a heat lamp.

TABLE 14-3
RECOMMENDED ENVIRONMENTAL CONDITIONS FOR HORSES

Age	Temperature				Acceptible Humidity	Commonly Used Ventilation Rates[1]					Drinking Water			
	Comfort Zone		Optimum			Basis	Winter[2]		Summer		Winter		Summer	
	(°F)	(°C)	(°F)	(°C)	(%)		(cfm)	(cu mm/min.)	(cfm)	(cu mm/min.)	(°F)	(°C)	(°F)	(°C)
Horse, mature	50–75	10–24	55	13	50–75	1,000 lb (or 454 kg)	60	1.7	160	4.5	40–45	4–7	60–75	16–24
Newborn foal	75–80	24–27												

[1]Generally two different ventilating systems are provided; one for winter, and an additional one for summer. Hence, as shown in Table 14-3, the winter ventilating system in a horse barn should be designed to provide 60 cfm (cubic feet/minute) for each 1,000 lb horse. Then, the summer system should be designed to provide an added 100 cfm, thereby providing a total of 160 cfm for summer ventilation.

In practice, in many horse barns, added summer ventilation is provided by opening (1) barn doors, and (2) high-up hinged walls.

[2]Provide approximately one-fourth the winter rate continuously for moisture removal.

■ **Humidity**—A range of 50 to 75% relative humidity is acceptable, with 60% preferred.

■ **Insulation and ventilation**—These needs will vary from area to area. Where a wide spread between summer and winter temperatures exists, and where horses are confined much of the time, proper insulation and ventilation are of prime importance. Under such circumstances, for moisture control in winter and temperature control in summer, horse barns should have at least 2 in. of insulation on the ceiling or roof, and the sidewalls should be insulated, also.

■ **Ventilation**—The barn should have as little moisture and odor as possible, and it should be free from drafts. In a properly ventilated barn, the ventilation system should provide 60 cu ft per minute (cfm) for each 1,000 lb of horse in winter and 160 cfm per 1,000 lb of horse in summer. In warm weather, satisfactory ventilation usually can be achieved by opening barn doors and by installing hinged doors or panels near the ceiling that swing open. Then, on extremely hot or quiet days, the natural ventilating system may be augmented with the fan ventilating system.

The design of the barn, and the temperature of the area, will determine the best type of ventilating system to use. Also, the requirements for summer and winter are so different that it is best to use two different ventilating systems—one for winter, and the other for summer.

A professional engineer should always be engaged to design the ventilating system. Generally, summer exhaust fans should be placed high, and winter exhaust fans low. Whatever the ventilating system, drafts on horses should be avoided.

■ **Light**—Windows should be provided in the ratio of 1 sq ft for each 30 sq ft of floor area. They should be protected from horses and screened to keep flies out. Additionally, artificial light should be provided for the convenience of the caretaker. One 60-watt bulb, properly recessed and protected, in each stall, plus lighting in the aisle, should suffice.

■ **Water temperature**—In the winter months, water for horses should be warmed to 40 to 45°F; in the summer, it should be within the range of 60 to 75°F.

HORSE BARN POINTERS

The care of horses differs from the care accorded cattle, sheep, swine, or poultry; they require more individual attention. But just as the needs are unique, meeting them requires greater imagination and creativity.

AREA ARRANGEMENT

Whether planning a new horse layout or altering an old one, all buildings, fences, corrals, and trees should be added according to a master plan, for once established they are usually difficult and expensive to move. The entire arrangement should make for the best use of the land and require a minimum of walking when caring for horses.

LOCATION

The barn should be located so as to be:

1. **Accessible.** It should be on an all-weather roadway or lane, thereby facilitating the use of horses, the delivery of feed and bedding, and removal of manure. Also, it should be adjacent, or in near proximity, to a corral, paddock, or pasture.

2. **High and dry.** It should be on high ground, with drainage away from it, thereby making for dryness.

3. **Expandable.** There should be provision for easy expansion, if and when the time comes. Often a building can be expanded in length provided no other structures or utilities interfere.

4. **Convenient to water and electricity.** Water

should be available and plentiful, and electricity should be in near proximity.

REQUISITES OF HORSE BARNS

All horse barns—regardless of kind, use, and purposes—should meet the following requisites:

1. **Environmental control.** Modify winter and summer temperatures for horses; protect them from rain, snow, sun, and wind; and minimize stress.

Also, barns should provide good ventilation. This refers to the changing of air—the replacement of foul air with fresh air. There should be a minimum of moisture and odor, and the barn should be free from drafts. Horse barn ventilation may be achieved through one or more of the following: an opening under the roof, a ridge vent, hinged windows, Dutch doors, and/or fans.

2. **Reasonable cost, along with minimum maintenance.** Initial cost is important, but consideration should also be given to durability and maintenance, and to such intangible values as pride and satisfaction, influence on the children, and advertising value.

3. **Adequate space.** Too little space may jeopardize the health and well-being of horses, whereas more space than needed makes for unnecessary expense.

4. **Storage for feed, bedding, and tack.** These are generally stored in the same building where used.

5. **Attractiveness.** An attractive horse barn makes for a *heap of living* and enhances the sale value of the property. A horse barn that has utility value, is in good proportions, and is in harmony with the natural surroundings, will have aesthetic value. Good design

is never achieved by indulgence in fads, frills, or highly ornamental features.

6. **Minimum fire risk.** The use of fire-resistant materials gives added protection to horses. Also, fire-retarding paints and sprays are available.

7. **Safety.** Safety features should be observed, such as no projections on which horses may become injured, and arrangements for feeding and watering without walking behind horses.

8. **Saving of labor.** This is a must in any commercial horse establishment. Also, where horses are kept for pleasure, it is well to minimize drudgery and eliminate unnecessary labor in feeding, cleaning, and handling.

9. **Horse health protection.** Healthy horses are superior and efficient performers; hence, horse barns should provide healthful living conditions for the occupants.

10. **Rodent and bird control.** Feed and tack storage areas should be rodent-proof and bird-proof.

11. **Suitable corrals and paddocks nearby.** Horse barns should be provided with well-drained, safe, and durably and attractively fenced corrals or paddocks, either adjacent to or in close proximity.

12. **Flexibility.** Both technological development and possible shifts in use make it desirable that horse barns be as flexible as possible—even to the point that they can be, cheaply and easily, converted into cabins, garages, storage buildings, and whatnot. Also, for suburbanites and renters, permanent barns that are portable are advantageous.

MATERIALS

Technology has evolved with new building materials and forced the improvement of old ones. In selecting horse barn building materials, consideration should be given to (1) initial cost, (2) durability and minimum maintenance, (3) attractiveness, and (4) fire resistance.

Among the materials available, and being used, are:

1. Wood, including plywood.
2. Metal.
3. Masonry, including concrete block, cinder, pumice block, brick, and stone.
4. Plastics.

PREFABRICATED HORSE BARNS

Preengineered and prefabricated horse barns are finding a place of increasing importance, especially on smaller horse establishments. Fabricators of such buildings have the distinct advantages of (1) price

Fig. 14-3. A Kentucky horse barn of great charm and beauty. (Courtesy, Kentucky Department of Travel Development, Frankfort)

savings due to purchase of materials in quantity lots, (2) economical and controlled fabricating, and (3) well-trained personnel for developing the best in plans and specifications.

FEED AND WATER FACILITIES

These are an important part of each barn. They may be either built-in or detached. For sanitary and flexibility reasons, as well as greater suitability, more and more good caretakers favor specialty feed and watering facilities, over old-time wood mangers and concrete or steel tanks. Bulk tank feed storage may well be considered on larger horse establishments, thereby eliminating sacks, lessening rodent and bird problems, and making it possible to obtain more favorable feed prices with larger orders.

KINDS OF HORSE BARNS

The needs for housing horses and storing materials vary according to the intended use of the building. Broadly speaking, horse barns are designed to serve (1) small horse establishments—the owner with one to a few head, (2) large horse breeding establishments, or (3) riding academies and training and boarding stables. A summary of the space requirements of buildings for horses is presented later in this chapter, under the section headed "Space Requirements," in Table 14-5.

SMALL HORSE ESTABLISHMENTS

When one or two riding horses or ponies are kept, they are usually stabled close to the house, which makes for greater convenience in their care and use. In most cases, box stalls are built in a row and provision is made for limited feed, bedding and tack storage; usually a combination feed and tack room for units with 1 to 2 stalls, and separate feed and tack rooms with 3 or more stalls. Fig. 14-4 shows an attractive small barn that is used as a private stable.

Building plans for a small horse barn are shown in Fig. 14-5.

Complete working drawings of small horse barns may be obtained through county agricultural agents or from extension agricultural engineers at most state agricultural colleges.

Fig. 14-4. An attractive small stable, along with limited feed storage and tack room. (Courtesy, *Sunset Magazine*, Menlo Park, CA)

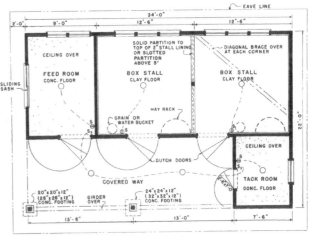

Fig. 14-5. Riding horse barn above and floor plan below. Barn has two box stalls, a feed room, and a tack room.

LARGE HORSE ESTABLISHMENTS

With large horse breeding establishments, specifically designed buildings are generally provided for different purposes. Because of the importance of horses for recreation and sport—and the further fact that the same principles of building construction apply to the one or two riding horse unit and the large breeding establishment—a brief discussion will be presented relative to each of the following types of buildings found on many of the larger breeding establishments throughout America: (1) broodmare and foaling barn, (2) barren mare barn, (3) stallion barn and paddocks, (4) breeding shed, (5) weanling and yearling quarters, and (6) isolation (quarantine) quarters.

BROODMARE AND FOALING BARNS

The building designed as the broodmare barn may also be used for mares in foal, mares with suckling foals, weanlings, and barren mares. Whatever their size or style, there are two basic rectangular arrangements of multiple stall barns. The most common is a central aisle with a row of stalls along each side. The other is the *island* type, which consists of two rows of stalls, back to back, surrounded by an alley or runway. The island type is preferred when an indoor exercising ring is desired.

Fig. 14-6. Broodmare and foaling barn, and nearby pasture paddock, at Walmac International, Lexington, Kentucky. (Courtesy, Thoroughbred Publications, Inc., Lexington, KY)

Maternity stalls should be 12 by 12 ft in size, or larger, and located so as to secure the most direct sunlight possible. When feasible, the maternity stalls should be adjacent to an office or some service room, so that at parturition time the caretaker may observe the mare through a peephole without being in sight. With this arrangement, it is preferable that the foaling stall have a double light switch, with one switch at the observation window and the other at the stall door.

For convenience and economy in operation, the broodmare barn should have ample quarters for the storage of a considerable supply of hay, bedding, and grain. Usually, hay and straw are stored in an overhead hay mow, and grain may be stored either overhead or on the ground-floor level. In the latter case, extra precaution should be taken to prevent animals from taking advantage of an open grain-bin door; otherwise, founder probably will result.

A record or office room, toilet facilities, hot water supply, veterinary supply room, and tack room are usually an integral part of the broodmare barn. In many cases, a reception room for visitors is also provided.

Fig. 14-7. Broodmare shed, opening onto a pasture, designed to accommodate a band of mares and their foals. (Courtesy, Kentucky Department of Travel Development, Frankfort)

BARREN MARE BARN OR SHED

The same type of barn as used for in-foal mares is entirely satisfactory for barren mares. Generally speaking, however, these mares do not require such careful attention or elaborate quarters. In large breeding establishments, usually they are run in bands of as many as 20 and are required to *rough it* to a considerable extent.

During inclement weather, a shelter should be available for barren mares. This may consist of either an open shed or a rectangular barn of the required size—allowing approximately 150 sq ft per animal—with a combination hay rack and trough down the center or along either wall. If the barn is closed, it should have a large sliding door opening out, away from the direction of the prevailing winds. Ample hay, grain, and bedding should be stored in the barn.

Fig. 14-8. Barren mare shed on the Morgan breeding establishment of Voorhis Farm, Red Hook, New York. (Photo by Fred J. Sass; courtesy, Fred Herrick, Manager, Voorhis Farm, Red Hook, NY)

STALLION BARN AND PADDOCK

This barn provides quarters for one or more stallions. It should have a small tack and equipment room, and it may or may not have feed storage. The stalls should be 14 ft square, or larger.

Stallion barns almost always face away from broodmare barns, and preferably in the direction of the prevailing winds. Some stud managers prefer that the topography or plantings be such as to prevent the stallion from seeing mares or other mature horses at a distance. In general, English and French managers subscribe to this type of arrangement, keeping their stallions so they cannot see any other horses. On the other hand, many good managers in this country insist that such isolation usually makes for a mean, nervous

Fig. 14-9. Stallion barns at Gainway Farm, Lexington, Kentucky—a masterly example of great beauty and elegance in horse barns. (Courtesy, Thoroughbred Publications, Lexington, KY)

horse. The latter advocates feel that stallions are better satisfied if they can see other horses off at a distance or even fairly close to them.

As in the broodmare barn, it is more practical and convenient to have feed and bedding storage within the stallion barn. Also a small tack and equipment room should be provided.

Stallion paddocks and the stallion barn are a necessary adjunct to each other. The stallion barn may open directly into the paddock or be separated from it by a runway. The former arrangement is the more convenient and is quite desirable when a vicious stallion must be handled. Many good stud managers insist, however, that a paddock immediately adjacent to the stallion barn—where the horse can go in and out of his quarters at will—encourages the animal to remain in the stall too much. These caretakers also believe that merely closing the stall door will not prevent the stallion from unnecessary loitering before the barn. Those subscribing to this school of thought insist that paddocks be located a short distance from the stallion barn and be separated from it by runways.

Regardless of the proximity of the stallion paddock to the barn, a large paddock helps considerably in keeping in fit condition horses that are not otherwise exercised regularly. Although paddock exercise is not as good as that given under saddle or in harness, it helps to guard against filled hocks, azoturia, and other trouble.

Sodded paddocks that provide succulent and nutritious grass are also preferable to barren areas which merely serve as gymnasiums for stallions. A 2- to 4-acre area is desirable. Every effort should be made to build the stallion paddock at least 300 ft on a side.

Care should be taken to see that paddock fences are free from projections that might cause injury. Fences should be constructed of wood or metal, rather than wire. A double fence should separate nearby stallion paddocks, or a stallion paddock from a broodmare pasture. The paddock fence should be a minimum of 6 ft high and should be constructed of 2- by 6-in. lumber or good strong poles.

Water should be available in the stallion paddock at all times. Shade is also very desirable.

BREEDING SHED AND BREEDING CORRAL

The breeding shed is nothing more than a large, roofed enclosure with a high ceiling in which mares may be handled and served under sanitary conditions. Most stud managers prefer to have the breeding shed in close proximity to the stallion barn, thus making for greater ease in handling nervous stallions.

The shed should be dust proof, high and without projections overhead that might possibly injure a rearing horse, well lighted, and should have a clay or tanbark floor (preferably the latter, as it lessens the dust problem). Most breeding sheds are a minimum of 24 by 24 ft in size and have a 15 to 20 ft ceiling. The breeding shed should be served by two wide doors located on opposite sides of the shed. With this arrangement, the stallion and mare can be taken out opposite doors. This will aid in preventing accidents when handling vicious or nervous animals.

The larger establishments generally include the following facilities in addition to the center court which serves as the breeding shed: laboratory for the veterinarian or technician, hot water facilities, and stalls in which mares are prepared for breeding. Formerly, many breeding sheds had a small stall for the young foal that usually accompanied the mare at the time of service. At the present time, however, these are seldom used, the foals being left at home.

When the cost of a breeding shed may be excessive, a high spacious corral built of boards may be used satisfactorily.

Fig. 14-10. An open shed for weanlings. This type of building furnishes a desirable place in which to winter young stock and idle horses unless the weather becomes too severe. (Courtesy, USDA)

WEANLING AND YEARLING QUARTERS

The same type of quarters is adapted to both weanlings and yearlings. In all cases, however, the different age groups should be kept separated from each other, for older animals are likely to crowd the younger ones away from the feed and may inflict injury. It is also best to separate the sexes, at least by the January following foaling. Either small separate barns should be provided for the different age and sex groups of weanlings and yearlings or a larger building and adjacent paddocks may be adapted for such handling.

Weanlings and yearlings may be housed satisfactorily in either a stable or open shed; the main requisites being that the quarters are dry, sanitary, and well bedded and that they provide fairly good protection from winds. When stalls are used, two weanlings or two yearlings may be kept together. Stalls should be 10 ft square. It must be remembered that in its native environment the horse is hardy and rugged and that diseases and unsoundnesses begin when there is too close confinement, improper feeding, and lack of exercise. This does not imply that such young animals should be neglected. Handling and gentling the animals at an early age is quite desirable.

It must be realized also that such animals will not develop and grow out satisfactorily unless they are well fed. The good caretaker, therefore, seeks a happy medium between stabling and ranging in the handling of young stock realizing that there are benefits to be derived from each and that losses occur if either is carried to an extreme. The main point to remember is that lots of fresh air and exercise are invaluable. Do not worry about young stock getting cold.

ISOLATION (QUARANTINE) QUARTERS

New animals that have been brought into a stable should always be kept isolated for a minimum of 21 days before being taken into the herd. This applies to newly purchased animals, boarders, or animals being returned from showing or racing. Mares requiring treatment for infection of the genital tract should be quartered separately and run in special fields or paddocks.

A small barn designed for this purpose, with 12 by 12 ft stalls and adjacent paddocks is considered an essential part of large breeding establishments. Separate feed and water facilities should also be provided for animals in isolation. Moreover, the caretaker must use discretion in going from the quarantine quarters to the rest of the stables or herd. The quarters should be cleaned thoroughly and disinfected following the removal of each animal that has been stabled therein.

When possible, the isolation quarters should be so located that horses can be taken to them and removed without either the animals themselves or the vehicles in which they are transported passing through the rest of the breeding farm. It is also desirable that the drainage from the isolation quarters be away from the rest of the farm.

RIDING, TRAINING, AND BOARDING STABLES

For this purpose, the quarters may consist of (1) stalls constructed back to back in the center of the barn with an indoor ring around the stalls, (2) stalls built around the sides of the barn with the ring in the center, or (3) stalls on either side of a hallway or alleyway and the ring outdoors. Box stalls should be 10 ft to 12 ft square and tie stalls should be 5 ft wide and 10 to 12 ft long.

SHEDS

In the wild state (as nature ordained it), the horse augmented its shaggy winter coat by seeking the protection afforded by hills, ravines, and trees. But domestication changed all this—and not always for the better. Diseases and unsoundnesses began with too close confinement and lack of exercise. Through mistaken kindness, horses are often subjected to lack of ventilation and high humidity.

Fig. 14-11. A horse shed; open to the south, away from the direction of the prevailing winds and toward the sun. (Photo by Ernst Peterson, Hamilton, MT; courtesy, Bitterroot Stock Farm, Hamilton, MT)

For broodmares and horses not in constant use, an open shed, with access to a pasture or corral, is preferred. Horses kept in an open shed, even in the colder areas, are healthier and suffer fewer respiratory diseases than horses kept in enclosed barns.

Sheds are usually open to the south or east, preferably opposite to the direction of the prevailing winds and toward the sun. They are enclosed on the ends and sides. Sometimes the front is partially closed, and in severe weather drop-doors may be used. The latter arrangement is especially desirable when the ceiling height is sufficient to accommodate a power manure loader.

In order that the bedding may be kept reasonably dry, it is important that sheds be located on high, well-drained ground; that eave troughs and downspouts drain into suitable tile lines, or surface drains; and that the structure have sufficient width to prevent rain and snow from blowing to the back end. Sheds should be a minimum of 24 ft in depth, front to back, with depths of up to 36 ft preferable. As a height of 8½ ft is necessary to accommodate some power operated manure loaders, when this type of equipment is to be used in the shed, a minimum ceiling height of 9 ft is recommended. The extra 6 in. allow for the accumulation of manure. Lower ceiling heights are satisfactory when it is intended to use a blade or pitchfork in cleaning the building.

The length of the shed can be varied according to the needed capacity. Likewise, the shape may be either a single long shed or in the form of an L or T. The long arrangement permits more corral space. When an open shed is contemplated, thought should be given to feed storage and feeding problems.

Sometimes hayracks are built along the back wall of sheds, or next to an alley, if the shed is very wide or if there is some hay storage overhead. Most generally, however, hayracks, feed bunks, and watering troughs are placed outside the structure.

SHADES

A shade, either trees or constructed should be provided for horses that are in the hot sun.

The most satisfactory constructed horse shades are (1) oriented with a north-south placement, (2) at least 12 to 15 ft in height (in addition to being cooler, high shades allow a mounted rider to pass under), and (3) open all around.

STALLS

Stalls are of two general types: (1) box stalls; and (2) tie, straight, standing, or slip stalls. As tie stalls differ primarily in the width of the area and their use is less common in breeding establishments, the discussion will be confined to loose or box stalls. The latter are preferred because they allow the horses more liberty, either when standing or lying down.

Adequate quarters for horses should be: (1) ample in size and height for the particular type of animal; (2) properly finished and without projections; (3) dry with good footing; (4) equipped with suitable doors; (5) provided with ample windows for proper lighting; (6) well ventilated; (7) cool in summer and warm in winter; (8) equipped with suitable mangers, grain containers, watering facilities, and mineral boxes; and (9) easy to keep clean.

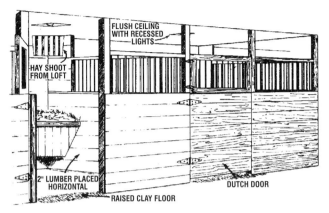

Fig. 14-12. A satisfactory type of box stall for horses. (Drawing by Steve Allured)

FLOOR OF STALL

A raised clay floor covered with a good absorbent bedding with proper drainage away from the building, is the most satisfactory flooring for horse stables. Clay

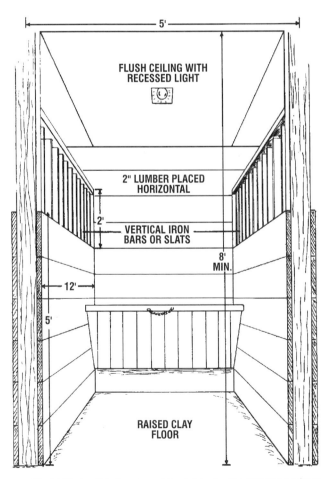

Fig. 14-13. A satisfactory type of tie stall for horses. (Drawing by Steve Allured)

floors are noiseless and springy, keep the hoofs moist and afford firm natural footing unless wet; but they are difficult to keep clean and level. To lessen the latter problems, the top layer should be removed each year, replaced with fresh clay, and leveled. Also, a semicircular concrete apron extending into each stall at the doorway will prevent horses from digging a hole in the clay floor at this point. This arrangement is particularly desirable in barns for yearlings, as they are likely to fret around the door.

Rough wooden floors furnish good traction for animals and are warm to lie upon; but they are absorbent and unsanitary, they often harbor rats and other rodents, and they lack durability.

Concrete, asphalt, or brick floors are durable, impervious to moisture, easily cleaned, and sanitary; but they are rigid and without resilient qualities, slippery when wet, hazardous to horses, and cold to lie upon. It is noteworthy that concrete and asphalt, generously covered with bedding, are widely used for stable floors throughout eastern and western Europe.

There is great need for an improved stall floor covering material for horses—one which will lessen (1) the amount of bedding needed, and (2) the labor and drudgery of cleaning.

Fig. 14-14. Box stall and door arrangement of the Al Blackburn Stable, Ojai, California. Note concrete footing of partition; walls boarded up solid with smooth, hard 20 in. lumber placed horizontally to a height of 5 ft, and slatted upper portion of partition and alleyway front of vertical iron slats. (Courtesy, *Sunset Magazine*, Menlo Park, CA)

Fig. 14-15. Box stalls in the stable of Mr. and Mrs. C. G. Furlong, Ojai, CA. (Courtesy, *Sunset Magazine*, Menlo Park, CA)

CONCRETE FOOTINGS

Concrete footings and foundation walls are recommended as they are both durable and noncorrosive. The foundation should be a minimum of 8 in. high, so as to be above the manure level.

SIZE AND HEIGHT OF STALL

Except for foaling mares and for stallions, there is no advantage in having box stalls larger than 12 ft square. The maternity stall should be at least 12 by 12 ft so that the attendant may get about the mare readily to accommodate the foal. Moreover, the stall should be without low hayracks (high hayracks may be used in a foaling stall), feed boxes, or other objects under which the mare might get caught or on which she might otherwise injure herself during parturition. The box stall for the stallion should be at least 14 by 14 ft in size.

It is also important that every part of a stall be of sufficient height so that the animal will not strike its head. A minimum clearance of 8 ft is essential, and it is preferable that the ceiling over all stalls be 9 ft or more in height.

PARTITIONS AND INTERIOR OF STALL

Regardless of the type of stall or the use made of it, there should be no projections (or ill-advised equipment) on which the horse may injure itself. Rough lumber, such as commonly used in the construction of stables on ordinary farms, has no place in the finishing of stables for breeding establishments.

In general, the walls of the stable should be boarded up solid with smooth, hard lumber placed horizontally to a height of 5 ft, using either (1) durable plywood of adequate thickness and strength, or (2) 2-in. hard lumber (such as oak) placed horizontally. Hollow concrete blocks encourage stall kicking; hence, when used they should either be filled with concrete or lined with wood. Breaks in any part of the stall, caused by kicking, create a hazard for the animal. Stallion stalls are sometimes padded to a height of approximately 5 ft. All walls and partitions should be on concrete footings.

Above 5 ft, and extending to a minimum of 7 ft (or even to the ceiling), stall partitions and the hallway (or alleyway) front of the stall may be slatted, preferably with metal, to allow for better air circulation and companionship with other horses.

A smooth ceiling should finish the interior of every stall. If electric lights are installed, they should be placed under protective cover and flush with the ceiling.

Tailboards are necessary for certain horses.

Stall doors may be either (1) the sliding type suspended by overhead rollers or rails (preferably sliding within the stall, so horses cannot push them out), or (2) the swinging Dutch type, with the top part swinging down or to the side.

Weather protection over the stall door is important. It can be easily and simply achieved by an over-hanging roof.

HALLWAYS OR ALLEYWAYS

The hallways or alleyways of stables should be a minimum of 8 ft in width[3] and height. Unlike stalls, they are usually not ceiled over, and they are usually higher.

The numerous types of flooring used in stalls are also used in hallways. In general, however, a clay floor is less popular than the hard-surfaced materials for this purpose.

Usually the hallway separates two rows of stables on either side. In northern areas, however, very often a hallway goes around the outside of the barn with two rows of stalls, back to back, down the center. In this arrangement, the alleyway is a very desirable

---

[3]The width should be increased if wide vehicles are to be accommodated. With wide trucks, 10 to 12 ft may be desirable.

Fig. 14-16. Hallway in the stable of L. Chase Grover, Woodside, California. Note the traditional wide hallway separates two rows of stables, and that the hallway is not ceiled over. (Courtesy, *Sunset Magazine*, Menlo Park, CA)

Fig. 14-17. The tack room of the Ella Mae Shofner stable, Montebello, California, is both attractive and practical for serving saddle horses. Note plastic harness cover on the wall, and the convenient saddle cleaning stand that holds all the necessary equipment for saddles, harness, and bridles. (Photo by John H. Williamson, Arcadia, CA)

place in which to exercise horses during inclement weather. This system, however, has one real disadvantage: It is difficult to arrange for direct sunlight in stalls that are located on the interior of the barn.

TACK ROOM

A tack room is an essential part of any barn. With one or two stall units, a combination tack and feed room is usually used, for practical reasons. On large establishments, the tack room is frequently the showplace of the stable. As such, the owner takes great pride in its equipment and arrangement. Also, depending upon the use of the horses, the tack room takes on an air and personality that represents the horses in their stalls.

Generally, the tack rooms in stables where there are American Saddle Horses, harness horses, or hunters are rather formal. In the vernacular of the *horsey set*, they maintain the *Boston touch*. On the other hand, where Western-style riding prevails, generally the formal tack rooms have been replaced by more practical, simple rooms.

Tack rooms should be floored, rodent-proof and bird-proof, and ceiled over.

Figs. 14-17 through 14-21 present some tack rooms that are rather characteristic of stables wherein there are different types and classes of light horses.

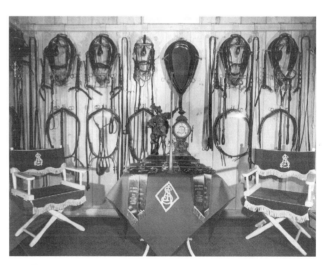

Fig. 14-18. The impeccable formal tack room of the J. A. Smith stable, El Monte, California, contains special tack for Hackney and harness show ponies of different sizes and classifications. Since appointments in harness show classes are very important, each set of harness is made for a particular class and rig. The bugle on the table is used to call classes at the shows. (Photo by John H. Williamson, Arcadia, CA)

Fig. 14-19. The tack room of the C. M. Deardorff stables, Santa Ana, California. This tack room presents an interesting and attractive display of pictures of winning horses, trophies and ribbons won in shows, and beautiful silver saddles used for parade. This tack room has been in active service for many years. (Photo by John H. Williamson, Arcadia, CA)

Fig. 14-21. The tack room of the Bob Egan stable, Pacific Palisades, California, is rather typical for owners of hunters, jumpers, and polo ponies. The tack box holds coolers, rub rags, cleaning equipment, hammers, nails, and other gear necessary in taking the horses to the shows. (Photo by John H. Williamson, Arcadia, CA)

FIRE PROTECTION

Barns in which valuable horses are stabled should be posted with "no smoking" signs. Additionally, they should be equipped with (1) fire hoses in recessed areas, (2) an automatic fire alarm system, and (3) an automatic sprinkler system.

The fire hazard can also be minimized by storing nothing but properly cured hay and by making sure that all wiring is in accord with strict electrical codes.

HORSE EQUIPMENT

Although the design of horse equipment is likely to be dominated by the fads and fancies of the owner, the basic needs are merely for simple but effective equipment with which to provide hay, concentrates, minerals, and water—without waste, and without hazard to the horse. Whenever possible, it is desirable that feed and water facilities be located so that they can be filled without necessitating that the caretaker enter the stall or corral, from the standpoint of both convenience and safety. In any event, it should not be

Fig. 14-20. Tack room of Dwight Murphy's San Marcos Ranch, Santa Ynez Valley, California. Note the large natural color painting by Nicholas S. Ferfires, depicting the different costumes and saddles of riders and the beautiful silver decorated saddles used in parades on the noted Palominos of San Marcos Ranch. (Photo by John H. Williamson, Arcadia, CA)

necessary to walk behind horses in order to feed and water them.

Feed and water equipment may be built in or detached. Because specialty feed and water equipment is more sanitary, flexible, and suitable, many equestrians favor it over old-style wood mangers and concrete or steel tanks. Bulk-tank feed storage may be used to advantage on large horse establishments to eliminate sacks, lessen rodent and bird problems, and make it possible to obtain feed at lower prices by ordering large amounts.

A discussion of each of the common types of horse equipment follows. The specifications of feed and water equipment for horses are given in Table 14-5, under the section headed "Space Requirements."

HAYRACKS AND MANGERS

Some authorities advocate feeding the hay from the floor, inasmuch as horses feed from the ground while grazing naturally. This system has the advantage of reducing the cost of construction, economizing in stall space, and enhancing the security of the horse in the stable. But it requires a careful allotment of hay in order to prevent waste. Moreover, some horses acquire the habit of pawing whatever is in front of them, so that they either eat contaminated hay or waste a considerable part of it.

The author favors the use of hayracks because they (1) alleviate the problem of contaminated hay and lessen parasites, and (2) lessen pawing and waste. In barns with haylofts, there should be a chute above each hayrack, so that the hay can be dropped directly from the loft. Racks should open at the bottom so that dirt, chaff, and trash may be removed or will fall out. For stallions and broodmares, high racks should be used to eliminate injury hazards.

Fig. 14-22. Steel hayrack in paddock at Murrieta Stud, Murrieta, California. (Courtesy, *The Thoroughbred of California*, Arcadia, CA)

Fig. 14-23. A good outdoor hayrack in a well-fenced horse paddock. (Courtesy, *Sunset Magazine*, Menlo Park, CA)

A stall rack may be made of metal, fiber, or plastic. A rack for horses should hold 25 to 30 lb of hay and a rack for ponies, 10 to 15 lb. It should be in a corner of the stall. The bottom of the rack should be the same height as the horse or pony at the withers.

A wooden manger may be used. It should be 30 in. wide and 24 to 30 in. long for horses and 20 in. square for ponies. Put the manger in the front or in a corner of the stall. The height should be 30 to 42 in. for horses and 20 to 24 in. for ponies.

A corral rack may be made of wood, steel, or aluminum. It should be large enough to hold a one-day supply of hay for the intended number of horses. Put the rack in the fence line of the corral if horses feed from one side only. Put it on high ground if horses feed from both sides. The top of the rack may be 1 to 2 ft higher than the horses at the withers. Corral hayracks that feed from both sides should be portable.

GRAIN CONTAINERS

There is hardly any limit to the number of types of grain containers, both patented and homemade, that are used for feeding horses. These containers range all the way from very simple, inexpensive boxes to elaborate and costly equipment. Regardless of the type, the concentrate containers should be removed easily and cleaned by scrubbing. Such cleaning is especially important after a wet mash has been fed. Also, they should not constitute a hazard to horses.

A pail or tub can be made of metal, plastic, or rubber. Usually it has screw eyes and hooks or snaps

Fig. 14-24. Feed bucket with snap hook, used in the stable of Mr. and Mrs. Edwin Knowles, Montecito, California. (Courtesy, *Sunset Magazine*, Menlo Park, CA)

Fig. 14-25. Automatic waterer, placed at one side of manger. (Courtesy, *Sunset Magazine*, Menlo Park, CA)

so it can be suspended. The capacity should be 16 to 20 qt for horses and 14 to 16 qt for ponies.

In a stall, the pail or tub should be at the front. The height should be two-thirds the height of the animal at the withers, or 38 to 42 in. for horses and 28 to 32 in. for ponies.

In a corral, put the tub or pail along a fence line and at the same height as in a stall.

A wooden box for horses should be 12 to 16 in. wide, 24 to 30 in. long, and 8 to 10 in. deep. A box for ponies should be 10 to 12 in. wide, 20 to 24 in. long, and 6 to 8 in. deep.

The location and height of a box in a stall are the same as for a pail or tub. Do not use a wooden box in a corral.

If desired, a wedge-shaped metal pan set on a wooden shelf can be mounted in a front corner of the stall and pivoted so it can be pulled out for filling and cleaning and then pushed back into the stall and locked in place.

WATERING FACILITIES

As in feed containers, there is a bountiful supply of types of watering facilities from which to select, some stationary, and others removable. Whatever the type, the water container should be one that can be drained and cleaned frequently. All animals in stalls should be provided with water, and each paddock should have a suitable tank or waterer.

Water pails or automatic waterers are commonly used in stalls. Pails come in different materials—metal, plastic, or rubber. Automatic waterers are made of metal. Pails or waterers should be located in a front corner of the stall and, preferably, considerable distance from feed containers. Otherwise, horses will

carry feed to the waterer or drip water in the concentrate container. Pails or waterers should be stationed at a height equal to two-thirds the height of the horse at the withers, or about 38 to 42 in. for horses and 28 to 32 in. for ponies.

Automatic waterers or water tanks may be used in corrals. A 2-cup waterer will accommodate 12 horses; a large 20- by 30-in. automatic waterer will accommodate 25 horses.

Water tanks, which may be made of concrete or steel, should be 30 to 36 in. high, with 1 linear foot of tank space allowed for each five horses. Tanks should be equipped with float valves that are protected from the horses. When used in a corral, a water tank should

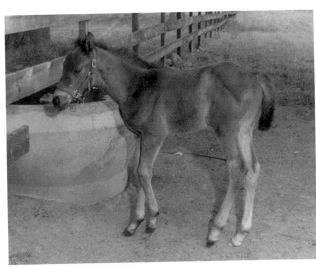

Fig. 14-26. Water tank set in fence line and rounded (no protruding corners), to protect horses from injury. (Courtesy, Kentucky Department of Public Information, Frankfort)

be set in the fence line, and there should not be any protruding corners. If a tank is in a pasture and away from a fence, it should be painted so the horses can see it at night.

The daily water requirements for horses are: mature horse, 12 gal.; foal to 2-year-old, and pony, 6 to 8 gal. In cold areas, waterers should be heated and equipped with thermostatic controls. A satisfactory water temperature range in winter is 40 to 45° F and in summer 60 to 75° F. Automatic waterers should be checked daily, to make sure that they are working.

MINERAL BOX OR SELF-FEEDER

All horses should have free access to (1) salt, and (2) suitable mineral mix at all times, with these placed in separate areas of a two-compartment mineral box or self-feeder.

A box may be made of wood and a self-feeder may be made of metal or wood. In a stall, the box or self-feeder should be in a corner and located at the same height as the box or pail used for concentrates.

In a corral, mineral containers should be in a fence corner. The height should be two-thirds the height of the horse at the withers. If a mineral container is in the open, it should be protected from wind and rain.

OTHER HORSE EQUIPMENT

In addition to the basic equipment needed for feeding and watering horses, there is hardly any limit to the other kinds of ingenious equipment used in the care and management of horses on breeding establishments. Some of these items of equipment, with

illustrated methods of use in some cases are presented in Fig. 14-27.

FENCES FOR HORSES

Good fences (1) maintain boundaries, (2) make horse operations possible, (3) reduce losses to both animals and crops, (4) increase property values, (5) promote better relationships between neighbors, (6) lessen accidents from animals getting on roads, and (7) add to the attractiveness and distinctiveness of the premises.

Large pastures, in which the concentration of horses is not too great, may be fenced with woven wire. The mesh of the woven wire fence should be small so that horses cannot get their feet through it. Corrals, paddocks, and smaller pastures require more rigid materials. The deficiencies of board and pole fences are generally recognized. They are chewed by horses; they splinter and break, which may injure a horse; they must be painted and repainted; they're expensive to maintain; and they rot.

Until recently, metal fences—conventional steel, aluminum, wrought iron, chain link, cable, and others—possessed one or more deficiencies; to most people all of them were cold, unimaginative and unattractive in color; some could not be painted; some sagged from side to side; some corroded; some lacked resilience—when bumped they stayed bent; and most of them were difficult to construct. But metal fences have been greatly improved in recent years. Also, polymer plastic or polyvinyl chloride (PVC) fences are now on the market.

Table 14-4 lists the common materials for horse fences and gives the specifications for their use.

TABLE 14-4
HORSE FENCES

Post and Fencing Material	Post Length and Diameter	Size of Rails, Boards, or Poles, and Gauge of Wire	Fence Height	Number of Rails, Boards, or Poles, and Mesh of Wire	Distance Between Posts on Centers
			(in.)		(ft)
Steel or aluminum posts and rails[1]	7½ ft	10 or 20 ft long	60	3 rails	10
	7½ ft	10 or 20 ft long	60	4 rails	10
	8½ ft	10 or 20 ft long	72	4 rails	10
Wooden posts and boards	7½ ft; 4 to 8 in.	2 × 6 or 2 × 8 in. boards	60	4 boards	8
	8½ ft; 4 to 8 in.	2 × 6 or 2 × 8 in. boards	72	5 boards	8
Wooden posts and poles	7½ ft; 4 to 8 in.	4 to 6 in. diameter	60	4 poles	8
	8½ ft; 4 to 8 in.	4 to 6 in. diameter	72	5 poles	8
Wooden posts and woven wire[2]	7½ ft; 4 to 8 in.	9 or 11 gauge stay wire	55 to 58	12-in. mesh	12

[1]Because of the strength of most metal, fewer rails and posts are necessary than when wood is used.

[2]Locate one strand of barbed wire—with 4 points, 5 in. apart—2 to 3 in. above the top of the woven wire. This will prevent horses from breaking down the woven wire by leaning on the fence.

Fig. 14-27. Various means of restraining a horse: **A**, knee strap; **B**, side sling; **C**, casting harness; **D**, humane nose twitch; **E**, stocks; and **F**, a breeding chute. The essential features of such methods and equipment are (1) thorough restraint of the animal, without the hazard of injury, and (2) convenience and protection for the operator. (Courtesy, USDA)

Fig. 14-28. Polyvinyl chloride (PVC) fence at Harris Farms, Coalinga, California, being evaluated by David McGlothlin, Manager, Horse Division. (Photo by Audrey H. Ensminger)

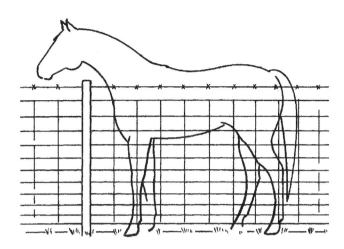

Fig. 14-30. A suitable wire fence where the concentration of animals is not too great. The woven wire should be 55 to 58 in. high, with No. 9 top and bottom wire and No. 9 or 11 stay wire, and 12-in. mesh. One strand of barbed wire—with 4 points, 5 in. apart—2 in. to 3 in. above the top of the woven wire will prevent horses from breaking down the woven wire by leaning over the fence. This type of fence is also satisfactory for all other farm animals except young pigs.

SPACE REQUIREMENTS

One of the first, and frequently one of the most difficult, problems confronting the horse owner who wishes to construct a building or item of equipment is that of arriving at the proper size or dimensions.

Fig. 14-29. A strong pole fence. Fences for valuable horses should always be constructed of metal, poles, or 2-in. lumber, and there should not be any projections that might cause injury. Barbed wire fence is always hazardous to horses. (Courtesy, *Sunset Magazine*, Menlo Park, CA)

Fig. 14-31. Pasture paddock enclosed with a metal fence for the Thorough-bred stallion, *Russian Ballet*, at Harris Farms, Coalinga, California, David McGlothlin, Manager, Horse Division (Photo by Audrey H. Ensminger)

SPACE REQUIREMENTS OF BUILDINGS AND EQUIPMENT FOR HORSES

Some conservative average figures of the building and equipment space requirements of horses are herewith presented. Table 14-5 shows the space requirements for buildings, and Table 14-6 shows the specifications for feed and water. In general, less space than indicated may jeopardize the health and well-being of animals, whereas more space makes the buildings and equipment more expensive than necessary.

Fig. 14-32. Stallion barn at Claiborne Farm, Paris, Kentucky. (Photo by J. Noye, Versailles, KY. Courtesy, Dr. W. C. Kaufman)

TABLE 14-5
SPACE REQUIREMENTS OF BUILDINGS FOR HORSES

Kinds, Uses and Purposes	Recommended Plan	Box Stalls or Shed Areas				Tie Stalls (size)
		Size	Height of Ceiling	Height of Doors	Width of Doors	
Smaller Horse Establishments:						
Horse barns for pleasure horses, ponies, and/or raising a few foals.	12 ft × 12 ft stalls in a row; combination tack-feed room for 1- and 2-stall units; separate tack and feed rooms for 3-stall units or more. Generally, not more than a month's supply of feed is stored at a time. Use of all-pelleted rations (hay and grain combined) lessens feed storage space requirements.	Horses: 12 ft × 12 ft Ponies: 10 ft × 10 ft[1]	8 – 9 ft	8 ft	4 ft	5 ft wide; 10 – 12 ft long
Larger Horse Breeding Establishments: *The following specially designed buildings may be provided for different purposes.*						
Broodmare and foaling barn	A rectangular building, either (1) with a central aisle, and a row of stalls along each side, or (2) of the *island* type, with two rows of stalls, back to back, surrounded by an alley or runway. Ample quarters for storage of hay, bedding, and grain. A record or office room, toilet facilities, hot water supply, veterinary supply room, and tack room are usually an integral part of a broodmare barn.	12 ft × 12 ft to 16 ft × 16 ft	9 ft	8 ft	4 ft	
Stallion barn	Quarters for one or more stallions, with or without feed storage. A small tack and equipment room. Stallion paddocks, at least 300 ft on a side, adjacent or in close proximity.	14 ft × 14 ft	9 ft	8 ft	4 ft	
Barren mare barn	An open shed or rectangular building, with a combination rack and trough down the center or along the wall. Storage space for ample hay, grain, and bedding.	150 sq ft per animal	9 ft	8 ft	4 ft	
Weanling or yearling quarters	Open shed or stalls. The same type of building is adapted to both weanlings and yearlings; but different ages and sex groups should be kept separate. When stalls are used, two weanlings or two yearlings may be placed together.	10 ft × 10 ft	9 ft	8 ft	4 ft	
Breeding shed	A large roofed enclosure with a high ceiling; should include laboratory for the veterinarian, hot water facilities, and stalls for preparing mares for breeding and holding foals.	24 ft × 24 ft	15 – 20 ft	8 ft	9 ft	
Isolation (quarantine) quarters	Small barn, with feed and water facilities and adjacent paddock; for occupancy by new or sick animals.	12 ft × 12 ft	9 ft	8 ft	4 ft	
Riding Academies; Training and Boarding Stables:	Either (1) stalls constructed back to back in the center of the barn, with an indoor ring around the outside; (2) stalls around the outside and a ring in the center; or (3) stalls on either side of a hallway or alleyway, and an outdoor ring.	12 ft × 12 ft	9 ft	8 ft	4 ft	5 ft wide; 10 – 12 ft long

[1]Even for ponies, a 12 × 12 ft stall is recommended since (1) it costs little more than a 10 × 10 ft, and (2) it affords more flexibility—it can be used for bigger horses when and if the occasion demands.

TABLE 14-6
SPECIFICATIONS OF FEED AND WATER EQUIPMENT FOR HORSES

Equipment for	Kind of Equipment	Materials and Design	Sizes for		In Stall		In Corral		Remarks
			Horses	Ponies	Location	Height	Location	Height	
Concentrates	Pail; tub	Metal, plastic, or rubber; usually with screw-eyes, hooks, or snaps for suspending.	16–20 qt	14–16 qt	Front of stall.	Two-thirds height of horse at withers; or 38–42 in. for horses, and 28–32 in. for ponies.	Along fence line	Same height as stall.	For sanitary reasons, removable concentrate containers are preferable so that they can be taken out and easily and frequently cleaned—which is especially important after a wet bran mash has been fed.
	Box	Wood	Width 12–16 in. Length 24–30 in. Depth 8-10 in.	10–12 in. 20–24 in. 6–8 in.	Front of stall.	Two-thirds height of horse at withers; or 38–42 in. for horses, and 28–32 in. for ponies.			If desired, a pie-shaped metal pan set in a wooden shelf can be mounted in a front corner of the stall and pivoted in such manner that it can be pulled outward for filling and cleaning, then returned into the stall and locked in place.
Hay	Stall rack	Metal, fiber, or plastic	25–30 lb	10–15 lb	Corner of stall; in trailer or van.	Bottom of rack, same height as horse or pony at withers.			Hayracks (1) eliminate contaminated hay and lessen parasite infestation, and (2) lessen pawing and waste. Racks should open at bottom so that dirt, chaff, and trash may be removed or will fall out. For stallions and broodmares, always use high racks to avoid injury hazards.
	Manger	Wood	Width 30 in. Length 24–30 in.	20 in. 20 in.	Front or corner of stall.	30–42 in. for horses; 20–24 in. for ponies.			
	Corral rack	Wood	Large enough to provide one day's supply of hay for intended number of horses.				In fence line if it feeds from one side only. On high ground if it feeds from both sides.	Top of rack may be 1 in. to 2 in. higher than height of horse at withers.	Corral hayracks that feed from both sides should be portable.
Mineral	Box	Wood			Corner of stall.	Same height as concentrate box.	Fence corner	Two-thirds height of horse at withers.	If mineral container is stationed in the open—in a corral, or in a pasture—it should be protected from wind and rain. Mineral containers should have two compartments—one for mineral mix, and the other for salt.
	Self-feeder	Metal or wood				Same height as concentrate box.	Fence corner		

(Continued)

TABLE 14-6 (Continued)

Equipment for	Kind of Equipment	Materials and Design	Sizes for		In Stall		In Corral		Remarks
			Horses	Ponies	Location	Height	Location	Height	
Water	Stall, automatic	Metal; 1 cup or 2 cups			Front corner of stall.	24–30 in.			The daily water requirements are: Mature horse, 12 gal.; foals to two-year-olds; 6–8 gal.; and ponies 6–8 gal. In colder areas, waterers should be heated, and equippped with thermostatic controls. A satisfactory water temperature range in the winter is 40–45°F; in summer, 60–80°F. Watering facilities should be designed so as to facilitate draining and cleaning. Also, they should be located a proper distance from feed containers; otherwise, horses will (1) carry feed to the waterer, or (2) slobber water into the concentrate container. A 20 × 30 in. automatic waterer will accommodate about 25 horses, and a 2-cup waterer will serve 12 head. Automatic waterers should be checked daily.
	Corral, automatic				In fence corner.	24–30 in.			
	Pail	Metal, plastic, or rubber			Front of stall.	Two-thirds height of horse at withers; or 38–42 in. for horses, and 28–32 in. for ponies.			
	Tank	Concrete, steel					Set in fence so that there are no protruding corners; or painted white out in corral or pasture.	30–36 in.	One linear foot of tank space should be allowed for each five horses. Tanks should be equipped with a float valve, which should be protected.

RECOMMENDED MINIMUM WIDTH OF SERVICE PASSAGES

In general, the requirements for service passages are similar, regardless of the kinds of animals. Accordingly, the suggestions contained in Table 14-7 are equally applicable to horse, sheep, cattle, and swine barns.

TABLE 14-7
RECOMMENDED MINIMUM WIDTHS FOR SERVICE PASSAGES

Kind of Passage	Use	Minimum Width
Feed alley	For feed cart	4 ft
Driveway	For wagon, spreader, or truck	9–12 ft
Doors and gate	Drive-through	8–9 ft

STORAGE SPACE REQUIREMENTS FOR FEED AND BEDDING

The space requirements for feed storage for horses vary so widely that it is difficult to provide a suggested method of calculating space requirements applicable to such diverse conditions. The amount of feed to be stored depends primarily upon (1) the length of pasture season, (2) the method of feeding and management, (3) the kind of feed, (4) the climate, (5) the proportion of feeds produced on the farm or ranch in comparison with those purchased, and (6) the number of horses. Normally, the storage capacity should be sufficient to handle all feed grown on the farm and to hold purchased supplies.

Table 14-8 gives the storage space requirements for feed and bedding. This information may be helpful to the individual operator who desires to compute the barn space required for a specific horse enterprise. Also, it provides a convenient means of estimating the amount of feed or bedding in storage.

Many factors—other than kind of hay/straw, such as form (loose, baled, chopped), and period of settling—affect the density of hay/straw in a stack or in a barn, including (a) moisture content at haying time, and (b) texture and foreign material.

TABLE 14-8
STORAGE SPACE REQUIREMENTS FOR FEED AND BEDDING[1]

Kind of Feed or Bedding	Pounds per Cubic Foot	Cubic Feet per Ton	Pounds per Bushel of Grain
Hay/Straw:[2]			
1. Loose			
Alfalfa	4.4–4.0	450–500	
Nonlegume	4.4–3.3	450–600	
Straw	3.0–2.0	670–1,000	
2. Baled			
Alfalfa	10.0–6.0	200–330	
Nonlegume	8.0–6.0	250–330	
Straw	5.0–4.0	400–500	
3. Chopped			
Alfalfa	7.0–5.5	285–360	
Nonlegume	6.7–5.0	300–400	
Straw	8.0–5.7	250–350	
Corn:			
15½% moisture			
Shelled	44.8		56
Ear	28.0		70
Shelled, ground	38.0		48
Ear, ground	36.0		45
30% moisture			
Shelled	54.0		67.5
Ear, ground	35.8		89.6
Barley, 15%	38.4		48.0
ground	28.0		37.0
Flax, 11%	44.8		56.0
Oats, 16%	25.6		32.0
ground	18.0		23.0
Rye, 16%	44.8		56.0
ground	38.0		48.0
Sorghum, grain 15%	44.8		56.0
Soybeans, 14%	48.0		60.0
Wheat, 14%	48.0		60.0
ground	43.0		50.0

[1]*Housing and Equipment Handbook*, MWPS-6, Midwest Plan Service, Iowa State University, Ames.

[2]Many factors—other than kind of hay/straw, such as form (loose, baled, chopped), and period of settling—affect the density of hay/straw in a stack or in a barn. including (a) moisture content at haying time, and (b) texture and foreign material.

SHOW-RING

There are no standard specifications relative to size, type of construction, and maintenance of show-rings. Yet all the better rings meet certain basics.

For most purposes, the author recommends a ring 125 by 250 ft in size. It is recognized, however, that many good show-rings are either smaller or larger than these dimensions.

In order to allow plenty of room for such classes as working hunters and jumpers, in which as many as 12 separate jumps may be used, a number of shows have copied the famous Devon Horse Show for ring size. It measures 150 by 300 ft. But some equestrians consider it too big.

Those favoring smaller rings point out that the Spanish Riding School ring, in Vienna, in which the famous Lipizzans perform, is only 180 ft long, 59 ft wide and 56 ft high; and that New York's Madison Square Garden ring, in which the National Horse Show is held, is slightly under 100 ft wide.

In addition to ring size, consideration must be given to proper footing—to achieving resilience, yet firmness and freedom from dust. With an outdoor ring, establishing proper drainage and constructing a good track base are requisite to all-weather use. Drainage is usually secured by (1) locating the ring so that it is high, with the runoff away from it, and (2) installing a perforated steel pipe (with perforations toward the bottom side), or drainage tile, underneath the track if necessary.

Resilience, with firmness, is usually secured by mixing organic matter with dirt or sand. For example, the entire ring at the Spanish Riding School is covered with a mixture of two-thirds sawdust and one-third sand, which is sprinkled at intervals to keep the dust down.

In many indoor rings of the United States, 6 to 8 in. of tanbark on a dirt base are used. Unless tanbark is sprinkled at frequent intervals, it tends to pulverize and give poor footing. Others mix shavings and/or sawdust with dirt or sand to obtain a covering of 18 to 24 in. of the material. One good ring with which the author is familiar was prepared by laying down 9 in. of wood shavings, 2 in. of sawdust, and 4 in. of sand—all of which were mixed together, then oiled. Still others add a bit of salt, because it holds moisture when wetted down, thereby minimizing dust.

For outdoor rings, needed organic matter for resilience is sometimes secured by seeding rye, or other small grain, on the track during the off season, then disking the green crop under.

No matter how good the construction, a show-ring must be maintained, both before the show and between events. It must be smoothed and leveled, and holes must be filled; and, when it gets too hard, it must be penetrated. A flexible, chain-type harrow is recommended for show-ring maintenance.

In addition to ring size, construction, and maintenance, consideration must be given to layout for facilitating reversing a performance class in a ring that has turf or other decorative material in the center; attractiveness of the ring; spectator seating capacity, comfort, and visibility; nearby parking; and handling the crowd.

DEPRECIATION ON BUILDINGS AND EQUIPMENT

Since 1988, single-purpose agricultural structures (such as horse barns) may normally be depreciated in 10 years. Automobiles, pick-up trucks, and certain technological and research equipment, may be depreciated in 5 years.

SELECTED REFERENCES

Title of Publication	Author(s)	Publisher
Agricultural Engineers Yearbook	Ed. by R. H. Hahn, Jr.	American Society of Agricultural Engineers, St. Joseph, MI, annual
Breeding and Raising Horses, Ag. Hdbk. No. 394	M. E. Ensminger	Agricultural Research Service, USDA, Washington, DC, 1972
Farm Builder's Handbook, Second Edition	R. J. Lytle	Structures Publishing Company, Farmington, MI, 1973
Farm Building Design	L. W. Neubauer H. B. Walker	Prentice-Hall, Inc., Englewood Cliffs, NJ, 1961
Farm Buildings	R. E. Phillips	Doane-Western, St. Louis, MO, 1981
Farm Service Buildings	H. E. Gray	McGraw-Hill Book Company, New York, NY, 1955
Farm Structures	H. J. Barre L. L. Sammet	John Wiley & Sons, Inc., New York, NY, 1950
Handbook of Livestock Equipment	E. M. Juergenson	The Interstate Printers & Publishers, Inc., Danville, IL, 1971
Horse, The	J. W. Evans, et al.	W. H. Freeman and Co., New York, NY, 1990
Horse Breeding Farm, The	L. C. Willis	A. S. Barnes & Co., Inc., Cranbury, NJ, 1973
Horse Science Handbook, Vols. 1-3	Ed. by M. E. Ensminger	Agriservices Foundation, Clovis, CA, 1963, 1964, 1966
Horsemanship and Horse Care, Ag. Info. Bull. No. 353	M. E. Ensminger	Agricultural Research Service, USDA, Washington, DC, 1972
Housing of Animals	A. Maton, et al.	Elsevier, Amsterdam, 1985
Latest Developments in Livestock Housing	Seminar	University of Illinois, Urbana-Champaign, 1987
Light Horses, Farmers' Bull. No. 2127	M. E. Ensminger	Agricultural Research Service, USDA, Washington, DC
Livestock Waste Management and Pollution Abatement	Symposium	American Society of Agricultural Engineers, St. Joseph, MI, 1971
Livestock Waste Management System Design Conference for Consulting and SCS Engineers		University of Nebraska Cooperative Extension Service, Lincoln, 1973
Practical Farm Buildings	J. S. Boyd	The Interstate Printers & Publishers, Inc., Danville, IL, 1973
Principles of Animal Environment	M. L. Esmay	Avi Publishing Co., Westport, CT, 1969
Stockman's Handbook, The, Seventh Edition	M. E. Ensminger	Interstate Publishers, Inc., Danville, IL, 1992
Structures and Environment Handbook		Midwest Plan Service, Iowa State University, Ames, 1972

Plans and specifications for horse buildings and equipment can also be obtained from the local county agricultural agent, your state college of agriculture, and materials and equipment manufacturers and dealers.

Signs of good health—bright-eyed and bushy-tailed. (Courtesy, Ruth White, White Horse Ranch, Naper, NE)

15

HORSE HEALTH, DISEASE PREVENTION, AND PARASITE CONTROL[1]

by
DR. MELISSA T. HINES, D.V.M., Ph.D.,

Assistant Professor, Large Animal Medicine, Department of Veterinary Clinical Sciences, Washington State University, Pullman Washington

and

DR. M. E. ENSMINGER, Ph.D.,
President, Agriservices Foundation, 648 West Sierra Avenue, P.O. Box 429, Clovis, California 93613

[1]The material presented in this chapter is based on factual information believed to be accurate, but it is not guaranteed. Where the instructions and precautions given herein are in disagreement with those of competent local authorities or reputable manufacturers, always follow the latter two.

Horses are generally quite valuable and, in the case of horses in training or competition, they must be in top shape. Hence, they merit well-informed owners. When disease is encountered, they require the best care and treatment that a competent veterinarian can administer.

With the advent of the automobile and truck, most draft horses and mules were automatically quarantined on the farm or ranch where they had less opportunity to rub noses, less need to eat out of livery stable mangers and feed boxes, and none of the hazards of the community hitching post and the town watering tank. But the rise of light horses for certain recreation and sport, along with their international movement for (1) sales, (2) breeding, and (3) competitive events, has brought new diseases, parasites, and ailments to plague horses.

In recent years, science has moved with rapid and far-reaching strides in the field of horse health, disease prevention, and parasite control; and new and important advances are being made almost daily. Progressive equestrians and veterinarians will wish to follow these modern developments with care, constantly improving upon present information and recommendations. Besides, horse health, disease prevention, and parasite control are costly.

It is estimated that animal diseases and parasites in the U.S. inflicting all classes of animals including horses (1) decrease animal productivity by 15 to 20%, and (2) make for annual losses of $10 billion. In the developing countries, diseases and parasites take an even greater toll—they decrease animal productivity by 30 to 40%.

SIGNS OF GOOD HEALTH

Equestrians need to be familiar with the behavioral norms of horses in order to detect and treat abnormalities, especially illnesses.

At the outset, it should be recognized that it is difficult to enumerate all the signs of good health, along with the departures therefrom that constitute ill health. It may be even more difficult to determine whether an illness is due to faulty nutrition or communicable disease. This ability, inborn and honed by experience, sets the expert caretaker apart from the novice. If in doubt, the veterinarian should be called.

The signs of good horse health, any departure from which constitutes a warning signal, follow:

1. **Contentment.** Healthy horses are contented. They look completely unworried when resting.

2. **Alertness.** In horse vernacular, healthy horses

are "bright-eyed and bushy-tailed." They are alert and will prick up their ears on the slightest provocation.

3. **Eating with relish.** In healthy horses, the appetite is good and the feed is attacked with relish (as indicated by eagerness to get to the feed—pawing, nickering, etc.).

4. **Normal productivity.** Healthy horses maintain their normal level of production—in weight and in work.

5. **Sleek coat and pliable and elastic skin.** Sleek, glossy coats of hair and pliable and elastic skins characterize healthy horses. When the coat loses its luster and the skin becomes dry, scurfy, and hidebound, there is usually trouble.

6. **Bright eyes and pink eye membranes.** In healthy horses, the eyes are bright and the membranes—which can be seen when the lower lid is pulled down—are whitish pink in color and moist.

7. **Normal feces and urine.** The consistency of the feces varies with the diet; for example, when horses are first turned on lush grass they will be loose. Normally, they should be firm but not dry. There should not be large quantities of undigested feed, blood, mucus, or pus. The urine should be clear or slightly cloudy, but free from blood or pus. Both the feces and urine should be passed without effort.

8. **Maintaining social organization.** Healthy animals whose movements are not restricted by close confinement maintain a normal social organization in the herd—they move about in a certain pattern.

9. **Normal temperature, pulse rate, and breathing rate.** Table 15-1 gives the normal temperature, pulse rate, and breathing rate of animals (for comparative purposes, species other than the horse are listed). In general, any marked and persistent deviations from these norms may be looked upon as a sign of ill health.

Every equine caretaker should have an animal thermometer, which is heavier and more rugged than the ordinary human thermometer. The temperature is measured by inserting the thermometer full length in the rectum, where it should be left a minimum of three minutes. Prior to inserting the thermometer, a long string should be tied to the end.

In general, infectious diseases are ushered in with a rise in body temperature, but it must be remembered that body temperature is affected by stable or outside temperature, exercise, excitement, age, feed, etc. It is lower in cold weather, in older animals, and at night. In young foals, the temperature may be higher than in adults, normally ranging from 100 to 102°F.

The pulse rate indicates the rapidity of the heart action. The pulse of a horse is taken either at the margin of the jaw where an artery winds around from the inner side, at the inside of the elbow, or under the tail. It should be pointed out that the younger, the smaller, and the more nervous the animal, the higher the pulse rate. Also, the pulse rate increases with exercise, excitement, digestion, and high outside temperatures.

The breathing rate can be determined by placing the hand on the flank, by observing the rise and fall of the flank, or, in the winter, by watching the breath condensate in coming from the nostrils. Rapid breathing due to recent exercise, excitement, hot weather, or poorly ventilated buildings should not be confused with disease. Respiration is accelerated in pain and in febrile conditions. Also, in foals the normal respiratory rate may approach 40 breaths per minute.

SIGNS OF ILL HEALTH

Most sicknesses, both nutritional and communicable, are ushered in by one or more departures from the signs of good health. They are foretold by signs of poor health, by indicators that tell expert caretakers that all is not well—that tell them that their horses will go off feed tomorrow; signs which cause experienced caretakers to do something about it today.

Among the signs of horse ill health are: off feed—the animal does not eat and graze normally; listlessness; droopy ears; sunken eyes; humped-up appearance; abnormal dung—either very hard or cow-like dung suggests an upset in the water balance or some intestinal disturbance following infection; abnormal urine—repeated attempts to urinate without success or off-colored urine should be cause for suspicion; abnormal discharges from the nose, mouth, and eyes, or a swelling under the jaw; unusual posture—such as standing with the head down or extreme nervousness; persistent rubbing or licking; dull hair coat and dry scurfy, hidebound skin; pale, red, or purple mucous membranes lining the eyes and gums; reluctance to move or unusual movements; higher than normal temperature; labored breathing—increased rate and depth; altered social behavior such as leaving the herd and

TABLE 15-1
NORMAL TEMPERATURE, PULSE RATE, AND
BREATHING RATE OF FARM ANIMALS[1]

Animal	Normal Rectal Temperature		Normal Pulse Rate	Normal Respiration Rate
	Average	Range		
	(°F)	(°F)	(rate/min.)	(rate/min.)
Horses	100.5	99.0–100.8	32–44	8–16
Cattle	101.5	100.4–102.8	60–70	10–30
Sheep	102.3	100.9–103.8	70–80	12–20
Goats	103.8	101.7–105.3	70–80	12–20
Swine	102.6	102.0–103.6	60–80	8–13
Poultry	106.0	105.0–107.0	200–400	15–36

[1]To convert degrees Fahrenheit (F) to degrees centigrade (C), subtract 32, then multiply by 5/9.

going off alone; and sudden drop in production—weight gains or work.

A PROGRAM OF HORSE HEALTH, DISEASE PREVENTION, AND PARASITE CONTROL

In addition to following programs embracing superior breeding, sound management, and scientific feeding, good caretakers adhere to strict sanitation and disease prevention programs designed to protect the health of animals. Although the exact program will differ from farm to farm, the basic principles will remain the same. With this thought in mind, the following program of horse health, disease prevention, and parasite control is presented with the hope that the caretakers will use it (1) as a yardstick with which to compare their existing programs, and (2) as a guide so that they and their local veterinarians, and other advisors, may develop similar and specific programs for their enterprises.

I. GENERAL HORSE HEALTH PROGRAM

The following health program is recommended for all horses:

1. Feed each horse a nutritious and well-balanced ration.
2. Provide regular dental care and farrier service.
3. Know the signs of ill-health and the signs of good health.
4. Have on hand first aid supplies, and know when and how to use them in case of accident or sudden illness.
5. Vaccinate against the most common diseases (Table 15-2).
6. Avoid public feeding and watering facilities.
7. When signs of infectious disease are encountered, promptly isolate affected animals, provide them with separate water and feed containers, and follow the instructions and prescribed treatment of the veterinarian.
8. Prevent or control parasites by adhering to the following program:
   a. Provide good sanitary practices and a high level of nutrition.
   b. Have adequate acreage; use temporary seeded pasture rather than permanent pasture, and practice rotation grazing.
   c. Pasture young stock on clean pasture, never allowing them to graze on an infested area unless the area has been either plowed or left idle for a year in the interim.
   d. Do not spread fresh horse manure on pastures grazed by horses; either store the manure in a suitable pit for an extended period or spread it on fields that are to be plowed and cropped.
   e. Pick up the droppings from pastures and paddocks twice a week.
   f. Keep pastures mowed.
   g. Prevent fecal contamination of feed and water.
   h. Follow a worming program and schedule to control internal parasites.
   i. When external parasites are present, apply the proper insecticide.
   j. If cattle and/or sheep are on the farm, alternate the use of pastures between cattle/sheep and horses, which will assist in the control of most parasites.
   k. Avoid overgrazing, because there are more parasites on the bottom inch of the grass.

II. BREEDING AND FOALING HEALTH PROGRAM

The following health program is recommended where horses are bred and foals are produced.

1. Mate only healthy mares to healthy stallions and observe scrupulous cleanliness at the time of service and examination. Never breed a mare from which there is a discharge.
2. Provide plenty of exercise for stallions and pregnant mares; in harness, under the saddle, or in roaming over a large pasture in which plenty of shade and water are available.
3. Protect foals against the most common diseases (for example, tetanus, influenza, rhinopneumonitis, and sleeping sickness; but rely on your veterinarian for advice) by immunizing pregnant mares about 30 days before foaling, thereby providing a high concentration of antibodies in the colostrum and protecting foals.
4. During the spring and fall months when the weather is warm, allow the mare to foal in a clean, open pasture, away from other livestock. During inclement weather, place the mare in a roomy, well-lighted, well-ventilated box stall—which first should be cleaned carefully and disinfected thoroughly with a lye solution (made by adding one can of lye to 12 to 15 gal. of water), and provided with clean straw (not shavings) for the occasion. Active delivery of the foal should not take more than 20 to 30 minutes. Any difficulty in delivering the foal should be treated as an emergency. After foaling, all wet, stained, or soiled bedding should be removed and the floor lightly dusted

with lime (excessive lime is irritating to the eyes and nasal passages of foals). The afterbirth (placenta) should be passed within three hours. Retained placenta should be treated by a veterinarian as it may result in serious complications such as uterine infection and founder. The afterbirth should be burned or buried in lime; and the mare should be kept isolated until all discharges have ceased.

5. To lessen the danger of navel infection, promptly treat the navel cord of the newborn foal with tincture of iodine; taking care to apply the iodine only to the umbilical stump as it can produce severe irritation of the skin.

III. HEALTH PROGRAM FOR NEW HORSES AND VISITING MARES

The following health program is recommended where new horses and visiting mares are brought into the herd.

1. Isolate new animals for a period of three weeks before adding them to the herd. During this period, the veterinarian may (a) administer sleeping sickness vaccine (in season), tetanus toxoid, and perhaps other vaccines; (b) make a thorough general and parasitic examination; and (c) give a genital examination of breeding animals, and treat where necessary.

2. Require that any horses brought in be accompanied by a health certificate issued by a veterinarian. Beware of mares that have had trouble in foaling or have lost foals.

3. If feasible, breed visiting mares near their own isolation quarters, using tack and equipment that is not interchanged with that used for mares kept on the establishment.

VACCINATION SCHEDULE

In no case should the vaccination program be used as a crutch for poor management. Likewise, no vaccination program is entirely successful without strict management practices to limit possible spread of infections.

For guidance purposes, a suggested vaccination program and schedule is given in Table 15-2.

FIRST AID FOR HORSES

First aid for horses, as for humans, refers to the immediate and temporary care given in the case of accident or sudden illness before the veterinarian arrives. Its purposes: (1) to prevent accidents, (2) to avoid further injury and unnecessary suffering in case

of injury, (3) to recognize serious trouble if and when it strikes, (4) to assist the veterinarian in carrying out the prescribed treatment, and (5) to teach simple remedies and treatments which may be used safely if it is not possible to get a practitioner.

First aid does not alleviate the need for professional assistance; rather, a well thought-out plan in advance of a possible emergency may save the horse's life and usefulness. To this end, caretakers should (1) have on hand first aid supplies and be knowledgeable relative to their use, and (2) know what to do in case of an accident or sudden illness.

■ **First aid supplies**—First aid supplies should be conveniently available, but they should be stored where neither children nor horses have access to them. The following items are rather basic; but equestrians are admonished to seek the counsel and advice of their local veterinarians relative to these and additional supplies:

Adhesive tape	Metal syringe
Bandages	Physiologic saline (sterile
Blanket	solution)
Boric Acid	Plastic ice bag
Bucket	Potassium iodide
Clippers	Scalpel
Disinfectants	Scissors
Epsom Salts	Screwworm preparation
Eyedropper	Splints
Germicidal soap	Sterile absorbent cotton
Hoof knife	Stomach tube
Hot-water bottle	Thermometer
Liniment	Tourniquet

■ **Liniment for the horse**—A good liniment, properly used, will hasten and assist nature in returning an injured part to normal and relieve fatigue, overexertion, and soreness.

Liniment is a mild stimulant. Its use, along with massage, stimulates circulation, assists the body in removing waste products of muscle metabolism, and hastens nature in returning an injured part to normal.

The use of liniment is recommended for the following conditions: lameness, stiffness, soreness, strained tendons, sore shins, certain types of arthritis, and swellings, bumps, and bruises. It hastens recovery time and helps to prevent everyday injuries from turning into serious problems.

Also, liniment may be used, according to manufacturer's directions, as a body wash or brace after strenuous workouts or transportation, especially on the horse's legs, to relieve fatigue and overexertion, and to prevent soreness.

■ **Wounds**—Accidents do happen; horses are more injury prone and subject to a more awesome variety of wounds than any other class of domestic animal. They are thin-skinned; and they cut, tear, and bruise

TABLE 15-2
EQUINE DISEASE VACCINATION PROGRAM AND SCHEDULE

Disease	Type	Initial Immunization		Booster	Age First Given to Foals
Encephalomyelitis: 1. Eastern (EEE) and Western (WEE)	Bivalent (EEE and WEE) and trivalent (EEE, WEE, and VEE) vaccines given IM.	One month before mosquito season.	Repeat within the year if mosquito season is long.	Both injections should be repeated annually.	2–3 months.
2. Venezuelan (VEE)	Attenuated virus cell culture, given IM.	One injection only. *Do not give to pregnant mares.*		One annually.	3 months.
Equine influenza (flu)	Bivalent inactivated vaccine.	1st injection.	2nd injection—4–12 weeks after the first.	One annually is usually sufficient, but every 60 to 90 days in highly susceptible horses.	3–4 months.
Potomac horse fever—vaccinate if present in state or area	Inactivated *Ehrlichia risticii.*	2 doses, 21 days apart.		Annual. Biannual in endemic areas.	
Rabies	Intramuscular vaccines. Inactivated cell line origin.	1st injection.	2nd injection—30 days after the first.	One annually.	3 months.
Strangles (distemper)	In the U.S., three vaccines confer comparable immunity and have similar complications.	Vaccination lasts 6 to 12 months.		Every 6 to 12 months.	3 months.
Tetanus (lockjaw)	Toxoid—horse builds immunity lasting for at least 6–18 months after vaccination.	1st injection—intramuscular.	2nd injection—intramuscular, 2–4 weeks after 1st injection.	One annually.	2–3 months.
	Antitoxin (1,500 to 3,000 IU)—produces passive immunity which lasts for about 7–14 days.	Given to horses with puncture wounds if they have not been previously immunized with tetanus toxoid.			
Viral rhinopneumonitis (equine herpesvirus)	Killed vaccines for both equine herpesvirus 1 (predominantly virus abortion) and equine herpesvirus 4 (predominantly respiratory disease).	• Pregnant mares—5th, 7th, and 9th month of pregnancy. • Young animals—2 doses, 4 to 6 weeks apart.		Followed by booster vaccination at intervals of 6 months.	
	Modified live virus (EHV-4).	• All horses except pregnant mares—2 doses 4 to 8 weeks apart.		Followed by booster vaccination at intervals of 6 months.	

easily. For this reason, maximum wound preventative measures should be an integral part of horse management procedure. Such things as loose wire, sticks, sharp rocks, machinery, loose or broken boards, and trash have no place in horse pastures or corrals; and stables and trailers should be periodically examined for loose boards, protruding nails, or any other sharp objects.

Despite all possible precautions, however, as long as there are horses, there will be such things as wire cuts, saddle galls, cinch sores, rope burns, and other abrasions. Hence, it is important that the caretaker have on hand at all times a good first aid powder, as an aid in (1) stopping bleeding, (2) killing microbes, (3) drying the wound, thereby discouraging flies and other insects from congregating around it and speeding the healing process; and (4) lessening proud flesh.

The horse, more than any other species of animal, must receive proper care and treatment of wounds. Mistreatment will result in slow healing, excessive scarring, blemishing, and sometimes unsoundness. Wounds below the knees and hocks are especially sensitive; hence, they require careful treatment, and sometimes bandaging to prevent complications.

Wounds take a variety of forms, sizes, and severity; and, in turn, these determine the treatment. Generally speaking, there are five classes of wounds: (1) *cut wounds* (incised) produced by sharp objects, such as glass or sharp metal, where there is a minimum of tissue damage and little bruising; (2) *torn wounds* (lacerated) produced by irregular objects, such as barbed wire and horn gores, characterized by extensive damage to underlying tissues; (3) *puncture wounds* (penetrating) produced by sharp objects, such as nails and pitchforks, characterized by small punctures and a considerable amount of deep injury; (4) *abrasions* caused by such things as rope burns and rubbing against a door or trailer, characterized by oozing of the serum and little bleeding; and (5) *bruises* (contusions) caused by a blow, such as a kick or fall, which do not break the skin, but which cause bleeding and fluid loss deep down.

If the wound is serious, such as a deep puncture wound, or where swelling or irritation persists, a veterinarian should be consulted. With minor wounds, however, the caretaker may administer first aid. At the outset, it should be recognized that only nature can produce living cells and heal a wound; hence, a person can merely aid the process.

Although wound treatment will vary according to form and severity, the following steps may be involved:

Step 1—Stop the bleeding. If it is severe, pressure may be applied by placing a pad on the wound and bandaging over it. When a large artery is severed, as evidence by bright red blood spurting with a pulsing action, it may be necessary to control the loss of blood by applying a tourniquet on the side of the wound nearest the heart, until the arrival of the veterinarian. A tourniquet must be released after about 20 minutes for a minute or two, but it can be reapplied.

Step 2—Clean the wound by washing it with cotton swabs soaked in warm saline (salt) solution. Remove all foreign material (objects and dirt), hair, and torn tissue. Cleanliness is of great importance.

Step 3—Clip or shave long hair (it is often best not to remove short hair, because of the danger of contamination) from around the wound, to a distance of about ½ in.

Step 4—Apply first aid powder according to the directions on the label.

Step 5—Suture incised and lacerated wounds if necessary, with this decision being left to, and the work done by, a veterinarian. Proper wound drainage should always be established.

Step 6—Protect against tetanus by administering (a) a tetanus antitoxin if the animal is not already on a toxoid program, or (b) a toxoid booster when the horse has been immunized previously with this product. Also, the veterinarian may inject an antibiotic(s).

Step 7—Switch from powder to salve. As soon as a scab has formed over the wound, switch from first aid powder to first aid salve. *Continue to keep the wound clean.*

It should be recognized that poor nutrition of the horse will delay healing of a wound. Hence, poorly balanced or inadequate rations, bad teeth, and parasitism may contribute to delayed wound healing.

Some common illnesses of horses, which should receive first aid treatment, follow.

■ **Azoturia**—When the characteristic wine-colored urine, sweating distress, and stiffness are noted, (1) stop all exercise, (2) rub the horse dry and blanket it, (3) apply hot-water bottles or heated blankets or clothes to the swollen and hardened muscles, and (4) secure professional help as quickly as possible.

■ **Bleeders**—Bleeders are horses afflicted by blood flowing from their nostrils or bronchial tubes, but originating in the lungs following strenuous exercise. Furosemide, popularly known by the trade name LASIX, which may reduce bleeding, is permitted as a raceday medication in some states.

■ **Bruises and swellings**—Blows may produce hemorrhages in the tissues under the skin. First aid for such injuries consists in (1) measures to stop the hemorrhage—cold applications together with firm, even pressure, (2) cold-water showers and cold-water bandages until the swelling stops, and (3) heat or liniment applied after the swelling has stopped.

■ **Colic**—When colicky symptoms appear, walk the horse slowly and quietly, by leading; but keep the animal from rolling.

■ **Founder (laminitis)**—Treatment of horses developing laminitis should be considered an emergency. Pending the arrival of the veterinarian, the horse should be provided with support to the feet in the form of sand or a well bedded stall. Antiinflammatory agents, such as phenylbutazone, are often recommended.

■ **Fractures**—In all cases of fracture, professional assistance should be secured as quickly as possible. Until help arrives, keep the horse as quiet as possible. With leg fractures, it may be necessary to splint the affected limb with wood or pipe to hold the break in place; then wrap it with towels or other padding.

■ **Impaction**—Impaction is a form of colic caused by obstruction of the gastrointestinal tract (frequently in the large colon or cecum) by sand, or by ingestion of such high-fiber feeds as straw or cornstalks, along with lack of water intake. Impaction may cause distention of the bowel and acute abdominal pain, accompanied by the usual signs described for colic. Medical treatments, which should be administered by a veterinarian, meet with variable success. Mineral oil or magnesium sulfate, administered by stomach tube, are popular treatments. In some cases, surgical treatment is required.

Common sense should always prevail when administering first aid; and the caretakers should realize their limitations and consult a professional when they are unsure of themselves or of their ability.

POISONS (TOXINS)

Horses are subject to many poisons. *A poison is a substance which in sufficient quantities and/or over a period of time kills or harms living things.* Many poisons are called toxins. The study of poisons is called *toxicology*. For most poisons, there is both a safe level and a poisonous level; and the severity of the effect depends upon (1) the amount taken, (2) the period of time over which the substance is taken (certain poisons are cumulative), and (3) the age and physical condition of the animal. This lends credence to the toxicological adage: "Only the dose makes the poison."

■ **National Poison Control Center**—This is located at the University of Illinois, Urbana-Champaign. It is open 24 hours a day, every day of the week. The **hot-line number** is: 1-800-548-2423.

Preventing toxicities by limiting exposure to toxins is an important part of good management. Treatment of most toxicities requires veterinary care, which may or may not be effective.

A list, along with a brief summary of each, of the most common potentially toxic substances to horses, both synthesized and naturally occurring, most of which are feed or stable related, follows:

■ **Arsenic poisoning**—Arsenic is sometimes used to control insects and weeds, and to defoliate crops. When consumed in excess by horses, it may be toxic. Signs of acute arsenic toxicity include salivation, abdominal pain, diarrhea, weakness, incoordination, and often death. Treatment should be handled by a veterinarian.

■ **Avocado poisoning**—Avocado leaves (even wilted leaves blown into a pasture during a storm), fruit, or bark may poison horses. The signs are swelling around the mouth and head, which may extend to the neck and chest; inflammation (swelling) of the mammary glands; depression; loss of appetite; and perhaps colic. Afflicted horses are uncomfortable, but they generally recover.

■ **Black walnut toxicosis**—This malady is caused by black walnut shavings and sawdust used as bedding. Only skin contact is necessary; the material need not be eaten. Founder (laminitis) occurs within 12 to 24 hours after horses are exposed to black walnut shavings or sawdust bedding. Treatment consists in removing black walnut bedding material. The veterinarian may administer medical treatment.

■ **Blister beetle poisoning**—This is caused by three-striped blister beetles (*Epicauta* spp.) which contain the poisonous substance *cantharidin* in their tissues. Blister beetle feed on the leaves of alfalfa, with the result that they may be in alfalfa hay. Blister beetle poison is very irritating to the digestive tract of the horse, and it also causes severe kidney damage. Large doses may cause shock and death within a few hours. Treatment of blister beetle toxicity is most successful if the diagnosis and treatment are made early. Treatment consists in administering mineral oil and/or activated charcoal. The veterinarian may also administer analgesics, antiinflammatories, and electrolyte solutions to combat pain, dehydration, and shock.

■ **Botulism**—Botulism is a poisoning caused by ingestion of feed containing *Clostridium botulinum.* There are eight different botulinum toxins, with horses being most susceptible to types B and C. The toxins formed from these bacteria are the most potent poisons known—the most lethal being 10,000 times more deadly than cobra venom and millions of times more potent than strychnine or cyanide. Botulism may result in death, usually due to nerve paralysis and respiratory or cardiac paralysis, of horses of all ages. *Clostridium botulinum* causes shaker foal syndrome, characterized by depression or lethargy; muscle weakness and trembling when standing (hence, the term *shaker foal*); and inability to swallow, resulting in milk running out of the mouth and nose. In the mid-1980s, a safe and effective vaccine which prevents some types of botulism in

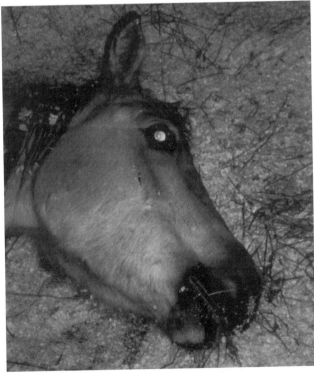

Fig. 15-1. Horse with botulism. There is a flaccid paralysis, often resulting in difficulty in eating, as seen in this case. (Courtesy, Department of Veterinary Clinical Sciences, College of Veterinary Medicine, Washington State University, Pullman)

horses and foals, and an antiserum that reverses the disease, were released. Prior to these developments, 90% of the horses that became ill because of botulism died. There are two problems with the antiserum: (1) the animal must live long enough for the new nerve growth—which requires about six days; and (2) its high cost.

In Kentucky, it is commonly recommended that mares shipped into the state for foaling and breeding be vaccinated in three doses, one month apart, with the last dose administered approximately four weeks prior to foaling; thereby giving the mare enough time to produce antibodies to the botulism vaccine and have a high titer of antibodies in the colostrum available for the newborn foal. Then, a yearly booster shot should follow.

■ **Ergot poisoning (ergotism)**—Ergot poisoning is caused by a parasite fungus which replaces the seeds in heads of grasses and cereal grains. Acute ergot poisoning, caused by consuming large quantities of ergot at one time, may produce paralysis of the limbs and tongue, disturbance of the gastrointestinal tract, and abortion. Chronic poisoning produces gangrene of the extremities, with subsequent sloughing off of the hoofs, ears, and tail. Treatment consists in removing the affected feed, and providing supportive care.

■ **Fluorine poisoning (fluorosis)**—Fluorosis is caused by ingesting excessive quantities of fluorine through the feed, water, or air, or a combination of these. The symptoms and signs are: abnormal teeth (especially mottled enamel) and bones, roughened hair coat, stiffness of joints, loss of appetite, emaciation, reduction of milk flow, diarrhea, delayed maturity, and salt hunger. Any damage may be permanent, but animals which have developed symptoms may be helped by eliminating the excess fluorine.

■ **Mercury poisoning**—Mercury poisoning may be caused by the consumption of seed grains treated with fungicides that contain mercury, for the control of fungus diseases of oats, wheat, barley, and flax. Mercury poisoning in horses causes gastrointestinal, renal, and nervous disturbances; but it is impossible on the basis of symptoms to differentiate mercury from other poisons. Case history of horses consuming mercury-treated grains is the best evidence. Usually, treatment is not successful. Protein (milk, eggs, serum) may reduce G.I. absorption, and selenium given at carefully controlled levels appears to be helpful.

■ **Monensin (Rumensin)**—Monensin is an antibiotic fermentation product produced by a strain of *Streptomyces cinnamonensis*, which alters the metabolism within the rumen. Monensin is an effective improver of feed efficiency in feedlot cattle, stocker and feeder cattle, and beef and dairy replacement heifers on pasture. *However, monensin is toxic to horses.* It causes damage to the heart muscles, and some animals go into cardiac arrest. When death does not result, the damage to the heart may be permanent.

■ **Mycotoxins (toxin-producing fungi or molds)**—Certain molds which produce toxins are associated with cereals, hay, and grasses. The mold *Fusarium moniliforme* is of considerable concern to the horse industry as it produces brain damage. Affected horses wander aimlessly, walk in circles, and may press their heads against an obstacle such as a fence. Some affected horses may fall down and paddle, with death following soon thereafter. After the onset of signs, death may result within six hours, although 72 hours is considered the average survival time after the onset of signs.

■ **Nitrate/Nitrite poisoning (oat hay poisoning, cornstalk poisoning)**—Acute nitrate/nitrite poisoning is caused by the presence of nitrite in the blood at a level sufficient to cause anoxia (internal suffocation). Nitrate (NO_3) may be reduced to nitrite (NO_2) by microorganisms in the gastrointestinal tract of the horse at a rate which overwhelms the body's defense system. Nitrite combines with the hemoglobin of the red blood cells to form methemoglobin, which cannot transport oxygen to the body tissues. The three principal sources of nitrate are plants, water, and air. Nitrate poisoning of horses can result from ingesting plants or water high in nitrate content, commonly one or more of the following sources: (1) forages under stress (drought, insufficient sunlight, or after spraying with weed killer), or following heavy nitrate fertilization of soils; (2) in organic nitrate or nitrite salts, or fertilizer, left where horses may consume them; or (3) pond or shallow well water from surface runoff from a barnyard or well-fertilized field. Death from nitrate/nitrite poisoning is usually sudden; and few treated animals recover. The most common treatment is methylene blue, administered by a veterinarian intravenously.

■ **Pesticide poisoning**—Pesticides are chemicals used to destroy, prevent, or control pests, but they can also be toxic (poisonous) to horses and other animals. When properly used, pesticides are beneficial; when improperly used, they may be harmful. The symptoms and signs of pesticide poisoning vary with each pesticide. The first and most important precaution to observe when using any pesticide is to read and heed the directions on the label. In the event of an accident, the label becomes extremely important in remedial measures.

■ **Phenylbutazone ("bute") toxicity**—Phenylbutazone is a safe, effective, and widely used pain-killing drug in horses when administered at recommended levels. However, it is relatively easy to produce toxicity with phenylbutazone if the dose is too large, the treatment prolonged, or the animal dehydrated. Signs of toxicity are loss of appetite, depression, ulceration in the mouth and gastrointestinal tract, ventral edema, diarrhea, and death. Once a horse is suspected of showing toxicity to phenylbuta-zone, administration of the drug should be ceased at once. The same precautions that apply to the use of phenylbutazone should be observed in the use of other pain-killing drugs to treat lameness in horses.

■ **Poisonous plants**—Many plants are poisonous to horses. Some are deadly in small amounts; others are toxic only if the horses consume large amounts. The list of poisonous plants is so extensive that no attempt is made herein to describe them in detail. Nevertheless, both equestrians and veterinarians should have a working knowledge of the principal poisonous species in the area in which they operate. Unfortunately, plant-poisoned horses are not generally discovered in sufficient time to avoid loss. So, prevention is decidedly superior to treatment. Following identification of the poisonous plant, treatment should be left to the veterinarian. Rapid and proper treatment may save an animal.

■ **Urea toxicity (ammonia toxicity)**—Ammonia is the actual toxic agent in urea poisoning. When urea is fed at excessive levels, large amounts of ammonia are liberated in the gastrointestinal tract, causing toxicity, evidenced by nervousness, excessive salivation, muscular tremors, respiratory difficulty, and tetanic spasms. Death occurs in ½ to 2½ hours. Young equines are more susceptible to urea toxicity than older horses. Mature horses can usually consume limited urea (such as access to protein blocks containing urea); however, the efficiency of the nitrogen utilization from nonprotein nitrogen is considerably less than that of nitrogen from intake protein. (Also, see Chapter 13, section on "Urea.")

DISEASES OF HORSES

Every good equestrian knows that keeping animals healthy is a major responsibility. In the discussion that follows, an attempt is made to give a combination of practical and scientific information relative to the most important diseases affecting horses. It is intended that this should enhance the services of the veterinarian, for caretakers can do a better job in controlling animal diseases if they have enlightened information at their disposal. Effective animal health programs call for full cooperation between caretakers and their veterinarians. Perhaps it is also a fair statement of fact to add that superstition, myth, and secret formulas are used more extensively in treating the diseases of horses than in treating the ailments of any other class of livestock.

Disease prevention calls for vaccinating horses against the most common diseases. It calls for establishing and following a vaccination program and schedule, as insurance against heavy losses from certain diseases (see Table 15-2). The program and schedule will vary somewhat from area to area and from herd to herd. Hence, it should be worked out in consultation with the local veterinarian. At the outset, it should be recognized that horses should not be vaccinated against every disease for which there is a vaccine. Rather, they should be vaccinated against those diseases which are the greatest hazard in a given herd and area, then a calculated risk should be assumed relative to the rest.

Vaccines should always be used according to the instructions of the manufacturer, in both time and method. Also, they should be kept cool before being opened, and they should be used immediately after they are opened.

ANTHRAX (SPLENIC FEVER, CHARBON)

Anthrax, also referred to as splenic fever or charbon, is an acute infectious disease affecting horses and other warm-blooded animals and people; but cattle are most susceptible. It usually occurs as scattered outbreaks or cases, but hundreds of animals may be involved. Certain sections are known as anthrax districts because of the repeated appearance of the disease. Grazing animals are particularly subject to anthrax, especially when pasturing closely following a drought or pasturing land that has been recently flooded. In the United States, human beings get the disease mostly from handling diseased or dead animals on the farm, or from handling hides, hair, and wool in factories.

Historically, anthrax is of great importance. It is one of the first scourges to be described in ancient and Biblical literature; it marks the beginning of modern bacteriology, being described by Koch in 1876; and it is the first disease in which immunization was effected by means of an attenuated culture, Pasteur having immunized against anthrax in 1881.

SYMPTOMS AND SIGNS[2]

The mortality is usually quite high. It runs a very short course and is characterized by a blood poisoning (septicemia). The first indication of the disease may

---

[2]Currently, many veterinarians prefer the word *signs* rather than *symptoms*, but throughout this chapter the author accedes to the more commonly accepted terminology among equestrians and includes the word *symptoms*.

be the presence of severe symptoms of colic accompanied by high temperature, loss of appetite, muscular weakness, depression, and the passage of blood-stained feces. Swellings may be observed over the body, especially around the neck region; and in the horse they may appear around the mammary gland or sheath. There may be a bloody discharge from all body openings. In very acute anthrax, the animal may die without having shown any noticeable symptoms.

CAUSE, PREVENTION, AND TREATMENT

The disease is identified by a microscopic examination of the blood in which will be found *Bacilli anthracis*, the typical, large rod-shaped organism causing anthrax. These bacilli can survive for years in a spore stage, resisting all destructive agents. As a result, they may remain in the soil for extremely long periods.

This disease can be prevented by immunization. In the so-called anthrax regions, vaccination should be performed well in advance of the time when the disease normally makes its appearance. Several types of biologics (serums, bacterins, and vaccines) are available for use in anthrax prevention. The choice of the one to be used should be left to the local veterinarian or state livestock sanitary official. In infested areas, vaccination should be repeated each year. Herds that are infected should be quarantined. Lay persons should never open the carcass of a dead animal suspected of having died from anthrax; instead, the veterinarian should be summoned at the first sign of an outbreak.

When the presence of anthrax is suspected or proved, all carcasses and contaminated materials should be completely burned or deeply buried, preferably on the spot. This precaution is important because the disease can be spread by dogs, coyotes, buzzards, and other flesh eaters and by flies and other insects.

When an outbreak of anthrax is discovered, all sick animals should be isolated promptly and treated. All exposed healthy animals should be vaccinated; pastures should be rotated; the premises should be quarantined; and a rigid program of sanitation should be carried out under the supervision of a veterinarian.

Massive doses of antibiotics (10 to 20 million units for an adult horse) may be effective if used in the early stages of the disease. Penicillin or streptomycin are commonly used. Likewise, if used at the first signs, antianthrax serum may also be helpful, although its use is limited by availability and cost.

CONTAGIOUS EQUINE METRITIS (CEM)

This is a highly contagious venereal disease of horses, which caused national and international equine problems in the late 1970s and early 1980s; and which still persists worldwide. In infected stallions, the causative bacteria reside in the smegma of the prepuce and on the surface of the penis, without producing clinical symptoms. Infection is transmitted by mares and stallions at breeding.

SYMPTOMS AND SIGNS

Severely affected mares manifest a profuse, sticky, mucopurulent, vulval discharge 2 to 6 days after service, while in other mares the signs are less severe or insignificant; conception rate is low; fertility is regained at ensuing estrual periods. Diestrus may be shortened. Normally, infected mares do not abort. Foals may be exposed to infection at birth and retain infection until breeding age.

CAUSE, PREVENTION, AND TREATMENT

The disease is caused by a gram-negative coccobacillus, designated *Taylorella equigenitalis* (previously designated *Haemophilus equigenitalis*).

The most effective prevention involves safeguards designed to prevent the introduction of CEM into the United States.

Treatment consists in teasing the stallion, then washing the extended penis and sheath thoroughly with Chlorhexidine, removing the smegma from the urethral fossa; after two minutes, washing the antiseptic off; and then drying the penis, fossa, and sheath, followed by smearing them liberally with nitrofurazone cream. This is repeated daily for five days. Acute CEM infection in most mares will resolve without treatment in about three weeks, but many retain infection in the clitoral fossa and sinuses. Cleansing the fossa of smegma and local application of chlorhexidine and antibiotic creams to the fossa and sinuses often is successful in overcoming residual infection.

DIARRHEA IN FOALS

Diarrhea is one of the most common disorders seen in foals, occurring in 70 to 80% of foals under six months of age.

SYMPTOMS AND SIGNS

The symptoms and signs of foal diarrhea are depression, diarrhea, dehydration, and loss of appetite. In severe diarrhea, the foal may have fever and reddened mucous membranes.

CAUSE, PREVENTION, AND TREATMENT

Various factors may cause diarrhea, including the mare's first heat after foaling, dietary changes, parasites, and infectious agents such as bacteria or viruses. Most cases are mild and self-limiting, but the infectious diarrheas can be life-threatening and cause significant economic loss.

The most common diarrhea in foals occurs at about 7 to 12 days of age and coincides with the mare's first heat cycle. Usually, the only treatment needed is to wash the feces off the buttocks and apply petroleum jelly to the area.

The cause of foal heat diarrhea is not known. The observation that diarrhea develops in orphan foals of this age raised on a consistent diet makes it unlikely that changes in milk composition due to hormonal changes in the mare are responsible. It may be that change in microorganisms in the foal's digestive tract is involved. The diarrhea is seldom serious, and it generally subsides within a week. In foals with diarrhea that are less than one week of age or that are depressed, causes other than foal heat diarrhea, such as infection, should be considered. These cases may require aggressive treatment.

Recently, equine rotavirus has emerged as a significant cause of foal diarrhea. Rotavirus-induced diarrhea is generally seen in foals under three months of age and is of particular concern in the very young foal where the ensuing dehydration can be fatal. Sanitation constitutes the best prevention. Foaling stalls should be thoroughly cleaned prior to each foaling, and the mare's udder should be washed. Staff hygiene should be strictly enforced. Foals should receive adequate colostrum. To date, no equine vaccine has been developed for the prevention of rotavirus.

Diarrhea can most effectively be treated if discovered early. Treatment should be determined by the cause. If severe diarrhea persists for more than a day, fluids and electrolytes should be administered before the foal becomes too dehydrated. The veterinarian may also administer an antibiotic and/or a gut-soother such as Kaopectate.

ENCEPHALOMYELITIS (SLEEPING SICKNESS; OR EASTERN, WESTERN, OR VENEZUELAN EQUINE ENCEPHALOMYELITIS)

This brain disease, which affects both horses and people, is known as equine encephalomyelitis, or sleeping sickness. Both horses and people are dead-end hosts of Eastern and Western equine encephalomyelitis, infected only by the mosquito.

Since 1930, the Eastern and Western types of the disease have assumed alarming proportions in the United States. Then, in 1971, the Venezuelan equine encephalomyelitis first occurred in the United States, with an outbreak reported in Texas. The Venezuelan type was first diagnosed in Venezuela in 1936 and was reported in several South and Central American countries prior to appearing in the United States. Equine encephalomyelitis is seasonal in character, extending from early summer until the first sharp frost of fall, when it invariably disappears.

SYMPTOMS AND SIGNS

The initial signs of viral encephalomyelitis are often nonspecific and include fever, loss of appetite, and stiffness. In the early stages, the horse walks aimlessly about, crashing into objects. Later, the animal may appear sleepy, standing with a depressed head. Grinding of the teeth may be noted. Local paralysis may develop, causing the animal to go down. Inability to swallow, paralysis of the lips and bladder, and blindness may be observed. If the affected animal does not recover, death usually occurs in two to four days following the onset of symptoms. Those animals which recover, but which are unable to react to normal stimuli, are referred to as *dummies*. Some animals make full recovery.

In mild cases, the horse may merely yawn a few times; and this may be the only clinical sign of the disease.

CAUSE, PREVENTION, AND TREATMENT

The disease is caused by several distinct viruses. The three most active types in the United States are: Eastern equine encephalomyelitis, Western equine en-

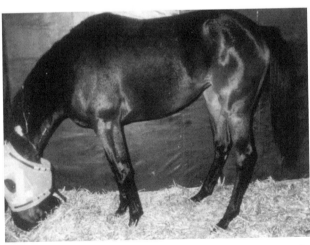

Fig. 15-2. Horse with encephalomyelitis (sleeping sickness). Note the sleepy attitude and the depressed head. (Courtesy, Department of Clinical Sciences, College of Veterinary Medicine, University of Florida, Gainesville)

cephalomyelitis, and Venezuelan equine encephalomyelitis. All three viruses may be spread from animals to people with mosquitoes serving as the primary means of transport. Wild birds, rodents, and wild animals in all areas of the country are reservoirs of the disease, which enters the body of a mosquito when it feeds on infected creatures. While in the mosquito, the virus multiplies and becomes highly concentrated in the salivary glands. The infected mosquito then transmits the virus to a horse or a human whichever is handy at its next feeding. In the Venezuelan type, horses can spread the disease directly since the virus is present in their saliva and nasal discharges.

Generally speaking, mortality from the Western type does not exceed 50%, whereas that from the Eastern and Venezuelan types is 90% or higher.

Prevention entails vaccination of all horses. Monovalent, bivalent (EEE and WEE), and trivalent (EEE, WEE, VEE) vaccines are available. Monovalent VEE vaccine is an attenuated virus of cell culture origin and should not be used in pregnant mares or young foals. The attenuated VEE vaccine has been largely replaced by a formalinized product incorporated into a trivalent vaccine with EEE and WEE antigens. Vaccine should be given about one month before the mosquito season and, where the mosquito season is long, should be repeated within the year. A veterinarian should administer the vaccine in keeping with the manufacturer's directions. Other preventive measures include the isolation of infected animals in screened cages or the application of insect repellent; prompt disposal of all infected carcasses; destruction, if possible, of insect breeding grounds; and discouragement of movement of animals from an epizootic area to a clean one. Fly and mosquito control seems to be very effective, since most outbreaks of the disease do not extend to racetracks and stables where insect control is practiced.

Treatment is not very effective, because of the rapid course of the disease. Since the Western type progresses more slowly and results in a lower mortality rate than the Eastern and Venezuelan types, it lends itself to more supportive treatment. Good nursing is perhaps the best and most important treatment. The maintenance of fluid and electrolyte balance is recommended. No specific therapeutic agent is known to influence the course of the disease.

Horses are considered to be dead-end hosts for WEE and EEE virus. In VEE, however, horses can spread the disease since the virus is present in saliva and nasal discharges.

EQUINE ABORTION

Abortion is the expulsion of the impregnated ovum at any period prior to the time the foal can survive out of the uterus. If the foal is advanced enough to live,

it is known as premature parturition, and in the mare this may occur as early as the tenth month.

It is estimated that 20 to 30% of all equine conceptions end in abortions.

SYMPTOMS AND SIGNS

Abortion symptoms vary according to the stage of pregnancy in which it occurs, whether it is early or late. Sometimes, especially during the first two months of pregnancy, the mare may miscarry without observable symptoms, and the fact only becomes known by her coming back in heat. At other times, a small clot of blood, containing the rudiments of the foal, may be found behind the mare if she is under close observation. If the occurrence is somewhat later in gestation, there will be some general disturbance, loss of appetite, neighing, and straining; and the small body of the fetus is expelled, enveloped in its membranes. In later stages of pregnancy, abortions are attended by greater constitutional disturbance; and the process resembles normal parturition, with the aggravation that more effort and straining is required to force the fetus through the comparatively undilatable cervix mouth of the uterus. The vulva becomes swollen, with mucus or even bloody discharge; the abdomen droops; the udder fills; the mare paws with the forefeet and kicks with the hind feet, switches the tail, moves around uneasily, lies down and rises, strains, and, as in natural foaling, expels first mucus and blood, then "the waters," and finally the fetus. These signs of approaching abortion may last an hour or two, or they may last for a day or more. The symptoms subside for a time, only to reappear with renewed energy.

CAUSE, PREVENTION, AND TREATMENT

Causes of abortion in mares may be grouped into two types: (1) infectious agents, such as viruses, bacteria, and fungi; and (2) noninfectious abortions, such as twinning, hormonal deficiencies, congenital anomalies, and miscellaneous causes. Some of the more common causes are discussed in the sections that follow.

■ **Infectious causes of abortion**—The effect of infection may be either (1) indirect, where there is destruction of large areas of the placenta causing fetal death through starvation and toxemia; and (2) direct, where the microorganisms invade the fetus.

A discussion of each of the infectious abortions follows:

1. **Virus abortions.** The most common cause of abortion in mares is due to infection by equine herpesvirus 1 (rhinopneumonitis). Most abortions due to this virus occur between the eighth and eleventh

months of gestation, but they may occur as early as the fifth month. Although this virus and the related virus, equine herpesvirus 4, can cause respiratory disease, abortions are usually not associated with a clinical respiratory infection. Sometimes the foal is born alive at term, but dies 2 to 3 days of age due to infection by the virus. There is usually no mammary development; the fetal membranes are seldom retained; and the genital tract returns to normal as quickly as it does following normal parturition. The abortion rate may approach 100% in a herd of susceptible mares. An effective vaccine will prevent rhinopneumonitis and should be used in areas subject to the disease. Additionally, the following management practices should be followed on all farms regardless of size: (1) isolate all pregnant mares from all other horses, including foals and yearlings; (2) isolate all horses coming onto the premises; and (3) train all farm personnel in the application of sanitary practices.

Equine viral arteritis may also cause abortions, but it is less frequent than equine herpesvirus abortion. However, it has become a problem in some areas. It produces more obvious signs of illness than equine rhinopneumonitis, including discharge from the eyes and nose, fever (102 to 106°F), and filling (edema) of the limbs. A laboratory examination is necessary to establish conclusively the presence of the specific virus. Up to 50% of affected pregnant mares may abort. The name *arteritis* is derived from the particular type of arterial damage that this disease inflicts; it results in degeneration of the middle layer of arterial walls, especially in the small arteries. Treatment consists in absolute rest and good nursing, augmented by antibiotics to prevent or combat secondary bacterial infections. A vaccine is available, but its use is subject to state regulations.

[3]In 1996, the American Horse Council (AHC), Washington, DC, was asked to address the issue of Equine Viral Arteritis (EVA) because of its continuing economic impact on U.S. horse owners. They developed a voluntary, industry-driven protocol that will assist stallion owners in preventing establishment of the carrier state in stallions and minimize the risk of EVA-related abortion in mares, and which will also serve to limit the liability associated with the use of stallions which shed equine arteritis virus or infect semen.

The American Horse Council continued: "Adoption of the protocol could greatly lessen the likelihood that the disease be driven underground; which, were it to occur, would greatly hinder horse owners being able to protect their horses effectively against the disease."

2. **Bacterial abortion.** Sporadic abortions in mares can be caused by bacterial infection of the

---

[3]Information for the rest of this section was obtained from a report dated May 5, 1997 which the author received from the American Horse Council.

placenta, acquired either through the cervix or the bloodstream. Several species of bacteria have been incriminated, including *S. zooepidemicus*, *E. coli*, *K. pneumonial*, *K. Pneumoniae*, *Staphylococcus aureus*, and *Leptospira species*. They may cause abortion at any stage of pregnancy. Bacterial abortion is often characterized by retention of the placenta, as well as by metritis or inflammation of the uterus. Treatment of the mare may be necessary before she can be rebred successfully. It is good practice to culture mares before rebreeding, to determine if harmful bacteria are present in the uterus. The latter precaution is especially important where it is the intent to rebreed mares on the ninth day after foaling.

Adherence to the following program will materially reduce bacterial abortions:

a. Breed mares only when the genital tract has returned to normal.

b. Mate only healthy (bacteriologically clean) mares to healthy stallions and be scrupulously clean at the time of breeding.

c. Give a mare foaling abnormally in any respect plenty of time to return to the normal state.

d. Remember that infection is ever present in the filth of the external genitals of both the stallion and the mare.

e. Suturing the lips of the vulva (Caslick's operation) will control this type of abortion in many mares. But this should be done by and on the advice of the veterinarian.

When a mare is found to have a severe genital infection, she should be treated properly and should have sexual rest for from six months to a year.

3. **Mycotic abortions.** Abortions may result from infection of the placenta by various types of fungi, including *Mucor* and *Aspergillus* spp. Fungi probably enter the uterus during the heat period at which conception occurs, or soon after birth in the case of foaling mares. Fungi do not attack the fetus directly; rather, they cause degeneration of the placenta so that the fetus has insufficient nourishment. For this reason, the aborted fetus is often small and only a fraction of the normal weight for its gestational age. If abortion does not occur, the foal may be carried to full term and be born in a reasonably vigorous, but undersized and undernourished state. Most mycotic abortions occur during the second half of pregnancy. There is no vaccine. Like bacterial abortions, mycotic abortions can be prevented by good breeding hygiene, treatment of genital disease prior to breeding, and corrective surgery (Caslick's operation).

■ **Noninfectious causes of abortion**—The common noninfectious causes of abortion are:

1. **Twinning.** The birth of healthy twin foals is unusual. The generally accepted theory relative to the

inability of the mare to carry twin foals successfully to term is that it is due to placental insufficiency—meaning that there are not enough fetal membranes to accommodate and provide nutrition for two developing fetuses.

2. **Hormone failure.** The hormone progesterone plays a dominant role in the maintenance of pregnancy, preparing the uterus for reception of the fertilized egg and the attachment of the placenta. It is responsible for the necessary changes in the uterus for the continuance of pregnancy and nourishment of the fetus. Other hormones, such as estrogen and cortisone, are also involved in the process and can contribute to abortion. Thus, the maintenance of pregnancy is a matter of hormone balance. Although there are many gaps in our knowledge of reproductive physiology, it appears that some abortions are caused by failure of the glands that control hormonal balance.

3. **Congenital defects.** Early embryonic deaths, which may be mistaken for failure of conception or silent heats, frequently occur. Some of these are presumed to be due to genetic or chromosomal defects resulting in improper development of the embryo, followed by rejection by the dam.

4. **Miscellaneous causes.** This embraces all cases of abortion that cannot be definitely classified in any of the categories discussed above. In the category of miscellaneous causes of abortions are nutritional deficiencies, certain drugs, accidents and injury—such as a severe kick that disturbs the uterus, and noninfectious pathological lesions in the uterus of the mare. Causes of this type are so numerous and general that aside from good breeding, feeding, and management practices not much can be done to prevent them; but these three practices are vital in prevention of abortion as well as other diseases. The mare may abort from almost any cause that very profoundly disturbs the system.

It is important to recognize an impending abortion as early as possible, for sometimes it may be prevented. When a pregnant mare shows any general indefinable illness, she should be examined closely for abortion indications. Any suggestive indications should prompt the caretaker to call the veterinarian immediately.

Preventive measures embrace avoidance of all possible causes. It begins with mating only healthy mares to healthy stallions, and with being scrupulously clean at the time of breeding. New horses should always be isolated as a preventive measure, and aborting mares should be quarantined. Where abortions have occurred in the broodmare band, the special cause in the matter of feed, water, exposure to injuries, overwork, lack of exercise, and so forth may often be identified and removed. Avoid constipation, diarrhea, indigestion, bloating, violent purgatives or other potent medicines—including administering cortisones in late pregnancy, painful operations, and slippery roads.

The following points are pertinent in controlling abortion in a band of broodmares:

1. Prevent rhinopneumonitis by following a planned immunization program under the direction of a veterinarian.

2. Prevent equine arteritis, in areas where the disease is a problem, by administering the vaccine.

3. Control and prevent bacterial and mycotic abortions by mating only healthy mares to healthy stallions and observing scrupulous cleanliness at the time of service and examination. Suture mares when necessary.

4. Keep broodmares healthy and in good flesh, and feed a ration that contains all the essential elements of nutrition.

When a case of abortion is encountered, the following procedure is recommended: (1) Gather up the fetus and afterbirth with great care and arrange through the local veterinarian for diagnosis by the state diagnostic laboratory; (2) isolate the mare in a place where she can be kept in quarantine; (3) burn or bury the bedding; and (4) thoroughly disinfect the stall with a 5% Lysol solution.

One of the most important factors to remember about abortion is that a veterinarian should be called for diagnosis, prevention, treatment, and cure. To forget this is to invite trouble and to pave the way for possible spreading of the infection.

EQUINE INFECTIOUS ANEMIA— E.I.A. (SWAMP FEVER)

Equine infectious anemia (E.I.A.) is a very serious blood disease of horses and mules. It is sometimes referred to as swamp fever, mountain fever, slow fever, or malarial fever. Very early, the name swamp fever was given to the disease in the United States because of its prevalence in moist locations—such as on the coastal plains of Texas, and in the lowlands of the Platte and Mississippi Rivers—but it is now known that altitude is not a factor. The disease is found in the higher altitudes, far removed from any swamps. This infectious disease was first reported in France as early as 1843, and it has existed in the United States for many years. It is characterized by a great variation in symptoms and course. There is a marked tendency for the disease to localize on certain farms or areas, and it does not spread rapidly.

SYMPTOMS AND SIGNS

Symptoms vary, but some of the following are usually seen: high and intermittent fever, depression, stiffness, and weakness (especially in the hindquarters), anemia, jaundice, edema and swelling of the

lower body and legs, unthriftiness, and loss of condition and weight—even though the appetite remains
good. Affected animals may die within two to four
weeks. However, many animals recover from the clinical signs, but remain lifelong carriers of the virus.

It is an unfortunate truth, however, that neither the
symptoms nor the postmortem findings relative to infectious anemia are sufficiently characteristic to make
a definite diagnosis possible. Currently, there are two
tests available for the diagnosis of E.I.A., both of which
depend on the detection of antibodies (modified globulins) to the E.I.A. virus. Testing for E.I.A. is regulated
by the U.S. Department of Agriculture, and blood
should be sampled by a veterinarian and sent to an
approved laboratory.

The most frequently used test to diagnose E.I.A.
is the Coggins test, an agar gel immunodiffusion
(AGID) test developed by Dr. Leroy Coggins of the
New York State Veterinary College, Cornell University;
hence, the common name. The Coggins test is a
specific and accurate indicator of E.I.A. virus infection.
Infected horses become positive to this test 2 to 4
weeks after the onset of the initial infection and remain
test positive the rest of their lives. Since foals receive
large quantities of antibodies from their dams by way
of colostrum, a nursing foal born of an E.I.A. positive
dam may be positive for the first 4 to 6 months of its
life but not actively infected. Such foals can be considered free from the disease if they test negative at
about seven months of age.

The test is usually repeated to confirm all positive
reactions because horses are often destroyed on the
basis of the test. Positive reactors are identified with
an A in a visible body brand or lip tattoo, which stands
for anemia. It does not indicate Grade A as some
buyers have belatedly discovered after acquiring
horses at what they thought were bargain prices. Animals branded with an A are quarantined and cannot
be moved except for slaughter or approved research
purposes.

In 1994, 0.18% of the 1,057,377 U.S. horses
tested were positive. However, since not all horses
were tested, these figures may not accurately reflect
the true prevalence of the disease. Most of the horses
are healthy inapparent carriers of the virus.

CAUSE, PREVENTION, AND TREATMENT

Equine infectious anemia is caused by infection
with a retrovirus of the subfamily lentiviruses. The virus
is commonly carried in the blood of infected animals
over long periods of time, even though these carrier
animals may have made a temporary or even a rather
lasting apparent recovery. It is spread chiefly by biting
insects, especially flies, but it may also be spread by

contaminated hypodermic needles. Studies show that
any debilitating factors that lower the animal's resistance not only may predispose the animal to disease,
but may greatly influence its progress.

There is no vaccination. The following preventive
measures are recommended:

1. Use disposable hypodermic needles (one needle to one horse) and sterilize all other skin penetrating
instruments by boiling at least 15 minutes.
2. Practice good sanitation and eliminate or reduce biting insects as much as possible.
3. Be on the alert for sick horses and get a
veterinary diagnosis on them.

When a positive diagnosis has been made, a
quarantine is imposed and slaughter of reactors is
advised. Infected mares or stallions should not be used
for breeding purposes.

After horse owners test and eliminate all infected
animals from their herd, the Coggins Test can be used
to protect their stock from reinfection, (1) by buying
horses only after they have been tested and found free
from the disease, (2) by not allowing untested horses
to be stabled or pastured with their own, and (3) by
not taking their horses to any assembly point (show,
sale, racetrack, trail ride, etc.) where prior testing is
not required.

In 1976, the U.S. Department of Agriculture
amended the animal import regulations to require that
imported horses pass the Coggins Test to assure that
they are free of equine infectious anemia. In addition,
most states require a recent negative Coggins test for
entry.

The treatment of the disease has been unsuccessful because at the present time no method is known
to destroy the virus in the bloodstream.

EQUINE INFLUENZA (FLU)

Equine influenza is a highly contagious disease
which has been recognized for many years and which
is widespread throughout the world. It frequently appears where a number of horses are assembled, such
as racetracks, sales, and horse shows.

While the mortality or death rate from influenza is
low, the economic loss is high. The disease may
interrupt training programs and racing schedules for
weeks or months; and it may force the withdrawal of
animals from sales, thereby delaying and/or making
for less favorable disposal.

Although both horses and people are subject to
influenza and the clinical symptoms are similar in the
two species, there appears to be no transmission of
the disease between them.

SYMPTOMS AND SIGNS

Young animals (except for very young foals, which have passive immunity from the dam's milk) are particularly susceptible to influenza. For this reason, outbreaks of epidemic proportions are rather common at racetracks where large numbers of yearlings and two-year-olds are shipped for training and racing purposes. Older animals are usually immune, probably due to repeated exposure to the disease. Symptoms develop as early as 2 days or as late as 10 days after exposure.

The onset of influenza in horses is marked by rapidly rising temperature, which may reach 106°F and persist for 2 to 10 days. Other signs include loss of appetite, extreme weakness and depression, rapid breathing, a dry cough, and watery discharges from the eyes and nostrils, which are followed by a white- to yellow-colored nasal discharge.

Since one of the first symptoms of equine influenza is a rapidly rising temperature, it is recommended that the temperature of young horses be taken twice daily under the following circumstances:

1. For a period of 4 to 5 days prior to shipment.
2. For 2 to 10 days after arrival at a new location.
3. When horses are stabled in an area where influenza, coughs, and colds are known to exist.

CAUSE, PREVENTION, AND TREATMENT

Influenza is caused by a group of related viruses. Currently, there are two important equine influenza viruses.

Conditions incident to shipment, exposure to cold, sudden changes in climate, and fatigue appear to lower the resistance of horses so as to make them more susceptible to the disease.

It is believed that the most common method of transmission of influenza is by way of the respiratory tract, and that the virus itself is carried on contaminated feed, bedding, water, buckets, brooms, on the clothing and hands of attendants, and on transportation facilities.

Effective prevention is obtained by vaccination, initially using two doses, with the second injection given 4 to 8 weeks after the first. For continued protection, each vaccinated animal must receive (1) a booster at intervals of six months, or (2) a booster when there is exposure or an epizootic condition. Also, all new animals should be isolated for three weeks, and sick animals should be quarantined.

Treatment should be handled by the veterinarian. No exercise, no matter how mild, should be permitted during the period of elevated temperature. The early use of antibiotics and/or sulfa drugs may prevent secondary bacterial complications.

GLANDERS (FARCY)

This is a very old disease, commonly referred to as farcy or *malleus*. It was described as early as 400 B.C., at which time it received the Greek name *malleus* from Aristotle. Glanders is an acute or chronic infectious disease of horses, mules, and donkeys; but it can be transmitted to other animals and to human beings through close contact.

Although glanders was worldwide at one time, it has been eliminated in many countries, including the United States.[4] Nevertheless, horses are now transported widely and quickly, with the result that there is danger of diseased horses being brought in from glanders-infected areas. To alleviate the latter hazard, all horses coming from any area where the disease exists are tested.

SYMPTOMS AND SIGNS

The disease usually manifests itself either in the acute or chronic form. The chronic form is most often observed in the horse, while the acute form is seen more in mules and donkeys. The incubation period varies from weeks to months. The chronic symptoms may be manifested in the lungs, skin, or nasal passages. In the nasal form, there is a nasal discharge which later becomes pus. Hard red nodules, which break down into abscesses and then ulcers, will be seen. When the ulcers heal, they leave a star-shaped scar. The skin form is often seen with the nasal form. It is characterized by the development of nodules and ulcers in the skin and subcutaneous tissue. Both the skin and nasal forms are thought to originate in the lungs. The lungs are the most common location for the lesions of glanders. Evidence of infection consists in a loss in condition and lack of endurance, with sudden bleeding from the nose. Coughing followed by a mucous discharge may be noted. At this stage, there are nodules and abscesses in the lung tissue. In the acute form of the disease, death usually occurs within a week after many or all of the symptoms noted above have been in evidence.

CAUSE, PREVENTION, AND TREATMENT

The cause of this disease is the bacterium *Malleomyces mallei*. It is transmitted by inhalation or ingestion of the exudate containing the causative organism.

Any suspected animal should be subjected to the *mallein test*. Positive diagnosis is cause for immediate

---

[4]Glanders is one of the success stories relative to the eradication of livestock diseases in the United States; it was completely eradicated in 1934.

destruction of the animal and the careful cleaning and disinfection of the contaminated equipment and premises. All exposed animals should be tested at frequent intervals.

No method of immunization is available. Treatment with sulfadiazine, given daily for 20 days, has proven fairly effective.

LYME DISEASE

Lyme disease was first recognized in people in Old Lyme, Connecticut in 1975; hence, the name. At that time, the outbreak was traced to the bite of a small deer tick, *Ixodes dammini*. (In California, the vector is the western black-legged tick, *Ixodes pacificus*.) But Lyme disease can strike any mammal—horses, cattle, dogs, rodents, raccoons, opossums, and others. The first case in equines was diagnosed in a pony, in Wisconsin, in 1985.

SYMPTOMS AND SIGNS

The most common symptoms/signs in horses are lameness (arthritis), fever, muscle aches and pains, limb swelling, eye inflammation, encephalitis, hepatitis, nephritis, and abortion. A positive diagnosis of Lyme disease is based on clinical signs, opportunity for infection, antibody titers, and response to treatment. Many horses may be exposed to the agent without developing clinical disease.

CAUSE, PREVENTION, AND TREATMENT

In 1981, the disease agent (a spirochete) was isolated from the tick and named *Borrelia burgdorferi*.

The best prevention is a diligent tick and fly control program. In the meantime, research is in progress to develop a vaccine.

Once diagnosed, Lyme disease is fairly simple to treat. Penicillin and tetracycline have been shown to be effective, particularly in the early stages of the disease; response to early treatment can be dramatic, often overnight. However, chronic cases may require treatment with antibiotics for a long time, up to six months.

NEONATAL INFECTION (SEPTICEMIA, NAVEL ILL, JOINT ILL)

Infection is one of the leading causes of morbidity and mortality in neonatal foals. In neonatal septicemia, infection is generalized in the bloodstream. Infection may also become localized in various tissues, such as the joints or umbilicus, resulting in the terms *joint ill* or *navel ill.*

SYMPTOMS AND SIGNS

Neonatal infection is characterized by loss of appetite and general listlessness. The body temperature may be either elevated (>102°F), subnormal (<100°F), or normal. If infection is localized, signs may include swelling, soreness and stiffness in the joints, or umbilical swelling and discharge. Signs may develop slowly in some cases.

CAUSE, PREVENTION, AND TREATMENT

Neonatal infection can be caused by several kinds of bacteria, including *Escherichia coli, Klebsiella pneumoniae, Actinobacillus equuli*, and *Salmonella species*. Although infection may be acquired in utero, it is often acquired at or after birth through inhalation, ingestion, or umbilical contamination.

The recommended preventive measures are: good hygiene at mating and parturition, dipping the navel of the newborn animal with iodine, and ensuring adequate passive transfer of antibody through the colostrum. Lack of sanitation is an important factor in the cause of this disease.

Treatment of neonatal infection involves the administration of systemic antibiotics. In addition, treatment for infected joints often includes flushing the joint with fluid to remove the accumulated pus cells and debris, and local antibiotics. In some cases of navel infection, surgical removal of the umbilicus may be required. Also, antiinflammatory drugs may be given to relieve pain and restore mobility, but caution should be used due to the risk of gastrointestinal ulcers and kidney disease.

POTOMAC HORSE FEVER

An acute, often fatal, diarrhea was first noticed in a number of horses in Montgomery County, Maryland, in the summer of 1979. At first the disorder was called *acute equine diarrhea syndrome*, but soon it became known as *Potomac horse fever*, after the region where it was first recognized.

SYMPTOMS AND SIGNS

Signs are: fever (102 to 108°F), depression, loss of appetite, colic, edema of the underline, and stocking of the limbs. These symptoms are usually followed within 48 hours by the onset of diarrhea which, in severe cases, is watery and explosive. A high percentage of horses with Potomac horse fever develop founder, or laminitis. The fatality rate may approach 30%, with death occurring primarily from dehydration and shock. Correct diagnosis is important since the symptoms of Potomac horse fever often mimic those of salmonellosis, yet the drug tetracycline, which is helpful against Potomac horse fever, may sometimes worsen other diarrheal disorders.

CAUSE, PREVENTION, AND TREATMENT

The causative agent is named *Ehrlichia risticii* after its discoverer. *E. risticii* is a member of the class of microorganisms called rickettsia, which are between bacteria and viruses in size. To date, researchers have not been able to determine how the disease is transmitted, but biting insects are strongly suspected.

A vaccine is available, which is administered intramuscularly in two doses, repeated 21 days apart, followed by an annual booster shot. So, if Potomac horse fever is present in a state or area, all horses therein should be vaccinated against the disease.

Treatment consists of large volumes of intravenous fluids, tetracycline, and supportive treatment to control fever and reduce laminitis.

RABIES (HYDROPHOBIA, MADNESS)

Rabies is an acute infectious disease of horses and all other warm-blooded animals, including humans. It is characterized by deranged consciousness and paralysis, and it terminates fatally. This disease is one that is far too prevalent, and, if present knowledge were applied, it could be controlled and even eradicated.

When a human being is bitten by a dog that is suspected of being rabid, the first impulse is to kill the dog immediately. This is a mistake. Instead, it is important to confine the animal under the observation of a veterinarian until the disease, if it is present, has a chance to develop and run its course. If no recognizable symptoms appear in the animal within a period of two weeks after it inflicted the bite, it is safe to assume that there was no rabies at the time. Death occurs within a few days after symptoms appear, and the dog's brain can then be examined for specific evidence of rabies. With this procedure, unless the bite is in the region of the neck or head, there will usually be ample time in which to administer treatment to exposed human beings. As the virus has been found in the saliva of a dog at least five days before the appearance of the clinically recognizable symptoms, the bite of a dog should always be considered potentially dangerous until proven otherwise. In any event, when people are bitten or exposed to rabies, they should see their local doctor, who will select and use the proper vaccine.

SYMPTOMS AND SIGNS

Less than 10% of the rabies cases appear in horses, cattle, swine, and sheep. The disease usually manifests itself in two forms: the furious, irritable, or violent form, or the dumb or paralytic form. It is often difficult to distinguish between the two forms, however. The furious type usually merges into the dumb form because paralysis always occurs just before death.

The signs of rabies virus infection in horses are highly variable. In comparison with other animals, the horse may be more violent and can be exceedingly dangerous. In some cases, the disease is characterized by lameness and abdominal pain (colic).

CAUSE, PREVENTION, AND TREATMENT

Rabies is caused by a filtrable virus which is usually carried into a bite wound by the infected saliva. The malady is generally transmitted to farm animals by dogs and certain wild animals such as the fox, skunk, bat, and raccoon.

Rabies can be best prevented by attacking it at its chief source, the dog. Effective vaccines are available, and it should be a requirement that all dogs be immunized. This should be supplemented by regulations governing the licensing, quarantine, and transportation of dogs. Also, the control of wild carnivores and bats is of increasing importance in the eradication of rabies.

When horses are bitten or exposed to rabies, they should be seen by a veterinarian. There are now several approved vaccines for horses; so, a program for rabies vaccination may be developed by the veterinarian.

SALMONELLOSIS

Salmonellosis is an important bacterial disease affecting multiple species, including horses and human beings. The disease has worldwide distribution.

SYMPTOMS AND SIGNS

The most common signs in adult horses are diarrhea, depression, dehydration, and fever. There may be abdominal pain, and in some cases, it is difficult to distinguish salmonellosis from other causes of colic. Foals may show lameness or stiffness in the joints with or without diarrhea; these warning signs indicate that a veterinarian should be called immediately.

CAUSE, PREVENTION, AND TREATMENT

There are over 2,200 serotypes of *Salmonella*, most of which can cause disease. *Salmonella* infection is most frequently transmitted by fecal-oral contamination. Stress may contribute to the development of clinical disease.

Fatality rates among horses vary considerably, depending on the type of *Salmonella* involved, the horse's immune system, and how aggressively the disease is treated. Treatment, which should be under the direction of a veterinarian, involves fluid therapy to correct the acid-base balance and dehydration and antiinflammatory drugs. In some cases, antibacterial drugs are indicated, especially in foals.

Prevention primarily depends on good management and avoiding contaminated feed. New animals should be quarantined.

STRANGLES (DISTEMPER)

This is a widespread communicable disease of horses and mules. It is also referred to as distemper or infectious adenitis. Although it is most common in young animals, all ages are susceptible. Animals that have previously had the disease are not always immune for life.

SYMPTOMS AND SIGNS

In a week or less following exposure, the disease may manifest itself suddenly in the form of depression and loss of appetite. There will be a high fever followed by a discharge of pus from the nose. By the third or fourth day of the disease, the glands under the jaw start to enlarge, become sensitive, and eventually

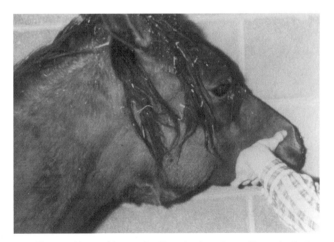

Fig. 15-3. Horse with strangles. Note the dramatic swelling under the jaw caused by abscessation of the lymph nodes. (Courtesy, College of Veterinary Medicine, The Ohio State University, Columbus)

break open and discharge pus. Because the pharynx is also involved, a cough is present that is easily initiated. The disease may spread to other lymph glands of the body, producing the condition known as bastard strangles. As soon as the abscesses are drained, healing usually takes place.

CAUSE, PREVENTION, AND TREATMENT

The disease is caused by the bacterium *Streptococcus equi*, which, typically, infects only horses. Transmission is usually by the ingestion or inhalation of the infected discharges. The disease seems to spread rapidly when young horses are brought together. The organism is capable of existence outside the animal's body for as long as six months.

Prevention consists in avoiding contact with infected animals or contaminated feeds, premises, or equipment. Public stables and watering troughs are to be avoided. At the first sign of symptoms, the affected animals should be put in strict quarantine. The contaminated quarters and premises should be thoroughly cleaned and disinfected. All excreta and contaminated bedding should be burned or buried.

Three types of vaccine are available, which confer similar immunity and have similar complications (see Table 15-2).

Good nursing is the most important treatment. This includes clean, fresh water, good feed, and shelter with uniform temperature away from drafts. The veterinarian may prescribe one of the antibiotics or sulfas, or both. Early treatment is of the utmost importance in strangles.

TETANUS (LOCKJAW)

Tetanus is chiefly a wound-infection disease that attacks horses (and other equines) and humans, and less frequently swine, cattle, sheep, and goats. It is generally referred to as lockjaw.

The disease is worldwide in distribution. In the United States it occurs most frequently in the South, where precautions against tetanus are an essential part of the routine treatment of wounds.

SYMPTOMS AND SIGNS

The incubation period of tetanus varies from one to four weeks, but may be from one day to many months. It is usually associated with a wound, but may not directly follow an injury. The first noticeable sign of the disease is a stiffness first observed about the head. The animal often chews slowly and weakly and swallows awkwardly. The third eyelid is seen protruding over the forward surface of the eyeball (haws). The

Fig. 15-4. Horse with tetanus. Notice the stiff-legged condition and partly raised tail. (Courtesy, Department of Veterinary Pathology and Hygiene, College of Veterinary Medicine, University of Illinois)

animal then shows violent spasms or contractions of groups of muscles brought on by the slightest movement or noise. It usually attempts to remain standing throughout the course of the disease. If recovery occurs, it will take a month or more. In over 80% of the cases, however, death ensues—usually because of sheer exhaustion or paralysis of vital organs.

CAUSE, PREVENTION, AND TREATMENT

The disease is caused by an exceedingly powerful toxin (more than 100 times as toxic as strychnine) liberated by the tetanus organism *(Clostridium tetani)*. This organism is an anaerobe (lives in absence of oxygen) which forms the most hardy spores known. It may be found in certain soils, horse dung, and sometimes in human excreta. The organism usually causes trouble when it gets into a wound that rapidly heals or closes over it. In the absence of oxygen, it then grows and liberates the toxin which follows up nerve trunks. Upon reaching the spinal cord, the toxin excites the symptoms noted.

Immunity against tetanus can be obtained through inoculation with either toxoid or antitoxin. The administration of toxoid, which is an inactivated form of tetanus toxin, stimulates the horse to build its own antibodies. Active immunization is achieved through two injections of tetanus toxoid at 2 to 4 week intervals, followed by annual booster injections. If an immunized horse is wounded six months or more following such immunization, it is recommended that the veterinarian administer another toxoid injection at that time.

Antitoxin is a concentrated serum with tetanus toxin antibodies taken from another horse, which will give passive protection for up to two weeks following administration. In some cases, the administration of tetanus antitoxin has been associated with the development of a severe liver disease (Theiler's disease) approximately 1 to 3 months later; therefore, it is now recommended that the use of tetanus antitoxin should be limited to unvaccinated horses with tetanus prone wounds, such as puncture wounds, and to the treatment of tetanus.

Once the disease develops, the horse should be placed under the care of a veterinarian. Early in the course of the disease, massive doses of antitoxin—100,000 to 200,000 units or more—may be helpful. Also, tranquilizing drugs are effective in reducing the extent and severity of muscular spasms, and antibiotics are helpful.

Horses with tetanus should be confined to darkened box stalls in which the feeding and watering facilities are placed high enough so that the animal is capable of gaining access to them without lowering its head. Support by slinging should be given wherever possible.

VESICULAR STOMATITIS (VS)

Vesicular stomatitis (VS) is a viral disease which affects several species, including horses, cattle, and pigs. The disease is seen in the U.S., Mexico, and Central and South America. It is primarily important from a regulatory standpoint, as the clinical signs can be indistinguishable from those of foot-and-mouth disease, which is currently not found in the U.S. However, foot-and-mouth disease does not affect horses.

SYMPTOMS AND SIGNS

Infected animals typically develop a fever and oral lesions following an incubation period of 3 to 14 days. The oral lesions, which begin as vesicles (blisters) that rupture and become ulcers, often result in excess salivation and reluctance to eat. Vesicles may occur in locations other than the mouth, such as on the teats.

CAUSE, PREVENTION, AND TREATMENT

The disease is caused by a rhabdovirus. The natural reservoir of the virus and modes of transmission remain unclear, but transmission can occur between animals. Outbreaks are often associated with the movement of animals.

State and federal regulatory veterinarians should be contacted immediately when VS is suspected, so that quarantine and disease identification can take place. During an outbreak of VS, quarantine of the premises and isolation of sick animals are required.

There is no specific treatment for the virus, but the majority of animals recover in 2 to 21 days, depending on the severity of the lesions. Supportive care, including soft feed, should be given.

PARASITES OF HORSES[5]

The term *parasite* refers to a form of animal life that lives in or on the body of a host animal, deriving its food therefrom. Parasites kill some horses, but, by and large, the main damage is insidious and results in lowered efficiency—*i.e.*, something less than the best performance of which the animal is capable.

Until the 1980s, parasite control programs were relatively standardized throughout the equine industry. But biotechnology changed all this! Even the parasites changed—some of them developed resistance to long-used chemicals. New drugs were developed; and the rotation of drug treatments, long held sacred, was challenged. And that was not all! Pollution, from whatever source, became a dirty word; and environmental control, sustainable agriculture, biological control of parasites, and animal behavior and welfare were in vogue. A basic understanding of all these forces is essential to establishing effective parasite control programs for the horses of tomorrow.

For guidance in the selection of an anthelmintic or insecticide, the user should seek the counsel of the veterinarian, county agent, extension entomologist, or agricultural consultant; and for instruction on the use of an anthelmintic or insecticide, the user should follow the directions on the label.

INTERNAL PARASITES OF HORSES

Some 150 different kinds of internal parasites infest horses throughout the world,[6] and probably no individual animal is ever entirely free from them. Although equines are not unique among herbivorous animals in their susceptibility to parasitism, they do harbor many diverse species of pests. Probably this can be attributed to the fact that horses, perhaps more than other domestic animals, have been transported widely for service and breeding purposes. Fortunately, comparatively few of these parasites inflict serious

Fig. 15-5. Same horse before (upper picture) and after (bottom picture) treatment for internal parasites. Parasites retard the foal's development and lower the efficiency of mature horses. Also, feed is always too costly to give to parasites. (Courtesy, College of Veterinary Medicine, University of Illinois)

damage upon their host; but those few can be extremely harmful and even deadly.

As would be expected, the kinds of parasites and the degree of infestation in horses vary in different parts of the world, and also among individual horses. Then, too, some of the parasites are distributed more or less regionally, primarily because of differences in development cycles, climatic conditions, and husbandry practices.

The internal parasites may be located in practically every tissue and cavity of the body. However, most of them locate in the alimentary tract, lungs, body cavity, or bloodstream. Those which inhabit the digestive system usually become localized in specific parts of it. Still others are migratory or wandering in their habits, traveling throughout different parts of the body.

Also, internal parasites play major roles in colic, enteritis, respiratory tract diseases, dermatitis, and

---

[5]The use of the trade names of wormers and insecticides in this section does not imply endorsement, nor is any criticism implied of similar products not named; rather, it is recognition of the fact that equestrians, and those who counsel them, are generally more familiar with the trade names than the generic names.

[6]Some 80 species commonly parasitize horses in this country.

poor growth and development of young horses; and parasites may interfere with nutrition, decrease performance, and cause disturbances in internal organs.

GENERAL SYMPTOMS

Usually the symptoms of parasites are marked by a slowly progressive chain of events that the owner may overlook entirely or confuse with other conditions. The general symptoms of parasitic infestation in the horse are: weakness, unthrifty appearance and emaciation, tucked-up flanks, distended abdomen (potbelly), rough coat, paleness of the membranes of the eyes and mouth, in some cases frequent colic and diarrhea, and stunted growth and development in young animals. Affected animals usually eat well, and the temperature remains normal; but there is always a loss in the functional efficiency of the individual as a working unit.

With certain types of parasitic infestations, the specific effects are very pronounced. This is true, for example, of the protozoan parasite *Savcocytis neurona*, which causes neurological signs.

GENERAL PREVENTIVE AND CONTROL BASICS

Most parasitic infestations of equines may be attributed to the fact that, under domestication, horses (as well as all other animal species) have been forced to sleep and eat in close proximity to their own feces—being either confined and fed in a stall or fenced within limited grazing areas or pastures. By contrast, in the wild state, animals roamed over vast areas, seldom eating, watering, or sleeping in the same spot. As the feces of the horse are the primary source of infestation of internal parasites, it should be obvious that the most important requisite of successful control measures is that they be designed to separate the animal from its own excrement.

An effective program for the prevention and control of internal parasites on all horse establishments, big or small and of whatever kind, calls for (1) good management, (2) superior sanitation, (3) periodic treatments with the proper anthelmintics, and (4) routine fecal examinations conducted by a veterinarian or skilled technician to determine the numbers and types of parasites present. A brief discussion of some of the basics of internal parasite control programs follows.

ANTHELMINTIC (DEWORMER) RESISTANCE

In recent years, many horse owners have noticed diminished effectiveness of certain anthelmintics (dewormers). This resistance is not due to a change in the drug itself; rather, it is due to biochemical and physiological adaptations by the parasites to combat the action of the dewormer. Worms can achieve resistance by absorbing less drug, breaking it down with new enzymes, or bypassing the chemical pathways that normally are blocked by the dewormer. Whatever biochemical mechanisms make for resistance, those traits become part of the parasite's genetic composition and are inherited in the offspring.

Resistance to certain anthelmintics has been demonstrated in several species of small strongyles in the United States. Once resistance has been demonstrated on a farm, these drugs should never be used again on that premises. A complete history of anthelmintic use on a farm is essential to detect anthelmintic resistance.

ANTHELMINTICS ABOUND

In the first half of the 20th century, the accepted means of deworming horses was with tobacco. Later, phenothiazine, piperazine, and carbon disulfide were added to the anthelmintic arsenal. Currently, ivermectin is in widespread use. Today, there is a great array of equine anthelmintics from which to choose, and more are continually being developed.

BIOLOGICAL CONTROL

There is little cross-infestation of parasites between horses and ruminants, so either (1) mixed grazing of horses, cattle, and sheep, or (2) rotation grazing of horses, alternated with cattle/sheep, constitutes effective biological control, with one exception. The small stomach worm, *Trichostrongulus axei*, infests horses, cattle, and sheep.

Biological control with dung beetles is theoretically feasible, but to date it has been of little practical benefit. Increasing use will be made of the biological control of parasites as an alternate to polluting the environment with pesticides.

CLEAN PASTURES

Treating the horse while ignoring the pasture is of little value!

The parasites in horse pastures can be reduced dramatically by picking up the manure twice a week. An Ohio State University study showed that a pasture routinely cleaned in this manner has 18 times fewer parasites than an uncleaned pasture. Manure can be removed manually or mechanically. In England, a power sweeper is available, consisting of a small trailer fitted with a vacuum pump powered by a tractor or small engine. A scoop shovel is just as effective. In damp or wet conditions, a harrow should not be used to break up the manure; it will merely spread the parasite larvae into the grazing area. If pasture harrowing is done in hot dry weather, it will effectively break up feces and expose larvae to death by desiccation.

Typically, horses divide pastures into (1) defecating areas, and (2) grazing areas. However, if manure piles are completely removed from the pasture twice a week, either by hand or machine, horses will utilize the entire area for grazing.

MONITORING CONTROL PROGRAMS

Monitoring the control program by fecal egg count is just as important as the choice of anthelmintic and the timing of treatments. It enables the veterinarian to compare the efficacy of different anthelmintics, to detect the development of drug resistance, and to assess the effectiveness of the program in reducing pasture contamination.

ROTATION OF ANTHELMINTICS

Until the mid-1980s, the rotation of dewormers was recommended as the best defense against resistance. Yet, those who rotate too frequently within the same drug class may be selecting, unwittingly, for resistance to more than one type of drug and further limiting the success of their deworming program.

Some researchers are now recommending a less frequent rotation regimen, one that uses a single product for at least a year at a time. Also, it is very important that rotation be between drug classes; for example, rotation among the benzimidazoles (BZD) is not effectively combating resistance because each wormer in this class works by the same mechanism.

OTHER BASICS OF AN INTERNAL PARASITE CONTROL PROGRAM

1. Make the program all inclusive (i.e., every horse on the farm that will share common ground should be treated simultaneously).

2. Isolate and treat newly added horses before allowing them to share pastures, paddocks, pens, or stalls with resident horses.

3. Control the parasites in the mare, thereby greatly reducing exposure of the foal.

4. Take periodic fecal examinations at random to determine efficacy of the therapeutic/treatment program and to survey for potential parasite drug-resistance. (Sample day of treatment to compare to two-week post-treatment samples.)

5. Rotate drug therapy wisely and sparingly. Use a product for at least a year, then rotate between chemically unrelated drug classes—and not within drug classes.

6. Remember that route of administration plays no part in the success of the program, as long as the total calculated dose is consumed by the horse(s) (i.e., feed administration, paste preparations, stomach tubing, and injection are equally effective if the horse receives its recommended dose of the drug).

7. Read and follow all label directions explicitly; if there are any questions, call the veterinarian or the manufacturer for assistance.

8. Devise the program to suit your needs and desired goals.

9. Adjust the drug treatment interval to the environmental factors present in the area.

10. Eliminate potential of repeated/recurrent reinfestation by sensible husbandry; avoid overcrowding, remove fecal contamination of stall once or twice daily, avoid ground feeding, and remove manure from pastures twice a week.

11. Plan the program with flexibility to incorporate all age groups, yet be able to concentrate on the special concerns of each age group present on the farm.

12. Remember that it costs less to maintain a routine and effective parasite control program on a year-round basis than it does to waste feed on a parasitized horse; the money spent on a routine program is better invested than money spent on life-saving treatment or surgery when the horse colics due to accumulated internal parasite damage.

13. Be a drum major for biological control, pollution and environmental control, sustainable agriculture, and horse behavior and welfare.

COMMON INTERNAL PARASITES AND THEIR CONTROL

In North America, horses are affected by more than 80 internal parasites, which inhabit nearly every organ. These parasites are so widespread that no horse escapes all of them.

Because there are so many kinds of internal parasites, only the most common and damaging ones are summarized in Table 15-3 and discussed at length in the narrative that follows. Strongyles, ascarids, and bots are generally the most injurious of internal parasites, although other kinds are capable of producing severe injury on occasion and generally contribute to the overall picture of parasitism wherever they occur.

■ **Choice of drug (anthelmintic)**—Knowing what internal parasites are present within a horse is the first requisite to the choice of the proper drug, or anthelmintic. Since no drug is appropriate or economical for all conditions, the next requisite is to select the right one; the one which, when used according to directions, will be most effective and produce a minimum of side effects on the animal treated. So, coupled with knowl-

TABLE 15-3
INTERNAL PARASITES OF HORSES

Parasite	Where Found	Damage	Signs
Ascarids *(Parascaris),* (Roundworms)	Small intestine.	Irritate intestinal wall, possible obstruction (impaction) and rupture of small intestine.	Digestive upsets (colic), diarrhea, weight loss, retarded growth, rough hair coat, pot bellied, death (ruptured intestine), more common in young horses.
Bots *(Gastrophilus)*	Larvae embedded in lining of mouth and tongue. Stomach.	Irritation and nervousness during the botfly egg laying season. Sore mouth and tongue. Inflammation, ulceration, perforation of stomach wall.	Excitement (caused by flies), evidence of pain when eating, digestive upsets (colic), retarded growth, poor condition, death (stomach rupture).
Pinworm *(Oxyuris)*	Large intestine. Rectum.	Irritation of anal region.	Rubbing of tail and anal regions, resulting in broken hairs and bare patches around tail and buttocks.
Stomach worm *(Habronema* adult), *(Habronema* larvae)	Stomach, attached to wall or free.	Stomach inflammation and colic. Larvae produce summer sores.	Gastritis, digestive disorders, and summer sores—which often heal spontaneously after first frost.
Strongyles, large (Bloodworm)	Adult strongyles are found in large intestine, attached to walls or free. Larvae migrate extensively to various organs and arteries.	Adults suck blood, cause anemia, and produce ulcers and mucosa. Larvae interfere with blood flow to the intestine, damage arteries, and cause aneurisms which may burst.	Anemia, rough hair coat, colic, loss of appetite, retarded growth, depression, soft feces with a foul odor. In large infestations, legs and abdomen swell.
Strongyles, small (*Triodontophorus, Poteriostomum, Trichonema,* and others)	Large intestine and cecum, attached to walls and free.	Injury to the large intestine.	Anemia, loss of appetite, retarded growth, dark or black manure, soft feces with a foul odor. In large infestations, legs and abdomen swell.
Tapeworm *(Anoplocephala)*	Varies according to species: *A. magna* and *P. mamillana* in small intestine and stomach. *A. perfoliata* mostly in cecum.	Ulceration of mucosa in area of attachment.	Unthriftiness, digestive disturbances, and anemia.
Threadworm *(Strongyloides)*	Small intestine.	Erosion of intestinal mucosa, enteritis.	Loss of appetite, loss of weight, diarrhea, worms disappear by time foals are 6 months old.

edge of the kind of parasites present, an individual assessment of each animal is necessary. Among the factors to consider are age, pregnancy, other illnesses and medications, and the method by which the drug is to be administered. Some drugs characteristically put horses off performance for several days after treatment, whereas others have less tendency to do so. Some drugs are unnecessarily harsh or expensive for the problem at hand, whereas a safe inexpensive alternative would be equally suitable.

Anthelmintics are constantly being improved, and new ones are becoming available. So the caretakers should consult their local veterinarian relative to the choice of drug to use on their horses at the time.

■ **Program and schedule**—A general understanding of parasite life cycles is necessary in order to time treatments to the best advantage. Several general types of treatment schedules have evolved. Probably the most common are suppressive or interval treatment regimes, where dewormings are regularly scheduled at fixed intervals. Typically, intervals of 4 to 8 weeks are recommended, based on the length of suppression of fecal strongyle egg production after anthelmintic administration. In some regions, strategic regimes are being used, in which schedules are determined by seasonal transmission factors. Recently, a formulation of pyrantel tartrate has been developed to be fed on a daily basis, providing continuous control.

Each horse establishment should, in cooperation with the local veterinarian and/or other advisors, develop an internal parasite control program. Also, it is recommended that an equine practitioner or parasitology laboratory do periodic fecal examinations to help assess the effectiveness of the parasite control program.

ASCARIDS (LARGE ROUNDWORMS, WHITE WORMS)

The ascarid, *Parascaris equorum*, is found in the small intestine of equines. The female roundworm varies from 6 to 22 in. in length and the male from 5 to 13 in. When full grown, both are about the diameter of a lead pencil.

Distribution and Losses Caused by Ascarids

Roundworms are fairly widely distributed throughout the United States. They especially affect foals and young animals, but are rarely important in horses over two years of age. This decreased susceptibility as age increases is credited to an acquired immunity resulting from earlier infestations. Roundworms are particularly damaging to their equine host because of the destruction that the migrating larvae inflict upon the liver and lungs and the partial or complete obstruction and possible rupture of the small intestine caused by the large size and numbers of worms.

Life History and Habits

Although it pursues a migratory route in the host, the roundworm usually comes to rest in the upper part of the small intestine; but sometimes it is found in the middle and terminal portions of the small intestine. The complete life cycle of the parasite may be summarized as follows:

1. In the small intestine, each female worm may deposit 100,000 eggs per day which pass to the outside with the feces. Ascarid eggs are very resistant to environmental conditions and may live for years in stalls, paddocks, and pastures. Thus, the source of infestation for young horses is the contaminated ground that was seeded down by ascarid eggs by preceding crops of infested foals.

2. Under favorable conditions—warm weather and dampness—the eggs develop embryos and are infestive to horses in 10 to 14 days.

3. The infestive eggs are swallowed with feed and water, especially by grazing horses, and the larvae are liberated in the stomach and intestine.

4. The larvae then take the following migratory route: They penetrate the gut wall and enter the bloodstream, thence travel via the blood through the liver, heart, and lungs, leave the bloodstream in the lungs and migrate up the trachea to the pharynx, and finally are again swallowed and develop to maturity in the small intestine.

Damage Inflicted; Symptoms and Signs of Affected Animals

The injury produced by ascarids covers a wide range, from light infestations producing moderate effects to heavy infestations which may be the cause of death. Death from ascarid infestation is usually due to a ruptured intestine. Serious lung damage caused by migrating ascarid larvae may result in pneumonia. More common, and probably more important, are retarded or impaired growth and development manifested by potbellies, rough hair coats, and digestive disturbances.

Prevention, Control, and Treatment

Prevention consists primarily in sanitary measures. The foaling barn and paddocks must be kept clean, manure must be disposed of properly, and clean feed and water must be supplied. Young foals should be placed on clean pasture.

In addition to selecting the particular drug(s) for ascarid control, the caretaker should set up a definite treatment schedule, then follow it. The advice of the veterinarian should be sought on both points. Then, the drug of choice should be given according to the manufacturer's directions.

The first ascarid infestations in foals mature when the foals are about 11 weeks of age; hence, the first treatment should be given at 8 to 10 weeks of age so as to remove the initial infestation just before the

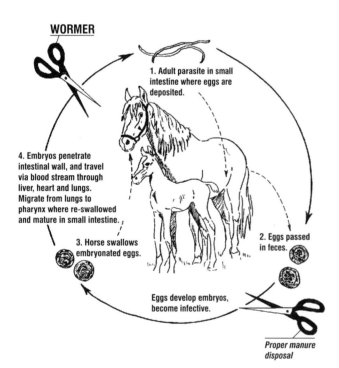

WORMER

1. Adult parasite in small intestine where eggs are deposited.

4. Embryos penetrate intestinal wall, and travel via blood stream through liver, heart and lungs. Migrate from lungs to pharynx where re-swallowed and mature in small intestine.

3. Horse swallows embryonated eggs.

2. Eggs passed in feces.

Eggs develop embryos, become infective.

Proper manure disposal

Fig. 15-6. Diagram showing the life history and habits of the ascarid (large roundworm). As noted (see scissors), effective control and treatment (cutting the cycle of the parasite) consist in (1) proper manure disposal, and (2) administering an effective wormer. (Drawing by Prof. R. F. Johnson)

ascarids mature. If ascarids are allowed to mature, and the foal is subsequently treated with an effective wormer, intestinal blockage and death may result.

BOTS

Horse bots are highly specialized parasites—attacking horses, mules, asses, and perhaps zebras, but not molesting other classes of livestock.

Three species of horse bot flies are pests of horses in the United States: the common horse bot or nit fly *(Gastrophilus intestinalis)*, the throat bot or chin fly *(G. nasalis)*, and the nose bot or nose fly *(G. hemorrhoidalis)*.

Fig. 15-8. Horses rubbing their noses on each other in an effort to avoid the nose bot fly *(G. hemorrhoidalis)*. Though the bot fly does not sting the animal, deposition of the eggs on the lips causes a tickling sensation. (Courtesy, USDA)

Fig. 15-7. The nose bot fly, *G. hemorrhoidalis.* (Courtesy, USDA)

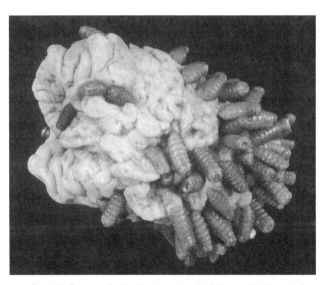

Fig. 15-9. Bots attached to the stomach wall of a horse. At this stage they remain attached to the lining of the stomach and intestines for several months, feeding on blood until they are about ¾ in. in length, after which they release their hold and pass out with the feces. (Courtesy, Department of Veterinary Pathology and Hygiene, College of Veterinary Medicine, University of Illinois)

Distribution and Losses Caused by Bots

As horse bots are found in different sections of the world, it is reasonable to surmise that they were introduced to this country with the first horses imported from Europe. The most common horse bot and the throat bot are now distributed throughout the United States wherever horses are found, but the nose bot fly is usually found only in the northwestern United States and in the midwestern states.

Broadly speaking, the losses inflicted by horse bots are of three types: (1) the annoyance to the animal caused by the flies at the time they deposit the eggs, (2) the burrowing of the bots into the lining of the cardiac or pyloric portions of the stomach and, in the case of *G. nasalis*, to the mucosa of the first part of the small intestine, resulting in irritation and a place of entry for microorganisms, and (3) interfering with the passage of food materials through the pyloric

region of the stomach. Contrary to the common belief of many persons, bot flies do not sting the animal.

Life History and Habits

Like other flies, the four distinct stages of the horse bot are: the egg, the larva (bot), the pupa, and the adult fly. It requires one year in which to complete the entire life cycle of the horse bot. Further details concerning the habits and life histories of the bot are as follows:

1. The eggs are attached to the hairs of the host.

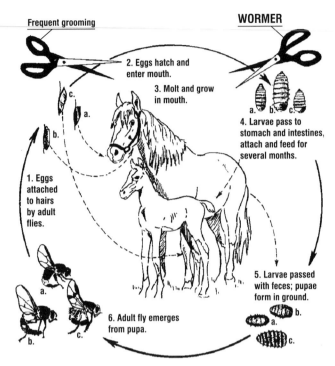

Fig. 15-10. Diagram showing the life history and habits of horse bots, of which three species are serious pests. As noted (see scissors), effective control and treatment (cutting the cycle of the parasite) consist in (1) frequent grooming, washing, and clipping to remove the eggs that are attached to the hairs of the host; and (2) administering an effective wormer. (Drawing by Prof. R. F. Johnson)

The common bot fly may deposit its eggs on various parts of the animal, but particularly about the fetlocks and on the inside of the knees; the throat bot fly attaches its eggs on the hairs beneath the jaws; and the nose bot fly deposits its eggs on the short hairs of the lips. Usually a single egg is laid at each strike.

2. Although varying somewhat according to the particular species of bot fly, the eggs usually hatch within 2 to 7[7] days' time, and the young larvae soon enter the horse's mouth.

3. Again varying according to species, the larvae remain in the mouth from 2 to 4 weeks, during which time they molt and grow.

4. Next the larvae pass to the stomach and intestine where they attach themselves to the lining for several months, feeding until they are about ¾ in. in length.

5. When grown, the bots release their hold on the lining of the alimentary canal and pass out with the feces; the nose bots reattach themselves to the rectum for a few days before dropping to the ground.

6. The larvae, or bots, then enter the pupal or

---

[7]As the eggs of the common bot fly must be rubbed first by the warm lips of the horse in order to hatch, they may lay quietly in the egg stage for as long as 90 days.

resting stage for a period of 20 to 70 days, the exact time varying according to the species. Finally, they change into the adult or fly stage at which time they are again ready to lay eggs. The adult fly is unable to take food, but enough is stored in its body in the bot stage to develop 150 to 300 eggs to be deposited during its short life, the sole purpose of which is reproduction. The flies are smaller than honeybees, which they somewhat resemble.

Damage Inflicted; Symptoms and Signs of Affected Animals

Even though the bot fly does not sting the animal, cementing of its eggs to the hairs causes a tickling sensation, particularly evident in the case of the nose bot fly. Attacked animals may toss their heads in the air, strike the ground with their front feet, and rub their noses on each other or on any convenient object.

Infested animals may show frequent digestive upsets and even colic, lowered vitality and emaciation, and reduced work output. The most serious effect is general debility of the animal caused by toxic excretions from the parasites. Occasionally, heavy infestations have caused rupture of the stomach.

Prevention, Control, and Treatment

Working animals may be given fair protection against the annoyance resulting from the deposition of eggs by throat and nose bots through the application of a cover to the jaws and nose, respectively. Frequent

Fig. 15-11. Washing to remove the eggs of adult bot flies attached to the hairs of the horse. (Courtesy, USDA)

grooming, washing, and clipping are also helpful control measures.

Horses should be treated for bots as follows:

1. In the late fall or early winter, at least one month after the first killing frost, administer one of the recommended drugs according to manufacturer's directions.

2. Thirty days prior to administering a drug, the eggs of the common bot fly, which may be clinging to the body, should be destroyed by either (a) vigorously applying warm water at 120°F, or (b) clipping the hair of the horse. The insides of the knees and the fetlocks especially should be treated in this manner.

3. Prevention of reinfestation is best assured through community campaigns in which all horses within the area are thus treated.

Caretakers should seek the advice of their local veterinarian, county agent, extension entomologist, or consultant in arriving at the wormer of choice. Also, they are admonished to follow the labeled directions of the manufacturer.

DOURINE

This is a chronic venereal disease of horses and asses, caused by the microscopic parasite *Trypanosoma equiperdum*. It is also referred to as *mal du coit* or equine syphilis, because it is similar to syphilis in humans.

Distribution and Losses Caused by Dourine

It is still quite frequent in many countries, but it was eradicated in the United States in 1942.

Life History and Habits

The causative agent is a protozoan parasite, which is transmitted primarily from animal to animal by the act of copulation. Transmission by biting insects may also occur. Following an incubation period of 8 days to 2 months, the characteristic symptoms appear in infested animals.

Damage Inflicted; Symptoms and Signs of Affected Animals

There are two stages usually described for the disease. The primary symptoms are a redness and swelling of the external genitalia of both the mare and stallion. There are frequent attempts at urination, and increased sexual excitement is observed in both sexes. A pussy discharge may be noted. The secondary stage is initiated by the appearance of firm, round, flat swellings (dollar plaques) on the body and neck. In the advanced stages, nervous symptoms may also be manifest. They consist of paralysis of the face, knuckling of the joints of the hind limbs, and dragging of the feet.

Prevention, Control, and Treatment

The complement fixation test is used in diagnosis.

The most effective method of eradication is the prompt destruction of all the infested animals. Often in areas of heavy infestation, the castration of stallions and spaying of mares is practiced with only a small degree of success. The most effective prevention consists in avoiding coition with infested animals, and in the application of modern hygiene.

No successful treatment is known.

EQUINE PIROPLASMOSIS (BABESIASES)

This disease is tick-borne and caused by either of two protozoans, *Babesia caballi* or *B. equi*, which invade the red blood cells.

Distribution and Losses Caused by Equine Piroplasmosis

The disease is worldwide. It was first diagnosed in the United States in 1961, in Florida. The death rate may be as high as 10 and 15%.

Life History and Habits

Horses usually acquire the infection from ticks, although occasionally it is introduced through intrauterine infection.

After the tick attaches itself to the host horse, the protozoan leaves it, enters the bloodstream, invades a red blood cell, multiplies (by simple division) and destroys the invaded red blood cell, following which each new protozoan invades different blood cells and repeats the performance.

Damage Inflicted; Symptoms and Signs of Affected Animals

The signs are very similar to equine infectious anemia (or swamp fever), but a positive diagnosis can be made by demonstrating the presence of the protozoa in the red blood cells or by an antigen-antibody serum test. Clinical signs include fever (103 to 106°F), anemia, depression, thirst, tears, and swelling of the eyelids. Constipation and colic may occur. The urine is yellow to reddish colored. The incubation period is 1 to 3 weeks. Many horses become inapparent carriers of the parasite.

Fig. 15-12. Horse with equine piroplasmosis. (Courtesy, USDA)

Prevention, Control, and Treatment

Tick control is the most effective approach to the prevention of equine piroplasmosis. There are several potential tick vectors in the United States, including the tropical horse tick, *Dermacentor nitens.*

Also, extreme caution should be exercised in the use of all syringes, needles, and medical instruments.

In general, isolation of affected animals is considered optimal. In the case of *B. equi*, infected horses probably remain carriers for life, and treatment does not consistently eliminate the carrier state. However, for *B. caballi*, the length of persistence has not been definitively established, but treatment is generally effective in clearing the organism. Several drugs may be used in the treatment of piroplasmosis.

The current principal significance of this disease is its impact on the international movement of horses. Horses with antibody to either *B. equi* or *B. caballi* are restricted from entering a number of countries, including the U.S.

EQUINE PROTOZOAL MYELOENCEPHALITIS (EPM)

Equine protozoal myeloencephalitis (EPM) is a neurological disease of horses caused by a protozoan parasite, currently identified as *Sarcocystis neurona.*

Distribution and Losses Caused by Equine Protozoal Myeloencephalitis

The disease has only been reported in North America, though it may have occurred in Central and South America.

Recently, the prevalence of this disease appears to be increasing, although it is unclear whether this is due to an actual increase in the disease or improved diagnostic capabilities.

Life History and Habits

The complete life cycle of the parasite is not fully understood. However, it appears that EPM probably cannot be transferred from horse to horse. Carnivorous wildlife that eat infected horse flesh may be involved in the spread of the disease; hence, they should be controlled.

Damage Inflicted; Symptoms and Signs of Affected Animals

The parasite can attack any part of the central nervous system, resulting in a wide variety of neurological signs. Most commonly, incoordination (ataxia) and weakness are seen. In mild cases, the only clinical sign might be a vague lameness, while in severe cases, the horse may be unable to stand or may have seizures. It appears that although exposure to *S. neurona* is relatively high, the majority of exposed horses do not develop clinical disease.

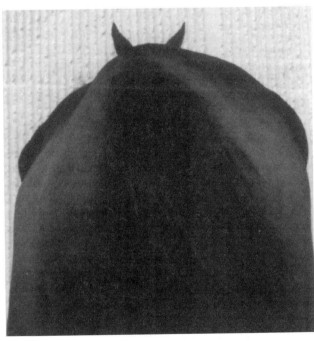

Fig. 15-13. Horse with equine protozoal myeloencephalitis (EPM). Note the marked asymmetric muscle atrophy in this case. (Courtesy, Department of Clinical Sciences, College of Veterinary Medicine, University of Florida, Gainesville)

Prevention, Control, and Treatment

There are now specific diagnostic tests to aid in the diagnosis of EPM. Horses with compatible clinical signs should be evaluated by a veterinarian, and if EPM is diagnosed an appropriate treatment plan should be established. Specific treatment for the disease includes oral sulfa-trimethoprim and pyrimethamine. Approximately 55 to 60% of EPM cases will demonstrate a good clinical response to treatment.

The parasites can be eliminated, but the damage they cause to the central nervous system is usually permanent.

PINWORMS (RECTAL WORMS)

Two species of pinworms are frequently found in horses; namely *Oxyuris equi* and *Probstmyria vivipara.* The former are whitish worms with long, slender tails, whereas the latter are so small as to be scarcely visible to the naked eye.

Distribution and Losses Caused by Pinworms

Pinworms are widely distributed in horses throughout the United States. The large species, *Oxyuris equi,* are the most damaging to the host.

Life History and Habits

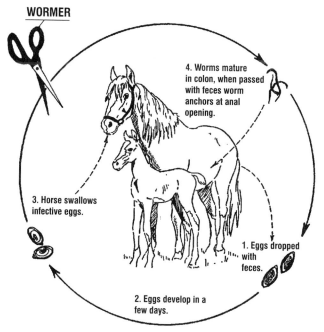

WORMER

4. Worms mature in colon, when passed with feces worm anchors at anal opening.

3. Horse swallows infective eggs.

1. Eggs dropped with feces.

2. Eggs develop in a few days.

Fig. 15-14. Diagram showing the life history and habits of the pinworm. As noted (see scissors),the common treatment for the removal of pinworms consists in administering a suitable wormer, thus cutting the cycle of the parasite. Prevention and control involve sanitation and keeping the animal separated from its own excrement. (Drawing by Prof. R. F. Johnson)

The life history of the larger of the two species of pinworms, *Oxyuris equi,* may be summarized as follows:

1. The female worms pass out with the feces, either depositing their eggs with the droppings or around the anal region. The latter type of deposition results when the female worms of *O. equi* anchor themselves at the anal opening and deposit their eggs.
2. Outside the body, the eggs develop and reach the infestive stage in a few days.
3. Horses become infested by swallowing the eggs with feed or water.
4. The worms mature in the large intestine, principally in the dorsal colon.

The small pinworm, *Probstmyria vivipara,* are—as the name indicates—viviparous worms. Their young are produced alive, and presumably they can complete their entire life cycle of development within the ventral colon of the host.

Damage Inflicted; Symptoms and Signs of Affected Animals

Frequently the best evidence of the presence of the larger pinworms is that the worms are seen in the feces of heavily infested animals. Irritation of the anus and tail rubbing are also symptoms. Heavy infestations may also cause digestive disturbances and produce anemia.

Prevention, Control, and Treatment

As with other intestinal parasites, the prevention and control of pinworms involves sanitation and keeping the animal separated from its own excrement.

The drug of choice should be administered in keeping with the labeled directions of the manufacturer.

In case of severe itching, ointment may be applied around the tail beneath the anus.

STOMACH WORMS

Stomach worms of horses consist of a group of different kinds of parasitic worms that are responsible for inflammation in the stomach or for a condition referred to as *summer sores.* Three species of large stomach worms are capable of producing severe gastritis in horses. Diagnosis is difficult because the eggs are not ordinarily detected by flotation examination of feces; thus, the importance of these worms tends to be minimized.

The minute stomach worm *(Trichostrongylus axei)* is a common parasite of cattle, sheep, and a number of other hosts, in addition to the horse.

Distribution and Losses Caused by Stomach Worms

Workers in both Europe and the United States have expressed the opinion that probably no other ailment of horses is so regularly associated with a sudden loss of condition as is infestation with stomach worms. Wasted feed and lowered efficiency are the chief losses when horses are infested with stomach worms.

Life History and Habits

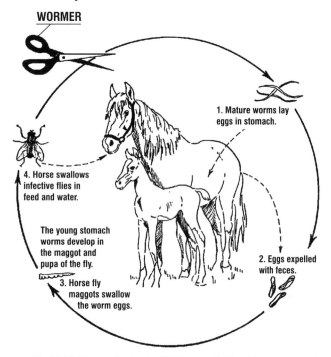

Fig. 15-15. Diagram showing the life history and habits of the large stomach worm. As noted (see scissors), a suitable wormer may be used for removal of stomach worms, thus cutting the cycle of the parasite. (Drawing by Prof. R. F. Johnson)

The life history of the horse stomach worm varies somewhat, according to the particular kind. The cycle of the large stomach worm, *Habronema muscae*, is as follows:

1. The mature worms in the stomach lay many eggs.
2. The eggs containing young worms are expelled from the digestive tract with manure.
3. The eggs are swallowed by fly maggots; the young worms develop in the maggot and in the pupa and are infestive when the adult fly emerges.
4. Horses become infested after swallowing infested flies or the larvae that escapes from flies while the latter are feeding on the moisture of the lips.

Damage Inflicted; Symptoms and Signs of Affected Animals

Sometimes, the larvae of the larger stomach worms are responsible in part for a relatively common skin disease of horses called summer sores.

Heavy infestations may cause a rapid loss of condition associated with extensive and severe catarrhal gastritis. Long-standing infestations result in chronic inflammatory changes.

Prevention, Control, and Treatment

Houseflies and stable flies are the vectors. Hence, the control of flies is the best method of preventing and controlling stomach worms.

Several wormers are effective when used according to manufacturer's directions.

Many different treatments have been used for summer sores, with varying success.

STRONGYLES (LARGE STRONGYLES, SMALL STRONGYLES)

Of the several hundred parasites affecting horses, the most serious threat to the health and life of the horse kept under conditions found on breeding farms the world over is the strongyle.

There are approximately 40 different species of strongyles. Although not all of these kinds have ever been found in any one horse, almost every animal that has had access to pasture, and has not been treated at intervals for their removal, harbors several of them. The different species vary considerably in size, some being scarcely visible to the naked eye; whereas others reach a length of 2 in.

The large strongyle—also variously referred to as palisade worms, bloodworms, sclerostomes, and red worms—include only three species, but these forms are the most injurious parasites of the horse. The balance of the species—the vast majority of strongyles—are the small strongyles. The latter are generally regarded as being much less pathogenic than the large strongyles. In a heavily infested animal, one or more of the three species of large strongyles may be present, along with 15 to 25 species of small strongyles.

Distribution and Losses Caused by Strongyles

Strongyles are found throughout the United States wherever horses are pastured. Naturally, the degree of infestation varies according to the extent of exposure; and this in turn depends upon the sanitation, feeding, medication, season, and climate. Heavy infestations with strongyles may result in marked unthriftiness, loss in capacity to perform work, and even death. The harmful effects are greatest with younger animals.

As a single deposit of manure from an infested horse may contain hundreds of thousands of strongyle eggs, and with the life cycle of the parasite being what it is, it is easy to understand why pastured horses are almost always infested.

Life History and Habits

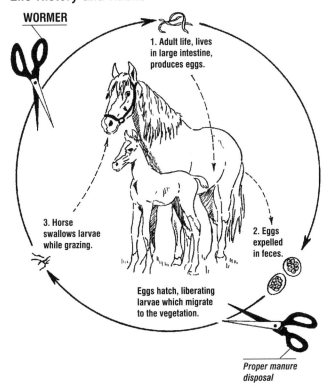

Fig. 15-16. Diagram showing the life history and habits of strongyles. As noted (see scissors), a wormer may be used for removing strongyles, thus cutting the cycle of the parasite. First and foremost, however, it is important that there be a barrier between the horse and its excrement. (Drawing by Prof. R. F. Johnson)

The life cycle of *Strongylus vulgaris* follows:

1. The eggs are passed in the feces.
2. The eggs embryonate on the ground or herbage.
3. The eggs hatch into the first stage larvae, thence they develop to second stage larvae, and finally to third stage infestive larvae. This process takes about seven days under favorable temperature and moisture conditions.
4. The larvae crawl onto vegetation.
5. The infestive larvae are ingested in feed and water.
6. After years of divergent opinions, there is now general agreement relative to the migratory route of

the parasite. The larvae penetrate the wall of the small intestine, cecum, and ventral colon; thence they invade the walls of the small arteries and migrate toward the anterior mesentric artery, and produce thrombosis and aneurysm. Thence the larvae break out of the thrombus and are carried by the bloodstream to the ventral colon and cecum, where they migrate back through the walls to become adult worms attached to mucosa of the cecum and colon. All this migration and development takes six months, during which time the larvae are inaccessible to ordinary doses of anthelmintics.

The small strongyles migrate to a lesser extent, passing directly to the large intestine after being swallowed. Large numbers of infective larvae may become encysted in the lining of the large colon and cecum, subsequently emerging and returning to the gut as mature adults. As adult worms, some of them attach themselves to the wall of the large intestine, much the same as the large strongyles. Most of them, however, are found free and unattached in the contents of the large intestine or cecum.

Damage Inflicted; Symptoms and Signs of Affected Animals

Severe infestation with large and small strongyles—and such infestations are especially common with animals grazed on permanent pastures— result in lack of appetite, anemia, progressive emaciation, a rough hair coat, sunken eyes, digestive disturbances including colic and diarrhea, a tucked-up appearance, and sometimes posterior incoordination or weakness. Collectively, these diverse and severe symptoms constitute the disease known as strongylosis.

Fig. 15-17. Horse with strongyle infestation. (Courtesy, Department of Veterinary Pathology and Hygiene, College of Veterinary Medicine, University of Illinois)

The presence of the characteristic eggs in the feces is evidence of strongyle infestation, and, combined with the marked symptoms indicated above, should be considered as evidence of strongylosis.

Prevention, Control, and Treatment

Unfortunately, the infestive larvae of the strongyle can withstand unfavorable environmental influences to a remarkable degree. Neither low temperatures nor air drying will harm them. As a result, when pastures are infested, they will so remain for a year or more, even when held idle or grazed by some other class of livestock. For these and other reasons, the control of strongyles involves more than average difficulties.

All the general control measures previously recommended for parasites may well be applied to the control of strongyles. First and foremost, it is important that there be a barrier between the horse and its excrement. Gathering up manure from pastures and barns and storing it in a pit for a period of time, allowing it to be subjected to its own generated heat, is a sure way to reduce infestations. Moist pastures and overstocking should be avoided. Medications should supplement rather than replace wholesome feed and water and clean surroundings.

TAPEWORMS

There are three species of horse tapeworms, but *Anoplocephala perfoliata* is both the most common and most damaging of the three. It tends to form clusters at the ileocecal valve region of the cecum and produce ulcerative lesions, which may perforate.

Many commonly used dewormers are not effective against tapeworms. However, pyrantel pamoate at twice the label dose can be safely used.

THREADWORMS (STRONGYLOIDS)

Infestations by the small intestinal threadworm *(Strongyloides westeri)* are quite common in foals. Little is known of the actual effects of this worm on foals other than the association of diarrhea with infestation and the self-limiting aspects in which the worms disappear by the time the foals are six months of age.

EXTERNAL PARASITES (ECTOPARASITES) OF HORSES

Horses are subject to infestation by a number of external parasites. Their effects vary according to the kind of parasite, the degree of infestation, and the health of the horse. Generally speaking, they cause irritation, restlessness, and rubbing; result in a dull coat, loss of hair, and harsh skin; make for a loss in weight; lower the vitality and spirit of the horse; and produce a general unthrifty condition. In extreme cases, they may even cause death.

External parasites are also responsible for the spread of several serious diseases of horses which exact a heavy toll each year in sickness and death. Thus, equine piroplasmosis (or babesiases) is transmitted by ticks *(Dermacentor species)*; and mosquitoes *(Culicidae)* are vectors of equine infectious anemia (swamp fever) and equine encephalomyelitis (sleeping sickness).

The cost of controlling external parasites on horses with insecticides is usually very small compared with the losses incurred when the infestations go uncontrolled. A good program for controlling external parasites of horses should (1) be initiated during the early stages of infestation, (2) include the use of good sanitation practices and manipulation of standing water in addition to the application of insecticides (not all external parasites can be controlled with insecticides), and (3) require use of insecticides in complete accordance with the labels and instructions.

INSECTICIDES

In the sections that follow, pertinent information is presented relative to the forms, application, precautions in the use, and drug withdrawal in insecticides. This is followed by a discussion of each of the common external parasites of horses. Strengths and application directions are not given for the recommended insecticides because of (1) the diversity of environments and management practices represented by this group; (2) the varying restrictions on the use of insecticides from area to area; (3) the fact that registered uses of insecticides change from time to time; and (4) the fact that the final choice of a specific insecticide will probably be made on the basis of what the local merchant, supplier, or veterinarian has available. Information about the choice and registered uses of insecticides in a particular area may be obtained from the local county agent, extension entomologist, or livestock consultant.

FORMS OF INSECTICIDES

Insecticides for use on horses may be purchased in several forms. The most common are emulsifiable concentrates, dusts, wettable powders, and oil solutions.

APPLICATION OF INSECTICIDES

The type of application for treating horses may be

based upon (1) the target pest; (2) the management and use of the horses; and (3) the available product and formulation. Horses tend to be more excitable than cattle, so when insecticides are applied as sprays, especially with high-pressure sprayers, care should be taken to avoid startling the animals. For this reason, many horse owners prefer to apply insecticides by hand, either as dusts or as dilute sprays wiped on with a sponge (wipe-on).

When sprays are used, wettable powder formulations are usually preferred because the oils and solvents in emulsifiable concentrates may cause hair damage and skin irritation in some horses.

In addition, insecticides may be purchased in aerosol applicators, and some insecticides may be added to the feed (feed additive) for treatment of some pests.

Another problem peculiar to insecticidal treatment of horses, one not usually encountered with other livestock, is that the excessive sweating of horses being ridden or exercised may render the insecticide ineffective and greatly shorten its residual life on the animal.

Timing of the application of insecticides is very important. Treatment should begin when the parasite is in a weak stage, not when the animal is in a weakened stage. Control measures should be initiated at the beginning of the season of the pest, before populations become annoying and more harmful. The objective is to break the life cycle of the pest early in life, before it becomes an adult.

PRECAUTIONS ON THE USE OF INSECTICIDES

Certain basic precautions should be observed when insecticides are used because, when used improperly, they can be injurious to people, animals, wildlife, and beneficial insects. Follow the directions and heed all the precautions on the labels. Some basic precautions in the use of insecticides follow:

■ **Selecting insecticides**—Always select the formulation and insecticide labeled for the purpose for which it is to be used.

■ **Storing insecticides**—Always store insecticides in original containers. Never transfer them to unlabeled containers or to food or beverage containers. Store insecticides in a dry place out of reach of children, animals, or unauthorized persons.

■ **Disposing of empty containers and unused insecticides**—Properly and promptly dispose of all empty insecticide containers. Do not reuse. Break and bury glass containers. Chop holes in, crush, and bury metal containers. Bury containers and unused insecticides at least 18 in. deep in the soil in a sanitary landfill or dump. Check with local authorities to determine specific procedures for the area.

■ **Mixing and handling**—Mix and prepare insecticides in the open or in a well-ventilated place. Wear rubber gloves and clean dry clothing (respirator device may be necessary with some products). If any insecticide is spilled on clothing, wash with soap and water immediately and change clothing. Avoid prolonged inhalation. Do not smoke, eat, or drink when mixing and handling insecticides.

■ **Applying**—Use only amounts recommended. Although horses are usually not considered for human consumption, the recommended insecticide may cause harmful residues in food or feed products if not handled in full accordance with the label. Avoid retreating more often than label restrictions. Avoid prolonged contact with all insecticides. Do not eat, drink, or smoke until all operations have ceased and hands and face are thoroughly washed. Change and launder clothing after extensive use of an insecticide.

DRUG WITHDRAWAL

The insecticide recommendations given in this chapter are for horses not used for food. Where horses are to be slaughtered for food, the tolerance levels and withdrawal period given on the manufacturer's label should be followed with care.

GENERAL PREVENTIVE AND CONTROL MEASURES

Effective prevention and control of external parasites of horses involves both the animals and their surroundings. It calls for good nutrition and grooming, avoiding too heavy concentration of horses, and the selection of the right insecticide and its application on the animals in accordance with the manufacturer's directions. It calls for sanitary stalls and paddocks, augmented by the choice of the right insecticide(s) for the control of flies, chiggers, and ticks, and its proper use—as a bait, dust, emulsifiable concentrate, spray, and/or wettable powder—in barns and holding areas.

COMMON EXTERNAL PARASITES

Flies and lice are the most common external parasites of horses, although some of the others are capable of producing more severe injury when they occur. A discussion of each of the most common and troublesome external parasites of horses follows.

BLOWFLIES

The flies of the blowfly group include a number of species that find their principal breeding ground in dead and putrifying flesh, although sometimes they infest wounds or unhealthy tissues of live animals and fresh or cooked meat. All the important species of blowflies except the flesh flies, which are grayish and have three dark stripes on their backs, have a more or less metallic luster.

Distribution and Losses Caused by Blowflies

Although blowflies are widespread, they present the greatest problem in the Pacific Northwest and in the South and southwestern states. Death losses from blowflies are not excessive, but they cause much discomfort to affected animals, and they lower production.

Life History and Habits

With the exception of the group known as gray flesh flies, which deposit tiny living maggots instead of eggs, the blowflies have a similar life cycle to the screwworm, although the cycle is completed in about one-half the time.

Damage Inflicted; Symptoms and Signs of Affected Animals

The blowfly causes its greatest damage by infesting wounds and the soiled hair of living animals. Such damage, which is largely limited to the black blowfly (or wool-maggot fly), is similar to that caused by screwworms. The maggots spread over the body, feeding on the dead skin and exudates, where they produce severe irritation and destroy the ability of the skin to function. Infested animals rapidly become weak and fevered; and, although they recover, they may remain in an unthrifty condition for a long period.

Prevention, Control, and Treatment

Prevention of blowfly damage consists of eliminating the pest and decreasing the susceptibility of animals to infestations.

As blowflies breed principally in dead carcasses, the most effective control consists in promptly destroying all dead animals by burning or deep burial. The use of traps, poisoned baits, and electrified screens is also helpful in reducing trouble from blowflies.

Daily dusting of the irritated or infested area with a recommended insecticide will control the flies. Puff-bottle applicators containing insecticides are available and provide an effective means of application. Also it is important to keep wounds clean.

FLIES AND MOSQUITOES

Flies and mosquitoes are probably the most important insect pests of horses. They lower the vitality of horses, mar the hair coat and skin, produce a general unthrifty condition, lower performance, and make for hazards when riding or using horses. Also, they may temporarily or permanently impair the development of foals and young stock. Even more important, they can be the vector (carrier) of serious diseases. Because of their varying habits, along with different materials and methods required for their control, flies have been classed as either biting or nonbiting in the discussion that follows.

Biting Flies and Mosquitoes

Several species of biting (bloodsucking) flies and mosquitoes attack horses, but the following are the most common: Horse flies (*Tabanus* spp.), deer flies (*Chrysops* spp.), stable flies *(Stomoxys calcitrans)*, horn flies *(Haematobia irritans)*, mosquitoes (species of the genera *Aedes, Anopheles, Culex*, and *Psorophora*), black flies (family *Simuliidae*), and biting midges (genus *Culicoides*). Because these flies suck blood, several of them may transmit such diseases as anthrax, encephalomyelitis (Eastern, Western, and Venezuelan), and swamp fever. All of them are pests—that is, they cause considerable annoyance to horses.

Fig. 15-18. Stable fly, *Stomaxys calcitrans.* (Courtesy, USDA)

Distribution and Losses Caused by Biting Flies and Mosquitoes

Biting (bloodsucking) flies and mosquitoes are found wherever there are horses, with the highest population occurring during warm weather and where there is lack of sanitation. They annoy horses—on pastures, in stalls, and in paddocks. They cause pain and discomfort to the animal, and, at times, they make them unmanageable when they are being worked.

Horse and deer flies attack horses pastured in or near areas with a marsh, swamp, creek, or irrigation ditch.

Stable flies are found wherever there are horses, people, or other mammals—their usual victims.

Horn flies are found near cattle. So, horses are attacked when they are pastured with cattle, kept in areas near cattle, or ridden near cattle.

Mosquitoes cause special discomfort to horses particularly during early spring and wet years.

Life History and Habits

Horse flies and deer flies breed in standing water that is fairly shallow and has an abundance of organic matter. Stable flies breed in horse manure, soiled bedding, feed wastes, decomposed fruit and vegetable matter, and compost piles and clippings. Horn flies breed in single, fresh droppings of cow manure. Mosquitoes breed on water, in such places as water-holding low spots in corrals and paddocks, infrequently used drinking troughs, irrigated pastures, drainage ditches, natural flooded meadows, swamps, creeks, tree holes, leaf choked rain gutters, and poorly covered septic tanks and drains.

The usual life cycle of flies from egg to adult is shown in Fig. 15-19.

The life cycles of all mosquitoes consist of four stages: egg, larva (wiggler), pupa (tumbler), and adult (Fig. 15-20).

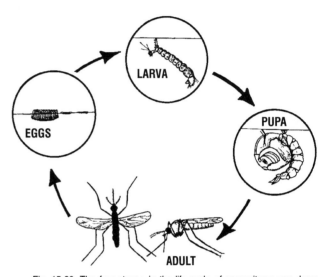

Fig. 15-20. The four stages in the life cycle of mosquitoes: egg, larva (wiggler), pupa (tumbler), and adult.

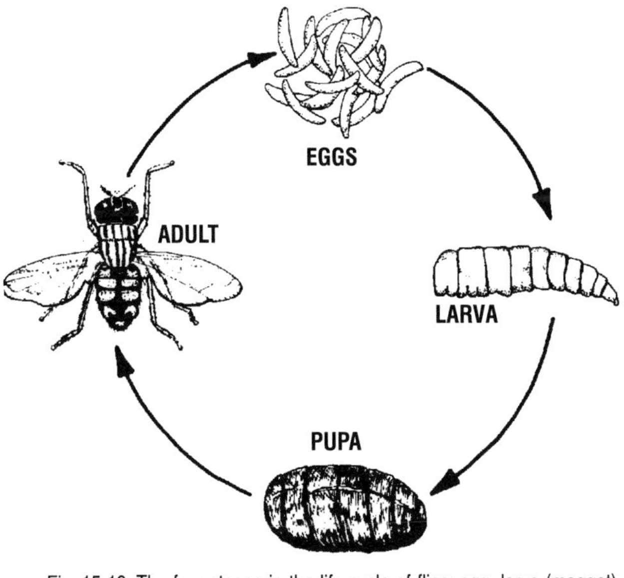

Fig. 15-19. The four stages in the life cycle of flies: egg, larva (maggot), pupa, and adult. Under optimum conditions during warm weather, the various species complete their life cycles in the following number of days: housefly, 7; stable fly, 21; face fly, 8; black blowfly, 11; green blowfly, 8; screwworm fly, 14.

Damage Inflicted; Symptoms and Signs of Affected Animals

Horse flies and deer flies possess sharp, scissor-like mouth parts, which slice into the skin and make for a good flow of blood.

The stable fly sucks blood and is a vicious biter, especially in the early evening hours when the weather is warm and humid. Severe attacks irritate horses and cause restlessness and the stamping of feet. Because stable flies crawl over horse manure and then suck blood from the horse, they readily transmit stomach worms *(Habronema)*.

Horn flies feed primarily on the back of the head, the sides of the neck, shoulders, withers, along the back, around the navel, and on the legs. They remain on the horse day and night.

In addition to their vicious biting habits, mosquitoes are of particular concern to equestrians because they transmit the virus causing encephalomyelitis (Eastern, Western, and Venezuelan).

Prevention, Control, and Treatment

Sanitation—the destruction of the breeding areas of the pests—is the key to the control of biting flies and mosquitoes. Do not allow manure or other breeding areas to accumulate. Spread manure in fields (to dry) every day or two. Control horse flies, deer flies, and mosquitoes by filling low spots in corrals or paddocks and draining all water-holding areas.

As a supplement to sanitation, use insecticide (of which there are several) according to the manufacturer's directions. Treat manure piles and buildings for fly control; and treat wet areas that harbor mosquitoes.

Fly repellents which last four to eight hours after application have been developed for the control of horse flies and deer flies on horses.

Nonbiting Flies

Horses may be annoyed by the face fly *(Musca autumnalis)* and the housefly *(M. domestica)*, neither of which suck blood.

Distribution and Losses Caused by
Nonbiting Flies

Face flies are serious pests of horses (and cattle) in the eastern, midwestern, and certain western states.

Houseflies are widely distributed throughout the world and are one of the principal pests around horse stables.

Life History and Habits

The face fly breeds only in single, fresh animal droppings, and only from cattle on rangeland or pasture. The life cycle from egg to adult takes 8 days during warm summer months (Fig. 15-19) and up to 2 to 3 weeks in cooler weather.

Houseflies are attracted to waste materials, where they feed and deposit their eggs. This includes stacked horse manure, soiled bedding, wet feed, and decomposed plant material (grass clippings, vegetable and fruit wastes). Houseflies do not normally develop in single manure droppings; rather they use piles of manure or other organic matter. Under favorable conditions—warm weather and plenty of food—the usual life cycle from egg to adult fly is one week (Fig. 15-19).

Damage Inflicted; Symptoms and Signs
of Affected Animals

Face flies congregate about the nose and eyes of horses, where they sponge up liquids. The feeding of face flies causes excessive flow of tears and saliva—and irritation. Infested horses usually stand about restlessly switching their tails and not grazing naturally. Almost complete freedom from face flies can be obtained by keeping horses confined to stables during the daytime.

The housefly, which feeds twice daily, regurgitates liquid through its proboscis while depositing fecal matter as it crawls over its food. In this manner it can transmit human and animal diseases, and it transmits stomach worms *(Habronema)* to horses. The dark spots on walls, ceilings, corral fences, etc., are the characteristic fly specks of vomit and fecal material.

Houseflies are attracted to the moist areas of the horse's face.

Prevention, Control, and Treatment

Good face fly control is difficult to achieve. Pyrethrin repellents applied to the horse's face and head will repel nonbiting flies for 8 to 12 hours. A variety of face masks and nets are now available that protect the horse's eyes from face flies when on pasture. Residual sprays, when applied to the sunny surfaces of barns, shelters, and fences where face flies congregate reduce population.

Sanitation is the most efficient method of reducing population of houseflies. Sanitation may be additionally important if the horses are located near an urban area, in order to avoid complaints from neighbors. Residual sprays will eliminate many houseflies. Also, houseflies are attracted to baits (insecticides mixed with sugar or other attractive material), which are effective housefly killers.

LICE

The louse is a small, flattened, wingless insect parasite of which there are several species. Most species of lice are specific for a particular species of animal. Horses are commonly infested with two species of lice, the horse-sucking louse *(Haematopinus asini)* and the horse-biting louse *(Bovicola equi)*. The sucking louse obtains blood and lymph from horses by puncturing the skin with piercing-sucking mouth parts. The biting louse feeds on scales, hair, and skin exudate and does not pierce the skin or suck blood. Of the two groups, sucking lice are the most injurious.

Lice are always more abundant on weak, unthrifty animals and are more troublesome during the winter months than during the rest of the year.

Distribution and Losses Caused by Lice

The presence of lice upon animals is almost universal, but the degree of infestation depends largely upon the state of animal nutrition and the extent to which the owner will tolerate parasites. The irritation caused by the presence of lice on horses retards growth, gains, and/or production of milk.

Life History and Habits

Lice spend their entire life cycle—eggs (nits), nymphs, and adults—on the host's body. They attach their eggs or nits to the hair near the skin where they hatch in about two weeks. Two weeks later the young females begin laying eggs, and after reproduction they die on the host. Lice do not survive more than a week when separated from the host; but, under favorable conditions, eggs clinging to detached hairs may continue to hatch for two or three weeks.

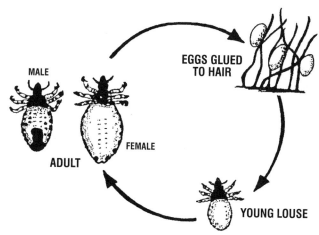

Fig. 15-21. Life cycle of long-nosed, bloodsucking lice showing nits (eggs) glued to hair, young louse, female with developing egg, and male.

Damage Inflicted; Symptoms and Signs of Affected Animals

Lice infestation shows up most commonly in winter on ill-nourished and neglected animals. There is intense irritation, restlessness, and loss of condition. As many lice are blood-suckers, they devitalize their host. There may be severe itching and the animal may be seen scratching, rubbing, and gnawing at the skin. The hair may be rough and thin, and lack luster; patches of hair may be rubbed off; and scabs may be evident. In horses, favorite locations for lice are the root of the tail, on the inside of the thighs, over the fetlock region, and along the neck and shoulders. In some cases, the symptoms may resemble those of mange; and it must be kept in mind that the two may occur simultaneously. With the coming of spring, when the hair sheds and the animals go to pasture, lousiness is greatly diminished.

Prevention, Control, and Treatment

Lice are easily controlled by periodic applications, according to the directions on the label, of one of several suitable insecticides, including the anthelmintic ivermectin.

MITES (MANGE)

Mites produce a specific contagious disease known as mange (or scabies, scab, or itch). These small insectlike parasites, which are almost invisible to the naked eye, constitute a very large group. They attack members of both the plant and animal kingdom.

Each species of domesticated animals has its own peculiar species of mange mites; and, with the exception of the sarcoptic mites, the mites from one species of animals cannot live normally and propagate permanently on a different species. The sarcoptic mites are transmissable from one class of animals to another and, in the case of the sarcoptic mite of the horse and cow, from animals to people. There are two chief forms of mange: sarcoptic mange, caused by burrowing mites, and psoroptic mange, caused by mites that bite the skin and suck blood but do not burrow. The sarcoptic form is most damaging; for, in addition to their tunneling, the mites secrete an irritating poison. This combination results in severe itching.

Horses may become infested with three species of mange mites—*Sarcoptes scabiei equi*, *Psoroptes equi*, and *Chorioptes equi*. These minute parasites live on the skin of horses; and each species produces a particular type of mange.

Mites are responsible for the condition known as mange (scabies) in horses, sheep, cattle, and swine. The disease appears to spread most rapidly among young and poorly nourished animals.

Distribution and Losses Caused by Mites

Injury from mites is caused by irritation and blood sucking and the formation of scabs and other skin problems. In a severe attack, the growth of young animals may be retarded.

Life History and Habits

All stages of the life cycle of mange mites are found on the host—the horse. The mites will live for only 2 or 3 weeks when removed from the animal. The female mite which produces sarcoptic mange—the most severe form of scabies—lays from 10 to 25 eggs during the egg-laying period, which lasts about two weeks. At the end of another two weeks, the eggs have hatched and the mites have reached maturity. A new generation of mites may be produced every 15 days.

The disease is more prevalent during the winter months, when animals are confined and in closer contact with each other.

Damage Inflicted; Symptoms and Signs of Affected Animals

Heavy infestation of mites, which are a source of constant annoyance to horses, result in a characteristic hairless, scaly appearance.

When the mite pierces the skin to feed on cells and lymph, there is marked irritation, itching, and scratching. Exudate forms on the surface, and this coagulates, crusting over the surface. The crusting is often accompanied or followed by the formation of thick, tough, wrinkled skin. Often there are secondary skin infections. The only certain method of diagnosis is to demonstrate the presence of mites.

Prevention, Control, and Treatment

Prevention consists in avoiding contact with diseased animals or infested premises. In the case of an outbreak, the local veterinarian or livestock sanitation officials should be contacted.

Ivermectin is generally effective in controlling mites on horses. In addition, lime sulfur, and, where permitted by FDA, both lindane and toxaphene are effective for the control of mites when used according to directions.

RINGWORM

Ringworm, or barn itch, is a contagious disease of the outer layers of skin. It is caused by certain microscopic molds or fungi in horses, primarily *Trichophyton equinum* and *Microsporum equinum*. All animals and humans are susceptible.

Distribution and Losses Caused by Ringworm

Ringworm is widespread throughout the United States. Though it may appear among animals on pasture, it is far more prevalent as a stable disease. It is unsightly, and affected animals may experience considerable discomfort; but the actual economic losses attributed to the disease are not too great.

Life History and Habits

The period of incubation for this disease is about one week. The fungi form seed or spores that may live 18 months or longer in barns and elsewhere.

Damage Inflicted; Symptoms and Signs of Affected Animals

Round, scaly areas almost devoid of hair appear mainly in the vicinity of the eyes, ears, side of the neck, or the root of the tail. Crusts may form, and the skin may have a gray, powdery, asbestos-like appearance. The infested patches, if not checked, gradually increase in size. Mild itching usually accompanies the disease.

Fig. 15-22. Horse with ringworm. Note the round scaly areas almost devoid of hair. (Courtesy, Department of Veterinary Clinical Sciences, College of Veterinary Medicine, Washington State University, Pullman)

Prevention, Control, and Treatment

The organisms are spread from animal to animal or through the medium of contaminated fence posts, currycombs, and brushes. Thus, prevention and control consists of disinfecting everything that has been in contact with infested animals. The affected animals should also be isolated. Strict sanitation is an essential in the control of ringworm.

Ringworm often regresses without specific therapy. However, either a variety of topical treatments or systemic therapy can be used. The hair should be clipped, the scabs removed, and the area cleaned. Some commonly used topical agents include tamed iodine shampoos, lime sulfur, hypochlorite solution, and Captan, a plant fungicide.

SCREWWORM (FLIES)

Among all the insect pests on this earth, those which raise their maggots in the living flesh of animals—such as the screwworm fly (*Cochliomyia hominivorax*)—are peculiarly loathsome. True screwworms seldom get through the unbroken skin, but will penetrate moist pockets like the prepuce of a gelding.

They are not found in cold-blooded animals such as turtles, snakes, and lizards.

Wounds resulting from branding and castrating horses afford a breeding ground for this parasite. Add to this the wounds from some types of vegetation, from fighting, and from bloodsucking insects; and ample places for propagation are provided.

Distribution and Losses Caused by Screwworms

The screwworm fly was eradicated from southeastern United States in the late 1950s. Today, infestations occur occasionally in certain areas of Arizona, New Mexico, and Texas; and infestations frequently occur in Mexico. Sometimes under exceptionally favorable weather conditions or through the shipping of infested animals from further south, destructive outbreaks of the pest occur in areas to the north and east.

The screwworm fly may infest horses through wounds, or through lesions caused by ticks, horse flies, or horn flies. In infested areas, it is undoubtedly the greatest enemy of all the insect species with which the livestock owner must contend. For example, in the Southwest, prior to the use of sterile flies for eradication, many ranchers reported that 50% of their normal annual livestock losses were caused by this parasite.

Life History and Habits

The primary screwworm fly is bluish green in color, with three dark stripes on its back and reddish orange color below the eyes. The fly generally deposits its eggs in shinglelike masses on the edges of the dry portion of wounds. From 50 to 300 eggs are laid at one time, with a single female being capable of laying about 3,000 eggs in a lifetime. Hatching of the egg occurs in 11 hours, and the young whitish worms (larvae or maggots) immediately burrow into the living flesh. There they feed and grow for a period of 4 to 7 days, shedding their skins twice during this period.

When the larva has reached its full growth, it assumes a pinkish color, leaves the wound, and drops to the ground, where it digs beneath the surface of the soil and undergoes a transformation to the hard-skinned, dark brown, motionless pupa. It is during the pupa stage that the maggot changes to the adult fly.

After the pupa has been in the soil from 7 to 60 days, the fly emerges from it, works its way to the surface of the ground, and crawls up on some nearby object (bush, weed, etc.) to allow its wings to unfold and otherwise mature. Under favorable conditions, the newly emerged female fly becomes sexually mature and will lay eggs 5 days later. During warm weather, the entire life cycle is usually completed in 21 days,

but under cold, unfavorable conditions, this cycle may take as many as 80 days or longer.

Damage Inflicted; Symptoms and Signs of Affected Animals

The injury caused by this parasite is inflicted chiefly by the maggots. Unless proper treatment is administered, the great destruction of tissues kills the host in a few days.

Prevention, Control, and Treatment

Prevention in infested areas consists mainly of keeping the animal wounds to a minimum and of protecting those that do materialize.

As the primary screwworm must have living warm-blooded animals in which to breed and so that it may survive, it must produce a new generation during each four-month period. It is evident, therefore, that the most effective control measures can be effected during the winter months. During this season, the life cycle is slowed down, and it is difficult for the fly to live and breed. Thus, the most effective control consists in preventing infestation of wounds and of killing all possible maggots during the winter and spring months. Additional control is effected through timing, as much as possible, those farm and ranch operations that necessarily produce wounds. The winter season is preferable, being the time when the flies are least abundant and least active. The eradication of plants that cause injuries, breeding so that the young will arrive during the season of least fly activity, and avoidance of anything else that might produce wounds will aid greatly in screwworm control. In brief, the elimination of wounds or injuries to the host constitutes effective control.

The screwworm eradication program, by sterilization, has been effective. This consists in sterilizing male screwworms, in the pupal stages with gamma rays. Male screwworms mate repeatedly, but females mate only once. Thus, when female mates with a sterilized male, only infertile eggs are laid. The release of millions of sterilized males has led to the near eradication of screwworms from most of the United States.

When maggots (larvae) infest the flesh of an animal, a sample of the larvae should be sent to proper authorities for identification, and the animal should be treated with a proper insecticide. Additional control measures will be supervised by inspection personnel if the larvae are screwworms.

TICKS

The numbers and species of ticks infesting horses

varies with the geographical area. Each region has its own group of ticks.

Basically, ticks can be classified into two groups: the hard ticks, and the soft ticks. Horses are parasitized by a number of hard ticks, most of which are three-host ticks (they utilize three hosts during the life cycle) that detach after feeding as larvae and as nymphs and molt on the ground.

Distribution and Losses Caused by Ticks

Ticks are particularly prevalent on horses in the southern and western parts of the United States. In severe infestations, they reduce the vitality of horses through constant irritation and loss of blood.

Life History and Habits

All ticks have life cycles that are generally similar; that is, the females lay eggs, and the six-legged larvae (or seed ticks) hatch, engorge on a host, and molt to eight-legged nymphs; the nymphs also engorge and then molt to adults. The adults usually mate on a host. The females engorge, drop off, and lay eggs, and the males remain on the host to mate with other females.

The lone star tick (Amblyomma americanum), the Gulf Coast tick (Amblyomma maculatum), the Pacific Coast tick (Dermacentor occidentalis), the American dog tick (D. variabilis), and the Rocky Mountain wood tick (D. andersoni) are all three-host ticks, and all are limited in distribution to certain areas. Immature stages (larvae and nymphs) engorge on small mammals and birds, and adults are usually found on horses in the spring and summer. Another three-host species, the blacklegged tick (Ixodes scapularis), is found on horses in the late winter and early spring.

Of special interest to horse owners are two species of one-host ticks, the winter tick (D. albipictus) and the tropical horse tick (D. nitens). These ticks are called one-host ticks because they molt from larva to nymph to adult while still attached to the same host. Thus, they utilize only one host during the life cycle.

The winter tick is widely distributed throughout the United States. As the name indicates, it is found on horses and other large animals in the fall and winter months. Females lay eggs in the winter and spring, and the larvae hatch, remain quiet through the summer, and then become active and attach to hosts in the fall. Winter ticks are often found in large numbers on horses.

The tropical horse tick is found in Florida, Georgia, and the southern tip of Texas. It is unusual because all the parasitic stages are found in the ears of horses. However, in cases of heavy infestation, they may also be found in the nasal diverticulae and on the mane and belly. The engorging female eliminates large amounts of wastes so the ears of horses may become full of ticks and their excrement. Anocentor nitens is of considerable importance to horse owners because it is the vector of equine piroplasmosis.

Two other one-host ticks are the closely related cattle tick (Boophilus annulatus) and the southern cattle tick (B. microplus). They have been eradicated from the United States and are subjects of stringent quarantine to prevent reintroduction from Mexico.

The only soft tick found on horses is the ear tick (Otobius megnini). The ear tick is a one-host species commonly found deep in the ears of livestock in the southwestern states though it is widely distributed in the United States and is established as far north as British Columbia, Canada. Larvae engorge in the ears of livestock and molt there to nymphs. After feeding slowly in the ear for as long as six months, nymphs engorge fully and leave the host. (The stage most commonly seen is the engorging spiny nymphs.) Fed nymphs seek shelter under sheds, salt troughs, and other cover where they molt to the adult stage. Unlike other tick species, the adults do not feed. After mating off the host, the female lays small batches of eggs intermittently for more than six months. Newly hatched larvae seek hosts and make their way to the animal's ears.

Damage Inflicted; Symptoms and Signs of Affected Animals

Ticks are important because they may transmit diseases such as equine piroplasmosis (carried by Anocentor nitens) or cattle fever (carried by the Boophilus species). Also, most of the ticks mentioned may be vectors of anaplasmosis, and several species can cause tick paralysis in hosts. Massive infestations may cause anemia, loss of weight, and even death. Head heaviness is often associated with massive infestations of ear ticks. Other losses may result from the simple presence of the ticks on the animals, a factor called tick worry.

Prevention, Control, and Treatment

Because most species of ticks, except the ear tick and tropical horse tick, attach to the external surfaces of horses, an application of the recommended insecticide by spray or wipe-on will give effective control. Ear ticks and tropical horse ticks should be treated by applying the chemical into the ears of the horses. Since horses are often confined to rather small areas, treatment of the premises may also help control heavy infestations of ticks.

SWIMMING HORSES THERAPEUTICALLY

Equestrians have long known that horses can swim. The Romans swam their battle steeds to give them endurance. Napoleon's troops swam their horses in competitive events. Some tribes of American Indians swam their mounts for sport. In the late 1920s, *Golden Prince*, a Thoroughbred, swam his way from a back injury back to the track. His trainer used California beaches for his swim to health. In his first start following swimming therapy, *Golden Prince* won the $100,000 added Coffroth Handicap at Tijuana, setting a new track record and collecting $98,250. Following this success, therapeutic swimming was here to stay.

Fig. 15-23. Horse swimming pool. This pool is 40 ft in diameter and 13 ft deep and is equipped with a complete filtering system. (Courtesy, El Rancho, Murrieta, CA)

Swimming pools have a place, and their use will increase. But they are expensive to construct and operate, and they're not a panacea. Thus, the therapeutic value of horse swimming should be placed in perspective. We need to know more about physiologic effect, injuries in the pool, health hazards, therapeutic value, and special needs in pool design and engineering; and we need more research on therapeutic horse swimming. Based on presently available information, the following points are pertinent to horse swimming pools and therapeutic swimming.

1. **Pool broke.** It takes 2 to 4 days to train a horse to enter the pool and swim in the proper direction.

2. **Wash before swim.** Most pool operators wash (or hose) horses off before putting them into the pool. It keeps the pool cleaner and prepares the horse for the swim.

3. **Usefulness.** Training by swimming is especially useful for horses with minor leg injuries; it allows exercising them back to condition without placing premature strain on the injury or ailment. Also, it is reported that many chronic cases of tying up improve after swimming.

4. **Pool construction.** Special construction is required for horse pools.

Pools may be either circular or canal type (linear). Circular pools range from 25 to 66 ft in diameter and average about 10 ft deep. Canal-type pools are usually about 100 ft long, 10 ft wide, and 10 ft deep. Each pool has advantages and disadvantages.

The main advantage of a circular pool with a tangential entry chute is that horses may exit without turning if they swim clockwise. The disadvantages: Some horses will swim only in one direction, regardless of lameness or track experience; and, too, a sharp turn must be negotiated after the animal enters the pool. In circular pools with a radial entry chute, horses must make turns both on entry and exit. With a center island in a round pool, the attendant does a minimum of walking.

Canal-type pools are most useful for stationary swimming.

Where a pond or lake is used, horses are usually led by motorboat, by the attendant swimming, or by the attendant standing on a floating dock, with the horse swimming around it.

Entry pens and chutes must be properly constructed and swimming horses must be kept away from the edge of the pool to avoid leg injury. The latter may be accomplished either by having an over-hanging ledge—walkway, or by putting a head pole to hold the animal away from the edge of the pool.

5. **Filter—Chlorination—Heating.** A special filter system is required for an equine pool, since horses routinely defecate during swimming. Floating manure must be removed with long-handled nets. Other contamination—hair, skin excretions, and debris carried on the hoofs—must also be removed. Vacuum cleaning and special filters are necessary.

A pH of 7.2 to 7.4 is recommended, with muriatic acid (hydrochloric acid) used for this purpose. Chlorine levels are held at 2 to 4 parts per million by most pool operators. Insufficient chlorine will result in infectious dermitoses; excessive chlorine may cause dermatitis.

During the winter months in colder climates, a water heater is necessary. Most horse pools are held at about 70°F.

6. **Leg movement.** The leg movements of most equine swimmers are similar to a three-beat gait—much like the gallop. However, it is noteworthy that many Standardbred horses mimic their gaits—they

either trot or pace in the pool. All horses can stay afloat, but some are better swimmers than others.

7. **Stationary swimming.** When a horse is held in one spot, slightly more exertion is required than when free swimming; hence, it's a way in which to increase the exercise.

8. **Length of swim.** The usual plan is to swim 1 to 3 minutes the first day, then increase the swim by 1 minute daily up to 15 to 25 minutes per day per swim. Many combinations of swimming, track work, and hot-walking are used.

9. **After the swim is over.** After the swim, horses are usually scraped, then walked for 20 to 30 minutes.

10. **Stifle lameness.** It is reported that stifle lameness is worsened by swimming.

11. **Maintain fitness.** Swimming offers a way in which to maintain fitness during convalescence.

12. **Psychosomatic therapy.** Swimming constitutes psychosomatic therapy for track-sour horses; following two to three weeks of swimming, they're ready to run and win.

13. **Physiological effect.** Pool advocates feel that a portion of a horse's training can be achieved in a swimming pool, but there is general agreement that the training of a racehorse must be finished on the track.

From the above, it may be concluded that swimming exercise is not a panacea, nor is it a totally trial-and-error lameness therapy. Further, it is obvious that much research is needed, particularly in the areas of pool design, filtration, chlorination, safety, and effect on the horse. It would appear, however, that equine swimming pools may come to mean to horses what swimming pools have always meant to people—a fine way in which to condition, or exercise, especially where there are minor leg weaknesses.

ACUPUNCTURE

Acupuncture has a history in China going back over 4,000 years. During the Tang dynasty (618–907 A.D.), a special acupuncture department was set up in the Imperial Medical Institute. In 1027 (during the Sung dynasty), two bronze figures were cast with acupuncture points clearly marked. In China, acupuncture specialists use fine needles of stainless steel, which are inserted into the body at predetermined points, and which may be manipulated gently by a twirling motion, either by hand or electricity; and acupuncture is used both as a pain killer and as an anesthetic, on both people and animals.

Today, a limited number of United States equine veterinarians use acupuncture in treating ailments when conventional methods have failed. Generally, these practitioners do not claim that acupuncture is a miracle method; rather, they argue persuasively that it is a valuable tool at both the diagnostic and therapeutic levels.

The underlying principle of acupuncture is the belief that there is an energy flow through the body. When the flow is uninterrupted, the body is healthy. When it is interrupted, there is a manifestation of an ailment. The goal of the acupuncturist is to restore the normal energy flow and allow the body to heal itself. To achieve this, fine, smooth needles are inserted into the body at key acupuncture points.

There is a growing positive attitude about acupuncture on the part of both veterinarians and horse owners/trainers, with acupuncture used, increasingly, for both diagnostic and treatment purposes.

DISINFECTANTS

A disinfectant is a bactericidal or microbicidal agent that frees from infection (usually a chemical agent which destroys disease germs or other microorganisms, or inactivates viruses).

The high concentration of animals and continuous use of modern livestock buildings often results in a condition referred to as disease buildup. As disease-producing organisms—viruses, bacteria, fungi, and parasite eggs—accumulate in the environment, disease problems can become more severe and be transmitted to each succeeding group of animals raised on the same premises. Under these circumstances, cleaning and disinfection become extremely important in breaking the life cycle. Also, in the case of a disease outbreak, the premises must be disinfected.

Under ordinary conditions, proper cleaning of barns removes most of the microorganisms, along with the filth, thus eliminating the necessity of disinfection.

Effective disinfection depends on five things:

1. Thorough cleaning before application.

2. The phenol coefficient of the disinfectant, which indicates the killing strength of a disinfectant as compared to phenol (carbolic acid). It is determined by a standard laboratory test in which the typhoid fever germ often is used as the test organism.

3. The dilution at which the disinfectant is used.

4. The temperature; most disinfectants are much more effective if applied hot.

5. Thoroughness of application, and time of exposure.

Disinfection must in all cases be preceded by a very thorough cleaning, for organic matter serves to protect disease germs and otherwise interferes with the activity of the disinfecting agent.

Sunlight possesses disinfecting properties, but it

is variable and superficial in its action. Heat and some of the chemical disinfectants are more effective.

The application of heat by steam, by hot water, by burning, or by boiling is an effective method of disinfection. In many cases, however, it may not be practical to use heat.

A good disinfectant should (1) have the power to kill disease-producing organisms, (2) remain stable in the presence of organic matter (manure, hair, soil), (3) dissolve readily in water and remain in solution, (4) be nontoxic to animals and humans, (5) penetrate organic matter rapidly, (6) remove dirt and grease, and (7) be economical to use.

The number of available disinfectants is large because the ideal universally applicable disinfectant does not exist. Table 15-4 gives a summary of the limitations, usefulness, and strength of some common disinfectants.

When using a disinfectant, *always read and follow the manufacturer's directions.*

TABLE 15-4
DISINFECTANT GUIDE[1]

Kind of Disinfectant	Usefulness	Strength	Limitations and Comments
Alcohol (ethyl-ethanol, isopropyl, methanol)	Primarily as skin disinfectant and for emergency purposes on instruments.	70% alcohol—the content usually found in rubbing alcohol.	They are too costly for general disinfection. They are ineffective against bacterial spores.
Boric acid[2]	As a wash for eyes, and other sensitive parts of the body.	1 oz in 1 pt water (about 6% solution).	It is a weak antiseptic. It may cause harm to the nervous system if absorbed into the body in large amounts. For this and other reasons, antibiotic solutions and saline solutions are replacing it.
Chlorines (sodium hypo-chlorate, chloramine-T)	They will kill all kinds of bacteria, fungi, and viruses, providing the concentration is sufficiently high. Used as a deodorant.	Generally used at about 200 ppm.	They are corrosive to metals and neutralized by organic materials. Not effective against TB organisms and spores.
Cresols (many commercial products available)	A generally reliable class of disinfectant. Effective against brucellosis, shipping fever, swine erysipelas, and tuberculosis. Cresols give good results in foot baths.	Cresol is usually used as a 2 to 4% solution (1 cup to 2 gal. of water makes a 4% solution).	Effective on organic material. Cannot be used where odor may be absorbed.
Formaldehyde	Formaldehyde will kill anthrax spores, TB organisms, and animal viruses in a 1 to 2% solution. It is often used to disinfect buildings following a disease outbreak.	As a liquid disinfectant, it is usually used as a 1 to 2% solution. As a gaseous disinfectant (fumigant), use 1½ lb of potassium permanganate plus 3 pt of formaldehyde. Also, gas may be released by heating paraformaldehyde.	It has a disagreeable odor, destroys living tissue, and can be extremely poisonous. The bactericidal effectiveness of the gas is dependent upon having the proper relative humidity (above 75%) and temperature (above 86°F and preferably near 140°F, above 30°C and preferably near 60°C).
Heat (by steam, hot water, burning, or boiling)	In the burning of rubbish or articles of little value, and in disposing of infected body discharges. The steam "Jenny" is effective for disinfection *if properly employed*, particularly if used in conjunction with a phenolic germicide.	10 minutes' exposure to boiling water is usually sufficient.	Exposure to boiling water will destroy all ordinary disease germs, but sometimes fails to kill the spores of such diseases as anthrax and tetanus. Moist heat is preferred to dry heat, and steam under pressure is the most effective. Heat may be impractical or too expensive.
Iodine[2] (tincture)	Extensively used as skin disinfectant, for minor cuts and bruises.	Generally used as tincture of iodine, either 2% or 7%.	Never cover with a bandage. Clean skin before applying iodine. It is corrosive to metals.
Iodophors (tamed iodine)	Effective against all bacteria (both gram-negative and gram-positive), fungi, and most viruses.	Usually used as disinfectants at concentrations of 50 to 75 ppm titratable iodine, and as sanitizers at levels of 12.5 to 25 ppm. At 12.5 ppm titratable iodine, they can be used as an antiseptic in drinking water.	Iodophors are a combination of iodine and detergents. They are inhibited in their activity by organic matter. They are quite expensive. They should not be used near heat.

(Continued)

TABLE 15-4 (Continued)

Kind of Disinfectant	Usefulness	Strength	Limitations and Comments
Lime (quicklime, burnt lime, calcium oxide)	As a deodorant when sprinkled on manure and animal discharges; or as a disinfectant when sprinkled on the floor or used as a newly made "milk of lime" or as a whitewash.	Use as a dust; as "milk of lime"; or as a whitewash, but *use fresh*.	Not effective against anthrax or tetanus spores. Wear goggles when adding water to quicklime.
Lye (sodium hydroxide, caustic soda)	On concrete floors; against microorganisms of brucellosis and the viruses of foot-and-mouth disease, hog cholera, and vesicular exanthema. In strong solution (5%), effective against anthrax.	Lye is usually used as either a 2% or a 5% solution. To prepare a 2% solution, add 1 can of lye to 5 gal. of water. To prepare a 5% solution, add 1 can of lye to 2 gal. of water. A 2% solution will destroy the organisms causing foot-and-mouth disease, but a 5% solution is necessary to destroy the spores of anthrax.	Damages fabrics, aluminum, and painted surfaces. Be careful, for it will burn the hands and face. Not effective against organisms of TB or Johne's disease. Lye solutions are most effective when used hot. It is relatively cheap. *Diluted vinegar can be used to neutralize lye.*
Lysol (the brand name of a product of cresol plus soap)	For disinfecting surgical instruments and instruments used in castrating and tattooing. Useful as a skin disinfectant before surgery, and for use on the hands before castrating.	0.5 to 2.0%	Has a disagreeable odor. Does not mix well with hard water. Less costly than phenol.
Phenols (carbolic acids): 1. Phenolics—coal tar derivatives 2. Synthetic phenols	They are ideal general-purpose disinfectants. Effective and inexpensive. They are very resistant to the inhibiting effects of organic residue; hence, they are suitable for barn disinfection, and foot and wheel dip-baths.	Both phenolics (coal tar) and synthetic phenols vary widely in efficacy from one compound to another. So, note and follow manufacturers' directions. Generally used in a 5% solution.	They are corrosive, and they are toxic to animals and humans. Ineffective on fungi and viruses. Effective against all bacteria, including TB organisms.
Quarternary ammonium compounds (QAC)	Very water soluble, ultra-rapid kill rate, effective deodorizing properties, and moderately priced. Good detergent characteristics and harmless to skin.	Follow manufacturers' directions.	They can corrode metal. Not very potent in combating viruses. Adversely affected by organic matter; hence, they are of limited use for disinfecting livestock facilities. Not effective against TB organisms and spores. Not effective against anthrax and tetanus.
Sal soda	It may be used in place of lye against foot-and-mouth disease and vesicular exanthema.	10½% solution (13½ oz to 1 gal. water).	
Sal soda and soda ash (or sodium carbonate)	They may be used in place of lye against foot-and-mouth disease and vesicular exanthema.	4% solution (1 lb to 3 gal. water). Most effective in hot solution.	Commonly used as cleansing agents, but have disinfectant properties, especially when used as a hot solution.
Soap	Its power to kill germs is very limited. Greatest usefulness is in cleansing and dissolving coatings from various surfaces, including the skin, prior to application of a good disinfectant.	As commercially prepared.	Although indispensable to sanitizing surfaces, soaps should not be used as disinfectants. They are not regularly effective; staphlococci and organisms which cause diarrheal disease are resistant.

[1]For metric conversions, see the Appendix, "Section III—Weights and Measures."

[2]Sometimes loosely classed as a disinfectant but actually an antiseptic and useful only on living tissue.

SELECTED REFERENCES

Title of Publication	Author(s)	Publisher
Adams' Lameness in Horses	Ed. by T. S. Stashok	Lea & Febiger, Philadelphia, PA, 1987
Animal Disease and Human Health	J. H. Steele	Food and Agriculture Organization of the United Nations, Rome, Italy, 1962
Animal Diseases: Yearbook of Agriculture, 1956	Ed. by A. Stefferud	U.S. Department of Agriculture, Washington, DC, 1956
Animal Parasitism	C. P. Read	Prentice-Hall, Inc., Englewood Cliffs, NJ, 1972
Control of Ticks on Livestock, The	S. F. Barnett	Food and Agriculture Organization of the United Nations, Rome, Italy, 1968
Diseases of the Horse	Bureau of Animal Industry	U.S. Department of Agriculture, Washington, DC, 1942
Diseases of Livestock, Sixth Edition	T. G. Hungerford	Angus & Robertson, Ltd., Sydney, Australia, 1967
Diseases Transmitted from Animals to Man, Fifth Edition	T. G. Hull	Charles C. Thomas, Publisher, Springfield, IL, 1963
Disinfection, Sterilization, and Preservation	C. A. Lawrence S. S. Block	Lea & Febiger, Philadelphia, PA, 1968
Emerging Diseases of Animals	Veterinary Research Laboratory, Onderstepoort, South Africa	Food and Agriculture Organization of the United Nations, Rome, Italy, 1968
Equine Medicine & Surgery, Fourth Edition	Ed. by P. T. Colahan I. G. Mayhew A. M. Merrick J. N. Moore	American Veterinary Publications, Inc., Goleta, CA, 1991
Equine Pathology	J. R. Rooney J. L. Robertson	Iowa State University Press, Ames, IA, 1996
First Aid Hints for the Horse Owner	W. E. Lyon	Collins, St. James's Place, London, England, 1971
Hagan and Bruner's Microbiology and Infectious Diseases of Domestic Animals, Eighth Edition	J. F. Timoney J. J. Gillespie F. W. Scott J. E. Barlough	Comstock Publishing Associates, Ithaca, NY, 1988
Handbook of Veterinary Procedures and Emergency Treatment, Sixth Edition	R. W. Kirk S. I. Bistner	W. B. Saunders Company, Philadelphia, PA, 1995
Horse, The, Second Edition	J. W. Evans A. Barton H. Hintz L. D. Van Vleck	W. H. Freeman and Co., New York, NY, 1990
Horse from Conception to Maturity, The	P. Rossdale	California Thoroughbred Breeders, Assn., Arcadia, CA, 1972
Horse Owner's Vet Book, The	E. C. Straiton	J. B. Lippincott Co., New York, NY, 1973
Horsemen's Veterinary Adviser	J. B. Davidson	Horse Publications, Columbus, OH, 1966
Horse's Health From A to Z, The, Eleventh Impression	P. D. Rossdale S. M. Wreford	Billings & Sons Ltd., Worcester, for David & Charles Publishers, London, 1989
Horses' Injuries	C. L. Strong	Arco Publishing Co., Inc., New York, NY, 1973

Illustrated Veterinary Encyclopedia for Horsemen, The	Staff	Equine Research Publications, Grapevine, TX, 1975
Livestock Health Encyclopedia, Third Edition	R. Seiden	Springer Publishing Co., Inc., New York, NY, 1968
Merck Veterinary Manual, The, Seventh Edition	Ed. by C. M. Fraser J. A. Bergeron A. Mays S. E. Aiello	Merck & Co., Inc., Rahway, NJ, 1991
Nationwide System for Animal Health Surveillance, A	National Research Council	National Academy of Sciences, Washington, DC, 1974
New Zealand Farmers' Veterinary Guide	D. G. Edgar, *et al.*	The New Zealand Dairy Exporter, Wellington, New Zealand, 1962
Practical Parasitology: General Laboratory Techniques and Parasitic Protozoa	C. J. Price J. E. Reed	United Nations Development Programme, and Food and Agriculture Organization of the United Nations, Rome, Italy, 1970
Preventive Medicine and Public Health, Ninth Edition	Ed. by P. E. Sartwell	Appleton-Century-Crofts, New York, NY, 1965
Progress in Equine Practice, Vol. I	Ed. by E. J. Catcott J. F. Smithcors	American Veterinary Publications, Inc., Santa Barbara, CA, 1966
Progress in Equine Practice, Vol. II	Ed. by E. J. Catcott J. F. Smithcors	American Veterinary Publications, Inc., Santa Barbara, CA, 1966
Some Diseases of Animals Communicable to Man in Britain	Ed. by O. Graham-Jones	Pergamon Press, Ltd., London, England, 1968
Some Important Animal Diseases in Europe: Papers Presented at the Animal Disease Meeting, Warsaw, 1948	K. V. Kesteven	Food and Agriculture Organization of the United Nations, Rome, Italy, 1952
Stockman's Handbook, The, Seventh Edition	M. E. Ensminger	Interstate Publishers, Inc., Danville, IL, 1992
Vet Horse Book, The	TV Vet	Farming Press Ltd., Ipswich Suffolk, England, 1973
Veterinary Encyclopedia	Staff	Equine Research Publications, Grapevine, TX, 1975
Veterinary Medicine, Eighth Edition	Ed. by O. M. Radostits D. C. Blood C. C. Gay	Bailliare Tindall, Philadelphia, PA, 1994
Veterinary Notes for Horse Owners	Rev. by J. F. Tutt	Arco Publishing Company, Inc., New York, NY, 1972
Veterinary Parasitology, Second Edition	G. Lapage	Charles C. Thomas, Publisher, Springfield, IL, 1968
Veterinary Treatments & Medications for Horses	Staff	Equine Research Publications, Grapevine, TX, 1977

In addition to the above selected references, valuable publications on different subjects pertaining to animal diseases, parasites, disinfectants, and poisonous plants can be obtained from the following sources:

1. Division of Publications
   Office of Information
   U.S. Department of Agriculture
   Washington, DC 20250

2. Your state agricultural college.

3. Several biological, pharmaceutical, and chemical companies.

16

HORSE BEHAVIOR/ TRAINING/ ENVIRONMENT

Horse Behavior! (Photo of Spanish Mustangs by Mrs. Buddy Banner, Willow Springs Ranch, Oracle, AZ)

Horse behavior, training, and environment are interrelated. A good understanding of each of them will enhance the performance and pleasure of horses.

Horse behavior is the reaction of the horse to certain stimuli or its environment.

Horse training is the educating and controlling of the mental faculties of the horse so that the desired performance may be obtained.

Horse environment is all of the conditions, circumstances, and influences surrounding and affecting the growth, development, and performance of the horse.

PART I. HORSE BEHAVIOR

Fig. 16-1. Investigative behavior. (Photo by Ernst Peterson, Hamilton, Montana. Courtesy, Margit Sigray Bessenyey)

The marvels and mysteries of horse behavior are ages old, yet 21st century new. Modern domestic horses paw the ground when excited in much the same manner as did Przewalsky's horse. During the last round of the barn at night, horses keep up a running conversation as the caretaker gives a handful of hay to one still-hungry horse or treats a favorite mount to an apple. In a sign language that speaks louder than words, they tell how they feel and what they want. Every movement and every sound conveys a message of well-being, distress, or disease. Lack of interest, dull eyes, sluggishness, rough coat, poor appetite, and/or abnormal droppings spell trouble. Alertness, stretching, yawning, vocalizing, eating with relish, and frisking are good omens and tell that all is well in the barn.

Written observations of animal behavior date to the writings of the ancient Greeks, Aristotle in particular, about 350 B.C.

Prior to animal domestication, the very survival of the human race depended upon knowledge of animal habits as people hunted for their food. Primitive people understood the behavior of wild horses; they knew where to find them, how to get close enough to kill them, and where they would run when frightened. But the behavioral information needed—first to hunt game, and later to domesticate animals—did not assume primary scientific significance for many years after the writings of Aristotle and of subsequent hunters, explorers, naturalists, and agriculturalists. Finally, in two classical books—*The Origin of Species by Means of Natural Selection*, published in 1859; and *The Descent of Man and Selection* in Relation to Sex, published in 1871, Charles Darwin laid the foundation for modern animal behavior. For many years thereafter, however, conditions were ripe for unscrupulous "animal behavior practitioners" to turn a "quick buck" as they made all sorts of claims for the reasoning powers of their charges. The most notable show on the road of this type involved *Clever Hans*, a horse in Germany, about 1900, billed as the wonder horse who could add, multiply, divide, and even spell out words and sentences. *Hans* would stand in front of his trainer, and by pawing the ground with his hoof the appropriate number of times, answer questions put to him. If asked, "How much is 2 + 2?" he would paw the ground 4 times. If asked to spell out words or sentences, he would paw the proper number of times for each letter of the alphabet. Finally, a committee of scientists was appointed to study the celebrated horse. They found that *Hans* did, indeed paw out the correct answers. But, close observation revealed that the trainer cued the horse through a slight movement of his head. Hence, by watching his trainer, the horse would always stop when he observed the head signal. Both horse and trainer were amply rewarded; the horse by treats and affection, the trainer by another stellar performance before a large and satisfied audience. Both maintained their behavior.

Despite some charlatans along the way, caretakers applied their knowledge of horse behavior from the remote day of their domestication forward. It required knowledge of basic behavior patterns to capture, confine, and herd horses; and to breed, feed, water, and shelter them. Without this understanding, domestication would have failed and horses would not have survived. By 1900, the groundwork had been laid for the scientific work that followed; and the study of animal behavior became a distinct discipline. In recent years, it has advanced rapidly.

Modern horse breeding, feeding, and management have brought renewed interest in horse behavior, especially as a factor in their training, performance, and efficiency. Also, with increased confinement, or stabling, of horses, many abnormal behaviors have evolved to plague those who raise them, including finicky appetites, degenerate sexual behavior, cribbing, and a host of other behavioral disorders. Confinement has not only limited space, but it has interfered with the habitat and social organization to which, through thousands of years of evolution, the species became adapted and best suited.

We now know that controlled environment must embrace far more than an air-conditioned chamber, along with ample feed and water. Equestrians need to concern themselves more with the natural habitat of horses. Nature ordained that they do more than eat, sleep, and reproduce. Evidently, environmental deficiencies are manifested by abnormal behaviors.

Preventing cribbing by using choke collars on horses is not unlike trying to control malaria fever in humans by the use of drugs without getting rid of mosquitoes. Rather, we need to recognize these disorders for what they are—warning signals that conditions are not right. Correcting the cause of the disorder is the best solution. Unfortunately, this is not easy. Rectifying the cause may involve trying to emulate the natural conditions of the species, such as altering space per animal and group size, providing training and experience at opportune times, promoting exercise, and gradually changing rations. Over the long pull, selection provides a major answer to correcting confinement and other behavioral problems; we need to breed horses adapted to unnatural environments.

This chapter is for the purpose of presenting some of the principles and applications of behavior in horse care and training. Those who have grown up around horses and dealt with them in practical ways have already accumulated substantial workaday knowledge about horse behavior. Those who are less familiar with horses may need to familiarize themselves with their behavior, better to feed, care for, and train them, and to recognize the early signs of illness. To all, the principles and applications of horse behavior depend on understanding, which is the intent of this chapter.

BEHAVIORAL SYSTEMS

Each animal species has characteristic ways of performing certain functions and rarely departs therefrom. The horse is no exception. Horses exhibit the following nine behavioral systems:[1]

1. Protective behavior.
2. Ingestive (eating and drinking) behavior.
3. Eliminative behavior.
4. Sexual behavior.
5. Care-giving and care-seeking (mother-young) behavior.
6. Agonistic behavior (combat).
7. Allelomimetic behavior (gregarious behavior).
8. Shelter-seeking behavior.
9. Investigative behavior.

---

[1]Adapted by the author from Scott, J. P., *Animal Behavior*, 2nd ed., The University of Chicago Press, Chicago, IL, 1972.

PROTECTIVE BEHAVIOR

The basic behavior of modern horses reflects the millions of years that they survived as creatures of the prairies, where they often grazed long distances from water and fled from their enemies in their struggle to survive.

Even today, horses retain their built-in environmental control—their self-protection from the elements. In cold weather, they augment their shaggy coats by seeking the protection of such natural windbreaks as trees, hills, and valleys. Also, they will turn their rear ends toward a storm. The latter instinct makes it difficult to ride a horse into a driving rain or snowstorm, because it wants to protect its eyes and ears by facing away from the elements.

Following a frosty night, horses will stand broadside to the sun, so as to expose as much of their bodies as possible to the sun's warmth. In hot weather, they will seek shade; they may even travel to the top of a hill or ridge to benefit from a cooling breeze. If no shade is to be had on a hot day, they will usually line up with the sun, thereby exposing a minimum of their bodies to the sun's heat.

Most wild animals respond to predator attack in one of two ways—by fight or flight. Wild horses were almost totally dependent upon flight. They fought only when cornered. The evolution in length and structure of the foot made for greater speed, agility, and endurance for escape. This explains much of their behavior today. They have well-developed senses of hearing, sight, and smell to warn them of the approach of danger. They are fearful of any type of confinement or restraint, because this meant death to their ancestors. This explains why untrained horses are skeptical about entering a barn or being loaded on a trailer for the first time. It's why unbroken horses are frightened by halters, foot ropes, and hobbles. It's why a gentle horse will even mutilate a foot in order to free itself from a wire fence.

The wild horse had an additional, and even greater, fear—the fear of something on its back. This stems from the fact that anything that jumped on its back was there to kill it (see Fig. 16-2). During the opening up of the western range of the United States, it was not uncommon for mountain lions to kill horses, particularly foals, in this manner. Even today, it occurs in remote parts of the world. This innate fear of something on its back explains the natural instinct of horses to buck off a rider. Even after 5,000 years of domestication, and almost constant association with people, an untrained horse is apt to revert to the wild and try to dislodge a rider. Today, training is designed to keep a horse from bucking. To accomplish this, the trainer must assure the horse that a saddle and a rider on its back are friends—not mortal enemies.

Fig. 16-2. The lion, a mortal enemy of the horse, has preyed on it for millions of years.

Fig. 16-3. It remembers! The horse must be assured that the saddle and the rider on its back are friends—not mortal enemies.

INGESTIVE (EATING AND DRINKING) BEHAVIOR

This type of behavior includes eating and drinking; hence, it is characteristic of animals of all species and ages. It is very important because animals cannot live without feed and water.

The first ingestive behavior trait, common to all young mammals, including foals, is suckling.

Each animal species is distinct in its eating and drinking habits. The following points are unique to horses and pertinent to an understanding of their eating and drinking habits:

1. As the horse was transformed to a creature of the prairie, its teeth grew longer, stronger, and more roughened—suited for grinding grasses. Thus, the modern horse has teeth that are well suited to masticating its common feeds.

2. As the horse's legs lengthened in the evolutionary process, it was necessary that its head and neck also became longer in order to enable it to feed on low-growing plants. This process of proportionate elongation of the legs and of the head and the neck is not always perfect. Thus, a foal may have difficulty in getting its head to the ground. As a result, it may have to spread its front legs in order to get its mouth to the grass. As the foal grows, its head and neck grow faster than its legs with the result that the anatomy problem is soon solved.

3. The horse possesses incisor teeth in both the upper and lower jaws. But the mobile upper lip is used in gathering in grass and other feed, in the same way that a cow uses her tongue or an elephant uses its trunk. The upper lip is very sensitive. So, in addition to being well adapted to ingesting food, the application of a twitch to the upper lip of the horse provides a way in which to restrain it.

4. When snow covers the pasture or range, horses will paw (with either their right or left front foot) through the snow and clear an area so that they can reach the grass. (Buffalo and elk also feed in this manner.) This behavior of horses allows them to winter in northern range areas without supplemental feed.

5. The horse has a blind spot that extends in front of its nose. Thus it cannot see the feed as it eats.

6. Horses rarely browse; that is, they will not eat the leaves of trees and shrubs provided grass is available.

7. Strange as it may seem, horses can injure themselves by eating natural feed; they will founder on lush grass, particularly when confined to small areas.

8. Horses prefer grazing in an open area, where they can watch for enemies. Also, they prefer young tender grass to coarse-stemmed plants, a preference which often causes them to overgraze certain areas.

9. The horse evolved to graze small amounts almost continuously, rather than large amounts infrequently. This explains why modern horses do better if fed small amounts—often. An understanding of ingestive behavior allows the horse owner to approach natural feeding. Irregular and inadequate hand feeding is directly related to such abnormal behavior patterns as wood chewing, stall weaving, pawing, and kicking.

10. The habit of foals nibbling the feces or droppings of older horses is usually condemned as unsanitary. However, it has been postulated that nature ordained this behavior as a means of inoculating the digestive tract (colon) of the foal with microorganisms. Apparently there is little danger of parasitism in this manner because most parasite eggs must go through an incubation period of about two weeks before they can infest a foal.

11. In areas where water is scarce, wild horses usually graze 6 to 8 miles from water and come to water once each day. Horses prefer clean, clear water from deep pools. A thirsty horse may lower its head deep enough to cover the nostrils, but there is no danger of drowning because it won't draw water into its lungs.

12. Grazing horses will meet their water needs by eating snow in the wintertime.

13 Where water is supplied to horses, it is best to use fountains or troughs with fresh running water available at all times. If horses are hand watered in buckets, they should be given water at least twice daily.

Fig. 16-4. A long-legged foal with a short head and neck standing with its front legs spread apart in order to reach the ground.

ELIMINATIVE BEHAVIOR

In recent years, elimination has become a most important phenomenon, and pollution has become a dirty word. Nevertheless, nature ordained that if animals eat, they must eliminate.

A full understanding of the eliminative behavior will make for improved animal building design and give a big assist in handling manure. Right off, it should be recognized that the eliminative behavior in farm animals tends to follow the general pattern of their wild ancestors; but it can be influenced by the method of management.

Horses tend to deposit their feces and urine in certain areas, then graze in other areas. This is particularly noticeable in small pastures where some areas may be grazed quite closely with few droppings present, whereas other areas have tall, rank grass with a greater concentration of droppings.

Stallions are much more prone to deposit droppings on the same old mound than mares or geldings. Mares and geldings are inclined to use the border of the defecating area, with the result that they enlarge it each time.

The defecating behavior of horses probably evolved for two reasons:

1. As a means of stallions marking their areas or territories, much as dogs stake out their areas with urine scent posts. Apparently, such markings serve to warn rival stallions that they are encroaching on the territory of another stallion.

2. To provide some protection for horses from infestation by internal parasites. Because many internal parasites are spread from one horse to another by grazing pastures contaminated with parasite eggs from the droppings of infested horses, it is conjectured that wild horses may have reduced this opportunity for the spread of internal parasites by defecating in certain areas and grazing in others. Horses in confinement cannot effectively employ this type of protection from parasites; hence, horse owners must use other methods to keep parasites under control (see Chapter 15).

SEXUAL BEHAVIOR

Reproduction is the first and most important requisite of horse breeding. Without young being born and born alive, the other economic traits are of academic interest only. Thus, it is important that all those who breed horses should have a working knowledge of sexual behavior.

Sexual behavior involves courtship and mating. It is largely controlled by hormones, although stallions that are castrated after reaching sexual maturity (known as *stags*) usually retain considerable sex drive and exhibit sexual behavior. This suggests that psychological, or learned, as well as hormonal factors may be involved in sexual behavior.

Each animal has a specific pattern of sexual be-

Fig. 16-5. Stallion (in the rear) cutting out his harem. (Photo by Jeff Edwards, Spanish Barb Wild Horse Research Farm, Porterville, CA)

havior. As a result, interspecies matings do not often occur. There is a notable exception however: The best-known cross between animal species is the mule, a hybrid, which is a cross between the horse family and the ass family.

Stallions detect females in heat by sight or smell. Also, it is noteworthy that courtship is more intense on pasture or range than under confinement, and that captivity has the effect of producing many distortions of sexual behavior in wild animals. Perhaps this explains the high percentage foal crop of wild bands of mares, where conception and foaling rates of 90% or better were commonplace, in comparison with the average 50% foaling rate under domestication.

The signs of estrus in the mare are (1) the relaxation of the external genitalia; (2) frequent urination in small quantities; (3) the teasing of other mares; (4) the apparent desire for company; (5) a slight mucous discharge from the vulva; (6) allowing the stallion to smell and bite her; (7) spreading the hind legs; and (8) lifting the tail sideways. But many mares are shy breeders. Thus, when there is any question about a mare being in season, she should be tried with the stallion. When possible, it is usually good business regularly to present mares to the teaser every day or every other day as the breeding season approaches. A systematic plan of this sort will save much time and trouble.

Horses (both mares and stallion) tend to be seasonal breeders, with the greatest sexual activity in the spring and early summer, although they will breed and are fertile any time of the year. This is due to hormone levels, which are influenced by the length of day. This nature-ordained phenomena of spring breeding and spring foaling was a biological necessity for wild horses. It meant that mares foaled in the spring when conditions were favorable (1) for the newborn, because

Fig. 16-6. Sexual behavior in the stallion, showing extended head and upcurled upper lip. The stallion is trying to detect an odor indicating estrus in a mare.

of the mild climate; (2) for milk production, for which nutritious green grass was available; and (3) for flushing and rebreeding the mare.

The courtship (teasing) of the stallion, which prepares him physically and mentally for mating, is characterized by neighing; smelling the external genitalia of the mare, followed by extended head and upcurled upper lip; and pinching the mare with his teeth by grasping the folds of her skin in the loin-croup area. Wild stallions, and range stallions, always carefully approach the mare from the front to avoid being kicked or struck.

CARE-GIVING AND CARE-SEEKING (MOTHER-YOUNG) BEHAVIOR

The care-giving behavior is largely confined to females among domestic animals, where it is usually described as *maternal*. The care-seeking behavior is normal for young animals. This type of behavior begins at birth and extends until the young are weaned.

The preference of the mare to foal away from other horses apparently evolved in their evolution for two reasons: (1) to provide the foal with the opportunity to identify or imprint itself with its mother, and (2) to protect against predators.

Imprinting occurs in many species of animals. At the time of birth, a newborn foal will follow any moving object, including humans. If other horses are present, a foal may follow a mare other than its own mother. Conditions are ripe for a dominant mare without a foal of her own to steal the new foal. So, by going off alone

to give birth, foal stealing is alleviated and the foal will imprint or learn to identify its mother in a short time.

The other reason that mares instinctively prefer to foal alone is that the chances of being found by predators is far less where a single mare is involved than where there is a group.

At birth, a mare identifies her foal partly by odor. As the foal grows older, recognition by sight and sound becomes more important.

Mares show the same maternal behavior toward their young as is exhibited by females of other species of farm animals. Thus, a mare calls for her foal with a neigh or whinny and exhibits nervousness and distress when her young is disturbed. When mares are separated from their foals, such as sometimes happens when they are worked or taken away for rebreeding, there is usually a noisy exchange of whinnying between mother and foal when they are put back together again and the foal is allowed to nurse.

Mares and foals will never willingly lose sight of each other. Thus, a mare will not leave her foal sleeping while she grazes at a distance, as cows do. This is due to the fact that there is no effective means for reuniting the two following a separation. Thus, if a wild mare is away from her foal, and if during her absence the foal is disturbed by a predator and runs off, the mare and foal are not likely to find each other again—except by chance. Of course, domesticated mares and foals in fenced pastures will eventually locate each other.

It is noteworthy that a mare will devote as much attention and affection to a mule colt—a hybrid (ass X horse) as she will to a horse foal.

All healthy foals exhibit an amazing ability to get on their feet and travel within a short time after birth.

Fig. 16-7.Care-giving and care-seeking—mother and yearling. (Courtesy, Kentucky Department of Information, Frankfort)

No other young of farm animals are as precocious. The newborn foal nurses frequently, usually once or twice each hour. If another horse or person approaches, the foal will seek the protection of the mare by moving to her side opposite the approacher.

AGONISTIC BEHAVIOR (COMBAT)

This type of behavior includes fighting, flight, and other related reactions associated with conflict. Among all species of farm mammals, males are more likely to fight than females. Nevertheless, females may exhibit fighting behavior under certain conditions. Castrated males are usually quite passive, which indicates that hormones (especially testosterone) are involved in this type of behavior. Thus, for centuries castration has been used as a means of producing docile males (geldings or stags).

Stallions that are run together from a very young age seldom fight. Perhaps they have already settled their social rank. On the other hand, bringing together sexually mature strange stallions almost always results in a vicious fight. Stallions fight by biting, kicking, and striking. Generally they fight head to head and most of the biting is on the neck, shoulders, and front legs. Although fighting rarely results in death, it usually continues until one gives up—battle scarred by teeth and hoof marks.

Fighting among mares is less vicious than between stallions. Body biting and kicking are used as a means of establishing social order. Geldings may fight much like mares.

Jacks are usually vicious fighters. They rely on their teeth, rather than kicking. Sometimes wild jacks killed a rival by cutting his windpipe or jugular vein.

Fig. 16-8. Agonistic behavior (combat), showing two stallions fighting viciously with their teeth and feet.

Also, it is reported that the dominant jack occasionally castrated the weaker jacks with his teeth.

Agonistic behavior is of practical importance when strange horses are first put together. One way or another, a social order must be established. Hence, there is always the potential of injury until rank is settled. Also, agonistic behavior may create a potentially dangerous situation to both horses and riders in group riding. To reduce the hazard of such accidents, all horses should be spaced well apart when standing or moving.

Wild bands of horses and bands of domestic horses on the range behave very much alike. The stallions have keen sight, hearing and smell; and each stallion leader is very good at protecting his harem, which usually includes 10 to 20 mares. When frightened or facing danger, the stallion warns his band with snorting and restless movements and takes his place ready for battle if necessary.

ALLELOMIMETIC BEHAVIOR (GREGARIOUS BEHAVIOR)

Allelomimetic behavior is mutual mimicking behavior. Thus, when one member of a group does something, another tends to do the same thing; and because others are doing it, the original individual continues. Horses moving across a pasture toward water often display allelomimetic behavior. One horse starts toward the water, and others follow. Because the rest of the herd is following, the first horse proceeds on. Even a timid horse will follow behind the group, in order not to be left behind.

In the wild state, this trait was advantageous in detecting the enemy, and in providing protection therefrom. Under domestication, animals are usually protected from predators.

Allelomimetic behavior is closely related to gregarious behavior; for if animals imitate each other, they must stay together. Thus, for animals that normally live in herds (like horses), the presence of other animals also provides companionship and has a quieting effect. When kept alone, such animals may become lonely, depressed, frightened, and/or irritated. The best-known animal companionship of all pertains to high-strung racehorses and stallions, in which all sorts of companions are used—a goat, a sheep, a chicken, a duck, or a pony. Such companions are commonly referred to as mascots. The expression "to get his goat" was born of the common custom of having goats for mascots. Back in the days when skullduggery was as important as form in winning races, the grooms of one stable sometimes plotted to kidnap the goat mascot of a rival horse. By "getting the goat" of a favorite, they cleaned up by betting against a horse that was odds-on to win, but too upset to run at its best.

The great *Stymie*, the Thoroughbred winner of $918,485, became attached to a hen of nondescript breeding who came to dinner one day and never left.

Probably the most publicized mascot of all times was the pony, *Peanuts*, constant companion to the Thoroughbred racehorse *Exterminator*. *Peanuts* died three years ahead of the great old gelding. When his pony pal failed to appear in the stall the next morning, *Exterminator* stopped eating. He would likely have died of a broken heart had his handlers not acted wisely. They left the remains of *Peanuts* in the Thoroughbred's stall one night, to demonstrate to him that his mate was dead. All night long, *Exterminator* lay with his head over the pony's body. By morning he was resigned to the situation. A new pony was brought to him, and the old warrior carried on.

SHELTER-SEEKING BEHAVIOR

All species of animals seek shelter—protection from the sun, wind, rain, and snow, insects, and predators.

Horses are not very sensitive to either heat or cold. In the wild state, they developed a shaggy coat of hair in the wintertime and sought shelter from storms under trees and in the valleys. They even pawed to get their feed supply when the ground was covered with snow. Like cattle, horses face away from the direction of a severe storm.

INVESTIGATIVE BEHAVIOR

Investigative behavior is closely related to fear—to self-protective behavior.

All animals are curious and have a tendency to explore their environment. Investigation takes place through seeing, hearing, smelling, tasting, and touching. Whenever an animal is introduced into a new area (stall, paddock, or pasture), its first reaction is to explore it. When a horse that is being ridden is spooked, it should be made to go near the spooky object where it can smell it. Usually this will cause it to lose its fear of the object.

Foals are more curious than older horses. Young equines spend much of their time looking at and sniffing objects in their pastures or stalls. As the foal grows older, it may exhibit fear of certain objects. At this stage, it may even move away from its caretaker. When this happens, the handler should never run after the foal. Rather, stand still; very soon the foal's curiosity will get the best of it, and it will return. A mare frequently becomes very nervous as she watches her offspring investigate, fearful that it may get hurt in the process.

HOW HORSES BEHAVE

Fig. 16-9. Even when grazing, the eyes of a horse allow it to see what's going on all around it—to the front, the side, and the back—all at the same time. By turning very slightly to the left, the horse shown above was able to keep an eye on the photographer who was standing behind it. (Courtesy, Wild Horse Research Farm, Porterville, CA)

A knowledge of horse behavior is necessary in order to feed, care for, and manage them successfully. Pertinent behavioral characteristics of horses follow.

■ **Grazing**—When grasses are available, horses prefer to feed on them. They manipulate the plants with their mobile and very sensitive upper lip, nip the blades off with their incisors, and use their tongue to ingest the material. When grazing, foals spread their forelegs in order to compensate for their long legs and short necks.

The amount of time spent in grazing depends on the quality and quantity of forage available, along with such factors as temperature, precipitation, and pests. But grazing time averages about 12 hours per day, although horses may graze up to 18 hours per day when feed is scarce. Horses are selective grazers and will eat a wide range of pasture plants, herbs, shrubs, and weeds.

Horses are notorious for overgrazing certain areas and for defecating and urinating in other areas. Moreover, defecating and urinating rituals are an important means of communicating on the range. Stallions routinely defecate on stud piles, but they are more likely to urinate on the excrement of mares.

Fig. 16-10. *Marking His Range*, painting by artist Tom Phillips. (Courtesy, Roscoe E. Dean, M.D., Washington Springs, SD)

■ **Feeding behavior**—Stall fed horses learn to anticipate their feed; so, they should be fed regularly and at the same time each day. Usually the concentrate ration is fed first. Little time is spent eating concentrate feeds, but they need time in which to eat bulky roughages more leisurely.

If given the opportunity, horses prefer to eat small amounts of feed throughout the day. When kept on pasture, they are able to eat in this manner. When kept in stalls and small paddocks, however, they must eat at the convenience of the caretaker. If fed concentrates *ad libitum*, they usually overeat and get digestive disturbances.

Horses practicing coprophagy—the eating of feces. Young foals will eat the feces of mares. Adult horses will eat their own feces or the feces of other horses.

■ **Control of feed intake**—When given all the feed that they will consume, mature horses will generally eat an amount equivalent to about 2.5% of their body weight daily. Growing foals and lactating mares eat more heartily—they will consume up to 3% of their body weight.

The horse is not adapted to self-feeding of high-energy rations. Overeating may result in two conse-

quences: If done suddenly, it may cause founder (laminitis); if prolonged, it will likely result in obesity.

Because the horse has rather limited digestive capacity, the amount of concentrate must be increased and the roughage decreased when the energy needs rise with the greater amount, severity, and speed of work. Additional factors affecting the quantity of grain and hay required by horses are: (1) the individuality and temperament of the horse; (2) the age, size, and condition of the animal; and (3) the weather. The total allowance of concentrate and hay should be within the range of 2.0 to 2.5 lb daily per 100 lb liveweight. No grain should be left from one feeding to the next, and all edible forage should be cleaned up at the end of the day.

■ **Drinking**—Przewalski Horses, the wild species discovered by the Russian explorer in Mongolia, sometimes went for 2 to 3 days without water. Feral horses walk to a water hole once each day, and on days of extreme heat they usually return a second time.

Domestic horses drink 10 to 12 gal. of water daily, the amount varying according to weather, amount of work and sweating, ration fed, and size of horse.

Free access to water is desirable. When this is not possible, horses should be watered at approximately the same times daily. Opinions vary among caretakers as to the proper times and methods of watering horses. However, most caretakers agree that water may be given before, during, and after feeding.

Frequent, small waterings between feedings are desirable during warm weather or when the animal is being put to hard use. Horses should not be allowed to drink heavily when they are hot, because they may founder; and they should not be allowed to drink heavily just before being put to work.

Automatic waterers are the modern way to provide water for stall-fed horses at all times, as nature intended.

■ **Nursing**—Care-giving behavior toward the foal is displayed by the mare from the time of birth; it seems to be triggered by the taste and smell of the allantoic fluid.

The mare generally licks the newborn foal, starting at the head. A strong, healthy foal will usually be up and ready to nurse within 30 minutes to 2 hours after birth. Some mares facilitate the first nursing by maintaining a position which makes it easy for the foal to locate the teats and suckle. Others resent the foal's activity around their sensitive udders. Occasionally, an awkward foal needs the assistance and guidance of the caretaker during its first time to nurse; such assistance should consist of coaxing, forcing is useless. The very weak foal should be given the mare's first milk even if it must be drawn in a bottle and fed by nipple for a time or two. The colostrum contains antibodies that temporarily protect the foal against certain infections, especially those of the digestive tract. Because of this, it is important that foals nurse within 10 to 12 hours after birth, preferably much sooner. Also, colostrum serves as a natural purgative, removing fecal matter (meconium) that has accumulated in the digestive tract. Suckling is frequent early in life; studies have recorded 3 to 4 feedings per hour during the first week of life. But frequency of nursing gradually decreases until it occurs about once every 2 hours at weaning time. A mare is very protective of her foal; she dissuades it from other herd members, she threatens intruders, and she shelters it by keeping it alongside, when standing and moving. Foals are usually weaned at about 6 months of age. Natural weaning takes place at about 9 months of age.

■ **Fostering (adopting)**—Occasionally a mare dies during or immediately after parturition, leaving an orphan foal to be raised. Also, there are times when a mare rejects her foal or fails to give sufficient milk to sustain it. Sometimes there are twins. In such cases, it may be necessary to resort to other milk supplies. The problem will be simplified if the foal has received colostrum from its mother.

If at all possible, the foal should be fostered on another mare. Some horse breeding establishments follow the practice of breeding a mare that is a good milk producer, but whose foal is expected to be of little value. Her own foal is either destroyed or raised on a bottle, and the mare is used as a foster mother, or nurse mare, for a more valuable foal. Generally foals can be fostered on other mares for up to 2 to 4 days after birth. If there is resistance, a foster gate may be used to protect the orphan foal.

■ **Handling**—A round pen is a valuable handling facility. It is the best place in which to conduct training lessons: restraint, sacking out, longeing, ground driving, saddling, ponying, and first rides. The size and construction of the round pen depends somewhat on its intended uses. With planning, a design can suit a variety of needs. A *breaking pen* that is built solely for initial gentling and first rides should be about 35 ft in diameter with solid 7 ft walls to assure maximum control in unpredictable training situations. A *training pen* that is built for routine longeing, driving, or riding should be 66 ft in diameter to allow the horses enough space for balanced movement.

Horses are big and strong, and fleet; hence, it is best that they want to do something, rather than be forced. Also, frequent and improper use of such artificial aids as whips, spurs, reins, and bits makes them less effective; worse yet, it will make for a mean horse. So, proper and modern handling calls for knowledge of horse behavior and the judicious use of rewards (a praising voice, a gentle stroking with the hand, and/or a lump of sugar or carrot) and punishment (spur or whip).

Handling should begin soon after birth, with the caretaker speaking to the foal softly and gently caressing it about the neck, as a result of which the foal will habituate better and be more self-confident when older. Subsequent training should progress to more difficult tasks. The foal should become accustomed to the halter, to being tied, and to being led. The yearling should be given the following intermediate training: to respond to "whoa" and its name; to stand when hobbled; to become accustomed to the saddle blanket; to get used to the saddle; to drive, turn, stop, and back up; to flex its neck and set its head; to respond to the bosal; and to being ridden, and to leg pressure. The two-year-old should be given the following advanced training: to respond to the aids; to pivot (if a western horse); and to make a sliding stop (if a western horse).

The good caretaker who has followed a program of training and educating the foal from soon after birth has already eliminated the word *breaking*. To such a trainer, the saddling and/or harnessing of the young horse is merely another step in the training program, which is carried out with ease and satisfaction.

When handling horses, always try kindness first; pat the animal and speak to it reassuringly. If this fails, and the horse is uncontrollable, try one of the following techniques as a last resort:

1. If the horse is unruly, especially if it is tossing its head about, apply a twitch to the upper lip.
2. If the horse is very excited and is about to break away, either (a) blindfold it, or (b) dash a bucket of water in its face. Usually, the animal will calm down following such treatment.
3. If the horse will not move or is kicking, grab its tail and push it over its back. In this position, the horse cannot kick, but can be pushed along.

CAUSES OF HORSE BEHAVIOR

Horse behavior is caused by, or is the result of, three forces: (1) heredity, (2) training and experience, and (3) intelligence.

HEREDITY

Genes determine all the hereditary characteristics of horses, from the body type to the color of the hair.

Progressive horse breeders influence horse behavior by propagating genetically superior animals. They locate such horses by observing their type and performance (individuality), along with the type and performance of their relatives.

SIMPLE LEARNING

No horse—whether it be used for saddle, race, or other purposes—reaches a high degree of proficiency without an education. Thus, if the offspring of *Man O'War* and six of the fastest mares ever to grace the tracks had merely worked on laundry trucks until six years old, then if they were suddenly—without warning or other preparation—placed upon a racetrack, the immediate results would have been disappointing. Their natural aptitude and conformation in breeding would not have been enough. Schooling and training would still have been necessary in order to bring out their inherent abilities.

In general, the behavior of animals depends upon the particular reaction patterns with which they were born. These are called *instincts* and *reflexes*. They are unlearned forms of behavior. Thus, all horses instinctively like to run. But how well and how fast they run depends upon the training to which they are subjected. They learn by experience. However, the training is only as effective as the inherited neural pathways. Several types of learned behavior are known; among them are those that follow.

■ **Trial and error (rewards and punishment)**—This is a method by which horses learn. It is reinforced through the judicious employment of rewards and punishments. This doesn't mean that a horse is rewarded each time it obeys, or that it is beaten when it refuses to do something. But horses are big and strong; hence, it's best that they want to do something, rather than have to be forced. Also, too frequent or improper use of such artificial aids as whips, spurs, reins, and bits makes them less effective; worse yet, it will likely make for a mean horse. However, horses appreciate a pat on the shoulder or a word of praise. Even better results may be obtained by working on the greediness of equines—their fondness for such things as carrots or a sugar cube. Also, treats may be used effectively as rewards to teach some specific thing such as posing, or to cure a vice like moving while the rider is mounting; but this should not be overdone.

■ **Imprinting (socialization)**—This is a form of early learning which occurs in foals. It is the phenomenon that causes newborn foals to follow any moving object, including humans. (Also see section on "Care-Giving and Care-Seeking (Mother-Young Behavior.")

COMPLEX LEARNING

Complex learning is the capacity to acquire and apply knowledge—the ability to learn from experience and to solve problems. It is the ability to solve complex problems by something more than simple trial-and-error, habit, or stimulus-response modifications. In people we recognize this capacity as the ability to develop concepts, to behave according to general principles, and to put together elements from past experience into a new organization.

Animals learn to do some things, whereas they inherit the ability to do others. The latter is often called instinct. Thus, ducks do not have to learn to swim—instinctively, they take to water.

Some folks judge the intelligence of animals by the size of their brain in relation to body size. Others rank them according to their ability to solve a maze (a pathway complicated by at least one blind alley, used in learning experiments and intelligence tests) in order to get food.

Generally speaking, behavioral scientists are agreed that each species has its own special abilities and capacities, and that it should only be tested on these. For example, the dog, pig, and rat, are more adept at solving a maze than the horse. Hence, solving a maze in order to find food favors the scavengers (and the dog, the pig, and the rat are all scavengers)—they have connived for their food since the beginning of time. However, the horse, whose natural feed was the grass that lay around it, never had to develop this kind of intelligence. It was a plains-living animal, highly specialized for speed as a means of escape from its enemies and with almost no powers of manipulation. Thus, a horse should be good at any problem that can be solved by running, including racing, polo, pole bending, calf roping, etc. Indeed, had equines not been smart and adapted to their particular environment, they would never have made it through 58 million years. Thus, each species is uniquely adapted to only one ecological niche. Moreover, a niche is filled by the particular species that can solve food finding therein, and that is best adapted under the conditions that prevail. It follows that intelligence comparisons between species are not meaningful, and that it is absurd to say that one species is smarter than another.

■ **Insight learning (reasoning)**—This type of learning is most prevalent in the highest mammals. It refers to the ability to respond correctly the first time that an animal encounters a certain situation or experience. It alleviates trial and error.

The most important single factor to remember in training animals is that none of them (horses included) can reason things out. An animal's mind functions by intuition, not logic. Moreover, it has no conscious sense of right and wrong. Thus, it is one of the trainer's tasks to teach a horse the difference between right and wrong—between good and bad. Although the horse cannot utilize pure reason, it can remember, and it has the ability to use the memory of one situation as it applies to another.

Of course, the intelligence of people is generally recognized. In fact, were it not for their superior mental faculties, along with their limited muscular force, they might find themselves under saddles or between shafts, instead of horses.

The horse's intelligence has been tested by two methods: (1) the detour method (Fig. 16-11), and (2) the reading signs method (Fig.16-12).

Fig. 16-11. Testing a horse for detour problem-solving ability. Horse X has been separated from its companions, Y and Z. Faced with this problem, X will not likely find the way back to its companions through the open gates, unless it accidentally encounters the gaps in its excitement and galloping. Instead, it will probably try to jump the fence at the point separating them. It is difficult to know whether X's failure to find the detour is due to its lack of intellect or because of its good training.

Fig. 16-12. Horse reading a sign. Two cards are used; one with a cross on it, the other with a triangle (other symbols, such as a square or a circle may be used if desired). The cross is placed in front of an open bucket with grain. The triangle is placed in front of a bucket about 10 ft away that has grain covered with a screen. The horse is allowed to walk to the buckets. If it selects the right one it is rewarded with feed; if it selects the wrong one, it goes hungry. An intelligent horse soon learns to look for and "read" the cross.

The following additional points are submitted in support of the intelligence of the horse:

■ **The horse has primeval instincts and a highly developed, but very specialized, degree of intelligence**—The horse learned to be ever alert—to interpret the slightest rustle of a leaf and the faintest whiff of an unknown scent. It remembered the best grazing areas, the freshest waterholes, and the most protected areas; these it returned to with the seasons. It learned

to free itself when trapped in boggy or craggy country. It learned to communicate warnings concerning danger and movement, so that the herd could stick together in its flight and fight.

■ **The horse has the intelligence to untie knots and open latches**—Horses will figure out how to undo knots and latches of the most intricate kinds.

■ **The horse has an excellent memory**—To a very considerable degree the horse's aptitude for training is due to its memory, for it remembers or recognizes the indications given it, the manner in which it responded, and the rewards or punishments that follow its actions. Many examples substantiating the excellent memory of horses could be cited, but only one will be related.

In the days of Mohammed, intelligence and obedience were the main requisites of the Arab's horse. For war purposes, only the most obedient horses were used, and they were trained to follow the bugle. Legend has it that the Prophet himself had need for some very obedient horses, so he inspected a certain herd to make personal selections. The horses from which he wished to make selections were pastured in a large area bordering on a river. The Prophet gave orders that the animals should be fenced off from the river until their thirst became very great. He then ordered the fence removed, and the horses rushed for the water. When they were just about to dash into the river to quench their thirst, a bugle was sounded. All but 10 of the horses ignored the call of the bugle. The obedient 10 turned and answered the call of duty, despite their great thirst. The whimsical story goes on to say that these 10 head constituted the foundation of the *Prophet Strain*.

SOCIAL RELATIONSHIPS OF HORSES

Social behavior of horses may be defined as any behavior caused by or affecting another horse or, in some cases, another species.

Social organization may be defined as an aggregation of individuals into a fairly well integrated and self-consistent group in which the unity is based upon the interdependence of the separate organisms and upon their responses to one another.

The social structure and infrastructure in wild and feral herds of horses are of great practical importance. Equestrians should be knowledgeable relative to these social relationships. Then, if this social relationship is disturbed and/or modified under intensive, confined conditions, they will be better able to feed, care, and manage the animals with maximum consideration accorded to both economy of production and animal welfare.

■ Social relationships of wild or feral horses— Przewalsky's Horse, a wild species, discovered in 1879 in the northwestern corner of Mongolia, has been preserved and propagated in captivity in Europe and America. Also, feral horses thrive in semiarid environments in western United States and southwestern Canada. Studies of feral horses, along with historical records of wild horses, give clear evidence of the social organization of horses in their natural habitat; It centers on a dominant stallion and his harem of 1 to 3 mares and their immature offspring. Each group has an alpha or leading female, and the other members respond as followers. However, the stallion maintains his patriarchal position until displaced by another adult male; sometimes he is at the front of his group, at other times he assumes a defensive position between intruders and his band, and at still other times he herds or drives his harem during the breeding season. Immature males are very submissive to the dominant stallion. The stallion and his harem are a closed society; animals not belonging to a group are rejected by either the dominant stallion or the mares.

Excess stallions live apart from the family/harem groups, either singly or in bachelor groups of up to eight males. The groups are organized with the dominant individual herding the other stallions in the same manner as the harem stallion herds mares.

Home range behavior exists, with each home range including at least one watering hole and a large grazing area. But there is considerable overlapping of the home ranges, with more than one group using the same area. The spacing between groups is controlled primarily by dominating stallions, which approach each other with threats, which occasionally result in pushing and kicking matches, during which time the animals within groups move closer together. Following such encounters, the stallions return to their respective harems and move them apart. When approaching a watering hole, the group whinneys; if the watering site is already occupied by a band, they await their turn until the watering group moves away.

Wild and feral mares commonly foal in the spring and summer and usually mate a few days after foaling. In an amazingly short time after birth, foals run almost as fast as their mothers—and on legs almost as long. Foals stay near the sides of their mothers; and the mares are very protective of their young. Harem stallions also look after the foals and herd them back to the group when they become separated. Barren mares are sometimes protective of other mares' foals.

■ Social relationships of domesticated horses— Each of the behavioral systems has a tendency to draw horses together, with the exception of agonistic

Fig. 16-13. Horses need other horses. This shows weanlings nuzzling each other, at Claiborne Farm, Paris, KY. (Courtesy, Thoroughbred Publications, Inc., Lexington, KY)

behavior, which has the effect of keeping them at a distance or driving them apart.

Through millions of years of evolution, horses have developed a very strong need for the company of other horses, primarily for protective reasons. A group of horses has many more eyes, ears, and nostrils to detect danger than one lone horse. Thus, a group imparts a feeling of security, whereas one individual feels insecure.

A horse's desire for companionship with other horses is deep seated and may create many problems in training and handling. Thus, the separation of a foal from its dam is a trying experience. Taking a mature horse away from its mates may be even more traumatic. Basically, the lone animal fears for its life. It may not eat, and it almost always becomes nervous and uneasy. Fortunately, most horses soon calm down after they learn that they have nothing to fear from being alone.

Although horses prefer the company of other members of their species, when no other horses are available they will accept other species as friends (see section entitled "Interspecies Relationships"). They will even replace the security of horse company with the security of the barn. Their feeling of security around the barn may be so strong that a horse in an adjacent corral or paddock may lose its life by running into a barn that is on fire.

Group living—in a herd or band—has resulted in the development of a form of social structure in horses, the unique features of which are discussed under the following headings: (1) social order (dominance); (2) leader-follower; (3) interspecies relationships; and (4) animal-people relationships.

SOCIAL ORDER (DOMINANCE)

Most species of animals which live in groups establish a social order, based on dominance and submissive relationships. This explains why one horse in a group seems to be the boss and will bite and kick others, always with authority—and sometimes with ferocity. By studying any group of horses, it is possible to rank them, numerically, by dominance, or social order. One method of accomplishing this is to place a tub of grain in a corral and remove one horse at a time as it is determined which of the remaining horses eats from the tub first. Thus, with a group of 10 horses, it will be found that Number 1 is dominant over the other 9; Number 2 is dominant over all horses from 3 to 10, and so on down the line. Number 10 is at the bottom of the totem pole and is not dominant over any horse. Depending on their disposition, some horses will inflict injury as they enforce their social strata; others merely lay back their ears or push a lower horse out of the feed box with their nose.

Fig. 16-14. Dominant mare using her teeth to put a submissive mare in her proper place.

Sometimes a horse high in the dominance order pairs up with a horse near the bottom of the scale. As long as the dominant horse is present, other horses will not be aggressive toward its partner. If the dominant horse is removed, however, the partner will very promptly be put in its proper place in the social order.

Animals respect the order in their relationship just as carefully as protocol demands that it be observed at a Department of State dinner. In chickens, in which this phenomenon was first observed, the social order is called the *peck order*.

Among wild horses, social order is nature's way of giving mating priority to the top ranking stallions. Hence, they leave behind more of their progeny than do the less dominant (bachelor) males. In domesticated horses, the social rank order is usually important only in mares and young stock, because mature stallions are seldom run together in groups.

Social order among horses is of little consequence as long as they are on pasture or range and there is plenty of feed and water, but it becomes of very great importance when animals are placed in confinement. It is doubly important if feed is limited. Under the latter circumstances, the dominant individuals crowd the subordinate ones away from the feed, with the result that they may go hungry.

■ **Establishing social order**—When unacquainted (strange) horses are brought together, they engage in some form of aggression (kicking, biting, etc.) until one submits and the other becomes the socially dominant one. After all have had their contacts, the dominance order is initiated. Each must now be able to recognize all the others and remember the dominance relationships. The larger the group of horses and the greater the space (as on the range), the less frequently the pairs meet and the longer it takes to reduce the strife—that is, to firm up the social relationship. Once the social order is established, it results in a peaceful coexistence of the herd. Thereafter, when the dominant animal merely threatens by some trait or stance, the subordinate animal submits and avoids conflict. The usual posture and signals of horses are kicking, attempting to bite with bared teeth, and ears laid back. Of course, there are some pairs that fight every time they chance to meet. Also, if strange animals are introduced into such a group, social disorganization results in the outbreak of new fighting, as a new social rank order is established.

Several factors influence social rank; among them, (1) age—both young animals and those that are senile rank toward the bottom; (2) early experience—once a subordinate, usually always a subordinate; (3) weight and size; and (4) aggressiveness or timidity.

It is noteworthy that a mature horse (be it mare, gelding, or stallion) will seldom fight a foal or short yearling to establish dominance. They appear to recognize that the foal is no threat to their position and, therefore disregard it.

■ **Maintaining social order**—The more frequent the meetings of pairs of horses under noncompetitive situations, the better the memory of individuals, and, it follows, the better the social dominance relationships. Too many individuals in the group stress the memory and lessen individual recognition. Too large a space (individual distances and personal spaces) reduces the chances of competitive encounters and the enforcement of social relationships. Too small a space, (extreme density) restricts social activity, creates stress, and promotes boredom.

■ **Stability in social order**—The ideal horse group is socially stable because procedures in activities (called mannerisms in people) are well developed. Hunger increases sensitivity to stimuli and results in threats and fights; hence, adequate and available feed facilitates stability. Adding strange horses to a group is always disruptive.

LEADER-FOLLOWER

For a group of horses to function effectively, there must be a leader. This implies that there are followers, too.

Fig. 16-16. Leader or follower—winner or loser?

Fig. 16-15. Lead mare taking off for a new area, with the stallion bringing up the rear. When on the move, horses always follow the leader in Indian file—never abreast. (Courtesy, Wild Horse Research Farm, Porterville, CA)

In wild bands, the stallion was not the leader. He was the defender-protector of his harem of mares from rival stallions and predators. He herded and kept the mares together, fought off other studs and chased other horse groups from his territory, and brought up the rear. But he was not the leader. Generally, a dominant mare, with special qualities of leadership, served as the leader of the band. She possessed an intimate knowledge of the area in which the group lived; she knew the location of the best grass and water; she knew where to seek protection from storms and predators; and she knew the trails and the best escape routes.

The lead mare in wild bands established and maintained her position by ample use of her teeth and feet. When a new mare was added to the band, a test of dominance ensued and the winner became the leader. In this manner, a new leader evolved from time to time. Thus, in wild bands, the best fighter (the dominant mare) was always the leader, but the leader was not necessarily the mare with the most knowledge of the area and the greatest ability to lead the band safely.

Domesticated groups of horses also exhibit the leader-follower relationship. But there may be one great difference. The leader of a domestic band is not always the dominant mare. The leader may be one of the smaller or younger mares. Taking a page from history and people, it is noteworthy that one of the world's greatest leaders, Napoleon, was small in stature, but he was adventuresome and smart. So it is with the leader of domestic horses; the leader may not be the strongest, but she must be adventuresome and smart.

The leader-follower relationship may be important in racehorses. At least, it merits further study. There is some evidence that a horse's natural inclination to be a leader or a follower is involved in winning or losing a race. It appears that the leader has a driving urge to take the lead out of the starting gate and never relinquish it. If not held back, it may use up too much energy—spend itself—early in the race and fade in the stretch. If it can be taught (without fighting the jockey) to stay off the lead at the start and conserve its energy for a drive to the front at the end of the race, it may be a great racehorse. On the other hand, if it is a natural follower, it may lack the heart to win—it may be reluctant to pass horses. Such a horse usually brings up the rear. Some trainers feel that follower-type horses must be in the lead all the way in order to win—that they must be front-runners.

INTERSPECIES RELATIONSHIPS

Social relationships are normally formed between members of the same species. However, they can be developed between two different species. In domestication this tendency is important (1) because it permits several species to be kept together in the same pasture or corral (horses and cattle, for example), and (2) because of the close relationship between animals and people. Such interspecies relationships can be produced artificially, especially by taking advantage of the maternal instinct of females and using them as foster mothers.

ANIMAL-PEOPLE RELATIONSHIPS

Social relationships can also be transferred to human beings. Thus, animal-caretakers usually form care-dependency relationships. This is particularly true with horses.

One of the best-known stories of a horse-human relationship pertained to the great Thoroughbred, *Man O' War* ("Big Red") and his groom, Will Harbut. When training, *Man O' War*'s morning came early. Will Harbut gave him his first meal at 3:30 a.m.; at 7:30 a.m., he was groomed. "Big Red" was very fond of his caretaker; he liked to snatch his hat and carry it around as he showed off for visitors. Will Harbut, who had quite a way with words as well as with horses, never tired of telling the thousands of visitors who came to see *Man O' War* that, "He was the mostest horse that ever was."

Without doubt, the most fantastic animal-people relationship of all time is the story pertaining to the wolf that suckled Romulus and Remus. Anulius, who was on the throne of Alban, ordered a mother to be buried alive (because she had broken her vestal vows) and her two children to be thrown into the Tiber River. The legendary story goes on to say that the river received the babies kindly and bore them to a little bank, where they were cast ashore at the foot of a fig tree. Here they were found by a she-wolf, who cared for them until they were discovered by the shepherd Faustulus, who took them into his home and reared them. Romulus later became the legendary first king of Rome and the founder of the city.

COMMUNICATION

Although horses cannot speak like people, they do communicate with each other very effectively. Without doubt, this trait accounts, in part at least, for the foundation stock of the American Indians and the hardy bands of Mustangs—the feral horses of the Great Plains. In some mysterious manner, the abandoned and stray horses of the expeditions of de Soto and Coronado communicated with and found each other; otherwise, they would not have reproduced.

VOCAL SIGNALS

Horses can detect sounds above and below the frequencies that a human is capable of hearing. They have a very acute sense of hearing, perceiving higher and fainter noises than the human ear.

Horses use sounds in many ways; among them, (1) feeding, in sounds of hunger by young, or food finding, and of hunting cries; (2) distress calls, which announce the approach or presence of an enemy and the all-clear signal following the departure of a predator; (3) sexual behavior, courting songs, and related fighting; (4) mother-young interrelations to establish contact and evoke care behavior; and (5) maintaining the group in its movements and assembly. Experienced equestrians always listen for such sounds and know how to interpret them. For example, if they hear horses squealing, they will investigate to see which horses are fighting and if there is any real danger of one of them being injured.

Horses use a variety of vocal, or voice communications, of which the following are most common:

1. **Snort.** This is a warning signal, used to alert a group of horses of impending danger. It is made by blowing air out through the nostrils. A horse will snort when he sees something that frightens him. In wild horses, the snort was used primarily as a warning of the presence of predators.

2. **Neigh or whinny.** This is a distress call. It is a loud piercing sound used by a horse to express great concern, anxiety, and even terror. It is never used to express pain or anger. The neigh is the call made by a horse when it finds itself unexpectedly alone.

3. **Nicker.** This is a greeting, used to greet other horses, other animal friends, the barn, and even people. It is the sound of pleasure emitted upon seeing an old friend.

4. **Squeal.** This is a sound of anger, most often heard when horses are fighting. Sometimes horses squeal when bucking. Also, stallions and mares may squeal during breeding season.

5. **Stallion or mating call.** This is the sound of a stallion. It is loud, shrill, and threatening. Wild stallions used it as a challenge or warning to other stallions. In domestic horses, it is considered a mating call, made by a stallion when he sees or hears another horse.

6. **Mare talk.** A mare talks to her foal in soft nickers, probably to reassure it that all is well.

VISUAL SIGNALS

The horse makes visual signals with its ears, tail, mouth and lips, eyes and nostrils. A brief description of each of these follows:

1. **Ears.** The ears of a horse are the most easily understood visual signs with which it communicates its feelings to humans (see Fig. 16-17). The eyes and ears of a horse function together.

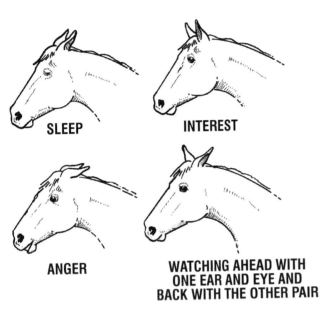

SLEEP   INTEREST

ANGER   WATCHING AHEAD WITH ONE EAR AND EYE AND BACK WITH THE OTHER PAIR

Fig. 16-17. Ear signals of horses.

Thus, the direction that a horse is looking can be determined by its ears. It is noteworthy, too, that a horse can, simultaneously, look and listen to the front with the ear and eye on one side and to the back with the ear and eye on the other side.

Good equestrians always watch the ears of a horse as a means of being aware of its moods.

2. **Tail.** The tail of a horse may be used as a signal (see Fig. 16-18).

If a horse has a kink in its tail on a cold morning, you better beware—it will likely test your riding ability.

When the tail is held high, it indicates that the horse is feeling good. When the tail is tucked between the legs, it indicates that the horse is badly frightened

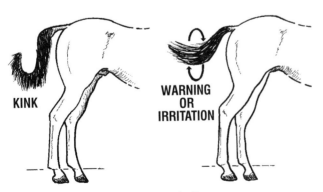

KINK   WARNING OR IRRITATION

Fig. 16-18. Tail signals of horses.

or is preparing to kick. Tail switching is a sign of irritation about something, such as flies or the actions of the rider.

3. **Mouth and lips.** A foal communicates its immaturity by mouth. It will cautiously approach a strange horse with its head extended and rapidly open and close its mouth. Usually this signal avoids attack and a test of dominance.

The lips are used to express the following three emotions which reflect the feeling of a horse: (1) A raised upper lip of a horse that is eating may express displeasure at the taste or odor of the feed; (2) a raised upper lip may express discomfort or pain in the digestive tract; (3) a stallion's curled upper lip with the head held high and extended is part of his mannerism in smelling horse droppings or in determining if a mare is in estrus.

4. **Eyes.** The eyes are not too communicative. The only visible change is in the opening of the eyelids; a frightened horse has its eyelids wide open.

5. **Nostrils.** When excited or frightened, the nostrils of a horse will flare out to allow greater intake of air into the lungs. Sometimes this is accompanied by a snort.

CHEMICAL INDICATORS

Females in estrus secrete a substance that attracts males. Hence, stallions locate mares that are in heat by the sense of smell.

On the range, it has been observed that each stallion usually stakes out a territory for himself and his harem of mares, with the outside boundary thereof marked by his feces.

SPECIAL SENSES

Horses are endowed with some special senses of importance in their behavior and training. These are listed in the sections that follow.

SIGHT

In its natural habitat, the adult horse keeps a sharp lookout for its enemies, even while grazing. It is rare to see all members of a herd lying down together; one horse is almost always on the lookout.

Horses have monocular vision; that is, each eye is independent of the other and can see different pictures. This gives them a panoramic view—to the sides, the front, and the back—virtually at the same time. When a horse wants to see an object very clearly, it will face the object and use both eyes in a binocular manner. By contrast, humans have binocular vision and see the same picture with both eyes.

The lens of the horse's eye is nonelastic, but the retina is arranged on a slope, the bottom part being nearer the lens than the top part. Thus, in order to focus on objects at different distances, the horse has to raise or lower its head so that the image is brought to that part of the retina at the correct distance to achieve a sharp image.

Because of its monocular vision, it is difficult for a horse to judge distance accurately. In its evolution, it was more important that horses see a wide area around them as they watched for predators than to judge distance. With domesticated horses, however, being able to judge distances is very important in certain types of performance. Thus, a roping horse must accurately judge the distance between itself and the animal it is following; a barrel racing horse must accurately judge the distance to the barrel as it prepares for the turn; and a jumping horse must accurately determine distance to the jump in order to select the take-off point, and it must determine the height and spread of the jump. Of course, top performing horses used for these purposes possess the ability to learn to judge distances, and they receive expert training.

Also, it is noteworthy that the horse has good vision in darkness. It's not as good as a cat's night vision, but it is considerably better than that of people. Thus, a horse may be ridden at night with reasonable safety, particularly if it is familiar with the area.

COLOR

Most authorities maintain that color vision in horses has not been established. However, color tests conducted at Montana State University by one of the author's former students showed that horses are able to recognize colors with considerable accuracy. The Montana workers devised a very simple test consisting of two buckets of equal size, but different colors. One had oats in it, the other was empty. The buckets were placed about 10 ft apart in a corral, and the horses were allowed to walk toward the buckets from a distance of 30 ft. It was found that all the horses tested had the ability to recognize colors, although some horses learned faster than others.

HEARING

The horse has excellent hearing, which undoubtedly evolved as part of its protective mechanism during its long evolution. Today, the acute hearing of the horse is very useful in training. The horse can be taught to

respond to such commands as walk, trot, canter (lope), as well as conventional start and stop cues.

SMELL

The horse has a good sense of smell. However, it is not as well developed in the horse as it is in some of its enemies.

Wild horses used smell for protection, to identify companions that may have been separated from the group, and to identify the home range. Stallions, in particular, smell fecal deposits, apparently to determine if they are on their home range and if there are any trespassers.

Domestic horses use the sense of smell in the following ways: (1) to identify one another, (2) to recognize humans, (3) to detect when mares come in heat, (4) to avoid drugs and other additives in feeds. Mares also use odor to identify their newborn foals.

TOUCH

Like all higher animals, the horse has a well-developed sense of touch. Certain areas of its body are more sensitive to touch than others. Among the most sensitive areas are: the nose, eyes, and ears, all of which are very essential parts; the legs; the rear flank; the withers; and the frog.

Touch is the most important sense used in cueing horses; it is used far more extensively than sight and sound. Thus, riders touch horses, through the mouth and neck; and they touch horses with their legs in the rib area and with their weight at its withers. Almost all horses will learn to respond to lighter and lighter touch cues. Response to light cues of the hands, legs, and weight is the ultimate in both training and horsemanship.

TRAITS OF HORSES

Certain traits of horses are pertinent in their behavior and training; among them, those listed in the sections which follow.

HOMING OR BACKTRACKING

The mystery of pathfinding is possessed by many species, great and small. The homing pigeon is noted for its ability to find its way home from great distances. Ants that go in groups usually travel a narrow trail that is chemically saturated by their passing; when one of them comes upon such a trail it is easily identified as the right roadway. When baby green turtles hatch from their eggs, they must dig upward through the sand in which the mother deposited the eggs, and head for water. Then, there are the migrating birds for which no single explanation is really satisfying. But it is the wide-roaming salmon whose navigational feats are the most fantastic. Horses also possess this trait. Through sound, scent, a photographic memory, or some sense of which we do not know, they often find their way back home when moved to very distant places.

The wild horse's best defense from predators was flight. In escape, it was often necessary for them to run for miles—to leave the home range far behind. If the home range possessed some definite survival advantages—in such things as feed, water, and shelter—it was in the best interest of the horses to return, thus necessitating a homing instinct. This behavioral instinct was usually most pronounced in the lead mare; hence, she was the one most determined to return to the home range.

Domestic horses have little opportunity to test the homing instinct. Today, most land areas are fenced, with the result that it is impossible for a stray horse to make its way for any distance. Also, most horses are hauled to new locations, rather than trailed; hence, they have no way of knowing which way is home.

Sometimes a riding horse exhibits the homing instinct—the urge to return to the home range by wanting to return to the barn, where it will feel safe and secure. Such behavior is commonly called *barn sour*.

A horse's homing or backtracking ability can be easily tested as follows: Ride for a considerable distance into an area that is new and unfamiliar to your horse. Take the most winding route possible, preferably not over distinct trails. When it is time to start back, give the horse his head and see what happens. Most horses will head back in the right direction. A few will backtrack almost step by step.

SLEEPING AND RESTING

The mature horse sleeps and rests standing up. This is made possible by a system of ligaments, which do not get tired like muscles, and which take the weight off muscles during rest. When asleep, the head droops, the eyes are closed, and the horse invariably stands on three legs. One hind leg is cocked, while the other three legs carry the weight. Unless a horse is lame, it will alternate the hind legs between resting and carrying weight. Most mature horses do not lie down regularly, although a few sleep and rest in this position.

Foals sleep lying flat and stretched out on one side. They spend a good part of their time sleeping. As they grow older, they lie down and sleep less.

In contrast to cattle and sheep which sleep very little, the horse may sleep soundly for as much as 7 hours out of each 24 hours, mostly during the warmest part of the day. But not all of the 7 hours sleep are taken at one time; rather, it is short and irregular, depending on the degree of hunger and the climatic conditions.

In a wild band, not all horses will sleep at the same time, either day or night. Domestic horses are different; all of them will eat at the same time, and all of them will sleep at the same time.

ROLLING (GROOMING)

The horse grooms itself by rolling in the dust. Unlike the cat or the cow, the horse's tongue is not suited for grooming. Instead, it rolls, preferably in dry, soft dirt—the dustier the better. After rolling, a horse shakes itself vigorously to remove as much dust as possible. Horses particularly like to roll after a hard day's work and much sweating. In addition to relaxing the horse, rolling gives an assist in controlling external parasites and in removing winter hair.

Other species groom themselves, too. Chickens take dust baths, whereas pigs wallow in the mud.

ABNORMAL HORSE BEHAVIOR (VICES)

Abnormal behaviors of domestic animals are not fully understood. As with human behavioral disorders, more experimental work is needed. However, we have learned from studies of captured wild animals that when the amount and quality, including variability, of the surroundings of an animal are reduced, there is increased probability that abnormal behaviors will develop. Also, it is recognized that confinement of animals makes for lack of space which often leads to unfavorable changes in habitat and social interactions for which the species have become adapted and best suited over thousands of years of evolution.

Few animals have undergone such drastic change through evolution as equines. Little *Eohippus* (the dawn horse of 58 million years ago) was a denizen of the swamp. Later, through evolution, the horse became a creature of the prairie. Even though the natural habitat of the horse shifted during this long predomestication period, until it was domesticated and confined, it gleaned the feeds provided by nature. Inevitably, this occupied its time and provided exercise.

But, domestication and confinement of horses has spawned many abnormal behaviors, which are commonly referred to as *vices* (bad habits). Horses have more abnormal behaviors than any other species; not because they are naturally bad, but because there are a lot of spoiled horses—horses that have received too much tender, loving care (including lumps of sugar and carrots) and too little discipline.

■ **Barn sour**—This refers to a horse that refuses to leave the barn—the horse refuses to leave home, friends, security, and feed. There are no easy cures for barn-sour horses; and each individual is different. But the most used, and the most successful, treatment for barn-sour horses consists of giving a bit of feed along the trail, with the feed given farther and farther from the barn.

■ **Biting**—This vice is acquired as a result of incompetent handling. Generally, it is started in either of two ways: (1) The horse has been accustomed to treats (such as a lump of sugar), and nips as an expression of disappointment when there is no treat (treats should always be placed in the feed manger); or (2) as a result of rubbing the horse's nose while petting it (never rub the nose; it teaches horses to bite).

■ **Bolting feed**—Bolting feed is the name given to the habit of eating too fast (gulping the feed down without chewing). This condition can be controlled by spreading the concentrate thinly over the bottom of the grain box, so that the horse cannot get a large mouthful; by adding chopped hay to the grain ration; or by placing some large, round stones, as big or bigger than baseballs, in the feed box.

■ **Charging (attacking)**—This refers to a deliberate attack on a person, with the horse's mouth wide open. In the beginning stage, this vice can usually be corrected. The technique is to discipline without inflicting pain. The horse must be taught to obey, but it must have confidence in the handler. If mature stallions have had this vice for a long time, it is difficult, and perhaps impossible, to break.

■ **Cribbing (wind-sucker, stump-sucker)**—A horse that has the vice of biting or setting the teeth against some object, such as the manger or a post, while sucking air is known as a cribber. This causes a bloated appearance and hard keeping; and such horses are more subject to colic. The common remedy for a cribber is a cribbing strap buckled around the neck in such a way that it will compress the larynx when the head is flexed, but not cause any discomfort when the horse is not indulging in the vice. A surgical operation to relieve cribbing has been developed and used with some success.

■ **Eating bedding**—Sometimes gluttonous horses eat their bedding. This is undesirable because (1) most bedding materials are low in nutritional value, and (2) feces soiled bedding will likely add to the parasite problem. This habit can be prevented by muzzling the horse.

Fig. 16-19. Cribbing (wind-sucker, stump-sucker) in action. This is the vice of biting or setting the teeth against some object (in this case, a post), and sucking in air. (Courtesy, Southern Illinois University, Carbondale)

■ **Halter pulling**—A confirmed halter puller breaks halters and lead ropes (straps) as it pulls back, then escapes. Either of two methods of tying will likely break the habit: (1) Tie a strong rope that the horse cannot break around the throatlatch, using a bowline knot so that the rope cannot slip and choke the horse; or (2) run a strong rope around the chest just back of the withers (some prefer to run it around the back area of the rear flanks), using a bowline knot. After a few struggles and attempts to break away, the horse will give up.

■ **Handler aversion**—As an aversion to handlers, some horses display aggressive vices such as bucking, or objection to catching, harnessing, saddling, and grooming. Flight responses occur in the form of backing, balking, bolting, or running away. Most of these vices originate with incompetent handling. Nevertheless, they may be difficult to cope with or to correct, especially in older animals.

■ **Kicking**—Two types of kickers are encountered: (1) the kicker that kicks the stall wall or door, and (2) the kicker that kicks people. The stall kicker kicks for no other excuse or satisfaction than to strike something and make a noise (kicking hollow tile makes a loud noise). Padding the stall will stop some stall kickers. Also, a chain or stick strapped to the back of the leg will usually break the habit; when the horse kicks, the chain or stick strikes the leg.

A horse that kicks people is dangerous, In the formative stage, usually the vice can be eliminated by prompt attention. But it is difficult to correct a confirmed and seasoned kicker.

■ **Pawing**—This refers to a horse that digs at the stall floor with its front feet. Heavy rubber mats on the stall floor and under the bedding will discourage stall digging.

■ **Pica**—This refers to a depraved appetite, or the eating of unnatural materials. This type of behavior is most common among horses that are kept in stalls and fed highly concentrated rations.

■ **Rearing**—Rearing is a very dangerous vice. When the horse rears up, the flailing forelegs can inflict injury on the handler. Such horses can usually be corrected by proper use of a lead shank or whip.

A horse that rears while being ridden should be handled by an experienced trainer, who can usually find the cause and correct the vice.

■ **Shying**—Shying at unfamiliar objects makes a horse dangerous to ride. The only solution is, patiently and gently, to take the horse over new trails and in new surroundings, again and again until there is no more shyness.

■ **Stall walking**—This is a stereotypic movement about the stall. A mascot, *e.g.*, a goat, may calm a stall walker.

■ **Striking**—Striking with the front feet is a dangerous vice, because the handler is always vulnerable. The handler should always stay at the side of such a horse, never in front of it. Each time that a horse attempts to strike, it should be punished with a war bridle or whip.

■ **Tail rubbing**—This refers to persistent rubbing of the tail against the side of the stall or other objects, resulting in the loss of hair and an unsightly tail. Tail rubbing is a common vice of Saddlebred horses that wear tail sets. Also, the presence of parasites may cause animals to acquire this vice. Installation of a tail board (a 2 in. × 12 in. shelf that runs around the stall at a height just above the point of the horse's buttock), or an electric wire similarly placed, may be necessary to break an animal of this habit.

■ **Weaving**—This is a rhythmical swaying back and forth while standing at the stall door. The prevention and cure are exercise, ample room, and freedom from stress. A mascot, *e.g.* a goat, may calm a weaver.

■ **Wood chewing**—This is the chewing of wood, usually a wood manger or a board fence. It is generally caused by (1) boredom, (2) nutritional inadequacies, or (3) psychological stress and habit. There is only one foolproof way in which to prevent wood chewing; to have no wood on which horses can chew—to use metal, or other similar materials, for barns and fences. But wood chewing can be lessened, although it cannot be entirely prevented, through one or more of the following practices:

1. Stepping up the exercise.
2. Feeding three times daily, rather than the normal two times; without increasing the total daily allowance.
3. Spreading out the feed in a large feed container and placing a few large, smooth stones about the size of a baseball in the feed container, thereby making the horse work longer and harder to obtain its feed.
4. Providing 2 to 4 lb of straw or coarse grass hay per animal per day, thereby giving the horse something to nibble on.

BEHAVIOR SUMMARY

Gradually, people adopted a more settled mode of life, and with this came the desire to safeguard their food supply for times when hunting was poor and to have their food close at hand; at this stage, nearly all our modern animals were tamed or confined, or, as we say, domesticated.

In domesticating animals, people recognized the importance of behavior; they selected those species which could both be tamed and used to satisfy their needs. However, in the breeding, care, and management that followed, behavior received less attention than the quality and quantity of meat, milk, eggs, fiber, and power produced. The race was on for greater rate and efficiency of production. Animals in forced production were confined and automated. Then, suddenly, animals told us that all was not well in the barnyard. They told us that something was missing—something as vital to them as an essential amino acid, mineral, or vitamin—something as important as disease prevention and environmental control. They told us that consideration of their habitat and social organization had not kept pace with advances in genetics, nutrition, environmental control, and other areas of animal care. They told us what was wrong and what they wanted through a whole host of abnormal behaviors, including cannibalism, loss of appetite, poor parental care, overaggressiveness, dullness, degenerate sexual behavior, and cribbing. These warning signals are being heeded. Today, there is renewed interest in the study and application of animal behavior; we are trying to make it right with animals by correcting the causes of the disorders. For the time being, this calls for emulating the natural conditions of the species.

At the outset of this chapter, it was stated that the application of animal behavior depends upon understanding. The presentation to this point (Part I) has been for the purpose of understanding. Part II, which follows, pertains to the practical applications of animal behavior—the training of horses.

PART II. HORSE TRAINING

Fig. 16-20. A well-trained horse! (Photo by Dean G. Miller, Elma, NY. Courtesy, The American Morgan Horse Assn., Shelburne, VT)

A well-mannered horse may be said to be the combined result of desirable heredity, skillful training, and vigilant control. Once conception has taken place, it is too late to change the genetic makeup—the native intelligence—of the animal. However, the eventual training and control of the horse are dependent upon how well the trainer understands equine behavior and mental faculties as well as methods of utilizing them so that the desired performance may be obtained.

There are as many successful ways to train horses as there are to train children. The author has observed several top professional trainers. Each used a different technique, yet all ended up with the same result—a champion. Most of them follow the basic principles given herein.

The good trainers who have followed programs of training and educating foals from the time they were a few days old have already eliminated the word *breaking*. To them, the saddling and/or harnessing of young horses is merely another step in the training program, which is done with apparent ease and satisfaction.

CONTROLLING THE HORSE

Horses have whims and ideas of their own. Always, however, riders should be the boss, with mounts promptly carrying out their wishes. With the experienced equestrian, this relationship is clear cut, for the rider is able to relay feelings to the horse instantly and unmistakably.

Purebred horse breeding establishments have long been aware, consciously or unconsciously, of the equine mental faculties. As a result, most breeders have substituted gradual and early training programs for the so-called breaking of animals at 3 to 5 years of age. Even on some of the more progressive ranches, the cowboy and bucking bronco are fast passing into permanent oblivion. The owners of the famous King Ranch in Texas report that they have discarded the former method of breaking three-year-olds in favor of starting training at three months of age. It has been their experience that the latter method has materially reduced injuries to both cowboys and horses, has resulted in more really gentle mounts, and has cost less in time, labor, and money.

For complete control and a finished performance, the horse should have a proud and exalted opinion of itself; but at the same time it should subjugate those undesirable traits that make a beast of its size and strength so difficult to handle by a comparatively frail and small human. Complete control, therefore, is based on mental faculties rather than muscular force.

The faculties of the horse that must be understood and played upon to obtain skillful training and control at all times are summarized briefly in the sections that follow.

MEMORY

To a considerable degree, the horse's aptitude for training is due to its memory; for it remembers or recognizes the indications given it, the manner in which it responded, and the rewards or punishments that followed its actions. These facts must be taken into consideration both in training the young horse and in retaining control of the trained animal.

Discipline and reward must be administered very soon after the act (some competent equestrians say that it should be within three seconds) in order for the horse to associate and remember.

CONFIDENCE AND FEAR

In the wild state, the horse was its own protector; and its very survival was often dependent upon rapidity of escape. In a well-mannered horse, it is necessary that confidence in the rider replace fear. Thus, it is best to approach the horse from the front. It should be spoken to in a quiet, calm voice, and it should be patted by using comparatively slow movement of the hands to avoid exciting the animal. Above all, when approaching a horse, one should make certain that the animal knows of his/her presence. Startling a horse often causes accidents for which the animal is blameless.

During moments of fright, the good equestrian utilizes the means by which the horse is calmed. However, when the horse is voluntarily and knowingly disobedient, the proper degree of punishment should be administered immediately.

ASSOCIATION OF IDEAS

Horses are creatures of habit; for example, when the grain bin door is heard to open, the horse regularly anticipates its feed. For this reason, the schooling of a horse should be handled by the same competent trainer who allows the animal an opportunity to associate the various commands with the desired response. A well-trained horse may become confused and ill mannered when poorly handled by several persons.

WILLINGNESS

A willing worker or performer is to be desired. Some animals submit to the handler's subjugation with little trouble and hesitation, whereas others offer resistance to the point of being stubborn. Complete control over the mount at all times is achieved through the judicious employment of rewards and punishments.

REWARDS

The two most common rewards given horses are a praising voice and a gentle stroking with the hand. Satisfying the horse's greediness for such things as a lump of sugar is also most effective, but this may make for great disappointment if the reward is not available at all times. To be effective, rewards must not be given promiscuously, but only when deserved. It is also important that the same word always be used for the same thing and that the handlers mean what they say.

PUNISHMENT

The two common types of equine punishment are the spur and the whip. Punishment should be administered only when the handler is certain that the animal is being disobedient and not when the horse lacks sufficient training, has not understood some command, or has done something wrong because of the rider. When necessary, however, the punishment should be administered promptly, so that the animal understands why it is given; and it should be given with justice and with the handler retaining a cool head at all times.

Following punishment, the animal should be made to carry out the original command that it failed to follow, and then it should be properly rewarded.

TRAINING THE FOAL

The foal should be given daily lessons of 15 to 30 minutes each, for 7 to 10 days. If trained early in life, it will be a better disciplined, more serviceable horse. Give it one lesson at a time, and in sequence; that is, be sure the pupil masters each learning experience before it is given the next one.

Put a well-fitted halter on the foal when it is 10 to 14 days old. When it has become accustomed to the halter, in a day or so, tie it securely in the stall beside the mare. Try to keep the foal from freeing itself from the rope or from becoming tangled up in it.

Leave the foal tied 15 to 30 minutes each day for 2 to 3 days. Groom the animal carefully while it is tied. Rub each leg and handle each foot so that the foal becomes accustomed to having its feet picked up. After it has been groomed, lead it around with the mare for a few days and then lead it by itself. Lead it at both the walk and the trot. Many breeders teach a foal to lead simply by leading it with the mare from the stall to the paddock and back again.

At this stage of the training, be sure the foal executes your commands to stop and go as soon as you give them. When halted, make sure it stands in show position—squarely on all four legs with its head up.

Use all your patience, gentleness, and firmness in training the foal. Never let your temper get the best of you.

Fig. 16-21. Teaching the foal to lead. After the foal has been gentled to a halter, a nonskid loop slipped over the hindquarters will teach it to move forward promptly.

TRAINING THE YEARLING

The yearling should be given daily lessons of 30 minutes each, repeated until each learning experience is mastered. The horse learns by repetition. Thus, teach only one thing at a time, and repeat it in the same manner daily until mastered; then proceed to the next learning experience. Teach the yearling the following, in order:

1. **The meaning of "Whoa" and its name.** The yearling should be taught that "whoa" means stop. Always give the command, then call its name, as "Whoa, Duke."

2. **To stand when hobbled.** Next the young horse should be hobbled; first the two front feet, then sideline (tie a front foot and a hind foot on the same side together). Hobbling is for the purpose of teaching the horse to stand still (as if tied) and not get excited if it gets caught in a fence. Many a valuable horse has mutilated itself for lack of this kind of training.

Fig. 16-22. Front feet of yearling hobbled with a large, soft cotton rope. This training lesson is designed to teach the young horse to stand still (as if tied) and not get excited if it gets caught in a fence.

3. **To become accustomed to the saddle blanket.** Gently put the saddle blanket on the young horse's back, and move it from head to tail, until the yearling is not afraid of having an object on its back. Repeat this training for two days.

4. **To get used to the saddle.** Next, ease a saddle on the yearling. Put it on and off several times. Then, tighten the girth moderately and lead the yearling around. Repeat this procedure for five or six days.

Thus, the gentling of the yearling is for the purposes of teaching it the meaning of the word "whoa"; to stand patiently when hobbled or caught in a wire

fence; and to get used to the saddle. After a few days of gentling like this, the yearling may be turned out to pasture for a time.

TRAINING AT 18 MONTHS OF AGE

At 18 months of age, the young horse should receive additional training. At this stage, each lesson should be 30 minutes daily, with each step mastered before moving on to the next. The trainer should always be gentle, but firm; and should not make a pet out of the horse. Let it know who is boss. When it must be punished for wrongdoing, use the whip—one time only; and do so immediately after the horse commits the act. Never discipline a horse by gouging it with spurs. When it does well, reward it by stroking its neck or shoulder and calling its name; "That's a good boy, Duke." At 18 months of age, teach the following:

1. **To drive, turn, stop, and back up, by using plowlines.** Tie the stirrups together under the horse, then run plowlines through them. Stand behind the horse and use the plowlines to drive, turn, stop, and back up.

Fig. 16-23. When the horse is approximately 18 months of age, use plowlines to teach it to drive, turn, stop, and back up.

2. **To flex the neck and set the head.** This may be accomplished either by (a) tying the reins to the stirrups, or (b) using rubber reins made from strips of old inner tubes. Then turn the young horse loose in the corral or training ring for 30 minutes, where it can't hurt itself.

Also, a dumb jockey bitting rig—a contrivance fastened on a young horse—may be used to train it to place its head in the desired position. The rigging consists of surcingle, back strap, crupper, side reins, overcheck or sidecheck, standing martingale, and some sort of projection above the top of the surcingle to which reins may be attached.

3. **To respond to the bosal, ride the horse;**

introduce leg pressure. During the first few months of riding, use a bosal; it will alleviate the hazard of hurting the mouth with bits. Do some light riding; introduce leg pressure.

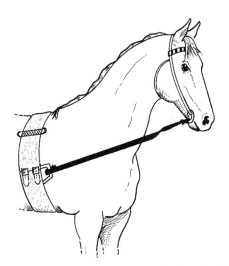

Fig. 16-24. When the horse is about 18 months of age, teach it to flex its neck and set its head. This shows rubber reins, made from strips of an old inner tube, being used for this purpose.

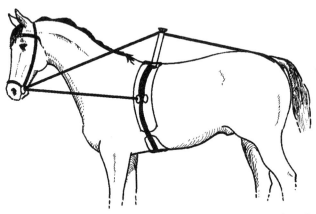

Fig. 16-25. Dumb jockey, a bitting contrivance for training a young horse to place his head in the desired position.

TRAINING THE TWO-YEAR-OLD

At this stage, each lesson should be of 30 minutes duration daily, repeated until mastered. The two-year-old is ready for the following advanced training:

1. **To respond to the aids.** Mount the horse and put him in motion by use of the aids—the legs, hands and reins, and voice. After riding the horse for 5 to 6 days at the walk and trot, move it into the lope or canter, always on the proper lead—a right foot lead when going clockwise, a left foot lead when moving counterclockwise.

2. **To back.** From the ground, teach the horse to back. Hold the reins near the bosal or bit; push back (push and release) and command "Back, Duke." If necessary, push on the animal's shoulder and/or switch it on the forelegs. Next, mount the horse and, from its back, teach it to stop and back up. If it won't back when you're mounted, have a friend stand in front of it and switch it back while you pull (pull and release) on the reins and command "Back, Duke." Backing teaches the horse to get the feet under the body which is essential for pivots and sharp turns.

3. **To pivot (Western horse).** Each time the horse is stopped and backed up, pause for a few seconds, then collect it (with the reins, and apply a little leg pressure), and pivot. Always teach the young horse to turn on its hind feet; pull it back until its hind feet are under the body, then pull diagonally on the reins.

4. **To make a sliding stop (Western horse).** Teach the horse to make a proper sliding stop—to "stick its tail in the ground." When properly done, the rider's reining hand is low, the horse's head is low and its front feet are near the ground. Most judges prefer a stop with 3 or 4 feet on the ground, rather than the more spectacular 2-hind-leg stop. If the stop is on 3 feet, one forefoot is up slightly, ready to run or roll back either way. Most expert Western riders don't like a sliding stop with both front feet up in the air because the horse is not balanced and can fall over backward.

It takes months of training to get a horse to do the sliding stop right. First it should be stopped at the walk, then the trot, next the short lope, and finally when wide open.

In executing the sliding stop, the Western rider uses his/her aids as follows: (a) squeezes with the legs; (b) says "Ho"; (c) sits back deep in the saddle; and (d) pulls up on the reins. The leg pressure is to alert the horse. Throwing the rider's weight back when properly timed, drives the horse's hind feet up under it. The reins are pulled no harder than necessary, then

Fig. 16-26. A sliding stop. World's Champion Reining Horse in action. (Courtesy, *The Quarter Horse Journal*, Amarillo, TX)

the pressure is released so that the horse can use its head to maintain its balance.

Proper timing is important. The rider squeezes when the lead foot is off the ground and the hind feet are getting ready to come off. As the hind feet come up, the rider shifts his/her weight back and starts making contact with the horse's mouth. The rider does not jerk, for jerking hurts the horses mouth, and makes its head fly up and its mouth gape open. Another important thing relative to timing is this: If the rider applies the brakes when the horse is stretched out and its front feet are in the air, it forces the horse to throw all its weight on its front feet and it will bounce. The really good sliding stop is performed with rhythm and balance, and is easy and smooth.

Some good trainers teach horses on the longe line—a light strap of webbing or leather 30 ft long. When the author visited the Spanish Riding School of Vienna, where the famed Lipizzaner stallions perform, he learned that all basic training—including gaits, leads, stops, rollbacks, etc.—is given on the longe. Starting at age four, these horses are worked from the ground for one year before they are ever mounted.

The only exception to use of the longe line in training is a roping horse, because, when on the end of a rope, a roping horse is taught to run straight back from the trainer, rather than around the trainer.

SORING HORSES

Soring is the use of painful methods and devices to enhance a horse's gait in the show-ring. It involves the use of caustic liquid, commonly called *scooter juice,* along with chains or shackles, to make a walking horse's front ankles sore. This process, combined with 7 or more in. long, heavy shoes, and some drastic training, creates the desired show-ring gait. Both the Horse Protection Act of 1970 and the rules of the American Horse Shows Association prohibit soring.

Soring evolved as a means of producing a fast, flashy gait in Tennessee Walkers, for the show-ring.

A true running walk is executed at a speed of 6 to 8 miles per hour and will not exceed 10 miles per hour. It is done with economy of effort to both the horse and the rider and is not very showy. In an effort to increase the speed to 15 to 18 miles per hour and obtain high action in front, yet keep the gait from being classed as a rack, horses are sometimes sored by means of blisters, chains, and whatnot, so that they scoot their hind feet far under them in order to keep the weight off their sore front feet. The soreness, along with accompanying long toes and heavy shoes (secured by bands over the feet, in addition to nails), cause the horse to pick its front feet up very high as it leaps through the air. Actually, the fast artificial gait

that results more nearly resembles a rack than a running walk.

The U.S. Department of Agriculture, Animal Plant Health Inspection Service, is charged with enforcing the Horse Inspection Act. The regulations provide that—

1. Boots and collarlike devices of any weight may be used so long as they are properly constructed and do not sore the feet of the horse that wears them.

2. Bracelets made of properly constructed chains may be used as long as they do not weigh more than 10 oz including the fastener.

3. Rollers may be used if made from hardwood or aluminum as long as they don't weigh more than 14 oz.

4. All other devices, including beads and bangles, are outlawed.

5. No substance may be applied to a horse's leg above the hoof and below the fetlock when the horse is brought for preshow inspection. After inspection, a clear, transparent lubricant (like glycerin, petrolatum, or mineral oil) may be applied, but only under supervision of horse show management.

Any person violating any provision of the Act or the regulations is subject to a civil penalty of up to $1,000 or criminal penalties up to $2,000 and 6 months imprisonment for each violation.

Note: In 1996, the U.S. Department of Agriculture held a series of public meetings to discuss proposed enforcement changes in the Horse Protection Act. So, the USDA is still looking at the soring rules. In the meantime, the practice of soring Tennessee Walking Horses continues.

BLOOD TESTING FOR FITNESS

Blood testing (hematology) is a means of evaluating physical fitness.

All body cells require oxygen. With strenuous exercise, as in racing, the oxygen requirement increases. Oxygen is transported by hemoglobin, the protein-iron coloring matter in blood. It follows that any reduction in the hemoglobin content, or in total blood volume, will lower the oxygen-carrying capacity of the blood. When this condition is marked, anoxia (or anemia) develops, fatigue sets in, and there is lowered stamina and endurance.

Anoxia may be caused by many conditions. Usually it is due either to (1) nutritional deficiency, or (2) bloodworms—both of which may be aggravated by the stress and strain of racing, endurance trials, and showing.

Most trainers accept one or more of the following as indicative of the lack of fitness: loss of appetite; loss of weight; excessive blowing following work; a dry, harsh cough; rough coat; dull eyes; watery instead of beady sweating; and blowing up over the loins. In an effort to be more exacting, some veterinarians who attend to racing stables, endurance trials, and show strings now use blood examination as a means of evaluating physical fitness.

It appears that, although there are breed differences, most horses which show consistent, good racing form have hemoglobin levels between 14 and 16 g per milliliter, red cell counts between 9 and 11 million per cu millimeter, and packed cell volumes between 40 and 45%. Also, other blood determinations are sometimes made. The blood testing approach is interesting and appealing. However, much more information on the subject is needed. Proof of this assertion becomes evident when it is realized that all horses whose blood pictures fall within the above range are not necessarily good performers; neither are horses with blood pictures outside this range incapable of winning. Some horses do respond to treatment, but, generally, the results have been inconsistent and disappointing. One needs to know if horses which have lower blood values, but which do not respond to treatment, carry all of the red cells and hemoglobin that they are capable of developing—whether they have less poten-

tial for racing. Even more perplexing is the fact that this blood count can be too high, producing polycythemia. A horse with polycythemia frequently loses appetite, fails to thrive in the stable, performs unsatisfactorily, and may show cyanosis (dark bluish or purple coloration of the skin and mucous membranes due to lack of oxygen). It is also noteworthy that absolute polycythemia occurs at high altitudes or when there is heart disease or fibrosis of the lungs.

Racehorses with anemia are sometimes treated by either (1) injecting iron and/or vitamin B-12, or (2) giving orally (in the feed or water) one of several iron preparations. Sometimes vitamin C (ascorbic acid), folic acid, and other B complex vitamins are added.

At this time, there is insufficient knowledge of equine anemia, or of ways of stimulating the making of blood (hematopoiesis), to make a winner. The true role of therapy, if any, remains unknown.

The most that can be said at this time is that prevailing treatments usually satisfy the owner or trainer who insists that they "get the works." Most scientists are agreed, however, that quickie miracle shots or concoctions will never replace sound nutrition and parasite control on a continuous basis.

PART III. HORSE ENVIRONMENT

A horse is the result of two forces—heredity and environment. Heredity has already made its contribution at the time of fertilization, but environment works ceaselessly away until death. Since most animal traits are only 30 to 50% heritable, the expression of the rest (more than 50%) depends on the quality of all of the components of the environment. Thus, it is very

Fig. 16-27. A perfect match, giving evidence of a perfect environment. (Courtesy, The American Morgan Horse Assn., Inc., Shelburne, VT)

important that equestrians have enlightened knowledge of, and apply expert management to the environment of horses. The branch of science concerned with the relation of living things to their environment and to each other is known as *ecology.*

Among horses, environmental control involves space requirements, light, air temperature, relative humidity, air velocity, wet bedding, ammonia buildup, dust, odors, and manure disposal, and proper feed and water. Control or modification of these factors offers possibilities for improving animal performance. Although there is still much to be learned about environmental control, the gap between awareness and application is becoming smaller. Research on animal environment has lagged, primarily, because it requires a melding of several disciplines—nutrition, physiology, genetics, engineering, and climatology.

ENVIRONMENTAL FACTORS AFFECTING HORSES

We know that controlled environment must embrace far more than an air-conditioned chamber, along with ample feed and water. The producer needs to be concerned more with the natural habitat of animals. Nature ordained that they do more than eat, sleep, and reproduce.

Over the long pull, selection provides a major answer to correcting confinement and other behavioral problems; we need to breed animals adapted to people-made environments.

The following are of special importance in any discussion of horse environmental factors affecting horses:

1. Feed
2. Water
3. Weather
4. Facilities
5. Health
6. Stress

FEED/ENVIRONMENTAL INTERACTIONS

Horses may be affected by either (1) too little or too much feed, (2) rations that are too low in one or more nutrients, (3) an imbalance between certain nutrients, or (4) objection to the physical form of the ration—for example, it may be ground too finely.

Forced production (such as growth, and racing 2-year-old horses) and feeding of forages and grains, which are often produced on leached and depleted soils, have created many problems in nutrition. These conditions have been further aggravated through the increased confinement of horses, many animals being confined to stalls or paddocks all or a large part of the year. Under these unnatural conditions, nutritional diseases and ailments have become increasingly common.

The following additional feed/environmental factors are pertinent:

■ **Appetite/intake.** Horses control their feed intake through a combination of the following mechanisms:

1. **The hypothalamus.** The two primary theories pertaining to hypothalamic control are: (a) the chemostatic hypothesis, which reasons that when blood nutrient levels, such as sugar and liquid, become too low, the hypothalamus sends signals to begin feeding; and (b) the thermostatic hypothesis, which theorizes that a decrease in hypothalamic temperature will induce feeding.

2. **The physical size of the digestive tract.** Generally, animals eat to satisfy their energy requirements. However, if the caloric density of the ration is low, as in the case of certain roughages, the bulk may limit the animal's ability to hold sufficient of the feed to meet its energy needs.

3. **The thermostatic control.** According to the thermostatic theory, in hot environments horses reduce metabolic rate by reducing feed intake; and in cold environments they increase metabolic rate by increasing feed intake.

4. **The fiber content of the ration.** Low-fiber high-energy rations stimulate horse growth and production in hot environments, whereas high-fiber rations increase the heat increment and keep the body warm in cold weather.

5. **Disease.** Feed intake is reduced quickly during most metabolic diseases. Also, most gastrointestinal disorders of either infectious or parasitic origin as well as many systemic diseases result in decreased feed intake.

■ **Familiarity of feed**—When given a choice, horses usually continue eating those feeds with which they are familiar. However, by gradually adding new and novel feeds, they learn to accept them (animals adapt). Also, early exposure of young animals to a feed may result in ready consumption of the feed later in life.

■ **Feed as a reward**—Feed rewards are particularly common with horses.

Satisfying a horse's liking for a lump of sugar or a carrot can be most effective. However, to be effective, rewards must not be given promiscuously, only when deserved; for example, after carrying out a training command.

■ **Nutrient deficiencies**—The nutrient requirement tables (feeding standards) presented for horses, in Chapter 13 in this book, list values for animals under conditions presumed to be relatively free from environmental stress and for animals expected to perform near their genetic potential. In practice, environmental factors are not always ideal. Stresses are produced by weather (temperature, humidity, air movement, and solar radiation); diseases and parasites; surgery and castrating; altitude; sound; density and confinement; and pollution. As a result, horse performance often falls short of genetic potential. Shelters and housing are intended to eliminate or moderate the impact of some of the environment, but if they are poorly designed, they may create a new array of stresses with which the horse must contend.

So, although nutrient requirement tables are excellent and needed guides, nutrient deficiencies may result even when they are followed because the environment in which the animals are produced can modify the requirements. For this reason, along with making provisions for variations in feed composition, nutrient allowances, which provide margins of safety for horses are presented in Chapter 13 in this book, in addition to the requirements.

■ **Overfeeding**—Too much feed is wasteful. Besides, it creates a health hazard; there is usually lowered reproduction in breeding animals, and higher incidence of digestive disturbances (colic, founder, and scours)—and even death. Horses that suffer from mild digestive disturbances are commonly referred to as *off feed*.

■ **Palatability**—*Palatability refers to the combination of factors that result in a feed being well-liked and eaten with relish.* If horses don't eat their feed, they won't produce; and if they don't eat enough feed, production efficiency will be poor. Only an animal can assess the palatability of a feed. Palatability is the result of the following factors: taste, appearance, odor, texture, and temperature.

■ **Regularity of feeding**—Horses are creatures of habit; hence, they should be fed at regular times each day.

■ **Selective grazing**—Different species of animals have different habits of grazing; they show preference for different plants and graze to different heights. Horses prefer young, tender grass to coarse-stemmed plants, a preference which often causes them to over-graze certain areas. Because of selective preference grazing, grazing by two or more classes of animals makes for more uniform pasture utilization and fewer weeds and parasites, providing the area is not over-stocked.

■ **Stress**—Stress should be considered when formulating horse rations. All environmental stressors, whether physiological, immunological, or behavioral in nature, require energy expenditure on the part of the animal. Stress especially increases the animal's need for metabolizable energy, which, in turn, affects the optimal ratio of metabolizable energy to protein and other nutrients. So, when under extreme stress, nutrients will be diverted to maintenance, which is high priority, with the result that production, reproduction, and disease resistance will be reduced. So, it is important that rations be formulated to meet the stressful conditions.

■ **Underfeeding**—Too little feed results in slow and stunted growth of young equines; in loss of weight, poor condition, and excessive fatigue of mature horses; and in poor reproduction, failure of some females to show heat, more services per conception, lowered foal crop, and light birth weights.

WATER/ENVIRONMENTAL INTERACTIONS

Horses can survive for a longer period without feed than without water. Water is one of the largest constituents in the animal body, ranging from 40% in

Fig. 16-28. Clear, cool mountain water. (Courtesy, American Quarter Horse Assn., Amarillo, TX)

very fat, mature horses to 80% in newborn foals. Deficits or excesses of more than a few percent of the total body water are incompatible with health, and large deficits of about 20% of the body weight lead to death.

The total water requirement of horses varies primarily with the weather (temperature and humidity); feed (kind and amount); the species, age, and weight of animal; and the physiological state. The need for water increases with increased intakes of protein and salt, and with increased milk production of lactating mares. Water quality is also important, especially with respect to the content of salts and toxic compounds.

Pertinent details relative to important water/environmental interactions follow:

■ **Air temperature**—Numerous experiments have shown a very positive correlation between water intake and ambient temperature. Thus, horses consume more water in summer than in winter.

■ **Feed**—The water content of feeds ranges from about 10% in air-dry feeds to more than 80% in fresh, green forage. Feeds containing more than 20% water are known as wet feeds.

The water content of feeds is especially important for horses which do not have ready access to drinking water. Also, the water on the surface of plants, such as dew, may serve as an important source for horses on arid ranges, but this supply is rarely sufficient to meet their needs.

■ **Frequency of watering**—Home range behavior exists among most wild and feral horses, with each home range including at least one watering hole—generally a stream, spring, lake, or pond. The frequency of watering wild and feral horses, as well as domestic horses on extensive pasture or ranges, is determined primarily by temperature and humidity—the higher the temperature and humidity, the more frequent the watering. However, under average conditions, horses usually drink once each day, but during extreme heat they may return a second time. Under practical conditions, the frequency of watering is best determined by horses, by allowing them access to clean, fresh water at all times.

■ **Water excretion**—Water is excreted from the body through three routes: (1) urine, (2) feces, and (3) evaporation from the body surfaces and respiratory tract.

Urine provides a means whereby water-soluble products of metabolism can be excreted. Generally, when rations are high in protein and mineral content, urine flow is increased.

The amount of water lost in the feces is highly dependent on the animal species and the ration. Horse feces contain only 60 to 65% water and are relatively dry.

Water loss from the respiratory tract is very variable, depending on humidity and respiration rate. Expired air is over 90% saturated; hence, when the humidity is low, respiratory losses are high. Conversely, respiratory losses are low when inhaled air is near saturation. When respiration rate is increased in response to high temperatures or other behavioral stimulus, the rate of respiratory water loss is increased.

There are large differences among species in the importance of sweating, with animals ranked in descending order as follows: horses, donkeys, cattle, buffalo, goats, sheep, and swine.

WEATHER/ENVIRONMENTAL INTERACTIONS

Weather is a state of the atmosphere with respect to heat or cold, wetness or dryness, calm or storm, clearness or cloudiness.

Extreme weather can cause wide fluctuations in horse performance. The difference in weather impact from one year to the next, and between areas of the country, causes difficulty in making a realistic analysis of building management techniques used to reduce weather stress.

The research data clearly show that winter shelters and summer shades improve production and feed efficiency. The issue is clouded only because the additional costs incurred by shelters have frequently exceeded the benefits gained by improved performance, particularly in those areas with less severe weather and climate.

The maintenance requirement of horses increases as temperature, humidity, and air movement depart from the comfort zone. Likewise, the heat loss from horses is affected by these three factors. Horses adapt to weather as follows.

In cold weather, the heating mechanisms are employed, including (1) increased insulation from growth of hair and more subcutaneous fat; (2) increase in thyroid activity; (3) seeking protective shelter and warming solar radiations (the animals sun themselves); (4) consumption of more feed, which increases the heat increment and warms animals; and (5) increasing activity. The most important animal body heating mechanisms are amount of feed consumed and body activity, which are also evidenced in people. For example, after skiing in bitter cold weather, a skier feels comfortable after eating a beefsteak; and during a marathon race, a runner may feel quite warm when the temperature is near freezing (32°F).

In hot weather, the cooling mechanisms are employed, including (1) moisture vaporization (from skin and lungs), (2) avoidance of the heating solar radiation (horses seek shade), (3) depression of thyroid activity, and (4) loafing.

THERMONEUTRAL ZONE (COMFORT ZONE)

Fig. 16-29 and the definitions that follow it are pertinent to an understanding of thermal zones.

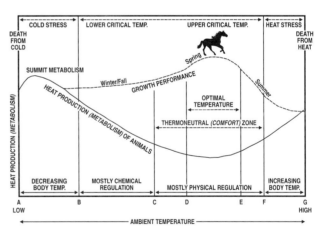

Fig. 16-29. Diagram showing (1) the influence of thermal zones and temperature on homeotherms (warm-blooded animals), and (2) the peak of growth/performance in the spring, followed by the summer slump due to high (hot) summer temperature and lignification of forage.

In Fig. 16-29, *heat production (metabolism)* is plotted against *ambient temperature* to depict the relationship between chemical and physical heat regulation. Note, too, the broad range of accommodation to low (cool) temperatures in contrast to the restricted range of accommodation of high (warm) temperatures. Definitions of terms pertaining to Fig. 16-29 follow.

■ *Thermoneutral (comfort) zone (C to F) is the range in temperature within which the horse may perform with little discomfort, and in which physical temperature regulation is employed.*

■ *Optimum temperature (D to E) is the temperature at which the horse responds most favorably, as determined by maximum production (gains, work, and feed efficiency).*

■ *Lower critical temperature (B) is the low point of the cold temperature beyond which the horse cannot maintain normal body temperature.* The chemical temperature regulation is employed in the zone below C. When the environmental temperature reaches point B, the chemical-regulating mechanism is no longer able to cope with the cold, and the body temperature drops, followed by death. The French physiologist, Giaja, used the term *summit metabolism* (maximum sustained heat production) to indicate the point beyond which a decreased ambient temperature causes the homeothermic mechanism to break down, resulting in a decline in both heat production and body temperature and eventually death of the animal.

■ *Upper critical temperature (F) is the high point on the range of the comfort zone, beyond which horses are heat stressed and physical regulation comes into play to cool them.* When the environmental temperature goes above the upper critical temperature (see Fig. 16-29), the horse is *heat stressed* and employs physical regulation, especially evaporative heat loss mechanisms such as sweating. Also, the immediate response of animals to heat stress is reduced feed intake, to attempt to bring heat production in line with heat dissipation capabilities. Evaporation of moisture from the skin surface or respiratory tract is the primary mechanism used by horses to lose excess body heat in a hot environment; this mechanism is limited by air vapor pressure, but enhanced by air movement.

The comfort zone, optimum temperature, and both upper and lower critical temperatures vary with different species, breeds, ages, body sizes, physiological and productive status, acclimatization, feed consumed (kind and amount), the activity of the animal, and the opportunity for evaporative cooling. The temperature varies according to age, too.

Animals that consume large quantities of roughage or high-protein feeds produce more heat during digestion; hence, they have a different critical temperature than the same animals fed a high-concentrate, moderate-protein ration.

Stresses at both high and low temperatures are increased with high humidity. The cooling effect of evaporating sweat is minimized and the respired air has less cooling effect. As humidity of the air increases, discomfort at any temperature, and nutrient utilization, decreases proportionately.

Air movement (wind) results in body heat being removed at a more rapid rate than when there is no wind. In warm weather, air movement may make the horse more comfortable, but in cold weather it adds to the stress temperature. At low temperatures, the nutrients required to maintain body temperature are increased as the wind velocity increases. In addition to the wind, a drafty condition where the wind passes through small openings directly onto some portion or all of the animal's body will usually be more detrimental to comfort and nutrient utilization than the wind itself.

ADAPTATION, ACCLIMATION, ACCLIMATIZATION, AND HABITUATION OF HORSES TO THE ENVIRONMENT

Every discipline has developed its own vocabulary. The study of adaptation/environment is no exception. So, the following definitions are pertinent to discussion of this subject:

Adaptation refers to the adjustment of horses to changes in their environment.

Acclimation refers to the short-term (over days or weeks) response of horses to their immediate environment.

Acclimatization refers to evolutionary changes of horses to a changed environment which may be passed on to succeeding generations.

Habituation is the act or process of making horses familiar with, or accustomed to, a new environment through use or experience.

Species differences in response to environment factors result primarily from the kind of thermoregulatory mechanism provided by nature, such as type of coat (hair, wool, feathers), and sweat glands. Thus, hogs, which have a light coat of hair, are very sensitive to extremes of heat and cold. On the other hand, nature gave horses an assist through growing more hair for winter and shedding hair for summer, with the result that they can withstand higher and lower temperatures than hogs.

Also, there are breed differences, which make it possible to select animals well adapted to specific environments. Thus, the Shetland Pony, native to the Shetland Isles, not more than 400 miles from the Arctic Circle, evolved in the rigors of the northland climate and on sparse vegetation, which imparted that hardiness for which the stocky breed is famed. The long-legged donkey is adapted to hot, desert areas.

Wild horses were little affected by their environment as long as they roamed pastures and ranges. But the domestication of horses and their confinement into smaller spaces has introduced a whole set of environmental influences.

Properly designed horse barns and other shelters, shades, insulation, ventilation, and air conditioning can be used to approach the most suitable environment. Naturally, the investment in environmental control facilities must be balanced against the expected increased returns; and there is a point beyond which further expenditures for environmental control will not increase returns sufficiently to justify the added cost. This point of diminishing returns will differ among sections of the country, quality of the horses (the more valuable the animals, the higher the expenditures for environmental control can be), and operators; and labor and feed costs will enter into the picture, also.

Environmentally controlled buildings are costly to construct, but they make for the ultimate in animal comfort, health, and efficiency of feed utilization. Also, they lend themselves to automation, which results in a saving in labor; and, because of minimizing space requirements, they effect a saving in land cost. Today, environmental control is rather common in poultry and swine housing, and it is on the increase for horses.

Environmental control is of particular importance in horse barn construction, because many horses spend the majority of their lives in stalls—for example, race and show horses may be confined as much as 95% of the time.

A temperature range of 50 to 75°F is considered the comfort zone for the horse, with 55°F considered optimum. Until a newborn foal is dry, it should be warmed to 75 to 80°F, which can be accomplished by means of a heat lamp.

Unfortunately, few experiments have been conducted on the effect of temperature on the well being of horses.

EFFECT OF TEMPERATURE ON HORSES

Horses react differently to cold weather and hot weather. A summary of their response to temperature follows:

■ **Cold weather response of horses**—Horses are not very sensitive to cold. In the wild state, they developed a long, shaggy coat of hair in the wintertime, sought shelter from storms under trees and in the valleys, and pawed the snow to obtain forage. Horses face away from the direction of a severe storm.

Although clipping and daily grooming make the horse more attractive, they remove the animal's natural protection against cold. So, when the weather is cold, idle horses should be blanketed.

Horses react to cold weather as follows:

1. **Voluntary feed intake is increased.** Feed intake is influenced by weather. For example, under ideal (optimum) weather conditions in October, a horse may eat 14 lb of 60% TDN feed daily, whereas in the same area the horse may eat 20 lb in the winter. Thus, feed consumption is increased with lower than optimum temperature.

2. **A higher proportion of their feed is used for maintenance.** A mature horse must have heat to maintain body temperature, sufficient energy to cover the internal work of the body and the minimum movement of the animal, and a small amount of proteins, minerals, and vitamins for the repair of body tissues. Normally, about half of all the feed consumed by horses is used in meeting the body maintenance requirements. The harder horses work and the more they eat, the smaller the proportion of the ration that is used for maintenance. For example, during brief periods when racing, horses use up to 100 times the energy utilized at rest, with the result that a much smaller proportion of their energy is used for maintenance than when idle.

In cold weather, horses eat more to keep warm, with the result that a high proportion of their feed is used for maintenance.

3. **They adapt to cold weather.** The lower critical temperature of horses is not known. Their shaggy coats of hair and a layer of fat under the skin, along with a windbreak and feed, equip them to withstand very low temperatures. If the environment becomes too cold, the demand for heat production may exceed the animal's metabolic capacity, and the animal may die of hypothermia (excessively low body temperature).

■ **Hot weather response of horses**—The horse is very tolerant to hot weather provided (1) plenty of salt and water are provided, and (2) it is not allowed to gorge on water when hot.

The salt requirements vary with work and temperature. Normally, the horse needs about 2 oz of salt daily, or less than 1 lb per week. However, when at hard work during hot weather—conditions accompanied by profuse perspiration and consequent loss of salt in the sweat—even greater quantities may be required. The white, encrusted sides of a horse after work are evidence of the large amount of salt drawn from the body through sweat (2 g of salt/pound of sweat). Horses at moderate work may lose 50 to 60 g of salt in the sweat and 35 g in the urine daily. Unless this salt is replaced, the animal will soon exhibit signs of excessive fatigue.

Frequent, small waterings between feedings are desirable during warm weather or when the horse is being put to hard use. Horses should not be allowed to drink heavily when they are hot, because they may founder; and they should not be allowed to drink heavily just before being put to work.

Horses react to hot weather as follows:

1. **Voluntary feed intake is reduced.** Feed consumption is reduced as the ambient temperature rises. Thus, the nutrients provided in the ration are subject to variation because they vary with the consumption of the ration. For example, if the horse eats half as much feed as recommended, the percent of nutrients (proteins, mineral, vitamins) must be doubled in order

that an adequate amount of each nutrient will be consumed daily.

2. **A lower proportion of their feed is used for maintenance.** Warmer temperatures reduce the basal metabolic rate and maintenance energy requirement. Also, both body weight and degree of work affect the feed required by horses.

3. **They adapt to hot weather.** Although the higher critical temperature of horses is not known, when extremely hot they employ physical means of cooling, including profuse sweating, increased blood flow to the skin and underlying tissue, decreased feed consumption, and decreased activity. Also, horses shed their winter coats with the coming of warm weather. Horses have more defense against cold than against heat.

4. **They are subject to heat stroke (sun stroke).** When being exercised very vigorously during hot, humid weather, horses may suffer from heat stroke. The symptoms: rapid breathing and heartbeat, weakness, dry skin, and no sweating. First aid consists of the immediate lowering of the body temperature by placing the horse in a cool place and spraying or sponging its head, lower side of the neck, and legs with cold water. In extreme cases, ice packs may be used and ice may be placed in the rectum. It may be necessary for the veterinarian to restore lost body fluids (the electrolytes).

FACILITIES/ENVIRONMENTAL INTERACTIONS

Optimum facility environments can only provide the means for horses to express their full genetic potential of production, but they do not compensate for poor management, health problems, or improper rations.

Research has shown that horses are more productive and feed-efficient when raised in an ideal environment. The primary reason for having facilities, therefore, is to modify the environment. Proper barns and other shelters, shades, sprinklers, insulation, ventilation, heating, air conditioning, and lighting can be used to approach the desired environment. Also, increasing attention needs to be given to other stress sources such as space requirements, and the grouping of animals as affected by class, age, size, and sex.

The principal scientific and practical criteria for decision making relative to the facilities for horses in modern, intensive operations is the productivity and cost of production, which can be achieved only by healthy animals under minimal stress. So the investment in environmental control facilities is usually balanced against the expected increased returns. (See Chapter 14 for the recommended environmental controls for horses.)

MODIFICATION OF FACILITIES

In recent years, there has been a trend to modify the environmental control facilities for horses as much as possible; among such modifications designed for maximum horse comfort and efficiency of production are fans and lights. (See Chapter 14 for modifications by shades and ventilation.)

FANS

Generally, the ventilation system of environmentally controlled horse buildings involves the use of fans, to maintain oxygen; keep carbon dioxide levels low; remove dust, moisture, and ammonia from the building; and maintain suitable temperature. Rate of production and feed efficiency are lowered when horses must endure excess stresses, such as temperatures appreciably below or above the comfort zone. Cold horses eat more and gain less, while heat stressed horses eat less and gain less.

There are two basic types of fans: (1) exhaust fans, and (2) pressure or intake fans.

In an exhaust system, fans force air out of the building, which creates a partial vacuum. Then, air comes in through intake openings and equalizes pressure. Where fresh air inlets appear uniformly around the building, fresh air distribution should occur uniformly.

In a pressure fan system, fans draw fresh air from the outside and build up enough pressure to push stale, moisture laden air out through exhaust ports and any other openings.

Fan capacity is important. Fans are rated in cu ft per minute (cfm) of air they move. By selecting and using different numbers and sizes of fans, the needed variable rate, or flexibility, of ventilation can be achieved. The amount of ventilation required depends upon (1) the inside-of-building temperature desired, (2) the outside air temperature, (3) the relative humidity, (4) the number and size of horses in the building, (5) the amount of insulation, and (6) the size of the building.

LIGHTS

In modern livestock operations, both the length of day and the intensity of light may be altered artificially.

The number of hours of light in the day affects the initiation of the normal breeding season of mares, who are seasonal breeders.

The ratio of hours of daylight to darkness throughout the year acts on nerves in the region of the pituitary gland, and stimulates or inhibits the release of the follicle-stimulation hormone (FSH). Lengthening the daylight hours activates the pituitary, and causes it to release increasing amounts of the FSH which stimulates ovarian function. Thus, sometime after the daylight period increases, the estrous cycle begins in mares. Artificial lighting will accomplish the same thing as daylight.

Normally, the natural breeding season of mares begins in March and extends to late July or August.

Artificial lighting of broodmares enables breeders to bring mares into season about 6 weeks earlier than normal. By the use of the artificial light technique, a mare that would normally conceive on March 15 may get in foal sometime in January. By avoiding the necessity of skipping a year due to late breeding, this technique may actually result in obtaining two additional foals during the lifetime of a mare.

The procedure consists in using a 200-watt light bulb in a box stall to extend the hours of light to 16 hours daily. By beginning the light treatment of mares about December 1, they may be bred the latter part of January.

Slight adjustments in the schedule will need to be made in different locations, depending upon the sunrise and sunset times of the particular area.

HEALTH/ENVIRONMENTAL INTERACTIONS

Health is the state of complete well-being, and not merely the absence of disease.

Environment embraces the forces and conditions, both physical and biological, that (1) surround horses, and (2) interact with heredity to determine behavior, growth, and development.

Disease is defined as any departure from the state of health.

Parasites are organisms living in, on, or at the expense of another living organism.

Feed, air quality, lighting, noise, other animals, and weather are among the many factors that constitute the environment of the horse. Extremes or alterations in the environment may subject an animal to stress; and stress may affect the health and lead to more diseases and parasites.

Some important health/environmental interactions not covered elsewhere in this book are discussed in the sections that follow.

ANTIBODY PRODUCTION

An antibody is a protein substance (a modified type of blood-serum globulin) developed or synthe-sized by lymphoid tissue of the body in response to an antigenic stimulus.

Antigens may be (1) components of certain drugs or feed; (2) infectious microorganisms or parasites; (3) substances from the environment, such as chemicals, dusts, pollen, grains, etc.; or (4) tissues of the body itself.

Each antigen elicits production of a specific antibody. In disease defense, the horse must have an encounter with the pathogen (antigen) before a specific antibody is developed in its blood.

Normally, antibodies react with antigens and render them harmless. However, certain antibodies may attack body tissue. This abnormal condition is called autoimmunity. Generally, repeated exposure to a specific type of antigen increases the rate at which antibodies against the substance are produced.

Antibody production may be impaired under such conditions as (1) malnutrition, (2) oversecretion of stress hormones, (3) advanced aging, or (4) inherited inability to produce certain antibodies.

DISEASE DEFENSE

Pathogens affecting horses are ever present in the environment. But, in order to produce disease, they must overcome the body's first line of defense—they must first gain entrance to the animal by one of the body openings or through the skin. Then, they usually multiply and attack the tissues. To accomplish this, they must be sufficiently powerful (virulent) to overcome the defenses of the animal body. The defenses of the animal body vary and may be weak or entirely lacking, especially under conditions of a low nutritional plane and poor management and sanitation practices.

Pathogens commonly gain entrance into the body through one or more of the following channels:

1. Respiratory tract
2. Digestive tract
3. Genital tract, especially during mating or parturition
4. Wounds
5. Mucous membranes of the eye, *e.g.*, pinkeye and leptospirosis (the latter may be acquired when the urine of the infected animal gets into the eye)
6. Teat canal, especially in lactating females
7. Navel cord in the newborn
8. Contaminated syringes or surgical instruments
9. Insect bites

If the pathogen gains entrance to the horse's body, they are usually subjected to one or more of the following reactive defenses; inflammatory reactions, febrile reactions, or immune reactions.

■ **Inflammatory reactions**—Inflammatory reactions are characterized by the following four cardinal signs: (1) an increase in blood supply (redness), (2) increased temperature of the part (heat), (3) swelling of the part (edema), and (4) increased sensitivity (tenderness and pain).

■ **Febrile reactions**—Febrile reactions are characterized by (1) an overall increase in body temperature, and (2) an increase in metabolic activity.

■ **Immune reactions**—Immune reactions are characterized by the ability of horses to resist and/or overcome disease either through (1) natural (inherited) immunity, or (2) acquired immunity. Immunity is very important; hence, further elucidation of its protective mechanisms against disease follows:

The horse's body is remarkably equipped to fight disease. Chief among this equipment are large white blood cells, called phagocytes, which are able to overcome many invading organisms.

The body also has the ability, when properly stimulated by a given organism or toxin, to produce antibodies and/or antitoxins. When a horse has enough antibodies to overcome particular disease-producing organisms, it is said to be immune to that disease.

When immunity to a disease is inherited, it is referred to as a *natural immunity*.

Acquired immunity or resistance is either active or passive. When the animal is stimulated in such a manner as to cause it to produce antibodies, it is said to have acquired active immunity. On the other hand, if an animal is injected with the antibodies (or immune bodies) produced by an actively immunized animal, it is referred to as an *acquired passive immunity*. Such immunity is usually conferred by the infection of blood serum from immunized animals, the serum carrying with it the substances by which the protection is conferred. Passive immunization confers immunity upon its injection, but the immunity disappears within 3 to 6 weeks.

In active immunity, resistance is not developed until after 1 or 2 weeks; but it is far more lasting, for the animal apparently keeps on manufacturing antibodies. It can be said, therefore, that active immunity has a great advantage.

It is noteworthy that young suckling mammals obtain a passive immunity from the colostrum that they obtain from their mothers following birth.

■ **Vaccination**—*Vaccination may be defined as the injection of some agent (such as bacteria or vaccine) into an animal for the purpose of preventing disease.*

In regions where a disease appears season after season, it is recommended that healthy susceptible horses be vaccinated before being exposed and before there is a disease outbreak. This practice is recommended not only because it takes time to produce an active immunity, but also because some horses may be about to be infected with the disease. The delay of vaccination until there is an outbreak may increase the seriousness of the infection. In addition, a new outbreak will "reseed" the premises with the infective agent.

In vaccination, the object is to produce in the animal a reaction that in some cases is a mild form of the disease.

It is a mistake, however, to depend on vaccination alone for disease prevention. One should always ensure its success by the removal of all interfering adverse conditions. It may also be said that varying degrees of immunity or resistance result when horses are actively immunized. Individual horses vary widely in their response to similar vaccinations. Heredity also plays a part in the determination of the level of resistance. In addition, nutritional management practices play important parts in degrees of resistance displayed by horses.

COLOSTRAL DEFENSE

Colostrum is the first milk secreted by mammalian females following parturition.

Newborn foals are unable to produce antibodies within their own bodies for some time after birth; they acquire these antibodies from their mothers either while in the uterus before birth or through colostrum after birth. Newborn foals should receive colostrum during the first 12 to 24 hours after birth if they are to acquire passive immunity. After about 24 hours following birth, gut closure occurs, following which the newborn foal digests these proteins, which then lose their immunization properties. Apparently, this results from the newborn not being able to absorb the large protein molecule.

IMMUNE SUPPRESSION (ALTERED IMMUNE RESPONSE)

People blush when they are embarrassed, and their hearts race when they are frightened—reactions that show the linkage of the brain and body. Recent studies in both humans and animals link the brain to the body's immune system—the complex array of organs, glands, and cells that comprise the body's principal mechanisms for repelling invaders.

Studies show that people's emotions have a great impact on their health—that people stressed by bereavement (such as the loss of a loved one) or by loneliness (social isolation) suffer high incidences of disease and mortality. Also, research has shown that chronic stress causes the adrenal gland to pump increased amounts of corticosteroids into the bloodstream, and that these chemical messengers inhibit immune action.

Although horses do not blush, they react to stress. Thus, for many years, caretakers have tried to minimize stress among their horses by providing a clean sanitary environment, and by keeping them warm in the winter and cool in the summer. Yet, horses still experience unavoidable and harmful stresses, especially during weaning and shipping. Following such stressful times, outbreaks of diseases are more common.

Stress suppresses the horse's immune system and leaves it more vulnerable to bacterial and viral infections and all other immune disorders. Here is how: When a horse is stressed, the secretion of a hormone, called corticosteroid (cortisol, corticosterone), by the adrenal gland, is increased. The main purpose of the corticosteroids is to increase the horse's immediate chances for survival by producing more energy to withstand the current stressful condition. They are the frontline warriors. However, corticosteroids also decrease immunity and suppress the subsequent ability of the horse to fight infection.

Many stressors increase corticosteroid production and alter the horse's immune system by depressing antibody production and leucocyte levels in the blood, both of which are important in fighting diseases. The most common stressors that can alter the horse's immune systems are: heat, cold, crowding, mixing, weaning, fatigue, limit-feeding, noise, and restraint.

If the stress is brief, detrimental effects are not generally observed. However, if the response to stress exceeds a few hours, the catabolic effects cause reduced feed efficiency, growth, performance, and disease resistance.

Based on the above concept, blood corticosteroid levels may be used as one of the measures of stress.

HEAVES

Heaves are an environmentally related disease of horses and mules. The disease is associated with (1) the feeding of damaged, dusty, or moldy hay; and/or (2) the use of dusty bedding or paddocks. Heaves are characterized by difficulty in forcing air out of the lungs, resulting in jerking of the flanks and coughing. Heaves in equines is similar to emphysema in people. Control consists of providing an environment that is as nearly dust-free as possible.

PESTS AND PESTICIDES

Pests are counterproductive—they make for an adverse environment and cause an estimated 30% annual loss in the worldwide potential production of crops, livestock, and forests.[2]

─────────
[2]Ennis, W. B., Jr., W. M. Dowler, and W. Klassen, "Crop Production to Increase Food Supplies," *Science*, Vol. 188, No. 4188, pp. 593-598. The authors are staff scientists on the National Program Staff, Agricultural Research Service, U.S. Department of Agriculture, Beltsville, MD.

This means that a worldwide annual loss of 30% potential food productivity occurs despite the use of advanced farming technology and mechanized agriculture. This also means that the losses in many of the developing countries greatly exceed this figure.

Among the pests that cause high losses are: (1) plant disease, caused by more than 160 bacteria, 250 viruses, and 8,000 fungi; (2) insects, of which 10,000 species in the United States are destructive; (3) weeds and brush of which some 2,000 species in the United States cause losses in crops and animals; (4) rats, mice, gophers, and other rodents, which consume and damage feed, destroy property, and spread disease; and (5) certain birds, such as starlings, which consume and contaminate feed and spread many diseases.

A pesticide is any substance that is used to control pests. Pesticides are an integral part of modern agricultural production and contribute greatly to the quality of food, clothing, and forest products that we enjoy. Also, they protect our health from disease and vermin. Pesticides have been condemned, however, for polluting the environment, and in some cases for posing human health hazards. Unfortunately, opinions relative to pesticides tend to become polarized.

No pest control system is perfect; and new pests keep evolving. So, research and development on a wide variety of fronts should be continued. We need to develop safer and more effective pesticides, both chemical and nonchemical. In the meantime, there is need for prudence and patience.

POLLUTION

Anything that defiles, desecrates, or makes impure or unclean the surroundings pollutes the environment and can have a detrimental effect on horse health and performance. Thus, gases, odorous vapors, and dust particles from animal waste (feces and urine) in buildings directly affect the quality of the environment. For healthy and productive animals, each of the pollutants must be maintained at an acceptable level.

DUST

Dust may be defined as a mixture of small particles of different sizes of dry matter.

Dust is a contributing factor to both animal and human health, especially with respect to respiratory diseases. Thus, it should be considered a significant contaminant that adversely affects environmental quality of horse facilities.

Dust may be present in significant amounts both inside and outside horse buildings.

GASES AND ODORS FROM ANIMAL WASTES

In closed buildings, gases arise from manure decomposition, respiratory excretion, and fuel burning heaters. Some gases are poisonous.

Odors arise predominantly from manure decomposition. They consist mostly of hydrocarbons containing sulfur or nitrogen. Most states use a nuisance theory to control odor. However, in advance of designing and constructing animal facilities, it is important to know how much abatement equipment is necessary to prevent the neighbors from being offended.

The animal's respiratory system is in continuous contact with the environmental air; hence, if the air contains excessive pollutants, respiratory diseases may occur.

The principal gases generated by stored manure are carbon dioxide, ammonia, hydrogen sulfide, and methane.

FOAL ULCERS

Gastric ulcers are of special importance among foals.

In a five-year study conducted at the University of Florida, gastric and/or duodenal ulcers were found in 25% (129) of the 511 foals that were presented for necropsy. A single cause of foal ulcer was not found, although stress and diet seemed to be especially important. At the University of Kentucky's Department of Veterinary Science, where gastric ulcers in foals have been studied for many years, the three main presdisposing factors causing the gastric ulcer syndrome in foals, in order of incidence, were: (1) excessive milk from the mare, (2) stress on the foal, and (3) drug-induced ulcers. The mares that produced the most milk tended to have the most foals with ulcers—the foals overindulged in milk. Stress-related ulcers were caused by sudden weather changes, especially the onset of hot weather, by mares coming into heat or being bred, and by weaning. Drug-induced ulcers tended to follow the drug treatments of foals for diseases, especially diarrhea and pneumonia.

STRESS/ENVIRONMENTAL INTERACTION

Stress is defined by Hans Selye, M.D., the world's leading authority on stress, as *the nonspecific response of the body to any demand.*

The term *stress* is used to indicate an environmental condition that is adverse to the well-being, either external (nutritional, weather, social) or internal (diseases, parasites).

Stresses of many kinds affect horses; among them, cold stress, heat stress, drafts, poor ventilation, excitement, presence of strangers, fatigue, mixing horses, number of horses together, space, changing corral and corral mates, weaning, previous nutrition, hunger, thirst, poor sanitation, disease, parasites, surgical operations, injury, and management.

Race and show horses are always under stress; and the greater the speed and the more tired they become, the greater the stress. Also, the greater the stress, the more exacting the nutritive requirements. Thus, the ration of race and show horses should be scientifically formulated.

Horses can be prepared, or adapted to the environment, in such a manner as to reduce stress.

In the life of an animal, some stresses are normal, and they may even be beneficial—they can stimulate favorable action on the part of an individual. Thus, we need to differentiate between stress and distress. Distress—not being able to adapt—is responsible for the harmful effects. The trick is to manage stress so that it doesn't become distress and cause damage, and to recognize the warning signals of distress.

The principal criteria used to evaluate, or measure, the well-being or stress of people are: increased blood pressure, increased muscle tension, body temperature, rapid heart rate, rapid breathing, and altered endocrine gland function. In the whole scheme, the nervous system and the endocrine system are intimately involved in the response to stress and the effects of stress.

The principal criteria used to evaluate, or measure, the well-being or stress of horses are: growth rate, efficiency of feed use, reproduction, body temperature, pulse rate, breathing rate, mortality, and morbidity. Other signs of horse well-being, any departure from which constitutes a warning signal, are: contentment, alertness, eating with relish, sleek coat and pliable, elastic skin, bright eyes and pink eye membranes, and normal feces and urine.

Stress is unavoidable. Wild animals were often subjected to great stress; there were no caretakers to modify their weather, often their range was overgrazed, and sometimes malnutrition, predators, disease, and parasites took a tremendous toll.

Domestic horses are subject to different stresses than their wild ancestors, especially to more restricted areas and greater animal density. However, in order to be profitable, their stresses must be minimal.

BLEEDERS

Stress triggers different syndromes in different individuals. When subjected to heavy exercise, such as in racing, horses are prone to a condition known as *bleeders.*

It has been estimated that 70 to 80% of Thoroughbred racehorses are bleeders. In a recent major U.S. race, it was reliably reported that 5 horses in the field of 11 ran with the aid of Lasix, a diuretic used to combat bleeding. So bleeders are a serious problem!

Bleeders are horses afflicted by blood flowing from their nostrils or bronchial tubes, but originating in the lungs following strenuous exercise. But the problem is not confined to Thoroughbreds, nor is it limited to racehorses. It also afflicts Quarter Horses and Standardbreds, and it afflicts horses when they are subjected to maximum stress by strenuous physical activity of whatever kind; for example, in endurance rides. But it does not affect racing dogs or humans who race competitively. The species dissimilarity is attributed to the difference in the horse's anatomy. The horse has a sloping diaphragm and is primarily an abdominal breather, inhaling by movement of the diaphragm. This type of breathing appears to create stress in the equine lung.

Bleeders among horses racing or training have been recognized for at least 300 years. One of the earliest reported bleeders was a horse named *Bleeding Childers*, so named because of his frequent bleeding from the nostrils. Retired to stud because of training and racing difficulties associated with bleeding, the horse was tactfully renamed *Bartlet's Childers* and went on to gain fame as the grandsire of *Eclipse*, England's undefeated racing champion of the 18th century. The story goes that another famous English Thoroughbred stallion, *Herod*, raced in the Great Subscription Purse at York "but broke a blood vessel and was beaten off."

Until recently, one of the major difficulties in determining the source of blood in bleeders has been the lack of an adequate diagnostic instrument to examine safely the horse's upper respiratory tract. The advent of the flexible fiberoptic endoscope revolutionized diagnosis.

Current indicators are that the blood originates in the lung tissue, and not within the nasal cavity. Recent findings indicate that the bleeding is caused by ruptured capillaries (pulmonary hemorrhaging) rather than nosebleed; and that, although a large number of horses bleed from the lungs following racing, only a small percentage actually show external evidence of blood at the nostrils—it is swallowed into the gastrointestinal tract.

Bleeding appears to affect the performance of racehorses. But the cause and cure remain elusive. The condition is exercise-induced; and there appears to be a higher frequency of bleeders among older horses. When bleeding is excessive, the most common treatment is to discontinue training and racing temporarily or permanently.

While scientists work to find the cause and effective treatment of bleeders, among the remedies, mostly highly secretive, attempted by distraught horse owners and caretakers, with little documented success, are copper bands around the tail, coins in water buckets, bloodletting, and a variety of folk remedies. Based on studies to date, supplementation with vitamin K, vitamin C, or bioflavinoids does not appear to be beneficial. Furosemide, popularly known by the trade name Lasix, which reduces (but does not prevent) pulmonary edema almost instantly, was approved by the FDA as an equine medication in 1967, and is a regulated raceday medication permitted in a majority of states. According to the researchers at Washington State University, Lasix promotes the clotting of blood.

Research studies indicate that bleeders are a stress/environmental interaction of equines induced by heavy exercise, but the findings do not signal any restriction in racing horses, because galloping is a very natural behavior in horses, inherited from their wild ancestors who escaped from the attacks of their predators by flight.

SUSTAINABLE AGRICULTURE

Today, the slashing and burning of the Amazon rain forest, greenhouse effect, toxicities, and polluted streams are among the warnings of environmental catastrophes. Worldwide, environmental quality and economic efficiency are in vogue. In the United States, this movement is called *sustainable agriculture*.

Sustainable agriculture is often described as farming that is ecologically sound and economically viable. It may be high or low input, large scale or small scale, a single crop or diversified farm, and use either organic or conventional inputs and practices. Obviously, the actual practices will differ from farm to farm; for example, on a horse farm manure disposal is a major problem, whereas on a fruit farm the use of pesticides is of concern. A definition of sustainable agriculture follows.

A sustainable agriculture is farming with reduced off-farm purchased inputs of pesticides, herbicides, and fertilizers, along with reduced negative impact on natural resources and improved environmental quality and economic efficiency.

Typically, such farms rely more on biological resources and management than on nonrenewable inputs of energy and chemicals.

Many of the practices advocated under a sustainable agriculture are not new; they involve such timeless agricultural practices as soil erosion control, the protection of ground water, the use of legumes as a source of nitrogen, biological insect and weed control, and the use of pastures as a primary feed source.

ANIMAL WELFARE/
ANIMAL RIGHTS

In recent years, the behavior and environment of animals in confinement have come under increased scrutiny of animal welfare/animal rights groups all over the world.

Animal welfarists see many modern practices as unnatural, and not conducive to the welfare of animals. In general, they construe animal welfare as the well-being, health, and happiness of animals; and they believe that certain intensive production systems are cruel and should be outlawed. The animal rightists go further; they maintain that humans are animals, too, and that all animals should be accorded the same moral protection. They contend that animals have essential physical and behavioral requirements, which, if denied, lead to privation, stress, and suffering; and they conclude that all animals have the right to live.

Equestrians know that abuse of horses in intensive/confinement systems leads to lowered performance and income—a case in which decency and profits are on the same side of the ledger. They recognize that husbandry that reduces labor and housing costs often results in physical and social conditions that increase animal problems. Nevertheless, means of reducing behavioral and environmental stress are needed so that decreased labor and housing costs are not offset by losses in productivity. The welfarists/rightists counter with the claim that the evaluation of animal welfare must be based on more than productivity; they believe that there should be behavioral, physiological, and environmental evidence of well being, too. And so the arguments go!

But wild horses were often more severely stressed than domesticated horses. They didn't have caretakers to store feed for winter or to irrigate during droughts; to provide protection against storms, extreme temperatures, and predators; and to control diseases and parasites. Often survival was grim business. In America, the entire horse population died out during the Pleistocene Epoch. Fossil remains prove that members of the horse family roamed the plains of America (especially the area that is now known as the Great Plains of the United States) during most of tertiary period, beginning about 58 million years ago. Yet no horses were present on this continent when Columbus discovered America in 1492. Why they perished, only a few thousand years before, is still one of the unexplained mysteries. As the disappearance was so complete and so sudden, many scientists believe that it must have been caused by some contagious disease or some fatal parasite. Others feel that perhaps it was due to multiple causes, including (1) climatic changes, (2) competition, and/or failure to adapt. Regardless of why horses disappeared, it is known that conditions

Fig. 16-30. Horses that are kept for recreation and sport are generally showered with love and affection. This shows the Norwegian Fjord Horse, *Evon*, ridden by Jennifer Jo Hansen, owned by Joe and Meg Hempel, Skoal Farm, Gilmanton Iron Works, NH. (Courtesy, Norwegian Fjord Horse Registry, Acworth, NJ)

were favorable to them at the time of their reestablishment by the Spanish conquistadors about 500 years ago.

To all equine caretakers, the principles and application of animal behavior and environment depend on understanding; and on recognizing that they should provide as comfortable an environment as feasible for their horses, for both humanitarian and economic reasons. This requires that attention be paid to environmental factors that influence the behavioral welfare of their animals as well as their physical comfort, with emphasis on the two most important influences of all in animal behavior and environment—feed and confinement.

Animal welfare issues tend to increase with urbanization. Moreover, fewer and fewer urbanites have farm backgrounds. As a result, the animal welfare gap between town and country widens. Also, both the news media and the legislators are increasingly informed from urban centers. It follows that the urban views that are propounded will have greater and greater impact in the years ahead.

■ **Commercial Transportation of Equine for Slaughter Act**—In 1996, Congress passed this Act as part of the Farm Bill. The legislation provides the Secretary of Agriculture with the authority to regulate individuals regularly engaged in the business of transporting equines to slaughter facilities. According to the Act, in writing regulations the Secretary shall review, among other issues, the feed, water, and rest provided to equines in transit, and the segregation of stallions from other equines. The Secretary may also require transporters to maintain appropriate records and reports, conduct such investigations and inspections as necessary, and establish and enforce appropriate and effective civil penalties. It does not authorize the Secretary to regulate the routine and regular transportation of horses not being transported to slaughter. In brief, the Act gives the Secretary of Agriculture the authority to develop sound regulations that will protect the well-being of horses transported for slaughter.

SELECTED REFERENCES

Title of Publication	Author(s)	Publisher
Agricultural Waste Utilization and Management, Proceedings	F. J. Humenik, Chairman Executive Committee	American Society of Agricultural Engineers, St. Joseph, MI, 1985
Agriculture and Groundwater Quality	P. F. Pratt, Chairman	Council for Agricultural Sciences and Technology, Ames, IA, 1985
Agriculture and the Environment in a Changing World Economy	Report	The Conservation Foundation, Washington, DC, 1986
Animal Behavior, Second Edition	J. P. Scott	The University of Chicago Press, Chicago, IL, 1972
Animal Behavior, Third Edition	V. G. Dethier E. Stellar	Prentice-Hall, Inc., Englewood Cliffs, NJ, 1970
Animal Behavior	N. Tinbergen	Time Incorporated, New York, NY, 1965
Animal Behavior and Its Application	D. V. Ellis	Lewis Publishers, Inc., Chelsea, MI, 1986
Animal Behavior in Laboratory and Field	A. W. Stokes	W. H. Freeman and Company, San Francisco, CA, 1968
Animal Behavior, The Marvels of	T. B. Allen, Editor	National Geographic Society, Washington, DC, 1972
Animal Behavior: A Synthesis of Ethology and Comparative Psychology	R. A. Hinde	McGraw-Hill Publishing Co., New York, NY, 1970
Animal Wastes	E. P. Taiganides	Applied Science Publishers, Ltd., Fosel, England, 1977
Applied Animal Ethology	W. R. Stricklin, Guest Editor	Elsevier Science Publishers B. V., Amsterdam, The Netherlands, Vol. II, No. 4, Feb., 1984
Behavior of Domestic Animals, The, Third Edition	E. S. E. Hafez, Editor	The Williams and Wilkens Company, Baltimore, MD, 1975
Bibliography of Livestock Waste Management	J. R. Miner D. Bundy G. Christenbury	Office of Research and Monitoring, U.S. Environmental Protection Agency, Washington, DC, 1972
Biology of Stress In Farm Animals: an integrative approach	P. R. Wiepkema P. W. M. van Adrichem	Kluwer Academic Publishers, Hingham, MA, 1987
"Brazil's Imperiled Rain Forest, Rondonia's Settlers Invade"	W. S. Ellis	National Geographic, Vol. 174, No. 6, pp. 772-799, Dec., 1988
Care and Training of the Trotter and Pacer	J. C. Harrison, *et al.*	The United States Trotting Association, Columbus, OH, 1970
Development and Evolution of Behavior	Ed. by L. R. Aronson, *et al.*	W. H. Freeman and Company, San Francisco, CA, 1970
Domestic Animal Behavior	J. V. Craig	Prentice-Hall, Inc., Englewood Cliffs, NJ, 1981

Dust in the Animal Environment	H. F. Honey J. B. Puitty	Department of Agricultural Engineering, University of Alberta, Edmonton, 1976
Effect of Environment on Nutrient Requirements of Animals	D. R. Ames, Chairman	NRC, National Academy Press, Washington, DC, 1981
Effects of Air Temperature, Air Humidity, and Air Movement On Heat Loss from the Pig	T. Kamada I. Notsuki	Proc. 3rd AAAP Anim. Sci. Cong. 2:1174, Seoul, S. Korea, 1985
Elements of Environmental Health	D. F. Newton	Charles E. Narrill Pub. Co., Columbus, OH, 1974
Environmental and Functional Engineering of Agricultural Buildings	H. J. Barre L. L. Sammet G. L. Nelson	Van Nostrand Reinhold Co., New York, NY, 1988
Environmental Biology	P. L. Altman D. S. Dittmer	Federation of American Societies for Experimental Biology, Bethesda, MD, 1966
Environmental Control for Agricultural Buildings	M. L. Esmay J. E. Dixon	The AVI Publishing Company, Inc., Westport, CT, 1986
Environmental Management in Animal Agriculture	S. E. Curtis	Animal Environment Services, Mahomet, IL, 1981
Environmental Quality	R. W. Peterson, Chairman	U.S. Government Printing Office, Washington, DC, 1976
Ethology of Free-Ranging Domestic Animals	G. W. Arnold M. L. Dudzinski	Elsevier Scientific Publishing Company, Amsterdam, The Netherlands, 1978
Ethology: The Biology of Behavior, Second Edition	I. Eibl-Eibesfeldt	Holt, Rinehart, and Winston, New York, NY, 1975
Farm Animal Manures: an overview of their role in the agricultural environment	J. Azevedo P. R. Stout	Agricultural Publications, University of California, Berkeley, CA, 1974
First Horse	R. Hapgood	Chronicle Books, San Francisco, CA, 1972
Groundwater Protection	The Conservation Foundation	The Conservation Foundation, Washington, DC, 1987
Guide to Environmental Research on Animals, A	R. G. Yeck, Chairman	NRC, National Academy of Sciences, Washington, DC, 1971
Health Issues Related to Chemicals in the Environment: A Scientific Perspective	A. L. Craigmill, Chairman	Council for Agricultural Sciences and Technology, Ames, IA, 198
Impact of Stress, The, Proceedings	Ed. by R. E. Moreng	Colorado State University, Ft. Collins, CO, 1986
Introduction to Animal Behavior, An,: ethology's first century, Second Edition	P. H. Klopfer	Prentice-Hall, Inc., Englewood-Cliffs, NJ, 1974
Kinships of Animals and Man	A. H. Morgan	McGraw-Hill Book Company, Inc., New York, NY, 1955
Livestock Behaviour, a practical guide	R. Kilgour C. Dalton	Westview Press, Boulder, CO, 1984
Livestock Environment, Proceedings, Second International Livestock Environment Symposium	D. S. Bundy, Planning Chairman	American Society of Agricultural Engineers, St. Joseph, MI, 1982
Managing Livestock Wastes	Proceedings	American Society of Agricultural Engineers, St. Joseph, MI, 1975

Manure Gases in the Animal Environment	G. A. Nordstrom J. B. McPuitty	University of Alberta, Edmonton, Alberta, 1976
Marvels & Mysteries of Our Animal World		Reader's Digest Association, Pleasantville, NY, 1964
Mechanisms of Animal Behavior	P. Parler W. J. Hamilton, III	John Wiley & Sons, New York, NY, 1966
NFEC Directory of Environmental Information Sources	M. M. Kessler C. E. Thibeau P. W. Taligberro	National Foundation for Environmental Control, Boston, MA, 1972
Organic Farming: current technology and its role in a sustainable agriculture	D. M. Kral, Editor	American Society of Agronomy, Madison, WI, 1984
Our Friendly Animals and Whence They Came	K. P. Schmidt	M. A. Donohue & Co., Chicago, IL, 1938
Portraits in the Wild	C. Moss	Houghton Mifflin Company, Boston, MA, 1975
Principles of Animal Behavior	W. N. Tavolga	Harper & Row, New York, NY, 1969
Principles of Animal Environment	M. L. Esmay	The AVI Publishing Company, Inc., Westport, CT, 1978
Readings in Animal Behavior	T. E. McGill, Editor	Holt, Rinehart and Winston, New York, NY, 1973
Saddle Up!	C. E. Ball	J. B. Lippincott Co., Philadelphia, PA, 1970
Safe and Effective Use of Pesticides, The	P. J. Marer	University of California, Publications, Oakland, CA, 1988
Scientific Aspects of the Welfare of Food Animals	F. H. Baker, Chairman	Council for Agricultural Science and Technology, Ames, IA, 1981
Social Hierarchy and Dominance	Ed. by M. W. Schein	Dowden, Hutchinson & Ross, Inc., Stroudsburg, PA, 1975
Social Space for Domestic Animals	R. Zayan, Editor	Kluwer Academic Publishers, Hingham, MA, 1985
Social Structure in Farm Animals	G. J. Syme L. A. Syme	Elsevier Scientific Publishing Co., Amsterdam, The Netherlands, 1979
Stress Physiology in Livestock Vol. 1, Basic Principles Vol. 2, Ungulates Vol. 3, Poultry	M. K. Yousef	CRC Press, Inc., Boca Raton, FL, 1985
Structures and Environment Handbook		Midwest Plan Service, Iowa State University, Ames, IA, 1972
Training the Arabian Horse	H. H. Reese	The Cruse Publishing Company, Inc., Fort Collins, CO, 1961
Training Horses for Races	G. W. Meredith	Constable and Company Ltd., London, England, 1926
Training the Quarter Horse Jumper	H. P. Levings	A. S. Barnes & Co., Inc., Cranbury, NJ, 1968
Training Tips for Western Riders	L. N. Sikes	The Texas Horseman Company, Houston, TX, 1960
Understanding and Training Horses	A. J. Ricci	J. B. Lippincott Co., Philadelphia, PA, 1964
Utilization, Treatment, and Disposal of Waste on Land, Proceedings	E. C. A. Runge, President of Society	Soil Science Society of America, Inc., Madison, WI, 1986

Western Equitation, Horsemanship and Showmanship	D. Stewart	Vantage Press, New York, NY, 1973
Western Horse Behavior & Training	R. W. Miller	Doubleday & Company, Inc., Garden City, NY, 1975
Wild Animals in Captivity	H. Hediger	Dover Publications, Inc., New York, NY, 1964

Horses adapt to cold weather by (1) growing more hair, (2) increasing thyroid activity, and (3) consuming more feed. (Courtesy, Thoroughbred Publications, Inc., Lexington, KY)

Western Pleasure Horses. *Left:* Lee Brown and *Two T Choctaw. Right:* William Brown and *PCG Skip Shi Sequel.* (Courtesy, Mike Carter Quarter Horses, Goodlettsville, TN)

17

HORSEMANSHIP[1]

[1]This chapter was authoritatively reviewed by, and suggestions were received from, Miss Carla Wennberg, who has expertise in both English and Western riding. Miss Wennberg is a member of the staff in the Equine Science Program at Colorado State University, Fort Collins, Colorado.

416

Riding has become increasingly popular in recent years because it offers pleasant and helpful outdoor recreation, beneficial to both body and mind. Furthermore, it is a sport that can be indulged in at any time by those who like it. Also, it can be enjoyed alone or with groups. Nor is it confined to any age, rank, or profession. Business executives value riding because they can get vigorous exercise and obtain relaxation from professional troubles. A good horse is companion enough, is always good humored, and has no worries or business troubles to talk about.

Women can ride at such times as may suit their convenience. Children build character through riding, automatically acquiring confidence, self-control, and patience—all through companionship with their good friend and stout companion, the horse.

For greatest enjoyment, one should learn to ride correctly. It is an unfortunate truth that many people think they can ride if only they can stick on a horse. Although these same people may pay well for instruction in golf, swimming, tennis, and other sports, it never occurs to them that a competent riding instructor may be essential in learning to ride. The word competent is used with reference to riding instructor; for, what is even more tragic, many people think that they are qualified to instruct others as soon as they have learned a few things about riding.

Equitation is a very difficult subject to teach. In the first place, no two horses nor two riders are alike. Then there is hardly any limit to the types of available equipment, and there are the different gaits; and, in addition, riding to hounds and riding on a city bridle path present entirely different problems. Moreover, riding cannot be taught by merely reading a set of instructions. It can be mastered only after patient practice under a competent instructor. The amateur, therefore, should be under no illusions about achieving horsemanship and horsemastership merely through reading what follows. Rather, it is proposed to present here some of the basic principles of equitation and information pertaining to equipment, with the hope that beginners may better understand the why and wherefore of the instructions given them. Also, through reading this presentation it is hoped that the experienced equestrian may be less likely to suffer relapse.

It must be recognized also that there are many schools of riding, and each riding instructor will proceed along different lines. Yet, the end result will always be the same—training riders to get the maximum pleasure with the least exertion to themselves and their mounts. Regardless of the method of instruction, the first requisite is that of instilling confidence in the amateur. Confidence is usually obtained through first becoming familiar with the horse and equipment and then by riding a gentle and obedient horse at the walk in an enclosed ring, while keeping the mount under control at all times.

In instructing the beginner, the author favors a simple approach of first becoming familiar with the horse and equipment and then learning to use that equipment properly. Knowledge of correct grooming and care of the horse, care of equipment, saddling and bridling, and leading is also essential.

SELECTION OF THE MOUNT

The mount should be carefully selected by a competent person. In addition to obtaining a sound horse of desirable conformation, one should give the following points careful consideration:

1. The mount should be purchased within a price range that the rider can afford.

2. The amateur or child should have a quiet, gentle, well-broken horse that is neither headstrong nor unmanageable. The horse should never be too spirited for the rider's skill. It is best that the beginner select a horse (a) with manners, rather than looks, and (b) that is older, rather than a two- or three-year-old.

3. The size of the horse should be in keeping with the size and weight of the rider. Very small children should have a small horse or pony, whereas a heavy person should have a horse of the weight-carrying type. An exceedingly tall rider also looks out of place if not mounted on a horse with considerable height.

4. Usually the novice will do best to start with a three-gaited horse and first master three natural gaits before attempting to ride a horse executing the more

Fig. 17-1. The mount should be selected carefully for the individual rider—keeping in mind (1) the purchase price that the rider can afford, (2) the skill of the rider, (3) the size of the rider, and (4) the type of work to be performed. (Courtesy, International Arabian Horse Assn., Denver, CO)

complicated five gaits, should a five-gaited horse be desired.

5. Other conditions being equal, the breed and color of horse may be decided on the basis of preference.

6. When one wants a horse that is to be used for business purposes—an animal such as is desired by ranchers—the mount should be well suited to the type of work to be performed.

7. Before buying, take every possible precaution to avoid a horse that has undesirable traits or vices; question the owner, and observe the horse in its stall and when being ridden.

After the horse has been selected, it is important that it and the rider become acquainted with each other. Just as every automobile driver knows the major parts of a car—the steering wheel, tires, wheels, hood, fenders, windows, etc.—the rider should be familiar with the important parts of a horse. This information may be secured by studying Fig. 4-1 in Chapter 4.

TACK

Each horse should have its own saddle, bridle, halter, and lead shank. Then, the equipment can be adjusted to fit the particular horse.

Equipment should be selected so as to suit the intended purpose, as well as to fit both the horse and the rider. As in buying almost anything—food, a suit of clothes, and whatnot—you generally get what you pay for. In the long run, it is usually cheaper to buy superior quality tack. Then, by taking good care of it, one can derive satisfaction for many years.

The sections that follow give pertinent facts about some common tack items.

BITS

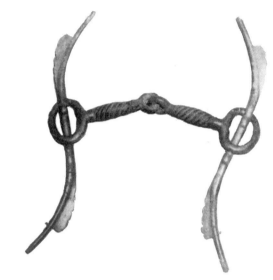

Fig. 17-3. Gold-gilded, winged snaffle bit, made and used 113 B.C., in Western Han Dynasty. On display in the Exhibit of Cultural Relics, Peking, China. (Photo by A. H. Ensminger)

The bit is the most important part of the bridle; in fact, the chief use of the bridle is to hold the bit in its place in the horse's mouth. There are more types of bits than of any other article of horse equipment. In this connection, it is interesting to note that the snaffle bit—which is still the most widely used of all varieties—was the first type to which historians make reference, having been developed by the early Greek equestrians. The bit provides communication between the hands of the rider or driver and the mouth of the horse.

Figs. 17-4, 17-5, and 17-6 show the common types of bits. It must be remembered, however, that there is hardly any limit to the number of variations in each of these kinds of bits.

The proper fit and adjustment of the bit is most essential, regardless of type. It should rest easily in the mouth, being sufficiently wide so as not to pinch the cheeks or cause wrinkles in the corners of the mouth. As a rule, curb-type bits rest lower in the mouth than the snaffle. All bits should be supplied with large rings or other devices to prevent them from passing through the mouth when either rein is drawn in turning.

Fig. 17-2. Western tack. Elizabeth Ross on Western Pleasure Horse. Matching sand pants, chaps, and gloves with taupe boots and a buckskin hat make this a striking outfit with a sorrel horse. (Courtesy, *The Quarter Horse Journal*, Amarillo, TX)

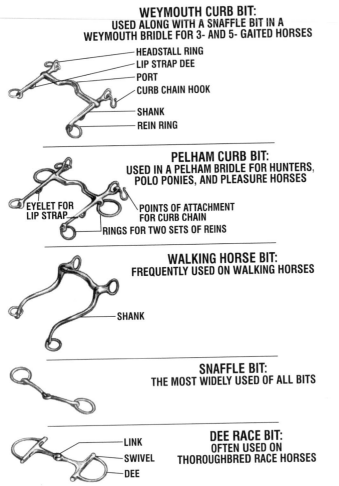

WEYMOUTH CURB BIT:
USED ALONG WITH A SNAFFLE BIT IN A
WEYMOUTH BRIDLE FOR 3- AND 5- GAITED HORSES

- HEADSTALL RING
- LIP STRAP DEE
- PORT
- CURB CHAIN HOOK
- SHANK
- REIN RING

PELHAM CURB BIT:
USED IN A PELHAM BRIDLE FOR HUNTERS,
POLO PONIES, AND PLEASURE HORSES

EYELET FOR LIP STRAP
POINTS OF ATTACHMENT FOR CURB CHAIN
RINGS FOR TWO SETS OF REINS

WALKING HORSE BIT:
FREQUENTLY USED ON WALKING HORSES

- SHANK

SNAFFLE BIT:
THE MOST WIDELY USED OF ALL BITS

- LINK
- SWIVEL
- DEE

DEE RACE BIT:
OFTEN USED ON
THOROUGHBRED RACE HORSES

Fig. 17-4. Five common types of English riding bits, and the parts of each.

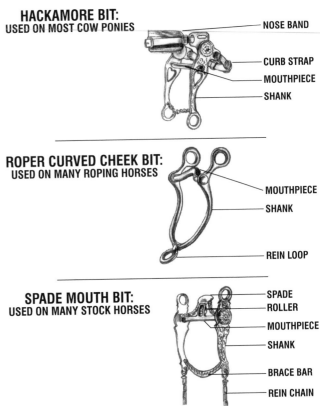

HACKAMORE BIT:
USED ON MOST COW PONIES

- NOSE BAND
- CURB STRAP
- MOUTHPIECE
- SHANK

ROPER CURVED CHEEK BIT:
USED ON MANY ROPING HORSES

- MOUTHPIECE
- SHANK
- REIN LOOP

SPADE MOUTH BIT:
USED ON MANY STOCK HORSES

- SPADE
- ROLLER
- MOUTHPIECE
- SHANK
- BRACE BAR
- REIN CHAIN

Fig. 17-5. Three common types of Western riding bits, and the parts of each.

The following additional points are pertinent to bits:

1. The snaffle bit is usually used when starting a horse in training.

2. The hunting (or egg butt) snaffle is used on hunters and jumpers.

3. The curb bit is a more severe bit, which may be used either alone or with a snaffle bit.

4. The Pelham bit is one bit, which is used with two reins and a curb chain. It is a combination of a snaffle and a curb bit and is used in park or pleasure riding and hunting.

5. The Weymouth bit, along with a snaffle bit, is known as a bit and bradoon.

6. Western bits are made similar to the curb bit, but they have longer shanks and are larger. They are usually used with a leather curb strap, although a leather curb strap with a small amount of chain in the middle is sometimes used.

BRIDLES AND HACKAMORES

Light bridles and bits usually indicate competent equestrians and well-mannered horses. Bridles may be either single or double. A single bridle is equipped with one bit, whereas a double bridle is ordinarily equipped with both a snaffle and a curb bit, two headstalls, and two pairs of reins. Only one rein is used with Western bridles.

All bridles should be properly fitted, and the headstall should be located so that it neither slides back on the horse's neck nor pulls up against the ears. The cheek straps should be adjusted in length so that the bit rests easily in the mouth without drawing up the corners; and the throat latch should be buckled loosely enough to permit the hand, when held in a vertical position, to pass between it and the horse's throat.

Both the bosal hackamore and the hackamore bit bridle are used as a training device for Western horses and on horses with tender mouths. The bosal hackamore consists of an ordinary headstall which holds in place a braided rawhide or rope noseband knotted under the horse's jaw, and a pair of reins. It is an excellent device for controlling and training a young horse without injuring its mouth. The hackamore is used extensively on the western ranges in the

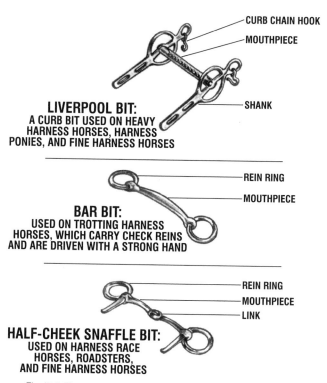

LIVERPOOL BIT:
A CURB BIT USED ON HEAVY HARNESS HORSES, HARNESS PONIES, AND FINE HARNESS HORSES

CURB CHAIN HOOK
MOUTHPIECE
SHANK

BAR BIT:
USED ON TROTTING HARNESS HORSES, WHICH CARRY CHECK REINS AND ARE DRIVEN WITH A STRONG HAND

REIN RING
MOUTHPIECE

HALF-CHEEK SNAFFLE BIT:
USED ON HARNESS RACE HORSES, ROADSTERS, AND FINE HARNESS HORSES

REIN RING
MOUTHPIECE
LINK

Fig. 17-6. Three common types of driving bits, and the parts of each.

training of cow ponies, and is used equally widely in the early training of polo ponies.

When properly adjusted, the hackamore should rest on the horse's nose, about 4 in. from the top of the nostrils (or a little below the base of the cheekbones of the horse's head). It should also permit the passage of two finger breadths between it and the branches of the jaw.

The hackamore bridle bit is a "fake" bit—it has the shanks on each side, but there is no mouthpiece.

Figs. 17-7 and 17-8 show the most common types of bridles and hackamores. The type of bridle and bit or hackamore will depend on the horse's previous training and intended use.

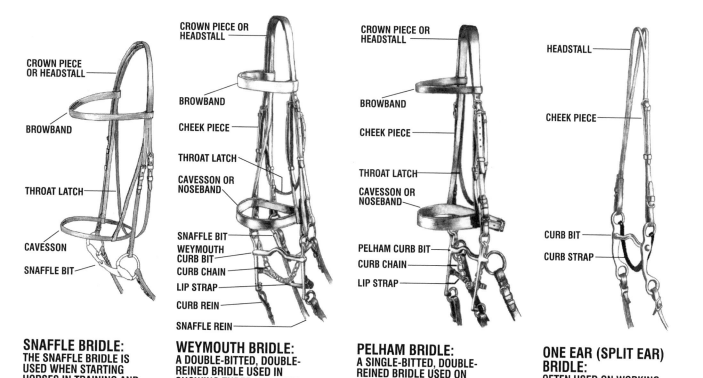

SNAFFLE BRIDLE:
THE SNAFFLE BRIDLE IS USED WHEN STARTING HORSES IN TRAINING AND ON MANY SPORT HORSES

WEYMOUTH BRIDLE:
A DOUBLE-BITTED, DOUBLE-REINED BRIDLE USED IN SHOWING THREE- AND FIVE-GAITED SADDLE HORSES

PELHAM BRIDLE:
A SINGLE-BITTED, DOUBLE-REINED BRIDLE USED ON HUNTERS, POLO PONIES, AND PLEASURE HORSES

ONE EAR (SPLIT EAR) BRIDLE:
OFTEN USED ON WORKING STOCK HORSES

Fig. 17-7. Four types of bridles, and the parts of each.

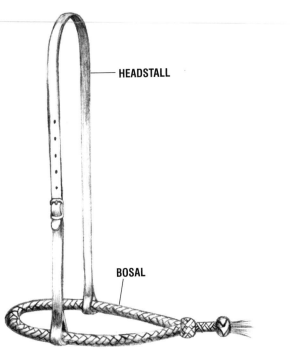

BOSAL HACKAMORE:
POPULAR FOR BREAKING HORSES

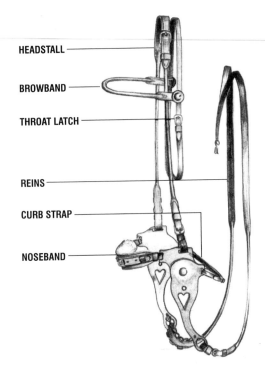

HACKAMORE BIT BRIDLE (REMOVABLE MOUTHPIECE):
USED ON WESTERN COW PONIES, AND ON YOUNG HORSES
WHEN THEY ARE BEING BROKEN, BECAUSE IT ELIMINATES
THE POSSIBILITY OF INJURING THE MOUTH

Fig. 17-8. Two types of hackamores, and the parts of each.

SADDLES

Horses were ridden long before there were saddles. The so-called *horse cloth* was first used about 800 B.C., but the use of saddles with trees did not exist until the 4th century A.D. Anne of Bohemia is credited with introducing the ladies' sidesaddle in the latter part of the 14th century.

Although considerable styling and individuality exist, the English saddle and the Western saddle are the two most common types.

ENGLISH SADDLE

The English saddle includes the flat type of saddle in which certain modifications are made specifically to adapt them for use in pleasure riding, training, racing, jumping, and polo. The English saddle is characterized by its relatively flat seat and its generally light construc-

tion. Its advocates claim that its use is a mark of distinction of the finished rider, as it permits the best in riding form, skill, and balance.

The following additional points are pertinent to the use of English saddles:

1. For show horses, use a white web or linen girth with the saddle.

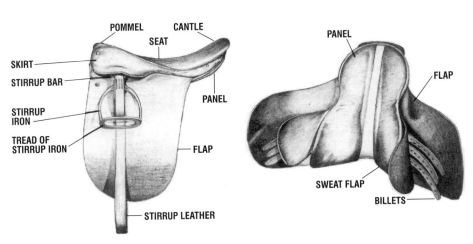

Fig. 17-9. An English saddle, and its parts. *Left:* upright position; *right:* underside.

2. Saddle blankets are usually not necessary.

3. For English pleasure riding or showing, select an English saddle; then use a double bit or Pelham bridle.

4. For hunting or jumping, use a forward seat English saddle, with a bridle having a hunting snaffle or Pelham bit.

WESTERN SADDLE

Western saddles were first developed and used by the Spaniards in Old Mexico. They constructed them with horns, and they liked them roomy, heavy, and ornate. Subsequently, American ranchers made some changes; they lightened them and made them less cumbersome, and they added the high pommel and swelled fork—better to provide extra leg grip should the horse buck or rear.

The Western saddle is the common saddle used by the cowboy. The essential features are: a steel, light metal, or wooden tree; a pommel varying in height and surmounted with a horn for roping; a comparatively deep seat; a cantle varying in height (the variation in the height of the pommel and cantle is determined by the uses to which the saddle is to be put and the personal preference of the rider); heavy square, or round, skirts; double cinch (though a single cinch may be used); and heavy stirrups that may be either hooded or open. This is primarily a work saddle and is designed to afford comfort for all-day riding and to provide enough strength to stand up under the strain of calf roping. The Western saddle often has strong appeal to the novice because it is the saddle of the romantic, adventurous cowboy and because its deep seat and heavy construction impart a feeling of security. Some riders claim that for pleasure riding, the Western saddle is too heavy, is hot in summer, and offers too much temptation to "pull leather" as a substitute for skill and balance. The average Western saddle weighs from 35 to 40 lb, but they may range up to 65 or 70 lb.

Additional pertinent facts about Western saddles are:

1. They're used for Western riding of all kinds, both work and pleasure.

2. Western saddles are utilitarian. They're designed to provide all-day comfort, and the horn is a convenient and secure post around which the lariat can be tied or quickly wound when handling cattle.

3. The design of Western saddles—especially of pommel and cantle—is determined by use and personal preference.

Westerners take pride in their saddles. To them, they're much more than something to throw over a horse's back, or to use in working cattle. They're symbolic of the development of the range, of trailing, and of the transition from the Texas longhorn to the

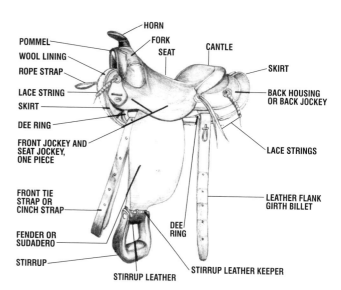

Fig. 17-10. A Western saddle and its parts.

prime bullock. Most makes and styles of Western saddles are accorded meaningful names, with such selections suggestive of their historical significance, their construction, and/or their use.

To reputable manufacturers and proud owners alike, the names of Western saddles are symbols of service, pledges of integrity, and assurances of courage, character, and wisdom.

HARNESS

It is not within the scope of this book to cover all types and parts of harness. But some conception of the subject may be obtained by studying Figs. 17-11 and 17-12, showing the standard harness and rigging used on trotters and pacers.

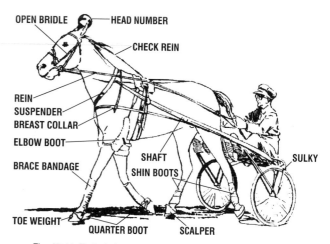

Fig. 17-11. Trotter's harness and rigging. (Courtesy, The United States Trotting Assn., Columbus, OH)

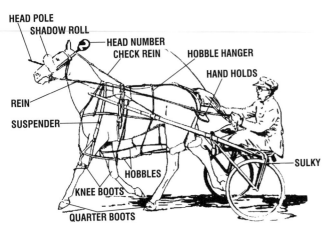

Fig. 17-12. Pacer's harness and rigging. (Courtesy, The United States Trotting Assn., Columbus, OH)

HORSE-DRAWN VEHICLES

Primitive people made much use of saddle horses and pack-horses before the carriage came into general use. Also, primitive sliding vehicles preceded the use of wheels. The coming of the wheel made as big an impact on civilization as did the internal combustion engine years later. The Egyptians are believed to have been the original makers of wheels; the first vehicles were probably the wagons and chariots referred to in the old testament.

The earliest carriage, still in perfect condition, to be found today is the State Chariot of Tutankhamen (1361–1352 B.C.) in the Cairo Museum, in Egypt. The first known carriage to be built in Great Britain was made by William Rippon for the second Earl of Rutland in 1555.

Originally, horse-drawn vehicles evolved to meet practical needs, following which they were embellished to meet individual tastes. There was the dignified family carriage with the fringe on top; the buckboard with its jump seat—the pickup truck of grandfather's time; the governess cart, with its door at the rear and two seats facing each other; the high two-wheeled dog cart, for transporting hounds to the hunt; the high-seated rig of the society matron; the old-fashioned top buggy of the country doctor; and the roadster of the young gallant.

The golden age of the carriage arrived in the 18th century. Many different styles of vehicles were built. The high phaeton was a popular vehicle of the period. Later, it was succeeded by the pony phaeton—a long, low vehicle. The names of different types of carriages often came from the name of the builder or the place in which they were made. Although carriages were built throughout the world, it was generally accepted that French and British carriage builders were the masters of their craft.

Even hitches evolved for practical reasons. Tandem driving, for example, was originated by the hunters of Old England. Wishing to spare their hunting mount as they traveled to and from the meet, these ingenious fox hunters devised the method of driving it ahead, where it trotted between slack traces, while the horse to the rear did all the work.

Today, most horse-drawn vehicles are used for recreation and sport—drawn by heavy harness horses, fine harness horses, roadsters, or ponies, or are of historical significance only—they are reminiscent of the horse-and-buggy era.

KINDS OF VEHICLES

There are many kinds of horse-drawn vehicles. Table 17-1 shows some appropriate vehicles for different uses. Other types of vehicles are illustrated and described in Figs. 17-14 through 17-18.

Fig. 17-13. A Stanhope Phaeton drawn by two Morgans striding in unison. (Courtesy, The American Morgan Horse Assn., Inc., Shelburne, VT)

TABLE 17-1
APPROPRIATE HORSE-DRAWN VEHICLES

Use	Breed	Appropriate Vehicle	Comments
Racing:	Standardbred Shetland	Sulky; a light vehicle with bicycle wheels. 	The pneumatic tire racing sulky was first introduced in 1892. Sulkies weigh from 29 to 37 lb, and usually have hardwood shafts, although aluminum and steel sulkies have been introduced in recent years.
Roadster: Horses	Standardbred, predominately; although other breeds may be used.	Cart or bike; buggy or road wagon. 	Roadster vehicles must be attractive and light, but strong.
Ponies		(same as above)	
Hackney (or heavy harness horses): Horses	Hackney	Viceroy, miniature side rail buggy of type used for fine harness horses, or gig. Tandem Hackneys may be shown with either a 2- or 4-wheeled vehicle; a gig or viceroy.	The vehicles pulled by Hackneys are of heavy construction, elegant design, and devoid of shiny parts.
Ponies		(same as above)	
Fine Harness: Horses	American Saddlebred, predominately; although other breeds are also used.	Preferably a small side rail buggy with 4 wire wheels, but without a top.	A fine harness horse is exactly what the name implies—a fine horse presented in fine harness. The entire ensemble is elegant and represents the ultimate in grace and charm.
Ponies	Hackney, Welsh, Shetland	(same as above)	
Pleasure driving	Any breed.	Any 2-wheeled or 4-wheeled vehicle. 	In olden times, the buckboard was usually a one-seater with a bed behind.
Breaking or training cart	Any breed.	2-wheeled training cart. 	When training green horses, 2-wheeled training carts should be used, because (1) they are strong and (2) they will not tip over easily.

Fig. 17-14. Four-wheeled dogcart. Dogcarts were so named because they were used for carrying sporting dogs, under the seat. They carried four passengers, back to back, plus the hounds. At first they were two-wheeled. Later, they were built with four wheels. Usually they were pulled by one horse, but the bigger four-wheeled dogcarts sometimes required two horses.

Fig. 17-17. The Victoria. Introduced from the Continent by the Prince of Wales in 1869, where it was known as a milord, the Victoria quickly achieved popularity. Essentially a summer vehicle (it has no doors), the Victoria was much favored by ladies of fashion because of the ease with which the carriage could be entered and the elegant setting for the display of finery. Initially designed for two passengers facing the front, the Victoria was later modified to accommodate four; sometimes there is a rumble seat for a groom. The Victoria is coachman-driven to a single horse or to a pair.

Fig. 17-15. Landau, the convertible of great grandfather's time. It was named after Landau, Germany, where it was first manufactured about 1790. It was a four-wheeled covered carriage with the top divided into two sections. The back section could be let down or thrown back while the front section could be removed or left stationary. Landaus held four people and were usually drawn by two horses. This vehicle was very popular in England from mid-Victorian times onward.

Fig. 17-18. Stagecoach, a heavy, enclosed, four-wheeled vehicle, usually drawn by four horses, formerly used for carrying passengers and goods.

DRIVING CUSTOMS

The history of some driving customs follows.

■ **Heavy harness vehicles**—Heavy harness horses (Hackneys) in horse shows are harnessed with heavy leather and hitched to heavy vehicles. The heavy leather used on these animals was first decreed by fashion in England, where it stemmed from the idea that to drive handsomely one had to drive heavily. In this country, heavy harness horses are reminiscent of the Gay Nineties, when bobtailed Hackneys hitched to high-seated rigs made a dashing picture as they pranced down the avenue.

Vehicles for Hackneys must be of heavy construc-

Fig. 17-16. The park phaeton. The phaeton was a four-wheeled vehicle of which there were many varieties. The early phaetons were built very high. But those of the 19th century were considerably lower and were made in many different shapes and sizes. There was the pony phaeton made in 1824 for King George IV. Then in 1828 came the massive male phaeton driven exclusively by men. Elegant ladies' phaetons followed.

tion, elegant design, and devoid of shiny parts (the latter tends to blind spectators).

■ **Driving to the right**—The American custom of driving to the right on the road, instead of to the left as is the practice in some parts of the world, originated among the Conestoga (named after the Conestoga Valley, a German settlement in Pennsylvania) wagon drivers of the 1750s, who transported freight overland to and from river flatboats and barges along the Ohio, Cumberland, Tennessee, and Mississippi Rivers. The drivers of these four- and six-horse teams either sat on the left wheel horse or on the left side of the seat, the better to wield their whip hand (the right hand) over the other horses in the team. Also, when two Conestoga drivers met, they pulled over to the right so that, sitting on the left wheel horse or on the left side of the seat, they could see that the left wheels of their wagons cleared each other. Lighter vehicles naturally followed the tracks of the big Conestoga wagons. Even with the development of highways and automobiles, the American custom of driving to the right persisted.

Fig. 17-19. World Champion Park Harness Horse, *Carlyle Command.* (Courtesy, The American Morgan Horse Assn., Shelburne, VT)

OTHER TACK

There is hardly any limit to the number of items and adaptations of tack. No attempt is made herein to describe, or even to mention, all of them. However, the most generally used types, in addition to those already described, are covered in the sections that follow.

BLINKERS (BLINDERS OR WINKERS)

Blinkers are an attachment to the bridle or hood, designed to restrict the vision of the horse from the sides and rear and to focus the vision forward. Driving blinkers (or winkers) are made of leather, often with a crest or embellishment on the outside. Racing blinkers are in the form of a hood with leather cups that act as shields.

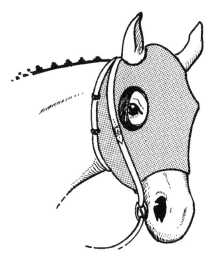

Fig. 17-20. Racing blinkers—a hood with leather cups.

BOOTS (FOR HORSES)

Boots are used to protect the legs or feet against injuries. The most common injuries requiring such protection are those caused (1) by brushing when the inside of the leg, usually on or in the region of the fetlock joint, is knocked by the opposite foot, (2) by overreaching when the hind toes strike into the rear of the foreleg, or (3) by speedy cutting when the inside of the leg is struck high above the joint, usually under the hock. The shins (either front or hind) may also be endangered as a result of striking an obstacle when jumping.

Various types of boots are available to protect the horse from the different kinds of injuries listed above—among them, the quarter boots to prevent bruising of a front heel from a hind toe, worn by five-gaited saddle horses, Tennessee Walking Horses, and harness horses; the shin boots worn by the polo pony to guard cannons from injury by the mallet; and many others.

The quarter boot is a flexible boot attached above the coronet which extends down over the hoof. It is designed to protect the quarter of the front heel from the hind toe.

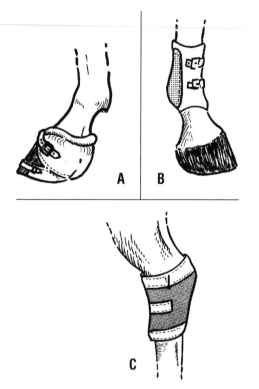

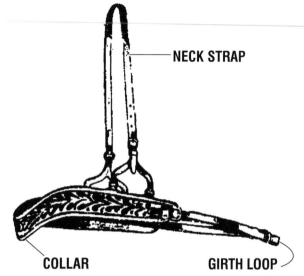

NECK STRAP

COLLAR   **GIRTH LOOP**

Fig. 17-22. The breast collar. It is frequently used on slender-bodied horses and on horses which require some special security to prevent the saddle from slipping to the rear (such as racehorses). The breastplate may be used for the same purposes as the breast collar.

Fig. 17-21. Three types of boots; **A**, quarter boot; **B**, ankle boot; and **C**, hock boot.

CAVESSON

The breaking or longeing cavesson consists of a heavy headstall, except that it has an additional strap known as the *jowl strap*—and a hinged, jointed, heavily padded, metal noseband with a ring at the top for the attachment of the longe. The cavesson (with the longe) is used for exercising, disciplining, and training horses.[2]

HALTER (HEAD COLLAR)

A halter is used for leading a horse or tying it. There are many types of halters made from a number of different materials. The rope halter (formerly made of cotton, now made of nylon) is very strong and inexpensive. It will outlast most leather halters, and it is easy to put on and take off. But care must be taken to fit it loosely, otherwise it will rub the cheekbones.

Leather halters are also widely used. The better ones are mounted with brass. Show halters are of finer, lighter leather than the ordinary stable halter, and usually they have brow bands.

BREASTPLATE; BREAST COLLAR

The breastplate usually consists of a short, wide strap that passes over the neck in front of the withers, two adjustable straps that run from each end of the short strap back to the saddle, two adjustable straps that run down the shoulders to a ring on the breastplate, and another adjustable strap that runs from this ring and attaches to the girth after passing between the forelegs. Sometimes this type is equipped with a strap that runs from the ring on the breastplate to the noseband, and acts as a martingale.

The breast collar serves the same purpose as the breastplate. Fig. 17-22 shows a breast collar.

Either the breastplate or the breast collar is frequently used on slender-bodied horses and on horses which require some special security to prevent the saddle from slipping to the rear (such as racehorses). With both articles, it is important that they be adjusted as loosely as possible consistent with holding the saddle in place, with proper allowance made for motion and movement of the horse's neck.

---

[2]Another type of cavesson is used on many bridles. It consists of a narrow strap around the nose which is held in place by another strap which goes over the head and behind the ears. The cavesson-type bridle was originally designed to prevent the horse from opening its mouth too wide when the reins are pulled, thereby getting away from the discipline of the bit.

Sometimes the novice has difficulty figuring out how to put on a halter. The following procedure will alleviate this problem:

Take the buckle in the left hand and the strap in the right hand, making sure that the three short parallel straps are on the bottom; slip the horse's nose through the noseband; swing the strap over from the far side, place it behind the ears, catch it with the left hand, bring the right hand back, and buckle the strap snugly enough to prevent the horse from getting it over its head.

Never leave the halter on a horse in the pasture. Although a haltered horse may be easier to catch, there is a risk of the halter getting caught on some object and the animal not being able to free itself.

Fig. 17-23. A leather halter.

LONGE (LUNGE)

The longe is a strong light strap (usually made of webbing or leather) about 30 ft long, one end of which is attached by a swivelled snap to the noseband of the cavesson. The young horse can begin training at an early age by means of the longe line. It can be circled to the left and to the right; made to walk, trot, canter, and halt; and trained to get used to and obey words of command. The longe is especially useful for urban raised foals, who are limited in space for exercising on natural footing.

Although young horses can do all kinds of gymnastics without injury when running loose in a corral or pasture, they can be injured by improper use of the longe line. If their head is pulled at the wrong time, or too quickly or too severely, their balance will be destroyed and they may injure a foreleg or foot, throw a curb, or be stifled.

LONGEING WHIP

A typical longeing whip has a stock about 4 ft long and a lash 6 to 8 ft long. It is used when exercising and disciplining the horse in longeing.

MARTINGALES

Martingales are of two types: standing (or sometimes called a tie-down) and running (or ring). The standing martingale consists of a strap which extends from around the girth, between the forelegs, to the noseband and a light neck strap to keep the martingale from getting under the horse's feet when the head is lowered. When properly adjusted, it has the effect of preventing the elevation of the head beyond a certain level without cramping the horse. The standing martingale is most generally employed on saddle horses that rear and on polo ponies and stock horses that endanger their riders by throwing their heads up in response to a severe curb when pulled up sharply. On the other hand, some competent equestrians prefer the use of a running martingale on horses that habitually rear. They feel that the standing martingale sets the head too high.

The running martingale is not attached to the horse's head, but terminates in two rings through which the reins pass. It is used for the same purpose as the standing martingale, but permits more freedom of movement. Thus, it is better adapted to and more frequently used for jumping than the standing martingale.

Proper adjustment of the running martingale is obtained when, with the horse's head in a normal position, the snaffle reins stretched from the pommel form a straight line from bit to pommel.

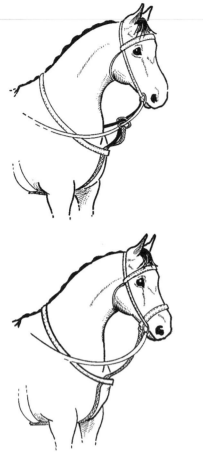

Fig. 17-24. The two types of martingales. *Upper:* standing martingale; also called a tie-down. It is sometimes used on saddle horses that rear and polo ponies and stock horses that endanger their riders by throwing their heads up in response to a severe curb when pulled up sharply. *Lower:* a running martingale. It is used for the same purposes as the standing martingale, but permits more freedom of movement; thus it may be used on jumpers.

after each ride, when the rider uses a balanced seat, and when the mount is properly groomed. When kept clean and when properly used, however, a blanket will prevent a sore back. For this reason, even with English saddles, many good equestrians always insist on the use of a saddle blanket.

A saddle blanket or corona is almost always used with Western saddles.

Felt, mohair, or pad blankets that are adapted to the various types of saddles may be secured. Many good riders even prefer a folded Navajo blanket, with a hair pad inside. The corona is a blanket cut to the shape of the saddle and has a large colorful roll around the edge that is quite showy for use with a stock saddle.

The saddle pad or blanket should be placed well forward on the horse's neck and then slid back into position so as to smooth down the hair. It should come to rest smoothly and in such manner that 2½ to 4 in. of it will show in front of the saddle. After being used, the blanket or pad should be hung up to dry. It then should be brushed thoroughly to eliminate hair and dried sweat.

TWITCH

A twitch is a rope run through the end of a stick, used on the horse's upper lip; it is tightened by twisting in order to attract the horse's attention so it will stand still.

NOSEBAND

The noseband is a wide leather band which passes around the nose below the cheekbones. It is used to keep the mouth shut and the bit in position, as a means for attaching the standing martingale, or to enhance the appearance of the bridle. Heavy harness and most riding bridles are equipped with nosebands. The noseband should be adjusted so that it is about 1½ in. below the cheekbone and loose enough so that two fingers may be placed under it.

SADDLE BLANKET (NUMNAH, PAD, OR CORONA)

With English saddles, saddle blankets are usually not necessary when the saddle is thoroughly cleaned

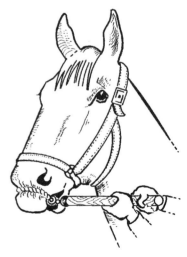

Fig. 17-25. Twitch, used in restraining a horse.

CLOTHES FOR RIDERS

There is hardly any limit to the variety or cost of clothes that may be and are worn by riders. In general, riding attire is utilitarian. Close fitting legs eliminate wrinkles that might cause chafing, and chamois leather lining inside the knees and calves prevents pinching of the muscles of the leg under the stirrup leathers and increases firmness of the leg grip. Boots or jodhpurs protect the ankle from the stirrup iron; and high boots also protect the breeches from being snagged on objects along the trail, shield the trouser leg from the saddle straps and the horse's sides, and protect the legs from rain and cold. For the most comfortable ride, breeches (either regulation or jodhpur type) should be made to order.

Appropriate clothes for riding for the most common occasions are shown in Fig. 17-26 and described in Table 17-2. The time of day, the type of riding horse, and the class in which shown determine the riding attire. In addition to selecting proper clothes, well-groomed and experienced riders place emphasis on fine tailoring, good materials, and proper fit. Also, when saddle horses are being ridden, gaudy colors, excess jewelry, and sequins are to be discouraged except in parade classes.

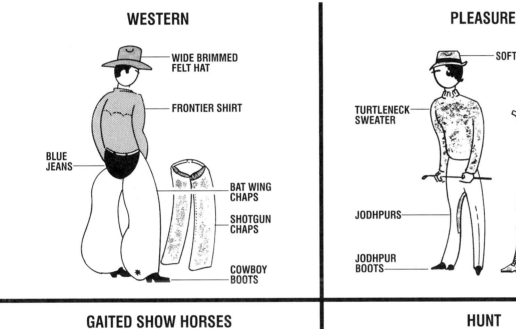

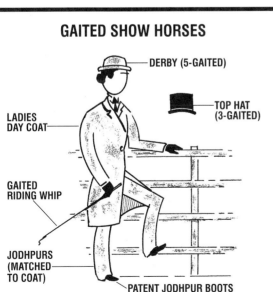

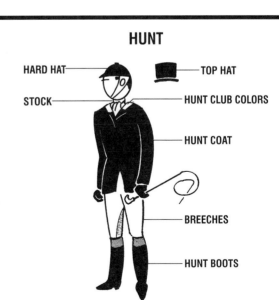

Fig. 17-26. Proper riding attire.

TABLE 17-2

| | Western Riding | Pleasure Classes | | Gaited Show Horse Classes | |
		Informal Park or School Riding, Morning or Afternoon Classes	Semiformal, Afternoon, or Evening Classes	Five-gaited	Three-gaited
Coat	Fitted jacket and vest. Button down shirt and jeans.	Any conservative color, tweeds or checks, usually light in weight.	Gabardine, wool gabardine, or dress worsted, or other menswear materials. Inverted pleats in back. Dark colors preferred. Summer—linen or tropical worsted.	One button, inverted pleats, black or midnight blue tuxedo style riding coat. Gentlemen usually wear dark suits instead of tuxedos. Conservative colors are required. In addition to black and midnight blue, the rider may wear gray, green, beige, or brown.	Tuxedo style in black, dark gray, dark brown, or midnight blue. Soft pastel-colored coats can be worn. White coat in summer. Shawl collar with satin lapels. *Equitation classes:* Must wear (1) dark tuxedo style with silk top hat in evening and (2) matched suit with derby in daytime.
Jodhpurs or breeches	Western cut, bell-bottom pants of gabardine, cotton twill, cavalry twill, or wool; with chaps, shotgun chaps, or chinks. Conservative in color and well tailored.	Jodhpurs of stretch gabardine, whipcord, corduroy, or stretch twill in colors to match or in contrast to coat. Kentucky style—no flare at hip and with bell-bottoms.	Jodhpurs of same material as coat (riding habit). Kentucky style—bell-bottom, no flare at hip and no cuff.	Material and color to match coat.	Material and color to match coat (riding habit). Satin stripe down outside of jods.
Vest	Leather or cloth (optional)	Optional. Light, solid color or tattersall check.	Solid color or tattersall check, to match outfit or to contrast.	Solid colors to match habit.	White pique or cummerbund (optional).
Shirt	Western type; color to match or contrast with Western pants (solid or patterned fabric acceptable). It is trim fitting with long sleeves.	Man's shirt, white or colored, broadcloth or oxford, cloth, or a long-sleeved sweater.	Man's shirt in white or light color to match suit.	Man's shirt.	Formal style, white stiff front tuxedo. Shirt with wing collar and pleated front.
Neckwear	Knotted kerchief; dogger-type tie; choker; or silk scarf tied ascot style and tucked into open neck of shirt.	Contrasting 4-in-hand tie, or bow tie.	Matching or contrasting color man's 4-in-hand tie.	4-in-hand tie, or bow tie.	Black, white, or midnight blue bow tie.
Hat	Western hat; felt or straw; wide brimmed.	A soft Panama hat.	Saddle derby to match suit.	Saddle derby or soft hat.	Silk top hat.
Boots	Western boots.	Black or brown strap or elastic jodhpur boots, casual style.	Black or brown jodhpur boots.	Black patent jodhpur boots with tuxedo; brown or black with a suit.	Black leather or patent leather jodhpur boots.
Gloves	Leather (optional).	Leather gloves to blend with habit (optional).	Leather in a natural shade or to match suit (optional).	Leather to match habit.	Leather to match habit.
Jewelry or other accessories	Hand carved belt and Western belt buckle. Carry a rope or riata. If closed reins are used in trail and pleasure horse classes, hobbles must be carried. Spurs (optional).	Cuff links, tie pin, belt. Spurs of unrowelled type, whip or crop (optional).	Tie clasp, cuff links, belt. Spurs and riding whip (optional).	Cuff links, tie pin, gaited riding whip and spurs (optional).	Formal shirt studs. Walk, trot stick (optional).

Other Occasions:

1. **Side Saddle Forward Seat for Hunting**—Hunting silk hat, hat guard required. Dark melton habit with matching skirt, black boots without tops. Spurs (optional). White or colored rain gloves, neckwear, coat collar, vest, sandwich case and flask same as member of a hunt.

[1]For information on the subject of clothes for riders for specific show classes, see the current (issued yearly) *Rule Book* of the American Horse Shows Association.

CLOTHES FOR RIDERS[1]

Hunting and Jumping

Hunting (informal)	Hunt Seat Equitation	Member of a Hunt (formal)	Jumping
Black oxford or English tweed.	Black (or conservative color) oxford or tweed hunt coat. Conservative wash jacket in season.	Black hunt coat of melton or English cavalry twill. May wear black or midnight blue coat of shadbelly or other cutaway-type scarlet hunt livery. Collar: Same material and color as coat, unless rider has been invited to wear hunt-club colors, in which case collar should conform to hunt livery.	Any color of hunt coat in solid or checks. Jumping attire can be of any informal forward seat type.
Brick, tan, beige, or canary breeches or jods, with peg and cuff.	Buff, brick, or canary breeches.	No-flare, in beige, brick, white, or canary with black coat. *Men:* White breeches with scarlet coat.	No-flare breeches of a contrasting color to coat.
Hunting yellow or tattersal (optional).	Canary with black coat (optional).	Buff or yellow, or hunt colors, if member.	Checkered or solid color.
Stock shirt or ratcatcher in white, light blue, maize, mint, pink, gray, or rust.	Stock shirt.	White stock shirt.	Ratcatcher shirt with stock. Man's shirt.
Choker, stock, or ratcatcher tie.	White stock or choker.	White stock, fastened with plain gold safety pin worn straight across stock.	4-in-hand tie, or stock.
Brown or black hunting derby; hunting cap if 18 years or under, with head harness and sponge rubber head cushion.	Hunting derby; hunting cap if 18 years or under.	Silk or velveteen hunting hat, hat guard required with scarlet coat or black shadbelly. Hunt caps for staff members and juniors. Derby with hat guard with black coat for adults.	Hunting derby, or hunt cap.
Black or brown boots, high or jodhpur.	Black or brown hunt boots.	Regular hunting boots with tabs; black calf. Black patent tops permissible for ladies; brown tops for men on staff.	Black or brown hunting boots.
Brown leather or rain gloves of string.	Optional.	Brown leather or rain gloves of white or yellow string.	Optional.
Stock or choker pin, belt, hunting crop, and spurs with straps to match boots.	Spurs of unrowelled type (optional). Crop or hat (optional). Stock pin worn straight across on stock tie or choker.	Sandwich case and flask. Regulation hunting whip. Spurs of heavy pattern with moderately short neck. Preferably without rowels. Worn high on heel. Boot garter: Plain black or black patent leather with patent leather boot tops. Brown with patent leather boot tops. White with white breeches.	Stock pin, belt, jumping bat, spurs optional.

2. **Side Saddle Show Seat**—Habit of dark blue, black, or oxford gray with matching or contrasting skirt. Black jodhpur boots. Bow tie or 4-in-hand. White shirt. Hard derby. White or pigskin gloves.
3. **Plantation Walking Horses** (Tennessee Walking Horse)—Attire should be same as listed for 3- or 5-gaited. Ladies seldom wear hats; men can wear soft felt.

■ **Western Boots**—Western boots are more than a handsome trademark of the range. They're practical. The high heel is designed to give the wearer protection against losing the stirrups at critical moments; it prevents the foot from slipping through when pressure is applied for quick stops and turns. The top protects the ankles and calves of the legs against inclement weather, brush, insects, and snakes.

Modern Western boots possess two added fea- tures; namely, (1) comfort, and (2) adaptation for walk- ing, so that the wearer can walk without it being a painful experience.

BRIDLING THE HORSE

Bridling is made easy by the procedure that fol- lows.

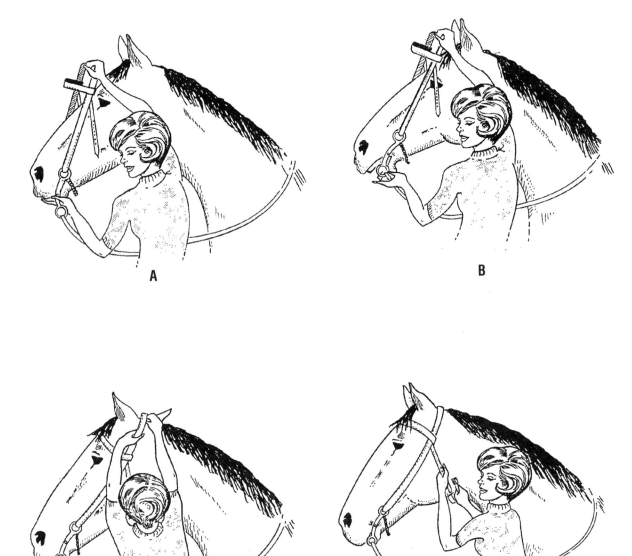

Fig. 17-27. Steps in bridling a horse:

A. Bridle in position—with the nose between the cheek pieces, the crownpiece in front of the ears, and the bit dangling against the teeth.
B. Mouth open.
C. Bridle on, with the bit in mouth and crownpiece over ears.
D. Throatlatch buckled.

Take the crownpiece of the bridle in the left hand and the reins in the right. Approach the horse from the left side opposite the shoulder. With your right hand slip the reins over the head, allowing them to rest on the crest directly behind the ears. Remove the halter—if there is one. Place yourself just behind the horse's head, facing front. Then, step by step, bridle it as follows:

■ **Step A**—Take the crownpiece of the bridle in your right hand and slip the horse's nose between the cheek pieces (and in the cavesson or noseband, if the bridle is so equipped). Raise the bridle with the right hand, until the crownpiece of headstall is just in front of the ears and the bit is dangling against the teeth. With your left hand, cup the horse's chin firmly, holding the bar of the bit across the palm and keeping it against the teeth with your thumb.

■ **Step B**—Slip the ends of your fingers between the horse's lips on the far side and into the animal's mouth. Thereupon, it will open the mouth and curl back the lips.

■ **Step C**—With a quick pull on the crownpiece, bring the bridle into position—that is, the bit in the mouth and the crownpiece slipped over the ears.

■ **Step D**—Buckle the throatlatch.

From these steps and the accompanying figure, the novice should not get the impression that in bridling a horse each step is so distinct and different as to be marked by intermittent pauses. Rather, when properly executed, bridling is a series of rhythmic movements, and the entire operation is done so smoothly and gracefully that it is difficult to discern where one stage ends and the next one begins.

SADDLING THE MOUNT

Regardless of the type of saddle—English or Western—it should be placed on the horse's back so that the girth will come about 4 in. to the rear of the point of the horse's elbow.

When first adjusted, the girth should be loose enough to admit a finger between it and the horse's belly. After tightening the saddle, it is always a good practice to untrack the horse—that is, to lead it ahead several paces before mounting. This procedure serves two purposes: First, if the horse is the kind that "blows up" so that it cannot be cinched snugly, the untracking will usually cause it to relax; and second, if a horse has any bad habits, it will often get them out of its system before the rider mounts.

After the horse has been ridden a few minutes, the girth should always be reexamined and tightened if necessary. The saddle should always be cinched

tightly enough so that it will not turn when the horse is being mounted, but not so tight as to cause discomfort to the horse.

The length of stirrups will depend upon the type of riding. It may vary from very short on running horses to quite long on stock horses. The stirrup leather on English saddles should always be turned so that the flat side of the leather comes against the leg of the rider.

For correct posting, the stirrup straps or stirrup leathers must be adjusted to the right length. If stirrups are too short, posting will be high and exaggerated. For English riding, the stirrups can be adjusted to the approximate correct length before mounting by making them about 1 in. shorter than the length of the rider's arm with fingers extended. When the rider is sitting in the saddle, with the legs relaxed downward and the feet out of the stirrups, the bottom of the stirrup iron should touch just below the ankle bone. For Western riding, the length of stirrups may be considered about right when there is approximately a 3 in. clearance between the saddle tree and the crotch of the mounted rider standing in the stirrups.

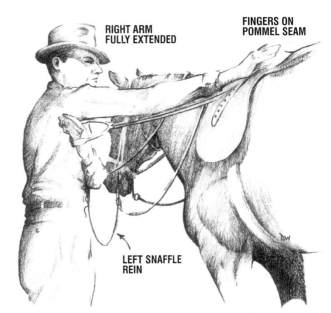

STIRRUP SHOULD JUST REACH INTO RIGHT ARMPIT . . . ADJUST ACCORDINGLY . . . REVERSE ARM ARRANGEMENT WHEN ADJUSTING RIGHT, OR OFF STIRRUP.

Fig. 17-28. Method of checking the stirrup straps of an English saddle for proper length.

MOUNTING AND DISMOUNTING ENGLISH

Before mounting, two precautions should be taken:

always check the cinch (or saddle girth) for tightness and the stirrup straps or leathers for length. A loose girth may let the saddle slip down on the horse's side or belly, especially when one is mounting and dismounting. When the girth is adjusted properly, one should be able to get only the first half of the fingers under it without considerable forcing.

When all precautions have been taken, the steps for mounting and dismounting a horse English style are as follows (see Fig. 17-29).

1. MOUNT FROM LEFT OR "NEAR" SIDE, GATHER REINS IN LEFT HAND, AND PLACE LEFT HAND ON OR JUST IN FRONT OF WITHERS.

2. TURN STIRRUP IRON ONE-QUARTER TURN, STEADY STIRRUP WITH RIGHT HAND AND SHOVE LEFT FOOT INTO IT.

3. HOP OFF THE RIGHT FOOT, SWING AROUND TO FACE THE HORSE, GRASP THE CANTLE (HORN IN WESTERN RIDING) WITH RIGHT HAND, AND SPRING UPWARD UNTIL STANDING POSITION IS REACHED.

4. LEAN ON LEFT ARM, SHIFT RIGHT HAND FROM CANTLE TO POMMEL (USUALLY RIGHT-HAND SIDE OF POMMEL) OF SADDLE; THEN SWING EXTENDED RIGHT LEG OVER HORSE'S BACK AND CROUP.

5. EASE DOWN INTO THE SADDLE; THEN SHOVE RIGHT FOOT INTO RIGHT STIRRUP WITHOUT LOOKING DOWN.

6. SIT EASILY, BE ALERT AND KEEP HEAD UP, AND ALLOW LEGS TO HANG COMFORTABLY WITH HEELS WELL DOWN AND TOES TURNED OUT SLIGHTLY.

7. DISMOUNTING: GATHER REINS IN LEFT HAND, PLACE LEFT HAND ON HORSE'S WITHERS AND RIGHT HAND ON POMMEL, STAND UP IN THE STIRRUPS. THEN PROCEED AS INSTRUCTED IN POINT NUMBER 7 OF THE NARRATIVE.

Fig. 17-29. Diagrams showing the steps in mounting and dismounting a horse English style. (Drawings based on photos made especially for this book by Mrs. Fern P. Bittner, noted equestrian, instructor, horse show manager, and horse show judge.)

1. Always mount from the left or near side of the horse. Stand beside the horse's left front leg and face diagonally toward the croup.[3] Then gather the reins in the left hand, adjusting them so that a gentle pressure (restraining, but not backing the animal) is applied equally on each side of the horse's mouth, and place the left hand on or immediately in front of the horse's withers. Without letting go of the reins, open the fingers of your left hand and get a handful of the horse's mane; this will give you more stability and avoid jerking the horse's mouth.

2. Turn the stirrup iron one-quarter turn toward you, steady the stirrup with the right hand and shove the left into it.

3. Hop off the right foot, swing around to face the horse, grasp the cantle (rear) of the saddle (in Western riding, the right hand is usually placed on the horn instead of the cantle) with the right hand, and spring upward until a standing position is reached, with the leg straight and facing the saddle and the left knee against the horse.

4. Lean on the left arm, shift the right hand from the cantle to the pommel (usually right-hand side of the pommel) of saddle. Then, at the same time, swing the fully extended right leg slowly over the horse's back and croup, being careful not to kick him.

5. Ease down into the saddle; avoid punishing or frightening the horse by suddenly dropping the entire weight of the body into the saddle. Then shove the right foot into the right stirrup without looking down. Adjust both stirrups under the balls of the feet, and simultaneously, gather the reins. Hold the reins as indicated in the section entitled "Holding the Reins."

6. Sit easily in the saddle, be alert and keep the head up, and allow the legs to hang comfortably with the heels well down and the toes turned out slightly. This position permits proper leg contact with the horse and a more secure seat.

7. Essentially, correct *dismounting* is just the reverse of mounting. In succession, the rider should carefully gather the reins in the left hand, place the left hand on the horse's withers and the right hand on the pommel of the saddle, stand up in the stirrups, kick the right foot free from the stirrup, transfer the weight to the left foot as the right leg is swung backward across the horse's back and croup, shift the right hand to the cantle of the saddle (or in Western riding, grasp the horn with the right hand), descend to the ground, and remove the left foot from the stirrup.

---

[3]Another common method of mounting begins with facing the front of the horse while standing opposite the left stirrup. The method given in Point 1 above is considered safer for the beginner, however; for if the horse should start to move as he is being mounted, the rider is automatically swung into the saddle and is not left behind. Also, the person mounting is out of the way of a horse that "cow kicks."

Another accepted way of dismounting from the English saddle consists in removing the left foot from the stirrup and sliding down with relaxed knees. The rider will never get hung in the stirrups when dismounting in this manner, and small children can get off a horse easily and without assistance.

From the above outline the novice should not gain the impression that in mounting and dismounting each step is so distinct and different as to be marked by intermittent pauses. Rather, when properly executed, mounting or dismounting is a series of rhythmic movements, and the entire operation is done so smoothly and gracefully that it is difficult to discern where one stage ends and the next begins.

MOUNTING AND DISMOUNTING WESTERN

Fig. 17-30. Mounting Western.

The steps in mounting a horse in Western riding are as follows: (1) Take the reins in the left hand and place the left hand on the horse's neck in front of the withers; (2) keep the romal or end of the reins on the near side; (3) grasp the stirrup with the right hand and place the left foot in the stirrup with the ball of the foot resting securely on the tread; (4) brace the left knee against the horse, grasp the saddle horn with the right hand, and spring upward and over; and (5) settle into the saddle and slip the right foot into the off stirrup. Dismounting is the same as described for dismounting English (see Point 7), except that, in Western riding, the horn is grasped with the right hand.

HOLDING THE REINS

In English riding, the rider may hold the reins

either in the left hand alone or in both hands. In Western riding, only one hand, usually the left, is permitted, and the hands cannot be changed.

When holding the reins with both hands—as is usual in English show-ring riding and training—toss the bight (ends) of the reins to the right (off) side of the horse's neck; in hunting and jumping, toss the bight to the left.

When holding the reins in one hand, the left for example—as in English style, cross-country riding, or Western riding—the bight should fall to the left side of the horse's neck and the right hand should be dropped loosely down the side or placed comfortably on the thigh of the right leg. The free hand should never be placed on the pommel of an English saddle or on the pommel or horn of a Western saddle.

Figs. 17-31 and 17-32 illustrate better than words the correct methods of holding the reins.

In no case should the rein pressure be more vigorous than absolutely necessary, nor should the reins be used as a means of staying on the horse. A horse's mouth is tender, but it can be toughened by unnecessary roughness. Good hands appear to be in proper rhythm with the head of the horse. Beginners are likely to let the hands bob too much, thus jerking the horse's mouth unnecessarily and using the reins as a means of hanging on to the horse. The desired light hands exist when a light feeling extends to the horse's mouth via the reins.

METHODS OF HOLDING THE REINS ENGLISH STYLE

DOUBLE – REIN BRIDLE

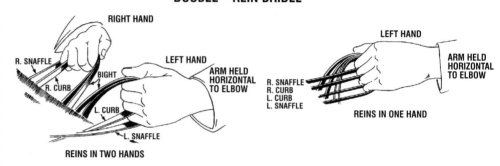

SINGLE – REIN BRIDLE

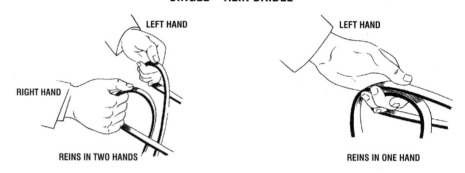

Fig. 17-31. Holding the reins English style. *Top:* double-rein bridle; *bottom:* single-rein bridle.

HOLDING THE REINS WESTERN STYLE

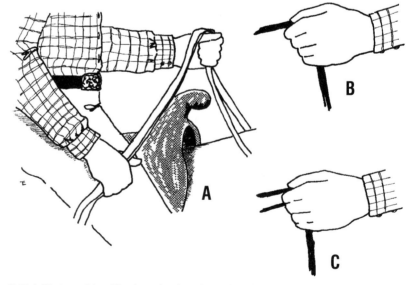

Fig. 17-32. In Western reining, (1) only one hand can be used and hands cannot be changed, and (2) the hand is to be around the reins (as shown in A and B above). When using split reins, one finger between the reins is permitted (as shown in C above).

SEAT

As in any type of sport, correct riding must include rhythm and balance. The rider's movements must be in complete harmony with the horse's movements, for this assures greater security for the rider and freedom of action for the horse.

The balanced seat may be defined as that position of the mounted rider that requires the minimum of muscular effort to remain in the saddle and which interferes least with the horse's movements and equilibrium. In essence, it means that the rider must be *with the horse*, rather than ahead of or behind it. When a balanced seat is maintained, the center of gravity of the rider is directly over the center of gravity of the horse. With the proper seat, the minimum use of the aids will be necessary to get immediate and correct response from the horse at any gait.

The balanced seat is obtained largely through shifting the point of balance of the upper body from the hips up; the knees, legs, ankles, and to a great extent the thighs remain in fixed position. Thus, the degree of forward inclination of the upper body will vary according to the speed and gait of the horse; but always the rider should remain in balance over the base of support. The eyes, chin, and chest are lifted, thus permitting clear vision ahead and normal posture of the back. It must also be remembered that the greater the speed and the inclination of the body forward, the shorter the stirrups. Jockeys, therefore, ride their mounts with very short stirrups and reins

and a pronounced forward position. They rise out of their saddle and support themselves almost entirely with the stirrups, knees, and legs. In steeplechasing, the position of the rider is less extreme than in flat racing; for in this type of riding, it is necessary to combine speed with security.

From what has been said, it can be readily understood that there are different seats or positions for different styles of riding. Fashion, particularly in the show-ring, also decrees that certain form be followed.

When riding a three- or five-gaited horse, at all gaits and either on the bridle path or in the show-ring, the rider assumes the show or park seat—sitting erect and well back in the saddle (leaving a space of at least a hand's breadth between the back of the jodhpurs and the cantle). The ball of the foot rests directly over the stirrup iron; knees are in; heels are lower than the toes; and the hands and reins are in such position that the horse will carry its head high and its neck arched. In this position, the body is easily erect and balanced on a base consisting of seat, thighs, knees, and stirrups; the chest is high and just forward of the true vertical; and the back is hollow, the waist relaxed, the head erect, and the shoulders square. Figs. 17-34 through 17-36 show the correct seat and riding attire for a three-gaited horse, a five-gaited horse, and a Plantation Walking Horse, respectively.

When using a stock saddle and riding Western style, the rider should sit straight, keep the legs fairly straight—or bent slightly forward at the knees—and rest the balls of the feet on the stirrup treads with the

LINE OF BODY

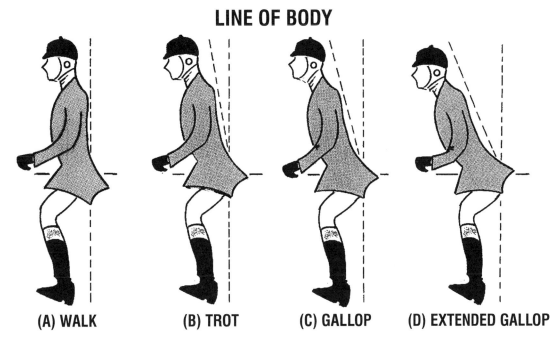

(A) WALK   **(B) TROT**   **(C) GALLOP**   **(D) EXTENDED GALLOP**

Fig. 17-33. The balanced seat, obtained by shifting the center of gravity of the rider over the center of gravity of the horse. The greater the forward speed of the horse, the greater the forward inclination of the rider.

heels down. The left hand with the reins should be carried in a relaxed manner slightly above and ahead of the horn. The right hand should be placed on the thigh, or it may be dropped loosely down the side, or held about waist high without resting it on anything. In cutting horses or in barrel racing, the left hand may rest on the saddle horn. Sitting the saddle is required at all gaits. Neither posting the trot (jog) nor standing in the stirrups at the trot or gallop (lope) is accepted

Fig. 17-34. Correct show seat and riding attire for a three-gaited horse. (Drawing by artist based on photo made especially for this book.)

Fig. 17-35. Correct show seat and riding attire for a five-gaited horse. (Drawing by artist based on photo made especially for this book.)

Fig. 17-36. Correct show seat and riding attire at the running walk. (Drawing by artist based on photo made especially for this book.)

Fig. 17-37. Correct Western seat and riding attire.

in Western style riding. Because speed and agility are required of stock horses, a firm seat and superior balance are important. Fig. 17-37 shows the correct Western Seat and riding attire.

In riding hunters (including cross-country riding) and jumpers, the stirrups are shortened; the foot is shot home farther than when working at slower gaits (but with some portion of the ball of the foot still resting on the stirrup, and with the heel slightly down); the upper part of the rider's body is thrust forward, giving the *forward seat*; and a comparatively loose rein is kept. The higher the jumps are, the shorter the stirrups should be and the more pronounced the forward incli-

Fig. 17-38. Correct hunter seat. The eyes should be up and the shoulders back. The toes should be out at an angle best suited to the rider's comfort; ankles flexed in, heels down, calf of leg in contact with horse and slightly behind girth. Iron may be either on toe, ball of foot, or home. Rider is wearing a metal-lined black velvet hunting cap.

nation of the body. Fig. 17-38 shows the correct saddle position for hunting and jumping.

Most polo players prefer to use medium-length stirrups, with feet shot home in the stirrups. This permits a good grip when turning at full speed. The stirrups are also sufficiently short to allow the player to stand up in the stirrup irons when making a long reach for the ball.

Each of these styles of riding differs in appearance, but the end result is the same—balanced riding. An accomplished equestrian can and does change the seat to meet the style of riding.

PUTTING THE HORSE IN MOTION

After being properly mounted, the rider is ready to put the horse in motion. This is accomplished by means of the aids, which are really the only mutual language between the horse and rider.

NATURAL AIDS

The natural aids to retaining equilibrium and controlling the horse's movements are the legs, the hands and the reins, the weight of the rider, and the voice.

When necessary, these may be assisted by the artificial aids; spurs and crop. For a finished performance, all of the natural aids must be invoked in unison, and the artificial aids must be used sparingly—if at all.

■ **Action of the legs**—The rider's legs are used primarily for the purposes of producing impulsion (forward movement) and increasing the gait. These results are obtained by a simple pressure on the horse by the inner calf muscles of the rider. Should this prove inadequate, it is proper to resort to the use of spurs or the whip. One of the rider's legs may be used with greater force than the other, thus displacing the horse's hindquarters laterally to prevent it from sidestepping, to straighten it, or to change direction in a cramped space.

■ **Action of the reins**—The reins are an intermediary between the rider and the mount; they afford direct contact between the hands and the horse's mouth. The reins regulate the impulsion—slowing, stopping, or backing the horse. The reins, acting through the mouth and neck, are also used to change direction of travel or to turn the horse to either the right or the left.

■ **Action of the weight**—By shifting the position of the body from the hips up—a weight of approximately 100 lb in the average person—the rider can contribute materially to variations in the balance of the horse. When moving, stopping, or turning, riders may facilitate and hasten the obedience of their mounts by slightly displacing their weight in the direction of desired movement.

ARTIFICIAL AIDS

Ingenious equestrians have devised many artificial aids which, when judiciously used by experienced riders may supplement effectively the natural aids. In addition to the whip and spur, the following equipment may be listed under this category: longeing whip, link straps, martingales, nosebands, various types of reins, and innumerable types of bits.

Such artificial aids should be used sparingly—particularly the spur and whip. Perhaps for the most part, they should be used only when there has been disobedience to the natural aids.

STARTING

In starting, horse riders should simultaneously invoke the use of the natural aids. They should slightly tighten the reins to awake the mount to attention, bring slight pressure with the inner calf muscles, and incline the body forward. Finally, as a last resort, they may use judiciously one or more of the artificial aids.

STOPPING

The rider stops the horse by pulling back on the reins in slow and repeated movements, by releasing the pressure the instant the animal shows signs of obedience, and by repeating the action as often as necessary to bring him to a dead stop. At the same time, the rider, without standing up, puts weight evenly into both stirrups and leans slightly backward.

TURNING

In turning, the rider must pull the rein on the side toward which it is desired that the horse shall go; at the same time the pressure on the opposite side must be slackened. Simultaneously, more weight is shifted to the stirrup on the side of the turn. Adequate rein pressure should be applied, but it is not necessary to jerk or pull hard.

EXECUTING THE GAITS

After the rider has mastered the art of starting, stopping, and turning the mount, attention may be given to the gaits.

The amateur had best use only the three natural gaits: the walk, trot, and canter. A description of these gaits, together with additional gaits and defects in the way of going, is found in Chapter 7. Knowledge of the different gaits should be mastered before one attempts to execute them.

WALK

Before trying the faster gaits, it is wise that the beginner first learn to walk. The balanced seat and correct posture must be mastered. The back should be erect, but the waist should be supple. Often it is helpful to have the beginner walk the horse with the feet out of the stirrups while keeping the knee and hip joints relaxed, the shoulders square, the head back, the legs down, and the ankles relaxed.

TROT

Trotting is the roughest of all the gaits to the beginner, but correct riding at this gait must be acquired. There are two ways of riding at the trot: the *close* or *cowboy seat*, in which the rider remains firmly seated in the saddle at all times; and the *posting seat*, in which the rider's body goes slightly up in the air in unison with the horse.

The beginner should not attempt to fast trot or to post until the balanced seat has been thoroughly mastered at the slow trot. Moreover, the slow trot (about six miles per hour) is not, as a rule, ridden by posting, nor do riders post when riding Western. The posting seat is used by most park-riding civilians and horse-show exhibitors.

■ **Posting the Trot**—Posting may be described as the rising and descending of the rider with the rhythm of the trot. This action reduces the shock or jar of the trot for both the horse and the rider. Posting is accomplished by rising easily in the saddle in rhythm at one beat, of the two-beat trot, and settling back at the next beat. In posting, the rider inclines the upper part of the body slightly forward (while at the same time keeping the shoulders back, the chin up, and the legs under the body, with the heels down); presses the knees inward against the horse for body support; and then permits the body to be impelled upward by the thrust of one of the hind legs (the left, for example). The rider remains up during the stride of the other hind leg (the right) and returns the seat nearly to the saddle only to be impelled upward again by the next thrust of the hind leg. Sitting back in the saddle each time the right forefoot strikes the ground is known as posting on the right diagonal; whereas returning to the saddle when the left fore strikes the ground is known as posting on the left diagonal.

Some competent and experienced equitation instructors[4] report that they prefer to teach posting the correct diagonal as follows:

1. Watch the horse's shoulder and knee.
2. Rise in the saddle as the shoulder and knee of the outside foreleg come forward. The rider will then be posting to the outside foreleg or the one nearest the rail.

To change diagonals, the rider should learn to sit 1, 3, or 5 beats of the trot—preferably 1 beat.

The rider should frequently alternate the diagonals used in posting as this makes for greater ease on the horse. When riding in a ring, the rider should post on the outside diagonal so that the work of the hindquarters will be equalized. For correct posting, the stirrups should be sufficiently short to permit the rider to carry most of the weight on the ball of the foot. Only a small portion of the weight should be carried on the inside of the thighs and knees. Correct posting is one of the most difficult phases of riding.

CANTER (LOPE)

The canter is a slow, restrained gallop. In the

---

[4]This is the system used by the late Ms. Claud H. Drew, Columbia, Missouri and Mrs. Fern P. Bittner, St. Charles, Missouri—noted equestrians, instructors, and judges—who very kindly reviewed this book.

show-ring or on the bridle path, this gait is started from the walk rather than from the trot, although some equestrians recommend that the canter be demanded from the trot.

The horse is made to canter (1) by drawing his head up and his nose in with the reins, and with the nose held slightly to the opposite direction of the desired lead (thus, the nose should be slightly to the left for a right lead), (2) by shifting the weight of the rider slightly to the front and to the side of the desired lead, and (3) by applying the legs in such a manner as to urge the horse to go forward. When cantering, the rider should stay with the saddle and keep the knees and calves of the legs close to the horse. When cantering in a circular ring, the horse should lead or step out with the right forefoot when traveling to the right and with the left forefoot when traveling to the left. A well-trained animal should be capable of and willing to take either lead upon command. Moreover, to avoid tiring the animal, the lead should be shifted at intervals.

The lope is the western adaptation of a very slow canter. It is a smooth, slow gait in which the head is carried low.

ADDITIONAL GAITS

In addition to the three natural gaits (walk, trot, and canter) five-gaited horses are expected to take one of the slow gaits—running walk, fox-trot, or stepping pace (stepping pace is the preferred slow gait in the show-ring)—and the rack. The amateur should not attempt to ride the added gaits until the three basic gaits have been mastered.

SOME RULES OF GOOD HORSEMANSHIP

Good riders observe the following rules:

1. Approach a horse from its left. Never walk or stand behind a horse unannounced; let it know that you are there by speaking to and placing your hand on it. Otherwise, you may get kicked.

2. Pet a horse by first placing your hand on its shoulder or neck. Do not dab at the end of the nose.

3. Grasp the reins close to the bit on the left side when leading a horse.

4. Walk the horse to and from the stable; this prevents it from running home and refusing to leave the stable.

5. See that the saddle blanket, numnah, pad or corona is clean and free from dried sweat, hair, caked dirt, or any rough places—any of which will cause a sore back.

6. Check the saddle and bridle (or hackamore) before mounting. The saddle should fit and be placed just back of the withers; it should not bear down on or rub the withers, nor should it be placed too far back. The girth should be fastened snugly and should not be too close to the forelegs. Be sure that the bridle (or hackamore) fits comfortably and that the curb chain or strap is flat in the chin groove and fastened correctly.

7. Mount and dismount from the left side. Make a horse stand until the rider is properly seated in the saddle or has dismounted.

8. Assume the correct seat for the style of riding intended.

9. Retain the proper tension on the reins; avoid either tight or dangling reins.

10. Keep the hands and voice quiet when handling your horse. Avoid clacking to the horse, loud laughing or screaming (never scream—no matter how excited or frightened you may be; it will only make matters worse), and slapping it with the ends of the reins; such things are unnecessary and in poor taste.

11. Warm up the horse gradually; walk it first, then jog it slowly.

12. Keep to the right side of the road except when passing, and never allow your horse to wander all over the road. Give right-of-way courteously.

13. Walk the horse across bridges, through underpasses, and over pavements and slippery roads.

14. Slow down when making a sharp turn.

15. Walk the horse when going up or down hill; running may injure its legs and wind. Do not race horses; when so handled, they form bad habits and may get out of control.

16. Keep the horse moving when a car passes. If you stop, it may act up or back into the passing vehicle.

17. Anticipate such distractions as cars, stones, paper, trees, bridges, noises, dogs, children, etc.; in other words, think ahead of your horse.

18. Vary the gaits; and do not force the horse to take a rapid gait—canter, rack, or trot—for more than a half mile at a time without allowing a breathing spell in the interim.

19. Keep the horse under control at all times. If you are riding a runaway horse, try to stop it by sawing the bit back and forth in its mouth so as to break (a) its hold on the bit, and (b) its stride; if in an open space, pull one rein hard enough to force it to circle.

20. Practice firmness with the horse and make it obey your wishes; it will have more respect for you. At the same time, love and understand it and it will reward you with the finest friendship and the grandest sport.

21. Never lose your temper and jerk a horse; a bad-tempered person never makes for a good-tempered horse.

22. Lean forward and loosen the reins if a horse rears. If you lean back and pull, the horse may fall over backwards.

23. Pull up the reins of a bucking horse; keep its head up.

24. Loosen the reins and urge the horse forward with your legs if it starts backing. Don't hold the reins too tightly when the horse is standing still.

25. Bring the horse in cool; walk him at the end of a ride.

26. Do not allow the horse to gorge on water when hot; water a warm horse slowly—just a few swallows at a time.

27. Do not turn the horse loose at the stall entrance. Walk into the stall with the horse, turn it around, so that it is facing the door, then depart. In a tie stall, make certain that the horse is tied securely with proper length rope.

28. Groom the horse thoroughly after each ride.

29. Wash the bit off carefully before it is hung in the tack room; remove hair and sweat from the saddle and girth before putting them on the rack; and wash all leather equipment with saddle soap at frequent intervals, thereby preserving the leather and keeping it pliable.

In addition to observing the above rules, good riders show consideration for other riders by observing the following additional practices—whether on the bridle path or on the trail, in the show-ring, or under other circumstances.

1. Keep abreast (about 5 ft apart), or keep a full horse's length behind other mounts, to prevent kicking.

2. Never dash up to another horse or group of horses at a gallop; to do so invites injury to yourself and the horses.

3. Never rush past riders who are proceeding at a slower gait; this may startle both horses and riders and cause an accident. Instead, approach slowly and pass cautiously on the left side.

4. Wait quietly when one person has to dismount, as when closing a gate. Do not run off and leave that person.

5. Never race after a mounted runaway horse—to do so will only make it run faster; instead, if possible, another rider should circle and come up in front of it. In case a rider is thrown, stop the other horses and keep quiet; generally the loose horse will return to the group where it may be caught.

6. Do not trespass on private property.

7. Leave gates the way you found them; otherwise, livestock may get out.

HOW TO CLEAN AND CARE FOR TACK

As used herein, tack, gear, and equipment embrace all articles used on, or attached to, riding and driving horses.

Good tack, gear, and equipment are expensive; hence, they merit good care. If properly cared for, they will last for years.

Ideally, each article should be cleaned thoroughly every time it is used on a horse. However, the owner and/or caretaker of pleasure horses may not be able to devote this amount of time. For the busy person, therefore, it is recommended that the vital parts be cleaned following each use—that the bottom of the saddle and the inside of the bridle be cleaned, that the bit be washed, and that the pad or blanket (if used) be brushed after drying out and before reusing. Then a thorough cleaning should be administered to all tack and equipment once each week.

The tack, gear, and equipment used on race and show horses, where maximum performance is all-important, should be thoroughly cleaned after each usage.

The general principles presented in the accompanying discussion also apply to the equipment used on race and show horses, with the following changes:

Do not use soap (or cream) on leather boots used on horses; it tends to deteriorate the stitching and catch a film of dirt. Instead, brush (preferably with a circular brush) to eliminate the sweat, dirt, and grime; wipe dry with a cloth, rub in petroleum jelly or liquid preservative; and, before using, dust with talcum powder or cornstarch, either of which will absorb moisture and smooth out minor rough or chafing spots.

■ **Why Clean**—Good tack is expensive. Proper cleaning will do the following:

1. Extend the life of leather and metal.

2. Impart softness and pliability to leather.

3. Make for comfort to the horse. It will lessen saddle and harness sores from the use of dirty, crusted, and stiff leather; and avoid irritation and infection from a rusty, moldy and dirty bit.

4. Assure that minor tack defects will be noticed and repaired promptly, before they become serious.

5. Protect the user, by minimizing the breaking of a rein or line, girth, girth straps, stirrup leathers, or other vital parts.

6. Impart pride and pleasure in ownership and use of equipment. Your equipment, your horse, and you will look smart and feel smart.

■ **Cleaning Equipment**—The following items of cleaning equipment are commonly used:

1. A saddle rack on which to rest the saddle when it's being cleaned. Preferably, the rack should be designed so that it will also hold the saddle upside down, to facilitate cleaning the underside as well as the top.

2. A bridle rack, peg, or hook on which to hang the bridle for cleaning.

3. A harness rack for cleaning (if you have harness).

4. A bucket for warm water.

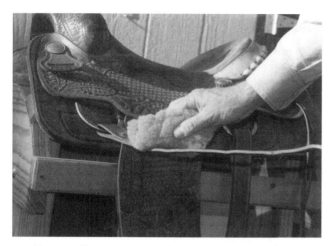

Fig. 17-39. Cleaning the saddle. (Courtesy, *The Quarter Horse Journal*, Amarillo, TX)

5. Three sponges, preferably (although one sponge will suffice if rinsed properly):

a. One for washing—for cleaning off sweat, dirt, mud, etc.

b. The second for applying leather preservative or glycerine soap.

c. The third for occasional application of neatsfoot or other similar oil.

6. A chamois cloth for drying off leather.

7. Cheesecloth (about a yard) for applying metal polish.

8. A flannel rag for polishing metal.

■ **Cleaning Materials**—The usual cleaning materials are:

1. Saddle soap, or a bar of castile soap, for cleaning.

2. A leather preservative, or bar of glycerine soap, for finishing.

3. Neatsfoot oil.

4. Metal polish.

5. Petroleum jelly.

■ **Order of Cleaning**—To assure that all tack and all parts are cleaned (that none is overlooked), it is important that some logical, practical, and regular order be followed, automatically and routinely. Any order that accomplishes this purpose will be satisfactory.

The following is suggested for articles used in riding, and is perhaps most common:

1. Clean the saddle.

a. Remove and clean girth.

b. Clean underside of saddle.

c. Get topside of saddle.

d. Clean nearside (left).

e. Clean offside (right).

2. Clean the bridle.

3. Clean the martingale, etc. if used.

4. If a saddle pad or blanket is used, brush it after it has dried.

A similar procedure should be used for articles used in driving.

■ **How to Clean Tack**—Once a week, wash with saddle soap or with castile soap as described and apply light neatsfoot oil or other leather dressing to all leather parts. Avoid excess oil, which will darken new leather and soil clothing. Proceed as follows:

1. **Saddle.** The steps in cleaning the saddle are:

a. Remove girth; clean as described under Point "c" below.

b. Turn saddle upside down.

c. Wash panel (that part of saddle in contact with horses back) and gullet (underside center). With sponge wetted in warm water and wrung out, apply saddle soap to leather, and rub to work up a stiff lather to remove sweat and dirt before it hardens. The amount of dirt will determine how much soap, water, and elbow grease are necessary.

d. Wash rest of saddle in same manner, following the order given under "Order of Cleaning."

e. Dry entire saddle with chamois.

f. Take second sponge, dampen slightly, and apply leather preservative or glycerin soap without suds to all parts of saddle, following the order given.

2. **Bridle.** First, wash the bit in warm water. Then—

a. On the leather part, follow exactly the same procedure given for the saddle; wash thoroughly with warm water and saddle soap or castile soap, dry with chamois, and apply either a preservative or glycerine soap with slightly damp sponge.

b. Using cheesecloth, apply metal polish to all metal parts; then polish with flannel. If the bridle is not to be used for a time, clean and dry the bit, and apply a light coat of petroleum jelly, to prevent pitting or rusting.

3. **Harness.** Follow the same procedure as given for saddle and bridle.

4. **Blankets and Pads.** Hang up or spread out to dry; then brush off hair and dried sweat.

5. **Vehicles.** Carts, sulkies, buckboards, and viceroys should be kept clean at all times. If vehicles are to be used in the show-ring, they should be washed a few hours ahead. Then apply metal polish to chrome, and wipe enamel wood finish with soft, dry flannel. Upholstering should be brushed, vacuumed, or washed—according to material.

■ **After Cleaning**—After cleaning, tack should be handled as follows:

1. Store in a cool, dry place.
2. Hang the bridle on its rack, neatly and so that all parts drape naturally without bending.
3. Place the saddle on its rack.
4. Hang the harness on a rack.
5. Cover the saddle, bridle and harness.
6. Protect vehicles from weather, and use dust covers.

GROOMING AND WASHING

Proper grooming is necessary to (1) make and keep the horse attractive, and (2) maintain good health and condition.

Grooming cleans the hair, keeps the skin functioning naturally, lessens skin diseases and parasites, and improves the condition and fitness of the muscles.

Wild horses groomed themselves by rolling and taking dust baths. Domesticated horses will do the same thing when turned into a corral.

HOW TO GROOM A HORSE

Grooming should be rapid and thorough, but not so rough or severe as to cause irritation, either to the horse's skin or temper.

Horses that are stabled or in small corrals should be groomed thoroughly at least once daily. Those that are worked or exercised should be groomed both before leaving the stable and immediately upon their return. Heated, wet, or sweating animals should be handled as follows:

1. Remove the equipment as fast as possible; wipe it off, and put it away.
2. Remove excess perspiration with a sweat scraper; then rub briskly with a grooming or

drying cloth to dry the coat partially.
3. Blanket and walk the horse until cool.
4. Allow a couple of swallows of water every few minutes while cooling out.

The needed articles of grooming equipment, and instructions on how to use them, are given in Table 17-3.

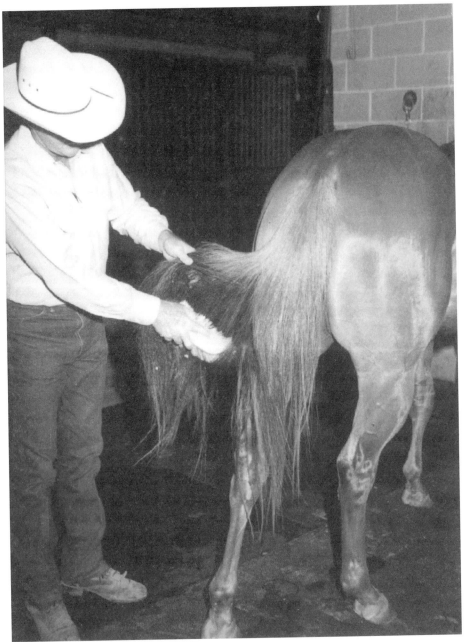

Fig. 17-40. Combing the tail; part of the grooming job. (Courtesy, *The Quarter Horse Journal*, Amarillo, TX)

TABLE 17-3
GROOMING EQUIPMENT AND HOW TO USE IT

Article	What It Is: How to Use It:	Used For	Grooming Procedure: How to Do It
Hoof pick	A metal pick for cleaning the feet.	To clean out the feet.	To assure that the horse will be groomed thoroughly and that no body parts will be missed, follow a definite order. This may differ according to individual preference, but the following procedure is most common: 1. **Clean out the feet**—Use the hoof pick. Work from the heel toward the toe. Clean thoroughly the depressions between the frog and the bars. Inspect for thrush and loose shoes
Curry comb (rubber or metal)	Use gently and in small circles, rather than with pressure and long strokes. Do not use the metal curry comb below the knees or hocks, about the head, or over bony predominances. Nor should it be used on horses that have been clipped recently, or that have a thin coat of hair.	To groom horses that have long, thick coats. To remove caked mud. To loosen matted scurf and dirt in the hair. To clean the brush.	2. **Groom the body**—Hold the curry comb in the right hand and the brush in the left hand, and proceed as follows: a. Start with the left side. b. Follow this order: the neck, breast, withers, shoulders, foreleg down to the knee, back, side, belly, croup, and hind legs down to the hock. Then brush from the knee and hock down toward the hoofs. At frequent intervals, clean the dust and hair from the brush with the curry comb, and knock the curry comb against your heel or the back of the brush to free it from dirt. Curry gently, but brush vigorously. Brush the hair in the direction of its natural lay. Brush with care in the regions of the flanks, between the fore and hind legs, at the point of the elbows, and in the fetlocks. After grooming the left side, transfer the brush to the right hand and the curry comb to the left hand; then groom the right side in the same order as described above.
Body brush	The body brush is the principal tool used for grooming.	To brush the entire body.	
Dandy brush	The dandy brush is made of stiff fiber usually about 2 in. in length.	To remove light dirt from the skin. To brush the mane and tail.	3. **Brush the head; comb and brush the mane and tail**—Use the body brush on the head. Groom the mane and tail as follows: a. Brush downward, using either the body brush or the dandy brush. b. Clean the tail by: (1) Brushing upward, a few strands of hair at a time; or by (2) Picking or separating out a few hairs at a time by hand, (3) Occasionally, washing with warm water and soap.
Mane and tail comb	Use as directed in last column.	To comb out matted mane and tail.	
Sweat scraper	A metal or wood scraper for removing sweat or water.	To remove excess perspiration from heated, wet, and sweating animals.	Place edge against horse's body and scrape with the grain of hair. Do not use on bony areas.
Grooming cloth	The grooming cloth can be made from old toweling or blankets. It should be about 18 to 24 in. square.	To remove dirt and dust from the coat. To wipe out the eyes, ears, nostrils, lips and dock. To give the coat a final sheen or polish. To dry or ruffle the coat before brushing.	4. **Wipe with the grooming cloth**—Use the grooming cloth to: a. Wipe about the ears, face, eyes, nostrils, lips, sheath, and dock, and b. Give a final polish to the coat. 5. **Check the grooming**—Pass the fingertips against the natural lay of the hair. If the coat and skin are not clean, the fingers will be dirtied and gray lines will show on the coat where the fingers passed. Also, inspect the ears, face, eyes, nostrils, lips, sheath, and dock. 6. **Wash and disinfect grooming equipment**—Wash with soap and warm water often enough to keep clean. Disinfect as necessary as precaution against the spread of diseases.

HOW TO CLIP AND SHEAR

In addition to routine grooming, horses should be sharpened up by shearing and clipping at such intervals as necessary.

Show-ring custom decrees certain breed differences in haircuts and hairdos. These are illustrated in Fig. 17-41.

1. **Protect inside of ears**—Place a wad of cotton in the ears, to cut down on noise from clippers and prevent hair from falling into ears.

2. **Clip long hairs**—Remove long hairs from about the head, the inside of the ears, on the jaw, and around the fetlocks.

Fig. 17-41. Some haircuts and hairstyles of different breeds and uses of horses.

But haircuts and hairstyles are changing! Today, five-gaited Saddlebred horses are being shown with braided manes and full-length and unset tails (see Chapter 8, Fig. 8-4); three-gaited Saddlebred horses are being shown with the mane shaved and the tail unset and full-length and flowing (see Chapter 8, Fig. 8-3); Hackneys are being shown with a short (or docked) tail, or a long tail; and Tennessee Walking Horses are being shown with unset tails.

HOW TO WASH (SHAMPOO) A HORSE

Following strenuous exercise, the horse should receive a welcome and refreshing bath. Washing will make the horse look better and feel better. Horses like to be clean.

Shampooing (1) cleans the animal—it removes dirt, stains, and sweat that cannot be removed by grooming; (2) makes for a fine hair coat with a good sheen; and (3) keeps the skin smooth and mellow.

Formerly, there was strong prejudice against washing horses, perhaps stemming from the use of old-fashioned, harsh detergents and strong soaps, followed by poor rinsing. But, baths are good for horses, just as they are good for people; and horses like to be shampooed.

Shampoo the horse as frequently as necessary, as determined by soiling, work, and weather conditions. For example, always wash it following use on a sloppy, muddy ring, trail, or track—when it comes back covered with mud from head to tail; or after using it when it's hot and muggy and all lathered up with sweat.

In preparation for shampooing, (1) groom the horse carefully, (2) secure the animal for washing either by having someone hold it by the shank or by tying, and (3) have shampoo concentrate, warm water, and sponges available.

Step 1—Wet the animal thoroughly all over with water alone. For this purpose, fill one bucket with warm water (and refill if necessary), then apply the water to the horse by means of a large sponge which may be dipped into the bucket as fast and frequently as desired.

To assure that the horse will be washed thoroughly and that no body parts will be missed, follow a definite order. This may differ somewhat according to individual preference, but the following procedure is most common: Start with the head, wetting between the ears and on the foretop (but do not get water in the ears; either hold them down or shut them off with the hand as the head is washed), over the face and cheeks, and around the eyes, muzzle and nostrils.

Next, proceed to the left side. While carrying the bucket in your left hand and holding the sponge in your right hand, with long strokes wet the neck, withers, shoulder, back, side, and croup. Return to the front, and with sponge in the left hand, wash the chest. Return the sponge to the right hand and wash under the elbow and down the foreleg. Then, take the sponge in the left hand, set the bucket down as near as possible, and sponge the belly thoroughly. Hold onto the hind leg on the outside above the hock (this precaution will keep a restive horse from pawing, kicking, or stepping on your foot) while sponging the sheath (of stallions and geldings) and the inside of the hind leg down to the hoof.

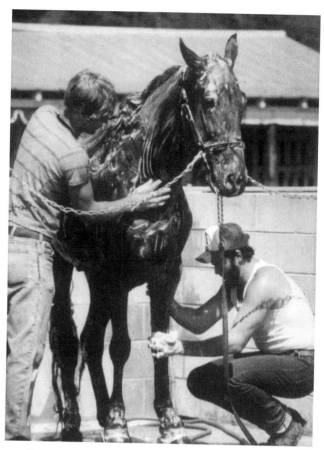

Fig. 17-42. Shampooing the horse. (Courtesy, Tennessee Walking Horse Breeders Assn., Lewisburg, TN)

Station yourself to the left of the horse near the hind leg, facing the rear. Set the bucket nearby. Take the sponge in the right hand and wash behind the hind legs and in the groove between the thighs. Since many horses fuss about this operation, be careful so as to avoid getting kicked or stepped on.

Hold the tail with the left hand and wash under it with the right hand. The tail is best washed by sponging with plenty of water at the tailhead, then putting the full length of the tail into the bucket of water, lifting the bucket to the bone and sloshing the tail around in the water. Set the bucket down, grip the tail near the top and draw the squeezed sponge down the full length of the hair; then give the tail a snap from side to side to swish out the water that is left.

After wetting the near (left) side and the rear end, get a bucket of fresh water. Then, while holding the bucket in your right hand and the sponge in your left hand, wet the off (right) side of the horse in the same order as described above, starting with the neck.

Step 2—Shampoo the horse. Put in a bucket or other suitable container shampoo concentrate and water in the amounts and proportions recommended on the shampoo label, then stir it vigorously with your hand to form suds. Sponge the shampoo solution over the animal, following exactly the same procedure and order as outlined for wetting. Scrub against the hair with the sponge and your hands until a rich, thick lather covers all parts.

Step 3—Rinse the horse with warm water, using either a bucket and sponge or a hose (if the horse is used to the latter), follow the procedure and order given in Step 1. Rinse thoroughly.

Step 4—Scrape with a sweat scraper held snugly against the hair to remove excess water, using long sweeping strokes and following the procedure and order given in Step 1, except do not scrape the head and legs.

Step 5—Dry with a clean dry sponge or coarse towel, squeezing it out at intervals; following the procedure and order given in Step 1.

Step 6—Blanket the horse and walk it until the coat is completely dry.

Step 7—Apply a coat dressing if desired.

■ **Coat Dressing**—"Trifles make perfection, but perfection is no trifle," is an old and well-known adage among equestrians. This philosophy prompts experienced caretakers to use a good coat dressing to achieve the all-important bloom or eye appeal in show, parade, and sale animals. Also, they use a coat dressing because they take pride in the everyday appearance of their charges, for how horses look is indicative of the kind of caretakers back of them.

A coat dressing will not take the place of natural conditioning of the horse, which can be achieved only through proper feeding, health, grooming, and shampooing.

Proper grooming should always precede the use of coat dressing. Coat dressing is best applied by means of a heavy cloth (preferably terry cloth). Moisten the rag with the dressing and rub the coat vigorously in the direction of natural lay of the hair; then brush to bring out the bloom.

Coat dressing should always be used following washing, and for show, parade, or sale. It is best to apply a heavier application of coat dressing 12 to 24 hours ahead of the event, then go over the horse with a lightly dressed rag just ahead.

SHOWING HORSES

Horse shows provide entertainment for spectators, and recreation, sport, and competition for the exhibitors. Also, the show-ring has been, and will continue to be, an important medium for getting horses and people together in one place and at one time to compare, design, and engineer the most desirable models.

There is no higher artistic accomplishment than that of breeding and showing a championship horse—an animal representing an ideal which has been produced through intelligent breeding and then trained and fitted to the height of perfection.

But the educational value of horse shows has not been exploited. Many people who attend a horse show for the first time are bewildered by the procedure and the many breeds and classes that they see. Others may have never gone to a horse show because they feel that their lack of knowledge would prevent them from enjoying it. It is the author's fond hope that this book will result in more people enjoying more horse shows with informed appraisal.

Horse shows have increased in recent years, on all levels—local, state, and national. Also, they have grown in terms of quality and prize money.

In addition to spectator entertainment, horse shows stimulate improved breeding, for winning horses (and their relatives) bring good prices.

The American Horse Shows Association (AHSA) regulates the rules and schedules of all the big shows. Recognized shows include all regular shows, local shows, combined training events, and dressage competitions which are members of the AHSA.

The successful exhibitor knows the rules of the classes and follows the correct showing techniques. Broadly speaking, this calls for knowledge of both performance and breeding (in hand) divisions, as well as of the several classes within each division.

SHOWING IN HAND (AT HALTER)

Breeding classes are discussed here. They are *shown in hand*, which means the horses are exhibited wearing a halter, preferably, or a bridle. The halter should be clean, properly adjusted, and fitted with a fresh looking leather or rope lead.

If the horse is shown wearing a bridle, the exhibitor should not jerk on the reins hard enough to injure the mouth.

Many exhibitors lack knowledge of the correct showing technique for breeding classes, even though they may be quite professional in exhibiting in performance classes.

The following practices are recommended for showing in hand, or at halter:

1. Train the horse early.
2. Groom the horse thoroughly.
3. Dress neatly for the show.
4. Enter the ring promptly and in tandem when the class is called. Line up at the location indicated

by the ringmaster or judge unless directed to continue around the ring in tandem.

5. Stand the horse squarely on all four feet with the forefeet on higher ground than the hind feet if possible. The standing position of the horse should vary according to the breed. For example, Arabians are not stretched, but American Saddlers are trained to stand with their front legs straight under them and their hind legs stretched behind them. Other breeds generally stand in slightly stretched position, somewhat intermediate between these two examples. When standing and facing the horse, hold the lead strap or rope in the left hand 10 to 12 in. from the halter ring. Try to make the horse keep its head up.

Fig. 17-43. Quarter Horses shown at halter, competing for the World's Championship. (Courtesy, American Quarter Horse Assn., Amarillo, TX)

6. Unless the judge directs otherwise, the horse should first be shown at the walk and then the trot. Move the horse as follows:

a. Reduce the length of the lead strap or rope by a series of figure 8 folds or by coils held in the left hand. Hold the upper part of the lead strap or rope in the right hand and lead from the left side of the horse. If the horse is well mannered, give it 2 to 3 ft of lead so it can keep its head, neck, and body in a straight line as it moves forward. But keep the lead taut so the horse is always under control. Do not look back.

b. The exhibitor should keep the horse's head up and briskly move the horse forward in a straight line for 50 to 100 ft as directed.

c. At the end of the walk, turn to the right. That is, the horse should be turned away from the exhibitor, then the exhibitor should walk around the horse. If the horse is turned toward the exhibitor, the horse is more likely to step on the exhibitor. Make the turn in as small a space as practical, and as effortless as possible. When showing at

the trot, bring the horse to a walk and move it slightly in the direction of the exhibitor before turning.

d. Exhibitors should lift their knees a little higher than usual when they are showing in the ring.

e. Trail the horse with a whip if it is permitted and desired. Most light horses are given early training by trailing with the whip, but usually they are shown without this aid. If a trailer is used he/she should follow at a proper distance. The distance should not be so near as to be in danger of getting kicked, but not so far as to be ineffective. The trailer should keep the animal in a straight line, avoid getting between the judges and the horse, and always cross in front of the horse at the turn.

7. Walk the horse down about 50 ft and walk back; then trot down about 100 ft and trot back. To save time, the judge may direct the horse to be walked down and trotted back, which is a proper procedure. After the horse has been walked and trotted, stand it promptly in front of the judge. After the judge has made a quick inspection, move to the location in the line indicated by the ringmaster or judge.

8. Keep the horse posed at all times; keep one eye on the judge and the other on the horse.

9. When the judge signals to change positions, the exhibitor should back the horse out of line, or if there is more room, turn it to the rear of the line and approach the new position from behind.

10. Try to keep the horse from kicking when it is close to other horses.

11. Keep calm; a nervous exhibitor creates an unfavorable impression.

12. Work in close partnership with the horse.

13. Be courteous and respect the rights of other exhibitors.

14. Do not stand between the judge and the horse.

15. Be a good sport; win without bragging and lose without complaining.

SHOWING IN PERFORMANCE CLASSES

Performance classes for horses are so numerous and varied that it is not practical to describe them here. Instead, the exhibitor should refer to the official rule book of the American Horse Shows Association and to the rules printed in the program of local horse shows.

COMBINED TRAINING (THREE-DAY EVENT)

Combined training or three-day event, is the modern English term for what the French have always known as *concours complet*—the complete test. It is perhaps the most demanding and rewarding of any equestrian activity. In order to do well, a horse must combine speed, stamina, obedience, and considerable jumping ability; and the rider must be knowledgeable and expert in three distinct branches of horsemanship—dressage, cross-country riding, and show-jumping. The object of combined training is to test the all-around quality and versatility of the horse.

Through the centuries, the great equestrians evolved a system of training and riding horses which were adopted in whole or in part by the cavalry, which placed emphasis upon endurance.

In Sweden, a military three-day event was held at the cavalry school at Stronsholm in 1907; Belgium followed suit in 1910; and Switzerland held its first event in 1921. The growing international interest was partly responsible for the introduction, at the 1912 Olympic games, of equestrian events. All the competition at this time was still drawn from military sources. It was not until after World War II that civilian participation in three-day events began.

Combined training competitions are usually held over three days, though the various phases of the competition have been modified to produce one-day events.

In any combination training competition, there are the following three phases:

1. **Dressage**—This test is designed to show that the horse is educated, balanced, supple, and obedient. Although many of the movements included in the test form part of the schooling program of any horse, others set out to demand from the horse and rider a greater degree of schooling and a more polished performance than the average hunter, for example, would require.

2. **Speed and endurance test**—The second part of the competition in three-day events, the speed and endurance test, consists of several phases. There are two on roads and tracks, with these separated by a steeplechase course. Finally, there is the greatest test of all—the cross country phase, a grueling course of some 30 obstacles spread over 4 to 5 miles of open country. The whole speed and endurance section of the competition will cover some 20 miles; the roads and tracks being taken at a brisk trot or easy canter, the steeplechase course at a good gallop, and the cross-country to be ridden at speed—allowing for the individual horse's ability over solid, and sometimes tricky, obstacles. Only bold, clever horses with confidence in and obedience to their riders, and at the peak of fitness, can hope to compete successfully in the second day—and without undue exhaustion.

3. **Show jumping**—The third day involves a show-jumping course designed as a final test of fitness for both horse and rider.

Any good hunter who is temperate enough to perform a dressage test and jump a course of artificial fences in addition to galloping across country tackling big fences at speed can succeed in combined training provided it has sufficient quality and heart.

In all countries where horses and riding are featured, the demands of versatility in achievement of combined training are a particularly popular challenge. Each year, the sport is becoming more popular all over the world.

Fig. 17-44. A hunter in action, and well-ridden. (Courtesy, Polaris Farm, Charlottesville, VA)

CAPARISONED HORSE WITH BOOTS IN REVERSE POSITION

In the funeral processions of former general officers and cavalry officers, there may be a riderless horse led by a person in uniform. The horse is properly saddled, but the stirrups are held in reverse position by a pair of polished cavalry boots with spurs. A glittering saber is hung to the right side of the saddle. Also, this consideration may be accorded to a U.S. President, as Commander-in-Chief.

The practice of having the caparisoned (or decked out) charger of the deceased military officer led in the funeral procession stems from an ancient custom surrounding the burial of warriors. The horse bore a saddle with the stirrups inverted and a sword through them to symbolize that the warrior had fallen and would ride no more. Also, the horse was sacrificed at the time, because it was believed that the equine spirit would find its master in the hereafter; otherwise, the departed warrior would have to walk. Horses are no longer sacrificed. But a riderless horse, with boots and spurs reversed, is still led in the funeral procession to symbolize that the warrior has fallen.

SELECTED REFERENCES

Title of Publication	Author(s)	Publisher
Bit by Bit	D. Tuke	J. A. Allen & Co. Ltd., London, England, 1965
Breeding and Raising Horses, Ag. Hdbk. No. 394	M. E. Ensminger	Agricultural Research Service, USDA, Washington, DC, 1972
Carts and Wagons	J. Vince	Spurbooks Ltd., Buckinghamshire, England, 1975
Cavalletti	R. Klimke Trans. by D. M. Goodall	J. A. Allen & Co. Ltd., London, England, 1973
Elegant Carriage, The	M. Watney	J. A. Allen & Co. Ltd., London, England, 1969
English Pleasure Carriages	W. B. Adams	Adams & Dart, Bath, Somerset, England, 1971
First Horse	R. Hapgood	Chronicle Books, San Francisco, CA, 1972
Grooming Horses	R. W. Collins	*The Blood Horse*, Lexington, KY, 1959; reprinted under special arrangement by *The Thoroughbred Record*, Lexington, KY, 1971
Grooming Your Horse	N. Haley	A. S. Barnes & Co., Inc., Cranbury, NJ, 1974
Guide to American Horse Shows, A	D. A. Spector	Arco Publishing Co., Inc., New York, NY, 1973
Horse, The	J. M. Kays	A. S. Barnes & Co., Inc., Cranbury, NJ, 1969
Horse Psychology	M. Williams	A. S. Barnes & Co., Inc., Cranbury, NJ, 1969
Horse Show, At the	M. C. Self	Arco Publishing Co., Inc., New York, NY, 1973
Horsemanship	A. W. Jasper	Boy Scouts of America, New Brunswick, NJ, 1963
Horsemanship and Horse Care, Ag. Info Bull. No. 353	M. E. Ensminger	Agricultural Research Service, USDA, Washington, DC, 1972
Horsemanship and Horsemastership	Ed. by G. Wright	Doubleday & Company, Inc., Garden City, NY, 1962
Horses	M. C. Self	A. S. Barnes & Co., Inc., Cranbury, NJ, 1953
Horses and Horsemanship	L. E. Walraven	A. S. Barnes & Co., Inc., Cranbury, NJ, 1970
Horses, Horses, Horses	M. E. Ensminger	M. E. Ensminger, Clovis, CA, 1969
Horses, Horses, Horses	S. Wilding	Van Nostrand Reinhold Company, New York, NY, 1970
Horses: Their Selection, Care and Handling	M. C. Self	A. S. Barnes & Co., Inc., Cranbury, NJ, 1943
Leg at Each Corner, A	N. Thelwell	E. P. Dutton & Co., Inc., New York, NY, 1963
Light Horse Management	R. C. Barbalace	Caballus Publishers, Fort Collins, CO, 1974
Light Horses, Farmers' Bull. No. 2127	M. E. Ensminger	Agricultural Research Service, USDA, Washington, DC, 1965

Manual of Horsemanship of The British Horse Society and The Pony Club		The British Horse Society, Warwickshire, England, 1968
Practical Dressage for Amateur Trainers	J. M. Ladendorf	A. S. Barnes & Co., Inc., Cranbury, NJ, 1973
Rule Book		The American Horse Shows Association, Inc., New York, NY, annual
Saddle Up!	C. E. Ball	J. B. Lippincott Co., Philadelphia, PA, 1970
Saddlery	E. H. Edwards	A. S. Barnes & Co., Inc., Cranbury, NJ, 1963
Shetland Pony, The	L. F. Bedell	Iowa State University Press, Ames, IA, 1959
Shetland Pony, The	M. C. Cox	A & C Black Ltd., London, England, 1965
Spanish Riding School, The	H. Handler	McGraw-Hill Book Company, Ltd., Maidenhead, England, 1972
Stagecoaches & Carriages	I. Sparkes	Spurbooks Ltd., Buckinghamshire, England, 1975
Western Equitation, Horsemanship and Showmanship	D. Stewart	Vantage Press, Inc., New York, NY, 1973

Management will largely determine the future of the foal! Standardbred mare and foal at Castleton Farm, Lexington, Kentucky. (Courtesy, The United States Trotting Assn., Columbus, OH)

Although horse management practices vary from area to area, and farm to farm, according to the size of the enterprise—whether one horse or several are involved—and between caretakers, the principles of good management are the same under all conditions.

SOME MANAGEMENT PRACTICES

Without attempting to cover all management practices, some facts relative to, and methods of accomplishing, common horse management practices are discussed in this chapter.

MARKING OR IDENTIFYING HORSES

The method of marking or identifying animals varies according to the class of animals and the objectives sought. Thus, some methods of marking are well adapted to one class of animals but not to another; ear notches, for example, are commonly used for identifying swine, but are seldom used for horses at the present time. On the western range, marking by branding is primarily a method of establishing ownership.

Until the 16th century (and even later in some parts of England), the ears of horses were cut in various ways as a means of identification. For example, a bitted ear was bitten (a piece was cut out) from the inner edge, and a cropped ear was cut straight across halfway down the ear. Eventually, cropped ears became fashionable, much as they are with certain breeds of dogs today, with the result that the practice persisted into the 18th century. This explains why early paintings of horses frequently showed the animals with tiny ears, scarcely 2 in. long.

With a purebred herd of horses, marking is a means of ascertaining ancestry or pedigree. This is particularly important where only one person knows the individuals in a given herd, and, suddenly and without warning, that person is no longer available. Under such circumstances, many a valuable registered horse has been sold as a grade, simply because positive identification could not be established.

In racehorses, an infallible means of identification is necessary in order to prevent ringers. *A ringer is a horse that is passed off under false identity, with the idea of entering it in a race below its class where it is almost certain to win.* In the early 1920s the most common camouflage for a ringer was a coat of paint—hence the terms *dark horse* and *horse of another color.* Formerly, the ringer's nemesis was rain; today, it is the lip tattoo system, which must accompany horses of most breeds to every major racing meet.

One of the duties of a steward, through the horse identification assistant, is that of assuring that each starter in a race is actually the horse named in the entry. This is necessary because only a relatively small percentage of the more prominent racehorses are fondly recognized on sight by the public; the vast majority of racehorses are known only by names and past performances.

A lip tattoo method of identifying horses was developed by the old Army Remount Service (now extinct) at Pomona, California. The Thoroughbred Racing Protective Bureau (TRPB), Inc., perfected this method and utilizes it so that the member tracks of the Thoroughbred Racing Association (TRA) are able to guarantee to the public the identity of each and every horse running at their tracks. The system consists of tattoo branding, with forgery-proof dyes, The Jockey Club serial number (the registry number) under the upper lip of the horse, with a prefix letter added to denote the age of the horse (see Fig. 18-1). The process is both simple and painless. It is applied by expert crews of the TRPB to two-year-olds as they come to each TRA track.

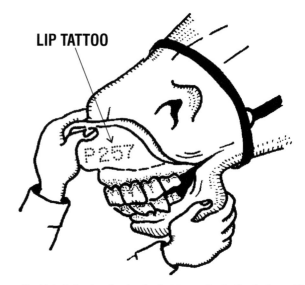

LIP TATTOO

Fig. 18-1. A drawing showing the lip tattoo under the lip of a horse. The prefix letter denotes the age of the horse, and the number denotes The Jockey Club registry number. (Drawing by Prof. R. F. Johnson)

Pinkerton's National Detective Agency, The Jockey Club, and others have also developed a method of identifying horses which corresponds to the human system of fingerprinting employed by the FBI and police departments throughout the world. A horse can be identified by its chestnuts or night-eyes; these consist of a horny growth on each of the four legs.[1] Studies reveal (1) that no two chestnuts are exactly alike, and (2) that from the yearling stage on, these chestnuts retain their distinctive sizes and shapes. The

---

[1]Chestnuts occur on the inside of each front leg above the knee and on the back legs below the hock. In rare instances, a horse lacks a chestnut on one or both hind limbs.

chestnuts are photographed, and then classified according to (1) size, and (2) distinctive pattern.

"Fingerprinting" horse chestnuts is both costly and complex. Also, except as a means of establishing herd ownership on range horses (where all animals in a specific herd are given the owner's registered brand), hot-iron hide brands are seldom used as a means of marking or identifying horses because they tend to damage the appearance of the animal and decrease its salability. However, the following two methods of individual identification are available for use by horse owners:

1. **The lip tattoo**—Lip tattoo equipment and ink similar to that used by the Thoroughbred Racing Protective Bureau is manufactured and sold commercially. The manufacturer's step-by-step instructions relative to the use of one commercially available tattoo gun reads as follows:

a. After the digits are placed in the head of the tattoo gun, place the gun head with the digits in a dish of antiseptic (such as Zephiran chloride, available at any drugstore).

b. Roll and hold upper lip back with fingers; do not place anything back of lip.

c. Wipe upper lip clean with cotton saturated with rubbing alcohol.

d. Shake gun to dry off excess antiseptic.

e. Apply tattoo gun, making sure gun and digits are square with lip. Hold gun rigidly and with sufficient pressure to withstand recoil action of gun.

f. Apply ink and rub into perforations with thumb. Use more ink if bleeding persists. Leave any excess ink on lip.

2. **Freeze marking (cold branding)**—This method of identifying horses, known as *freeze marking* (cold branding), was developed at Washington State University. Called the Angle System, it is derived from the ancient Arabic numeral system. It utilizes the basic principle that straight lines are easy to make with crude instruments. It offers simplicity, preciseness, universal application, and good visual communication. Also, it lends itself to a computerized data retrieval system. Freeze marking is now used to identify horses in the United States, and in several other countries.

Called *freeze marking* to escape painful association with the term *branding*, the technique utilizes heavy copper stamps, or marking rods, chilled in either liquid nitrogen (at −300°F) or dry ice, and 95% alcohol. The area to be marked is shaved and scrubbed with a 95% alcohol wetting solution to aid in conducting the intense cold and to withdraw body heat.

Placing the copper stamp against the animal's body for 10 to 20 seconds destroys pigment-producing cells (melanocytes) and produces a pigment-free skin area. Hairs growing back in this area will be white.

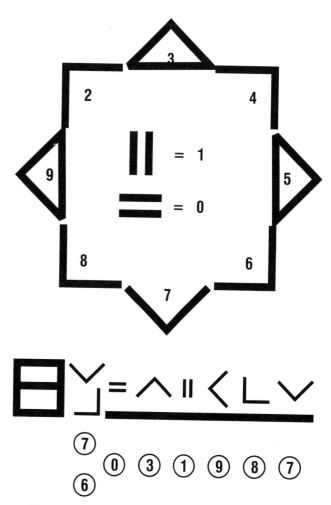

Fig. 18-2. Above is a series of right angles developed at Washington State University. The number that each angle represents is written inside the angle.

Below is a freeze brand as it would actually appear under the mane of a horse. The encircled numbers do not appear in the brand; they are used in this illustration and caption merely to enhance readability. The first symbol, the capital A, denotes that the horse is a purebred Arabian. The stacked symbols in the second position indicate the year of birth of the horse. The remaining symbols are the horse's registration number: 031987.

Longer application times result in more balding, a condition necessary for producing legible marks on white or light-colored animals.

A freeze mark that produces white hair causes only minimal changes in the hide and does not seriously impair leather properties. Freeze marks that produce baldness cause some permanent scarring and hide damage. Severe freeze mark damage, however, is minimal compared with fire brand damage.

Freeze marking is more legible than fire branding. Marks are much more distinct, and last just as long. No open wound is produced, which eliminates disease and insect infestations, and freeze marking is relatively painless.

Fig. 18-3. Cold (freeze) branded horse. Note that the identity is placed on the neck under the mane, as is preferred by some exhibitors. (Courtesy, USDA)

Fig. 18-4. *Peter Pan*, a Shetland Pony, before and after foot trimming. *Top:* Hoofs turned grotesquely upward like wooden shoes—the results of three years' neglect while confined to a small corral. *Bottom:* Six months later, following trimming by master farrier, M. I. Rasmussen, New Mexico State University, Las Cruces. (Courtesy, Mr. Rasmussen)

Because some equestrians, particularly those who show horses, object to a visible mark, the mark is usually placed on the neck under the mane. It is applied approximately 2 in. below the eruption of the mane and about midway between the poll and withers. An area approximately 12 in. × 7 in. is clipped close to the skin and washed with alcohol. The iron is then applied to the clipped area of the neck.

3. **Parentage verification.** To achieve parentage verification it is necessary that the stallion, mare, and foal be genotyped. Currently, genotyping for the American Quarter Horse Association is conducted through DNA analysis of a few strands of hair from the horse's mane. Because DNA is unique to each horse and cannot be altered, it is the most accurate identification known.

CARE OF THE FEET

The value of a horse lies chiefly in its ability to move; hence, good feet and legs are necessary. The Greeks alluded to this age-old axiom: "no foot, no horse."

Of course, nature didn't intend that the horse be used on hard surfaces or have a person on its back. When it is realized that the horse has been transplanted from its natural environment and soft, mother-earth footing to be used in carrying and drawing loads over hard, dry-surfaced topography by day and then stabled on hard, dry floors at night, it is not surprising that foot troubles are commonplace. Thus, when people domesticated horses, they assumed certain responsibilities for their care in an unnatural environ-

ment—including trimming, shoeing, and caring for their feet.

The important points in the care of a horse's feet are to keep them clean, prevent them from drying out, trim them so they retain proper shape and length, and shoe them correctly when shoes are needed.

Each day, the feet of horses that are shod, stabled, or used should be cleaned and inspected for loose shoes and thrush. Thrush is a fungus disease of the foot, caused by a necrotic fungus, and characterized by a pungent odor. It causes a deterioration of tissues in the cleft of the frog or in the junction between the frog and bars. This disease produces lameness and, if not treated, can be serious.

HORSESHOEING

Horseshoeing is a time-honored profession. In the golden age of the horse, which extends from the Gay Nineties to the mechanization of American agriculture, every schoolchild knew and respected the village blacksmith who plied his trade "under the spreading chestnut tree."

It is not necessary that horse owners and managers be expert farriers. Yet, they should be knowledgeable relative to (1) the anatomy and nomenclature of the foot, (see Fig. 3-4 and Table 3-1, Chapter 3), (2) what constitutes proper stance and motion, and how

Fig. 18-7. Master horseshoer at work.

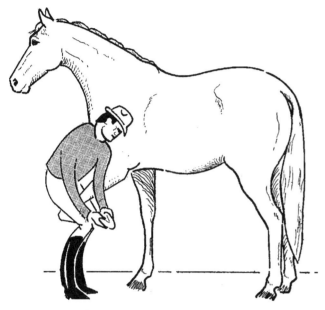

Fig. 18-5. Correct way to pick up and examine the front foot.

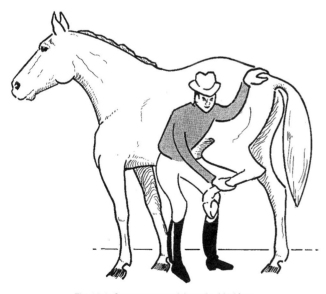

Fig. 18-6. Correct way to pick up the hind foot.

to correct some common faults through trimming, (3) the basic horseshoeing tools and how to use them, (4) how to recognize good and faulty shoeing, (5) kinds of shoes, and (6) the treatment of dry hoofs.

PROPER STANCE; CORRECTING COMMON FAULTS

Before trimming the feet or shoeing a horse, it is important to know what constitutes both proper and faulty conformation. This is pictured in Chapter 4, Figs. 4-17 and 4-18.

Fig. 18-8 shows the proper posture of the hoof and incorrect postures caused by hoofs grown too long in either toe or heel. The slope is considered normal when the toe of the hoof and the pastern have the same direction. This angle should always be kept in mind and changed only as a corrective measure. If it should become necessary to correct uneven wear of the hoof, the correction should be made gradually over a period of several trimmings.

Prior to the trimming of the feet, the horse should be inspected while standing squarely on a level area—preferably a hard surface. Then it should be seen in action, both at the walk and the trot.

The hoofs should be trimmed every month or six weeks, whether the animal is shod or not. If shoes are left on too long, the hoofs grow out of proportion. This

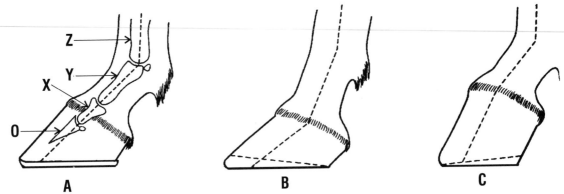

Fig. 18-8. **(A)** Properly trimmed hoof with normal foot axis: O—coffin bone; X—short pastern bone; Y—long pastern bone; Z—cannon bone. **(B)** Toe too long, which breaks the foot axis backward. Horizontal dotted line shows how hoof should be trimmed to restore normal posture. **(C)** Heel too long, which breaks the foot axis forward. Horizontal dotted line shows how trimming will restore the correct posture.

may throw the horse off balance and place extra stress upon the tendons. Hence, the hoofs should always be kept at the proper length and the correct posture. They should be trimmed near the level of the sole; otherwise, they will split off if the horse remains unshod. The frog should be trimmed carefully, with only ragged edges removed that allow the filth to accumulate in the crevices, and the sole should be trimmed sparingly, if at all. The wall of the hoof should never be rasped.

Table 18-1 shows the common faults and how to correct them through proper trimming.

and wearing away faster than the growth of the horn. Also, shoes may be used to change gaits and action, to correct faulty hoof structure or growth, and to protect the hoof itself from such conditions as corns, contraction, or cracks. When properly done, shoes should interfere as little as possible with the physiological functions of the different structures of the foot or with the gaits of the horse.

Just as do-it-yourself woodworkers, mechanics, and whatnot usually have a shop and some tools, so equestrians should have certain basic horseshoeing tools, and know how to use them. Table 18-2 may be used as a guide in selecting tools.

TABLE 18-1
COMMON FOOT FAULTS, AND HOW TO CORRECT THEM

Fault	How It Looks	How to Trim
Splayfoot	Front toes turned out, heels turned in.	Trim the outer half of the foot.
Pigeon-toed	Front toes turned in, heels turned out—the opposite of splayfoot.	Trim the inner half of foot more heavily; leave the outer half relatively long.
Quarter crack	Vertical crack on side of hoof.	Keep the hoof moist, shorten the toes, and use a corrective shoe.
Cocked ankles	Standing bent forward on fetlocks—most frequently the hind ones.	Lower the heels to correct. However, raising the heels makes for more immediate horse comfort.
Contracted heels	Close at the heels.	Lower the heels and allow the frog to carry more of the weight, which tends to spread the heels apart.

TABLE 18-2
HORSESHOEING TOOLS AND THEIR USE

Tools	Use
Anvil	As a block to shape shoes, and as the farrier's work bench.
Forge	To heat steel or shoes in preparation for shaping them for the horse being shod.
Vise	To finish shoes, and to hold metal.
Knife	To remove dirt and trim excess frog and sole from the foot. The hook on the end is used to trim the frog and clean the crevice between the bar and frog.

(Continued)

HORSESHOEING TOOLS, AND HOW TO USE THEM

Horses are shod to protect the foot from breaking

TABLE 18-2 (Continued)

Tools	Use
Nippers or parers	To trim the wall of the hoof and other parts that are too hard for the knife. There is hardly any limit to the sizes and descriptions of these items; some are one-sided, others are two-sided.
Hoof level	To determine the angle of the hoof relative to the ground surface.
Clinch cutter	To cut clinches prior to pulling shoes.
Rasp	To level the foot after trimming; one side is coarse, and the other side fine.
Driving hammer	To drive nails into hoof.
Hardy	As a wedge in the anvil hole, in cutting steel of the desired length and in cutting off shoes.
Hammers	To shape shoes. Various kinds of hammers may be used.
Tongs	To hold hot metal.
Nails	Assorted sizes of nails are available for different types of horseshoes.
Apron	To protect the horseshoer from sparks, from cuts that might otherwise be inflicted by slips of the knife or rasp, and from possible nail injury of nervous horses.

HOW TO RECOGNIZE GOOD AND FAULTY SHOEING

The following checklist may be used as a means by which to evaluate a shoeing job, whether plied by the caretaker or owner, or by a professional farrier:

1. As viewed from the front—

Yes No

- ☐ ☐ Are the front feet the same size, the toes the same length, and the heels the same height?
- ☐ ☐ Is the foot in balance in relation to the leg?
- ☐ ☐ Is the foot directly under the leg, is the axis of the foot in prolongation to the axis of the up-per leg bones, and is the weight of the body equally distributed over the foot structure?

2. As viewed from the side—

Yes No

- ☐ ☐ Does the axis of the foot coincide with the axis of the pastern?
- ☐ ☐ Does the slope of the wall from the coronet to the lower border parallel the slope of the pastern?
- ☐ ☐ Has the lower outer border of the wall been rasped?
- ☐ ☐ Does the conformation of the foot and the type of shoe used warrant the amount of rasping done?

3. As the height and strength of nailing are inspected closely—

Yes No

- ☐ ☐ Do the nails come out of the wall at the proper height and in sound horn?
- ☐ ☐ Are the nails driven to a greater height in the wall than necessary?
- ☐ ☐ Is the size of the nail used best suited for the size and condition of the foot and the weight of the shoe?
- ☐ ☐ Are the clinches of sufficient thickness where the nail comes out of the wall to ensure strength?
- ☐ ☐ Are the clinches smooth and not projecting above the surface of the wall?

4. As the outline and size of the shoe are scrutinized—

Yes No

- ☐ ☐ Is the toe of the shoe fitted with sufficient fullness to give lateral support to the foot at the moment of breaking over and leaving the ground?
- ☐ ☐ Are the branches of the shoe from the bend of the quarter to the heel fitted fuller than the outline of the wall to provide for expansion of the foot and normal growth of horn between shoeing periods?
- ☐ ☐ Are the heels of the shoe of sufficient length and width to cover the buttresses?
- ☐ ☐ Are the heels finished without sharp edges?
- ☐ ☐ Does the shoe rest evenly on the bearing surface of the hoof, covering the lower border of the wall, white line, and buttresses?
- ☐ ☐ Is the shoe concaved so that it does not rest upon the horny sole?
- ☐ ☐ Are the nail heads properly seated?
- ☐ ☐ Is the shoe the correct size for the foot?
- ☐ ☐ Will the weight of the shoe provide reasonable wear and protection to the foot?
- ☐ ☐ Have the ragged particles of the horny frog been removed?

KINDS OF SHOES

A number of factors should be considered when selecting the shoes for a given horse; among them:

1. **The proper size**—The shoe should fit the hoof, rather than any attempt being made to trim the hoof to fit the shoe.

Shoes come in sizes. The old size compared to the Multi-Product shoe (a popular Japanese-made shoe) which is widely used in the United States, follows:[2]

Old Standard Shoe (Size)	Multi-Product (Japanese) (Size)
00	3
0	4
1	5
Half size	6
2	7
Half size	8
3	9

2. **Front vs hind shoes**—Front shoes are more nearly circular and wider at the heels than hind shoes.

3. **The individual horse**—His weight, the shape and texture of his hoof, and the set of his legs should be considered.

4. **The use to which the horse is put, and the kind of ground**—A plain shoe or rim shoe is satisfactory for most horses used for pleasure, cutting, roping, barrel racing, polo, and jumping; whereas racing plates, to aid in gripping the track, are needed on running horses. Also, there are many corrective shoes, a few of which are listed in Table 18-3.

Shoes may be either handmade or ready-made (factory-made). The latter are becoming increasingly popular because they (1) require a minimum of work, and (2) are ideal for the do-it-yourselfer. Both steel and aluminum shoes are available. Fig. 18-9 shows four common types of horseshoes.

TABLE 18-3
SOME CORRECTIVE SHOES, AND THEIR USE

Kind of Corrective Shoe	Purpose or Use
Bar shoe	To apply pressure to the frog of the foot, or to relieve pressure on any part of it.
Rocker toe shoe	For use on horses that stumble, that forge, or that have ringbone or sidebones.
Squared toe shoe with trailer	For cow-hocked horses.
Lateral extension toed shoe	For horses that either toe out or toe in.

---

[2]Several good brands of shoes are available from which selections may be made.

A READY-MADE SHOE IS SUITED FOR MOST RIDING AND DRIVING HORSES.

READY-MADE SHOE

A SELF-CLEANING RIM SHOE IS SUITED FOR HORSES USED FOR RIDING, CUTTING, ROPING, BARREL RACING, POLO, AND JUMPING.

RIM SHOE

A HOT SHOE IS ONE THAT MUST BE HEATED AND SHAPED PRIOR TO BEING USED.

HOT SHOE

A RACING PLATE MEETS THE EXACTING NEEDS OF RACEHORSES—IT IS LIGHT IN WEIGHT, AND IT GRIPS THE TRACK.

RACING PLATE

Fig. 18-9. Common types of horseshoes.

■ **Toe Grabs**[3]—*Toe grabs are common racing shoes, which elevate the toe and increase the traction on the track.*

Toe grabs may be low, regular, or high. They are used mostly on Thoroughbreds; it is estimated that 90% of the Thoroughbred racehorses in California compete in toe grabs.

A recent study conducted by the University of California, Davis, Veterinary Orthopedic Research Laboratory, showed that you can have too much traction. In a study involving 201 horses, the scientists found that toe grabs are associated with a markedly increased risk of sustaining suspensory apparatus injury. The odds of being hurt were 16 times greater for a horse wearing regular toe grabs, which extend six millimeters from the bottom of shoes, than for horses shod without grabs. For horses wearing low toe grabs, which extend four millimeters, the odds of

---

[3]Biles, D. B., *The Blood-Horse*, Lexington, KY, July 20, 1996, p. 3562.

injury were six times greater. The researchers postulated two reasons why toe grabs cause problems: (1) a toe grab elevates the toe and changes the geometry of the horse's hoof as well as the geometry of the bones all the way up the leg; and (2) a toe grab increases, excessively, the amount of traction that a horse gets on the track. In addition to pinpointing a potential shoeing problem, the University of California, Davis researchers came up with a possible solution: Rim shoes, they discovered, seemed to decrease the risk of injury. The odds of suffering suspensory apparatus failure for horses wearing such shoes were one-third of those for horses without rim shoes. Like the toe grab, a rim shoe helps improve a horse's traction but with one important difference. The toe grab's traction device is located only on the front of the shoe, while the rim shoe's extended part goes all the way around the bottom surface. There are inner rims and outer rims, the researchers continued, with their preference expressed for inner rims. The researchers concluded: "As the height of the toe grabs increases, the odds of injury also increase."

TREATMENT OF DRY HOOFS

In the wild state, horses roved over the prairies and moistened their hoofs frequently as they drank deep from the streams and lakes. But domestication changed all this. Today, the vast majority of horses spend much of their time in a dry stall or corral; stand dry footed as they drink from a bucket, fountain, or tank; are shod; and are exercised on a hard, dry surface—conditions which make for dry, brittle hoofs. With the domestication of horses, therefore, people entered into an unwritten contract with them—to replace nature's way of keeping the hoofs moist.

When hoofs become dry and brittle, they sometimes split and cause lameness. The frogs lose their elasticity and are no longer effective shock absorbers. If the dryness is prolonged, the frogs shrink and the heels contract.

Dry hoofs usually can be prevented by keeping the ground wet around the watering tank, attaching wet burlap sacks around the hoofs, or applying a hoof dressing.

A good hoof dressing will restore and maintain necessary flexibility and elasticity of the hoof. It will (1) penetrate the hoof structure readily; (2) allow the hoof to breathe; (3) regulate the absorption and evaporation of moisture; and (4) accentuate the natural luster of the hoof, without leaving a sticky residue or sealing off the hoof wall. When applied daily, a hoof dressing will penetrate the hoof and prevent evaporation of the moisture that is already within the hoof, thereby imparting suppleness (elasticity). Several satisfactory commercial hoof dressings are on the market. Also, a good homemade product may be made as follows:

    6 parts fish oil (cod liver oil)
    1 part pine tar oil
    1 part Creolin
    2 parts glycerin

The above mix should be stirred well before using and applied daily. If fish oil is not available, raw linseed oil may be substituted.

When it comes to preventing dry hoofs, "an ounce of prevention is worth a pound of cure"—then some. Each day, the feet of shod horses that are confined to a stable (or corral) should be cleaned thoroughly, then treated with a hoof dressing. By means of a brush or cloth, apply the hoof dressing to the coronet, the wall, and the bottom surface (including the frog), of freshly cleaned feet. Because most of the moisture within the hoof rises through the sole (like sap rises in a tree), be sure to apply plenty of hoof dressing to the bottom area.

The telltale symptoms of too dry feet are: hardness and drying of the horny frog, contracted heels, corns, brittle hoofs, and sometimes cracks and lameness. When these conditions prevail, good nursing and first aid treatment are essential. The first step is to correct any errors in shoeing and trimming, and the second is to restore and maintain the normal moisture content of the horn. Treating the wall and the bottom of the feet daily with hoof dressing will accomplish the latter.

Hoof dressing is not designed to take the place of proper trimming and shoeing by an experienced farrier; rather, it should go hand in hand with them.

GELATIN AS PREVENTIVE FOR DRY, BRITTLE HOOFS

Although it is true that the major protein in the hoofs of horses is gelatin, the author is not aware of any experimental evidence that the feeding of gelatin as such will improve the structure, toughness, and moisture of the hoof.

Hoof tissue is synthesized in the body primarily from the amino acids contained in the bloodstream, and these can be derived from any good source of protein for horses, such as linseed meal and soybean meal. Of course, a deficiency of protein in the horse's ration would tend to produce poor hoofs, but this protein can be furnished from sources other than gelatin and the same results obtained.

From the standpoint of other tissue in the body, gelatin is a rather incomplete protein, notably deficient in the amino acids lysine and tryptophan. From an overall metabolism standpoint, therefore, gelatin would appear to be a poorer source of protein than the oilseed proteins—linseed, soybean, cottonseed, peanut, and canola meal.

For the above reasons, before buying and feeding gelatin instead of one of the oilseed proteins, the feeder is admonished to see research data, conducted by a reputable independent research laboratory, in support of the gelatin theory.

CARE OF THE FOAL'S FEET

Foals may become unsound of limb when the wear and tear is not equally distributed due to an unshapely hoof. On the other hand, faulty limbs may be helped or even corrected by regular and persistent trimming. Such practice also tends to educate the foal and make shoeing easier at maturity. If the foal is run on pasture, trimming the feet may be necessary long before weaning time. A good practice is to check the feet regularly every month or six weeks and to trim a small amount each time if trimming is needed rather than trim too much at any one time. Tendons should not receive undue strain by careless trimming of the feet. Usually, only the outer rim should be trimmed, though sometimes it is necessary to cut down the heel or frog to shorten the toes. The necessary trimming may be done with the rasp, farrier's knife, and nippers (using the rasp for the most part.)

Before the feet are trimmed, the foal should be inspected first while standing squarely on a hard surface. Then it should be seen in action, both at the walk and the trot.

WEANING THE FOAL

Weaning of the foal is more a matter of preparation than of absolute separation from the dam. The simplicity with which it is accomplished depends very largely upon the thoroughness of the preparation.

AGE OF WEANING

Foals are usually weaned at 4 to 6 months of age, depending on conditions. When either the foal or the mare is not doing well, when the mare is being given heavy work, or when the dam has been rebred on the ninth day after foaling, it may be advisable to wean the foal at a comparatively early age. On the other hand, when both the mare and the foal seem to be doing well, when the mare is idle, when breeding has been delayed following foaling, or when it is desirable to develop the foal to the maximum, the weaning may very well be delayed until 6 months of age.

If by means of the creep or a separate grain box, the foal has become accustomed to the consumption of considerable grain and hay (about ¾ lb of grain per each 100 lb liveweight daily), weaning will result in very little disturbance or setback. Likewise, if the ration of the dam has been decreased (lessened by one-half) a few days before the separation, usually her udder will dry up with no difficulty.

SEPARATION OF MARE AND FOAL

When all preliminary precautions and preparations for weaning have been made, the separation should be accomplished. This should be complete and final with no opportunity for the foal to see, hear, or smell its dam again. Otherwise, all which has been gained up to this time will be lost, and it will be necessary to begin all over again. Perhaps the best arrangement is to shut the foal in the stall to which it has been accustomed and to move the mare away to new quarters, making certain that all obstructions have first been removed so that there is no possibility of injury to the foal while it is fretting over the separation.

After weanlings have remained in the stable for a day or two and have quieted down, they should be turned out to pasture. Where a group of weanlings is involved, undue running and possible injury hazard may be minimized in this transition by the following procedure: First turn two or three of the least valuable animals out and let them tire themselves out, and then turn the rest of the weanlings out and they will do very little running.

With a great number of weanlings, it is advisable to separate the sexes, and even to place some of the more timid ones to themselves. In all cases, it is best not to run weanlings with older horses.

DRYING UP THE MARE

The following procedure for drying up the mare is recommended:

1. Rub an oil preparation (such as camphorated oil or a mixture of lard and spirits of camphor) on the bag. Take the mare from the foal and place her on less lush pasture or grass hay.

2. Examine the udder and rub oil on it at intervals, but do not milk it out for 5 to 7 days. It will fill up and get tight, *but do not milk it out*. At the end of 5 to 7 days, when the bag is soft and flabby, milk out what little secretions remain (probably not more than a half a cup).

CASTRATION

Regardless of age or time, the operation is best performed by an experienced veterinarian. A colt may be castrated when only a few days old, but most equestrians prefer to delay the operation until the animal is about one year of age. Although there is less real danger to the animal and much less setback with early altering, the practice results in imperfect development of the foreparts. On the other hand, leaving the colt entire for a time will result in more muscular, bold features and better carriage of the foreparts. Therefore, weather and management conditions permitting, the time of altering should be determined by the development of the individual animal. Thus, underdeveloped colts may be left entire six months or even a year longer than overdeveloped ones. Breeders of Thoroughbred horses usually prefer to have the horse's first race as an entire.

There is less danger of infection if colts are castrated in the spring of the year soon after they are turned out on a clean pasture. Naturally, this should be done sufficiently early so as to avoid hot weather and fly time.

EXERCISE

Regular exercise is essential to strong, sound feet and legs and to health.

Except during times of inclement weather and when being worked heavily, horses should be out in the open where they can romp and play on natural footing as much as possible. For this purpose, pastures are ideal, especially for young animals.

Where exercise on pasture is not feasible, mature animals should be exercised for an hour daily under saddle or hitched to a cart.

When handled carefully, the broodmare should be exercised within a day or two of foaling. Above all, when not receiving forced exercise or on idle days, she should not be confined to a stable or a small dry lot.

Frequently, in light horses, bad feet exclude exercise on roads, and faulty tendons exclude exercise

Fig. 18-10. Correct method of longeing a horse, with a longeing cavesson and long web tape longe line in use.

under saddle. Under such conditions, one may have to depend upon (1) exercise taken voluntarily in a large paddock, (2) longeing or exercise on a 30- to 40-ft. rope, or (3) leading.

TRANSPORTING HORSES

Horses are transported via trailer, van, truck, rail, boat, and plane. Today, transportation by motor (trailer, van, or truck) is most common because of the distinct advantage of door-to-door movement. Regardless of the method, however, the objectives are the same: to move them safely, with a maximum of comfort, and as economically as possible. To this end, selection of equipment is the first requisite. But equipment alone, no matter how good, will not suffice.

Fig. 18-11. Front view of a horse in a trailer, showing animal properly blanketed, double tied, and with hay in the manger. Trailers are a very popular means of transporting one or two horses. (Courtesy, USDA)

The trip must be preceded by proper preparation including conditioning of horses; and horses must receive proper care, including smooth movement, *en route*.

The discussion which follows presents, in summary form, the requisites of good transportation, with special emphasis on motor transportation. The same principles also apply to plane, boat, and rail shipments, although each method of transportation has certain peculiarities and presents special problems.

■ **Provide good footing**—The floor of the vehicle should be covered with heavy coco matting made for the purpose, sand covered with straw or other suitable bedding material, or rubber mats. Clean the floor covering at frequent intervals while in transit to avoid ammonia and heat.

■ **Drive carefully**—Drive at a moderate, constant speed as distinguished from fast or jerky driving, which causes added stress and tiring. If weather conditions make the roads unsafe, the vehicle should be stopped.

■ **Make nurse stops**—Nurse stops should be made at about three-hour intervals when mares and foals are transported together.

■ **Provide proper ventilation**—Provide plenty of fresh air without drafts.

■ **Teach horses to load early in life**—When horses will be transported later in life, they should be accustomed to transportation as youngsters before they get too big and strong. This can be done by moving them from one part of the farm to another.

■ **Provide health certificate and statement of ownership**—A health certificate signed by a licensed veterinarian is required for most interstate shipments. Foreign shipments must be accompanied by a health certificate that has been approved by a government veterinarian. The latter takes several days. Branded horses must be accompanied by a brand certificate, and all horses should be accompanied by a statement of ownership.

■ **Schedule properly**—Schedule the transportation so that animals will arrive on time. Show, sale, and race animals should arrive a few days early.

■ **Have the horses relaxed**—Horses ship best when they are relaxed and not overtired before they are moved.

■ **Clean and disinfect public conveyance**—Before using any type of public conveyance, thoroughly clean and disinfect it. Steam is excellent for this purpose. Remove nails or other hazards that might cause injury.

■ **Have a competent caretaker accompany horses**—Valuable horses should not be shipped in the care of an inexperienced person.

■ **Use shanks except on stallions**—When animals are tied, use a ⅝-inch cotton rope shank that is 5 ft long and has a big swivel snap at the end. Chain shanks are too noisy. Always tie the shank with a knot that can easily and quickly be released in case of an emergency.

■ **Feed lightly**—Allow horses only a half feed of grain before they are loaded for shipment and at the first feed after they reach their destination. In transit, horses should be fed alfalfa, to keep the bowels open, but no concentrates should be fed. Commercial hay nets or homemade burlap containers may be used to hold the hay in transit, but they should not be placed too high.

■ **Water liberally**—When transporting horses, give them all the fresh, clean water they will drink at frequent intervals unless the weather is extremely hot

and there is danger of gorging. A tiny bit of molasses may be added to each pail of water, beginning about a week before the horses are shipped, and the addition of molasses to the water may be continued in transit. This prevents any taste change in the water.

■ **Pad the stalls**—Many experienced shippers favor padding the inside of the vehicle to lessen the likelihood of injury, especially when a valuable animal is shipped. Coco matting or a sack of straw properly placed may save the horse's hocks from injury.

■ **Take along tools and supplies**—The following tools and supplies should be taken along in a suitable box: pinch bar, hammer, hatchet, saw, nails, pliers, flashlight, extra halters and shanks, twitch, canvas slapper or short piece of hose, pair of gloves, fork and broom, fire extinguisher, and medicine for colic and shipping fever provided by a veterinarian.

■ **Check shoes, blankets, and bandages**—Whenever possible, ship horses barefoot. Never allow them to wear calked shoes during a long shipment. They may wear smooth shoes. In cool weather, horses may be blanketed if an attendant is present in case a horse gets entangled. The legs of racehorses in training should be bandaged to keep the ankles from getting scuffed or the tendons bruised. Bandages are not necessary on breeding stock except for valuable stallions and young animals. When bandages are used, they should be reset often.

■ **Be calm when loading and unloading**—In loading and unloading horses, always be patient and never show anger. Try kindness first; pat the horse and speak to it to reassure it. If this fails, it may be necessary to use one of the following techniques:

1. Sometimes the use of a twitch at the right time is desirable, especially if the horse is tossing its head about.

Fig. 18-12. Easy does it! This shows an easy way in which to load a "green" horse into a trailer.

2. When a horse must be disciplined, a canvas slapper or a short rubber hose can be used effectively; these make a lot of noise without inflicting much hurt.

3. If a horse gets very excited and is about to break out, dash a bucket of water in its face; usually it will back off and calm down.

4. A nervous, excitable horse may be calmed by a tranquilizer, which should be administered by a veterinarian.

5. If a horse will not move or is kicking, grab its tail and push it over its back. In this position, it cannot kick but can be pushed along.

■ **Control insects**—In season, flies and other insects molest animals in transit. When necessary, use a reliable insecticide to control insects. Follow directions on the container label.

Trailers, vans, and trucks have the very great advantage of being able to load from in front of one stable and unload in front of another.

The trailer is usually a one- or two-horse unit, which is drawn behind a car or truck. Generally speaking, this method of transportation is best adapted to short distances—less than 500 miles. Horses are trailered to shows, races, endurance rides, breeding establishments, to new owners, and from one work area to another on the range; in fact, it may well be said that today's horses are well traveled.

The van or vanlike trailer is a common and satisfactory method of transportation where three to eight horses are involved. There is hardly any limit to the kinds of vans, ranging from rather simple to very palatial pieces of equipment.

Most experienced horse shippers frown upon shipping horses in an open truck.

Rail shipments are seldom used anymore. But during the heyday of the draft horse and mule—until the 1930s—rail shipments were the common mode of horse transportation. Old-time caretakers, who have used various methods of transportation, are generally agreed that horses ship more comfortably by rail, either by freight or express, than in any other way.

Like rail shipments, boat shipments have declined in importance in recent years. Where valuable horses are involved, they have given way to the greater speed and flexibility of plane transportation.

Plane shipments are a specialty, the details of which had best be left in the hands of an experienced person or agency, such as an importing or exporting company or the representative of the airline. At the present time, such shipments are largely confined to valuable racehorses, polo ponies, and breeding horses, with both national and international movements involved.

Fig. 18-13. A horse being boarded on a cargo liner in Kennedy Airport, New York, for transport to Hollywood Park. (Courtesy, United Airlines)

BEDDING HORSES

A soft comfortable bed will ensure proper rest and make for a cleaner animal and easier grooming. But bedding has the following added values from the standpoint of manure:

1. It soaks up the urine, which contains about one-half to total plant food of manure.

2. It makes manure easier to handle.

3. It absorbs plant nutrients, fixing both ammonia and potash in relatively insoluble forms that protect them against losses by leaching. This characteristic of bedding is especially important in peat moss, but of little significance with sawdust and shavings.

KIND AND AMOUNT OF BEDDING

The kind of bedding material selected should be determined primarily by (1) availability and price, (2) absorptive capacity, (3) cleanness (this excludes dirt or dust which might cause odors or stain horses), (4) ease of handling, (5) ease of cleanup and disposal, (6) nonirritability from dust or components causing allergies, (7) texture or size, and (8) fertility value or plant nutrient content. In addition, a desirable bedding should not be excessively coarse, and should remain well in place and not be too readily kicked aside.

Table 18-4 lists some common bedding materials and gives the average water absorptive capacity of each. Cereal straw and wood shavings are the favorite bedding materials for horses.

TABLE 18-4
WATER ABSORPTION OF BEDDING MATERIALS

Material	Lb of Water Absorbed per Cwt of Air-Dry Bedding
Barley straw	210
Cocoa shells	270
Corn stover (shredded)	250
Corncobs (crushed or ground)	210
Cottonseed hulls	250
Flax straw	260
Hay (mature, chopped)	300
Leaves (broadleaf)	200
(pine needles)	100
Oat hulls	200
Oat straw (long)	280
(chopped)	375
Peanut hulls	250
Peat moss	1,000
Rye straw	210
Sand	25
Sawdust (top quality pine)	250
(run-of-the-mill hardwood)[1]	150
Sugarcane bagasse	220
Tree bark (dry, fine)	250
(from tanneries)	400
Vermiculite[2]	350
Wheat straw (long)	220
(chopped)	295
Wood chips (top quality pine)	300
(run-of-the-mill hardwood)[1]	150
Wood shavings (top quality pine)	200
(run-of-the-mill hardwood)[1]	150

[1]*CAUTION:* Do not use black walnut shavings or sawdust. They may cause acute laminitis—even death.

[2]This is a micalike mineral and mined chiefly in South Carolina and Montana.

Naturally, the availability and price per ton of various bedding materials vary from area to area, and from year to year. Thus, in the New England states shavings and sawdust are available, whereas other forms of bedding are scarce, and straws are more plentiful in the central and western states.

Other facts of importance, relative to certain bedding materials and bedding uses, are:

1. **Wood products (sawdust, shavings, tree bark, chips, etc.)**—The suspicion that wood products will hurt the land is rather widespread but unfounded. It is true that shavings and sawdust decompose slowly, but this process can be expedited by the addition of nitrogen fertilizers. Also, when plowed under, they increase soil acidity, but the change is both small and temporary.

Softwood (on weight basis) is about twice as absorptive as hardwood, and green wood has only 50% the absorptive capacity of dried wood.

But, *beware of black walnut shavings and sawdust.* Although the black walnut *(Juglans nigra)* is the aristocrat of U.S. hardwoods for making furniture, numerous cases of laminitis in horses exposed to black walnut shavings or sawdust have been reported. The laminitis occurs within 12 to 24 hours of contact with fresh bedding containing black walnut shavings or sawdust. Skin contact will trigger the onset of laminitis; horses need not eat the bedding. Swelling of the fetlocks and hocks have been reported in some cases—and there have been some deaths. Although the toxic element has not been identified, some researchers are studying a chemical component unique to black walnut known as *juglone.*

2. **Cut straw**—Cut straw will absorb more liquid than long straw; cut oats or wheat straw will take up about 25% more water than long straw from comparable material. But there are disadvantages to chopping—chopped straw may be dusty.

From the standpoint of the value of plant food nutrients per ton of air-dry material, peat moss is the most valuable bedding and wood products the least valuable.

The minimum desirable amount of bedding to use is the amount necessary to absorb completely the liquids in the manure. For 24-hour confinement, the minimum daily bedding requirements of horses, based on uncut wheat or oats straw, is 10 to 15 lb. With other bedding materials, these quantities will vary according to their absorptive capacities (see Table 18-4). Also, more than minimum quantities of bedding may be desirable where cleanliness and comfort of the horse are important.

In most areas, bedding materials are becoming scarcer and higher in price, primarily because (1) geneticists are breeding plants with shorter straws and stalks, (2) there are more competitive and numerous uses for some of the materials, and (3) the current trend toward more confinement rearing of livestock requires more bedding.

Owners and caretakers may reduce bedding needs and costs as follows:

1. **Chop bedding.** Chopped straw, waste hay, fodder, or cobs will go further and do a better job of keeping horses dry than long materials.

2. **Ventilate quarters properly.** Proper ventilation lowers the humidity and keeps the bedding dry.

3. **Provide exercise area.** Where possible and practical, provide for exercise in well-drained, dry pastures or corrals, without confining horses to stalls more than necessary.

STABLE MANAGEMENT

The following stable management practices are recommended:

1. Remove the top layer of clay floors yearly; replace with fresh clay, and level and tamp. Also, keep the stable floor slightly higher than the surrounding area, thereby making for dryness.

2. Keep stalls well lighted.

3. Use properly constructed hayracks to lessen waste and contamination of hay, with the possible exception of maternity stalls.

4. Scrub concentrate containers at such intervals as necessary, and after feeding a wet mash.

5. Work over bedding daily, removing excrement and wet, stained or soiled material, and provide fresh bedding.

6. Practice rigid stable sanitation to prevent fecal contamination of feed and water.

7. Lead foals when taking them from stall to the paddock and back, as a way in which to further their training.

8. Restrict the ration when horses are idle, and provide either a wet bran mash the evening before an idle day or turn idle horses to pasture.

9. Provide proper ventilation at all times—by means of open doors, windows that open inwardly from the top, or stall partitions slatted at the top.

10. Keep stables in repair at all times, so as to lessen injury hazards.

MINIMIZE ELECTRICAL HAZARDS

Electrical storms and electrical lines can, and do, kill horses.

Horses tend to bunch together for protection during an electrical storm. In a pasture, horses often seek shelter under a large tree. Trees are frequently located near water troughs and/or wire fences, making them extremely good conductors of electricity. This arrangement, along with wet ground and steel horseshoes on the horses' feet, put horses in a precarious position.

Electricity in the form of lighting will follow low metal fencing for a considerable distance. Also, it travels along power lines and comes down poles or brace wires; and it can also strike tall trees and spread to the animals sheltered beneath the branches.

Although electrical storms cannot be prevented, the following things can be done to lessen the hazard of horses being struck by lightning:

1. House horses in a safe well-grounded building during electrical storms. A wooden barn is best, but a well-grounded metal barn is pretty safe.

2. Ground well conduit and water pipes.

3. Install wooden or vinyl fencing and posts rather than wire fencing.

4. Do not put horses in a pasture having one lone tree under which they can group during a storm.

5. Do not put horses in pastures having power line towers.

6. Avoid horse contact with 110-volt electrical lines or shortened electrical appliances such as mechanical walkers, clippers, blowers, heating tape for water lines, or any other electrical equipment.

MANURE

The term manure refers to a mixture of animal excrements (consisting of undigested feeds plus certain body wastes) and bedding.

The rise in light horse numbers, along with the shift of much of the horse population from the nation's farms and ranches to stables and small enclosures in suburban areas, created disposal problems. Surplus manure came during an era when chemical fertilizers were relatively abundant and cheap, with the result that most equestrians forgot that horses can provide manure for the fields.

No doubt, the manure pollution problems, suspicioned or real, will persist. However, the energy crisis, accompanied by high chemical fertilizer prices, has caused manure to be looked upon as a resource and not a waste that presents a disposal problem. At current fertilizer prices (per lb: nitrogen (N) = 25¢; phosphorus (P) = 20¢; and potassium (K) = 10¢), 1 ton of average horse manure is worth $5.05 (Table 18-5). As a result, a growing number of American farmers are returning to organic farming—they're using more manure—the unwanted barnyard centerpiece of the past 50 years. They are discovering that they are just as good reapers of the land and far better stewards of the soil.

In the future, as fertilizer and feed become increasingly scarce and expensive, the economic value of horse manure will increase.

From the standpoint of the soils and crops, barnyard manure contains the following valuable ingredients:

■ **Organic matter**—It supplies valuable organic matter which cannot be secured in chemical fertilizers. Organic matter—which constitutes three to six percent, by weight, of most soils—improves soil tilth, increases water-holding capacity, lessens water and wind erosion, improves aeration, and has a beneficial effect on soil microorganisms and plants. It is the lifeblood of the land.

■ **Plant food**—It supplies plant food or fertility—especially nitrogen, phosphorous, and potassium. In addition to these three nutrients, manure contains calcium, and trace elements such as boron, manganese, copper, and zinc. A ton of well-preserved horse manure, free of bedding, contains plant food nutrients equal to about 100 lb of 13-2-12 fertilizer (see Table 18-5). Thus, spreading manure at the rate of 8 tons per acre supplies the same amounts of nutrients as 800 lb of a 13-2-12 commercial fertilizer.

AMOUNT, COMPOSITION, AND VALUE OF MANURE PRODUCED

The quantity, composition, and value of horse manure produced vary according to weight of animal, kind and amount of feed, and kind and amount of bedding. The author's computations in Table 18-5 are on fresh manure (exclusive of bedding) basis and per 1,000 lb liveweight. As indicated, a 1,000 lb horse will produce about 8 tons of manure, free of bedding, per year.

The data in Table 18-5 are based on animals confined to stalls the year around. Actually, the manure recovered and available to spread where desired is considerably less than indicated because (1) animals are kept on pasture and along roads and lanes much of the year, where the manure is dropped, and (2) losses in weight often run as high as 60% when manure is exposed to the weather for a considerable time.

Fig. 18-14 shows the tons of manure (free of bedding) produced by different species per year per 1,000 lb weight. As noted, on comparable body weight basis, horses rank fourth in manure production, being exceeded by swine, dairy cows, and beef cattle.

About 75% of the nitrogen, 80% of the phosphorus, and 85% of the potassium contained in horse feeds are returned as manure. In addition, about 40% of the organic matter in feeds is excreted as manure. As a rule of thumb, it is commonly estimated that 80% of the total nutrients in feeds are excreted by horses as manure.

The urine makes up 20% of the total weight of the excrement of horses. Also, it is noteworthy that the nutrients in liquid manure are more readily available to plants than the nutrients in solid excrement. These are the reasons why it is important to conserve the urine.

The actual monetary value of manure can and should be based on (1) increased crop yields, and (2)

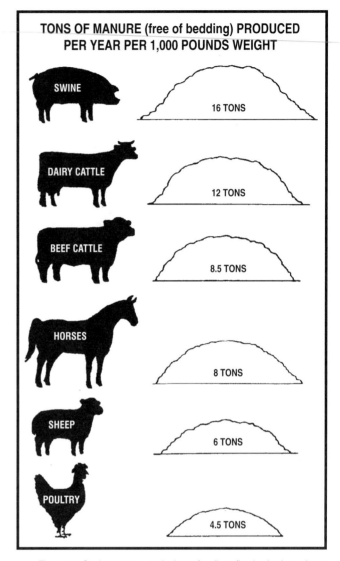

Fig. 18-14. On the average, each class of stall-confined animals produces per year per 1,000 lb weight the tonnages shown above.

equivalent cost of a like amount of commercial fertilizer. Numerous experiments and practical observations have shown the measurable monetary value of manure in increased crop yields. Tables 18-5 and 18-6 give the equivalent cost of a like amount of commercial fertilizer.

Currently, we are producing equine manure (exclusive of bedding) at the rate of 31,552,000 tons annually (see Table 18-6). Based on equivalent fertilizer prices (see Table 18-5, right hand column), and horse and mule numbers (Table 18-6), the yearly equine manure crop is worth $159,338,000.

Of course, the value of manure cannot be measured in terms of increased yearly crop yields and equivalent cost of a like amount of commercial fertilizer. It has additional value for the organic matter which it

TABLE 18-5
QUANTITY, COMPOSITION, AND VALUE OF FRESH HORSE MANURE
(FREE OF BEDDING) EXCRETED PER 1,000 LB LIVEWEIGHT

Tons Excreted/Year/ 1,000 Lb Liveweight[1]	Composition and Value of Manure on a Tonnage Basis[2]						
	Excrement	Lb/Ton[3]	Water	N	P[4]	K[4]	Value/Ton[5]
			(%)	(lb)	(lb)	(lb)	($)
8	Liquid	400					
	Solid	1,600					
	Total	2,000	60	13.8	2.0	12.0	5.05

[1]*Manure Is Worth Money—It Deserves Good Care*, University of Illinois Circ. 595, 1953, p. 4.

[2]Last 5 columns on the right from *Farm Manures*, University of Kentucky Circ. 595, 1964, p. 5, Table 2.

[3]From reference material for 1951 Saddle and Sirloin Essay Contest, p. 43, compiled by M. E. Ensminger; data from *Fertilizers and Crop Production*, by Van Slyke, published by Orange Judd Publishing Co.

[4]Phosphorus (P) can be converted to P_2O_5 by multiplying the figure given above by 2.29, and potassium (K) can be converted to K_2O by multiplying by 1.2.

[5]Calculated on the assumption that nitrogen (N) retails at 25¢, phosphorus (P) at 20¢, and potassium (K) at 10¢ per lb in commercial fertilizers.

TABLE 18-6
TONNAGE AND VALUE OF MANURE (EXCLUSIVE OF BEDDING)
EXCRETED BY U.S. HORSES AND MULES IN 1994[1]

No. of Horses and Mules in U.S.[2]	Average Liveweight	Tons Manure Excreted/Year/ 1,000 Lb Liveweight[3]	Total Manure Production	Total Value of Manure
	(lb)	(tons)	(tons)	($)
3,944,000	1,000	8	31,552,000	159,338,000

[1]In these computations, no provision was made for animals that died during the year. Rather, it was assumed that their places were taken by younger animals, and that the population was stable throughout the year.

[2]From Chapter 2, Table 2-2 of this book.

[3]*Manure Is Worth Money—It Deserves Good Care*, University of Illinois Circ. 595, 1953, p. 4.

[4]Computed on the basis of the value per ton given in the right hand column of Table 18-5.

contains, which almost all soils need, and which farmers and ranchers cannot buy in a sack or tank.

Also, it is noteworthy that, due to the slower availability of its nitrogen and to its contribution to the soil humus, manure produces rather lasting benefits which may continue for many years. Approximately one-half of the plant nutrients in manure are available to and effective upon the crops in the immediate cycle of rotation to which the application is made. Of the unused remainder, about one-half in turn, is taken up by the crops in the second cycle of the rotation; one-half of the remainder is the third cycle, etc. Likewise, the continuous use of manure through several rounds of a rotation builds up a backlog which brings additional benefits, and a measurable climb in yield levels.

Managers sometimes fail to recognize the value of this barnyard crop because (1) it is produced whether or not it is wanted, and (2) it is available without cost. Most of all, no one is selling it. Whoever heard of a traveling manure sales person?

MODERN WAYS OF HANDLING MANURE

Clay floors cannot be cleaned by flushing with water, and hard stable floors of concrete, asphalt, or wood require considerable bedding to provide softness and comfort. These conditions make it impractical to handle horse manure as a liquid. But horse manure is relatively dry and well adapted to handling as a solid.

Modern handling of manure involves maximum automation and a minimum of loss of nutrients. Among the methods of handling manure being used are: scrapers; power loaders; conveyors; industrial-type vacuums; slotted floors; storage vats; spreaders; dehydrators; and lagoons. Actually, there is no best manure management system for all situations; rather, it is a matter of designing and using the system which will be most practical for a particular set of conditions.

Both small and large horse establishments face the problem of what to do with horse manure, once it is removed from the stable. Because the feces of horses are the primary source of infestation of internal parasites, fresh horse manure should never be spread on pastures grazed by horses. The following alternatives for disposing of horse manure exist:

1. Spread the fresh manure on those fields that will be plowed and cropped, where there is sufficient land and this is feasible.

2. Contract with a nearby mushroom or vegetable grower, on a mutually satisfactory basis.

3. Store the manure in a suitable tightly constructed pit for a period of time prior to spreading, allowing the spontaneously generated heat to destroy the parasites.

4. Compost it in an area which will neither pollute a stream nor be offensive to the neighbors; then spread it on the land.

■ **Composting horse manure**—By composting horse manure, owners can create a valuable humus soil additive, for their own use or for sale.

Composting is the breaking down of biodegradable waste material into a nutrient rich soil mix with less offensive odor.

Temperature, air, and moisture are the main ingredients needed for composting. During the first three weeks, the pile needs to be turned 2 or 3 times a week. After the third week most of the break-down phase is over and the pile can be turned once a week.

Temperatures generated in the pile of 150 to 160°F are not unusual. The high temperatures destroy weed seeds, insect larvae, and disease pathogens. If the temperature gets any hotter, however, the temperature will kill the helpful microbes. When the pile is fully composted, it will level off at about 100°F.

The pile needs air because the process is aerobic; the microbes need air to continue breaking down the contents.

Water should be added as needed to keep the moisture content of the pile at about 55 to 60%—about as wet as a squeezed-out sponge.

HOW MUCH MANURE CAN BE APPLIED TO THE LAND?

With today's heavy animal concentration in one location, the question is being asked: How much manure can be applied to the land without depressing crop yields, making for salt problems in the soil, making for nitrate problems in feed, or contributing excess nitrate to groundwater or surface streams?

Based on earlier studies in midwestern United States, before the rise of commercial fertilizers, it would appear that one can apply from 5 to 20 tons of manure per acre, year after year, with benefit. Heavier applications can be made, but probably

should not be repeated every year. With rates higher than 20 tons per annum, there may be excess salt and nitrate buildup. Excess nitrate from manure can pollute streams or groundwater and result in toxic levels of nitrate in crops. Without doubt the maximum rate at which manure can be applied to the land will vary widely according to soil type, rainfall, and temperature.

OBJECTIONABLE FEATURES OF MANURE

Despite the recognized value of horse manure, it does possess the following objectionable features:

1. **It may propagate insects.** Unless precautions are taken, often manure is the preferred breeding place for flies and other insects.

2. **It may spread diseases and parasites.** Where animals are allowed to come in contact with their own excrement, there is always danger of infections from diseases and parasites.

3. **It may produce undesirable odors.** Where manure is stored improperly, there may be a nuisance from odors.

4. **It may scatter weed seeds.** Even when fermented, manure usually contains a certain quantity of viable weed seeds which may be scattered over the land.

MANAGEMENT OF SUBHUMID, HUMID, AND IRRIGATED PASTURES

Many good pastures have been established only to be lost through careless management. Good pasture management in the subhumid, humid, and irrigated areas involves the following practices:

Fig. 18-15. Standardbred mares and foals on pasture in Kentucky. Good equestrians, good pastures, and good horses go hand in hand. (Courtesy, United States Trotting Assn., Columbus, OH)

1. **Controlled grazing.** Nothing contributes more to good pasture management than controlled grazing. At its best, it embraces the following:

a. **Protect first year seedings.** First year seedings should be grazed lightly or not at all in order that they may get a good start in life. Where practical, instead of grazing, it is preferable to mow a first year seeding about 3 in. above the ground and to utilize it as hay or silage, provided there is sufficient growth to justify this procedure.

b. **Rotation or alternate grazing.** Rotation or alternate grazing is accomplished by dividing a pasture into fields (usually two to four) of approximately equal size, so that one field can be grazed while the others are allowed to make new growth. This results in increased pasture yields, more uniform grazing, and higher quality forage.

Generally speaking, rotation or alternate grazing is (1) more practical and profitable on rotation and supplemental pastures than on permanent pastures, and (2) more beneficial where parasite infestations are heavy than where little or no parasite problems are involved.

c. **Shift the location of salt, shade, and water.** Where portable salt containers are used, more uniform grazing and scattering of the droppings may be obtained simply by the practice of shifting the location of the salt to the less grazed areas of the pasture. Where possible and practical, the shade and the water should be shifted likewise.

d. **Defer spring grazing.** Allow six to eight inches of growth before turning horses out to pasture in the spring, thereby giving grass a needed start. Anyway, the early spring growth of pastures is high in moisture and washy.

e. **Avoid close late fall grazing.** Pastures that are grazed closely late in the fall start late in the spring. With most pastures, three to five inches of growth should be left for winter cover.

f. **Avoid overgrazing.** Never graze more closely than two to three inches during the pasture season. Continued close grazing reduces the yield, weakens the plants, allows weeds to invade, and increases soil erosion. The use of temporary and supplemental pastures may "spell off" regular pastures through seasons of drought and other pasture shortage, and alleviate overgrazing.

g. **Avoid undergrazing.** Undergrazing seeded pastures should be avoided, because (1) mature forage is unpalatable and of low nutritional value, (2) tall-growing grasses may drive out such low-growing plants as white clover due to shading, and (3) weeds, brush, and coarse grasses are more apt to gain a foothold when the pasture is grazed insufficiently. It is a good rule, therefore, to graze the pasture fairly close at least once a year.

2. **Clipping pastures and controlling weeds.** Pastures should be clipped at such intervals as necessary to control weeds (and brush) and to get rid of uneaten clumps and other unpalatable coarse growth left after incomplete grazing. Pastures that are grazed continuously may be clipped at or just preceding the usual haymaking time; rotated pastures may be clipped at the close of the grazing period. Weeds and brush may also be controlled by chemicals, by burning, etc.

3. **Topdressing (fertilizing).** Like animals, for best result grasses and legumes must be fed properly throughout a lifetime. It is not sufficient that they be fertilized (and limed if necessary) at or prior to seeding time. In addition, in most areas it is desirable and profitable to topdress pastures with fertilizer annually, and, at less frequent intervals, with reinforced manure and lime (lime to maintain a pH of about 6.5). Such treatments should be based on soil tests, and are usually applied in the spring or fall.

Properly used, inorganic fertilizers will make for more sound horses. Of course, improper fertilization of pasture or hayland can result in an imbalance of the mineral content of the forage, which in turn, will affect the animal. But when soil samples are properly taken and analyzed, then used as a guide for fertilizer application, the mineral content of the forage will be improved.

Remember that it's the total mineral intake of the horse that counts. This calls for (1) soil testing, with the fertilizer application based thereon, (2) forage testing, and (3) ration testing, with the mineral supplement balancing out the needs of the horse.

4. **Clean pastures.** The parasites in a pasture can be reduced dramatically by picking up the manure twice a week. Manure can be removed manually or mechanically; by using a muscle-powered shovel, or by using a vacuum pump powered by a tractor or small engine. But, in wet or damp conditions, a harrow should not be used to break up the manure; it will merely spread the parasite larvae into the grazing area. If pasture harrowing is done in hot, dry weather, it will effectively break up feces and expose larvae to death by desiccation.

5. **Grazing by more than one class of animals.** Grazing by two or more classes of animals makes for more uniform pasture utilization and fewer weeds and parasites, provided the area is not overstocked. Different kinds of livestock have different habits of grazing; they show preference for different plants and graze to different heights. Also, with the exception of the small stomach worm, horse parasites die in cattle and sheep. For these reasons, horses and cattle are commonly grazed on the same pastures in the great horse breeding centers of the world.

6. **Irrigating where practical and feasible.**

Fig. 18-16. Picking up pasture manure twice a week will reduce parasites dramatically. Manure may be removed with a hand shovel or by using a vacuum pump powered by a tractor or engine. (Courtesy, Commonwealth of Kentucky Department of Travel Development, Frankfort)

Where irrigation is practical and feasible, it alleviates the necessity of depending on the weather.

7. **Supplementing to provide needed nutrients.** Although the horse ration should be as economical as possible, condition and results in show, sale, and use are the primary objectives, even at somewhat added expense. Generally, this calls for supplemental feeding on pasture—for providing added energy, protein, minerals, and vitamins.

EXTENDING THE GRAZING SEASON

In the South and in Hawaii, year-round grazing is a reality on many a successful farm. By careful planning and by selecting the proper combination of crops, the areas can approach this desired goal.

In addition to lengthening the grazing season through the selection of species, earlier spring pastures can be secured by avoiding grazing too late in the fall and by the application of a nitrogen fertilizer in the fall or early spring. Nitrogen fertilizers will often stimulate the growth of grass so that it will be ready for grazing 10 days to 2 weeks earlier than unfertilized areas.

POINTERS ON CARING FOR HORSE PASTURES AND RECREATIONAL AREAS

There is a paucity of information on the care of horse pastures, turfs, and recreational areas. Few college courses even mention them, and precious little authoritative literature has been published on the subject.

Table 18-7 tells how successful operators maintain, renovate, and seed horse pastures, and how they care for racetracks, show-rings, bridle paths, and other like areas. These areas can no longer be taken for granted. They're big and important—and they'll get bigger. Hence, they merit the combined best recommendations of scientists and practical operators.

TABLE 18-7
GUIDE FOR CARING FOR HORSE PASTURES AND RECREATIONAL AREAS

For	When	How to Do It	Comments
Pasture maintenance	Twice a week.	Pick up manure from pasture, using a shovel or a mechanically powered vacuum.	Researchers at Ohio State reported that twice a week cleaning of pastures resulted in 18 times fewer parasites than uncleaned pastures.
	When it's hot and dry.	Use a chain-type tine harrow to— 1. Tear out the old, dead material. 2. Stimulate growth through gentle cultivating action. 3. Prevent a sod-bound condition. 4. Increase moisture penetration. 5. Scatter horse feces and expose larvae to death by drying, *only in hot, dry weather.*	Altogether too many horse pastures are merely gymnasiums or exercising grounds. This need not be so. Through improved pasture maintenance, caretakers can— 1. Produce higher yields of nutritious forage. 2. Extend the grazing season from early in the spring to late in the fall. 3. Provide a fairly uniform supply of feed throughout the entire season.
Pasture renovation	Spring or fall.	Use a chain-type tine harrow to work the fertilizer and seed into the soil, and yet destroy a minimum of the existing sod.	Run-down pastures can be brought back into production without plowing and reseeding.

(Continued)

TABLE 18-7 (Continued)

For	When	How to Do It	Comments
Preparing new pasture seedbed	Spring or fall.	Use a chain-type tine harrow to— 1. Level. 2. Smooth down. 3. Pack.	When properly prepared, a seedbed should be so firm that you barely leave a footprint when you walk across it. The firmer the better from the standpoint of moisture conservation and small seeds.
Racetracks; show-rings	Whenever the track or ring becomes bedded.	Set a chain-type tine harrow for maximum or light penetration, depending on the condition of the ring or track.	Good racetracks and show-rings must be firm, yet resilient.
	Just before the race or show; and between races or show events.	Use a chain-type tine harrow as a drag mat to smooth and fill holes.	Because it's flexible, this harrow can be pulled at good speed, as is necessary between races or show events, and yet do an excellent job of smoothing and filling holes.
Bridle paths; farm lanes; dirt roads	Whenever they become rough or uneven.	Use maximum penetration of chain-type tine harrow to put in shape; then turn harrow over to level and fill up holes.	

SELECTED REFERENCES

Title of Publication	Author(s)	Publisher
Art and Science of Horseshoeing, The	R. G. Greeley	J. B. Lippincott Co., Philadelphia, PA, 1970
Breeding and Raising Horses, Ag. Hdbk. No. 394	M. E. Ensminger	Agricultural Research Service, USDA, Washington, DC, 1972
Care and Training of the Trotter and Pacer	J. C. Harrison, *et al.*	The United States Trotting Association, Columbus, OH, 1970
Complete Horseshoeing Guide, The	R. F. Wiseman	University of Oklahoma Press, Norman, OK, 1968
Elements of Farrier Science	D. M. Canfield	Enderes Tool Co., Inc., Albert Lea, MN, 1966
First Horse	R. Hapgood	Chronicle Books, San Francisco, CA, 1972
Horse Science Handbook, Vol. 1-3	Ed. by M. E. Ensminger	Agriservices Foundation, Clovis, CA, 1963, 1964, 1966
Horsemanship and Horse Care	M. E. Ensminger	Agricultural Research Service, USDA, Washington, DC, 1972
Horsemanship and Horsemastership, Vol. II	The Cavalry School, Fort Riley, KS, 1946	
Horses: Their Selection, Care and Handling	M. C. Self	A. S. Barnes & Co., Inc., New York, NY, 1943
Horseshoeing	A. Lungwitz Trans. by J. W. Adams	Oregon State University Press, Corvallis, OR, 1966
Introduction to Light Horse Management, An	R. C. Barbalace	Caballus Publishers, Fort Collins, CO, 1974
Light Horses, Farmers' Bull. No. 2127	M. E. Ensminger	Agricultural Research Service, USDA, Washington, DC, 1965
Master Farrier, The	B. Beaston	Oklahoma Farrier's College, Sperry, OK, 1975

Principles of Horseshoeing, The	D. Butler	D. Butler, Ithaca, NY, 1985
Saddle Up!	C. E. Ball	J. B. Lippincott Co., Philadelphia, PA, 1970
Stable Management and Exercise, Sixth Edition	M. H. Hayes	Stanley Paul & Co., Ltd., London, England, 1968
Stockman's Handbook, The, Seventh Edition	M. E. Ensminger	Interstate Publishers, Inc., Danville, IL, 1992
Stud Managers' Course (Lectures)		Stud Managers' Course, Lexington, KY, intermittent since 1951
Stud Managers' Handbook	Ed. by M. E. Ensminger	Agriservices Foundation, Clovis, CA, annually 1965 to 1981
Top Form Book of Horse Care	F. Harper	Popular Library, New York, NY, 1966

19

BUSINESS ASPECTS OF HORSE PRODUCTION

Horses are big business! The U.S. horse industry produces goods and services valued at $25.3 billion, annually. This shows yearlings at famed Clairborne Farms, Paris, Kentucky. (Photo by Dell Hancock, Clairborne)

In the present era, many horse enterprises are owned and operated as businesses, with a profit motive—just as other owners have cattle, sheep, or swine enterprises. These owners must treat their operations as businesses and become more sophisticated; otherwise, they won't be in business very long. Other owners keep horses as a hobby—for much the same reason that some folks play golf, hunt, fish, or go boating. When kept for the latter purpose, their cost should be looked upon much like that of any other hobby or an evening's entertainment; that is, decide in advance how much you can afford to spend, then stop when that amount has been spent.

There was a time when equestrian-hobbyists operated much like most anglers and hunters, who do not wish to be reminded of the cost per lb of their catch or quarry. The guiding philosophy of these hobbyists is similar to that of the story attributed to J. Pierpont Morgan, who once admonished an inquiring friend that, "If you have to ask what it costs to maintain a yacht, you can't afford it." But this attitude among horse owner-hobbyists has changed, primarily because of (1) inheritance taxes making it increasingly difficult to pass wealth from one generation to the next, and (2) closer scrutiny of tax write-offs. Also, even when horses are kept primarily for the fun of it, most owners derive more pleasure therefrom when the operation pays, or nearly pays, its way—it's a matter of pride and a challenge. For these reasons, more and more folks who keep horses primarily for pleasure, like those who keep horses for profit, are interested in improving the business aspects of their enterprises.

CAPITAL

Equestrians who are in business to make a profit should never invest money, either their own or borrowed, unless they are reasonably certain that it will make money. Capital will be needed for land, buildings, machinery and equipment, horses, feed, supplies, labor, and miscellaneous items.

Whether establishing or enlarging a horse enterprise, the most common question, a two-pronged one, is—how much money will it take, and how much money will it make? This information is needed by both investors and lenders. Unfortunately, a simple answer cannot be given. However the following guides will be helpful:

1. **Land, buildings, machinery and equipment, and horse and labor costs.** Generally speaking, it is not too difficult to arrive at these costs.

The investor can easily determine the prevailing price of land in the area under consideration, either by inquiring of local land owners or reputable realtors. Where new buildings must be constructed, local architects can quote approximate costs on a square foot basis. Likewise, dealers can give prices on major items of machinery and equipment.

Horse prices vary widely, by breed and age, and according to quality. Nevertheless, auction or private treaty sales, or a knowledgeable equestrian will aid one in establishing the prevailing price for the breed, age, and quality desired. Also, going wages usually can be determined rather easily for a particular area.

2. **Feed, tack, and drug costs.** Where no pasture whatsoever is available, a 1,000-lb horse will consume about 30 lb of feed (hay and grain) daily, or about 5½ tons per year. Where an all-pelleted ration is used, 20% less feed will suffice, primarily because there is practically no wastage; hence, the allowance of a 1,000 lb horse on an all-pelleted ration may be computed on the basis of 25 lb per day, or 4½ tons per year.

Certainly, feed, tack, and drug costs will vary widely from area to area and farm to farm.

3. Size of the horse enterprise. Generally speaking, larger horse enterprises contribute to increased profits for the following reasons:

a. They result in fewer hours of labor per horse.

b. They are more apt to be used to capacity. For example, if for an establishment producing 20 foals per year the depreciation, interest, repairs, insurance and taxes cost $12,000 annually, that's $600 per foal. If the same facilities were used to produce 40 foals per year, the cost would be lessened to $300 per foal. This shows how increased numbers can reduce the building and equipment cost per foal.

GUIDELINES RELATIVE TO FACILITY AND EQUIPMENT COSTS

Overinvestment is a mistake. Some owners invest more in land and buildings than reasonably can be expected to make a satisfactory return; others invest too much in feed mills and equipment. Sometimes operators of small establishments fail to recognize that it may cost half as much to mechanize for 10 horses as it does for 60.

In order to lessen the hazard of overinvestment, guidelines are useful. Here are two:

Guideline No. 1. The break-even point on how much you can afford to invest in equipment to replace hired labor can be arrived at by the following formula:

$$\frac{\text{Annual saving in hired labor from new equipment}}{\text{(divide by) 0.15}} = \begin{array}{l}\text{amount you can}\\\text{afford to invest}\end{array}$$

Example:

If hired labor costs $10,000 per year, this becomes—

$$\frac{\$10,000}{0.15} = \$66,667: \text{the break-even point on new equipment}$$

Since labor costs are going up faster than machinery and equipment costs, it may be good business to exceed this limitation under some circumstances. Nevertheless, the break-even point, $66,667 in this case, is probably the maximum expenditure that can be economically justified at this time.

Guideline No. 2. Assuming an annual cost plus operation of power machinery and equipment equal to 20% of new cost, the break-even point to justify replacement of one hired person is as follows:

If annual cost of one hired person is[1]	The break-even point on new investment is
8,000 (20%) × 5	$40,000
10,000 (20%) × 5	50,000
12,000 (20%) × 5	60,000

In the above figures, it is assumed that the productivity of laborers at different salaries is the same, which may or may not be the case.

Example:

Assume that the new cost of added equipment comes to $10,000, that the annual cost is 20% of this amount, and that the new equipment would save 2 hours of labor per day for 6 months of the year. Here's how to figure the value of labor to justify an expenditure of $10,000 for this item:

$10,000 (new cost) × 20% = $2,000, which is the annual ownership use cost

$2,000 ÷ 360 hours (labor saved) = $5.56/hour

So, if labor costs less than $5.56/hour, you probably shouldn't buy the new item.

CREDIT IN THE HORSE BUSINESS

In 1993, U.S. agricultural assets totaled $888 billion, while total farm debt was $141.9 billion.[2] This means that, in the aggregate, farmers had 84% equity in their business, and 16% borrowed capital. Perhaps they have been too conservative, for it is estimated that one-fourth to one-third of American farmers could profit from the use of more credit in their operation.

Credit is an integral part of today's horse business.

Wise use of it can be profitable, but unwise use of it can be disastrous. Accordingly, owners should know more about it. They need to know something about the lending agencies available to them, the types of credit, how to go about obtaining a loan, and methods of computing interest.

The common lending sources of farm credit are: commercial banks, individuals and other private lenders, Farm Credit Administration, Farm Home Administration, and Commodity Credit Corp. Grain companies, feed companies, and various other suppliers are also important sources of credit to horse owners.

TYPES OF CREDIT OR LOANS

Following are the three general types of agriculture credit to consider, based on length of life and type of collateral needed:

1. **Short-term or production loans.** These loans are for up to one year. They are used for purchase of feed and operating expenses.

2. **Intermediate-term loans.** These loans may be for one to seven years. They are used for the purchase of breeding stock, machinery, equipment, and semipermanent investments. Repayment is made from the profits over several production periods.

3. **Long-term loans.** These loans are used for land and major farm building, and for physical plant construction. They may be for as long as 40 years. Usually they are paid off in regular annual or semiannual payments. The best source of long-term loans are: an insurance company, the Federal Land Bank, the Farm Home Administration, or an individual.

CREDIT FACTORS CONSIDERED AND EVALUATED BY LENDERS

Potential money borrowers sometimes make their first big mistake by going in cold to see a lender—without adequate facts and figures—with the result that they already have two strikes against them regarding their getting the loan. Moreover, equestrians should realize that bankers have a long-standing fear of loans on horses and feathers (poultry).

When considering and reviewing horse loan requests, the lender tries to arrive at the repayment ability of the potential borrower. Likewise, the borrower has no reason to obtain money unless it will make money.

Lenders need certain basic information in order to evaluate the soundness of a loan request. To this end, the following information should be submitted:

1. **Analysis and feasibility study.** Lenders are

---

[1]This is assuming that the productivity of people at different salaries is the same, which may or may not be the case.

[2]Statistical Abstracts of the United States, 1995, Table 1116.

impressed with borrowers who have written down feasibility studies, showing where they are now, where they're going, and how they expect to get there. In addition to spelling out the goals, feasibility reports should give assurance of the necessary management skills to achieve them. Such an analysis of the present and projection into the future is imperative in big operations.

2. **The applicant, farm, and financial statement.** It is the borrower's obligation, and in his best interest, to present the following information to the lender:

    a. **The applicant:**

        (1) Name of applicant and spouse; age of applicant.

        (2) Number of children (minors, legal age).

        (3) Partners in business, if any.

        (4) Years in area.

        (5) References.

    b. **The farm:**

        (1) Owner or tenant.

        (2) Location; legal description and county, and direction and distance from nearest town.

        (3) Type of enterprise: breeding, racing, riding stable, etc.

    c. **Financial statement:** This document indicates the financial record and current financial position of borrowers, their potential ahead, and their liability to others. Borrowers should always have sufficient slack to absorb reasonable losses due to such unforeseen happenstances as storms, droughts, diseases, and poor markets, thereby permitting lenders to stay with them in adversity and give them a chance to recoup their losses in the future. The financial statement should include the following:

        (1) **Current assets:**

            (a) Horses and other animals.

            (b) Feed.

            (c) Machinery.

            (d) Cash—there should be reasonable cash reserves, to cut interest costs, and to provide a cushion against emergencies.

            (e) Bonds and other investments.

            (f) Cash value of life insurance.

        (2) **Fixed assets:**

            (a) Real property, with estimated value.

            (b) Farm property.

            (c) City property.

            (d) Long-term contracts.

        (3) **Current liabilities:**

            (a) Mortgages.

            (b) Contracts.

            (c) Open account—to whom owed.

            (d) Cosigner or guarantor on notes.

            (e) Any taxes due.

            (f) Current portion of real estate indebtedness due.

        (4) **Fixed liabilities**—amount and nature of real estate debt:

            (a) Date due.

            (b) Interest rate.

            (c) To whom payable.

            (d) Contract or mortgage.

3. **Other factors.** Shrewd lenders usually ferret out many things, among them:

    a. The potential borrower. Most lenders will tell potential borrowers that they are the most important part of the loan. Lenders consider their:

        (1) Character.

        (2) Honesty and integrity.

        (3) Experience and ability.

        (4) Moral and credit rating.

        (5) Age and health.

        (6) Family cooperation.

        (7) Continuity, or line of succession.

Lenders are quick to sense "high-livers"—persons who live beyond their income; the poor managers—the kind who would have made it except for hard luck, and to whom the hard luck happened many times; and those who are dishonest, lazy, and incompetent.

In recognition of the importance of the person back of the loan, key insurance on the owner or manager should be considered by both the lender and the borrower.

    b. **Production records.** This refers to a good set of records showing efficiency of production. On a horse breeding establishment, for example, such records should show prices of horses sold, percent foal crop, filly replacement program, depreciation schedule, average crop yield, and other pertinent information. Lenders will increasingly insist on good records.

    c. **Progress with previous loans.** Has the borrower paid back previous loans plus interest? Has he/she reduced the amount of the loan, thereby giving evidence of progress?

    d. **Profit and loss (P & L).** This serves as a valuable guide to the potential ahead. Preferably, this should cover the previous three years. Also, most lenders prefer that this be on an accrual basis (even if the owner is on a cash basis in reporting to the Internal Revenue Service).

    e. **Physical plant.**

        (1) Is it an economic unit?

        (2) Does it have adequate water, and is it well balanced in feed and horses?

        (3) Is there adequate diversification?

        (4) Is the right kind of horse enterprise being conducted?

(5) Are the right crops and varieties grown; and are approved methods of tillage and fertilizer practices being followed?

(6) Is the farmstead neat and well kept?

f. **Collateral (or security).**

(1) Adequate to cover loan, with margin.

(2) Quality of security.

(a) Grade and age of horses.

(b) Type and condition of machinery.

(c) If grain storage is involved, adequacy of protection from moisture and rodents.

(d) Government participation.

(3) Identification of security.

(a) Tattoo or brand on horses.

(b) Serial number on machinery.

4. **The loan request.** Horse investors are in competition for money with other agriculturalists and with urban businesses. Hence, it is important that their request for a loan be well presented and supported. The potential borrower should tell the purpose of the loan, how much money is needed, when it's needed, the soundness of the venture, and the repayment schedule.

CREDIT FACTORS CONSIDERED BY BORROWERS

Credit is a two-way street; it must be good for both borrowers and lenders. If borrowers are the right kind of people and on a sound basis, more than one lender will want their business. Thus, it is usually well that borrowers shop around a bit; that they be familiar with several sources of credit and what they have to offer. There are basic differences in length and type of loan, repayment schedules, services provided with the loan, interest rate, and the ability and willingness of lenders to stick by the borrower in emergencies and times of adversity. Thus, interest rates and willingness to loan are only two of the several factors to consider. Also, if at all possible, all borrowing should be done from one source; a one-source lender will know more about the borrower's operations and be in a better position to help.

HELPFUL HINTS FOR BUILDING AND MAINTAINING A GOOD CREDIT RATING

Equestrians who wish to build up and maintain good credit are admonished to do the following:

1. **Keep credit in one place, or in a few places.** Generally, lenders frown upon split financing. Shop around for a creditor (a) who is able, willing, and interested in extending the kind and amount of credit needed, and (b) who will lend at a reasonable rate of interest; then stay with the borrower.

2. **Get the right kind of credit.** Don't use short-term credit to finance long-term improvements or other capital investments.

3. **Be frank with the lender.** Be completely open and aboveboard. Mutual confidence and esteem should prevail between borrower and lender.

4. **Keep complete and accurate records.** Complete and accurate records should be kept by enterprises. By knowing the cost of doing business, decision making can be on a sound basis.

5. **Keep annual inventory.** Take an annual inventory for the purpose of showing progress made during the year.

6. **Repay loans when due.** Borrowers should work out a repayment schedule on each loan, then meet payments when due. Sale proceeds should be promptly applied on loans.

7. **Plan ahead.** Analyze the next year's operation and project ahead.

CALCULATING INTEREST

The charge for the use of money is called interest. The basic charge is strongly influenced by the following.

1. The *basic cost* of money in the money market.

2. The *servicing costs* of making, handling, collecting, and keeping necessary records on loans.

3. The *risk* of loss.

Interest rates vary among lenders and can be quoted and applied in several different ways. The quoted rate is not always the basis for proper comparison and analysis of credit costs. Even though several lenders may quote the same interest rate, the effective or simple annual rate of interest may vary widely. The more common procedures for determining the actual interest rate, or the equivalent of simple interest on the unpaid balance, follow:

1. **Simple or true annual interest on the unpaid balance.** A $1,200 note payable at maturity (12 months) with 12% interest:

Interest paid . . . . $0.12 \times \$1,200 = \$144$

Average use of the money $1,200 for the entire year

Actual rate of interest . . . $\dfrac{\$144 \text{ (interest)}}{\$1,200 \text{ (used for one year)}} = 12\%$

2. **Installment loan (with interest on unpaid balance).**[3] A $1,200 note payable in 12 monthly installments with 12% interest on the unpaid balance:

Interest paid ranges from:

First month . . . . $\dfrac{0.12 \times \$1,200}{12}$ = $12

to

Twelfth month . . . . . $\dfrac{0.12 \times \$100}{12}$ = $1.00

Total for 12 months is $78

Average use of the money ranges from $1,200 for the first month down to $100 for the twelfth month, an average of $650 for 12 months.

Effective rate of interest $\dfrac{\$78}{\$650}$ = 12%

3. **Add-on installment loan (with interest on face amount).** A $1,200 note payable in 12 monthly installments with 12% interest on face amount of loan:

Interest paid . . . . . .   0.12 × $1,200 = $144

Average use of the money ranges from $1,200 for the first month down to $100 for the twelfth month, an average of $650 for 12 months.

Effective rate of interest $\dfrac{\$144}{\$650}$ = 22.15%

4. **Points and interest.** Some lenders now charge points. *A point is 1% of the face value of the loan.* Thus, if 4 points are being charged on a $1,200 loan, $48 will be deducted and the borrower will receive only $1,152. But the borrower will have to repay the full $1,200. Obviously, this means that the actual interest rate will be more than the stated rate. But how much more?

Assume that a $1,200 loan is for 1 year and the annual rate of interest is 12%. Then the payment by the borrower of 4 points would make the actual interest rate as follows:

Interest . . . . 0.12 × $1,200 = $144

Average use of money $1,152 for one year

Effective rate of interest $\dfrac{\$144 \ (\text{interest})}{\$1,152 \ (\text{used for one year})}$ = 12.5%

5. **If interest is not stated, use this formula to determine the effective annual interest rate:**

Effective rate of interest =

$$\dfrac{\substack{\text{Number of} \\ \text{payment periods} \\ \times 2 \text{ in 1 year}[4]} \quad \times \quad \substack{\text{Finance} \\ \text{charges}[5]}}{\substack{\text{Balance owed}[6] \qquad \text{Number of payments in} \\ \text{contract plus one}}}$$

For example, a store advertises an article for $500. It can be purchased on the installment plan for $80 down and monthly payments of $35 for 12 months. What is the actual rate of interest if you buy on the time payment plan?

Effective rate of interest =

$$\dfrac{2 \times 12 \times \$35}{\$420 \times (12 \text{ plus } 1)} = \dfrac{\$840}{\$5,460} = 15.4\%$$

BUDGETS IN THE HORSE BUSINESS

A budget is a projection of records and accounts and a plan for organizing and operating ahead for a specific period of time. A short-time budget is usually for one year, whereas a longtime budget is for a period of years. The principal value of a budget is that it provides a working plan through which the operation can be coordinated. Changes in prices, droughts, and other factors make adjustments necessary. But these adjustments are more simply and wisely made if there is a written budget to use as a reference.

HOW TO SET UP A BUDGET

It's unimportant whether a printed form (of which there are many good ones) is used or a form is made up on an ordinary ruled 8½ by 11 in. sheet placed sideways. The important things are that (1) a budget is kept, (2) it be on a monthly basis, and (3) the operator be comfortable with whatever form or system is to be used.

An important part of any budget, or any system of accounting, is that there shall be a listing, or chart, of classifications or categories under which the owner wants the transactions accumulated. In a horse operation that breeds and races, there may be 150 or more such classifications. From the standpoint of facilitating record keeping, each classification is usually given a

---

[3]This method is used for amortized loans.

[4]Regardless of the total number of payments to be made, use 12 if the payments are monthly, use 6 if payments are every other month, or use 2 if payments are semiannual.

[5]Use either the time payment price less the cash price, or the amount you pay the lender less the amount you received if negotiating for a loan.

[6]Use cash price less down payment or, if negotiating for a loan, the amount you receive.

number for identification purposes. Then the farm bookkeeper, or the farm manager, codes or classifies each transaction into proper category.

No budget is perfect. But it should be as good an estimate as can be made—despite the fact that it will be affected by such things as droughts, diseases, markets, and many other unpredictables.

A simple, easily kept, and adequate budget can be evolved by using forms such as those shown in Tables 19-1, 19-2, and 19-3.

TABLE 19-1
ANNUAL CASH EXPENSE BUDGET

_____ for _____
(name of farm)   (date)

Item	Total	Jan.	Feb.	Mar.	Apr.	May	June	July	Aug.	Sept.	Oct.	Nov.	Dec.
Labor hired													
Feed purchased													
Stud fees													
Gas, fuel, grease													
Taxes													
Insurance													
Interest													
Utilities													
Etc.													
Total													

TABLE 19-2
ANNUAL CASH INCOME BUDGET

_____ for _____
(name of farm)   (date)

Item	Total	Jan.	Feb.	Mar.	Apr.	May	June	July	Aug.	Sept.	Oct.	Nov.	Dec.
30 yearlings													
30 stud fees, @ $1,000 each													
490 bu. wheat													
Etc.													
Total													

TABLE 19-3
ANNUAL CASH EXPENSE AND INCOME BUDGET (Cash Flow Chart)

_____ for _____
(name of farm)   (date)

Item	Total	Jan.	Feb.	Mar.	Apr.	May	June	July	Aug.	Sept.	Oct.	Nov.	Dec.
Gross income	25,670					1,000	1,000	etc.					
Gross expense	13,910					575	2,405	etc.					
Difference	11,760					425	1,405	etc.					
Surplus (+) or Deficit (−)	+					+	−						

The Annual Cash Expense Budget should show the monthly breakdown of various recurring items—everything except the initial loan and capital improvements. It includes, labor, feed, supplies, fertilizer, taxes, interest, utilities, etc.

The Annual Cash Income Budget is just what the name implies—an estimated cash income by months.

The Annual Cash Expense and Income Budget is a cash flow chart obtained from the first two forms. It's a money flow summary by months. From this, it can be ascertained when money will need to be borrowed, how much will be needed, and the length of the loan along with a repayment schedule. It makes it possible to avoid tying up capital unnecessarily, and to avoid unnecessary interest.

HOW TO FIGURE NET INCOME

Table 19-3 shows a gross income statement. There are other expenses that must be taken care of before net profit is determined, namely:

1. **Depreciation on buildings and equipment.** It is suggested that the useful life of horse buildings and equipment be as follows, with depreciation accordingly:

Buildings—10 years.
Machinery and equipment—5 years.

Sometimes a higher depreciation, or amortization, is desirable because it produces tax savings and is protection against obsolescence due to scientific and technological developments.

2. **Interest on owner's money invested in farm and equipment.** This should be computed at the going rate in the area, say 12%.

Here's an example of how these work:

Let's assume that on a given horse establishment there was a gross income of $200,000 and a gross expense of $125,000, or a surplus of $75,000. Let's further assume that there are $60,000 worth of machinery, $60,000 worth of buildings, and $200,000 of the owner's money invested in farm and equipment. Let's further assume that buildings are being depreciated in 10 years and machinery in 5 years. Here is the result:

```
Gross profit . . . . . . . . . . . . . . . . . . . . . $75,000

Depreciation—
  Machinery:   $ 60,000 @ 20%  = $12,000
  Buildings    $ 60,000 @ 10%  =   6,000
                                 _____
                                 $18,000
  Interest:    $200,000  @   12%= 24,000
                                 _____
              Total . . . . . . . . . . .  42,000
                                           _____
Return to labor and management . . . . . . $33,000
```

Some people prefer to measure management by return on invested capital, and not wages. This approach may be accomplished by paying management wages first, then figuring return on investment.

ENTERPRISE ACCOUNTS

When one has a diversified horse enterprise—for example when producing yearlings for sale, having a racing or showing stable, standing stallions for public service, and growing corn—enterprise accounts should be kept; in this case four different accounts for four different enterprises. The reason for keeping enterprise accounts are:

1. It makes it possible to determine which enterprises have been most profitable, and which least profitable.

2. It makes it possible to compare a given enterprise with competing enterprises of like kind, from the standpoint of ascertaining comparative performance.

3. It makes it possible to determine the profitableness of an enterprise at the margin (the last unit of production). This will give an indication as to whether to increase the size of a certain enterprise at the expense of an alternative existing enterprise when both enterprises are profitable in total.

ANALYZING A HORSE BUSINESS; IS IT PROFITABLE?

Most people are in business to make money—and horse owners are people. In some areas, particularly near cities where population is dense, land values may appreciate so as to be a very considerable profit factor. Also, a tax angle may be important. But neither of these should be counted upon. The horse operation should make a reasonable return on the investment; otherwise, the owner should not consider it a business.

The owner or manager of a horse establishment needs to analyze the business—to determine how well it's doing. With big operations, it's no longer possible to base such an analysis on the bank balance statement at the end of the year. In the first place, once a year is not frequent enough, for it is possible to go broke, without really knowing it, in that period of time. Secondly, a balance statement gives no basis for analyzing an operation—for ferreting out its strengths and weaknesses. In large horse enterprises, it is strongly recommended that progress be charted by means of monthly or quarterly closings of financial records.

Also, owners must not only compete with other owners down the road, but they must compete with themselves—with their record last year and the year before. They must work ceaselessly at making progress and lowering costs of production.

To analyze a horse business, three things are essential: (1) good records, (2) enterprise accounts—that is, with such categories as boarding horses, racing stable, breaking and training yearlings, etc., and (3) profit indicators.

Through enterprise accounts, the owner or farm manager can get answers to such questions as the following:

1. How much does it cost me to board horses of different ages each month during the year?

2. How much is it costing to run a racing stable (or show stable)?

3. What is the actual cost of breaking and training a yearling?

4. Are grooms producing at or below standard rates of performance?

5. Is it possible for me to produce crops along with my breeding operation?

6. Should I rent my crop land on a cash rental or sharecropping arrangement, or should we do the farming ourselves?

7. Should I produce or buy hay?

Profit indicators are a gauge for measuring the primary factors contributing to profit. In order for horse farm owners to determine how well they are doing, they must be able to compare their own operation with something else, for example: (1) their own historical five-year average, (2) the average for the United States or for their particular area, or (3) the top five percent. The author favors the latter, for high goals have a tendency to spur superior achievement.

Admittedly, profit indicators are not perfect, simply because no two horse enterprises are the same. Nationally, there are wide area differences in climate, feeds, land costs, salaries and wages, and other factors. Nevertheless, indicators as such serve as a valuable yardstick. Through them, it is possible to measure how well a given operation is doing—to ascertain if it is out of line in any one category, and, if so, the extent to which it is out of line.

After a few years of operation, it is desirable that horse operators evolve with their own yardstick and profit indicators, based on their own historical records and averages. Even with these, there will be year-to-year fluctuations due to seasonal differences, horse and feed price changes, disease outbreaks, changes in managers, wars and inflation, and other happenstances.

COMPUTERS IN THE HORSE BUSINESS

Accurate and up-to-the-minute records and controls have taken on increasing importance in all agriculture, including the horse business, as the investment required to engage therein has risen. Today's successful horse owners and managers must have, and use, as complete records as any other business. Also, records must be kept current.

Big and complex enterprises have outgrown hand record keeping. It's too time consuming, with the result that it doesn't allow management enough time for planning and decision making. Additionally, it does not permit an all-at-once consideration of the complex interrelationships which affect the economic success of the business. This has prompted a new computer technique known as linear programming.

Fig. 19-1. Portable computer. Computers in modern horse businesses are aiding in decisions and enhancing profits. (Courtesy, California State University, Fresno)

Linear programming is similar to budgeting, in that it compares several plans simultaneously and chooses from among them the one likely to yield the highest returns. It is a way in which to analyze a great mass of data and consider many alternatives. It is not a managerial genie, nor will it replace decision-making managers. However, it is a modern and effective tool in the present age, when just a few dollars per head or per acre can spell the difference between profit and loss.

There is hardly any limit to what computers can do if fed the proper information. Among the difficult questions that they can answer for a specific operation are:

1. **How is the entire operation doing so far?** It is preferable to obtain quarterly or monthly progress

reports, often making it possible to spot trouble before it's too late.

2. **What enterprises are making money; which ones are freeloading or losing?** By keeping records by enterprises—breeding horses, racing stable, wheat, corn, etc.—it is possible to determine strengths and weaknesses, then either to rectify the situation or shift labor and capital to a more profitable operation. Through enterprise analysis, some operators have discovered that one part of the business may earn $10, or more, per hour for labor and management, whereas another may earn only $5 per hour, and still another may lose money.

3. **Is each enterprise yielding maximum returns?** By having profit or performance indicators in each enterprise, it is possible to compare these (a) with the historical average of the same establishment, or (b) with the same indicators of other operations.

4. **How does this operation stack up with its competition?** Without revealing names, the computing center (local, state, area, or national) can determine how a given operation compares with others—either the average, or the top (say 5%).

5. **How can you plan ahead?** By using projected prices and costs, computers can show what moves to make for the future—they can be a powerful planning tool. They can be used in determining when to plant, when to schedule farm machine use, etc.

6. **How can income taxes be cut to the legal minimum?** By keeping accurate record of expenses and figuring depreciation accurately, computers make for a saving in income taxes on most establishments.

7. **What is the least-cost ration formulation and the best buy in ingredients?** Many large horse breeding establishments, and most commercial feed companies, now use computers for ration formulation and as a buying and selling aid for feed ingredients. An electronic computer can't do a thing that a good mathematician can't, but it can do it a lot faster and check all possible combinations. It alleviates the endless calculations and hours common to hand calculations. For example, it is estimated that there may be as many as 500 practical solutions when as many as 6 quality specifications and 10 feedstuffs are considered. For these reasons, the use of computers in horse ration formulation and in the buying and selling of feed ingredients will increase.

For providing answers to these questions, and many more, computer accounting costs an average of 1% of the gross income.

There are three requisites for linear programming a horse establishment, namely:

1. Access to a computer.
2. Computer know-how, so as to set the program up properly and be able to analyze and interpret the results.

3. Good records.

The pioneering computer services available to farmers were operated by universities, trade associations, and government; most of them were on an experimental basis. Subsequently, others have entered the field, including commercial data processing firms, banks, machinery companies, feed and fertilizer companies, and farm suppliers. They are using it as a service sell, as a replacement for the days of hard sell.

Programmed farming is here to stay, and it will increase in the horse business.

COMPUTERS IN HORSE BREEDING OPERATIONS

In the past, the biggest deterrent to adequate records on a horse breeding establishment has been the voluminous and time-consuming record keeping involved. Keeping records as such does not change what an animal will transmit, but records must be used to locate and propagate the genetically superior animals if genetic improvement is to be accomplished.

Performance testing has been covered elsewhere in this book (see Chapter 12); thus, repetition at this point is unnecessary.

In addition to their use in performance testing; computerized records can be used for breeding record purposes—as a means of keeping management up-to-date and as an alert on problems to be solved or work to be done. Each animal must be individually identified. Reports can be obtained at such intervals as desired, usually monthly or every two weeks. Also, the owner can keep as complete or as few records as desired. Here are several of the records that can be kept by computer:

1. Pedigrees.

2. Records of animals that need attention, such as:
   a. Animals 4 months old that are unregistered.
   b. Animals ready for inspection or scoring.
   c. Mares that have been bred 2 consecutive times.
   d. Mares that have not conceived 2 months after foaling.
   e. Mares due to foal in 30 days.
   f. Foals 7 months of age that haven't been weaned.
   g. Animals that have not received their seasonal vaccinations; for example, that have not been vaccinated against sleeping sickness by May 1.
   h. Animals that have not been treated for parasites at the scheduled time.

3. A running or cumulative inventory of the herd, by sex; including foals dropped, foals due, and purchases and sales—in number of animals and dollars.

4. The depreciation of purchased animals according to the accounting method of choice.

MANAGEMENT

According to Webster, *management is "the act, art, or manner of managing, or handling, controlling, directing, etc."*

Three major ingredients are essential to success in the horse business: (1) good horses, (2) a sound feed and care program, and (3) good management.

Management gives point and purpose to everything else. The skill of the manager materially affects how well horses are bought and sold, the health of the animals, the results of the rations, the stresses of the horses, the growth rate of young stock, the performance of labor, the public relations of the establishment, and even the expression of the genetic potential of the horses. Indeed, managers must wear many hats—and they must wear each of them well.

The bigger and the more complicated the horse operation, the more competent the management required. This point merits emphasis because, currently, (1) bigness is a sign of the times, and (2) the most common method of attempting to bail out of an unprofitable horse venture is to increase its size. Although it's easier to achieve efficiency of equipment, labor, purchases, and marketing in big operations, bigness alone will not make for greater efficiency as some owners have discovered to their sorrow, and others will experience. Management is still the key to success. When in financial trouble, owners should have no illusions on this point.

In manufacturing and commerce, the importance and scarcity of top managers are generally recognized and reflected in the salaries paid to persons in such positions. Unfortunately, agriculture as a whole has lagged; and although too many owners still subscribe to the philosophy that the way to make money out of the horse business is to hire a manager cheap, with the result that they usually get what they pay for—*a cheap manager.*

TRAITS OF A GOOD MANAGER

There are established bases for evaluating many articles of trade, including hay and grain. They are graded according to well-defined standards. Additionally, we chemically analyze feeds and conduct feeding trials. But no such standard or system of evaluation

has evolved for managers, despite their acknowledged importance.

The author has prepared the Manager Checklist given in Table 19-4, which (1) employers may find useful when selecting or evaluating a manager, and (2) managers may apply to themselves for self improvement purposes. No attempt has been made to assign a percentage score to each trait, because this will vary among horse establishments. Rather, it is hoped that this checklist will serve as a useful guide (1) to the traits of a good manager, and (2) to what the boss wants.

TABLE 19-4
MANAGER CHECKLIST

☐ **CHARACTER—**

    Has absolute sincerity, honesty, integrity, and loyalty; is ethical.

☐ **INDUSTRY—**

    Has enthusiasm, initiative, and aggressiveness; is willing to work, work, work.

☐ **ABILITY—**

    Has horse know-how and experience, business acumen—including ability systematically to arrive at the financial aspects and convert this information into sound and timely management decisions, knowledge of how to automate and cut costs, common sense, and growth potential. Is organized

☐ **PLANS—**

    Sets goals, prepares organization chart and job description, plans work, and works plans.

☐ **ANALYZES—**

    Identifies the problem, determines pros and cons, then comes to a decision.

☐ **COURAGE—**

    Has the courage to accept responsibility, to innovate, and to keep on keeping on.

☐ **PROMPTNESS AND DEPENDABILITY—**

    Is a self-starter, has "T.N.T."; which means doing it "today, not tomorrow."

☐ **LEADERSHIP—**

    Stimulates subordinates, and delegates responsibility.

☐ **PERSONALITY—**

    Is cheerful, not a complainer.

ORGANIZATION CHART AND JOB DESCRIPTION

It is important that all workers know to whom they are responsible and for what they are responsible; and the bigger and the more complex the operation, the more important this becomes. This should be written down in an organization chart and a job description.

Fig. 19-2 shows an Organization Chart and Fig. 19-3 gives a Job Description.

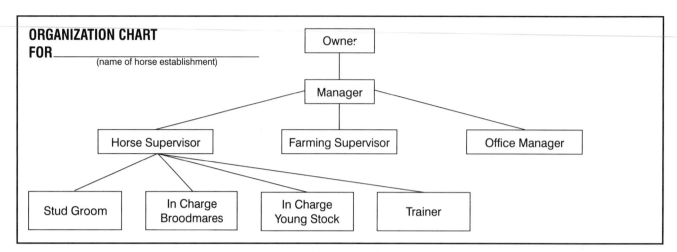

Fig. 19-2. Organization Chart.

JOB DESCRIPTIONS ON _____
(name of horse establishment)

Owner . . . . Responsible for:
    1. Making policy decisions.
    2. Borrowing capital.
    (List other.)

Manager . . . . Responsible for:
    1. Supervising all staff.
    2. Preparing proposed longtime plan.
    3. Budgets.

Horse Supervisor . . . . . Responsible for:
    1. All horse operations.
    2. Directing staff.

Stud Groom . . . . Responsible for:
    1. Care of stallions.
    2. Teasing and breeding mares.
    3. Breeding records.

In Charge Broodmares Responsible for:
    1. Care of broodmares.
    2. Foaling.

In Charge Young Stock Responsible for:
    1. Care of young stock, including—
      a. Feeding.
      b. Trimming feet.
      c. Gentling and green breaking.
    2. Sale of young stock.

Trainer . . . . Responsible for:
    1. Preparation of horses for the track.
    2. Care and training of horses on the track.

Farming Supervisor . . . Responsible for:
    1. Crop operations.
    2. Maintenance.

Office Manager . . . . Responsible for:
    1. Records.
    2. Budgets.

Fig. 19-3. Job Description.

INCENTIVE BASIS FOR THE HELP

Big horse establishments must rely on hired labor, all or in part. Good help—the kind that everyone wants—is hard to come by; it's scarce, in strong demand, and difficult to keep. And the horse farm labor situation is going to become more difficult in the years ahead. There is need, therefore, for some system that will (1) give a big assist in getting and holding top-flight help, and (2) cut costs and boost profits. An incentive basis that makes hired help partners in profit is the answer.

Many manufacturers have long had an incentive basis. Executives are frequently accorded stock option privileges, through which they prosper as the business prospers. Laborers may receive bonuses based on piecework or quotas (number of units, pounds produced). Also, most factory workers get overtime pay and have group insurance and a retirement plan. A few industries have a true profit-sharing arrangement based on net profit as such, a specified percentage of which is divided among employees. No two systems are alike. Yet, each is designed to pay more for labor, provided labor improves production and efficiency. In this way, both owners and laborers benefit from better performance.

Fig. 19-4. A good incentive basis makes hired help partners in profit.

Family-owned and family-operated horse enterprises have a built-in incentive basis; there is pride of ownership, and all members of the family are cognizant that they prosper as the business prospers. Also, there is an incentive basis in racehorses; both trainers and jockeys share in winnings. However, few horse breeding establishments or riding stables have evolved with an incentive basis for the help. They should give serious consideration to doing so.

Sometimes employers erroneously conclude that providing an incentive basis means that they are giving up a portion of their normal net. For a brief period of time, this may be true. But with the right kind of help, and over a period of time, it will make money for both owners and employees.

Many different incentive plans can be, and are, used. There is no best one for all operations. The various plans given in Table 19-5 are intended as guides only.

The incentive basis chosen should be tailored to fit the specific operation, with consideration given to kind and size of operation, extent of owner's supervision, present and projected productivity levels, mechanization, and other factors.

TABLE 19-5
INCENTIVE PLANS FOR HORSE ESTABLISHMENTS

Types of Incentives	Pertinent Provisions of Some Known Incentive Systems In Use	Advantages	Disadvantages	Comments
Bonuses	A flat, arbitrary bonus; at Christmas time, year-end, or quarterly or other intervals. A tenure bonus such as (1) 5 to 10% of the base wage or 2 to 4 weeks' additional salary paid at Christmas time or year-end, (2) 2 to 4 weeks' vacation with pay, depending on length and quality of service, or (3) $10.00 to $50.00 per week set aside and to be paid if employee stays on the job a specified time.	It's simple and direct.	Not very effective in increasing production and profits.	
Equity-building plan	Employee is allowed to own a certain number of horses. These are usually fed without charge.	It imparts pride of ownership to the employee.	The hazard that the owner may feel that the employee accords personally owned animals preferential treatment; suspected if not proved.	
Production sharing	$50 for every mare conceiving above 75%. $100 for every live foal born (foal standing and nursing) above 60%, based on mares bred.	It's an effective way to achieve higher conception and foal crop.	Net returns may suffer. If a high performance level already exists, further gains or improvements may be hard to achieve.	
Profit sharing:		It's an effective way to get hired help to cut costs.		
1. Percent of gross income in cash.	1 to 2% of the gross, with each employee sharing on a pro rata of salary basis.	It's a good plan for a hustler.	Percent of gross does not impart cost of production consciousness. Controversy may arise (1) over accounting procedure; e.g., from the standpoint of the owner a fast tax write-off may be desirable on new equipment, but this reduces the net shared with the worker; and (2) because some owners are prone to overbuild and overequip, thereby decreasing net.	There must be prior agreement on what constitutes gross or net receipts, as the case may be, and how it is figured. Generally, working owners should accord themselves salaries as part of the operating expense of the business, just as they pay salaries to other help. Then, all operating costs, including interest on the owner's money, should be deducted as expenses.

(Continued)

TABLE 19-5 (Continued)

Types of Incentives	Pertinent Provisions of Some Known Incentive Systems In Use	Advantages	Disadvantages	Comments
Profit sharing: (continued)				Books should not be opened to all employees. Access to books should be limited to supervisory personnel and the bookkeeper. Most laborers do not understand accounting principles; hence, opening up the books to them may lead to gossip, suspicion, and distrust.
2. Percent of net income in cash.	10 to 20% of the net after deducting all costs, with each employee sharing on a pro rata of salary basis.		There may not be any net some years.	
3. Percent of net income as investment in the business.	Giving employees an investment (stock) in the future growth and expansion of the business in an amount equal to 20% of the yearly net profit, with each employee sharing on a pro rata of salary basis.	Employees stand to profit if the business grows and prospers.		
4. Percent of net income placed in trust account.	A certain percent (say 20%) of the net earnings placed in a trust account, and (1) divided among the employees on a pro rata of salary basis, and (2) paid to employees upon retirement or completion of a specified number of years service.	Provides for retirement income and encourages continuity of service. There is a considerable saving in income tax paid.	Some employees do not wish to wait so long for their added compensation.	
Production sharing and prevailing price	Table 19-6 gives a proposed incentive basis for a breeding establishment that derives most of its income from the sale of yearlings. Table 19-7 gives a proposed incentive basis for a riding stable.	It embraces the best features of both production and profit sharing, without the major disadvantages of each. It (1) encourages high productivity and likely profits, (2) is tied in with prevailing prices, (3) does not necessitate opening the books, and (4) is flexible—it can be split between owner and employee on any basis desired, and the production part can be adapted to a sliding scale or escalator arrangement.	It is a bit more complicated than some other plans, and it requires more complete records.	When properly done, and all factors considered, this is the most satisfactory incentive basis for a horse establishment selling yearlings or operating a riding stable. Also, it can be adapted to any other type of horse enterprise.
Using a scorecard (rating)	The score is the basis for bonus, salary raise, and other considerations. The score method involves the preparation of a score card listing desired traits and performance, with a numerical value assigned to each according to its relative importance (see Fig. 19-5).	This method works well in an office in which the personnel are carefully selected.		

HOW MUCH INCENTIVE PAY?

After (1) reaching a decision to go on an incentive basis, and (2) deciding on the kind of incentive, it is necessary to arrive at how much the incentive should be. Here are some guidelines that may be helpful in determining this:

1. Pay the going base, or guaranteed, salary; then add the incentive pay above this.

2. Determine the total stipend (the base salary plus incentive) to which you are willing to go.

3. Before making any offers, always check the plan on paper to see (a) how it would have worked out in past years based on your records, and (b) how it will work out as you achieve the future projected production.

REQUISITES OF AN INCENTIVE BASIS

Owners who have not previously had experience with an incentive basis are admonished not to start with any plan until they are sure of both their plan and their help. Also, it is well to start with a simple plan; then a change can be made to a more inclusive and sophisticated plan after experience is acquired.

Regardless of the incentive plan adopted for a specific operation, it should encompass the following essential features:

1. Good owner (or manager) and good workers. No incentive basis can overcome a poor manager. A good manager must be a good supervisor and fair to the help. Also, on big establishments, the manager must prepare a written down organization chart and job description so the help knows (a) to whom they are responsible, and (b) for what they are responsible. Likewise, no incentive basis can spur employees who are not able, interested, and/or willing. This necessitates that employees must be selected with special care where they will be on an incentive basis. Hence, the three—good owner (manager), good employees, and good incentive—go hand in hand.

2. It must be fair to both employer and employees.

3. It must be based on and make for mutual trust and esteem.

4. It must compensate for extra performance, rather than substitute for a reasonable base salary and other considerations (house, utilities, and certain provisions).

5. It must be as simple, direct, and easily understood as possible.

6. It should compensate all members of the team, from top to bottom.

7. It must be put in writing, so that there will be no misunderstanding.

8. It is preferable, although not essential, that workers receive incentive payments (a) at frequent intervals, rather than annually, and (b) immediately after accomplishing the extra performance.

9. It should give the hired help a certain amount of responsibility, from the wise exercise of which they will benefit through the incentive arrangement.

10. It must be backed up by good records; otherwise, there is nothing on which to base incentive payments.

11. It should be a two-way street. If employees are compensated for superior performance, they should be penalized (or, under most circumstances, fired) for poor performance. It serves no useful purpose to reward the unwilling, the incompetent, and the stupid. No overtime pay should be given to employees who must work longer because of slowness or correcting mistakes of their own making. Likewise, if the reasonable break-even point on an operation is not reached because of obvious neglect (for example, not being on the job at foaling time), the employee(s) should be penalized (or fired).

INDIRECT INCENTIVES

Normally, we think of incentive as monetary in nature—as direct payments or bonuses for extra production or efficiency. However, there are other ways of encouraging employees to do a better job. The latter are known as indirect incentives. Among them are (1) good wages; (2) good labor relations; (3) an adequate house plus such privileges as the use of the farm truck or car, payment of the electric bill, use of a swimming pool, hunting and fishing, and the furnishing of meat, milk, and eggs; (4) good buildings and equipment; (5) vacation time with pay, time off, sick leave; (6) group health; (7) security; (8) the opportunities for self-improvement that can accrue from working for a top boss; (9) the right to invest in the business; (10) an all expense paid trip to a short course, show, or convention; and (11) a year-end bonus for staying all year. Such indirect incentives will be accorded to the help of more and more establishments, especially the big ones.

INCENTIVE BASIS FOR HORSE BREEDING ESTABLISHMENT

On horse breeding establishments there is need for some system which will encourage caretakers to (1) get a high conception rate; (2) be good attendants to newborn foals, though it may mean the loss of sleep; and (3) develop and sell surplus animals advantageously.

From the standpoint of the owner of a horse breeding establishment, production expenses remain practically unchanged regardless of the efficiency of the operation. Thus, the investment in land, buildings and equipment, stallion and broodmares, feed, and labor differs very little with a change (up or down) in the percent foal crop; and income above the break-even point is largely net profit. Yet, it must be remembered that owners take all the risks; hence, they should benefit most from profits.

On a horse breeding establishment, the author recommends that profit beyond the break-even point (after deducting all expenses, including the salary of the owner) be split on an 80:20 basis. This means that every dollar made above a certain level is split, with the owner taking 80 cents and employees getting 20 cents. Also, there is merit in an escalator arrangement, with the split changed to 70:30, for example, when a certain plateau of efficiency is reached. Moreover, that which goes to the employees should be divided on the basis of their respective contributions, all the way down the line; for example, 25% of it might go to the manager, 25% might be divided among the supervisors, and 50% of it divided among the rest of the help; or that which goes to the employees may be divided on a pro rata of salary basis.

Gross income in horse breeding operations is determined primarily by (1) percent conception on mares bred, (2) percent foal crop, and (3) prices on horses sold. The first two factors can easily be determined. Usually, enough horses are sold to establish prices or values; otherwise, the going price can be used.

The incentive basis proposed in Table 19-6 for horse breeding operations is simple, direct, and easily applied. As noted, it is based on the number and price of yearlings sold.

BREAK-EVEN POINT

Whenever possible, the break-even point on a horse establishment—the dollars gross necessary in order to break even—should be arrived at from actual records accumulated by the specific horse establishment, preferably over a period of years. Perhaps, too, break-even points should be moving averages, based on 5 to 10 years added from time to time, thereby reflecting improvements in efficiency due primarily to changing technology, rather than to the efforts of the caretakers.

With a new horse operation, on which there are no historical records from which to arrive at a break-even point, it is recommended that the figures of other similar operations be used at the outset. These can be revised as actual records on the specific enterprise become available. It is important, however, that the new operation start on an incentive basis, even though the break-even point must be arbitrarily assumed at the time.

INCENTIVE BASIS FOR RIDING STABLE

An incentive basis for riding stable help is needed for motivation purposes, just as it is in racing or breeding horses. It is the most effective way in which to lessen absenteeism; make for superior training, teaching, and public relations; and improve housekeeping.

A proposed incentive basis for a riding stable is shown in Table 19-7. For this incentive basis to work at its best, the organization should have each instructor-trainer under the supervision of the director of the riding stable, and responsible for a specific unit of 40 to 80 horses. This includes serving as a working

TABLE 19-6
A PROPOSED INCENTIVE BASIS FOR A BREEDER WHO SELLS YEARLINGS

Yearling Crop Sold Based on 100 Mares Bred to Produce	Price of Yearlings	How It Works
(no. of yearlings sold)	*($)*	
30	400	On this particular establishment, 100 mares are bred annually, and each year 15 top fillies are retained as herd replacements. Over and above this, the break-even point is 50 yearlings marketed annually. Thus, if 100 mares were bred in 1997, to break even there would have to be 65 yearlings in 1998, out of which 15 would be kept and 50 marketed.
35	600	
40	800	
45	1,000	
50 ← (break-even) →	1,200	Moreover, the historical records of this establishment show that $1,200/head is the break-even point, provided 50 yearlings are sold—or a total gross of $60,000.
55	1,400	
60	1,600	The sale of each yearling in excess of 50 head involves only $600 expense, primarily for added feed. Thus, if 60 yearlings are marketed at an average of $2,000, that's a gross of $120,000. The break-even point is $60,000 (50 yearlings @ $1,200), plus the added cost of $6,000 to produce 10 more yearlings (10 × $600), or a total of $66,000. Hence, the net is $54,000. With an escalator arrangement there might be an 80:20 split on a net up to $54,000; a 70:30 split on a net from $54,000 to $80,000, and a 65:35 split of a net in excess of $80,000.
65	1,800	
70	2,000	
75	2,200	
80	2,400	It is recommended that division among employees be on a pro rata of salary basis.

supervisor in their care, and handling all the instruction and training therewith.

This unit-responsibility-and-care arrangement is patterned after Grosbois in France, and Newmarket in England, where it has been highly successful for many years. It will require that the facilities be developed with the unit type of operation in mind. But it has the very great virtue of making each instructor-trainer responsible for the success of his/her division—horses, facilities, keep of premises, and instruction—thereby minimizing supervision and avoiding "passing the buck." In addition, each instructor-trainer is responsible for such assignments as delegated by the director, including record keeping.

In the operation of a riding stable, where teaching equitation and training horses are the two primary sources of income, there is need for instructor-trainers who are able to (1) keep their stables filled with horses in training, and (2) keep their classes filled with students; for, here again, the overhead cost is little different between well-filled and empty classrooms and stables. The incentive basis proposed in Table 19-7 will accomplish these objectives.

THE SCORECARD INCENTIVE BASIS

As the name implies, the scorecard method involves the preparation of a scorecard. In the scorecard, each major desired trait and performance is given a numerical value according to its relative importance.

A scorecard which the author developed and has used is herewith presented in Fig. 19-5.

Based on the average of two scorecards per year (Fig. 19-5), the following considerations are suggested for staff:

1. **Christmas Bonus.**

Score	Grade	Employee Should:	Christmas Bonus[7]
59 or under	Poor	Improve, work longer hours, and/or look for a job elsewhere.	None
60-74	Fair	Improve and work longer hours.	None
75-79	Good	Keep improving	$100
80-84	Good	Keep improving	$200
85-89	Good+	Keep improving	$300
90-94	Excellent	Keep improving	$400
95-100	Superior	Keep on keeping on	$500

2. **Health insurance; extra vacation time.** Full-time employees on appointment (not on hourly basis) exceeding (and maintaining) a minimum score of 75 after 6 months' service or 80 after 2 years' service, can be accorded the following considerations:

---

[7]Based on full-time employees and 12 months' prior service; regular half-time employees are accorded half these amounts. Those not on the job 12 months are accorded consideration on a proportion to 12 months' basis.

TABLE 19-7
A PROPOSED INCENTIVE BASIS FOR EACH INSTRUCTOR-TRAINER IN A RIDING STABLE

Yearly Gross from Boarding-Training Horses (@ $200/mo., $2,400/yr.)	Yearly Gross from Conducting Riding Classes (@ $10/student/2-hr. lesson)	How It Works
(no. horses; $ gross/yr.)	(students; class days; gross)	
2 horses; $4,800/yr.	One class of 6 students/day; 300 days/yr. instruction = $18,000 gross.	Instructors-trainers are responsible for their own unit. They receive a basic salary of $1,000/mo. plus living quarters.
3 horses; $7,200/yr. ◄—(break-even)—►	One class of 12 students/day; 300 days/yr. instruction = $36,000 gross.	To cover all expenses—the instructor-trainer's salary, grooms, horses, facilities, equipment, feed, insurance, and overhead, requires 3 horses being boarded-trained and one class of 12 students receiving 300 days instruction, or a total gross of $43,200 ($7,200 + $36,000). That's the break-even point.
5 horses; $12,000/yr.	Two classes of 12 students/day; 300 days/yr. instruction = $72,000 gross.	With 5 horses boarded-trained and two classes instead of one, the gross would be increased to $84,000. The added expense to generate $84,000 instead of $43,200 is small—only $1,200 more for keeping 2 horses. Hence, the net on the $84,000 is: $84,000—($43,200 + 1,200), or $39,600. With an 80-20 division, $31,680 would go to the owner, and $7,920 would be distributed among the employees. Or, if desired, the split could be on an escalator arrangement, with the employees getting a higher percentage as the net increases. Whatever the division, it is suggested that it be divided among them on a pro rata of salary basis.

PERSONAL SCORECARD

For _____

USE: This scorecard is applied by the owner-manager to each staff member every six months, then the results are discussed with each person in a private conference.

PURPOSE: To provide staff with an evaluation which they may use as a basis for self-improvement, and to recognize and reward superior performance.

	Pts or %	1997 June 30	1997 Dec. 31	1998 June 30	1998 Dec. 31	1999 June 30	1999 Dec. 31
CHARACTER: Absolute sincerity, honesty, integrity, loyalty; ethical.	10						
INDUSTRY: Works hard; has enthusiasm, initiative, and aggressiveness; a desire to get the job done, and a willingness to let the boss worry about raises; not afraid of long hours when necessary, not a clock watcher.	15						
ABILITY AND PERFORMANCE: Skilled and competent in area of work; is neat and accurate; turns out adequate work; has know-how, clarity, common sense, good judgment, and maturity; is organized; shows growth potential and self-improvement; not a know-it-all; accepts responsibility, masters the job assignments without being told "what to do next"; plans work, organizes, and keeps on top; is efficient and cuts costs; recognizes that the boss must make decisions and give directions.	40						
INTEREST: Genuine interest in work—not just payday and 5 o'clock.	10						
COURAGE: To innovate—to try the new, and to keep on keeping on.	5						
PROMPTNESS AND DEPENDABILITY: A self-starter, does it today and not tomorrow.	10						
PERSONALITY AND APPEARANCE: Cheerful; not a complainer; a member of the team.	10						
	100						

Fig. 19-5. Scorecard and incentive basis for staff.

After Year's Service	Consideration
½ year (6 mos.) . . .	Health insurance[8] for employee (not family), with employer and employee each paying 50% of premiums. (Employer will terminate health insurance upon termination of employee.)
2 years	Health insurance for employee (not family), with employer paying premiums. (Employer will terminate health insurance upon termination of employee.)
3 years	Added workday of paid vacation.[9]
4 years	Added workday of paid vacation.
5 years	Added workday of paid vacation.
6 years	Added workday of paid vacation.
7 years	Added workday of paid vacation.

[8]Health insurance is not accorded employees who already have such protection via the spouse.

[9]Thus, at the end of 7 years, employees meeting the stipulated score requisite will have health insurance and 3 weeks' (15 work days) vacation with pay.

3. **Merit increases.** Salary increases on a merit basis only, and determined by (a) average annual score of the employee, (b) how well the business is doing, and (c) going wages of the area for the particular assignment. Whatever salary increase is accorded will be on January 1 basis only, following the second six months' review.

SYNDICATED HORSES

Reduced to simple terms, *a syndicated horse is one that is owned by several people.* Most commonly, it's a stallion; although an expensive yearling or broodmare is sometimes syndicated. Also, any number of people can form a syndicate. However, there is a tendency to use the term *partnership* where two to four owners are involved, and to confine the word *syndicate* to a larger group of owners.

Each member of a syndicate owns a certain number of shares, depending on how much he/she

Fig. 19-6. *Aladdin*, National Champion Arabian Stallion, syndicated for $6.3 million. (Courtesy, Arabian Horse Assn., Denver, CO)

purchased or contributed. It's much like a stock market investor, who may own one or several shares in General Electric, IBM, or some other company. Sometimes one person may own as much as a half-interest in a horse. Occasionally, half-shares are sold.

Generally speaking, the number of shares in a stallion is limited to the number of mares that may reasonably be bred to him in one season—usually 30 to 35, with Thoroughbred stallions.

WHY AND HOW OWNERS SYNDICATE

The owner of a stallion that has raced successfully usually has the opportunity to choose between (1) continuing as sole owner of the horse, and standing him for service privately or publicly, or (2) syndicating him. In recent years, more and more owners of top stallions have elected to syndicate. The most common reasons for doing so are:

1. The stallion owner does not have a breeding farm or an extensive band of broodmares.

2. The owner believes that the stallion under consideration may not nick well with many of the mares; or perhaps the stallion is closely related to the mares.

3. The owner has need for immediate income. Moreover, if sole ownership is retained, considerable promotional and advertising expenses will be involved for approximately three years—until the stallion's get make their debut on the tracks; and, in the meantime,

practically no income can be expected until about a year from entering stud, at which time the usual live foal guarantee is met. Until this condition is fulfilled, any stud fees that are collected are generally held in escrow, as protection if they should have to be returned.

4. Syndicating spreads the risk, should the stallion get injured or die, or prove unsuccessful as a sire.

The owner may do the syndicating usually with competent legal advice; or, if preferred, the syndication can be turned over to a professional manager, who will generally take a free share for services rendered.

The following pointers are pertinent to successful syndication of stallions:

1. **Check fertility.** Before syndicating, it is a good idea to check the fertility by test-mating to a coldblood (draft) mare. Of course, if the stallion is still racing, and has not been retired to stud, this is impossible.

2. **Establish stud fee.** A common rule of thumb is that each syndicate share is worth four times the stud fee. Hence, if it is decided that the stallion under consideration will command a $10,000 stud fee, each share would be worth $40,000. If 30 shares are involved, the horse would have a value of $1,200,000 for syndication purposes.

3. **Determine time of payment.** In most cases, payment is due upon the signing of the syndicate contract, although some contracts (a) allow 30, 60, or 90 days, or (b) provide that the price of a share may be paid on the installment plan over a 2- or 3-year period.

4. **Put it in writing.** Syndication agreements should be clear, detailed, and in writing. In addition to identifying the horse, the agreement should state (a) the shareholder's proportionate interest (say $\frac{1}{32}$); (b) the breeding rights of a shareholder (for example, the right to breed one mare per season to the horse, so long as he is in good health and able to breed); (c) the method of distributing services by lot, should it be necessary to limit the number of mares bred during any given season; (d) the method of disposing of, and the price charged for, any extra services (over and above one per share, for example) during a given season; (e) the place where the horse shall stand, or how such determination will be made (usually by majority vote of the shareholders); and (f) how other policy matters not covered in the agreement will be determined (usually by majority vote).

Generally, such routine matters as the feed, care, and health of the stallion, and the scheduling of mares are left to the discretion of the syndicate manager, at a stated fee per month, with each shareholder billed proportionate to his number of shares. The manager also handles the promotion and advertising, insurance, and unusual veterinary expense, as stipulated by the syndicate, with the costs prorated among its members.

Normally, shareholders can barter their breeding service to another stallion. However, they cannot sell their share without prior approval of the manager and giving the shareholders the right to buy it at the price offered; and, normally, this same stipulation applies to the sale of a service during any season.

Also, provision is usually made for sale of the horse should the majority of the shareholders so desire, with them also determining, at the time of sale,

the price and whether sale shall be at private treaty or auction. Further, the contract usually provides for pensioning, or otherwise disposing of, a sire should he become sterile or overtaken by old age before dying.

In short, a syndicate agreement, like any good legal contract, attempts to spell out every foreseeable contingency that may arise during the stud's career, and to arrange for majority vote of the shareholders to settle any unforeseen contingencies.

STALLION BREEDING CONTRACTS

Stallion breeding contracts should always be in writing; and the higher the stud fee, the more important it is that good business methods prevail. Neither "gentlemen's agreements" nor barn door records will suffice.

From a legal standpoint, a stallion breeding contract is binding to the parties whose signatures are affixed thereto. Thus, it is important that the contract be carefully read and understood before signing.

A sample breeding contract[10] is presented in Fig. 19-7.

In addition to the provisions made in the sample stallion breeding contract presented here, and in most other similar contracts, the author suggests that the following matters be covered in the stallion breeding contract:

1. **Facts about the mare.** There should be a record of the mare's temperament; thereby lessening danger to her, to the stallion, and to the personnel. Also, historical information should be included about the mare's breeding record and peculiarities, and her health—preferably with the health record provided by the veterinarian who has looked after her.

2. **Some management understanding.** The parties to the contract should reach an understanding relative to the mare's veterinary care, parasite control, sea-

---

STALLION BREEDING CONTRACT

(To be executed in duplicate for each mare; one copy to be retained by each party.)
This Contract for the breeding season of _____ made and entered into by and between
(year)

_____   _____
(owner of stallion)   (address)
hereinafter designated "Stallion Owner," and

_____   _____
(owner of mare)   (address)
hereinafter designated "Mare Owner."
This contract covers _____

The stallion, _____, whose service fee is $ _____
(name of stallion)

$ _____ of which is paid with this contract, and the balance of

$ _____ will be paid before the mare leaves _____
(name of farm or ranch)

and
The mare, _____, Reg. No. _____, by _____
(name of mare)   (sire)

out of _____, age _____, color _____
(dam)

I. *The Mare Owner agrees that—*

Upon arrival, the mare will be (a) halter-broken, (b) have the hind shoes removed, and (c) be accompanied by a health certificate signed by a veterinarian, certifying that she is healthy and in sound breeding condition. Stallion Owner will not be responsible for accident, disease, or death to the mare, or to her foal (if she has a foal).
Stallion Owner may option to have a veterinarian (a) check and treat the mare for breeding condition or diseases, and (b) treat her for parasites if needed; with the expenses of such services charged to Mare Owner's account and paid when the mare leaves the farm or ranch.
Feed and facilities costs (mare care) shall be $ _____ per day (dry), or $ _____ per day if mare arrives with nursing foal (wet). Payment shall be made for feed/facilities/other charges at the time the mare leaves the farm or ranch.
Should the mare prove barren, or should the foal die at birth, notice of same, signed by a licensed veterinarian will be sent to the Stallion Owner within five days of such barren determination or death.
Should the mare not be delivered to the Stallion Owner's premises on or before _____,
(date)
Stallion Owner shall be under no further obligation with respect to any matter herein set forth.
This contract shall not be assigned nor transferred. In the event the mare is sold, any remaining unpaid fee shall immediately become due and payable and no refund shall be due anyone under the circumstances.

II. *The Stallion Owner agrees that—*

The mare will be provided with suitable facilities, feed, and care while on the premises of the Stallion Owner. Mare Owner will not be responsible for any disease, accident, or injury to Stallion Owner's horses.
A live foal is guaranteed—meaning a foal that can stand up alone and nurse within 24 hours.

III. *The Stallion Owner and Mare Owner mutually agree that—*

This contract is void unless completed in full.
Should the above-named stallion die or become unfit for service, or should the above-named mare die or become unfit to breed, this contract shall become null and void and money paid as part of this contract shall be refunded to Mare Owner.
Should the mare prove barren, or should the foal die at birth, with certification of same provided to Stallion Owner within the time specified, Stallion Owner has the option either to (a) rebreed the mare the following year, or (b) refund the $ _____ portion of the breeding fee, thereby cancelling this entire contract.
The mare will not receive more than _____ covers during the breeding season, and she will
(no.)
not be bred before _____ 19_____
(date)
or after _____ 19_____
(date)

_____   _____   _____
(date)   (signature; Mare Owner or Rep.)   (address)

_____   _____   _____
(date)   (signature; Stallion Owner or Rep.)   (address)

Fig. 19-7. Stallion breeding contract.

---

[10]Sample prepared by the author of this book.

sonal injections, foot trimming, etc., and then put it in writing.

3. **An incentive basis.** Generally, stallion owners guarantee a live foal, which means that the foal must stand and nurse; otherwise, the stud fee is either refunded or not collected, according to the stipulations. Of course, it is in the best interests of both parties that a strong, healthy foal be born. One well-known Quarter Horse establishment reports that their records reveal that of all mares settled during a particular three-year period, 19% of them subsequently either resorbed or aborted fetuses, or the foal or mare died. Further, their investigation of these situations showed that the vast majority of these losses could have been averted by better care and management. They found many things wrong—ranging from racing mares in foal to turning them to pastures where there was insufficient feed. To alleviate many, if not most, of these losses—losses that accrue after the mare has been examined and pronounced safe in foal, then taken away from the stallion owner's premises—the author suggests that an incentive basis be incorporated in the stallion breeding contract. For example, the stallion owner might agree to reduce the stud fee (1) by 10, 15, or 20% (state which), provided a live foal is born; or (2) by 25 to 33⅓% provided the mare owner's veterinarian certifies that the mare is safe in foal 30 days after being removed from the place where bred, with payment made at that time and based on conception rather than birth of a live foal.

BOARDING AGREEMENT

Today's tough zoning laws and antipollution campaigns are making it increasingly difficult to keep horses in towns and suburban areas. As a result, more and more horses are being stabled and cared for in boarding establishments out in the country, to which owners commute. This prompts the need for an agreement.

Boarding agreements should always be in writing, rather than verbal "gentlemen's agreements." From a legal standpoint, a boarding agreement is binding to the parties whose signatures are affixed thereto. Thus, it is important that the agreement be carefully filled out, read, and fully understood before signing. A sample boarding agreement is given in Fig. 19-8.

BOARDING AGREEMENT

(To be executed in duplicate; one copy to be retained by each party.)
This agreement made and entered into by and between ______ (owner of horse) ______ (address) hereinafter designated "Horse Owner," and ______ (owner of stable) ______ (address) hereinafter designated, "Stable Owner." This agreement covers the horse described as follows:

______ (name) (sex) ______ (age) ______ (color) ______

I. *Stable owner agrees to—*

1. Keep the horse in a stall and/or paddock described as follows:

2. Feed, water, and care for the horse in a good and husbandlike manner; feeding horse as follows:

	Amount of Feed		
Kind of Feed	Morning	Noon	Night
	(lbs)	*(lbs)*	*(lbs)*

3. Perform the following additional services:

a. *Grooming (specify):* ______

b. *Exercising (specify):* ______

c. *Parasite treatments (specify):* ______

d. *Others (list):* ______

II. *Horse Owner agrees to—*

1. Make all arrangements for the periodic shoeing of the horse, and assume the cost thereof. Any exception to this shoeing arrangement shall be in the space that follows:

2. Pay Stable Owner (a) for the foregoing facilities, feed, and services the sum of $ ______ per month, payable on the ______ day of each month in advance, and (b) for drugs and medications, at cost, the first of each month following invoicing.

3. Entitlement of Stable Owner to a lien against the boarded horse for the value of services rendered, and to enforce said lien according to the appropriate laws of the state, *provided* (a) Stable Owner performs the services herein specified, and (b) Horse Owner fails to make a scheduled payment.

III. *Horse Owner and Stable Owner mutually agree that—*

1. In the event the horse shall require the services of a Veterinarian, Stable Owner will immediately contact the Horse Owner. In the event Horse Owner cannot be reached, Stable Owner is hereby authorized, as agent for Horse Owner, (a) to call Dr. ______ DVM; and should Dr. ______ be unavailable, (b) to call any other licensed veterinarian of choice. All fees charged by said veterinarian shall be the sole and exclusive responsibility of the Horse Owner, with no liability whatsoever on the part of Stable Owner for such fees.

2. This document constitutes the entire agreement between the parties and there are no other agreements between them except as noted below.

______ (Signature of Horse Owner) ______ (date)

______ (Signature of Stable Owner) ______ (date)

Fig. 19-8. Boarding agreement.

Fig. 19-9. More and more horses are stabled and cared for in boarding establishments, under boarding agreements. (Courtesy, American Quarter Horse Assn., Amarillo, TX)

LIABILITY[11]

Most horse owners or managers are in such financial position that they are vulnerable to damage suits. Moreover, the number of damage suits arising each year is increasing at an almost alarming rate, and astronomical damages are being claimed. Studies reveal that about 95% of the court cases involving injury result in damages being awarded.

Comprehensive personal liability insurance protects an operator who is sued for alleged damages suffered from an accident involving his/her property or family. The kinds of situations from which a claim might arise are quite broad, including suits for personal injuries caused by animals, equipment, or personal acts.

Both workers' compensation insurance and employer's liability insurance protect operators against claims or court awards resulting from injury to hired help. Workers' compensation usually costs slightly more than straight employer's liability insurance, but it

carries more benefits to the worker. An injured employee must prove negligence by the employer before the company will pay a claim under employer's liability insurance, whereas workers' compensation benefits are established by state law, and settlements are made by the insurance company without regard to who was negligent in causing the injury. Conditions governing participation in workers' compensation insurance vary among the states.

Note: By mid-1996, three dozen states had passed "limited equine liability laws," and legislation was pending in another 10 states. While still untested in the courts, these laws are designed to create some immunity from lawsuits by acknowledging that there are risks associated with horses and horse related activities.

WORKERS' COMPENSATION

Workers' compensation laws, now in full force in every one of the 50 states, cover on-the-job injuries and protect disabled workers regardless of whether their disabilities are temporary or permanent. Although broad differences exist among the individual states in their workers' compensation laws, principally in their benefit provisions, all statutes follow a definite pattern as to employment covered, benefits, insurance and the like.

Workers' compensation is a program designed to provide employees with assured payment for medical expenses or lost income due to injury on the job. Whenever an employment-related injury results in death, compensation benefits are generally paid to the worker's surviving dependents.

Generally all employment is covered by workers' compensation, although a few states provide exemptions for farm labor, or exempt farm employers of fewer than 10 full-time employees, for example. Farm employers in these states, however, may elect workers' compensation protection. Livestock producers in these states may wish to consider coverage as a financial protection strategy because under workers' compensation, the upper limits for settlement of lawsuits are set by state law.

This government-required employee benefit is costly for horse operators. Costs vary among insurance companies due to dividends paid, surcharges and minimum premiums, and competitive pricing. Some companies, as a matter of policy, will not write workers' compensation in agricultural industries. Some states have a quasi-government provider of workers' compensation to assure availability of coverage for small businesses and high-risk industries.

For information, contact your area extension farm management or personnel management advisor and

---

[11]The sections on Liability, Workers' Compensation, Social Security Law, Tax Management and Reporting, and Estate Planning were authoritatively reviewed by Waymon E. Watts, CPA, Fresno, California.

an insurance agent experienced in marketing workers' compensation and liability insurance.

SOCIAL SECURITY LAW

The Social Security Law covers stipulated agricultural workers, including workers on horse operations. Thus, owners and managers of horse operations should be familiar with, and follow the pertinent provisions of the Social Security Law.

The number on the social security card is very important to the farm operator as well as to the hired farm worker. It identifies the individual's social security record and is key to future benefit payments. It is important, therefore, that a person's social security number is on the social security reports for both the self-employed farmer and the agricultural worker.

Those who expect to draw social security payments later should check with the Social Security Administration every three years, especially if they change jobs frequently, to make sure that their records are in order and that their correct earnings are credited to their individual social security records.

For a social security card—either a new card or a duplicate of one that has been lost—or for more information about retirement, survivors, and disability insurance, Medicare health insurance, or Supplemental Security Income, get in touch with the nearest social security office or call Social Security's toll-free number: 1-800-772-1213.

TAX MANAGEMENT AND REPORTING

Good tax management and reporting consists in complying with the law, but in paying no more tax than is required. It is the duty of revenue agents to see that taxpayers pay the correct amount, and it is the business of taxpayers to make sure that they do not pay more than is required. From both standpoints, it is important that farmers and ranchers should familiarize themselves with as many of the tax laws and regulations as possible.

The cardinal principles of good tax management are: (1) maintenance of adequate records, and (2) conduct of business affairs to the end that the tax required is no greater than necessary. Good tax management and good farm management do not necessarily go hand in hand, and may sometimes be in conflict. When the latter condition prevails, the advantages of one must be balanced against the disadvantages of the other to the end that there shall be the greatest net return.

It is recognized that tax matters constitute a highly specialized and complex field, and each farm or ranch will need separate considerations in appropriate planning. The recent rounds of federal tax legislation have made significant changes in the procedures horse farm operators must use in accounting, as well as in their approaches to financial and estate planning. More than ever, it is important that they consult competent professionals before embarking upon any business operation involving horses. It is noteworthy that, if a horse operator's return is to be audited, under the recently enacted Taxpayer Bill of Rights, the taxpayer is entitled to be represented at the audit by a representative. Though the IRS can require the taxpayer's attendance with a special summons, this is not likely to be used at the initial meeting.

Increasingly, as local governments must make up for decreased federal support, local tax matters become more important in planning; this also makes consultation with a specialist knowledgeable in state and local tax law, crucial for effective management.

Some tax pointers of particular interest to horse farm operators follow:

1. File an estimate or file your current return.
2. Keep adequate and accurate records and accounts.
3. Separate the farm home from the farm business.
4. Keep year-to-year income as steady as possible.
5. Select the best method of accounting—cash or accrual.

CASH BASIS

Under this system, farm income includes all cash or value of merchandise or other property received during the tax year. It includes all receipts from the sale of items produced on the farm and profits from the sales of items that have been sold. It does not include proceeds from sales if the proceeds were not actually available during the tax year.

Allowable deductions include those business expenses incurred that were actually paid during the year, and depreciation on depreciable items.

ACCRUAL BASIS

This system requires the keeping of complete annual inventories. Tax is paid on all income earned during the taxable year, regardless of whether payment was actually received, and on increases of inventory values of horses, crops, feed, produce, etc., at the end of the year as compared with the beginning of the year. All expenses incurred during the year's business are deducted from gross income regardless of whether payment is actually made, and deductions are made for any decrease in inventory values of livestock, etc., during the year.

Four methods of inventorying are available to the accrual basis farmer or rancher.

1. **Cost.** Inventory items are valued at the actual cost of producing or purchasing them.

2. **The lower of cost or market value.** The comparison is made separately for each item in the inventory, not for the entire inventory. The entire stock should *not* be valued at cost and then at market, with the lower selected.

3. **Farm price.** Each item, raised or purchased, is valued at its market price less estimated direct cost of disposition. This method must be used for the entire inventory, except that horses may be inventoried by the next method.

4. **Unit livestock price.** Horses are classified according to kind and age, and a standard unit price is used for each animal within a class. All raised livestock must be included in inventory under this method. Unit prices must reflect any costs required to be capitalized under the uniform capitalization rules. This method is usually chosen by many large operations. Producers using the unit-livestock method are permitted to elect a simplified production method for determining costs required to be capitalized.

The third and fourth methods are unique to farmers and ranchers.

DISTINGUISH CAPITAL GAINS FROM ORDINARY INCOME

There is a difference in the tax rates applied to ordinary income and capital gains. Income reported as capital gains will be taxed at a lower rate. Thus, livestock held for sale in inventory, and livestock held for breeding purposes, may produce different tax effects when sold, even if the sale prices are the same. But there continues to be developments in this area.

SET UP DEPRECIATION SCHEDULES PROPERLY

Depreciation is estimated operating expense covering wear, tear, exhaustion, and obsolescence of property used in a farm business.

Depreciation may be taken on all farm buildings (except the livestock producer's personal residence), and on everything from grain elevators to horse clippers, including tile drains, water systems, fences, machinery and equipment.

Those who file returns on a cash basis may also take depreciation on horses which were purchased, but they cannot take depreciation on horses they raised because all costs of raising are deducted as operating expenses. On the accrual basis, depreciation may be taken on purchased animals that are not included in inventory.

Taxpayers should list each building, and each piece of machinery on which depreciation is to be computed on the depreciation schedule. Such items as small implements may be grouped together, but such groupings should be derived from totaling of a detailed individual list kept current in a permanent farm record book.

Depreciation is not available for inventory, which would include animals held for sale to customers. After 1986, depreciable property is placed in specific classes. Because the period over which property is amortized affects the overall tax revenues. Congress has tended to lengthen recovery periods as a means of increasing tax collections without *raising* taxes.

1. **Three-year property.** This includes horses that are more than 12 years old when placed in service (racehorses more than two years old when placed in service).

2. **Five-year property.** This includes automobiles and light-general purpose trucks, certain technological equipment and research and experimentation property.

3. **Seven-year property.** This includes breeding and work horses, 12 years or younger, and any horse not in any other category.

4. **Ten-year property.** Horticultural or single-purpose agricultural structures were originally recovered over 7 years, but after 1988 have a 10-year recovery period. A companion requirement limits recovery on such items to the 150% declining balance method (discussed below). Orchards, groves and vineyards placed in service after 1988 are depreciated on a straight-line basis over 10 years.

5. **Fifteen-year property.** This includes equipment used for two-way exchange of voice and data communications.

6. **27.5-year property.** This covers residential rental property.

7. **31.5-year property.** This covers nonresidential real property. This will include most farm buildings.

For property in the 3-, 5-, 7-, and 10-year classes, depreciation was, prior to 1989, calculated on the double declining balance method, switching to the straight-line method at the time where depreciation is maximized. For property in the 15- and 20-year classes, the 150% declining balance method is used. For the 27.5- and 31.5-year classes, the straight-line method is used. However, for personal property (i.e., nonreal property) placed in service in a farming business after 1988, the 150% declining balance must be used regardless of the recovery period.

A horse owner can elect to depreciate a two-year-old race horse under the straight-line method provided the election is made for all property in the same class. Once the election is made it is irrevocable. Special provisions apply to property which is not placed in service at the beginning of the year. If property depreciated under certain methods is sold, the gain will be characterized as ordinary income, a factor which may become relevant if differential capital gains rates are reintroduced.

For purchased animals, the price paid will generally determine the amount which can be depreciated. Inherited or gift animals can be depreciated. However, their value may have to be established by a qualified appraiser, if the IRS contests the taxpayer's valuation.

DO NOT OVERLOOK ADDITIONAL DEDUCTIONS

■ **Annual expensing**—The annual expensing limitation is $10,000 for property placed in service after 1986. However, this election is not available for taxpayers whose aggregate cost of qualifying property exceeds $210,000 (reduced dollar-for-dollar over $200,000). The amount which can be expensed is limited to taxable income derived from the trade or business. The repeal of the Investment Tax Credit and the longer recovery periods for most classes of property increases the value of this provision for the livestock producer.

■ **Soil and water conservation**—Farmers can deduct soil and water conservation expenditures only if the expenditures are consistent with a conservation plan approved by the USDA or a comparable state agency. Such expenditures include treatment or movement of earth, such as leveling, terracing or restoration of fertility, construction and protection of diversion channels, drainage ditches and earthen dams, planting of windbreaks, etc. Though land clearing expenses are no longer deductible, ordinary maintenance, including brush clearing, remains deductible. Costs of fertilizing and other conditioning of land remain deductible. The amount deducted under this election can't exceed 25% of the taxpayer's gross income from farming for the year. Part of the amount deducted may be recovered if the land is sold within 10 years of the deduction.

■ **Education expenses**—Educational expenses, such as the cost of short courses, are deductible if they are taken to maintain or improve the skills of the person in conducting the operation, or, if the person is employed by a farming operation and they are taken as a requirement of continuing that employment. How-

ever, if taken to allow the person to enter another trade or business, such expenses will not be deductible. For instance, a physician who owns a few horses, who takes a course of study with the idea of eventually managing a horse operation, will not likely be able to deduct the education expenses.

■ **Pay children for farm work**—The farmer/rancher must be able to show that a true employer-employee relationship exists. To do so, children should, as much as possible, be treated as are other employees. They should be assigned definite jobs at agreed-upon wages, and paid regularly.

TREAT LOSSES APPROPRIATELY

On the cash basis, no death deduction can be made for an animal that was born and raised on the farm, because the cost of raising the animal has been deducted already with operating expenses. On the accrual basis, when the value of an animal appears in the beginning-of-year inventory but not in the end-of-year inventory, the loss is automatically accounted for in the change in inventory value. Any money received from insurance or indemnity is entered as other farm income. Other death losses are listed on line 34, Part II of Form 1040 F as "other deductions," with an explanation.

■ **Losses from destruction, theft, and condemnation**—Special treatment is available for certain gains or losses that are netted. The gains and losses can arise from the sale or exchange of property used in the trade or business, involuntary conversion or condemnation. If gains exceed losses, the net gain is treated as long-term capital gain. If losses exceed gains, the loss is ordinary. While this has limited significance as long as there is no tax differential between capital gain and ordinary income, the likelihood of a reintroduced capital gain preference makes the matter important to keep in mind. Gains and losses from these causes include those involving (1) cattle and horses, regardless of age, which are held for draft, breeding, dairy or sporting purposes, and held for at least 24 months from the date of acquisition, and (2) other livestock, regardless of age, held for draft, breeding, dairy or sporting purposes, and held at least 12 months from the date of acquisition. The fact the livestock is included in inventory doesn't prevent this treatment if the animal is held for the required purposes and for the specified time.

■ **Passive activity losses**—Perhaps the most complicated addition to tax law in recent years was the passive activity loss concept, a development which will take tax lawyers years to decipher, with untold questions yet to be answered. Under this concept, all income and losses are divided between passive and nonpassive activities. A passive activity is one which involves the trade or business in which the livestock producer does *not* materially participate. Losses and credits from passive trade or business activities are disallowed to the extent they exceed aggregate passive income. Passive income does not include portfolio income (interest, dividends or royalties). However, rental activities are (if within the definition provided in the Internal Revenue Code) always passive.

■ **Material participation**—The IRS has provided seven exclusive tests for meeting the material participation requirement as to a particular activity:

1. **The 500 hours test.** The livestock owner participates more than 500 hours in the operation during the year. Obviously, full-time livestock producers will not have significant difficulties in meeting this requirement.

2. **Substantially all test.** The producer's participation constitutes substantially all participation in the activity. Given the requirements for the care of animals, it is unlikely that this test is even necessary for producers, as they would then satisfy the first test in any case.

3. **The 100 hours test.** The individual participates for more than 100 hours and no other person participates for a greater number of hours. Again, this will not generally be relevant to livestock producers. Nevertheless, a physician who owns horses and has a full-time employee to take care of them will often fail to be an active participant under this test.

4. **The related activities test.** The livestock producer participates in a group of activities for more than 500 hours, more than 100 hours in each. This may apply where a producer has a number of operations, but only limited involvement in each.

5. **The 5 of 10 years test.** This allows a livestock producer who has materially participated in the particular activity in the past to qualify as materially participating presently, even if his/her direct involvement has fallen off somewhat.

6. **Personal service activities.** This would apply to consultants involved in the livestock industry, but not to livestock producers running their own operations.

7. **Facts and circumstances test.** This test is, according to many experts, essentially similar to the 100 hours test.

Also, certain retired livestock producers will qualify in the event of death during the year. Though these requirements will have no effect on the full-time producer, they are important factors in terms of investment planning for anyone who is considering investments in rental real estate activities and other ventures.

■ **At-risk rules**—Another provision in the Internal Revenue Code limits losses to the extent that a taxpayer is at risk with respect to a particular activity. This means generally that a taxpayer is limited to the amount of his/her personal investment and the amount as to which he/she is personally liable. This provision specifically applies to farming, which includes livestock activities. The provision was designed principally to preclude losses from tax shelters and other leveraged investments where there may be no real chance that the taxpayer will have to cover the losses. Thus, it will seldom affect livestock producers whose credit is generally limited to the amount of collateral they can provide.

AVOID OPERATING THE BUSINESS AS A HOBBY

If an activity is not engaged in for profit, deductions are generally not available for the conduct of the activity except to the extent of income from it. This requirement has often been applied when the IRS determines that a livestock operation is actually a hobby. Though the problem will generally not apply to full-time livestock producers, others who devote a smaller amount of their time to an operation may find their activity is classified by the IRS as a hobby.

The general presumption for activities is that if an activity is profitable for 3 of the 5 consecutive years before the year being audited, it will be presumed to be engaged in for profit. Recognizing that horse operations often depend on the success of a rare horse, in such an operation Congress has allowed the activity to be presumed to be engaged in for profit if only 2 of 7 years are profitable. The IRS has indicated that an activity cannot be considered as engaged in for profit until there is a profit year.

Horse owners can delay the determination of whether a horse operation is engaged in for profit until the seventh taxable year of the activity. This election also keeps open the statute of limitations for those years.

In determining whether a horse operation is a business or a hobby, the IRS will examine the following factors:

1. **The manner in which the operator carries on the activity.** The more businesslike the conduct of the activity, the more likely it is to be recognized as a business. This includes the keeping of accurate records of income and expenses. If the operation is conducted in a manner similar to other profit-making livestock operations, it is more likely to be recognized as a business. If operating methods and procedures are changed because of losses, the impression is enhanced that the operation is a business. If the operation is typical of the other operations in the

vicinity, it may indicate an attempt to fit into the live-stock industry.

2. **The expertise of the operator and the employees.** A study of the industry and of other successful operations indicates a profit-making approach. If operators tend to ignore advice, they may have to establish that their expertise is even greater than that of their advisors.

3. **Time and effort spent in carrying out the operation.** The more time the owner devotes to the activity as a business and not as a recreational pursuit, the more likely the Service will find that the operation is a business. If the owner hires a full-time assistant to run day-to-day operations, he/she will be in a stronger position to argue that an attempt is being made to turn a profit. If the assistant is an inexperienced family member, the owner's position may, on the other hand, be weakened. Proper and rigid culling of herds will enhance the evidence for business conduct.

4. **The expectation that assets used in the activity will appreciate in value.** Even if current operations do not produce much income, the investment in land and buildings may support an argument that the owner has taken other businesslike factors into consideration. If the primary focus of the operation is breeding, it may take considerable time to get the necessary stock.

5. **Prior successes of the livestock producer.** The more experienced the producer and the more successful his/her prior livestock operations, the more he/she is likely to be seen as a serious business person. It may be important that the producer comes from a family of successful livestock producers.

6. **The operation's history of income and losses.** If losses are due to unforeseen circumstances (drought, disease, fire, theft, weather damages or other involuntary conversions, or from depressed markets), it may be possible to argue that there was nevertheless a profit motive in the operation.

7. **Occasional profits.** An occasional profit may indicate a profit motive if the investment or the losses of other years are comparatively small. The more speculative the venture, the more the livestock producer may be able to show that the losses were not due to a lack of profit intent.

8. **Financial status of the livestock producer.** The more the producer relies on the livestock operation, the more likely the producer is able to justify it as a business. If there are substantial profits from other sources, it may appear that the operation is nothing more than a private tax shelter. If this is the case, the producer may also have to worry about the effect of the limits on passive activity losses.

9. **Elements of recreation or pleasure.** Though having fun does not mean an operation is a hobby, the more the recreational element dominates the horse operator's involvement, the more likely the livestock producer will have difficulty convincing the IRS that he/she is trying to make a profit. The presence of fishing holes, tennis courts and guest houses may indicate that the producer has a country club (a different sort of business, but not a practical horse farm).

ESTATE PLANNING

Human nature being what it is, most horse operators shy away from suggestions that someone help plan the disposition of their property and other assets after they are gone. Also, they have a long-standing distrust of lawyers, legal terms, and trusts; and to them the subject of taxes on death seldom makes for pleasant conversation.

If a horse farmer has prepared a valid will, or placed the property in joint tenancy, the estate will be distributed as intended. If not, it goes to the heirs, according to the laws governing intestate (without a will) succession. The heirs are those persons whom the law appoints to succeed to the property in the event of intestacy, and are not necessarily the persons to whom the horse farmer would want to leave the property. These laws vary somewhat from state to state.

If no plans are made, estate taxes and settlement costs often run considerably higher than if proper estate planning is done. Today, horse farm operations are big business; many have well over $1 million invested in land, animals and equipment. Thus, it is not a satisfying thought to one who has worked hard to build and maintain a good establishment during their lifetime to feel that the heirs will have to sell the facilities and animals to raise enough cash to pay estate and inheritance taxes. Therefore, horse operators should go to an estate planning specialist—a lawyer or company specializing in this work, or the trust department of a commercial bank. A limited discussion of some of the major considerations follows:

■ **Valuation can be based on farming use.** Owners of farms and small businesses have been granted an estate planning advantage by means of what is called *special use valuation*. Under this concept, a farm or ranch can escape valuation for estate tax purposes at the highest and best use. Thus, a farm located in an area undergoing development may be considerably more valuable to developers than it is as a farm. Nevertheless, if the family is willing to continue the farming use for ten years, the farm can be included in the estate at its value as a farm. The aggregate reduction in fair market value cannot exceed $750,000.

In order to qualify for special use valuation, the decedent must have been a U.S. citizen or resident and the farm must be located in the U.S. The farm must have been used by the decedent or a family member at the date of the decedent's death. A lease to a nonfamily member, if not dependent on production, will not satisfy this requirement. At least 50% of the value of the decedent's estate must consist of the farm and more than 25% of the estate must consist of the farm and real property. It may be possible to split up a farm and take the special valuation for only part of it, but this part must involve real property worth at least 25% of the estate.

The property must be passed to a qualified heir, including ancestors of the decedent, the spouse and lineal descendants, lineal descendants of the spouse or parents, and the spouse of any lineal descendant. Aunts, uncles and first cousins are excluded. Legally adopted children are included.

The property must have been owned by the decedent or a family member for five of the eight years preceding the decedent's death and used as a farm in that period. The decedent or a family member must have participated in the farming operation for such a period prior to the decedent's death or disability.

■ **Electing special use valuation.** Though the procedures are clear as to how special use valuation is elected, the frequency with which mistakes are made indicates the importance of having a competent tax attorney or CPA firm prepare the estate tax return. A procedural failure denying the estate the considerable savings that can be gained by the election may give sufficient grounds for a malpractice suit against the return preparer.

■ **Recapture tax.** If the farm ceases to be operated by the heir or a family member within ten years, an additional estate tax will be imposed and the advantage of the election will be substantially lost. Partition among qualified heirs will not bring about recapture. A recent change allows the surviving spouse of the decedent to lease a farm on a net cash basis to a family member without being subject to the recapture tax.

■ **Longer time to pay estate taxes.** Estates eligible for special use valuation may often be able to defer payment of estate taxes. Where more than 35% of an estate of a U.S. citizen or resident consists of a farm, the estate tax liability may be paid in up to ten annual installments beginning as late as 5 years from when the tax might otherwise be due. Thus, a portion of the estate taxes is deferred as much as 15 years. For purposes of the 35% requirement, the residential buildings and improvements on them which are on the farm are considered to be part of the farming operation.

If more than 50% of the decedent's interest in the farm is disposed of in the deferral period, then the entire unpaid portion of the estate tax liability is accelerated. The transfer of the decedent's interest in a closely held business on the death of the original heir will not cause an acceleration if the transferee is a family member of the transferor.

■ **Use the gift tax exclusion for lifetime transfers.** The nontaxable gift tax exclusion remains at $10,000 per donee per year. A husband and wife who elect gift-splitting may jointly give $20,000 per recipient per year. These gifts may be in the form of interests in the farming operation.

■ **Plan with the unlimited marital deduction.** An unlimited deduction is permitted for the value of all property included in the gross estate that passes to the decedent's surviving spouse in the specified manner. Certain *terminable* interests do not qualify for such a deduction—that is, interests as to which of the surviving spouse's interests will terminate on the happening of some event. Surviving spouses may be given *qualified terminable interests*. The most common arrangement involves the surviving spouse receiving a lifetime interest in the farm, with the remainder passing on the spouse's death to others, perhaps the children of the decedent. No marital deduction is allowed if the surviving spouse is not a U.S. citizen, unless a specific trust arrangement is used.

■ **Consult a professional.** The preparation of wills, trusts, redemption agreements (if the farm is incorporated), partnership agreements, etc., requires consideration of the effects of federal and state tax law, as well as state law governing the various potential arrangements. Consequently, it is strongly advised that competent professionals be consulted in order to achieve an effective and cost-saving estate plan.

WILLS

A will is a set of instructions drawn up by or for an individual which details how the individual wishes the estate to be handled after death.

Despite the importance of a will in distributing property in keeping with the individual's wishes, about 50% of farmers and ranchers pass away without having written a will. This means that state law determines property distribution in such cases.

Every horse operator should have a will. By so doing, (1) the property will be distributed in keeping with his/her wishes, (2) they can name the executor of the estate, and (3) sizable tax savings can be made by the way in which the property is distributed. Because technical and legal rules govern the preparation, validity, and execution of a will, it should be drawn up by an attorney. Wills can and should be changed and updated from time to time. This can be done either by (1) a properly drawn-up codicil (formal amendment to a will), or (2) a completely new will which revokes the old one.

The same attorney should prepare both the husband's and wife's wills so that a common disaster clause can be incorporated and the estate planning of each can be coordinated.

TRUSTS

A trust is a written agreement by which an owner of property (the trustor) transfers title to a trustee for the benefit of persons called beneficiaries. Both real and personal property may be placed in trust.

The trustee may be an individual(s), bank, or corporation, or a combination of two or three of these. Management skill should be considered carefully in choosing a trustee.

A trust can continue for any period of time set by the owner—for a lifetime, until the youngest child reaches age 21, etc. If the trust extends beyond a lifetime, there are limitations which should be explained by an attorney.

KINDS OF TRUSTS

Basically, there are two kinds of trusts, the *living* and the *testamentary*. The living or *inter vivos* trust is in essence an agreement between the trustor and the trustee and may be revocable or irrevocable.

The *revocable trust* can be terminated or altered; under it the trustor is concerned about the here and now, rather than only the hereafter. The trustor continues to make decisions, and can call off the whole arrangement (it's revocable) if it doesn't work out as expected. The revocable trust offers no special estate tax advantage; the assets of a revocable trust are included in the estate of the deceased creating the trust. However, it can be written in such a manner as to reduce substantially the estate taxes of the beneficiaries. Also, the revocable trust will eliminate the cost of probate—costs which may include executor's fees, attorney's fees, court costs, and appraisal fees.

The *irrevocable trust* cannot be amended, altered, revoked, or terminated. Under an irrevocable trust, the trustor must be willing to part with the trust property forever (irrevocably) and have nothing further to do with it and its administration. However, the irrevocable trust has many favorable aspects in estate planning; it will reduce estate taxes in both the estate of the trustor and the estate(s) of the life beneficiaries, and it avoids probate.

The *testamentary trust* is so-called because it is established under the provisions of the trustor's last will and testament. The testamentary trust does not become effective until after death of the trustor, fol-

lowed by probate. There is no tax saving in the trustor's estate. However, the trust may be drafted to save estate taxes in the estates of the beneficiaries. A testamentary trust is useful when the heirs are minors or inexperienced in money matters.

STRAY HORSES ON HIGHWAYS

Although state, county, and/or township laws vary, and it is not possible to predict with accuracy what damages, if any, may be recovered in particular instances, the following general rules apply:

■ If horse owners are negligent in maintaining their fences and allow their horses to get on the road, they can be held liable for damage or injury resulting to persons using the highway.

■ If horse owners have good fences that are well maintained, but have horses which they know are in the habit of breaking out, they may be held liable for damages caused by such horses.

■ If horses get out onto the highway, despite the facts that there are both good fences and the horses are not known habitually to get out, the owners may be held liable for any damage inflicted provided they knew that the horses were out and made no reasonable effort to get them in.

■ If horse owners are not negligent in any way, they may or may not be judged liable for the damage inflicted by their horses, depending on the state law.

■ If horse owners are driving their horses along or across a highway, they are not likely to suffer liability for any damage unless it can be proved that they were negligent. Stock-crossing signs usually increase the caution exercised by motorists, but such signs do not excuse a horse owner from exercising due care.

■ In some states, laws provide that horse owners may, under the supervision of and with varying amounts of assistance from highway authorities, construct underpasses for their horses and for general farm use.

HORSE INSURANCE

Few horse owners or managers examine closely or understand the insurance coverage that they buy, either on their horses or in the area of liability. To the end that they may be more knowledgeable on this subject, a section on horse insurance follows:

The ownership of a fine horse constitutes a risk, which means that there is a chance of financial loss. Unless owners are in such strong financial position that they can assume this risk, the animal should be insured.

Several good companies write horse insurance; and, in general, the policies and rates do not differ greatly. The provisions and rates which follow are those of American Live Stock Insurance Company, Geneva, Illinois, which is rated A+ (Superior), by A. M. Best Company, the independent rating service for all classes of livestock.

Conditions		Rate

AMERICAN SADDLEBREDS, MORGANS, AND ALL OTHER BREEDS OF SHOW, SADDLE HORSES AND PONIES

FOALS	Age 24 hours through 29 days	6.0%
	30 days through 89 days	5.0%
	90 days and older	4.5%
YEARLINGS		4.5%
BREEDING	Animals through age of 12 years only used exclusively for breeding	4.5%
PLEASURE and SHOW ages 2 through 12 years	Excluding geldings	4.5%
	Geldings	5.0%

ARABIANS

FOALS	Age 24 hours through 5 months	7.0%
	6 months to 12 months	5.5%
BREEDING	Animals 12 months through 12 years only	4.0%
SHOW	Animals 12 months through 12 years only	4.0%
PRIVATE RIDING	Ages 12 months through 12 years only	4.0%
OTHER USES	Except those noted above through age 12	4.5%

QUARTER HORSES and APPALOOSAS

FOALS	Age 24 hours through 7 days	7.0%
	8 days through 29 days	6.5%
	30 days through 89 days	6.0%
	90 days and older	5.5%
YEARLINGS		5.0%
BREEDING	Animals through age 12 used for breeding exclusively	4.5%
RACERS	Rates apply to animals through the age of 7 years only. All racing coverage subject to Claiming Race Inclusion Clause	
	Excluding geldings	
	Values up to $25,000	7.5%
	Values over $25,000	6.5%
	(minimum premium — $1,875)	
	Geldings of all values	8.5%
PLEASURE	Includes riding, excludes jumping through age 12	5.0%
OTHER USES	Except those noted above through age 12	5.5%

Conditions		Rate

STANDARDBREDS (TROTTERS AND PACERS)

FOALS	Age 24 hours through 7 days	8.0%
	8 days through 29 days	5.5%
	30 days through 89 days	5.0%
	90 days and older	4.5%
YEARLINGS		4.0%
BREEDING	Animals through 12 years of age	
	Stallions	4.0%
	Broodmares	4.5%
RACERS	Rates apply to animals through the age of 12 years only. All racing coverage subject to Claiming Race Inclusion Clause.	
	Excluding geldings	4.5%
	Geldings	7.0%

TENNESSEE WALKING HORSES

ALL USES	Age 24 hours through 7 days	7.0%
	8 days through 29 days	6.5%
	30 days through 89 days	6.0%
	90 days to 12 months	5.5%
	12 months through 12 years	6.5%

THOROUGHBREDS

FOALS	Age 24 hours through 7 days	7.0%
	8 days through 29 days	6.5%
	30 days through 89 days	6.0%
	90 days and older	5.5%
YEARLINGS	Insured prior to November 1	
	Values to $14,999	5.0%
	Values of $15,000 and over	4.0%
	Insured on or after November 1 use rates for Flat Racers	
BREEDING	Animals through age 12	4.5%
FLAT RACERS	Rates apply to Flat Racers only through the age of 7 years. All racing coverage subject to Claiming Race Inclusion Clause.	
	Excluding geldings	
	Values to $25,000	7.5%
	Values over $25,000	6.5%
	(minimum premium — $1,875)	
	Geldings of all values	8.5%

ALL BREEDS

SPECIFIED PERIL COVERAGE		
	Including racetracks and shows	1.0%
	Excluding racetracks and shows	0.6%
SPECIAL ACCIDENT — 60% of the normal mortality rate for the appropriate class of horse.		
SHORT TERM TRANSPORTATION		
	Excludes racing risk	normally 1.0%
PROSPECTIVE FOAL INSURANCE		Submit for rating
OVERAGE ANIMALS		Submit for rating
STABLE DISCOUNT		Submit for rating
GROUP RATES		Submit for rating

Conditions	Rate

HUNTERS, JUMPERS, POLO PONIES
　　　　12 year age limit 5.5%

HURDLERS
　　　　12 year age limit 8.5%

STEEPLECHASERS
　　　　12 year age limit 9.0%

Special stipulations and rates apply to (a) fire, lightning, windstorm and transportation losses only, (b) castration of colts and setting tails, (c) air and ocean transportation, and (d) group insurance. Also, reimbursement coverage for colic surgery is available. Depending on individual situations, discounts may apply. For information relative to these, the owner should see a livestock insurance agent.

In order to obtain insurance, the following information is generally required: Name, registry number, ear tag or tattoo number (markings on horse), breed, sex, date of birth, amount to be insured for and period of insurance required, and a statement of health examination (made not more than five days prior to insuring) by an approved federal or state veterinarian to the effect *that the animal(s) (referring to it by name) is at the time of applying for insurance in a state of good physical health and condition.*

It is recommended that the person desiring or having insurance confer with a broker who makes a specialty of horse insurance, read the policy with care, and change the provisions of the policy at such intervals as required or when special circumstances arise.

COST OF PRODUCING HORSES

Horses are kept for the following two reasons:

1. As a business—to make money.
2. To enhance the quality of life.

Those who produce horses as a business expect to make money; unless they make a reasonable return on their investment, they will not likely stay in business very long.

Those who keep horses to enhance the quality of life are of two types: (1) those who use horses for leisure/sports activities; and (2) young people (4-H, FFA), and other youth for whom horses serve (a) as an educational tool, and (b) as a living object/pet to keep them busy, and upon which to shower their love and affection.

Those who keep horses for leisure/sports, may not expect to turn a profit; like those who hunt and fish without computing the cost per lb of their catch, they may be in the horse business for the fun of it.

Fig. 19-10. The cost of producing horses may be lowered by utilizing pastures, keeping animals free from parasites, providing balanced rations, and attaining higher fertility in both mares and stallions. (Courtesy, Commonwealth of Kentucky, Department of Travel Development, Frankfort)

Most youth like to make money from their horse projects, but as educational and keep-occupied tools, no price tag can be put on their ownership of horses—they're invaluable.

■ Prior Horse Cost Studies

In 1960, the author of this book conducted a nationwide survey of selected breeders of the three major breeds used in racing—Thoroughbreds, Standardbreds, and Quarter Horses. This was the first independent, scientific survey of the economics of United States light horse production. The detailed results of this survey were reported in *The Thoroughbred of California*, March 1961, but a few significant findings follow: (1) there was only a 66% foal crop; (2) the average return on investment was only 1.2%; (3) it cost $1,391 per year to maintain an in-foal mare, and $1,019 per year to maintain a barren mare, (4) it cost $1,365 to raise a foal from birth to two years of age; and (5) of the animals raced, they raced 3.5 years, raced 42 times, and had lifetime earnings of $17,320.

In the mid-1970s, Lawrence and Downes analyzed the costs and returns of Maryland Standardbred breeders. They found (1) that only 19% of the breeders sampled showed a profit on their operations; (2) that the break-even prices on yearlings on farms with fewer than three mares was $5,900, and for farms with more than 10 mares it was $11,400.

OKLAHOMA STUDY

Oklahoma State University (OSU) researchers reported the results of a study in which the enterprise budgeting technique was used to estimate the total yearling break-even price.[12]

OVERVIEW OF OKLAHOMA HORSE INDUSTRY

Oklahoma ranks third in total number of horses per state, with California and Texas ranking first and second respectively. The average Oklahoma owner has 8 horses. The predominant breeds in the state, by rank, are Quarter Horse (which accounts for 55% of the equine population), Appaloosa and Paint Horses (11%), Thoroughbred (9%), other purebreds (13%), and non-purebreds (12%).

Like most states, Oklahoma has many kinds, sizes, and mixes of horse production. But the most common horse operations in the state are: (1) broodmare farms producing yearlings for sale and/or own use, (2) stallion farms offering breeding services and mare boarding, (3) yearling, weanling, and other horse sales preparation services (grooming, feeding, and basic training), (4) horse breaking and training farms for racing, showing, or working horses, and (5) horse owners/investors who place mares or performing horses at mare boarding or training farms.

FOCUS OF THE OKLAHOMA STUDY

The Oklahoma study focused on productive costs in the breeding/production of the following four types of horse farm operations:

1. Forty broodmares producing yearlings on pasture, two stallions plus overhead costs (see Table 19-8). Note that this shows a total yearling break-even price of $6,463.

2. Forty broodmares producing yearlings in drylot, 2 stallions, plus overhead costs (see Table 19-9). Note that this shows a total yearling break-even price of $6,392.

3. Forty broodmares producing yearlings on pasture, 2 stallions, 40 outside mares plus overhead costs (see Table 19-10). Note that this shows a total yearling break-even price of $5,533.

4. Forty broodmares producing yearlings in drylot, 2 stallions, 40 outside mares, plus overhead costs (see Table 19-11). Note that this shows a total yearling break-even price of $5,463.

For comparative purposes, the following assumptions were made relative to the above four types of horse farm operations: (1) a 40-head broodmare unit;

(2) an 80% yearling survival rate; and (3) yearlings kept until June 1, at which time 25% are culled and sold, 22% are sold at private treaty, and 53% are sent to a sales preparation farm and later (in September) sold in auction.

SUMMARY OF THE OKLAHOMA STUDY

The annual operating and fixed costs per mare of maintaining a broodmare on a pasture mare system on a typical Oklahoma horse production farm ranges from $3,621 to $3,667. (These per mare costs are not shown in Tables 19-8 to 19-11.)

As shown in Tables 19-8 to 19-11 it costs from $5,463 to $6,463 to produce a yearling. But, in a separate Oklahoma State University publication, it is reported that the average price for yearlings at the fall Heritage Place Sales in Oklahoma City is $8,600, $7,700, $5,200, $6,100, and $6,700 in 1984, 1985, 1986, 1987, and 1988 respectively.[13]

TABLE 19-8
ESTIMATED TOTAL YEARLING BREAK-EVEN PRICE OF 40 BROODMARES ON PASTURE, 2 STALLIONS, PLUS OVERHEAD COSTS

Inputs	Total Costs
Feed (including salt and minerals)	$ 10,267
Pasture (60 acres and bermuda; 80 acres small grain)	12,158
Veterinarian and medicine	12,890
Farrier	7,560
Bedding	865
Advertising	5,700
Marketing (consignment fees, fitting charges)	36,253
Papers and registration	480
Insurance	447
Utilities	4,800
Dues to organizations	70
Farm magazines	51
Labor	28,900
Annual operating capital	4,005
Carryover capital	1,567
Machinery and equipment repairs, fuel and lubrication	3,868
Machinery costs[1]	2,025
Facility and equipment costs[1]	22,933
Horse investment costs[1]	32,768
Land costs[2]	6,481
Total farm cost	**$194,088**
Cost per yearling	$ 6,065
5% sales company commission on 25 yearlings	237
5% agent fee on 17 yearlings sold in Sept.	161
Total yearling break-even price	**$ 6,463**

[1]includes interest, depreciation, taxes, and insurance.
[2]Includes interest and taxes.

[12]Goode, Jennifer C., Odell L. Walker, Donald R. Topliff, David W. Freeman, and Raleigh A. Jacobs, III, *Economic Analysis of Selected Horse Production Systems in Oklahoma*, Research Report P-905, Oklahoma State University, Stillwater, 1989.

[13]Freeman, David W., *Oklahoma Horse Industry Trends*, Current Report, CR-3987, 0689, Oklahoma State University, Stillwater, 1989.

TABLE 19-9
ESTIMATED TOTAL YEARLING BREAK-EVEN PRICE
OF 40 BROODMARES IN DRYLOT,
2 STALLIONS, PLUS OVERHEAD COSTS

Inputs	Total Costs
Feed (including salt and minerals)	$ 23,702
Veterinarian and medicine	12,890
Farrier	7,560
Bedding	865
Advertising	5,700
Marketing (consignment fees, fitting charges)	36,253
Papers and registration	480
Insurance	447
Utilities	4,800
Dues to organizations	70
Farm magazines	51
Labor	32,937
Annual operating capital	3,970
Carryover capital	2,339
Machinery and equipment repairs, fuel and lubrication	4,081
Machinery costs[1]	2,232
Facility and equipment costs[1]	18,259
Horse investment costs[1]	32,768
Land costs[2]	2,561
Total farm cost	**$191,965**
Cost per yearling	$ 5,999
5% sales company commission on 25 yearlings	234
5% agent fee on 17 yearlings sold in Sept.	159
Total yearling break-even price	**$ 6,392**

[1]includes interest, depreciation, taxes, and insurance.
[2]Includes interest and taxes.

Fig. 19-11. Hungarian mares at Bitterroot Stock Farm, Hamilton, MT. (Photo by Ernst Peterson, Hamilton, MT)

TABLE 19-10
ESTIMATED TOTAL YEARLING BREAK-EVEN PRICE
OF 40 BROODMARES ON PASTURE, 2 STALLIONS,
40 OUTSIDE MARES, PLUS OVERHEAD COSTS

Inputs	Total Costs
Feed (including salt and minerals)	$ 12,679
Pasture (60 acres and bermuda; 80 acres small grain)	12,158
Veterinarian and medicine	12,890
Farrier	7,560
Bedding	2,465
Advertising	5,700
Marketing (consignment fees, fitting charges)	36,253
Papers and registration	480
Insurance	447
Utilities	4,800
Dues to organizations	70
Farm magazines	51
Labor	33,046
Annual operating capital	4,225
Carryover capital	1,567
Machinery and equipment repairs, fuel and lubrication	4,018
Machinery costs[1]	2,100
Facility and equipment costs[1]	25,542
Horse investment costs[1]	32,768
Land costs[2]	6,524
Total farm cost	**$205,343**
Gross returns from outside mares[3]	−19,200
Stud fees earned[4]	−20,000
Adjusted farm cost	**$166,143**
Cost per yearling	$ 5,192
5% sales company commission on 25 yearlings	202
5% agent fee on 17 yearlings sold in Sept.	138
Total yearling break-even price	**$ 5,533**

[1]includes interest, depreciation, taxes, and insurance.
[2]Includes interest and taxes.
[3]Assuming a mare care rate of $8.00 per day for 40 mares.
[4]Assuming an average stud fee of $500 for 40 mares.

COST OF HORSE OWNERSHIP

Oklahoma State University reported that the annual cost of one mature hobby horse ownership in a confinement system totals $1,993.77, exclusive of overhead and risk. Then, they add: "Most people own horses for hobby interests related to family and youth development, enhancement of the quality of life, and/or entertainment."[14]

[14]Oklahoma State University, Stillwater, "First Time Horse Ownership: Selecting Horses and Budgeting Horse Interests." OSU Extension Facts, No. 4004. The $1,993.77 annual cost figure is in 1992 dollars.

TABLE 19-11
ESTIMATED TOTAL YEARLING BREAK-EVEN PRICE
OF 40 BROODMARES IN DRYLOT, 2 STALLIONS,
40 OUTSIDE MARES, PLUS OVERHEAD COSTS

Inputs	Total Costs
Feed (including salt and minerals)	$ 26,114
Veterinarian and medicine	12,890
Farrier	7,560
Bedding	2,465
Advertising	5,700
Marketing (consignment fees, fitting charges)	36,253
Papers and registration	480
Insurance	447
Utilities	4,800
Dues to organizations	70
Farm magazines	51
Labor	37,083
Annual operating capital	4,190
Carryover capital	2,339
Machinery and equipment repairs, fuel and lubrication . . .	4,284
Machinery costs[1]	2,307
Facility and equipment costs[1]	20,868
Horse investment costs[1]	32,768
Land costs[2]	2,604
Total farm cost	$203,273
Gross returns from outside mares[3]	−19,200
Stud fees earned[4]	−20,000
Adjusted farm cost	$164,073
Cost per yearling	$ 5,127
5% sales company commission on 25 yearlings	200
5% agent fee on 17 yearlings sold in Sept.	136
Total yearling break-even price	$ 5,463

[1]includes interest, depreciation, taxes, and insurance.

[2]Includes interest and taxes.

[3]Assuming a mare care rate of $8.00 per day for 40 mares.

[4]Assuming an average stud fee of $500 for 40 mares.

IMPACT OF THE U.S. HORSE INDUSTRY

In a study sponsored by the California Horsemen's Benevolent and Protective Association, it was found that the California horse industry was responsible for 28,200 full-time jobs and expenditures totaling $1.65 billion in the state. The review of racing's impact on jobs, revenue, and taxes showed that racing generated an estimated $246.4 million.[15]

---

[15]*The Blood Horse*, Lexington, Kentucky, Feb. 26, 1994, p. 980.

Fig. 19-12. A Standardbred mare and foal in a picturesque setting. (Courtesy, The United States Trotting Association, Columbus, OH)

With the exception of the 1995 Thoroughbred racing statistics, the following impact statistics are from the *1996 American Horse Council Horse Industry Directory*, p. 4. The 1995 Thoroughbred racing statistics are from *Preliminary Business Plan*, National Thoroughbred Association, 128 East Reynolds Road, Lexington, Kentucky, 1996.

■ There are 258,434 youths involved in 4-H horse and pony programs. Additionally, more than 13,000 young people are involved in the United States Pony Club.

■ Horse shows are increasing in numbers, size, and economic impact. In 1995, there were 14,000 sanctioned horse shows. Additionally, that same year there were thousands of local unsanctioned events. This included:

1. 2,500 events sanctioned by the American Horse Shows Association.

2. 2,288 events sanctioned by the American Quarter Horse Association.

3. 1,400 events sanctioned by the National Cutting Horse Association.

4. 2,100 events sanctioned by the National Barrel Horse Association.

5. 1,093 events sanctioned by the American Paint Horse Association.

Horse shows generate total revenues of about $119 million per year.

In 1995, 35.8 million people attended Thoroughbred racing in North America (down from 58.7 million in 1991), which had (1) a mutuel handle of $13.1 billion (up from $10.1 billion in 1991), and (2) a purse distribution of $796 million (up from $752 million in 1991).

(Also see Chapter 2, section headed "Present Status of the U.S. Horse Industry" for additional facts and figures relative to the impact of the U.S. horse industry.)

SELECTED REFERENCES

Title of Publication	Author(s)	Publisher
Business of Horses, The	K. A. Wood	Wood Publications, P.O. Box 963, Rancho Santa Fe, CA, 1973.
Depreciation for the Horse Industry	D. E. Rose	Equine Publications, Ltd., Lexington, OH, 1975
Farm Management Economics	E. O. Heady H. R. Jensen	Prentice-Hall, Inc., Englewood Cliffs, NJ, 1955
Kiplinger Agricultural Letter, The		The Kiplinger Washington Editors, Washington, DC, bi-weekly
Law and Your Horse	E. H. Greene	A. S. Barnes & Co., Inc., Cranbury, NJ, 1971
Midwest Farm Handbook		Iowa State University, Ames, IA, 1964
Stockman's Handbook, The, Seventh Edition	M. E. Ensminger	Interstate Publishers, Inc., Danville, IL, 1992
Stud Manager's Handbook	Ed. by M. E. Ensminger	Agriservices Foundation, Clovis, CA, annually, 1965–1981

Many horse enterprises are big business; hence, they should be operated as such. This shows the foaling barn at Walmac International, Lexington, Kentucky. (Courtesy, Thoroughbred Publications, Inc., Lexington, KY)

20

GLOSSARY OF HORSE TERMS

About the World of Animals. This is from an original painting by the noted artist, Tom Phillips (3333 17th Street, San Francisco, CA 94110), prepared especially for this book. It portrays the artist's conception of what is in Chapter 20, Glossary of Horse Terms.

A mark of distinction of good equestrians is that they speak the language—they use correct terms and know what they mean. Even though horse terms are used glibly by people in the horse and pony business, often they are baffling to the newcomer.

Many terms that are defined or explained elsewhere in this book are not repeated in this chapter. Thus, if a particular term is not listed herein, the reader should look in the index or in the particular chapter and section where it is discussed.

A

Across the board: A combination pari-mutuel (race) ticket on a horse is known as across the board, meaning that you collect something if your horse runs first, second, or third.

Actinobacillosis: See Navel infection.

Action: Movement of the feet and legs—it should be straight and true.

Aerobic: Dependent on oxygen for life and/or activity.

Aficionado: Ardent follower, supporter, or enthusiast; fan of bullfighting.

Aflatoxin: Class of toxins produced by certain molds.

Age: The age of a horse is computed from the first of January.

Aged horse: Correctly speaking, a horse 8 years of age or over; but the term is often used to indicate a horse that is smooth mouthed—that is, 12 years of age or older. Since one year of a horse's life corresponds to approximately 3 of a human's, it follows that at age 7 a horse comes of age, or attains maturity.

Aids: The legs, hands, weight and voice, as used in controlling a horse.

Allowance race: Event other than claiming for which the racing secretary drafts certain conditions.

Alter: To castrate a horse; to geld.

American Horse Council, Inc.: The American Horse Council, which represents all sectors of the U.S. horse industry, was formed in 1969. It is dedicated to the development of the American equine industry. It seeks a fair tax consideration for horse producers (farmers) and develops educational programs and activities designed to meet the needs of the horse industry. The address follows:

American Horse Council, Inc.
1770 "K" Street, N.W., Suite 300
Washington, DC 20006-3805

Anaerobic: Able to survive or function only where there is no oxygen.

Anatomy: The science of the structure of the animal body and the relation of its parts.

Anglo-Arab: An animal out of registered parents, one of which is a Thoroughbred and the other an Arabian.

Anthelmintic: Any of various classes of drugs used to destroy internal parasites.

Anthrax (splenic fever, charbon): An acute, infectious disease caused by *Bacillus anthracis*, a large, rod-shaped organism.

Antihistamine: A drug used to neutralize and treat allergic conditions in the body.

Antiseptic: An agent used in the treatment of wounds or disease to prevent the growth and development of microbes.

Appointments: Equipment and clothing used in showing.

Arab: Used interchangeably with Arabian; hence, a breed of horses.

Ascarids: See Roundworms, large.

Aseptic: Refers to something being free from pathogenic microorganisms.

Asterisk: Used in front of a horse's name, an asterisk (*) indicates imported. Used in front of a jockey's name, it indicates that the jockey is an apprentice rider.

Astringent: A drug, such as tannic acid, alum, and zinc oxide or sulphate, that causes contraction of tissues.

ATP (adenosine triphosphate): Chemical from which energy is released in the cell.

Atrophy: The wasting away of a body part or tissue.

At the end of the halter: Sold with no guarantee except title.

Azoturia (Monday morning disease, blackwater, tying up): A metabolic disease of unknown origin. It usually appears when the horse is worked following a period of idleness on full feed.

B

Babesiasis: See Equine piroplasmosis.

Back: The command to move backward.

Back stretch:

　1. Straightaway part of track on far side between turns.

　2. The stable area of a race track.

Balanced seat: That position of the mounted rider that requires the minimum of muscular effort to remain in the saddle and which interferes least with the horse's movement and equilibrium.

Bald face: A white face, including the eyes and the nostrils, or a portion thereof.

Balk: Refuse to go.

Balky horse: Any horse that stands still—refuses to

go. This vice was not uncommon in the draft horse and horse-and-buggy era. The causes of balking were numerous; among them, too severe punishment when overloaded, and sore shoulders. The legendary cures (none recommended by the author) included (1) pounding on one shoe to divert the balky horse's attention; (2) pouring sand in one ear, which was supposed to shake the idea of balking out of its head; and (3) building a fire under it.

In the old days, when selling a balky horse at auction, it was generally announced that "This horse sells at halter." Belatedly, some uninformed buyer learned that this meant that the horse was prone to balk, and that it wouldn't pull the hat off your head.

Bandage: Strips of cloth wound around lower part of horses' legs for support or protection against injury.

Banged: Hair of the tail cut off in a straight line.

Bangtail: Slang term for a racehorse, as in the old days running horses usually had banged tails, often banged close to the dock, or docked and banged. Also a wild horse.

Barefoot: Unshod.

Barrel racing: It is an excellent test of combined speed and agility of horseflesh, for it is a race against time coupled with ease of maneuverability. Each contestant must ride a cloverleaf pattern around three barrels.

Barren: A mare that is not in foal.

Bars: May refer either to the bars of the mouth, or of the hoof.

Base narrow: Standing with front or rear feet close together, yet standing with legs vertical.

Base wide: Standing with front or rear feet wide apart, yet with legs vertical.

Bean-shooter: A horse that throws its front feet violently forward at the trot, with little flexion, landing about 12 in. above the ground. A very undesirable trait.

Beefy hocks: Thick meaty hocks, lacking in quality.

Bell:

　1. Signal when starter opens gate.

　2. Signal for closing of betting.

Bell boots: Rubber protective boots that are bell-shaped, fitting over the coronet bands and down on the hoof.

Bellerophon: The Prince of Corinth in Greek mythology who tamed the winged horse, Pegasus. According to legend, Bellerophon used a golden bridle to coax the curious animal from his favorite meadow, then made him captive and rode him off to destroy the dragonlike monster, the Chimera. Success encouraged him to try to fly to Olympia to live with the gods.

However, Zeus, angered by this mortal's ambition, sent a gadfly to sting Pegasus, causing him to unseat his venerable and conceited master, who fell to earth crippled and blinded.

Big hitch: A heavy hitch of draft horses in 4s, 6s, 8s, or even more.

Bight of the reins: The part of the reins passing between thumb and fingers and out the top of the hand.

Biopsy: Surgical removal and examination of living tissue as an aid to precise diagnosis.

Bishoping: The practice of artificially altering the teeth of older horses in an attempt to make them sell as young horses.

Blaze: A broad white marking covering almost all of the forehead, but not including the eyes or nostrils.

Bleeder: Horse that bleeds after or during workout or race due to ruptured blood vessel(s).

Blemishes: Those abnormalities that do not affect the serviceability of the horse, including such things as wire cuts, rope burns, nail punctures, shoe boils, and capped hocks.

Blindness: Partial or complete loss of vision.

Blinker: An attachment to the bridle or hood, designed to restrict the vision of the horse from the sides and rear and to focus the vision forward.

Blister: An irritant applied as a treatment for unsoundness and blemishes.

Blistering: Blistering consists in applying an irritating substance such as Spanish fly and iodide of mercury (one common preparation consists of 15 parts Spanish fly, 8 parts iodide of mercury and 120 parts of lard) as treatment for a blemish or unsoundness. Before applying a blister, the hair should be closely clipped from the affected area, the scurf brushed from the skin, and the animal tied so that it cannot rub, lick, or bite the treated area. The blistering agent is then applied by rubbing it into the pores of the skin with the palm of the hand. Three days later the blistered area should be bathed with warm water and soap, dried, and treated with sweet oil or Vaseline to prevent cracking of the skin. Blistering increases the blood supply to the site of the blister and induces more rapid healing.

Blood-horse: A pedigreed horse. To most equestrians the term is synonymous with the Thoroughbred breed.

Blood spavin: A varicose vein enlargement which appears on the inside of the hock but immediately above the location of the bog spavin.

Bloodworms: See Strongyles.

Bloom: Hair that is clean and of healthy texture.

Blow: To blow wind after strenuous exercise.

Blowfly: The blowfly group consists of several species of flies that breed in animal flesh.

Blow out: To walk or exercise a horse either to loosen its muscles for further exercise, or to prevent chilling and stiffening after a hard workout.

Blue eye: An unsound eye with a blue appearance; the sight may or may not be entirely gone.

Bog spavin: A filling of the natural depression on the inside and front of the hock. A bog spavin is much larger than a blood spavin.

Bolting:

1. The name given to the habit that ravenous horses have of eating too fast. This condition may be controlled by adding chopped hay to the grain ration or by placing some large, round stones, as big or bigger than baseballs, in the feed box.

2. An animal breaking out of control or trying to run away is said to be bolting.

Bolus: Large pill.

Bone: The measurement of the circumference around the cannon bone about halfway between the knee and fetlock joints. Eight inches of bone is average for the Thoroughbred. *Flat bone* indicates that the cannon and the back tendon are parallel, with the tendon clean-cut and standing well away from the cannon bone. The word *flat* refers to the appearance of the cannon, which is wide and flat when viewed from the side although narrow from the front, and does not mean that the bone itself is flat.

Bone spavin (or jack spavin): Bone spavin is a bony enlargement that appears on the inside and front of the hind leg(s) below the hock at the point where the base of the hock tapers into the cannon part of the leg.

Boots: Protective covering for the legs or feet, generally used when exercising. Some types of boots are used for balance and perfection in gait.

Bosal: The braided rawhide or rope noseband of a bosal hackamore. The bosal is knotted under the horse's jaw.

Bots: The larva stage of highly specialized parasites that attack horses, mules, and perhaps zebras.

Bowed tendons: Enlarged tendons behind the cannon bones, in both the front and hind legs. Descriptive terms of *high* or *low* bow are used by equestrians to denote the location of the injury; the high bow appears just under the knee and the low bow just above the fetlock. This condition is often brought about by severe strains, such as heavy training or racing. When bowed tendons are pronounced, more or less swelling, soreness, and lameness are present. Treatment consists in blistering or firing. The object of blistering and firing is to convert a chronic into an acute inflammation. This hastens nature's processes by bringing more blood to the part, thus inducing a reparative process which renders the animal suitable for work sooner than would otherwise be the case.

Bowlegged: Wide at the knees, close at the feet.

Brace bandages: Resilient bandages on the legs of horses worn in some cases in an effort to support lame legs, and worn in other cases to protect a horse from cutting and skinning its legs while racing.

Brand: A mark used as a means of identification.

Break: To teach a young horse to obey commands, and accept direction and control.

Breaking: A horse's leaving its gait and breaking into a gallop. A trotter or pacer must remain on gait in a race. If it makes a break, the driver must immediately pull it back to its gait.

Break maiden: Horse or rider winning first race of career.

Breeder: Owner of the dam at the time of service who was responsible for the selection of the sire to which she was mated.

Breeding: An attempt to regulate the progeny through intensive selection of the parents.

Breedy: Smart and trim about the head and front part of the body.

Breezing: A race workout in which a horse is running at a controlled speed.

Bridoon: The correct name for the little snaffle bit in the full bridle.

Brittle hoofs: Hoofs that are abnormally dry and fragile.

Broke: Tamed and trained to a particular function, as halter-broke. Also, to leave or alter gait; *e.g.*, the trotter broke stride.

Broken crest: A heavy neck which breaks over and falls to one side.

Broken knees: Knees with scars on them, indicating that the horse has fallen. Often scars are an indication that the horse is awkward and inclined to stumble.

Bronchitis: A condition of the respiratory system, characterized by the inflammation of the bronchial tubes, with signs similar to heaves.

Broodmare: A mare kept for breeding or reproductive purposes.

Broomtail: A wild and untrained western range horse of inferior quality.

Brothers (or sisters):

Full brothers: By the same sire and out of the same dam.

Half brothers: Out of the same dam, by different sires. This is one of the most frequently misused terms. Horses by the same sire and out of different dams are referred to as *by the same sire*, or else the name of the sire is used, as *by Man O' War*. This distinction is for a definite purpose, for only a few horses can be half brothers (or half sisters) to a famous horse, but hundreds can be by the same sire. This restricted definition tends to give a little of the credit to good broodmares instead of leaving the meaning ambiguous.

Brothers in blood: By the same sire out of full sisters, or by full brothers out of the same dam, or any combination of exactly the same blood.

Three-quarter brothers: For example, horses having the same dam and whose sires have identical sires but different dams.

Seven-eighths brothers: The progeny of a horse and his son produced by the same mare, or similar combinations of lineage.

Brush: To force a horse to top speed over a short distance.

Brushing: Striking the fetlock with the other hoof, which may result in either roughing the fetlock hair or in an actual injury.

Bucked shins: A temporary racing unsoundness characterized by a very painful inflammation of the periosteum (bone covering along the greater part of the front surface of the cannon bone, caused by constant pressure from concussion during fast works or races.

Bucking: Springing with a quick leap, arching the back, and descending with the forelegs rigid and the head held as low as possible.

Buck-kneed: Standing with the knees too far forward.

Bug boy: An apprentice jockey.

Bull pen: Auction ring.

C

Calcium lactate: A calcium salt of lactic acid, used to induce thickening and more rapid clotting of the blood.

Calf-kneed: Standing with knees too far back; directly opposite to buck-kneed or knee-sprung. This condition causes more trouble than knee-sprung or buck-kneed.

Calf roping: A skill required of cowboys when branding and doctoring animals on the range.

Calico-pinto: A multicolored or spotted pony.

Calk: Grips on the heels and outside of the front shoes of horses, designed to give the horse better footing and prevent slipping.

Fig. 20-1. Calf roping—a team effort by a working cowboy and his horse. (Courtesy, American Quarter Horse Assn., Amarillo, TX)

Calking: Injury to the coronary band by the shoe of the horse. Usually incurred by horses whose shoes have calks, or by horses that are rough-shod, as for ice.

Canter: A slow, restrained, three-beat gait in which the two diagonal legs are paired, thereby producing a single beat which falls between the successive beats of the other unpaired legs.

Capped elbow: See Shoe boil.

Capped hock: An enlargement at the point of the hock; it is usually caused by bruising.

Capriole: An intricate movement performed by the Lipizzan horses in the Spanish Riding School in Vienna. It is considered the ultimate of all high school and classical training. The horse leaps into the air, and, while in the air, kicks out with the hind feet. The Capriole also, like so many other forms of high school work, belongs to the Medieval methods of combat, in which, by means of such jumps by the horse, the surrounded rider could rid himself of adversaries. By the horse's kicking out with the hind legs, the enemy was prevented from getting within striking distance with sword and lance.

Cast: Refers to a horse's falling or lying down close to a wall or fence so that it cannot get up without assistance.

Cat-hammed: Having long, relatively thin thighs and legs.

Cavesson: Head stall with a noseband (often quite large) used for exercising and training horses.

Centaurs: The centaurs were an ancient mythical Greek race dwelling in the mountains of Thessalay. They were imagined as men with the bodies of horses and half-bestial natures.

Champing: A term that describes the horse's playing with the bit. Its development is encouraged in bitting a young horse by using a bit with keys attached to the mouthpiece, which tends to make saliva flow and keep the mouth moist—an aid in producing a soft mouth.

Charbon: See Anthrax.

Check: Short for checkrein.

Checkrein: A strap coupling the bit of a bridle to the harness back band to keep the head up and in position.

Cheek: A cheek strap, a part of the bridle.

Chestnut: The horny growth on the inside of the horse's legs, above the knees and below the hocks.

Chromosome: Structure in the nucleus of a cell which carries genes. Each species has a constant set of chromosomes set in pairs. The horse has 64.

Chukker: A seven-and-one-half-minute period in a polo game. (From the Hindu language, meaning *a circle*.)

Cinch: Girth of a Western saddle.

Claiming race: A race in which all the horses are entered at stated prices and may be claimed (purchased) by any other owner or a starter in the race. In effect, all horses in a claiming race are offered for sale.

Clean legs: A term indicating that there are no blemishes or unsoundnesses on the legs.

Clicking: Striking the forefoot with the toe of the hind foot on the same side. Also known as forging.

Cluck: To move the tongue in such a way as to produce clucks. The command to go, proceed; the signal to increase speed.

Coarse: Lacking in quality—shown in texture of hair, hairy fetlocks, all-over lack of refinement, common head; flat and shelly feet, and gummy legs.

Cob: A close-knit horse, heavy boned, short coupled and muscular, but with quality, and not so heavy or coarse as to be a draft animal. A cob is usually small, standing under 15 hands.

Cobby: Close coupled, stoutly built. Like a cob.

Cocked ankles: A horse that stands bent forward on the fetlocks in a cocked position.

Cockhorse: An extra horse used with English stage-coaches, ridden behind the coach in ordinary going, but hitched before the team for added draft when approaching steep hills or heavy going. The cockhorse was usually of a flashy color.

Coffin bone: The bone of the foot of a horse, enclosed within the hoof.

Coggins test: A test for diagnosing equine infectious anemia. It was developed by Dr. Leroy Coggins, Cornell University, from whom it takes its common name.

Cold-backed: Describes a horse that humps his back and does not settle down until the saddle has been on a few minutes. Some cold-backed horses will merely tuck their tails and arch their backs when first mounted, but others will take a few crow hops until warmed up.

Coldblood: A horse of draft horse breeding.

Cold-jawed: Tough-mouthed.

Colic: A severe indigestion, which causes abdominal discomfort.

Collected: The term applied to a horse when ridden well up to its bit with its neck flexed, jaw relaxed, and hocks well under it. A collected horse has full control over its limbs at all gaits and is ready and able to respond to the signals or aids of its rider.

Colors: Racing silks, jacket, and cap worn by jockeys to denote ownership of horse.

Colostrum: Milk secreted by the mare at foal's birth. It contains globulin, a protein that provides the foal temporary immunity against infectious disease.

Colt: A young stallion under three years of age; in Thoroughbreds, the age is extended to include four-year-olds.

Combination horse: One used for saddle and driving.

Combined training: Competitions of this type are usually held over three days and involve dressage, speed and endurance test, and show jumping. In order to do well, a horse must combine speed, stamina, obedience, and considerable jumping ability; and the rider must be knowledgeable and expert in the three branches of horsemanship upon which the mount is tested.

Complete feed: A nutritionally adequate feed for animals other than humans; by specific formula compounded to be fed as the sole ration; and capable of maintaining life and/or promoting production without any additional substance, except water, being consumed.

Concentrate: A feed used with another to improve the nutritive balance of the total and intended to be further diluted and mixed to produce a supplement or a complete feed.

Condition: The state of health, as evidenced by the coat, state of flesh, and general appearance.

Conformation: Body shape or form.

Congenital: Acquired during development in the uterus and not through heredity.

Contracted feet: A condition characterized by a drawing in or contracting at the heels.

Cool out: To cause a horse to move about quietly after heavy exercise.

Coon footed: Having low pasterns and shallow heels.

Corn: A bruise of the soft tissue underlying the horny sole of the foot which manifests itself in a reddish discoloration of the sole immediately below the affected area.

Corticosteroids: An organic compound, used to stimulate the proper functioning of the adrenal gland.

Coupling: The section between the point of the hip and the last rib. A short-coupled horse is considered to be an easy keeper, while a long-coupled horse is said to "take a bale of hay a day." The width of four fingers is considered to constitute a short coupling.

Cow hocks, cow hocked: Standing with the joints of the hocks bent inward, with the toes pointing outward.

Crab bit: Bit with prongs extending at the horse's nose. Purpose is to tip the horse's head up and help prevent it from ducking its head, bowing its neck, and pulling hard on the reins.

Cracked heels, scratches: An inflamed state of the skin at the back of the pastern joint.

Cradle: A device made of wood or aluminum worn around the neck of the horse which prevents him from chewing at sores, blankets, bandages, etc.

Crest: The top part of the neck. This is very well developed in stallions.

Cribber (wind sucker, or stump sucker): A horse that has the vice of biting or setting the teeth against some object such as a manger, while sucking air.

Crop: A riding whip with a short, straight stock and a loop.

Crop-eared: Refers to an animal which has the tips of its ears either cut off or frozen off.

Crossbred: The offspring of a sire and a dam of different breeds.

Cross-firing: Cross-firing is a defect in the way of going, generally confined to pacers, which consists of a scuffing on the inside of the diagonal fore feet and hind feet.

Crow hops: Mild or playful bucking motions.

Crupper: A leather strap with a padded semicircular loop. The loop end goes under the tail and the strap end is affixed at the center of the back band of a harness or the cantle of a saddle to prevent the saddle from slipping over the withers.

Cryptorchid: A stallion with one or both testicles retained in the abdomen.

Curb:

1. An enlargement at the rear of the leg and below the point of the hock.

2. A bit mouthpiece designed to bring pressure to bear on the horse's bars.

Curry: Cleaning (grooming) with currycomb, dandy brush, body brush, sponge, rub rag, hoof pick, etc.

Cutback saddle: A long, flat saddle that rests low on the horse's back and is designed to place the rider's weight toward the rear. The name is derived from the U-shaped cutaway slot for the withers. It is used primarily for showing.

Cut-out: The cutting out of certain animals in a herd.

Cutting horse: A cow horse used in cutting cattle from the herd. To promote the cutting horse and establish uniform rules for its exhibition, cutting horse enthusiasts are banded together in the following association:

National Cutting Horse Assn.
4704 Highway 377 South
Fort Worth, TX 76116-8805

D

Daisy-cutter: A horse that seems to skim the surface of the ground at a trot. Such horses are often predisposed to stumbling.

Dam: The female parent of a horse.

Dapple: Small spots, patches, or dots contrasting color or shade with the background, such as dapple-gray.

Dash: Race decided in a single trial.

Dead heat: A racing term referring to two or more contestants that arrive simultaneously at the finish line.

Deerfly: A biting insect that inflicts a painful bite.

Denerving: The removal of part of the nerve trunk and/or nerves in certain areas.

Dental star: A marking on the incisor teeth of horses, used in judging their age. It first appears on the lower central and intermediate incisors when the horse is about eight years of age.

Derby: A word that stems from a classic race exclusively for three-year-olds which was initiated at Epsom Downs, in England, in 1780, by the Twelfth Earl of Derby. This race became so famous that, today, the word *derby* is considered synonymous with any well-known race; hence, there is the Kentucky Derby, the Japan Derby, etc. In England, the word is pronounced *darby*, whereas in the United States it is pronounced *derby*.

Diagonal: Refers to the forefoot moving in unison with its opposite hindfoot at the trot. If it is the left forefoot, it is called the left diagonal.

Dish-faced: A term used if the face is concave below the eyes, and, especially in Arabians, if the profile shows a definite depression below the level of the eyes. This term is also applied to some horses and many ponies that have flat or concave foreheads with prominent temples, but this type is the absolute opposite of the dish of the Arab, which has a prominent forehead.

Dishing: Carrying the foot forward in a lateral arc in a trot, but advancing the knee in a straight line.

Disqualification: A fault so serious that it disqualifies a horse for registry or show.

Distaff side: The female side, as in a pedigree.

Distemper: See Strangles.

Diuretic: Any agent that increases urine production.

Dock: The solid portion of the tail.

Docked: A tail in which part of the dock has been removed.

Docking and setting: Removing part of the dock of the tail, cutting the tendons, and setting the tail to make the horse carry it high.

Doping: The administering of a drug to a horse to increase or decrease its speed in a race. Racecourse officials run saliva tests, urine tests (urinalyses), etc., in order to try to detect any horses that have been doped. Usually such tests are conducted on the winners of every race and on the first three to finish in stakes races. Where doping is proven, the horse may be banned from the track for a period of time; the owner's entire stable may be banned from racing for a period of time; and/or the license of the trainer or jockey may be suspended; with the penalty determined by the circumstances.

Double-gaited: A term applied to a horse that can both trot and pace with good speed.

Drafty: Having the characteristics of a draft horse. Heavy and lacking in quality.

Drag hunt: A hunt staged on horseback with hounds following a laid trail, made by dragging a bag containing anise seed or litter from a fox's den.

Dressage: The guiding of a horse through natural maneuvers without emphasis on the use of reins, hands, and feet.

Drover: A word reminiscent of one of the most thrilling chapters in American history. Prior to the advent of railroads and improved highways, great herds of cattle, sheep, and hogs were driven on horseback over famous trails, often many hundreds of miles long. the crew of drovers usually consisted of the boss (often the owner of the herd), a person to ride along each side, and a fourth rider to lead.

The drovers—those who did the driving—were rugged, and their lives were filled with adventure. The work was accompanied by an almost ceaseless battle with the elements, clashes with thieves, and no small amount of bloodshed.

Dutchman's team: It is customary to hitch the smaller horse of a team on the left side. When a careless teamster hitches the larger horse on the near side, it is said to be a *Dutchman's team*.

Dwelling: A noticeable pause in the flight of the foot, as though the stride were completed before the foot reaches the ground. It is most noticeable in trick-trained horses.

E

Ear down: To restrain an animal by biting or twisting its ear.

Eastern: Applied to horses of Arab, Barb, or similar breeding.

Eczema: A condition involving the skin, inflammation of the skin with lesions of either dry or weeping nature. Allergies are probably the most common cause.

Edema: Abnormal collection of fluids in body tissues.

Electrolytes: Simple inorganic compounds which dissolve in water and are essential for many of the processes in the body.

Embryo transplant (ET): Process of recovering a fertilized egg from the uterus of one mare and transferring it to the uterus of another for gestation.

Encephalomyelitis (sleeping sickness): A virus, epizootic (epidemic) brain disease which affects both horses and people. It is caused by several distinct viruses. The three most common types in the United States are: Eastern equine encephalomyelitis, Western equine encephalomyelitis, and Venezuelan equine encephalomyelitis.

Endurance rides: Trials of speed and endurance. Eleven 300-mile endurance rides were held, 7 in New England and 4 in Colorado, but these were discontinued in 1926. Today, there are several well-known 50- to 100-mile competitive endurance rides in the United States. The time for the different courses varies according to the topography, elevation, and footing, but it is approximately 17 hours for 100 miles and 6 hours for 50 miles.

Entire: An ungelded male.

Enzyme: Chemical produced by living cells which acts as a catalyst by breaking down or "digesting" specific substances with which it comes in contact.

Epiphysitis: Swelling, leg pain, and/or collapse of the plates of cartilage near the ends of the long leg bones where lengthening of the bone occurs. Normally, the lengthening process involves the generation of new cartilage cells, which are steadily changed into bone. Epiphysitis occurs when there is an increase in cartilage-cell production or the material fails to change to bone in an orderly fashion.

Equestrian: A man or woman engaged in horse work or activities.

Equine: A horse. Correctly speaking, the term includes all members of the family *Equidae*—horses, zebras, and asses.

Equine abortion: The premature expulsion of the fetus.

Equine infectious anemia (swamp fever): An infectious virus disease.

Equine influenza: An infectious disease caused by a myxovirus that has properties of the Type A influenza viruses.

Equine piroplasmosis (babesiasis): Caused by *Babesia caballi* or *B. equi*, protozoan parasites that invade the red blood cells.

Equitation: The act or art of riding horseback.

Equus: Latin word for horse.

Ergot:

1. The horny growth at the back of the fetlock joint; the spurs of a horse's hoofs.

2. A fungus disease of plants.

Estrogen: Hormone responsible for the mare's outward sexual behavior and changes in sex cycle.

Estrus: The period of sexual excitement (heat) during which the female will accept the male in the act of mating.

Ewe neck: A neck like that of a sheep, with a dip between the poll and the withers. Also termed a *turkey neck* and *upside-down neck*.

Extended trot: Moving the horse at a very rapid, but collected, gait at the trot. To achieve this, the rider applies pressure with the calves of the legs as he/she comes down into the saddle while posting.

Exudate: Refers to the discharge of fluid and tissue material from an oozing sore or wound. This is usually characterized by a dry, crusty state of scablike sores.

F

Face fly: Flies that gather in large numbers on the faces of horses, especially around the eyes and nose.

Fallen neck: See Broken crest.

Family: The lineage of an animal as traced through

either the males or females, depending upon the breed.

Farcy: See Glanders.

Farrier: A horseshoer.

Far side: the right side of a horse.

Fast track: Footing at its best—dry, fast, and even.

Favoring a leg: To favor one leg; to limp slightly.

Feather: The long hairs that grow at the back of the pastern or fetlock.

Feather in eye: A mark across the eyeball, not touching the pupil; often caused by an injury, it may be a blemish or some other defect.

Feral: Describes a wild horse—one that has escaped from domestication and become wild, as contrasted to one originating in the wild.

Fetal: Relating to unborn animal.

Fetlock feather: Long hair which grows back of the fetlock.

Fetlock joint: The connection between the cannon and the pastern bones.

Fetus: The unborn animal as it develops in the uterus.

Figure-eight bandage: A style of bandaging, applied in a figure-eight fashion, which allows for expansion at the flexing of hocks and knees.

Filly: A young female horse under three years of age; in Thoroughbreds, it includes four-year-olds.

Film patrol: The practice of recording a race on film.

Firing: Applying a hot iron or needle to a blemish or unsoundness as a treatment.

First lock: The first lock of the mane on or in back of the poll (when the poll is clipped). The first lock is sometimes braided with a ribbon, as is the foretop.

Fistulous withers: An inflamed condition in the region of the withers, commonly thought to be caused by bruising.

Flat bone: See Bone.

Flat foot: A foot of which the angle is less than 45°, or one in which the sole is not concave, or one with a low, weak heel.

Flat race: A race without jumps.

Flat-sided: Lacking spring in ribs.

Flaxen: A light-colored mane and tail.

Flea-bitten: Describes a white horse covered with small, brown marks, or any mangy-looking animal.

Floating: Filing off the sharp edges of a horse's teeth.

Foal: A young, unweaned horse of either sex.

Foaling: Giving birth to a foal.

Follicle: A bubblelike structure on the ovary which contains an egg.

Forage: Vegetable material in a fresh, dried, or ensiled state which is fed to livestock (pasture, hay, silage).

Forehand: The front of the horse, including head, neck, shoulders, and forelegs—in other words, that portion of the horse in front of the center of gravity.

Foretop, forelock: The lock of hair falling forward over the face.

Forging: See Clicking.

Form: The past performance of a racehorse; often a table giving details relating to a horse's past performance.

Founder: See Laminitis.

Four-in-hand: A hitch of four horses, consisting of two pairs, with one pair in front of the other.

Fox hunt: A hunt with hounds, staged on horseback, after a live fox. The fox may have been released from captivity or racked and flushed out of hiding by the hounds.

Fox trot: A slow, short, broken type of trot in which the head usually nods. In executing the fox trot, the horse brings each hind foot to the ground an instant before the diagonal forefoot.

Frog: A triangular-shaped, elastic like formation in the sole of the horse's hoof.

Full bridle: Another term for either a Weymouth or show bridle.

Full brothers (or sisters): Horses having the same sire and the same dam.

Funeral procession horse(s): U.S. Armed Service horse(s) used in funeral processions, either as a team to draw a caisson or as a riderless horse.

Fungi: Certain vegetable organisms such as molds, mushrooms, and toadstools.

Furlong: A racing distance of one-eighth mile, 220 yards, or 660 feet.

Futurity race: A race in which the horses entered were nominated before birth. As in any other stake race, a fee must accompany the entry of the mare's unborn produce, and further payments must be made to keep the youngster eligible. All these fees go into the winner's kitty.

G

Gait: A particular way of going, either natural or acquired, which is characterized by a distinctive rhythmic movement of the feet and legs.

Gallop: See Run.

Galloping boot: A protective leg support, put on the front legs covering the tendon, cannon bone, and upper portion of the ankle joint.

Galton's law: The theory of inheritance expounded by Sir Francis Galton (1822–1911). According to this genetic theory, the individual's inheritance is determined as follows: one-fourth by its sire and one-fourth by its dam; one-sixteenth by each of the four grandparents; and on and on, with each ancestor contributing just one-fourth as much to the total inheritance as did the one a generation nearer to the individual. Galton's law is correct in the sense that the relationship between ancestor and descendant is halved with each additional generation which intervenes between them. It is not correct in the sense that the individual's heredity is completely determined by the heredity of its ancestors. Rather, in a random-bred population, the individual is one-fourth determined by each parent and one-half determined by chance in Mendelian segregation. Determination by more remote ancestors is included in the determination by the parent. Galton's law is often used as a stamina index by Thoroughbred breeders.

Gamete: A mature sex cell (sperm or egg.)

Gaucho: The South American cowboy. In particular, the term is used in the Pampas area of Argentina. The gaucho is considered by many to be the world's finest roughrider.

Gear: The equipment and accessories used in harness driving (except the vehicle) and in polo playing (except the bridles and saddles). See tack.

Gee: The teamster's term signaling a turn to the right.

Geld: To cut or castrate a male horse.

Gelding: A male horse that was castrated before reaching maturity.

Gene: Unit of hereditary material present in the nucleus of a cell, which carries the necessary protein code for the development of a specific trait or characteristic in offspring cells.

Genotype selection: Selection of breeding stock not necessarily from the best appearing animals but from the best breeding animals, according to genetic makeup.

Germ plasm: Germ cells and their precursors, bearers of hereditary characters.

Get: Progeny or offspring.

Get-up: The command to go; proceed; move forward. When repeated, it means to increase speed. "Giddap," slang.

Gimpy: Lame, or sore.

Girth: The strap or webbing that holds the saddle or backband in place.

Girth-place: The place for the girth, as the name implies, it is marked by a depression in the underline just in back of the front legs.

Glanders (or farcy): An acute or chronic infectious disease caused by *Malleomyces mallei*, a bacterium.

Glass-eyed: The term applied to an eye that is devoid of pigment.

Good mouth: Said of an animal 6 to 10 years of age.

Goose-rumped: An animal having a short, steep croup that narrows at the point of the buttocks.

Grade: An animal of unknown ancestry. If it shows some specific breed characteristics, it may be suffixed with the name of the breed; *e.g.*, grade Shetland.

Grain: Harvested cereals or other edible seeds, including oats, corn, milo, barley, etc.

Granulation: The formation of excess or scar tissue in early wound healing and repair.

Gravel: A condition which is usually caused by penetration of the protective covering of the hoof by small bits of gravel or dirt. Access to the sensitive tissue is usually gained by the white line or junction of the sole and wall, where the horn is somewhat softer. Once in the soft tissue inside the wall or sole, bacterial infection carried by the foreign material develops rapidly, producing pus and gas that create pressure and intense pain in the foot. In untreated cases, it breaks out at the top of the coronary band and the pus and gas are forced out through this opening.

Grease heel (or scratches): A low-grade infection affecting the hair follicles and skin at the base of the fetlock joint, most frequently the hind legs. It is similar to scratches, but in a more advanced stage.

Green broke: A term applied to a horse that has been hitched or ridden only one or two times.

Groom: A person who tends and cares for horses; an attendant, caretaker, hostler, swipe (not preferred).

Gummy-legged: Having legs in which the tendons lack definition, or do not stand out clearly.

Gymkhana: A program of games on horseback.

H

Hack: A horse used for riding at an ordinary gait over roads, trails, etc.

Hackney pony: Cannot exceed 14.2 hands in height.

Hair: A slender outgrowth of the epidermis which performs a thermoregulatory function, to protect the animal from cold or heat. It becomes long and shaggy during the winter months in cold areas, especially if the horse is left outside. Then, during the warm season, or when the animal is blanketed, the horse sheds and the coat becomes short.

Hair colors: The five basic horse coat colors are bay, black, brown, chestnut, and white. Additionally, there are five major variations of these colors: dun (buckskin), gray, palomino, pinto (calico or paint), and roan.

Half-bred: When capitalized, this denotes a horse sired by a Thoroughbred and registered in the Half-Bred Stud Book.

Half stocking: White extends from the coronet to the middle of the cannon.

Halter puller: A horse that pulls back on the halter rope.

Hammerhead: A coarse-headed animal.

Hamstrung: Disabled by an injury to the tendon above the hock.

Hand: A 4-in. unit of measurement.

Hand-canter: A semiextended canter, midway between a promenade canter and a gallop.

Hand gallop: An extended canter, but the horse remains collected, unlike the flat-out run when the horse's gait almost returns to a four-beat status.

Handicap: A race in which chances of winning are equalized by assigned weights; heaviest weights are given to the best horses, and lightest weights to the poorest.

Handle (mutuel): Amount of money bet on a race, the daily card, or during the meeting, season, or year.

Hard-mouthed: Term used when the membrane of the bars of the mouth where the bit rests have become toughened and the nerves deadened because of the continued pressure of the bit.

Hat rack: An emaciated animal.

Haute ecole: *High school,* the highest form of specialized training of the riding horse.

Haw: The teamster's term signaling a turn to the left.

Hay belly: Having a distended barrel due to the excessive feeding of bulky rations, such as hay, straw, or grass. Also called *grass belly.*

Heat:

1. One trip in a race that will be decided by winning two or more trials.

2. A common term for estrus.

Heaves: Difficulty in forcing air out of the lungs. It is characterized by a jerking of the flanks (double-flank action) and coughing after drinking cold water.

Height: Tallness of a horse as measured from the withers to the ground. It is expressed in hands, each hand being 4 in.

Heredity: Characteristics transmitted to offspring from parents and other ancestors.

Hernia (or rupture): The protrusion of any internal organ through the wall of its containing cavity, but it usually means the passage of a portion of the intestine through an opening in the abdominal muscle.

Herring gutted: Lacking depth of flank, which is also termed *single gutted.*

Heterozygous: Having like genes which can be present for any of the characteristics such as coat color, size, etc.

Hidebound: A tight hide over the body.

High school: The highest form of specialized training of riding horses.

Hippology: The study of the horse.

Hitch:

1. To fasten a horse; *e.g.,* when hitched to a rail.

2. A connection between a vehicle and a horse.

3. A defect in gait noted in the hind leg, which seems to skip at the trot.

Hitching:

1. Having a shorter stride in one hind leg than in the other.

2. Fastening a horse to an object or vehicle.

Hives: Small swellings under or within the skin similar to human hives. They appear suddenly over large portions of the body and can be caused by a change in feed.

Hobbles: Straps which encircle the pasterns or fetlock joints on the front legs of the horse and are connected with a short strap or chain, to prevent it from roaming too far when turned out to graze. Another type of hobble is used on the hind legs (often around the hocks) of a mare in breeding, to prevent her from kicking the stallion.

Hogged mane: A hogged mane is one that has been clipped short.

Homo sapiens: Scientific name for modern man.

Homozygous: Having like genes in a horse which can be present for any of the characteristics of the animal such as coat color, size, etc.

Honda: A ring of rope, rawhide, or metal on a lasso through which the loop slides.

Hopples: The term applied to hobbles (leather or plastic straps with semicircular loops) used in harness racing, which are placed on the gaskin and forearm, connecting the fore and hind legs of the same side in pacers, and running diagonally in trotters, connecting the diagonal fore and hind legs. Such hopples, which were invented by a railroad conductor named John Browning in 1885, are used to keep a horse on gait; *i.e.*, to prevent trotters from pacing and pacers from trotting.

Hormone: A body-regulating chemical secreted by a gland into the bloodstream.

Horn fly: Primarily pests of cattle, but they sometimes seriously annoy horses.

Horse: In the restricted sense this applies to an entire (an ungelded male), not a gelding or mare.

Horsemanship: The art of riding horseback.

Horsemeat: In France and Belgium, and other parts of the world, horsemeat is considered a delicacy for human consumption. In this country, many horses that have outlived their usefulness or that are less valuable for other purposes are processed in modern, sanitary slaughtering plants for pet food.

Horsepower: Originally, horsepower was a measure of the power that a horse exerts in pulling. Technically speaking, a horsepower is the rate at which work is accomplished when a resistance (weight) of 33,000 lb moved 1 foot in 1 minute, or 550 lb is moved 1 foot in 1 second. Despite their sophistication, modern motors are rated in horsepower, based on tests made on a machine known as the dynamometer.

Hot-blooded: Of Eastern or Oriental blood.

Hot-walker: A mechanical, labor-saving device that leads horses in a circle at a slow walk in order to cool them after training.

Housefly: Nonbiting, nuisance insect.

Hunt: Pursuit of game. As used by equestrians, the term usually implies a hunt on horseback with hounds.

Hunt seat saddle: Much like the jump saddle, but with less incline in the cantle.

Hybrids: Crosses of species, not breeds. The mule is a hybrid, cross between the horse family and the ass family. Most mules are infertile.

I

Import: To bring horses from another country.

Importing: In registering horses from another country in the U.S. stud book or their respective breeds, the certificates of registration issued bear the abbreviation Imp. and the country of export; *e.g.*, *Imp. Hydroplane* (Eng.). When a name, such as *Hydroplane* has been previously granted to a horse foaled (born) in this country, a symbol is added; *e.g.*, *Imp. Hydroplane II* (Eng.). Imported is also denoted by an asterisk in front of the name; *e.g.*, **Hydroplane II* (Eng.).

Indian broke: Horses trained to allow mounting from the off side.

Indian pony: A horse of pinto color.

Influenza: A contagious virus disease, characterized by respiratory inflammation, fever, muscle soreness, and often a loss of appetite.

In hand: Refers to horses shown in halter classes.

Interfering: The striking of the fetlock or cannon by the opposite foot that is in motion is known as interfering. This condition is predisposed in horses with base-narrow, toe-wide, or splay-footed standing positions.

Iodoform: A light yellow crystalline compound, used as an antiseptic medicine.

Irons: Stirrups.

Itch: See Mange.

J

Jack spavin: See Bone spavin.

Jennet: Female of the ass family.

Jerk line: A single rein, originally used in western United States. It was fastened to the brake handle and ran through the driver's hand to the bit of the lead animal.

Jockey Club: Probably the most exclusive club in America, with fewer than 100 members. The Jockey Club is custodian of the American Stud Book, registry of Thoroughbred horses.

Jockeys: Professional riders of horses in races. Jockeys are both born and made. They were born to be small people; and they are made as jockeys if they possess courage and intelligence. Jockeys weigh anywhere from 94 to 116 lb, with an average of about 105 lb. A famous observation, which the author once overheard in a jockey's room before a race, was "What would we all be if it weren't for racing? We'd all be bellhops." But the jockey might well have added that they would be bellhops anyway if they didn't have the courage to ride down a track at 40 miles an hour, delicately balanced in a pair of short stirrups, amid 48 flying steel plates (shoes) and 6 thundering tons of horseflesh—calmly, but in a split second, planning every move as they ride.

Jockey stick: A stick fastened to the hame of the near horse and the bit of the off horse for use in driving with a single rein to prevent crowding.

Jog cart: A cart longer and heavier than a racing sulky, used in warm-up miles because it's more comfortable for the driver than a sulky.

Jogging: A slow warm-up exercise of several miles with the horse going the wrong way of the track.

Joint ill: See Navel infection.

Jughead: A stupid horse. Also one with a large, ugly head.

Jump seat saddle: A saddle with a high cantle (back) which inclines the rider's weight forward to keep in balance with the horse when going over jumps. It usually has knee rolls to help maintain balance.

Juvenile: Two-year-old horse.

K

Kick: Movement by a horse of the back or front leg, or legs, with intent to hit a person or other object.

Knee-sprung: See Buck-kneed.

L

Lameness: A defect that can be detected when the affected foot is favored when standing. In action, the load on the ailing foot is eased, and there is a characteristic bobbing of the head of the horse as the affected foot strikes the ground.

Laminae: The flat tissue in the sole or base of the hoof.

Laminitis (or founder): An inflammation of the sensitive laminae under the horny wall of the hoof. All feet may be affected, but the front feet are most susceptible. It is characterized by ridges running around the hoof.

Lampas: Referring to the membranes of the upper hard plate of the mouth, just behind the upper incisor teeth.

Laser: Device producing a narrow, focused, very intense light beam.

Lasix: An intravenous diuretic used for bleeders.

Lead: The leading foot (leg) of a horse under saddle. When cantering circularly, the foot to the inner arc of the circle—clockwise, a right foot lead; and counter clockwise, a left foot lead.

Leaders: The head team in 4- 6- or 8-horse hitch.

Lead line: A chain, rope, or strap, or combination thereof, used for leading a horse.

Lead pony: Horse or pony that leads parade of field from paddock to starting gate. Also, horse or pony that accompanies a starter to the post to quiet him.

Leathers: The straps running from the saddle to the irons on an English saddle.

Left lead: Left front foot and left rear foot lead on the canter.

Leg bracer: A solution, lotion, or liniment, containing a large amount of alcohol used as a stimulant for the legs, causing increased blood circulation to the applied area.

Legs out of the same hole: Very narrow-fronted. Such horses usually stand basewide; *i.e.*, the front feet stand wider apart than the distance across the legs at the chest.

Levade: An exercise of the *haute ecole*, especially as performed in the Spanish Riding School at Vienna. In the Levade the horse is in a half rearing position, with the forelegs well bent and the hind legs in a crouching position.

Lice: Small, flattened, wingless insect parasites.

Lineback: An animal having a stripe of distinctive color along the spine.

Lines, reins: A leather, webbing, or rope attached to the bit or bits for control and direction. In driving, lines are sometimes called reins. In riding, reins are never called lines.

Lip strap: The small strap running through the curb chain from one side of the bit shank to the other. Its primary function is to keep the horse from taking the shank or the bit in its teeth.

Live foal: A foal that must stand and nurse.

Lockjaw: See Tetanus.

Long-coupled: Too much space between the last rib and the point of the hip.

Longe: See Lunge.

Lope: The western adaptation of a very slow canter. It is a smooth, slow gait in which the head is carried low.

Lop-neck, fallen-neck, or broken crest: A heavy neck that breaks over or falls to one side.

Lugger: A horse that pulls at the bit.

Lugging and pulling: Some horses pull on the reins, lug on one rein, or bear out or in with the driver, making it hard to drive them and to rate the mile at an even clip.

Lunge (longe): The act of exercising a horse on the end of a long rope, usually in a circle.

Lungworms *(Dictyocaulus arnfieldi):* Parasites which may be found in the air passages of the horse and other equines. The male worm reaches a length of about 1 in. and the female may be about 2 in. long. The equine lungworm is very rare in the United States.

Luteinizing hormone (LH): Hormone released by the pituitary gland. It causes ovulation and change of the follicle to corpus luteum.

M

Maiden:

1. A mare that has never been bred.

2. On the racetrack, it refers to a horse (stallion, mare, or gelding) that has not won a race on a recognized track. In the show-ring, it refers to a horse that has not won a first ribbon in a recognized show in the division in which it is showing.

Mane: Long hair on the top of the neck.

Mange (scabies, scab, or itch): A specific contagious disease caused by mites.

Manners: A way of behaving.

Mare: A mature female four years or older; in Thoroughbreds, five years or older.

Mascot: A companion for a horse. The most common mascots are ponies, goats, dogs, cats, and chickens.

Matron: A mare that has produced a foal.

Mites: Very small parasites that cause mange (scabies, scab, or itch).

Mixed-gaited: Said of a horse that will not adhere to any one true gait at a time.

Mohammed's ten horses: In the days of Mohammed, intelligence and obedience were the main requisites of the Arab's horse. For war purposes, only the most obedient horses were used, and they were trained to follow the bugle.

Legend has it that the Prophet himself had need for some very obedient horses, so he inspected a certain herd to make personal selections. The horses from which he wished to make selections were pastured in a large area bordering on a river. The Prophet gave orders that the animals should be fenced off from the river until their thirst became very great. Then he ordered the fence removed, and the horses rushed for the water. When they were just about to dash into the river to quench their thirst, a bugle was sounded.

All but 10 of the horses ignored the call of the bugle. The obedient 10 turned and answered the call of duty, despite their great thirst. The whimsical story goes on to say that these 10 head constituted the foundation of the Prophet Strain.

Moon blindness (periodic ophthalmia): An eye disease which causes a cloudy or inflamed condition of the eyes.

Morning glory: A horse that works out in record time in the morning, but does not live up to its promise in the afternoon race.

Mosquito: A biting insect.

Mottled: Marked with spots of different colors: dappled, spotted.

Mounting: The act of getting on a horse.

Mouthing: Determining the approximate age of a horse by examining the teeth.

Mudder: A horse that runs well on a track that is wet, sloppy, or heavy.

Mustang: Native horse of the western plains.

Mutation: A sudden variation which is later passed on through inheritance and which results from changes in a gene or genes.

Mutton-withered: Being low in the withers, with heavy shoulder muscling.

Muzzle: The lower end of the nose which includes the nostrils, lips, and chin.

N

Narragansett pacer: A fast type of pacer, descended from the indigenous horse of the Narragansett Bay area of Rhode Island, which evolved during the time of the Revolutionary War (1775–1781). During this period, racing was illegal except in Rhode Island.

Navel ill: See Navel infection.

Navel infection (joint ill, navel ill, actinobacillosis): An infectious disease of newborn animals caused by several kinds of bacteria.

Navicular disease: An inflammation of the small navicular bone and bursa of the front foot. It is often impossible to determine the exact cause of the disease. Affected animals go lame; have a short stubby stride; and usually point the affected foot when standing. Few animals completely recover from the disease. Treatment consists in special shoeing. In cases of persistent and severe lameness, unnerving may be performed by a veterinarian to destroy the sensation of the foot.

Near side: The left side of a horse. The custom of working from the left side of the horse evolved quite logically in two ways:

1. In the days when riders wore swords, they hung to the left. Hence, the sword would have interfered with the rider by hanging between his legs had he tried mounting from the right.

2. In England, traffic keeps to the left. Therefore, when working around horses the coachman stood on the left side if possible in order to be on the side of the road and out of the line of traffic.

In both the above situations equestrians were most often on the left side of horses; hence, logically it became known as the near side, and the right side became the off side. With a team of horses, the one on the left is the near horse, the one on the right is the off horse.

Neck rein: To guide or direct a horse by pressure of the rein on the neck.

Necrotic: Containing dead or dying tissue.

Neigh: The loud, prolonged call of a horse.

Neolithic: New stone age.

O

Off side: The right side of a horse.

Open bridle: Bridle without blinds or blinkers covering the eyes. Some bridles are rigged with blinds that shut off vision to the rear and side and a few horses are raced with goggles or peekaboo blinds.

Open-hocked: Wide apart at the hocks with the feet close together.

Organophosphates: Class of insecticides widely used to fight parasitic infestation.

Oriental: See Eastern.

Orloff trotter: A breed of horses originating in Russia in the 18th century, principally through the interest of Count Alexis Gregory Orloff Chesminski. Used in the Soviet Union for light work, pleasure driving and riding, exhibition at fairs in various forms of competition including dressage, and extensively in harness racing.

Osselets: A rather inclusive term used to refer to a number of inflammatory conditions around the ankle joints. Generally it denotes a swelling that is fairly well defined and located slightly above or below the actual center of the joint, and, ordinarily, a little to the inside or outside of the exact front of the leg. When touched, it imparts the feeling of putty or mush, and it may be warm to hot. The pain will be in keeping with the degree of inflammation as evidenced by swelling and fever. Afflicted horses travel with a short, choppy stride and show evidence of pain when the ankle is flexed.

Outlaw: A horse that cannot be broken.

Ovary: The female organ that produces the eggs. There are two ovaries.

Overreach: The hitting of the forefoot with the hind foot.

Overshot jaw: The upper jaw protruding beyond the lower jaw. Same as parrot mouth.

Ovulation: The time when the follicle bursts and the egg is released.

Ovum: Scientific name for egg, the female reproductive cell.

P

Pace: A fast, two-beat gait in which the front and hind feet on the same side start and stop simultaneously.

Packed cell volume (PCV): The percentage of a blood sample that is composed of cells. The blood of a healthy, resting horse is made up of approximately 40% cells and 60% fluid.

Paddling: Throwing the front feet outward as they are picked up. This condition is predisposed in horses with toe-narrow or pigeon-toed standing positions.

Pair: Two horses hitched abreast. Also, used in reference to two horses ridden side by side, together as in pair classes.

Paleolithic: Old stone age.

Palisade worms: See Strongyles.

Pari-mutuels: Machine-controlled pool betting, invented in France in 1865, by a perfume shop proprietor name Pierre Oller, who, embittered by a losing streak with the bookies, worked out the idea of the betting pool and began selling tickets over his store counter. His take was five percent; the rest was divided equally among the winners.

Parrot mouth: See Overshot jaw.

Passage: A movement of the *haute ecole*. This is a slow, cadenced, rather than high trot with a fairly long period of suspension, giving the impression that the horse is on springs, or trotting on air. Also a term for diagonal movement of the horse while facing straight forward, at the walk or trot.

Pastern: That part of the leg between the fetlock joint and the coronary band of the hoof.

Pedigree: A record of the ancestry of the animal.

Pedigree breeding: Selection on the combined bases of the merits of the individual and the average merits of its ancestry.

Pegasus: A word of Greek origin, meaning strong. Legend has it that the winged horse, Pegasus, was fashioned from the body of Medusa, daughter of a sea god who, in her youth, was as mortal as she was beautiful. At his birth, the frisky colt flew to Mount Helicon, where he created a fountain (Horsewell) with one swift blow of his hoof. Using a golden bridle, Bellerophon coaxed the curious animal from his favorite meadow, made him captive, and rode him off. Later, Pegasus unceremoniously dumped his venerable and conceited master and flew into outer space where he became the constellation that bears his name.

Pelham bit: A one-piece bit equipped to handle four reins. Two are snaffle reins, used for guiding the horse and lifting the head; and two are curb reins, used for control and for setting the head. Snaffle reins are always heavier than curb reins.

Periodic ophthalmia: See Moon blindness.

Piaffe: A dressage movement in which the horse does

Fig. 20-2.   Pegasus, the strong, fleet, winged horse of Greek mythology.

a cadenced trot in place, without moving from the spot. It is the foundation of all high school movements.

Piebald: Refers to a black-and-white coat color.

Pigeon-toed: Pointing toes inward and heels outward.

Pig-eyed: Having small, narrow, squinty eyes, set back in the head; also, having thick eyelids.

Pin-firing: A method of using an electric needle to insert into an injured area. This induces healing at the site.

Pinto: A multicolored, spotted horse.

Pinworms *(Oxyuris equi, Probstmyria vivipara):* Two species of pinworms, or rectal worms, frequently found in horses. *Oxyuris equi* are whitish worms with long, slender tails. *Probstmyria vivipara* are so small they are scarcely visible to the eye.

Pirouette: A dressage exercise in which the horse holds its forelegs more or less in place while it moves its hindquarters around them.

Pivot: A movement in dressage in which the horse pivots around its hindquarters, holding one hind leg more or less in place and side-stepping with the other hind foot.

Place: To finish second in a race.

Placebo: Preparation containing no medication, administered in order to simulate treatment.

Placenta: The membrane by which the fetus is attached to the uterus. Nutrients from the mother pass into the placenta and then through the navel cord to the fetus. When the animal is born, the placenta is expelled. It is commonly called the *afterbirth.*

Plug: A horse of common breeding and poor conformation.

Point: The team in back of the leaders in an eight-horse hitch.

Pointing:

1. Perceptible extension of the stride with little flexion is called pointing. This condition is likely to occur in the Thoroughbred and Standardbred breeds—animals bred and trained for great speed with a long stride.

2. Referring to a standing position when one of the front legs is extended ahead of the other. This occurs when a horse with a sore foot places the ailing foot ahead in order to take the weight off it.

Points: Black coloration from the knees and hocks down, as in most bays and browns, and in some buckskins, roans, and grays.

Poll evil: An inflamed condition in the region of the poll (the area on top of the neck and immediately behind the ears), usually caused by bruising the top of the head.

Polo pony: A pony used for polo. Polo ponies of today are mostly of Thoroughbred breeding. They must be fast, and tough and courageous enough to stand the bumping, riding-off, and the many quick stops and turns.

Pony: An equine under 14.2 hands (58 in.) at the withers.

Pop-eyed: Refers to a horse whose eyes are generally more prominent or bulge out a little more than normal; also to a horse that is spooky or attempts to see everything that goes on.

Popped knee: A general term describing inflammatory conditions affecting the knees, so named because of the sudden swelling that accompanies it.

Post: The starting point of a race.

Posting: The rising and descending of the rider with the rhythm of the trot.

Post position: Refers to race starting position. Beginning with position No. 1 nearest the rail, horses line up at the starting gate according to number.

Poultice: A moist, mealy mass, applied hot to a sore or inflamed part of the body.

Pounding: A heavy foot contact with the ground, common in high-going horses.

Premix: A uniform mixture of one or more microingredients with dilutent and/or carrier. Premixes are used to facilitate uniform dispersion of the microingredients in a large mix.

Prepotency: Refers to breeding power, as measured by the degree in which parent likeness is transmitted to offspring.

Primary feed: A feed mixed with individual feed ingredients, sometimes with the addition of a premix at the rate of up to 100 lb per ton of finished feed.

Produce: Offspring.

Progenitor: One that originates or precedes.

Progeny: Refers to offspring or descendents of one or both parents.

Progesterone: Female hormone secreted by the corpus luteum of the ovary, preceding the implantation of the fertilized egg. Progesterone maintains pregnancy by stopping the estrus cycle.

Prostaglandin: Released by the uterine lining. Causes regression or death of the corpus lutea; and signals that the mare is not pregnant.

Proud flesh: Excess tissue rising above the edges of a wound, forming a raw mound which makes further healing impossible without medication or surgery.

Puffs: Windgalls, bog spavins, or thoroughpins.

Pulled tail: A tail thinned by hairs being pulled.

Pulling record, world: The world's record in a pulling contest was established at the 1965 Hillsdale County Fair, in Michigan. It is held jointly by Frank Vurckio, Sun Down, New York; and Fowler Bros., Montgomery, Michigan. It was made on a dynamometer with a tractive pull of 4,350 lb (equal to 56,493 lb, or over 28 ton, on a wagon).

Purebred: An animal descended from a line of ancestors of the same breed, but not necessarily registered. This should not be confused with Thoroughbred, a breed of horses.

Purse: Race prize money to which the owners of horses in the race do not contribute.

Q

Quality: Refinement, as shown in a neat and well-chiselled head, fine texture of hair with little or no fetlock, clean bone, good texture of hoof, etc.

Quarter crack (sand crack): A vertical split in the horny wall of the inside of the hoof (in the region of the quarter), which extends from the coronet or hoof head downward.

Quittor: A deep-seated running sore which occurs on the coronet band or hoof head. It is caused initially be an injury or puncture wound in the area of the sole of the foot.

R

Rack (single-foot): A fast, flashy, unnatural, four-beat gait in which each foot meets the ground separately at equal intervals; hence, it was originally known as the *single foot*, a designation now largely discarded.

Radiation therapy: Use of radioactive rays to reduce inflammation, treat skin disease, or kill damaged or cancerous cells.

Random: Three horses hitched in single file, usually to a dogcart.

Rangy: Elongated, lean, muscular, of slight build.

Rat tail: A tail with a short-hair coat.

Rattlers: Rattlers (wooden, rubber, or plastic balls) or links of light chain fastened about the pasterns of high-going harness and saddle horses and ponies. Weighted boots are also used to enhance action.

Reata: Spanish for lariat.

Recessive character: A characteristic which appears only when both members of a pair of genes are alike. Opposite of dominant.

Red worms: See Strongyles.

Reins: See Lines.

Remuda: A collection of riding horses at a roundup from which are chosen those used for the day. A relay of mounts.

Ribbed-up: Said of a horse on which the back ribs are well arched and incline well backwards, bringing the ends closer to the point of the hip and making the horse shorter in coupling.

Ridgeling: A horse with at least one testicle in the abdomen. A ridgeling is difficult to geld, and often retains the characteristics of a stallion.

Right lead: Right front foot and right rear lead on the canter.

Ringbone: A bony growth on the pastern bone in the area of the coronet. It is generally on the forefoot, although occasionally the hind foot is affected.

Ringer: A horse passed off under false identity, with the idea of entering it in a race below its class where it is almost certain to win. With today's systems of identification, ringers are a thing of the past.

Ringworm: This is a contagious infection of the outer layers of skin caused by an infestation of microscopic fungi.

Roach-backed: Arched-backed, razor-backed.

Roached mane: A mane that has been cut short and tapered so that it stands upright. It is not so short as a clipped mane.

Roarer: A wind-broken animal that makes a loud noise in drawing air into the lungs.

Rollers, rattlers: Wooden balls on a cord, encircling a horse's pastern to give the horse more action.

Rolling: Excessive lateral shoulder motion, characteristic of horses with protruding shoulders, is known as rolling.

Roman-nosed: Refers to a horse having a profile that is convex from poll to muzzle.

Rope-walking: See Winding.

Roundworms, large (ascarids; *Parascaris equorum*): The female varies from 6 to 22 in. long and the male from 5 to 13 in. When full grown, both are about the diameter of a lead pencil.

Rubdown: A rubbing of the body with a rough towel, usually given after exercise to promote circulation and remove fatigue.

Run (gallop): The run, or gallop, is a fast, four-beat gait where the feet strike the ground separately—first one hind foot, then the other hind foot, then the front foot on the same side as the first hind foot, then the other front foot which decides the lead.

Running walk: A slow, four-beat gait, intermediate in speed between the walk and rack. The hind foot oversteps the front foot from a few to as many as 18 in., giving the motion a smooth gliding effect. It is characterized by a bobbing or nodding of the head, a flopping of the ears, and a snapping of the teeth in rhythm with the movement of the legs.

Rupture: See Hernia.

S

Saline: Consisting of or containing salt.

Saliva test: The testing of saliva for the presence of drugs or narcotics.

Sand crack: See Quarter crack.

Scab: See Mange.

Scabies: See Mange.

Scalping: That condition in which the hairline at the top of the hind foot hits the toe of the forefoot as it breaks over.

Schooling: Training and developing natural characteristics in a pony.

Sclerostomes: See Strongyles.

Scoring: Preliminary warming up of horses before the start. The horses are turned near the starting point and hustled away as they will be in the race.

Scotch collar: Housing over the collar of draft show harness.

Scraper: A metal or wooden, slightly concave, tool shaped like a hook at the upper end and used with one hand for scraping sweat and liquid from the body. Also, a thin metal strip with handles affixed at either end, used with both hands for scraping sweat and liquid from the body.

Scratches: See Grease heel.

Screwworm: Maggots of the screwworm fly, which require living flesh of animals on which to feed.

Scrotum: The saclike pouch that suspends the testicles outside the male animal.

Scrub: A low-grade animal.

Self-colored: A term applied to the mane and tail when they are the same color as the body coat.

Sell at halter: To sell with no guarantee except title.

Semen: Sperm mixed with fluids from the accessory glands.

Serviceably sound: Said of a horse that has nothing wrong that will materially impair its value for the intended use.

Sesamoid fractures: The fracture of one or both of the two pyramidlike bones that form a part of the fetlock or ankle joints (on both front and rear legs) and articulate with the posterior part of the lower end of the cannon bone.

Set tail: A tail in which the cords have been cut or nicked and the tail put in a set.

Sex cells: The egg and the sperm, which unite to create life. They transmit genetic characteristics from the parents to the offspring.

Shadbelly: See Herring gutted.

Shipping fever (distemper, strangles): An infectious, febrile disease. Frequently abscesses will develop under the lower jaw, along the neck or anywhere on the body. To begin with, similar signs are shown as with a cold and later the abscesses develop. One should be most cautious and observant of the disease developing in young horses.

Shoe boil (capped elbow): A soft, flabby swelling at the point of the elbow; hence, the other name *capped elbow*. It is usually caused by contact with the shoe when the horse is lying down.

Short-coupled: Describes a horse having a short distance (usually not more than four fingers' width) between the last rib and the point of the hip.

Show: Finishing third in a race.

Show bridle: Same as Weymouth bridle, but the leather usually is cut finer and the bits often are more severe.

Sickle-hocked: The hind legs set too far forward, giving the impression of a sickle when viewed from the side.

Sidebones: Ossified lateral cartilages immediately above and toward the rear quarter of the hoof head. They occur most commonly in the forefeet.

Sidestep: See Traverse.

Sign: The word used when speaking of animal symptoms. Animals show signs of abnormality, whereas people can relate their symptoms of ill health. In horses, one must observe these signs.

Single-foot: Now called a *rack*. See Rack.

Sire: The male parent.

Sisters: See Brothers.

Skewbald: Refers to coat color other than black—such as bay, brown, or chestnut—combined with white.

Skirt: The part of the saddle against which the knees and calves of the rider are placed.

Slab-sided: Flat ribbed.

Sleeping sickness: See Encephalomyelitis.

Sloping shoulders: Shoulders properly angulated and laid back.

Slow gait: A slow, animated, four-beat gait, similar to the rack.

Slow pace: See Stepping pace.

Smoky eye: A whitish-clouded eye. See Wall eye.

Smooth: Unshod, barefoot.

Smooth coat: Short, hard, close-fitting coat of hair.

Smooth-mouthed: No cups in the teeth. Indicates a horse 12 years of age or older.

Snaffle bit: A mouthpiece with a joint in the center. The ring may be either circular or D-shaped. The most widely used of all bits.

Snip: A white mark between the nostrils or on the lip.

Snorter: An excitable horse.

Soft: Easily fatigued.

Solid color: Having no white markings.

Sound: Said of a horse free from injury, flaw, mutilation, or decay; also one that is guaranteed free from blemishes and unsoundnesses.

Spavin: See Blood spavin, Bog spavin, and Bone spavin.

Spay: To remove a mare's ovaries.

Speck in eye: A spot in the eye, but not covering the pupil. It may or may not impair the vision. See Feather in eye.

Speedy cutting: A condition of a horse at speed in which a hind leg above the scalping mark hits against the shoe of a breaking-over forefoot. In trotters, legs on the same side are involved. In pacers, diagonal legs are involved.

Sperm, sperm cell: Male sex cell produced in the testicles.

Spider bandage: A style of bandaging, using a tying method which resembles a spider lock. Applied to either the hocks or the knees, allowing expansion at the flexing points.

Splenic fever: See Anthrax.

Splints: Abnormal body growths found on the cannon bone, usually on the inside surface, but occasionally on the outside. They are most common on the front legs.

Spooky: Nervous.

Sprinter: A horse who performs best at distances of a mile or under.

Spurs: The artificial aid worn over a boot, used to achieve a desired result when riding.

Stable fly: Biting insect that bites principally on the legs.

Stag: A male horse that is castrated after reaching maturity.

Stake race: A stake race, short for sweepstake, is just what the name implies. Each owner puts up an equal amount of money (nominating fees, fees for keeping them eligible, and starting fees) and the winner takes all. Also, the track usually puts up added money. Actually, few stake races are run on a winner-take-all basis; rather, the money is divided among the first four horses.

Stall: Space or compartment in which an animal is placed or confined. It may be a straight stall with the animal tied at the front end (a tie stall) or a compartment with the animal loose inside (a box stall).

Stallion: A male horse four years old or over; in Thoroughbreds, five years old or over.

Standing halter: Similar to a martingale, it is a strap that runs from the girth to a tight halter on the horse's head. It helps keep the horse from throwing its head up and going into a break.

Star: Any white mark on the forehead located above a line running from eye to eye.

Stargazer: A horse that holds its head high in an awkward position.

Starting gate: Mechanical device with partitions for horses into which they are confined until starter releases doors in front to start race.

Steeplechaser: A horse used in cross-country racing with jumps.

Stepping pace (slow pace): A modified pace in which the objectionable side or rolling motion of the true pace is eliminated because the 2 feet on each side do not move exactly together. Instead, it is a 4-beat gait with each of the 4 feet striking the ground separately.

Sterile: A term used to designate a stallion that is infertile.

Steroid: Artificially produced drug which is similar to the natural hormone that controls inflammation.

Steward: Top official of racing.

Stifle: The counterpart of the knee joint in humans. The junction of the horse's tibia and patella in the hind leg.

Stifled: A horse is said to be stifled when the patella (or kneecap) slips out of place and temporarily locks in a location above and to the inside of its normal location.

Stirrup iron: The metal D-shaped device on the saddle through which the leather runs and on which the foot rests.

Stock horse:

1. In the West this term designates a cow horse.

2. In some places, it refers to a stallion used as a stud.

Stocking: White extends from the coronet to the knee. When the white includes the knee, it is known as a full stocking.

Stocking up: Thickening of the lower legs due to collection of fluid in and under the skin.

Stomach worms (*Habronemia spp., Trichostrongylus axei*): A group of parasitic worms that produce inflammation of the stomach.

Straight shoulder: Said of shoulder lacking sufficient angulation.

Strangles (distemper): A widespread contagious disease of horses, especially among young animals, caused by *Streptococcus equi*, a bacterium.

Stride: The distance covered by one foot when in motion. *Greyhound*, with a trotting record of 1:55;m, had a stride of more than 27 ft.

Stringhalt: A condition characterized by excessive flexing of the hind legs. It is most easily detected when backing a horse.

Stripe: A narrow white marking that extends from about the line of the eyes to the nostrils.

Strongyles, large and small (*Strongylus spp.* and others.): There are about 60 species of strongyles. Three are large worms that grow up to 2 in. long. The rest are small and sometimes barely visible to the eye. Large strongyles are variously called bloodworms (*Strongylus vulgaris*), palisade worms, sclerostomes, and red worms.

Stud:

1. A male horse (stallion) kept for breeding.

2. An establishment or farm where animals are kept for breeding.

Stud book: The permanent book of breeding records.

Stump sucker: See Cribber.

Substance: A combination of good bone, muscularity, and width and depth of body.

Suckling: A foal that is not weaned.

Sulky or bike: Light racing rig with bicycle-type wheels used in harness races. The sulkies weigh from 29 to 37 lb, and usually have hardwood shafts, although aluminum and steel sulkies have been introduced recently:

Summer sores: Sores caused by the larvae of the stomach worm being deposited in wounds by flies.

Supplement: A feed used with another to improve the nutritive balance or performance of the total and intended to be (1) fed undiluted as a supplement to other feeds, (2) offered free-choice with other parts of the ration separately available, or (3) further diluted and mixed to produce a complete feed.

Surcingle: A belt, band, or girth passing over a saddle or over anything on a horse's back to bind the saddle fast.

Suspensory ligament sprain: The suspensory ligament is situated over the back of the leg and passes over the fetlock or ankle joint, both in the forelegs and hind legs. Its principal function is to support the fetlock. This ligament is frequently the object of severe strain; the swelling begins just above the ankle and extends obliquely downward and forward over the sides of the ankle. Should the injury be further up on the leg, the exact location at first may appear obscure as the ligament is covered by the flexor tendons.

When the suspensory ligament is affected, the swelling will be found right up against the bone. If it is the flexor tendons that are involved, the swelling will be further back near the surface on the back of the leg.

Swamp fever: See Equine infectious anemia.

Swan neck: A long, slim, swanlike neck.

"Swap horses in midstream": The origin of the saying, "Don't swap horses in midstream," appears to be clouded in obscurity.

Upon being congratulated when renominated for the presidency, Lincoln said: "I do not allow myself to suppose that either the convention or the league have concluded to decide that I am either the greatest or the best man in America, but rather they have concluded it is not best to swap horses while crossing the river, and have further concluded that I am not so poor a horse that they might not make a botch of it in trying to swap." One historian of that period credited the utterance to a Dutch farmer; and H. L. Mencken reports that the phrase was used some 24 years earlier than when Lincoln used it.

Swaybacked: Having a decided dip in the back. Also termed *easy-backed* and *saddle-backed*.

Sweat scraper: An instrument used for removing excess sweat from a hard worked horse.

Sweeney: A depression in the shoulder due to atrophied muscles.

Sweet feed: Refers to a horse feed which is characterized by its sweetness due to the addition of molasses, usually a commercial horse feed mixture.

Swing team: The middle team in a six-horse hitch, or the team in front of the wheelers in an eight-horse hitch.

Swipe: Racetrack slang for a groom, stable hand, or exercise boy.

Synovial fluid: The fluid that lubricates the joint.

T

Tack: Equipment used in riding and driving horses, such as saddles, bridles, etc.

Tack room: Place for storage of bridles, saddles, other equipment and accessories used in horseback riding. Also a display room for pictures, prizes, ribbons, trophies, and the like.

Tail (banged or thin): A tail is banged if the hair is cut off in a straight line below the dock; it is thinned if it is shortened; and it is thinned and tapered if the hairs are pulled and broken.

Tail female: The female, or bottom line of a pedigree.

Tail male: The sire line, or top line in a pedigree.

Tail rubbing: Persistent rubbing of the tail against the side of the stall or other objects.

Tail-set: A crupperlike contrivance, with a shaped section for the tail, which brings the tail high so that it can be doubled and tied down, to give it an arch and extremely high carriage; but a tail so set must first be nicked to give such results. The set is worn most of the time while the horse is in the stable, and until a short time before the horse is to be shown. Horses with set tails are usually gingered (an herb which is

used as a stimulant) before entering the ring, in order to assure high tail carriage while being shown.

Tally ho: The cry of the hunt once the fox is sighted.

"Tamed" iodine: Iodine solution from which the usual burning effect has been removed.

Tandem: Said of two horses, one hitched in front of the other.

Tapadera: A long, decorative covering over the stirrup used in parade classes.

Tapeworms *(Anoplocephala magna, A. perfoliata, Paranoplocephala mamillana):* Internal parasites of horses, of which there are three species. *Anoplocephala perfoliata* is the most common and most damaging.

Teaser: A horse, usually a stallion or a ridgeling, used to test the response of a mare prior to breeding, or used to determine if a mare is in heat and ready to breed.

Temperament: Refers to the horse's suitability for the job it is to perform.

Temperature: Normal rectal temperature for the horse is 100.5°F.

Testicle: A male gland which produces sperm. There are two testicles.

Testosterone: Male sex hormone secreted by the testes and adrenal glands.

Tetanus (lockjaw): Chiefly a wound-infection disease caused by a powerful toxin, more than 100 times as toxic as strychnine, that is liberated by the bacterium *Clostridium tetani*, an anaerobe.

Thick wind: Difficulty in breathing.

Thong: The lash of the whip.

Thoroughpin: A puffy condition in the web of the hock. It can be determined by movement of the puff, when pressed, to the opposite side of the leg. The swelling is more or less rounded or oval in shape and can be observed from both sides.

Threadworms *(Strongyloides westeri):* They are known as *strongyloids*.

Three-day event: See Combined training.

Thrifty condition: Healthy, active, vigorous.

Throat latch: The narrow strap of the bridle, which goes under the horse's throat and is used to secure the bridle to the head.

Thrush: A disease of the foot, caused by a necrotic fungus characterized by a pungent odor. It is most commonly found in the hind feet and is caused by unsanitary conditions in the animal's stall. Thrush causes a deterioration of tissues in the cleft of the frog or in the junction between the frog and the bars. This disease produces lameness and, if not treated, can be serious.

Ticks: External insects, several kinds of which may be found on horses. The most common ones are the winter tick, *Dermacentor albipictus*; the lone star tick, *Amblyomma americanum*; and the spinose ear tick, *Otobius megnini*.

Tie: To attach or fasten by use of a halter and a shank.

Tie weight (drop weight, ground weight): An iron weight formerly used for ground-tying a horse. They were either (1) rounded, but flat on the ground side, or (2) square; and they usually weighed about eight pounds.

Toe weight: A metal weight (knob) fitted to a spur previously placed on the front hoof to induce a change or balance in motion. Used extensively in the training and racing of harness horses.

Tongue-loller: A horse whose tongue hangs out.

Tooth rasp: A file with a long handle, used for floating or removing sharp edges from the teeth.

Totalisator: The mechanical brains of the pari-mutuel system.

Tote board: The indicator of the totalisator on which is flashed all pari-mutuel information before or after a race.

Tout: A low-order con man who peddles tips, betting systems, etc. to the unwary racegoer.

Traces: The parts of a harness which run from the collar to the single-tree.

Tracheotomy: An operation on the throat to cure roaring, or to keep a horse from suffocating in an emergency.

Trail ride: A cross-country ride over paths or unimproved roads, requiring that the horse work over or through obstacles.

Trappy action: A short, quick stride.

Traverse (sidestep): The traverse or sidestep is simply a lateral movement of the animal to the right or left as desired, without moving forward or backward.

Triple Crown:

  1. In the U.S., the Kentucky Derby, The Preakness, and Belmont Stakes.

  2. In England, the Two Thousand Guineas, Epsom Derby, and St. Leger.

Troika: The word *troika* is a Russian word meaning trio or three. A troika hitch is a three-horse combination team hitched to a vehicle: *e.g.*, a carriage, wagon, sleigh, or sled. The carriage is the vehicle of common use and it is known as a charaban. It is a light

Fig. 20-3. Trail ride. (Courtesy, The American Morgan Horse Assn., Shelburne, VT)

four-wheeled, two-passenger vehicle with an elevated seat for the driver.

Trot: A natural, rapid, two-beat, diagonal gait in which the front foot and the opposite hind foot take off at the same split second and strike the ground simultaneously.

Tucked-up: Having the belly under the loin. Refers also to a small-waisted horse. Differs from herring gutted and similar conditions, in that a horse may be tucked-up temporarily due to hard work, lack of water, lack of bulk in the diet, etc. Also, called *gaunted-up* or *ganted-up*.

Turf course: Grass racing course.

Twitch: A rope run through the end of a stick, used on the horse's upper lip; it is tightened by twisting in order to attract the horse's attention so it will stand still.

Two-track: The horse moves forward and diagonally at the same time.

Tying up: The tying up syndrome is characterized by muscle rigidity and lameness affecting the muscles of the croup and loin, accompanied by pain, disinclination to move, a variable temperature, and brownish-colored urine. The cause is unknown, although it does seem to be associated with nervousness.

Type: Type may be defined as an ideal or standard of perfection combining all the characteristics that contribute to the animal's usefulness for a specific purpose.

U

Ultrasound: High frequency sound waves (above the range of human hearing).

Underpinning: The legs and feet of the horse.

Undershot jaw: The lower jaw is longer than the upper jaw.

Unicorn: An unusual three-horse hitch with two horses hitched as a pair and the third hitched in front of the pair.

Unsoundnesses: Those more serious abnormalities that affect the serviceability of the horse.

Urinalysis: Laboratory test of urine to determine whether horse has been drugged.

Utility saddle: A saddle that is between the jump seat and the show seat and is designed for general purpose use, except jumping.

V

Vesicular stomatitis: A contagious disease of the mouth caused by a virus.

Veterinarian: One who treats diseases or affliction of animals medically and surgically; a practitioner of veterinary medicine or surgery.

Vice: Any of a multitude of bad habits that a horse may acquire.

Viceroy: A lightweight, cut under, wire-wheeled show vehicle with curved dash, used for some heavy harness classes, and especially for Hackney ponies, Shetlands, and harness show ponies.

W

Walk: A natural, slow, flatfooted, four-beat gait, the latter meaning that each foot takes off from and strikes the ground at a separate interval.

Wall-eye: Also termed glass, blue, china, or crockery eye; refers to lack of color in a horse's eye.

Warm-up, warming-up:

1. The process or routine of graduated exercise until the horse is properly conditioned for a strenuous effort.

2. Galloping horse on way to post.

Weanling: A weaned foal.

Weaving: A rhythmical swaying back and forth while standing in the stall. The prevention and cure are exercise, with ample room and freedom from stress.

Weymouth bridle: A bridle in which the snaffle bit and the curb bit are separate.

Wheelers: The team on the pole or tongue, hitched directly in front of a rig or wagon in a four or more horse hitch.

Whinny: The horse's sound that denotes happiness, or anticipation of more pleasure.

Whip: An instrument or device of wood, bone, plastic, leather, fiberglass, metal, or combination thereof with a loop or cracker of leather or cord at the upper end; used for disciplining or goading an animal. Sometimes a required accessory when exhibiting (driving), as in a horse show. Also, one who handles a whip expertly, one who drives a horse in harness other than racing, or one who whips in or manages the hounds of a hunt club.

Whip in the Senate: The term *whip* is derived from the British fox hunting term *whipper-in*, the Huntsman's principal assistant whose job is to keep the hounds from leaving the pack. The principal job of the whip in the U.S. Senate is to round up the party's Senators for important votes and to try to make sure that they vote in keeping with the wishes of the party leaders.

White line: The union between the sole and the wall of the foot.

Whoa: The command to stop; stand. When repeated softly, means to slow down, but may also mean attention.

Windgall: See Wind-puffs.

Winding (rope-walking): A twisting of the striding leg around in front of the supporting leg so as to make contact in the manner of a rope-walking artist is known as *winding* or *rope-walking*. This condition most often occurs in horses with very wide fronts.

Wind-puffs (windgall): An enlargement of the fluid sac (bursa) located immediately above the pastern joints on the fore and rear legs. They are usually the result of too fast or too hard road work, especially on hard surfaces.

Wind sucker: See Cribber.

Windy, or wind-broken: Said of an animal that whistles or roars when exerted.

Winging: Winging is an exaggerated paddling, particularly noticeable in high-going horses.

Winner-take-all: Winner receiving all the purse or stakes.

Wrangling: Rounding up range horses.

Y

Yearling: A horse between one and two years of age.

Fig. 20-4.   Cutting horse in action at world-famed King Ranch, Kingsville, Texas. (Photo by Ruth K. Hapgood)

21
CAREERS IN THE WORLD OF HORSES

Contents	Page

Contents	Page

Wherever humans have left their footprints in their long climb from barbarism to civilization, the footprints of horses are beside them. Indeed, the history and development of horses and people are inseparable; they are part of each other. Without horses, people would neither be what, or where, they are today. Thus, the unique thing about the horse business, not found in any other industry, is the human values back of it. It's a people business, and a way of life for many.

PROFESSIONAL OPPORTUNITIES IN THE HORSE INDUSTRY

Professional opportunities in horse work abound for those who possess a great love and aptitude for horses, along with knowledge, a good attitude, judgment, and experience; and who are willing to work and to succeed.

The first and most important requisite for a successful career in the equine field is that the person must possess a great love for horses. This appears to be an inborn trait, for some people never acquire a natural ability to work with horses—no matter how long or how hard they try. When such love for horses exists, the animals are more docile and easier to handle, for caretaker's feelings are relayed to their charges. Also, a great love for horses appears to be essential if caretakers are to feed them regularly and cheerfully, with enjoyment and without regard to long hours and Sundays or holidays; if they are to provide clean, dry bedding, despite the fact that a driving storm may make it necessary to repeat the same operation the next day; if they are to serve as nursemaids to newborn foals or sick horses, though it may mean loss of sleep and working with cold, numb fingers; and if they are to remain calm and collected, though striking animals or otherwise giving vent to their feelings might at first appear to be warranted.

Next to having a great love for horses, to be successful in the equine field it is important that the person have adequate knowledge, both scientific and practical. Also, owners and managers of large operations must have skill in money management and knowledge of the business aspects. A college education is important. If they are good students, serious consideration should also be given to completing a veterinary or Ph.D. degree. Additionally, those who have not grown up with horses should learn the rudiments of the business by working two years on a good horse establishment. Most young folks entering the horse field aspire higher than being a groom and mucking out stalls. Nevertheless, this is a good place to start.

Finally, attitude, industry, and good judgment are very necessary requisites for success in the horse business. These words carry the same connotation in all industries and are self-explanatory.

Among the professional opportunities in the multi-billion dollar horse industry are the following:

■ Owning, managing, or working on a horse breeding establishment.

■ Training horses.

■ Operating a boarding stable.

■ Veterinarians in private practice, or with drug manufacturers, or with large horse establishments.

■ In research, sales, and public relations with companies that manufacture and distribute feed, tack, and other products for the horse industry.

■ As farriers (horseshoers).

■ On the staffs of horse magazines and breed registry associations.

■ In college teaching.

■ As riding school instructors.

■ With racing stables; and as racing officials and jockeys.

■ With hunt clubs.

■ With summer camps.

■ Horse shows.

■ Buying and selling horses.

■ Rodeo riding.

■ As secretaries, office managers, and executive assistants, to administrators and associations engaged in the horse field.

■ Consultants.

MAGNITUDE AND IMPORTANCE OF THE U.S. HORSE INDUSTRY

The United States horse industry is big and important business. The following facts and figures attest to the magnitude and importance of the industry:

■ There are 6 million equine in the United States.[1]

■ The United States horse industry is a $15.2 billion industry. It accounts for 16% of the gross national product (GNP) of the agriculture, forestry, and fisheries of the U.S. economy.[2]

■ There are 258,434 youths involved in 4-H horse and pony programs. Additionally, more than 13,000 young people are involved in the United States Pony Club.[3]

■ Horse shows are increasing in numbers, size, and economic impact.[4] In 1995, there were 14,000 sanctioned horse shows. Additionally, that same year there were thousands of local unsanctioned events. This included:

1. 2,500 events sanctioned by the American Horse Shows Association.

2. 2,288 events sanctioned by the American Quarter Horse Association.

---

[1]Statistics from *FAO Production Yearbook*, 1996, Vol. 50, p. 187.

[2]Statistics from 1996 American Horse Council, *Horse Industry Directory*, Washington, DC, latest figures available.

[3]*Ibid.,* 1994 statistics, latest figures available.

[4]*Ibid.,* 1975 statistics.

COLLEGE INSTRUCTION

Fig. 21-1. Texas A&M University Students receive instruction in both the art and the science of horses and horse care. (Courtesy, Texas A&M University, College Station)

Fig. 21-4. Students receiving instruction in equitation. (Courtesy, Texas A&M University, College Station)

Fig. 21-2. Instruction in Western Equitation at Mississippi State University. Riding, care of horses and equipment. (Courtesy, Mississippi State University, Mississippi State)

Fig. 21-5. A horse judging class at the University of Connecticut. (Courtesy, University of Connecticut, Storrs)

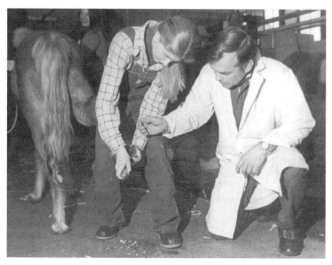

Fig. 21-3. Student receiving instruction on foot care. (Courtesy, University of Delaware, Newark)

Fig. 21-6. Students at the University of Delaware being instructed in equine dental care. (Courtesy, University of Delaware, Newark)

SHOWING HORSES

Fig. 21-7. Saddle Seat Equitation Class. (Courtesy, International Arabian Horse Assn., Aurora, CO)

Fig. 21-9. An American Saddlebred jumper. (Photo by Mary Ciskell. Courtesy, American Saddlebred Horse Assn., Lexington, KY)

Fig. 21-8. *Diamonds Toronado*, Reserve World Champion Hunter Hack. (Courtesy, International Buckskin Horse Assn., Shelby, IN)

Fig. 21-10. Dressage. (Photo by Mary Phelps. Courtesy, *Appaloosa Journal*, Moscow, ID)

SHOWING HORSES

Fig. 21-11. A student competing in a jumping class. (Courtesy, Washington State University, Pullman)

Fig. 21-13. Palomino trail horse. (Courtesy, Palomino Horse Breeders of America, Tulsa, OK)

Fig. 21-12. Hackney Harness Pony. (Photo by Jamie Donaldson. Courtesy, American Hackney Horse Society, Lexington, KY)

Fig. 21-14. Exhibition horse. (Courtesy, International Andalusian Assn., Shoal Creek, AL)

3. 1,400 events sanctioned by the National Cutting Horse Association.

4. 2,100 events sanctioned by the National Barrel Horse Association.

5. 1,093 events sanctioned by the American Paint Horse Association.

Horse shows generate total revenues of about $119 million per year.

■ Horse racing is a leading U.S. spectator sport.[5] In 1994, approximately 42.6 million people went to the U.S. horse races, and wagered an estimated $14 billion. That same year, race track wagering contributed $452 million in state tax revenue and helped create hundreds of thousands of jobs in the industry.

■ Saddle clubs are springing up everywhere, and more people are riding horses for pleasure than ever before.

■ On the western range, cow ponies are still used in the traditional manner.

■ Horses are benefactors of humankind in numerous other ways. Limited numbers of them are used by the Forest Service; others are used as pack animals into remote areas not otherwise accessible by surface travel. They are still the show in many motion pictures and parades. Those responsible for law enforcement have found that mounted patrols are one of the most effective ways in which to handle crowds and riots.

In the laboratory, horses serve as a factory for the manufacture of antitoxins that are used for rendering animals and people immune to certain diseases, such as tetanus. Also, medical doctors use equine produced estrogens (female sex hormones), obtained from the urine of pregnant mares, to relieve the menopause (change of life) of women.

FUNCTIONS OF HORSES

The various uses that people have made of horses through the ages, in order of period of time, are (1) as a source of food; (2) for military purposes; (3) in the pastimes and sports of nations; (4) in agricultural and commercial pursuits; and (5) as cow ponies, and for recreation, sport, and/or a way of life. Horses are still used for these various purposes in different parts of the world. But, in the United States, horse have come up fast as cow ponies, and for recreation, sport, and enhancing the quality of living.

Those who produce horses as a business expect to make money—they expect to make a reasonable return from their time and investment; otherwise, they are not likely to stay in business very long.

Generally, those who engage in horses as a busi-

ness enterprise produce them either (1) for cow pony purposes, or (2) for recreation and sport. Within each of these two major categories, there are many kinds, sizes, and mixes of horse operations, but the most common types are: (1) broodmare farms producing yearlings for sale and/or their own use; (2) stallion farms offering breeding services and mare boarding; (3) yearling, weanling, and other horse sales preparation services (grooming, feeding, and basic training); (4) horse breaking and training farms for racing, showing, or working horses; and (5) horse owners/investors who place mares or performing horses at mare boarding or training farms.

Those who produce or keep horses for recreation, sports, and/or a way of life are of two types: (1) those who produce or use horses for leisure or sports activities; and (2) those who keep horses to enhance the quality of life—those who ride or drive horses for health purposes, and young people (4-H, FFA, and other youth) for whom horses are an educational tool and a living object/pet to keep them busy, and upon which to shower their love and affection. Those who keep horses for leisure, sports, and/or to enhance the quality of life may not expect to make a profit; they may be in the same position as those who hunt and fish for the fun of it, without figuring the cost per lb of their catch. No price tag can be put on the ownership of horses for enhancing the quality of human life.

FUTURE OF THE
U.S. HORSE INDUSTRY

This generation has more money to spend and more leisure time in which to spend it than any population in history. In 1993, leisure time spending in the United States consumed an average of 8.8% of personal income, or an amount of $304 billion.

A shorter workweek, increased automation, and the continued recreation and sports surge, with emphasis on physical fitness and the out-of-doors, will require more horses and support more shows, and other horse events.

It is expected that the estimated 500,000 horses on the ranges in the 17 western states will continue to hold their own. Even the Jeep is not sufficiently versatile for use in roping a steer on the range. It is reasonable to assume, therefore, that the cow pony will continue to furnish needed assistance to ranchers in the West.

Horse racing will continue to be a popular spectator sport, although there will be increased competition for the recreation and sports dollar in the years ahead.

In the final analysis, the dominant factors that will determine the future of the horse industry are (1) the

---

[5] *Ibid.*, 1994 statistics, latest figures available.

USES OF HORSES

Fig. 21-15. Harness racing. (Courtesy, The United States Trotting Assn., Columbus, OH)

Fig. 21-18. Running racehorse—a Thoroughbred. (Photo by Anne M. Eberhardt. Courtesy, *The Blood Horse*, Lexington, KY)

Fig. 21-16. Welsh Ponies. (Courtesy, Welsh Pony Society of America, Winchester, VA)

Fig. 21-19. Fine harness horse—an American Saddlebred. (Photo by James Donaldson. Courtesy, American Saddlebred Horse Assn., Lexington, KY)

Fig. 21-17. Dr. John L. Merrill, XXX Ranch, Crowley, Texas, and Range Management Specialist, Texas Christian University, Ft. Worth, checking range vegetation. (Courtesy, Dr. Merrill)

Fig. 21-20. Cowboy and cutting horse sorting cattle on world-famed King Ranch, Kingville, Texas. (Courtesy, King Ranch)

FOR THE FUN OF IT!

Fig. 21-21. A little girl showering her love and affection on an Arabian. (Photo by Rob Hess. Courtesy, International Arabian Horse Assn., Aurora, CO)

Fig. 21-22. Horses enhance the quality of living for people. (Courtesy, American Morgan Horse Assn., Shelburne, VT)

Fig. 21-23. Trail riders on a range. Trail rides are popular and a source of income for ranchers.

Fig. 21-24. Standardbred yearlings on pasture. (Courtesy, The United States Trotting Assn., Columbus, OH)

FOR THE FUN OF IT!

Fig. 21-25. Horses enhance the quality of life—they're precious and priceless. (Courtesy, Kentucky Department of Travel Development, Frankfort)

Fig. 21-27. Suzanne Hayes riding an endurance champion—a Morab gelding. (Courtesy, International Morab Breeder's Assn., Eagle, WI)

Fig. 21-26. Friends! (Courtesy, USDA)

Fig. 21-28. Adam Boldig, preparing for a local show and ready to meet the challenges of youth achievement. (Courtesy, North American Morab Horse Assn., Hilbert, WI)

need for the cow pony, and (2) the use of horses for recreation, sport, and enhancing the quality of life.

Horse production will, in common with most businesses, encounter increasing competition in the years ahead. Competition will be keen for land, labor, and capital, as well as from other sports.

Skilled management and production programs geared to produce horses that meet more exacting market demands will be the two essential ingredients for success. Also, it will require greater skill and understanding of fundamental relationships to take care of highly bred, sensitive animals in forced production.

Never has there been so much reason to have confidence in, and to be optimistic about, the future. The years ahead will be the most rewarding in the history of the horse industry.

WHY GO TO SCHOOL?

Practical young people graduate from high school and college for four primary reasons:

1. Because it takes trained people to operate high-tech; which is already here in the form of such things as computer-controlled environments, robots, gene transfers that make animals resistant to disease, and laser-guided machinery.

2. Because in many cases a diploma is a requisite to getting a position. There are fewer unskilled agricultural jobs; more positions for managers, technicians, and scientists.

3. Because it increases earning power. As a re-

sult, they can enjoy a higher standard of living and some of the finer things of life. Indeed, a college education is a big key to financial success (see Fig. 21-29). But remember that a job is more than a paycheck! It reflects who you are, your success in life, and your position in the community. It also affects your well-being. Remember, too, that when work is play and play is work, the job changes from an eight hour per day task to an *exciting career*.

4. Most people like to do some good in the world. Certainly everyone wants to make money; and there's no doubt that an education is most helpful from this standpoint. But an education also enhances those things of the spirit and intellect that do not wear dollar marks—the pure enjoyment from living and the enlarged contribution to society. Generally speaking, those who command respect as leaders, and whose lives are fullest and most productive, are college graduates.

FOR MORE INFORMATION CONTACT

1. The Animal Science Department of the Land Grant or State University.

2. The American Society of Animal Science, 111 N. Dunlap Ave., Savoy, IL 61874.

3. The local County Extension Agent or FFA Instructor.

4. The career offices in local colleges.

5. The state employment service.

6. The public libraries.

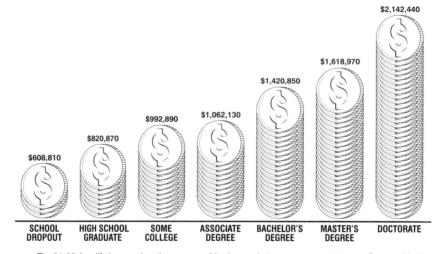

Fig. 21-29. In a lifetime, and on the average, this shows what you may expect to earn. Prepared by the author from the most current data available: *Lifetime Earning Estimates for Men and Women in the United States*. U.S. Bureau of the Census (*Current Population Reports*, Series P-60, Number 139, page 3). The data are for 18-year-old, year-round, full-time, male workers. Subsequent to the above data, lifetime earnings have been affected by (1) supply of, and demand for, the educated labor force, and (2) inflation/value of the dollar. In the decades to come, it is expected that these same factors will affect lifetime earnings, that lifetime earnings of each group will be higher, and that the gap between the least and most educated will grow wider. (Compiled by Career Opportunities News, based on data from the U.S. Bureau of the Census)

SOME EXCITING EQUINE CAREERS

Fig. 21-31. Carla Wennberg is the Equine Instructor in the Animal and Dairy Science Department at the University of Georgia, Athens, where she coaches students in horse judging and teaches horsemanship. She has judged the Quarter Horse Open World Show three times; and the Youth and Amateur World Show once. Carla Wennberg has judged shows in Australia, Austria, Denmark, and Germany, including the Quarter AMA twice, and the European Nationals twice.

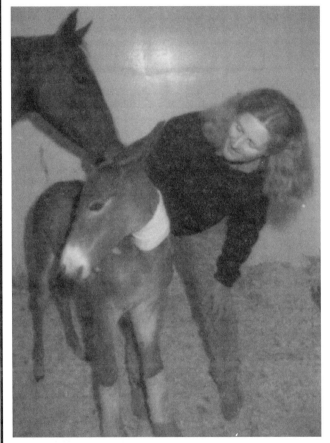

Fig. 21-30. Dr. Melissa T. Hines, D.V.M., Ph.D., Assistant Professor, Department of Veterinary Clinical Sciences, Washington State University, Pullman. Dr. Hines completed undergraduate studies at Michigan State University; the D.V.M. at Ohio State University, Columbus, *summa cum laude*; and the Ph.D. at the University of Florida, College of Medicine, Department of Immunology and Medical Microbiology. Since 1990, she has served as Section Head for Equine Medicine Service, Department of Veterinary Clinical Sciences, Washington State University. This photo shows Dr. Hines examining a mule foal with renal disease.

Fig. 21-32. Fern Palmer Bittner is one of the best known and most highly respected horse show people in America, with great proficiency in showing horses, teaching horsemanship, lecturing, judging, and managing horse shows.

SOME EXCITING EQUINE CAREERS

Fig. 21-33. David McGlothlin, Manager, Horse Division, Harris Farms, Coalinga, California, shown with a mare and foal. David McGlothlin has a B.S. degree in Animal Science and a Masters Degree in Reproductive Physiology; both degrees are from Colorado State University, Fort Collins. David McGlothlin is a successful horse farm manager—he loves horses, he's knowledgeable, and he's a great worker.

Fig. 21-34. Lee Eaton: (a) partner in Eaton Farms, Inc., and Red Bull Stable, 4454 Mt. Horeb, Lexington, KY 40505; and (b) proprietor of Eaton and Thorne, 4454 Mt. Horeb, Lexington, KY 40505. Lee Eaton attended the University of Kentucky, where he majored in general agriculture and commerce. Today, he is one of the most successful and respected horsemen in America.

A rare triple dead heat of Quarter Horses, which occurred at the Alameda County Fair Grounds, Pleasanton, California. (Photo by Photo-Patrol, Inc., San Mateo, CA, Courtesy American Quarter Racing Assn., Tucson, AZ)

COMPOSITION OF HORSE FEEDS

In addition to the discussion that follows pertaining to composition of feeds, the reader is referred to Chapter 13, Feeding Horses.

Both those who feed and care for horses and nutritionists have need for accurate and up-to-date composition of feedstuffs in order to formulate rations. In recognition of this need and its importance, the author spared no time nor expense in compiling the feed composition tables presented in this section. At the outset, a survey of the industry was made in order to determine what kind of feed composition tables would be most useful, in both format and content. Secondly, it was decided to utilize, to the extent available, the feed compositions which, for many years, were compiled by Lorin Harris, Utah State University, now carried forward by the USDA, National Agricultural Library, Feed Composition Bank. These data were augmented by the author with feed compositions from the National Academy of Sciences, NRC, and from experimental reports, industries, and other reliable sources.

FEED NAMES

Ideally, a feed name should conjure up the same meaning to all those who use it, and it should provide helpful information. This was the guiding philosophy of the author when choosing the names given in the Feed Composition Tables. Genus and species—Latin names—are also included. To facilitate worldwide usage, the International Feed Number of each feed is given. To the extent possible, consideration was also given to source (or parent material), variety or kind, stage of maturity, processing, part eaten, and grade.

Where feeds are known by more than one name, cross-referencing was used.

MOISTURE CONTENT OF FEEDS

It is necessary to know the moisture content of feeds in ration formulation and buying. Usually, the composition of a feed is expressed according to one or more of the following bases:

1. **As-fed; A-F (wet, fresh).** This refers to feed as normally fed to horses. As-fed may range from near 0% to 100% dry matter.

2. **Air-dry (approximately 90% dry matter).** This refers to feed that is dried by means of natural air movement, usually in the open. It may either be an actual or an assumed dry matter content; the latter is approximately 90%. Most feeds are fed in an air-dry state.

3. **Moisture-free; M-F (oven-dry, 100% dry matter).** This refers to a sample of feed that has been dried in an oven at 221°F until all the moisture has been removed.

In this book, feed compositions are presented on both As-Fed (A-F) and Moisture-Free (M-F) bases.

ADJUSTING MOISTURE CONTENT

The simplest way to avoid errors in ration formulation is to formulate on a 100% dry matter basis.

The multipliers in Table A-1 may be used to convert feeds of various moisture contents to a 100% dry matter basis.

The majority of feed composition tables are listed on an "as-fed" basis, while most of the National Research Council nutrient requirement tables are on either an "approximate 90% dry matter" or "moisture-free basis." Since feeds contain varying amounts of dry matter, it would be much simpler, and more accurate, if both feed composition and nutrient requirement tables were on a dry basis. In order to facilitate ration formulation, the author lists both the "as-fed" and

TABLE A-1
CORRECTION FACTORS TO USE WHEN COVERTING FEEDS OF VARIOUS MOISTURE CONTENTS TO A 100% DRY MATTER BASIS (0% MOISTURE)

% Moisture	100% DM Basis Multiplier	% Moisture	100% DM Basis Multiplier	% Moisture	100% DM Basis Multiplier
0	1.0000	29	1.4084	58	2.3809
1	1.0101	30	1.4285	59	2.4390
2	1.0204	31	1.4492	60	2.5000
3	1.0309	32	1.4705	61	2.5641
4	1.0416	33	1.4925	62	2.6315
5	1.0526	34	1.5151	63	2.7020
6	1.0638	35	1.5384	64	2.7777
7	1.0752	36	1.5625	65	2.8571
8	1.0869	37	1.5873	66	2.9411
9	1.0989	38	1.6129	67	3.0303
10	1.1111	39	1.6393	68	3.1250
11	1.1235	40	1.6666	69	3.2258
12	1.1363	41	1.6949	70	3.3333
13	1.1494	42	1.7241	71	3.4482
14	1.1627	43	1.7543	72	3.5714
15	1.1765	44	1.7857	73	3.7037
16	1.1904	45	1.8181	74	3.8461
17	1.2048	46	1.8518	75	4.0000
18	1.2195	47	1.8867	76	4.1666
19	1.2345	48	1.9231	77	4.3478
20	1.2500	49	1.9607	78	4.5454
21	1.2658	50	2.0000	79	4.7619
22	1.2820	51	2.0408	80	5.0000
23	1.2987	52	2.0833	81	5.2631
24	1.3157	53	2.1276	82	5.5555
25	1.3333	54	2.1739	83	5.8824
26	1.3513	55	2.2222	84	6.2500
27	1.3698	56	2.2727	85	6.6666
28	1.3889	57	2.3255		

"moisture-free" contents of feeds in Table A-4, Feed Composition Tables.

The significance of water content of feeds becomes obvious in the examples given in Table A-2. When using total digestible nutrients (TDN) as a measure of energy, three of the high-moisture feeds, carrots, melons, and milk, have a higher energy value than oats on a moisture-free basis. The same principle applies to other nutrients, also.

As shown, dry matter becomes a common denominator for the comparison of feeds, particularly as to energy value; but this applies to other nutrients, also.

The following formulas may be used for adjusting moisture contents:

From Dry to As-Fed
To be used in converting the amounts of ingredi-

TABLE A-2
COMPARATIVE ENERGY VALUE OF FIVE FEEDS
BASED ON (1) AS-FED, AND (2) MOISTURE-FREE BASIS

| Feed | Water | Dry Matter | Energy Value (TDN) | |
			As-Fed	Moisture-Free Basis
	(%)	(%)	(%)	(%)
Apples	82	18	13	74
Carrots, roots	84	16	12	78
Melons	94	6	5	80
Milk	88	12	16	128
Oats, grain	11	89	69	77

ents of a dry diet[1] to a wet diet having a given percentage of dry matter.

Formula 1

$$\text{Parts of ingredient in wet diet} = \frac{\text{\% ingredient in dry diet} \times \text{\% dry matter wanted in diet}}{\text{\%dry matter in ingredient}}$$

Total the parts and add enough water to make 100 parts (or 100%).

From Wet to Dry

To be used in calculating the amount of an ingredient that should be contained in a dry diet if the amount required in a wet diet having a given percent of dry matter is known.

Formula 2

$$\text{\% of ingredient in wet diet} = \frac{\text{\% of ingredient in wet diet}}{\text{\% dry matter wanted in diet} \times \text{\% dry matter of ingredient}} = \text{\% of ingredient in dry diet}$$

From Wet to Dry

To be used if the diet is on an as-fed basis and it is desired to change the amounts of the ingredients to a dry basis.

Formula 3

Parts on wet basis = % ingredient in wet diet × % dry matter of ingredient

Perform this calculation for each ingredient; then add the products and divide each product by the sum of the products.

From Wet to Dry

To be used if the diet is on an as-fed basis and

---

[1]The term *dry diet* means a diet calculated on a dry (moisture-free) basis; *as-fed* means a diet calculated to contain the amount of dry matter as it is fed to the animal.

it is desired to compare the nutrient content of the diet with dry basis requirements.

Formula 4

$$\text{\% nutrient in dry diet (total)} = \frac{\text{\% nutrient in wet diet (total)}}{\text{\% dry matter in diet (total)}}$$

CAROTENE

Different species of animals convert B-carotene to vitamin A with varying degrees of efficiency. The conversion rate of the rat has been used as the standard value, with 1 mg of B-carotene equal to 1,667 IU of vitamin A. Based on this standard, the comparative efficiency of each animal species is as shown in table A-3, Conversion of Beta Carotene to Vitamin A for Different Species.

TABLE A-3
CONVERSION OF BETA-CAROTENE TO VITAMIN A
FOR DIFFERENT SPECIES[1]

Species	Conversion of mg of Beta-Carotene to IU of Vitamin A		IU of Vitamin A Activity (calculated from carotene)
	(mg)	(IU)	(%)
Standard (rat)	1	1,667	100
Horses			
Growth	1	555	33.3
Pregnancy	1	333	20.0
Cattle	1	400	24.0
Dairy cattle	1	400	24.0
Sheep	1	400–500	24.0–30.0
Swine	1	500	30.0
Poultry	1	1,667	100
Mink	Carotene not utilized		—
Humans	1	556	33.3

[1]Adapted from the *Atlas of Nutritional Data on United States and Canadian Feeds*, NRC-National Academy of Sciences, 1972, p. XVI, Table 6.

PERTINENT INFORMATION ABOUT DATA

The information which follows is pertinent to the feed composition tables presented in this section.

■ **Variations in composition**—Feeds vary in their composition. Thus, actual analysis of a feedstuff should be obtained and used whenever possible, especially where a large lot of feed from one source is involved. Many times, however, it is either impossible to determine actual compositions or there is insufficient time to obtain such analysis. Under such circumstances, tabulated data may be the only information available.

■ **Feed compositions change**—Feed compositions

change over a period of time, primarily due to (1) the introduction of new varieties, and (2) modifications in the manufacturing process from which byproducts evolve.

■ **Biological value**—The response of animals when fed a feed is termed the biological value, which is a function of its chemical composition and the ability of the animal to derive useful nutrient value from the feed. The latter relates to the digestibility, or availability, of the nutrients in the feed. Thus, soft coal and shelled corn may have the same gross energy value in a bomb calorimeter, but markedly different useful energy values when consumed by an animal. Biological tests of feeds are more laborious and costly than chemical analysis, but they are much more accurate in predicting the response of animals to a feed.

■ **Where information is not available**—Where information is not available or reasonable estimates could not be made, no values are shown. Hopefully, such information will become available in the future.

■ **Calculated on a dry matter (DM) basis**—All data were calculated on a 100% dry matter basis (moisture-free), then converted to an as-fed basis by multiplying the decimal equivalent of the DM content times the compositional value shown in the table.

■ **Fiber**—Four values relating to dietary fiber are given in the feed composition tables—crude fiber, neutral detergent fiber (NDF), acid detergent fiber (ADF), and lignin.

Crude fiber, methods for the determination of which were developed more than 100 years ago, is declining as a measure of low digestible material in the more fibrous feeds. The newer method of forage analysis, developed by Van Soest and associates of the U.S. Department of Agriculture, separates feed dry matter into two fractions: a neutral detergent fibrous fraction; and an acid detergent fibrous fraction. Also the amount of lignin in the ADF may be determined.

1. **Crude fiber (CF).** This fraction is an indicator of the relative indigestibility and bulkiness of the sample. It is the residue that remains after boiling a feed in a weak acid, and then in a weak alkali, in an attempt to imitate the process that occurs in the digestive tract. This procedure is based on the supposition that carbohydrates which are readily dissolved also will be readily digested by animals, and that those not soluble under such conditions are not readily digested. Unfortunately, the treatment dissolves much of the lignin, a nondigestible component. Hence, crude fiber is only an approximation of the indigestible material in feedstuffs. Nevertheless, it is a rough indicator of the energy value of feeds. Also, the crude fiber value is needed for the computation of TDN.

2. **Neutral detergent fiber (NDF).** This is the fraction of the feed which is not soluble in neutral detergent. It consists of plant cell walls, including lignin, cellulose, and hemicellulose. NDF is closely related to feed intake because it contains all the fiber components that occupy space in the digestive tract and are slowly digested. The lower the NDF, the more forage the animal will eat; hence, a low percentage of NDF is desirable.

3. **Acid detergent fiber (ADF).** This is the fraction of the feed which is not soluble in acid detergent. It consists of cellulose (digestible) and lignin (indigestible). ADF is an indicator of forage digestibility because it contains a high proportion of lignin which is the indigestible fiber fraction. The lower the ADF, the more feed an animal can digest; hence, a low percentage of ADF is desirable.

4. **Lignin.** This fraction is essentially indigestible by all animals and is the substance that limits the availability of cellulose carbohydrates in the plant cell wall to rumen bacteria.

The acid detergent fiber procedure is used as a preparatory step in determining the lignin content of a forage sample. Hemicellulose is solubilized during this procedure, while the lignocellulose fraction of the feed remains insoluble. Cellulose is then separated from lignin by the addition of sulfuric acid. Only lignin and acid-insoluble ash remain upon completion of this step. This residue is then ashed, and the difference of the weights before and after ashing yields the amount of lignin present in the feed.

■ **Nitrogen-free extract**—The nitrogen-free extract was calculated with mean data as: mean nitrogen-free extract (%) = 100 – % ash – % crude fiber – % ether extract – % protein.

■ **Protein values**—Both crude protein and digestible protein values are given. Crude protein is determined by finding the nitrogen content and multiplying the result by 6.25. The nitrogen content of proteins averages about 16% (100 ÷ 16 = 6.25).

■ **Energy**—Many of the energy values given in the feed composition tables were derived from complex formulas developed by L. E. Harris and other animal scientists.

The following three measures of energy are shown:

1. **Total digestible nutrients (TDN).** This value is given because there are more of them, and because it has been the standard method of expressing the energy value of feeds for many years. However, the following disadvantages are inherent in the TDN system: (a) Only digestive losses are considered—it does not take into account other important losses, such as those in the urine, gases, and increased heat production; (b) there is a poor relationship between crude fiber and NFE digestibility in certain feeds; and (c) it

overestimates roughages in relation to concentrates when animals are fed for high rates of production, due to the higher heat loss per pound of TDN in high-fiber feeds.

2. **Digestible energy (DE).** Digestible energy is that portion of the gross energy in a feed that is not excreted in the feces. It is roughly comparable to TDN.

3. **Metabolizable energy (ME).** Metabolizable energy represents that portion of the gross energy that is not lost in the feces, urine, and gas (mainly methane). It does not take into account the energy lost as heat, commonly called heat increment. As a result, it overevaluates roughages compared with concentrates, as do TDN and DE.

■ **Minerals**—The level of minerals in forages is largely determined by the mineral content of the soil on which the feeds are grown. Calcium, phosphorus, iodine, and selenium are well-known examples of soil nutrient—plant nutrient relationships.

■ **Vitamins**—Generally speaking, it is unwise to rely on harvested feeds as a source of carotene (vitamin A value), unless the forage being fed is fresh (pasture or green chop) or of a good green color and not over a year old.

The author is very grateful to Lorin E. Harris, Ph.D., and Clyde R. Richards, Ph.D., Utah State University, Logan, for their interest and invaluable assistance in preparing the Feed Composition Tables for this book. Also, in the preparation of Table A-4, Composition of Mineral Supplements, the author acknowledges with appreciation the review and added values provided by International Minerals and Chemical Corporation, Northbrook, Illinois; and R. F. Klay, Ph.D., Research Department, Moorman Mfg. Co., Quincy, Illinois.

FEED COMPOSITION TABLES

To facilitate quick and easy use, the feeds in Table A-4 are classified and separated into the following subtables:

1. **Table A-4a, Energy Feeds.** This includes feeds which are high in energy and low in fiber (under 18%), and which generally contain less than 20% protein.

2. **Table A-4b, Protein Feeds.** This includes feeds that contain more than 20% protein or protein equivalent.

3. **Table A-4c, Dry Forages.** This includes feeds which are bulky, low in weight per unit volume, and relatively low in energy, and which in the dry state contain more than 18% crude fiber.

4. **Table A-4d, Silages and Haylages.** Silage (ensilage) is fermentable high-moisture forage stored under anaerobic conditions in a silo, consisting of either green crops or crops to which moisture has been added, chopped when stored, and containing 65 to 70% moisture.

Haylages are low-moisture silages, made from grasses and/or legumes that are wilted to 40 to 55% moisture content before ensiling.

5. **Table A-4e, Pasture and Range Plants.** This includes grass, browse, and other plants that are harvested by grazing animals.

6. **Table A-4f, Mineral Supplements.** This includes rich natural and synthetic sources of inorganic elements needed to perform certain essential body functions.

7. **Table A-4g, Vitamin Supplements.** This includes rich synthetic or natural feed sources of one or more complex compounds, called vitamins, that are required by horses in minute amounts for normal growth, performance, reproduction, and/or health.

8. **Table A-4h, Amino Acids.** This gives the known amino acid composition of certain feeds.

Some feeds fit the criteria of more than one of the above classes. For example, whole soybeans are used as both an energy feed and a protein feed; hence, they are listed in both Table A-4a and Table A-4b.

In Tables A-4a to A-4e, and A-4g, covering 6 of the respective feedstuff classifications indicated above, values for each feed are presented in tabular form on 3 pages.

Note well: Each of the following tables is a three-page spread: Tables A-4a, A-4b, A-4c, A-4d, A-4e, and Table A-4g. (Table A-4f is a two-page spread.) Thus, the composition of entry No. 1, *Animal, Fat, hydrolyzed,* is given on three consecutive pages (see pages with black borders). Then, after the first three-page spread is filled by alphabetically listed entries (feeds), a second three-page spread is filled in like manner (see pages with gray borders). This same three-page pattern, with similar border changes each three pages, applies to Tables A-4a through A-4e, and to Table A-4g.

Fig. A-1. Horse feeds should make for a nutritionally complete and balanced ration. Except for idle horses, it is generally advisable to provide supplemental feed for horses on pasture. (Photo by Dell Hancock, Claiborne, Paris, KY)

ENERGY FEEDS

TABLE A–4a ENERGY FEEDS FOR HORSES, COMPOSITION OF FEEDS, DATA EXPRESSED **AS-FED** AND **MOISTURE-FREE** (See footnote at end of table.)

Entry Number	Feed Name Description	International Feed Number	Moisture Basis: A-F (as-fed) or M-F (moisture-free)	Dry Matter %	Ash %	Crude Fiber %	Neutral Det. Fib. (NDF) %	Acid Det. Fib. (ADF) %	Lignin %	Ether Extract (Fat) %	N-Free Exract %	Crude Protein %	Digestible Protein %	TDN %	Digestible Energy Mcal lb	kg	Metabolizable Energy Mcal lb	kg
1	**ANIMAL** FAT, HYDROLYZED	5-00-376	A-F	99	–	–	–	–	–	98.4	–	–	–	–	–	–	–	–
			M-F	100	–	–	–	–	–	99.2	–	–	–	–	–	–	–	–
2	**ANIMAL-POULTRY** FAT	4-00-409	A-F	99	–	–	–	–	–	98.4	–	–	–	–	–	–	–	–
			M-F	100	–	–	–	–	–	100.0	–	–	–	–	–	–	–	–
3	**BARLEY** *Hordeum vulgare* GRAIN, ALL ANALYSES	4-00-549	A-F	88	2.4	5.0	16.8	10.7	1.5	1.7	67.7	11.7	9.6	73	1.31	2.88	1.07	2.36
			M-F	100	2.7	5.7	19.0	12.1	1.7	1.9	76.5	13.2	10.8	82	1.48	3.26	1.21	2.67
4	GRAIN, PACIFIC COAST	4-07-939	A-F	89	2.5	6.5	–	–	–	2.0	68.2	9.5	6.7	66	1.20	2.64	0.98	2.16
			M-F	100	2.8	7.3	–	–	–	2.2	76.9	10.8	7.6	74	1.35	2.98	1.11	2.44
5	MALT SPROUTS, DEHY	4-00-545	A-F	93	5.6	14.2	–	–	–	1.4	48.8	22.9	17.2	–	–	–	–	–
			M-F	100	6.1	15.3	–	–	–	1.5	52.6	24.6	18.6	–	–	–	–	–
6	**BEET, SUGAR** *Beta vulgaris, altissima* MOLASSES, MORE THAN 48% INVERT SUGAR, MORE THAN 79.5 DEGREES BRIX	4-00-668	A-F	78	8.9	–	–	–	–	0.2	62.2	6.6	4.5	–	–	–	–	–
			M-F	100	11.4	–	–	–	–	0.2	79.9	8.5	5.8	–	–	–	–	–
7	PULP, DEHY	4-00-669	A-F	91	4.8	18.2	53.6	26.3	4.5	0.5	58.4	8.8	6.2	59	1.09	2.40	0.89	1.97
			M-F	100	5.3	20.1	59.0	29.0	5.0	0.6	64.3	9.7	6.8	65	1.20	2.64	0.98	2.17
8	PULP WITH MOLASSES, DEHY	4-00-672	A-F	92	5.7	15.2	–	24.5	2.4	0.6	61.1	9.3	6.5	62	1.13	2.50	0.93	2.05
			M-F	100	6.2	16.6	–	26.6	2.6	0.6	66.5	10.1	7.1	67	1.23	2.72	1.01	2.23
9	**BREWERS** GRAINS, DEHY	5-02-141	A-F	92	3.6	13.0	38.7	23.9	4.6	6.6	41.6	27.3	21.0	48	–	–	–	–
			M-F	100	4.0	14.1	42.0	26.0	5.0	7.1	45.2	29.6	22.8	52	–	–	–	–
10	**CARROT** *Daucus* spp ROOTS, FRESH[1]	4-01-145	A-F	11	1.0	1.1	1.0	0.9	–	0.2	8.1	1.2	0.8	8	0.14	0.31	0.12	0.26
			M-F	100	8.4	9.5	9.0	8.0	–	1.3	70.7	10.0	7.0	67	1.23	2.72	1.01	2.23
11	**CITRUS** *Citrus* spp PULP WITHOUT FINES, DEHY (DRIED CITRUS PULP)[1]	4-01-237	A-F	91	6.0	11.6	20.9	20.0	–	3.4	63.9	6.1	4.0	48	–	–	–	–
			M-F	100	6.6	12.8	23.0	22.0	–	3.7	70.2	6.7	4.4	53	–	–	–	–
12	SYRUP (MOLASSES)	4-01-241	A-F	67	5.1	–	–	–	–	0.2	55.7	5.8	3.9	–	–	–	–	–
			M-F	100	7.6	–	–	–	–	0.3	82.7	8.5	5.8	–	–	–	–	–
13	**CORN, DENT YELLOW** *Zea mays, indentata* GRAIN, ALL ANALYSES	4-02-935	A-F	88	1.3	2.3	–	3.8	–	3.6	71.0	9.9	7.0	64	1.17	2.57	0.96	2.11
			M-F	100	1.5	2.6	–	4.3	–	4.1	80.7	11.2	7.9	73	1.32	2.92	1.09	2.39
14	GRAIN, GRADE 2, 54 lb/bu (69.5 kg/hl)	4-02-931	A-F	87	1.2	2.1	–	–	–	4.0	71.3	8.9	6.2	61	1.11	2.45	0.91	2.01
			M-F	100	1.4	2.4	–	–	–	4.5	81.5	10.2	7.1	70	1.27	2.81	1.04	2.30
15	DISTILLERS GRAINS, DEHY[1]	5-02-842	A-F	93	2.2	11.5	40.0	15.8	–	8.9	43.1	27.8	22.7	–	–	–	–	–
			M-F	100	2.4	12.3	43.0	17.0	–	9.5	46.2	29.7	24.3	–	–	–	–	–
16	DISTILLERS SOLUBLES, DEHY[1]	5-28-237	A-F	93	7.2	4.6	21.4	6.5	–	8.8	45.2	27.4	22.3	–	–	–	–	–
			M-F	100	7.7	4.9	23.0	7.0	–	9.3	48.6	29.5	24.1	–	–	–	–	–
17	EARS, GROUND (CORN AND COB MEAL)[1]	4-28-238	A-F	87	1.7	8.2	24.4	9.6	–	3.2	65.7	7.8	5.4	56	1.03	2.28	0.85	1.87
			M-F	100	1.9	9.4	28.0	11.0	–	3.7	75.9	9.0	6.2	65	1.20	2.64	0.98	2.16
18	GLUTEN, MEAL, 60% PROTEIN[1]	5-28-242	A-F	90	1.7	1.8	12.6	4.5	–	2.1	23.7	60.8	-0.4	–	–	–	–	–
			M-F	100	1.9	2.0	14.0	5.0	–	2.3	26.3	67.5	-0.5	–	–	–	–	–
19	GLUTEN FEED[1]	5-28-243	A-F	90	6.6	8.7	40.5	10.8	–	2.1	49.4	23.0	17.7	–	–	–	–	–
			M-F	100	7.4	9.7	45.0	12.0	–	2.4	55.0	25.6	19.6	–	–	–	–	–
20	GRITS (HOMINY GRITS)[1]	4-03-011	A-F	90	2.8	4.8	49.5	11.7	–	6.5	65.8	10.3	7.3	49	0.91	2.01	0.75	1.65
			M-F	100	3.1	5.3	55.0	13.0	–	7.2	72.9	11.4	8.1	54	1.01	2.23	0.83	1.83
21	OIL	4-16-450	A-F	99	–	–	–	–	–	99.0	–	–	–	–	–	–	–	–
			M-F	100	–	–	–	–	–	100.0	–	–	–	–	–	–	–	–
22	**CORN, OPAQUE 2, HIGH LYSINE** *Zea mays* GRAIN	4-11-445	A-F	90	1.6	3.0	–	–	–	4.4	71.0	10.1	7.2	61	1.12	2.47	0.92	2.03
			M-F	100	1.7	3.3	–	–	–	4.9	78.8	11.2	8.0	68	1.25	2.75	1.02	2.25
23	**COTTON** *Gossypium* spp SEEDS[1]	5-13-749	A-F	91	4.7	19.4	40.0	30.9	–	20.4	24.5	21.8	16.2	–	–	–	–	–
			M-F	100	5.2	21.4	44.0	34.0	–	22.5	27.0	24.0	17.9	–	–	–	–	–
24	**DISTILLERS PRODUCTS** (ALSO SEE CORN; RYE; SORGHUM; WHEAT) GRAINS, DEHY	5-02-144	A-F	93	1.5	12.8	–	–	–	7.4	43.5	27.3	22.3	–	–	–	–	–
			M-F	100	1.6	13.8	–	–	–	8.0	47.0	29.5	24.1	–	–	–	–	–
25	SOLUBLES, DEHY	5-02-147	A-F	92	6.2	3.4	–	–	–	8.9	44.8	28.8	24.0	31	0.62	1.37	0.51	1.12
			M-F	100	6.7	3.7	–	–	–	9.7	48.6	31.3	26.1	34	0.68	1.49	0.56	1.22
26	**FATS AND OILS** FAT, ANIMAL, HYDROLYZED	4-00-376	A-F	99	–	–	–	–	–	98.4	–	–	–	–	–	–	–	–
			M-F	100	–	–	–	–	–	99.2	–	–	–	–	–	–	–	–
27	FAT, ANIMAL-POULTRY	4-00-409	A-F	99	–	–	–	–	–	99.1	–	–	–	–	–	–	–	–
			M-F	100	–	–	–	–	–	100.0	–	–	–	–	–	–	–	–
28	**FLAX, COMMON** *Linum usitatissimum* SEEDS	5-02-042	A-F	96	5.0	6.3	–	–	–	35.9	30.7	17.8	11.2	–	–	–	–	–
			M-F	100	5.2	6.6	–	–	–	37.5	32.1	18.6	11.7	–	–	–	–	–
29	**HOMINY GRITS (CORN, DENT YELLOW, GRITS)** *Zea mays, indentata*	4-03-011	A-F	90	2.8	4.8	–	–	–	6.5	65.8	10.3	7.3	49	0.91	2.01	0.75	1.65
			M-F	100	7.2	5.3	–	–	–	7.2	72.9	11.4	8.1	54	1.01	2.23	0.83	1.83

ENERGY FEEDS FOR HORSES

Entry Number	Calcium (Ca) %	Phosphorus (P) %	Sodium (Na) %	Chlorine (Cl) %	Magnesium (Mg) %	Potassium (K) %	Sulfur (S) %	Cobalt (Co) ppm or mg/kg	Copper (Cu) ppm or mg/kg	Iodine (I) ppm or mg/kg	Iron (Fe) %	Manganese (Mn) ppm or mg/kg	Selenium (Se) ppm or mg/kg	Zinc (Zn) ppm or mg/kg	A (1 mg Carotene = 1667 IU Vit A) IU/g	Carotene (Provitamin A) ppm or mg/kg	D IU/kg	E ppm or mg/kg	K ppm or mg/kg
1	–	–	–	–	–	–	–	–	–	–	–	–	–	–	–	–	–	–	–
	–	–	–	–	–	–	–	–	–	–	–	–	–	–	–	–	–	–	–
2	–	–	–	–	–	0.23	–	–	–	–	–	–	–	–	–	–	–	7.9	–
	–	–	–	–	–	0.23	–	–	–	–	–	–	–	–	–	–	–	7.9	–
3	0.05	0.34	0.03	0.12	0.13	0.46	0.15	0.171	7.6	0.044	0.008	16.0	0.158	39.3	3.4	2.0	–	23.2	0.22
	0.06	0.39	0.03	0.13	0.15	0.52	0.17	0.193	8.6	0.050	0.009	18.1	0.179	44.4	3.8	2.3	–	26.2	0.24
4	0.05	0.34	0.02	0.15	0.12	0.51	0.14	0.087	8.1	–	0.009	16.0	0.101	15.2	–	–	–	26.2	–
	0.06	0.39	0.02	0.17	0.14	0.58	0.16	0.098	9.1	–	0.010	18.0	0.114	17.1	–	–	–	29.6	–
5	0.18	0.63	0.88	0.36	0.17	0.25	0.79	–	5.9	–	0.018	29.4	0.416	56.4	–	–	–	3.7	–
	0.19	0.68	0.95	0.39	0.18	0.27	0.85	–	6.3	–	0.020	31.7	0.448	60.7	–	–	–	4.0	–
6	0.12	0.03	1.16	1.28	0.23	4.73	0.46	0.362	16.8	–	0.007	4.5	–	14.0	–	–	–	4.0	–
	0.16	0.03	1.48	1.64	0.29	6.07	0.60	0.465	21.6	–	0.009	5.8	–	18.0	–	–	–	5.1	–
7	0.63	0.09	0.19	0.04	0.26	0.18	0.20	0.074	12.5	–	0.027	34.2	–	0.7	0.4	0.2	1	–	–
	0.70	0.10	0.21	0.04	0.28	0.20	0.22	0.081	13.7	–	0.030	37.7	–	0.8	0.4	0.2	1	–	–
8	0.56	0.09	0.48	–	0.15	1.63	0.39	0.209	14.7	–	0.017	18.4	–	5.1	0.4	0.2	–	–	–
	0.61	0.10	0.53	–	0.16	1.78	0.42	0.227	16.0	–	0.018	20.1	–	5.5	0.4	0.2	–	–	–
9	0.30	0.51	0.21	0.15	0.15	0.09	0.30	0.076	21.7	0.066	0.024	37.2	–	27.3	0.8	0.5	–	26.7	–
	0.33	0.55	0.23	0.17	0.17	0.09	0.32	0.083	23.6	0.072	0.026	40.4	–	29.6	0.8	0.5	–	29.0	–
10	0.05	0.04	0.06	0.06	0.02	0.32	0.02	–	1.2	–	0.002	3.6	–	–	129.9	77.9	–	6.9	–
	0.40	0.35	0.48	0.50	0.20	2.80	0.17	–	10.4	–	0.013	31.5	–	–	1129.4	677.5	–	60.2	–
11	1.69	0.12	0.07	–	0.15	0.71	0.17	0.169	5.0	–	0.033	6.6	–	13.7	0.4	0.2	–	–	–
	1.86	0.13	0.08	–	0.17	0.78	0.19	0.185	5.4	–	0.036	7.3	–	15.1	0.4	0.2	–	–	–
12	1.18	0.09	0.28	0.07	0.14	0.09	0.16	0.109	72.8	–	0.035	40.9	–	92.4	–	–	–	–	–
	1.76	0.13	0.41	0.11	0.21	0.14	0.23	0.162	108.0	–	0.051	60.7	–	137.1	–	–	–	–	–
13	0.05	0.28	0.01	0.05	0.11	0.33	0.11	0.378	3.5	–	0.004	5.7	0.127	19.4	9.5	5.7	–	20.9	0.22
	0.05	0.31	0.01	0.06	0.13	0.37	0.13	0.429	4.0	–	0.004	6.4	0.144	22.0	10.8	6.5	–	23.8	0.25
14	0.02	0.29	0.02	0.04	0.11	0.31	0.12	0.029	3.8	–	0.003	5.3	–	13.7	2.9	1.7	–	21.6	–
	0.03	0.33	0.02	0.05	0.13	0.36	0.14	0.033	4.3	–	0.003	6.1	–	15.6	3.3	2.0	–	24.7	–
15	0.09	0.39	0.09	0.07	0.07	0.16	0.43	0.076	38.9	0.048	0.020	19.3	0.352	41.7	5.2	3.1	–	–	–
	0.10	0.42	0.09	0.08	0.07	0.18	0.46	0.082	41.7	0.051	0.021	20.7	0.377	44.7	5.6	3.3	–	–	–
16	0.30	1.30	0.23	0.26	0.60	1.70	0.37	0.167	77.9	0.079	0.052	72.0	0.371	88.0	1.1	0.7	–	45.9	–
	0.32	1.40	0.24	0.28	0.65	1.83	0.40	0.180	83.9	0.085	0.056	77.6	0.400	94.8	1.2	0.7	–	49.4	–
17	0.06	0.24	0.02	0.04	0.12	0.46	0.14	0.273	6.8	0.023	0.008	19.9	0.074	12.1	5.3	3.2	–	17.5	–
	0.07	0.27	0.02	0.05	0.14	0.53	0.16	0.315	7.9	0.026	0.010	23.0	0.086	14.0	6.1	3.7	–	20.2	–
18	0.07	0.45	0.05	0.09	0.08	0.18	0.65	0.045	26.1	0.018	0.023	6.3	0.829	30.6	–	–	–	14.6	–
	0.08	0.50	0.05	0.10	0.09	0.20	0.72	0.051	29.0	0.020	0.026	7.0	0.921	34.0	–	–	–	16.2	–
19	0.32	0.74	0.12	0.22	0.33	0.57	0.21	0.087	47.1	0.066	0.043	23.1	0.272	64.6	9.8	5.9	–	12.1	–
	0.36	0.82	0.14	0.25	0.36	0.64	0.23	0.097	52.3	0.074	0.048	25.7	0.302	71.8	10.9	6.5	–	13.5	–
20	0.05	0.51	0.08	0.05	0.24	0.59	0.03	0.055	13.6	–	0.007	14.5	–	–	15.4	9.2	–	–	–
	0.05	0.57	0.09	0.06	0.26	0.65	0.03	0.061	15.1	–	0.008	16.1	–	–	17.0	10.2	–	–	–
21	–	–	–	–	–	–	–	–	–	–	–	–	–	–	–	–	–	–	–
	–	–	–	–	–	–	–	–	–	–	–	–	–	–	–	–	–	–	–
22	0.03	0.20	–	–	0.13	0.35	0.10	–	–	–	–	–	–	–	7.8	4.7	–	–	–
	0.03	0.22	–	–	0.14	0.39	0.11	–	–	–	–	–	–	–	8.6	5.2	–	–	–
23	0.14	0.69	0.03	–	0.32	1.11	0.24	–	49.0	–	0.014	11.1	–	–	–	–	–	–	–
	0.16	0.76	0.03	–	0.35	1.22	0.26	–	53.9	–	0.016	12.2	–	–	–	–	–	–	–
24	0.12	0.54	0.05	0.05	0.09	0.20	0.46	0.092	47.9	–	0.027	35.0	–	–	13.0	7.8	–	30.5	–
	0.13	0.59	0.05	0.06	0.10	0.21	0.49	0.099	51.7	–	0.029	37.8	–	–	14.0	8.4	–	32.9	–
25	0.24	1.35	0.45	–	0.53	1.97	–	0.196	71.6	–	0.031	64.1	–	138.0	1.9	1.1	–	–	–
	0.26	1.47	0.49	–	0.58	2.14	–	0.213	77.9	–	0.034	69.7	–	150.0	2.0	1.2	–	–	–
26	–	–	–	–	–	–	–	–	–	–	–	–	–	–	–	–	–	–	–
	–	–	–	–	–	–	–	–	–	–	–	–	–	–	–	–	–	–	–
27	–	–	–	–	–	0.23	–	–	–	–	–	–	–	–	–	–	–	7.9	–
	–	–	–	–	–	0.23	–	–	–	–	–	–	–	–	–	–	–	7.9	–
28	0.28	0.55	–	–	–	–	–	–	–	–	–	–	–	–	–	–	–	–	–
	0.29	0.58	–	–	–	–	–	–	–	–	–	–	–	–	–	–	–	–	–
29	0.05	0.51	0.08	0.05	0.24	0.59	0.03	0.055	13.6	–	0.007	14.5	–	–	15.4	9.2	–	–	–
	0.05	0.57	0.09	0.06	0.26	0.65	0.03	0.061	15.1	–	0.008	16.1	–	–	17.0	10.2	–	–	–

(Continued)

ENERGY FEEDS

TABLE A–4a ENERGY FEEDS FOR HORSES, COMPOSITION OF FEEDS, DATA EXPRESSED **AS-FED** AND **MOISTURE-FREE** (Continued)

Entry Number	Feed Name Description	Moisture Basis: A-F (as-fed) or M-F (moisture-free)	Dry Matter %	B-12 ppb or mcg/kg	Biotin ppm or mg/kg	Choline ppm or mg/kg	Folacin (Folic Acid) ppm or mg/kg	Niacin ppm or mg/kg	Pantothenic Acid (B-3) ppm or mg/kg	Pyridoxine (B-6) ppm or mg/kg	Riboflavin (B-2) ppm or mg/kg	Thiamin (B-1) ppm or mg/kg
1	**ANIMAL** FAT, HYDROLYZED	A-F	99	–	–	–	–	–	–	–	–	–
		M-F	100	–	–	–	–	–	–	–	–	–
2	**ANIMAL-POULTRY** FAT	A-F	99	–	–	–	–	–	–	–	–	–
		M-F	100	–	–	–	–	–	–	–	–	–
3	**BARLEY** *Hordeum vulgare* GRAIN, ALL ANALYSES	A-F	88	–	0.15	1036	0.57	76	7.9	5.80	1.6	4.5
		M-F	100	–	0.17	1171	0.64	86	9.0	6.55	1.8	5.0
4	GRAIN, PACIFIC COAST	A-F	89	–	0.15	976	0.50	47	7.1	2.89	1.5	4.2
		M-F	100	–	0.17	1102	0.56	53	8.0	3.26	1.7	4.7
5	MALT SPROUTS, DEHY	A-F	93	–	4.09	1591	0.20	55	9.0	8.62	2.8	8.3
		M-F	100	–	4.40	1713	0.22	59	9.6	9.28	3.0	8.9
6	**BEET, SUGAR** *Beta vulgaris, altissima* MOLASSES, MORE THAN 48% INVERT SUGAR, MORE THAN 79.5 DEGREES BRIX	A-F	78	–	–	827	–	41	4.5	–	2.3	–
		M-F	100	–	–	1062	–	53	5.8	–	2.9	–
7	PULP, DEHY	A-F	91	–	–	820	–	17	1.4	–	0.7	0.4
		M-F	100	–	–	902	–	18	1.5	–	0.8	0.4
8	PULP WITH MOLASSES, DEHY	A-F	92	–	–	814	–	16	1.5	–	0.7	–
		M-F	100	–	–	887	–	18	1.7	–	0.7	–
9	**BREWERS** GRAINS, DEHY	A-F	92	3.6	0.44	1651	0.22	44	8.2	1.03	1.5	0.6
		M-F	100	3.9	0.48	1792	0.24	47	8.9	1.11	1.6	0.7
10	**CARROT** *Daucus* spp ROOTS, FRESH	A-F	11	–	0.01	–	0.14	7	3.5	1.39	0.6	0.7
		M-F	100	–	0.07	–	1.21	58	30.1	12.05	4.9	5.8
11	**CITRUS** *Citrus* spp PULP WITHOUT FINES, DEHY (DRIED CITRUS PULP)	A-F	91	–	–	789	–	22	14.0	–	2.1	1.5
		M-F	100	–	–	867	–	24	15.4	–	2.3	1.6
12	SYRUP (MOLASSES)	A-F	67	–	–	–	–	27	17.2	–	6.2	–
		M-F	100	–	–	–	–	40	25.5	–	9.2	–
13	**CORN, DENT YELLOW** *Zea mays, indentata* GRAIN, ALL ANALYSES	A-F	88	–	0.07	504	0.31	23	5.1	6.16	1.1	3.7
		M-F	100	–	0.08	573	0.35	26	5.8	7.01	1.2	4.2
14	GRAIN, GRADE 2, 56 ib/bu (69.5 kg/hl)	A-F	87	–	0.06	569	0.35	24	3.9	6.88	1.3	3.5
		M-F	100	–	0.07	650	0.40	28	4.5	7.87	1.5	4.0
15	DISTILLERS GRAINS, DEHY	A-F	93	0.3	0.41	1113	1.00	38	11.3	4.22	5.0	1.8
		M-F	100	0.3	0.44	1191	1.07	41	12.1	4.51	5.3	1.9
16	DISTILLERS SOLUBLES, DEHY	A-F	93	4.2	1.49	4751	1.34	124	23.3	9.41	15.1	6.8
		M-F	100	4.5	1.61	5116	1.45	133	25.0	10.14	16.3	7.3
17	EARS, GROUND (CORN AND COB MEAL)	A-F	87	–	0.03	357	0.24	17	4.2	5.97	0.9	2.9
		M-F	100	–	0.04	412	0.28	20	4.8	6.89	1.0	3.3
18	GLUTEN, MEAL, 60% PROTEIN	A-F	90	–	–	–	–	–	–	6.39	–	–
		M-F	100	–	–	–	–	–	–	7.10	–	–
19	GLUTEN FEED	A-F	90	–	0.33	1514	0.27	70	13.6	13.93	2.2	2.0
		M-F	100	–	0.36	1684	0.30	78	15.1	15.49	2.5	2.2
20	GRITS (HOMINY GRITS)	A-F	90	–	0.13	1154	0.31	47	8.2	10.95	2.1	8.1
		M-F	100	–	0.15	1280	0.34	52	9.1	12.14	2.4	8.9
21	OIL	A-F	99	–	–	–	–	–	–	–	–	–
		M-F	100	–	–	–	–	–	–	–	–	–
22	**CORN, OPAQUE 2, HIGH LYSINE** *Zea mays* GRAIN	A-F	90	–	–	518	–	19	4.7	–	1.1	–
		M-F	100	–	–	575	–	22	5.2	–	1.2	–
23	**COTTON** *Gossypium* spp SEEDS	A-F	91	–	–	–	–	–	–	–	–	–
		M-F	100	–	–	–	–	–	–	–	–	–
24	**DISTILLERS PRODUCTS** (ALSO SEE CORN; SORGHUM; WHEAT) GRAINS, DEHY	A-F	93	–	–	2645	–	47	11.9	6.00	6.6	2.5
		M-F	100	–	–	2858	–	51	12.9	6.48	7.1	2.6
25	SOLUBLES, DEHY	A-F	92	2.9	2.84	4992	–	143	25.3	8.66	11.3	6.9
		M-F	100	3.1	3.09	5425	–	155	27.5	9.42	12.3	7.5
26	**FATS AND OILS** FAT, ANIMAL, HYDROLYZED	A-F	99	–	–	–	–	–	–	–	–	–
		M-F	100	–	–	–	–	–	–	–	–	–
27	**FAT, ANIMAL-POULTRY**	A-F	99	–	–	–	–	–	–	–	–	–
		M-F	100	–	–	–	–	–	–	–	–	–
28	**FLAX, COMMON** *Limum usitatissimum* SEEDS	A-F	96	–	–	–	–	–	–	–	–	–
		M-F	100	–	–	–	–	–	–	–	–	–
29	**HOMINY GRITS (CORN, DENT YELLOW, GRITS)** *Zea mays, indentata*	A-F	90	–	0.13	1154	0.31	47	8.2	10.95	2.1	8.1
		M-F	100	–	0.15	1280	0.34	52	9.1	12.14	2.4	8.9

ENERGY FEEDS FOR HORSES

Entry Number	Feed Name Description	International Feed Number	Moisture Basis: A-F (as-fed) or M-F (moisture-free)	Dry Matter %	Ash %	Crude Fiber %	Neutral Det. Fib. (NDF) %	Acid Det. Fib. (ADF) %	Lignin %	Ether Extract (Fat) %	N-Free Extract %	Crude Protein %	Digestible Protein %	TDN %	Digestible Energy Mcal lb	Digestible Energy Mcal kg	Metabolizable Energy Mcal lb	Metabolizable Energy Mcal kg
30	KAFIR SORGHUM *Sorghum bicolor, caffrorum* — GRAIN	4-04-428	A-F	89	1.5	2.0	–	1.8	–	2.8	72.0	10.8	7.7	70	1.26	2.77	1.03	2.27
			M-F	100	1.7	2.2	–	2.0	–	3.1	80.8	12.1	8.7	78	1.41	3.11	1.16	2.55
31	KELP (SEAWEED) *Laminariales* (order), *(Fucales* (order) — WHOLE, DEHY	1-08-073	A-F	91	35.0	6.5	–	–	–	0.5	42.4	6.5	3.4	–	–	–	–	–
			M-F	100	38.6	7.1	–	–	–	0.5	46.7	7.1	3.7	–	–	–	–	–
32	MILLET *Setaria* spp — GRAIN	4-03-098	A-F	90	2.7	5.8	–	–	–	4.0	65.2	12.1	8.7	61	1.11	2.46	0.91	2.01
			M-F	100	3.1	6.4	–	–	–	4.5	72.6	13.5	9.7	68	1.24	2.73	1.02	2.24
33	MILLET, FOXTAIL *Setaria italica* — GRAIN	4-03-102	A-F	89	3.4	7.4	–	–	–	4.1	63.0	11.4	8.2	57	1.04	2.30	0.86	1.89
			M-F	100	3.8	8.3	–	–	–	4.6	70.6	12.8	9.2	64	1.17	2.58	0.96	2.12
34	MILO SORGHUM *Sorghum bicolor, subglabrescens* — GRAIN	4-04-444	A-F	89	1.6	2.2	20.6	4.7	–	2.8	71.9	10.1	7.1	68	1.23	2.71	1.01	2.23
			M-F	100	1.8	2.5	23.2	5.3	–	3.1	81.2	11.4	8.1	77	1.39	3.06	1.14	2.51
	MOLASSES AND SYRUP																	
35	BEET, SUGAR, MOLASSES, MORE THAN 48% INVERT SUGAR, MORE THAN 79.5° BRIX	4-00-668	A-F	78	8.9	–	–	–	–	0.2	62.2	6.6	4.5	–	–	–	–	–
			M-F	100	11.4	–	–	–	–	0.2	79.9	8.5	5.8	–	–	–	–	–
36	CITRUS, SYRUP (CITRUS MOLASSES)	4-01-241	A-F	67	5.1	–	–	–	–	0.2	55.7	5.8	3.9	–	–	–	–	–
			M-F	100	7.6	–	–	–	–	0.3	82.7	8.5	5.8	–	–	–	–	–
37	SUGAR CANE, MOLASSES, DEHY	4-04-695	A-F	94	12.5	6.3	–	–	–	0.9	65.0	9.7	6.8	61	1.12	2.48	0.92	2.03
			M-F	100	13.3	6.7	–	–	–	0.9	68.8	10.3	7.2	65	1.19	2.62	0.98	2.15
38	SUGAR CANE, MOLASSES, MORE THAN 46% INVERT SUGAR, MORE THAN 79.5 DEGREES BRIX (BLACKSTRAP)	4-04-696	A-F	74	9.8	0.4	–	0.3	0.2	0.2	59.7	4.3	2.7	–	–	–	–	–
			M-F	100	13.2	0.5	–	0.4	0.3	0.2	80.2	5.8	3.7	–	–	–	–	–
	OATS *Avena sativa***																	
39	GRAIN, ALL ANALYSES	4-03-309	A-F	89	3.1	10.7	26.4	14.2	2.7	4.7	58.9	11.9	9.1	65	1.19	2.63	0.98	2.15
			M-F	100	3.4	11.9	29.6	15.9	3.0	5.2	66.1	13.3	10.2	73	1.34	2.94	1.10	2.41
40	CEREAL BY-PRODUCT (FEEDING OAT MEAL; OAT MIDDLINGS)	4-03-303	A-F	91	2.3	3.6	–	–	–	6.4	63.7	14.8	10.8	57	1.04	2.30	0.86	1.89
			M-F	100	2.5	4.0	–	–	–	7.0	70.2	16.3	11.9	62	1.15	2.54	0.95	2.08
41	GROATS	4-03-331	A-F	90	2.1	2.5	–	–	–	6.2	63.0	15.8	11.6	59	1.08	2.39	0.89	1.96
			M-F	100	2.4	2.8	–	–	–	6.9	70.3	17.6	13.0	66	1.21	2.66	0.99	2.18
	PEARL MILLET *Pennisetum glaucum*																	
42	GRAIN	4-03-118	A-F	90	2.2	3.7	–	–	–	4.3	67.2	13.0	9.4	64	1.16	2.57	0.96	2.11
			M-F	100	2.5	4.1	–	–	–	4.7	74.4	14.3	10.4	71	1.29	2.84	1.06	2.33
	PINEAPPLE *Ananas comosus*																	
43	CANNERY RESIDUE, DEHY (PINEAPPLE BRAN)[1]	4-03-722	A-F	87	3.0	18.2	63.5	32.2	–	1.3	60.5	4.0	2.4	50	0.93	2.04	0.76	1.67
			M-F	100	3.5	20.9	73.0	37.0	–	1.5	69.5	4.6	2.7	57	1.06	2.34	0.87	1.92
	RICE *Oryza sativa*																	
44	GRAIN, GROUND (GROUND ROUGH RICE; GROUND PADDY RICE)	4-03-938	A-F	89	5.3	8.6	–	–	–	1.6	65.9	7.5	5.1	59	1.09	2.39	0.89	1.96
			M-F	100	6.0	9.7	–	–	–	1.8	74.1	8.4	5.7	67	1.22	2.69	1.00	2.21
45	BRAN WITH GERM (RICE BRAN)	4-03-928	A-F	91	11.3	11.9	28.0	25.7	3.6	13.5	41.0	13.0	9.4	–	–	–	–	–
			M-F	100	12.5	13.1	30.9	28.4	4.0	14.9	45.2	14.3	10.4	–	–	–	–	–
	RYE *Secale cereale*																	
46	GRAIN, ALL ANALYSES	4-04-047	A-F	87	1.6	2.2	–	–	–	1.5	70.0	12.0	8.7	75	1.35	2.96	1.10	2.43
			M-F	100	1.9	2.5	–	–	–	1.7	80.1	13.8	9.9	86	1.54	3.39	1.26	2.78
	SAFFLOWER *Carthamus tinctorius*																	
47	SEEDS	4-07-958	A-F	93	3.0	23.6	–	37.2	–	30.8	20.9	14.9	10.9	–	–	–	–	–
			M-F	100	3.2	25.3	–	40.0	–	33.1	22.4	16.0	11.7	–	–	–	–	–
	SORGHUM *Sorghum bicolor*																	
48	GRAIN, ALL ANALYSES	4-04-383	A-F	90	1.8	2.6	16.2	8.1	1.2	2.7	71.6	11.5	8.2	71	1.28	2.82	1.05	2.31
			M-F	100	1.9	2.8	18.0	9.0	1.3	2.9	79.5	12.8	9.2	79	1.42	3.13	1.17	2.57
49	KAFIR, GRAIN	4-04-428	A-F	89	1.5	2.0	–	1.8	–	2.8	72.0	10.8	7.7	70	1.26	2.77	1.03	2.27
			M-F	100	1.7	2.2	–	2.0	–	3.1	80.8	12.1	8.7	78	1.41	3.11	1.16	2.55
50	MILO, GRAIN	4-04-444	A-F	89	1.6	2.2	20.6	4.7	–	2.8	71.9	10.1	7.1	68	1.23	2.71	1.01	2.23
			M-F	100	1.8	2.5	23.2	5.3	–	3.1	81.2	11.4	8.1	77	1.39	3.06	1.14	2.51
	SOYBEAN *Glycine max*																	
51	SEEDS[1]	5-04-610	A-F	92	5.1	5.4	–	10.1	–	17.2	25.9	38.4	34.9	–	–	–	–	–
			M-F	100	5.6	5.8	–	11.0	–	18.7	28.1	41.7	37.9	–	–	–	–	–
52	OIL	4-07-983	A-F	100	0.3	–	–	–	–	95.0	7.3	1.4	0.2	–	–	–	–	–
			M-F	100	0.3	–	–	–	–	95.5	7.3	1.4	0.2	–	–	–	–	–
	SUGARCANE *Saccharum officinarum*																	
53	MOLASSES, DEHY	4-04-695	A-F	94	12.5	6.3	–	–	–	0.9	65.0	9.7	6.8	61	1.12	2.48	0.92	2.03
			M-F	100	13.3	6.7	–	–	–	0.9	68.8	10.3	7.2	65	1.19	2.62	0.98	2.15
54	MOLASSES, MORE THAN 46% INVERT SUGAR, MORE THAN 79.5 DEGREES BRIX	4-04-696	A-F	74	9.8	0.4	–	0.3	0.2	0.2	59.7	4.3	2.7	–	–	–	–	–
			M-F	100	13.2	0.5	–	0.4	0.3	0.2	80.2	5.8	3.7	–	–	–	–	–
	SUNFLOWER *Helianthus* spp																	
55	SEEDS	5-08-530	A-F	94	3.7	22.7	–	–	–	32.3	14.4	20.9	14.9	–	–	–	–	–
			M-F	100	4.0	24.1	–	–	–	34.4	15.3	22.2	15.8	–	–	–	–	–

*The chemical composition and feeding value of oats are quite variable, due to the wide spread in hull content and weight per bushel.

(Continued)

E N E R G Y   F E E D S

TABLE A–4a ENERGY FEEDS FOR HORSES, COMPOSITION OF FEEDS, DATA EXPRESSED **AS-FED** AND **MOISTURE-FREE** (Continued)

Entry Number	Feed Name Description	Moisture Basis: A-F (as-fed) or M-F (moisture-free)	Dry Matter	Calcium (Ca)	Phos-phorus (P)	Sodium (Na)	Chlo-rine (Cl)	Mag-nesium (Mg)	Potas-sium (K)	Sulfur (S)	Cobalt (Co)	Copper (Cu)	Iodine (I)	Iron (Fe)	Man-ganese (Mn)	Sele-nium (Se)	Zinc (Zn)
			%	%	%	%	%	%	%	%	ppm or mg/kg	ppm or mg/kg	ppm or mg/kg	%	ppm or mg/kg	ppm or mg/kg	ppm or mg/kg
30	**KAFIR SORGHUM** *Sorghum bicolor, caffrorum* GRAIN	A-F	89	0.03	0.31	0.05	0.10	0.15	0.34	0.16	0.387	7.0	–	0.007	15.8	0.797	13.5
		M-F	100	0.04	0.35	0.06	0.11	0.17	0.38	0.18	0.435	7.8	–	0.008	17.8	0.894	15.2
31	**KELP (SEAWEED)** *Laminariales* (order), *Fucales* (order) WHOLE, DEHY	A-F	91	2.47	0.28	–	–	0.85	–	–	–	–	–	–	–	–	–
		M-F	100	2.72	0.31	–	–	0.93	–	–	–	–	–	–	–	–	–
32	**MILLET** *Setaria* spp GRAIN	A-F	90	0.05	0.29	0.04	0.14	0.16	0.43	0.13	0.044	21.8	–	0.007	29.9	–	13.9
		M-F	100	0.05	0.32	0.04	0.16	0.18	0.48	0.14	0.049	24.3	–	0.008	33.3	–	15.4
33	**MILLET, FOXTAIL** *Setaria italica* GRAIN	A-F	89	–	0.41	–	–	–	0.31	–	–	–	–	0.010	–	–	–
		M-F	100	–	0.46	–	–	–	0.35	–	–	–	–	0.011	–	–	–
34	**MILO SORGHUM** *Sorghum bicolor, subglabrescens* GRAIN	A-F	89	0.04	0.30	0.04	0.08	0.13	0.31	0.11	0.471	4.3	0.061	0.005	15.8	0.201	16.9
		M-F	100	0.05	0.34	0.04	0.09	0.14	0.35	0.12	0.531	4.9	0.069	0.006	17.9	0.227	19.1
35	**MOLASSES AND SYRUP** BEET, SUGAR, MOLASSES, MORE THAN 48% INVERT SUGAR, MORE THAN 79.5 ° BRIX	A-F	78	0.12	0.03	1.16	1.28	0.23	4.73	0.46	0.362	16.8	–	0.007	4.5	–	14.0
		M-F	100	0.16	0.03	1.48	1.64	0.29	6.07	0.60	0.465	21.6	–	0.009	5.8	–	18.0
36	CITRUS, SYRUP (CITRUS MOLASSES)	A-F	67	1.18	0.09	0.28	0.07	0.14	0.09	0.16	0.109	72.8	–	0.035	40.9	–	92.4
		M-F	100	1.76	0.13	0.41	0.11	0.21	0.14	0.23	0.162	108.0	–	0.051	60.7	–	137.1
37	SUGAR CANE, MOLASSES, DEHY	A-F	94	1.04	0.42	0.19	–	0.44	3.40	0.43	1.145	74.9	–	0.024	54.1	–	31.2
		M-F	100	1.10	0.45	0.20	–	0.47	3.60	0.46	1.213	79.4	–	0.025	57.3	–	33.0
38	SUGAR CANE, MOLASSES, MORE THAN 46% INVERT SUGAR, MORE THAN 79.5 DEGREES BRIX (BLACKSTRAP)	A-F	74	0.74	0.08	0.16	2.26	0.31	2.98	0.35	1.180	48.9	1.564	0.020	43.7	–	15.6
		M-F	100	1.00	0.11	0.22	3.04	0.42	4.01	0.47	1.587	65.7	2.103	0.027	58.8	–	20.9
39	**OATS** *Avena sativa** GRAIN, ALL ANALYSES	A-F	89	0.08	0.34	0.05	0.09	0.14	0.40	0.21	0.056	6.0	0.112	0.007	35.8	0.215	34.9
		M-F	100	0.09	0.38	0.06	0.10	0.16	0.45	0.23	0.063	6.7	0.125	0.008	40.1	0.241	39.2
40	CEREAL BY-PRODUCT (FEEDING OAT MEAL; OAT MIDDLINGS)	A-F	91	0.07	0.44	0.09	0.05	0.14	0.50	0.22	0.046	5.2	–	0.039	43.8	–	139.5
		M-F	100	0.08	0.48	0.10	0.06	0.16	0.55	0.24	0.051	5.7	–	0.043	48.3	–	153.8
41	GROATS	A-F	90	0.08	0.43	0.05	0.08	0.11	0.35	0.20	–	6.0	0.108	0.008	27.8	–	0.0
		M-F	100	0.08	0.48	0.06	0.09	0.13	0.39	0.22	–	6.7	0.120	0.009	31.0	–	0.1
42	**PEARL MILLET** *Pennisetum glaucum* GRAIN	A-F	90	0.05	0.31	0.04	0.14	0.16	0.43	0.13	0.045	22.1	–	0.006	31.0	–	13.3
		M-F	100	0.05	0.34	0.04	0.16	0.18	0.48	0.14	0.049	24.5	–	0.007	34.3	–	14.7
43	**PINEAPPLE** *Ananas comosus* CANNERY RESIDUE, DEHY (PINEAPPLE BRAN)	A-F	87	0.20	0.11	–	–	–	–	–	–	–	–	0.049	–	–	–
		M-F	100	0.23	0.13	–	–	–	–	–	–	–	–	0.057	–	–	–
44	**RICE** *Oryza sativa* GRAIN, GROUND (GROUND ROUGH RICE; GROUND PADDY RICE)	A-F	89	0.07	0.32	0.06	0.07	0.13	0.47	0.05	–	–	–	–	18.0	–	15.0
		M-F	100	0.07	0.36	0.07	0.08	0.14	0.53	0.05	–	–	–	–	20.2	–	16.9
45	BRAN WITH GERM (RICE BRAN)	A-F	91	0.07	1.44	0.03	0.07	0.85	1.69	0.18	1.383	11.0	–	0.019	337.6	–	37.4
		M-F	100	0.08	1.59	0.04	0.08	0.94	1.87	0.20	1.526	12.1	–	0.021	372.4	–	41.3
46	**RYE** *Secale cereale* GRAIN, ALL ANALYSES	A-F	87	0.06	0.31	0.02	0.03	0.12	0.46	0.15	–	7.5	–	0.007	72.0	–	28.1
		M-F	100	0.07	0.36	0.03	0.03	0.14	0.52	0.17	–	8.6	–	0.008	82.3	–	32.2
47	**SAFFLOWER** *Carthamus tinctorius* SEEDS	A-F	93	0.24	0.57	0.06	–	0.34	0.74	0.06	–	10.0	–	0.032	1.1	–	30.0
		M-F	100	0.26	0.61	0.06	–	0.36	0.79	0.06	–	10.7	–	0.035	1.2	–	32.2
48	**SORGHUM** *Sorghum bicolor* GRAIN, ALL ANALYSES	A-F	90	0.05	0.32	0.03	0.08	0.14	0.35	0.15	0.275	9.7	–	0.007	9.8	–	42.4
		M-F	100	0.06	0.35	0.03	0.09	0.16	0.38	0.17	0.305	10.8	–	0.007	10.9	–	47.1
49	KAFIR, GRAIN	A-F	89	0.03	0.31	0.05	0.10	0.15	0.34	0.16	0.387	7.0	–	0.007	15.8	0.797	13.5
		M-F	100	0.04	0.35	0.06	0.11	0.17	0.38	0.18	0.435	7.8	–	0.008	17.8	0.894	15.2
50	MILO, GRAIN	A-F	89	0.04	0.30	0.04	0.08	0.13	0.31	0.11	0.471	4.3	0.061	0.005	15.8	0.201	16.9
		M-F	100	0.05	0.34	0.04	0.09	0.14	0.35	0.12	0.531	4.9	0.069	0.006	17.9	0.227	19.1
51	**SOYBEAN** *Glycine max* SEEDS	A-F	92	0.25	0.60	0.00	0.03	0.27	1.66	0.22	–	18.2	–	0.009	36.4	0.111	56.9
		M-F	100	0.27	0.65	0.00	0.03	0.29	1.80	0.24	–	19.8	–	0.010	39.6	0.120	61.8
52	OIL	A-F	100	–	–	–	–	–	–	–	–	–	–	–	–	–	–
		M-F	100	–	–	–	–	–	–	–	–	–	–	–	–	–	–
53	**SUGARCANE** *Saccharum officinarum* MOLASSES, DEHY	A-F	94	1.04	0.42	0.19	–	0.44	3.40	0.43	1.145	74.9	–	0.024	54.1	–	31.2
		M-F	100	1.10	0.45	0.20	–	0.47	3.60	0.46	1.213	79.4	–	0.025	57.3	–	33.0
54	MOLASSES, MORE THAN 46% INVERT SUGAR, MORE THAN 79.5 DEGREES BRIX	A-F	74	0.74	0.08	0.16	2.26	0.31	2.98	0.35	1.180	48.9	1.564	0.020	43.7	–	15.6
		M-F	100	1.00	0.11	0.22	3.04	0.42	4.01	0.47	1.587	65.7	2.103	0.027	58.8	–	20.9
55	**SUNFLOWER** *Helianthus* spp SEEDS	A-F	94	0.16	0.67	0.02	–	0.37	0.68	0.28	–	23.5	–	0.006	21.9	–	68.6
		M-F	100	0.17	0.71	0.02	–	0.39	0.72	0.29	–	25.0	–	0.006	23.3	–	73.0

ENERGY FEEDS FOR HORSES

Entry Number	Fat-Soluble Vitamins					Water-Soluble Vitamins								
	A (1 mg Carotene = 1667 IU Vit A)	Carotene (Provitamin A)	D	E	K	B-12	Biotin	Choline	Folacin (Folic Acid)	Niacin	Pantothenic Acid (B-3)	Pyridoxine (B-6)	Riboflavin (B-2)	Thiamin (B-1)
	IU/g	ppm or mg/kg	IU/kg	ppm or mg/kg	ppm or mg/kg	ppb or mcg/kg	ppm or mg/kg	ppm or mg/kg	ppm or mg/kg	ppm or mg/kg	ppm or mg/kg	ppm or mg/kg	ppm or mg/kg	ppm or mg/kg
30	0.6	0.4	—	—	—	—	0.24	439	0.20	38	12.0	6.68	1.2	3.8
	0.7	0.4	—	—	—	—	0.27	493	0.22	43	13.4	7.50	1.4	4.3
31	—	—	—	—	—	—	—	—	—	—	—	—	—	—
	—	—	—	—	—	—	—	—	—	—	—	—	—	—
32	—	—	—	—	—	—	—	739	0.22	48	9.0	—	1.5	6.6
	—	—	—	—	—	—	—	822	0.25	54	10.1	—	1.6	7.3
33	—	—	—	—	—	—	—	—	—	33	—	—	1.1	3.8
	—	—	—	—	—	—	—	—	—	37	—	—	1.2	4.3
34	0.4	0.2	0	12.1	0.22	—	0.23	638	0.21	37	11.0	4.69	1.1	4.1
	0.5	0.3	0	13.7	0.25	—	0.26	720	0.23	42	12.4	5.29	1.3	4.7
35	—	—	—	4.0	—	—	—	827	—	41	4.5	—	2.3	—
	—	—	—	5.1	—	—	—	1062	—	53	5.8	—	2.9	—
36	—	—	—	—	—	—	—	—	—	27	17.2	—	6.2	—
	—	—	—	—	—	—	—	—	—	40	25.5	—	9.2	—
37	—	—	—	5.2	—	—	—	—	—	—	—	—	—	—
	—	—	—	5.5	—	—	—	—	—	—	—	—	—	—
38	—	—	—	5.4	—	—	0.69	764	0.11	36	37.4	4.21	2.8	0.9
	—	—	—	7.3	—	—	0.92	1027	0.15	49	50.3	5.67	3.8	1.2
39	0.2	0.1	—	14.9	—	—	0.27	967	0.39	14	9.9	2.53	1.4	6.0
	0.2	0.1	—	16.8	—	—	0.30	1084	0.44	16	11.1	2.84	1.5	6.8
40	—	—	—	23.7	—	—	0.22	1157	0.46	24	17.6	—	1.7	7.0
	—	—	—	26.1	—	—	0.24	1277	0.51	26	19.4	—	1.9	7.7
41	—	—	—	14.8	—	—	—	1132	0.51	10	13.8	1.00	1.2	6.5
	—	—	—	16.5	—	—	—	1264	0.57	11	15.4	1.12	1.3	7.2
42	4.3	2.6	—	—	—	—	—	790	—	52	8.8	—	1.8	7.1
	4.8	2.9	—	—	—	—	—	874	—	57	9.7	—	2.0	7.9
43	78.4	47.0	—	—	—	—	—	—	—	—	—	—	—	—
	90.0	54.0	—	—	—	—	—	—	—	—	—	—	—	—
44	—	—	—	14.0	—	—	—	926	0.25	40	7.1	—	0.7	—
	—	—	—	15.7	—	—	—	1041	0.28	45	8.0	—	0.8	—
45	—	—	—	60.4	—	—	0.43	1230	2.20	299	22.8	13.24	2.6	22.4
	—	—	—	66.7	—	—	0.47	1357	2.42	330	25.2	14.61	2.8	24.8
46	0.1	0.1	—	14.5	—	—	0.06	419	0.62	14	7.5	—	1.7	4.1
	0.2	0.1	—	16.6	—	—	0.06	479	0.71	16	8.5	—	1.9	4.7
47	—	—	—	—	—	—	—	—	—	—	—	—	—	—
	—	—	—	—	—	—	—	—	—	—	—	—	—	—
48	2.0	1.2	—	—	—	—	0.26	686	0.22	47	10.2	5.41	1.2	4.5
	2.2	1.3	—	—	—	—	0.29	762	0.24	52	11.3	6.00	1.4	5.0
49	0.6	0.4	—	—	—	—	0.24	439	0.20	38	12.0	6.68	1.2	3.8
	0.7	0.4	—	—	—	—	0.27	493	0.22	43	13.4	7.50	1.4	4.3
50	0.4	0.2	0	12.1	0.22	—	0.23	638	0.21	37	11.0	4.69	1.1	4.1
	0.5	0.3	0	13.7	0.25	—	0.26	720	0.23	42	12.4	5.29	1.3	4.7
51	1.5	0.9	—	33.7	—	—	0.38	2931	—	23	16.0	11.04	2.9	11.3
	1.6	1.0	—	36.6	—	—	0.42	3184	—	24	17.4	12.00	3.2	12.2
52	—	—	—	—	—	—	—	—	—	—	—	—	—	—
	—	—	—	—	—	—	—	—	—	—	—	—	—	—
53	—	—	—	5.2	—	—	—	—	—	—	—	—	—	—
	—	—	—	5.5	—	—	—	—	—	—	—	—	—	—
54	—	—	—	5.4	—	—	0.69	764	0.11	36	37.4	4.21	2.8	0.9
	—	—	—	7.3	—	—	0.92	1027	0.15	49	50.3	5.67	3.8	1.2
55	—	—	—	—	—	—	—	—	—	—	—	—	3.3	0.4
	—	—	—	—	—	—	—	—	—	—	—	—	3.5	0.5

(Continued)

TABLE A–4a ENERGY FEEDS FOR HORSES, COMPOSITION OF FEEDS, DATA EXPRESSED **AS-FED** AND **MOISTURE-FREE** *(Continued)*

Entry Number	Feed Name Description	International Feed Number	Moisture Basis: A-F (as-fed) or M-F (moisture-free)	Proximate Analysis: Dry Matter	Ash	Crude Fiber	Neutral Det. Fib. (NDF)	Acid Det. Fib. (ADF)	Lignin	Ether Extract (Fat)	N-Free Exract	Crude Protein	Digestible Protein	TDN	Digestible Energy		Metabolizable Energy	
				%	%	%	%	%	%	%	%	%	%	%	Mcal lb	Mcal kg	Mcal lb	Mcal kg
	WHEAT *Tritricum aestivum*																	
56	GRAIN, ALL ANALYSES[1]	**4-05-211**	**A-F**	**89**	**1.8**	**2.6**	**–**	**7.1**	**–**	**1.8**	**69.7**	**13.1**	**9.5**	**76**	**1.36**	***2.99***	**1.11**	***2.45***
			M-F	100	2.0	2.9	–	8.0	–	2.0	78.4	14.7	10.7	85	1.53	*3.36*	1.25	*2.76*
57	BRAN	**4-05-190**	**A-F**	**89**	**5.9**	**10.0**	**40.9**	**12.0**	**2.6**	**4.0**	**53.6**	**15.5**	**13.1**	**44**	**0.84**	***1.84***	**0.69**	***1.51***
			M-F	100	6.7	11.2	45.9	13.5	3.0	4.5	60.2	17.5	14.7	50	0.94	*2.07*	0.77	*1.70*
58	MIDDLINGS, LESS THAN 9.5% FIBER[1]	**4-05-205**	**A-F**	**89**	**4.7**	**7.7**	**32.9**	**8.9**	**–**	**4.3**	**55.7**	**16.4**	**12.1**	**59**	**1.08**	***2.39***	**0.89**	***1.96***
			M-F	100	5.3	8.7	37.0	10.0	–	4.9	62.7	18.5	13.7	66	1.22	*2.69*	1.00	*2.20*
59	MILL RUN, LESS THAN 9.5% FIBER	**4-05-206**	**A-F**	**90**	**5.1**	**8.2**	**–**	**9.9**	**–**	**4.1**	**57.4**	**15.1**	**11.0**	**58**	**1.07**	***2.35***	**0.88**	***1.93***
			M-F	100	5.7	9.1	–	11.0	–	4.6	63.9	16.7	12.3	65	1.19	*2.62*	0.97	*2.15*

[1]Neutral Detergent Fiber (NDF) and Acid Detergent Fiber (ADF) values taken from *Nutrient Requirements of Dairy Cattle*, 6th rev. ed., NRC, National Academy Press, 1988, pp. 90–110, Table 7–1.

TABLE A–4b PROTEIN FEEDS FOR HORSES, COMPOSITION OF FEEDS, DATA EXPRESSED **AS-FED** AND **MOISTURE-FREE** (See footnote at end of table.)

Entry Number	Feed Name Description	International Feed Number	Moisture Basis: A-F (as-fed) or M-F (moisture-free)	Proximate Analysis: Dry Matter	Ash	Crude Fiber	Neutral Det. Fib. (NDF)	Acid Det. Fib. (ADF)	Lignin	Ether Extract (Fat)	N-Free Exract	Crude Protein	Digestible Protein	TDN	Digestible Energy		Metabolizable Energy	
				%	%	%	%	%	%	%	%	%	%	%	Mcal lb	Mcal kg	Mcal lb	Mcal kg
	BARLEY *Hordeum vulgare*																	
1	MALT SPROUTS, DEHY[1]	**5-00-545**	**A-F**	**93**	**5.6**	**14.2**	**43.7**	**16.7**	**–**	**1.4**	**48.8**	**22.9**	**17.2**	**–**	**–**	**–**	**–**	**–**
			M-F	100	6.1	15.3	47.0	18.0	–	1.5	52.6	24.6	18.6	–	–	–	–	–
	BLOOD																	
2	MEAL	**5-00-380**	**A-F**	**91**	**5.3**	**1.0**	**–**	**–**	**–**	**1.3**	**3.1**	**80.5**	**82.5**	**–**	**–**	**–**	**–**	**–**
			M-F	100	5.8	1.1	–	–	–	1.5	3.4	88.2	90.4	–	–	–	–	–
	BREWERS																	
3	GRAINS, DEHY	**5-02-141**	**A-F**	**92**	**3.6**	**13.0**	**38.7**	**23.9**	**4.6**	**6.6**	**41.6**	**27.3**	**21.0**	**48**	**–**	**–**	**–**	**–**
			M-F	100	4.0	14.1	42.0	26.0	5.0	7.1	45.2	29.6	22.8	52	–	–	–	–
	COCONUT *Cocos nucifera*																	
4	KERNELS WITH COATS, MEAL MECH EXTD (COPRA MEAL)	**5-01-572**	**A-F**	**92**	**6.4**	**12.1**	**–**	**18.3**	**–**	**6.8**	**45.0**	**21.2**	**15.4**	**–**	**–**	**–**	**–**	**–**
			M-F	100	7.0	13.2	–	20.0	–	7.4	49.2	23.1	16.9	–	–	–	–	–
	CORN *Zea mays*																	
5	DISTILLERS GRAINS, DEHY	**5-02-842**	**A-F**	**93**	**2.2**	**11.5**	**–**	**–**	**–**	**8.9**	**43.1**	**27.8**	**22.7**	**–**	**–**	**–**	**–**	**–**
			M-F	100	2.4	12.3	–	–	–	9.5	46.2	29.7	24.3	–	–	–	–	–
6	DISTILLERS SOLUBLES, DEHY	**5-02-844**	**A-F**	**93**	**7.2**	**4.6**	**–**	**–**	**–**	**8.6**	**45.2**	**27.4**	**22.3**	**–**	**–**	**–**	**–**	**–**
			M-F	100	7.7	4.9	–	–	–	9.3	48.6	29.5	24.1	–	–	–	–	–
7	GERM MEAL, WET MILLED, SOLV EXTD	**5-02-898**	**A-F**	**92**	**3.9**	**12.2**	**–**	**–**	**–**	**1.5**	**53.5**	**20.7**	**14.9**	**–**	**–**	**–**	**–**	**–**
			M-F	100	4.2	13.3	–	–	–	1.6	58.3	22.6	16.2	–	–	–	–	–
8	GLUTEN FEED	**5-02-903**	**A-F**	**90**	**6.6**	**8.7**	**–**	**–**	**–**	**2.1**	**49.4**	**23.0**	**17.7**	**–**	**–**	**–**	**–**	**–**
			M-F	100	7.4	9.7	–	–	–	2.4	55.0	25.6	19.6	–	–	–	–	–
9	GLUTEN MEAL[1]	**5-02-900**	**A-F**	**91**	**3.1**	**4.5**	**33.7**	**8.2**	**–**	**2.2**	**38.4**	**43.2**	**40.3**	**–**	**–**	**–**	**–**	**–**
			M-F	100	3.4	4.9	37.0	9.0	–	2.4	42.0	47.3	44.1	–	–	–	–	–
	COTTON *Gossypium* spp																	
10	SEEDS WITHOUT LINT	**5-13-749**	**A-F**	**91**	**4.7**	**19.4**	**–**	**–**	**–**	**20.4**	**24.5**	**21.8**	**16.2**	**–**	**–**	**–**	**–**	**–**
			M-F	100	5.2	21.4	–	–	–	22.5	27.0	24.0	17.9	–	–	–	–	–
11	SEEDS, MEAL MECH EXTD, 41% PROTEIN	**5-01-617**	**A-F**	**93**	**6.1**	**11.9**	**25.9**	**18.5**	**5.6**	**4.7**	**28.9**	**41.0**	**37.7**	**–**	**–**	**–**	**–**	**–**
			M-F	100	6.6	12.9	28.0	20.0	6.0	5.0	31.2	44.3	40.8	–	–	–	–	–
12	SEEDS, MEAL SOLV EXTD, 41% PROTEIN	**5-01-621**	**A-F**	**91**	**6.5**	**12.1**	**23.6**	**18.4**	**5.5**	**1.5**	**29.6**	**41.2**	**38.2**					
			M-F	100	7.1	13.4	26.0	20.2	6.0	1.6	32.5	45.4	42.0	–	–	–	–	–
13	SEEDS, MEAL SOLV EXTD, 46% PROTEIN[1]	**5-26-100**	**A-F**	**92**	**7.2**	**8.9**	**25.8**	**19.3**	**–**	**1.6**	**26.8**	**47.6**	**45.2**	**–**	**–**	**–**	**–**	**–**
			M-F	100	7.8	9.6	28.0	21.0	–	1.8	29.1	51.7	49.1	–	–	–	–	–
14	SEEDS, MEAL SOLV EXTD, 48% PROTEIN	**5-26-101**	**A-F**	**90**	**7.4**	**7.0**	**–**	**–**	**–**	**1.9**	**24.7**	**49.3**	**47.4**	**–**	**–**	**–**	**–**	**–**
			M-F	100	8.2	7.7	–	–	–	2.1	27.4	54.7	52.5	–	–	–	–	–
15	SEEDS WITHOUT HULLS, MEAL, PREPRESSED, SOLV EXTD, 50% PROTEIN	**5-07-874**	**A-F**	**93**	**6.6**	**8.2**	**–**	**–**	**–**	**1.3**	**26.8**	**50.3**	**48.2**	**–**	**–**	**–**	**–**	**–**
			M-F	100	7.1	8.8	–	–	–	1.4	28.8	54.0	51.8	–	–	–	–	–
	COTTON, GLANDLESS *Gossypium* spp																	
16	SEEDS, MEAL SOLV EXTD	**5-08-979**	**A-F**	**95**	**7.3**	**2.5**	**–**	**–**	**–**	**1.9**	**23.8**	**59.8**	**58.7**	**–**	**–**	**–**	**–**	**–**
			M-F	100	7.6	2.7	–	–	–	2.0	25.0	62.7	61.6	–	–	–	–	–
	DISTILLERS PRODUCTS (ALSO SEE CORN; RYE; SORGHUM; WHEAT)																	
17	GRAINS, DEHY	**5-02-144**	**A-F**	**93**	**1.5**	**12.8**	**–**	**–**	**–**	**7.4**	**43.5**	**27.3**	**22.3**	**–**	**–**	**–**	**–**	**–**
			M-F	100	1.6	13.8	–	–	–	8.0	47.0	29.5	24.1	–	–	–	–	–

ENERGY FEEDS FOR HORSES

Entry Number	Calcium (Ca) %	Phosphorus (P) %	Sodium (Na) %	Chlorine (Cl) %	Magnesium (Mg) %	Potassium (K) %	Sulfur (S) %	Cobalt (Co) ppm or mg/kg	Copper (Cu) ppm or mg/kg	Iodine (I) ppm or mg/kg	Iron (Fe) %	Manganese (Mn) ppm or mg/kg	Selenium (Se) ppm or mg/kg	Zinc (Zn) ppm or mg/kg	A (1 mg Carotene = 1667 IU Vit A) IU/g	Carotene (Provitamin A) ppm or mg/kg	D IU/kg	E ppm or mg/kg	K ppm or mg/kg
56	0.05	0.35	0.06	0.08	0.14	0.41	0.18	0.442	5.8	0.090	0.006	41.5	0.256	31.4	—	—	—	15.5	—
	0.06	0.39	0.06	0.09	0.15	0.15	0.20	0.497	6.5	0.101	0.006	46.7	0.288	35.2	—	—	—	17.4	—
57	0.13	1.16	0.06	0.05	0.58	1.23	0.22	0.075	11.0	0.066	0.015	114.9	0.641	94.6	4.4	2.6	—	14.3	—
	0.14	1.30	0.06	0.06	0.65	1.38	0.25	—	12.4	0.074	0.017	129.0	0.719	106.2	4.9	2.9	—	16.0	—
58	0.13	0.89	0.01	0.04	0.34	0.98	0.17	0.502	15.9	0.109	0.009	114.0	0.736	96.9	5.1	3.1	—	23.8	—
	0.15	1.00	0.01	0.04	0.38	1.10	0.19	0.565	17.9	0.123	0.011	128.3	0.828	109.1	5.8	3.5	—	26.9	—
59	0.10	1.02	—	—	0.48	1.20	0.30	0.209	18.5	—	0.010	104.1	—	—	—	—	—	31.9	—
	0.11	1.13	—	—	0.53	1.34	0.34	0.232	20.6	—	0.011	115.8	—	—	—	—	—	35.5	—

PROTEIN FEEDS FOR HORSES

Entry Number	Calcium (Ca) %	Phosphorus (P) %	Sodium (Na) %	Chlorine (Cl) %	Magnesium (Mg) %	Potassium (K) %	Sulfur (S) %	Cobalt (Co) ppm or mg/kg	Copper (Cu) ppm or mg/kg	Iodine (I) ppm or mg/kg	Iron (Fe) %	Manganese (Mn) ppm or mg/kg	Selenium (Se) ppm or mg/kg	Zinc (Zn) ppm or mg/kg	A (1 mg Carotene = 1667 IU Vit A) IU/g	Carotene (Provitamin A) ppm or mg/kg	D IU/kg	E ppm or mg/kg	K ppm or mg/kg
1	0.18	0.63	0.88	0.36	0.17	0.25	0.79	—	5.9	—	0.018	29.4	0.416	56.4	—	—	—	3.7	—
	0.19	0.68	0.95	0.39	0.18	0.27	0.85	—	6.3	—	0.020	31.7	0.448	60.7	—	—	—	4.0	—
2	0.29	0.25	0.32	0.30	0.22	0.09	0.34	0.088	12.6	—	0.372	5.3	0.731	4.4	—	—	—	—	—
	0.32	0.28	0.35	0.33	0.24	0.10	0.37	0.097	13.8	—	0.407	5.8	0.801	4.8	—	—	—	—	—
3	0.30	0.51	0.21	0.15	0.15	0.09	0.30	0.076	21.7	0.066	0.024	37.2	—	27.3	0.8	0.5	—	26.7	—
	0.33	0.55	0.23	0.17	0.17	0.09	0.32	0.083	23.6	0.072	0.026	40.4	—	29.6	0.8	0.5	—	29.0	—
4	0.19	0.60	0.04	—	0.30	1.65	0.34	0.127	16.7	—	0.068	70.1	—	48.5	—	—	—	—	—
	0.21	0.65	0.04	—	0.33	1.80	0.37	0.139	18.2	—	0.075	76.6	—	53.0	—	—	—	—	—
5	0.09	0.39	0.09	0.07	0.07	0.16	0.43	0.076	38.9	0.048	0.020	19.3	0.352	41.7	5.2	3.1	—	—	—
	0.10	0.42	0.09	0.08	0.07	0.18	0.46	0.082	41.7	0.051	0.021	20.7	0.377	44.7	5.6	3.3	—	—	—
6	0.30	1.30	0.23	0.26	0.60	1.70	0.37	0.167	77.9	0.079	0.052	72.0	0.371	88.0	1.1	0.7	—	45.9	—
	0.32	1.40	0.24	0.28	0.65	1.83	0.40	0.180	83.9	0.085	0.056	77.6	0.400	94.8	1.2	0.7	—	49.4	—
7	0.04	0.51	0.04	0.04	0.16	0.35	0.31	—	4.5	—	0.034	3.8	0.340	104.8	3.4	2.0	—	85.8	—
	0.04	0.55	0.04	0.04	0.17	0.38	0.34	—	4.9	—	0.037	4.1	0.370	114.2	3.7	2.2	—	93.5	—
8	0.32	0.74	0.12	0.22	0.33	0.57	0.21	0.087	47.1	0.066	0.043	23.1	0.272	64.6	9.8	5.9	—	12.1	—
	0.36	0.82	0.14	0.25	0.36	0.64	0.23	0.097	52.3	0.074	0.048	25.7	0.302	71.8	10.9	6.5	—	13.5	—
9	0.15	0.46	0.09	0.06	0.06	0.03	0.20	0.077	27.7	—	0.039	7.7	1.015	173.7	27.3	16.3	—	29.3	—
	0.16	0.51	0.10	0.07	0.06	0.03	0.22	0.085	30.3	—	0.043	8.5	1.111	190.2	29.8	17.9	—	32.0	—
10	0.14	0.69	0.03	—	0.32	1.11	0.24	—	49.0	—	0.014	11.1	—	—	—	—	—	—	—
	0.16	0.76	0.03	—	0.35	1.22	0.26	—	53.9	—	0.016	12.2	—	—	—	—	—	—	—
11	0.19	1.07	0.04	0.04	0.53	1.33	0.40	0.626	18.5	—	0.018	22.3	—	61.8	0.4	0.2	—	32.3	—
	0.21	1.16	0.05	0.05	0.57	1.44	0.43	0.676	20.0	—	0.019	24.1	—	66.8	0.4	0.2	—	34.9	—
12	0.17	1.11	0.04	0.04	0.54	1.37	0.25	0.483	19.5	—	0.019	20.6	—	60.7	—	—	—	14.6	—
	0.19	1.22	0.05	0.05	0.59	1.51	0.27	0.531	21.4	—	0.021	22.7	—	66.7	—	—	—	16.1	—
13	—	—	—	—	—	—	—	—	—	—	—	—	—	—	—	—	—	—	—
	—	—	—	—	—	—	—	—	—	—	—	—	—	—	—	—	—	—	—
14	0.20	1.20	—	—	—	—	—	—	—	—	—	—	—	—	—	—	—	—	—
	0.22	1.33	—	—	—	—	—	—	—	—	—	—	—	—	—	—	—	—	—
15	0.18	1.16	0.05	0.05	0.46	1.45	0.52	0.042	14.5	—	0.012	23.0	—	73.8	—	—	—	11.3	—
	0.19	1.24	0.06	0.05	0.50	1.56	0.56	0.046	15.6	—	0.012	24.8	—	79.4	—	—	—	12.1	—
16	—	—	—	—	—	—	—	—	—	—	—	—	—	—	—	—	—	—	—
	—	—	—	—	—	—	—	—	—	—	—	—	—	—	—	—	—	—	—
17	0.12	0.54	0.05	0.05	0.09	0.20	0.46	0.092	47.9	—	0.027	35.0	—	—	13.0	7.8	—	30.5	—
	0.13	0.59	0.05	0.06	0.10	0.21	0.49	0.099	51.7	—	0.029	37.8	—	—	14.0	8.4	—	32.9	—

ENERGY FEEDS

PROTEIN FEEDS

(Continued)

TABLE A–4a ENERGY FEEDS FOR HORSES, COMPOSITION OF FEEDS, DATA EXPRESSED **AS-FED** AND **MOISTURE-FREE** (Continued)

Entry Number	Feed Name Description	Moisture Basis: A-F (as-fed) or M-F (moisture-free)	Dry Matter	Water-Soluble Vitamins								
				B-12	Biotin	Choline	Folacin (Folic Acid)	Niacin	Pantothenic Acid (B-3)	Pyri-doxine (B-6)	Ribo-flavin (B-2)	Thiamin (B-1)
			%	ppb or mcg/kg	ppm or mg/kg	ppm or mg/kg	ppm or mg/kg	ppm or mg/kg	ppm or mg/kg	ppm or mg/kg	ppm or mg/kg	ppm or mg/kg
56	**WHEAT** *Triticum aestivum* GRAIN, ALL ANALYSES	A-F	89	0.9	0.10	918	0.43	59	11.3	3.74	1.3	4.3
		M-F	100	1.0	0.11	1032	0.49	66	12.7	4.20	1.4	4.8
57	BRAN	A-F	89	–	0.38	1232	1.77	197	28.0	10.34	3.6	8.4
		M-F	100	–	0.42	1383	1.98	221	31.4	11.61	4.0	9.4
58	MIDDLINGS, LESS THAN 9.5% FIBER	A-F	89	–	0.24	1246	1.24	95	17.8	9.14	2.0	14.2
		M-F	100	–	0.27	1403	1.39	107	20.0	10.29	2.3	15.9
59	MILL RUN, LESS THAN 9.5% FIBER	A-F	90	–	0.31	1005	1.08	116	13.7	11.09	2.1	15.2
		M-F	100	–	0.34	1118	1.20	129	15.2	12.33	2.4	17.0

TABLE A–4b PROTEIN FEEDS FOR HORSES, COMPOSITION OF FEEDS, DATA EXPRESSED **AS-FED** AND **MOISTURE-FREE** (Continued)

Entry Number	Feed Name Description	Moisture Basis: A-F (as-fed) or M-F (moisture-free)	Dry Matter	Water-Soluble Vitamins								
				B-12	Biotin	Choline	Folacin (Folic Acid)	Niacin	Pantothenic Acid (B-3)	Pyri-doxine (B-6)	Ribo-flavin (B-2)	Thiamin (B-1)
			%	ppm or mg/kg	ppm or mg/kg	ppm or mg/kg	ppm or mg/kg	ppm or mg/kg	ppm or mg/kg	ppm or mg/kg	ppm or mg/kg	ppm or mg/kg
1	**BARLEY** *Orbignya* spp MALT SPROUTS, DEHY	A-F	93	–	4.09	1591	0.20	55	9.0	8.62	2.8	8.3
		M-F	100	–	4.40	1713	0.22	59	9.6	9.28	3.0	8.9
2	**BLOOD** MEAL	A-F	91	44.3	0.09	780	0.10	31	2.3	4.41	2.0	0.3
		M-F	100	48.5	0.09	854	0.11	34	2.6	4.83	2.2	0.4
3	**BREWERS** GRAINS, DEHY	A-F	92	3.6	0.44	1651	0.22	44	8.2	1.03	1.5	0.6
		M-F	100	3.9	0.48	1792	0.24	47	8.9	1.11	1.6	0.7
4	**COCONUT** *Cocus nucifera* KERNELS WITH COATS, MEAL MECH EXTD (COPRA MEAL)	A-F	92	–	–	1046	1.08	27	6.1	–	3.3	0.8
		M-F	100	–	–	1143	1.18	30	6.6	–	3.6	0.9
5	**CORN** *Zea mays* DISTILLERS GRAINS, DEHY	A-F	93	0.3	0.41	1113	1.00	38	11.3	4.22	5.0	1.8
		M-F	100	0.3	0.44	1191	1.07	41	12.1	4.51	5.3	1.9
6	DISTILLERS SOLUBLES, DEHY	A-F	93	4.2	1.49	4751	1.34	124	23.3	9.41	15.1	6.8
		M-F	100	4.5	1.61	5116	1.45	133	25.0	10.14	16.3	7.3
7	GERM MEAL, WET MILLED, SOLV EXTD	A-F	92	–	0.22	1586	0.20	39	4.2	–	3.8	4.5
		M-F	100	–	0.24	1728	0.22	42	4.6	–	4.1	4.9
8	GLUTEN FEED	A-F	90	–	0.33	1514	0.27	70	13.6	13.93	2.2	2.0
		M-F	100	–	0.36	1684	0.30	78	15.1	15.49	2.5	2.2
9	GLUTEN MEAL	A-F	91	–	0.19	360	0.30	50	10.0	7.98	1.5	0.2
		M-F	100	–	0.21	394	0.33	55	10.9	8.73	1.6	0.2
10	**COTTON** *Gossypium* spp SEEDS WITHOUT LINT	A-F	91	–	–	–	–	–	–	–	–	–
		M-F	100	–	–	–	–	–	–	–	–	–
11	SEEDS, MEAL MECH EXTD, 41% PROTEIN	A-F	93	–	0.91	2753	2.45	35	10.2	5.00	5.2	7.1
		M-F	100	–	0.99	2974	2.65	38	11.0	5.41	5.6	7.6
12	SEEDS, MEAL SOLV EXTD, 41% PROTEIN	A-F	91	–	0.55	2780	2.55	41	13.7	5.41	4.7	7.3
		M-F	100	–	0.61	3058	2.81	45	15.1	5.95	5.2	8.0
13	SEEDS, MEAL SOLV EXTD, 46% PROTEIN	A-F	92	–	–	–	–	–	–	–	–	–
		M-F	100	–	–	–	–	–	–	–	–	–
14	SEEDS, MEL SOLV EXTD, 48% PROTEIN	A-F	90	–	–	3316	–	51	15.5	–	6.0	–
		M-F	100	–	–	3674	–	56	17.1	–	6.6	–
15	SEEDS WITHOUT HULLS, MEAL, PREPRESSED, SOLV EXTD, 50% PROTEIN	A-F	93	–	0.44	2962	0.93	45	14.3	6.29	4.9	8.2
		M-F	100	–	0.48	3184	1.00	48	15.4	6.76	5.3	8.8
16	**COTTON, GLANDLESS** *Gossypium* spp SEEDS, MEAL SOLV EXTD	A-F	95	–	–	–	–	–	–	–	–	–
		M-F	100	–	–	–	–	–	–	–	–	–
17	**DISTILLERS PRODUCTS** (ALSO SEE CORN; RYE; SORGHUM; WHEAT) GRAINS, DEHY	A-F	93	–	–	2645	–	47	11.9	6.00	6.6	2.5
		M-F	100	–	–	2858	–	51	12.9	6.48	7.1	2.6

PROTEIN FEEDS FOR HORSES

Entry Number	Feed Name Description	Inter-national Feed Number	Moisture Basis: A-F (as-fed) or M-F (moisture-free)	Proximate Analysis									Digestible Protein	TDN	Digestible Energy (Mcal)		Metabolizable Energy (Mcal)	
				Dry Matter	Ash	Crude Fiber	Neutral Det. Fib. (NDF)	Acid Det. Fib. (ADF)	Lignin	Ether Extract (Fat)	N-Free Exract	Crude Protein			lb	kg	lb	kg
				%	%	%	%	%	%	%	%	%	%	%				
18	**DISTILLERS PRODUCTS** (Continued) SOLUBLES, DEHY	5-02-147	A-F	92	6.2	3.4	—	—	—	8.9	44.8	28.8	24.0	—	—	—	—	—
			M-F	100	6.7	3.7	—	—	—	9.7	48.6	31.3	26.1	—	—	—	—	—
19	**FISH, ANCHOVY** *Engraulis ringen* MEAL MECH EXTD	5-01-985	A-F	92	14.7	1.0	—	—	—	4.1	6.7	65.4	65.4	—	—	—	—	—
			M-F	100	16.0	1.1	—	—	—	4.5	7.3	71.1	71.1	—	—	—	—	—
20	**FISH, MENHADEN** *Brevoortia tyrannus* MEAL MECH EXTD	5-02-009	A-F	92	19.1	0.9	—	—	—	9.6	0.8	61.2	60.7	—	—	—	—	—
			M-F	100	20.9	1.0	—	—	—	10.5	0.8	66.8	66.2	—	—	—	—	—
21	**FLAX, COMMON** *Linum usitatissimum* SEEDS, MEAL SOLV EXTD, 35% PROTEIN (LINSEED MEAL)	5-26-090	A-F	90	5.8	8.9	—	—	—	1.7	38.2	35.7	32.0	—	—	—	—	—
			M-F	100	6.4	9.9	—	—	—	1.9	42.3	39.6	35.4	—	—	—	—	—
	LINSEED—SEE FLAX																	
	MILK																	
22	FRESH (CATTLE *Bos taurus*)	5-01-168	A-F	12	0.8	—	—	—	—	3.6	4.7	3.3	2.6	—	—	—	—	—
			M-F	100	6.2	—	—	—	—	29.5	37.6	26.7	20.9	—	—	—	—	—
23	SKIMMED, FRESH (CATTLE *Bos taurus*)	5-01-170	A-F	10	0.7	—	—	—	—	0.1	5.8	3.0	2.5	—	—	—	—	—
			M-F	100	6.9	—	—	—	—	1.0	60.6	31.2	26.0	—	—	—	—	—
24	SKIMMED, DEHY (CATTLE *Bos taurus*)	5-01-175	A-F	94	8.0	0.2	0.0	—	—	1.1	51.6	33.3	28.9	—	—	—	—	—
			M-F	100	8.4	0.2	0.0	—	—	1.2	54.8	35.4	30.7	—	—	—	—	—
25	**MOLASSES AND SYRUP** *Saccharum officinarum* SUGARCANE, MOLASSES, AMMONIATED	5-04-702	A-F	65	5.9	—	—	—	—	—	—	26.3	23.7	—	—	—	—	—
			M-F	100	9.1	—	—	—	—	—	—	40.5	36.5	—	—	—	—	—
26	**PEANUT** *Arachis hypogaea* SEEDS WITHOUT HULLS, MEAL MECH EXTD (PEANUT MEAL)	5-03-649	A-F	93	5.0	6.2	13.2	5.6	1.0	5.6	26.7	49.2	47.0	—	—	—	—	—
			M-F	100	5.4	6.7	14.2	6.1	1.1	6.0	28.8	53.1	50.7	—	—	—	—	—
27	**RAPE** (CANOLA) *Brassica napus* SEEDS, MEAL SOLV EXTD, 34% PROTEIN	5-26-092	A-F	90	7.0	13.0	—	—	—	2.5	33.5	34.0	—	—	—	—	—	—
			M-F	100	7.8	14.4	—	—	—	2.8	37.2	37.8	—	—	—	—	—	—
28	**SAFFLOWER** *Carthamus tinctorius* SEEDS, MEAL SOLV EXTD, 20% PROTEIN	5-26-095	A-F	92	4.6	32.2	—	39.6	—	1.1	32.7	21.6	15.8	—	—	—	—	—
			M-F	100	5.0	34.9	—	43.0	—	1.2	35.5	23.4	17.2	—	—	—	—	—
29	SEEDS WITHOUT HULLS, MEAL SOLV EXTD, 42% PROTEIN	5-26-094	A-F	92	6.5	14.6	—	19.2	—	1.3	26.3	42.7	39.8	—	—	—	—	—
			M-F	100	7.2	16.0	—	21.0	—	1.5	28.8	46.7	43.5	—	—	—	—	—
30	**SESAME** *Sesamum indicum* SEEDS, MEAL SOLV EXTD, 44% PROTEIN	5-26-096	A-F	92	13.1	6.8	—	—	—	1.4	25.8	45.0	42.3	—	—	—	—	—
			M-F	100	14.2	7.4	—	—	—	1.5	28.0	48.9	46.0	—	—	—	—	—
31	**SORGHUM** *Sorghum bicolor* DISTILLERS GRAINS, DEHY	5-04-374	A-F	94	4.3	12.1	—	—	—	8.3	38.3	30.8	26.1	—	—	—	—	—
			M-F	100	4.6	12.9	—	—	—	8.8	40.8	32.9	27.9	—	—	—	—	—
32	GLUTEN MEAL	5-04-388	A-F	90	1.7	4.9	—	—	—	4.4	34.9	44.4	41.8	—	—	—	—	—
			M-F	100	1.9	5.4	—	—	—	4.8	38.7	49.2	46.3	—	—	—	—	—
33	**SOYBEAN** *Glycine max* SEEDS[1]	5-04-610	A-F	92	5.1	5.4	—	9.2	—	17.2	25.9	38.4	34.9	—	—	—	—	—
			M-F	100	5.6	5.8	—	10.0	—	18.7	28.1	41.7	37.9	—	—	—	—	—
34	SEEDS, MEAL SOLV EXTD, 44% PROTEIN	5-20-637	A-F	89	6.4	6.2	12.5	8.9	—	1.5	30.6	44.4	41.9	—	—	—	—	—
			M-F	100	7.2	6.9	14.0	10.0	—	1.7	34.3	49.9	47.1	—	—	—	—	—
35	SEEDS WITHOUT HULLS, MEAL SOLV EXTD, 49% PROTEIN	5-20-638	A-F	90	6.1	3.7	6.6	6.2	—	1.2	29.8	49.0	47.1	—	—	—	—	—
			M-F	100	6.8	4.1	7.4	6.9	—	1.4	33.2	54.6	52.4	—	—	—	—	—
36	**SUNFLOWER, COMMON** *Helianthus annuus* SEEDS WITHOUT HULLS, MEAL SOLV EXTD, 44% PROTEIN	5-26-098	A-F	93	7.7	11.0	—	—	—	2.9	24.6	46.8	—	—	—	—	—	—
			M-F	100	8.3	11.8	—	—	—	3.1	26.5	50.3	—	—	—	—	—	—
37	**WHEAT** *Triticum aestivum* DISTILLERS GRAINS, DEHY	5-05-193	A-F	93	3.0	11.8	—	—	—	6.7	40.2	31.6	27.1	—	—	—	—	—
			M-F	100	3.3	12.6	—	—	—	7.2	43.0	33.9	29.0	—	—	—	—	—
38	DISTILLERS SOLUBLES, DEHY	5-05-195	A-F	94	6.8	3.4	—	—	—	2.2	50.5	31.1	—	—	—	—	—	—
			M-F	100	7.2	3.6	—	—	—	2.3	53.7	33.1	—	—	—	—	—	—
39	GERM MEAL	5-05-218	A-F	88	4.3	3.1	—	4.4	—	8.5	48.1	24.4	19.4	—	—	—	—	—
			M-F	100	4.9	3.5	—	5.0	—	9.6	54.4	27.6	21.9	—	—	—	—	—
40	GLUTEN	5-05-221	A-F	91	0.9	0.4	—	—	—	0.8	9.8	79.0	80.9	—	—	—	—	—
			M-F	100	1.0	0.4	—	—	—	0.9	10.8	86.9	88.9	—	—	—	—	—
41	**WHEY, CATTLE** *Bos taurus* DEHY	4-01-182	A-F	93	8.8	0.2	0.3	0.2	—	0.8	70.2	13.3	9.6	—	—	—	—	—
			M-F	100	9.4	0.2	0.3	0.2	—	0.8	75.3	14.2	10.3	—	—	—	—	—
42	**YEAST, BREWERS** *Saccharomyces cerevisiae* DEHY	7-05-527	A-F	93	6.5	3.0	—	3.7	—	0.9	38.8	43.8	—	—	—	—	—	—
			M-F	100	7.0	3.2	—	4.0	—	1.0	41.7	47.1	—	—	—	—	—	—

PROTEIN FEEDS

TABLE A–4b PROTEIN FEEDS FOR HORSES, COMPOSITION OF FEEDS, DATA EXPRESSED **AS-FED** AND **MOISTURE-FREE** *(Continued)*

Entry Number	Feed Name Description	Moisture Basis: A-F (as-fed) or M-F (moisture-free)	Dry Matter	Macrominerals							Microminerals						
				Calcium (Ca)	Phosphorus (P)	Sodium (Na)	Chlorine (Cl)	Magnesium (Mg)	Potassium (K)	Sulfur (S)	Cobalt (Co)	Copper (Cu)	Iodine (I)	Iron (Fe)	Manganese (Mn)	Selenium (Se)	Zinc (Zn)
			%	%	%	%	%	%	%	%	ppm or mg/kg	ppm or mg/kg	ppm or mg/kg	%	ppm or mg/kg	ppm or mg/kg	ppm or mg/kg
	DISTILLERS PRODUCTS (Continued)																
18	SOLUBLES, DEHY	A-F	92	0.24	1.35	0.45	–	0.53	1.97	–	0.196	71.6	–	0.031	64.1	–	138.0
		M-F	100	0.26	1.47	0.49	–	0.58	2.14	–	0.213	77.9	–	0.034	69.7	–	150.0
	FISH, ANCHOVY *Engraulis ringen*																
19	MEAL MECH EXTD	A-F	92	3.74	2.48	0.88	1.00	0.25	0.72	0.78	0.173	9.1	3.137	0.022	11.0	1.355	105.0
		M-F	100	4.07	2.70	0.95	1.08	0.27	0.78	0.84	0.188	9.9	3.411	0.024	11.9	1.473	114.2
	FISH, MENHADEN *Brevoortia tyrannus*																
20	MEAL MECH EXTD	A-F	92	5.19	2.88	0.41	0.55	0.15	0.70	0.56	0.153	10.3	1.091	0.055	37.0	2.147	144.2
		M-F	100	5.67	3.14	0.45	0.60	0.17	0.77	0.61	0.167	11.3	1.191	0.060	40.4	2.344	157.5
	FLAX, COMMON *Linum usitatissimum*																
21	SEEDS, MEAL SOLV EXTD, 35% PROTEIN (LINSEED MEAL)	A-F	90	0.40	0.82	0.14	–	0.60	1.37	0.39	–	–	–	–	–	–	–
		M-F	100	0.44	0.91	0.15	–	0.66	1.52	0.43	–	–	–	–	–	–	–
	LINSEED–SEE FLAX																
	MILK																
22	FRESH (CATTLE *Bos taurus*)	A-F	12	0.12	0.09	0.05	0.11	0.01	0.14	0.04	0.001	0.1	–	0.002	–	–	2.3
		M-F	100	0.93	0.75	0.38	0.92	0.10	1.13	0.32	0.005	0.8	–	0.010	–	–	23.0
23	SKIMMED, FRESH (CATTLE *Bos taurus*)	A-F	10	0.13	0.10	0.04	0.05	0.01	0.12	0.03	0.011	1.1	–	0.001	0.2	–	4.9
		M-F	100	1.31	1.04	0.47	0.54	0.12	1.29	0.32	0.111	11.6	–	0.009	2.3	–	51.0
24	SKIMMED, DEHY (CATTLE *Bos taurus*)	A-F	94	1.28	1.02	0.51	0.90	0.12	1.60	0.32	0.113	11.7	–	0.001	2.1	0.124	38.5
		M-F	100	1.36	1.09	0.54	0.96	0.13	1.70	0.34	0.120	12.4	–	0.001	2.3	0.131	40.9
	MOLASSES AND SYRUP *Saccharum officinarum*																
25	SUGARCANE, MOLASSES, AMMONIATED	A-F	65	0.79	0.13	–	–	–	–	–	–	–	–	–	–	–	–
		M-F	100	1.22	0.20	–	–	–	–	–	–	–	–	–	–	–	–
	PEANUT *Arachis hypogaea*																
26	SEEDS WITHOUT HULLS, MEAL MECH EXTD (PEANUT MEAL)	A-F	93	0.20	0.56	0.12	0.03	0.26	1.16	0.22	0.111	15.4	0.067	0.030	25.5	–	33.0
		M-F	100	0.22	0.61	0.13	0.03	0.28	1.25	0.24	0.119	16.6	0.072	0.033	27.6	–	35.6
	RAPE (CANOLA) *Brassica napus*																
27	SEEDS, MEAL SOLV EXTD, 34% PROTEIN	A-F	90	–	–	–	–	–	–	–	–	–	–	–	–	–	–
		M-F	100	–	–	–	–	–	–	–	–	–	–	–	–	–	–
	SAFFLOWER *Carthamus tinctorius*																
28	SEEDS, MEAL SOLV EXTD, 20% PROTEIN	A-F	92	0.31	0.61	–	–	0.32	0.74	0.20	–	9.6	–	0.043	17.7	–	39.6
		M-F	100	0.34	0.66	–	–	0.35	0.80	0.22	–	10.4	–	0.046	19.2	–	43.0
29	SEEDS WITHOUT HULLS, MEAL SOLV EXTD, 42% PROTEIN	A-F	92	0.38	1.08	–	–	1.18	1.18	0.34	1.832	80.6	–	0.091	36.6	–	168.5
		M-F	100	0.41	1.18	–	–	1.29	1.29	0.38	2.000	88.0	–	0.100	40.0	–	184.0
	SESAME *Sesamum indicum*																
30	SEEDS, MEAL SOLV EXTD, 44% PROTEIN	A-F	92	2.01	1.28	–	–	–	–	–	–	–	–	–	47.5	–	–
		M-F	100	2.18	1.39	–	–	–	–	–	–	–	–	–	51.6	–	–
	SORGHUM *Sorghum bicolor*																
31	DISTILLERS GRAINS, DEHY	A-F	94	0.15	0.69	0.05	–	0.18	0.36	0.17	–	–	–	0.005	–	–	–
		M-F	100	0.16	0.74	0.05	–	0.19	0.38	0.18	–	–	–	0.005	–	–	–
32	GLUTEN MEAL	A-F	90	0.03	0.27	–	–	0.16	0.48	–	–	–	–	–	15.6	–	–
		M-F	100	0.04	0.30	–	–	0.17	0.53	–	–	–	–	–	17.3	–	–
	SOYBEAN *Glycine max*																
33	SEEDS	A-F	92	0.25	0.60	0.00	0.03	0.27	1.66	0.22	–	18.2	–	0.009	36.4	0.111	56.9
		M-F	100	0.27	0.65	0.00	0.03	0.29	1.80	0.24	–	19.6	–	0.010	39.6	0.120	61.8
34	SEEDS, MEAL SOLV EXTD, 44% PROTEIN	A-F	89	0.35	0.64	0.03	–	0.27	1.98	0.41	1.381	19.9	–	0.017	31.6	0.486	50.5
		M-F	100	0.40	0.71	0.04	–	0.31	2.22	0.47	1.550	22.3	–	0.019	35.5	0.546	56.6
35	SEEDS WITHOUT HULLS, MEAL SOLV EXTD, 49% PROTEIN	A-F	90	0.25	0.63	0.00	0.07	0.37	1.79	0.41	2.693	13.5	0.152	0.010	49.5	–	51.1
		M-F	100	0.28	0.70	0.00	0.08	0.41	1.99	0.46	3.000	15.0	0.169	0.011	55.2	–	56.9
	SUNFLOWER, COMMON *Helianthus annuus*																
36	SEEDS WITHOUT HULLS, MEAL SOLV EXTD, 44% PROTEIN	A-F	93	–	–	–	–	–	–	–	–	–	–	–	–	–	–
		M-F	100	–	–	–	–	–	–	–	–	–	–	–	–	–	–
	WHEAT *Triticum aestivum*																
37	DISTILLERS GRAINS, DEHY	A-F	93	0.11	0.58	–	–	–	–	–	–	–	–	–	15.0	–	–
		M-F	100	0.12	0.63	–	–	–	–	–	–	–	–	–	16.1	–	–
38	DISTILLERS SOLUBLES, DEHY	A-F	94	–	–	–	–	–	–	–	–	–	–	–	–	–	–
		M-F	100	–	–	–	–	–	–	–	–	–	–	–	–	–	–
39	GERM MEAL	A-F	88	0.06	0.95	0.02	0.06	0.25	0.94	0.27	0.120	9.2	–	0.006	132.5	0.463	119.4
		M-F	100	0.06	1.07	0.03	0.07	0.28	1.06	0.30	0.136	10.4	–	0.007	149.9	0.524	135.1
40	GLUTEN	A-F	90	0.06	0.23	0.06	–	0.04	0.02	0.95	0.049	11.6	0.058	0.006	18.1	3.753	38.5
		M-F	100	0.07	0.25	0.07	–	0.04	0.02	1.06	0.054	12.8	0.064	0.007	20.1	4.158	42.6
	WHEY, CATTLE *Bos taurus*																
41	DEHY	A-F	93	0.86	0.76	0.62	0.07	0.13	1.11	1.04	0.111	46.5	–	0.017	5.9	–	3.2
		M-F	100	0.92	0.82	0.66	0.08	0.14	1.19	1.11	0.119	49.9	–	0.019	6.3	–	3.4
	YEAST, BREWERS *Saccharomyces cerevisiae*																
42	DEHY	A-F	93	0.14	1.36	0.07	0.07	0.24	1.69	0.43	0.506	38.4	0.358	0.009	6.7	0.911	39.0
		M-F	100	0.15	1.47	0.08	0.08	0.26	1.82	0.46	0.544	41.3	0.384	0.009	7.2	0.979	41.9

PROTEIN FEEDS

PROTEIN FEEDS FOR HORSES

	Fat-Soluble Vitamins					Water-Soluble Vitamins								
Entry Number	A (1 mg Carotene = 1667 IU Vit A)	Carotene (Provitamin A)	D	E	K	B-12	Biotin	Choline	Folacin (Folic Acid)	Niacin	Pantothenic Acid (B-3)	Pyridoxine (B-6)	Riboflavin (B-2)	Thiamin (B-1)
	IU/g	ppm or mg/kg	IU/kg	ppm or mg/kg	ppm or mg/kg	ppm or mg/kg	ppm or mg/kg	ppm or mg/kg	ppm or mg/kg	ppm or mg/kg	ppm or mg/kg	ppm or mg/kg	ppm or mg/kg	ppm or mg/kg
18	1.9	1.1	–	–	–	2.9	2.84	4992	–	143	25.3	8.66	11.3	6.9
	2.0	1.2	–	–	–	3.1	3.09	5425	–	155	27.5	9.42	12.3	7.5
19	–	–	–	3.7	–	214.5	0.20	3700	0.16	81	10.0	4.71	7.3	0.5
	–	–	–	4.0	–	233.2	0.21	4023	0.17	88	10.9	5.12	8.0	0.6
20	–	–	–	6.8	–	122.0	0.18	3112	0.15	55	8.6	3.80	4.8	0.6
	–	–	–	7.4	–	133.2	0.20	3398	0.17	60	9.4	4.15	5.3	0.6
21	–	–	–	5.9	–	–	–	1216	2.85	30	–	9.93	2.9	9.4
	–	–	–	6.5	–	–	–	1346	3.15	33	–	10.99	3.2	10.4
22	–	–	–	–	–	–	–	904	–	1	8.4	–	1.7	0.3
	–	–	–	–	–	–	–	7311	–	10	68.0	–	13.8	2.4
23	–	–	–	–	–	–	–	–	–	1	3.5	–	2.0	0.4
	–	–	–	–	–	–	–	–	–	12	36.9	–	20.8	4.6
24	–	–	0	9.1	–	50.9	0.33	1394	0.62	11	36.4	4.10	19.1	3.7
	–	–	0	9.6	–	54.1	0.35	1480	0.66	12	38.6	4.35	20.3	3.9
25	–	–	–	–	–	–	–	–	–	–	–	–	–	–
	–	–	–	–	–	–	–	–	–	–	–	–	–	–
26	–	–	–	2.4	–	–	0.33	1975	0.66	173	47.6	6.12	9.1	5.7
	–	–	–	2.6	–	–	0.36	2132	0.71	186	51.4	6.61	9.8	6.2
27	–	–	–	–	–	–	–	–	–	–	–	–	–	–
	–	–	–	–	–	–	–	–	–	–	–	–	–	–
28	–	–	–	0.9	–	–	–	1541	–	12	36.2	474.43	2.2	–
	–	–	–	1.0	–	–	–	1673	–	13	39.3	515.00	2.4	–
29	–	–	–	0.6	–	–	1.56	3156	1.47	21	38.2	10.71	2.3	4.2
	–	–	–	0.7	–	–	1.70	3447	1.60	23	41.7	11.70	2.5	4.6
30	–	–	–	–	–	–	–	1517	–	–	6.3	–	3.7	–
	–	–	–	–	–	–	–	1649	–	–	6.8	–	4.0	–
31	–	–	–	–	–	–	0.31	805	–	–	–	–	–	–
	–	–	–	–	–	–	0.33	858	–	–	–	–	–	–
32	–	–	–	–	–	–	–	680	–	37	9.3	–	1.5	–
	–	–	–	–	–	–	–	754	–	41	10.4	–	1.7	–
33	1.5	0.9	–	33.7	–	–	0.38	2931	–	23	16.0	11.04	2.9	11.3
	1.6	1.0	–	36.6	–	–	0.42	3184	–	24	17.4	12.00	3.2	12.2
34	–	–	–	3.0	0.22	2.0	0.36	2706	0.69	26	13.8	5.90	3.0	6.6
	–	–	–	3.4	0.25	2.2	0.41	3036	0.77	29	15.5	6.62	3.4	7.4
35	–	–	0	3.3	–	2.0	0.38	2772	0.59	24	14.1	5.59	2.9	3.5
	–	–	0	3.7	–	2.2	0.42	3089	0.66	27	15.7	6.23	3.3	3.9
36	–	–	–	–	–	–	–	–	–	–	–	–	–	–
	–	–	–	–	–	–	–	–	–	–	–	–	–	–
37	1.8	1.1	–	–	–	–	–	–	–	56	8.2	–	3.7	2.0
	2.0	1.2	–	–	–	–	–	–	–	60	8.7	–	4.0	2.1
38	–	–	–	–	–	–	–	–	–	–	–	–	–	–
	–	–	–	–	–	–	–	–	–	–	–	–	–	–
39	–	–	–	141.2	–	–	0.22	3062	2.12	68	18.6	9.97	6.0	23.1
	–	–	–	159.7	–	–	0.24	3465	2.40	77	21.0	11.28	6.8	26.2
40	–	–	0	34.1	–	73.1	0.00	577	0.74	74	5.8	2.26	0.7	0.9
	–	–	0	37.7	–	81.0	0.00	640	0.82	82	6.4	2.51	0.7	1.0
41	–	–	–	0.2	–	18.9	0.35	1790	0.85	11	46.2	3.21	27.4	4.0
	–	–	–	0.2	–	20.3	0.38	1921	0.91	11	49.6	3.45	29.4	4.3
42	–	–	–	2.1	–	1.1	1.04	3847	9.69	443	81.5	36.67	34.1	85.2
	–	–	–	2.3	–	1.1	1.12	4134	10.41	476	87.6	39.40	36.6	91.6

PROTEIN FEEDS

TABLE A–4c DRY FORAGES FOR HORSES, COMPOSITION OF FEEDS, DATA EXPRESSED **AS-FED** AND **MOISTURE-FREE** (See footnote at end of table.)

Entry Number	Feed Name Description	International Feed Number	Moisture Basis: A-F (as-fed) or M-F (moisture-free)	Dry Matter %	Ash %	Crude Fiber %	Neutral Det. Fib. (NDF) %	Acid Det. Fib. (ADF) %	Lignin %	Ether Extract (Fat) %	N-Free Exract %	Crude Protein %	Digestible Protein %	TDN %	Digestible Energy Mcal lb	Digestible Energy Mcal kg	Metabolizable Energy Mcal lb	Metabolizable Energy Mcal kg
	ALFALFA (LUCERNE) *Medicago sativa*																	
1	HAY, SUN-CURED, ALL ANALYSES	1-00-078	A-F	90	8.6	28.2	35.4	30.9	8.9	1.7	35.9	16.0	11.9	48	0.90	1.98	0.74	1.62
			M-F	100	9.5	31.2	39.2	34.2	9.8	1.9	39.7	17.7	13.2	53	0.99	2.19	0.81	1.79
2	HAY, PREBLOOM, SUN-CURED	1-00-054	A-F	90	8.3	20.7	38.3	29.6	5.5	4.1	36.4	20.2	14.0	48	0.90	1.98	0.74	1.63
			M-F	100	9.2	23.1	42.7	33.0	6.1	4.5	40.6	22.5	15.6	54	1.00	2.21	0.82	1.82
3	HAY, EARLY BLOOM, SUN-CURED	1-00-059	A-F	91	8.4	25.8	36.8	29.0	5.8	2.6	35.8	17.9	12.2	48	0.90	1.99	0.74	1.63
			M-F	100	9.2	28.5	40.7	32.0	6.4	2.9	39.6	19.8	13.5	53	1.00	2.19	0.82	1.80
4	HAY, MIDBLOOM, SUN-CURED	1-00-063	A-F	91	7.8	25.5	43.2	33.4	6.7	3.3	37.4	17.1	11.6	46	0.86	1.90	0.71	1.56
			M-F	100	8.6	28.0	47.4	36.7	7.4	3.6	41.1	18.8	12.7	50	0.95	2.09	0.78	1.71
5	HAY, FULL BLOOM, SUN-CURED	1-00-068	A-F	91	7.1	27.3	45.0	35.2	6.9	3.1	37.9	15.5	10.3	44	0.83	1.83	0.68	1.50
			M-F	100	7.8	30.1	49.5	38.7	7.6	3.4	41.7	17.0	11.3	48	0.91	2.01	0.75	1.65
6	HAY, MATURE, SUN-CURED	1-00-071	A-F	91	6.7	29.3	50.1	40.1	11.3	2.9	37.0	15.2	10.1	43	0.82	1.81	0.67	1.48
			M-F	100	7.4	32.1	55.0	44.0	12.4	3.2	40.6	16.7	11.1	47	0.90	1.98	0.74	1.63
7	HAY, RAINED ON, SUN-CURED	1-00-130	A-F	89	6.6	33.5	–	–	–	0.8	30.4	17.9	12.2	50	0.94	2.07	0.77	1.70
			M-F	100	7.4	37.6	–	–	–	0.9	34.1	20.0	13.6	56	1.05	2.32	0.86	1.90
8	MEAL, DEHY, 17% PROTEIN	1-00-023	A-F	92	9.7	24.0	41.3	31.5	9.7	2.8	37.8	17.4	11.8	47	0.89	1.96	0.73	1.61
			M-F	100	10.6	26.2	45.0	34.3	10.6	3.0	41.2	18.9	12.8	51	0.97	2.14	0.80	1.75
9	MEAL, DEHY, 20% PROTEIN [1]	1-00-024	A-F	92	10.2	20.8	38.6	28.5	–	3.3	37.1	20.2	14.0	50	0.94	2.08	0.77	1.70
			M-F	100	11.1	22.7	42.0	31.0	–	3.6	40.5	22.1	15.2	55	1.03	2.27	0.84	1.86
10	MEAL, DEHY, 22% PROTEIN [1]	1-07-851	A-F	93	10.2	18.3	36.3	26.0	–	4.1	38.1	22.2	15.5	52	0.98	2.15	0.80	1.76
			M-F	100	11.0	19.8	39.0	28.0	–	4.4	41.0	23.9	16.6	56	1.05	2.32	0.86	1.90
	ALFALFA-BROMEGRASS, SMOOTH *Medicago sativa-Bromus inermis*																	
11	HAY, SUN-CURED	1-00-255	A-F	91	6.1	31.0	–	–	–	2.1	37.7	14.1	9.2	45	0.85	1.88	0.70	1.54
			M-F	100	6.7	34.1	–	–	–	2.3	41.5	15.5	10.2	49	0.94	2.06	0.77	1.69
	ALFALFA-GRASS *Medicago sativa-grass*																	
12	HAY, SUN-CURED	1-08-331	A-F	91	6.7	30.3	–	36.6	–	2.1	37.8	14.5	9.5	45	0.86	1.89	0.70	1.55
			M-F	100	7.4	33.2	–	40.0	–	2.3	41.3	15.9	10.4	50	0.94	2.07	0.77	1.70
	ALFALFA-ORCHARDGRASS *Medicago sativa-Dactylis glomerata*																	
13	HAY, SUN-CURED	1-00-322	A-F	89	7.3	28.7	–	–	–	1.9	36.8	14.8	9.8	47	0.88	1.93	0.72	1.58
			M-F	100	8.1	32.0	–	–	–	2.2	41.2	16.5	11.0	52	0.98	2.16	0.80	1.77
	BARLEY *Hordeum vulgare*																	
14	HAY, SUN-CURED	1-00-495	A-F	88	6.6	23.6	–	–	–	1.9	48.5	7.8	4.4	42	0.81	1.77	0.66	1.46
			M-F	100	7.5	26.7	–	–	–	2.1	54.9	8.8	5.0	48	0.91	2.01	0.75	1.65
15	STRAW	1-00-498	A-F	91	6.7	37.9	77.5	51.1	6.9	1.7	41.1	4.0	1.4	28	0.57	1.26	0.47	1.03
			M-F	100	7.3	41.5	84.8	55.9	7.6	1.9	44.9	4.4	1.6	31	0.63	1.38	0.51	1.13
	BERMUDAGRASS *Cynodon dactylon*																	
16	HAY, SUN-CURED	1-00-703	A-F	91	8.0	28.4	–	–	–	1.8	43.7	9.2	5.4	40	0.77	1.70	0.63	1.40
			M-F	100	8.8	31.2	–	–	–	2.0	48.0	10.0	6.0	44	0.85	1.87	0.70	1.53
	BERMUDAGRASS, COASTAL *Cynodon dactylon*																	
17	HAY, SUN-CURED [1]	1-00-716	A-F	91	6.3	27.0	69.2	34.6	–	2.0	43.9	11.7	7.4	46	0.86	1.90	0.71	1.56
			M-F	100	6.9	29.7	76.0	38.0	–	2.2	48.3	12.8	8.1	50	0.95	2.10	0.78	1.72
	BIRDSFOOT TREFOIL *Lotus corniculatus*																	
18	HAY, SUN-CURED	1-05-044	A-F	91	6.7	29.3	–	–	–	1.9	38.9	13.9	9.1	46	0.87	1.91	0.71	1.56
			M-F	100	7.4	32.3	–	–	–	2.1	42.9	15.3	10.0	51	0.96	2.11	0.78	1.73
	BLUEGRASS, CANADA *Poa compressa*																	
19	HAY, SUN-CURED	1-00-762	A-F	92	6.5	27.6	–	–	–	2.4	45.8	9.5	5.7	41	0.79	1.75	0.65	1.43
			M-F	100	7.0	30.1	–	–	–	2.6	49.9	10.3	6.2	45	0.86	1.90	0.71	1.56
	BLUEGRASS, KENTUCKY *Poa pratensis*																	
20	HAY, SUN-CURED	1-00-776	A-F	89	5.9	26.8	–	–	–	3.0	44.3	9.1	5.4	37	0.73	1.60	0.60	1.31
			M-F	100	6.6	30.0	–	–	–	3.4	49.7	10.2	6.1	42	0.81	1.80	0.67	1.47
	BROMEGRASS *Bromus* spp																	
21	HAY, SUN-CURED	1-00-890	A-F	91	7.1	29.8	–	31.7	4.3	1.9	43.3	8.7	5.1	39	0.75	1.65	0.61	1.35
			M-F	100	7.8	32.9	–	34.9	4.7	2.1	47.7	9.5	5.6	43	0.83	1.82	0.68	1.49
	CANADA BLUEGRASS–SEE BLUEGRASS, CANADA																	
	CLOVER, ALSIKE *Trifolium hybridum*																	
22	HAY, SUN-CURED	1-01-313	A-F	88	7.6	26.2	–	–	–	2.4	39.1	12.4	8.0	41	0.78	1.72	0.64	1.41
			M-F	100	8.7	29.9	–	–	–	2.8	44.5	14.2	9.1	46	0.89	1.96	0.73	1.60
	CLOVER, ALYCE *Alysicarpus vaginalis*																	
23	HAY, SUN-CURED	1-00-361	A-F	90	5.7	36.2	–	–	–	1.6	35.3	10.9	6.8	38	0.74	1.63	0.61	1.34
			M-F	100	6.4	40.3	–	–	–	1.7	39.3	12.2	7.6	43	0.83	1.82	0.68	1.49
	CLOVER, LADINO *Trifolium repens*																	
24	HAY, SUN-CURED	1-01-378	A-F	89	8.4	18.5	32.1	28.5	5.9	2.4	39.9	20.0	13.8	57	1.05	2.31	0.86	1.89
			M-F	100	9.4	20.8	36.0	32.0	6.6	2.7	44.7	22.4	15.5	64	1.17	2.59	0.96	2.12
	CLOVER, RED *Trifolium pratense*																	
25	HAY, SUN-CURED, ALL ANALYSES	1-01-415	A-F	88	6.7	27.1	49.5	36.2	8.8	2.5	39.2	13.0	8.4	42	0.81	1.78	0.66	1.46
			M-F	100	7.5	30.7	56.0	41.0	10.0	2.8	44.3	14.7	9.5	48	0.91	2.01	0.75	1.65
	CLOVER, RED-GRASS *Trifolium pratense-grass*																	
26	HAY, FULL BLOOM, SUN-CURED	1-01-532	A-F	89	5.9	29.9	–	–	–	1.6	37.4	14.0	9.2	47	0.88	1.93	0.72	1.59
			M-F	100	6.6	33.7	–	–	–	1.8	42.2	15.8	10.4	53	0.99	2.18	0.81	1.79

DRY FORAGES FOR HORSES

Entry Number	Macrominerals							Microminerals							Fat-Soluble Vitamins				
	Calcium (Ca)	Phosphorus (P)	Sodium (Na)	Chlorine (Cl)	Magnesium (Mg)	Potassium (K)	Sulfur (S)	Cobalt (Co)	Copper (Cu)	Iodine (I)	Iron (Fe)	Manganese (Mn)	Selenium (Se)	Zinc (Zn)	A (1 mg Carotene = 1667 IU Vit A)	Carotene (Provitamin A)	D	E	K
	%	%	%	%	%	%	%	ppm or mg/kg	ppm or mg/kg	ppm or mg/kg	%	ppm or mg/kg	ppm or mg/kg	ppm or mg/kg	IU/g	ppm or mg/kg	IU/kg	ppm or mg/kg	ppm or mg/kg
1	1.28	0.24	0.07	0.33	0.30	1.85	0.25	0.250	10.0	–	0.019	41.4	–	21.9	45.0	27.0	2	55.9	–
	1.42	0.26	0.08	0.37	0.33	2.05	0.28	0.277	11.0	–	0.020	45.8	–	24.3	49.8	29.9	2	61.9	–
2	1.34	0.30	0.10	0.31	0.19	2.25	0.48	0.256	10.2	–	0.021	42.2	–	33.5	300.2	180.1	–	–	–
	1.50	0.33	0.12	0.34	0.21	2.51	0.54	0.285	11.4	–	0.024	47.1	–	37.4	335.1	201.0	–	–	–
3	1.48	0.20	0.14	0.34	0.31	2.32	0.27	0.264	11.4	–	0.021	32.8	0.497	27.3	210.9	126.5	2	23.5	–
	1.63	0.22	0.15	0.38	0.34	2.56	0.30	0.292	12.6	–	0.023	36.2	0.549	30.2	233.0	139.8	2	26.0	–
4	1.27	0.22	0.11	0.34	0.32	1.42	0.26	0.359	16.1	–	0.021	55.1	–	28.1	50.5	30.3	1	–	–
	1.39	0.24	0.12	0.38	0.35	1.56	0.28	0.394	17.7	–	0.023	60.5	–	30.9	55.5	33.3	2	–	–
5	1.08	0.22	0.06	–	0.25	1.42	0.27	0.210	9.0	–	0.015	38.5	–	23.7	98.5	59.1	–	–	–
	1.19	0.24	0.07	–	0.27	1.56	0.30	0.230	9.9	–	0.016	42.3	–	26.1	108.4	65.0	–	–	–
6	1.07	0.19	0.07	–	0.20	1.88	0.23	0.370	12.5	–	0.015	35.1	–	20.1	17.6	10.6	1	–	–
	1.18	0.21	0.08	–	0.22	2.07	0.25	0.406	13.7	–	0.017	38.5	–	22.1	19.3	11.6	1	–	–
7	2.04	0.21	0.05	–	0.24	2.16	–	–	2.5	–	0.026	22.1	–	23.8	–	–	1	–	–
	2.29	0.23	0.06	–	0.27	2.42	–	–	2.8	–	0.029	24.8	–	26.6	–	–	1	–	–
8	1.40	0.23	0.10	0.47	0.29	2.38	0.23	0.302	8.6	0.148	0.041	31.0	0.335	19.3	200.3	120.2	–	105.7	8.24
	1.52	0.25	0.11	0.52	0.32	2.60	0.25	0.329	9.3	0.162	0.045	33.8	0.365	21.1	218.5	131.1	–	115.3	8.98
9	1.59	0.28	0.11	0.47	0.33	2.41	0.50	0.259	12.2	0.135	0.036	45.2	0.285	21.8	265.4	159.2	–	143.3	14.19
	1.74	0.31	0.13	0.51	0.36	2.63	0.55	0.283	13.3	0.147	0.039	49.4	0.311	23.8	289.7	173.8	–	156.4	15.50
10	1.69	0.30	0.12	0.52	0.31	2.40	0.30	0.311	9.8	0.166	0.036	36.4	0.534	19.5	391.4	234.8	–	221.3	11.65
	1.82	0.33	0.13	0.56	0.33	2.58	0.32	0.336	10.5	0.179	0.039	39.2	0.576	21.0	421.8	253.0	–	238.4	12.55
11	1.02	0.25	0.21	0.43	0.52	1.77	0.21	0.079	15.5	–	0.012	36.2	–	–	39.4	23.7	–	–	–
	1.12	0.28	0.23	0.47	0.57	1.94	0.23	0.086	17.1	–	0.013	39.8	–	–	43.4	26.0	–	–	–
12	1.33	0.23	0.11	–	0.28	2.31	0.22	–	11.4	–	0.020	60.7	–	20.1	28.9	17.3	–	–	–
	1.45	0.25	0.12	–	0.30	2.53	0.24	–	12.4	–	0.022	66.4	–	22.0	31.6	18.9	–	–	–
13	–	–	–	–	–	–	–	–	–	–	–	–	–	–	–	–	–	–	–
	–	–	–	–	–	–	–	–	–	–	–	–	–	–	–	–	–	–	–
14	0.21	0.25	0.12	–	0.14	1.30	0.15	0.059	3.9	–	0.027	34.8	–	–	77.4	46.4	1	–	–
	0.24	0.28	0.14	–	0.16	1.47	0.17	0.067	4.4	–	0.030	39.4	–	–	87.5	52.5	1	–	–
15	0.27	0.07	0.13	0.61	0.21	2.16	0.16	0.061	4.9	–	0.019	15.1	–	6.8	3.5	2.1	1	–	–
	0.30	0.07	0.14	0.67	0.23	2.37	0.17	0.067	5.4	–	0.021	16.6	–	7.4	3.9	2.3	1	–	–
16	0.43	0.16	0.07	–	0.16	1.40	0.19	0.111	24.3	0.105	0.027	99.4	–	53.0	87.5	52.5	–	–	–
	0.47	0.17	0.08	–	0.17	1.53	0.21	0.122	26.6	0.115	0.029	109.0	–	58.1 96.0	57.6	–	–	–	–
17	0.38	0.17	–	–	0.16	1.46	0.19	–	–	–	0.028	–	–	18.2	123.7	74.2	–	–	–
	0.42	0.18	–	–	0.17	1.61	0.21	–	–	–	0.030	–	–	20.0	136.2	81.7	–	–	–
18	1.54	0.21	0.06	–	0.46	1.74	0.23	0.100	8.4	–	0.021	26.0	–	69.9	217.8	130.6	1	–	–
	1.70	0.23	0.07	–	0.51	1.92	0.25	0.111	9.3	–	0.023	28.7	–	77.2	240.4	144.2	2	–	–
19	0.28	0.24	0.10	–	0.30	1.73	0.12	–	–	–	0.028	84.9	–	–	378.4	227.0	–	–	–
	0.30	0.26	0.11	–	0.33	1.88	0.13	–	–	–	0.030	92.6	–	–	412.6	247.5	–	–	–
20	0.40	0.27	0.10	0.55	0.19	1.66	0.12	–	8.8	–	0.025	76.2	–	–	–	–	–	–	–
	0.45	0.30	0.11	0.62	0.21	1.87	0.13	–	9.9	–	0.028	85.6	–	–	–	–	–	–	–
21	0.32	0.15	0.03	–	0.09	1.49	0.18	–	–	–	0.019	–	–	–	50.3	30.2	–	–	–
	0.36	0.16	0.03	–	0.10	1.64	0.20	–	–	–	0.020	–	–	–	55.4	33.2	–	–	–
22	1.14	0.22	0.40	0.68	0.40	1.95	0.17	–	5.3	–	0.023	60.5	–	–	272.1	163.2	–	–	–
	1.30	0.25	0.46	0.78	0.45	2.22	0.19	–	6.0	–	0.026	69.0	–	–	310.1	186.0	–	–	–
23	–	–	–	–	–	–	–	–	–	–	–	–	–	–	–	–	–	–	–
	–	–	–	–	–	–	–	–	–	–	–	–	–	–	–	–	–	–	–
24	1.30	0.30	0.12	0.27	0.42	2.17	0.19	0.144	8.4	0.268	0.042	109.7	–	15.2	239.5	143.7	–	–	–
	1.45	0.34	0.13	0.30	0.47	2.44	0.21	0.161	9.4	0.301	0.047	123.1	–	17.0	268.7	161.2	–	–	–
25	1.22	0.22	0.16	0.28	0.34	1.60	0.15	0.138	18.8	0.217	0.022	95.2	–	32.5	40.5	24.3	–	–	–
	1.38	0.25	0.18	0.32	0.38	1.81	0.16	0.156	21.2	0.245	0.024	107.7	–	36.7	45.9	27.5	–	–	–
26	–	–	–	–	–	–	–	0.137	–	–	–	–	–	–	16.6	10.0	–	–	–
	–	–	–	–	–	–	–	0.155	–	–	–	–	–	–	18.7	11.2	–	–	–

(Continued)

DRY FORAGES

TABLE A-4c DRY FORAGES FOR HORSES, COMPOSITION OF FEEDS, DATA EXPRESSED **AS-FED** AND **MOISTURE-FREE** (Continued)

Entry Number	Feed Name Description	Moisture Basis: A-F (as-fed) or M-F (moisture-free)	Dry Matter	B-12	Biotin	Choline	Folacin (Folic Acid)	Niacin	Pantothenic Acid (B-3)	Pyridoxine (B-6)	Riboflavin (B-2)	Thiamin (B-1)
			%	ppm or mg/kg	ppm or mg/kg	ppm or mg/kg	ppm or mg/kg	ppm or mg/kg	ppm or mg/kg	ppm or mg/kg	ppm or mg/kg	ppm or mg/kg
	ALFALFA (LUCERNE) *Medicago sativa*											
1	HAY, SUN-CURED, ALL ANALYSES	A-F	90	–	0.18	892	3.07	43	18.1	–	9.5	3.1
		M-F	100		0.20	988	3.40	48	20.1	–	10.5	3.4
2	HAY, PREBLOOM, SUN-CURED	A-F	90	–	–	–	–	–	–	–	–	–
		M-F	100	–	–	–	–	–	–	–	–	–
3	HAY, EARLY BLOOM, SUN-CURED	A-F	91	–	–	–	–	–	–	–	–	–
		M-F	100	–	–	–	–	–	–	–	9.6	–
4	HAY, MIDBLOOM, SUN-CURED	A-F	91	–	–	–	–	–	–	–	9.6	–
		M-F	100	–	–	–	–	–	–	–	10.6	–
5	HAY, FULL BLOOM SUN-CURED	A-F	91	–	–	–	–	–	–	–	–	–
		M-F	100	–	–	–	–	–	–	–	–	–
6	HAY, MATURE, SUN-CURED	A-F	91	–	–	–	–	–	–	–	–	–
		M-F	100	–	–	–	–	–	–	–	–	–
7	HAY, RAINED ON, SUN-CURED	A-F	89	–	–	–	–	–	–	–	–	–
		M-F	100	–	–	–	–	–	–	–	–	–
8	MEAL, DEHY, 17% PROTEIN	A-F	92	–	0.33	1369	4.37	37	29.7	7.18	12.9	3.4
		M-F	100	–	0.36	1494	4.77	40	32.4	7.83	14.1	3.7
9	MEAL, DEHY, 20% PROTEIN	A-F	92	–	0.35	1417	2.96	48	35.5	8.72	15.2	5.4
		M-F	100	–	0.39	1547	3.24	52	38.8	9.52	16.6	5.9
10	MEAL, DEHY, 22% PROTEIN	A-F	93	–	0.33	1605	5.15	50	39.0	8.28	17.6	5.9
		M-F	100	–	0.36	1729	5.55	54	42.0	8.92	19.0	6.3
	ALFALFA-BROMEGRASS, SMOOTH *Medicago sativa-Bromus inermis*											
11	HAY, SUN-CURED	A-F	91	–	–	–	–	25	21.4	–	6.1	–
		M-F	100	–	–	–	–	27	23.5	–	6.7	–
	ALFALFA-GRASS *Medicago sativa-grass*											
12	HAY, SUN-CURED	A-F	91	–	–	–	–	–	–	–	–	–
		M-F	100	–	–	–	–	–	–	–	–	–
	ALFALFA-ORCHARDGRASS *Medicago sativa-Dactylis glomerata*											
13	HAY, SUN-CURED	A-F	89	–	–	–	–	–	–	–	–	–
		M-F	100	–	–	–	–	–	–	–	–	–
	BARLEY *Hordeum vulgare*											
14	HAY, SUN-CURED	A-F	88	–	–	–	–	–	–	–	–	–
		M-F	100	–	–	–	–	–	–	–	–	–
15	STRAW	A-F	91	–	–	–	–	–	–	–	–	–
		M-F	100	–	–	–	–	–	–	–	–	–
	BERMUDAGRASS *Cynodon dactylon*											
16	HAY, SUN-CURED	A-F	91	–	–	–	–	–	–	–	–	–
		M-F	100	–	–	–	–	–	–	–	–	–
	BERMUDAGRASS, COASTAL *Cynodon dactylon*											
17	HAY, SUN-CURED	A-F	91	–	–	–	–	–	–	–	–	–
		M-F	100	–	–	–	–	–	–	–	–	–
	BIRDSFOOT TREFOIL *Lotus corniculatus*											
18	HAY, SUN-CURED	A-F	91	–	–	–	–	–	–	–	14.6	6.2
		M-F	100	–	–	–	–	–	–	–	16.1	6.8
	BLUEGRASS, CANADA *Poa compressa*											
19	HAY, SUN-CURED	A-F	92	–	–	–	–	–	–	–	–	–
		M-F	100	–	–	–	–	–	–	–	–	–
	BLUEGRASS, KENTUCKY *Poa pratensis*											
20	HAY, SUN-CURED	A-F	89	–	–	–	–	–	–	–	9.9	–
		M-F	100	–	–	–	–	–	–	–	11.1	–
	BROMEGRASS *Bromus spp*											
21	HAY, SUN-CURED	A-F	91	–	–	–	–	–	–	–	–	–
		M-F	100	–	–	–	–	–	–	–	–	–
	CANADA BLUEGRASS–SEE BLUEGRASS, CANADA											
	CLOVER, ALSIKE *Trifolium hybridum*											
22	HAY, SUN-CURED	A-F	88	–	–	–	–	–	–	–	15.1	4.2
		M-F	100	–	–	–	–	–	–	–	17.2	4.8
	CLOVER, ALYCE *Alysicarpus vaginalis*											
23	HAY, SUN-CURED	A-F	90	–	–	–	–	–	–	–	–	–
		M-F	100	–	–	–	–	–	–	–	–	–
	CLOVER, LADINO *Trifolium repens*											
24	HAY, SUN-CURED	A-F	89	–	–	–	–	10	1.0	–	15.2	3.7
		M-F	100	–	–	–	–	11	1.1	–	17.0	4.2
	CLOVER, RED *Trifolium pratense*											
25	HAY, SUN-CURED, ALL ANALYSES	A-F	88	–	0.09	–	–	38	9.9	–	15.7	2.0
		M-F	100	–	0.11	–	–	43	11.2	–	17.8	2.2
	CLOVER, RED-GRASS *Trifolium pratense-grass*											
26	HAY, FULL BLOOM, SUN-CURED	A-F	89	–	–	–	–	–	–	–	–	–
		M-F	100	–	–	–	–	–	–	–	–	–

DRY FORAGES

DRY FORAGES FOR HORSES

Entry Number	Feed Name Description	International Feed Number	Moisture Basis: A-F (as-fed) or M-F (moisture-free)	Dry Matter	Ash	Crude Fiber	Neutral Det. Fib. (NDF)	Acid Det. Fib. (ADF)	Lignin	Ether Extract (Fat)	N-Free Exract	Crude Protein	Digestible Protein	TDN	Digestible Energy Mcal		Metabolizable Energy Mcal	
				%	%	%	%	%	%	%	%	%	%	%	lb	kg	lb	kg
27	**CLOVER, WHITE** *Trifolium repens* HAY, SUN-CURED	1-01-464	A-F M-F	90 100	9.0 9.9	21.9 24.2	– –	– –	– –	2.4 2.6	40.1 44.4	16.9 18.8	11.5 12.7	50 56	0.94 1.04	2.07 2.30	0.77 0.86	1.70 1.88
28	**CLOVER-TIMOTHY** *Trifolium spp-Phleum pratense* HAY, FULL BLOOM, SUN-CURED	1-01-484	A-F M-F	90 100	5.7 6.3	32.2 35.8	– –	– –	– –	3.1 3.4	39.6 44.0	9.5 10.5	5.7 6.3	34 38	0.67 0.74	1.47 1.63	0.55 0.61	1.21 1.34
29	**CORN** *Zea mays* COBS, GROUND [1]	1-02-782	A-F M-F	90 100	1.6 1.8	32.2 35.8	80.1 89.0	31.5 35.0	– –	0.6 0.7	52.7 58.7	2.8 3.1	0.4 0.5	28 31	0.57 0.63	1.25 1.39	0.46 0.52	1.02 1.14
30	**CRESTED WHEATGRASS** *Agropyron desertorum* HAY, SUN-CURED	1-05-418	A-F M-F	92 100	6.4 7.0	30.8 33.6	– –	33.2 36.2	5.1 5.5	2.1 2.3	42.2 46.0	10.3 11.2	6.3 6.8	41 44	0.78 0.85	1.73 1.88	0.64 0.70	1.42 1.54
31	**CRIMSON CLOVER** *Trifolium incarnatum* HAY, SUN-CURED	1-01-328	A-F M-F	88 100	7.8 8.9	28.1 31.9	– –	– –	– –	2.0 2.3	35.2 40.1	14.7 16.8	9.8 11.1	43 49	0.82 0.94	1.81 2.06	0.67 0.77	1.49 1.69
32	**FESCUE, TALL (ALTA)** *Festuca arundinacea* HAY, SUN-CURED	1-05-684	A-F M-F	89 100	5.9 6.6	32.6 36.6	61.7 69.3	35.6 40.0	– –	2.0 2.2	41.4 46.5	7.2 8.1	3.9 4.4	41 46	0.78 0.87	1.71 1.92	0.64 0.72	1.40 1.58
33	**GRASS** HAY, SUN-CURED, ALL ANALYSES	1-02-250	A-F M-F	89 100	7.3 8.1	29.7 33.2	– –	34.4 38.5	– –	2.3 2.5	41.2 46.1	8.9 10.0	5.7 6.4	40 44	0.76 0.85	1.68 1.88	0.63 0.70	1.38 1.54
34	**GRASS-LEGUME** HAY, SUN-CURED	1-02-301	A-F M-F	89 100	5.6 6.2	31.6 35.4	– –	33.9 38.0	– –	2.3 2.5	39.5 44.3	10.3 11.5	6.3 7.1	38 43	0.74 0.83	1.64 1.83	0.61 0.68	1.34 1.50
35	**JOHNSONGRASS SORGHUM** *Sorghum halepense* HAY, SUN-CURED	1-04-407	A-F M-F	91 100	7.7 8.6	30.4 33.6	– –	– –	– –	2.0 2.2	43.7 48.3	6.7 7.5	3.6 4.0	35 39	0.68 0.76	1.51 1.66	0.56 0.62	1.24 1.37
36	**KELP (SEAWEED)** *Laminariales* (order), *Fucales* (order) WHOLE, DEHY	1-08-073	A-F M-F	91 100	35.0 38.6	6.5 7.1	– –	– –	– –	0.5 0.5	42.4 46.7	6.5 7.1	3.4 3.7	– –	– –	– –	– –	– –
37	**KENTUCKY BLUEGRASS** *Poa pratensis* HAY, SUN-CURED	1-00-776	A-F M-F	89 100	5.9 6.6	26.8 30.0	– –	– –	– –	3.0 3.4	44.3 49.7	9.1 10.2	5.4 6.1	37 42	0.73 0.81	1.60 1.80	0.60 0.67	1.31 1.47
38	**LESPEDEZA, COMMON** *Lespedeza striata* HAY, SUN-CURED, ALL ANALYSES	1-08-591	A-F M-F	89 100	4.7 5.3	28.4 32.0	– –	– –	– –	2.5 2.8	39.4 44.4	13.8 15.6	9.1 10.2	45 51	0.86 0.97	1.89 2.13	0.70 0.79	1.55 1.75
39	**LESPEDEZA, SERICEA (CHINESE LESPEDEZA)** *Lespedeza cuneata* HAY, SUN-CURED, ALL ANALYSES	1-02-607	A-F M-F	90 100	4.8 5.3	29.9 33.1	– –	– –	– –	2.0 2.2	42.9 47.5	10.7 11.8	6.6 7.4	44 49	0.83 0.92	1.84 2.03	0.68 0.76	1.51 1.67
40	**MILLET, FOXTAIL** *Setaria italica* HAY, SUN-CURED	1-03-099	A-F M-F	87 100	7.5 8.6	25.7 29.6	– –	– –	– –	2.5 2.9	43.7 50.3	7.5 8.6	4.2 4.8	35 40	0.68 0.78	1.49 1.72	0.56 0.64	1.22 1.41
41	**OATS** *Avena sativa* HAY, SUN-CURED, ALL ANALYSES	1-03-280	A-F M-F	91 100	7.2 7.9	29.1 32.0	– –	34.8 38.4	– –	2.2 2.4	43.6 48.1	8.6 9.5	5.0 5.5	38 42	0.74 0.81	1.62 1.79	0.60 0.67	1.33 1.47
42	STRAW	1-03-283	A-F M-F	92 100	7.2 7.8	37.2 40.4	65.7 71.3	43.1 46.8	7.0 7.6	2.0 2.2	41.6 45.2	4.1 4.4	2.4 2.6	44 48	0.84 0.91	1.85 2.01	0.69 0.75	1.52 1.65
43	**ORCHARDGRASS** *Dactylis glomerata* HAY, SUN-CURED	1-03-438	A-F M-F	89 100	6.5 7.3	31.0 34.7	64.1 71.8	36.0 40.3	– –	2.8 3.1	39.7 44.4	9.4 10.5	5.6 6.3	40 45	0.77 0.86	1.69 1.89	0.63 0.70	1.38 1.55
44	**PEANUT** *Arachis hypogaea* HAY, SUN-CURED	1-03-619	A-F M-F	91 100	8.2 9.0	30.3 33.4	– –	37.2 41.0	– –	3.3 3.6	39.1 43.1	9.9 10.9	6.0 6.6	32 35	0.64 0.70	1.41 1.55	0.52 0.58	1.15 1.27
45	**PEARL MILLET** *Pennisetum glaucum* HAY, SUN-CURED	1-03-112	A-F M-F	87 100	8.9 10.2	32.2 36.9	– –	– –	– –	1.8 2.0	37.2 42.5	7.3 8.4	4.1 4.7	30 35	0.61 0.69	1.33 1.53	0.50 0.57	1.09 1.25
46	**PRAIRIE GRASS, MIDWEST (PRAIRIE HAY)** HAY, SUN-CURED	1-03-191	A-F M-F	91 100	7.2 8.0	30.7 33.7	– –	– –	– –	2.1 2.3	45.2 49.6	5.8 6.4	2.9 3.1	34 37	0.67 0.74	1.48 1.62	0.55 0.60	1.21 1.33
47	**REDTOP** *Agrostis alba* HAY, SUN-CURED	1-03-885	A-F M-F	92 100	6.0 6.6	28.4 30.9	– –	– –	– –	2.8 3.1	47.4 51.5	7.4 8.1	4.1 4.4	37 40	0.73 0.79	1.60 1.74	0.60 0.65	1.31 1.42
	RICE *Oryza sativa* :S	1-08-075	A-F M-F	92 100	19.0 20.6	38.9 42.2	71.9 78.0	62.3 67.6	9.6 10.4	1.0 1.1	30.3 32.9	3.0 3.2	0.6 0.7	12 13	0.30 0.33	0.67 0.72	0.25 0.27	0.55 0.59

(Continued)

D R Y   F O R A G E S

TABLE A–4c DRY FORAGES FOR HORSES, COMPOSITION OF FEEDS, DATA EXPRESSED **AS-FED** AND **MOISTURE-FREE** (Continued)

Entry Number	Feed Name Description	Moisture Basis: A-F (as-fed) or M-F (moisture-free)	Dry Matter %	Calcium (Ca) %	Phos-phorus (P) %	Sodium (Na) %	Chlo-rine (Cl) %	Mag-nesium (Mg) %	Potas-sium (K) %	Sulfur (S) %	Cobalt (Co) ppm or mg/kg	Copper (Cu) ppm or mg/kg	Iodine (I) ppm or mg/kg	Iron (Fe) %	Man-ganese (Mn) ppm or mg/kg	Sele-nium (Se) ppm or mg/kg	Zinc (Zn) ppm or mg/kg
27	CLOVER, WHITE _Trifolium repens_ HAY, SUN-CURED	A-F	90	1.71	0.29	–	–	–	–	–	–	–	–	–	–	–	–
		M-F	100	1.90	0.32	–	–	–	–	–	–	–	–	–	–	–	–
28	CLOVER-TIMOTHY _Trifolium spp-Phleum pratense_ HAY, FULL BLOOM, SUN-CURED	A-F	90	–	–	–	–	–	–	–	–	–	–	–	–	–	–
		M-F	100	–	–	–	–	–	–	–	–	–	–	–	–	–	–
29	CORN _Zea mays_ COBS, GROUND	A-F	90	0.11	0.04	–	–	0.06	0.78	0.42	0.117	6.6	–	0.021	5.6	–	–
		M-F	100	0.12	0.04	–	–	0.07	0.87	0.47	0.130	7.3	–	0.023	6.2	–	–
30	CRESTED WHEATGRASS _Agropyron desertorum_ HAY, SUN-CURED	A-F	92	0.24	0.14	–	–	–	–	–	0.219	–	–	–	–	–	–
		M-F	100	0.26	0.15	–	–	–	–	–	0.239	–	–	–	–	–	–
31	CRIMSON CLOVER _Trifolium incarnatum_ HAY, SUN-CURED	A-F	88	1.23	0.19	0.34	0.55	0.25	2.10	0.25	–	–	0.059	0.062	183.3	–	–
		M-F	100	1.40	0.22	0.39	0.63	0.28	2.40	0.28	–	–	0.067	0.070	208.7	–	–
32	FESCUE, TALL (ALTA) _Festuca arundinacea_ HAY, SUN-CURED	A-F	89	0.35	0.21	0.05	–	0.20	2.12	–	–	–	–	–	–	–	–
		M-F	100	0.39	0.24	0.06	–	0.23	2.38	–	–	–	–	–	–	–	–
33	GRASS HAY, SUN-CURED, ALL ANALYSES	A-F	89	0.44	0.18	0.01	–	0.20	1.38	0.19	0.133	6.5	–	0.013	75.4	–	15.1
		M-F	100	0.49	0.20	0.01	–	0.22	1.55	0.21	0.149	7.3	–	0.015	84.4	–	16.9
34	GRASS-LEGUME HAY, SUN-CURED	A-F	89	0.66	0.19	0.06	–	0.23	1.62	0.13	0.118	5.0	–	0.014	42.5	–	23.2
		M-F	100	0.74	0.22	0.07	–	0.26	1.82	0.14	0.132	5.6	–	0.015	47.7	–	26.0
35	JOHNSONGRASS SORGHUM _Sorghum halepense_ HAY, SUN-CURED	A-F	91	0.80	0.27	0.01	–	0.31	1.22	0.09	–	–	–	0.054	–	–	–
		M-F	100	0.89	0.30	0.01	–	0.35	1.35	0.10	–	–	–	0.059	–	–	–
36	KELP (SEAWEED) _Laminariales_ (order), _Fucales_ (order) WHOLE, DEHY	A-F	91	2.47	0.28	–	–	0.85	–	–	–	–	–	–	–	–	–
		M-F	100	2.72	0.31	–	–	0.93	–	–	–	–	–	–	–	–	–
37	KENTUCKY BLUEGRASS _Poa pratensis_ HAY, SUN-CURED	A-F	89	0.40	0.27	0.10	0.55	0.19	1.66	0.12	–	8.8	–	0.025	76.2	–	–
		M-F	100	0.45	0.30	0.11	0.62	0.21	1.87	0.13	–	9.9	–	0.028	85.6	–	–
38	LESPEDEZA, COMMON _Lespedeza striata_ HAY, SUN-CURED, ALL ANALYSES	A-F	89	0.78	0.25	–	–	0.20	1.21	0.21	–	7.1	–	0.019	99.6	–	21.3
		M-F	100	0.88	0.29	–	–	0.23	1.37	0.24	–	8.0	–	0.022	112.3	–	24.0
39	LESPEDEZA, SERICEA (CHINESE LESPEDEZA) _Lespedeza cuneata_ HAY, SUN-CURED, ALL ANALYSES	A-F	90	0.93	0.22	–	–	0.20	0.99	–	–	–	–	0.027	91.1	–	–
		M-F	100	1.03	0.25	–	–	0.22	1.10	–	–	–	–	0.030	100.8	–	–
40	MILLET, FOXTAIL _Setaria italica_ HAY, SUN-CURED	A-F	87	0.29	0.16	0.09	0.11	0.20	1.69	0.14	–	–	–	–	120.1	–	–
		M-F	100	0.33	0.18	0.10	0.13	0.23	1.94	0.16	–	–	–	–	138.1	–	–
41	OATS _Avena sativa_ HAY, SUN-CURED, ALL ANALYSES	A-F	91	0.29	0.23	0.17	0.47	0.26	1.35	0.21	0.067	4.4	–	0.037	89.6	–	40.8
		M-F	100	0.32	0.25	0.18	0.52	0.29	1.49	0.23	0.073	4.8	–	0.041	98.7	–	45.0
42	STRAW	A-F	92	0.22	0.06	0.39	0.72	0.16	2.35	0.21	–	9.5	–	0.016	29.0	–	5.5
		M-F	100	0.24	0.07	0.42	0.78	0.17	2.55	0.23	–	10.3	–	0.017	31.5	–	5.9
43	ORCHARDGRASS _Dactylis glomerata_ HAY, SUN-CURED	A-F	89	0.34	0.23	0.01	0.37	0.16	2.68	0.23	0.339	12.9	–	0.014	162.7	–	32.0
		M-F	100	0.38	0.26	0.02	0.41	0.18	3.00	0.26	0.379	14.5	–	0.015	182.3	–	35.8
44	PEANUT _Arachis hypogaea_ HAY, SUN-CURED	A-F	91	1.12	0.14	–	–	0.44	1.25	0.21	0.072	–	–	–	–	–	–
		M-F	100	1.23	0.16	–	–	0.49	1.38	0.23	0.080	–	–	–	–	–	–
45	PEARL MILLET _Pennisetum glaucum_ HAY, SUN-CURED	A-F	87	–	–	–	–	–	–	–	–	–	–	–	–	–	–
		M-F	100	–	–	–	–	–	–	–	–	–	–	–	–	–	–
46	PRAIRIE GRASS, MIDWEST (PRAIRIE HAY) HAY, SUN-CURED	A-F	91	0.32	0.13	–	–	0.24	0.98	–	–	–	–	0.008	–	–	–
		M-F	100	0.35	0.14	–	–	0.26	1.08	–	–	–	–	0.009	–	–	–
47	REDTOP _Agrostis alba_ HAY, SUN-CURED	A-F	92	0.39	0.20	0.06	0.06	0.20	1.74	0.23	0.134	3.6	0.092	0.015	207.7	–	–
		M-F	100	0.43	0.22	0.07	0.07	0.22	1.89	0.25	0.146	3.9	0.100	0.016	225.5	–	–
48	RICE _Oryza sativa_ HULLS	A-F	92	0.11	0.10	0.02	0.07	0.41	0.64	0.08	2.046	3.1	–	0.010	295.0	–	22.0
		M-F	100	0.12	0.10	0.02	0.08	0.45	0.69	0.09	2.220	3.4	–	0.010	320.1	–	23.9

DRY FORAGES FOR HORSES

Entry Number	Fat-Soluble Vitamins					Water-Soluble Vitamins								
	A (1 mg Carotene = 1667 IU Vit A)	Carotene (Provitamin A)	D	E	K	B-12	Biotin	Choline	Folacin (Folic Acid)	Niacin	Pantothenic Acid (B-3)	Pyri-doxine (B-6)	Ribo-flavin (B-2)	Thiamin (B-1)
	IU/g	ppm or mg/kg	IU/kg	ppm or mg/kg	ppm or mg/kg	ppm or mg/kg	ppm or mg/kg	ppm or mg/kg	ppm or mg/kg	ppm or mg/kg	ppm or mg/kg	ppm or mg/kg	ppm or mg/kg	ppm or mg/kg
27	**92.1** 102.2	**55.3** 61.3	− −	**115.5** 128.1	− −	− −	− −	− −	− −	− −	− −	− −	− −	− −
28	− −	− −	− −	− −	− −	− −	− −	− −	− −	− −	− −	− −	− −	− −
29	**1.0** 1.2	**0.6** 0.7	− −	− −	− −	− −	− −	− −	− −	**7** 8	**3.8** 4.2	− −	**1.0** 1.1	**0.9** 1.0
30	**34.2** 37.2	**20.5** 22.3	− −	− −	− −	− −	− −	− −	− −	− −	− −	− −	− −	− −
31	**32.9** 37.5	**19.8** 22.5	− −	− −	− −	− −	− −	− −	− −	− −	− −	− −	− −	− −
32	**30.8** 34.6	**18.5** 20.7	− −	− −	− −	− −	− −	− −	− −	− −	− −	− −	− −	− −
33	**40.8** 45.7	**24.5** 27.4	− −	− −	− −	− −	− −	− −	− −	− −	− −	− −	− −	− −
34	**18.0** 20.2	**10.8** 12.1	**2** 3	− −	− −	− −	− −	− −	− −	− −	− −	− −	− −	− −
35	**58.8** 64.9	**35.3** 38.9	− −	− −	− −	− −	− −	− −	− −	− −	− −	− −	− −	− −
36	− −	− −	− −	− −	− −	− −	− −	− −	− −	− −	− −	− −	− −	− −
37	− −	− −	− −	− −	− −	− −	− −	− −	− −	− −	− −	− −	**9.9** 11.1	− −
38	**73.9** 83.3	**44.3** 50.0	− −	− −	− −	− −	− −	− −	− −	− −	− −	− −	**8.7** 9.8	− −
39	**59.3** 65.6	**35.6** 39.4	− −	− −	− −	− −	− −	− −	− −	− −	− −	− −	**8.7** 9.7	− −
40	**86.9** 100.0	**52.1** 60.0	− −	− −	− −	− −	− −	− −	− −	− −	− −	− −	− −	− −
41	**45.0** 49.6	**27.0** 29.7	**1** 2	− −	− −	− −	− −	− −	− −	− −	− −	− −	− −	− −
42	**5.8** 6.3	**3.5** 3.8	**1** 1	− −	− −	− −	− −	− −	− −	− −	− −	− −	− −	− −
43	**28.9** 32.4	**17.3** 19.4	− −	**170.7** 191.1	− −	− −	− −	− −	− −	− −	− −	− −	**6.1** 6.8	**2.6** 2.9
44	**52.6** 58.0	**31.5** 34.8	− −	− −	− −	− −	− −	− −	− −	− −	− −	− −	**8.8** 9.7	− −
45	− −	− −	− −	− −	− −	− −	− −	− −	− −	− −	− −	− −	− −	− −
46	− −	− −	**1** 1	− −	− −	− −	− −	− −	− −	− −	− −	− −	− −	− −
47	**6.1** 6.6	**3.7** 4.0	− −	− −	− −	− −	− −	− −	− −	− −	− −	− −	− −	− −
48	− −	− −	− −	**7.5** 8.1	− −	− −	− −	− −	− −	**28** 31	**7.9** 8.6	**0.07** 0.08	**0.5** 0.6	**2.2** 2.4

(Continued)

TABLE A–4c DRY FORAGES FOR HORSES, COMPOSITION OF FEEDS, DATA EXPRESSED **AS-FED** AND **MOISTURE-FREE** (Continued)

Entry Number	Feed Name Description	International Feed Number	Moisture Basis: A-F (as-fed) or M-F (moisture-free)	Dry Matter %	Ash %	Crude Fiber %	Neutral Det. Fib. (NDF) %	Acid Det. Fib. (ADF) %	Lignin %	Ether Extract (Fat) %	N-Free Exract %	Crude Protein %	Digestible Protein %	TDN %	Digestible Energy Mcal lb	Digestible Energy Mcal kg	Metabolizable Energy Mcal lb	Metabolizable Energy Mcal kg
49	**RYEGRASS** Lolium spp HAY, SUN-CURED [1]	1-04-057	A-F	88	7.1	25.3	56.3	37.0	—	1.8	46.2	7.5	4.2	40	0.76	1.68	0.62	1.38
			M-F	100	8.1	28.8	64.0	42.0	—	2.1	52.5	8.5	4.8	45	0.87	1.91	0.71	1.56
50	**SEAWEED (KELP)** Laminariales (order), Fucales (order) WHOLE, DEHY	1-08-073	A-F	91	35.0	6.5	—	—	—	0.5	42.4	6.5	3.4	—	—	—	—	—
			M-F	100	38.6	7.1	—	—	—	0.5	46.7	7.1	3.7	—	—	—	—	—
51	**SOYBEAN** Glycine max HAY, SUN-CURED	1-04-558	A-F	89	7.2	30.6	—	35.7	—	2.3	35.0	14.1	9.3	41	0.79	1.74	0.65	1.43
			M-F	100	8.0	34.3	—	40.0	—	2.5	39.3	15.8	10.4	46	0.89	1.95	0.73	1.60
52	**STARGRASS** Cynodon plectostachyus HAY, SUN-CURED	1-13-407	A-F	90	8.6	28.8	—	—	—	1.5	44.4	7.7	2.8	35	0.65	1.44	0.53	1.17
			M-F	100	9.6	32.0	—	—	—	1.7	49.3	8.6	3.1	39	0.73	1.60	0.59	1.30
53	**TIMOTHY** Phleum pratense HAY, SUN-CURED, ALL ANALYSES [1]	1-04-893	A-F	91	4.6	30.3	63.7	36.4	—	2.4	47.3	6.8	3.3	43	0.81	1.79	0.67	1.47
			M-F	100	5.1	33.2	70.0	40.0	—	2.6	51.8	7.4	3.6	47	0.89	1.96	0.73	1.61
54	HAY, EARLY BLOOM, SUN-CURED	1-04-882	A-F	89	5.1	30.3	54.4	30.4	3.8	2.6	41.7	9.5	5.8	38	0.74	1.63	0.61	1.34
			M-F	100	5.7	33.9	61.0	34.1	4.3	2.9	46.8	10.7	6.5	43	0.83	1.83	0.68	1.50
55	HAY, MIDBLOOM, SUN-CURED	1-04-883	A-F	89	5.6	30.3	58.0	33.6	4.4	2.3	42.1	8.6	4.7	51	0.94	2.08	0.77	1.70
			M-F	100	6.3	34.0	65.3	37.8	4.9	2.6	47.4	9.7	5.3	57	1.06	2.34	0.87	1.92
56	HAY, FULL BLOOM, SUN-CURED [1]	1-04-884	A-F	89	4.6	31.1	60.5	33.8	—	2.7	43.4	6.8	1.4	39	0.75	1.65	0.62	1.36
			M-F	100	5.2	35.1	68.0	38.0	—	3.0	48.9	7.7	1.6	44	0.85	1.87	0.69	1.53
57	**TIMOTHY-CLOVER** Phleum pratense-Trifolium spp HAY, SUN-CURED	1-04-973	A-F	89	5.1	31.7	—	—	—	2.0	42.7	7.8	4.4	38	0.73	1.60	0.60	1.31
			M-F	100	5.7	35.5	—	—	—	2.2	47.8	8.7	4.9	42	0.81	1.79	0.67	1.47
58	**TREFOIL, BIRDSFOOT** Lotus corniculatus HAY, SUN-CURED [1]	1-05-044	A-F	91	6.7	29.3	42.8	32.8	—	1.9	38.9	13.9	9.1	46	0.87	1.91	0.71	1.56
			M-F	100	7.4	32.3	47.0	36.0	—	2.1	42.9	15.3	10.0	51	0.96	2.11	0.78	1.73
59	**WHEAT** Triticum aestivum STRAW	1-05-175	A-F	90	6.9	37.4	70.3	47.7	8.4	1.8	40.4	3.2	0.6	36	0.71	1.56	0.58	1.28
			M-F	100	7.7	41.7	78.4	53.2	9.4	2.0	45.0	3.6	0.7	40	0.79	1.73	0.65	1.42
60	**WHEATGRASS, CRESTED** Agropyron desertorum HAY, SUN-CURED	1-05-418	A-F	92	6.4	30.8	—	33.2	5.1	2.1	42.2	10.3	6.3	41	0.78	1.73	0.64	1.42
			M-F	100	7.0	33.6	—	36.2	5.5	2.3	46.0	11.2	6.8	44	0.85	1.88	0.70	1.54
61	**WHITE CLOVER** Trifolium repens HAY, SUN CURED	1-01-464	A-F	90	9.0	21.9	—	—	—	2.4	40.1	16.9	11.5	50	0.94	2.07	0.77	1.70
			M-F	100	9.9	24.2	—	—	—	2.6	44.4	18.8	12.7	56	1.04	2.30	0.86	1.88

[1]Neutral Detergent Fiber (NDF) and Acid Detergent Fiber (ADF) values taken from *Nutrient Requirements of Dairy Cattle,* 6th rev. ed., NRC, National Academy Press, 1988, pp. 90–110, Table 7–1.

TABLE A–4d SILAGES AND HAYLAGES FOR HORSES, COMPOSITION OF FEEDS, DATA EXPRESSED **AS-FED** AND **MOISTURE-FREE** (See footnote at end of table.)

Entry Number	Feed Name Description	International Feed Number	Moisture Basis: A-F (as-fed) or M-F (moisture-free)	Dry Matter %	Ash %	Crude Fiber %	Neutral Det. Fib. (NDF) %	Acid Det. Fib. (ADF) %	Lignin %	Ether Extract (Fat) %	N-Free Exract %	Crude Protein %	Digestible Protein %	TDN %	Digestible Energy Mcal lb	Digestible Energy Mcal kg	Metabolizable Energy Mcal lb	Metabolizable Energy Mcal kg
1	**ALFALFA-BROMEGRASS, SMOOTH, SILAGE** Medicago sativa-Bromus inermis ALL ANALYSES	3-00-268	A-F	26	2.0	9.4	—	—	—	1.1	10.4	3.6	—	—	—	—	—	—
			M-F	100	7.4	35.6	—	—	—	4.1	39.3	13.6	—	—	—	—	—	—
2	**CORN, SILAGE** Zea mays ALL ANALYSES	3-02-822	A-F	26	1.5	6.6	—	8.9	1.2	0.8	15.2	2.2	—	—	—	—	—	—
			M-F	100	5.6	25.1	—	34.0	4.4	3.2	57.8	8.3	—	—	—	—	—	—
3	MOLASSES ADDED	3-02-834	A-F	29	1.9	6.8	—	—	—	0.8	17.2	2.3	—	—	—	—	—	—
			M-F	100	6.4	23.4	—	—	—	2.9	59.3	8.0	—	—	—	—	—	—
4	**GRASS, SILAGE** EARLY BLOOM	3-02-218	A-F	23	2.1	7.3	—	—	—	0.6	10.6	2.8	—	—	—	—	—	—
			M-F	100	9.1	31.0	—	—	—	2.7	45.1	12.1	—	—	—	—	—	—
5	MOLASSES ADDED	3-02-261	A-F	27	3.8	6.4	—	—	—	1.4	10.6	4.3	—	—	—	—	—	—
			M-F	100	14.4	24.1	—	—	—	5.3	40.0	16.1	—	—	—	—	—	—
6	**GRASS-LEGUME, SILAGE** ALL ANALYSES	3-02-303	A-F	31	2.5	10.1	18.1	12.4	3.1	1.1	13.6	3.7	—	—	—	—	—	—
			M-F	100	8.0	32.6	58.4	40.0	10.0	3.6	43.8	11.9	—	—	—	—	—	—
7	BARLEY GRAIN ADDED	3-02-305	A-F	34	2.2	8.6	—	—	—	1.4	16.7	5.2	—	—	—	—	—	—
			M-F	100	6.4	25.4	—	—	—	4.0	49.0	15.2	—	—	—	—	—	—
8	MOLASSES ADDED	3-02-309	A-F	28	2.0	9.1	—	—	—	1.1	12.8	3.4	—	—	—	—	—	—
			M-F	100	7.0	32.0	—	—	—	4.0	45.2	11.8	—	—	—	—	—	—

DRY FORAGES FOR HORSES

Entry Number	Calcium (Ca) %	Phosphorus (P) %	Sodium (Na) %	Chlorine (Cl) %	Magnesium (Mg) %	Potassium (K) %	Sulfur (S) %	Cobalt (Co) ppm or mg/kg	Copper (Cu) ppm or mg/kg	Iodine (I) ppm or mg/kg	Iron (Fe) %	Manganese (Mn) ppm or mg/kg	Selenium (Se) ppm or mg/kg	Zinc (Zn) ppm or mg/kg	A (1 mg Carotene = 1667 IU Vit A) IU/g	Carotene (Provitamin A) ppm or mg/kg	D IU/kg	E ppm or mg/kg	K ppm or mg/kg
49	–	–	–	–	–	–	–	–	–	–	–	–	–	–	175.8	105.5	1	–	–
	–	–	–	–	–	–	–	–	–	–	–	–	–	–	199.9	119.9	–	–	–
50	2.47	0.28	–	–	0.85	–	–	–	–	–	–	–	–	–	–	–	–	–	–
	2.72	0.31	–	–	0.93	–	–	–	–	–	–	–	–	–	–	–	–	–	–
51	1.13	0.22	0.10	0.13	0.71	0.92	0.25	0.083	8.0	0.216	0.026	94.3	–	21.5	53.1	31.8	1	26.3	–
	1.26	0.24	0.11	0.15	0.81	1.04	0.28	0.093	9.0	0.242	0.029	105.8	–	24.1	59.5	35.7	1	29.5	–
52	–	–	–	–	–	–	–	–	–	–	–	–	–	–	–	–	–	–	–
	–	–	–	–	–	–	–	–	–	–	–	–	–	–	–	–	–	–	–
53	0.38	0.17	0.03	0.49	0.11	1.43	0.11	0.071	4.3	0.034	0.010	45.2	–	15.5	39.8	23.8	2	57.6	–
	0.41	0.19	0.03	0.53	0.12	1.57	0.12	0.077	4.7	0.037	0.011	49.5	–	17.0	43.5	26.1	2	63.1	–
54	0.46	0.25	0.09	–	0.11	2.14	0.12	–	57.1	–	0.019	91.8	–	55.3	78.0	46.8	–	11.6	–
	0.51	0.29	0.10	–	0.13	2.41	0.13	–	64.0	–	0.021	103.0	–	62.0	87.5	52.5	–	13.0	–
55	0.32	0.20	0.08	–	0.12	1.61	0.12	–	14.3	–	0.014	49.9	–	38.2	79.0	47.4	2	–	–
	0.36	0.23	0.10	–	0.13	1.82	0.13	–	16.0	.	0.015	56.1	–	43.0	88.9	53.3	2	–	–
56	0.36	0.21	0.11	0.55	0.10	1.77	0.12	.	25.7	–	0.013	82.4	–	47.9	–	–	–	–	–
	0.41	0.24	0.12	0.62	0.11	2.00	0.13	–	29.0	–	0.014	93.0	–	54.0	–	–	–	–	–
57	0.62	0.17	0.17	0.48	0.17	1.33	0.13	–	6.3	–	0.011	48.7	–	–	39.7	23.8	–	–	–
	0.69	0.19	0.19	0.54	0.20	1.49	0.14	–	7.0	–	0.013	54.5	–	–	44.5	26.7	–	–	–
58	1.54	0.21	0.06	–	0.46	1.74	0.23	0.100	8.4	–	0.021	26.0	–	69.9	217.8	130.6	1	–	–
	1.70	0.23	0.07	–	0.51	1.92	0.25	0.111	9.3	–	0.023	28.7	–	77.2	240.4	144.2	2	–	–
59	0.16	0.05	0.13	0.29	0.11	1.27	0.17	0.041	3.2	–	0.015	36.7	–	5.8	3.3	2.0	1	–	–
	0.18	0.05	0.14	0.32	0.12	1.41	0.19	0.046	3.6	–	0.016	40.9	–	6.5	3.7	2.2	1	–	–
60	0.24	0.14	–	–	–	–	–	0.219	–	–	–	–	–	–	34.2	20.5	–	–	–
	0.26	0.15	–	–	–	–	–	0.239	–	–	–	–	–	–	37.2	22.3	–	–	–
61	1.71	0.29	–	–	–	–	–	–	–	–	–	–	–	–	92.1	55.3	–	115.5	–
	1.90	0.32	–	–	–	–	–	–	–	–	–	–	–	–	102.2	61.3	–	128.1	–

SILAGES AND HAYLAGES FOR HORSES

Entry Number	Calcium (Ca) %	Phosphorus (P) %	Sodium (Na) %	Chlorine (Cl) %	Magnesium (Mg) %	Potassium (K) %	Sulfur (S) %	Cobalt (Co) ppm or mg/kg	Copper (Cu) ppm or mg/kg	Iodine (I) ppm or mg/kg	Iron (Fe) %	Manganese (Mn) ppm or mg/kg	Selenium (Se) ppm or mg/kg	Zinc (Zn) ppm or mg/kg	A (1 mg Carotene = 1667 IU Vit A) IU/g	Carotene (Provitamin A) ppm or mg/kg	D IU/g	E ppm or mg/kg	K ppm or mg/kg
1	0.17	0.05	–	–	0.05	0.49	–	0.030	3.0	–	0.004	8.0	–	–	–	–	–	–	–
	0.64	0.20	–	–	0.20	1.86	–	0.113	11.2	–	0.015	30.2	–	–	–	–	–	–	–
2	0.08	0.07	0.01	0.05	0.06	0.32	0.03	0.026	2.4	–	0.005	10.8	–	5.5	15.2	9.1	0	–	–
	0.31	0.27	0.03	0.18	0.22	1.22	0.12	0.097	9.2	–	0.018	41.1	–	21.2	58.1	34.9	0	–	–
3	0.07	0.09	–	–	–	–	–	–	–	–	–	–	–	–	–	–	–	–	–
	0.25	0.30	–	–	–	–	–	–	–	–	–	–	–	–	–	–	–	–	–
4	–	–	–	–	–	–	–	–	–	–	–	–	–	–	–	–	–	–	–
5	0.28	0.07	–	–	–	–	–	–	–	–	–	–	–	–	–	–	–	–	–
	1.04	0.28	–	–	–	–	–	–	–	–	–	–	–	–	–	–	–	–	–
6	0.26	0.08	0.02	0.33	0.08	0.57	0.17	0.040	1.9	–	0.013	18.0	–	8.7	102.4	61.4	0	–	–
	0.84	0.26	0.07	1.06	0.25	1.83	0.54	0.126	6.0	–	0.041	58.1	–	28.0	329.5	197.6	0	–	–
7	0.26	0.12	–	–	–	–	–	–	–	–	–	–	–	–	–	–	–	–	–
	0.75	0.35	–	–	–	–	–	–	–	–	–	–	–	–	–	–	–	–	–
8	0.30	0.10	0.04	–	0.09	0.55	0.07	–	–	–	0.015	–	–	–	–	–	–	–	–
	1.07	0.34	0.13	–	0.32	1.92	0.24	–	–	–	0.053	–	–	–	–	–	–	–	–

DRY FORAGES SILAGES AND HAYLAGES

(Continued)

TABLE A–4d SILAGES AND HAYLAGES FOR HORSES, COMPOSITION OF FEEDS, DATA EXPRESSED **AS-FED** AND **MOISTURE-FREE** (Continued)

Entry Number	Feed Name Description	Moisture Basis: A-F (as-fed) or M-F (moisture-free)	Dry Matter	Water-Soluble Vitamins								
				B–12	Biotin	Choline	Folacin (Folic Acid)	Niacin	Pantothenic Acid (B–3)	Pyri-doxine (B–6)	Ribo-flavin (B–2)	Thiamin (B–1)
			%	ppm or mg/kg	ppm or mg/kg	ppm or mg/kg	ppm or mg/kg	ppm or mg/kg	ppm or mg/kg	ppm or mg/kg	ppm or mg/kg	ppm or mg/kg
49	**RYEGRASS** *Lolium* spp HAY, SUN-CURED	A-F	88	–	–	–	–	–	–	–	–	–
		M-F	100	–	–	–	–	–	–	–	–	–
50	**SEAWEED (KELP)** *Laminariales* (order), *Fucales* (order) WHOLE, DEHY	A-F	91	–	–	–	–	–	–	–	–	–
		M-F	100	–	–	–	–	–	–	–	–	–
51	**SOYBEAN** *Glycine max* HAY, SUN-CURED	A-F	89	–	–	–	–	–	–	–	–	–
		M-F	100	–	–	–	–	–	–	–	–	–
52	**STARGRASS** *Cynodon plectostachyus* HAY, SUN-CURED	A-F	90	–	–	–	–	–	–	–	–	–
		M-F	100	–	–	–	–	–	–	–	–	–
53	**TIMOTHY** *Phleum pratense* HAY, SUN-CURED, ALL ANALYSES	A-F	91	–	0.06	741	2.09	31	7.2	–	9.2	1.5
		M-F	100	–	0.07	811	2.29	34	7.9	–	10.1	1.7
54	HAY, EARLY BLOOM, SUN-CURED	A-F	89	–	–	–	–	–	–	–	–	–
		M-F	100	–	–	–	–	–	–	–	–	–
55	HAY, MIDBLOOM, SUN-CURED	A-F	89	–	–	–	–	–	–	–	–	–
		M-F	100	–	–	–	–	–	–	–	–	–
56	HAY, FULL BLOOM, SUN-CURED	A-F	89	–	–	–	–	–	–	–	–	–
		M-F	100	–	–	–	–	–	–	–	–	–
57	**TIMOTHY-CLOVER** *Phleum pratense-Trifolium* spp HAY, SUN-CURED	A-F	89	–	–	–	–	–	–	–	–	–
		M-F	100	–	–	–	–	–	–	–	–	–
58	**TREFOIL, BIRDSFOOT** *Lotus corniculatus* HAY, SUN-CURED	A-F	91	–	–	–	–	–	–	–	14.6	6.2
		M-F	100	–	–	–	–	–	–	–	16.1	6.8
59	**WHEAT** *Triticum aestivum* STRAW	A-F	90	–	–	–	–	–	–	–	2.2	–
		M-F	100	–	–	–	–	–	–	–	2.4	–
60	**WHEATGRASS, CRESTED** *Agropyron desertorum* HAY, SUN-CURED	A-F	92	–	–	–	–	–	–	–	–	–
		M-F	100	–	–	–	–	–	–	–	–	–
61	**WHITE CLOVER** *Trifolium repens* HAY, SUN-CURED	A-F	90	–	–	–	–	–	–	–	–	–
		M-F	100	–	–	–	–	–	–	–	–	–

TABLE A–4d SILAGES AND HAYLAGES FOR HORSES, COMPOSITION OF FEEDS, DATA EXPRESSED **AS-FED** AND **MOISTURE-FREE** (Continued)

Entry Number	Feed Name Description	Moisture Basis: A-F (as-fed) or M-F (moisture-free)	Dry Matter	Water-Soluble Vitamins								
				B–12	Biotin	Choline	Folacin (Folic Acid)	Niacin	Pantothenic Acid (B–3)	Pyri-doxine (B–6)	Ribo-flavin (B–2)	Thiamin (B–1)
			%	ppm or mg/kg	ppm or mg/kg	ppm or mg/kg	ppm or mg/kg	ppm or mg/kg	ppm or mg/kg	ppm or mg/kg	ppm or mg/kg	ppm or mg/kg
1	**ALFALFA-BROMEGRASS, SMOOTH, SILAGE** *Medicago sativa-Bromus inermis* ALL ANALYSES	A-F	26	–	–	–	–	–	–	–	–	–
		M-F	100	–	–	–	–	–	–	–	–	–
2	**CORN, SILAGE** *Zea mays* ALL ANALYSES	A-F	26	–	–	–	–	11	–	–	–	–
		M-F	100	–	–	–	–	43	–	–	–	–
3	MOLASSES ADDED	A-F	29	–	–	–	–	–	–	–	–	–
		M-F	100	–	–	–	–	–	–	–	–	–
4	**GRASS, SILAGE** EARLY BLOOM	A-F	23	–	–	–	–	–	–	–	–	–
		M-F	100	–	–	–	–	–	–	–	–	–
5	MOLASSES ADDED	A-F	27	–	–	–	–	–	–	–	–	–
		M-F	100	–	–	–	–	–	–	–	–	–
6	**GRASS-LEGUME, SILAGE** ALL ANALYSES	A-F	31	–	–	–	–	14	–	–	–	–
		M-F	100	–	–	–	–	46	–	–	–	–
7	BARLEY GRAIN ADDED	A-F	34	–	–	–	–	–	–	–	–	–
		M-F	100	–	–	–	–	–	–	–	–	–
8	MOLASSES ADDED	A-F	28	–	–	–	–	–	–	–	–	–
		M-F	100	–	–	–	–	–	–	–	–	–

SILAGES AND HAYLAGES FOR HORSES

Entry Number	Feed Name Description	International Feed Number	Moisture Basis: A-F (as-fed) or M-F (moisture-free)	Proximate Analysis									Digestible Protein	TDN	Digestible Energy		Metabolizable Energy	
				Dry Matter	Ash	Crude Fiber	Neutral Det. Fib. (NDF)	Acid Det. Fib. (ADF)	Lignin	Ether Extract (Fat)	N-Free Exract	Crude Protein						
				%	%	%	%	%	%	%	%	%	%	%	Mcal lb	kg	Mcal lb	kg
	KAFIR SORGHUM–SEE SORGHUM, SILAGE																	
	MILO SORGHUM–SEE SORGHUM, SILAGE																	
	OATS, SILAGE *Avena sativa*																	
9	DOUGH STAGE	3-03-296	A-F	35	2.4	11.6	–	–	–	1.4	16.1	3.5	–	–	–	–	–	–
			M-F	100	6.9	33.0	–	–	–	4.1	46.0	10.0	–	–	–	–	–	–
10	MOLASSES ADDED	3-03-300	A-F	33	2.5	10.4	–	–	–	1.2	15.8	2.9	–	–	–	–	–	–
			M-F	100	7.5	31.7	–	–	–	3.8	48.3	8.8	–	–	–	–	–	–
	SORGHUM, SILAGE *Sorghum bicolor*																	
11	DOUGH STAGE	3-04-321	A-F	29	2.5	8.3	19.2	10.9	1.9	0.9	15.1	2.3	–	–	–	–	–	–
			M-F	100	8.5	28.6	66.2	37.4	6.5	3.1	52.0	7.9	–	–	–	–	–	–
12	KAFIR	3-04-425	A-F	30	2.2	8.1	–	–	–	1.0	16.1	2.1	–	–	–	–	–	–
			M-F	100	7.6	27.3	–	–	–	3.3	54.6	7.2	–	–	–	–	–	–
13	MILO	3-04-437	A-F	31	2.5	5.5	–	–	–	0.5	20.0	2.3	–	–	–	–	–	–
			M-F	100	8.2	17.9	–	–	–	1.8	64.7	7.4	–	–	–	–	–	–

[1]Neutral Detergent Fiber (NDF) and Acid Detergent Fiber (ADF) values taken from *Nutrient Requirements of Dairy Cattle,* 6th rev. ed., NRC, National Academy Press, 1988, pp. 90–110, Table 7–1.

TABLE A–4e PASTURE AND RANGE PLANTS FOR HORSES, COMPOSITION OF FEEDS, DATA EXPRESSED AS-FED AND MOISTURE-FREE (See footnote at end of table.)

Entry Number	Feed Name Description	International Feed Number	Moisture Basis: A-F (as-fed) or M-F (moisture-free)	Proximate Analysis									Digestible Protein	TDN	Digestible Energy		Metabolizable Energy	
				Dry Matter	Ash	Crude Fiber	Neutral Det. Fib. (NDF)	Acid Det. Fib. (ADF)	Lignin	Ether Extract (Fat)	N-Free Exract	Crude Protein						
				%	%	%	%	%	%	%	%	%	%	%	Mcal lb	kg	Mcal lb	kg
	ALFALFA (LUCERNE) *Medicago sativa*																	
1	FRESH, ALL ANALYSES	2-00-196	A-F	26	2.5	6.0	11.8	–	–	1.0	11.2	5.3	–	–	–	–	–	–
			M-F	100	9.5	23.0	45.4	–	–	3.8	43.1	20.5	–	–	–	–	–	–
	ALFALFA-BROMEGRASS *Medicago sativa-Bromus* spp																	
2	FRESH	2-08-328	A-F	23	2.2	5.3	–	–	–	0.8	9.4	4.8	–	–	–	–	–	–
			M-F	100	9.8	23.6	–	–	–	3.6	41.8	21.3	–	–	–	–	–	–
	ALFALFA-BROMEGRASS, SMOOTH *Medicago sativa-Bromus inermis*																	
3	FRESH	2-00-262	A-F	22	2.1	5.5	–	–	–	0.8	9.0	4.2	–	–	–	–	–	–
			M-F	100	9.8	25.3	–	–	–	3.6	41.7	19.6	–	–	–	–	–	–
	ALFALFA-ORCHARDGRASS *Medicago sativa-Dactylis glomerata*																	
4	FRESH	2-00-323	A-F	25	–	–	–	–	–	–	–	–	–	–	–	–	–	–
			M-F	100	–	–	–	–	–	–	–	–	–	–	–	–	–	–
	ALFILERIA, REDSTEM (FILAREE) *Erodium cicutarium*																	
5	FRESH	2-00-356	A-F	18	2.4	3.6	–	5.3	–	0.6	8.2	2.8	–	–	–	–	–	–
			M-F	100	13.7	20.4	–	30.0	–	3.5	46.4	15.9	–	–	–	–	–	–
	ALTA (TALL) FESCUE *Festuca arundinacea*																	
6	FRESH	2-01-889	A-F	28	2.5	7.5	19.5	–	–	0.9	14.3	2.7	–	–	–	–	–	–
			M-F	100	9.0	26.7	69.9	–	–	3.3	51.2	9.8	–	–	–	–	–	–
	BAHIAGRASS *Paspalum notatum*																	
7	FRESH [1]	2-00-464	A-F	30	3.3	9.0	20.4	11.4	–	0.5	14.2	2.6	–	–	–	–	–	–
			M-F	100	11.1	30.4	68.0	38.0	–	1.6	48.0	8.9	–	–	–	–	–	–
	BERMUDAGRASS, COASTAL *Cynodon dactylon*																	
8	FRESH	2-00-719	A-F	29	1.8	8.3	–	–	–	1.1	13.6	4.4	–	–	–	–	–	–
			M-F	100	6.3	28.4	–	–	–	3.8	46.6	15.0	–	–	–	–	–	–
	BLUEGRASS, CANADA *Poa compressa*																	
9	FRESH	2-00-764	A-F	31	2.8	8.3	–	–	–	1.2	13.8	5.3	–	–	–	–	–	–
			M-F	100	8.9	26.4	–	–	–	3.7	44.0	17.0	–	–	–	–	–	–
	BLUEGRASS, KENTUCKY *Poa pratensis*																	
10	IMMATURE, FRESH [1]	2-00-777	A-F	31	2.9	7.8	17.1	9.0	–	1.1	13.7	5.4	–	–	–	–	–	–
			M-F	100	9.4	25.2	55.0	29.0	–	3.6	44.4	17.4	–	–	–	–	–	–
11	EARLY BLOOM, FRESH [1]	2-00-779	A-F	35	2.5	9.6	22.8	11.2	–	1.4	15.7	5.8	–	–	–	–	–	–
			M-F	100	7.1	27.4	65.0	32.0	–	3.9	44.9	16.6	–	–	–	–	–	–
	BLUEGRASS, KENTUCKY-CLOVER, WHITE *Poa pratensis-Trifolium repens*																	
12	FRESH	2-08-356	A-F	24	2.7	4.5	–	–	–	0.9	11.3	5.0	–	–	–	–	–	–
			M-F	100	11.0	18.3	–	–	–	3.5	46.5	20.6	–	–	–	–	–	–
	BROMEGRASS *Bromus* spp																	
13	IMMATURE, FRESH [1]	2-00-892	A-F	34	3.8	7.5	19.0	10.5	–	1.2	15.5	5.8	–	–	–	–	–	–
			M-F	100	11.4	22.1	56.0	31.0	–	3.7	45.8	17.1	–	–	–	–	–	–
	CLOVER, ALSIKE *Trifolium hybridum*																	
14	FRESH	2-01-316	A-F	22	2.1	5.2	–	–	–	0.8	10.3	4.1	–	–	–	–	–	–
			M-F	100	9.3	23.3	–	–	–	3.6	45.7	18.1	–	–	–	–	–	–

(Continued)

TABLE A–4d SILAGES AND HAYLAGES FOR HORSES, COMPOSITION OF FEEDS, DATA EXPRESSED **AS-FED** AND **MOISTURE-FREE** (Continued)

Entry Number	Feed Name Description	Moisture Basis: A-F (as-fed) or M-F (moisture-free)	Dry Matter	Calcium (Ca)	Phosphorus (P)	Sodium (Na)	Chlorine (Cl)	Magnesium (Mg)	Potassium (K)	Sulfur (S)	Cobalt (Co)	Copper (Cu)	Iodine (I)	Iron (Fe)	Manganese (Mn)	Selenium (Se)	Zinc (Zn)
			%	%	%	%	%	%	%	%	ppm or mg/kg	ppm or mg/kg	ppm or mg/kg	%	ppm or mg/kg	ppm or mg/kg	ppm or mg/kg
	KAFIR SORGHUM—SEE SORGHUM, SILAGE																
	MILO SORGHUM—SEE SORGHUM, SILAGE																
9	**OATS, SILAGE** *Avena sativa* DOUGH STAGE	A-F	35	0.17	0.12	—	—	—	—	—	—	—	—	—	—	—	—
		M-F	100	0.47	0.33	—	—	—	—	—	—	—	—	—	—	—	—
10	MOLASSES ADDED	A-F	33	0.10	0.09	—	—	—	0.31	—	—	—	—	—	—	—	—
		M-F	100	0.31	0.28	—	—	—	0.94	—	—	—	—	—	—	—	—
11	**SORGHUM, SILAGE** *Sorghum bicolor* DOUGH STAGE	A-F	29	—	—	—	—	—	—	—	—	—	—	—	—	—	—
		M-F	100	—	—	—	—	—	—	—	—	—	—	—	—	—	—
12	KAFIR	A-F	30	0.07	0.05	—	—	0.08	0.50	—	—	—	—	—	—	—	—
		M-F	100	0.24	0.17	—	—	0.27	1.68	—	—	—	—	—	—	—	—
13	MILO	A-F	31	0.11	0.06	—	—	—	—	—	—	—	—	—	—	—	—
		M-F	100	0.34	0.19	—	—	—	—	—	—	—	—	—	—	—	—

TABLE A–4e PASTURE AND RANGE PLANTS FOR HORSES, COMPOSITION OF FEEDS, DATA EXPRESSED **AS-FED** AND **MOISTURE-FREE** (See footnote at end of table.)

Entry Number	Feed Name Description	Moisture Basis: A-F (as-fed) or M-F (moisture-free)	Dry Matter	Calcium (Ca)	Phosphorus (P)	Sodium (Na)	Chlorine (Cl)	Magnesium (Mg)	Potassium (K)	Sulfur (S)	Cobalt (Co)	Copper (Cu)	Iodine (I)	Iron (Fe)	Manganese (Mn)	Selenium (Se)	Zinc (Zn)
			%	%	%	%	%	%	%	%	ppm or mg/kg	ppm or mg/kg	ppm or mg/kg	%	ppm or mg/kg	ppm or mg/kg	ppm or mg/kg
1	**ALFALFA (LUCERNE)** *Medicago sativa* FRESH, ALL ANALYSES	A-F	26	0.40	0.07	0.05	0.12	0.09	0.83	0.10	0.092	3.2	—	0.009	24.1	—	9.4
		M-F	100	1.52	0.28	0.17	0.46	0.34	3.18	0.38	0.352	12.4	—	0.032	92.7	—	36.1
2	**ALFALFA-BROMEGRASS** *Medicago sativa-Bromus spp* FRESH	A-F	23	0.28	0.07	—	—	—	0.63	—	—	—	—	—	—	—	—
		M-F	100	1.24	0.31	—	—	—	2.80	—	—	—	—	—	—	—	—
3	**ALFALFA-BROMEGRASS, SMOOTH** *Medicago sativa-Bromus inermis* FRESH	A-F	22	0.33	0.08	0.09	—	0.08	0.84	0.05	—	—	—	0.003	—	—	—
		M-F	100	1.52	0.37	0.42	—	0.35	3.87	0.23	—	—	—	0.013	—	—	—
4	**ALFALFA-ORCHARDGRASS** *Medicago sativa-Dactylis glomerata* FRESH	A-F	25	0.10	0.13	—	—	0.06	—	—	—	—	—	—	—	—	—
		M-F	100	0.40	0.52	—	—	0.24	—	—	—	—	—	—	—	—	—
5	**AFILERIA REDSTEM (FILAREE)** *Erodium cicutarium* FRESH	A-F	18	0.35	0.08	—	—	—	0.59	—	—	—	—	—	—	—	—
		M-F	100	1.99	0.43	—	—	—	3.37	—	—	—	—	—	—	—	—
6	**ALTA (TALL) FESCUE** *Festuca arundinacea* FRESH	A-F	28	0.13	0.05	0.03	—	0.07	0.70	—	0.113	1.0	—	0.003	18.0	—	5.9
		M-F	100	0.48	0.19	0.12	—	0.25	2.51	—	0.401	3.4	—	0.011	64.4	—	21.0
7	**BAHIAGRASS** *Paspalum notatum* FRESH	A-F	30	0.14	0.06	—	—	0.07	0.43	—	—	—	—	—	—	—	—
		M-F	100	0.46	0.22	—	—	0.25	1.45	—	—	—	—	—	—	—	—
8	**BERMUDAGRASS, COASTAL** *Cynodon dactylon* FRESH	A-F	29	0.14	0.08	—	—	—	—	—	—	—	—	—	—	—	—
		M-F	100	0.49	0.27	—	—	—	—	—	—	—	—	—	—	—	—
9	**BLUEGRASS, CANADA** *Poa compressa* FRESH	A-F	31	0.12	0.12	0.04	—	0.05	0.64	0.05	—	—	—	0.010	24.8	—	—
		M-F	100	0.39	0.39	0.14	—	0.16	2.04	0.17	—	—	—	0.030	79.1	—	—
10	**BLUEGRASS, KENTUCKY** *Poa pratensis* IMMATURE, FRESH	A-F	31	0.15	0.14	0.04	—	0.05	0.70	0.05	—	—	—	0.010	—	—	—
		M-F	100	0.50	0.44	0.14	—	0.18	2.27	0.17	—	—	—	0.030	—	—	—
11	EARLY BLOOM, FRESH	A-F	35	0.16	0.14	0.05	—	0.04	0.70	0.06	—	—	—	0.011	—	—	—
		M-F	100	0.46	0.39	0.14	—	0.11	2.01	0.17	—	—	—	0.030	—	—	—
12	**BLUEGRASS, KENTUCKY-CLOVER, WHITE** *Poa pratensis-Trifolium repens* FRESH	A-F	24	0.31	0.11	—	—	—	—	—	—	—	—	—	—	—	—
		M-F	100	1.29	0.46	—	—	—	—	—	—	—	—	—	—	—	—
13	**BROMEGRASS** *Bromus spp* IMMATURE, FRESH	A-F	34	0.20	0.13	0.01	—	0.06	1.46	0.07	—	—	—	0.007	—	—	—
		M-F	100	0.59	0.37	0.02	—	0.18	4.30	0.20	—	—	—	0.020	—	—	—
14	**CLOVER, ALSIKE** *Trifolium hybridum* FRESH	A-F	22	0.31	0.06	0.10	0.17	0.07	0.61	0.05	—	1.3	—	0.010	26.3	—	—
		M-F	100	1.36	0.29	0.45	0.77	0.32	2.70	0.22	—	6.0	—	0.044	117.1	—	—

SILAGES AND HAYLAGES PASTURE AND RANGE PLANTS

SILAGES AND HAYLAGES FOR HORSES

Entry Number	Fat-Soluble Vitamins					Water-Soluble Vitamins								
	A (1 mg Carotene = 1667 IU Vit A)	Carotene (Provitamin A)	D	E	K	B–12	Biotin	Choline	Folacin (Folic Acid)	Niacin	Pantothenic Acid (B–3)	Pyri- doxine (B–6)	Ribo- flavin (B–2)	Thiamin (B–1)
	IU/g	ppm or mg/kg	IU/kg	ppm or mg/kg	ppm or mg/kg	ppm or mg/kg	ppm or mg/kg	ppm or mg/kg	ppm or mg/kg	ppm or mg/kg	ppm or mg/kg	ppm or mg/kg	ppm or mg/kg	ppm or mg/kg
9	35.1 100.0	21.1 60.0	– –	– –	– –	– –	– –	– –	– –	– –	– –	– –	– –	– –
10	– –	– –	– –	– –	– –	– –	– –	– –	– –	– –	– –	– –	– –	– –
11	– –	– –	– –	– –	– –	– –	– –	– –	– –	– –	– –	– –	– –	– –
12	5.3 18.0	3.2 10.8	– –	– –	– –	– –	– –	– –	– –	– –	– –	– –	– –	– –
13	– –	– –	– –	– –	– –	– –	– –	– –	– –	– –	– –	– –	– –	– –

PASTURE AND RANGE PLANTS FOR HORSES

Entry Number	Fat-Soluble Vitamins					Water-Soluble Vitamins								
	A (1 mg Carotene = 1667 IU Vit A)	Carotene (Provitamin A)	D	E	K	B–12	Biotin	Choline	Folacin (Folic Acid)	Niacin	Pantothenic Acid (B–3)	Pyri- doxine (B–6)	Ribo- flavin (B–2)	Thiamin (B–1)
	IU/g	ppm or mg/kg	IU/kg	ppm or mg/kg	ppm or mg/kg	ppm or mg/kg	ppm or mg/kg	ppm or mg/kg	ppm or mg/kg	ppm or mg/kg	ppm or mg/kg	ppm or mg/kg	ppm or mg/kg	ppm or mg/kg
1	101.3 389.3	60.8 233.5	0 0	– –	– –	– –	0.13 0.49	374 1439	0.64 2.47	15 59	8.9 34.3	1.66 6.38	4.6 17.5	1.7 6.4
2	– –	– –	– –	– –	– –	– –	– –	– –	– –	– –	– –	– –	– –	– –
3	– –	– –	– –	– –	– –	– –	– –	– –	– –	– –	– –	– –	– –	– –
4	– –	– –	– –	– –	– –	– –	– –	– –	– –	– –	– –	– –	– –	– –
5	– –	– –	– –	– –	– –	– –	– –	– –	– –	– –	– –	– –	– –	– –
6	– –	– –	– –	– –	– –	– –	– –	– –	– –	– –	– –	– –	– –	– –
7	89.7 304.2	53.8 182.5	– –	– –	– –	– –	– –	– –	– –	– –	– –	– –	– –	– –
8	160.3 550.9	96.1 330.5	– –	– –	– –	– –	– –	– –	– –	– –	– –	– –	– –	– –
9	199.9 637.6	119.9 382.5	– –	– –	– –	– –	– –	– –	– –	– –	– –	– –	– –	– –
10	247.6 803.4	148.5 481.9	– –	47.8 155.0	– –	– –	– –	– –	– –	– –	– –	– –	– –	– –
11	163.4 466.8	98.0 280.0	– –	– –	– –	– –	– –	– –	– –	– –	– –	– –	– –	– –
12	– –	– –	– –	– –	– –	– –	– –	– –	– –	– –	– –	– –	– –	– –
13	259.6 765.9	155.7 459.4	– –	– –	– –	– –	– –	– –	– –	– –	– –	– –	– –	– –
14	– –	– –	– –	– –	– –	– –	– –	– –	– –	– –	– –	– –	4.4 19.6	2.0 8.8

(Continued)

TABLE A–4e PASTURE AND RANGE PLANTS FOR HORSES, COMPOSITION OF FEEDS, DATA EXPRESSED **AS-FED** AND **MOISTURE-FREE** (Continued)

Entry Number	Feed Name Description	International Feed Number	Moisture Basis: A-F (as-fed) or M-F (moisture-free)	Dry Matter	Ash	Crude Fiber	Neutral Det. Fib. (NDF)	Acid Det. Fib. (ADF)	Lignin	Ether Extract (Fat)	N-Free Exract	Crude Protein	Digestible Protein	TDN	Digestible Energy (Mcal)		Metabolizable Energy (Mcal)	
				%	%	%	%	%	%	%	%	%	%	%	lb	kg	lb	kg
15	CLOVER, LADINO *Trifolium repens* FRESH	2-01-383	A-F	18	1.9	2.5	–	–	–	0.9	8.1	4.4	–	–	–	–	–	–
			M-F	100	10.5	14.2	–	–	–	4.8	45.7	24.7	–	–				
16	CLOVER, RED *Trifolium pratense* EARLY BLOOM, FRESH[1]	2-01-428	A-F	20	2.0	4.6	8.0	6.2	–	1.0	8.3	3.8	–	–	–	–	–	–
			M-F	100	10.2	23.3	40.0	31.0	–	5.0	42.3	19.4	–					
17	CLOVER, WHITE *Trifolium repens* FRESH	2-01-468	A-F	18	2.1	2.8	–	–	–	0.6	7.2	5.0	–	–	–	–	–	–
			M-F	100	11.9	15.7	–	–	–	3.3	40.9	28.2	–					
18	CRESTED WHEATGRASS *Agropyron desertorum* EARLY BLOOM, FRESH	2-05-422	A-F	41	–	8.9	–	–	–	1.7	–	4.8	–	–	–	–	–	–
			M-F	100	–	21.7	–	–	–	4.1	–	11.7	–					
19	FESCUE, TALL (ALTA) *Festuca arundinacea* FRESH	2-01-889	A-F	28	2.5	7.5	19.5	–	–	0.9	14.3	2.7	–	–	–	–	–	–
			M-F	100	9.0	26.7	69.9	–	–	3.3	51.2	9.8	–					
20	GRASS-LEGUME FRESH	2-08-439	A-F	24	2.5	5.6	–	–	–	0.8	10.4	4.2	–	–	–	–	–	–
			M-F	100	10.5	23.9	–	–	–	3.4	44.4	17.8	–					
	KENTUCKY BLUEGRASS–SEE BLUEGRASS, KENTUCKY																	
21	LESPEDEZA, COMMON-KOREAN *Lespedeza striata-stipulacea* MATURE, FRESH	2-26-032	A-F	35	2.6	15.8	–	–	–	0.7	11.8	4.4	2.9	–	–	–	–	–
			M-F	100	7.4	45.1	–	–	–	2.1	33.7	12.7	8.3					
22	MILLET, PEARL (PEARL MILLET) *Pennisetum glaucum* FRESH	2-03-115	A-F	21	1.9	6.5	–	–	–	0.6	9.7	2.1	–	–	–	–	–	–
			M-F	100	9.2	31.1	–	–	–	2.9	46.8	10.1	–					
	MILO SORGHUM–SEE SORGHUM																	
23	OATGRASS, TALL *Arrhenatherum elatius* FRESH	2-03-267	A-F	30	2.0	10.5	–	–	–	0.9	14.3	2.6	–	–	–	–	–	–
			M-F	100	6.6	34.7	–	–	–	3.0	47.2	8.6	–					
24	OATS *Avena sativa* IMMATURE, FRESH	2-03-286	A-F	16	1.7	4.0	–	–	–	0.4	7.4	2.5	–	–	–	–	–	–
			M-F	100	10.6	24.9	–	–	–	2.6	46.3	15.6	–					
25	ORCHARDGRASS *Dactylis glomerata* FRESH, ALL ANALYSES	2-03-451	A-F	26	2.6	6.4	13.9	–	–	1.6	11.3	3.9	–	–	–	–	–	–
			M-F	100	10.0	24.8	54.0	–	–	6.4	43.8	15.0	–					
26	REDTOP *Agrostis alba* FULL BLOOM, FRESH[1]	2-03-891	A-F	26	1.8	6.6	16.6	–	–	0.9	14.8	2.1	–	–	–	–	–	–
			M-F	100	7.0	25.1	64.0	–	–	3.5	56.3	8.1	–					
27	RYEGRASS, ITALIAN *Lolium muliflorum* FRESH	2-04-073	A-F	23	3.9	4.7	–	–	–	0.9	9.0	4.0	–	–	–	–	–	–
			M-F	100	17.4	20.9	–	–	–	4.1	39.8	17.9	–					
28	SORGHUM *Sorghum bicolor* KAFIR, FRESH	2-04-424	A-F	24	1.9	6.6	–	–	–	0.7	12.0	2.4	–	–	–	–	–	–
			M-F	100	8.1	28.0	–	–	–	3.0	50.8	10.2	–					
29	MILO, FRESH[1]	2-04-436	A-F	30	1.8	7.6	19.5	12.0	–	0.5	17.2	2.6	–	–	–	–	–	–
			M-F	100	6.2	25.7	65.0	40.0	–	1.8	57.8	8.6	–					
30	TALL (ALTA) FESCUE *Festuca arundinacea* FRESH	2-01-889	A-F	28	2.5	7.5	19.5	–	–	0.9	14.3	2.7	–	–	–	–	–	–
			M-F	100	9.0	26.7	69.9	–	–	3.3	51.2	9.8	–					
31	TIMOTHY *Phleum pratense* FRESH	2-04-912	A-F	28	2.3	7.5	19.4	–	–	1.1	13.4	3.4	–	–	–	–	–	–
			M-F	100	8.2	27.0	69.9	–	–	4.1	48.4	12.3	–					
32	TREFOIL, BIRDSFOOT (DEERVETCH, BIRDSFOOT) *Lotus corniculatus* FRESH	2-20-786	A-F	19	2.2	4.1	9.5	–	–	0.8	8.5	3.7	–	–	–	–	–	–
			M-F	100	11.2	21.2	49.4	–	–	4.0	44.3	19.3	–					
33	WHEAT *Triticum aestivum* IMMATURE, FRESH	2-05-176	A-F	22	3.0	3.9	10.2	6.3	1.0	1.0	8.3	6.1	–	–	–	–	–	–
			M-F	100	13.3	17.4	46.2	28.4	4.5	4.4	37.5	27.4	–					
34	WHEATGRASS, CRESTED *Agropyron desertorum* IMMATURE, FRESH	2-05-420	A-F	28	2.9	6.2	–	–	–	0.6	12.9	6.0	–	–	–	–	–	–
			M-F	100	10.0	21.6	–	–	–	2.2	45.2	21.0	–					
	WHITE CLOVER–SEE CLOVER, WHITE																	

[1]Neutral Detergent Fiber (NDF) and Acid Detergent Fiber (ADF) values taken from *Nutrient Requirements of Dairy Cattle*, 6th rev. ed., NRC, National Academy Press, 1988, pp. 90–110, Table 7-1.

PASTURE AND RANGE PLANTS FOR HORSES

Entry Number	Macrominerals							Microminerals							Fat-Soluble Vitamins				
	Calcium (Ca)	Phos-phorus (P)	Sodium (Na)	Chlo-rine (Cl)	Mag-nesium (Mg)	Potas-sium (K)	Sulfur (S)	Cobalt (Co)	Copper (Cu)	Iodine (I)	Iron (Fe)	Man-ganese (Mn)	Sele-nium (Se)	Zinc (Zn)	A (1 mg Carotene = 1667 IU Vit A)	Carotene (Provitamin A)	D	E	K
	%	%	%	%	%	%	%	ppm or mg/kg	ppm or mg/kg	ppm or mg/kg	%	ppm or mg/kg	ppm or mg/kg	ppm or mg/kg	IU/g	ppm or mg/kg	IU/kg	ppm or mg/kg	ppm or mg/kg
15	0.22	0.07	0.02	–	0.09	0.33	0.02	–	–	–	0.007	12.7	–	–	96.2	57.7	–	–	–
	1.27	0.42	0.12	–	0.48	1.87	0.12	–	–	–	0.037	71.7	–	–	545.2	327.0	–	–	–
16	0.45	0.08	0.04	–	0.10	0.49	0.03	–	–	–	0.006	–	–	–	81.5	48.9	–	–	–
	2.26	0.38	0.20	–	0.51	2.49	0.17	–	–	–	0.030	–	–	–	412.6	247.5	–	–	–
17	0.25	0.09	0.07	0.11	0.08	0.38	0.06	–	–	–	0.006	54.4	–	–	44.0	26.4	–	54.6	–
	1.40	0.51	0.39	0.61	0.45	2.14	0.33	–	–	–	0.034	307.1	–	–	248.4	149.0	–	308.6	–
18	0.09	0.07	–	–	–	–	–	–	–	–	–	–	–	–	–	–	–	–	–
	0.22	0.18	–	–	–	–	–	–	–	–	–	–	–	–	–	–	–	–	–
19	0.13	0.05	0.03	–	0.07	0.70	–	0.113	1.0	–	0.003	18.0	–	5.9	–	–	–	–	–
	0.48	0.19	0.12	–	0.25	2.51	–	0.401	3.4	–	0.011	64.4	–	21.0	–	–	–	–	–
20	0.15	0.08	–	–	0.08	0.40	–	–	–	–	–	–	–	–	–	–	–	–	–
	0.62	0.34	–	–	0.32	1.70	–	–	–	–	–	–	–	–	–	–	–	–	–
21	0.35	0.07	–	–	–	–	–	–	–	–	–	–	–	–	–	–	–	–	–
	1.00	0.20	–	–	–	–	–	–	–	–	–	–	–	–	–	–	–	–	–
22	–	–	–	–	–	–	–	–	–	–	–	–	–	–	63.0	37.8	–	–	–
	–	–	–	–	–	–	–	–	–	–	–	–	–	–	304.2	182.5	–	–	–
23	0.12	0.14	–	–	–	0.91	–	–	–	–	–	–	–	–	–	–	–	–	–
	0.40	0.46	–	–	–	3.00	–	–	–	–	–	–	–	–	–	–	–	–	–
24	–	–	0.02	0.02	–	–	0.01	–	–	–	–	–	–	–	150.0	90.0	–	–	–
	–	–	0.11	0.10	–	–	0.08	–	–	–	–	–	–	–	934.4	560.5	–	–	–
25	0.09	0.05	0.03	–	0.06	0.74	–	0.055	2.5	–	0.003	28.5	–	5.3	137.1	82.2	–	112.3	–
	0.37	0.18	0.13	–	0.24	2.88	–	0.212	9.8	–	0.010	110.4	–	20.6	531.8	319.0	–	435.6	–
26	0.16	0.10	0.01	–	0.07	0.62	0.04	–	–	–	0.006	–	–	–	66.9	40.1	–	–	–
	0.62	0.37	0.05	–	0.25	2.35	0.16	–	–	–	0.020	–	–	–	254.4	152.6	–	–	–
27	0.15	0.09	0.00	–	0.08	0.45	0.02	–	–	–	0.023	–	–	–	–	–	–	–	–
	0.65	0.41	0.01	–	0.35	2.00	0.10	–	–	–	0.101	–	–	–	–	–	–	–	–
28	0.09	0.04	–	–	–	0.40	–	–	–	–	–	–	–	–	6.9	4.2	–	–	–
	0.38	0.17	–	–	–	1.70	–	–	–	–	–	–	–	–	29.4	17.6	–	–	–
29	0.09	0.05	–	–	–	0.81	–	–	–	–	–	–	–	–	–	–	–	–	–
	0.30	0.17	–	–	–	2.73	–	–	–	–	–	–	–	–	–	–	–	–	–
30	0.13	0.05	0.03	–	0.07	0.70	–	0.113	1.0	–	0.003	18.0	–	5.9	–	–	–	–	–
	0.48	0.19	0.12	–	0.25	2.51	–	0.401	3.4	–	0.011	64.4	–	21.0	–	–	–	–	–
31	0.14	0.08	0.03	0.14	0.06	0.69	0.04	0.041	2.2	–	0.004	24.6	–	7.5	103.2	61.9	–	42.6	–
	0.51	0.27	0.11	0.51	0.23	2.47	0.13	0.147	8.0	–	0.012	89.0	–	26.9	372.7	223.6	–	153.9	–
32	0.34	0.05	0.02	–	0.08	0.63	0.05	0.094	2.5	–	0.006	16.0	–	6.0	–	–	–	–	–
	1.74	0.26	0.11	–	0.40	3.26	0.25	0.487	12.8	–	0.031	82.9	–	31.1	–	–	–	–	–
33	0.09	0.09	0.04	–	0.05	0.78	0.05	–	–	–	0.003	–	–	–	192.5	115.4	–	–	–
	0.42	0.40	0.18	–	0.21	3.50	0.22	–	–	–	0.010	–	–	–	866.9	520.1	–	–	–
34	0.13	0.10	–	–	0.08	–	–	–	–	–	–	–	–	–	205.8	123.4	–	–	–
	0.44	0.33	–	–	0.28	–	–	–	–	–	–	–	–	–	722.9	433.6	–	–	–

(Continued)

PASTURE AND RANGE PLANTS

TABLE A–4e PASTURE AND RANGE PLANTS FOR HORSES, COMPOSITION OF FEEDS, DATA EXPRESSED **AS-FED** AND **MOISTURE-FREE** (Continued)

Entry Number	Feed Name Description	Moisture Basis: A-F (as-fed) or M-F (moisture-free)	Dry Matter	Water-Soluble Vitamins								
				B-12	Biotin	Choline	Folacin (Folic Acid)	Niacin	Pantothenic Acid (B-3)	Pyridoxine (B-6)	Riboflavin (B-2)	Thiamin (B-1)
			%	ppm or mg/kg	ppm or mg/kg	ppm or mg/kg	ppm or mg/kg	ppm or mg/kg	ppm or mg/kg	ppm or mg/kg	ppm or mg/kg	ppm or mg/kg
15	**CLOVER, LADINO** *Trifolium repens* FRESH	A-F	18	–	–	–	–	–	–	–	4.2	–
		M-F	100	–	–	–	–	–	–	–	24.1	–
16	**CLOVER, RED** *Trifolium pratense* EARLY BLOOM, FRESH	A-F	20	–	–	–	–	–	–	–	–	–
		M-F	100	–	–	–	–	–	–	–	–	–
17	**CLOVER, WHITE** *Trifolium repens* FRESH	A-F	18	–	–	–	–	11	–	–	16.0	2.5
		M-F	100	–	–	–	–	63	–	–	90.2	14.1
18	**CRESTED WHEATGRASS** *Agropyron desertorum* EARLY BLOOM, FRESH	A-F	41	–	–	–	–	–	–	–	–	–
		M-F	100	–	–	–	–	–	–	–	–	–
19	**FESCUE, TALL (ALTA)** *Festuca arundinacea* FRESH	A-F	28	–	–	–	–	–	–	–	–	–
		M-F	100	–	–	–	–	–	–	–	–	–
20	**GRASS-LEGUME** FRESH	A-F	24	–	–	–	–	–	–	–	–	–
		M-F	100	–	–	–	–	–	–	–	–	–
	KENTUCKY BLUEGRASS–SEE BLUEGRASS, KENTUCKY											
21	**LESPEDEZA, COMMON-KOREAN** *Lespedeza striata-stipulacea* MATURE, FRESH	A-F	35	–	–	–	–	–	–	–	–	–
		M-F	100	–	–	–	–	–	–	–	–	–
22	**MILLET, PEARL (PEARL MILLET)** *Panicum miliaceum* FRESH	A-F	25	–	–	–	–	–	–	–	–	–
		M-F	100	–	–	–	–	–	–	–	–	–
	MILO SORGHUM–SEE SORGHUM											
23	**OATGRASS, TALL** *Arrhenatherum elatius* FRESH	A-F	30	–	–	–	–	–	–	–	–	–
		M-F	100	–	–	–	–	–	–	–	–	–
24	**OATS** *Avena sativa* IMMATURE, FRESH	A-F	16	–	–	–	–	–	–	–	–	–
		M-F	100	–	–	–	–	–	–	–	–	–
25	**ORCHARDGRASS** *Dactylis glomerata* FRESH, ALL ANALYSES	A-F	26	–	–	–	–	–	–	–	–	1.9
		M-F	100	–	–	–	–	–	–	–	–	7.3
26	**REDTOP** *Agrostis alba* FULL BLOOM, FRESH	A-F	26	–	–	–	–	–	–	–	–	–
		M-F	100	–	–	–	–	–	–	–	–	–
27	**RYEGRASS, ITALIAN** *Lolium muliflorum* FRESH	A-F	23	–	–	–	–	–	–	–	–	–
		M-F	100	–	–	–	–	–	–	–	–	–
28	**SORGHUM** *Sorghum bicolor* KAFIR, FRESH	A-F	24	–	–	–	–	9	3.3	1.41	1.0	–
		M-F	100	–	–	–	–	39	14.1	5.95	4.2	–
29	MILO, FRESH	A-F	30	–	–	–	–	–	–	–	–	–
		M-F	100	–	–	–	–	–	–	–	–	–
30	**TALL (ALTA) FESCUE** *Fesuca arundinacea* FRESH	A-F	28	–	–	–	–	–	–	–	–	–
		M-F	100	–	–	–	–	–	–	–	–	–
31	**TIMOTHY** *Phleum pratense* FRESH	A-F	28	–	–	–	–	–	–	–	3.2	0.8
		M-F	100	–	–	–	–	–	–	–	11.5	2.9
32	**TREFOIL, BIRDSFOOT (DEERVETCH, BIRDSFOOT)** *Lotus corniculatus* FRESH	A-F	19	–	–	–	–	–	–	–	–	–
		M-F	100	–	–	–	–	–	–	–	–	–
33	**WHEAT** *Triticum aestivum* IMMATURE, FRESH	A-F	22	–	–	–	–	13	4.7	–	6.1	–
		M-F	100	–	–	–	–	57	21.2	–	27.6	–
34	**WHEATGRASS, CRESTED** *Agropyron desertorum* IMMATURE, FRESH	A-F	28	–	–	–	–	–	–	–	–	–
		M-F	100	–	–	–	–	–	–	–	–	–
	WHITE CLOVER–SEE CLOVER, WHITE											

Care-giving/care-seeking behavior of mare and foal, which exists until after weaning. (Courtesy, Mr. and Mrs. R. H. Adams, Vancouver, WA)

TABLE A–4f MINERAL SUPPLEMENTS FOR HORSES, COMPOSITION OF FEEDS, DATA EXPRESSED **AS-FED** AND **MOISTURE-FREE** (See footnote at end of table.)

Entry Number	Feed Name Description	International Feed Number	Moisture Basis: A-F (as-fed) or M-F (moisture-free)	Dry Matter	Ash	Crude Fiber	Ether Extract (Fat)	N-Free Exract	Crude Protein (6.25 × N)	Digestible Protein
				%	%	%	%	%	%	%
1	BONE MEAL, STEAMED*	6-00-400	A-F	95	67.3	1.9	3.6	3.8	18.6	—
			M-F	100	70.7	2.0	3.8	4.0	19.5	—
2	CALCIUM CARBONATE*	6-01-069	A-F	100	97.1	—	—	—	—	—
			M-F	100	97.5	—	—	—	—	—
3	CALCIUM PHOSPHATE, DIBASIC, FROM DEFLUORINATED PHOSPHORIC ACID*	6-01-080	A-F	97	89.7	—	—	—	—	—
			M-F	100	92.5	—	—	—	—	—
4	CALCIUM PHOSPHATE, DIBASIC, FROM FURNACED PHOSPHORIC ACID*	6-26-335	A-F	97	85.6	—	—	—	—	—
			M-F	100	88.2	—	—	—	—	—
5	COPPER (CUPRIC) SULFATE, PENTAHYDRATE*	6-01-719	A-F	99	—	—	—	—	—	—
			M-F	100	—	—	—	—	—	—
6	COPPER (CUPROUS) OXIDE*	6-28-224	A-F	99	—	—	—	—	—	—
			M-F	100	—	—	—	—	—	—
7	FERROUS (IRON) CARBONATE*	6-01-863	A-F	99	—	—	—	—	—	—
			M-F	100	—	—	—	—	—	—
8	FERROUS (IRON) SULFATE, MONOHYDRATE*	6-01-869	A-F	98	98.0	—	—	—	—	—
			M-F	100	100.0	—	—	—	—	—
9	KELP (SEAWEED) *Laminariales* (order), *Fucales* (order) WHOLE, DEHY	1-08-073	A-F	91	35.0	6.5	0.5	42.4	6.5	3.4
			M-F	100	38.6	7.1	0.5	46.7	7.1	3.7
10	LIMESTONE, GROUND*	6-02-632	A-F	100	93.8	—	—	—	—	—
			M-F	100	94.1	—	—	—	—	—
11	LIMESTONE, MAGNESIUM (DOLOMITE), GROUND*	6-02-633	A-F	100	—	—	—	—	—	—
			M-F	100	—	—	—	—	—	—
12	MAGNESIUM OXIDE*	6-02-756	A-F	98	98.3	—	—	—	—	—
			M-F	100	100.0	—	—	—	—	—
13	MAGNESIUM SULFATE (EPSOM SALTS)*	6-02-758	A-F	99	—	—	—	—	—	—
			M-F	100	—	—	—	—	—	—
14	MANGANOUS (MANGANESE) OXIDE*	6-03-054	A-F	99	—	—	—	—	—	—
			M-F	100	—	—	—	—	—	—
15	MANGANOUS (MANGANESE) SULFATE*	6-26-136	A-F	100	—	—	—	—	—	—
			M-F	100	—	—	—	—	—	—
16	OYSTER SHELLS, GROUND (FLOUR)*	6-03-481	A-F	99	79.0	1.8	0.3	17.0	0.7	—
			M-F	100	79.9	1.8	0.3	17.2	0.7	—
17	PHOSPHATE, DEFLUORINATED	6-01-780	A-F	100	99.3	—	—	—	—	—
			M-F	100	99.7	—	—	—	—	—
18	PHOSPHATE ROCK, LOW FLUORINE*	6-03-946	A-F	—	—	—	—	—	—	—
			M-F	100	—	—	—	—	—	—
19	PHOSPHORIC ACID, FEED GRADE (ORTHO)*	6-03-707	A-F	75	—	—	—	—	—	—
			M-F	100	—	—	—	—	—	—
20	POTASSIUM CHLORIDE*	6-03-755	A-F	100	98.9	—	—	—	—	—
			M-F	100	99.0	—	—	—	—	—
21	POTASSIUM IODIDE*	6-03-759	A-F	—	—	—	—	—	—	—
			M-F	100	—	—	—	—	—	—
22	SODIUM BICARBONATE*	6-04-272	A-F	100	—	—	—	—	—	—
			M-F	100	—	—	—	—	—	—
23	SODIUM CHLORIDE*	6-04-152	A-F	97	93.0	—	—	—	—	—
			M-F	100	95.9	—	—	—	—	—
24	SODIUM IODIDE*	6-04-279	A-F	—	—	—	—	—	—	—
			M-F	100	—	—	—	—	—	—
25	SODIUM PHOSPHATE, MONOBASIC*	6-04-288	A-F	97	96.9	—	—	—	—	—
			M-F	100	99.8	—	—	—	—	—
26	SODIUM SELENATE*	6-26-014	A-F	99	—	—	—	—	—	—
			M-F	100	—	—	—	—	—	—
27	SODIUM SELENITE*	6-26-013	A-F	99	—	—	—	—	—	—
			M-F	100	—	—	—	—	—	—
28	SODIUM SULFATE, DECAHYDRATE	6-04-291	A-F	97	—	—	—	—	—	—
			M-F	100	—	—	—	—	—	—
29	SODIUM TRIPOLYPHOSPHATE*	6-08-076	A-F	97	89.7	—	—	—	—	—
			M-F	100	92.8	—	—	—	—	—
30	SULFUR*	6-04-705	A-F	99	—	—	—	—	—	—
			M-F	100	—	—	—	—	—	—
31	ZINC OXIDE*	6-05-553	A-F	—	—	—	—	—	—	—
			M-F	100	—	—	—	—	—	—
32	ZINC SULFATE, MONOHYDRATE*	6-05-555	A-F	99	—	—	—	—	—	—
			M-F	100	—	—	—	—	—	—

*Sources most commonly used in commercial feeds.

MINERAL SUPPLEMENTS FOR HORSES

Entry Number	Macrominerals							Microminerals							
	Calcium (Ca)	Phosphorus (P)	Sodium (Na)	Chlorine (Cl)	Magnesium (Mg)	Potassium (K)	Sulfur (S)	Cobalt (Co)	Copper (Cu)	Fluorine (F)	Iodine (I)	Iron (Fe)	Manganese (Mn)	Selenium (Se)	Zinc (Zn)
	%	%	%	%	%	%	%	ppm or mg/kg	ppm or mg/kg	ppm or mg/kg	ppm or mg/kg	%	ppm or mg/kg	ppm or mg/kg	ppm or mg/kg
1	25.98 27.31	11.80 12.40	0.40 0.42	0.01 0.01	0.78 0.82	0.18 0.19	0.34 0.36	0 0	162 170	637 669	29 31	0.085 0.089	37 39	– –	362 381
2	37.97 38.13	0.04 0.04	0.07 0.07	0.04 0.04	0.41 0.41	0.04 0.04	0.08 0.08	– –	14 14	0 0	– –	0.059 0.059	159 160	0.07 0.07	17 17
3	22.00 22.67	18.43 19.00	1.56 1.61	– –	0.51 0.52	0.10 0.10	0.69 0.71	8 9	9 9	940 969	– –	0.844 0.870	253 261	– –	122 126
4	23.00 23.71	18.50 19.07	0.08 0.08	– –	0.60 0.62	0.07 0.07	– –	– –	80 82	1150 1186	– –	1.000 1.031	300 309	0.60 0.62	220 227
5	– –	– –	– –	– –	– –	– –	13.25 13.32	– –	250976 252257	– –	– –	0.010 0.011	2 2	– –	9 9
6	– –	– –	– –	– –	– –	– –	– –	– –	879318 888200	– –	– –	– –	– –	– –	– –
7	1.24 1.25	0.01 0.01	– –	– –	0.33 0.33	– –	1.77 1.79	200 202	3000 3030	– –	– –	40.667 41.077	9000 9091	– –	– –
8	– –	– –	– –	– –	0.50 0.51	– –	17.80 18.16	– –	– –	– –	– –	31.000 31.633	– –	– –	– –
9	2.47 2.72	0.28 0.31	– –	– –	0.85 0.93	– –	– –	– –	– –	– –	– –	– –	– –	– –	– –
10	37.12 37.22	0.21 0.22	0.06 0.06	0.03 0.03	1.13 1.13	0.11 0.11	0.04 0.04	– –	11 11	– –	– –	0.357 0.358	269 270	– –	19 19
11	20.61 20.65	0.02 0.02	0.38 0.38	0.12 0.12	10.37 10.39	0.27 0.27	0.01 0.01	– –	20 20	– –	– –	0.053 0.053	– –	– –	– –
12	1.66 1.69	– –	– –	– –	55.19 56.15	– –	0.10 0.10	501 510	5 5	251 255	– –	1.048 1.066	80 82	0.35 0.35	9 9
13	0.02 0.02	– –	– –	0.01 0.01	9.60 9.68	– –	13.00 13.11	– –	– –	– –	– –	– –	– –	10.12 10.20	– –
14	0.16 0.16	0.10 0.10	0.06 0.06	– –	0.70 0.71	0.58 0.59	0.01 0.01	300 303	724 731	– –	– –	3.436 3.470	620217 626482	– –	1349 1363
15	– –	– –	– –	– –	0.30 0.30	– –	19.01 19.10	– –	– –	– –	– –	0.040 0.041	250000 251256	– –	– –
16	35.85 36.27	0.10 0.10	0.21 0.21	0.01 0.01	0.24 0.24	0.10 0.10	– –	– –	15 15	– –	– –	0.254 0.257	178 180	– –	7 7
17	31.99 32.10	17.07 17.13	3.26 3.27	– –	0.29 0.29	0.10 0.10	0.13 0.13	10 10	40 41	1794 1800	– –	0.840 0.843	496 498	– –	90 90
18	– 36.00	– 14.00	– –	– –	– –	– –	– –	– –	– –	4500	– –	– –	– –	– –	– –
19	0.14 0.18	20.88 27.84	0.18 0.23	– –	0.40 0.53	0.06 0.08	1.56 2.08	– –	17 22	1900 2533	– –	0.913 1.217	500 667	– –	210 280
20	0.05 0.05	– –	1.00 1.00	46.88 46.93	0.23 0.23	51.31 51.37	0.32 0.32	– –	7 7	– –	– –	0.061 0.061	7 7	– –	9 9
21	– –	– –	– 0.01	– –	– –	21.00	– –	– –	– –	– –	681700	– –	– –	– –	– –
22	– –	– –	26.87 27.00	– –	– –	0.01 0.01	– –	– –	– –	450138 452400	– –	0.001 0.002	– –	– –	– –
23	– –	– –	38.17 39.34	58.46 60.26	– –	– –	– –	– –	– –	– –	– –	– –	– –	– –	– –
24	– –	– –	– 15.33	– –	– –	– –	– –	– –	– –	– –	– –	– –	– –	– –	– –
25	0.04 0.04	24.84 25.60	18.65 19.23	– –	– –	0.14 0.14	– –	– –	7 7	– –	– –	– –	– –	– –	5 5
26	– –	– –	24.18 24.42	– –	– –	– –	– –	– –	– –	– –	– –	– –	– –	415898.96 420100.00	– –
27	– –	– –	26.40 26.60	– –	0.01 0.01	– –	– –	– –	10 10	– –	– –	0.031 0.031	– –	452927.78 456386.34	– –
28	– –	– –	31.33 32.30	– –	– –	– –	9.66 9.96	– –	– –	– –	– –	0.001 0.002	– –	– –	– –
29	– –	24.53 25.38	30.18 31.23	– –	– –	– –	– –	– –	– –	247 256	– –	0.004 0.004	– –	– –	– –
30	– –	– –	– –	– –	– –	– –	99.00 100.00	– –	– –	– –	– –	– –	– –	– –	291951 294900
31	– 4.29	– –	– –	– –	0.30	– –	1.00	1500	500	– –	– –	0.551	800	– –	724968
32	0.05 0.05	– –	– –	0.20 0.20	– –	– –	17.62 17.76	– –	55 56	– –	– –	0.053 0.053	169 171	99.24 100.00	359073 361815

TABLE A–4g VITAMIN SUPPLEMENTS FOR HORSES, COMPOSITION OF FEEDS, DATA EXPRESSED AS-FED AND MOISTURE-FREE

Entry Number	Feed Name Description	International Feed Number	Moisture Basis: A-F (as-fed) or M-F (moisture-free)	Dry Matter %	Ash %	Crude Fiber %	Neutral Det. Fib. (NDF) %	Acid Det. Fib. (ADF) %	Lignin %	Ether Extract (Fat) %	N-Free Exract %	Crude Protein %	Digestible Protein %	TDN %	Digestible Energy Mcal lb	kg	Metabolizable Energy Mcal lb	kg
	ALFALFA (LUCERNE) *Medicago sativa*																	
1	MEAL, DEHY, 17% PROTEIN	1-00-023	A-F	92	9.7	24.0	41.3	31.5	9.7	2.8	37.8	17.4	11.8	47	0.89	1.96	0.73	1.61
			M-F	100	10.6	26.2	45.0	34.3	10.6	3.0	41.2	18.9	12.8	51	0.97	2.14	0.80	1.75
2	MEAL, DEHY, 20% PROTEIN	1-00-024	A-F	92	10.2	20.8	—	27.0	—	3.3	37.1	20.2	14.0	50	0.94	2.08	0.77	1.70
			M-F	100	11.1	22.7	—	29.4	—	3.6	40.5	22.1	15.2	55	1.03	2.27	0.84	1.86
3	MEAL, DEHY, 22% PROTEIN	1-07-851	A-F	93	10.2	18.3	—	25.3	—	4.1	38.1	22.2	15.5	52	0.98	2.15	0.80	1.76
			M-F	100	11.0	19.8	—	27.3	—	4.4	41.0	23.9	16.6	56	1.05	2.32	0.86	1.90
	ANIMAL																	
4	LIVER, MEAL	5-00-389	A-F	93	6.3	1.4	—	—	—	15.7	3.2	66.1	66.1	—	—	—	—	—
			M-F	100	6.8	1.5	—	—	—	17.0	3.5	71.4	71.4	—	—	—	—	—
	BREWERS GRAINS																	
5	DEHY	5-02-141	A-F	92	3.6	13.0	38.7	23.9	4.6	6.6	41.6	27.3	21.0	48	—	—	—	—
			M-F	100	4.0	14.1	42.0	26.0	5.0	7.1	45.2	29.6	22.8	52	—	—	—	—
	CARROT *Daucus* spp																	
6	ROOTS, FRESH	4-01-145	A-F	11	1.0	1.1	—	—	—	0.2	8.1	1.2	0.8	8	0.14	0.31	0.12	0.26
			M-F	100	8.4	9.5	—	—	—	1.3	70.7	10.0	7.0	67	1.23	2.72	1.01	2.23
	CATTLE *Bos taurus*																	
7	WHEY, DEHY	4-01-182	A-F	93	8.8	0.2	0.3	0.2	—	0.8	70.2	13.3	9.6	—	—	—	—	—
			M-F	100	9.4	0.2	0.3	0.2	—	0.8	75.3	14.2	10.3	—	—	—	—	—
	COD, FISH *Gadus morrhua, Gadus macrocephalus*																	
8	LIVER, MEAL	5-08-423	A-F	93	2.9	0.7	—	—	—	28.9	9.6	50.4	48.4	—	—	—	—	—
			M-F	100	3.1	0.8	—	—	—	31.2	10.4	54.5	52.3	—	—	—	—	—
9	LIVER OIL	7-01-993	A-F	100	—	—	—	—	—	99.5	—	—	—	—	—	—	—	—
			M-F	100	—	—	—	—	—	100.0	—	—	—	—	—	—	—	—
	CORN *Zea mays*																	
10	DISTILLERS GRAINS WITH SOLUBLES, DEHY	5-02-843	A-F	92	4.5	9.1	—	—	—	9.2	41.9	27.1	22.1	—	—	—	—	—
			M-F	100	4.9	9.9	—	—	—	10.1	45.7	29.5	24.1	—	—	—	—	—
	DISTILLERS PRODUCTS (ALSO SEE CORN)																	
11	GRAINS, DEHY	5-02-144	A-F	93	1.5	12.8	—	—	—	7.4	43.5	27.3	22.3	—	—	—	—	—
			M-F	100	1.6	13.8	—	—	—	8.0	47.0	29.5	24.1	—	—	—	—	—
12	SOLUBLES, DEHY	5-02-147	A-F	92	6.2	3.4	—	—	—	8.9	44.8	28.8	24.0	—	—	—	—	—
			M-F	100	6.7	3.7	—	—	—	9.7	48.6	31.3	26.1	—	—	—	—	—
	FATS AND OILS																	
13	GERM OIL (WHEAT)	7-05-207	A-F	100	—	—	—	—	—	99.5	—	—	—	—	—	—	—	—
			M-F	100	—	—	—	—	—	100.0	—	—	—	—	—	—	—	—
14	LIVER OIL (COD)	7-01-993	A-F	100	—	—	—	—	—	99.5	—	—	—	—	—	—	—	—
			M-F	100	—	—	—	—	—	100.0	—	—	—	—	—	—	—	—
	FISH																	
15	SOLUBLES, DEHY	5-01-971	A-F	93	12.7	2.0	—	—	—	9.0	8.7	60.4	59.7	—	—	—	—	—
			M-F	100	13.7	2.1	—	—	—	9.7	9.4	65.1	64.3	—	—	—	—	—
	FISH, COD *Gadus morrhua, Gadus macrocephalus*																	
16	LIVER, MEAL	5-08-423	A-F	93	2.9	0.7	—	—	—	28.9	9.6	50.4	48.4	—	—	—	—	—
			M-F	100	3.1	0.8	—	—	—	31.2	10.4	54.5	52.3	—	—	—	—	—
17	LIVER OIL	7-01-993	A-F	100	—	—	—	—	—	99.5	—	—	—	—	—	—	—	—
			M-F	100	—	—	—	—	—	100.0	—	—	—	—	—	—	—	—
	FISH, SARDINE *Clupea* spp, *Sardinops* spp																	
18	MEAL MECH EXTD	5-02-015	A-F	93	15.8	1.0	—	—	—	5.0	6.1	65.2	65.1	—	—	—	—	—
			M-F	100	17.0	1.1	—	—	—	5.4	6.5	70.0	69.8	—	—	—	—	—
19	SOLUBLES, CONDENSED	5-02-014	A-F	50	10.2	—	—	—	—	9.4	0.6	29.5	28.7	—	—	—	—	—
			M-F	100	20.5	—	—	—	—	18.9	1.2	59.4	57.8	—	—	—	—	—
	MEAT																	
20	SOLUBLES, DEHY	5-00-393	A-F	90	5.7	—	—	—	—	—	—	80.0	82.0	—	—	—	—	—
			M-F	100	6.3	—	—	—	—	—	—	88.9	91.2	—	—	—	—	—
	OATS *Avena sativa*																	
21	IMMATURE, FRESH	2-03-286	A-F	16	1.7	4.0	—	—	—	0.4	7.4	2.5	—	—	—	—	—	—
			M-F	100	10.6	24.9	—	—	—	2.6	46.3	15.6	—	—	—	—	—	—
	WHEAT *Triticum aestivum*																	
22	GERM MEAL	5-05-218	A-F	88	4.3	3.1	—	4.4	—	8.5	48.1	24.4	19.4	—	—	—	—	—
			M-F	100	4.9	3.5	—	5.0	—	9.6	54.4	27.6	21.9	—	—	—	—	—
23	GERM OIL	7-05-207	A-F	100	—	—	—	—	—	99.5	—	—	—	—	—	—	—	—
			M-F	100	—	—	—	—	—	100.0	—	—	—	—	—	—	—	—
	WHEY, CATTLE *Bos taurus*																	
24	DEHY	4-01-182	A-F	93	8.8	0.2	0.3	0.2	—	0.8	70.2	13.3	9.6	—	—	—	—	—
			M-F	100	9.4	0.2	0.3	0.2	—	0.8	75.3	14.2	10.3	—	—	—	—	—
	YEAST, BREWERS *Saccharomyces cerevisiae*																	
25	DEHY	7-05-527	A-F	93	6.5	3.0	—	3.7	—	0.9	38.8	43.8	—	—	—	—	—	—
			M-F	100	7.0	3.2	—	4.0	—	1.0	41.7	47.1	—	—	—	—	—	—
	YEAST, PRIMARY *Saccharomyces cerevisiae*																	
26	DEHY	7-05-533	A-F	93	8.0	3.1	—	—	—	1.0	32.5	48.0	—	—	—	—	—	—
			M-F	100	8.6	3.3	—	—	—	1.1	35.1	51.8	—	—	—	—	—	—
	YEAST, TORULA *Torulopsis utilis*																	
27	DEHY	7-05-534	A-F	93	8.0	2.5	—	3.7	—	1.6	31.5	49.6	—	—	—	—	—	—
			M-F	100	8.6	2.7	—	4.0	—	1.7	33.8	53.3	—	—	—	—	—	—

VITAMIN SUPPLEMENTS FOR HORSES

Entry Number	Macrominerals							Microminerals							Fat-Soluble Vitamins				
	Calcium (Ca)	Phosphorus (P)	Sodium (Na)	Chlorine (Cl)	Magnesium (Mg)	Potassium (K)	Sulfur (S)	Cobalt (Co)	Copper (Cu)	Iodine (I)	Iron (Fe)	Manganese (Mn)	Selenium (Se)	Zinc (Zn)	A (1 mg Carotene = 1667 IU Vit A)	Carotene (Provitamin A)	D	E	K
	%	%	%	%	%	%	%	ppm or mg/kg	ppm or mg/kg	ppm or mg/kg	%	ppm or mg/kg	ppm or mg/kg	ppm or mg/kg	IU/g	ppm or mg/kg	IU/kg	ppm or mg/kg	ppm or mg/kg
1	1.40	0.23	0.10	0.47	0.29	2.38	0.23	0.302	8.6	0.148	0.041	31.0	0.335	19.3	200.3	120.2	–	105.7	8.24
	1.52	0.25	0.11	0.52	0.32	2.60	0.25	0.329	9.3	0.162	0.045	33.8	0.365	21.1	218.5	131.1	–	115.3	8.98
2	1.59	0.28	0.11	0.47	0.33	2.41	0.50	0.259	12.2	0.135	0.036	45.2	0.285	21.8	265.4	159.2	–	143.3	14.19
	1.74	0.31	0.13	0.51	0.36	2.63	0.55	0.283	13.3	0.147	0.039	49.4	0.311	23.8	289.7	173.8	–	156.4	15.50
3	1.69	0.30	0.12	0.52	0.31	2.40	0.30	0.311	9.8	0.166	0.036	36.4	0.534	19.5	391.4	234.8	–	221.3	11.65
	1.82	0.33	0.13	0.56	0.33	2.58	0.32	0.336	10.5	0.179	0.039	39.2	0.576	21.0	421.8	253.0	–	238.4	12.55
4	0.56	1.26	–	–	0.10	–	–	0.135	89.4	–	0.064	8.8	–	61.8	–	–	–	–	–
	0.61	1.36	–	–	0.11	–	–	0.146	96.5	–	0.069	9.5	–	66.8	–	–	–	–	–
5	0.30	0.51	0.21	0.15	0.15	0.09	0.30	0.076	21.7	0.066	0.024	37.2	–	27.3	0.8	0.5	–	26.7	–
	0.33	0.55	0.23	0.17	0.17	0.09	0.32	0.083	23.6	0.072	0.026	40.4	–	29.6	0.8	0.5	–	29.0	–
6	0.05	0.04	0.06	0.06	0.02	0.32	0.02	–	1.2	–	0.002	3.6	–	–	129.9	77.9	–	6.9	–
	0.40	0.35	0.48	0.50	0.20	2.80	0.17	–	10.4	–	0.013	31.5	–	–	1129.4	677.5	–	60.2	–
7	0.86	0.76	0.62	0.07	0.13	1.11	1.04	0.111	46.5	–	0.017	5.9	–	3.2	–	–	–	0.2	–
	0.92	0.82	0.66	0.08	0.14	1.19	1.11	0.119	49.9	–	0.019	6.3	–	3.4	–	–	–	0.2	–
8	0.16	0.69	–	–	–	–	–	–	–	–	–	–	–	–	–	–	–	–	–
	0.17	0.75	–	–	–	–	–	–	–	–	–	–	–	–	–	–	–	–	–
9	–	–	–	–	–	–	–	–	–	–	–	–	–	–	845.8	–	–	39.5	–
	–	–	–	–	–	–	–	–	–	–	–	–	–	–	850.0	–	–	39.7	–
10	0.16	0.69	0.47	0.17	0.18	0.47	0.31	0.152	52.6	0.051	0.024	24.0	0.331	80.7	6.2	3.7	1	39.8	–
	0.17	0.76	0.52	0.18	0.20	0.51	0.33	0.165	57.3	0.055	0.026	26.1	0.361	87.9	6.8	4.1	1	43.4	–
11	0.12	0.54	0.05	0.05	0.09	0.20	0.46	0.092	47.9	–	0.027	35.0	–	–	13.0	7.8	–	30.5	–
	0.13	0.59	0.05	0.06	0.10	0.21	0.49	0.099	51.7	–	0.029	37.8	–	–	14.0	8.4	–	32.9	–
12	0.24	1.35	0.45	–	0.53	1.97	–	0.196	71.6	–	0.031	64.1	–	138.0	1.9	1.1	–	–	–
	0.26	1.47	0.49	–	0.58	2.14	–	0.213	77.9	–	0.034	69.7	–	150.0	2.0	1.2	–	–	–
13	–	–	–	–	–	–	–	–	–	–	–	–	–	–	–	–	–	–	18.66
	–	–	–	–	–	–	–	–	–	–	–	–	–	–	–	–	–	–	18.75
14	–	–	–	–	–	–	–	–	–	–	–	–	–	–	845.8	–	–	39.5	–
	–	–	–	–	–	–	–	–	–	–	–	–	–	–	850.0	–	–	39.7	–
15	0.40	1.27	1.70	–	0.30	2.50	0.45	–	20.0	–	0.095	50.4	2.692	76.7	–	–	–	6.1	–
	0.43	1.37	1.83	–	0.32	2.69	0.48	–	21.5	–	0.102	54.3	2.901	82.6	–	–	–	6.5	–
16	0.16	0.69	–	–	–	–	–	–	–	–	–	–	–	–	–	–	–	–	–
	0.17	0.75	–	–	–	–	–	–	–	–	–	–	–	–	–	–	–	–	–
17	–	–	–	–	–	–	–	–	–	–	–	–	–	–	845.8	–	–	39.5	–
	–	–	–	–	–	–	–	–	–	–	–	–	–	–	850.0	–	–	39.7	–
18	4.61	2.68	0.18	0.41	0.10	0.32	–	0.183	20.2	–	0.030	23.2	1.772	–	–	–	–	–	–
	4.95	2.88	0.19	0.44	0.11	0.35	–	0.197	21.7	–	0.033	24.9	1.903	–	–	–	–	–	–
19	0.14	0.83	0.18	0.28	–	0.18	0.11	–	25.8	4.934	0.002	24.9	–	–	–	–	–	–	–
	0.28	1.67	0.36	0.56	–	0.36	0.22	–	51.9	9.928	0.005	50.1	–	–	–	–	–	–	–
20	0.45	0.67	–	–	–	–	–	–	–	–	–	–	–	–	–	–	–	–	–
	0.50	0.74	–	–	–	–	–	–	–	–	–	–	–	–	–	–	–	–	–
21	–	–	0.02	0.02	–	–	0.01	–	–	–	–	–	–	–	150.0	90.0	–	–	–
	–	–	0.11	0.10	–	–	0.08	–	–	–	–	–	–	–	934.4	560.5	–	–	–
22	0.06	0.95	0.02	0.06	0.25	0.94	0.27	0.120	9.2	–	0.006	132.5	0.463	119.4	–	–	–	141.2	–
	0.06	1.07	0.03	0.07	0.28	1.06	0.30	0.136	10.4	–	0.007	149.9	0.524	135.1	–	–	–	159.7	–
23	–	–	–	–	–	–	–	–	–	–	–	–	–	–	–	–	–	–	18.66
	–	–	–	–	–	–	–	–	–	–	–	–	–	–	–	–	–	–	18.75
24	0.86	0.76	0.62	0.07	0.13	1.11	1.04	0.111	46.5	–	0.017	5.9	–	3.2	–	–	–	0.2	–
	0.92	0.82	0.66	0.08	0.14	1.19	1.11	0.119	49.9	–	0.019	6.3	–	3.4	–	–	–	0.2	–
25	0.14	1.36	0.07	0.07	0.24	1.69	0.43	0.506	38.4	0.358	0.009	6.7	0.911	39.0	–	–	–	2.1	–
	0.15	1.47	0.08	0.08	0.26	1.82	0.46	0.544	41.3	0.384	0.009	7.2	0.979	41.9	–	–	–	2.3	–
26	0.36	1.72	–	0.02	0.36	–	0.57	–	–	–	0.030	3.7	–	–	–	–	–	–	–
	0.39	1.86	–	0.02	0.39	–	0.62	–	–	–	0.033	4.0	–	–	–	–	–	–	–
27	0.55	1.61	0.01	0.02	0.14	1.92	0.55	0.031	11.9	2.502	0.011	9.3	–	99.5	–	–	–	–	–
	0.59	1.73	0.01	0.02	0.15	2.06	0.59	0.033	12.8	2.689	0.012	10.0	–	107.0	–	–	–	–	–

(Continued)

VITAMIN SUPPLEMENTS

TABLE A–4g VITAMIN SUPPLEMENTS FOR HORSES, COMPOSITION OF FEEDS, DATA EXPRESSED **AS-FED** AND **MOISTURE-FREE** (Continued)

VITAMIN SUPPLEMENTS

Entry Number	Feed Name Description	Moisture Basis: A-F (as-fed) or M-F (moisture-free)	Dry Matter	Water-Soluble Vitamins								
				B-12	Biotin	Choline	Folacin (Folic Acid)	Niacin	Pantothenic Acid (B-3)	Pyridoxine (B-6)	Riboflavin (B-2)	Thiamin (B-1)
			%	ppm or mg/kg	ppm or mg/kg	ppm or mg/kg	ppm or mg/kg	ppm or mg/kg	ppm or mg/kg	ppm or mg/kg	ppm or mg/kg	ppm or mg/kg
	ALFALFA (LUCERNE) *Medicago sativa*											
1	MEAL, DEHY, 17% PROTEIN	A-F	92	–	0.33	1369	4.37	37	29.7	7.18	12.9	3.4
		M-F	100	–	0.36	1494	4.77	40	32.4	7.83	14.1	3.7
2	MEAL, DEHY, 20% PROTEIN	A-F	92	–	0.35	1417	2.96	48	35.5	8.72	15.2	5.4
		M-F	100	–	0.39	1547	3.24	52	38.8	9.52	16.6	5.9
3	MEAL, DEHY, 22% PROTEIN	A-F	93	–	0.33	1605	5.15	50	39.0	8.28	17.6	5.9
		M-F	100	–	0.36	1729	5.55	54	42.0	8.92	19.0	6.3
	ANIMAL											
4	LIVER, MEAL	A-F	93	501.3	0.02	11370	5.56	205	29.2	–	36.2	0.2
		M-F	100	541.5	0.02	12281	6.01	221	31.5	–	39.1	0.2
	BREWERS GRAINS											
5	DEHY	A-F	92	3.6	0.44	1651	0.22	44	8.2	1.03	1.5	0.6
		M-F	100	3.9	0.48	1792	0.24	47	8.9	1.11	1.6	0.7
	CARROT *Daucus* spp											
6	ROOTS, FRESH	A-F	11	–	0.01	–	0.14	7	3.5	1.39	0.6	0.7
		M-F	100	–	0.07	–	1.21	58	30.1	12.05	4.9	5.8
	CATTLE *Bos taurus*											
7	WHEY, DEHY	A-F	93	18.9	0.35	1790	0.85	11	46.2	3.21	27.4	4.0
		M-F	100	20.3	0.38	1921	0.91	11	49.6	3.45	29.4	4.3
	COD, FISH *Gadus morrhua, Gadus macrocephalus*											
8	LIVER, MEAL	A-F	93	–	–	–	–	132	46.1	32.85	33.3	18.1
		M-F	100	–	–	–	–	143	49.8	35.51	36.0	19.5
9	LIVER OIL	A-F	100	–	–	–	–	–	–	–	–	–
		M-F	100	–	–	–	–	–	–	–	–	–
	CORN *Zea mays*											
10	DISTILLERS GRAINS WITH SOLUBLES, DEHY	A-F	92	1.5	0.69	2582	0.91	73	13.8	4.74	8.5	3.0
		M-F	100	1.6	0.75	2813	0.99	80	15.1	5.17	9.2	3.3
	DISTILLERS PRODUCTS (ALSO SEE CORN)											
11	GRAINS, DEHY	A-F	93	–	–	2645	–	47	11.9	6.00	6.6	2.5
		M-F	100	–	–	2858	–	51	12.9	6.48	7.1	2.6
12	SOLUBLES, DEHY	A-F	92	2.9	2.84	4992	–	143	25.3	8.66	11.3	6.9
		M-F	100	3.1	3.09	5425	–	155	27.5	9.42	12.3	7.5
	FATS AND OILS											
13	GERM OIL (WHEAT)	A-F	100	–	–	–	–	–	–	–	–	–
		M-F	100	–	–	–	–	–	–	–	–	–
14	LIVER OIL (COD)	A-F	100	–	–	–	–	–	–	–	–	–
		M-F	100	–	–	–	–	–	–	–	–	–
	FISH											
15	SOLUBLES, DEHY	A-F	93	485.9	0.40	5525	0.57	256	50.4	19.71	13.5	7.4
		M-F	100	523.6	0.43	5953	0.62	276	54.3	21.24	14.6	8.0
	FISH, COD *Gadus morrhua, Gadus macrocephalus*											
16	LIVER, MEAL	A-F	93	–	–	–	–	132	46.1	32.85	33.3	18.1
		M-F	100	–	–	–	–	143	49.8	35.51	36.0	19.5
17	LIVER OIL	A-F	100	–	–	–	–	–	–	–	–	–
		M-F	100	–	–	–	–	–	–	–	–	–
	FISH, SARDINE *Clupea* spp, *Sardinops* spp											
18	MEAL MECH EXTD	A-F	93	238.0	0.10	3277	–	75	11.0	–	5.4	0.3
		M-F	100	255.5	0.11	3518	–	81	11.8	–	5.8	0.3
19	SOLUBLES, CONDENSED	A-F	50	1041.0	0.13	3009	–	356	41.2	–	16.8	4.0
		M-F	100	2094.6	0.27	6054	–	716	82.9	–	33.7	8.0
	MEAT											
20	SOLUBLES, DEHY	A-F	90	881.6	–	–	–	–	–	–	–	–
		M-F	100	979.7	–	–	–	–	–	–	–	–
	OATS *Avena sativa*											
21	IMMATURE, FRESH	A-F	16	–	–	–	–	–	–	–	–	–
		M-F	100	–	–	–	–	–	–	–	–	–
	WHEAT *Triticum aestivum*											
22	GERM MEAL	A-F	88	–	0.22	3062	2.12	68	18.6	9.97	6.0	23.1
		M-F	100	–	0.24	3465	2.40	77	21.0	11.28	6.8	26.2
23	GERM OIL	A-F	100	–	–	–	–	–	–	–	–	–
		M-F	100	–	–	–	–	–	–	–	–	–
	WHEY, CATTLE *Bos taurus*											
24	DEHY	A-F	93	18.9	0.35	1790	0.85	11	46.2	3.21	27.4	4.0
		M-F	100	20.3	0.38	1921	0.91	11	49.6	3.45	29.4	4.3
	YEAST, BREWERS *Saccharomyces cerevisiae*											
25	DEHY	A-F	93	1.1	1.04	3847	9.69	443	81.5	36.67	34.1	85.2
		M-F	100	1.1	1.12	4134	10.41	476	87.6	39.40	36.6	91.6
	YEAST, PRIMARY *Saccharomyces cerevisiae*											
26	DEHY	A-F	93	6.2	1.61	–	31.13	301	312.0	–	38.8	6.4
		M-F	100	6.7	1.74	–	33.62	325	336.9	–	41.9	6.9
	YEAST, TORULA *Torulopsis utilis*											
27	DEHY	A-F	93	4.0	1.19	2981	25.66	512	107.5	34.48	47.7	6.8
		M-F	100	4.3	1.27	3203	27.58	550	115.6	37.06	51.3	7.3

Range cattle branding scene. Note cattle, horse, cowboys, and branding irons heating in the fire. (Courtesy, *The Quarter Horse Journal*, Amarillo, TX)

A M I N O   A C I D S

TABLE A-4h AMINO ACIDS FOR HORSES, COMPOSITION OF FEEDS, DATA EXPRESSED **AS-FED** AND **MOISTURE-FREE**

Entry Number	Feed Name Description	International Feed Number	Moisture Basis: A-F (as-fed) or M-F (moisture-free)	Dry Matter %	Crude Protein %	Arginine %	Cystine %	Glycine %	Histidine %	Iso-leucine %	Leucine %	Lysine %	Methi-onine %	Phenyl-alanine %	Serine %	Threo-nine %	Trypto-phan %	Tyrosine %	Valine %
	ENERGY FEEDS																		
	BARLEY *Hordeum vulgare*																		
1	GRAIN	4-00-549	A-F	88	11.7	0.51	0.20	0.37	0.25	0.46	0.75	0.40	0.16	0.58	0.46	0.36	0.15	0.35	0.57
			M-F	100	13.2	0.58	0.23	0.42	0.28	0.52	0.85	0.45	0.18	0.65	0.52	0.41	0.17	0.39	0.64
2	GRAIN, PACIFIC COAST	4-07-939	A-F	89	9.5	0.44	0.19	0.30	0.21	0.40	0.60	0.26	0.14	0.47	0.32	0.31	0.12	0.31	0.46
			M-F	100	10.8	0.50	0.22	0.34	0.23	0.45	0.67	0.30	0.16	0.53	0.36	0.35	0.14	0.34	0.52
3	MALT SPROUTS, DEHY	5-00-545	A-F	93	22.9	1.05	0.23	0.81	0.43	0.88	1.36	1.12	0.31	0.80	0.47	0.85	0.41	0.46	1.16
			M-F	100	24.6	1.13	0.25	0.87	0.46	0.95	1.47	1.21	0.33	0.87	0.51	0.91	0.44	0.49	1.25
	BEET, SUGAR *Beta vulgaris, altissima*																		
4	PULP, DEHY	4-00-669	A-F	91	8.8	0.30	0.01	—	0.20	0.30	0.60	0.60	0.01	0.30	—	0.40	0.10	0.40	0.40
			M-F	100	9.7	0.33	0.01	—	0.22	0.33	0.66	0.66	0.01	0.33	—	0.44	0.11	0.44	0.44
	CITRUS *Citrus spp*																		
5	PULP WITHOUT FINES, DEHY (DRIED CITRUS PULP)	4-01-237	A-F	91	6.1	0.25	0.11	—	0.09	0.18	0.31	0.20	0.09	0.18	—	0.18	0.06	—	0.25
			M-F	100	6.7	0.28	0.12	—	0.10	0.20	0.34	0.22	0.09	0.20	—	0.20	0.07	—	0.28
	CORN, DENT WHITE *Zea mays, indentata*																		
6	GRAIN	4-02-928	A-F	90	10.8	0.27	0.09	—	0.18	0.45	0.90	0.27	0.09	0.36	—	0.36	0.09	0.45	0.36
			M-F	100	11.9	0.30	0.10	—	0.20	0.50	1.00	0.30	0.10	0.40	—	0.40	0.10	0.50	0.40
	CORN, DENT YELLOW *Zea mays, indentata*																		
7	GRAIN, ALL ANALYSES	4-02-935	A-F	88	9.9	0.43	0.12	0.37	0.27	0.35	1.19	0.30	0.18	0.46	0.49	0.36	0.09	0.31	0.48
			M-F	100	11.2	0.49	0.13	0.42	0.31	0.40	1.35	0.34	0.20	0.52	0.55	0.41	0.10	0.35	0.54
8	GRAIN, GRADE 2, 54 lb/bu 69.5 kg/hl	4-02-931	A-F	87	8.9	0.45	0.11	0.45	0.20	0.40	1.00	0.19	0.11	0.45	—	0.35	0.09	0.43	0.35
			M-F	100	10.2	0.52	0.13	0.52	0.23	0.46	1.15	0.22	0.13	0.52	—	0.40	0.10	0.49	0.40
9	GRAIN, FLAKED	4-28-244	A-F	89	9.9	0.44	0.25	0.36	0.28	0.34	1.24	0.25	0.15	0.44	0.48	0.35	—	0.39	0.47
			M-F	100	11.2	0.49	0.28	0.40	0.31	0.38	1.40	0.28	0.17	0.50	0.54	0.39	—	0.44	0.53
10	DISTILLERS SOLUBLES, DEHY	5-28-237	A-F	93	27.4	0.99	0.44	1.12	0.67	1.32	2.38	0.92	0.55	1.47	1.22	1.01	0.25	0.88	1.53
			M-F	100	29.5	1.06	0.48	1.21	0.73	1.42	2.56	0.99	0.59	1.58	1.32	1.09	0.27	0.95	1.65
11	EARS, GROUND (CORN-AND-COB MEAL)	4-28-238	A-F	87	7.8	0.36	0.12	0.31	0.16	0.35	0.86	0.17	0.14	0.39	0.28	0.28	0.07	0.32	0.31
			M-F	100	9.0	0.42	0.14	0.36	0.19	0.40	1.00	0.20	0.16	0.45	—	0.33	0.08	0.38	0.36
12	GERM MEAL, WET MILLED, SOLV EXTD	5-28-240	A-F	91	20.7	1.31	0.40	1.10	0.70	0.70	1.81	0.90	0.58	0.90	1.00	1.09	0.20	0.70	1.20
			M-F	100	22.6	1.43	0.44	1.20	0.76	0.76	1.97	0.98	0.64	0.98	1.09	1.19	0.21	0.76	1.31
13	GRITS (HOMINY GRITS)	4-03-011	A-F	90	10.3	0.47	0.15	0.35	0.20	0.39	0.85	0.38	0.16	0.33	—	0.39	0.11	0.50	0.49
			M-F	100	11.4	0.52	0.16	0.38	0.22	0.44	0.94	0.42	0.18	0.36	—	0.44	0.12	0.55	0.55
	CORN, OPAQUE 2 (HIGH LYSINE) *Zea mays*																		
14	GRAIN	4-11-445	A-F	90	10.1	0.64	0.19	0.48	0.35	0.33	0.98	0.42	0.16	0.43	0.46	0.37	0.12	0.40	0.48
			M-F		11.2	0.71	0.21	0.53	0.38	0.37	1.09	0.46	0.18	0.48	0.51	0.42	0.13	0.44	0.54
	DISTILLERS PRODUCTS (ALSO SEE CORN; WHEAT)																		
15	SOLUBLES, DEHY	5-02-147	A-F	92	28.8	1.06	0.40	1.20	0.66	1.21	2.35	0.95	0.50	1.24	0.93	1.00	0.24	0.93	1.40
			M-F	100	31.3	1.15	0.44	1.30	0.72	1.32	2.55	1.03	0.54	1.35	1.01	1.09	0.26	1.01	1.52
	HOMINY GRITS (CORN, DENT YELLOW, GRITS) *Zea mays, indentata*																		
16		4-03-011	A-F	90	10.3	0.47	0.15	0.35	0.20	0.39	0.85	0.38	0.16	0.33	—	0.39	0.11	0.50	0.49
			M-F	100	11.4	0.52	0.16	0.38	0.22	0.44	0.94	0.42	0.18	0.36	—	0.44	0.12	0.55	0.55
	MAIZE—SEE CORN																		
	OATS *Avena sativa*																		
17	GRAIN	4-03-309	A-F	89	11.9	0.71	0.19	0.51	0.17	0.48	0.87	0.40	0.18	0.57	0.50	0.38	0.15	0.45	0.62
			M-F	100	13.3	0.80	0.21	0.57	0.19	0.54	0.97	0.45	0.20	0.64	0.56	0.43	0.17	0.50	0.69
18	GRAIN, GRADE 1, 34 lb/bu 43.8 kg/hl	4-03-313	A-F	88	11.2	0.79	0.22	0.49	0.19	0.52	0.89	0.49	0.18	0.59	—	0.39	0.16	0.52	0.69
			M-F	100	12.7	0.89	0.25	0.56	0.22	0.59	1.01	0.56	0.20	0.67	—	0.45	0.18	0.59	0.78
19	GRAIN, PACIFIC COAST	4-07-999	A-F	91	9.1	0.58	0.17	0.40	0.17	0.38	0.70	0.33	0.13	0.43	0.40	0.30	0.12	0.70	0.49
			M-F	100	10.0	0.63	0.18	0.44	0.18	0.42	0.77	0.37	0.14	0.47	0.44	0.33	0.13	0.77	0.54

TABLE A–4h AMINO ACIDS FOR HORSES, COMPOSITION OF FEEDS, DATA EXPRESSED **AS-FED** AND **MOISTURE-FREE** (Continued)

Entry Number	Feed Name Description	International Feed Number	Moisture Basis: A-F (as-fed) or M-F (moisture-free)	Dry Matter %	Crude Protein %	Arginine %	Cystine %	Glycine %	Histidine %	Iso-leucine %	Leucine %	Lysine %	Methionine %	Phenyl-alanine %	Serine %	Threonine %	Trypto-phan %	Tyrosine %	Valine %
	OATS (Continued)																		
20	GROATS	4-03-331	A-F	90	15.8	0.89	0.21	0.61	0.27	0.54	1.04	0.54	0.20	0.70	0.62	0.44	0.19	0.51	0.74
			M-F	100	17.6	0.99	0.23	0.68	0.31	0.60	1.16	0.61	0.23	0.78	0.69	0.49	0.21	0.57	0.83
	RICE *Oryza sativa*																		
21	GRAIN, GROUND (GROUND ROUGH RICE; GROUND PADDY RICE)	4-03-938	A-F	89	7.5	0.54	0.12	0.62	0.16	0.27	0.54	0.25	0.14	0.30	0.50	0.23	0.10	0.63	0.40
			M-F	100	8.4	0.61	0.14	0.69	0.18	0.30	0.60	0.28	0.15	0.34	0.56	0.26	0.12	0.71	0.45
22	BRAN WITH GERMS (RICE BRAN)	4-03-928	A-F	91	13.0	0.82	0.16	0.81	0.29	0.50	0.84	0.54	0.26	0.53	0.73	0.44	0.10	0.59	0.75
			M-F	100	14.3	0.91	0.18	0.90	0.32	0.56	0.93	0.60	0.29	0.58	0.81	0.49	0.11	0.65	0.83
23	POLISHINGS	4-03-943	A-F	90	12.0	0.57	0.14	0.65	0.19	0.37	0.73	0.51	0.22	0.43	0.49	0.35	0.11	0.45	0.68
			M-F	100	13.3	0.63	0.16	0.72	0.21	0.41	0.81	0.57	0.24	0.47	0.54	0.39	0.12	0.50	0.76
	RYE *Secale cereale*																		
24	GRAIN	4-04-047	A-F	87	12.0	0.52	0.19	0.44	0.25	0.48	0.68	0.42	0.17	0.56	0.61	0.35	0.12	0.26	0.58
			M-F	100	13.8	0.60	0.21	0.50	0.29	0.55	0.77	0.48	0.20	0.64	0.70	0.40	0.13	0.30	0.66
	SORGHUM *Sorghum bicolor*																		
25	GRAIN, ALL ANALYSES	4-04-383	A-F	90	11.5	0.39	0.21	0.34	0.24	0.42	1.47	0.26	0.14	0.56	0.49	0.36	0.09	0.40	0.50
			M-F	100	12.8	0.43	0.23	0.38	0.26	0.47	1.63	0.29	0.15	0.62	0.54	0.40	0.10	0.45	0.56
26	GRAIN, LESS THAN 9% PROTEIN	4-08-138	A-F	89	8.9	0.28	0.14	0.27	0.19	0.46	1.40	0.19	0.12	0.47	—	0.36	0.12	0.60	0.53
			M-F	100	10.1	0.32	0.16	0.31	0.22	0.52	1.58	0.22	0.14	0.53	—	0.41	0.14	0.68	0.60
27	DARSO, GRAIN	4-04-357	A-F	90	10.1	0.36	0.16	—	0.18	0.45	1.23	0.19	0.11	0.48	—	0.31	0.11	—	0.48
			M-F	100	11.2	0.40	—	—	0.20	0.51	1.38	0.21	0.12	0.53	—	0.34	0.12	—	0.53
28	FETERITA, GRAIN	4-04-369	A-F	89	11.7	0.46	—	—	0.26	0.58	1.78	0.20	0.18	0.67	—	0.46	0.17	—	0.67
			M-F	100	13.0	0.51	—	—	0.29	0.65	1.99	0.23	0.21	0.75	—	0.51	0.19	—	0.75
29	HEGARI, GRAIN	4-04-398	A-F	89	10.4	0.29	0.17	—	0.18	0.47	1.40	0.17	0.12	0.54	—	0.36	0.11	—	0.55
			M-F	100	11.7	0.33	0.19	—	0.21	0.52	1.56	0.20	0.13	0.61	—	0.41	0.12	—	0.61
30	KAFIR, GRAIN	4-04-428	A-F	89	10.8	0.38	0.13	0.30	0.27	0.55	1.62	0.26	0.19	0.64	—	0.45	0.15	—	0.62
			M-F	100	12.1	0.43	0.15	0.33	0.30	0.62	1.81	0.29	0.21	0.71	—	0.50	0.17	—	0.69
31	MILO, GRAIN	4-04-444	A-F	89	10.1	0.37	0.20	0.35	0.24	0.44	1.32	0.23	0.16	0.49	0.49	0.35	0.10	0.37	0.53
			M-F	100	11.4	0.42	0.23	0.39	0.27	0.50	1.49	0.26	0.18	0.55	0.56	0.40	0.11	0.41	0.60
32	MILO, GLUTEN WITH BRAN, MEAL	5-08-089	A-F	89	23.2	0.90	0.23	0.68	0.60	1.00	2.51	0.70	0.40	1.00	—	0.80	0.20	0.90	1.30
			M-F	100	26.0	1.01	—	0.77	0.68	1.13	2.81	0.79	0.45	1.13	—	0.90	0.23	1.01	1.46
33	SHALLU, GRAIN	4-04-456	A-F	90	11.5	0.31	—	—	0.19	0.38	0.97	0.19	0.17	0.40	—	0.30	0.10	—	0.46
			M-F	100	12.7	0.34	—	—	0.21	0.42	1.08	0.21	0.18	0.44	—	0.33	0.11	—	0.51
	SOYBEAN *Glycine max*																		
34	SEEDS	5-04-610	A-F	92	38.4	2.63	0.42	1.42	0.92	1.62	2.72	2.32	0.48	1.76	1.99	1.46	0.56	1.29	1.61
			M-F	100	41.7	2.86	0.45	1.55	1.00	1.76	2.95	2.52	0.52	1.91	2.16	1.58	0.61	1.40	1.75
	WHEAT *Triticum aestivum*																		
35	GRAIN, ALL ANALYSES	4-05-211	A-F	89	13.1	0.61	0.22	0.59	0.30	0.49	0.90	0.39	0.18	0.61	0.63	0.40	0.15	0.37	0.61
			M-F	100	14.7	0.69	0.25	0.66	0.34	0.55	1.01	0.44	0.20	0.69	0.71	0.45	0.17	0.41	0.69
36	GRAIN, HARD RED WINTER	4-05-268	A-F	89	12.8	0.65	0.30	0.58	0.30	0.53	0.87	0.36	0.22	0.63	0.59	0.37	0.17	0.46	0.58
			M-F	100	14.5	0.74	0.34	0.65	0.34	0.60	0.98	0.41	0.24	0.71	0.66	0.42	0.19	0.52	0.66
37	GRAIN, SOFT WHITE WINTER, PACIFIC COAST	4-08-555	A-F	89	10.0	0.45	0.24	0.50	0.20	0.40	0.75	0.30	0.14	0.48	0.49	0.31	0.12	0.36	0.46
			M-F	100	11.2	0.50	0.27	0.56	0.22	0.45	0.84	0.34	0.16	0.54	0.54	0.34	0.13	0.41	0.52
38	BRAN	4-05-190	A-F	89	15.5	0.85	0.26	0.77	0.33	0.55	0.89	0.54	0.17	0.50	0.68	0.40	0.25	0.38	0.67
			M-F	100	17.5	0.96	0.29	0.86	0.37	0.62	1.00	0.61	0.19	0.56	0.76	0.45	0.28	0.43	0.76
39	DISTILLERS GRAINS, DEHY	5-05-193	A-F	93	31.6	1.10	—	—	0.80	2.01	1.71	0.70	—	1.71	—	0.90	—	0.50	1.71
			M-F	100	33.9	1.18	—	—	0.86	2.15	1.83	0.75	—	1.83	—	0.97	—	0.54	1.83
	WHEAT, DURUM *Triticum durum*																		
40	GRAIN	4-05-224	A-F	88	13.8	0.58	0.13	0.46	0.27	0.48	1.40	1.05	0.14	0.53	0.45	0.37	0.26	0.29	0.54
			M-F	100	15.7	0.67	0.15	0.52	0.31	0.55	1.60	1.19	0.16	0.61	0.51	0.42	0.30	0.33	0.62

AMINO ACIDS

A M I N O   A C I D S

TABLE A–4h **AMINO ACIDS FOR HORSES,** COMPOSITION OF FEEDS, DATA EXPRESSED **AS-FED** AND **MOISTURE-FREE** (Continued)

Entry Number	Feed Name Description	International Feed Number	Moisture Basis: A-F (as-fed) or M-F (moisture-free)	Dry Matter %	Crude Protein %	AMINO ACIDS													
						Arginine %	Cystine %	Glycine %	Histidine %	Iso-leucine %	Leucine %	Lysine %	Methionine %	Phenyl-alanine %	Serine %	Threo-nine %	Trypto-phan %	Tyrosine %	Valine %
	PROTEIN FEEDS																		
	ANIMAL																		
41	BLOOD, MEAL	5-00-380	A-F	91	80.5	3.23	1.25	3.45	3.93	0.85	10.07	6.43	0.94	5.56	3.95	3.59	1.01	1.94	6.56
			M-F	100	88.2	3.54	1.37	3.78	4.31	0.94	11.03	7.04	1.03	6.09	4.32	3.93	1.10	2.12	7.19
42	LIVER, MEAL	5-00-389	A-F	93	66.1	4.04	0.94	5.61	1.48	3.11	5.31	5.22	1.22	2.92	2.50	2.50	0.69	1.70	4.15
			M-F	100	71.4	4.37	1.01	6.05	1.60	3.36	5.74	5.63	1.32	3.15	2.70	2.70	0.74	1.84	4.49
	BLOOD																		
43	MEAL	5-00-380	A-F	91	80.5	3.23	1.25	3.45	3.93	0.85	10.07	6.43	0.94	5.56	3.95	3.59	1.01	1.94	6.56
			M-F	100	88.2	3.54	1.37	3.78	4.31	0.94	11.03	7.04	1.03	6.09	4.32	3.93	1.10	2.12	7.19
	CASEIN																		
44	ACID PRECIPITATED, DEHY	5-01-162	A-F	91	84.0	3.49	0.31	1.61	2.59	5.72	8.80	7.14	2.81	4.81	5.46	3.91	1.08	4.90	6.71
			M-F	100	92.7	3.85	0.34	1.77	2.86	6.32	9.71	7.88	3.10	5.31	6.03	4.32	1.19	5.41	7.40
	CATTLE *Bos taurus*																		
45	MILK, DEHY	5-01-167	A-F	95	25.3	0.92	—	—	0.71	1.32	2.54	2.24	0.61	1.32	—	1.02	0.41	1.32	1.73
			M-F	100	26.6	0.96	—	—	0.75	1.39	2.67	2.35	0.64	1.39	1.08	1.07	0.43	1.39	1.81
46	SKIM MILK, DEHY	5-01-175	A-F	94	33.3	1.16	0.45	0.29	0.86	2.18	3.33	2.54	0.90	1.57	1.67	1.57	0.43	1.14	2.29
			M-F	100	35.4	1.23	0.48	0.31	0.92	2.32	3.53	2.70	0.96	1.66	1.78	1.66	0.46	1.22	2.43
47	WHEY, DEHY	4-01-182	A-F	93	13.3	0.33	0.30	0.44	0.17	0.78	1.18	0.94	0.19	0.35	0.47	0.90	0.20	0.25	0.67
			M-F	100	14.2	0.36	0.32	0.47	0.18	0.83	1.26	1.00	0.20	0.37	0.50	0.97	0.21	0.26	0.72
	COCONUT *Cocos nucifera*																		
48	KERNELS WITH COATS, MEAL MECH EXTD (COPRA MEAL)	5-01-572	A-F	92	21.2	2.30	0.21	1.05	0.33	0.90	1.35	0.55	0.31	0.81	—	0.60	0.20	0.58	0.98
			M-F	100	23.1	2.52	0.23	1.15	0.36	0.99	1.48	0.60	0.34	0.88	—	0.66	0.22	0.63	1.07
	CORN *Zea mays*																		
49	DISTILLERS GRAINS, DEHY	5-02-842	A-F	93	27.8	0.99	0.23	0.75	0.62	1.00	3.01	0.76	0.42	0.99	1.01	0.56	0.20	0.84	1.21
			M-F	100	29.7	1.06	0.25	0.80	0.66	1.07	3.23	0.81	0.44	1.06	1.08	0.60	0.21	0.89	1.29
50	DISTILLERS SOLUBLES, DEHY	5-02-844	A-F	93	27.4	0.99	0.44	1.12	0.67	1.32	2.38	0.92	0.55	1.47	1.22	1.01	0.25	0.88	1.53
			M-F	100	29.5	1.06	0.48	1.21	0.73	1.42	2.56	0.99	0.59	1.58	1.32	1.09	0.27	0.95	1.65
51	GLUTEN FEED	5-02-903	A-F	90	23.0	0.87	0.42	0.85	0.61	0.88	2.20	0.64	0.37	0.81	0.85	0.78	0.15	0.72	1.10
			M-F	100	25.6	0.97	0.47	0.94	0.68	0.98	2.44	0.71	0.41	0.90	0.94	0.87	0.17	0.81	1.22
52	GLUTEN MEAL	5-02-900	A-F	91	43.2	1.40	0.67	1.51	0.97	2.25	7.38	0.80	1.03	2.85	1.70	1.43	0.21	1.01	2.23
			M-F	100	47.3	1.53	0.73	1.65	1.06	2.46	8.08	0.88	1.13	3.12	1.86	1.56	0.23	1.11	2.44
	COTTON *Gossypium* spp																		
53	SEEDS, MEAL MECH EXTD, 36% PROTEIN	5-01-625	A-F	92	37.2	3.55	0.79	1.83	0.91	1.32	—	1.22	0.55	1.88	—	1.12	0.46	—	2.84
			M-F	100	40.5	3.86	0.86	1.99	0.99	1.44	—	1.33	0.60	2.04	—	1.21	0.50	—	3.09
54	SEEDS, MEAL MECH EXTD, 41% PROTEIN	5-01-617	A-F	93	41.0	4.20	0.71	1.87	1.07	1.42	2.30	1.60	0.57	2.19	1.70	1.33	0.52	0.97	1.89
			M-F	100	44.3	4.54	0.77	2.02	1.15	1.54	2.49	1.73	0.62	2.36	1.84	1.44	0.57	1.05	2.04
55	SEEDS, MEAL PREPRESSED, SOLV EXTD, 41% PROTEIN	5-07-872	A-F	90	41.3	4.32	0.78	1.89	1.14	1.42	2.42	1.80	0.56	2.05	1.80	1.34	0.50	1.14	1.97
			M-F	100	45.7	4.78	0.87	2.09	1.26	1.57	2.67	1.99	0.61	2.27	1.99	1.48	0.56	1.27	2.18
56	SEEDS, MEAL SOLV EXTD, 41% PROTEIN	5-01-621	A-F	91	41.2	4.24	0.76	1.95	1.10	1.50	2.46	1.69	0.58	2.23	1.76	1.37	0.55	1.04	1.97
			M-F	100	45.4	4.66	0.84	2.14	1.22	1.65	2.70	1.86	0.64	2.46	1.93	1.51	0.60	1.15	2.17
	DISTILLERS PRODUCTS (ALSO SEE CORN; RYE)																		
57	GRAINS, DEHY	5-02-144	A-F	93	27.3	1.04	0.42	0.56	0.53	1.16	2.66	0.81	0.46	1.03	0.70	0.81	0.21	0.73	1.22
			M-F	100	29.5	1.13	0.45	0.61	0.57	1.25	2.88	0.87	0.50	1.12	0.75	0.88	0.22	0.79	1.32
58	SOLUBLES, DEHY	5-02-147	A-F	92	28.8	1.06	0.40	1.20	0.66	1.21	2.35	0.95	0.50	1.24	0.93	1.00	0.24	0.93	1.40
			M-F	100	31.3	1.15	0.44	1.30	0.72	1.32	2.55	1.03	0.54	1.35	1.01	1.09	0.26	1.01	1.52

TABLE A–4h AMINO ACIDS FOR HORSES, COMPOSITION OF FEEDS, DATA EXPRESSED **AS-FED** AND **MOISTURE-FREE** (Continued)

Entry Number	Feed Name Description	International Feed Number	Moisture Basis: A-F (as-fed) or M-F (moisture-free)	Dry Matter %	Crude Protein %	Arginine %	Cystine %	Glycine %	Histidine %	Iso-leucine %	Leucine %	Lysine %	Methionine %	Phenyl-alanine %	Serine %	Threo-nine %	Trypto-phan %	Tyrosine %	Valine %
59	**FISH** MEAL MECH EXTD	5-01-977	A-F	92	64.3	31.28	0.62	3.99	1.46	3.27	4.90	5.26	1.63	2.60	2.42	2.59	0.75	1.79	3.14
			M-F	100	70.2	34.16	0.68	4.35	1.59	3.57	5.35	5.74	1.78	2.84	2.64	2.83	0.82	1.96	3.43
60	**FISH, ANCHOVY** *Engraulis ringen* MEAL MECH EXTD	5-01-985	A-F	92	65.4	3.78	0.60	3.69	1.60	3.11	4.99	5.02	1.99	2.78	2.42	2.76	0.75	2.24	3.50
			M-F	100	71.1	4.10	0.66	4.01	1.74	3.38	5.42	5.46	2.16	3.03	2.63	3.01	0.81	2.44	3.81
61	**FISH, MENHADEN** *Brevoortia tyrannus* MEAL MECH EXTD	5-02-009	A-F	92	61.2	3.74	0.58	4.19	1.44	2.85	4.48	4.74	1.75	2.46	2.25	2.51	0.65	1.93	3.19
			M-F	100	66.8	4.08	0.63	4.57	1.58	3.11	4.89	5.17	1.91	2.68	2.45	2.74	0.71	2.11	3.48
62	**FISH, TUNA** *Thunnus thynnus, Thunnus albacares* MEAL MECH EXTD	5-02-023	A-F	93	59.0	3.43	0.47	4.09	1.75	2.45	3.79	4.06	1.47	2.15	2.08	2.31	0.57	1.69	2.77
			M-F	100	63.6	3.69	0.50	4.41	1.89	2.64	4.09	4.37	1.58	2.32	2.25	2.49	0.62	1.82	2.98
63	**FISH, WHITE** *Gadidae (family), Lophiidae (family), Rajidae (family)* MEAL MECH EXTD	5-02-025	A-F	91	62.6	4.26	0.77	5.15	1.38	2.85	4.65	4.70	1.79	2.44	3.44	2.56	0.67	2.27	3.25
			M-F	100	68.8	4.68	0.84	5.66	1.52	3.13	5.11	5.16	1.97	2.68	3.78	2.82	0.73	2.49	3.57
64	**FLAX, COMMON** *Linum usitatissimum* SEEDS, MEAL MECH EXTD (LINSEED MEAL)	5-02-048	A-F	90	34.6	2.94	0.61	1.74	0.69	1.68	2.02	1.16	0.54	1.46	1.93	1.22	0.51	1.09	1.74
			M-F	100	38.4	3.25	0.67	1.93	0.77	1.87	2.24	1.28	0.60	1.62	2.13	1.35	0.56	1.21	1.93
65	SEEDS, MEAL SOLV EXTD (LINSEED MEAL)	5-02-045	A-F	91	34.3	2.81	0.61	1.64	0.65	1.69	1.92	1.18	0.58	1.38	1.90	1.14	0.51	0.96	1.61
			M-F	100	37.8	3.10	0.67	1.80	0.71	1.86	2.11	1.30	0.64	1.53	2.09	1.25	0.56	1.06	1.77
	MAIZE—SEE CORN																		
	MILK																		
66	FRESH (CATTLE *Bos taurus*)	5-01-168	A-F	12	3.3	—	—	—	—	0.32	0.25	0.28	0.18	0.07	—	0.16	0.05	—	0.25
			M-F	100	26.7	—	—	—	—	2.58	2.03	2.27	1.43	0.55	—	1.33	0.39	—	2.03
67	DEHY (CATTLE *Bos taurus*)	5-01-167	A-F	95	25.3	0.92	—	—	0.71	1.32	2.54	2.24	0.61	1.32	—	1.02	0.41	1.32	1.73
			M-F	100	26.6	0.96	—	—	0.75	1.39	2.67	2.35	0.64	1.39	—	1.07	0.43	1.39	1.81
68	SKIMMED, DEHY (CATTLE *Bos taurus*)	5-01-175	A-F	94	33.3	1.16	0.45	0.29	0.86	2.18	3.33	2.54	0.90	1.57	1.67	1.57	0.43	1.14	2.29
			M-F	100	35.4	1.23	0.48	0.31	0.92	2.32	3.53	2.70	0.96	1.66	1.78	1.66	0.46	1.22	2.43
69	FRESH (HORSE *Equus caballus*)	5-02-401	A-F	17	4.2	—	—	—	0.11	0.25	0.34	0.25	0.07	0.18	—	0.16	0.05	—	0.29
			M-F	100	24.7	—	—	—	0.64	1.49	2.02	1.49	0.43	1.06	—	0.96	0.32	—	1.70
70	**PEANUT** *Arachis hypogaea* SEEDS WITHOUT HULLS, MEAL MECH EXTD (PEANUT MEAL)	5-03-649	A-F	93	49.2	5.08	0.96	2.49	1.03	1.78	3.13	1.69	0.50	2.38	1.44	1.27	0.46	1.59	2.29
			M-F	100	53.1	5.49	1.04	2.69	1.11	1.92	3.38	1.83	0.54	2.56	1.56	1.37	0.49	1.72	2.47
71	**RAPE (CANOLA), SUMMER** *Brassica napus, annua* SEEDS, MEAL, PREPRESSED, SOLV EXTD	5-08-135	A-F	92	40.5	2.23	—	1.94	1.09	1.46	2.71	2.15	0.77	1.54	1.70	1.70	0.49	0.85	1.94
			M-F	100	44.0	2.42	—	2.11	1.19	1.59	2.95	2.33	0.84	1.67	1.85	1.85	0.53	0.92	2.11
72	**SAFFLOWER** *Carthamus tinctorius* SEEDS WITHOUT HULLS, MEAL MECH EXTD	5-08-499	A-F	91	42.0	5.44	—	2.52	—	—	—	1.31	0.71	—	—	0.81	—	—	—
			M-F	100	46.1	5.97	—	2.76	—	—	—	1.44	0.77	—	—	0.88	—	—	—
73	SEEDS WITHOUT HULLS, MEAL SOLV EXTD	5-07-959	A-F	91	42.8	3.67	0.71	2.36	0.97	1.58	2.42	1.26	0.67	1.73	—	1.30	0.59	1.01	2.17
			M-F	100	47.0	4.03	0.78	2.59	1.07	1.73	2.66	1.38	0.74	1.90	—	1.43	0.65	1.11	2.39
74	**SESAME** *Sesamum indicum* SEEDS, MEAL MECH EXTD	5-04-220	A-F	93	45.0	4.55	0.59	3.96	1.07	1.96	3.20	1.26	1.37	2.14	2.94	1.60	0.71	1.87	2.32
			M-F	100	48.6	4.91	0.64	4.28	1.16	2.12	3.45	1.36	1.48	2.31	3.18	1.72	0.76	2.02	2.51

AMINO ACIDS

A M I N O A C I D S

TABLE A–4h AMINO ACIDS FOR HORSES, COMPOSITION OF FEEDS, DATA EXPRESSED **AS-FED** AND **MOISTURE-FREE** *(Continued)*

Entry Number	Feed Name Description	International Feed Number	Moisture Basis: A-F (as-fed) or M-F (moisture-free)	Dry Matter %	Crude Protein %	Arginine %	Cystine %	Glycine %	Histidine %	Iso-leucine %	Leucine %	Lysine %	Methionine %	Phenyl-alanine %	Serine %	Threonine %	Trypto-phan %	Tyrosine %	Valine %
	SORGHUM *Sorghum bicolor*																		
75	GLUTEN MEAL	5-04-388	A-F	90	44.4	1.26	0.73	0.95	1.07	2.39	7.85	0.74	0.71	2.70	—	1.45	0.44	—	2.50
			M-F	100	49.2	1.39	0.81	1.05	1.19	2.65	8.70	0.82	0.78	2.99	—	1.61	0.48	—	2.77
	SOYBEAN *Glycine max*																		
76	MEAL, SOLV EXTD	5-04-612	A-F	90	49.7	3.67	0.70	2.27	1.20	2.13	3.63	3.12	0.71	2.36	2.49	1.90	0.69	1.71	2.47
			M-F	100	55.1	4.07	0.78	2.51	1.33	2.37	4.03	3.46	0.79	2.62	2.76	2.11	0.77	1.89	2.74
77	MEAL, SOLV EXTD, 44% PROTEIN	5-20-637	A-F	89	44.4	3.26	0.67	2.10	1.13	2.12	3.49	2.85	0.59	2.23	2.37	1.81	0.62	1.60	2.37
			M-F	100	49.8	3.65	0.75	2.36	1.27	2.38	3.92	3.20	0.67	2.51	2.66	2.03	0.69	1.80	2.66
78	MEAL, SOLV EXTD, 49% PROTEIN	5-20-638	A-F	90	49.0	3.62	0.75	2.39	1.28	2.34	3.77	3.08	0.66	2.47	2.76	2.00	0.70	1.96	2.49
			M-F	100	54.6	4.03	0.83	2.66	1.43	2.60	4.20	3.44	0.74	2.76	3.08	2.23	0.78	2.18	2.77
	WHEAT *Triticum aestivum*																		
79	GERM MEAL	5-05-218	A-F	88	24.4	1.83	0.47	1.46	0.62	0.95	1.47	1.53	0.41	0.93	1.12	0.94	0.30	0.74	1.16
			M-F	100	27.6	2.07	0.53	1.65	0.70	1.07	1.67	1.73	0.47	1.05	1.27	1.07	0.34	0.84	1.31
80	GLUTEN	5-05-221	A-F	90	63.4	2.97	1.74	2.77	1.64	3.39	5.54	1.54	1.23	4.21	4.10	2.15	0.72	2.36	3.90
			M-F	100	70.3	3.30	1.93	3.07	1.82	3.75	6.14	1.71	1.36	4.66	4.55	2.39	0.80	2.61	4.32
	WHEY (CATTLE) *Bos taurus*																		
81	DEHY	4-01-182	A-F	93	13.3	0.33	0.30	0.44	0.17	0.78	1.18	0.94	0.19	0.35	0.47	0.90	0.20	0.25	0.67
			M-F	100	14.2	0.36	0.32	0.47	0.18	0.83	1.26	1.00	0.20	0.37	0.50	0.97	0.21	0.26	0.72
82	LOW LACTOSE, DEHY (DRIED WHEY PRODUCT)	4-01-186	A-F	93	16.7	0.60	0.43	0.72	0.27	0.96	1.54	1.40	0.41	0.55	0.59	0.95	0.27	0.46	0.87
			M-F	100	17.9	0.64	0.46	0.77	0.29	1.03	1.65	1.50	0.43	0.59	0.63	1.01	0.29	0.49	0.93
	YEAST, IRRADIATED *Saccharomyces cerevisiae*																		
83	DEHY	7-05-529	A-F	94	48.1	2.46	—	—	1.00	2.94	3.56	3.70	1.00	2.77	—	2.41	0.73	—	3.06
			M-F	100	51.2	2.62	—	—	1.06	3.13	3.79	3.94	1.06	2.95	—	2.56	0.78	—	3.26
	YEAST, TORULA *Torulopsis utilis*																		
84	DEHY	7-05-534	A-F	93	49.6	2.52	0.59	2.54	1.34	2.69	3.39	3.65	0.76	2.63	2.75	2.67	0.52	1.94	2.88
			M-F	100	53.3	2.71	0.63	2.73	1.44	2.89	3.65	3.93	0.82	2.83	2.96	2.87	0.56	2.08	3.10
	DRY FORAGES																		
	ALFALFA (LUCERNE) *Medicago sativa*																		
85	HAY, SUN-CURED	1-00-078	A-F	90	16.0	0.81	—	—	0.28	0.87	1.12	1.00	0.12	0.71	—	0.62	0.18	0.50	0.69
			M-F	100	17.7	0.89	—	—	0.31	0.96	1.24	1.11	0.13	0.79	—	0.69	0.20	0.55	0.76
86	HAY, SUN-CURED, EARLY BLOOM, MEAL	1-00-108	A-F	92	22.5	—	—	—	—	—	—	—	—	—	—	—	—	—	—
			M-F	100	24.5	—	—	—	—	—	—	—	—	—	—	—	—	—	—
87	MEAL, DEHY, 15% PROTEIN	1-00-022	A-F	90	15.6	0.59	0.17	0.70	0.27	0.64	1.02	0.59	0.22	0.62	0.60	0.56	0.38	0.41	0.75
			M-F	100	17.3	0.65	0.19	0.78	0.30	0.71	1.13	0.66	0.24	0.69	0.67	0.62	0.42	0.45	0.83
88	MEAL, DEHY, 17% PROTEIN	1-00-023	A-F	92	17.4	0.77	0.29	0.84	0.33	0.81	1.28	0.85	0.27	0.80	0.71	0.71	0.34	0.54	0.88
			M-F	100	18.9	0.84	0.31	0.91	0.36	0.88	1.39	0.93	0.29	0.87	0.77	0.77	0.37	0.59	0.96
89	MEAL, DEHY, 20% PROTEIN	1-00-024	A-F	92	20.2	0.95	0.32	0.99	0.38	0.89	1.43	0.89	0.32	0.94	0.90	0.82	0.41	0.60	1.05
			M-F	100	22.1	1.04	0.35	1.08	0.41	0.97	1.56	0.97	0.34	1.03	0.98	0.89	0.45	0.66	1.15
90	MEAL, DEHY, 22% PROTEIN	1-07-851	A-F	93	22.2	0.96	0.30	1.09	0.44	1.06	1.63	0.97	0.34	1.13	0.97	0.97	0.49	0.64	1.29
			M-F	100	23.9	1.04	0.32	1.18	0.47	1.15	1.75	1.05	0.37	1.22	1.05	1.04	0.52	0.69	1.39
	ALFALFA-GRASS *Medicago sativa grass*																		
91	HAY, SUN-CURED	1-08-331	A-F	91	14.5	—	—	—	—	—	—	—	—	—	—	—	—	—	—
			M-F	100	15.9	—	—	—	—	—	—	—	—	—	—	—	—	—	—

TABLE A-4h AMINO ACIDS FOR HORSES, COMPOSITION OF FEEDS, DATA EXPRESSED **AS-FED** AND **MOISTURE-FREE** (Continued)

Entry Number	Feed Name Description	International Feed Number	Moisture Basis: A-F (as fed) or M-F (moisture-free)	Dry Matter %	Crude Protein %	AMINO ACIDS													
						Arginine %	Cystine %	Glycine %	Histidine %	Iso-leucine %	Leucine %	Lysine %	Methionine %	Phenyl-alanine %	Serine %	Threonine %	Trypto-phan %	Tyrosine %	Valine %
92	**CLOVER, LADINO** *Trifolium repens* HAY, SUN-CURED	1-01-378	A-F	89	20.0	—	—	—	—	—	—	—	—	—	—	—	—	—	—
			M-F	100	22.4	—	—	—	—	—	—	—	—	—	—	—	—	—	—
93	**LESPEDEZA, COMMON** *Lespedeza striata* HAY, SUN-CURED	1-08-591	A-F	89	13.8	—	—	—	—	—	—	—	—	—	—	—	—	—	—
			M-F	100	15.6	—	—	—	—	—	—	—	—	—	—	—	—	—	—
94	**OATS** *Avena sativa* HULLS	1-03-281	A-F	92	3.7	0.15	0.06	0.15	0.08	0.15	0.25	0.17	0.08	0.15	—	0.16	0.09	0.14	0.19
			M-F	100	4.0	0.16	0.07	0.16	0.08	0.16	0.27	0.18	0.09	0.16	—	0.17	0.09	0.15	0.21
	VITAMIN SUPPLEMENTS																		
95	**ALFALFA (LUCERNE)** *Medicago sativa* MEAL, DEHY, 20% PROTEIN	1-00-024	A-F	92	20.2	0.95	0.32	0.99	0.38	0.89	1.43	0.89	0.32	0.94	0.90	0.82	0.41	0.60	1.05
			M-F	100	22.1	1.04	0.35	1.08	0.41	0.97	1.56	0.97	0.34	1.03	0.98	0.89	0.45	0.66	1.15
96	MEAL, DEHY, 22% PROTEIN	1-07-851	A-F	93	22.2	0.96	0.30	1.09	0.44	1.06	1.63	0.97	0.34	1.13	0.97	0.97	0.49	0.64	1.29
			M-F	100	23.9	1.04	0.32	1.18	0.47	1.15	1.75	1.05	0.37	1.22	1.05	1.04	0.52	0.69	1.39
97	**BREWERS GRAINS** DEHY	5-02-141	A-F	92	27.3	1.27	0.35	1.09	0.53	1.57	2.53	0.88	0.46	1.46	1.30	0.93	0.37	1.16	1.58
			M-F	100	29.6	1.38	0.38	1.18	0.58	1.71	2.75	0.95	0.50	1.58	1.41	1.01	0.40	1.26	1.72
98	**CORN** *Zea mays* DISTILLERS GRAINS WITH SOLUBLES, DEHY	5-02-843	A-F	92	27.1	0.97	0.31	0.59	0.64	1.33	2.31	0.70	0.50	1.47	1.21	0.93	0.18	0.72	1.47
			M-F	100	29.5	1.05	0.34	0.64	0.69	1.45	2.52	0.77	0.54	1.60	1.31	1.01	0.19	0.78	1.60
99	**FISH** SOLUBLES, DEHY	5-01-971	A-F	93	60.4	3.06	0.62	5.75	2.10	2.05	2.98	3.52	1.18	1.53	2.03	1.35	0.60	0.85	2.10
			M-F	100	65.1	3.29	0.66	6.20	2.26	2.21	3.21	3.79	1.27	1.65	2.19	1.46	0.64	0.92	2.26
100	**FISH, SARDINE** *Clupea* spp, *Sardinops* spp MEAL MECH EXTD	5-02-015	A-F	93	65.2	2.70	0.80	4.50	1.80	3.34	—	5.91	2.01	2.00	—	2.60	0.50	2.79	4.10
			M-F	100	70.0	2.90	0.86	4.84	1.93	3.59	—	6.34	2.16	2.15	—	2.79	0.54	3.00	4.40
101	SOLUBLES, CONDENSED	5-02-014	A-F	50	29.5	1.50	0.20	—	2.00	0.90	1.60	1.60	0.90	0.80	—	0.80	0.10	—	1.00
			M-F	100	59.4	3.02	0.40	—	4.02	1.81	3.22	3.22	1.81	1.61	—	1.61	0.20	—	2.01
102	**RICE** *Oryza sativa* BRAN WITH GERMS, MEAL SOLV EXTD (RICE BRAN, SOLV EXTD)	4-03-930	A-F	91	14.0	0.98	0.21	0.91	0.33	0.52	1.02	0.61	0.26	0.57	0.70	0.53	0.21	0.55	0.76
			M-F	100	15.4	1.07	0.23	1.00	0.37	0.57	1.12	0.67	0.29	0.63	0.77	0.58	0.23	0.60	0.84
103	**YEAST, BREWERS** *Saccharomyces cerevisiae* DEHY	7-05-527	A-F	93	43.8	2.26	0.52	1.77	1.13	2.03	2.86	2.98	0.66	1.60	—	2.06	0.51	1.47	2.25
			M-F	100	47.1	2.43	0.56	1.90	1.21	2.18	3.07	3.20	0.71	1.72	—	2.22	0.54	1.58	2.42

AMINO ACIDS

WEIGHTS AND MEASURES

Weights and measures are the standards employed in arriving at weights, quantities, and volumes. Even among primitive people, such standards were necessary; and with the growing complexity of life, they become of greater and greater importance.

Weights and measures form one of the most important parts of modern agriculture. This section contains pertinent information relative to the most common standards used in the U.S. livestock industry.

METRIC SYSTEM[2]

The United States and a few other countries use standards that belong to the customary, or English, system of measurement. This system evolved in England from older measurement standards, beginning

[2]For additional conversion factors, or for greater accuracy, see *Misc. Pub. 223*, the National Bureau of Standards.

about the year 1200. All other countries—including England—now use a system of measurements called the *metric system*, which was created in France in the 1790s. Increasingly, the metric system is being used in the United States. Hence, everyone should have a working knowledge of it.

The basic metric units are the meter (length/distance), the gram (weight), and the liter (capacity). The units are then expanded in multiples of 10 or made smaller by one-tenth. The prefixes, which are used in the same way with all basic metric units, follow:

"milli-" = 1/1,000   "deca-" = 10
"centi-" = 1/100   "hecto-" = 100
"deci-" = 1/10   "kilo-" = 1,000

The following tables will facilitate conversion from metric units to U.S. customary, and vice versa:

Table A-5   Weights and Measures—
    Length
    Surface/Area
    Volume
    Weight

Table A-6   Temperature

Fig. A-2. Weights and measures are very important in modern horse production; used in measuring the growth and condition of horses, in the design and construction of facilities and equipment, in feeding, and in temperature control.

TABLE A-5
WEIGHTS AND MEASURES (METRIC AND U.S. CUSTOMARY)

LENGTH

Unit	Is Equal To	
Metric System		**(U.S. Customary)**
1 millimicron (mμ)	0.000000001 m	0.000000039 in.
1 micron (μ)	0.000001 m	0.000039 in.
1 millimeter (mm)	0.001 m	0.0394 in.
1 centimeter (cm)	0.01 m	0.3937 in.
1 decimeter (dm)	0.1 m	3.937 in.
1 meter (m)	1 m	39.37 in.; 3.281 ft; 1.094 yd
1 hectometer (hm)	100 m	328 ft, 1 in.; 19.8338 rd
1 kilometer (km)	1,000 m	3,280 ft, 10 in.; 0.621 mi
U.S. Customary		**(Metric)**
1 inch (in.)		25 mm; 2.54 cm
1 hand*	4 in.	
1 foot (ft)	12 in.	30.48 cm; 0.305 m
1 yard (yd)	3 ft	0.914 m
1 fathom** (fath)	6.08 ft	1.829 m
1 rod (rd), pole, or perch	16.5 ft; 5.5 yd	5.029 m
1 furlong (fur.)	220 yd; 40 rd	201.168 m
1 mile (mi)	5,280 ft; 1,760 yd; 320 rd; 8 fur.	1,609.35 m; 1.609 km
1 knot or nautical mile	6,080 ft; 1.15 land mi	
1 league (land)	3 mi (land)	
1 league (nautical)	3 mi (nautical)	

*Used in measuring height of horses.

**Used in measuring depth at sea.

CONVERSIONS

To Change	To	Multiply By
inches	centimeters	2.54
feet	meters	0.305
meters	inches	39.73
miles	kilometers	1.609
kilometers	miles	0.621

(To make opposite conversion, divide by the number given instead of multiplying)

(Continued)

TABLE A-5 (Continued)

SURFACE OR AREA

Unit	Is Equal To	
Metric System		**(U.S. Customary)**
1 square millimeter (mm^2)	0.000001 m^2	0.00155 in.^{2}
1 square centimeter (cm^2)	0.0001 m^2	0.155 in.^{2}
1 square decimeter (dm^2)	0.01 m^2	15.50 in.^{2}
1 square meter (m^2)	1 centare (ca)	1,550 in.^{2}; 10.76 ft^2; 1.196 yd^2
1 are (a)	100 m^2	119.6 yd^2
1 hectare (ha)	10,000 m^2	2.47 acres
1 square kilometer (km^2)	1,000,000 m^2	247.1 acres; 0.386 mi^2
U.S. Customary		**(Metric)**
1 square inch (in.^{2})	1 in. × 1 in.	6.452 cm^2
1 square foot (ft^2)	144 in.^{2}	0.093 m^2
1 square yard (yd^2)	1,296 in.^{2}; 9 ft^2	0.836 m^2
1 square rod (rd^2)	272.25 ft^2; 30.25 yd^2	25.29 m^2
1 rood	40 rd^2	10.117 a
1 acre	43,560 ft^2; 4,840 yd^2; 160 rd^2; 4 roods	4,046.87 m^2; 0.405 ha
1 square mile (mi^2)	640 acres	2.59 km^2; 259 ha
1 township	36 sections; 6 mi^2	

CONVERSIONS

To Change	To	Multiply By
square inches	square centimeters	6.452
square centimeters	square inches	0.155
square yards	square meters	0.836
square meters	square yards	1.196

(To make opposite conversion, divide by the number given instead of multiplying.)

VOLUME

Unit	Is Equal To		
Metric System Liquid and Dry		**(U.S. Customary)**	
		(Liquid)	**(Dry)**
1 milliliter (ml)	0.001 liter	0.271 dram (fl)	0.061 in.^{3}
1 centiliter (cl)	0.01 liter	0.338 oz (fl)	0.610 in.^{3}
1 deciliter (dl)	0.1 liter	3.38 oz (fl)	
1 liter (l)	1,000 cc	1.057 qt; 0.2642 gal (fl)	0.908 qt
1 hectoliter (hl)	100 liter	26.418 gal	2.838 bu
1 kiloliter (kl)	1,000 liter	264.18 gal	1,308 yd^3

(Continued)

TABLE A-5 (Continued)

VOLUME (Continued)

Unit		Is Equal To		
U.S. Customary *Liquid*		(Ounces)	(Cubic Inches)	(Metric)
1 teaspoon (t)	60 drops	0.1666		5 ml
1 dessert spoon	2 t			
1 tablespoon (T)	3 t	0.5		15 ml
1 fl oz		1	1.805	29.57 ml
1 gill (gi)	0.5 c	4	7.22	118.29 ml
1 cup (c)	16 T	8	14.44	236.58 ml; 0.24 l
1 pint (pt)	2 c	16	28.88	0.47 l
1 quart (qt)	2 pt	32	57.75	0.95 l
1 gallon (gal)	4 qt	8.34 lb	231	3.79 l
1 barrel (bbl)	31.5 gal			
1 hogshead (hhd)	2 bbl			
Dry		(Ounces)	(Cubic Inches)	(Metric)
1 pint (pt)	0.5 qt		33.6	0.55 l
1 quart (qt)	2 pt		67.20	1.10 l
1 peck (pk)	8 qt		537.61	8.81 l
1 bushel (bu)	4 pk		2,150.42	35.24 l
Solid **Metric System**		(Metric)	(U.S. Customary)	
1 cubic millimeter (mm^3)		0.001 cc		
1 cubic centimeter (cc)		1,000 mm^3	0.061 in.^{3}	
1 cubic decimeter (dm^3)		1,000 cc	61.023 in.^{3}	
1 cubic meter (m^3)		1,000 dm^3	35.315 ft^3; 1.308 yd^3	
U.S. Customary				(Metric)
1 cubic inch (in.^{3})				16.387 cc
1 board foot (fbm)		144 in.^{3}		2,359.8 cc
1 cubic foot (ft^3)		1,728 in.^{3}		0.028 m^3
1 cubic yard (yd^3)		27 ft^3		0.765 m^3
1 cord		128 ft^3		3.625 m^3

CONVERSIONS

To Change	To	Multiply By
ounces (fluid)	cubic centimeters	29.57
cubic centimeters	ounces (fluid)	0.034
quarts	liters	0.946
liters	quarts	1.057
cubic inches	cubic centimeters	16.387
cubic centimeters	cubic inches	0.061
cubic yards	cubic meters	0.765
cubic meters	cubic yards	1.308

(To make opposite conversion, divide by the number given instead of multiplying.)

(Continued)

TABLE A-5 (Continued)

WEIGHT

Unit	Is Equal To	
Metric System		**(U.S. Customary)**
1 microgram (mcg)	0.001 mg	
1 milligram (mg)	0.001 g	0.015432356 grain
1 centigram (cg)	0.01 g	0.15432356 grain
1 decigram (dg)	0.1 g	1.5432 grains
1 gram (g)	1,000 mg	0.03527396 oz
1 decagram (dkg)	10 g	5.643833 dr
1 hectogram (hg)	100 g	3.527396 oz
1 kilogram (kg)	1,000 g	35.274 oz; 2.2046223 lb
1 ton	1,000 kg	2,204.6 lb; 1.102 tons (short); 0.984 ton (long)
U.S. Customary		**(Metric)**
1 grain	0.037 dr	64.798918 mg; 0.064798918 g
1 dram (dr)	0.063 oz	1.771845 g
1 ounce (oz)	16 dr	28.349527 g
1 pound (lb)	16 oz	453.5924 g; 0.4536 kg
1 hundredweight (cwt)	100 lb	
1 ton (short)	2,000 lb	907.18486 kg; 0.907 (metric) ton
1 ton (long)	2,200 lb	1,016.05 kg; 1.016 (metric) ton
1 part per million (ppm)	1 microgram/gram; 1 mg/liter; 1 mg/kg	0.4535924 mg/lb; 0.907 g/ton
	0.0001%; 0.00013 oz/gal	
1 percent (%) (1 part in 100 parts)	10,000 ppm; 10 g/liter	
	1.28 oz/gal; 8.34 lb/100 gal	

CONVERSIONS

To Change	To	Multiply By
grains	milligrams	64.799
ounces (dry)	grams	28.35
pounds (dry)	kilograms	0.4535924
kilograms	pounds	2.2046223
milligrams/pound	parts/million	2.2046223
parts/million	grams/ton	0.90718486
grams/ton	parts/million	1.1
milligrams/pound	grams/ton	2
grams/ton	milligrams/pound	0.5
grams/pound	grams/ton	2,000
grams/ton	grams/pound	0.0005
grams/ton	pounds/ton	0.0022
pounds/ton	grams/ton	453.5924
grams/ton	percent	0.00011
percent	grams/ton	9,072
parts/million	percent	move decimal four places to left

(To make opposite conversion, divide by the number given instead of multiplying.)

TABLE A-6
TEMPERATURE

One Fahrenheit (F) degree is 1/180 of the difference between the temperature of melting ice and that of water boiling at standard atmospheric pressure. One Fahrenheit degree equals 0.556°C.

One Centigrade (C) degree is 1/100 the difference between the temperature of melting ice and that of water boiling at standard atmospheric pressure. One Centigrade degree equals 1.8°F.

To Change	To	Do This
Degrees Fahrenheit	Degrees Centigrade	Subtract 32, then multiply by 0.556 (5/9)
Degrees Centigrade	Degrees Fahrenheit	Multiply by 1.8 (9/5) and add 32

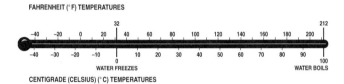

FAHRENHEIT (°F) TEMPERATURES

CENTIGRADE (CELSIUS) (°C) TEMPERATURES

Fig. A-3. Fahrenheit-Centigrade scale for direct conversion and reading.

WEIGHTS AND MEASURES OF COMMON FEEDS

In calculating rations and mixing concentrates, it is usually necessary to use weights rather than measures. However, in practical feeding operations it is often more convenient for the farmer or rancher to measure the concentrates by volume. Table A-7 will serve as a guide in feeding by measure.

STORAGE SPACE REQUIREMENTS FOR FEED AND BEDDING

The space requirements for feed storage for the livestock enterprise—whether it be for cattle, sheep, hogs, or horses, or, as is more frequently the case, a combination of these—vary so widely that it is difficult to provide a standard method of calculating space requirements applicable to such diverse conditions. The amount of feed to be stored depends primarily upon (1) length of pasture season, (2) method of feeding and management, (3) kind of feed, (4) climate, and (5) the proportion of feeds produced on the farm or ranch in comparison with those purchased. Normally, the storage capacity should be sufficient to handle all feed grain and silage grown on the farm and to hold purchased supplies. Forage and bedding may or may not be stored under cover. In those areas where weather conditions permit, hay and straw are frequently stacked in the fields or near the barns in

TABLE A-7
WEIGHTS AND MEASURES OF COMMON FEEDS

Feed	Approximate Weight	
	Lb per Quart[1]	Lb per Bushel
Alfalfa meal	0.6	19
Barley	1.5	48
Beet pulp (dried)	0.6	19
Brewers' grain (dried)	0.6	19
Buckwheat	1.6	50
Buckwheat bran	1.0	29
Corn, husked ear	—	70
Corn, cracked	1.6	50
Corn, shelled	1.8	56
Corn meal	1.6	50
Corn-and-cob meal	1.4	45
Cottonseed meal	1.5	48
Cowpeas	1.9	60
Distillers' grain (dried)	0.6	19
Fish meal	1.0	35
Gluten feed	1.3	42
Linseed meal (old process)	1.1	35
Linseed meal (new process)	0.9	29
Meat scrap	1.3	42
Milo (grain sorghum)	1.7	56
Molasses feed	0.8	26
Oats	1.0	32
Oats, ground	0.7	22
Oat middlings	1.5	48
Peanut meal	1.0	32
Rice bran	0.8	26
Rye	1.7	56
Sorghum (grain)	1.7	56
Soybeans	1.7	60
Tankage	1.6	51
Velvet beans, shelled	1.8	60
Wheat	1.9	60
Wheat bran	0.5	16
Wheat middlings, standard	0.8	26
Wheat screenings	1.0	32

[1]32 qts per bushel.

loose, baled, or chopped form. Sometimes poled, framed sheds or a cheap cover of waterproof paper, grass, or cereal straw grass are used for protection. Other forms of low-cost storage include temporary upright silos, trench silos, temporary grain bins, and open-walled buildings for hay.

Table A-8 gives the storage space requirements for feed and bedding. This information may be helpful to the individual operator who desires to compute the barn storage space required for a specific livestock

TABLE A-8
STORAGE SPACE REQUIREMENTS FOR FEED AND BEDDING

Kind of Feed or Bedding	Pounds per Cubic Foot	Cubic Feet per Ton	Pounds per Bushel of Grain
Hay-Straw:[1]			
1. Loose			
Alfalfa	4.4–4.0	450–500	
Nonlegume	4.4–3.3	450–600	
Straw	3.0–2.0	670–1,000	
2. Baled			
Alfalfa	10.0–6.0	200–330	
Nonlegume	8.0–6.0	250–330	
Straw	5.0–4.0	400–500	
3. Chopped			
Alfalfa	7.0–5.5	285–360	
Nonlegume	6.7–5.0	300–400	
Straw	8.0–5.7	250–350	
Corn:			
15½% moisture:			
Shelled	44.8		56.0
Ear	28.0		70.0
Shelled, ground	38.0		48.0
Ear, ground	36.0		45.0
30% moisture:			
Shelled	54.0		67.5
Ear, ground	35.8		89.6
Barley, 15% moisture	38.4		48.0
Ground	28.0		37.0
Flax, 11% moisture	44.8		56.0
Oats, 16% moisture	25.6		32.0
Ground	18.0		23.0
Rye, 16% moisture	44.8		56.0
Ground	38.0		48.0
Sorghum grain, 15% moisture	44.8		56.0
Soybeans, 14% moisture . .	48.0		60.0
Wheat, 14% moisture	48.0		60.0
Ground	43.0		50.0

[1]Many factors—other than kind of hay-straw, form (loose, baled, chopped), and period of settling—affect the density of hay-straw in a stack or in a barn, including (a) moisture content at haying time, and (b) texture and foreign material.

enterprise. This table provides a convenient means of estimating the amount of feed or bedding in storage.

ESTIMATING HORSE WEIGHTS FROM BODY MEASUREMENTS

It is easy to estimate the weight of a horse from body measurements. Studies have revealed that the results obtained by the method herewith outlined are within three percent of the actual weight made on scales. The procedure is as follows:

1. Measure the heart girth in inches (C in Fig. A-4).

2. Measure the length of body from point of shoulder to point of buttocks (A to B in Fig. A-5).

3. Use the above two measurements to calculate the weight of the horse according to the following formula:

Heart girth × heart girth × length ÷ 300 + 50 lb = weight of horse

Example: A horse has a heart girth of 70 in. and a length of 65 in. What is its estimated weight?

Answer:

> 70 in. × 70 in. × 65 in. ÷ 300 + 50 lb = weight
> 4,900 × 65 = 318,500
> 318,500 ÷ 300 = 1,062 lb
> 1,062 + 50 = 1,112 lb body weight

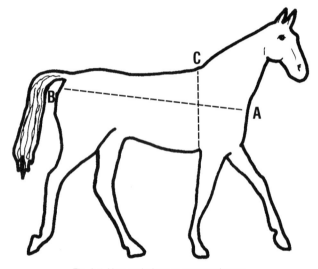

Fig. A-4. How and where to measure horses.

ANIMAL UNITS

An animal unit is a common animal denominator, based on feed consumption. It is assumed that one mature cow represents an animal unit. Then, the comparative (to a mature cow) feed consumption of other age groups or classes of animals determines the proportion of an animal unit which they represent. For example, it is generally estimated that the ration of one mature cow will feed five mature ewes, or that five mature ewes equal 1.0 animal unit.

The original concept of an animal unit included a weight stipulation—an animal unit referred to a 1,000-lb cow, with or without a calf at side. Unfortunately, in recent years, the 1,000-lb qualification has been dropped. Certainly, there is a wide difference in the daily feed requirements of a 900-lb cow and of a 1,500-lb cow. Both will consume dry matter on a daily basis at a level equivalent to about 2% of their body weight.

Hence, a 1,500-lb cow will consume 50% more feed than a 1,000-lb cow.

Also, the period of time to be grazed has an effect on the total carrying capacity. For example, if an animal is carried for 1 month only, it will take one-twelfth of the total feed required to carry the same animal 1 year. For this reason, the term *animal unit months* is becoming increasingly important. So, in addition to the weight factor, the time factor has a distinct bearing on the ultimate carrying capacity of a tract of land.

Table A-9 gives the animal units of different classes and ages of livestock.

TABLE A-9
ANIMAL UNITS

Type of Livestock	Animal Units
Cattle:	
Cow, with or without unweaned calf at side, or heifer 2 yrs. old or older	1.0
Bull, 2 yrs. old or older	1.3
Young cattle, 1 to 2 yrs. old	0.8
Weaned calves to yearlings	0.6
Horses:	
Horse, mature	1.3
Horse, yearling	1.0
Weanling colt or filly	0.75
Sheep:	
5 mature ewes, with or without unweaned lambs at side	1.0
5 rams, 2 yrs. old or older	1.3
5 yearlings	0.8
5 weaned lambs to yearlings	0.6
Swine:	
Sow	0.4
Boar	0.5
Pigs to 200 lb (91 kg)	0.2
Chickens:	
75 layers or breeders	1.0
325 replacement pullets to 6 mo. of age	1.0
650 8-week-old broilers	1.0
Turkeys:	
35 breeders	1.0
40 turkeys raised to maturity	1.0
75 turkeys to 6 mo. of age.	1.0

GESTATION TABLE

The horseman who has information relative to breeding dates can easily estimate parturition dates from Table A-10.

TABLE A-10
GESTATION TABLE—MARE

Date Bred	Date Due, 336 Days	Date Bred	Date Due, 336 Days
Jan. 1	Dec. 3	July 5	June 6
Jan. 6	Dec. 8	July 10	June 11
Jan. 11	Dec. 13	July 15	June 16
Jan. 16	Dec. 18	July 20	June 21
Jan. 21	Dec. 23	July 25	June 26
Jan. 26	Dec. 28	July 30	July 1
Jan. 31	Jan. 2	Aug. 4	July 6
Feb. 5	Jan. 7	Aug. 9	July 11
Feb. 10	Jan. 12	Aug. 14	July 16
Feb. 15	Jan. 17	Aug. 19	July 21
Feb. 20	Jan. 22	Aug. 24	July 26
Feb. 25	Jan. 27	Aug. 29	July 31
Mar. 2	Feb. 1	Sept. 3	Aug. 5
Mar. 7	Feb. 6	Sept. 8	Aug. 10
Mar. 12	Feb. 11	Sept. 13	Aug. 15
Mar. 17	Feb. 16	Sept. 18	Aug. 20
Mar. 22	Feb. 21	Sept. 23	Aug. 25
Mar. 27	Feb. 26	Sept. 28	Aug. 30
April 1	Mar. 3	Oct. 3	Sept. 4
April 6	Mar. 8	Oct. 8	Sept. 9
April 11	Mar. 13	Oct. 13	Sept. 14
April 16	Mar. 18	Oct. 18	Sept. 19
April 21	Mar. 23	Oct. 23	Sept. 24
April 26	Mar. 28	Oct. 28	Sept. 29
May 1	April 2	Nov. 2	Oct. 4
May 6	April 7	Nov. 7	Oct. 9
May 11	April 12	Nov. 12	Oct. 14
May 16	April 17	Nov. 17	Oct. 19
May 21	April 22	Nov. 22	Oct. 24
May 26	April 27	Nov. 27	Oct. 29
May 31	May 2	Dec. 2	Nov. 3
June 5	May 7	Dec. 7	Nov. 8
June 10	May 12	Dec. 12	Nov. 13
June 15	May 17	Dec. 17	Nov. 18
June 20	May 22	Dec. 22	Nov. 23
June 25	May 27	Dec. 27	Nov. 28
June 30	June 1		

UNITED STATES AND WORLD RECORDS FOR THOROUGHBREDS, STANDARDBREDS, AND QUARTER HORSES

The U.S. and world records for Thoroughbreds, Standardbreds, and Quarter Horses at some of the popular American distances are given in Tables A-11, A-12, and A-13, respectively.

Fig. A-5. Rounding the clubhouse turn at picturesque Saratoga Race Track. (Courtesy, The Jockey Club, New York, NY)

TABLE A-11
UNITED STATES AND WORLD NEW DIRT RECORDS FOR THOROUGHBREDS[1]

Distance	Name of Horse	Age of Horse	Weight Carried	Track	Year Record Established	Time
		(yrs.)	(lb)			
4f[2]	Midnite Mackee	5	116	Stampede Park	1992	0:44
4.5f	War of Aces	4	126	Kamloops (B.C.)	1992	0:48 2/5
5.5f	Silvey's Image	5	116	Turf Paradise	1992	1:01 1/5
6.5f	Native Paster	4	117	Del Mar	1988	1:13 3/5
9f	Simply Majestic	4	114	Golden Gate Fields	1988	1:45
11f	Timely Warning	6	112	Aqueduct	1991	2:14

[1]Data provided by The Jockey Club, 821 Corporate Drive, Lexington, KY 40503-2794

[2]A furlong is a measure of length equal to an eighth of a mile (or 40 rods, 220 yards, or 201.17 meters).

TABLE A-12
WORLD RECORDS FOR STANDARDBREDS[1]

Track Size	Sex[2]	Name of Horse	Track	Year Record Established	Time for One Mile
Pacing:					
1 mile	H	Silver Almahurst	Yonkers, NY	1993	1:50.4
1 mile	M	Pensive	Yonkers, NY	1993	1:52.2
1 mile	G	Majectic Osborne	Northfield, OH	1993	1:52.3
1 mile	G	Hotrod Falcon	Freehold, NJ	1993	1:52.3
5/8 mile	C	Riyadh	Meadowlands, NJ	1993	1:50.1
5/8 mile	M	Camourous	Meadowlands, NJ	1993	1:50.1
5/8 mile	G	Staying Together	Greenwood, Ontario	1993	1:50.4
1/2 mile	H	Silver Almahurst	Yonkers, NY	1993	1:50.4
1/2 mile	M	Pensive	Yonkers NY	1993	152.2
1/2 mile	G	Majectic Osborne	Northfield, OH	1993	152.3
1/2 mile	G	Hotrod Falcon	Freehold, NJ	1993	152.3
Trotting:					
1 mile	H	Pine Chip	Red Mile, KY	1994	1:51
1 mile	M	Beat the Wheel	Meadowlands, NJ	1994	1:51.4
1 mile	G	Champion on Tee	Springfield, IL	1994	153.2
1 mile	F	Fancy Crown	Springfield, IL	1984	1:53.4
5/8 mile	C	Mack Lobell	Pompano, FL	1987	1:54.1
5/8 mile	M	Peace Corps	Pompano, FL	1990	1:54.2
5/8 mile	G	No Sex Please	Pompano, FL	1990	1:55
1/2 mile	H	Pine Chip	Delaware, OH	1994	1:54
1/2 mile	F	Peace Corps	Delaware, OH	1989	1:56
1/2 mile	G	Comeover	Delaware, OH	1994	1:56.4
1/2 mile	F	Armbro Devona	Delaware, OH	1985	1:57

[1]Data provided by The United States Trotting Association, 750 Michigan Ave., Columbus, OH 43215.
[2]Sex: H = horse, G = gelding, C = colt, M = mare, F = filly.

TABLE A-13
WORLD RECORDS FOR QUARTER HORSES[1]

Distance	Name of Horse	Age of Horse	Weight Carried	Track	Year Record Established	Time
(yards)		(yrs.)	(lb)			
220	Junior Meyers	4	120	La Mesa Park, Raton, NM	1969	11.62
250	Dashing Scott	4	125	Pocatello Downs, Pocatello, ID	1994	12.92
300	The Prize	2	118	Hipodromo de las Americas, Mexico City, Mexico	1995	15.06
330	Pies Royal Request	4	125	Prescott Downs, Prescott, AZ	1995	16.43
330	Blue Blister	7	119	Prescott Downs, Prescott, AZ	1996	16.43
350	Bardella	3	113	Los Alamitos Race Course, Los Alamitos, CA	1953	17.10
400	Jack O Dash	2	120	Portland Meadows, Portland, OR	1996	20.50
440	Evening Snow	3	122	Turf Paradise, Phoenix, AZ	1996	20.94
550	Tuxer	5	122	Rillito Park, Tucson, AZ	1995	26.33
660	Deckum Larum	5	122	Illinois State Fair, Springfield, IL	1983	33.51
660S	Holme of the Count	4	121	Remington Park, Oklahoma, City, OK	1993	32.67
770	Miami Prince	3	120	Fair Meadows at Tulsa, Tulsa, OK	1994	39.53
870	Griswold	5	125	Los Alamitos Race Course, Los Alamitos, CA	1991	43.99

[1]Data provided by The Quarter Racing Journal.

LEADING MONEY-WINNING THOROUGHBREDS, STANDARDBREDS, AND QUARTER HORSES

The leading money-winning Thoroughbreds are listed, by rank, in Table A-14. Similar information for Standardbreds is given in Table A-15, and for Quarter Horses, in Table A-16.

Fig. A-6   Harness racing action at Lexington, Kentucky. (Courtesy, United States Trotting Association, Columbus, OH)

TABLE A-14
LEADING MONEY-WINNING THOROUGHBREDS[1]

Rank	Horse	Starts	1st	2nd	3rd	Total Earnings
1	Cigar, 1990	29	18	2	4	$9,999,815
2	Alysheba, 1984	26	11	8	2	6,679,242
3	John Henry, 1975	83	39	15	9	6,597,947
4	Best Pal, 1988	47	18	11	4	5,668,245
5	Sunday Silence, 1986	14	9	5	0	4,968,554
6	Easy Goer, 1986	20	14	5	1	4,873,770
7	Unbridled, 1987	24	8	6	6	4,489,475
8	Spend A Buck, 1982	15	10	3	2	4,220,689
9	Creme Fraiche, 1982	54	16	11	11	3,809,559
10	Ferdinand, 1983	28	8	9	6	3,722,978
11	Slew O'Gold, 1980	21	12	5	1	3,533,234
12	Precisionist, 1981	46	20	10	4	3,485,393
13	Strike The Gold, 1988	31	6	8	5	3,457,026
14	Snow Chief, 1983	24	13	3	5	3,383,210
15	Cryptoclearance, 1984	44	12	10	7	3,376,327

[1]Data provided by The Jockey Club, 821 Corporate Drive, Lexington, KY 40503-2794

TABLE A-15
LEADING MONEY-WINNING STANDARDBREDS[1]

Rank	Horse	Age	Record	Color	Sex	Sire	Years Raced	Total Earnings
Pacers:								
1	Nihilator	3	1:49.3	b	H	Niatross	1984–85	$3,225,653
2	Artsplace	4	1:49.2	b	H	Abercrombie	1990–92	3,085,083
3	Presidential Ball	3	1:50	br	C	Cam Fella	1992–93	3,021,363
4	Matt's Scooter	4	1:48.2	b	H	Direct Scooter	1987–89	2,944,591
5	On The Road Again	4	1:51.4	ch	H	Happy Motoring	1983–85	2,819,102
6	Beach Towel	3	1:50	b	C	French Chef	1989–90	2,570,357
7	Western Hanover	3	1:50.4	br	C	No Nukes	1991–92	2,541,647
8	Cam's Card Shark	3	1:50	b	C	Cam Fella	1993–94	2,498,204
9	Precious Bunny	3	1:49.4	b	C	Cam Fella	1990–91	2,281,142
10	Jake and Elwood	4	1:50.1	br	H	Samadhi	1989–92	2,273,187
11	Jate Lobell	3	1:51.2	b	C	No Nukes	1986–87	2,231,402
12	Die Laughing	3	1:51.1	br	C	No Nukes	1990–91	2,164,386
13	Camtastic	4	1:49.3	br	C	Cam Fella	1987–89	2,117,619
14	Cam Fella	4	1:53.1	b	H	Most Happy Fella	1981–83	2,041,367
15	Rambling Willie	7	1:54.3	b	G	Rambling Fury	1972–83	2,038,219
Trotters:								
1	Peace Corps	3	1:52.4	b	F	Baltic Speed	1988–93	4,907,307
2	Ourasi		none at mile	ch	H	Greyhound	1988–90	4,010,105
3	Mack Lobell	3	1:52.1	br	C	Mystic Park	1986–91	3,917,594
4	Reve d'Udon		none at mile	b	H	Eja Kval	1985–92	3,611,351
5	Ideal de Gazeau		none at mile	br	H	Alexis III	1976–83	2,744,777
6	Vrai Lutin		none at mile	br	H	Lutin d'Isigny	1991–93	2,612,429
7	Pracles Singing	4	1:57	br	M	Texas	1984–89	2,607,552
8	Embassy Lobell	3	1:54.4	b	C	Speedy Crown	1989–93	2,566,370
9	Napoletans	5	1:54.1	b	H	Super Bowl	1986–89	2,467,878
10	Sea Cove	3	1:56.2	b	C	Bonefish	1989–94	2,505,047
11	Jef's Spice	3	1:55.2	b	F	Super Bowl	1985–90	2,311,271
12	Lutin d'Isigny		none at mile	ch	H	Firefly	1985	2,017,554
13	Jorky		none at mile	b	H	Kerjacques	1982	1,970,432
14	Prakas	3	1:53.2	b	H	Speedy Crown	1984–85	1,956,056
15	No Sex Please	5	1:55	br	G	Brisco Hanover	1987–93	1,884,392

[1]Data provided by the United States Trotting Assn., Columbus, Ohio.

TABLE A-16
LEADING MONEY-WINNING QUARTER HORSES[1]

Rank	Horse	Sex	Starts	1st	2nd	3rd	Owner	Total Earnings
1	Refrigerator	G	36	22	8	3	James E. Helzer	$2,126,309
2	Eastex	G	31	13	4	5	Speedhorse Inc.	1,869,406
3	Mr. Master Bug	S	25	17	4	3	Bob G. Burke	1,793,718
4	Ronas Ryon	S	23	18	4	0	Ben Benham	1,777,977
5	Dashingly	M	25	18	5	0	J. B. Brinkmann	1,754,323
6	Winalota Cash	G	21	15	5	0	Andra D. Meridyth	1,709,204
7	Higheasterjet	G	30	20	2	2	G. D. Highsmith	1,633,035
8	Merganser	S	23	13	3	2	Bobby D. Cox	1,373,704
9	Strawberry Silk	M	17	11	3	0	Jackie Spencer	1,266,264
10	Dash For Speed	M	30	22	3	2	C. Scharbauer	1,225,337
11	Special Effort	S	14	13	0	1	Burnett Ranches	1,219,950
12	Elans Special	M	22	11	4	3	Edward C. Allred	1,186,540
13	On A High	S	22	9	6	4	On A High Joint Venture	1,167,234
14	Tolltac	S	18	12	4	0	Vessels Stallion Frm/D. E. Payne	1,143,043
15	Make Mine Cash	M	26	7	5	5	R. D. Hubbard, H. D. Farris	1,142,428
16	Streakin Flyer	G	6	4	1	0	Southern Rose Ranch	1,136,512
17	Florentine	M	30	16	6	2	A. K. Kawananakoa	1,123,102
18	Dashs Dreams	M	24	19	3	1	Joe Kirk	1,119,610

[1]Data provided by *The Quarter Racing Journal.*

BREED REGISTRY ASSOCIATIONS

A breed registry association consists of a group of breeders banded together for the purpose of (1) recording the lineage of their animals, (2) protecting the purity of the breed, (3) encouraging further improvement of the breed, and (4) promoting interest in the breed. A list of the horse breed registry associations is given in Table A-17, but no claim is made that all breed registries are listed therein.

TABLE A-17
HORSE BREED REGISTRY ASSOCIATIONS

Light Horses:

Akhal-Teke

Akhal-Teke Association of America, Inc., The
Shenandoah Farm, Route 5, Box 110
Staunton, VA 24401

American Bashkir Curly

American Bashkir Curly Registry
P.O. Box 453
Ely, NV 89301

American Creme

International American Albino Association
Box 194
Naper, NE 68755

American Mustang

American Mustang Association, Inc.
P.O. Box 338
Yucaipa, CA 92399

American Saddlebred

American Saddlebred Horse Association, Inc.
4093 Iron Works Pike
Lexington, KY 40511

American Warmblood

American Warmblood Society
6801 W. Romley
Phoenix, AZ 85043

American Warmblood Registry, Inc.
P.O. Box 15167
Tallahassee, FL 32317-5167

American White/American Creme

International American Albino Association
Route 1, Box 20
Naper, NE 68755

Andalusian

American Andalusian Horse Association

International Andalusian Horse Association
256 S. Robertson, No. 9378
Beverly Hills, CA 90211

(Continued)

TABLE A-17 (Continued)

Appaloosa

Appaloosa Horse Club, Inc.
5070 Hwy. 8 West
P.O. Box 8403
Moscow, ID 83843

International Colored Appaloosa Assn., Inc.
P.O. Box 99
Shipshewana, IN 46565

Arabian

Arabian Horse Registry of America, Inc.
12000 Zuni Street
Westminster, CO 80234

International Arabian Horse Registry of North America
12465 Brown-Moder Road
Marysville, OH 43040-9513

Association of Parti-Colored Arabians
37680 S.E. Fall Creek Road
Estacada, OR 97023

Belgian Warmblood

Belgian Warmblood Breeding Association
North American District
900 N. Mildred Street
Ransom, WV 25438

Buckskin

International Buckskin Horse Association, Inc.
P.O. Box 268
Shelby, IN 46377

Chickasaw

Chickasaw Horse Association, Inc., The
169 Henry Martin Trail
Love Valley, NC 28677

Cleveland Bay

Cleveland Bay Horse Society of North America, The
P.O. Box 221
South Windham, CT 06266

Dutch Warmblood

North American Department of the Royal Dutch
Warmblood Studbook of the Netherlands
P.O. Box 828
Winchester, OR 97475-0828

Galiceno

Galiceno Horse Breeders Association, Inc.
P.O. Box 219
Godley, TX 76044

Generic Horse

P.O. Box 6778-D
Dept. AHC
Rancho Palos Verdes, CA 90734-6778

Hackney

American Hackney Horse Society
4059 Iron Works Road #A
Lexington, KY 40511-8462

Haflinger

Haflinger Association of America
14570 Gratiot Road
Hemlock, MI 48626

Haflinger Registry of North America
14640 State Route 83
Coshocton, OH 43812-8911

Half Saddlebred

Half Saddlebred Registry of America, The
319 S. 6th Street
Coshocton, OH 43812

Hanoverian

American Hanoverian Society, The
4059 Iron Works Pike, Bldg. A
Lexington, KY 40511

Hungarian Horse

Hungarian Horse Association of America
HC 71, Box 108
Anselmo, NE 68813

Irish Draft Horse

Irish Draft Horse Society of North America
755 Tower Park Road, R.R. 1
Sidney, B.C., Canada V8C5C7

Lipizzan

Lipizzan Association of North America
P.O. Box 1133
Anderson, IN 46015-1133

Missouri Fox Trotting Horse

Missouri Fox Trotting Horse Breed Association, Inc.
P.O. Box 1027
Ava, MO 65608

Morab

International Morab Breeders Association and Registry
S. 101 W. 34628 Hwy. 99
Eagle, WI 53119-1857

North American Morab Horse Association, Inc.
W3174 Faro Springs Road
Hilbert, WI 54129

Mustang (Also see Spanish-Barb)

American Mustang Association
P.O. Box 338
Yucaipa, CA 93299

Gilbert H. Jones
Southwest Spanish Mustang Association
Finley, OK 45840

International Society for the Protection of
Mustangs and Burros
6212 E. Sweetwater Avenue
Scottsdale, AZ 85254

North American Mustang Association and Registry
P.O. Box 850906
Mesquite, TX 75185-0906

Spanish Mustang Registry, Inc.
Rt. 3, Box 7670
Willcox, AZ 85643

National Show Horse

National Show Horse Registry
11700 Commonwealth Dr., Suite 200
Louisville, KY 40299

National Spotted Saddle Horse

National Spotted Saddle Horse Association, Inc.
P.O. Box 898
Murfreesboro, TN 37133

(Continued)

TABLE A-17 (Continued)

Norwegian Fjord Horse

Norwegian Fjord Association of North America
24570 W. Chardon Road
Grayslake, IL 60030

Paint Horse

American Paint Horse Association
P.O. Box 961023
Ft. Worth, TX 76161-0023

Palomino

Palomino Horse Association, Inc., The
Box 24, Star Route
Dornsife, PA 17823

Palomino Horse Breeders of America, Inc.
15253 E. Skelly Dr.
Tulsa, OK 74116-2637

Paso Fino

Paso Fino Horse Association, Inc.
101 North Collins Street
Plant City, FL 33566-3311

Peruvian Paso

American Association of Owners & Breeders
of Peruvian Paso Horses
P.O. Box 30723
Oakland, CA 94604

Peruvian Paso Horse Registry of North America
3077 Wiljan Court, Suite A
Santa Rosa, CA 95407-5702

Peruvian Paso Part-Blood Registry
3077 Wiljan Court, Suite A
Santa Rosa, CA 95407-5702

Pintabian

Pintabian Horse Registry
P.O. Box 360
Karlstad, MN 56732-0360

Pinto Arabian

American Pinto Arabian Registry
P.O. Box 459
Ennis, TX 75119

Pinto Horse

National Pinto Horse Registry
P.O. Box 486
Oxford, NY 13830-0486

Quarter Horse

American Quarter Horse Association
P.O. Box 200
Amarillo, TX 79168

Foundation Quarter Horse Registry, The
Box 500
Akron, CO 80720

Selle Francais

North American Selle Francais Horse Association
P.O. Box 646
Winchester, VA 22604

Spanish-Barb (Also see Mustang)

Spanish-Barb Breeders Association
12284 Springridge Road
Terry, MS 39170

Standardbred

United States Trotting Association
750 Michigan Avenue
Columbus, OH 43215

Swedish Warmblood

Swedish Warmblood Association of North America, The
P.O. Box 1587
Coupeville, WA 98239

Tennessee Walking Horse

Tennessee Walking Horse Breeders' and
Exhibitors Association
P.O. Box 286
Lewisburg, TN 37091

Thoroughbred

Jockey Club, The
380 Madison Avenue
New York, NY 10017

Performance Horse Registry
P.O. Box 24710
821 Corporate Drive
Lexington, KY 40524-4710

Trakehner

American Trakehner Association, Inc.
1520 West Church St.
Newark, OH 43055

Welsh Cob

Welsh Cob Society of America
Grazing Field Farm
Head of the Bay Road
Buzzard Bay, MA 02532

Ponies:

American Walking Pony

American Walking Pony Association
P.O. Box 5282
Macon, GA 31208

Connemara Pony

American Connemara Pony Society
2360 Hunting Road
Winchester, VA 22603

Dales Pony

Canadian Mountain & Moorland Society
RR 4, Box 273
Amherst, Nova Scotia, Canada B4H3Y2

Exmoor Pony

Canadian Mountain & Moorland Society
RR 4, Box 273
Amherst, Nova Scotia, Canada B4H3Y2

Pony of the Americas

Pony of the Americas Club, Inc.
5240 Elmwood Ave.
Indianapolis, IN 46203

Shetland Pony

American Shetland Pony Club
6748 N. Frostwood Pkwy.
Peoria, IL 61615

(Continued)

TABLE A-17 (Continued)

Swedish Gotland Horse

American Livestock Breeds Conservatory
Box 477
Pittsboro, NC 27312

Welara Pony

American Welara Pony Society
P.O. Box 401
Yucca Valley, CA 92284

Welsh Pony and Cob

Welsh Pony and Cob Society of America
P.O. Box 2977
Winchester, VA 22604

Miniature Horse:

Miniature Horse

American Miniature Horse Association, Inc.
P.O. Box 129
Burleson, TX 76028

American Miniature Horse Registry
6748 North Frostwood Pkwy.
Peoria, IL 61615

Draft Horses:

American Cream

American Cream Draft Horse Association
2065 Noble Avenue
Charles City, IA 50616-9108

Belgian

Belgian Draft Horse Corporation of America
P.O. Box 335
Wabash, IN 46992

Clydesdale

Clydesdale Breeders Association of the United States
17378 Kelley Road
Pecatonica, IL 61063

Percheron

Percheron Horse Association of America
P.O. Box 141
Fredericktown, OH 43019

Shire

American Shire Horse Association, The
35380 County Road 31
Davis, CA 95616

Suffolk

American Suffolk Horse Association, Inc.
4240 Goehring Road
Ledbetter, TX 78946

Jacks, Donkeys, and Mules:

Jack and Jennet

American Mammoth Stock Registry
6513 W. Laurel Road
London, KY 40741

Donkeys

American Donkey Registry, The
(founded in 1967, all breeds)
American Donkey and Mule Society, The
2901 N. Elm Street
Denton, TX 76201

Mules

American Mule Registry, The (founded in 1967)
American Donkey and Mule Society, The
2901 N. Elm Street
Denton, TX 76201

Miniature Donkeys

Miniature Donkey Registry of the United States, The
(founded in 1958 for donkeys under 36 in.)
American Donkey and Mule Society, The
2901 N. Elm Street
Denton, TX 76201

Racing Mules

American Mule Racing Registry, The
American Donkey and Mule Society, The
2901 N. Elm Street
Denton, TX 76201

Spotted Asses

American Council of Spotted Asses, Inc.
Box 121
New Melle, MO 63365

All Horses and Half-Breeds

Any and all colors and types of horses (including animals not eligible for registry, eligible but not registered, or registered in existing associations) including both light and draft horses.

International American Albino Association
Box 194
Naper, NE 68755

All breeds and crossbreds

American Equine Registration Service
375 Burton Road
Reidsville, NC 27320

Generic horse—all horses and ponies, regardless of breed or type

P.O. Box 6778
Dept. AHC
Palos Verdes, CA 90734-6778

Half-bred Thoroughbreds

American Remount Association, Inc.
(Half-Thoroughbred Registry)[1]
HC O Box 4000
Lakeview, OR 97630

Section 1: The American Remount Half-Thoroughbred—Must have one Thoroughbred parent registered in the American (Jockey Club) Stud Book.

Section 2: The American Remount Anglo—Must have one Thoroughbred parent registered in the American (Jockey Club) Stud Book and the other parent registered in the Stud Book of a recognized breed.

Section 3: The American Remount Thoroughbred Kind—Must have one Thoroughbred parent of a recognized Foreign Registry or must have both parents registered in the American (Jockey Club) Stud Book but be ineligible for registry in the American (Jockey Club) Stud Book.

Section 4: The American Remount Hunter-Jumper— Must be a minimum of 36 months of age; be performance certified by an approved Equine Practitioner, a Master of Fox Hounds, an Official of the American Horse Show Association, or a Steward of the American Remount Association; and be ineligible for registry in the American (Jockey Club) Stud Book.

(Continued)

TABLE A-17 (Continued)

Section 5: The American Remount Polo Pony—Must be performance certified by an approved Equine Practitioner, a five-goal rated player, an Officer of the U.S. Polo Association, or a Steward of the American Remount Association; and be ineligible for registry in the American (Jockey Club) Stud Book.

Section 6: The American Remount Endurance Horse— Must be performance certified by an approved Equine Practitioner, an Official of the American Show Horse Association, or a Steward of the American Remount Association; and be ineligible for registry in the American (Jockey Club) Stud Book

Section 7: The American Remount Record—This is an identification Certificate issued to a horse that has apparent Thoroughbred ancestry but is not otherwise eligible for registry in the American (Jockey Club) Stud Book or any other recognized Stud Book.

Half-bred Arabian

International Arabian Horse Association
P.O. Box 33696
Denver, CO 80233

1. Anglo-Arabs must carry not more than three-fourths and not less than one-fourth Arabian blood. May be either—

(a) By Thoroughbred stallions and out of registered Arabian mares;

(b) By registered Arabian stallions and out of registered Thoroughbred mares;

(c) By registered Thoroughbred or Arabian stallions and out of registered Anglo-Arab mares; or

(d) By Anglo-Arab stallions and out of either Anglo-Arab mares, registered Thoroughbred mares, or registered Arabian mares.

2. Half-Arabians are by registered Arabian stallions and out of mares that are not registered Thoroughbreds or Arabians.

Half-bred, grade, and crossbred horses of most of the light horse breeds

American Part-Blooded Horse Registry[2]
4120 S.E. River Drive
Portland, OR 97267

National Grade Horse Registry
P.O. Box 338
10221 Slater Ave., #103
Fountain Valley, CA 92708

[1]Formerly the Half-Bred Stud Book operated by the American Remount Association, but now a privately owned registry. It records only foals sired by registered Thoroughbred stallions and out of mares not registered in the American (Jockey Club) Stud Book, or in the Arabian Stud Book.

[2]The American Part-Blooded Registry was founded in 1939. In 1994, it registered 132 horses, bringing their total to 15, 280.

BREED MAGAZINES

The horse breed magazines publish news items and informative articles of special interest to equestrians. Also, many of them employ field representatives whose chief duty is to assist in the buying and selling of animals.

In the compilation of the list herewith presented, no attempt was made to list the general livestock magazines of which there are numerous outstanding ones, and no claim is made that all horse magazines are listed therein.

TABLE A-18
BREED MAGAZINES

General

Bridle & Bit
16619 N. Cave Creek Road
Phoenix, AZ 85032

California Horse Review
9560 SW Nimbus
Beaverton, OR 97008

Chronicle of the Horse, The
301 W. Washington St. (20117)
Box 46
Middleburg, VA 20118

Cutting Horse Chatter, The
4704 Highway 377, South
Ft. Worth, TX 76116-8805

Dressage & C.T.
6405 Flank Drive
Harrisburg, PA 17112

Dressage Today
656 Quince Orchard Road
Gaithersburg, MD 20878

Equestrian Trails
13741 Foothill Blvd., Suite 220
Sylmar, CA 91342

Equine Image, The
1003 Central Avenue
Fort Dodge, IA 50501

Equus
656 Quince Orchard Rd.
Gaithersburg, MD 20878

Horse, The
1736 Alexandria Drive
Lexington, KY 40504

Horse Illustrated
P.O. Box 57549
Boulder, CO 80322-7549

Horse World
P.O. Box 1007
730 Madison Street
Shelbyville, TN 37160

(Continued)

TABLE A-18 (Continued)

Horsemen's Corral
P.O. Box 110
211 W. Main Street
New London, OH 44851

Horseplay
P.O. Box 130
11 Park Avenue
Gaithersburg, MD 20884

Lariat, The
P.O. Box 229
Beaverton, OR 97075

Northeast Equine Journal
312 Marlboro Street
Keene, NH 03431

Performance Horse
2895 Chad Drive
Eugene, OR 97408

Record Horseman
P.O. Box 1209
Wheat Ridge, CO 80034

Southern Horseman, The
P.O. Box 71
Meridian, MS 39302

Spur
735 Broad Street
Augusta, GA 30901

West Coast Horse Review
9560 SW Nimbus
Beaverton, OR 97008

Western Horseman, The
3850 N. Nevada Avenue (80907)
P.O. Box 7980
Colorado Springs, CO 80933

American Bashkir Curly

Curly Cues
Box 453
Ely, NV 89301

American Cream

American Cream Newsletter
112 King Henry Way
Williamsburg, VA 23188-1904

American Saddlebred

American Saddlebred Magazine, The
Kentucky Horse Park
4093 Iron Works Pike
Lexington, KY 40511

Bluegrass Horseman, The
P.O. Box 389
Lexington, KY 40501

Saddle and Bridle
375 N. Jackson Ave.
St. Louis, MO 63130

Saddle Horse Report
P.O. Box 1007
Shelbyville, TN 37160

American Walking Pony

A Dream Walking
P.O. Box 5282
Macon, GA 31208

Andalusian

The Spanish Bit
1941 Old Mill Road
Springfield, OH 45502

Appaloosa

Appaloosa Journal
Box 8403
Moscow, ID 83843

Cal-Western Appaloosa
3097 Willow -15
Clovis, CA 93612

Arabian

Arabian Horse Country
P.O. Box 4607-A
Portland, OR 97208

Arabian Horse Express
P.O. Box 845
Coffeyville, KS 67337

Arabian Horse Times, The
1050 8th Street, N.E.
P.O. Box 1469
Waseca, MN 56093

Arabian Horse World
824 San Antonio Ave.
Palo Alto, CA 94303

Arabian Visions
Box 230
Platte City, MO 64079

Arabian Voice, The
12465 Brown-Modes Road
Marysville, OH 43040-9513

Belgian

Belgian Review (annual)
P.O. Box 335
Wabash, IN 46992

Buckskin

Horse Circuit News
8098 E. 4005
New Castle, IN 47362

Cleveland Bay

Baywatch
The Cleveland Bay Horse Society of North America
P.O. Box 221
South Windham, CT 06266

Connemara Pony

The American Connemara
32600 Fairmount Blvd.
Pepper Pike, OH 44124

(Continued)

TABLE A-18 (Continued)

Dutch Warmblood

WPN Newsletter
P.O. Box 828
Winchester, OR 97495-0828

Exmoor Pony

North American Exmoors
Canadian Mounted & Moorland Society
RR 4, Box 273
Amherst, Nova Scotia, Canada BH4 3Y2

Galiceno

Galiceno Newsletter
P.O. Box 219
Godley, TX 76044

Hackney

Hackney Journal, The
American Hackney Horse Society
4059 Iron Works Road #A
Lexington, KY 40511-8462

Haflinger

Haflinger Highlite
2061 Kenyon Ave., S.W.
Massillon, OH 44646

Hanoverian

American Hanoverian, The
3401 St. Johns Drive
Dallas, TX 75205

Irish Draft Horse

Blarney, The
201 Lake Ridge Drive
Goldsboro, NC 27530

Lipizzan

Haute Ecole
Lipizzan Association of North America
P.O. Box 1133
Anderson, IN 46015

Miniature Horse

Miniature Horse World, The
American Miniature Horse Association, The
P.O. Box 129
Burleson, TX 76028

Missouri Fox Trotting Horse

Journal, The
P.O. Box 1027
Ava, MO 65608

Morgan

Morgan Horse, The
American Morgan Horse Association, Inc., The
P.O. Box 960
3 Bostwick Road
Shelburn, VT 05482

Morab

Morab World, The
W3174 Faro Springs Rd.
Hilbert, WI 54129

Morab Perspective
International Morab Breeders Association
S. 101 W. 34628 Hwy. 99
Eagle, WI 53119

Mustang

American Mustang World
American Mustang Association
P.O. Box 338
Yucaipa, CA 92399

Namar
P.O. Box 850906
Mesquite, TX 75185-0906

Spanish Mustang (annual and newsletters—5 to 6 per year)
Spanish Mustang Registry
Rt. 3, Box 7670
Wilcox, AZ 85643

National Show Horse

National Show Horse Connection
340 Calle Sierpe
Sante Fe, NM 87501

National Spotted Saddle Horse

National Spotted Saddle Horse Journal
P.O. Box 898
Murfreesboro, TN 37133-0898

Norwegian Fjord Horse

Fjord Times, The
Norwegian Fjord Association of North America
24570 W. Chardon Rd.
Draplake, IL 60030

Paint Horse

Paint Horse Journal, The
P.O. Box 961023
Ft. Worth, TX 76161-0023

Palomino

Palomino Horses
15253 East Skelly Drive
Tulsa, OK 74116

Palomino Parade
HC63 – Box 24
Dornsife, PA 17823

Paso Fino

Paso Fino Horse World
101 North Collins Street
Plant City, FL 33566-3311

Percheron

Percheron Notes
P.O. Box 141
Fredericktown, OH 43019

(Continued)

TABLE A-18 (Continued)

Peruvian Paso

Caballo
P.O. Box 1049
Lake Elsinore, CA 92531-1049

Conquistador
1645 Ballard Canyon Road
Solvang, CA 93463

Pintabian

Pintabian Ink Spot
P.O. Box 360
Karlstad, MN 56732

Pinto Arabian

Top Spot
2230 Walkers Lane
Burlington, Ontario, Canada

Pinto Horse

Pinto Horse, The
101 North Collins Street
Plant City, FL 33566

Pony of the Americas

POA
5240 Elmwood Ave.
Indianapolis, IN 46203

Quarter Horse

Foundation Quarter Horse, The
Box 500
Akron, CO 80720

Quarter Horse Journal, The
P.O. Box 32470
Amarillo, TX 79120

Quarter Racing Journal, The
P.O. Box 32470
Amarillo, TX 79120

Shetland Pony

**Journal of the American Shetland Pony Club &
American Miniature Horse Registry**
P.O. Box 887
Warrenville, IL 60555

Spanish-Barb

Spanish Barb World/Journal, The
188 Springridge Rd.
Terry, MS 39170

Spotted Saddle Horse

Spotted Saddle Horse News
P.O. Box 1046
Shelbyville, TN 37160

Standardbred

Hoof Beats
750 Michigan Avenue
Columbus, OH 43215

Horseman and Fair World, The
904 N. Broadway
Lexington, KY 40505

Swedish Gotland Horse

Russ Review
370 Arden Road
Menlo Park, CA 94025

Swedish Warmblood

SWANA News
P.O. Box 1587
Coupeville, WA 98239

Tennessee Walking Horse

Voice of the Tennessee Walking Horse
P.O. Box 286
Lewisburg, TN 37091

Walking Horse Report
P.O. Box 1007
Shelbyville, TN 37160

Thoroughbred

American Turf Monthly
438 W. 37th St.
New York, NY 10018

Arizona Thoroughbred, The
1501 West Bell Rd.
Phoenix, AZ 85069

Backstretch, The
19363 James Couzens Hwy.
Detroit, MI 48235

Blood-Horse, The
Box 4038
Lexington, KY 40544-4038

Daily Racing Form
10 Lake Drive
Hightstown, NJ 08520

Florida Horse, The
P.O. Box 2106
Ocala, FL 32678

Maryland Horse, The
P.O. Box 427
Timonium, MD 21093

Texas Thoroughbred, The
P.O. Box 14967
Austin, TX 78761

Thoroughbred of California, The
201 Colorado Place
Arcadia, CA 91006

Thoroughbred Record, The
367 W. Short St.
Lexington, KY 40533

Thoroughbred Times
P.O. Box 8237
Lexington, KY 40533

Washington Thoroughbred, The
P.O. Box 88258
Seattle, WA 98138-2258

(Continued)

TABLE A-18 (Continued)

Trakehner

American Trakehner, The
American Trakehner Association
1520 West Church Street
Newark, OH 43055

Welara Pony

Welara Journal
P.O. Box 401
Yucca Valley, CA 92284

Welsh

Welsh Pony & Cob Society of America Newsletter (quarterly)
P.O. Box 2977
Winchester, VA 22604

Draft Horses (all breeds, and mules)

Draft Horse Journal, The
Box 670
Waverly, IA 50677

Donkey and Mule

Brayer, The
2901 N. Elm
Denton, TX 76201

Mules
American Mule Association
6725 Union Road
Paso Robles, CA 93446

Mules & More
P.O. Box 872
Carthage, MO 64836

U.S. STATE COLLEGES OF AGRICULTURE AND CANADIAN PROVINCIAL UNIVERSITIES

U.S. horse producers can obtain a list of available bulletins and circulars, and other information regarding horses by writing to (1) their state agricultural college (land-grant institution), and (2) the U.S. Superintendent of Documents, Washington, DC; or by going to the local county extension office (farm advisor) of the county in which they reside. Canadian producers may write to the Department of Agriculture of their province or to their provincial university. A list of U.S. land-grant institutions and Canadian provincial universities follows in Table A-19.

TABLE A-19
U.S. LAND-GRANT INSTITUTIONS AND CANADIAN PROVINCIAL UNIVERSITIES

State	Address
Alabama	School of Agriculture, Auburn University, Auburn, AL 36830
Alaska	Department of Agriculture, University of Alaska, Fairbanks, AK 99701
Arizona	College of Agriculture, The University of Arizona, Tucson, AZ 85721
Arkansas	Division of Agricutlure, University of Arkansas, Fayetteville, AR 72701
California	College of Agriculture and Environmental Sciences, University of California, Davis, CA 95616
Colorado	College of Agricultural Sciences, Colorado State University, Fort Collins, CO 80521
Connecticut	College of Agriculture and Natural Resources, University of Connecticut, Storrs, CT 06268
Delaware	College of Agricultural Sciences, University of Delaware, Newark, DE 19711
Florida	College of Agriculture, University of Florida, Gainesville, FL 32611
Georgia	College of Agriculture, University of Georgia, Athens, GA 30602
Hawaii	College of Tropical Agriculture, University of Hawaii, Honolulu, HI 96822
Idaho	College of Agriculture, University of Idaho, Moscow, ID 83843
Illinois	College of Agriculture, University of Illinois, Urbana–Champaign, IL 61801
Indiana	School of Agriculture, Purdue University, West Lafayette, IN 47907
Iowa	College of Agriculture, Iowa State University, Ames, IA 50010
Kansas	College of Agriculture, Kansas State University, Manhattan, KS 66506
Kentucky	College of Agriculture, University of Kentucky, Lexington, KY 40506
Louisiana	College of Agriculture, Louisiana State University and A&M College, University Station, Baton Rouge, LA 70803
Maine	College of Life Sciences and Agriculture, University of Maine, Orono, ME 04473

(Continued)

TABLE A-19 (Continued)

State	Address
Maryland	College of Agriculture, University of Maryland, College Park, MD 20742
Massachusetts	College of Food and Natural Resources, University of Massachusetts, Amherst, MA 01002
Michigan	College of Agriculture and Natural Resources, Michigan State University, East Lansing, MI 48823
Minnesota	College of Agriculture, University of Minnesota, St. Paul, MN 55101
Mississippi	College of Agriculture, Mississippi State University, Mississippi State, MS 39762
Missouri	College of Agriculture, University of Missouri, Columbia, MO 65201
Montana	College of Agriculture, Montana State University, Bozeman, MT 59715
Nebraska	College of Agriculture, University of Nebraska, Lincoln, NE 68503
Nevada	The Max C. Fleischmann College of Agriculture, University of Nevada, Reno, NV 89507
New Hampshire	College of Life Sciences and Agriculture, University of New Hampshire, Durham, NH 03824
New Jersey	College of Agriculture and Environmental Science, Rutgers University, New Brunswick, NJ 08903
New Mexico	College of Agriculture and Home Economics, New Mexico State University, Las Cruces, NM 88003
New York	New York State College of Agriculture, Cornell University, Ithaca, NY 14850
North Carolina	School of Agriculture, North Carolina State University, Raleigh, NC 27607
North Dakota	College of Agriculture, North Dakota State University, State University Station, Fargo, ND 58102
Ohio	College of Agriculture and Home Economics, The Ohio State University, Columbus, OH 43210
Oklahoma	College of Agriculture and Applied Science, Oklahoma State University, Stillwater, OK 74074
Oregon	School of Agriculture, Oregon State University, Corvallis, OR 97331
Pennsylvania	College of Agriculture, The Pennsylvania State University, University Park, PA 16802
Puerto Rico	College of Agricultural Sciences, University of Puerto Rico, Mayagüez, PR 00708
Rhode Island	College of Resource Development, University of Rhode Island, Kingston, RI 02881
South Carolina	College of Agricultural Sciences, Clemson University, Clemson, SC 29631
South Dakota	College of Agriculture and Biological Sciences, South Dakota State University, Brookings, SD 57006
Tennessee	College of Agriculture, University of Tennessee, P.O. Box 1071, Knoxville, TN 37901
Texas	College of Agriculture, Texas A&M University, College Station, TX 77843
Utah	College of Agriculture, Utah State University, Logan, UT 84321
Vermont	College of Agriculture, University of Vermont, Burlington, VT 05401
Virginia	College of Agriculture, Viriginia Polytechnic Institute and State University, Blacksburg, VA 24061
Washington	College of Agriculture, Washington State University, Pullman, WA 99163
West Virginia	College of Agriculture and Forestry, West Virginia University, Morgantown, WV 26506
Wisconsin	College of Agricultural and Life Sciences, University of Wisconsin, Madison, WI 53706
Wyoming	College of Agriculture, University of Wyoming, University Station, P.O. Box 3354, Laramie, WY 82070

Canada	Address
Alberta	University of Alberta, Edmonton, Alberta T6H 3K6
British Columbia	University of British Columbia, Vancouver, British Columbia V6T 1W5
Manitoba	University of Manitoba, Winnipeg, Manitoba R3T 2N2
New Brunswick	University of New Brunswick, Federicton, New Brunswick E3B 4N7
Ontario	University of Guelph, Guelph, Ontario N1G 2W1
Québéc	Faculty d'Agriculture, L'Université Laval, Québéc City, Québéc G1K 7D4; and Macdonald College of McGill University, Ste. Anne de Bellevue, Québéc H9X 1C0
Saskatchewan	University of Saskatchewan, Saskatoon, Saskatchewan S7N 0W0

POISON INFORMATION CENTERS

With the large number of chemical sprays, dusts, and gases now on the market for use in agriculture, accidents may arise because of operators being careless in their use. Also, there is always the hazard that a child may eat or drink something that may be harmful. Centers have been established in various parts of the country where doctors can obtain prompt and up-to-date information on treatment of such cases, if desired.

Local medical doctors have information relative to the Poison Information Centers of their area, along with some of the names of their directors, telephone numbers, and street numbers. When calling any of these centers, one should ask for the "Poison Information Center." If this information cannot be obtained locally, call the U.S. Public Health Service at Atlanta, Georgia; or Wenatchee, Washington.

Also, the National Poison Control Center is located at the University of Illinois, Urbana-Champaign. It is open 24 hours a day, every day of the week. The hot line number is: 1-800-548-2423. The toxicology group is staffed to answer questions about known or suspected cases of poisoning or chemical contaminations involving any species of animal. It is not intended to replace local veterinarians or state toxicology laboratories, but to complement them. Where consultation over the telephone is adequate, there is no charge to the veterinarian or producer. Where telephone consultation is inadequate or the problem is of major proportions, a team of veterinary specialists can arrive at the scene of a toxic or contamination problem within a short time. The cost of a personal visitation varies according to the distance traveled, personnel time, and laboratory services required.

Fig. A-7. Horse owners generally determine pasture needs on the basis of number of acres required per mature horse, which is called *carrying capacity*. It ranges from 1 to 5 acres of seeded pasture per horse. (Photo by Dell Hancock, Claiborne, Paris, KY)

INDEX